BUSINESS STATISTICS OF THE UNITED STATES

Patterns of Economic Change

27th Edition
2022

Edited by Susan Ockert

Lanham • Boulder • New York • London

Published by Bernan Press
An imprint of The Rowman & Littlefield Publishing Group, Inc.
4501 Forbes Boulevard, Suite 200, Lanham, Maryland 20706
www.rowman.com

86-90 Paul Street, London EC2A 4NE

ISBN 9781636710877 (cloth) | ISBN 9781636710884 (ebook)

CONTENTS

PREFACE

Business Statistics of the United States: Patterns of Economic Change, 27th Edition, 2022 is a basic desk reference for anyone requiring statistics on the U.S. economy. It contains over 3,000 economic time series portraying the period from World War II to December 2021 in industry, product, and demographic detail. Detailed information on how COVID-19 impacted the economy is included throughout the book. In the case of about 200 key series, the period from 1929 through 1948 is depicted as well.

Additionally, for three important statistical series that have been compiled monthly on a continuous basis, monthly and annual data are included going back to 1919 for industrial production and to 1913 for consumer and producer prices. Annual data for money and credit have also been taken back before 1929, including money supply figures back to 1892 and some interest rates back to 1919. Annual estimates of the unemployment rate from 1890 to 1929—not official but using a method similar to that used by BLS for its 1929–48 unemployment estimates—are also included.

The national income and product accounts (NIPAs) were comprehensively revised in July 2013, changing some measurement concepts, changing base periods for price indexes and real output, and as a result altering all the data back to 1929. *Business Statistics* incorporates fully revised data for over 700 series from this data set and productivity and costs series that are based on the revised NIPAs, all extended and updated through 2016. The important new concepts introduced in the NIPA revision are explained in the Notes and Definitions to Chapters 1, 4, 5, and 6. In all, this edition provides, in one volume, unparalleled, up-to-date background information on the course of the U.S. economy.

The data are predominantly from federal government sources. Of equal importance are the extensive background notes for each chapter, which help users understand the data, use them appropriately, and, if desired, seek additional information from the source agencies.

Chapters are organized according to subject matter. For most time series, users will find an initial page displaying the latest two years of monthly data, or three years of quarterly data, for the most recent completed years, along with annual averages for the last completed 40, 50, or even 60 years.

For the most important series for which we have long-term historical data, this initial page will be labeled with "A" after the table number, and identified in the title by the additional words "Recent Data." It will be immediately followed by pages labeled with "B" after the table number and identified by the words "Historical Data," which will show all available historical data annually back as far as possible, and monthly or quarterly back to the earliest available postwar year. In some cases, additional tables of historical data will be included.

The leading article "Cycle and Growth Perspectives" provides other information and techniques to assist in using and interpreting the data.

THE PLAN OF THE BOOK

The history of the U.S. economy is told in major U.S. government sets of statistical data: the national income and product accounts compiled by the Bureau of Economic Analysis (BEA); the data on labor force, employment, hours, earnings, and productivity compiled by the Bureau of Labor Statistics (BLS); the price indexes collected by BLS; and the financial market and industrial production data compiled primarily by the Board of Governors of the Federal Reserve System (FRB). All of these sets exist in annual and either monthly or quarterly form beginning at 1946, 1947, or 1948; many are available, at least annually, as far back as 1929, and a few even farther back; and three are available monthly back to the teens of the twentieth century.

In part A, *Business Statistics* presents the aggregate U.S. economy in a number of important dimensions. The presentations begin with the national income and product accounts, or NIPAs. The NIPAs comprise a comprehensive, thorough, and internally consistent body of data. They measure the value of the total output of the U.S. economy (gross domestic product, or GDP), and they allocate that value between its quantity, or "real," and price components. They show how the value of aggregate demand is generated by consumers, business investors, government, and foreign customers; how much of aggregate demand is supplied by imports and how much by domestic production; and how the income generated in domestic production is distributed between labor and capital.

Production estimates covering only the sectors of the economy traditionally labeled "industrial"—manufacturing, mining, and utilities—are shown in chapter 2, after the presentation of the overall NIPAs in chapter 1.

Median income—the best measure of the economic well-being of the typical American—income distribution, and poverty statistics from a Census household survey are presented in chapter 3.

Then, more detail from the NIPAs is presented for the demand components of economic activity. GDP, by its product-side definition, consists of the sum of consumption expenditures, business investment in fixed capital and inventories, government purchases of goods and services, and exports minus imports—as in the elementary economics blackboard identity "GDP = C + I + G + X − M." Chapters on each of these components—consumption, investment, government, and foreign trade—are presented in part A.

Following these chapters, there are a chapter on prices, two chapters on the compensation of labor and capital inputs and the amount and productivity of labor input, one chapter on energy inputs into production and consumption, and one chapter on money, interest, assets, and debt.

At the end of part A, comparisons of output, prices, and labor markets among major industrial countries are presented, along with statistics on the value of the dollar against other currencies.

While GDP is initially defined and measured by adding its demand categories and subtracting imports, this output is produced in industries—some in the old-line heavy industries such as manufacturing, mining, and utilities, but an increasing share in the huge and heterogeneous group known as "service-providing" industries. Part A gives a number of measures of activity classified by industry or industrial sector: industrial production, profits, and employment-related data. Further industry information is provided in part B, including new quarterly indicators of GDP by industry.

Industry data collection is important because demands for goods and services are channeled into demands for labor and capital through the industries responsible for producing the requested goods and services. These data are reported using the North American Industry Classification System (NAICS). This system, introduced in 1997 to replace the older Standard Industrial Classification System (SIC), delineates industries that are better defined in relation to today's demands and more closely related to each other by technology. Notable examples include more detailed data available on service industries, a more rational grouping of the computer and electronic product manufacturing subsector, and the creation of the information sector; see the references at the end of this preface.

NAICS industries are groupings of producing units—not of products as such—and are grouped according to similarity of production processes. This is done in order to collect consistent data on inputs and outputs, which are then used to measure important concepts, such as productivity and input-output parameters. Emphasis on the production process helps to explain a number of ways in which the NAICS differs from the SIC.

- Manufacturing activities at retail locations, such as bakeries, have been classified separately from retail activity and put into the food manufacturing industry.

- Central administrative offices of companies have a new sector of their own, management of companies and enterprises (sector 55). For example, the office headquarters of a food-producing corporation is considered part of the new sector instead of part of the food manufacturing industry.

- Reproduction of packaged software, which was classified as a business service in the SIC, is now classified as

a manufacturing process, in sector 334, computer and electronic product manufacturing.

- Electronic markets and agents and brokers, formerly undifferentiated components of wholesale trade industries, have a sector of their own (425).

- Retail trade in NAICS (sectors 44 and 45) now includes establishments such as office supply stores, computer and software stores, building materials dealers, plumbing supply stores, and electrical supply stores, that display merchandise and use mass-media advertising to sell to individuals as well as to businesses, which were formerly classified in wholesale trade.

In part B, *Business Statistics* shows GDP, income, employment, hours, and earnings by industry, followed by statistics for key sectors such as petroleum, housing, manufacturing, retail trade, and services.

NOTES AND DEFINITIONS

Productive use of economic data requires accurate knowledge about the sources and meaning of the data. The notes and definitions for each chapter, shown immediately after that chapter's tables, contain definitions, descriptions of recent data revisions, and references to sources of additional technical information. They also include information about data availability and revision and release schedules, which helps users to readily access the latest current values if they need to keep up with the data month by month or quarter by quarter.

A NOTE ON THE IMPORTANCE OF ECONOMIC STATISTICS

To retrieve money and credit data for earlier years, the editor of *Business Statistics* had to consult old printed volumes, where she encountered some inspiring prefatory words in the Federal Reserve Board volume *Banking and Monetary Statistics* (1943). These words were written by the Fed's longtime statistics chief E. A. Goldenweiser, in the stately cadences of an earlier era, about the financial statistics collected in that volume. But they well express the hope and expectation of statisticians and economists that their work can lead to better economic decisions: "These serried ranks of organized statistics on banking and finance, even though they may inspire awe, should also inspire confidence. They are an augury that credit policy can be based in the future, as in the past, on fact rather than on fancy."

THE HISTORY OF *BUSINESS STATISTICS*

The history of *Business Statistics* began with the publication, many years ago, of the first edition of a volume with the same name by the U.S. Department of Commerce's Bureau of Economic Analysis (BEA). After twenty-seven periodic editions, the last of which appeared in 1992, BEA found it necessary, for budgetary and other reasons, to discontinue both the publication and the maintenance of the database from which the publication was derived.

The individual statistical series gathered here are all publicly available. However, the task of gathering them from the numerous different sources within the government and assembling them into one coherent database is impractical for most data users. Even when current data are readily available, obtaining the full historical time series is often time-consuming and difficult. Definitions and other documentation can also be inconvenient to find. Believing that a *Business Statistics* compilation was too valuable to be lost to the public, Bernan Press published the first edition of the present publication, edited by Dr. Courtenay M. Slater, in 1995. The first edition received a warm welcome from users of economic data. Dr. Slater, formerly chief economist of the Department of Commerce, continued to develop *Business Statistics* through four subsequent annual editions. The current editor worked with Dr. Slater on the fourth and fifth editions. In subsequent editions, she has continued in the tradition established by Dr. Slater of ensuring high-quality data, while revising and expanding the book's scope to include significant new aspects of the U.S. economy and longer historical background.

Nearly all of the statistical data in this book are from federal government sources and all are available in the public domain. Sources are given in the applicable notes and definitions.

The data in this volume meet the publication standards of the federal statistical agencies from which they were obtained. Every effort has been made to select data that are accurate, meaningful, and useful. All statistical data are subject to error arising from sampling variability, reporting errors, incomplete coverage, imputation, and other causes. The responsibility of the editor and publisher of this volume is limited to reasonable care in the reproduction and presentation of data obtained from established sources.

The 2022 edition has been edited by Susan Ockert, who has worked as an economist in the military, for the federal government, and at regional and state levels. She earned her masters of economics at George Mason University in Fairfax, Virginia, as well as her masters of international management at the Thunderbird University in Glendale, Arizona. She currently teaches economics at the collegiate level.

REFERENCES

The NAICS is explained and laid out in *North American Industry Classification System: United States*, from the Executive Office of the President, Office of Management and Budget and Bernan Press. The North American Industry Classification System began in 1997 and is updated every five years with the most recent update occurring in 2022.

Information on differences between NAICS and SIC can be found in *North American Industry Classification System: United States, 1997*, from the Executive Office of the President, Office of Management and Budget (which contains matches between the 1997 NAICS and the 1987 SIC); and *North American Industry Classification System: United States, 2002* (which contains matches that show the relatively few changes from the 1997 NAICS to the 2002 NAICS).

These volumes fully describe the development and application of the new classification system and are the sources for the material presented in this volume. More detailed information is also available on the NAICS website at https://www.census.gov/naics.

CYCLE AND GROWTH PERSPECTIVES

This 27th edition of *Business Statistics of the United States* presents comprehensive and detailed data on U.S. economic performance through December 2021, going back to the early 20th century. These numbers show changes in many dimensions—economic growth, employment, inflation, income, the dramatic impact COVID-19 had on the economy in the United States and the world, to name a few. There are patterns of fluctuation, and, simultaneously, patterns of enduring change. This article will present some ways of looking at these movements and trying to make sense of them. In addition, policy instruments are also described.

The Federal Reserve conducts the nation's *monetary policy* by managing the level of short-term interest rates and influencing the overall availability and cost of credit in the economy. Monetary policy directly affects short-term interest rates; it indirectly affects longer-term interest rates, currency exchange rates, and prices of equities and other assets and thus wealth. Through these channels, monetary policy influences household spending, business investment, production, employment, and inflation in the United States.

Governments use spending and taxing powers to promote stable and sustainable growth. *Fiscal policy* is the use of government spending and taxation to influence the economy. Governments typically use fiscal policy to promote strong and sustainable growth and reduce poverty. Fiscal policy aims to stabilize economic growth, avoiding a boom and bust economic cycle. Fiscal policy is often used in conjunction with monetary policy. In fact, governments often prefer monetary policy for stabilizing the economy.

The U.S. economy, even in its infancy, experienced boom or bust periods. The first recorded downturn was the Panic of 1785, which followed the American Revolution when the economy changed from military to industrial. Attempts have been made to date recessions in America beginning in the late 18th century. Economists and historians, because of the lack of economic statistics, didn't always agree on the start and stop of recessions, but they agree that volatility in economic activity and unemployment did exist.

BUSINESS CYCLES IN THE U.S. ECONOMY: RECESSIONS AND EXPANSIONS

The study of economic fluctuations in the United States was pioneered by Wesley C. Mitchell and Arthur F. Burns early in the twentieth century, and was carried on subsequently by other researchers affiliated with the National Bureau of Economic Research (NBER). NBER is an independent, nonpartisan research organization founded in 1920 and is committed to providing unbiased economic research. These analysts observed that indicators of the general state of business activity tended to move up and down over periods that were longer than a year and were therefore not accounted for by seasonal variation. Although these periods of expansion and contraction were not uniform in length, and thus not "cycles" in any strict mathematical sense, their recurrent nature and certain generic similarities caused them to be called "business cycles." NBER has identified 32 complete peak-to-peak business cycles over the period beginning with December 1854.

The first NBER-established business cycle dates, identifying the months in which peaks and troughs in general economic activity occurred, were published in 1929. The dates of current cycles are established, typically within a year or so of their occurrence, by the NBER Business Cycle Dating Committee. This group, first formed in 1978, consists of eight economists who are university professors, associated with research organizations, or both. The peak of the cycle signals the start of a downturn of an economy while the trough signals the beginning of a upturn.

Business cycle dates are based on monthly data, and have been identified for periods long before the availability of quarterly data on real gross national product (GDP). It is important to understand that even in the period since 1947 for which quarterly real GDP exists, the NBER identification of a recession does not always coincide with the frequently cited definition, "two consecutive quarters of decline in real GDP." Because a recession is a broad contraction of the economy, NBER emphasizes economy-wide measures of economic activity such as production, employment, real income, real manufacturing, wholesale-retail sales, and many more indicators. Federal agencies collect the economic data used by NBER. Employment data is provided by the Department of Labor, Bureau of Labor Statistics while the Department of Commerce provides data from the Census Bureau and Bureau of Economic Analysis along with the Federal Reserve Board.

The NBER monthly and quarterly dates of the cycles from 1854 to the latest announced turning point—the June 2009 trough ending the recession that began in December 2007—are shown in Table A-1. The quarterly turning points are identified by Roman numerals. NBER considers that the trough month is both the end of the decline and the beginning of the expansion, based on the concept that the actual turning point was some particular day within that month. The longest running contraction, during the Great Depression, lasted from August 1929 to November 1933, for a total of 43 months. The latest recession ended in June 2009, after 19 months.

Meanwhile, an expansion began in June 2009 and ended in February 2020, the longest expansion in U.S. history, lasting for 10 years and 8 months. This expansionary period was followed by the shortest recession in U.S. history, lasting only two months from February 2020 to April 2020. Concerns of another recession have many people worried but the job market has remained strong through the first two quarters of 2022.

TABLE A-1. Business Cycle Reference Dates, 1854–2009

Peak (Recession)	Trough (Recovery)
	December 1854 (IV)
June 1857 (II)	December 1858 (IV)
October 1860 (III)	June 1861 (III)
April 1865 (I)	December 1867 (I)
June 1869 (II)	December 1870 (IV)
October 1873 (III)	March 1879 (I)
March 1882 (I)	May 1885 (II)
March 1887 (II)	April 1888 (I)
July 1890 (III)	May 1891 (II)
January 1893 (I)	June 1894 (II)
December 1895 (IV)	June 1897 (II)
June 1899 (III)	December 1900 (IV)
September 1902 (IV)	August 1904 (III)
May 1907 (II)	June 1908 (II)
January 1910 (I)	January 1912 (IV)
January 1913 (I)	December 1914 (IV)
August 1918 (III)	March 1919 (I)
January 1920 (I)	July 1921 (III)
May 1923 (II)	July 1924 (III)
October 1926 (III)	November 1927 (IV)
August 1929 (III)	March 1933 (I)
May 1937 (II)	June 1938 (II)
February 1945 (I)	October 1945 (IV)
November 1948 (IV)	October 1949 (IV)
July 1953 (II)	May 1954 (II)
August 1957 (III)	April 1958 (II)
April 1960 (II)	February 1961 (I)
December 1969 (IV)	November 1970 (IV)
November 1973 (IV)	March 1975 (I)
January 1980 (I)	July 1980 (III)
July 1981 (III)	November 1982 (IV)
July 1990 (III)	March 1991 (I)
March 2001 (I)	November 2001 (IV)
December 2007 (IV)	April 2020 (II)
February 2020 (I)	

Between 1854 to 2020, the American economy experienced over 30 separate recessions (contractions) and expansions (recoveries). Before the Great Depression, recessions occurred more frequently and in conjunction with financial panics. With such financial instability, the Federal Reserve System was established in 1913 to assert central control of the monetary system. Financial crises during the 1800s occurred due to crop failures, banking failures, drops in cotton prices, rapid speculation in land, sudden plunges in the stock market and currency and credit crises, The United States of America during this period was a very young nation and thus these panics devastated its economy.

THE U.S. ECONOMY, 1929–1948

While there has been much discussion in recent years of the Great Depression, there is surprisingly little familiarity with the basic statistical record of the period between 1929 and the end of World War II. Reproducing material from chapter 18 of the 15th edition of *Business Statistics*, we present here an explanation of that period from the NBER business cycle perspective, along with a graphic overview and narration of its economic developments as recorded in the statistics now presented in Part A of this volume.

The NBER chronology, presented in Table A-1 in the preceding article "Cycle and Growth Perspectives," may surprise readers who are looking for the Great Depression and are not familiar with the NBER approach to business cycles. As NBER perceives it, a downtrend in economic activity began in August 1929 (*before* the stock market crash) and lasted until March 1933. This 43-month period has been called the "Great Contraction": it was the longest period of economic decline since the 1870s, and more than double the length of the longest recession identified and completed since that time (the one from December 2007 to June 2009, which lasted 18 months). For the rest of the 1930s—excepting a 13-month recession in 1937–1938—the economy is viewed by the NBER as having been in an expansion phase. The NBER chronology does not use the term "depression."

However, the term "Great Depression" is often colloquially used for the entire 1929–1939 period, even though the economy was expanding for most of the period following March 1933. This is because economic activity during that time, though increasing, remained below the likely capacity of the economy, as is indicated in Figures A-1 and A-2 below.

It should also be noted that NBER construes the entire period from June 1938 through February 1945 as a business cycle expansion. The recovery from the 1937–1938 recession merged into a further, continued rise in activity that reflected the outbreak of war in Europe in September 1939, a consequent preparedness effort in the United States, and an increase in demand from abroad for U.S. output. The United States entered the war after being attacked by Japan in December 1941, launching an all-out war production effort at that time.

The February 1945 end of the "wartime expansion" (as NBER terms the period June 1938–February 1945) preceded the end of the war (the European war ended in May 1945 and the Pacific war concluded in August 1945). A brief recession associated with demobilization occurred from February to October 1945, followed by the first postwar expansion, which lasted from October 1945 to November 1948.

Figure A-1: Employment, 1929–1948

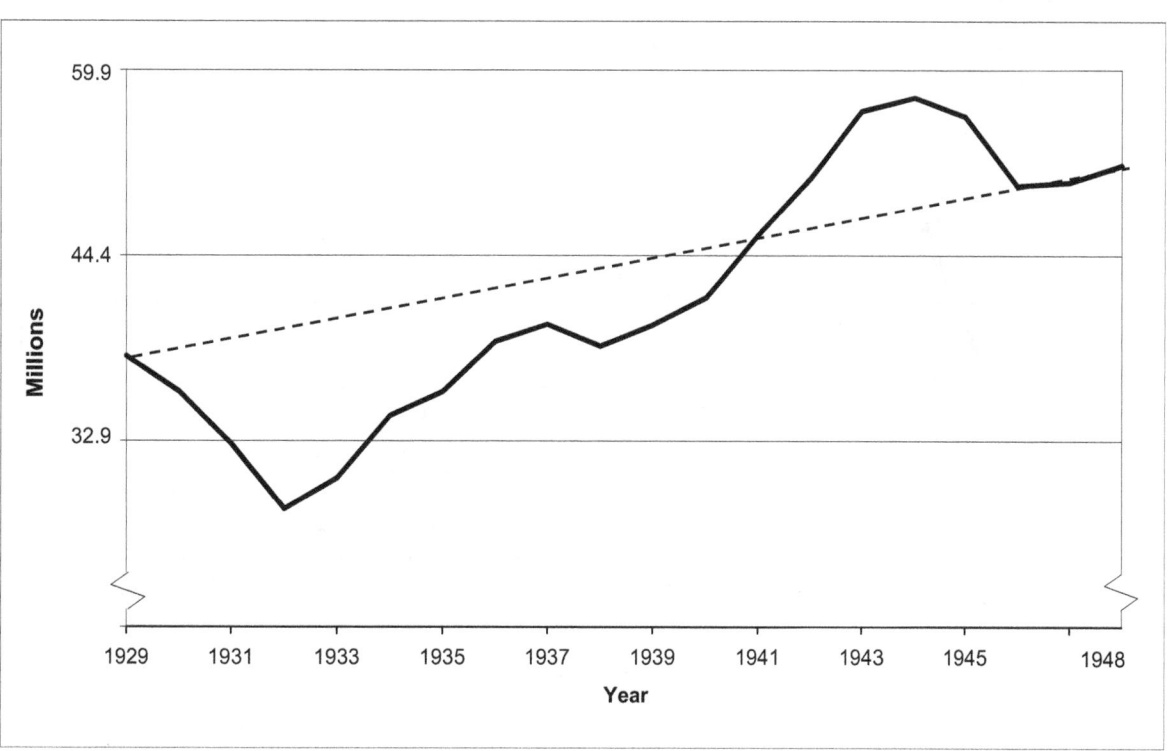

In the graphs that follow, summary annual statistics for the years 1929 through 1948 are presented, depicting the economy during two of its most tumultuous decades. This period encompasses the "great contraction," the economic collapse that began in August 1929 and lasted until March 1933; a subsequent period of recovery, which failed to return many important economic indicators to their expected trend levels and was interrupted by a new, though less severe, recession; apprehension of coming war, then the outbreak of war in Europe in September 1939, leading to increased war-related production; United States participation in all-out war, beginning with the Japanese attack on Pearl Harbor on December 7, 1941, and ending in 1945, with supercharged production and employment rates; then, rapid demobilization, and return to a high peacetime rate of economic activity by 1948.

For a first overall view of the economy during these decades, Figure A-1 shows total U.S. employment as calculated by the Bureau of Economic Analysis, including all private and government jobs, both civilian and military. In this graph a trend line is shown connecting the two peacetime high employment levels of 1929 and 1948.

- More than one-fifth of all the jobs held in the U.S. economy in 1929 were gone by 1932. In the subsequent recovery, total employment was back at the 1929 level by 1936, but only because of government employment, including over 3.5 million work relief jobs; private industry employment would not recover to its 1929 level until 1941.

- Because the recovery was incomplete and economic activity did not recover to a trend level until after the decade's end, the entire decade of the 1930s is often described as "The Great Depression."

- During the war, men were drafted into the armed forces, practically all of the unemployed were put back to work, and women were drawn into the labor force, resulting in a period of what might be called "super-employment." After the war, employment fell back to a more normal trend level.

- The unemployment rates for the prewar period calculated by the Bureau of Labor Statistics count people on government work relief programs as unemployed. By this reckoning, unemployment rose from 3.2 percent of the civilian labor force in 1929 to a peak of 24.9 percent in 1933, and got no lower than 14.3 percent for the rest of the 1930s, as shown in Figure A-2 (Table 10-1C).

- State and local governments started hiring people for work relief in 1930. The Federal government's programs began in 1933, and in 1936 and 1938 agencies such as the WPA and the CCC employed over 3.5 million people. When workers in these programs are counted as employed rather than unemployed, the high point for unemployment was 22.5 percent in 1932, and it was reduced to 9.1 percent in 1937, as shown by the dashed line in Figure A-2 see Notes and Definitions to chapter 10 for further explanation).

Figure A-2: Unemployment Rates, 1929–1948

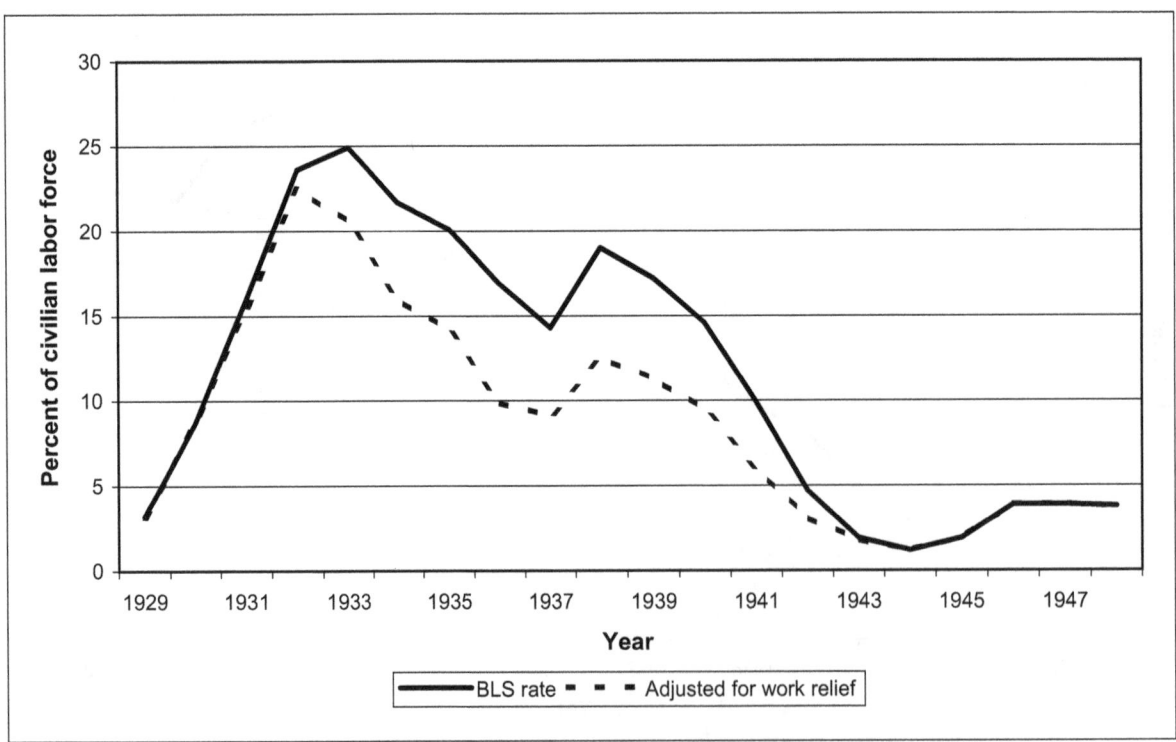

Figure A-3: Per Capita Real Output and Consumption, 1929–1948

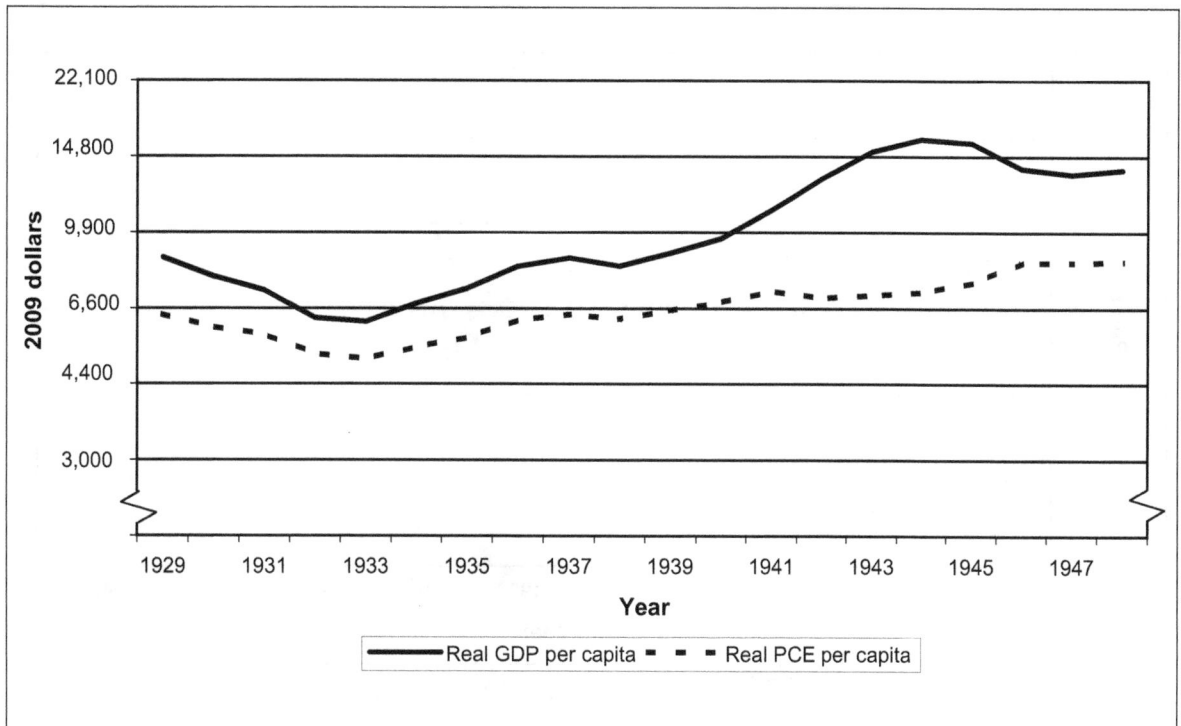

- By 1943, the economy reached a state of over-full employment, which would have been associated with runaway inflation if not for comprehensive price, wage, and production controls; the years of full wartime production, 1943 through 1945, all saw unemployment rates below 2 percent. After demobilization, the unemployment rate returned to just under 4 percent.

- Real GDP declined 26.7 percent from 1929 to 1933—28.9 percent on a per capita basis. Per capita output recovered almost to the 1929 level in 1937 but fell back 4.1 percent in the 1938 recession. Output then nearly doubled from 1939 to the peak war production year, 1944; the per capita annual growth rate was 12.4 percent. Output fell back during the demobilization, but in 1948 was still at a per capita level representing a 5.0 percent per year growth rate since 1939.

- Per capita personal consumption expenditures fell 20.9 percent from 1929 to 1933. The decline would have been greater if consumers had not dipped into their assets to keep their living standards from declining as steeply as their incomes; the personal saving rate was negative in 1932 and 1933. Real per capita consumption recovered to the 1929 level by 1937. Despite rationing and shortages, real per capita consumption spending declined little during the war years. In 1948, it was 29.3 percent above the 1939 level.

- Why was the 1929–33 contraction so deep and long-lasting? By some, blame is placed on U.S. government tax increases and imposition of new trade barriers (the Smoot-Hawley Tariff), which undoubtedly made their contribution. A substantial number of well-regarded economists, however, point primarily to deflation and its interaction with debt. The price index for personal consumption expenditures declined 27.2 percent from 1929 to 1933, for an annual average *deflation* rate of 7.6 percent. Current and prospective price declines make debt more burdensome and debtors more likely to default, as interest payments remain fixed while incomes and asset values decline.

- Current and prospective price declines also make borrowing prohibitively expensive; a low nominal interest rate becomes high in real terms (since the real rate is the nominal rate *minus* the inflation rate, and subtraction means changing the sign and adding). A dollar in the hands of a prospective lender will be worth more in terms of purchasing power if he simply holds on to it than if he invests it in some real economic asset or activity whose price will be lower at the end of the year. There is no feasible way for a central bank to lower interest rates below zero in order to reduce real rates in the presence of deflation. As Figure A-4 shows, real rates were high from 1930 through 1933 despite near-zero market nominal rates on Treasury bills (Tables 12-9B and 1-6B).

Figure A-4: Inflation and Nominal and Real Interest Rates, 1929–1948

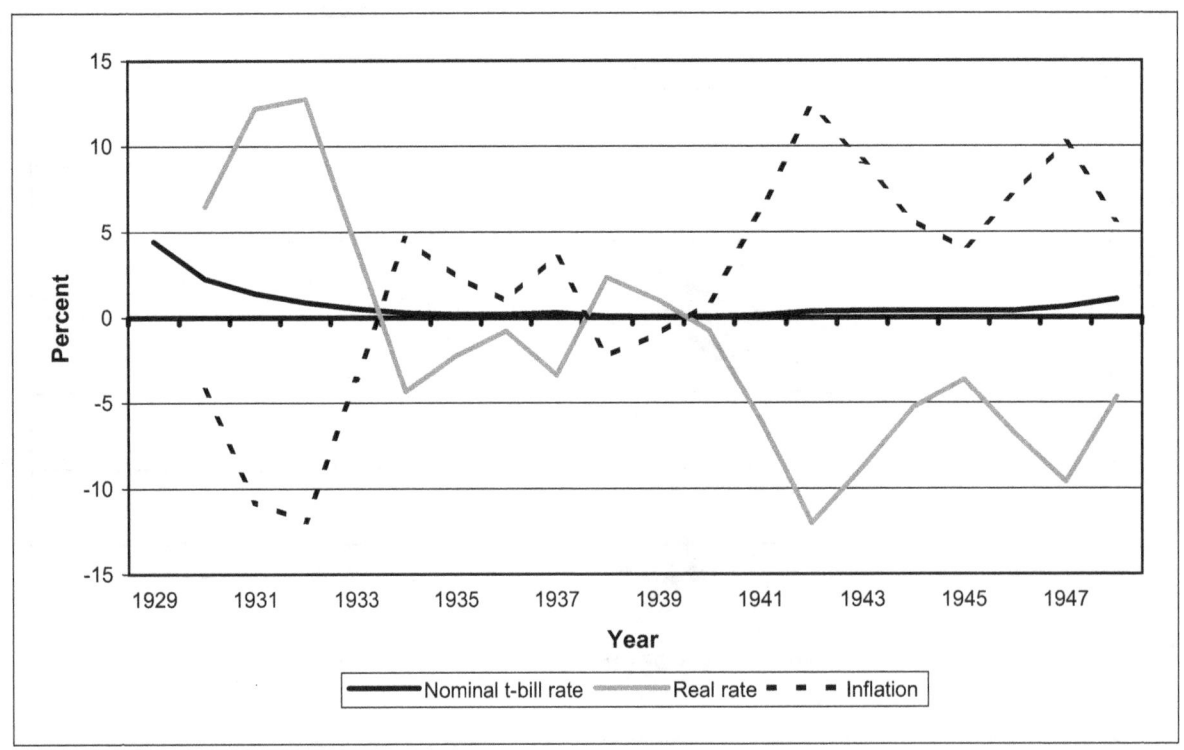

Figure A-5: Money and Credit Growth, 1930–1948

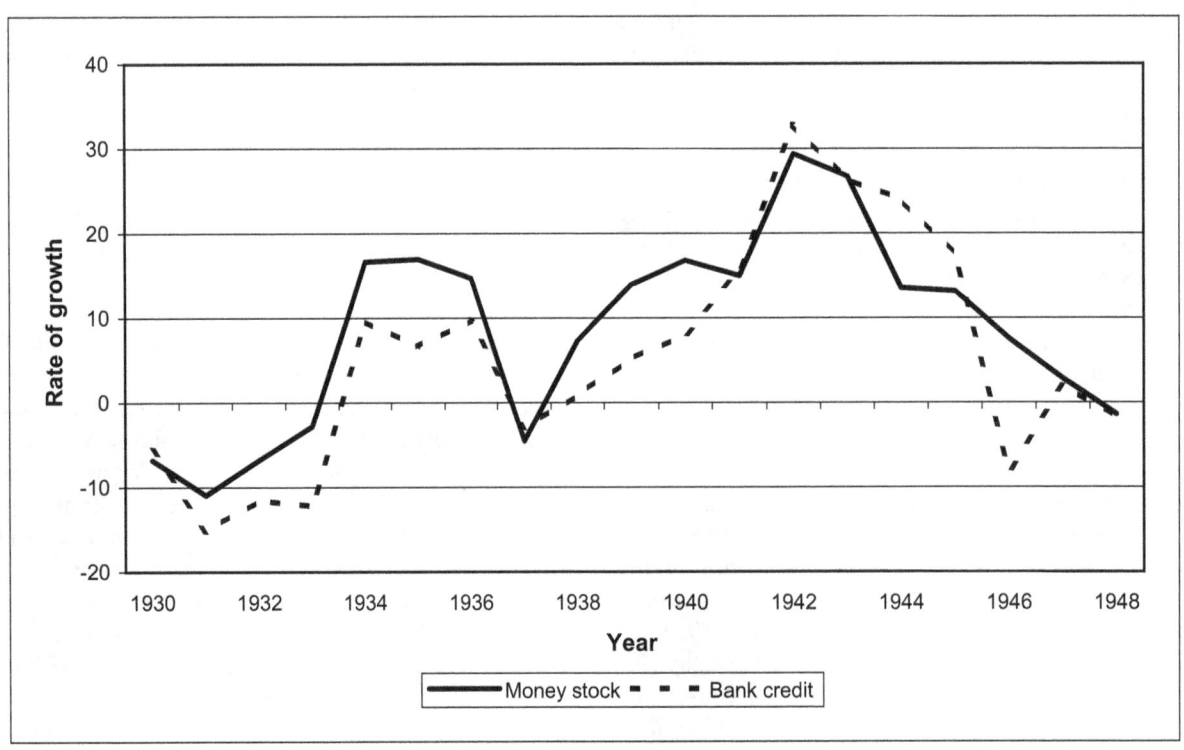

- Deflation was rooted in deep and sustained declines in the dollar volumes of money and credit, as illustrated in Figure A-5. The money stock (currency and demand deposits) declined 27 percent from June 30, 1929, to June 30, 1933. Loans and investments at all commercial banks declined 29 percent over the same period. Commercial paper outstanding plunged 76 percent between December 1929 and December 1932, and bankers' acceptances were down 59 percent.

- Positive money and credit growth after 1933 was reflected in moderate rates of price increase and moderately negative—which means stimulative—real interest rates. As can be seen in Figure A-5, there was a monetary component to the 1937–38 recession. There was also a premature federal budget retrenchment at that time (Table 6-14B).

- During the war, monetary policy was preempted by wartime needs. Interest rates were held low to facilitate the financing of huge federal deficits (Tables 6-14B and 12-9B).

- Worker incomes increased during the wartime boom as employment, average hours, and hourly wages all rose. But inflation and consumer spending were held down by price and production controls and rationing. Personal saving rates soared when there was little to buy and the government emphasized the sale of "war bonds"; the saving rate reached 26 percent in 1943 and 1944, then fell back to 4.2 percent in 1947, almost equal to its 1929 level.

COVID-19 AND THE ECONOMY

The World Health Organization (WHO) declared COVID-19 a pandemic on March 11, 2020. Five days later on March 16, President Trump announced "15 Days to Slow the Spread" essentially closing down the U.S. economy except essential employees including healthcare workers, first responders, truckers, grocery workers, and those in law enforcement. When businesses closed and stay-at-home orders were issued, demand dropped, and consumer spending declined precipitously. Events were cancelled, gasoline prices fell, and travel nearly came to a halt. Not surprisingly, the National Bureau of Economic Research (NBER) announced that the U.S. economy fell into a recession in February 2020—but recovered just two months later in April 2020—marking the shortest recession in U.S. history.

This troubled economy resulted in millions of people out of work, trying to register for unemployment compensation, and even waiting in long lines for food. Unemployment increased dramatically going from 5.7 million people in February 2020 to over 23 million people in April 2020 (see Chapter 10). With businesses closed, median household income fell for the first time since 2011 to $67,521. With millions of people unemployed, poverty increased to 11.4 percent in 2020, and the percentage of uninsured individuals increased to 8.6 percent as many people lost their employee-based health care coverage (see Chapter 3).

Gross domestic product (GDP), a comprehensive measure of U.S. economic activity, was naturally impacted. A change in GDP is the most popular indicator of the nation's overall economic health. In the second quarter of 2020, the economy fell 9.3 percent but rapidly rose 8.5 percent the following quarter (Chapter 1).

Finally, in early December 2020, a vaccine became available giving hope to everyone that the end of the pandemic was near.

As the number of COVID-19 cases fluctuated in the United States and the world due to variants, and concern about the vaccine, businesses began opening, but often operating with a new set of rules. Delivery was no longer just for restaurants as grocery stores increased "personal shoppers" who picked out your order, retail stores began curb-side pick-up, and restaurants built outdoor eating areas even in cold weather climates. Additionally, drone-delivery was tested and telemedicine became more commonplace. Although much of the economy slowed during COVID-19, one aspect of the economy that grew was e-commerce, growing from 11.9 percent of total sales in the first quarter of 2020 to 16.4 percent of total sales in the second quarter of 2020 (see Chapter 16).

Unemployment declined gradually in the second half of 2020 and continued to drop 2021. By December 2021, the unemployment rate declined to 3.9 percent, a massive reduction from 14.8 percent just sixteen months earlier in April 2020. As COVID-19 eased, more businesses opened, but many workers had left the labor force, resulting in a shortage of workers (see Chapter 10).

The Federal Reserve once again stepped in to support the U.S. economy, as they did during the Great Recession. Interest rates (federal funds rates) were kept near zero. Also, the Fed resumed purchases of securities from banks, called *quantitative easing* (see Chapter 12).

Initially when the pandemic started, demand decreased, and consumer spending plummeted. As conditions improved and the economy opened again, demand began to soar for goods and services. However, companies were not able to keep with demand as ports were overwhelmed with a shortage of containers, container ships waited days to off load their cargo, and production shut down in different parts of the world. Supply-chain disruptions were common in every industry from construction to publishing.

As demand continued to climb and supply slowed, prices increased. In December 2021, inflation increased to a 39-year high of 7.1 percent. The Producer Price Index (PPI), a measure of prices of materials used in the production of a final product, is often an early predictor of inflation. In 2019, the composite index was 118.2, it increased slightly to 118.4 in 2020 and by 2021, the index rose to 126.7 (Chapter 8).

Crude oil prices declined in 2020 as lockdowns, restricted travel, and millions of Americans working at home, all reduced demand. In 2020, the price of a barrel of oil dropped to its lowest rate the lowest price since 2004. Prices then skyrocketed in 2021 as restrictions eased and people began to travel again (Chapter 11). Gasoline prices have been highly volatile in recent years growing from $1.93 per gallon to a high of $5.33 in July 2022. Energy consumption is part of the market basket that is used to calculate the Consumer Price Index (CPI). Chapter 8 provides more information on the CPI and the PPI.

THE 2022 ECONOMY AND BEYOND

In 2022, there have been both signs of hope and areas of concern. Job creation continues to be strong through the third quarter of 2022, unemployment fell to its lowest level in years, and gasoline prices finally started to fall (see Chapters 10 and 11). However, inflation soared to a 40-year high of 9.1 percent in June 2022. In response to the rising inflation, the Federal Reserve decided to no longer keep the federal funds rate near zero but instead raise the rate to 2.5 percent in July 2022 (see Chapter 12). Real gross domestic product declined for the first two quarters of 2022 creating more concern about the state of the economy (see Chapter 1).

By 2027, the WHO is projecting growth in GDP at 3.3 percent and inflation at 3.2 percent. However, as we have seen in recent years, the world can change in instant and projections that are created today may change tomorrow.

GENERAL NOTES

These notes provide general information about the data in Tables 1-1 through 16-14. Specific notes with information about data sources, definitions, methodology, revisions, and sources of additional information follow the tables in each chapter.

MAIN DIVISIONS OF THE BOOK

The tables are presented in two parts:

Part A (Tables 1-1 through 13-2) pertains principally to the U.S. economy as a whole. Generally, each table presents, on its initial page, annual averages as far back as data availability and space permit, and quarterly or monthly values for the most recent year or years. For many important series, this initial page is followed by full annual and quarterly or monthly histories as far back as they are available on a continuous, consistent basis. Some chapters present data for the United States only in aggregate, while others—such as the chapters concerning industrial production and capacity utilization (Chapter 2), capital expenditures (Chapter 5), profits (Chapter 9), and employment, hours, and earnings (Chapter 10)—also have detail for industry groups.

Data by industry are classified using the North American Industry Classification System (NAICS), as far back as such data are made available by the source agencies.

Part B focuses on the individual industries that together produce the gross domestic product (GDP).

- Chapter 14 contains data on the value of GDP, quantity production trends, and factor income by NAICS industry group.

- Chapter 15 provides further detail on payroll employment, hours, and earnings classified according to NAICS.

- Chapter 16 presents various data sets for key economic sectors. Some of the tables are based on definitions of products, rather than of producing establishments, and are valid for either classification system. This is the case for Tables 16-1, Petroleum and Petroleum Products; 16-2, New Construction; 16-3, Housing Starts and Building Permits, New House Sales, and Prices; and 16-8, Motor Vehicle Sales and Inventories. Tables 16-4 through 16-7 and 16-9, 16-11, and 16-12, which cover manufacturing and retail and wholesale trade, show data classified according to NAICS. Table 16-15 presents data for services industries classified according to NAICS.

CHARACTERISTICS OF THE TABLES AND THE DATA

The subtitles or column headings for the data tables normally indicate whether the data are *seasonally adjusted, not seasonally adjusted*, or *at a seasonally adjusted annual rate.* These descriptions refer to the monthly or quarterly data, rather than the annual data; annual data by definition require no seasonal adjustment. Annual values are normally calculated as totals or averages, as appropriate, of unadjusted data. Such annual values are shown in either or both adjusted or unadjusted data columns.

Seasonal adjustment removes from a monthly or quarterly time series the average impact of variations that normally occur at about the same time each year, due to occurrences such as weather, holidays, and tax payment dates.

A simplified example of the process of seasonal adjustment, or deseasonalizing, can indicate its importance in the interpretation of economic time series. Statisticians compare actual monthly data for a number of years with "moving average" trends of the monthly data for the 12 months centered on each month's data. For example, they may find that in November, sales values are usually about 95 percent of the moving average, while in December, usual sales values are 110 percent of the average. Suppose that actual November sales in the current year are $100 and December sales are $105. The seasonally adjusted value for November will be $105 ($100 / 0.95) while the value for December will be $95 ($105 / 1.10). Thus, an apparent increase in the unadjusted data turns out to be a decrease when adjusted for the usual seasonal pattern.

The statistical method used to achieve the seasonal adjustment may vary from one data set to another. Many of the data are adjusted by a computer method known as X-12-ARIMA, developed by the Census Bureau. A description of the method is found in "New Capabilities and Methods of the X-12-ARIMA Seasonal Adjustment Program," by David F. Findley, Brian C. Monsell, William R. Bell, Mark C. Otto and Bor-Chung Chen (*Journal of Business and Economic Statistics*, April 1998). This article can be downloaded from the Bureau of the Census website at https://www.census.gov.

Production and sales data presented at *annual rates*—such as NIPA data in dollars, or motor vehicle data in number of units—show values at their annual equivalents: the values that would be registered if the seasonally adjusted rate of activity measured during a particular month or quarter were maintained for a full year. Specifically, seasonally adjusted monthly values are multiplied by 12 and quarterly values by 4 to yield seasonally adjusted annual rates.

Percent changes at seasonally adjusted annual rates for quarterly time periods are calculated using a compound interest formula, by raising the quarter-to-quarter percent change in a seasonally adjusted series to the fourth power. See the article

"Cycle and Growth Perspectives" for an explanation of compound annual growth rates.

Indexes. In many of the most important data sets presented in this volume, aggregate measures of prices and quantities are expressed in the form of indexes. The most basic and familiar form of index, the original Consumer Price Index, begins with a "market basket" of goods and services purchased in a base period, with each product category valued at its dollar prices— the amount spent on that category by the average consumer. The value weight ascribed to each component of the market basket is moved forward by the observed change in the price of the item selected to represent that component. These weighted component prices—which constitute the quantities in the base period repriced in the prices of subsequent periods—are aggregated, divided by the base period aggregate, and multiplied by 100 to provide an index number. An index calculated in this way is known as a *Laspeyres index*. In general, economists believe that Laspeyres price indexes have an upward bias, showing more price increase than they would if account were taken of consumers' ability to change spending patterns *and maintain the same level of satisfaction* in response to changing relative prices.

A *Paasche index* is one that uses the weights of the current period. Since the weights in the Paasche index change in each period, Paasche indexes only provide acceptable indications of change relative to the base period. Paasche indexes for two periods neither of which is the base period cannot be correctly compared: for example, a Paasche price index for a recent period might increase from the period just preceding even if no prices changed between those two periods, if there was a change in the composition of output toward prices that had previously increased more from the base period. When the national income and product account (NIPA) measures of real output were Laspeyres measures, using the weights of a single base year, the implicit deflators (current-dollar values divided by constant-dollar values) were Paasche indexes. Just as Laspeyres price indexes are upward-biased, Paasche price indexes are downward-biased because they overestimate consumers' ability to maintain the same level of satisfaction by changing spending patterns.

In recent years, government statisticians—with the aid of complex computer programs—have developed measures of real output and prices that minimize bias by using the weights of both periods and updating the weights for each period-to-period comparison. Such measures are described as chained indexes and are used in the NIPAs, the index of industrial production, and an experimental consumer price index. Chained measures are discussed more fully in the notes and definitions for Chapter 1, Chapter 2, and Chapter 8. The "Fisher Ideal" index, the "superlative" index, and the "Tornqvist formula" are all types of chained indexes that use weights for both periods under comparison.

Detail may not sum to totals due to rounding. Since annual data are typically calculated by source agencies as the annual totals or averages of not-seasonally-adjusted data, they therefore will not be precisely equal to the annual totals or averages of monthly seasonally adjusted data. Also, seasonal adjustment procedures are typically multiplicative rather than additive, which may also prevent seasonally adjusted data from adding or averaging to the annual figure. Percent changes and growth rates may have been calculated using unrounded data and therefore differ from those using the published figures.

The data in this volume are from federal government sources and may be reproduced freely. A list of data sources is shown below.

The tables in this volume incorporate data revisions and corrections released by the source agencies through mid-2014, including the July annual revision of the NIPAs and the resulting August revision of productivity and costs.

DATA SOURCES

The source agencies for the data in this volume are listed below. The specific source or sources for each particular data set are identified at the beginning of the notes and definitions for the relevant data pages.

Board of Governors of the Federal Reserve System
20th Street & Constitution Avenue NW
Washington, DC 20551

URL: https://www.federalreserve.gov

Quarterly Publication: As of 2006, the *Federal Reserve Bulletin* is available free of charge and only on the Federal Reserve website.

Data Inquiries and Publication Sales:
  Publications Services
  Mail Stop 127
  Board of Governors of the Federal Reserve System
  Washington, DC 20551
  (202) 452-3245

Census Bureau
U.S. Department of Commerce
4600 Silver Hill Road
Washington, DC 20233

URL: https://www.census.gov

Ordering Data Products: (301) 763-INFO (4636)

Questions: https://ask.census.gov

Bureau of Economic Analysis
U.S. Department of Commerce
Washington, DC 20230

URL: https://www.bea.gov

Data Inquiries: Public Information Office: (202) 606-9900

Monthly Publication, available online: *Survey of Current Business*

Bureau of Labor Statistics
U.S. Department of Labor
2 Massachusetts Avenue NE
Washington, DC 20212-0001
(202) 691-5200

URL: https://www.bls.gov

Data Inquiries: blsdata_staff@bls.gov

Monthly Publications, available online:
  Monthly Labor Review
  Employment and Earnings
  Compensation and Working Conditions
  Producer Price Indexes
  CPI Detailed Report

Employment and Training Administration
U.S. Department of Labor
200 Constitution Avenue NW
Washington, DC 20210
(877) US2-JOBS

URL: https://www.dol.gov/agencies/eta

Energy Information Administration
U.S. Department of Energy
1000 Independence Avenue SW
Washington, DC 20585

URL: https://www.eia.gov

Monthly Publication: *Monthly Energy Review* available only on the EIA website, free of charge
Data Inquiries and Publications:
  National Energy Information Center
  (202) 586-8800
  E-mail: infoctr@eia.doe.gov

Federal Housing Finance Agency
FHFAinfo@FHFA.gov
(202) 414-6921, 6922
(202) 414-6376

URL: https://www.fhfa.gov

U.S. Department of the Treasury
Office of International Affairs
Treasury International Capital System

URL: https://home.treasury.gov/data/treasury-international-capital-tic-system

PART A: THE U.S. ECONOMY

CHAPTER 1: NATIONAL INCOME AND PRODUCT

SECTION 1A: GROSS DOMESTIC PRODUCT: VALUES, QUANTITIES, AND PRICES

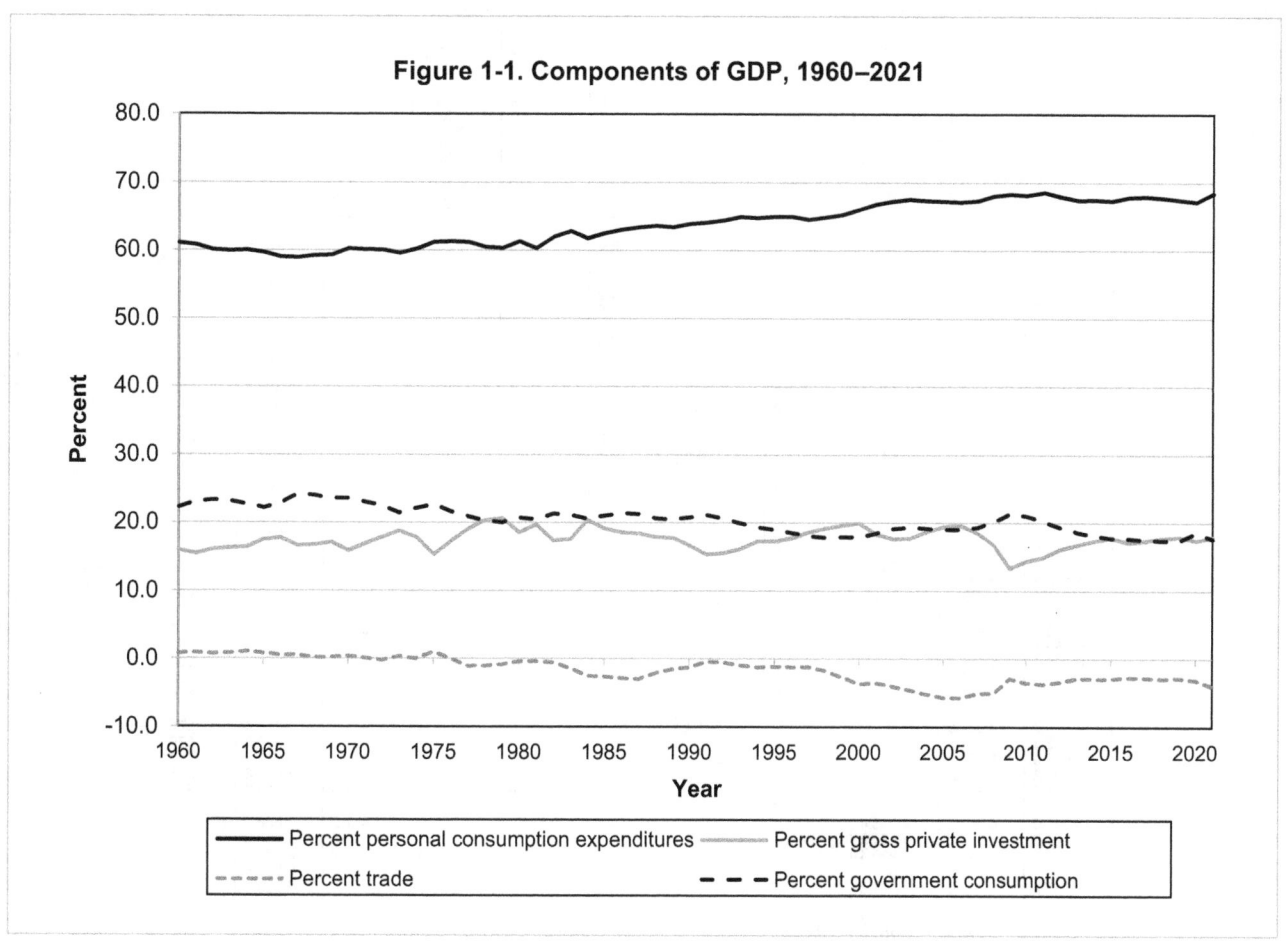

Figure 1-1. Components of GDP, 1960–2021

- After Gross Domestic Product (GDP) dropped sharply in 2020, it recovered and surpassed its pre-pandemic level in 2021. However, in 2022, the GDP declined again for two consecutive quarters.

- As the economy slowed in 2020, the federal government legislated several acts to help consumers, businesses, states, counties, and tribal nations keep afloat. For example, checks were sent directly to Americans. Another program was enhanced unemployment compensation, funding to governmental entities, and more.

- Towards the end of 2020 and throughout 2021 the economy grew as the nation began to recover from the effects of the pandemic. In 2021, GDP grew by 10 percent after decreasing the previous year 2.2 percent.

- Figure 1 illustrates the four components of GDP. Consumption's share of GDP rose from 61.1 percent in 1960 to nearly 68.5 percent in 2021. Government's percent share of GDP fell in the same period. (Table 1-1A)

Table 1-1A. Gross Domestic Product: Recent Data

(Billions of dollars, quarterly data are at seasonally adjusted annual rates.)

NIPA Tables 1.1.5, 1.2.5

Year and quarter	Gross domestic product	Personal consumption expenditures	Gross private domestic investment — Total	Fixed investment — Nonresidential	Fixed investment — Residential	Change in private inventories	Net exports	Exports	Imports	Government — Total	Federal	State and local	Addendum: final sales of domestic product
1960	542.4	331.2	86.5	56.4	26.9	3.2	4.2	27.0	22.8	120.5	72.9	47.6	539.1
1961	562.2	341.5	86.6	56.6	27.0	3.0	4.9	27.6	22.7	129.2	77.4	51.9	559.2
1962	603.9	362.6	97.0	61.2	29.6	6.1	4.1	29.1	25.0	140.3	85.5	54.8	597.8
1963	637.5	382.0	103.3	64.8	32.9	5.6	4.9	31.1	26.1	147.2	87.9	59.3	631.8
1964	684.5	410.6	112.2	72.2	35.1	4.8	6.9	35.0	28.1	154.8	90.3	64.5	679.6
1965	742.3	443.0	129.6	85.2	35.2	9.2	5.6	37.1	31.5	164.1	93.2	70.9	733.0
1966	813.4	479.9	144.2	97.2	33.4	13.6	3.9	40.9	37.1	185.4	106.6	78.9	799.8
1967	860.0	506.7	142.7	99.2	33.6	9.9	3.6	43.5	39.9	207.0	120.0	87.0	850.1
1968	940.7	556.9	156.9	107.7	40.2	9.1	1.4	47.9	46.6	225.5	128.0	97.6	931.6
1969	1 017.6	603.6	173.6	120.0	44.4	9.2	1.4	51.9	50.5	239.0	131.2	107.8	1 008.4
1970	1 073.3	646.7	170.0	124.6	43.4	2.0	3.9	59.7	55.8	252.6	132.8	119.8	1 071.3
1971	1 164.9	699.9	196.8	130.4	58.2	8.3	0.6	63.0	62.3	267.5	134.5	133.0	1 156.6
1972	1 279.1	768.2	228.1	146.6	72.4	9.1	-3.4	70.8	74.2	286.2	141.6	144.5	1 270.0
1973	1 425.4	849.6	266.9	172.7	78.3	15.9	4.1	95.3	91.2	304.8	146.2	158.6	1 409.5
1974	1 545.2	930.2	274.5	191.1	69.5	14.0	-0.8	126.7	127.5	341.4	158.8	182.5	1 531.3
1975	1 684.9	1 030.5	257.3	196.8	66.7	-6.3	16.0	138.7	122.7	381.1	173.7	207.4	1 691.2
1976	1 873.4	1 147.7	323.2	219.3	86.8	17.1	-1.6	149.5	151.1	404.2	184.8	219.4	1 856.3
1977	2 081.8	1 274.0	396.6	259.1	115.2	22.3	-23.1	159.3	182.4	434.3	200.3	234.0	2 059.5
1978	2 351.6	1 422.3	478.4	314.6	138.0	25.8	-25.4	186.9	212.3	476.3	218.9	257.4	2 325.8
1979	2 627.3	1 585.4	539.7	373.8	147.8	18.0	-22.5	230.1	252.7	524.8	240.6	284.2	2 609.3
1980	2 857.3	1 750.7	530.1	406.9	129.5	-6.3	-13.1	280.8	293.8	589.6	274.9	314.7	2 863.6
1981	3 207.0	1 934.0	631.2	472.9	128.5	29.8	-12.5	305.2	317.8	654.4	314.0	340.4	3 177.2
1982	3 343.8	2 071.3	581.0	485.1	110.8	-14.9	-20.0	283.2	303.2	711.5	348.3	363.1	3 358.7
1983	3 634.0	2 281.6	637.5	482.2	161.1	-5.8	-51.6	277.0	328.6	766.6	382.4	384.2	3 639.8
1984	4 037.6	2 492.3	820.1	564.3	190.4	65.4	-102.7	302.4	405.1	827.9	411.8	416.1	3 972.2
1985	4 339.0	2 712.8	829.7	607.8	200.1	21.8	-114.0	303.2	417.2	910.5	452.9	457.6	4 317.2
1986	4 579.6	2 886.3	849.1	607.8	234.8	6.6	-131.9	321.0	452.9	976.1	481.7	494.4	4 573.1
1987	4 855.2	3 076.5	892.2	615.2	249.8	27.1	-144.8	363.9	508.7	1 031.5	502.8	528.7	4 828.1
1988	5 236.4	3 330.0	937.0	662.3	256.2	18.5	-109.4	444.6	554.0	1 078.9	511.4	567.4	5 218.0
1989	5 641.6	3 576.8	999.7	716.0	256.0	27.7	-86.7	504.3	591.0	1 151.9	534.1	617.8	5 613.9
1990	5 963.1	3 809.0	993.4	739.2	239.7	14.5	-77.9	551.9	629.7	1 238.6	562.4	676.2	5 948.6
1991	6 158.1	3 943.4	944.3	723.6	221.2	-0.4	-28.6	594.9	623.5	1 299.0	582.9	716.0	6 158.5
1992	6 520.3	4 197.6	1 013.0	741.9	254.7	16.3	-34.7	633.1	667.8	1 344.5	588.5	756.0	6 504.0
1993	6 858.6	4 452.0	1 106.8	799.2	286.8	20.8	-65.2	654.8	720.0	1 364.9	580.2	784.8	6 837.7
1994	7 287.2	4 721.0	1 256.5	868.9	323.8	63.8	-92.5	720.9	813.4	1 402.3	574.7	827.6	7 223.5
1995	7 639.7	4 962.6	1 317.5	962.2	324.1	31.2	-89.8	812.8	902.6	1 449.4	576.7	872.7	7 608.6
1996	8 073.1	5 244.6	1 432.1	1 043.2	358.1	30.8	-96.4	867.6	964.0	1 492.8	579.2	913.7	8 042.3
1997	8 577.6	5 536.8	1 595.6	1 149.1	375.6	70.9	-102.0	953.8	1 055.8	1 547.1	583.3	963.8	8 506.6
1998	9 062.8	5 877.2	1 736.7	1 254.1	418.8	63.7	-162.7	953.0	1 115.7	1 611.6	585.5	1 026.1	8 999.1
1999	9 631.2	6 283.8	1 887.1	1 364.5	461.8	60.8	-259.6	992.9	1 252.5	1 719.9	610.7	1 109.2	9 570.4
2000	10 251.0	6 767.2	2 038.4	1 498.4	485.4	54.5	-381.1	1 096.1	1 477.2	1 826.4	633.1	1 193.4	10 196.4
2001	10 581.9	7 073.8	1 934.8	1 460.1	513.1	-38.3	-376.7	1 026.8	1 403.6	1 950.0	670.2	1 279.8	10 620.2
2002	10 929.1	7 348.9	1 930.4	1 352.8	557.6	20.0	-439.7	998.0	1 437.7	2 089.5	743.1	1 346.4	10 909.1
2003	11 456.5	7 740.7	2 027.1	1 375.9	637.1	14.1	-522.0	1 035.2	1 557.1	2 210.6	826.8	1 383.8	11 442.4
2004	12 217.2	8 232.0	2 281.3	1 467.4	749.8	64.1	-634.1	1 176.4	1 810.5	2 338.1	892.1	1 446.0	12 153.1
2005	13 039.2	8 769.1	2 534.7	1 621.0	856.2	57.5	-739.9	1 301.6	2 041.5	2 475.3	947.8	1 527.5	12 981.7
2006	13 815.6	9 277.2	2 701.0	1 793.8	838.2	69.0	-786.5	1 470.2	2 256.6	2 623.8	1 001.2	1 622.7	13 746.6
2007	14 474.2	9 746.6	2 673.0	1 948.6	690.5	34.0	-735.9	1 659.3	2 395.2	2 790.6	1 051.0	1 739.5	14 440.3
2008	14 769.9	10 050.1	2 477.6	1 990.9	516.0	-29.2	-740.9	1 835.3	2 576.2	2 983.0	1 152.0	1 831.1	14 799.1
2009	14 478.1	9 891.2	1 929.7	1 690.4	390.0	-150.8	-419.2	1 582.8	2 001.9	3 076.3	1 220.8	1 855.6	14 628.8
2010	15 049.0	10 260.3	2 165.5	1 735.0	376.6	53.9	-532.3	1 857.2	2 389.6	3 155.6	1 300.2	1 855.4	14 995.1
2011	15 599.7	10 698.9	2 332.6	1 907.5	378.8	46.3	-579.6	2 115.9	2 695.5	3 147.9	1 299.8	1 848.1	15 553.5
2012	16 254.0	11 047.4	2 621.8	2 118.5	432.0	71.2	-551.6	2 217.7	2 769.3	3 136.5	1 287.0	1 849.5	16 182.8
2013	16 843.2	11 363.5	2 826.0	2 211.5	510.0	104.5	-479.4	2 287.0	2 766.4	3 133.0	1 227.2	1 905.9	16 738.7
2014	17 550.7	11 847.7	3 044.2	2 400.1	560.2	84.0	-510.0	2 377.4	2 887.4	3 168.8	1 216.0	1 952.8	17 466.7
2015	18 206.0	12 263.5	3 237.2	2 466.6	633.8	136.8	-526.2	2 268.7	2 794.9	3 231.6	1 221.8	2 009.8	18 069.2
2016	18 695.1	12 693.3	3 205.0	2 469.3	699.4	36.3	-506.3	2 232.1	2 738.4	3 303.1	1 234.5	2 068.5	18 658.8
2017	19 479.6	13 239.1	3 381.4	2 591.6	760.3	29.5	-539.9	2 383.8	2 923.7	3 399.1	1 262.8	2 136.3	19 450.1
2018	20 527.2	13 913.5	3 637.8	2 780.6	798.5	58.7	-596.2	2 533.5	3 129.7	3 572.0	1 339.0	2 233.0	20 468.4
2019	21 372.6	14 428.7	3 826.3	2 938.7	813.9	73.6	-596.3	2 519.7	3 116.0	3 713.9	1 414.9	2 299.0	21 299.0
2020	20 893.7	14 047.6	3 637.8	2 799.6	897.8	-59.6	-651.2	2 123.4	2 774.6	3 859.5	1 501.8	2 357.8	20 953.3
2021	22 996.1	15 741.6	4 120.0	3 053.7	1 086.1	-19.9	-918.2	2 478.3	3 396.5	4 052.7	1 565.0	2 487.7	23 015.9
2019													
1st quarter	21 001.6	14 155.6	3 801.9	2 886.9	796.5	118.5	-606.4	2 524.6	3 131.0	3 650.5	1 387.0	2 263.5	20 883.1
2nd quarter	21 289.3	14 375.7	3 843.0	2 946.1	808.5	88.4	-632.3	2 533.4	3 165.7	3 702.9	1 406.9	2 296.0	21 200.8
3rd quarter	21 505.0	14 529.5	3 858.2	2 969.3	821.9	67.0	-614.0	2 512.1	3 126.1	3 731.3	1 424.1	2 307.2	21 438.0
4th quarter	21 694.5	14 653.9	3 801.9	2 952.6	828.8	20.6	-532.4	2 508.7	3 041.1	3 771.0	1 441.7	2 329.2	21 673.9
2020													
1st quarter	21 481.4	14 439.1	3 752.4	2 900.1	872.9	-20.6	-541.7	2 385.5	2 927.3	3 831.6	1 454.7	2 376.9	21 502.0
2nd quarter	19 477.4	12 989.7	3 167.0	2 659.1	797.8	-289.9	-538.9	1 807.9	2 346.7	3 859.6	1 525.0	2 334.6	19 767.4
3rd quarter	21 138.6	14 293.8	3 708.8	2 776.6	917.2	15.0	-725.7	2 079.6	2 805.3	3 861.7	1 515.1	2 346.5	21 123.6
4th quarter	21 477.6	14 467.6	3 923.2	2 862.7	1 003.2	57.3	-798.4	2 220.7	3 019.1	3 885.3	1 512.3	2 373.0	21 420.3
2021													
1st quarter	22 038.2	15 005.4	3 928.0	2 956.7	1 065.5	-94.2	-872.5	2 311.9	3 184.5	3 977.3	1 568.6	2 408.7	22 132.5
2nd quarter	22 741.0	15 681.7	3 925.1	3 029.2	1 070.2	-174.3	-881.7	2 461.5	3 343.2	4 015.9	1 563.3	2 452.6	22 915.3
3rd quarter	23 202.3	15 964.9	4 099.6	3 073.9	1 085.9	-60.2	-947.0	2 485.2	3 432.3	4 084.9	1 562.0	2 522.9	23 262.5
4th quarter	24 002.8	16 314.2	4 527.2	3 154.9	1 122.9	249.3	-971.4	2 654.5	3 625.9	4 132.9	1 566.2	2 566.7	23 753.5

Table 1-1B. Gross Domestic Product: Historical Data

(Billions of dollars, quarterly data are at seasonally adjusted annual rates.)

NIPA Tables 1.1.5, 1.2.5

Year and quarter	Gross domestic product	Personal consumption expenditures	Gross private domestic investment Total	Fixed investment Nonresidential	Fixed investment Residential	Change in private inventories	Net exports	Exports	Imports	Government Total	Government Federal	Government State and local	Addendum: Final sales of domestic product
1929	104.6	77.4	17.2	11.6	4.1	1.5	0.4	5.9	5.6	9.6	1.9	7.7	103.0
1930	92.2	70.1	11.4	9.2	2.5	-0.2	0.3	4.4	4.1	10.3	2.0	8.3	92.4
1931	77.4	60.7	6.5	5.8	1.9	-1.1	0.0	2.9	2.9	10.2	2.1	8.1	78.5
1932	59.5	48.7	1.8	3.3	0.9	-2.4	0.0	2.0	1.9	8.9	2.0	6.9	61.9
1933	57.2	45.9	2.3	3.0	0.7	-1.4	0.1	2.0	1.9	8.9	2.5	6.4	58.6
1934	66.8	51.5	4.3	3.8	1.0	-0.6	0.3	2.6	2.2	10.7	3.5	7.3	67.4
1935	74.2	55.9	7.4	4.8	1.4	1.1	-0.2	2.8	3.0	11.2	3.6	7.6	73.1
1936	84.8	62.2	9.4	6.4	1.8	1.2	-0.1	3.0	3.2	13.4	5.8	7.6	83.7
1937	93.0	66.8	13.0	8.2	2.2	2.6	0.1	4.0	4.0	13.1	5.3	7.8	90.4
1938	87.4	64.3	7.9	6.3	2.2	-0.6	1.0	3.8	2.8	14.2	5.9	8.3	87.9
1939	93.4	67.2	10.2	6.9	3.2	0.2	0.8	4.0	3.1	15.2	6.2	8.9	93.2
1940	102.9	71.3	14.6	8.5	3.6	2.4	1.5	4.9	3.4	15.6	6.8	8.7	100.5
1941	129.3	81.1	19.4	10.8	4.2	4.3	1.0	5.5	4.4	27.8	19.1	8.7	125.0
1942	166.0	89.0	11.8	7.5	2.4	1.9	-0.3	4.4	4.6	65.4	56.7	8.7	164.0
1943	203.1	99.9	7.4	6.6	1.6	-0.7	-2.2	4.0	6.3	98.0	89.5	8.5	203.8
1944	224.4	108.6	9.2	8.6	1.5	-0.9	-2.0	4.9	6.9	108.6	100.1	8.6	225.4
1945	228.0	120.0	12.4	12.1	1.8	-1.5	-0.8	6.8	7.5	96.4	87.2	9.2	229.5
1946	227.5	144.2	33.1	19.2	8.0	6.0	7.2	14.2	7.0	43.0	32.0	11.0	221.5
1947	249.6	161.9	37.1	25.5	12.2	-0.6	10.8	18.7	7.9	39.8	25.7	14.1	250.2
1948	274.5	174.9	50.3	28.9	15.8	5.7	5.5	15.5	10.1	43.8	27.0	16.7	268.8
1949	272.5	178.3	39.1	27.0	14.8	-2.7	5.2	14.5	9.2	49.8	30.4	19.4	275.2
1947													
1st quarter	243.2	156.2	35.9	24.8	10.5	0.5	10.9	18.4	7.5	40.3	27.0	13.3	242.7
2nd quarter	246.0	160.0	34.5	25.2	10.6	-1.2	11.3	19.5	8.2	40.1	26.4	13.7	247.2
3rd quarter	249.6	163.5	34.9	25.4	12.5	-2.9	11.8	19.4	7.7	39.4	25.0	14.3	252.5
4th quarter	259.7	167.7	43.3	26.5	15.3	1.5	9.3	17.6	8.3	39.5	24.5	15.0	258.3
1948													
1st quarter	265.7	170.4	47.2	28.2	15.3	3.6	7.3	16.9	9.6	40.9	25.4	15.5	262.1
2nd quarter	272.6	174.1	50.3	28.1	16.4	5.9	5.2	15.2	10.0	42.9	26.6	16.3	266.7
3rd quarter	279.2	177.1	52.5	29.1	16.3	7.2	4.9	15.4	10.5	44.7	27.5	17.2	272.0
4th quarter	280.4	177.9	51.3	30.2	15.2	6.0	4.5	14.6	10.1	46.6	28.7	17.9	274.4
1949													
1st quarter	275.0	176.8	43.1	28.6	14.2	0.4	6.5	16.1	9.6	48.6	30.2	18.4	274.6
2nd quarter	271.4	178.4	36.2	27.5	13.9	-5.1	6.3	15.6	9.4	50.4	31.2	19.1	276.5
3rd quarter	272.9	177.8	39.5	26.1	14.7	-1.3	5.2	14.1	8.9	50.4	30.5	19.9	274.2
4th quarter	270.6	180.2	37.5	25.6	16.5	-4.7	3.0	12.1	9.1	49.9	29.8	20.1	275.3
1950													
1st quarter	280.8	182.9	46.7	26.4	18.3	2.0	2.2	11.7	9.5	49.0	28.5	20.4	278.8
2nd quarter	290.4	186.8	52.3	28.9	20.6	2.8	1.6	11.9	10.2	49.6	28.9	20.7	287.6
3rd quarter	308.2	200.5	58.6	31.9	22.6	4.2	-0.7	12.3	13.0	49.7	28.4	21.3	304.0
4th quarter	319.9	197.9	68.4	32.9	21.5	14.0	-0.2	13.5	13.7	53.7	31.8	21.9	305.9
1951													
1st quarter	336.0	209.2	64.6	33.1	21.1	10.4	0.2	15.0	14.9	62.0	39.6	22.5	325.6
2nd quarter	344.1	204.9	67.4	34.1	18.5	14.8	1.9	17.1	15.2	69.8	46.6	23.2	329.3
3rd quarter	351.4	207.6	62.0	34.8	17.4	9.7	3.7	18.1	14.3	78.0	54.3	23.7	341.6
4th quarter	356.2	211.6	57.1	34.6	17.7	4.7	4.2	18.2	14.0	83.3	59.3	24.0	351.5
1952													
1st quarter	359.8	213.0	58.1	35.1	18.3	4.7	3.7	18.7	15.0	85.0	60.9	24.1	355.1
2nd quarter	361.0	217.1	53.0	35.8	18.8	-1.5	2.0	16.6	14.6	89.0	64.1	24.9	362.6
3rd quarter	367.7	219.6	57.2	32.9	18.8	5.6	0.0	15.2	15.3	90.9	66.2	24.8	362.1
4th quarter	380.8	227.7	60.7	35.8	19.6	5.3	-1.0	15.3	16.3	93.4	68.1	25.3	375.5
1953													
1st quarter	388.0	231.2	61.7	37.8	20.0	3.9	-0.7	15.1	15.8	95.8	69.7	26.1	384.1
2nd quarter	391.7	233.0	62.1	38.5	20.1	3.6	-1.3	15.2	16.4	97.9	72.0	26.0	388.2
3rd quarter	391.2	233.7	61.4	39.6	19.5	2.3	-0.6	15.8	16.3	96.6	70.0	26.7	388.8
4th quarter	386.0	233.1	56.4	39.2	19.3	-2.0	-0.3	15.2	15.5	96.7	69.5	27.2	388.0
1954													
1st quarter	385.3	235.2	55.7	38.3	19.4	-2.0	-0.4	14.4	14.8	94.8	66.7	28.1	387.3
2nd quarter	386.1	237.9	55.4	38.2	20.7	-3.4	0.3	16.4	16.2	92.5	63.7	28.8	389.5
3rd quarter	391.0	240.3	59.0	38.9	22.2	-2.1	0.6	15.9	15.3	91.1	61.4	29.8	393.1
4th quarter	399.7	245.1	62.1	38.9	23.6	-0.3	1.1	16.6	15.5	91.4	61.2	30.1	400.1
1955													
1st quarter	413.1	251.4	68.7	39.5	25.4	3.8	1.1	17.3	16.2	91.9	60.7	31.1	409.3
2nd quarter	421.5	256.5	72.7	42.1	26.0	4.6	-0.2	16.9	17.1	92.5	60.8	31.7	416.9
3rd quarter	430.2	260.7	74.7	44.8	25.6	4.3	0.7	18.1	17.4	94.1	61.9	32.2	425.9
4th quarter	437.1	264.6	78.9	47.1	24.6	7.2	0.2	18.3	18.1	93.3	60.6	32.8	429.9
1956													
1st quarter	439.7	266.2	78.3	47.8	24.1	6.4	0.4	19.4	18.9	94.8	61.0	33.9	433.3
2nd quarter	446.0	268.8	77.0	49.1	24.4	3.6	1.9	20.9	19.0	98.2	63.5	34.7	442.4
3rd quarter	451.2	272.1	78.3	50.7	24.0	3.6	2.6	21.8	19.3	98.3	62.8	35.5	447.6
4th quarter	460.5	277.4	77.1	51.4	23.5	2.2	4.5	23.1	18.5	101.3	65.2	36.2	458.2
1957													
1st quarter	469.8	281.9	77.7	52.5	23.1	2.2	4.8	24.9	20.1	105.3	67.9	37.5	467.6
2nd quarter	472.0	284.2	77.9	52.6	22.6	2.7	4.1	24.4	20.3	105.8	67.5	38.3	469.4
3rd quarter	479.5	288.8	79.3	54.1	22.5	2.8	4.0	23.8	19.8	107.4	68.4	39.1	476.7
4th quarter	474.9	290.4	71.0	53.2	22.3	-4.5	3.4	23.0	19.6	110.1	70.0	40.0	479.4
1958													
1st quarter	467.5	289.9	66.7	49.4	21.4	-4.0	1.1	20.5	19.5	109.8	68.7	41.1	471.5
2nd quarter	472.0	292.8	65.1	47.8	21.5	-4.2	0.5	20.5	20.1	113.6	71.5	42.1	476.2
3rd quarter	485.8	297.9	72.0	47.4	23.0	1.5	0.9	20.6	19.7	115.1	71.9	43.2	484.3
4th quarter	499.6	301.8	80.0	49.3	25.4	5.2	-0.3	20.6	20.8	118.0	73.9	44.1	494.3

Table 1-1B. Gross Domestic Product: Historical Data—*Continued*

(Billions of dollars, quarterly data are at seasonally adjusted annual rates.)

NIPA Tables 1.1.5, 1.2.5

Year and quarter	Gross domestic product	Personal consump-tion expen-ditures	Gross private domestic investment				Exports and imports of goods and services			Government consumption expenditures and gross investment			Addendum: Final sales of domestic product
			Total	Fixed investment		Change in private inventories	Net exports	Exports	Imports	Total	Federal	State and local	
				Nonresi-dential	Residential								
1959													
1st quarter	510.3	309.4	83.2	50.9	28.3	3.9	0.5	21.9	21.4	117.2	72.4	44.8	506.5
2nd quarter	522.7	315.5	89.4	52.7	29.4	7.3	-0.8	21.8	22.5	118.5	73.6	45.0	515.4
3rd quarter	525.0	320.7	83.6	54.4	28.8	0.4	1.2	24.1	22.9	119.5	74.5	45.0	524.7
4th quarter	528.6	322.8	86.5	54.4	28.0	4.1	0.6	23.1	22.5	118.6	73.8	44.8	524.5
1960													
1st quarter	542.6	326.4	96.5	56.3	29.0	11.2	2.9	26.1	23.3	117.0	71.0	46.0	531.4
2nd quarter	541.1	332.2	87.1	57.2	26.7	3.2	3.4	26.9	23.5	118.4	71.1	47.3	537.9
3rd quarter	545.6	332.1	86.4	56.2	25.9	4.3	4.7	27.6	22.9	122.4	74.2	48.3	541.3
4th quarter	540.2	334.0	76.0	55.9	25.9	-5.8	5.9	27.6	21.7	124.3	75.3	49.0	546.0
1961													
1st quarter	545.0	334.5	78.4	55.0	25.9	-2.5	5.9	27.6	21.7	126.2	75.3	50.9	547.6
2nd quarter	555.5	339.5	84.1	56.2	26.1	1.8	4.7	26.6	21.9	127.3	76.2	51.1	553.8
3rd quarter	567.7	342.3	90.9	56.7	27.6	6.7	4.5	27.8	23.3	130.0	78.1	51.8	561.0
4th quarter	580.6	349.6	92.9	58.5	28.5	6.0	4.6	28.4	23.9	133.5	79.9	53.6	574.6
1962													
1st quarter	594.0	354.8	98.1	59.7	29.0	9.4	4.0	28.3	24.3	137.1	83.3	53.8	584.6
2nd quarter	600.4	360.5	96.7	61.4	29.9	5.4	4.8	29.7	24.9	138.4	84.1	54.3	594.9
3rd quarter	609.0	364.3	98.2	62.1	29.9	6.2	4.5	29.6	25.1	142.1	87.0	55.0	602.8
4th quarter	612.3	370.6	95.0	61.8	29.8	3.4	3.1	28.7	25.6	143.6	87.6	56.0	608.9
1963													
1st quarter	621.7	374.3	99.7	62.0	30.8	6.9	4.0	29.2	25.2	143.7	86.2	57.5	614.8
2nd quarter	629.8	378.4	101.7	63.9	32.9	4.8	5.6	31.4	25.9	144.1	85.8	58.4	624.9
3rd quarter	644.4	385.4	104.6	65.7	33.2	5.7	4.5	31.2	26.7	149.9	89.9	60.1	638.7
4th quarter	653.9	390.0	107.2	67.7	34.5	5.1	5.7	32.5	26.8	151.0	89.7	61.3	648.9
1964													
1st quarter	669.8	399.6	110.5	69.1	36.2	5.1	7.2	34.2	27.0	152.6	90.1	62.5	664.7
2nd quarter	678.7	407.5	110.5	71.1	35.0	4.5	6.3	34.0	27.7	154.3	90.1	64.2	674.2
3rd quarter	692.0	416.4	112.6	73.4	34.5	4.7	6.9	35.4	28.4	156.0	90.8	65.2	687.3
4th quarter	697.3	419.0	115.0	75.3	34.6	5.0	7.2	36.5	29.3	156.2	90.0	66.2	692.3
1965													
1st quarter	717.8	429.7	126.5	80.2	34.8	11.5	4.5	33.0	28.5	157.0	89.5	67.5	706.2
2nd quarter	730.2	436.6	127.1	83.4	35.1	8.6	6.7	38.4	31.7	159.8	90.1	69.7	721.6
3rd quarter	749.3	445.8	131.2	86.7	35.3	9.3	5.5	37.6	32.0	166.8	94.5	72.3	740.0
4th quarter	771.9	459.7	133.8	90.6	35.5	7.6	5.8	39.7	33.9	172.6	98.7	73.9	764.3
1966													
1st quarter	795.7	470.1	144.2	94.4	35.9	13.9	4.4	39.4	35.0	177.0	101.2	75.8	781.9
2nd quarter	805.0	475.2	143.5	96.8	34.4	12.3	4.6	40.9	36.2	181.7	104.0	77.6	792.7
3rd quarter	819.6	484.3	143.2	98.3	33.0	11.9	2.7	40.9	38.2	189.5	109.9	79.5	807.8
4th quarter	833.3	490.1	145.9	99.2	30.2	16.5	3.8	42.6	38.8	193.6	111.2	82.5	816.8
1967													
1st quarter	844.2	494.3	142.8	98.0	29.4	15.4	4.5	43.9	39.4	202.6	117.9	84.7	828.7
2nd quarter	849.0	503.5	137.5	98.3	32.9	6.3	4.2	43.2	39.0	203.8	117.9	85.9	842.6
3rd quarter	865.2	510.7	142.8	98.8	34.8	9.3	3.3	42.8	39.5	208.4	121.0	87.4	856.0
4th quarter	881.4	518.2	147.7	101.7	37.5	8.4	2.2	43.9	41.7	213.3	123.2	90.1	873.0
1968													
1st quarter	909.4	536.3	152.3	105.6	38.3	8.4	1.1	45.5	44.4	219.7	126.4	93.3	900.9
2nd quarter	934.3	550.0	158.9	105.3	39.6	14.1	1.7	47.2	45.4	223.6	127.2	96.5	920.3
3rd quarter	950.8	566.1	155.7	107.6	40.4	7.7	1.7	49.9	48.2	227.4	128.5	98.8	943.1
4th quarter	968.0	575.0	160.8	112.2	42.6	6.0	0.9	49.1	48.2	231.3	129.7	101.6	962.0
1969													
1st quarter	993.3	587.0	172.4	116.0	44.9	11.5	0.2	44.0	43.8	233.7	129.6	104.1	981.8
2nd quarter	1 009.0	598.3	172.7	118.4	45.1	9.2	1.1	53.8	52.7	236.9	129.8	107.1	999.8
3rd quarter	1 030.0	608.6	177.6	122.4	45.0	10.2	1.2	53.6	52.4	242.5	133.4	109.1	1 019.8
4th quarter	1 038.1	620.6	171.6	123.3	42.5	5.8	3.1	56.3	53.1	242.8	132.0	110.8	1 032.4
1970													
1st quarter	1 051.2	631.7	168.1	123.8	42.5	1.8	3.5	57.0	53.5	247.9	133.6	114.3	1 049.4
2nd quarter	1 067.4	641.6	171.5	125.0	41.4	5.1	5.2	60.4	55.2	249.1	131.8	117.4	1 062.3
3rd quarter	1 086.1	653.5	173.9	126.3	42.6	5.1	4.1	60.5	56.4	254.6	132.4	122.2	1 081.0
4th quarter	1 088.6	660.2	166.8	123.5	47.2	-4.0	3.0	60.9	57.9	258.7	133.5	125.2	1 092.6
1971													
1st quarter	1 135.2	679.2	189.5	126.3	51.0	12.3	4.6	63.2	58.7	261.9	133.3	128.6	1 122.9
2nd quarter	1 156.3	693.2	197.3	129.5	57.0	10.9	-0.4	62.9	63.3	266.1	134.3	131.9	1 145.4
3rd quarter	1 177.7	705.6	202.1	131.2	60.7	10.2	0.2	65.7	65.5	269.8	135.6	134.2	1 167.5
4th quarter	1 190.3	721.7	198.4	134.7	64.0	-0.3	-1.9	60.0	61.9	272.1	134.7	137.4	1 190.6
1972													
1st quarter	1 230.6	738.9	213.0	140.6	69.2	3.2	-3.5	68.6	72.2	282.2	141.4	140.8	1 227.4
2nd quarter	1 266.4	757.4	226.8	144.0	70.8	12.0	-4.3	67.2	71.4	286.5	144.2	142.2	1 254.4
3rd quarter	1 290.6	775.8	233.1	147.0	72.4	13.7	-2.6	71.5	74.1	284.3	138.8	145.6	1 276.9
4th quarter	1 328.9	800.5	239.7	155.0	77.3	7.5	-3.1	76.1	79.2	291.7	142.2	149.6	1 321.4
1973													
1st quarter	1 377.5	825.0	254.3	162.8	80.9	10.6	-1.4	84.0	85.4	299.6	146.4	153.2	1 366.9
2nd quarter	1 413.9	840.5	268.2	171.3	78.7	18.2	2.5	91.9	89.5	302.7	146.5	156.2	1 395.7
3rd quarter	1 433.8	858.9	264.3	176.6	77.9	9.8	6.4	97.6	91.1	304.2	144.2	159.9	1 424.1
4th quarter	1 476.3	873.9	280.9	180.1	75.7	25.0	9.0	107.6	98.7	312.6	147.6	165.0	1 451.3
1974													
1st quarter	1 491.2	891.9	268.4	183.4	72.4	12.5	6.4	116.7	110.3	324.6	152.7	171.9	1 478.7
2nd quarter	1 530.1	920.4	277.4	188.8	71.2	17.4	-2.7	126.7	129.4	335.0	154.9	180.1	1 512.6
3rd quarter	1 560.0	949.3	271.0	194.5	70.9	5.6	-7.0	126.6	133.6	346.7	160.4	186.3	1 554.4
4th quarter	1 599.7	959.1	281.3	197.6	63.3	20.4	0.0	136.6	136.6	359.2	167.4	191.9	1 579.2

Table 1-1B. Gross Domestic Product: Historical Data—*Continued*

(Billions of dollars, quarterly data are at seasonally adjusted annual rates.) NIPA Tables 1.1.5, 1.2.5

Year and quarter	Gross domestic product	Personal consumption expenditures	Gross private domestic investment — Total	Fixed investment — Nonresidential	Fixed investment — Residential	Change in private inventories	Net exports	Exports	Imports	Government — Total	Government — Federal	Government — State and local	Addendum: Final sales of domestic product
1975													
1st quarter	1 616.1	985.2	244.3	193.1	61.2	-10.0	16.5	141.4	124.9	370.1	168.6	201.5	1 626.1
2nd quarter	1 651.9	1 013.6	243.3	193.3	64.0	-14.0	21.6	136.8	115.2	373.4	169.4	204.0	1 665.8
3rd quarter	1 709.8	1 047.2	265.2	197.8	68.8	-1.4	12.0	134.1	122.1	385.4	176.1	209.3	1 711.2
4th quarter	1 761.8	1 076.2	276.2	202.9	73.0	0.3	13.8	142.5	128.7	395.6	180.8	214.8	1 761.5
1976													
1st quarter	1 820.5	1 109.9	304.6	209.5	80.4	14.7	4.7	143.6	138.9	401.3	181.6	219.7	1 805.8
2nd quarter	1 852.3	1 129.5	322.3	215.0	84.8	22.4	-0.5	146.6	147.1	401.0	182.5	218.5	1 829.9
3rd quarter	1 886.6	1 158.8	328.3	222.6	84.9	20.8	-4.1	151.8	155.8	403.5	184.9	218.6	1 865.8
4th quarter	1 934.3	1 192.4	337.7	230.2	96.9	10.5	-6.6	156.1	162.7	410.8	190.2	220.6	1 923.8
1977													
1st quarter	1 988.6	1 228.2	360.3	243.3	102.2	14.8	-21.1	155.4	176.4	421.2	194.2	227.0	1 973.8
2nd quarter	2 055.9	1 256.0	389.7	253.7	116.5	19.5	-21.1	161.9	183.0	431.4	198.9	232.4	2 036.4
3rd quarter	2 118.5	1 286.9	414.1	263.3	120.0	30.9	-20.6	162.3	182.9	438.0	201.9	236.1	2 087.6
4th quarter	2 164.3	1 324.8	422.3	275.9	122.2	24.1	-29.6	157.8	187.4	446.7	206.3	240.5	2 140.1
1978													
1st quarter	2 202.8	1 354.1	434.8	282.4	126.9	25.5	-38.7	164.6	203.3	452.6	208.8	243.8	2 177.3
2nd quarter	2 331.6	1 411.4	470.6	309.4	137.0	24.3	-22.6	186.2	208.8	472.3	217.0	255.3	2 307.4
3rd quarter	2 395.1	1 442.2	492.4	325.1	142.3	25.0	-23.8	191.3	215.1	484.2	222.1	262.2	2 370.1
4th quarter	2 476.9	1 481.4	515.8	341.4	145.8	28.5	-16.4	205.4	221.8	496.2	227.8	268.4	2 448.5
1979													
1st quarter	2 526.6	1 517.1	525.8	356.7	145.3	23.9	-18.2	211.7	229.8	501.8	231.7	270.1	2 502.8
2nd quarter	2 591.2	1 557.6	539.3	364.3	147.6	27.4	-22.2	220.9	243.1	516.5	237.6	278.9	2 563.8
3rd quarter	2 667.6	1 611.9	545.6	383.0	150.5	12.1	-23.0	234.3	257.3	533.1	243.7	289.4	2 655.4
4th quarter	2 723.9	1 655.0	547.9	391.3	148.0	8.6	-26.8	253.7	280.5	547.8	249.3	298.4	2 715.3
1980													
1st quarter	2 789.8	1 702.3	554.6	404.5	140.2	9.9	-35.8	268.5	304.3	568.8	261.1	307.7	2 779.9
2nd quarter	2 797.4	1 704.7	519.3	394.7	116.9	7.8	-15.2	277.4	292.6	588.5	276.5	312.0	2 789.6
3rd quarter	2 856.5	1 763.8	495.1	405.7	123.2	-33.9	5.5	284.7	279.2	592.2	276.1	316.1	2 890.3
4th quarter	2 985.6	1 831.9	551.5	422.8	137.8	-9.1	-6.7	292.5	299.2	608.9	285.8	323.1	2 994.7
1981													
1st quarter	3 124.2	1 885.7	619.4	443.0	137.6	38.8	-14.3	305.5	319.7	633.4	297.2	336.1	3 085.5
2nd quarter	3 162.5	1 917.5	609.8	462.9	135.3	11.7	-13.5	308.5	322.0	648.7	311.9	336.8	3 150.8
3rd quarter	3 260.6	1 958.1	652.3	482.1	126.2	44.0	-7.6	302.3	309.9	657.8	317.4	340.3	3 216.7
4th quarter	3 280.8	1 974.4	643.4	503.8	114.8	24.8	-14.8	304.7	319.4	677.7	329.3	348.4	3 256.0
1982													
1st quarter	3 274.3	2 014.2	588.3	500.1	109.7	-21.5	-16.3	293.2	309.5	688.1	334.9	353.2	3 295.8
2nd quarter	3 332.0	2 039.6	593.6	490.1	107.7	-4.2	-4.4	294.7	299.1	703.1	342.9	360.2	3 336.1
3rd quarter	3 366.3	2 085.7	593.0	478.7	108.4	5.8	-29.6	279.6	309.3	717.3	351.5	365.8	3 360.5
4th quarter	3 402.6	2 145.6	549.2	471.5	117.5	-39.8	-29.6	265.3	294.9	737.4	364.1	373.3	3 442.4
1983													
1st quarter	3 473.4	2 184.6	565.5	462.1	138.5	-35.1	-24.5	270.7	295.3	747.9	370.5	377.4	3 508.5
2nd quarter	3 578.8	2 249.4	613.8	466.5	155.0	-7.7	-45.4	272.5	317.9	761.1	380.3	380.7	3 586.5
3rd quarter	3 689.2	2 319.9	652.3	485.4	171.1	-4.2	-65.2	278.2	343.4	782.2	394.4	387.8	3 693.4
4th quarter	3 794.7	2 372.5	718.5	514.7	179.9	23.9	-71.4	286.6	358.0	775.1	384.2	390.9	3 770.8
1984													
1st quarter	3 908.1	2 418.2	790.9	531.5	186.4	73.0	-95.0	293.0	388.0	794.0	392.4	401.6	3 835.1
2nd quarter	4 009.6	2 475.9	818.9	558.3	191.3	69.3	-104.3	302.2	406.5	819.1	408.3	410.8	3 940.3
3rd quarter	4 084.3	2 513.5	838.9	576.6	190.9	71.3	-103.8	305.7	409.6	835.7	414.0	421.7	4 012.9
4th quarter	4 148.6	2 561.8	831.7	590.9	192.9	48.0	-107.8	308.6	416.4	862.8	432.5	430.2	4 100.6
1985													
1st quarter	4 230.2	2 636.0	809.9	599.4	194.2	16.2	-91.3	306.0	397.3	875.6	434.8	440.8	4 213.9
2nd quarter	4 294.9	2 681.8	827.0	609.1	196.3	21.6	-114.4	304.1	418.6	900.5	447.3	453.2	4 273.2
3rd quarter	4 386.8	2 754.1	822.2	604.4	201.4	16.3	-116.9	297.3	414.2	927.4	463.1	464.3	4 370.5
4th quarter	4 444.1	2 779.4	859.5	618.1	208.4	33.1	-133.4	305.4	438.9	938.6	466.4	472.1	4 411.0
1986													
1st quarter	4 507.9	2 823.6	863.5	613.5	219.5	30.4	-126.0	313.4	439.4	946.8	464.0	482.8	4 477.5
2nd quarter	4 545.3	2 851.5	855.2	605.0	234.6	15.7	-128.9	315.1	444.0	967.5	477.8	489.7	4 529.7
3rd quarter	4 607.7	2 917.2	835.8	602.0	240.9	-7.0	-139.0	320.5	459.4	993.6	495.1	498.5	4 614.7
4th quarter	4 657.6	2 952.8	842.1	610.6	244.3	-12.8	-133.6	335.0	468.6	996.4	489.8	506.6	4 670.4
1987													
1st quarter	4 722.2	2 983.5	871.2	596.6	246.7	28.0	-141.2	336.5	477.7	1 008.7	492.1	516.5	4 694.2
2nd quarter	4 806.2	3 053.3	874.6	608.4	249.7	16.5	-147.0	355.4	502.3	1 025.2	501.2	524.0	4 789.6
3rd quarter	4 884.6	3 117.4	876.5	625.5	250.0	1.0	-145.5	371.9	517.3	1 036.2	504.1	532.1	4 883.5
4th quarter	5 008.0	3 150.9	946.5	630.6	252.8	63.1	-145.4	392.1	537.5	1 056.0	513.7	542.3	4 944.9
1988													
1st quarter	5 073.4	3 231.9	908.6	641.5	250.1	17.0	-124.0	418.7	542.7	1 056.9	505.8	551.1	5 056.4
2nd quarter	5 190.0	3 291.7	934.5	659.4	255.5	19.6	-106.6	439.5	546.1	1 070.4	506.9	563.5	5 170.4
3rd quarter	5 282.8	3 361.9	942.0	666.3	257.5	18.2	-99.3	453.6	552.8	1 078.2	507.4	570.8	5 264.7
4th quarter	5 399.5	3 434.5	962.7	681.9	261.7	19.1	-107.7	466.6	574.3	1 109.9	525.6	584.3	5 380.4
1989													
1st quarter	5 511.3	3 490.2	1 005.5	696.5	260.9	48.1	-101.0	485.2	586.2	1 116.6	519.9	596.7	5 463.1
2nd quarter	5 612.5	3 553.8	1 001.0	709.0	255.8	36.3	-88.2	507.2	595.4	1 145.8	534.3	611.5	5 576.2
3rd quarter	5 695.4	3 609.4	996.5	731.1	255.5	9.8	-75.1	509.4	584.4	1 164.6	541.4	623.2	5 685.5
4th quarter	5 747.2	3 653.7	995.8	727.4	251.9	16.6	-82.8	515.4	598.2	1 180.5	540.8	639.7	5 730.7
1990													
1st quarter	5 872.7	3 737.9	1 010.8	740.9	256.0	14.0	-88.5	538.2	626.8	1 212.5	553.7	658.8	5 858.7
2nd quarter	5 960.0	3 783.4	1 014.7	734.1	246.9	33.7	-68.8	545.9	614.8	1 230.7	563.9	666.8	5 926.3
3rd quarter	6 015.1	3 846.7	1 000.8	744.4	234.5	21.9	-75.0	555.1	630.1	1 242.6	562.2	680.3	5 993.3
4th quarter	6 004.7	3 867.9	947.5	737.5	221.3	-11.3	-79.1	568.2	647.3	1 268.5	569.7	698.8	6 016.1

Table 1-1B. Gross Domestic Product: Historical Data—*Continued*

(Billions of dollars, quarterly data are at seasonally adjusted annual rates.)   **NIPA Tables 1.1.5, 1.2.5**

| Year and quarter | Gross domestic product | Personal consumption expenditures | Gross private domestic investment | | | | Exports and imports of goods and services | | | Government consumption expenditures and gross investment | | | Addendum: Final sales of domestic product |
| | | | Total | Fixed investment | | Change in private inventories | Net exports | Exports | Imports | Total | Federal | State and local | |
				Nonresidential	Residential								
1991													
1st quarter	6 035.2	3 873.6	924.6	729.8	210.3	-15.5	-47.1	573.2	620.3	1 284.2	581.4	702.8	6 050.7
2nd quarter	6 126.9	3 926.9	926.5	726.8	217.8	-18.0	-23.2	590.7	613.9	1 296.6	586.6	709.9	6 144.9
3rd quarter	6 205.9	3 973.3	947.5	720.2	226.5	0.8	-21.1	600.6	621.7	1 306.3	586.3	719.9	6 205.1
4th quarter	6 264.5	4 000.0	978.8	717.6	230.1	31.1	-23.1	615.2	638.3	1 308.8	577.4	731.4	6 233.4
1992													
1st quarter	6 363.1	4 100.4	956.8	714.2	242.4	0.2	-20.5	625.3	645.8	1 326.4	580.3	746.1	6 362.9
2nd quarter	6 470.8	4 155.7	1 013.1	736.7	253.2	23.2	-32.8	626.2	659.0	1 334.8	580.9	753.9	6 447.6
3rd quarter	6 566.6	4 227.0	1 024.2	748.5	255.1	20.5	-38.5	639.4	677.9	1 354.0	594.2	759.8	6 546.1
4th quarter	6 680.8	4 307.2	1 058.0	768.3	268.3	21.3	-47.1	641.4	688.5	1 362.8	598.4	764.4	6 659.5
1993													
1st quarter	6 729.5	4 349.5	1 083.8	776.5	271.4	35.9	-55.7	643.6	699.3	1 351.8	580.3	771.5	6 693.5
2nd quarter	6 808.9	4 418.6	1 094.5	792.4	278.0	24.1	-63.2	653.1	716.3	1 359.1	576.7	782.3	6 784.8
3rd quarter	6 882.1	4 487.2	1 095.9	798.3	290.9	6.6	-68.4	650.9	719.3	1 367.4	578.7	788.7	6 875.5
4th quarter	7 013.7	4 552.7	1 153.1	829.6	306.9	16.6	-73.4	671.6	745.0	1 381.4	584.9	796.5	6 997.1
1994													
1st quarter	7 115.7	4 621.2	1 201.7	840.7	315.6	45.4	-80.6	681.2	761.8	1 373.4	567.0	806.3	7 070.3
2nd quarter	7 246.9	4 683.2	1 264.9	855.6	327.9	81.4	-90.6	707.0	797.6	1 389.4	569.4	820.0	7 165.5
3rd quarter	7 331.1	4 752.8	1 251.7	872.1	326.4	53.2	-96.9	736.9	833.8	1 423.4	586.5	836.9	7 277.9
4th quarter	7 455.3	4 826.7	1 307.6	907.0	325.4	75.1	-101.9	758.6	860.6	1 422.9	575.8	847.1	7 380.1
1995													
1st quarter	7 522.3	4 862.4	1 327.6	944.6	321.8	61.2	-105.3	781.6	886.9	1 437.6	579.1	858.5	7 461.1
2nd quarter	7 581.0	4 933.6	1 304.0	956.8	313.5	33.8	-109.5	798.9	908.3	1 452.9	581.0	871.9	7 547.2
3rd quarter	7 683.1	4 998.7	1 303.2	965.5	326.4	11.3	-74.4	831.4	905.8	1 455.7	579.3	876.3	7 671.8
4th quarter	7 772.6	5 055.7	1 335.1	982.1	334.6	18.4	-69.8	839.4	909.2	1 451.6	567.3	884.3	7 754.2
1996													
1st quarter	7 868.5	5 130.6	1 355.4	1 003.7	344.7	6.9	-88.8	847.9	936.7	1 471.3	579.8	891.5	7 861.6
2nd quarter	8 032.8	5 220.5	1 418.4	1 026.5	361.4	30.5	-93.7	859.0	952.8	1 487.7	582.1	905.5	8 002.3
3rd quarter	8 131.4	5 274.5	1 474.4	1 059.0	364.3	51.1	-114.2	859.6	973.8	1 496.7	577.8	919.0	8 080.3
4th quarter	8 259.8	5 352.8	1 480.1	1 083.6	361.8	34.7	-88.8	903.8	992.6	1 515.7	576.9	938.8	8 225.0
1997													
1st quarter	8 362.7	5 433.1	1 522.4	1 107.3	365.4	49.7	-108.8	918.4	1 027.2	1 516.0	570.7	945.3	8 312.9
2nd quarter	8 518.8	5 471.3	1 590.2	1 129.6	372.3	88.4	-85.2	954.5	1 039.7	1 542.5	587.2	955.4	8 430.5
3rd quarter	8 662.8	5 579.2	1 625.3	1 178.4	379.0	67.9	-96.8	974.1	1 070.9	1 555.2	586.0	969.2	8 594.9
4th quarter	8 765.9	5 663.6	1 644.5	1 181.1	385.8	77.7	-117.0	968.3	1 085.3	1 574.8	589.2	985.6	8 688.3
1998													
1st quarter	8 866.5	5 721.3	1 712.3	1 212.4	394.8	105.1	-135.2	963.0	1 098.2	1 568.0	572.2	995.9	8 761.4
2nd quarter	8 969.7	5 832.6	1 695.8	1 247.1	411.3	37.3	-162.3	947.3	1 109.6	1 603.7	587.1	1 016.6	8 932.4
3rd quarter	9 121.1	5 926.8	1 741.6	1 261.7	427.6	52.4	-174.6	935.3	1 109.9	1 627.3	588.6	1 038.6	9 068.7
4th quarter	9 294.0	6 028.2	1 797.0	1 295.4	441.5	60.0	-178.7	966.3	1 145.0	1 647.5	594.2	1 053.2	9 234.0
1999													
1st quarter	9 411.7	6 102.0	1 853.1	1 322.3	447.4	83.4	-212.6	960.8	1 173.3	1 669.1	595.1	1 074.0	9 328.3
2nd quarter	9 526.2	6 230.6	1 848.3	1 354.0	459.3	35.1	-247.5	974.6	1 222.1	1 694.8	599.2	1 095.5	9 491.1
3rd quarter	9 686.6	6 335.3	1 893.7	1 386.6	466.6	40.5	-276.4	1 005.3	1 281.7	1 734.0	614.2	1 119.8	9 646.1
4th quarter	9 900.2	6 467.0	1 953.1	1 395.0	473.8	84.2	-301.7	1 031.0	1 332.7	1 781.7	634.3	1 147.4	9 815.9
2000													
1st quarter	10 002.2	6 618.2	1 950.7	1 450.3	484.2	16.2	-356.6	1 052.9	1 409.5	1 789.9	619.4	1 170.5	9 986.0
2nd quarter	10 247.7	6 711.9	2 075.8	1 498.7	486.6	90.4	-362.5	1 093.4	1 455.9	1 822.5	641.2	1 181.3	10 157.3
3rd quarter	10 318.2	6 820.0	2 060.0	1 519.7	483.1	57.2	-393.9	1 125.0	1 518.9	1 832.1	633.6	1 198.5	10 260.9
4th quarter	10 435.7	6 918.6	2 067.2	1 525.1	487.8	54.3	-411.3	1 113.2	1 524.5	1 861.3	638.2	1 223.1	10 381.4
2001													
1st quarter	10 470.2	6 995.3	1 971.3	1 505.2	496.7	-30.6	-402.7	1 096.8	1 499.5	1 906.3	653.3	1 253.0	10 500.9
2nd quarter	10 599.0	7 042.3	1 973.0	1 473.6	511.0	-11.6	-364.0	1 058.0	1 422.0	1 947.7	666.2	1 281.5	10 610.6
3rd quarter	10 598.0	7 070.3	1 944.9	1 452.6	522.4	-30.1	-370.6	998.9	1 369.5	1 953.4	674.4	1 279.0	10 628.1
4th quarter	10 660.5	7 187.3	1 850.1	1 408.9	522.1	-80.8	-369.7	953.5	1 323.2	1 992.7	686.9	1 305.9	10 741.3
2002													
1st quarter	10 783.5	7 217.7	1 912.7	1 374.0	538.3	0.3	-386.9	969.2	1 356.0	2 040.0	714.0	1 326.0	10 783.2
2nd quarter	10 887.5	7 308.0	1 933.3	1 357.3	554.8	21.2	-428.3	1 004.2	1 432.4	2 074.5	734.8	1 339.7	10 866.3
3rd quarter	10 984.0	7 397.1	1 933.2	1 348.9	558.9	25.4	-447.5	1 015.6	1 463.1	2 101.3	748.4	1 352.9	10 958.6
4th quarter	11 061.4	7 473.0	1 942.5	1 331.2	578.3	33.0	-496.3	1 003.0	1 499.3	2 142.2	775.2	1 367.0	11 028.4
2003													
1st quarter	11 174.1	7 567.2	1 960.2	1 332.7	601.4	26.1	-525.3	1 004.2	1 529.5	2 172.0	792.7	1 379.3	11 148.0
2nd quarter	11 312.8	7 661.5	1 972.4	1 366.8	612.0	-6.5	-519.9	1 007.5	1 527.3	2 198.8	826.0	1 372.8	11 319.3
3rd quarter	11 566.7	7 820.9	2 044.3	1 392.1	651.7	0.4	-519.0	1 037.3	1 556.3	2 220.4	833.3	1 387.2	11 566.2
4th quarter	11 772.2	7 913.5	2 131.3	1 411.9	683.1	36.3	-523.7	1 091.7	1 615.4	2 251.2	855.1	1 396.0	11 735.9
2004													
1st quarter	11 923.4	8 048.8	2 154.1	1 401.8	706.2	46.0	-566.0	1 133.7	1 699.6	2 286.6	871.8	1 414.8	11 877.4
2nd quarter	12 112.8	8 147.1	2 262.6	1 445.5	743.2	74.0	-617.6	1 170.2	1 787.7	2 320.7	884.6	1 436.1	12 038.8
3rd quarter	12 305.3	8 283.3	2 318.3	1 490.5	763.6	64.2	-652.7	1 180.2	1 832.9	2 356.4	902.5	1 453.9	12 241.1
4th quarter	12 527.2	8 448.6	2 390.1	1 531.7	786.3	72.1	-700.3	1 221.4	1 921.8	2 388.8	909.6	1 479.2	12 455.1
2005													
1st quarter	12 767.3	8 551.7	2 486.1	1 568.3	815.3	102.5	-696.7	1 258.4	1 955.1	2 426.1	931.8	1 494.3	12 664.8
2nd quarter	12 922.7	8 701.1	2 476.5	1 603.8	843.8	28.8	-707.2	1 294.9	2 002.1	2 452.2	939.3	1 513.0	12 893.8
3rd quarter	13 142.6	8 868.1	2 531.1	1 643.1	875.6	12.4	-751.0	1 302.3	2 053.3	2 494.4	956.4	1 538.0	13 130.3
4th quarter	13 324.2	8 955.3	2 645.3	1 668.7	890.2	86.4	-804.8	1 350.7	2 155.5	2 528.4	963.7	1 564.8	13 237.8
2006													
1st quarter	13 599.2	9 100.2	2 709.7	1 735.3	896.2	78.2	-790.8	1 414.0	2 204.8	2 580.1	997.1	1 583.0	13 520.9
2nd quarter	13 753.4	9 227.6	2 709.3	1 774.4	859.3	75.5	-794.0	1 459.8	2 253.8	2 610.6	997.2	1 613.4	13 677.9
3rd quarter	13 870.2	9 353.8	2 709.4	1 815.9	814.7	78.8	-823.3	1 475.4	2 298.7	2 630.3	995.4	1 634.8	13 791.4
4th quarter	14 039.6	9 427.4	2 675.4	1 849.5	782.4	43.5	-737.7	1 531.5	2 269.2	2 674.5	1 015.1	1 659.4	13 996.1

Table 1-1B. Gross Domestic Product: Historical Data—*Continued*

(Billions of dollars, quarterly data are at seasonally adjusted annual rates.)

NIPA Tables 1.1.5, 1.2.5

Year and quarter	Gross domestic product	Personal consumption expenditures	Gross private domestic investment					Exports and imports of goods and services			Government consumption expenditures and gross investment			Addendum: Final sales of domestic product
			Total	Fixed investment			Change in private inventories	Net exports	Exports	Imports	Total	Federal	State and local	
				Nonresidential	Residential									
2007														
1st quarter	14 215.7	9 572.1	2 664.3	1 892.0	750.9	21.4	-739.3	1 578.0	2 317.3	2 718.5	1 017.5	1 700.9	14 194.3
2nd quarter	14 402.1	9 678.7	2 699.2	1 937.7	719.3	42.2	-745.8	1 622.8	2 368.6	2 770.0	1 042.5	1 727.5	14 359.9
3rd quarter	14 564.1	9 798.4	2 686.0	1 967.4	673.7	44.9	-729.0	1 685.7	2 414.7	2 808.7	1 058.8	1 749.9	14 519.2
4th quarter	14 715.1	9 937.1	2 642.6	1 997.1	618.2	27.3	-729.7	1 750.7	2 480.4	2 865.1	1 085.3	1 779.8	14 687.8
2008														
1st quarter	14 706.5	10 004.4	2 563.7	2 013.7	566.7	-16.7	-771.2	1 813.3	2 584.6	2 909.6	1 111.2	1 798.5	14 723.2
2nd quarter	14 865.7	10 129.9	2 540.6	2 024.0	538.8	-22.3	-776.4	1 905.3	2 681.7	2 971.6	1 146.6	1 825.0	14 888.0
3rd quarter	14 899.0	10 159.1	2 498.2	2 007.0	507.1	-15.8	-787.4	1 922.2	2 709.6	3 029.0	1 170.2	1 858.8	14 914.8
4th quarter	14 608.2	9 906.9	2 307.9	1 918.7	451.4	-62.2	-628.5	1 700.3	2 328.8	3 021.8	1 179.8	1 842.0	14 670.4
2009														
1st quarter	14 430.9	9 815.0	2 014.9	1 761.4	404.5	-151.0	-421.0	1 511.8	1 932.8	3 022.0	1 185.2	1 836.8	14 581.9
2nd quarter	14 381.2	9 805.5	1 863.7	1 685.0	374.7	-196.0	-358.4	1 521.1	1 879.5	3 070.5	1 213.5	1 857.0	14 577.2
3rd quarter	14 448.9	9 939.4	1 841.4	1 656.0	389.4	-204.0	-424.0	1 594.7	2 018.7	3 092.1	1 228.3	1 863.8	14 652.9
4th quarter	14 651.2	10 005.0	1 998.7	1 659.3	391.5	-52.1	-473.3	1 703.5	2 176.8	3 120.8	1 256.2	1 864.6	14 703.3
2010														
1st quarter	14 764.6	10 101.8	2 038.2	1 660.0	379.4	-1.2	-509.2	1 759.9	2 269.1	3 133.8	1 278.4	1 855.5	14 765.8
2nd quarter	14 980.2	10 208.1	2 148.8	1 715.7	396.3	36.7	-542.5	1 819.7	2 362.3	3 165.8	1 305.1	1 860.7	14 943.5
3rd quarter	15 141.6	10 300.8	2 236.5	1 762.4	361.2	112.9	-553.9	1 877.3	2 431.2	3 158.3	1 304.3	1 854.0	15 028.7
4th quarter	15 309.5	10 430.3	2 238.4	1 801.9	369.3	67.3	-523.6	1 972.1	2 495.7	3 164.3	1 312.9	1 851.4	15 242.2
2011														
1st quarter	15 351.4	10 558.2	2 206.0	1 805.1	368.8	32.1	-568.5	2 040.4	2 608.9	3 155.8	1 306.0	1 849.8	15 319.4
2nd quarter	15 557.5	10 673.0	2 297.4	1 862.0	374.3	61.0	-581.1	2 116.1	2 697.2	3 168.3	1 312.7	1 855.5	15 496.5
3rd quarter	15 647.7	10 755.0	2 322.8	1 953.8	381.1	-12.0	-567.1	2 156.8	2 723.9	3 136.9	1 288.7	1 848.3	15 659.7
4th quarter	15 842.3	10 809.2	2 504.1	2 009.0	391.2	104.0	-601.8	2 150.1	2 751.9	3 130.8	1 291.7	1 839.1	15 738.3
2012														
1st quarter	16 068.8	10 959.3	2 567.8	2 073.4	414.1	80.3	-602.3	2 190.0	2 792.3	3 144.0	1 296.1	1 847.9	15 988.5
2nd quarter	16 207.1	11 005.1	2 636.9	2 126.2	419.3	91.4	-565.2	2 215.6	2 780.8	3 130.5	1 288.6	1 841.8	16 115.7
3rd quarter	16 319.5	11 059.4	2 644.1	2 126.0	433.7	84.4	-523.1	2 227.7	2 750.8	3 139.1	1 293.8	1 845.3	16 235.1
4th quarter	16 420.4	11 165.7	2 638.3	2 148.6	460.9	28.7	-515.9	2 237.5	2 753.4	3 132.3	1 269.5	1 862.7	16 391.7
2013														
1st quarter	16 629.1	11 265.6	2 738.2	2 170.9	485.1	82.3	-500.2	2 255.1	2 755.3	3 125.4	1 240.5	1 884.9	16 546.8
2nd quarter	16 699.6	11 291.0	2 775.3	2 180.3	507.2	87.8	-499.3	2 260.4	2 759.8	3 132.6	1 232.9	1 899.8	16 611.8
3rd quarter	16 911.1	11 379.2	2 880.0	2 220.7	523.1	136.2	-483.0	2 284.2	2 767.2	3 134.8	1 219.0	1 915.8	16 774.9
4th quarter	17 133.1	11 518.4	2 910.5	2 274.0	524.6	111.9	-435.1	2 348.2	2 783.3	3 139.3	1 216.3	1 923.0	17 021.2
2014														
1st quarter	17 144.3	11 618.1	2 899.2	2 314.9	532.1	52.3	-511.3	2 342.4	2 853.7	3 138.2	1 211.8	1 926.4	17 092.0
2nd quarter	17 462.7	11 784.7	3 030.4	2 383.6	550.4	96.4	-506.5	2 394.1	2 900.6	3 154.1	1 210.0	1 944.1	17 366.3
3rd quarter	17 743.2	11 934.3	3 107.6	2 439.8	568.4	99.4	-490.5	2 398.1	2 888.5	3 191.8	1 229.3	1 962.5	17 643.8
4th quarter	17 852.5	12 053.8	3 139.5	2 462.0	589.7	87.8	-531.9	2 375.1	2 907.0	3 191.2	1 212.9	1 978.3	17 764.8
2015														
1st quarter	17 991.3	12 083.9	3 245.1	2 464.3	605.1	175.6	-526.9	2 297.4	2 824.4	3 189.3	1 216.0	1 973.3	17 815.7
2nd quarter	18 193.7	12 224.7	3 245.8	2 472.5	623.3	150.0	-508.8	2 298.7	2 807.5	3 232.0	1 220.6	2 011.4	18 043.7
3rd quarter	18 307.0	12 347.8	3 251.7	2 479.2	645.7	126.8	-543.0	2 258.4	2 801.4	3 250.6	1 221.2	2 029.4	18 180.2
4th quarter	18 332.1	12 397.5	3 206.1	2 450.3	661.1	94.7	-526.1	2 220.1	2 746.1	3 254.5	1 229.3	2 025.2	18 237.4
2016														
1st quarter	18 425.3	12 495.1	3 174.4	2 435.5	684.4	54.5	-514.4	2 179.2	2 693.6	3 270.2	1 229.3	2 040.9	18 370.8
2nd quarter	18 611.6	12 637.4	3 178.5	2 454.1	694.1	30.3	-491.7	2 218.9	2 710.6	3 287.4	1 225.8	2 061.6	18 581.3
3rd quarter	18 775.5	12 759.1	3 185.7	2 481.6	700.7	3.4	-485.1	2 265.4	2 750.5	3 315.8	1 238.1	2 077.7	18 772.0
4th quarter	18 968.0	12 881.6	3 281.5	2 506.2	718.6	56.8	-533.8	2 264.9	2 798.7	3 338.8	1 244.8	2 094.0	18 911.3
2017														
1st quarter	19 153.9	13 046.4	3 283.5	2 545.4	742.7	-4.6	-533.3	2 334.4	2 867.7	3 357.3	1 242.5	2 114.8	19 158.5
2nd quarter	19 322.9	13 144.4	3 357.4	2 579.7	756.7	21.0	-557.1	2 346.2	2 903.3	3 378.2	1 257.6	2 120.6	19 301.9
3rd quarter	19 558.7	13 268.1	3 413.3	2 592.7	761.5	59.1	-523.5	2 383.1	2 906.6	3 400.8	1 263.3	2 137.5	19 499.6
4th quarter	19 883.0	13 497.5	3 471.4	2 648.6	780.4	42.4	-545.8	2 471.3	3 017.1	3 459.9	1 287.7	2 172.2	19 840.5
2018														
1st quarter	20 143.7	13 667.4	3 550.8	2 716.0	789.0	45.9	-580.1	2 504.4	3 084.5	3 505.5	1 305.8	2 199.7	20 097.9
2nd quarter	20 492.5	13 864.8	3 603.2	2 770.1	808.9	24.2	-539.8	2 568.3	3 108.1	3 564.3	1 331.7	2 232.6	20 468.3
3rd quarter	20 659.1	14 002.6	3 679.6	2 798.1	804.3	77.1	-624.0	2 534.2	3 158.2	3 600.9	1 350.8	2 250.1	20 582.0
4th quarter	20 813.3	14 119.3	3 717.5	2 838.1	791.8	87.7	-640.9	2 527.1	3 168.1	3 617.4	1 367.7	2 249.7	20 725.7
2019														
1st quarter	21 001.6	14 155.6	3 801.9	2 886.9	796.5	118.5	-606.4	2 524.6	3 131.0	3 650.5	1 387.0	2 263.5	20 883.1
2nd quarter	21 289.3	14 375.7	3 843.0	2 946.1	808.5	88.4	-632.3	2 533.4	3 165.7	3 702.9	1 406.9	2 296.0	21 200.8
3rd quarter	21 505.0	14 529.5	3 858.2	2 969.3	821.9	67.0	-614.0	2 512.1	3 126.1	3 731.3	1 424.1	2 307.2	21 438.0
4th quarter	21 694.5	14 653.9	3 801.9	2 952.6	828.8	20.6	-532.4	2 508.7	3 041.1	3 771.0	1 441.7	2 329.2	21 673.9
2020														
1st quarter	21 481.4	14 439.1	3 752.4	2 900.1	872.9	-20.6	-541.7	2 385.5	2 927.3	3 831.6	1 454.7	2 376.9	21 502.0
2nd quarter	19 477.4	12 989.7	3 167.0	2 659.1	797.8	-289.9	-538.9	1 807.9	2 346.7	3 859.6	1 525.0	2 334.6	19 767.4
3rd quarter	21 138.6	14 293.8	3 708.8	2 776.0	917.2	15.0	-725.7	2 079.6	2 805.3	3 861.7	1 515.1	2 346.5	21 123.6
4th quarter	21 477.6	14 467.6	3 923.2	2 862.7	1 003.2	57.3	-798.4	2 220.7	3 019.1	3 885.3	1 512.3	2 373.0	21 420.3
2021														
1st quarter	22 038.2	15 005.4	3 928.0	2 956.7	1 065.5	-94.2	-872.5	2 311.9	3 184.5	3 977.3	1 568.6	2 408.7	22 132.5
2nd quarter	22 741.0	15 681.7	3 925.1	3 029.2	1 070.2	-174.3	-881.7	2 461.5	3 343.2	4 015.9	1 563.3	2 452.6	22 915.3
3rd quarter	23 202.3	15 964.9	4 099.6	3 073.9	1 085.9	-60.2	-947.0	2 485.2	3 432.3	4 084.9	1 562.0	2 522.9	23 262.5
4th quarter	24 002.8	16 314.2	4 527.4	3 154.9	1 122.9	249.3	-971.4	2 654.5	3 625.9	4 132.9	1 566.2	2 566.7	23 753.5

Table 1-2A. Real Gross Domestic Product: Recent Data

(Billions of chained [2012] dollars, quarterly data are at seasonally adjusted annual rates.)   NIPA Tables 1.1.6, 1.2.6

| Year and quarter | Gross domestic product | Personal consumption expenditures | Gross private domestic investment | | | | Exports and imports of goods and services | | | Government consumption expenditures and gross investment | | | Residual | Addendum: final sales of domestic product |
| | | | Total | Fixed investment | | Change in private inventories | Net exports | Exports | Imports | Total | Federal | State and local | | |
				Nonresidential	Residential									
1960	3 262.1	2 014.3	352.7	...	...	...	...	112.7	135.7	1 086.3	...	...	-183.6	3 268.6
1961	3 345.7	2 055.6	353.8	...	...	...	...	113.3	134.8	1 145.1	...	...	-201.1	3 354.6
1962	3 550.7	2 157.3	395.9	...	...	...	...	119.0	150.1	1 220.0	...	...	-219.8	3 542.5
1963	3 705.3	2 246.3	422.8	...	...	...	...	127.5	154.2	1 249.6	...	...	-212.9	3 701.0
1964	3 918.8	2 380.0	456.1	...	...	...	...	142.6	162.4	1 280.2	...	...	-200.0	3 920.6
1965	4 173.4	2 531.0	519.2	...	...	...	...	146.6	179.6	1 321.1	...	...	-207.4	4 151.9
1966	4 448.7	2 674.5	565.9	...	...	...	...	156.7	206.3	1 436.3	...	...	-239.2	4 405.7
1967	4 570.7	2 754.4	546.1	...	...	...	...	160.3	221.4	1 550.2	...	...	-262.8	4 549.6
1968	4 795.4	2 913.1	578.7	...	...	...	...	172.9	254.3	1 603.0	...	...	-257.9	4 780.2
1969	4 945.2	3 021.8	610.9	...	...	...	...	181.4	268.8	1 604.7	...	...	-243.9	4 931.0
1970	4 954.4	3 092.9	573.8	...	...	...	...	200.7	280.3	1 570.8	...	...	-210.7	4 975.2
1971	5 117.6	3 211.0	632.9	...	...	...	...	204.2	295.3	1 541.4	...	...	-208.9	5 111.6
1972	5 386.7	3 407.7	704.2	...	...	...	...	220.1	328.5	1 533.5	...	...	-183.4	5 379.4
1973	5 690.9	3 576.3	781.3	...	...	...	...	261.5	343.7	1 528.5	...	...	-163.5	5 659.1
1974	5 660.1	3 546.4	729.5	...	...	...	...	282.3	335.9	1 562.1	...	...	-161.9	5 643.0
1975	5 648.5	3 626.8	611.4	...	...	...	...	280.5	298.6	1 596.5	...	...	-151.6	5 701.7
1976	5 952.8	3 828.9	728.0	...	...	...	...	292.7	357.0	1 604.9	...	...	-189.0	5 929.6
1977	6 228.1	3 990.7	831.9	...	...	...	...	299.8	396.0	1 624.2	...	...	-178.2	6 191.7
1978	6 572.8	4 165.4	928.1	...	...	...	...	331.4	430.4	1 670.8	...	...	-151.4	6 530.7
1979	6 780.9	4 264.4	960.7	...	...	...	...	364.2	437.5	1 700.8	...	...	-107.9	6 766.0
1980	6 763.5	4 251.1	864.0	...	...	...	...	403.4	408.4	1 731.6	...	...	-66.1	6 809.1
1981	6 935.2	4 310.0	940.1	...	...	...	...	408.4	419.1	1 748.4	...	...	-103.0	6 904.6
1982	6 810.1	4 373.1	822.0	...	...	...	...	377.1	413.7	1 779.8	...	...	-102.7	6 869.9
1983	7 122.3	4 620.7	898.7	...	...	...	...	367.3	465.9	1 846.2	...	...	-134.6	7 164.6
1984	7 637.7	4 863.8	1 144.0	...	...	...	...	397.3	579.3	1 911.1	...	...	-199.6	7 546.4
1985	7 956.2	5 115.6	1 143.2	...	...	...	...	410.6	616.9	2 038.6	...	...	-167.3	7 945.4
1986	8 231.7	5 326.8	1 145.0	...	...	...	...	442.0	669.6	2 149.3	...	...	-172.5	8 246.4
1987	8 516.4	5 507.6	1 177.6	...	...	...	...	490.3	709.4	2 211.7	...	...	-204.1	8 498.0
1988	8 872.2	5 737.7	1 206.6	...	...	...	...	569.8	737.2	2 239.2	...	...	-171.9	8 866.3
1989	9 198.0	5 905.0	1 255.4	...	...	...	...	635.8	769.7	2 302.8	...	...	-170.3	9 178.2
1990	9 371.5	6 023.9	1 223.0	...	...	...	...	691.9	797.2	2 376.5	...	...	-167.7	9 371.2
1991	9 361.3	6 034.8	1 142.1	...	...	...	...	737.7	796.0	2 405.0	...	...	-159.9	9 385.0
1992	9 691.1	6 256.9	1 225.3	...	...	...	...	788.8	851.8	2 416.1	...	...	-167.0	9 689.4
1993	9 957.7	6 474.8	1 323.3	...	...	...	...	814.5	925.5	2 396.3	...	...	-154.0	9 949.9
1994	10 358.9	6 725.7	1 479.8	...	...	...	...	886.5	1 035.9	2 398.3	...	...	-184.0	10 290.7
1995	10 637.0	6 924.1	1 527.3	...	...	...	...	977.6	1 118.7	2 410.6	...	...	-124.4	10 615.2
1996	11 038.3	7 164.4	1 660.8	...	...	...	...	1 057.5	1 216.0	2 432.9	...	...	-101.0	11 015.6
1997	11 529.2	7 434.2	1 850.2	...	...	...	...	1 183.5	1 379.8	2 472.8	...	...	-127.1	11 449.5
1998	12 045.8	7 829.0	2 026.3	...	...	...	...	1 211.1	1 541.1	2 532.8	...	...	-104.1	11 974.5
1999	12 623.4	8 250.3	2 198.7	...	...	...	...	1 271.5	1 719.8	2 615.7	...	...	-80.4	12 556.0
2000	13 138.0	8 665.8	2 346.7	...	...	...	...	1 377.2	1 943.3	2 663.3	...	...	-50.3	13 075.1
2001	13 263.4	8 880.4	2 214.6	...	...	...	...	1 300.3	1 895.5	2 763.7	...	...	53.1	13 311.0
2002	13 488.4	9 106.2	2 195.5	1 472.7	692.6	24.3	-690.3	1 274.8	1 965.1	2 886.6	969.5	1 929.1	-86.6	13 471.8
2003	13 865.5	9 394.4	2 290.4	1 509.4	755.5	19.9	-764.2	1 301.6	2 065.8	2 945.7	1 033.1	1 920.3	-46.9	13 851.3
2004	14 399.7	9 748.6	2 502.6	1 594.0	830.9	82.6	-865.6	1 427.0	2 292.6	2 991.1	1 077.7	1 918.2	-5.2	14 329.2
2005	14 901.3	10 093.8	2 670.6	1 716.4	885.4	63.7	-915.4	1 526.1	2 441.4	3 013.8	1 099.2	1 918.3	36.0	14 841.2
2006	15 315.9	10 386.2	2 752.4	1 854.2	818.9	87.1	-927.6	1 670.5	2 598.2	3 061.8	1 125.3	1 939.6	33.3	15 240.9
2007	15 623.9	10 638.7	2 684.1	1 982.1	665.8	40.6	-847.9	1 816.9	2 664.8	3 116.9	1 147.3	1 972.7	26.8	15 586.7
2008	15 643.0	10 654.7	2 462.9	1 994.2	504.6	-32.7	-685.7	1 921.9	2 607.6	3 195.8	1 220.0	1 977.6	-1.7	15 678.0
2009	15 236.3	10 515.6	1 942.0	1 704.3	395.3	-177.3	-516.3	1 762.5	2 278.8	3 310.7	1 296.0	2 015.9	-15.3	15 400.3
2010	15 649.0	10 716.0	2 216.5	1 781.0	383.0	57.3	-589.4	1 989.5	2 578.9	3 308.0	1 348.4	1 959.8	-11.3	15 596.8
2011	15 891.5	10 898.3	2 362.1	1 935.4	382.5	46.7	-571.0	2 132.1	2 703.1	3 202.7	1 312.0	1 890.8	-3.7	15 847.4
2012	16 254.0	11 047.4	2 621.8	2 118.5	432.0	71.2	-551.6	2 217.7	2 769.3	3 136.5	1 287.0	1 849.5	0.0	16 182.8
2013	16 553.3	11 211.7	2 801.5	2 206.0	485.5	108.7	-519.3	2 283.6	2 802.9	3 060.7	1 215.8	1 844.4	-0.3	16 444.1
2014	16 932.1	11 515.3	2 959.2	2 365.3	504.1	86.3	-575.3	2 372.3	2 947.6	3 033.2	1 184.7	1 847.6	0.6	16 842.3
2015	17 390.3	11 892.9	3 121.8	2 420.3	555.4	137.6	-721.7	2 378.7	3 100.4	3 088.4	1 184.5	1 902.2	10.7	17 248.3
2016	17 680.3	12 187.7	3 089.9	2 442.0	592.1	35.7	-757.1	2 388.4	3 145.4	3 148.8	1 190.5	1 956.3	15.3	17 630.6
2017	18 079.1	12 483.7	3 212.5	2 541.4	615.9	33.6	-799.5	2 485.8	3 285.2	3 165.2	1 194.7	1 968.5	11.8	18 030.4
2018	18 606.8	12 845.0	3 394.8	2 704.4	612.3	65.7	-864.2	2 555.6	3 419.9	3 208.8	1 231.0	1 976.4	-7.2	18 528.8
2019	19 032.7	13 126.3	3 510.6	2 822.0	606.7	75.1	-905.3	2 554.0	3 459.2	3 279.5	1 277.2	2 001.5	-32.3	18 944.4
2020	18 384.7	12 629.9	3 316.2	2 671.1	648.0	-42.3	-942.7	2 207.6	3 150.3	3 360.2	1 340.7	2 019.9	-83.7	18 395.9
2021	19 427.3	13 624.8	3 640.0	2 868.5	707.7	-32.6	-1 284.3	2 307.5	3 591.9	3 376.3	1 348.9	2 027.8	-73.7	19 375.8
2019														
1st quarter	18 833.2	12 975.1	3 503.4	2 780.7	599.1	131.7	-906.7	2 565.3	3 472.0	3 235.2	1 248.7	1 985.4	-33.8	18 704.8
2nd quarter	18 982.5	13 088.8	3 526.0	2 826.0	605.2	84.3	-935.3	2 551.3	3 486.6	3 274.9	1 275.5	1 998.7	-20.7	18 881.4
3rd quarter	19 112.7	13 192.3	3 535.9	2 846.5	610.6	68.3	-931.5	2 545.9	3 477.4	3 291.7	1 286.8	2 004.3	-29.3	19 027.1
4th quarter	19 202.3	13 249.0	3 477.1	2 834.7	612.2	16.3	-847.6	2 553.3	3 400.9	3 316.3	1 298.0	2 017.6	-45.4	19 164.4
2020														
1st quarter	18 952.0	13 014.5	3 430.1	2 775.5	641.2	-30.4	-841.9	2 442.1	3 283.9	3 346.3	1 305.8	2 039.7	-25.5	18 940.1
2nd quarter	17 258.2	11 756.4	2 901.9	2 535.7	584.9	-252.8	-774.8	1 943.0	2 717.7	3 378.1	1 368.4	2 011.0	-95.1	17 471.0
3rd quarter	18 560.8	12 820.8	3 371.0	2 646.9	657.8	25.3	-1 021.3	2 166.3	3 187.5	3 360.2	1 349.6	2 011.4	-117.5	18 508.0
4th quarter	18 767.8	12 927.9	3 561.9	2 726.2	708.2	88.8	-1 132.8	2 279.0	3 411.8	3 356.0	1 338.8	2 017.6	-96.7	18 664.8
2021														
1st quarter	19 055.7	13 282.7	3 541.3	2 810.4	730.6	-88.3	-1 226.1	2 262.3	3 488.4	3 390.9	1 375.2	2 017.1	-91.5	19 076.1
2nd quarter	19 368.3	13 665.6	3 506.0	2 873.1	708.2	-168.5	-1 244.5	2 304.2	3 548.7	3 373.8	1 356.7	2 017.9	-101.7	19 449.3
3rd quarter	19 478.9	13 732.4	3 609.7	2 884.8	694.2	-66.8	-1 316.6	2 273.0	3 589.6	3 381.6	1 339.1	2 042.1	-57.1	19 453.4
4th quarter	19 806.3	13 818.4	3 903.0	2 905.5	697.9	193.2	-1 350.1	2 390.6	3 740.8	3 359.0	1 324.3	2 034.0	-44.4	19 524.3

Note: Chained (2012) dollar series are calculated as the product of the chain-type quantity index and the 2012 current-dollar value of the corresponding series, divided by 100. Because the formula for the chain-type quantity indexes uses weights from more than one period, the corresponding chained-dollar estimates are usually not additive. The residual column is the difference between the total and the sum of the most detailed components shown in the Bureau of Economic Analysis (BEA) published data.

. . . = Not available.

Table 1-2B. Real Gross Domestic Product: Historical Data

(Billions of chained [2012] dollars, quarterly data are at seasonally adjusted annual rates.)   **NIPA Tables 1.1.6, 1.2.6**

Year and quarter	Gross domestic product	Personal consump- tion expen- ditures	Gross private domestic investment				Exports and imports of goods and services			Government consumption expenditures and gross investment			Residual	Adden- dum: Final sales of domestic product
			Total	Fixed investment		Change in private inventories	Net exports	Exports	Imports	Total	Federal	State and local		
				Nonresi- dential	Residential									
1929	1 110.2	832.4	120.4	...	...	...	...	43.4	58.1	180.4	...	...	-21.6	1 122.0
1930	1 015.8	787.8	82.0	...	...	...	...	35.9	50.6	198.7	...	...	-32.2	1 046.3
1931	950.7	763.2	53.3	...	...	...	...	29.8	44.1	206.8	...	...	-44.7	985.5
1932	828.1	694.9	19.7	...	...	...	...	23.4	36.6	200.2	...	...	-42.7	874.6
1933	817.8	679.6	26.6	...	...	...	...	23.5	38.1	193.8	...	...	-51.7	848.7
1934	906.2	728.1	44.0	...	...	...	...	26.2	39.0	217.8	...	...	-63.3	929.1
1935	986.9	772.3	76.5	...	...	...	...	27.6	51.1	224.5	...	...	-72.8	987.2
1936	1 114.1	850.9	96.8	...	...	...	...	29.0	50.5	259.9	...	...	-82.0	1 116.0
1937	1 171.1	882.4	119.2	...	...	...	...	36.5	56.8	249.7	...	...	-76.5	1 162.8
1938	1 132.3	868.3	82.0	...	...	...	...	36.1	44.1	268.7	...	...	-74.6	1 147.4
1939	1 223.2	916.8	103.1	...	...	...	...	38.1	46.4	292.3	...	...	-82.8	1 231.7
1940	1 331.1	964.3	140.4	...	...	...	...	43.3	47.5	302.9	...	...	-93.3	1 316.2
1941	1 566.8	1 032.5	171.9	...	...	...	...	44.4	58.4	509.7	...	...	-167.4	1 536.3
1942	1 862.8	1 008.0	95.7	...	...	...	...	29.3	53.0	1 183.8	...	...	-414.4	1 862.6
1943	2 179.9	1 036.1	59.7	...	...	...	...	24.7	66.8	1 774.8	...	...	-643.9	2 208.7
1944	2 353.2	1 065.5	71.3	...	...	...	...	26.6	69.9	1 992.1	...	...	-726.8	2 384.9
1945	2 330.2	1 131.4	91.7	...	...	...	...	37.2	74.4	1 749.4	...	...	-594.8	2 368.7
1946	2 059.8	1 271.3	220.3	...	...	...	...	80.4	61.6	615.9	...	...	-99.4	2 030.6
1947	2 036.2	1 295.6	212.1	...	...	...	...	91.7	58.5	522.6	...	...	-22.6	2 066.5
1948	2 120.0	1 324.9	267.3	...	...	...	...	72.2	68.3	551.7	...	...	-52.8	2 100.8
1949	2 108.0	1 361.7	206.7	...	...	...	...	71.5	65.9	611.0	...	...	-63.9	2 148.4
1947														
1st quarter	2 034.5	1 277.4	218.1	...	...	...	...	97.6	60.4	524.0	...	...	-28.8	2 051.2
2nd quarter	2 029.0	1 298.7	201.4	...	...	...	...	96.4	61.6	523.6	...	...	-25.0	2 061.7
3rd quarter	2 024.8	1 302.9	195.5	...	...	...	...	91.5	54.6	523.5	...	...	-16.5	2 075.4
4th quarter	2 056.5	1 303.3	233.3	...	...	...	...	81.1	57.5	519.2	...	...	-20.0	2 077.7
1948														
1st quarter	2 087.4	1 309.8	257.2	...	...	...	...	77.4	64.9	527.0	...	...	-33.7	2 085.5
2nd quarter	2 121.9	1 325.1	273.1	...	...	...	...	70.2	67.5	545.6	...	...	-52.4	2 097.2
3rd quarter	2 134.1	1 327.0	275.9	...	...	...	...	71.8	71.0	556.9	...	...	-59.2	2 101.7
4th quarter	2 136.4	1 337.6	262.7	...	...	...	...	69.3	69.8	577.5	...	...	-66.0	2 118.6
1949														
1st quarter	2 107.0	1 339.8	223.5	...	...	...	...	77.6	67.7	592.5	...	...	-56.4	2 126.7
2nd quarter	2 099.8	1 360.3	193.8	...	...	...	...	76.9	66.7	618.5	...	...	-60.4	2 154.1
3rd quarter	2 121.5	1 363.4	209.9	...	...	...	...	70.5	64.0	621.8	...	...	-75.1	2 151.7
4th quarter	2 103.7	1 383.4	199.5	...	...	...	...	61.0	65.0	610.9	...	...	-63.6	2 161.2
1950														
1st quarter	2 186.4	1 406.4	246.9	...	...	...	...	60.0	66.8	599.6	...	...	-69.3	2 194.5
2nd quarter	2 253.0	1 429.6	273.3	...	...	...	...	60.8	70.5	610.5	...	...	-64.5	2 253.8
3rd quarter	2 340.1	1 503.0	296.8	...	...	...	...	62.3	87.0	600.7	...	...	-53.9	2 334.0
4th quarter	2 384.9	1 457.7	334.5	...	...	...	...	67.4	87.1	643.1	...	...	-88.9	2 313.5
1951														
1st quarter	2 417.3	1 492.9	300.4	...	...	...	...	70.8	87.2	711.5	...	...	-107.3	2 383.3
2nd quarter	2 459.2	1 450.8	307.3	...	...	...	...	77.7	84.3	806.4	...	...	-151.3	2 397.0
3rd quarter	2 509.9	1 467.7	284.7	...	...	...	...	79.6	77.1	895.0	...	...	-174.7	2 477.3
4th quarter	2 515.4	1 476.2	262.0	...	...	...	...	78.9	75.1	942.4	...	...	-183.8	2 514.6
1952														
1st quarter	2 542.3	1 479.6	268.9	...	...	...	...	83.1	83.8	970.4	...	...	-194.5	2 536.9
2nd quarter	2 547.8	1 508.6	248.6	...	...	...	...	74.0	83.4	1 003.5	...	...	-198.9	2 579.8
3rd quarter	2 566.2	1 515.6	261.9	...	...	...	...	68.1	88.5	1 013.6	...	...	-225.5	2 557.0
4th quarter	2 650.4	1 569.3	280.8	...	...	...	...	68.6	96.4	1 030.5	...	...	-223.1	2 641.3
1953														
1st quarter	2 699.7	1 587.7	286.8	...	...	...	...	67.4	94.1	1 063.2	...	...	-228.2	2 697.9
2nd quarter	2 720.6	1 597.3	288.4	...	...	...	...	67.8	98.9	1 085.0	...	...	-235.5	2 719.6
3rd quarter	2 705.3	1 593.5	282.4	...	...	...	...	70.6	98.6	1 073.4	...	...	-226.1	2 714.0
4th quarter	2 664.3	1 582.8	262.0	...	...	...	...	68.2	93.7	1 070.8	...	...	-217.3	2 699.8
1954														
1st quarter	2 651.6	1 588.7	260.1	...	...	...	...	65.2	88.3	1 042.9	...	...	-209.4	2 684.0
2nd quarter	2 654.5	1 609.3	259.5	...	...	...	...	74.5	96.2	1 007.6	...	...	-188.0	2 694.3
3rd quarter	2 684.4	1 631.1	272.0	...	...	...	...	72.1	90.4	985.8	...	...	-176.4	2 721.2
4th quarter	2 737.0	1 665.3	284.0	...	...	...	...	75.5	91.3	979.9	...	...	-172.8	2 765.5
1955														
1st quarter	2 815.1	1 702.7	312.3	...	...	...	...	78.3	96.7	980.5	...	...	-176.4	2 818.3
2nd quarter	2 860.9	1 735.3	331.3	...	...	...	...	76.4	102.2	970.9	...	...	-172.2	2 854.8
3rd quarter	2 899.6	1 756.2	336.4	...	...	...	...	81.5	103.9	977.1	...	...	-167.8	2 896.7
4th quarter	2 917.0	1 778.8	344.2	...	...	...	...	81.8	107.7	957.7	...	...	-164.8	2 904.4
1956														
1st quarter	2 905.7	1 781.7	334.4	...	...	...	...	85.7	112.2	957.4	...	...	-164.1	2 899.8
2nd quarter	2 929.7	1 787.6	331.8	...	...	...	...	91.5	111.6	976.8	...	...	-162.1	2 932.9
3rd quarter	2 927.0	1 791.6	328.8	...	...	...	...	94.5	112.6	968.2	...	...	-155.8	2 935.0
4th quarter	2 975.2	1 816.3	325.7	...	...	...	...	98.8	107.4	992.8	...	...	-161.9	2 986.0
1957														
1st quarter	2 994.3	1 829.0	320.7	...	...	...	...	105.2	115.9	1 014.1	...	...	-164.6	3 012.7
2nd quarter	2 987.7	1 832.1	320.4	...	...	...	...	102.1	116.8	1 008.9	...	...	-167.3	3 002.4
3rd quarter	3 017.0	1 846.6	327.7	...	...	...	...	99.2	114.6	1 017.4	...	...	-171.8	3 025.6
4th quarter	2 985.8	1 847.4	302.5	...	...	...	...	96.3	115.0	1 034.2	...	...	-168.1	3 024.6

Note: Chained (2012) dollar series are calculated as the product of the chain-type quantity index and the 2012 current-dollar value of the corresponding series, divided by 100. Because the formula for the chain-type quantity indexes uses weights from more than one period, the corresponding chained-dollar estimates are usually not additive. The residual column is the difference between the total and the sum of the most detailed components shown in the Bureau of Economic Analysis (BEA) published data.

. . . = Not available.

Table 1-2B. Real Gross Domestic Product: Historical Data—*Continued*

(Billions of chained [2012] dollars, quarterly data are at seasonally adjusted annual rates.)   **NIPA Tables 1.1.6, 1.2.6**

Year and quarter	Gross domestic product	Personal consumption expenditures	Gross private domestic investment				Exports and imports of goods and services			Government consumption expenditures and gross investment			Residual	Addendum: Final sales of domestic product
			Total	Fixed investment		Change in private inventories	Net exports	Exports	Imports	Total	Federal	State and local		
				Nonresidential	Residential									
1958														
1st quarter	2 908.3	1 821.8	282.1	...	...	...	...	86.7	116.7	1 025.2	...	...	-176.6	2 950.4
2nd quarter ...	2 927.4	1 836.9	276.4	...	...	...	...	87.1	121.7	1 050.8	...	...	-189.7	2 967.1
3rd quarter ...	2 995.1	1 867.4	297.6	...	...	...	...	87.4	119.8	1 056.9	...	...	-200.7	3 010.2
4th quarter	3 065.1	1 892.7	323.0	...	...	...	...	87.1	126.1	1 078.2	...	...	-206.4	3 068.9
1959														
1st quarter	3 124.0	1 927.4	340.6	...	...	...	...	93.4	129.4	1 067.2	...	...	-188.8	3 129.0
2nd quarter ...	3 194.4	1 957.2	367.1	...	...	...	...	92.6	135.7	1 080.4	...	...	-201.5	3 175.2
3rd quarter ...	3 196.7	1 977.6	343.4	...	...	...	...	101.6	137.0	1 089.7	...	...	-182.6	3 218.7
4th quarter	3 205.8	1 979.9	354.6	...	...	...	...	96.6	133.6	1 080.7	...	...	-192.5	3 205.2
1960														
1st quarter	3 277.8	1 998.8	390.2	...	...	...	...	109.0	138.6	1 062.3	...	...	-194.1	3 241.5
2nd quarter ...	3 260.2	2 024.0	353.8	...	...	...	...	112.1	139.6	1 074.2	...	...	-178.8	3 268.6
3rd quarter ...	3 276.1	2 015.9	352.9	...	...	...	...	114.6	135.5	1 100.5	...	...	-192.6	3 275.0
4th quarter	3 234.1	2 018.5	313.8	...	...	...	...	115.2	129.1	1 108.1	...	...	-168.9	3 289.2
1961														
1st quarter	3 255.9	2 017.8	322.0	...	...	...	...	114.4	128.5	1 124.6	...	...	-183.6	3 295.0
2nd quarter ...	3 311.2	2 047.8	344.5	...	...	...	...	109.1	130.1	1 127.4	...	...	-196.9	3 325.5
3rd quarter ...	3 374.7	2 057.8	371.3	...	...	...	...	114.0	138.7	1 151.5	...	...	-212.0	3 362.1
4th quarter	3 440.9	2 099.2	377.5	...	...	...	...	115.9	142.0	1 176.7	...	...	-211.9	3 435.7
1962														
1st quarter	3 502.3	2 121.4	397.8	...	...	...	...	115.2	146.3	1 199.4	...	...	-225.7	3 477.9
2nd quarter ...	3 533.9	2 147.5	394.7	...	...	...	...	121.8	149.5	1 205.5	...	...	-211.4	3 529.4
3rd quarter ...	3 577.4	2 164.8	401.4	...	...	...	...	121.6	151.4	1 233.3	...	...	-222.1	3 567.8
4th quarter	3 589.1	2 195.4	389.7	...	...	...	...	117.6	153.2	1 241.9	...	...	-219.9	3 595.0
1963														
1st quarter	3 628.3	2 210.8	410.2	...	...	...	...	119.4	149.7	1 225.0	...	...	-222.1	3 611.9
2nd quarter ...	3 669.0	2 231.7	416.7	...	...	...	...	129.0	153.2	1 225.9	...	...	-203.9	3 667.9
3rd quarter ...	3 749.7	2 261.9	429.5	...	...	...	...	128.3	157.1	1 280.3	...	...	-220.5	3 744.7
4th quarter	3 774.3	2 280.8	434.7	...	...	...	...	133.3	156.6	1 267.0	...	...	-204.9	3 779.4
1964														
1st quarter	3 853.8	2 325.6	451.0	...	...	...	...	140.1	156.5	1 271.0	...	...	-198.6	3 856.9
2nd quarter ...	3 895.8	2 366.7	449.4	...	...	...	...	139.5	160.0	1 282.4	...	...	-202.6	3 900.4
3rd quarter ...	3 956.7	2 410.4	459.9	...	...	...	...	143.9	164.3	1 283.9	...	...	-201.5	3 956.8
4th quarter	3 968.9	2 417.3	464.2	...	...	...	...	146.8	168.7	1 283.4	...	...	-197.4	3 968.4
1965														
1st quarter	4 064.9	2 471.2	508.5	...	...	...	...	129.7	162.6	1 281.9	...	...	-217.2	4 030.7
2nd quarter ...	4 116.3	2 498.5	509.8	...	...	...	...	151.4	181.8	1 297.1	...	...	-197.2	4 099.2
3rd quarter ...	4 207.8	2 541.4	527.6	...	...	...	...	148.0	182.6	1 340.1	...	...	-210.1	4 184.5
4th quarter	4 304.7	2 612.8	531.1	...	...	...	...	157.1	191.5	1 365.5	...	...	-205.1	4 293.2
1966														
1st quarter	4 409.5	2 651.4	573.5	...	...	...	...	153.2	196.4	1 390.9	...	...	-224.2	4 365.2
2nd quarter ...	4 424.6	2 658.2	565.0	...	...	...	...	157.8	201.3	1 417.2	...	...	-231.1	4 385.2
3rd quarter ...	4 462.1	2 688.5	560.8	...	...	...	...	155.9	212.6	1 455.9	...	...	-238.7	4 429.6
4th quarter	4 498.7	2 699.7	564.1	...	...	...	...	159.8	215.0	1 481.0	...	...	-262.9	4 442.7
1967														
1st quarter	4 538.5	2 715.3	550.3	...	...	...	...	161.8	218.3	1 543.6	...	...	-281.3	4 488.9
2nd quarter ...	4 541.3	2 752.4	530.4	...	...	...	...	159.6	216.6	1 537.2	...	...	-251.2	4 536.6
3rd quarter ...	4 584.2	2 766.5	545.9	...	...	...	...	158.4	219.5	1 554.2	...	...	-261.1	4 566.6
4th quarter	4 618.8	2 783.4	557.7	...	...	...	...	161.3	231.0	1 566.0	...	...	-257.4	4 606.4
1968														
1st quarter	4 713.0	2 850.2	568.9	...	...	...	...	165.9	244.6	1 594.0	...	...	-256.7	4 702.0
2nd quarter ...	4 791.8	2 893.6	590.6	...	...	...	...	168.6	248.4	1 602.3	...	...	-277.0	4 749.2
3rd quarter ...	4 828.9	2 947.8	574.5	...	...	...	...	180.6	263.3	1 607.1	...	...	-251.7	4 820.5
4th quarter	4 847.9	2 961.1	580.8	...	...	...	...	176.6	261.1	1 608.6	...	...	-246.2	4 848.9
1969														
1st quarter	4 923.8	2 993.9	615.0	...	...	...	...	156.1	236.5	1 612.2	...	...	-264.1	4 899.3
2nd quarter ...	4 938.7	3 013.2	611.4	...	...	...	...	190.3	283.1	1 607.2	...	...	-239.6	4 923.7
3rd quarter ...	4 971.3	3 027.9	623.8	...	...	...	...	187.1	279.4	1 610.5	...	...	-244.0	4 950.8
4th quarter	4 947.1	3 052.1	593.7	...	...	...	...	192.0	276.4	1 588.8	...	...	-227.7	4 950.1
1970														
1st quarter	4 939.8	3 071.1	576.0	...	...	...	...	194.5	275.5	1 581.1	...	...	-212.0	4 963.2
2nd quarter ...	4 946.8	3 085.0	577.2	...	...	...	...	202.1	280.9	1 562.8	...	...	-220.2	4 952.3
3rd quarter ...	4 992.4	3 112.0	586.6	...	...	...	...	202.9	280.3	1 569.4	...	...	-219.2	4 998.2
4th quarter	4 938.9	3 103.6	555.5	...	...	...	...	203.3	284.6	1 570.1	...	...	-191.5	4 987.0
1971														
1st quarter	5 073.0	3 163.1	620.2	...	...	...	...	205.2	281.2	1 547.1	...	...	-230.8	5 049.1
2nd quarter ...	5 100.4	3 192.2	637.8	...	...	...	...	203.6	302.5	1 543.6	...	...	-216.4	5 082.5
3rd quarter ...	5 142.4	3 217.7	645.5	...	...	...	...	213.8	309.2	1 542.8	...	...	-208.2	5 128.3
4th quarter	5 154.5	3 271.1	628.2	...	...	...	...	194.1	288.2	1 531.9	...	...	-180.2	5 186.4
1972														
1st quarter	5 249.3	3 314.2	669.6	...	...	...	...	216.1	330.3	1 540.4	...	...	-175.1	5 261.8
2nd quarter ...	5 368.5	3 377.3	707.6	...	...	...	...	209.8	318.6	1 546.6	...	...	-201.6	5 344.9
3rd quarter ...	5 419.2	3 429.4	717.6	...	...	...	...	222.5	325.2	1 517.1	...	...	-192.8	5 392.5
4th quarter	5 509.9	3 509.8	722.1	...	...	...	...	231.9	339.9	1 529.7	...	...	-164.1	5 518.3

Note: Chained (2012) dollar series are calculated as the product of the chain-type quantity index and the 2012 current-dollar value of the corresponding series, divided by 100. Because the formula for the chain-type quantity indexes uses weights from more than one period, the corresponding chained-dollar estimates are usually not additive. The residual column is the difference between the total and the sum of the most detailed components shown in the Bureau of Economic Analysis (BEA) published data.

. . . = Not available.

Table 1-2B. Real Gross Domestic Product: Historical Data—*Continued*

(Billions of chained [2012] dollars, quarterly data are at seasonally adjusted annual rates.)   NIPA Tables 1.1.6, 1.2.6

Year and quarter	Gross domestic product	Personal consumption expenditures	Gross private domestic investment				Exports and imports of goods and services			Government consumption expenditures and gross investment			Residual	Addendum: Final sales of domestic product
			Total	Fixed investment		Change in private inventories	Net exports	Exports	Imports	Total	Federal	State and local		
				Nonresidential	Residential									
1973														
1st quarter	5 646.3	3 573.9	764.5	...	...	...	...	248.9	355.6	1 542.9	...	...	-161.6	5 635.3
2nd quarter ...	5 707.8	3 572.3	797.0	...	...	...	...	260.9	345.3	1 532.0	...	...	-174.3	5 660.1
3rd quarter ...	5 677.7	3 584.9	768.1	...	...	...	...	261.7	335.8	1 514.0	...	...	-146.3	5 666.5
4th quarter ...	5 731.6	3 574.2	795.5	...	...	...	...	274.6	338.3	1 525.3	...	...	-171.8	5 674.2
1974														
1st quarter	5 682.4	3 542.2	750.1	...	...	...	...	278.2	326.8	1 552.9	...	...	-149.3	5 667.0
2nd quarter ...	5 695.9	3 555.0	747.1	...	...	...	...	291.7	344.1	1 560.7	...	...	-160.5	5 672.4
3rd quarter ...	5 642.0	3 570.2	708.4	...	...	...	...	276.0	338.1	1 563.8	...	...	-153.0	5 656.3
4th quarter ...	5 620.1	3 518.1	712.7	...	...	...	...	283.2	334.8	1 571.3	...	...	-184.7	5 576.3
1975														
1st quarter	5 551.7	3 547.6	597.9	...	...	...	...	285.2	301.2	1 588.4	...	...	-144.2	5 616.4
2nd quarter ...	5 591.4	3 605.9	580.1	...	...	...	...	276.9	277.1	1 574.9	...	...	-130.9	5 670.8
3rd quarter ...	5 687.1	3 657.2	625.0	...	...	...	...	272.2	300.1	1 604.4	...	...	-165.5	5 724.6
4th quarter ...	5 763.7	3 696.5	642.5	...	...	...	...	287.6	316.1	1 618.4	...	...	-165.6	5 794.8
1976														
1st quarter	5 893.3	3 770.4	704.5	...	...	...	...	285.6	335.9	1 621.0	...	...	-192.9	5 874.8
2nd quarter ...	5 936.5	3 805.1	732.4	...	...	...	...	288.5	350.5	1 602.9	...	...	-203.0	5 894.2
3rd quarter ...	5 969.1	3 845.1	734.9	...	...	...	...	296.9	364.8	1 598.2	...	...	-196.5	5 933.9
4th quarter ...	6 012.4	3 895.0	740.4	...	...	...	...	299.9	376.8	1 597.3	...	...	-163.6	6 015.7
1977														
1st quarter	6 083.4	3 940.9	774.7	...	...	...	...	295.1	394.7	1 610.8	...	...	-177.8	6 073.8
2nd quarter ...	6 201.7	3 962.3	830.3	...	...	...	...	303.0	398.3	1 625.6	...	...	-172.4	6 169.3
3rd quarter ...	6 313.6	3 999.8	872.3	...	...	...	...	305.4	392.8	1 632.1	...	...	-193.1	6 236.4
4th quarter ...	6 313.7	4 059.9	850.4	...	...	...	...	295.6	398.3	1 628.2	...	...	-169.4	6 287.5
1978														
1st quarter	6 333.8	4 082.7	867.0	...	...	...	...	302.6	425.1	1 628.6	...	...	-178.3	6 294.3
2nd quarter ...	6 578.6	4 170.0	923.3	...	...	...	...	334.1	426.4	1 669.5	...	...	-147.3	6 539.6
3rd quarter ...	6 644.8	4 187.5	950.2	...	...	...	...	337.8	432.0	1 684.9	...	...	-140.1	6 601.3
4th quarter ...	6 734.1	4 221.3	972.1	...	...	...	...	351.2	437.9	1 700.1	...	...	-139.9	6 687.7
1979														
1st quarter	6 746.2	4 243.2	973.8	...	...	...	...	351.5	436.7	1 683.3	...	...	-119.5	6 709.4
2nd quarter ...	6 753.4	4 240.4	972.9	...	...	...	...	352.4	439.1	1 699.7	...	...	-130.3	6 710.1
3rd quarter ...	6 803.6	4 281.7	956.5	...	...	...	...	365.1	432.4	1 704.6	...	...	-93.1	6 807.7
4th quarter ...	6 820.6	4 292.3	939.5	...	...	...	...	388.0	441.8	1 715.9	...	...	-88.6	6 836.8
1980														
1st quarter	6 842.0	4 286.2	933.1	...	...	...	...	398.8	442.1	1 741.0	...	...	-91.9	6 849.8
2nd quarter ...	6 701.0	4 189.7	853.8	...	...	...	...	406.4	410.0	1 744.5	...	...	-97.6	6 714.6
3rd quarter ...	6 693.1	4 235.6	797.4	...	...	...	...	405.5	380.5	1 720.7	...	...	-23.6	6 804.3
4th quarter ...	6 817.9	4 292.9	871.7	...	...	...	...	403.0	400.9	1 720.3	...	...	-51.5	6 867.7
1981														
1st quarter	6 951.5	4 307.2	952.4	...	...	...	...	410.6	418.0	1 743.3	...	...	-115.8	6 895.9
2nd quarter ...	6 900.0	4 307.6	912.9	...	...	...	...	412.8	418.6	1 746.7	...	...	-79.4	6 912.0
3rd quarter ...	6 982.6	4 327.5	964.4	...	...	...	...	404.1	413.8	1 740.7	...	...	-114.2	6 920.7
4th quarter ...	6 906.5	4 297.9	930.4	...	...	...	...	405.9	425.7	1 762.8	...	...	-102.4	6 889.8
1982														
1st quarter	6 799.2	4 329.5	842.4	...	...	...	...	388.3	413.5	1 760.8	...	...	-73.0	6 873.9
2nd quarter ...	6 830.3	4 342.7	841.8	...	...	...	...	390.6	406.8	1 767.5	...	...	-98.7	6 866.2
3rd quarter ...	6 804.1	4 371.8	834.1	...	...	...	...	373.3	425.6	1 781.7	...	...	-138.8	6 821.9
4th quarter ...	6 806.9	4 448.4	769.6	...	...	...	...	356.2	408.9	1 809.2	...	...	-100.1	6 917.8
1983														
1st quarter	6 896.6	4 492.4	796.3	...	...	...	...	361.9	418.3	1 826.6	...	...	-99.4	6 996.3
2nd quarter ...	7 053.5	4 583.9	866.8	...	...	...	...	363.0	450.5	1 841.6	...	...	-141.4	7 098.8
3rd quarter ...	7 194.5	4 666.1	921.1	...	...	...	...	368.5	485.6	1 873.4	...	...	-145.5	7 232.7
4th quarter ...	7 344.6	4 740.4	1 010.7	...	...	...	...	375.9	509.4	1 843.4	...	...	-152.1	7 330.5
1984														
1st quarter	7 488.2	4 779.8	1 108.3	...	...	...	...	383.7	550.5	1 863.0	...	...	-210.0	7 383.1
2nd quarter ...	7 617.5	4 846.7	1 144.4	...	...	...	...	393.3	573.4	1 903.4	...	...	-203.8	7 518.4
3rd quarter ...	7 691.0	4 882.7	1 169.1	...	...	...	...	401.9	588.2	1 918.8	...	...	-205.0	7 587.2
4th quarter ...	7 754.1	4 945.9	1 154.0	...	...	...	...	410.1	605.5	1 959.1	...	...	-179.8	7 697.0
1985														
1st quarter	7 829.3	5 030.0	1 122.3	...	...	...	...	411.2	592.1	1 980.5	...	...	-144.3	7 827.9
2nd quarter ...	7 898.2	5 076.1	1 141.4	...	...	...	...	410.3	621.2	2 024.4	...	...	-164.8	7 890.3
3rd quarter ...	8 018.8	5 172.6	1 133.7	...	...	...	...	404.3	615.2	2 070.6	...	...	-173.9	8 015.5
4th quarter ...	8 078.4	5 183.7	1 175.5	...	...	...	...	416.4	639.3	2 079.1	...	...	-186.2	8 047.8
1986														
1st quarter	8 153.8	5 229.0	1 175.1	...	...	...	...	429.5	638.6	2 095.5	...	...	-180.3	8 128.2
2nd quarter ...	8 190.6	5 286.0	1 154.6	...	...	...	...	434.1	665.8	2 139.2	...	...	-178.8	8 192.8
3rd quarter ...	8 268.9	5 379.5	1 123.5	...	...	...	...	444.0	684.3	2 185.8	...	...	-167.5	8 306.3
4th quarter ...	8 313.3	5 412.5	1 126.9	...	...	...	...	460.6	689.6	2 176.8	...	...	-163.5	8 358.2
1987														
1st quarter	8 375.3	5 417.9	1 157.3	...	...	...	...	461.0	685.5	2 189.5	...	...	-212.0	8 353.2
2nd quarter ...	8 465.6	5 491.8	1 157.9	...	...	...	...	480.0	702.7	2 206.5	...	...	-194.3	8 466.0
3rd quarter ...	8 539.1	5 554.5	1 158.1	...	...	...	...	500.8	716.4	2 208.8	...	...	-164.5	8 565.6
4th quarter ...	8 685.7	5 566.3	1 237.0	...	...	...	...	519.5	732.8	2 241.9	...	...	-245.3	8 607.2

Note: Chained (2012) dollar series are calculated as the product of the chain-type quantity index and the 2012 current-dollar value of the corresponding series, divided by 100. Because the formula for the chain-type quantity indexes uses weights from more than one period, the corresponding chained-dollar estimates are usually not additive. The residual column is the difference between the total and the sum of the most detailed components shown in the Bureau of Economic Analysis (BEA) published data.

. . . = Not available.

Table 1-2B. Real Gross Domestic Product: Historical Data—*Continued*

(Billions of chained [2012] dollars, quarterly data are at seasonally adjusted annual rates.)   NIPA Tables 1.1.6, 1.2.6

Year and quarter	Gross domestic product	Personal consump-tion expen-ditures	Gross private domestic investment				Exports and imports of goods and services			Government consumption expenditures and gross investment			Residual	Adden-dum: Final sales of domestic product
			Total	Fixed investment		Change in private inventories	Net exports	Exports	Imports	Total	Federal	State and local		
				Nonresi-dential	Residential									
1988														
1st quarter	8 730.6	5 664.6	1 177.6	...	...	...	...	548.4	729.4	2 223.2	...	...	-175.6	8 732.0
2nd quarter ...	8 845.3	5 706.4	1 205.7	...	...	...	...	563.7	721.0	2 229.9	...	...	-169.7	8 839.8
3rd quarter ...	8 897.1	5 757.1	1 212.4	...	...	...	...	574.9	738.0	2 230.1	...	...	-164.5	8 890.2
4th quarter	9 015.7	5 822.6	1 230.9	...	...	...	...	592.4	760.5	2 273.4	...	...	-177.7	9 003.3
1989														
1st quarter	9 107.3	5 849.6	1 272.6	...	...	...	...	610.1	764.0	2 263.4	...	...	-192.7	9 054.6
2nd quarter ...	9 176.8	5 876.9	1 260.3	...	...	...	...	636.8	767.6	2 298.2	...	...	-180.1	9 142.5
3rd quarter ...	9 244.8	5 933.8	1 249.0	...	...	...	...	643.3	766.6	2 318.9	...	...	-148.1	9 253.1
4th quarter ...	9 263.0	5 959.6	1 239.7	...	...	...	...	653.0	780.5	2 330.5	...	...	-160.4	9 262.6
1990														
1st quarter	9 364.3	6 009.7	1 252.1	...	...	...	...	681.4	805.2	2 367.8	...	...	-160.8	9 366.9
2nd quarter ...	9 398.2	6 028.0	1 252.4	...	...	...	...	689.9	803.9	2 371.5	...	...	-188.0	9 369.0
3rd quarter ...	9 404.5	6 051.9	1 228.2	...	...	...	...	695.1	800.6	2 375.3	...	...	-177.0	9 393.4
4th quarter ...	9 318.9	6 005.9	1 159.5	...	...	...	...	701.2	779.2	2 391.2	...	...	-144.9	9 355.6
1991														
1st quarter	9 275.3	5 983.3	1 120.9	...	...	...	...	705.5	770.3	2 405.4	...	...	-146.1	9 319.8
2nd quarter ...	9 347.6	6 032.9	1 120.9	...	...	...	...	731.2	784.0	2 415.2	...	...	-140.8	9 396.6
3rd quarter ...	9 394.8	6 063.0	1 143.1	...	...	...	...	748.5	806.0	2 408.5	...	...	-163.4	9 417.7
4th quarter ...	9 427.6	6 059.9	1 183.6	...	...	...	...	765.4	823.8	2 390.8	...	...	-189.2	9 406.0
1992														
1st quarter	9 540.4	6 173.4	1 161.7	...	...	...	...	779.2	829.8	2 412.0	...	...	-159.2	9 562.1
2nd quarter ...	9 643.9	6 215.3	1 227.4	...	...	...	...	779.6	843.5	2 407.4	...	...	-172.1	9 631.8
3rd quarter ...	9 739.2	6 281.9	1 237.2	...	...	...	...	796.1	856.8	2 422.7	...	...	-169.3	9 732.3
4th quarter ...	9 840.8	6 356.8	1 274.9	...	...	...	...	800.1	877.3	2 422.4	...	...	-167.5	9 831.4
1993														
1st quarter	9 857.2	6 381.2	1 305.0	...	...	...	...	801.9	896.3	2 392.4	...	...	-181.0	9 822.5
2nd quarter ...	9 914.6	6 439.2	1 312.5	...	...	...	...	811.5	914.8	2 392.6	...	...	-162.9	9 898.5
3rd quarter ...	9 961.9	6 510.9	1 303.6	...	...	...	...	809.3	926.8	2 396.0	...	...	-133.5	9 981.3
4th quarter ...	10 097.4	6 568.0	1 372.1	...	...	...	...	835.4	964.1	2 404.4	...	...	-138.8	10 097.4
1994														
1st quarter	10 195.3	6 643.2	1 424.4	...	...	...	...	843.6	986.5	2 374.7	...	...	-168.1	10 151.6
2nd quarter ...	10 333.5	6 694.8	1 494.4	...	...	...	...	872.1	1 023.3	2 386.5	...	...	-206.8	10 238.5
3rd quarter ...	10 393.9	6 745.9	1 470.0	...	...	...	...	904.7	1 052.0	2 426.7	...	...	-173.7	10 342.6
4th quarter ...	10 513.0	6 818.8	1 530.5	...	...	...	...	925.6	1 081.6	2 405.6	...	...	-187.5	10 430.0
1995														
1st quarter	10 550.3	6 835.8	1 546.5	...	...	...	...	943.4	1 105.4	2 414.0	...	...	-169.1	10 484.9
2nd quarter ...	10 581.7	6 895.7	1 514.4	...	...	...	...	956.6	1 115.9	2 422.1	...	...	-139.8	10 554.0
3rd quarter ...	10 671.7	6 958.2	1 505.4	...	...	...	...	998.0	1 119.7	2 415.7	...	...	-97.0	10 679.8
4th quarter ...	10 744.2	7 006.7	1 542.8	...	...	...	...	1 012.3	1 134.0	2 390.5	...	...	-91.8	10 742.3
1996														
1st quarter	10 824.7	7 071.4	1 567.6	...	...	...	...	1 024.5	1 170.9	2 406.2	...	...	-76.5	10 839.7
2nd quarter ...	11 005.2	7 147.4	1 642.9	...	...	...	...	1 041.1	1 197.1	2 436.2	...	...	-100.1	10 988.6
3rd quarter ...	11 103.9	7 190.7	1 717.5	...	...	...	...	1 049.5	1 235.9	2 436.2	...	...	-131.0	11 042.5
4th quarter ...	11 219.2	7 248.0	1 715.2	...	...	...	...	1 115.0	1 260.3	2 453.0	...	...	-96.5	11 191.5
1997														
1st quarter	11 291.7	7 324.4	1 749.9	...	...	...	...	1 136.2	1 314.1	2 440.2	...	...	-82.1	11 260.1
2nd quarter ...	11 479.3	7 357.4	1 857.0	...	...	...	...	1 181.6	1 358.2	2 471.9	...	...	-174.8	11 361.4
3rd quarter ...	11 622.9	7 482.7	1 883.0	...	...	...	...	1 208.9	1 408.3	2 483.3	...	...	-122.8	11 546.7
4th quarter ...	11 722.7	7 572.1	1 911.0	...	...	...	...	1 207.3	1 438.7	2 495.8	...	...	-128.6	11 629.8
1998														
1st quarter	11 839.9	7 648.7	1 994.4	...	...	...	...	1 212.9	1 492.6	2 486.8	...	...	-166.6	11 713.2
2nd quarter ...	11 949.5	7 783.4	1 982.1	...	...	...	...	1 199.5	1 526.8	2 530.4	...	...	-75.5	11 910.0
3rd quarter ...	12 099.2	7 884.9	2 033.0	...	...	...	...	1 193.9	1 547.4	2 549.4	...	...	-85.9	12 044.1
4th quarter ...	12 294.7	7 998.8	2 095.8	...	...	...	...	1 238.1	1 597.5	2 564.5	...	...	-88.4	12 230.7
1999														
1st quarter	12 410.8	8 081.0	2 153.3	...	...	...	...	1 234.5	1 642.6	2 582.9	...	...	-116.3	12 321.9
2nd quarter ...	12 514.4	8 204.8	2 154.7	...	...	...	...	1 249.6	1 689.8	2 592.2	...	...	-47.0	12 479.5
3rd quarter ...	12 680.0	8 297.0	2 213.8	...	...	...	...	1 287.2	1 750.9	2 623.4	...	...	-52.9	12 634.1
4th quarter ...	12 888.3	8 418.3	2 273.1	...	...	...	...	1 314.6	1 795.7	2 664.2	...	...	-105.6	12 788.7
2000														
1st quarter	12 935.3	8 545.6	2 257.1	...	...	...	...	1 333.7	1 863.5	2 645.3	...	...	-4.4	12 923.2
2nd quarter ...	13 170.7	8 625.4	2 390.7	...	...	...	...	1 374.3	1 922.9	2 671.4	...	...	-91.8	13 065.1
3rd quarter ...	13 183.9	8 708.1	2 367.3	...	...	...	...	1 407.3	1 992.0	2 660.1	...	...	-54.2	13 115.5
4th quarter ...	13 262.3	8 784.2	2 371.8	...	...	...	...	1 393.3	1 995.0	2 676.4	...	...	-50.9	13 196.7
2001														
1st quarter	13 219.3	8 816.0	2 264.2	...	...	...	...	1 375.8	1 969.2	2 718.3	...	...	59.7	13 257.7
2nd quarter ...	13 301.4	8 833.7	2 267.4	...	...	...	...	1 335.4	1 906.2	2 765.4	...	...	8.3	13 306.8
3rd quarter ...	13 248.1	8 864.5	2 218.4	...	...	...	...	1 267.0	1 863.0	2 762.7	...	...	45.3	13 289.4
4th quarter ...	13 284.9	9 007.5	2 108.5	...	...	...	...	1 222.9	1 843.7	2 808.5	...	...	99.0	13 390.2
2002														
1st quarter	13 394.9	9 027.5	2 170.7	1 492.6	675.9	-7.8	-646.4	1 249.6	1 896.0	2 857.3	946.8	1 923.7	-103.6	13 411.4
2nd quarter ...	13 477.4	9 073.2	2 206.4	1 475.8	692.6	33.1	-672.8	1 286.8	1 959.6	2 879.3	965.2	1 926.3	-92.4	13 452.5
3rd quarter ...	13 531.7	9 136.7	2 203.1	1 471.0	694.7	28.7	-693.6	1 290.9	1 984.5	2 894.2	974.7	1 931.3	-68.2	13 506.9
4th quarter ...	13 549.4	9 187.5	2 201.7	1 451.2	707.2	43.4	-748.3	1 271.8	2 020.1	2 915.6	991.3	1 935.3	-82.1	13 516.2

Note: Chained (2012) dollar series are calculated as the product of the chain-type quantity index and the 2012 current-dollar value of the corresponding series, divided by 100. Because the formula for the chain-type quantity indexes uses weights from more than one period, the corresponding chained-dollar estimates are usually not additive. The residual column is the difference between the total and the sum of the most detailed components shown in the Bureau of Economic Analysis (BEA) published data.

. . . = Not available.

Table 1-2B. Real Gross Domestic Product: Historical Data—*Continued*

(Billions of chained [2012] dollars, quarterly data are at seasonally adjusted annual rates.)   **NIPA Tables 1.1.6, 1.2.6**

| Year and quarter | Gross domestic product | Personal consumption expenditures | Gross private domestic investment | | | | Exports and imports of goods and services | | | Government consumption expenditures and gross investment | | | Residual | Addendum: Final sales of domestic product |
| | | | Total | Fixed investment | | Change in private inventories | Net exports | Exports | Imports | Total | Federal | State and local | | |
				Nonresidential	Residential									
2003														
1st quarter	13 619.4	9 232.8	2 218.7	1 458.4	720.2	39.9	-743.4	1 267.9	2 011.3	2 917.9	1 002.5	1 925.3	-79.6	13 589.3
2nd quarter	13 741.1	9 338.5	2 234.0	1 498.7	731.7	-9.2	-770.5	1 270.1	2 040.7	2 944.7	1 037.1	1 914.9	-48.5	13 751.1
3rd quarter	13 970.2	9 470.5	2 315.4	1 530.5	773.6	2.8	-767.8	1 304.8	2 072.6	2 951.2	1 036.8	1 921.9	-32.5	13 970.9
4th quarter	14 131.4	9 535.7	2 393.4	1 549.8	796.6	46.2	-774.9	1 363.5	2 138.4	2 969.1	1 056.1	1 919.2	-26.9	14 093.7
2004														
1st quarter	14 212.3	9 624.6	2 398.2	1 534.4	805.9	58.7	-804.0	1 394.3	2 198.3	2 982.7	1 067.6	1 920.6	-20.7	14 162.7
2nd quarter	14 323.0	9 677.2	2 493.9	1 572.8	831.4	97.7	-861.4	1 423.5	2 284.9	2 990.8	1 073.9	1 922.1	-13.3	14 239.4
3rd quarter	14 457.8	9 790.8	2 532.6	1 617.8	837.4	83.1	-888.4	1 428.2	2 316.6	2 996.3	1 085.7	1 914.9	0.6	14 387.8
4th quarter	14 605.6	9 901.6	2 585.5	1 651.0	848.9	91.1	-908.5	1 462.1	2 370.6	2 994.6	1 083.7	1 915.3	12.5	14 527.0
2005														
1st quarter	14 767.8	9 964.5	2 658.2	1 675.0	868.9	124.9	-901.5	1 489.5	2 391.0	3 009.6	1 095.8	1 917.6	11.7	14 658.3
2nd quarter	14 839.7	10 074.9	2 622.8	1 702.0	885.0	24.7	-900.2	1 522.7	2 423.0	3 007.8	1 094.6	1 917.0	38.9	14 815.3
3rd quarter	14 956.3	10 158.5	2 657.5	1 737.5	894.7	7.9	-914.2	1 522.4	2 436.6	3 017.8	1 103.1	1 918.2	55.0	14 943.6
4th quarter	15 041.2	10 177.2	2 743.8	1 750.9	892.9	97.4	-945.5	1 569.6	2 515.1	3 020.1	1 103.5	1 920.2	38.4	14 947.7
2006														
1st quarter	15 244.1	10 288.2	2 784.6	1 809.7	884.6	102.7	-933.7	1 633.2	2 566.9	3 058.5	1 132.2	1 928.9	33.5	15 160.5
2nd quarter	15 281.5	10 341.6	2 766.6	1 841.3	840.3	92.7	-929.0	1 663.4	2 592.5	3 057.6	1 124.4	1 936.2	33.4	15 201.6
3rd quarter	15 304.5	10 408.0	2 756.0	1 872.9	793.8	97.3	-957.1	1 661.2	2 618.4	3 053.1	1 114.3	1 942.4	34.1	15 217.5
4th quarter	15 433.6	10 507.2	2 702.5	1 892.7	756.9	55.7	-890.7	1 724.3	2 615.0	3 078.2	1 130.4	1 951.0	32.1	15 384.1
2007														
1st quarter	15 479.0	10 572.1	2 683.9	1 926.8	722.7	27.5	-894.6	1 758.4	2 653.1	3 082.5	1 123.7	1 962.4	41.3	15 447.1
2nd quarter	15 577.8	10 599.8	2 713.5	1 969.6	694.3	56.4	-882.1	1 785.1	2 667.2	3 110.7	1 142.1	1 971.8	28.8	15 527.4
3rd quarter	15 671.6	10 670.5	2 686.1	2 000.5	650.1	43.4	-841.3	1 840.8	2 682.1	3 124.9	1 152.1	1 975.8	22.2	15 634.2
4th quarter	15 767.1	10 712.6	2 653.1	2 031.3	596.1	35.0	-773.7	1 883.1	2 656.8	3 149.5	1 171.3	1 980.8	15.1	15 738.0
2008														
1st quarter	15 702.9	10 697.9	2 583.3	2 039.4	548.7	1.6	-753.7	1 913.0	2 666.7	3 156.9	1 189.1	1 970.0	4.8	15 705.2
2nd quarter ...	15 792.8	10 727.3	2 536.4	2 043.5	523.8	-25.4	-672.3	1 969.2	2 641.5	3 184.3	1 214.5	1 971.6	1.5	15 822.7
3rd quarter ...	15 709.6	10 644.7	2 485.5	2 005.4	497.2	-19.3	-647.8	1 960.4	2 608.2	3 210.0	1 230.3	1 981.5	5.6	15 724.6
4th quarter ...	15 366.6	10 548.9	2 246.4	1 888.6	448.8	-87.6	-668.9	1 845.0	2 513.8	3 231.9	1 246.3	1 987.3	-18.5	15 459.7
2009														
1st quarter	15 187.5	10 522.1	1 986.8	1 746.3	405.3	-179.0	-577.3	1 697.6	2 274.9	3 268.8	1 262.8	2 007.7	-23.5	15 359.8
2nd quarter	15 161.8	10 470.4	1 872.3	1 693.2	380.4	-228.3	-473.7	1 708.8	2 182.5	3 316.6	1 292.8	2 025.2	-21.0	15 371.4
3rd quarter	15 216.6	10 540.8	1 868.0	1 683.3	398.1	-245.1	-500.5	1 772.0	2 272.5	3 325.7	1 304.6	2 022.3	-1.0	15 437.6
4th quarter	15 379.2	10 529.2	2 040.7	1 694.5	397.2	-56.8	-513.6	1 871.5	2 385.1	3 331.6	1 324.0	2 008.4	-15.9	15 432.4
2010														
1st quarter	15 456.1	10 590.2	2 087.2	1 706.4	384.4	-5.0	-531.8	1 916.2	2 448.0	3 317.3	1 338.8	1 978.9	-13.7	15 460.9
2nd quarter	15 605.6	10 685.1	2 196.7	1 762.3	404.4	33.3	-601.3	1 958.4	2 559.7	3 327.6	1 356.4	1 971.3	-10.9	15 576.4
3rd quarter	15 726.3	10 761.4	2 294.7	1 810.1	368.6	128.8	-634.9	2 014.2	2 649.1	3 304.1	1 350.2	1 953.9	-14.3	15 609.5
4th quarter	15 808.0	10 827.3	2 287.4	1 845.2	374.7	72.1	-589.5	2 069.3	2 658.9	3 283.0	1 348.0	1 934.9	-6.4	15 740.4
2011														
1st quarter	15 769.9	10 868.7	2 244.2	1 842.7	373.4	32.8	-584.8	2 087.1	2 671.9	3 242.8	1 329.0	1 913.8	-5.3	15 742.1
2nd quarter	15 876.8	10 879.9	2 336.1	1 890.4	377.6	71.3	-559.5	2 122.3	2 681.9	3 220.8	1 323.9	1 896.9	-4.6	15 808.8
3rd quarter	15 870.7	10 913.0	2 343.8	1 978.9	384.4	-17.7	-560.1	2 151.5	2 711.6	3 174.8	1 295.1	1 879.8	-4.0	15 890.5
4th quarter	16 048.7	10 931.8	2 524.4	2 029.4	394.4	100.4	-579.6	2 167.7	2 747.2	3 172.5	1 299.9	1 872.6	-0.8	15 948.0
2012														
1st quarter	16 180.0	11 010.7	2 577.2	2 081.3	418.3	72.8	-566.7	2 194.1	2 760.7	3 158.9	1 299.9	1 859.0	4.6	16 102.3
2nd quarter	16 253.7	11 030.0	2 636.5	2 128.0	421.9	87.1	-555.3	2 215.8	2 771.0	3 142.4	1 289.5	1 852.9	-0.3	16 167.1
3rd quarter	16 282.2	11 052.4	2 648.5	2 120.9	432.7	98.0	-556.5	2 229.4	2 785.9	3 137.7	1 292.2	1 845.5	-2.8	16 187.3
4th quarter	16 300.0	11 096.4	2 624.9	2 144.0	455.2	27.0	-528.0	2 231.6	2 759.6	3 106.9	1 266.4	1 840.5	-1.5	16 274.3
2013														
1st quarter	16 441.5	11 155.5	2 722.8	2 171.6	471.8	81.2	-515.0	2 242.3	2 757.3	3 078.9	1 237.4	1 841.3	-3.1	16 362.5
2nd quarter	16 464.4	11 172.6	2 753.2	2 177.5	486.8	85.8	-534.8	2 262.5	2 797.3	3 073.7	1 227.4	1 846.0	2.3	16 376.4
3rd quarter	16 594.7	11 214.4	2 859.8	2 214.7	495.5	147.6	-535.4	2 282.0	2 817.4	3 057.2	1 209.6	1 847.0	0.8	16 446.7
4th quarter	16 712.8	11 304.3	2 870.1	2 260.0	487.7	120.0	-492.1	2 347.6	2 839.7	3 033.1	1 188.9	1 843.4	-1.0	16 591.0
2014														
1st quarter	16 654.2	11 347.6	2 838.3	2 291.7	484.3	58.3	-551.5	2 324.8	2 876.3	3 020.6	1 187.7	1 832.2	2.9	16 591.3
2nd quarter	16 868.1	11 453.0	2 958.1	2 353.3	499.8	98.6	-566.7	2 375.1	2 941.8	3 024.4	1 180.7	1 842.7	3.8	16 763.1
3rd quarter	17 064.6	11 565.7	3 018.6	2 400.8	507.1	106.3	-562.6	2 384.8	2 947.4	3 044.7	1 193.9	1 849.9	-1.4	16 953.8
4th quarter	17 141.2	11 694.9	3 021.9	2 415.5	525.2	82.0	-620.3	2 404.4	3 024.7	3 043.2	1 176.5	1 865.4	-2.9	17 061.0
2015														
1st quarter	17 280.6	11 772.9	3 127.3	2 412.6	535.5	177.3	-683.6	2 384.8	3 068.5	3 059.0	1 181.3	1 876.3	4.5	17 104.4
2nd quarter	17 380.9	11 852.7	3 136.7	2 423.6	548.9	156.5	-699.9	2 391.1	3 091.1	3 085.1	1 183.5	1 900.0	9.0	17 220.5
3rd quarter	17 437.1	11 943.0	3 130.4	2 432.4	563.7	125.2	-746.6	2 371.2	3 117.8	3 099.1	1 182.3	1 915.1	11.8	17 307.2
4th quarter	17 462.6	12 003.1	3 092.7	2 412.8	573.6	91.4	-756.7	2 367.7	3 124.4	3 110.3	1 191.1	1 917.5	17.4	17 361.0
2016														
1st quarter	17 565.5	12 091.2	3 079.4	2 410.4	591.2	59.1	-759.3	2 360.7	3 120.0	3 142.8	1 194.0	1 946.9	14.9	17 494.9
2nd quarter	17 618.6	12 152.6	3 063.3	2 426.1	592.0	23.0	-744.6	2 378.6	3 123.2	3 137.9	1 184.3	1 951.6	17.8	17 579.7
3rd quarter	17 724.5	12 223.8	3 069.3	2 457.8	588.9	-6.2	-730.4	2 415.6	3 146.0	3 153.9	1 191.5	1 960.4	19.4	17 706.5
4th quarter	17 812.6	12 283.1	3 147.6	2 473.6	596.3	66.9	-794.0	2 398.6	3 192.5	3 160.5	1 192.3	1 966.2	9.0	17 741.3
2017														
1st quarter	17 896.6	12 372.2	3 137.7	2 505.1	611.8	-13.0	-783.2	2 455.6	3 238.8	3 153.8	1 183.8	1 967.8	32.4	17 882.3
2nd quarter	17 996.8	12 430.1	3 192.8	2 531.0	615.7	18.5	-808.0	2 465.4	3 273.4	3 163.2	1 193.7	1 967.5	24.0	17 957.5
3rd quarter	18 126.2	12 500.4	3 241.0	2 538.7	612.7	83.4	-790.3	2 481.9	3 272.2	3 160.7	1 193.4	1 965.3	-9.6	18 043.5
4th quarter	18 296.7	12 632.0	3 278.4	2 590.5	623.2	45.6	-816.3	2 540.1	3 356.5	3 183.0	1 207.7	1 973.4	0.4	18 238.3
2018														
1st quarter	18 436.3	12 707.6	3 346.3	2 654.0	616.5	63.5	-826.4	2 551.6	3 378.0	3 189.7	1 213.0	1 974.9	-2.2	18 363.5
2nd quarter	18 590.0	12 816.4	3 352.5	2 698.0	621.5	11.1	-807.2	2 582.9	3 390.1	3 212.2	1 228.1	1 982.5	-4.5	18 558.0
3rd quarter	18 679.6	12 900.6	3 430.9	2 716.7	612.2	101.0	-896.9	2 542.5	3 439.4	3 220.0	1 238.5	1 980.2	-15.9	18 577.9
4th quarter	18 721.3	12 955.5	3 449.6	2 749.0	599.0	87.3	-926.5	2 545.6	3 472.1	3 213.4	1 244.2	1 968.1	-6.3	18 615.8

Note: Chained (2012) dollar series are calculated as the product of the chain-type quantity index and the 2012 current-dollar value of the corresponding series, divided by 100. Because the formula for the chain-type quantity indexes uses weights from more than one period, the corresponding chained-dollar estimates are usually not additive. The residual column is the difference between the total and the sum of the most detailed components shown in the Bureau of Economic Analysis (BEA) published data.

Table 1-3A. U.S. Population and Per Capita Product and Income: Recent Data

(Dollars, except as noted; quarterly data are at seasonally adjusted annual rates.)

NIPA Table 7.1

Year and quarter	Population (mid-period, thousands)	Current dollars							Chained (2012) dollars					
		Gross domestic product	Personal income	Disposable personal income	Personal consumption expenditures				Gross domestic product	Disposable personal income	Personal consumption expenditures			
					Total	Durable goods	Nondurable goods	Services			Total	Durable goods	Nondurable goods	Services
1960	180 760	3 001	2 335	2 080	1 832	252	727	853	18 046	12 654	11 144	444	4 024	7 232
1961	183 742	3 060	2 398	2 141	1 858	241	733	885	18 209	12 886	11 188	422	4 039	7 376
1962	186 590	3 237	2 513	2 236	1 943	265	748	930	19 029	13 307	11 562	463	4 099	7 607
1963	189 300	3 367	2 603	2 315	2 018	286	760	971	19 574	13 612	11 866	498	4 128	7 818
1964	191 927	3 566	2 752	2 481	2 140	310	796	1 034	20 418	14 378	12 400	537	4 262	8 169
1965	194 347	3 819	2 936	2 640	2 279	342	840	1 098	21 474	15 081	13 023	596	4 421	8 515
1966	196 599	4 137	3 155	2 818	2 441	365	905	1 171	22 628	15 702	13 604	638	4 614	8 834
1967	198 752	4 327	3 350	2 982	2 549	372	931	1 246	22 997	16 213	13 859	641	4 662	9 097
1968	200 745	4 686	3 641	3 208	2 774	423	995	1 356	23 888	16 781	14 512	705	4 811	9 485
1969	202 736	5 019	3 948	3 432	2 977	446	1 057	1 475	24 392	17 181	14 905	724	4 895	9 808
1970	205 089	5 233	4 218	3 715	3 153	439	1 116	1 599	24 157	17 768	15 081	697	4 947	10 077
1971	207 692	5 609	4 491	4 002	3 370	493	1 154	1 723	24 640	18 357	15 460	757	4 976	10 296
1972	209 924	6 093	4 880	4 291	3 659	555	1 226	1 878	25 660	19 036	16 233	842	5 123	10 770
1973	211 939	6 725	5 383	4 758	4 009	616	1 350	2 043	26 851	20 028	16 874	921	5 220	11 172
1974	213 898	7 224	5 852	5 146	4 349	609	1 502	2 238	26 462	19 621	16 580	854	5 046	11 282
1975	215 981	7 801	6 340	5 657	4 771	658	1 617	2 497	26 153	19 908	16 792	848	5 040	11 594
1976	218 086	8 590	6 890	6 098	5 262	773	1 732	2 757	27 296	20 346	17 557	945	5 229	11 975
1977	220 289	9 450	7 532	6 634	5 783	871	1 854	3 058	28 272	20 780	18 116	1 019	5 295	12 345
1978	222 629	10 563	8 371	7 340	6 388	958	2 022	3 408	29 524	21 497	18 710	1 061	5 428	12 776
1979	225 106	11 672	9 252	8 057	7 043	1 005	2 273	3 765	30 123	21 672	18 944	1 044	5 507	13 022
1980	227 726	12 547	10 204	8 888	7 688	994	2 518	4 176	29 700	21 584	18 668	950	5 434	13 082
1981	230 008	13 943	11 326	9 823	8 408	1 061	2 719	4 628	30 152	21 891	18 739	950	5 448	13 154
1982	232 218	14 399	12 021	10 494	8 919	1 090	2 783	5 047	29 326	22 156	18 832	939	5 452	13 299
1983	234 333	15 508	12 721	11 216	9 737	1 259	2 897	5 581	30 394	22 714	19 718	1 064	5 579	13 855
1984	236 394	17 080	13 929	12 330	10 543	1 447	3 052	6 043	32 309	24 062	20 575	1 205	5 759	14 261
1985	238 506	18 192	14 779	13 027	11 374	1 595	3 175	6 605	33 358	24 565	21 449	1 314	5 880	14 858
1986	240 683	19 028	15 510	13 691	11 992	1 751	3 217	7 024	34 201	25 268	22 132	1 427	6 035	15 179
1987	242 843	19 993	16 313	14 297	12 668	1 820	3 353	7 494	35 070	25 597	22 680	1 442	6 084	15 725
1988	245 061	21 368	17 479	15 414	13 589	1 939	3 519	8 131	36 204	26 559	23 413	1 511	6 187	16 283
1989	247 387	22 805	18 698	16 403	14 458	1 998	3 757	8 703	37 181	27 080	23 869	1 530	6 294	16 642
1990	250 181	23 835	19 641	17 264	15 225	1 987	3 974	9 264	37 459	27 303	24 078	1 506	6 297	16 939
1991	253 530	24 290	20 056	17 734	15 554	1 882	4 024	9 648	36 924	27 138	23 803	1 406	6 195	16 977
1992	256 922	25 379	21 099	18 714	16 338	1 978	4 107	10 253	37 720	27 895	24 353	1 467	6 232	17 423
1993	260 282	26 350	21 738	19 245	17 104	2 119	4 191	10 795	38 258	27 990	24 876	1 557	6 308	17 729
1994	263 455	27 660	22 574	19 943	17 919	2 305	4 325	11 290	39 320	28 411	25 529	1 661	6 475	18 052
1995	266 588	28 658	23 600	20 792	18 615	2 385	4 426	11 805	39 900	29 011	25 973	1 706	6 558	18 363
1996	269 714	29 932	24 762	21 658	19 445	2 507	4 603	12 335	40 926	29 586	26 563	1 812	6 669	18 675
1997	272 958	31 424	25 984	22 570	20 284	2 621	4 730	12 933	42 238	30 304	27 236	1 937	6 782	19 044
1998	276 154	32 818	27 545	23 806	21 283	2 822	4 813	13 647	43 620	31 712	28 350	2 145	6 953	19 679
1999	279 328	34 480	28 665	24 684	22 496	3 063	5 125	14 308	45 192	32 409	29 536	2 393	7 224	20 229
2000	282 398	36 300	30 651	26 274	23 963	3 232	5 455	15 276	46 523	33 645	30 687	2 570	7 373	21 001
2001	285 225	37 100	31 599	27 255	24 801	3 301	5 554	15 946	46 502	34 216	31 135	2 678	7 427	21 243
2002	287 955	37 954	31 814	28 160	25 521	3 422	5 603	16 496	46 842	34 894	31 624	2 848	7 493	21 422
2003	290 626	39 420	32 683	29 230	26 635	3 502	5 866	17 267	47 709	35 474	32 325	3 026	7 685	21 699
2004	293 262	41 660	34 250	30 674	28 070	3 685	6 211	18 175	49 102	36 325	33 242	3 247	7 865	22 159
2005	295 993	44 052	35 828	31 732	29 626	3 813	6 603	19 210	50 343	36 526	34 101	3 395	8 052	22 661
2006	298 818	46 234	38 099	33 558	31 046	3 876	6 965	20 205	51 255	37 570	34 758	3 512	8 238	23 001
2007	301 696	47 976	39 846	34 899	32 306	3 938	7 222	21 146	51 787	38 093	35 263	3 645	8 298	23 292
2008	304 543	48 498	40 971	36 021	33 001	3 608	7 436	21 957	51 365	38 188	34 986	3 403	8 091	23 494
2009	307 240	47 123	39 319	35 568	32 194	3 294	7 056	21 843	49 591	37 814	34 226	3 167	7 887	23 193
2010	309 839	48 570	40 649	36 654	33 115	3 386	7 323	22 407	50 507	38 282	34 586	3 316	7 944	23 336
2011	312 295	49 952	42 714	38 059	34 259	3 501	7 764	22 993	50 886	38 769	34 898	3 457	7 951	23 493
2012	314 725	51 645	44 529	39 732	35 102	3 636	7 923	23 543	51 645	39 732	35 102	3 636	7 923	23 543
2013	317 099	53 117	44 761	39 474	35 836	3 751	8 012	24 073	52 202	38 947	35 357	3 829	8 005	23 527
2014	319 601	54 914	46 860	41 276	37 070	3 886	8 200	24 984	52 979	40 118	36 030	4 072	8 152	23 821
2015	322 113	56 521	48 695	42 672	38 072	4 059	8 119	25 893	53 988	41 383	36 922	4 348	8 363	24 245
2016	324 609	57 593	49 589	43 556	39 103	4 144	8 153	26 806	54 466	41 821	37 546	4 547	8 504	24 548
2017	326 860	59 596	51 552	45 283	40 504	4 273	8 450	27 781	55 311	42 699	38 193	4 798	8 671	24 812
2018	328 794	62 432	53 851	47 536	42 317	4 468	8 773	29 075	56 591	43 886	39 067	5 104	8 831	25 261
2019	330 513	64 665	55 745	49 073	43 655	4 579	8 973	30 104	57 585	44 644	39 715	5 294	9 041	25 547
2020	331 761	62 978	59 162	52 544	42 342	4 872	9 155	28 315	55 415	47 241	38 069	5 680	9 285	23 536
2021	332 213	69 221	63 492	55 710	47 384	6 099	10 401	30 884	58 478	48 219	41 012	6 698	10 112	24 858
2019														
1st quarter	329 868	63 667	55 291	48 715	42 913	4 466	8 820	29 626	57 093	44 653	39 334	5 134	8 939	25 397
2nd quarter	330 245	64 465	55 551	48 820	43 530	4 570	8 994	29 967	57 480	44 450	39 633	5 261	9 040	25 497
3rd quarter	330 729	65 023	55 830	49 163	43 932	4 630	9 014	30 287	57 789	44 638	39 888	5 361	9 096	25 613
4th quarter	331 208	65 501	56 304	49 592	44 244	4 647	9 063	30 534	57 977	44 837	40 002	5 419	9 088	25 681
2020														
1st quarter	331 534	64 794	56 833	50 072	43 552	4 479	9 188	29 886	57 165	45 132	39 255	5 243	9 235	24 988
2nd quarter	331 692	58 722	61 348	55 020	39 162	4 427	8 688	26 048	52 031	49 796	35 444	5 221	8 891	21 759
3rd quarter	331 841	63 701	59 599	53 024	43 074	5 284	9 384	28 407	55 933	47 560	38 635	6 119	9 522	23 551
4th quarter	331 978	64 696	58 865	52 058	43 580	5 299	9 362	28 919	56 533	46 518	38 942	6 134	9 492	23 848
2021														
1st quarter	331 949	66 390	65 876	58 609	45 204	5 898	9 903	29 403	57 405	51 880	40 014	6 789	9 849	24 080
2nd quarter	332 021	68 493	62 225	54 627	47 231	6 301	10 354	30 576	58 335	47 604	41 159	6 976	10 172	24 740
3rd quarter	332 297	69 824	62 666	54 718	48 044	6 004	10 548	31 492	58 619	47 066	41 326	6 496	10 214	25 214
4th quarter	332 584	72 171	63 172	54 889	49 053	6 193	10 798	32 062	59 553	46 492	41 549	6 530	10 214	25 396

Table 1-3B. U.S. Population and Per Capita Product and Income: Historical Data

(Dollars, except as noted; quarterly data are at seasonally adjusted annual rates.)   NIPA Table 7.1

Year and quarter	Population (mid-period, thou-sands)	Current dollars							Chained (2012) dollars					
		Gross domestic product	Personal income	Dispos-able personal income	Personal consumption expenditures				Gross domestic product	Dispos-able personal income	Personal consumption expenditures			
					Total	Durable goods	Nondur-able goods	Services			Total	Durable goods	Nondur-able goods	Services
1929	121 878	858	700	686	635	81	278	276	9 109	7 375	6 830	251	2 769	4 074
1930	123 188	748	621	609	569	62	248	260	8 246	6 836	6 395	206	2 597	3 947
1931	124 149	623	529	521	489	48	208	233	7 658	6 552	6 148	177	2 549	3 817
1932	124 949	476	403	397	390	32	161	197	6 627	5 659	5 562	133	2 310	3 563
1933	125 690	455	376	369	366	30	159	177	6 507	5 463	5 407	129	2 288	3 411
1934	126 485	528	428	421	407	36	189	182	7 165	5 950	5 757	147	2 459	3 556
1935	127 362	583	478	469	439	43	205	191	7 749	6 481	6 064	177	2 582	3 655
1936	128 181	662	540	530	485	53	228	205	8 691	7 251	6 638	214	2 858	3 855
1937	128 961	721	579	564	518	57	240	221	9 081	7 451	6 842	224	2 911	4 011
1938	129 969	672	532	517	495	47	230	217	8 712	6 988	6 681	184	2 930	3 948
1939	131 028	713	562	551	513	55	235	224	9 335	7 511	6 997	217	3 039	4 069
1940	132 122	779	601	588	540	63	245	232	10 074	7 957	7 299	246	3 143	4 190
1941	133 402	969	734	716	608	77	279	252	11 745	9 123	7 740	281	3 299	4 397
1942	134 860	1 231	940	903	660	57	322	282	13 813	10 232	7 474	176	3 272	4 589
1943	136 739	1 485	1 142	1 020	731	55	357	319	15 942	10 576	7 577	156	3 248	4 887
1944	138 397	1 622	1 226	1 099	785	56	381	348	17 004	10 775	7 699	142	3 276	5 098
1945	139 928	1 629	1 256	1 117	857	65	418	374	16 653	10 537	8 086	156	3 441	5 312
1946	141 389	1 609	1 291	1 169	1 020	121	489	410	14 568	10 309	8 992	279	3 713	5 487
1947	144 126	1 732	1 349	1 212	1 123	151	538	433	14 128	9 702	8 989	322	3 621	5 404
1948	146 631	1 872	1 456	1 325	1 193	167	566	460	14 458	10 039	9 036	337	3 586	5 453
1949	149 188	1 826	1 415	1 303	1 195	178	546	471	14 130	9 947	9 128	358	3 577	5 488
1947														
1st quarter	143 143	1 699	1 325	1 191	1 091	145	523	423	14 213	9 746	8 924	311	3 603	5 395
2nd quarter	143 790	1 711	1 319	1 184	1 113	148	535	430	14 111	9 608	9 032	317	3 648	5 449
3rd quarter	144 449	1 728	1 369	1 233	1 132	151	544	437	14 018	9 820	9 020	319	3 648	5 413
4th quarter	145 122	1 790	1 383	1 240	1 155	162	551	443	14 171	9 637	8 981	339	3 584	5 360
1948														
1st quarter	145 709	1 824	1 417	1 272	1 169	162	560	448	14 326	9 777	8 989	336	3 581	5 395
2nd quarter	146 289	1 863	1 449	1 319	1 190	164	569	458	14 505	10 040	9 058	337	3 602	5 458
3rd quarter	146 921	1 900	1 480	1 356	1 205	172	568	465	14 525	10 160	9 032	341	3 565	5 464
4th quarter	147 607	1 899	1 478	1 353	1 205	169	567	469	14 474	10 170	9 062	334	3 595	5 493
1949														
1st quarter	148 254	1 855	1 430	1 310	1 193	165	558	470	14 212	9 926	9 037	327	3 593	5 503
2nd quarter	148 847	1 823	1 417	1 303	1 199	177	550	471	14 107	9 935	9 139	354	3 588	5 509
3rd quarter	149 485	1 826	1 408	1 299	1 189	183	537	470	14 192	9 957	9 121	369	3 542	5 474
4th quarter	150 167	1 802	1 404	1 299	1 200	189	539	472	14 009	9 968	9 212	382	3 583	5 465
1950														
1st quarter	150 786	1 862	1 501	1 391	1 213	195	540	478	14 500	10 693	9 327	395	3 614	5 511
2nd quarter	151 319	1 919	1 505	1 388	1 235	197	547	490	14 889	10 624	9 448	397	3 644	5 630
3rd quarter	151 973	2 028	1 553	1 429	1 319	246	570	503	15 398	10 711	9 890	489	3 691	5 693
4th quarter	152 658	2 096	1 604	1 457	1 297	218	568	511	15 623	10 728	9 549	426	3 592	5 704
1951														
1st quarter	153 291	2 192	1 658	1 499	1 365	232	600	532	15 769	10 694	9 739	438	3 643	5 836
2nd quarter	153 902	2 236	1 710	1 538	1 332	200	594	538	15 979	10 889	9 426	374	3 576	5 852
3rd quarter	154 610	2 273	1 730	1 551	1 343	195	603	545	16 234	10 962	9 493	365	3 634	5 898
4th quarter	155 344	2 293	1 752	1 561	1 362	196	614	552	16 192	10 891	9 503	362	3 659	5 885
1952														
1st quarter	155 976	2 307	1 758	1 561	1 365	197	608	561	16 299	10 842	9 486	363	3 614	5 935
2nd quarter	156 587	2 306	1 777	1 574	1 386	198	617	571	16 271	10 937	9 634	369	3 684	6 003
3rd quarter	157 267	2 338	1 814	1 609	1 396	187	626	583	16 317	11 109	9 639	345	3 733	6 056
4th quarter	157 986	2 410	1 848	1 639	1 441	213	635	593	16 776	11 296	9 933	403	3 770	6 113
1953														
1st quarter	158 574	2 447	1 869	1 658	1 458	222	634	602	17 025	11 387	10 013	415	3 779	6 150
2nd quarter	159 160	2 461	1 886	1 676	1 464	220	632	612	17 093	11 494	10 036	411	3 783	6 201
3rd quarter	159 889	2 447	1 877	1 670	1 461	216	624	621	16 920	11 386	9 966	407	3 731	6 209
4th quarter	160 639	2 403	1 868	1 663	1 451	210	622	619	16 586	11 295	9 853	393	3 719	6 133
1954														
1st quarter	161 328	2 389	1 860	1 673	1 458	204	628	626	16 436	11 304	9 847	379	3 739	6 165
2nd quarter	161 983	2 384	1 851	1 666	1 469	208	626	635	16 387	11 269	9 935	396	3 714	6 245
3rd quarter	162 731	2 403	1 854	1 670	1 477	204	628	644	16 496	11 336	10 023	396	3 744	6 324
4th quarter	163 524	2 445	1 878	1 692	1 499	214	633	652	16 737	11 498	10 184	418	3 788	6 369
1955														
1st quarter	164 204	2 516	1 909	1 718	1 531	234	636	661	17 144	11 636	10 369	454	3 812	6 417
2nd quarter	164 864	2 557	1 947	1 751	1 556	247	644	665	17 353	11 846	10 525	477	3 866	6 438
3rd quarter	165 612	2 598	1 983	1 782	1 574	256	646	672	17 508	12 010	10 607	490	3 875	6 474
4th quarter	166 419	2 626	2 004	1 799	1 590	249	655	686	17 528	12 091	10 688	475	3 934	6 571
1956														
1st quarter	167 109	2 632	2 029	1 817	1 593	237	661	694	17 388	12 162	10 662	451	3 962	6 607
2nd quarter	167 788	2 658	2 055	1 839	1 602	237	663	702	17 461	12 228	10 654	450	3 936	6 644
3rd quarter	168 573	2 677	2 077	1 858	1 614	235	667	712	17 364	12 234	10 628	440	3 921	6 682
4th quarter	169 416	2 718	2 112	1 888	1 638	245	671	722	17 562	12 361	10 721	452	3 932	6 736
1957														
1st quarter	170 172	2 761	2 129	1 903	1 656	250	678	728	17 595	12 345	10 748	458	3 939	6 733
2nd quarter	170 869	2 762	2 148	1 920	1 663	247	682	735	17 485	12 382	10 723	446	3 937	6 763
3rd quarter	171 638	2 794	2 165	1 937	1 682	244	695	743	17 578	12 388	10 759	441	3 974	6 781
4th quarter	172 417	2 754	2 150	1 925	1 684	241	690	753	17 317	12 250	10 715	433	3 930	6 824

Table 1-3B. U.S. Population and Per Capita Product and Income: Historical Data—*Continued*

(Dollars, except as noted; quarterly data are at seasonally adjusted annual rates.)   NIPA Table 7.1

Year and quarter	Population (mid-period, thousands)	Current dollars							Chained (2012) dollars					
		Gross domestic product	Personal income	Disposable personal income	Personal consumption expenditures				Gross domestic product	Disposable personal income	Personal consumption expenditures			
					Total	Durable goods	Nondurable goods	Services			Total	Durable goods	Nondurable goods	Services
1958														
1st quarter	173 064	2 702	2 145	1 925	1 675	228	693	755	16 805	12 096	10 527	403	3 880	6 789
2nd quarter	173 729	2 717	2 151	1 934	1 685	222	698	766	16 850	12 134	10 573	395	3 901	6 862
3rd quarter	174 483	2 784	2 193	1 970	1 707	226	705	776	17 166	12 347	10 702	402	3 955	6 927
4th quarter	175 288	2 850	2 215	1 990	1 722	232	708	782	17 486	12 479	10 798	415	3 991	6 942
1959														
1st quarter	176 045	2 899	2 238	2 006	1 758	248	716	794	17 745	12 497	10 949	435	4 025	6 998
2nd quarter	176 727	2 957	2 277	2 039	1 785	257	719	809	18 075	12 650	11 075	450	4 043	7 075
3rd quarter	177 481	2 958	2 280	2 040	1 807	261	722	824	18 011	12 579	11 143	457	4 041	7 140
4th quarter	178 268	2 965	2 302	2 057	1 811	247	726	837	17 983	12 613	11 106	433	4 048	7 195
1960														
1st quarter	179 319	3 026	2 324	2 071	1 820	253	723	844	18 279	12 683	11 147	444	4 035	7 217
2nd quarter	180 401	2 999	2 338	2 083	1 842	257	731	853	18 072	12 689	11 220	452	4 054	7 253
3rd quarter	181 301	3 009	2 341	2 084	1 832	253	726	853	18 070	12 650	11 119	446	4 010	7 209
4th quarter	182 019	2 968	2 339	2 084	1 835	246	727	862	17 768	12 595	11 090	433	3 997	7 250
1961														
1st quarter	182 634	2 984	2 355	2 101	1 832	231	730	870	17 828	12 671	11 048	408	4 008	7 296
2nd quarter	183 337	3 030	2 380	2 124	1 852	236	732	883	18 061	12 814	11 170	415	4 046	7 374
3rd quarter	184 103	3 083	2 409	2 151	1 859	242	731	886	18 331	12 931	11 177	423	4 032	7 366
4th quarter	184 894	3 140	2 446	2 186	1 891	252	736	902	18 610	13 126	11 353	442	4 069	7 465
1962														
1st quarter	185 553	3 201	2 475	2 209	1 912	257	743	912	18 875	13 209	11 433	449	4 088	7 508
2nd quarter	186 203	3 224	2 507	2 233	1 936	263	745	927	18 979	13 305	11 533	460	4 090	7 594
3rd quarter	186 926	3 258	2 522	2 242	1 949	265	749	935	19 138	13 324	11 581	461	4 106	7 629
4th quarter	187 680	3 262	2 546	2 260	1 975	275	754	946	19 124	13 389	11 698	480	4 113	7 694
1963														
1st quarter	188 299	3 302	2 566	2 279	1 988	279	757	952	19 269	13 461	11 741	488	4 122	7 703
2nd quarter	188 906	3 334	2 584	2 296	2 003	285	756	962	19 422	13 541	11 814	497	4 122	7 760
3rd quarter	189 631	3 398	2 611	2 323	2 032	288	766	978	19 774	13 637	11 928	501	4 144	7 865
4th quarter	190 362	3 435	2 651	2 361	2 049	293	763	993	19 827	13 806	11 981	507	4 123	7 942
1964														
1st quarter	190 954	3 508	2 693	2 411	2 093	304	778	1 010	20 182	14 032	12 179	525	4 181	8 043
2nd quarter	191 560	3 543	2 733	2 474	2 127	310	791	1 026	20 337	14 365	12 355	537	4 247	8 130
3rd quarter	192 256	3 600	2 773	2 505	2 166	319	806	1 041	20 580	14 499	12 537	553	4 314	8 208
4th quarter	192 938	3 614	2 809	2 533	2 172	308	808	1 056	20 571	14 613	12 529	534	4 307	8 293
1965														
1st quarter	193 467	3 710	2 858	2 564	2 221	336	815	1 070	21 011	14 744	12 773	582	4 336	8 365
2nd quarter	193 994	3 764	2 900	2 599	2 251	334	829	1 088	21 219	14 870	12 879	581	4 366	8 468
3rd quarter	194 647	3 850	2 964	2 671	2 290	343	843	1 105	21 618	15 225	13 056	599	4 417	8 555
4th quarter	195 279	3 953	3 022	2 724	2 354	354	873	1 127	22 044	15 482	13 380	622	4 566	8 672
1966														
1st quarter	195 763	4 065	3 080	2 765	2 402	369	889	1 143	22 525	15 596	13 544	650	4 587	8 740
2nd quarter	196 277	4 101	3 122	2 788	2 421	355	903	1 163	22 543	15 597	13 543	623	4 619	8 812
3rd quarter	196 877	4 163	3 180	2 835	2 460	367	913	1 179	22 664	15 739	13 656	641	4 638	8 857
4th quarter	197 481	4 220	3 239	2 882	2 482	368	913	1 200	22 780	15 875	13 671	639	4 611	8 927
1967														
1st quarter	197 967	4 264	3 286	2 926	2 497	359	921	1 217	22 926	16 075	13 716	625	4 651	8 986
2nd quarter	198 455	4 278	3 314	2 956	2 537	375	927	1 234	22 883	16 162	13 869	651	4 674	9 051
3rd quarter	199 012	4 348	3 375	3 004	2 566	375	933	1 257	23 035	16 270	13 901	644	4 657	9 149
4th quarter	199 572	4 417	3 423	3 043	2 597	379	941	1 276	23 144	16 343	13 947	643	4 665	9 200
1968														
1st quarter	199 995	4 547	3 513	3 120	2 682	404	968	1 310	23 566	16 580	14 251	682	4 746	9 326
2nd quarter	200 452	4 661	3 604	3 196	2 744	414	987	1 343	23 905	16 815	14 435	695	4 794	9 449
3rd quarter	200 997	4 731	3 688	3 231	2 817	436	1 009	1 372	24 025	16 823	14 666	724	4 857	9 543
4th quarter	201 538	4 803	3 759	3 283	2 853	436	1 017	1 400	24 054	16 908	14 692	718	4 845	9 622
1969														
1st quarter	201 955	4 919	3 824	3 316	2 907	446	1 034	1 427	24 380	16 915	14 825	730	4 889	9 686
2nd quarter	202 419	4 985	3 906	3 384	2 956	447	1 048	1 461	24 399	17 041	14 886	726	4 888	9 784
3rd quarter	202 986	5 074	3 998	3 485	2 998	446	1 064	1 488	24 491	17 340	14 917	722	4 893	9 835
4th quarter	203 584	5 099	4 061	3 542	3 048	446	1 079	1 523	24 300	17 421	14 992	717	4 911	9 928
1970														
1st quarter	204 086	5 151	4 124	3 612	3 095	439	1 100	1 556	24 204	17 561	15 048	705	4 941	10 010
2nd quarter	204 721	5 214	4 201	3 686	3 134	445	1 107	1 583	24 163	17 722	15 069	711	4 923	10 041
3rd quarter	205 419	5 287	4 258	3 768	3 181	448	1 118	1 615	24 303	17 944	15 150	711	4 941	10 120
4th quarter	206 130	5 281	4 287	3 795	3 203	424	1 138	1 641	23 960	17 839	15 056	661	4 982	10 137
1971														
1st quarter	206 763	5 490	4 371	3 895	3 285	474	1 141	1 670	24 535	18 140	15 298	730	4 987	10 176
2nd quarter	207 362	5 576	4 471	3 985	3 343	487	1 152	1 704	24 597	18 351	15 394	744	4 984	10 249
3rd quarter	208 000	5 662	4 525	4 033	3 392	497	1 156	1 739	24 723	18 390	15 470	762	4 958	10 314
4th quarter	208 642	5 705	4 598	4 092	3 459	514	1 168	1 777	24 705	18 547	15 678	792	4 977	10 443
1972														
1st quarter	209 142	5 884	4 717	4 144	3 533	529	1 181	1 823	25 099	18 588	15 847	808	4 981	10 594
2nd quarter	209 637	6 041	4 790	4 202	3 613	544	1 213	1 856	25 608	18 736	16 110	827	5 104	10 696
3rd quarter	210 181	6 140	4 901	4 310	3 691	559	1 237	1 894	25 783	19 051	16 316	846	5 161	10 813
4th quarter	210 737	6 306	5 111	4 507	3 799	586	1 272	1 941	26 146	19 763	16 655	888	5 244	10 977

Table 1-3B. U.S. Population and Per Capita Product and Income: Historical Data—*Continued*

(Dollars, except as noted; quarterly data are at seasonally adjusted annual rates.)

NIPA Table 7.1

Year and quarter	Population (mid-period, thousands)	Current dollars Gross domestic product	Personal income	Disposable personal income	Personal consumption expenditures Total	Durable goods	Nondurable goods	Services	Chained (2012) dollars Gross domestic product	Disposable personal income	Personal consumption expenditures Total	Durable goods	Nondurable goods	Services
1973														
1st quarter	211 192	6 522	5 185	4 587	3 906	624	1 304	1 978	26 735	19 870	16 923	943	5 264	11 094
2nd quarter	211 663	6 680	5 314	4 704	3 971	620	1 329	2 021	26 966	19 993	16 877	929	5 208	11 163
3rd quarter	212 191	6 757	5 432	4 800	4 048	616	1 366	2 065	26 758	20 033	16 895	919	5 220	11 209
4th quarter	212 708	6 940	5 598	4 940	4 108	603	1 399	2 106	26 946	20 203	16 803	895	5 186	11 223
1974														
1st quarter	213 144	6 996	5 662	4 992	4 184	594	1 449	2 141	26 660	19 827	16 619	872	5 106	11 179
2nd quarter	213 602	7 163	5 772	5 075	4 309	611	1 489	2 209	26 666	19 600	16 643	875	5 062	11 267
3rd quarter	214 147	7 285	5 926	5 203	4 433	637	1 530	2 266	26 347	19 568	16 672	878	5 060	11 298
4th quarter	214 700	7 451	6 048	5 314	4 467	592	1 541	2 334	26 177	19 492	16 386	792	4 957	11 384
1975														
1st quarter	215 135	7 512	6 128	5 394	4 579	613	1 563	2 404	25 806	19 423	16 490	808	4 956	11 467
2nd quarter	215 652	7 660	6 260	5 698	4 700	634	1 599	2 467	25 928	20 273	16 721	821	5 054	11 577
3rd quarter	216 289	7 905	6 410	5 704	4 842	679	1 646	2 517	26 294	19 919	16 909	870	5 088	11 597
4th quarter	216 848	8 125	6 561	5 830	4 963	707	1 659	2 597	26 579	20 023	17 046	893	5 063	11 734
1976														
1st quarter	217 314	8 377	6 701	5 953	5 107	751	1 691	2 665	27 119	20 222	17 350	936	5 154	11 845
2nd quarter	217 776	8 506	6 802	6 024	5 187	762	1 713	2 712	27 260	20 293	17 472	938	5 222	11 898
3rd quarter	218 338	8 641	6 954	6 148	5 307	778	1 743	2 786	27 339	20 399	17 611	946	5 249	12 011
4th quarter	218 917	8 836	7 102	6 268	5 447	801	1 780	2 866	27 464	20 474	17 792	959	5 290	12 144
1977														
1st quarter	219 427	9 063	7 241	6 380	5 597	838	1 807	2 952	27 724	20 472	17 960	993	5 274	12 264
2nd quarter	219 956	9 347	7 424	6 535	5 710	860	1 835	3 014	28 195	20 615	18 014	1 014	5 261	12 280
3rd quarter	220 573	9 604	7 606	6 706	5 834	879	1 858	3 096	28 623	20 843	18 134	1 026	5 272	12 376
4th quarter	221 201	9 784	7 854	6 912	5 989	907	1 915	3 167	28 543	21 181	18 354	1 044	5 370	12 458
1978														
1st quarter	221 719	9 935	8 020	7 063	6 107	894	1 944	3 269	28 567	21 297	18 414	1 014	5 381	12 623
2nd quarter	222 281	10 490	8 270	7 266	6 350	973	2 001	3 376	29 596	21 468	18 760	1 087	5 408	12 780
3rd quarter	222 933	10 743	8 490	7 430	6 469	972	2 044	3 453	29 806	21 572	18 784	1 069	5 434	12 835
4th quarter	223 583	11 078	8 704	7 598	6 626	994	2 099	3 532	30 119	21 651	18 880	1 075	5 488	12 865
1979														
1st quarter	224 152	11 272	8 947	7 815	6 768	996	2 162	3 610	30 096	21 857	18 930	1 059	5 499	12 966
2nd quarter	224 737	11 530	9 101	7 936	6 931	988	2 225	3 718	30 050	21 603	18 868	1 033	5 474	13 012
3rd quarter	225 418	11 834	9 364	8 145	7 151	1 024	2 317	3 809	30 182	21 636	18 994	1 058	5 521	13 021
4th quarter	226 117	12 046	9 593	8 331	7 319	1 013	2 385	3 921	30 164	21 607	18 983	1 028	5 533	13 089
1980														
1st quarter	226 754	12 303	9 843	8 587	7 507	1 023	2 469	4 014	30 174	21 621	18 902	1 009	5 515	13 075
2nd quarter	227 389	12 302	9 980	8 696	7 497	932	2 489	4 076	29 470	21 371	18 425	897	5 425	12 956
3rd quarter	228 070	12 525	10 297	8 972	7 733	988	2 528	4 218	29 347	21 546	18 572	934	5 396	13 066
4th quarter	228 689	13 055	10 690	9 296	8 010	1 033	2 585	4 392	29 813	21 784	18 772	960	5 402	13 230
1981														
1st quarter	229 155	13 634	10 948	9 504	8 229	1 074	2 680	4 476	30 335	21 709	18 796	986	5 439	13 128
2nd quarter	229 674	13 770	11 145	9 653	8 349	1 049	2 712	4 588	30 042	21 685	18 755	945	5 450	13 187
3rd quarter	230 301	14 158	11 546	9 997	8 502	1 094	2 732	4 677	30 319	22 093	18 791	971	5 448	13 153
4th quarter	230 903	14 209	11 661	10 134	8 551	1 026	2 753	4 772	29 911	22 059	18 613	899	5 454	13 147
1982														
1st quarter	231 395	14 150	11 789	10 265	8 704	1 065	2 765	4 874	29 384	22 066	18 711	926	5 453	13 188
2nd quarter	231 906	14 368	11 954	10 403	8 795	1 075	2 754	4 966	29 453	22 150	18 726	927	5 431	13 232
3rd quarter	232 498	14 479	12 097	10 591	8 971	1 084	2 795	5 092	29 265	22 199	18 804	932	5 441	13 301
4th quarter	233 074	14 599	12 244	10 714	9 205	1 134	2 818	5 254	29 205	22 214	19 086	972	5 483	13 473
1983														
1st quarter	233 546	14 872	12 385	10 882	9 354	1 151	2 813	5 389	29 530	22 378	19 236	980	5 490	13 625
2nd quarter	234 028	15 292	12 571	11 035	9 612	1 237	2 876	5 499	30 140	22 487	19 587	1 050	5 543	13 782
3rd quarter	234 603	15 725	12 793	11 320	9 889	1 289	2 934	5 665	30 667	22 769	19 889	1 087	5 613	13 951
4th quarter	235 153	16 137	13 134	11 622	10 089	1 358	2 962	5 769	31 233	23 221	20 159	1 138	5 668	14 062
1984														
1st quarter	235 605	16 587	13 493	11 960	10 264	1 407	2 998	5 858	31 783	23 640	20 287	1 179	5 672	14 097
2nd quarter	236 082	16 984	13 821	12 252	10 487	1 446	3 060	5 982	32 267	23 984	20 530	1 204	5 784	14 180
3rd quarter	236 657	17 258	14 102	12 479	10 621	1 445	3 062	6 114	32 498	24 241	20 632	1 201	5 774	14 323
4th quarter	237 232	17 487	14 297	12 628	10 799	1 492	3 089	6 218	32 686	24 380	20 848	1 237	5 805	14 445
1985														
1st quarter	237 673	17 798	14 538	12 720	11 091	1 548	3 124	6 419	32 941	24 271	21 163	1 278	5 829	14 680
2nd quarter	238 176	18 032	14 676	13 045	11 260	1 567	3 161	6 532	33 161	24 692	21 313	1 290	5 862	14 783
3rd quarter	238 789	18 371	14 838	13 072	11 534	1 660	3 185	6 689	33 581	24 551	21 662	1 369	5 895	14 944
4th quarter	239 387	18 564	15 062	13 270	11 610	1 603	3 231	6 777	33 746	24 749	21 654	1 319	5 933	15 026
1986														
1st quarter	239 861	18 794	15 291	13 513	11 772	1 633	3 249	6 891	33 994	25 025	21 800	1 343	5 997	15 058
2nd quarter	240 368	18 910	15 430	13 643	11 863	1 694	3 193	6 976	34 075	25 291	21 991	1 388	6 037	15 117
3rd quarter	240 962	19 122	15 592	13 768	12 106	1 850	3 200	7 057	34 316	25 390	22 325	1 502	6 035	15 206
4th quarter	241 539	19 283	15 728	13 839	12 225	1 826	3 225	7 173	34 418	25 368	22 408	1 475	6 069	15 336
1987														
1st quarter	242 009	19 512	15 933	14 071	12 328	1 729	3 295	7 304	34 607	25 552	22 387	1 385	6 065	15 555
2nd quarter	242 520	19 818	16 153	14 044	12 590	1 811	3 349	7 430	34 907	25 259	22 645	1 439	6 099	15 676
3rd quarter	243 120	20 091	16 406	14 394	12 822	1 894	3 376	7 552	35 123	25 648	22 847	1 494	6 089	15 776
4th quarter	243 721	20 548	16 758	14 678	12 928	1 846	3 392	7 690	35 638	25 930	22 839	1 450	6 081	15 892

Table 1-3B. U.S. Population and Per Capita Product and Income: Historical Data—*Continued*

(Dollars, except as noted; quarterly data are at seasonally adjusted annual rates.)   NIPA Table 7.1

Year and quarter	Population (mid-period, thousands)	Current dollars							Chained (2012) dollars					
		Gross domestic product	Personal income	Disposable personal income	Personal consumption expenditures				Gross domestic product	Disposable personal income	Personal consumption expenditures			
					Total	Durable goods	Nondurable goods	Services			Total	Durable goods	Nondurable goods	Services
1988														
1st quarter	244 208	20 775	17 037	14 981	13 234	1 926	3 433	7 875	35 751	26 258	23 196	1 516	6 135	16 077
2nd quarter	244 716	21 208	17 305	15 271	13 451	1 934	3 488	8 030	36 145	26 473	23 319	1 513	6 170	16 185
3rd quarter	245 354	21 531	17 633	15 568	13 702	1 917	3 549	8 236	36 262	26 659	23 465	1 490	6 197	16 386
4th quarter	245 966	21 952	17 937	15 834	13 963	1 977	3 603	8 384	36 654	26 844	23 672	1 525	6 246	16 482
1989														
1st quarter	246 460	22 362	18 410	16 166	14 161	1 974	3 662	8 526	36 953	27 095	23 734	1 515	6 262	16 561
2nd quarter	247 017	22 721	18 593	16 299	14 387	1 997	3 756	8 634	37 151	26 954	23 791	1 531	6 257	16 590
3rd quarter	247 698	22 993	18 767	16 459	14 572	2 041	3 780	8 750	37 323	27 059	23 956	1 562	6 302	16 653
4th quarter	248 374	23 139	19 018	16 684	14 710	1 980	3 830	8 900	37 295	27 213	23 994	1 510	6 356	16 764
1990														
1st quarter	248 936	23 591	19 358	17 018	15 016	2 070	3 913	9 032	37 617	27 361	24 142	1 570	6 334	16 813
2nd quarter	249 711	23 868	19 620	17 238	15 151	1 996	3 928	9 227	37 636	27 465	24 140	1 514	6 321	16 964
3rd quarter	250 595	24 003	19 787	17 390	15 350	1 970	4 003	9 378	37 529	27 359	24 150	1 493	6 309	17 040
4th quarter	251 482	23 877	19 797	17 408	15 380	1 912	4 051	9 417	37 056	27 030	23 882	1 447	6 224	16 939
1991														
1st quarter	252 258	23 925	19 791	17 489	15 356	1 870	4 020	9 465	36 769	27 014	23 719	1 403	6 207	16 874
2nd quarter	253 063	24 211	19 972	17 656	15 518	1 878	4 038	9 602	36 938	27 125	23 839	1 405	6 224	16 988
3rd quarter	253 965	24 436	20 109	17 785	15 645	1 907	4 034	9 704	36 993	27 139	23 873	1 422	6 212	17 001
4th quarter	254 835	24 583	20 351	18 001	15 697	1 874	4 005	9 818	36 995	27 271	23 780	1 394	6 138	17 044
1992														
1st quarter	255 585	24 896	20 728	18 424	16 043	1 941	4 060	10 042	37 328	27 739	24 154	1 444	6 211	17 272
2nd quarter	256 439	25 233	21 036	18 668	16 205	1 954	4 084	10 168	37 607	27 920	24 237	1 450	6 216	17 349
3rd quarter	257 386	25 513	21 199	18 805	16 423	1 990	4 122	10 311	37 839	27 947	24 407	1 475	6 230	17 468
4th quarter	258 277	25 867	21 430	18 957	16 677	2 025	4 161	10 490	38 102	27 977	24 612	1 499	6 271	17 601
1993														
1st quarter	259 039	25 979	21 467	19 085	16 791	2 038	4 166	10 587	38 053	27 999	24 634	1 509	6 259	17 616
2nd quarter	259 826	26 206	21 691	19 214	17 006	2 108	4 181	10 716	38 158	28 001	24 783	1 554	6 290	17 651
3rd quarter	260 714	26 397	21 777	19 249	17 211	2 135	4 191	10 886	38 210	27 930	24 973	1 566	6 330	17 795
4th quarter	261 547	26 816	22 014	19 432	17 407	2 194	4 226	10 987	38 606	28 034	25 112	1 598	6 354	17 853
1994														
1st quarter	262 250	27 133	22 147	19 578	17 621	2 245	4 259	11 117	38 876	28 144	25 331	1 632	6 422	17 952
2nd quarter	263 020	27 553	22 480	19 827	17 805	2 276	4 289	11 240	39 288	28 344	25 454	1 644	6 454	18 027
3rd quarter	263 870	27 783	22 657	20 021	18 012	2 309	4 357	11 346	39 390	28 417	25 565	1 656	6 488	18 089
4th quarter	264 678	28 167	23 007	20 342	18 236	2 387	4 394	11 455	39 720	28 737	25 763	1 709	6 537	18 141
1995														
1st quarter	265 388	28 344	23 291	20 561	18 322	2 341	4 397	11 584	39 754	28 905	25 758	1 670	6 543	18 217
2nd quarter	266 142	28 485	23 486	20 680	18 538	2 356	4 422	11 760	39 760	28 905	25 910	1 682	6 557	18 346
3rd quarter	267 000	28 776	23 705	20 888	18 722	2 407	4 433	11 882	39 969	29 076	26 061	1 724	6 559	18 421
4th quarter	267 820	29 022	23 913	21 038	18 877	2 435	4 449	11 992	40 117	29 157	26 162	1 748	6 572	18 466
1996														
1st quarter	268 487	29 307	24 288	21 302	19 109	2 458	4 511	12 141	40 317	29 359	26 338	1 763	6 599	18 603
2nd quarter	269 251	29 834	24 698	21 579	19 389	2 512	4 604	12 273	40 873	29 545	26 546	1 814	6 664	18 657
3rd quarter	270 128	30 102	24 899	21 776	19 526	2 515	4 614	12 396	41 106	29 687	26 620	1 821	6 690	18 697
4th quarter	270 991	30 480	25 158	21 971	19 753	2 545	4 680	12 527	41 401	29 750	26 746	1 850	6 723	18 742
1997														
1st quarter	271 709	30 778	25 540	22 220	19 996	2 597	4 715	12 685	41 558	29 954	26 957	1 895	6 745	18 858
2nd quarter	272 487	31 263	25 771	22 409	20 079	2 556	4 689	12 833	42 128	30 133	27 001	1 884	6 729	18 947
3rd quarter	273 391	31 687	26 099	22 657	20 407	2 644	4 745	13 018	42 514	30 387	27 370	1 961	6 814	19 110
4th quarter	274 246	31 964	26 520	22 991	20 652	2 688	4 769	13 195	42 745	30 739	27 611	2 005	6 840	19 259
1998														
1st quarter	274 950	32 248	27 040	23 417	20 809	2 683	4 752	13 373	43 062	31 305	27 819	2 016	6 872	19 431
2nd quarter	275 703	32 534	27 425	23 716	21 155	2 790	4 787	13 578	43 342	31 649	28 231	2 112	6 936	19 629
3rd quarter	276 564	32 980	27 726	23 954	21 430	2 839	4 826	13 765	43 748	31 868	28 510	2 165	6 965	19 801
4th quarter	277 400	33 504	27 984	24 134	21 731	2 975	4 885	13 871	44 321	32 024	28 835	2 286	7 039	19 852
1999														
1st quarter	278 103	33 842	28 260	24 384	21 942	2 948	4 980	14 013	44 627	32 292	29 058	2 286	7 151	19 982
2nd quarter	278 864	34 161	28 411	24 484	22 343	3 065	5 086	14 192	44 876	32 242	29 422	2 388	7 199	20 139
3rd quarter	279 751	34 626	28 734	24 728	22 646	3 114	5 148	14 384	45 326	32 385	29 658	2 438	7 209	20 294
4th quarter	280 592	35 283	29 248	25 136	23 048	3 123	5 284	14 641	45 932	32 720	30 002	2 460	7 334	20 500
2000														
1st quarter	281 304	35 556	30 015	25 718	23 527	3 274	5 305	14 949	45 983	33 208	30 379	2 590	7 252	20 759
2nd quarter	282 002	36 339	30 447	26 084	23 801	3 198	5 444	15 159	46 704	33 521	30 586	2 536	7 377	20 950
3rd quarter	282 769	36 490	30 933	26 521	24 119	3 224	5 508	15 387	46 624	33 863	30 796	2 572	7 406	21 083
4th quarter	283 518	36 808	31 206	26 766	24 403	3 230	5 564	15 608	46 777	33 983	30 983	2 583	7 457	21 211
2001														
1st quarter	284 169	36 845	31 704	27 122	24 617	3 261	5 533	15 822	46 519	34 182	31 024	2 620	7 396	21 253
2nd quarter	284 838	37 211	31 711	27 116	24 724	3 228	5 584	15 911	46 698	34 014	31 013	2 611	7 413	21 237
3rd quarter	285 584	37 110	31 548	27 649	24 758	3 235	5 572	15 950	46 390	34 665	31 040	2 634	7 428	21 213
4th quarter	286 311	37 234	31 434	27 132	25 103	3 478	5 525	16 100	46 400	34 003	31 461	2 847	7 472	21 271
2002														
1st quarter	286 935	37 582	31 511	27 764	25 155	3 402	5 526	16 226	46 683	34 725	31 462	2 809	7 487	21 319
2nd quarter	287 574	37 860	31 788	28 133	25 412	3 399	5 597	16 417	46 866	34 929	31 551	2 821	7 475	21 407
3rd quarter	288 303	38 099	31 870	28 249	25 658	3 475	5 608	16 575	46 936	34 892	31 691	2 898	7 469	21 439
4th quarter	289 007	38 274	32 084	28 491	25 857	3 412	5 681	16 764	46 883	35 028	31 790	2 865	7 540	21 524

Table 1-3B. U.S. Population and Per Capita Product and Income: Historical Data—*Continued*

(Dollars, except as noted; quarterly data are at seasonally adjusted annual rates.) NIPA Table 7.1

Year and quarter	Population (mid-period, thousands)	Current dollars							Chained (2012) dollars					
		Gross domestic product	Personal income	Disposable personal income	Personal consumption expenditures				Gross domestic product	Disposable personal income	Personal consumption expenditures			
					Total	Durable goods	Nondurable goods	Services			Total	Durable goods	Nondurable goods	Services
2003														
1st quarter	289 609	38 584	32 159	28 633	26 129	3 365	5 811	16 953	47 027	34 935	31 880	2 861	7 585	21 577
2nd quarter	290 253	38 976	32 474	28 957	26 396	3 472	5 754	17 170	47 342	35 295	32 174	2 985	7 629	21 656
3rd quarter	290 974	39 752	32 852	29 584	26 878	3 580	5 927	17 372	48 012	35 825	32 548	3 109	7 750	21 745
4th quarter	291 669	40 362	33 242	29 741	27 132	3 590	5 972	17 570	48 450	35 838	32 694	3 146	7 776	21 818
2004														
1st quarter	292 237	40 801	33 508	30 045	27 542	3 642	6 088	17 813	48 633	35 927	32 934	3 195	7 821	21 956
2nd quarter	292 875	41 358	34 000	30 494	27 818	3 640	6 156	18 022	48 905	36 221	33 042	3 196	7 835	22 052
3rd quarter	293 603	41 911	34 412	30 787	28 213	3 696	6 220	18 297	49 243	36 390	33 347	3 271	7 872	22 229
4th quarter	294 334	42 561	35 073	31 365	28 704	3 761	6 379	18 564	49 623	36 759	33 641	3 324	7 932	22 399
2005														
1st quarter	294 957	43 285	35 073	31 099	28 993	3 763	6 414	18 816	50 068	36 237	33 783	3 333	7 990	22 478
2nd quarter	295 588	43 718	35 579	31 532	29 437	3 850	6 494	19 093	50 204	36 510	34 084	3 414	8 036	22 634
3rd quarter	296 340	44 350	36 060	31 925	29 925	3 887	6 702	19 337	50 470	36 570	34 280	3 472	8 045	22 748
4th quarter	297 086	44 850	36 595	32 368	30 144	3 752	6 799	19 593	50 629	36 784	34 257	3 360	8 137	22 782
2006														
1st quarter	297 736	45 675	37 554	33 119	30 564	3 876	6 861	19 827	51 200	37 442	34 555	3 486	8 203	22 860
2nd quarter	298 408	46 089	37 989	33 461	30 923	3 851	6 960	20 112	51 210	37 500	34 656	3 479	8 201	22 973
3rd quarter	299 180	46 361	38 223	33 682	31 265	3 879	7 062	20 323	51 155	37 478	34 788	3 520	8 227	23 032
4th quarter	299 946	46 807	38 626	33 967	31 430	3 899	6 977	20 554	51 455	37 858	35 030	3 561	8 320	23 137
2007														
1st quarter	300 609	47 289	39 334	34 455	31 842	3 922	7 083	20 838	51 492	38 054	35 169	3 601	8 330	23 218
2nd quarter	301 284	47 802	39 792	34 827	32 125	3 935	7 190	21 000	51 705	38 141	35 182	3 630	8 293	23 231
3rd quarter	302 062	48 216	39 956	34 994	32 438	3 946	7 244	21 248	51 882	38 109	35 325	3 665	8 298	23 330
4th quarter	302 829	48 592	40 298	35 316	32 814	3 948	7 372	21 494	52 066	38 072	35 375	3 683	8 270	23 387
2008														
1st quarter	303 494	48 457	40 644	35 586	32 964	3 801	7 423	21 740	51 740	38 053	35 249	3 556	8 188	23 489
2nd quarter	304 160	48 875	41 654	36 550	33 304	3 741	7 581	21 983	51 923	38 706	35 269	3 523	8 183	23 554
3rd quarter	304 902	48 865	41 025	36 114	33 319	3 594	7 649	22 076	51 523	37 840	34 912	3 396	8 044	23 475
4th quarter	305 616	47 799	40 563	35 836	32 416	3 298	7 091	22 027	50 281	38 158	34 517	3 139	7 948	23 459
2009														
1st quarter	306 237	47 123	39 372	35 445	32 050	3 280	6 908	21 862	49 594	37 999	34 359	3 138	7 929	23 319
2nd quarter	306 866	46 865	39 390	35 704	31 954	3 241	6 973	21 739	49 408	38 124	34 120	3 109	7 866	23 172
3rd quarter	307 573	46 977	39 123	35 432	32 316	3 365	7 131	21 819	49 473	37 576	34 271	3 252	7 873	23 156
4th quarter	308 285	47 525	39 392	35 692	32 454	3 290	7 211	21 953	49 886	37 562	34 154	3 168	7 880	23 125
2010														
1st quarter	308 901	47 797	39 887	36 029	32 702	3 306	7 268	22 129	50 036	37 771	34 283	3 201	7 906	23 194
2nd quarter	309 460	48 408	40 537	36 617	32 987	3 373	7 262	22 352	50 429	38 328	34 528	3 296	7 935	23 309
3rd quarter	310 062	48 834	40 902	36 850	33 222	3 394	7 298	22 530	50 720	38 498	34 707	3 341	7 949	23 425
4th quarter	310 675	49 278	41 298	37 148	33 573	3 471	7 469	22 633	50 883	38 562	34 851	3 428	7 992	23 435
2011														
1st quarter	311 376	49 302	42 315	37 734	33 908	3 494	7 647	22 767	50 646	38 843	34 905	11 448	8 001	23 458
2nd quarter	311 940	49 873	42 574	37 939	34 215	3 472	7 795	22 948	50 897	38 674	34 878	11 385	7 969	23 494
3rd quarter	312 606	50 056	42 909	38 203	34 404	3 489	7 796	23 119	50 769	38 764	34 910	11 365	7 925	23 545
4th quarter	313 258	50 573	43 054	38 358	34 506	3 551	7 817	23 137	51 232	38 793	34 897	11 423	7 907	23 474
2012														
1st quarter	313 813	51 205	43 931	39 252	34 923	3 627	7 937	23 360	51 559	39 436	35 087	11 548	7 951	23 539
2nd quarter	314 373	51 554	44 361	39 629	35 006	3 606	7 898	23 503	51 702	39 719	35 086	11 525	7 927	23 561
3rd quarter	315 030	51 803	44 195	39 401	35 106	3 624	7 904	23 577	51 684	39 376	35 150	11 552	7 915	23 532
4th quarter	315 685	52 015	45 623	40 643	35 370	3 686	7 953	23 731	51 634	40 391	35 150	11 610	7 899	23 541
2013														
1st quarter	316 196	52 591	44 338	39 120	35 629	3 760	8 042	23 827	51 998	38 737	35 280	11 790	7 991	23 492
2nd quarter	316 733	52 724	44 684	39 372	35 648	3 743	7 937	23 969	51 982	38 960	35 275	11 779	7 969	23 498
3rd quarter	317 396	53 281	44 878	39 601	35 852	3 746	8 007	24 099	52 284	39 028	35 333	11 838	8 004	23 497
4th quarter	318 072	53 866	45 141	39 802	36 213	3 755	8 061	24 396	52 544	39 062	35 540	11 924	8 057	23 619
2014														
1st quarter	318 645	53 804	45 898	40 422	36 461	3 777	8 116	24 568	52 266	39 481	35 612	11 982	8 062	23 635
2nd quarter	319 228	54 703	46 596	41 087	36 916	3 883	8 218	24 815	52 840	39 931	35 877	12 175	8 124	23 712
3rd quarter	319 919	55 462	47 198	41 576	37 304	3 925	8 259	25 120	53 340	40 292	36 152	12 289	8 175	23 874
4th quarter	320 611	55 683	47 744	42 015	37 596	3 960	8 208	25 428	53 464	40 764	36 477	12 427	8 245	24 063
2015														
1st quarter	321 168	56 018	48 254	42 324	37 625	3 997	8 046	25 582	53 806	41 235	36 657	12 554	8 305	24 121
2nd quarter	321 744	56 547	48 610	42 571	37 995	4 070	8 136	25 789	54 021	41 275	36 839	12 664	8 335	24 198
3rd quarter	322 428	56 779	48 870	42 830	38 296	4 089	8 194	26 013	54 081	41 426	37 041	12 779	8 401	24 289
4th quarter	323 110	56 736	49 043	42 962	38 369	4 081	8 102	26 187	54 045	41 595	37 149	12 802	8 409	24 373
2016														
1st quarter	323 689	56 923	49 179	43 233	38 602	4 105	8 050	26 447	54 267	41 835	37 354	12 907	8 465	24 478
2nd quarter	324 265	57 396	49 349	43 356	38 972	4 120	8 169	26 684	54 334	41 693	37 477	12 997	8 518	24 517
3rd quarter	324 926	57 784	49 709	43 640	39 268	4 169	8 167	26 931	54 549	41 809	37 620	13 098	8 520	24 566
4th quarter	325 557	58 263	50 115	43 993	39 568	4 182	8 227	27 158	54 714	41 949	37 729	13 143	8 512	24 631
2017														
1st quarter	326 053	58 745	50 765	44 615	40 013	4 204	8 357	27 453	54 889	42 310	37 946	13 235	8 580	24 757
2nd quarter	326 554	59 172	51 262	45 115	40 252	4 217	8 387	27 648	55 111	42 663	38 064	13 355	8 656	24 768
3rd quarter	327 140	59 787	51 759	45 474	40 558	4 273	8 443	27 842	55 408	42 842	38 211	13 475	8 680	24 805
4th quarter	327 692	60 676	52 417	45 925	41 189	4 398	8 612	28 180	55 835	42 980	38 548	13 720	8 767	24 918
2018														
1st quarter	328 091	61 397	53 053	46 724	41 657	4 418	8 684	28 556	56 192	43 443	38 732	13 752	8 764	25 066
2nd quarter	328 526	62 377	53 568	47 329	42 203	4 478	8 776	28 949	56 586	43 750	39 012	13 877	8 813	25 226
3rd quarter	329 040	62 786	54 161	47 805	42 556	4 493	8 798	29 265	56 770	44 043	39 207	13 954	8 852	25 346
4th quarter	329 522	63 162	54 620	48 284	42 848	4 485	8 834	29 529	56 813	44 304	39 316	14 006	8 896	25 406

Table 1-4. Contributions to Percent Change in Real Gross Domestic Product: Recent Data

(Percent, percentage points.)   NIPA Table 1.1.2

| Year and quarter | Percent change at seasonally adjusted annual rate, real GDP | Personal consump-tion expen-ditures | Gross private domestic investment | | | | Exports and imports of goods and services | | | Government consumption expenditures and gross investment | | |
| | | | Total | Fixed investment | | Change in private inventories | Net exports | Exports | Imports | Total | Federal | State and local |
				Nonresi-dential	Residential							
1960	2.6	1.67	0.06	0.56	-0.37	-0.13	0.70	0.76	-0.06	0.14	-0.23	0.37
1961	2.6	1.25	0.05	0.08	0.02	-0.05	0.05	0.03	0.03	1.21	0.66	0.54
1962	6.1	3.00	1.82	0.81	0.46	0.55	-0.21	0.25	-0.45	1.51	1.24	0.27
1963	4.4	2.48	1.08	0.59	0.57	-0.07	0.23	0.34	-0.11	0.57	0.03	0.53
1964	5.8	3.57	1.27	1.09	0.31	-0.12	0.35	0.57	-0.22	0.57	-0.05	0.62
1965	6.5	3.80	2.26	1.76	-0.13	0.64	-0.29	0.14	-0.44	0.73	0.10	0.63
1966	6.6	3.38	1.56	1.40	-0.40	0.56	-0.28	0.35	-0.63	1.94	1.34	0.60
1967	2.7	1.76	-0.62	-0.04	-0.11	-0.47	-0.21	0.12	-0.33	1.81	1.32	0.49
1968	4.9	3.39	0.99	0.55	0.53	-0.09	-0.29	0.40	-0.68	0.82	0.21	0.61
1969	3.1	2.20	0.93	0.79	0.14	0.00	-0.03	0.25	-0.28	0.02	-0.34	0.36
1970	0.2	1.39	-1.03	-0.10	-0.23	-0.70	0.33	0.54	-0.21	-0.50	-0.80	0.30
1971	3.3	2.29	1.63	-0.01	1.08	0.56	-0.18	0.10	-0.28	-0.45	-0.80	0.35
1972	5.3	3.66	1.90	0.97	0.87	0.06	-0.19	0.42	-0.61	-0.12	-0.37	0.25
1973	5.6	2.97	1.95	1.51	-0.04	0.48	0.80	1.08	-0.28	-0.07	-0.39	0.32
1974	-0.5	-0.50	-1.24	0.10	-1.08	-0.26	0.73	0.56	0.17	0.47	0.06	0.41
1975	-0.2	1.36	-2.91	-1.13	-0.54	-1.24	0.86	-0.05	0.91	0.49	0.05	0.43
1976	5.4	3.41	2.91	0.66	0.88	1.37	-1.05	0.36	-1.41	0.12	0.01	0.10
1977	4.6	2.59	2.47	1.26	0.97	0.24	-0.70	0.19	-0.89	0.26	0.21	0.05
1978	5.5	2.68	2.22	1.72	0.38	0.12	0.05	0.80	-0.76	0.60	0.23	0.37
1979	3.2	1.44	0.72	1.34	-0.22	-0.40	0.64	0.80	-0.16	0.36	0.20	0.16
1980	-0.3	-0.19	-2.07	0.00	-1.19	-0.89	1.64	0.95	0.69	0.36	0.38	-0.02
1981	2.5	0.85	1.64	0.87	-0.37	1.13	-0.15	0.12	-0.26	0.20	0.43	-0.23
1982	-1.8	0.88	-2.46	-0.43	-0.72	-1.31	-0.59	-0.71	0.12	0.37	0.35	0.01
1983	4.6	3.51	1.60	-0.06	1.38	0.28	-1.32	-0.22	-1.10	0.79	0.65	0.14
1984	7.2	3.30	4.73	2.18	0.65	1.90	-1.54	0.61	-2.16	0.74	0.33	0.41
1985	4.2	3.20	-0.01	0.91	0.11	-1.03	-0.39	0.24	-0.63	1.37	0.78	0.59
1986	3.5	2.58	0.03	-0.24	0.58	-0.31	-0.29	0.53	-0.82	1.14	0.61	0.53
1987	3.5	2.15	0.53	0.01	0.10	0.41	0.17	0.77	-0.60	0.62	0.38	0.24
1988	4.2	2.65	0.45	0.63	-0.05	-0.13	0.81	1.23	-0.41	0.26	-0.15	0.42
1989	3.7	1.86	0.72	0.71	-0.16	0.17	0.51	0.97	-0.46	0.58	0.15	0.43
1990	1.9	1.28	-0.45	0.14	-0.38	-0.21	0.40	0.78	-0.37	0.65	0.20	0.45
1991	-0.1	0.12	-1.09	-0.48	-0.35	-0.26	0.62	0.61	0.01	0.25	0.01	0.24
1992	3.5	2.36	1.11	0.33	0.49	0.28	-0.04	0.66	-0.70	0.10	-0.15	0.25
1993	2.8	2.24	1.24	0.84	0.32	0.07	-0.56	0.31	-0.87	-0.17	-0.32	0.15
1994	4.0	2.51	1.90	0.91	0.38	0.61	-0.41	0.84	-1.25	0.02	-0.31	0.32
1995	2.7	1.91	0.55	1.15	-0.15	-0.44	0.12	1.02	-0.90	0.10	-0.21	0.31
1996	3.8	2.26	1.49	1.13	0.35	0.02	-0.15	0.86	-1.01	0.18	-0.09	0.27
1997	4.4	2.45	2.01	1.38	0.11	0.52	-0.31	1.26	-1.57	0.30	-0.06	0.36
1998	4.5	3.42	1.76	1.44	0.38	-0.07	-1.14	0.26	-1.39	0.44	-0.06	0.50
1999	4.8	3.49	1.62	1.36	0.29	-0.03	-0.90	0.52	-1.42	0.59	0.12	0.47
2000	4.1	3.29	1.31	1.31	0.03	-0.03	-0.85	0.86	-1.71	0.33	0.02	0.31
2001	1.0	1.63	-1.11	-0.31	0.04	-0.84	-0.24	-0.59	0.35	0.67	0.24	0.43
2002	1.7	1.70	-0.16	-0.94	0.29	0.48	-0.67	-0.19	-0.48	0.82	0.47	0.35
2003	2.8	2.13	0.76	0.30	0.47	-0.02	-0.49	0.19	-0.68	0.39	0.45	-0.06
2004	3.9	2.54	1.64	0.67	0.57	0.41	-0.63	0.88	-1.51	0.30	0.31	-0.01
2005	3.5	2.38	1.26	0.92	0.41	-0.07	-0.31	0.67	-0.98	0.15	0.15	0.00
2006	2.8	1.95	0.60	1.00	-0.50	0.10	-0.06	0.95	-1.01	0.30	0.17	0.13
2007	2.0	1.63	-0.48	0.89	-1.13	-0.25	0.52	0.94	-0.42	0.34	0.14	0.20
2008	0.1	0.10	-1.52	0.08	-1.14	-0.46	1.04	0.67	0.37	0.49	0.46	0.03
2009	-2.6	-0.88	-3.51	-1.95	-0.74	-0.82	1.07	-1.00	2.07	0.72	0.48	0.24
2010	2.7	1.31	1.85	0.52	-0.08	1.42	-0.43	1.43	-1.86	-0.02	0.34	-0.36
2011	1.5	1.16	0.94	0.99	0.00	-0.05	0.12	0.90	-0.79	-0.67	-0.23	-0.44
2012	2.3	0.94	1.64	1.16	0.31	0.17	0.12	0.54	-0.42	-0.42	-0.16	-0.26
2013	1.8	1.01	1.10	0.53	0.33	0.23	0.20	0.40	-0.20	-0.47	-0.44	-0.03
2014	2.3	1.82	0.95	0.95	0.12	-0.12	-0.31	0.52	-0.84	-0.17	-0.19	0.02
2015	2.7	2.20	0.95	0.32	0.33	0.31	-0.78	0.04	-0.81	0.33	0.00	0.33
2016	1.7	1.67	-0.18	0.12	0.23	-0.53	-0.17	0.05	-0.22	0.35	0.03	0.31
2017	2.3	1.65	0.68	0.53	0.15	-0.01	-0.16	0.49	-0.65	0.09	0.02	0.07
2018	2.9	1.96	0.98	0.85	-0.02	0.16	-0.27	0.35	-0.62	0.24	0.20	0.04
2019	2.3	1.48	0.60	0.59	-0.04	0.05	-0.18	-0.01	-0.17	0.38	0.25	0.14
2020	-3.4	-2.55	-0.99	-0.73	0.26	-0.52	-0.29	-1.57	1.28	0.43	0.33	0.10
2021	5.7	5.27	1.72	0.97	0.39	0.35	-1.40	0.47	-1.88	0.09	0.04	0.04
2019												
1st quarter	2.4	0.43	1.13	0.63	0.00	0.49	0.39	0.36	0.02	0.47	0.09	0.38
2nd quarter	3.2	2.37	0.48	0.90	0.15	-0.57	-0.50	-0.26	-0.24	0.86	0.57	0.29
3rd quarter	2.8	2.12	0.22	0.40	0.14	-0.32	0.07	-0.08	0.15	0.36	0.23	0.12
4th quarter	1.9	1.13	-1.18	-0.23	0.04	-0.99	1.43	0.17	1.26	0.52	0.23	0.28
2020												
1st quarter	-5.1	-4.79	-0.92	-1.14	0.73	-0.51	-0.05	-1.95	1.90	0.63	0.16	0.47
2nd quarter	-31.2	-24.10	-9.64	-4.28	-1.36	-4.01	1.53	-8.34	9.87	0.97	1.42	-0.45
3rd quarter	33.8	25.51	11.71	2.72	2.16	6.84	-3.25	4.64	-7.89	-0.19	-0.32	0.13
4th quarter	4.5	2.26	4.01	1.57	1.34	1.10	-1.65	2.07	-3.73	-0.09	-0.22	0.14
2021												
1st quarter	6.3	7.44	-0.37	1.65	0.60	-2.62	-1.56	-0.30	-1.26	0.77	0.78	-0.01
2nd quarter	6.7	7.92	-0.65	1.21	-0.60	-1.26	-0.18	0.80	-0.99	-0.36	-0.38	0.02
3rd quarter	2.3	1.35	2.05	0.22	-0.38	2.20	-1.26	-0.59	-0.68	0.17	-0.35	0.52
4th quarter	6.9	1.76	5.82	0.40	0.10	5.32	-0.23	2.24	-2.46	-0.46	-0.29	-0.17

Table 1-5A. Chain-Type Quantity Indexes for Gross Domestic Product and Domestic Purchases: Recent Data

(Index numbers, 2012 = 100.)   NIPA Tables 1.1.3, 1.4.3, 2.3.3

Year and quarter	Gross domestic product, total	Personal consumption expenditures		Private fixed investment			Exports and imports of goods and services		Government consumption expenditures and gross investment			Gross domestic purchases
		Total	Excluding food and energy	Total	Nonresidential	Residential	Exports	Imports	Total	Federal	State and local	
1960	20.1	18.2	14.9	13.9	8.8	49.9	5.1	4.9	34.6	41.5	27.7	19.8
1961	20.6	18.6	15.2	13.9	8.8	50.1	5.1	4.9	36.5	43.5	29.4	20.3
1962	21.8	19.5	16.2	15.1	9.5	54.9	5.4	5.4	38.9	47.4	30.3	21.6
1963	22.8	20.3	16.9	16.3	10.1	61.3	5.8	5.6	39.8	47.5	32.1	22.5
1964	24.1	21.5	18.1	17.8	11.2	65.0	6.4	5.9	40.8	47.3	34.2	23.7
1965	25.7	22.9	19.3	19.7	13.0	63.4	6.6	6.5	42.1	47.7	36.5	25.3
1966	27.4	24.2	20.5	20.9	14.6	58.0	7.1	7.5	45.8	52.8	38.7	27.1
1967	28.1	24.9	21.1	20.7	14.6	56.5	7.2	8.0	49.4	58.1	40.7	27.9
1968	29.5	26.4	22.4	22.1	15.3	64.2	7.8	9.2	51.1	59.0	43.1	29.3
1969	30.4	27.4	23.3	23.4	16.4	66.2	8.2	9.7	51.2	57.5	44.6	30.3
1970	30.5	28.0	23.7	23.0	16.2	62.7	9.1	10.1	50.1	54.0	45.9	30.2
1971	31.5	29.1	24.8	24.5	16.2	79.4	9.2	10.7	49.1	50.5	47.3	31.3
1972	33.1	30.8	26.5	27.3	17.6	93.2	9.9	11.9	48.9	48.9	48.4	33.0
1973	35.0	32.4	28.2	29.7	19.9	92.6	11.8	12.4	48.7	47.2	49.7	34.6
1974	34.8	32.1	28.1	28.0	20.1	74.5	12.7	12.1	49.8	47.5	51.5	34.1
1975	34.8	32.8	28.8	25.3	18.3	65.5	12.6	10.8	50.9	47.8	53.4	33.8
1976	36.6	34.7	30.4	27.8	19.3	80.0	13.2	12.9	51.2	47.8	53.9	36.0
1977	38.3	36.1	31.9	31.5	21.4	96.4	13.5	14.3	51.8	48.9	54.1	37.9
1978	40.4	37.7	33.6	35.2	24.4	102.8	14.9	15.5	53.3	50.0	55.9	39.9
1979	41.7	38.6	34.6	37.2	26.8	98.9	16.4	15.8	54.2	51.1	56.7	40.9
1980	41.6	38.5	34.6	35.0	26.8	78.2	18.2	14.7	55.2	53.3	56.6	40.1
1981	42.7	39.0	35.3	35.9	28.5	71.8	18.4	15.1	55.7	55.6	55.4	41.2
1982	41.9	39.6	35.8	33.7	27.6	58.8	17.0	14.9	56.7	57.6	55.5	40.7
1983	43.8	41.8	38.2	36.3	27.5	83.5	16.6	16.8	58.9	61.2	56.2	43.1
1984	47.0	44.0	40.5	42.1	32.1	95.8	17.9	20.9	60.9	63.2	58.4	46.8
1985	48.9	46.3	42.8	44.4	34.2	98.0	18.5	22.3	65.0	68.0	61.7	48.9
1986	50.6	48.2	44.8	45.2	33.6	110.1	19.9	24.2	68.5	72.0	64.8	50.7
1987	52.4	49.9	46.6	45.5	33.6	112.3	22.1	25.6	70.5	74.7	66.2	52.3
1988	54.6	51.9	48.6	47.0	35.3	111.3	25.7	26.6	71.4	73.5	68.7	54.0
1989	56.6	53.5	50.2	48.5	37.3	107.7	28.7	27.8	73.4	74.7	71.4	55.7
1990	57.7	54.5	51.3	47.8	37.7	98.6	31.2	28.8	75.8	76.3	74.4	56.5
1991	57.6	54.6	51.4	45.3	36.2	89.8	33.3	28.7	76.7	76.4	76.0	56.1
1992	59.6	56.6	53.6	47.8	37.3	102.2	35.6	30.8	77.0	75.2	77.6	58.1
1993	61.3	58.6	55.7	51.5	40.1	110.5	36.7	33.4	76.4	72.5	78.6	60.0
1994	63.7	60.9	58.0	55.7	43.2	120.4	40.0	37.4	76.5	69.9	80.8	62.7
1995	65.4	62.7	59.9	59.1	47.4	116.3	44.1	40.4	76.9	68.0	83.0	64.3
1996	67.9	64.9	62.2	64.3	51.7	125.9	47.7	43.9	77.6	67.2	84.9	66.8
1997	70.9	67.3	64.8	69.8	57.3	128.9	53.4	49.8	78.8	66.7	87.6	69.9
1998	74.1	70.9	68.6	77.0	63.5	140.0	54.6	55.6	80.8	66.1	91.5	73.8
1999	77.7	74.7	72.5	84.0	69.8	148.8	57.3	62.1	83.4	67.3	95.3	77.9
2000	80.8	78.4	76.5	89.9	76.3	149.8	62.1	70.2	84.9	67.5	97.8	81.6
2001	81.6	80.4	78.6	88.7	74.6	151.2	58.6	68.4	88.1	70.1	101.4	82.6
2002	83.0	82.4	80.8	85.6	69.5	160.3	57.5	71.0	92.0	75.3	104.3	84.5
2003	85.3	85.0	83.5	89.4	71.2	174.9	58.7	74.6	93.9	80.3	103.8	87.1
2004	88.6	88.2	86.9	95.7	75.2	192.3	64.3	82.8	95.4	83.7	103.7	90.9
2005	91.7	91.4	90.1	102.7	81.0	204.9	68.8	88.2	96.1	85.4	103.7	94.1
2006	94.2	94.0	92.9	105.3	87.5	189.5	75.3	93.8	97.6	87.4	104.9	96.7
2007	96.1	96.3	95.4	104.0	93.6	154.1	81.9	96.2	99.4	89.1	106.7	98.0
2008	96.2	96.4	95.9	98.0	94.1	116.8	86.7	94.2	101.9	94.8	106.9	97.2
2009	93.7	95.2	94.5	82.3	80.5	91.5	79.5	82.3	105.6	100.7	109.0	93.8
2010	96.3	97.0	96.4	84.9	84.1	88.7	89.7	93.1	105.5	104.8	106.0	96.6
2011	97.8	98.7	98.4	90.9	91.4	88.5	96.1	97.6	102.1	101.9	102.2	98.0
2012	100.0	100.0	100.0	100.0	100.0	100.0	100.0	100.0	100.0	100.0	100.0	100.0
2013	101.8	101.5	101.5	105.6	104.1	112.4	103.0	101.2	97.6	94.5	99.7	101.6
2014	104.2	104.2	104.4	112.5	111.6	116.7	107.0	106.4	96.7	92.1	99.9	104.2
2015	107.0	107.7	108.1	116.8	114.2	128.6	107.3	112.0	98.5	92.0	102.9	107.7
2016	108.8	110.3	110.8	119.2	115.3	137.1	107.7	113.6	100.4	92.5	105.8	109.6
2017	111.2	113.0	113.6	124.1	120.0	142.6	112.1	118.6	100.9	92.8	106.4	112.2
2018	114.5	116.3	116.9	130.0	127.7	141.7	115.2	123.5	102.3	95.6	106.9	115.7
2019	117.1	118.8	119.6	134.1	133.2	140.4	115.2	124.9	104.6	99.2	108.2	118.5
2020	113.1	114.3	114.2	130.5	126.1	150.0	99.5	113.8	107.1	104.2	109.2	114.9
2021	119.5	123.3	123.7	140.7	135.4	163.8	104.1	129.7	107.6	104.8	109.6	122.8
2019												
1st quarter	115.9	117.5	118.2	132.2	131.3	138.7	115.7	125.4	103.1	97.0	107.3	117.3
2nd quarter	116.8	118.5	119.3	134.2	133.4	140.1	115.0	125.9	104.4	99.1	108.1	118.3
3rd quarter	117.6	119.4	120.2	135.2	134.4	141.3	114.8	125.6	105.0	100.0	108.4	119.1
4th quarter	118.1	119.9	120.8	134.9	133.8	141.7	115.1	122.8	105.7	100.9	109.1	119.2
2020												
1st quarter	116.6	117.8	118.1	134.1	131.0	148.4	110.1	118.6	106.7	101.5	110.3	117.7
2nd quarter	106.2	106.4	105.5	122.4	119.7	135.4	87.6	98.1	107.7	106.3	108.7	107.4
3rd quarter	114.2	116.1	116.0	130.1	124.9	152.3	97.7	115.1	107.1	104.9	108.8	116.3
4th quarter	115.5	117.0	117.3	135.5	128.7	163.9	102.8	123.2	107.0	104.0	109.1	118.1
2021												
1st quarter	117.2	120.2	120.4	139.7	132.7	169.1	102.0	126.0	108.1	106.9	109.1	120.3
2nd quarter	119.2	123.7	124.1	140.9	135.6	163.9	103.9	128.1	107.6	105.4	109.1	122.2
3rd quarter	119.8	124.3	124.6	140.6	136.2	160.7	102.5	129.6	107.8	104.1	110.4	123.3
4th quarter	121.9	125.1	125.6	141.5	137.1	161.6	107.8	135.1	107.1	102.9	110.0	125.3

Table 1-5B. Chain-Type Quantity Indexes for Gross Domestic Product and Domestic Purchases: Historical Data

(Index numbers, 2012 = 100.)   NIPA Tables 1.1.3, 1.4.3, 2.3.3

Year and quarter	Gross domestic product, total	Personal consumption expenditures		Private fixed investment			Exports and imports of goods and services		Government consumption expenditures and gross investment			Gross domestic purchases
		Total	Excluding food and energy	Total	Nonresidential	Residential	Exports	Imports	Total	Federal	State and local	
1929	6.8	7.5	6.2	5.9	4.1	18.6	2.0	2.1	5.8	2.3	11.3	6.8
1930	6.2	7.1	5.8	4.6	3.4	11.5	1.6	1.8	6.3	2.5	12.4	6.2
1931	5.8	6.9	5.5	3.3	2.3	9.8	1.3	1.6	6.6	2.6	13.0	5.8
1932	5.1	6.3	5.0	2.0	1.4	5.5	1.1	1.3	6.4	2.6	12.4	5.1
1933	5.0	6.2	4.8	1.8	1.3	4.6	1.1	1.4	6.2	3.2	11.1	5.0
1934	5.6	6.6	5.1	2.3	1.7	6.0	1.2	1.4	6.9	4.2	11.6	5.6
1935	6.1	7.0	5.4	2.9	2.1	8.2	1.2	1.8	7.2	4.3	12.0	6.1
1936	6.9	7.7	5.9	3.8	2.7	10.2	1.3	1.8	8.3	6.4	12.0	6.9
1937	7.2	8.0	6.2	4.4	3.2	11.0	1.6	2.1	8.0	5.8	12.0	7.2
1938	7.0	7.9	6.0	3.6	2.5	11.0	1.6	1.6	8.6	6.4	12.7	6.9
1939	7.5	8.3	6.4	4.2	2.7	15.4	1.7	1.7	9.3	6.9	14.0	7.4
1940	8.2	8.7	6.7	5.0	3.3	17.3	2.0	1.7	9.7	7.8	13.6	8.1
1941	9.6	9.3	7.3	5.8	4.0	18.4	2.0	2.1	16.3	20.6	12.7	9.6
1942	11.5	9.1	7.1	3.4	2.5	9.5	1.3	1.9	37.7	61.6	11.6	11.5
1943	13.4	9.4	7.5	2.7	2.1	5.9	1.1	2.4	56.6	98.1	10.6	13.6
1944	14.5	9.6	7.7	3.2	2.6	5.1	1.2	2.5	63.5	111.6	10.2	14.6
1945	14.3	10.2	8.2	4.3	3.6	5.8	1.7	2.7	55.8	96.5	10.6	14.4
1946	12.7	11.5	9.1	7.6	5.2	23.5	3.6	2.2	19.6	27.0	11.6	12.2
1947	12.5	11.7	9.3	9.1	6.0	30.1	4.1	2.1	16.7	20.2	13.2	11.9
1948	13.0	12.0	9.6	9.9	6.3	35.9	3.3	2.5	17.6	21.3	14.0	12.7
1949	13.0	12.3	9.9	9.1	5.7	33.3	3.2	2.4	19.5	23.0	16.1	12.6
1947												
1st quarter	12.5	11.6	. . .	8.9	6.1	27.6	4.4	2.2	16.7	20.6	12.8	11.9
2nd quarter	12.5	11.8	. . .	8.7	6.0	26.2	4.3	2.2	16.7	20.4	13.0	11.9
3rd quarter	12.5	11.8	. . .	9.0	5.9	30.3	4.1	2.0	16.7	20.1	13.3	11.8
4th quarter	12.7	11.8	. . .	9.7	6.0	36.1	3.7	2.1	16.6	19.7	13.5	12.2
1948												
1st quarter	12.8	11.9	. . .	10.0	6.4	35.6	3.5	2.3	16.8	20.2	13.5	12.4
2nd quarter	13.1	12.0	. . .	10.0	6.2	37.7	3.2	2.4	17.4	21.0	13.9	12.7
3rd quarter	13.1	12.0	. . .	9.9	6.2	36.5	3.2	2.6	17.8	21.5	14.1	12.8
4th quarter	13.1	12.1	. . .	9.8	6.3	33.8	3.1	2.5	18.4	22.4	14.4	12.9
1949												
1st quarter	13.0	12.1	. . .	9.3	6.0	31.3	3.5	2.4	18.9	22.8	15.0	12.6
2nd quarter	12.9	12.3	. . .	9.0	5.8	30.8	3.5	2.4	19.7	23.7	15.9	12.5
3rd quarter	13.1	12.3	. . .	9.0	5.5	33.4	3.2	2.3	19.8	23.3	16.5	12.7
4th quarter	12.9	12.5	. . .	9.3	5.5	37.5	2.8	2.3	19.5	22.3	16.8	12.7
1950												
1st quarter	13.5	12.7	. . .	9.9	5.6	41.7	2.7	2.4	19.1	21.2	17.2	13.2
2nd quarter	13.9	12.9	. . .	10.7	6.1	45.7	2.7	2.5	19.5	21.8	17.4	13.6
3rd quarter	14.4	13.6	. . .	11.5	6.6	48.2	2.8	3.1	19.2	21.2	17.4	14.3
4th quarter	14.7	13.2	. . .	11.3	6.6	45.9	3.0	3.1	20.5	23.8	17.4	14.5
1951												
1st quarter	14.9	13.5	. . .	10.8	6.4	43.6	3.2	3.1	22.7	28.2	17.2	14.7
2nd quarter	15.1	13.1	. . .	10.4	6.5	37.7	3.5	3.0	25.7	33.8	17.5	14.8
3rd quarter	15.4	13.3	. . .	10.2	6.6	35.4	3.6	2.8	28.5	39.3	17.6	15.1
4th quarter	15.5	13.4	. . .	10.1	6.5	35.7	3.6	2.7	30.0	42.3	17.6	15.1
1952												
1st quarter	15.6	13.4	. . .	10.3	6.5	36.6	3.7	3.0	30.9	44.0	17.6	15.3
2nd quarter	15.7	13.7	. . .	10.5	6.6	37.3	3.3	3.0	32.0	45.8	18.0	15.4
3rd quarter	15.8	13.7	. . .	9.9	6.1	37.0	3.1	3.2	32.3	46.9	17.5	15.6
4th quarter	16.3	14.2	. . .	10.6	6.7	38.9	3.1	3.5	32.9	47.6	17.9	16.2
1953												
1st quarter	16.6	14.4	. . .	11.1	7.0	39.6	3.0	3.4	33.9	49.3	18.3	16.5
2nd quarter	16.7	14.5	. . .	11.2	7.1	39.7	3.1	3.6	34.6	50.7	18.3	16.6
3rd quarter	16.6	14.4	. . .	11.2	7.2	38.2	3.2	3.6	34.2	49.5	18.8	16.5
4th quarter	16.4	14.3	. . .	11.1	7.2	37.9	3.1	3.4	34.1	48.8	19.2	16.3
1954												
1st quarter	16.3	14.4	. . .	10.9	7.0	38.3	2.9	3.2	33.3	46.4	19.9	16.2
2nd quarter	16.3	14.6	. . .	11.1	6.9	40.8	3.4	3.5	32.1	44.1	20.0	16.2
3rd quarter	16.5	14.8	. . .	11.5	7.1	43.3	3.3	3.3	31.4	42.1	20.5	16.3
4th quarter	16.8	15.1	. . .	11.8	7.1	46.0	3.4	3.3	31.2	41.7	20.6	16.6
1955												
1st quarter	17.3	15.4	. . .	12.2	7.2	49.4	3.5	3.5	31.3	40.9	21.5	17.1
2nd quarter	17.6	15.7	. . .	12.7	7.7	50.1	3.4	3.7	31.0	40.0	21.8	17.4
3rd quarter	17.8	15.9	. . .	13.0	8.0	49.0	3.7	3.8	31.2	40.4	21.7	17.6
4th quarter	17.9	16.1	. . .	13.1	8.3	47.0	3.7	3.9	30.5	39.1	21.9	17.8

. . . = Not available.

Table 1-5B. Chain-Type Quantity Indexes for Gross Domestic Product and Domestic Purchases: Historical Data—*Continued*

(Index numbers, 2012 = 100.)   NIPA Tables 1.1.3, 1.4.3, 2.3.3

Year and quarter	Gross domestic product											Gross domestic purchases
	Gross domestic product, total	Personal consumption expenditures		Private fixed investment			Exports and imports of goods and services		Government consumption expenditures and gross investment			
		Total	Excluding food and energy	Total	Nonresidential	Residential	Exports	Imports	Total	Federal	State and local	
1956												
1st quarter	17.9	16.1	. . .	12.9	8.2	45.8	3.9	4.1	30.5	38.8	22.1	17.7
2nd quarter	18.0	16.2	. . .	13.0	8.3	45.6	4.1	4.0	31.1	39.8	22.4	17.8
3rd quarter	18.0	16.2	. . .	13.0	8.4	44.7	4.3	4.1	30.9	39.1	22.5	17.7
4th quarter	18.3	16.4	. . .	12.9	8.4	44.0	4.5	3.9	31.7	40.5	22.7	18.0
1957												
1st quarter	18.4	16.6	. . .	12.9	8.4	43.4	4.7	4.2	32.3	41.3	23.3	18.1
2nd quarter	18.4	16.6	. . .	12.8	8.4	42.4	4.6	4.2	32.2	40.7	23.4	18.1
3rd quarter	18.6	16.7	. . .	13.0	8.6	41.8	4.5	4.1	32.4	41.0	23.8	18.3
4th quarter	18.4	16.7	. . .	12.7	8.4	41.8	4.3	4.2	33.0	41.4	24.4	18.1
1958												
1st quarter	17.9	16.5	. . .	12.0	7.9	40.1	3.9	4.2	32.7	40.2	25.1	17.7
2nd quarter	18.0	16.6	. . .	11.7	7.6	40.3	3.9	4.4	33.5	41.5	25.4	17.9
3rd quarter	18.4	16.9	. . .	11.9	7.5	43.2	3.9	4.3	33.7	41.3	26.0	18.3
4th quarter	18.9	17.1	. . .	12.6	7.8	47.7	3.9	4.6	34.4	42.2	26.4	18.7
1959												
1st quarter	19.2	17.4	14.1	13.4	8.0	53.1	4.2	4.7	34.0	41.4	26.6	19.1
2nd quarter	19.7	17.7	14.4	13.8	8.2	54.9	4.2	4.9	34.4	42.2	26.6	19.5
3rd quarter	19.7	17.9	14.6	13.9	8.5	53.9	4.6	4.9	34.7	42.7	26.6	19.5
4th quarter	19.7	17.9	14.6	13.7	8.4	52.4	4.4	4.8	34.5	42.3	26.5	19.6
1960												
1st quarter	20.2	18.1	14.8	14.2	8.7	54.0	4.9	5.0	33.9	40.7	27.0	19.9
2nd quarter	20.1	18.3	15.0	13.9	8.9	49.5	5.1	5.0	34.3	40.8	27.6	19.8
3rd quarter	20.2	18.2	14.9	13.6	8.7	48.1	5.2	4.9	35.1	42.1	28.0	19.8
4th quarter	19.9	18.3	14.9	13.6	8.7	48.0	5.2	4.7	35.3	42.2	28.4	19.5
1961												
1st quarter	20.0	18.3	14.9	13.5	8.6	48.2	5.2	4.6	35.9	42.4	29.3	19.7
2nd quarter	20.4	18.5	15.1	13.7	8.8	48.4	4.9	4.7	35.9	42.8	29.1	20.1
3rd quarter	20.8	18.6	15.3	14.1	8.8	51.0	5.1	5.0	36.7	44.0	29.3	20.5
4th quarter	21.2	19.0	15.6	14.5	9.1	52.8	5.2	5.1	37.5	44.9	30.1	20.9
1962												
1st quarter	21.5	19.2	15.8	14.8	9.3	53.7	5.2	5.3	38.2	46.5	29.9	21.3
2nd quarter	21.7	19.4	16.1	15.2	9.6	55.4	5.5	5.4	38.4	46.7	30.1	21.4
3rd quarter	22.0	19.6	16.2	15.3	9.7	55.3	5.5	5.5	39.3	48.1	30.5	21.7
4th quarter	22.1	19.9	16.5	15.3	9.6	55.2	5.3	5.5	39.6	48.3	30.8	21.8
1963												
1st quarter	22.3	20.0	16.6	15.5	9.7	57.2	5.4	5.4	39.1	46.7	31.3	22.0
2nd quarter	22.6	20.2	16.8	16.2	10.0	61.3	5.8	5.5	39.1	46.5	31.6	22.2
3rd quarter	23.1	20.5	17.1	16.6	10.2	62.5	5.8	5.7	40.8	49.1	32.5	22.7
4th quarter	23.2	20.6	17.3	17.1	10.5	64.4	6.0	5.7	40.4	47.8	32.9	22.8
1964												
1st quarter	23.7	21.1	17.6	17.6	10.7	68.4	6.3	5.6	40.5	47.6	33.4	23.3
2nd quarter	24.0	21.4	18.0	17.6	11.0	65.0	6.3	5.8	40.9	47.6	34.1	23.6
3rd quarter	24.3	21.8	18.3	17.9	11.4	63.9	6.5	5.9	40.9	47.3	34.5	23.9
4th quarter	24.4	21.9	18.4	18.1	11.6	62.8	6.6	6.1	40.9	46.9	34.9	24.0
1965												
1st quarter	25.0	22.4	18.8	18.9	12.3	63.1	5.8	5.9	40.9	46.5	35.2	24.7
2nd quarter	25.3	22.6	19.0	19.4	12.8	63.7	6.8	6.6	41.4	46.6	36.1	24.9
3rd quarter	25.9	23.0	19.4	19.9	13.3	64.0	6.7	6.6	42.7	48.3	37.1	25.5
4th quarter	26.5	23.7	19.9	20.4	13.8	62.7	7.1	6.9	43.5	49.4	37.6	26.1
1966												
1st quarter	27.1	24.0	20.3	21.2	14.4	64.3	6.9	7.1	44.3	50.6	38.1	26.8
2nd quarter	27.2	24.1	20.3	20.9	14.6	59.3	7.1	7.3	45.2	52.0	38.3	26.9
3rd quarter	27.5	24.3	20.6	21.0	14.8	57.3	7.0	7.7	46.4	54.0	38.8	27.2
4th quarter	27.7	24.4	20.7	20.4	14.8	51.3	7.2	7.8	47.2	54.6	39.8	27.4
1967												
1st quarter	27.9	24.6	20.8	20.0	14.6	49.9	7.3	7.9	49.2	58.1	40.3	27.6
2nd quarter	27.9	24.9	21.1	20.5	14.5	55.6	7.2	7.8	49.0	57.5	40.5	27.7
3rd quarter	28.2	25.0	21.2	20.8	14.5	58.6	7.1	7.9	49.6	58.4	40.6	28.0
4th quarter	28.4	25.2	21.3	21.4	14.8	62.0	7.3	8.3	49.9	58.5	41.3	28.2
1968												
1st quarter	29.0	25.8	21.9	21.9	15.2	62.2	7.5	8.8	50.8	59.5	42.1	28.8
2nd quarter	29.5	26.2	22.2	21.8	15.0	63.7	7.6	9.0	51.1	59.2	42.9	29.3
3rd quarter	29.7	26.7	22.7	22.2	15.2	65.0	8.1	9.5	51.2	58.8	43.5	29.5
4th quarter	29.8	26.8	22.8	22.7	15.7	65.9	8.0	9.4	51.3	58.5	43.9	29.7

. . . = Not available.

Table 1-5B. Chain-Type Quantity Indexes for Gross Domestic Product and Domestic Purchases: Historical Data—Continued

(Index numbers, 2012 = 100.)

NIPA Tables 1.1.3, 1.4.3, 2.3.3

Year and quarter	Gross domestic product, total	Personal consumption expenditures		Private fixed investment			Exports and imports of goods and services		Government consumption expenditures and gross investment			Gross domestic purchases
		Total	Excluding food and energy	Total	Nonresidential	Residential	Exports	Imports	Total	Federal	State and local	
1969												
1st quarter	30.3	27.1	23.0	23.3	16.1	68.1	7.0	8.5	51.4	58.4	44.3	30.2
2nd quarter	30.4	27.3	23.2	23.4	16.2	67.5	8.6	10.2	51.2	57.6	44.7	30.2
3rd quarter	30.6	27.4	23.3	23.8	16.6	66.9	8.4	10.1	51.3	57.7	44.8	30.4
4th quarter	30.4	27.6	23.5	23.2	16.5	62.3	8.7	10.0	50.7	56.4	44.7	30.2
1970												
1st quarter	30.4	27.8	23.6	23.1	16.4	62.4	8.8	9.9	50.4	55.5	45.1	30.1
2nd quarter	30.4	27.9	23.7	22.6	16.3	58.5	9.1	10.1	49.8	54.0	45.4	30.2
3rd quarter	30.7	28.2	23.9	23.0	16.4	61.9	9.1	10.1	50.0	53.3	46.4	30.4
4th quarter	30.4	28.1	23.8	23.0	15.8	68.2	9.2	10.3	50.1	53.1	46.6	30.1
1971												
1st quarter	31.2	28.6	24.3	23.5	15.9	71.7	9.3	10.2	49.3	51.4	46.8	30.9
2nd quarter	31.4	28.9	24.6	24.4	16.1	78.6	9.2	10.9	49.2	50.8	47.2	31.2
3rd quarter	31.6	29.1	24.9	24.8	16.2	82.2	9.6	11.2	49.2	50.6	47.3	31.4
4th quarter	31.7	29.6	25.4	25.5	16.5	85.3	8.8	10.4	48.8	49.3	47.9	31.5
1972												
1st quarter	32.3	30.0	25.8	26.5	17.1	90.9	9.7	11.9	49.1	49.7	48.1	32.2
2nd quarter	33.0	30.6	26.2	27.0	17.3	92.6	9.5	11.5	49.3	50.2	48.0	32.9
3rd quarter	33.3	31.0	26.7	27.3	17.6	93.0	10.0	11.7	48.4	47.9	48.4	33.1
4th quarter	33.9	31.8	27.4	28.5	18.4	96.3	10.5	12.3	48.8	48.0	49.0	33.7
1973												
1st quarter	34.7	32.4	28.1	29.6	19.2	99.6	11.2	12.8	49.2	48.6	49.2	34.5
2nd quarter	35.1	32.3	28.2	29.8	19.9	94.4	11.8	12.5	48.8	47.8	49.3	34.7
3rd quarter	34.9	32.5	28.3	29.8	20.2	90.3	11.8	12.1	48.3	46.2	49.8	34.4
4th quarter	35.3	32.4	28.3	29.5	20.4	86.2	12.4	12.2	48.6	46.3	50.5	34.7
1974												
1st quarter	35.0	32.1	28.2	28.9	20.4	80.6	12.5	11.8	49.5	47.4	51.1	34.2
2nd quarter	35.0	32.2	28.3	28.5	20.3	77.4	13.2	12.4	49.8	47.2	51.7	34.3
3rd quarter	34.7	32.3	28.3	28.1	20.1	74.8	12.4	12.2	49.9	47.5	51.6	34.1
4th quarter	34.6	31.8	27.8	26.6	19.6	65.1	12.8	12.1	50.1	48.0	51.6	33.9
1975												
1st quarter	34.2	32.1	28.1	25.1	18.5	61.4	12.9	10.9	50.6	47.5	53.2	33.1
2nd quarter	34.4	32.6	28.5	24.8	18.0	63.1	12.5	10.0	50.2	47.0	52.8	33.3
3rd quarter	35.0	33.1	29.0	25.4	18.2	67.3	12.3	10.8	51.2	48.2	53.5	34.1
4th quarter	35.5	33.5	29.5	25.9	18.4	70.2	13.0	11.4	51.6	48.4	54.2	34.5
1976												
1st quarter	36.3	34.1	30.0	26.9	18.8	76.8	12.9	12.1	51.7	47.9	54.8	35.5
2nd quarter	36.5	34.4	30.2	27.4	19.1	78.7	13.0	12.7	51.1	47.7	53.8	35.8
3rd quarter	36.7	34.8	30.6	27.7	19.5	77.5	13.4	13.2	51.0	47.8	53.5	36.1
4th quarter	37.0	35.3	30.9	29.0	19.9	86.8	13.5	13.6	50.9	47.9	53.3	36.4
1977												
1st quarter	37.4	35.7	31.4	30.0	20.6	89.4	13.3	14.3	51.4	48.2	53.8	37.0
2nd quarter	38.2	35.9	31.7	31.6	21.2	99.2	13.7	14.4	51.8	48.9	54.2	37.7
3rd quarter	38.8	36.2	32.0	32.0	21.6	98.9	13.8	14.2	52.0	49.3	54.1	38.3
4th quarter	38.8	36.8	32.5	32.5	22.3	97.8	13.3	14.4	51.9	49.0	54.2	38.4
1978												
1st quarter	39.0	37.0	32.7	32.8	22.5	98.7	13.6	15.3	51.9	49.0	54.2	38.7
2nd quarter	40.5	37.7	33.7	35.1	24.2	103.4	15.1	15.4	53.2	50.0	55.8	39.9
3rd quarter	40.9	37.9	33.9	36.0	25.0	104.6	15.2	15.6	53.7	50.3	56.5	40.3
4th quarter	41.4	38.2	34.2	36.8	25.8	104.4	15.8	15.8	54.2	50.7	57.0	40.8
1979												
1st quarter	41.5	38.4	34.3	37.1	26.4	101.9	15.8	15.8	53.7	50.7	56.0	40.8
2nd quarter	41.5	38.4	34.4	36.9	26.4	100.1	15.9	15.9	54.2	51.2	56.6	40.9
3rd quarter	41.9	38.8	34.9	37.6	27.2	98.9	16.5	15.6	54.3	51.3	56.7	41.0
4th quarter	42.0	38.9	34.9	37.2	27.2	94.9	17.5	16.0	54.7	51.3	57.4	41.0
1980												
1st quarter	42.1	38.8	34.8	36.7	27.5	87.6	18.0	16.0	55.5	52.7	57.7	41.0
2nd quarter	41.2	37.9	33.9	33.7	26.3	71.4	18.3	14.8	55.6	53.8	56.9	39.8
3rd quarter	41.2	38.3	34.5	34.1	26.4	73.5	18.3	13.7	54.9	53.1	56.0	39.4
4th quarter	41.9	38.9	35.2	35.4	27.0	80.4	18.2	14.5	54.8	53.4	55.7	40.4
1981												
1st quarter	42.8	39.0	35.4	35.7	27.5	78.4	18.5	15.1	55.6	54.5	56.2	41.3
2nd quarter	42.5	39.0	35.3	36.0	28.1	75.9	18.6	15.1	55.7	55.9	55.1	41.0
3rd quarter	43.0	39.2	35.5	36.0	28.8	70.0	18.2	14.9	55.5	55.6	54.9	41.5
4th quarter	42.5	38.9	35.1	35.9	29.4	62.7	18.3	15.4	56.2	56.6	55.4	41.1

Table 1-5B. Chain-Type Quantity Indexes for Gross Domestic Product and Domestic Purchases: Historical Data—*Continued*

(Index numbers, 2012 = 100.)

NIPA Tables 1.1.3, 1.4.3, 2.3.3

Year and quarter	Gross domestic product, total	Personal consumption expenditures		Private fixed investment			Exports and imports of goods and services		Government consumption expenditures and gross investment			Gross domestic purchases
		Total	Excluding food and energy	Total	Nonresidential	Residential	Exports	Imports	Total	Federal	State and local	
1982												
1st quarter	41.8	39.2	35.4	34.9	28.8	59.1	17.5	14.9	56.1	56.7	55.2	40.5
2nd quarter	42.0	39.3	35.5	33.8	27.9	57.2	17.6	14.7	56.4	56.9	55.4	40.7
3rd quarter	41.9	39.6	35.9	33.0	27.1	57.2	16.8	15.4	56.8	57.8	55.4	40.8
4th quarter	41.9	40.3	36.6	33.1	26.6	61.7	16.1	14.8	57.7	59.2	55.8	40.9
1983												
1st quarter	42.4	40.7	37.0	33.8	26.2	72.3	16.3	15.1	58.2	60.1	56.0	41.4
2nd quarter	43.4	41.5	37.9	35.1	26.6	80.7	16.4	16.3	58.7	61.2	55.9	42.6
3rd quarter	44.3	42.2	38.5	37.0	27.7	88.6	16.6	17.5	59.7	62.8	56.4	43.7
4th quarter	45.2	42.9	39.3	39.1	29.4	92.3	16.9	18.4	58.8	60.8	56.4	44.7
1984												
1st quarter	46.1	43.3	39.8	40.3	30.3	95.1	17.3	19.9	59.4	61.3	57.2	45.8
2nd quarter	46.9	43.9	40.3	41.9	31.8	96.7	17.7	20.7	60.7	63.2	57.9	46.7
3rd quarter	47.3	44.2	40.7	42.7	32.7	95.6	18.1	21.2	61.2	63.1	58.9	47.2
4th quarter	47.7	44.8	41.3	43.5	33.5	95.7	18.5	21.9	62.5	65.1	59.5	47.6
1985												
1st quarter	48.2	45.5	42.0	43.9	33.9	95.9	18.5	21.4	63.1	65.7	60.3	48.0
2nd quarter	48.6	45.9	42.5	44.5	34.4	96.7	18.5	22.4	64.5	67.5	61.3	48.6
3rd quarter	49.3	46.8	43.4	44.3	34.0	98.5	18.2	22.2	66.0	69.5	62.3	49.3
4th quarter	49.7	46.9	43.4	45.1	34.6	100.7	18.8	23.1	66.3	69.5	62.8	49.8
1986												
1st quarter	50.2	47.3	43.9	45.2	34.2	104.8	19.4	23.1	66.8	69.3	64.0	50.1
2nd quarter	50.4	47.8	44.4	45.3	33.5	110.8	19.6	24.0	68.2	71.6	64.6	50.5
3rd quarter	50.9	48.7	45.4	45.1	33.2	112.3	20.0	24.7	69.7	74.0	65.2	51.0
4th quarter	51.1	49.0	45.6	45.4	33.5	112.6	20.8	24.9	69.4	73.2	65.4	51.2
1987												
1st quarter	51.5	49.0	45.7	44.6	32.7	112.4	20.8	24.8	69.8	73.6	65.7	51.5
2nd quarter	52.1	49.7	46.4	45.3	33.3	112.8	21.6	25.4	70.4	74.6	65.9	52.1
3rd quarter	52.5	50.3	47.1	46.1	34.3	111.9	22.6	25.9	70.4	74.5	66.1	52.4
4th quarter	53.4	50.4	47.2	46.1	34.2	112.1	23.4	26.5	71.5	75.8	67.0	53.3
1988												
1st quarter	53.7	51.3	48.0	46.1	34.5	110.1	24.7	26.3	70.9	73.6	67.7	53.3
2nd quarter	54.4	51.7	48.3	47.0	35.3	111.4	25.4	26.0	71.1	73.1	68.6	53.8
3rd quarter	54.7	52.1	48.8	47.2	35.5	111.5	25.9	26.6	71.1	72.7	68.9	54.2
4th quarter	55.5	52.7	49.4	47.8	36.0	112.2	26.7	27.5	72.5	74.7	69.7	54.9
1989												
1st quarter	56.0	53.0	49.7	48.2	36.6	111.1	27.5	27.6	72.2	73.4	70.3	55.3
2nd quarter	56.5	53.2	50.0	48.3	37.1	107.7	28.7	27.7	73.3	74.9	71.1	55.6
3rd quarter	56.9	53.7	50.5	49.1	38.0	107.2	29.0	27.7	73.9	75.5	71.7	55.9
4th quarter	57.0	53.9	50.6	48.5	37.6	104.9	29.4	28.2	74.3	75.1	72.7	56.1
1990												
1st quarter	57.6	54.4	51.3	49.0	38.1	105.8	30.7	29.1	75.5	76.4	73.8	56.6
2nd quarter	57.8	54.6	51.3	48.1	37.6	101.6	31.1	29.0	75.6	76.5	74.0	56.8
3rd quarter	57.9	54.8	51.5	47.7	37.9	96.2	31.3	28.9	75.7	76.1	74.4	56.7
4th quarter	57.3	54.4	51.2	46.4	37.3	90.6	31.6	28.1	76.2	76.2	75.3	56.0
1991												
1st quarter	57.1	54.2	51.0	45.2	36.5	85.8	31.8	27.8	76.7	77.1	75.4	55.7
2nd quarter	57.5	54.6	51.3	45.3	36.3	88.5	33.0	28.3	77.0	77.4	75.7	56.0
3rd quarter	57.8	54.9	51.6	45.4	36.0	91.5	33.8	29.1	76.8	76.4	76.1	56.3
4th quarter	58.0	54.9	51.7	45.6	36.0	93.3	34.5	29.7	76.2	74.5	76.7	56.5
1992												
1st quarter	58.7	55.9	52.9	46.1	35.9	98.6	35.1	30.0	76.9	74.8	77.7	57.1
2nd quarter	59.3	56.3	53.2	47.6	37.0	102.0	35.2	30.5	76.8	74.6	77.6	57.8
3rd quarter	59.9	56.9	53.9	48.1	37.6	102.0	35.9	30.9	77.2	75.6	77.6	58.4
4th quarter	60.5	57.5	54.5	49.5	38.6	105.9	36.1	31.7	77.2	75.7	77.5	59.1
1993												
1st quarter	60.6	57.8	54.8	49.9	39.0	106.0	36.2	32.4	76.3	73.2	77.8	59.3
2nd quarter	61.0	58.3	55.4	50.8	39.7	107.4	36.6	33.0	76.3	72.4	78.4	59.7
3rd quarter	61.3	58.9	56.0	51.6	40.1	111.4	36.5	33.5	76.4	72.2	78.8	60.1
4th quarter	62.1	59.5	56.5	53.7	41.5	117.2	37.7	34.8	76.7	72.3	79.2	61.0
1994												
1st quarter	62.7	60.1	57.2	54.3	41.9	118.9	38.0	35.6	75.7	69.8	79.5	61.7
2nd quarter	63.6	60.6	57.6	55.4	42.6	122.8	39.3	37.0	76.1	69.5	80.5	62.5
3rd quarter	63.9	61.1	58.2	55.8	43.3	121.0	40.8	38.0	77.4	71.1	81.4	62.9
4th quarter	64.7	61.7	58.9	57.2	45.0	119.1	41.7	39.1	76.7	69.3	81.7	63.6
1995												
1st quarter	64.9	61.9	59.1	58.4	46.7	116.4	42.5	39.9	77.0	69.1	82.3	63.9
2nd quarter	65.1	62.4	59.6	58.4	47.1	112.8	43.1	40.3	77.2	68.8	83.0	64.1
3rd quarter	65.7	63.0	60.2	59.2	47.4	117.0	45.0	40.4	77.0	68.3	83.1	64.3
4th quarter	66.1	63.4	60.7	60.3	48.3	119.2	45.6	41.0	76.2	66.0	83.5	64.8

Table 1-5B. Chain-Type Quantity Indexes for Gross Domestic Product and Domestic Purchases: Historical Data—*Continued*

(Index numbers, 2012 = 100.)   NIPA Tables 1.1.3, 1.4.3, 2.3.3

Year and quarter	Gross domestic product, total	Personal consumption expenditures		Private fixed investment			Exports and imports of goods and services		Government consumption expenditures and gross investment			Gross domestic purchases
		Total	Excluding food and energy	Total	Nonresidential	Residential	Exports	Imports	Total	Federal	State and local	
1996												
1st quarter	66.6	64.0	61.2	61.9	49.6	122.3	46.2	42.3	76.7	67.3	83.4	65.4
2nd quarter	67.7	64.7	61.9	63.8	50.9	127.7	46.9	43.2	77.7	67.9	84.6	66.5
3rd quarter	68.3	65.1	62.5	65.2	52.5	127.4	47.3	44.6	77.7	67.0	85.3	67.3
4th quarter	69.0	65.6	63.0	66.3	53.8	126.0	50.3	45.5	78.2	66.7	86.5	67.7
1997												
1st quarter	69.5	66.3	63.7	67.5	55.1	126.6	51.2	47.5	77.8	65.7	86.5	68.4
2nd quarter	70.6	66.6	64.1	68.8	56.2	128.4	53.3	49.0	78.8	67.2	87.2	69.5
3rd quarter	71.5	67.7	65.3	71.2	58.7	129.6	54.5	50.9	79.2	66.9	88.0	70.5
4th quarter	72.1	68.5	66.1	71.8	59.1	131.0	54.4	52.0	79.6	66.8	88.8	71.3
1998												
1st quarter	72.8	69.2	66.9	73.9	61.0	133.7	54.7	53.9	79.3	65.1	89.6	72.2
2nd quarter	73.5	70.5	68.1	76.4	63.0	138.3	54.1	55.1	80.7	66.4	91.1	73.2
3rd quarter	74.4	71.4	69.1	77.9	64.0	142.4	53.8	55.9	81.3	66.2	92.4	74.2
4th quarter	75.6	72.4	70.3	80.0	65.9	145.7	55.8	57.7	81.8	66.6	92.9	75.4
1999												
1st quarter	76.4	73.1	70.9	81.4	67.4	146.3	55.7	59.3	82.4	66.5	94.0	76.4
2nd quarter	77.0	74.3	72.0	83.4	69.1	148.6	56.3	61.0	82.6	66.4	94.6	77.2
3rd quarter	78.0	75.1	72.9	85.3	71.1	149.7	58.0	63.2	83.6	67.4	95.6	78.3
4th quarter	79.3	76.2	74.1	85.8	71.4	150.8	59.3	64.8	84.9	68.8	96.8	79.7
2000												
1st quarter	79.6	77.4	75.5	88.2	74.1	151.5	60.1	67.3	84.3	66.5	97.5	80.2
2nd quarter	81.0	78.1	76.1	90.2	76.4	150.8	62.0	69.4	85.2	68.6	97.4	81.7
3rd quarter	81.1	78.8	76.9	90.6	77.2	148.4	63.5	71.9	84.8	67.3	97.7	82.0
4th quarter	81.6	79.5	77.5	90.8	77.5	148.6	62.8	72.0	85.3	67.5	98.5	82.6
2001												
1st quarter	81.3	79.8	77.9	90.3	76.8	149.2	62.0	71.1	86.7	69.0	99.7	82.3
2nd quarter	81.8	80.0	78.2	89.2	75.2	151.5	60.2	68.8	88.2	70.0	101.6	82.7
3rd quarter	81.5	80.2	78.5	88.6	74.3	152.5	57.1	67.3	88.1	70.4	101.1	82.5
4th quarter	81.7	81.5	79.9	86.6	72.2	151.5	55.1	66.6	89.5	71.2	103.1	82.9
2002												
1st quarter	82.4	81.7	80.2	85.8	70.5	156.4	56.3	68.5	91.1	73.6	104.0	83.7
2nd quarter	82.9	82.1	80.5	85.7	69.7	160.3	58.0	70.8	91.8	75.0	104.2	84.3
3rd quarter	83.3	82.7	81.1	85.6	69.4	160.8	58.2	71.7	92.3	75.7	104.4	84.7
4th quarter	83.4	83.2	81.5	85.2	68.5	163.7	57.3	72.9	93.0	77.0	104.6	85.2
2003												
1st quarter	83.8	83.6	81.9	86.0	68.8	166.7	57.2	72.6	93.0	77.9	104.1	85.6
2nd quarter	84.5	84.5	83.0	88.1	70.7	169.4	57.3	73.7	93.9	80.6	103.5	86.4
3rd quarter	85.9	85.7	84.3	91.0	72.2	179.1	58.8	74.8	94.1	80.6	103.9	87.8
4th quarter	86.9	86.3	84.9	92.6	73.2	184.4	61.5	77.2	94.7	82.1	103.8	88.8
2004												
1st quarter	87.4	87.1	85.7	92.4	72.4	186.5	62.9	79.4	95.1	83.0	103.8	89.4
2nd quarter	88.1	87.6	86.2	94.9	74.2	192.5	64.2	82.5	95.4	83.4	103.9	90.4
3rd quarter	89.0	88.6	87.4	96.9	76.4	193.8	64.4	83.7	95.5	84.4	103.5	91.3
4th quarter	89.9	89.6	88.4	98.7	77.9	196.5	65.9	85.6	95.5	84.2	103.6	92.3
2005												
1st quarter	90.9	90.2	88.9	100.4	79.1	201.1	67.2	86.3	96.0	85.1	103.7	93.3
2nd quarter	91.3	91.2	89.9	102.1	80.3	204.9	68.7	87.5	95.9	85.1	103.7	93.7
3rd quarter	92.0	92.0	90.7	103.9	82.0	207.1	68.6	88.0	96.2	85.7	103.7	94.5
4th quarter	92.5	92.1	90.9	104.3	82.6	206.7	70.8	90.8	96.3	85.7	103.8	95.1
2006												
1st quarter	93.8	93.1	92.2	106.3	85.4	204.8	73.6	92.7	97.5	88.0	104.3	96.3
2nd quarter	94.0	93.6	92.5	105.7	86.9	194.5	75.0	93.6	97.5	87.4	104.7	96.5
3rd quarter	94.2	94.2	93.1	105.0	88.4	183.7	74.9	94.5	97.3	86.6	105.0	96.8
4th quarter	95.0	95.1	94.1	104.3	89.3	175.2	77.8	94.4	98.1	87.8	105.5	97.2
2007												
1st quarter	95.2	95.7	94.6	104.2	91.0	167.3	79.3	95.8	98.3	87.3	106.1	97.4
2nd quarter	95.8	95.9	95.0	104.7	93.0	160.7	80.5	96.3	99.2	88.7	106.6	98.0
3rd quarter	96.4	96.6	95.7	104.1	94.4	150.5	83.0	96.9	99.6	89.5	106.8	98.3
4th quarter	97.0	97.0	96.2	103.1	95.9	138.0	84.9	95.9	100.4	91.0	107.1	98.5
2008												
1st quarter	96.6	96.8	96.1	101.5	96.3	127.0	86.3	96.3	100.7	92.4	106.5	98.0
2nd quarter	97.2	97.1	96.6	100.7	96.5	121.2	88.8	95.4	101.5	94.4	106.6	98.0
3rd quarter	96.7	96.4	96.1	98.1	94.7	115.1	88.4	94.2	102.3	95.6	107.1	97.4
4th quarter	94.5	95.5	94.9	91.7	89.1	103.9	83.2	90.8	103.0	96.8	107.5	95.4
2009												
1st quarter	93.4	95.2	94.6	84.4	82.4	93.8	76.5	82.1	104.2	98.1	108.6	93.8
2nd quarter	93.3	94.8	94.1	81.3	79.9	88.1	77.1	78.8	105.7	100.4	109.5	93.1
3rd quarter	93.6	95.4	94.8	81.6	79.5	92.1	79.9	82.1	106.0	101.4	109.3	93.6
4th quarter	94.6	95.3	94.5	82.0	80.0	92.0	84.4	86.1	106.2	102.9	108.6	94.6

Table 1-5B. Chain-Type Quantity Indexes for Gross Domestic Product and Domestic Purchases: Historical Data—*Continued*

(Index numbers, 2012 = 100.)   NIPA Tables 1.1.3, 1.4.3, 2.3.3

Year and quarter	Gross domestic product, total	Personal consumption expenditures		Private fixed investment			Exports and imports of goods and services		Government consumption expenditures and gross investment			Gross domestic purchases
		Total	Excluding food and energy	Total	Nonresidential	Residential	Exports	Imports	Total	Federal	State and local	
2010												
1st quarter	95.1	95.9	95.1	82.0	80.5	89.0	86.4	88.4	105.8	104.0	107.0	95.1
2nd quarter	96.0	96.7	96.1	85.0	83.2	93.6	88.3	92.4	106.1	105.4	106.6	96.4
3rd quarter	96.8	97.4	96.8	85.4	85.4	85.3	90.8	95.7	105.3	104.9	105.6	97.3
4th quarter	97.3	98.0	97.4	87.0	87.1	86.7	93.3	96.0	104.7	104.7	104.6	97.6
2011												
1st quarter	97.0	98.4	98.0	86.9	87.0	86.4	94.1	96.5	103.4	103.3	103.5	97.3
2nd quarter	97.7	98.5	98.2	88.9	89.2	87.4	95.7	96.8	102.7	102.9	102.6	97.8
3rd quarter	97.6	98.8	98.5	92.7	93.4	89.0	97.0	97.9	101.2	100.6	101.6	97.8
4th quarter	98.7	99.0	98.8	95.0	95.8	91.3	97.7	99.2	101.2	101.0	101.3	98.9
2012												
1st quarter	99.5	99.7	99.8	98.0	98.2	96.8	98.9	99.7	100.7	101.0	100.5	99.7
2nd quarter	100.0	99.8	99.7	100.0	100.4	97.6	99.9	100.1	100.2	100.2	100.2	100.0
3rd quarter	100.2	100.0	99.9	100.1	100.1	100.2	100.5	100.6	100.0	100.4	99.8	100.2
4th quarter	100.3	100.4	100.5	101.9	101.2	105.4	100.6	99.7	99.1	98.4	99.5	100.1
2013												
1st quarter	101.2	101.0	100.9	103.7	102.5	109.2	101.1	99.6	98.2	96.1	99.6	100.9
2nd quarter	101.3	101.1	101.1	104.5	102.8	112.7	102.0	101.0	98.0	95.4	99.8	101.2
3rd quarter	102.1	101.5	101.6	106.3	104.5	114.7	102.9	101.7	97.5	94.0	99.9	101.9
4th quarter	102.8	102.3	102.3	107.7	106.7	112.9	105.9	102.5	96.7	92.4	99.7	102.4
2014												
1st quarter	102.5	102.7	102.6	108.8	108.2	112.1	104.8	103.9	96.3	92.3	99.1	102.4
2nd quarter	103.8	103.7	103.9	111.8	111.1	115.7	107.1	106.2	96.4	91.7	99.6	103.7
3rd quarter	105.0	104.7	105.1	114.0	113.3	117.4	107.5	106.4	97.1	92.8	100.0	104.9
4th quarter	105.5	105.9	106.2	115.3	114.0	121.6	108.4	109.2	97.0	91.4	100.9	105.7
2015												
1st quarter	106.3	106.6	106.8	115.6	113.9	124.0	107.5	110.8	97.5	91.8	101.5	106.8
2nd quarter	106.9	107.3	107.7	116.6	114.4	127.1	107.8	111.6	98.4	92.0	102.7	107.5
3rd quarter	107.3	108.1	108.6	117.6	114.8	130.5	106.9	112.6	98.8	91.9	103.5	108.1
4th quarter	107.4	108.7	109.3	117.3	113.9	132.8	106.8	112.8	99.2	92.5	103.7	108.3
2016												
1st quarter	108.1	109.4	110.0	118.0	113.8	136.9	106.4	112.7	100.2	92.8	105.3	109.0
2nd quarter	108.4	110.0	110.4	118.6	114.5	137.0	107.3	112.8	100.0	92.0	105.5	109.2
3rd quarter	109.0	110.6	111.1	119.7	116.0	136.3	108.9	113.6	100.6	92.6	106.0	109.8
4th quarter	109.6	111.2	111.7	120.6	116.8	138.0	108.2	115.3	100.8	92.6	106.3	110.6
2017												
1st quarter	110.1	112.0	112.7	122.5	118.2	141.6	110.7	117.0	100.6	92.0	106.4	111.0
2nd quarter	110.7	112.5	113.0	123.7	119.5	142.5	111.2	118.2	100.9	92.8	106.4	111.8
3rd quarter	111.5	113.2	113.7	123.8	119.8	141.8	111.9	118.2	100.8	92.7	106.3	112.5
4th quarter	112.6	114.3	114.8	126.3	122.3	144.3	114.5	121.2	101.5	93.8	106.7	113.6
2018												
1st quarter	113.4	115.0	115.6	128.3	125.3	142.7	115.1	122.0	101.7	94.3	106.8	114.5
2nd quarter	114.4	116.0	116.6	130.2	127.4	143.9	116.5	122.4	102.4	95.4	107.2	115.3
3rd quarter	114.9	116.8	117.5	130.5	128.2	141.7	114.6	124.2	102.7	96.2	107.1	116.3
4th quarter	115.2	117.3	117.9	131.1	129.8	138.6	114.8	125.4	102.5	96.7	106.4	116.7
2019												
1st quarter	115.9	117.5	118.2	132.2	131.3	138.7	115.7	125.4	103.1	97.0	107.3	117.3
2nd quarter	116.8	118.5	119.3	134.2	133.4	140.1	115.0	125.9	104.4	99.1	108.1	118.3
3rd quarter	117.6	119.4	120.2	135.2	134.4	141.3	114.8	125.6	105.0	100.0	108.4	119.1
4th quarter	118.1	119.9	120.8	134.9	133.8	141.7	115.1	122.8	105.7	100.9	109.1	119.2
2020												
1st quarter	116.6	117.8	118.1	134.1	131.0	148.4	110.1	118.6	106.7	101.5	110.3	117.7
2nd quarter	106.2	106.4	105.5	122.4	119.7	135.4	87.6	98.1	107.7	106.3	108.7	107.4
3rd quarter	114.2	116.1	116.0	130.1	124.9	152.3	97.7	115.1	107.1	104.9	108.8	116.3
4th quarter	115.5	117.0	117.3	135.5	128.7	163.9	102.8	123.2	107.0	104.0	109.1	118.1
2021												
1st quarter	117.2	120.2	120.4	139.7	132.7	169.1	102.0	126.0	108.1	106.9	109.1	120.3
2nd quarter	119.2	123.7	124.1	140.9	135.6	163.9	103.9	128.1	107.6	105.4	109.1	122.2
3rd quarter	119.8	124.3	124.6	140.6	136.2	160.7	102.5	129.6	107.8	104.1	110.4	123.3
4th quarter	121.9	125.1	125.6	141.5	137.1	161.6	107.8	135.1	107.1	102.9	110.0	125.3

Table 1-6A. Chain-Type Price Indexes for Gross Domestic Product and Domestic Purchases: Recent Data

(Index numbers, 2012 = 100.)   **NIPA Tables 1.1.4, 1.6.4, 2.3.4**

Year and quarter	Gross domestic product											Gross domestic purchases
	Gross domestic product, total	Personal consumption expenditures		Private fixed investment			Exports and imports of goods and services		Government consumption expenditures and gross investment			
		Total	Excluding food and energy	Total	Nonresidential	Residential	Exports	Imports	Total	Federal	State and local	
1960	16.6	16.4	17.2	24.5	30.4	12.5	24.0	16.8	11.1	13.7	9.3	16.2
1961	16.8	16.6	17.4	24.5	30.3	12.5	24.4	16.8	11.3	13.8	9.5	16.4
1962	17.0	16.8	17.6	24.5	30.3	12.5	24.4	16.6	11.5	14.0	9.8	16.5
1963	17.2	17.0	17.8	24.4	30.3	12.4	24.4	17.0	11.8	14.4	10.0	16.8
1964	17.5	17.3	18.1	24.6	30.5	12.5	24.6	17.3	12.1	14.8	10.2	17.0
1965	17.8	17.5	18.3	25.0	30.9	12.8	25.3	17.6	12.4	15.2	10.5	17.3
1966	18.3	17.9	18.7	25.5	31.3	13.3	26.1	18.0	12.9	15.7	11.0	17.8
1967	18.8	18.4	19.3	26.1	32.1	13.8	27.1	18.0	13.4	16.0	11.6	18.3
1968	19.6	19.1	20.1	27.1	33.2	14.5	27.7	18.3	14.1	16.9	12.2	19.1
1969	20.6	20.0	21.1	28.4	34.6	15.5	28.6	18.8	14.9	17.7	13.1	20.0
1970	21.7	20.9	22.1	29.6	36.3	16.0	29.8	19.9	16.1	19.1	14.1	21.1
1971	22.8	21.8	23.1	31.1	38.0	16.9	30.8	21.1	17.4	20.7	15.2	22.2
1972	23.7	22.5	23.9	32.4	39.3	18.0	32.2	22.6	18.7	22.5	16.2	23.1
1973	25.0	23.8	24.8	34.2	40.9	19.6	36.4	26.5	19.9	24.1	17.2	24.5
1974	27.3	26.2	26.7	37.6	44.9	21.6	44.9	37.9	21.9	26.0	19.2	27.0
1975	29.8	28.4	29.0	42.1	50.8	23.6	49.5	41.1	23.9	28.3	21.0	29.4
1976	31.5	30.0	30.7	44.4	53.6	25.1	51.1	42.3	25.2	30.0	22.0	31.0
1977	33.4	31.9	32.7	47.7	57.1	27.7	53.2	46.1	26.7	31.9	23.4	33.1
1978	35.8	34.1	34.9	51.5	60.9	31.1	56.4	49.3	28.5	34.0	24.9	35.4
1979	38.7	37.2	37.4	56.1	65.8	34.6	63.2	57.8	30.9	36.6	27.1	38.5
1980	42.3	41.2	40.8	61.4	71.6	38.3	69.6	71.9	34.0	40.1	30.1	42.6
1981	46.2	44.9	44.4	67.1	78.5	41.4	74.7	75.8	37.4	43.8	33.2	46.5
1982	49.1	47.4	47.3	70.7	82.9	43.6	75.1	73.3	40.0	47.0	35.4	49.2
1983	51.0	49.4	49.7	70.9	82.8	44.7	75.4	70.5	41.5	48.5	37.0	50.9
1984	52.9	51.2	51.8	71.7	83.0	46.0	76.1	69.9	43.3	50.6	38.5	52.6
1985	54.5	53.0	53.9	72.5	83.9	47.3	73.9	67.6	44.7	51.7	40.1	54.1
1986	55.6	54.2	55.8	74.2	85.4	49.4	72.6	67.6	45.4	52.0	41.3	55.3
1987	57.0	55.9	57.5	75.7	86.3	51.5	74.2	71.7	46.6	52.3	43.2	56.8
1988	59.0	58.0	60.0	77.6	88.5	53.3	78.0	75.1	48.2	54.0	44.6	58.9
1989	61.3	60.6	62.5	79.6	90.6	55.0	79.3	76.8	50.0	55.5	46.8	61.2
1990	63.6	63.2	65.0	81.3	92.5	56.3	79.8	79.0	52.1	57.3	49.2	63.6
1991	65.8	65.3	67.3	82.6	94.3	57.0	80.7	78.3	54.0	59.3	51.0	65.6
1992	67.3	67.1	69.4	82.6	94.0	57.7	80.3	78.4	55.6	60.8	52.7	67.1
1993	68.9	68.8	71.3	83.6	94.2	60.1	80.4	77.8	57.0	62.2	54.0	68.6
1994	70.3	70.2	72.9	84.9	94.9	62.2	81.3	78.5	58.5	63.9	55.4	70.1
1995	71.8	71.7	74.5	86.2	95.8	64.5	83.1	80.7	60.1	65.8	56.9	71.6
1996	73.1	73.2	75.9	86.2	95.3	65.9	82.0	79.3	61.4	66.9	58.2	72.8
1997	74.4	74.5	77.2	86.2	94.7	67.4	80.6	76.5	62.6	68.0	59.5	73.9
1998	75.2	75.1	78.2	85.6	93.2	69.2	78.7	72.4	63.6	68.9	60.6	74.4
1999	76.3	76.2	79.2	85.7	92.3	71.8	78.1	72.8	65.8	70.5	63.0	75.5
2000	78.0	78.1	80.6	86.8	92.7	75.0	79.6	76.0	68.6	72.9	66.0	77.5
2001	79.8	79.7	82.2	87.6	92.3	78.6	79.0	74.0	70.6	74.2	68.3	79.0
2002	81.0	80.7	83.5	87.8	91.9	80.5	78.3	73.2	72.4	76.6	69.8	80.1
2003	82.6	82.4	84.9	88.6	91.2	84.3	79.5	75.4	75.0	80.0	72.1	81.8
2004	84.8	84.4	86.5	91.1	92.1	90.2	82.4	79.0	78.2	82.8	75.4	84.2
2005	87.5	86.9	88.4	94.8	94.4	96.7	85.3	83.6	82.1	86.2	79.6	87.1
2006	90.2	89.3	90.6	98.2	96.7	102.4	88.0	86.9	85.7	89.0	83.7	89.9
2007	92.7	91.6	92.6	99.7	98.3	103.7	91.3	89.9	89.5	91.6	88.2	92.3
2008	94.4	94.3	94.4	100.5	99.8	102.2	95.5	98.8	93.3	94.4	92.6	94.9
2009	95.0	94.1	95.3	99.3	99.2	98.7	89.8	87.9	92.9	94.2	92.0	94.5
2010	96.2	95.7	96.7	97.7	97.4	98.3	93.4	92.7	95.4	96.4	94.7	96.0
2011	98.2	98.2	98.2	98.7	98.6	99.0	99.2	99.7	98.3	99.1	97.7	98.3
2012	100.0	100.0	100.0	100.0	100.0	100.0	100.0	100.0	100.0	100.0	100.0	100.0
2013	101.8	101.4	101.5	101.0	100.3	105.1	100.1	98.7	102.4	100.9	103.3	101.5
2014	103.7	102.9	103.2	102.9	101.5	111.1	100.2	98.0	104.5	102.6	105.7	103.2
2015	104.7	103.1	104.5	103.5	101.9	114.1	95.4	90.1	104.6	103.1	105.7	103.5
2016	105.7	104.1	106.1	103.5	101.1	118.1	93.5	87.1	104.9	103.7	105.7	104.2
2017	107.7	106.1	107.9	105.2	102.0	123.5	95.9	89.0	107.4	105.7	108.5	106.2
2018	110.3	108.3	110.1	107.2	102.8	130.4	99.1	91.5	111.3	108.8	113.0	108.6
2019	112.3	109.9	112.0	108.9	104.1	134.1	98.7	90.1	113.2	110.8	114.9	110.3
2020	113.7	111.2	113.6	110.2	104.8	138.5	96.2	88.1	114.9	112.0	116.7	111.7
2021	118.5	115.5	117.3	113.8	106.4	153.7	107.5	94.6	120.0	116.0	122.7	116.0
2019												
1st quarter	111.5	109.1	111.1	108.4	103.8	132.9	98.4	90.2	112.8	111.1	114.0	109.6
2nd quarter	112.1	109.8	111.8	108.9	104.3	133.6	99.3	90.8	113.1	110.3	114.9	110.2
3rd quarter	112.5	110.1	112.3	109.1	104.3	134.6	98.7	89.9	113.4	110.7	115.1	110.5
4th quarter	112.9	110.6	112.6	109.1	104.2	135.4	98.3	89.4	113.7	111.1	115.4	110.9
2020												
1st quarter	113.4	111.0	113.1	109.6	104.5	136.2	97.8	89.2	114.5	111.4	116.5	111.3
2nd quarter	113.0	110.5	112.9	109.7	104.9	136.5	93.2	86.4	114.3	111.4	116.1	111.0
3rd quarter	114.0	111.5	113.9	110.5	104.9	139.6	96.2	88.1	114.9	112.3	116.7	111.9
4th quarter	114.6	111.9	114.3	111.0	105.0	141.8	97.6	88.6	115.8	113.0	117.6	112.4
2021												
1st quarter	115.8	113.0	115.0	111.8	105.2	146.0	102.4	91.4	117.3	114.1	119.4	113.5
2nd quarter	117.5	114.8	116.7	112.6	105.4	151.3	107.0	94.3	119.0	115.2	121.5	115.1
3rd quarter	119.3	116.3	118.0	114.3	106.5	156.6	109.5	95.7	120.8	116.6	123.5	116.7
4th quarter	121.3	118.1	119.5	116.7	108.6	161.1	111.2	97.0	123.0	118.3	126.2	118.7

Table 1-6B. Chain-Type Price Indexes for Gross Domestic Product and Domestic Purchases: Historical Data

(Index numbers, 2012 = 100.)   NIPA Tables 1.1.4, 1.6.4, 2.3.4

Year and quarter	Gross domestic product, total	Personal consumption expenditures		Private fixed investment			Exports and imports of goods and services		Government consumption expenditures and gross investment			Gross domestic purchases
		Total	Excluding food and energy	Total	Nonresidential	Residential	Exports	Imports	Total	Federal	State and local	
1929	9.4	9.3	9.6	14.0	13.5	5.1	13.7	9.6	5.3	6.6	3.7	9.1
1930	9.0	8.9	9.2	13.4	12.8	5.0	12.4	8.1	5.2	6.3	3.6	8.8
1931	8.1	7.9	8.5	12.3	11.9	4.5	9.7	6.6	4.9	6.2	3.4	7.9
1932	7.2	7.0	7.5	10.4	10.8	3.7	8.4	5.3	4.5	5.9	3.0	7.0
1933	7.0	6.8	7.2	9.5	10.6	3.6	8.4	5.1	4.6	6.0	3.1	6.8
1934	7.4	7.1	7.3	9.5	10.9	4.0	9.8	5.7	4.9	6.4	3.4	7.1
1935	7.5	7.2	7.4	9.4	11.0	4.0	10.0	5.8	5.0	6.4	3.4	7.3
1936	7.6	7.3	7.5	9.5	11.0	4.1	10.4	6.3	5.2	7.0	3.4	7.4
1937	7.9	7.6	7.8	10.2	11.9	4.5	11.1	7.0	5.3	7.1	3.5	7.6
1938	7.7	7.4	7.8	9.9	12.0	4.7	10.6	6.4	5.3	7.1	3.5	7.5
1939	7.6	7.3	7.7	9.9	11.9	4.7	10.4	6.8	5.2	7.0	3.5	7.4
1940	7.7	7.4	7.8	10.1	12.1	4.9	11.3	7.2	5.1	6.8	3.5	7.5
1941	8.2	7.9	8.2	10.8	12.9	5.3	12.3	7.6	5.5	7.2	3.7	7.9
1942	8.9	8.8	9.1	12.0	14.3	5.7	14.9	8.7	5.5	7.2	4.1	8.6
1943	9.3	9.6	9.8	12.6	14.9	6.2	16.3	9.4	5.5	7.1	4.4	9.0
1944	9.5	10.2	10.5	13.1	15.4	6.8	18.4	9.9	5.5	7.0	4.5	9.2
1945	9.8	10.6	11.0	13.4	15.8	7.2	18.2	10.1	5.5	7.0	4.7	9.4
1946	11.0	11.3	11.7	14.7	17.4	7.8	17.6	11.3	7.0	9.2	5.1	10.7
1947	12.2	12.5	12.7	17.4	20.1	9.4	20.4	13.6	7.6	9.9	5.8	11.9
1948	12.9	13.2	13.4	18.8	21.8	10.2	21.5	14.7	7.9	9.9	6.5	12.6
1949	12.9	13.1	13.4	19.0	22.3	10.3	20.2	14.0	8.2	10.3	6.5	12.6
1947												
1st quarter	12.0	12.2	. . .	16.5	19.3	8.9	18.8	12.4	7.7	10.2	5.6	11.6
2nd quarter	12.1	12.3	. . .	17.2	19.9	9.4	20.1	13.3	7.7	10.1	5.7	11.8
3rd quarter	12.3	12.6	. . .	17.7	20.4	9.6	21.2	14.0	7.5	9.7	5.8	11.9
4th quarter	12.6	12.9	. . .	18.0	20.8	9.8	21.7	14.5	7.6	9.7	6.0	12.2
1948												
1st quarter	12.7	13.0	. . .	18.2	20.9	10.0	21.8	14.8	7.8	9.8	6.2	12.3
2nd quarter	12.9	13.1	. . .	18.6	21.5	10.1	21.7	14.9	7.9	9.8	6.4	12.5
3rd quarter	13.1	13.3	. . .	19.1	22.2	10.3	21.5	14.7	8.0	9.9	6.6	12.7
4th quarter	13.1	13.3	. . .	19.2	22.5	10.4	21.1	14.5	8.1	10.0	6.7	12.7
1949												
1st quarter	13.0	13.2	. . .	19.1	22.4	10.5	20.8	14.2	8.2	10.3	6.6	12.7
2nd quarter	13.0	13.1	. . .	19.1	22.3	10.4	20.4	14.0	8.1	10.3	6.5	12.6
3rd quarter	12.9	13.0	. . .	18.9	22.3	10.2	20.0	14.0	8.1	10.2	6.5	12.5
4th quarter	12.9	13.0	. . .	18.8	22.1	10.2	19.8	14.0	8.2	10.4	6.5	12.5
1950												
1st quarter	12.8	13.0	. . .	18.8	22.2	10.2	19.5	14.3	8.2	10.4	6.4	12.5
2nd quarter	12.9	13.1	. . .	19.1	22.4	10.5	19.5	14.6	8.1	10.3	6.4	12.6
3rd quarter	13.2	13.3	. . .	19.6	22.8	10.9	19.7	15.1	8.3	10.4	6.6	12.9
4th quarter	13.4	13.6	. . .	20.0	23.6	10.8	20.1	15.8	8.4	10.4	6.8	13.1
1951												
1st quarter	13.8	14.0	. . .	20.8	24.4	11.2	21.3	17.1	8.7	10.9	7.0	13.5
2nd quarter	13.9	14.1	. . .	21.1	24.8	11.3	22.1	18.0	8.7	10.7	7.2	13.6
3rd quarter	13.9	14.1	. . .	21.2	25.0	11.4	22.7	18.5	8.7	10.7	7.3	13.7
4th quarter	14.1	14.3	. . .	21.4	25.3	11.5	23.1	18.6	8.8	10.9	7.4	13.8
1952												
1st quarter	14.1	14.4	. . .	21.5	25.4	11.5	22.5	17.8	8.8	10.7	7.4	13.8
2nd quarter	14.2	14.4	. . .	21.5	25.4	11.6	22.4	17.5	8.9	10.9	7.5	13.9
3rd quarter	14.3	14.5	. . .	21.5	25.4	11.8	22.4	17.2	9.0	11.0	7.6	14.0
4th quarter	14.3	14.5	. . .	21.4	25.4	11.7	22.4	16.9	9.1	11.1	7.6	14.0
1953												
1st quarter	14.4	14.6	. . .	21.4	25.4	11.7	22.4	16.8	9.0	11.0	7.7	14.0
2nd quarter	14.4	14.6	. . .	21.5	25.6	11.7	22.4	16.6	9.0	11.0	7.7	14.1
3rd quarter	14.5	14.7	. . .	21.7	25.8	11.8	22.3	16.5	9.0	11.0	7.7	14.1
4th quarter	14.5	14.7	. . .	21.6	25.8	11.8	22.2	16.6	9.0	11.1	7.7	14.2
1954												
1st quarter	14.6	14.8	. . .	21.7	25.9	11.7	22.1	16.7	9.1	11.2	7.6	14.2
2nd quarter	14.6	14.8	. . .	21.7	26.0	11.7	22.1	16.8	9.2	11.2	7.8	14.3
3rd quarter	14.6	14.7	. . .	21.7	25.8	11.9	22.0	16.9	9.2	11.3	7.9	14.2
4th quarter	14.6	14.7	. . .	21.7	25.9	11.9	22.0	16.9	9.3	11.4	7.9	14.3
1955												
1st quarter	14.6	14.8	. . .	21.7	25.8	11.9	22.1	16.7	9.4	11.5	7.8	14.3
2nd quarter	14.7	14.8	. . .	21.9	26.0	12.0	22.2	16.7	9.5	11.8	7.9	14.4
3rd quarter	14.8	14.8	. . .	22.1	26.4	12.1	22.3	16.8	9.6	11.9	8.0	14.5
4th quarter	14.9	14.9	. . .	22.4	26.9	12.1	22.4	16.8	9.7	12.0	8.1	14.6
1956												
1st quarter	15.1	14.9	. . .	22.9	27.6	12.2	22.6	16.9	9.9	12.2	8.3	14.7
2nd quarter	15.2	15.0	. . .	23.1	27.9	12.4	22.8	17.0	10.1	12.4	8.4	14.9
3rd quarter	15.4	15.2	. . .	23.5	28.5	12.4	23.1	17.1	10.2	12.5	8.5	15.0
4th quarter	15.5	15.3	. . .	23.7	28.9	12.4	23.4	17.3	10.2	12.5	8.6	15.1
1957												
1st quarter	15.7	15.4	. . .	23.9	29.3	12.3	23.7	17.3	10.4	12.8	8.7	15.3
2nd quarter	15.8	15.5	. . .	24.0	29.5	12.3	23.9	17.4	10.5	12.9	8.8	15.4
3rd quarter	15.9	15.6	. . .	24.1	29.7	12.4	23.9	17.2	10.6	13.0	8.9	15.5
4th quarter	16.0	15.7	. . .	24.2	29.9	12.4	23.9	17.1	10.6	13.1	8.9	15.6

. . . = Not available.

Table 1-6B. Chain-Type Price Indexes for Gross Domestic Product and Domestic Purchases: Historical Data—*Continued*

(Index numbers, 2012 = 100.)

NIPA Tables 1.1.4, 1.6.4, 2.3.4

Year and quarter	Gross domestic product, total	Personal consumption expenditures		Private fixed investment			Exports and imports of goods and services		Government consumption expenditures and gross investment			Gross domestic purchases
		Total	Excluding food and energy	Total	Nonresidential	Residential	Exports	Imports	Total	Federal	State and local	
1958												
1st quarter	16.1	15.9	. . .	24.0	29.6	12.3	23.7	16.7	10.7	13.3	8.9	15.7
2nd quarter	16.2	15.9	. . .	24.1	29.8	12.3	23.6	16.5	10.8	13.4	9.0	15.8
3rd quarter	16.2	16.0	. . .	24.2	29.9	12.3	23.6	16.5	10.9	13.5	9.0	15.8
4th quarter	16.2	15.9	. . .	24.2	30.0	12.3	23.6	16.5	10.9	13.6	9.0	15.8
1959												
1st quarter	16.3	16.1	16.7	24.2	30.0	12.4	23.5	16.5	11.0	13.6	9.1	15.9
2nd quarter	16.4	16.1	16.8	24.3	30.2	12.4	23.5	16.6	11.0	13.6	9.1	15.9
3rd quarter	16.4	16.2	16.9	24.4	30.3	12.4	23.7	16.7	11.0	13.6	9.1	16.0
4th quarter	16.5	16.3	17.0	24.5	30.4	12.4	24.0	16.8	11.0	13.6	9.1	16.1
1960												
1st quarter	16.5	16.3	17.1	24.5	30.4	12.4	24.0	16.8	11.0	13.5	9.2	16.1
2nd quarter	16.6	16.4	17.1	24.5	30.4	12.5	23.9	16.8	11.0	13.5	9.3	16.2
3rd quarter	16.7	16.5	17.2	24.5	30.4	12.5	24.1	16.9	11.1	13.7	9.3	16.2
4th quarter	16.7	16.5	17.2	24.5	30.3	12.5	24.0	16.8	11.2	13.9	9.4	16.3
1961												
1st quarter	16.8	16.6	17.3	24.5	30.3	12.4	24.1	16.9	11.2	13.8	9.4	16.3
2nd quarter	16.8	16.6	17.3	24.5	30.3	12.5	24.4	16.8	11.3	13.8	9.5	16.3
3rd quarter	16.8	16.6	17.4	24.5	30.3	12.5	24.4	16.8	11.3	13.8	9.6	16.4
4th quarter	16.9	16.7	17.4	24.5	30.3	12.5	24.5	16.8	11.3	13.8	9.6	16.4
1962												
1st quarter	16.9	16.7	17.5	24.5	30.3	12.5	24.6	16.6	11.4	13.9	9.7	16.5
2nd quarter	17.0	16.8	17.6	24.5	30.3	12.5	24.4	16.6	11.5	14.0	9.8	16.5
3rd quarter	17.0	16.8	17.6	24.5	30.3	12.5	24.3	16.6	11.5	14.1	9.8	16.6
4th quarter	17.1	16.9	17.7	24.5	30.3	12.5	24.4	16.7	11.6	14.1	9.8	16.6
1963												
1st quarter	17.2	16.9	17.7	24.5	30.3	12.5	24.4	16.8	11.7	14.3	9.9	16.7
2nd quarter	17.2	17.0	17.8	24.4	30.3	12.4	24.4	16.9	11.8	14.3	10.0	16.7
3rd quarter	17.2	17.0	17.9	24.4	30.3	12.3	24.3	17.0	11.7	14.2	10.0	16.7
4th quarter	17.3	17.1	18.0	24.4	30.3	12.4	24.4	17.1	11.9	14.6	10.1	16.9
1964												
1st quarter	17.4	17.2	18.0	24.4	30.4	12.3	24.4	17.2	12.0	14.7	10.1	16.9
2nd quarter	17.4	17.2	18.1	24.6	30.5	12.5	24.4	17.3	12.0	14.7	10.2	17.0
3rd quarter	17.5	17.3	18.1	24.6	30.5	12.5	24.6	17.3	12.2	14.9	10.2	17.1
4th quarter	17.6	17.3	18.2	24.8	30.7	12.8	24.9	17.4	12.2	14.9	10.3	17.1
1965												
1st quarter	17.7	17.4	18.2	24.8	30.7	12.8	25.4	17.5	12.3	15.0	10.4	17.2
2nd quarter	17.7	17.5	18.3	24.9	30.8	12.8	25.3	17.4	12.3	15.0	10.5	17.3
3rd quarter	17.8	17.5	18.4	24.9	30.9	12.8	25.4	17.5	12.4	15.2	10.5	17.3
4th quarter	17.9	17.6	18.4	25.2	31.0	13.1	25.3	17.7	12.6	15.5	10.6	17.5
1966												
1st quarter	18.0	17.7	18.5	25.1	31.0	12.9	25.7	17.8	12.7	15.6	10.8	17.6
2nd quarter	18.2	17.9	18.7	25.5	31.3	13.4	25.9	18.0	12.8	15.6	11.0	17.7
3rd quarter	18.4	18.0	18.8	25.5	31.4	13.3	26.2	18.0	13.0	15.8	11.1	17.9
4th quarter	18.5	18.2	19.0	25.8	31.6	13.6	26.7	18.1	13.1	15.8	11.2	18.0
1967												
1st quarter	18.6	18.2	19.1	25.9	31.8	13.6	27.1	18.1	13.1	15.8	11.4	18.1
2nd quarter	18.7	18.3	19.2	26.0	32.0	13.7	27.1	18.0	13.3	15.9	11.5	18.2
3rd quarter	18.9	18.5	19.4	26.1	32.2	13.8	27.1	18.0	13.4	16.1	11.6	18.3
4th quarter	19.1	18.6	19.6	26.4	32.5	14.0	27.2	18.0	13.6	16.4	11.8	18.5
1968												
1st quarter	19.3	18.8	19.8	26.7	32.7	14.3	27.4	18.2	13.8	16.5	12.0	18.7
2nd quarter	19.5	19.0	20.0	26.9	33.1	14.4	28.0	18.3	14.0	16.7	12.2	18.9
3rd quarter	19.7	19.2	20.3	27.1	33.3	14.4	27.6	18.3	14.1	17.0	12.3	19.1
4th quarter	20.0	19.4	20.5	27.7	33.8	15.0	27.8	18.5	14.4	17.2	12.5	19.4
1969												
1st quarter	20.2	19.6	20.7	28.0	34.1	15.3	28.2	18.5	14.5	17.3	12.7	19.6
2nd quarter	20.4	19.9	21.0	28.3	34.4	15.5	28.3	18.6	14.7	17.5	13.0	19.8
3rd quarter	20.7	20.1	21.2	28.5	34.8	15.5	28.7	18.7	15.1	17.9	13.2	20.1
4th quarter	21.0	20.3	21.5	28.9	35.2	15.8	29.3	19.2	15.3	18.2	13.4	20.4
1970												
1st quarter	21.3	20.6	21.7	29.1	35.6	15.8	29.3	19.4	15.7	18.7	13.7	20.7
2nd quarter	21.6	20.8	21.9	29.7	36.2	16.3	29.9	19.7	15.9	19.0	14.0	21.0
3rd quarter	21.8	21.0	22.2	29.7	36.4	15.9	29.8	20.1	16.2	19.3	14.3	21.2
4th quarter	22.0	21.3	22.5	30.0	36.9	16.0	29.9	20.3	16.5	19.5	14.5	21.4
1971												
1st quarter	22.4	21.5	22.8	30.5	37.4	16.5	30.8	20.9	16.9	20.1	14.8	21.8
2nd quarter	22.7	21.7	23.0	31.0	37.9	16.8	30.9	20.9	17.2	20.5	15.1	22.1
3rd quarter	22.9	21.9	23.3	31.3	38.2	17.1	30.7	21.2	17.5	20.8	15.3	22.3
4th quarter	23.1	22.1	23.4	31.6	38.5	17.4	30.9	21.5	17.8	21.2	15.5	22.5
1972												
1st quarter	23.5	22.3	23.6	31.9	38.9	17.6	31.8	21.9	18.3	22.1	15.8	22.8
2nd quarter	23.6	22.4	23.8	32.2	39.2	17.7	32.0	22.4	18.5	22.3	16.0	23.0
3rd quarter	23.8	22.6	23.9	32.5	39.4	18.0	32.1	22.8	18.7	22.5	16.3	23.2
4th quarter	24.1	22.8	24.1	33.0	39.7	18.6	32.9	23.3	19.1	23.0	16.5	23.5

. . . = Not available.

Table 1-6B. Chain-Type Price Indexes for Gross Domestic Product and Domestic Purchases: Historical Data—*Continued*

(Index numbers, 2012 = 100.)   NIPA Tables 1.1.4, 1.6.4, 2.3.4

| Year and quarter | Gross domestic product, total | Personal consumption expenditures | | Private fixed investment | | | Exports and imports of goods and services | | Government consumption expenditures and gross investment | | | Gross domestic purchases |
		Total	Excluding food and energy	Total	Nonresidential	Residential	Exports	Imports	Total	Federal	State and local	
1973												
1st quarter	24.4	23.1	24.3	33.3	40.0	18.8	33.8	24.0	19.4	23.4	16.8	23.8
2nd quarter	24.8	23.5	24.6	33.8	40.6	19.3	35.3	25.9	19.8	23.8	17.1	24.2
3rd quarter	25.3	24.0	24.9	34.6	41.2	19.9	37.4	27.1	20.1	24.3	17.4	24.7
4th quarter	25.7	24.4	25.3	35.0	41.7	20.3	39.3	29.1	20.5	24.8	17.7	25.2
1974												
1st quarter	26.2	25.2	25.7	35.7	42.5	20.7	42.0	33.8	20.9	25.0	18.2	25.8
2nd quarter	26.8	25.9	26.3	36.8	43.8	21.2	43.4	37.6	21.5	25.5	18.8	26.5
3rd quarter	27.6	26.6	27.1	38.2	45.6	21.9	45.9	39.6	22.2	26.2	19.5	27.3
4th quarter	28.5	27.3	27.8	39.6	47.6	22.5	48.2	40.8	22.9	27.1	20.1	28.1
1975												
1st quarter	29.1	27.8	28.3	41.0	49.3	23.1	49.6	41.5	23.3	27.6	20.5	28.7
2nd quarter	29.5	28.1	28.7	41.9	50.6	23.5	49.4	41.6	23.7	28.0	20.9	29.2
3rd quarter	30.1	28.6	29.2	42.4	51.2	23.7	49.3	40.6	24.0	28.4	21.2	29.6
4th quarter	30.6	29.1	29.6	43.0	51.9	24.1	49.6	40.7	24.4	29.0	21.4	30.1
1976												
1st quarter	30.9	29.4	30.1	43.4	52.5	24.3	50.3	41.4	24.8	29.5	21.7	30.5
2nd quarter	31.2	29.7	30.4	44.1	53.2	25.0	50.8	42.0	25.0	29.7	21.9	30.8
3rd quarter	31.6	30.1	30.9	44.7	53.9	25.4	51.1	42.8	25.2	30.0	22.1	31.2
4th quarter	32.1	30.6	31.4	45.4	54.7	25.8	52.0	43.2	25.7	30.9	22.4	31.7
1977												
1st quarter	32.7	31.2	31.9	46.3	55.7	26.5	52.6	44.7	26.1	31.3	22.8	32.3
2nd quarter	33.2	31.7	32.4	47.2	56.6	27.2	53.4	46.0	26.5	31.6	23.2	32.8
3rd quarter	33.6	32.2	33.0	48.1	57.6	28.1	53.2	46.6	26.8	31.8	23.6	33.3
4th quarter	34.2	32.6	33.4	49.1	58.6	29.0	53.4	47.0	27.4	32.7	24.0	33.9
1978												
1st quarter	34.8	33.2	34.0	50.0	59.4	29.8	54.5	47.8	27.8	33.1	24.3	34.4
2nd quarter	35.5	33.9	34.6	51.0	60.4	30.7	55.8	49.0	28.3	33.7	24.7	35.1
3rd quarter	36.1	34.4	35.1	52.0	61.4	31.5	56.7	49.8	28.7	34.3	25.1	35.7
4th quarter	36.8	35.1	35.8	53.1	62.5	32.3	58.6	50.7	29.2	34.9	25.5	36.4
1979												
1st quarter	37.5	35.8	36.3	54.2	63.8	33.0	60.3	52.6	29.8	35.5	26.1	37.1
2nd quarter	38.4	36.7	37.1	55.5	65.2	34.1	62.8	55.4	30.4	36.1	26.7	38.1
3rd quarter	39.2	37.7	37.7	56.9	66.6	35.2	64.2	59.5	31.3	36.9	27.6	39.0
4th quarter	39.9	38.6	38.5	58.0	67.8	36.1	65.4	63.5	31.9	37.7	28.1	39.9
1980												
1st quarter	40.8	39.7	39.5	59.4	69.3	37.0	67.3	68.8	32.7	38.5	28.9	41.0
2nd quarter	41.7	40.7	40.4	60.8	70.9	37.9	68.3	71.2	33.7	40.0	29.6	42.1
3rd quarter	42.7	41.6	41.3	62.0	72.4	38.8	70.2	73.3	34.4	40.4	30.5	43.0
4th quarter	43.8	42.7	42.3	63.4	73.9	39.6	72.6	74.5	35.4	41.6	31.3	44.1
1981												
1st quarter	45.0	43.8	43.2	65.2	76.0	40.6	74.4	76.4	36.3	42.4	32.3	45.3
2nd quarter	45.8	44.5	44.0	66.6	77.8	41.2	74.7	76.9	37.1	43.4	33.0	46.1
3rd quarter	46.7	45.2	44.8	67.7	79.2	41.7	74.8	74.9	37.8	44.4	33.5	46.9
4th quarter	47.5	45.9	45.6	69.0	80.9	42.3	75.1	75.1	38.5	45.2	34.0	47.6
1982												
1st quarter	48.2	46.5	46.3	69.8	81.9	42.9	75.5	74.8	39.1	45.9	34.6	48.3
2nd quarter	48.8	47.0	46.9	70.6	82.9	43.6	75.5	73.5	39.8	46.8	35.2	48.9
3rd quarter	49.5	47.7	47.7	71.1	83.3	43.9	74.9	72.7	40.3	47.2	35.7	49.5
4th quarter	50.0	48.2	48.3	71.2	83.5	44.1	74.5	72.1	40.8	47.8	36.2	50.0
1983												
1st quarter	50.4	48.6	49.0	71.0	83.1	44.4	74.8	70.6	40.9	47.9	36.4	50.3
2nd quarter	50.7	49.1	49.3	70.8	82.7	44.5	75.1	70.6	41.3	48.3	36.8	50.6
3rd quarter	51.3	49.7	50.1	70.8	82.6	44.7	75.5	70.7	41.8	48.8	37.2	51.1
4th quarter	51.7	50.1	50.5	71.0	82.6	45.1	76.2	70.3	42.1	49.1	37.5	51.4
1984												
1st quarter	52.2	50.6	51.0	71.2	82.7	45.4	76.3	70.5	42.6	49.7	38.0	52.0
2nd quarter	52.6	51.1	51.6	71.6	83.0	45.8	76.8	70.9	43.0	50.2	38.4	52.4
3rd quarter	53.1	51.5	52.1	71.9	83.2	46.2	76.1	69.6	43.6	51.0	38.7	52.8
4th quarter	53.5	51.8	52.5	72.0	83.3	46.6	75.2	68.8	44.0	51.6	39.1	53.2
1985												
1st quarter	54.0	52.4	53.2	72.2	83.5	46.9	74.4	67.1	44.2	51.4	39.6	53.6
2nd quarter	54.4	52.8	53.6	72.3	83.7	47.0	74.1	67.4	44.5	51.5	40.0	54.0
3rd quarter	54.7	53.3	54.2	72.6	84.0	47.3	73.5	67.3	44.8	51.8	40.3	54.3
4th quarter	55.0	53.6	54.6	73.1	84.4	47.9	73.3	68.7	45.1	52.1	40.7	54.7
1986												
1st quarter	55.3	54.0	55.2	73.4	84.6	48.5	73.0	68.8	45.2	52.0	40.8	55.0
2nd quarter	55.5	53.9	55.5	73.9	85.1	49.0	72.6	66.7	45.2	51.9	41.0	55.0
3rd quarter	55.7	54.2	55.9	74.5	85.7	49.7	72.2	67.1	45.5	52.0	41.4	55.4
4th quarter	56.1	54.6	56.4	75.0	86.1	50.2	72.7	67.9	45.8	52.0	41.9	55.7
1987												
1st quarter	56.4	55.1	56.7	75.3	86.1	50.8	73.0	69.7	46.1	51.9	42.5	56.2
2nd quarter	56.8	55.6	57.3	75.5	86.1	51.2	74.1	71.5	46.5	52.2	43.0	56.6
3rd quarter	57.2	56.1	57.8	75.7	86.1	51.7	74.3	72.3	46.9	52.5	43.5	57.1
4th quarter	57.6	56.6	58.4	76.4	87.0	52.2	75.5	73.4	47.1	52.7	43.8	57.5

Table 1-6B. Chain-Type Price Indexes for Gross Domestic Product and Domestic Purchases: Historical Data—Continued

(Index numbers, 2012 = 100.)

NIPA Tables 1.1.4, 1.6.4, 2.3.4

Year and quarter	Gross domestic product, total	Personal consumption expenditures Total	Personal consumption expenditures Excluding food and energy	Private fixed investment Total	Private fixed investment Nonresidential	Private fixed investment Residential	Exports and imports of goods and services Exports	Exports and imports of goods and services Imports	Government consumption expenditures and gross investment Total	Government consumption expenditures and gross investment Federal	Government consumption expenditures and gross investment State and local	Gross domestic purchases
1988												
1st quarter	58.1	57.1	58.9	76.9	87.8	52.6	76.4	74.4	47.5	53.4	44.0	58.0
2nd quarter	58.7	57.7	59.7	77.4	88.2	53.1	78.0	75.7	48.0	53.9	44.4	58.6
3rd quarter	59.4	58.4	60.3	77.7	88.6	53.5	78.9	74.9	48.4	54.2	44.8	59.1
4th quarter	59.9	59.0	61.0	78.5	89.4	54.0	78.8	75.5	48.8	54.6	45.3	59.7
1989												
1st quarter	60.5	59.7	61.7	78.9	89.9	54.3	79.5	76.7	49.3	55.1	45.9	60.3
2nd quarter	61.2	60.5	62.2	79.4	90.3	55.0	79.6	77.6	49.9	55.5	46.5	61.0
3rd quarter	61.6	60.8	62.7	79.8	90.8	55.2	79.2	76.2	50.2	55.7	47.0	61.4
4th quarter	62.0	61.3	63.3	80.2	91.3	55.6	78.9	76.6	50.7	55.9	47.6	61.9
1990												
1st quarter	62.7	62.2	64.0	80.7	91.8	56.0	79.0	77.8	51.2	56.3	48.3	62.6
2nd quarter	63.4	62.8	64.7	81.0	92.1	56.2	79.1	76.4	51.9	57.3	48.8	63.2
3rd quarter	64.0	63.6	65.4	81.5	92.8	56.4	79.9	78.7	52.3	57.4	49.4	63.9
4th quarter	64.5	64.4	65.9	81.8	93.4	56.5	81.0	83.0	53.0	58.1	50.2	64.6
1991												
1st quarter	65.1	64.7	66.5	82.6	94.3	56.7	81.2	80.5	53.4	58.6	50.4	65.0
2nd quarter	65.5	65.1	67.0	82.7	94.4	57.0	80.8	78.3	53.7	58.9	50.7	65.3
3rd quarter	66.1	65.5	67.6	82.8	94.3	57.3	80.2	77.1	54.2	59.6	51.1	65.8
4th quarter	66.4	66.0	68.2	82.5	94.1	57.1	80.4	77.5	54.7	60.2	51.6	66.2
1992												
1st quarter	66.7	66.4	68.7	82.4	94.0	56.9	80.2	77.8	55.0	60.3	51.9	66.5
2nd quarter	67.1	66.9	69.2	82.5	93.9	57.5	80.3	78.1	55.4	60.5	52.6	66.9
3rd quarter	67.4	67.3	69.6	82.7	94.0	57.9	80.3	79.1	55.9	61.1	53.0	67.3
4th quarter	67.9	67.8	70.1	83.0	94.0	58.6	80.2	78.5	56.3	61.4	53.3	67.7
1993												
1st quarter	68.3	68.2	70.6	83.2	94.1	59.3	80.3	78.0	56.5	61.6	53.6	68.1
2nd quarter	68.7	68.6	71.1	83.6	94.1	59.9	80.5	78.3	56.8	61.9	53.9	68.5
3rd quarter	69.0	68.9	71.5	83.8	94.1	60.4	80.4	77.6	57.1	62.3	54.1	68.8
4th quarter	69.5	69.3	71.9	84.0	94.4	60.6	80.4	77.3	57.5	62.9	54.4	69.1
1994												
1st quarter	69.8	69.6	72.2	84.5	94.6	61.4	80.8	77.2	57.8	63.2	54.8	69.5
2nd quarter	70.1	70.0	72.7	84.7	94.8	61.8	81.1	78.0	58.2	63.7	55.1	69.8
3rd quarter	70.5	70.5	73.1	85.0	95.0	62.5	81.5	79.3	58.7	64.1	55.6	70.3
4th quarter	70.9	70.8	73.5	85.4	95.1	63.3	82.0	79.6	59.2	64.6	56.1	70.7
1995												
1st quarter	71.3	71.1	73.9	85.9	95.5	64.0	82.9	80.2	59.6	65.1	56.4	71.1
2nd quarter	71.7	71.5	74.3	86.2	95.8	64.3	83.5	81.4	60.0	65.6	56.8	71.5
3rd quarter	72.0	71.8	74.6	86.5	96.1	64.6	83.3	80.9	60.3	65.9	57.0	71.7
4th quarter	72.3	72.2	75.0	86.4	95.9	65.0	82.9	80.2	60.7	66.8	57.3	72.0
1996												
1st quarter	72.7	72.6	75.3	86.2	95.6	65.2	82.7	80.0	61.1	67.0	57.8	72.4
2nd quarter	73.0	73.0	75.7	86.0	95.2	65.5	82.5	79.6	61.1	66.6	57.9	72.6
3rd quarter	73.3	73.4	76.0	86.3	95.2	66.2	81.9	78.8	61.4	67.0	58.3	73.0
4th quarter	73.6	73.9	76.5	86.2	95.0	66.5	81.0	78.7	61.8	67.2	58.7	73.3
1997												
1st quarter	73.9	74.2	76.8	86.2	94.9	66.8	80.8	78.1	62.1	67.5	59.1	73.6
2nd quarter	74.3	74.4	77.2	86.3	94.9	67.1	80.8	76.5	62.4	67.9	59.3	73.8
3rd quarter	74.5	74.6	77.3	86.3	94.8	67.7	80.6	76.0	62.6	68.1	59.5	74.0
4th quarter	74.8	74.8	77.6	86.2	94.4	68.2	80.2	75.4	63.1	68.5	60.0	74.2
1998												
1st quarter	74.9	74.8	77.8	85.8	93.8	68.4	79.4	73.5	63.1	68.2	60.1	74.1
2nd quarter	75.1	74.9	78.0	85.6	93.4	68.8	79.0	72.7	63.4	68.7	60.3	74.2
3rd quarter	75.4	75.2	78.3	85.5	93.0	69.5	78.3	71.7	63.8	69.1	60.8	74.5
4th quarter	75.6	75.4	78.6	85.6	92.8	70.1	78.0	71.7	64.2	69.4	61.3	74.7
1999												
1st quarter	75.8	75.5	78.8	85.6	92.7	70.8	77.8	71.5	64.6	69.6	61.8	74.9
2nd quarter	76.1	75.9	79.0	85.7	92.4	71.6	78.0	72.4	65.4	70.1	62.6	75.3
3rd quarter	76.4	76.4	79.3	85.6	92.0	72.2	78.1	73.2	66.1	70.8	63.4	75.7
4th quarter	76.8	76.8	79.7	85.8	92.2	72.7	78.4	74.2	66.9	71.6	64.1	76.2
2000												
1st quarter	77.3	77.5	80.1	86.4	92.4	74.0	79.0	75.7	67.7	72.3	64.9	76.8
2nd quarter	77.8	77.8	80.4	86.7	92.6	74.7	79.6	75.7	68.2	72.6	65.6	77.2
3rd quarter	78.3	78.3	80.8	87.0	92.9	75.3	79.9	76.3	68.9	73.1	66.3	77.7
4th quarter	78.7	78.8	81.2	87.2	92.9	76.0	79.9	76.4	69.5	73.5	67.1	78.2
2001												
1st quarter	79.2	79.3	81.7	87.2	92.5	77.1	79.7	76.2	70.1	73.6	67.9	78.7
2nd quarter	79.8	79.7	82.0	87.5	92.5	78.1	79.3	74.6	70.4	74.0	68.2	79.0
3rd quarter	80.0	79.8	82.2	87.7	92.3	79.3	78.9	73.6	70.7	74.5	68.4	79.1
4th quarter	80.3	79.8	82.6	87.8	92.1	79.8	78.0	71.8	71.0	74.9	68.5	79.2
2002												
1st quarter	80.5	80.0	82.9	87.9	92.1	79.7	77.6	71.6	71.4	75.4	68.9	79.4
2nd quarter	80.8	80.5	83.3	87.7	92.0	80.1	78.0	73.1	72.1	76.1	69.6	79.9
3rd quarter	81.2	81.0	83.8	87.6	91.7	80.5	78.7	73.7	72.6	76.8	70.1	80.3
4th quarter	81.6	81.3	84.1	88.1	91.7	81.8	78.9	74.2	73.5	78.2	70.6	80.7

Table 1-6B. Chain-Type Price Indexes for Gross Domestic Product and Domestic Purchases: Historical Data—*Continued*

(Index numbers, 2012 = 100.)   NIPA Tables 1.1.4, 1.6.4, 2.3.4

Year and quarter	Gross domestic product, total	Personal consumption expenditures		Private fixed investment			Exports and imports of goods and services		Government consumption expenditures and gross investment			Gross domestic purchases
		Total	Excluding food and energy	Total	Nonresidential	Residential	Exports	Imports	Total	Federal	State and local	
2003												
1st quarter	82.1	82.0	84.3	88.5	91.4	83.5	79.2	76.0	74.4	79.1	71.6	81.4
2nd quarter	82.3	82.0	84.7	88.4	91.2	83.7	79.3	74.8	74.7	79.7	71.7	81.5
3rd quarter	82.8	82.6	85.1	88.4	91.0	84.3	79.5	75.1	75.2	80.4	72.2	81.9
4th quarter	83.3	83.0	85.4	89.0	91.1	85.8	80.1	75.5	75.8	81.0	72.7	82.4
2004												
1st quarter	83.9	83.6	85.9	89.8	91.4	87.7	81.3	77.3	76.7	81.7	73.7	83.1
2nd quarter	84.6	84.2	86.4	90.8	91.9	89.4	82.2	78.3	77.6	82.4	74.7	83.8
3rd quarter	85.1	84.6	86.7	91.6	92.1	91.2	82.6	79.2	78.6	83.1	75.9	84.4
4th quarter	85.8	85.3	87.2	92.4	92.8	92.7	83.6	81.1	79.8	83.9	77.2	85.2
2005												
1st quarter	86.4	85.8	87.8	93.4	93.6	93.9	84.5	81.8	80.6	85.0	77.9	85.9
2nd quarter	87.1	86.4	88.2	94.3	94.2	95.4	85.0	82.7	81.5	85.8	78.9	86.6
3rd quarter	87.9	87.3	88.6	95.3	94.6	97.9	85.6	84.3	82.7	86.7	80.2	87.5
4th quarter	88.6	88.0	89.2	96.4	95.3	99.7	86.1	85.7	83.7	87.3	81.5	88.4
2006												
1st quarter	89.2	88.5	89.7	97.3	95.9	101.3	86.6	85.9	84.4	88.1	82.1	88.9
2nd quarter	90.0	89.2	90.4	97.9	96.4	102.2	87.8	86.9	85.4	88.7	83.3	89.7
3rd quarter	90.7	89.9	90.9	98.4	97.0	102.6	88.8	87.8	86.2	89.3	84.2	90.4
4th quarter	91.0	89.7	91.3	99.2	97.7	103.3	88.8	86.8	86.9	89.8	85.1	90.5
2007												
1st quarter	91.9	90.5	91.9	99.7	98.2	103.9	89.8	87.3	88.2	90.6	86.7	91.4
2nd quarter	92.5	91.3	92.3	99.7	98.4	103.6	90.9	88.8	89.1	91.3	87.6	92.0
3rd quarter	92.9	91.8	92.7	99.7	98.3	103.6	91.6	90.0	89.9	91.9	88.6	92.5
4th quarter	93.3	92.8	93.4	99.6	98.3	103.7	93.0	93.4	91.0	92.7	89.9	93.3
2008												
1st quarter	93.7	93.5	93.9	99.7	98.7	103.4	94.8	97.0	92.2	93.4	91.3	94.1
2nd quarter	94.1	94.4	94.3	99.8	99.0	102.9	96.8	101.6	93.3	94.4	92.6	94.9
3rd quarter	94.8	95.4	94.8	100.3	100.0	102.1	98.1	104.0	94.4	95.1	93.8	95.8
4th quarter	95.0	93.9	94.7	102.1	101.6	100.6	92.2	92.7	93.5	94.7	92.7	94.9
2009												
1st quarter	95.0	93.3	94.7	101.3	100.9	99.8	89.1	85.0	92.5	93.9	91.5	94.2
2nd quarter	94.9	93.7	95.0	99.7	99.5	98.5	89.0	86.2	92.6	93.9	91.7	94.2
3rd quarter	94.9	94.3	95.4	98.3	98.4	97.8	90.0	88.9	93.0	94.2	92.2	94.6
4th quarter	95.3	95.0	96.0	98.0	97.9	98.5	91.1	91.3	93.7	94.9	92.8	95.2
2010												
1st quarter	95.5	95.4	96.3	97.6	97.3	98.7	91.9	92.7	94.5	95.5	93.8	95.5
2nd quarter	96.0	95.5	96.6	97.6	97.4	98.0	93.0	92.3	95.1	96.2	94.4	95.7
3rd quarter	96.3	95.7	96.7	97.6	97.4	98.0	93.2	91.8	95.6	96.6	94.9	96.0
4th quarter	96.9	96.3	97.0	98.0	97.7	98.6	95.3	93.9	96.4	97.4	95.7	96.6
2011												
1st quarter	97.3	97.1	97.4	98.2	98.0	98.8	97.8	97.6	97.3	98.3	96.7	97.3
2nd quarter	98.0	98.1	98.0	98.7	98.5	99.1	99.7	100.6	98.4	99.2	97.8	98.2
3rd quarter	98.6	98.6	98.5	98.9	98.7	99.1	100.3	100.5	98.8	99.5	98.3	98.7
4th quarter	98.7	98.9	98.8	99.0	99.0	99.2	99.2	100.2	98.7	99.4	98.2	98.9
2012												
1st quarter	99.3	99.5	99.4	99.4	99.6	99.0	99.8	101.1	99.5	99.7	99.4	99.5
2nd quarter	99.7	99.8	99.8	99.9	99.9	99.4	100.0	100.4	99.6	99.9	99.4	99.8
3rd quarter	100.3	100.1	100.1	100.3	100.2	100.3	99.9	98.7	100.0	100.1	100.0	100.1
4th quarter	100.7	100.6	100.6	100.4	100.2	101.3	100.3	99.8	100.8	100.2	101.2	100.6
2013												
1st quarter	101.1	101.0	101.0	100.5	100.0	102.8	100.6	99.9	101.5	100.2	102.4	101.0
2nd quarter	101.4	101.1	101.3	100.8	100.1	104.2	99.9	98.7	101.9	100.4	102.9	101.2
3rd quarter	102.0	101.5	101.7	101.1	100.3	105.6	100.1	98.2	102.5	100.8	103.7	101.6
4th quarter	102.6	101.9	102.2	101.6	100.6	107.6	100.0	98.0	103.5	102.3	104.3	102.1
2014												
1st quarter	103.0	102.4	102.5	102.3	101.0	109.9	100.7	99.2	103.9	102.0	105.1	102.6
2nd quarter	103.6	102.9	103.0	102.6	101.3	110.2	100.8	98.6	104.3	102.5	105.5	103.1
3rd quarter	104.0	103.2	103.4	103.2	101.6	112.1	100.6	98.0	104.8	103.0	106.1	103.5
4th quarter	104.1	103.1	103.7	103.6	101.9	112.3	98.8	96.1	104.9	103.1	106.1	103.5
2015												
1st quarter	104.1	102.6	103.9	103.6	102.1	113.0	96.3	92.0	104.3	102.9	105.2	103.1
2nd quarter	104.7	103.1	104.4	103.5	102.0	113.6	96.1	90.8	104.8	103.1	105.9	103.5
3rd quarter	104.9	103.4	104.7	103.6	101.9	114.6	95.2	89.8	104.9	103.3	106.0	103.7
4th quarter	104.9	103.3	104.9	103.4	101.6	115.3	93.8	87.9	104.6	103.2	105.6	103.5
2016												
1st quarter	104.9	103.3	105.4	102.9	101.0	115.8	92.3	86.3	104.1	103.0	104.8	103.4
2nd quarter	105.6	104.0	105.9	103.4	101.2	117.3	93.3	86.8	104.8	103.5	105.6	104.0
3rd quarter	105.9	104.4	106.4	103.6	101.0	119.0	93.8	87.4	105.1	103.9	106.0	104.4
4th quarter	106.5	104.9	106.8	104.1	101.3	120.5	94.4	87.7	105.6	104.4	106.5	104.9
2017												
1st quarter	107.0	105.5	107.3	104.5	101.6	121.4	95.1	88.6	106.5	105.0	107.5	105.5
2nd quarter	107.4	105.8	107.7	105.1	101.9	122.9	95.2	88.7	106.8	105.4	107.8	105.8
3rd quarter	107.9	106.1	108.1	105.5	102.1	124.3	96.0	88.8	107.6	105.9	108.8	106.3
4th quarter	108.7	106.9	108.6	105.8	102.2	125.2	97.3	89.9	108.7	106.6	110.1	107.0
2018												
1st quarter	109.3	107.6	109.3	106.4	102.3	128.0	98.2	91.3	109.9	107.7	111.4	107.8
2nd quarter	110.2	108.2	109.9	107.0	102.7	130.2	99.4	91.7	111.0	108.4	112.6	108.5
3rd quarter	110.6	108.5	110.3	107.5	103.0	131.4	99.7	91.8	111.8	109.1	113.6	108.9
4th quarter	111.2	109.0	110.8	107.8	103.2	132.2	99.3	91.2	112.6	109.9	114.3	109.4

Table 1-7. Final Sales

(Quarterly dollar data are at seasonally adjusted annual rates.)   **NIPA Tables 1.4.4, 1.4.5, 1.4.6**

Year and quarter	Final sales of domestic product			Final sales to domestic purchasers		
	Billions of dollars	Billions of chained (2012) dollars	Chain-type price index, 2012 = 100	Billions of dollars	Billions of chained (2012) dollars	Chain-type price index, 2012 = 100
1960	539.1	3 268.6	16.5	534.9	3 329.7	16.1
1961	559.2	3 354.6	16.7	554.3	3 416.2	16.2
1962	597.8	3 542.5	16.9	593.7	3 616.5	16.4
1963	631.8	3 701.0	17.1	626.9	3 770.8	16.6
1964	679.6	3 920.6	17.3	672.7	3 982.8	16.9
1965	733.0	4 151.9	17.7	727.4	4 232.1	17.2
1966	799.8	4 405.7	18.2	795.9	4 505.0	17.7
1967	850.1	4 549.6	18.7	846.5	4 662.8	18.2
1968	931.6	4 780.2	19.5	930.2	4 913.7	18.9
1969	1 008.4	4 931.0	20.5	1 007.0	5 070.6	19.9
1970	1 071.3	4 975.2	21.5	1 067.4	5 099.3	20.9
1971	1 156.6	5 111.6	22.6	1 156.0	5 248.9	22.0
1972	1 270.0	5 379.4	23.6	1 273.4	5 533.7	23.0
1973	1 409.5	5 659.1	24.9	1 405.4	5 776.2	24.3
1974	1 531.3	5 643.0	27.1	1 532.1	5 717.1	26.8
1975	1 691.2	5 701.7	29.7	1 675.2	5 726.9	29.3
1976	1 856.3	5 929.6	31.3	1 857.9	6 018.6	30.9
1977	2 059.5	6 191.7	33.3	2 082.6	6 326.5	32.9
1978	2 325.8	6 530.7	35.6	2 351.2	6 666.1	35.3
1979	2 609.3	6 766.0	38.6	2 631.9	6 860.2	38.4
1980	2 863.6	6 809.1	42.1	2 876.7	6 791.5	42.4
1981	3 177.2	6 904.6	46.0	3 189.8	6 896.3	46.3
1982	3 358.7	6 869.9	48.9	3 378.7	6 902.7	48.9
1983	3 639.8	7 164.6	50.8	3 691.4	7 287.8	50.7
1984	3 972.2	7 546.4	52.6	4 074.9	7 781.8	52.4
1985	4 317.2	7 945.4	54.3	4 431.2	8 213.1	54.0
1986	4 573.1	8 246.4	55.5	4 704.9	8 539.3	55.1
1987	4 828.1	8 498.0	56.8	4 972.8	8 778.2	56.7
1988	5 218.0	8 866.3	58.9	5 327.3	9 078.1	58.7
1989	5 613.9	9 178.2	61.2	5 700.6	9 345.3	61.0
1990	5 948.6	9 371.2	63.5	6 026.5	9 501.3	63.4
1991	6 158.5	9 385.0	65.6	6 187.1	9 456.7	65.4
1992	6 504.0	9 689.4	67.1	6 538.7	9 765.8	67.0
1993	6 837.7	9 949.9	68.7	6 902.9	10 081.6	68.5
1994	7 223.5	10 290.7	70.2	7 315.9	10 464.2	69.9
1995	7 608.6	10 615.2	71.7	7 698.3	10 777.2	71.4
1996	8 042.3	11 015.6	73.0	8 138.7	11 195.6	72.7
1997	8 506.6	11 449.5	74.3	8 608.6	11 666.5	73.8
1998	8 999.1	11 974.5	75.2	9 161.8	12 328.5	74.3
1999	9 570.4	12 556.0	76.2	9 829.9	13 026.4	75.5
2000	10 196.4	13 075.1	78.0	10 577.5	13 658.6	77.4
2001	10 620.2	13 311.0	79.8	10 997.0	13 928.6	79.0
2002	10 909.1	13 471.8	81.0	11 348.9	14 180.8	80.0
2003	11 442.4	13 851.3	82.6	11 964.3	14 630.8	81.8
2004	12 153.1	14 329.2	84.8	12 787.3	15 201.7	84.1
2005	12 981.7	14 841.2	87.5	13 721.6	15 761.3	87.1
2006	13 746.6	15 240.9	90.2	14 533.0	16 172.3	89.9
2007	14 440.3	15 586.7	92.6	15 176.2	16 439.9	92.3
2008	14 799.1	15 678.0	94.4	15 540.0	16 368.5	94.9
2009	14 628.8	15 400.3	95.0	15 048.0	15 922.7	94.5
2010	14 995.1	15 596.8	96.1	15 527.4	16 186.2	95.9
2011	15 553.5	15 847.4	98.1	16 133.1	16 418.5	98.3
2012	16 182.8	16 182.8	100.0	16 734.4	16 734.4	100.0
2013	16 738.7	16 444.1	101.8	17 218.1	16 963.8	101.5
2014	17 466.7	16 842.3	103.7	17 976.8	17 415.7	103.2
2015	18 069.2	17 248.3	104.8	18 595.4	17 957.7	103.6
2016	18 658.8	17 630.6	105.8	19 165.1	18 374.6	104.3
2017	19 450.1	18 030.4	107.9	19 990.1	18 809.7	106.3
2018	20 468.4	18 528.8	110.5	21 064.6	19 365.4	108.8
2019	21 299.0	18 944.4	112.4	21 895.2	19 822.0	110.5
2020	20 953.3	18 395.9	113.9	21 604.5	19 319.8	111.8
2021	23 015.9	19 375.8	118.8	23 934.1	20 582.0	116.3
2019						
1st quarter	20 883.1	18 704.8	111.6	21 489.5	19 578.0	109.8
2nd quarter	21 200.8	18 881.4	112.3	21 833.1	19 781.9	110.4
3rd quarter	21 438.0	19 027.1	112.7	22 052.0	19 928.0	110.7
4th quarter	21 673.9	19 164.4	113.1	22 206.3	20 000.2	111.0
2020						
1st quarter	21 502.0	18 940.1	113.5	22 043.7	19 777.4	111.5
2nd quarter	19 767.4	17 471.0	113.2	20 306.3	18 264.4	111.2
3rd quarter	21 123.6	18 508.0	114.1	21 849.3	19 498.9	112.1
4th quarter	21 420.3	18 664.8	114.8	22 218.8	19 738.3	112.6
2021						
1st quarter	22 132.5	19 076.1	116.0	23 005.0	20 233.6	113.7
2nd quarter	22 915.3	19 449.3	117.8	23 797.0	20 625.1	115.4
3rd quarter	23 262.5	19 453.4	119.6	24 209.6	20 691.8	117.0
4th quarter	23 753.5	19 524.3	121.7	24 724.9	20 777.7	119.0

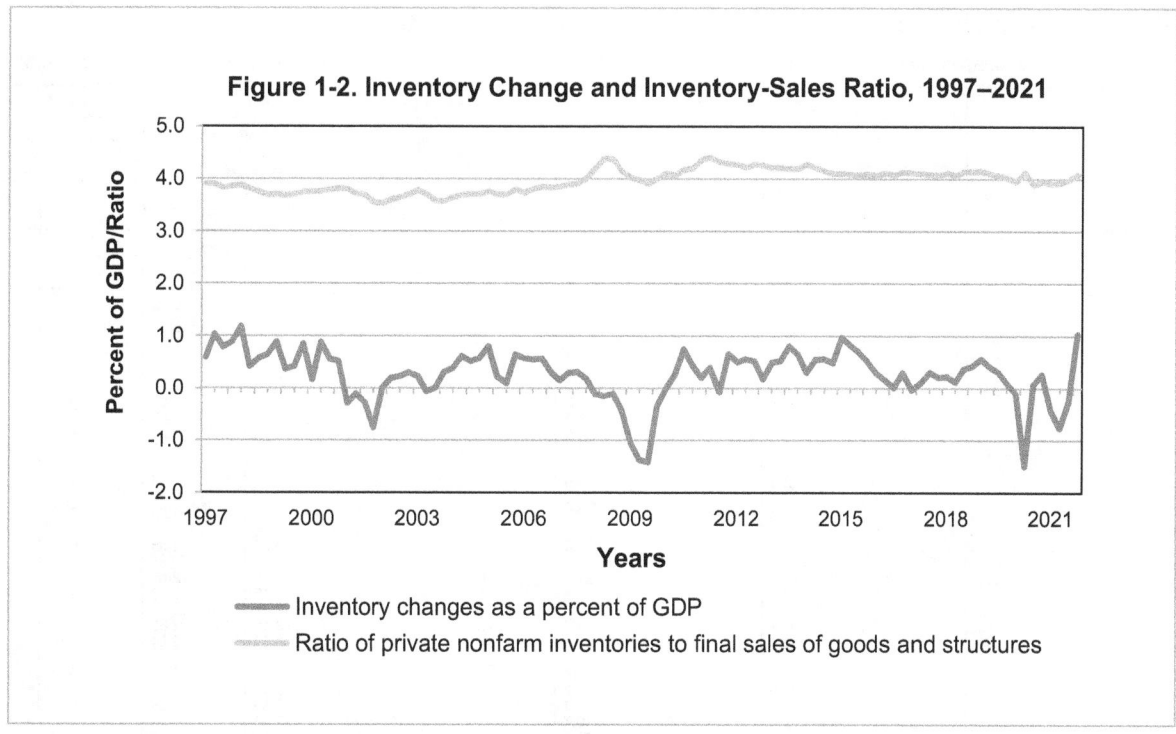

Figure 1-2. Inventory Change and Inventory-Sales Ratio, 1997–2021

- The change in inventories is part of business investment component that, although small, can be volatile and even negative, reflecting the fact that production is frequently more variable than sales. When inventory change is positive, the economy is producing more than is sold. This is the normal condition, as inventories grow to accommodate a growing level of sales. When inventory change is negative, production is below the rate of sales—which could be because sales rose faster than anticipated, causing involuntary inventory reduction, or on the other hand because production was deliberately cut back in order to get rid of unwanted stocks. Furthermore, it is the change in inventory —the change in an already volatile number—that drives the GDP's growth rate.

- In 2020 and throughout 2021, supply chain disruptions led to shortages of many inputs, such as computer chips, toys, steel, etc. Supply chain shortages affected everything from cars to toilet paper. Ports suffered from a lack of containers, the inability to upload fast enough, and from port congestion. Private inventories fell dramatically in 2020 to-59.6 and -19.9 in 2021. (Table 1-1A)

- The impact that COVID-19 had on industrial production is illustrated starting in the 2nd quarter of 2020. This disruption to production hampered supply chains in 2021. (Tables 1-8A and B)

- In 2009, following a rapid and unwanted rise in inventories, stocks were reduced at a record rate of $144 billion (2012 dollars), contributing to the 2.0 percent decline in GDP. In 2010, the resumption of inventory-building contributed significantly to the 3.9 percent GDP increase. (Tables 1-2A, 1-8A and 1-4A).

Table 1-8A. Inventory Change and Inventory-Sales Ratios: Recent Data

(Quarterly dollar data are at seasonally adjusted annual rates.)   **NIPA Tables 5.7.5B, 5.7.6B, 5.8.5B, 5.8.6B**

Year and quarter	Change in private inventories				Ratio, inventories at end of quarter to monthly rate of sales during the quarter					
	Billions of current dollars		Billions of chained dollars [1]		Total private inventories to final sales of domestic business		Nonfarm inventories to final sales of domestic business		Nonfarm inventories to final sales of goods and structures	
	Farm	Nonfarm	Farm	Nonfarm	Current dollars	Chained dollars[1]	Current dollars	Chained dollars[1]	Current dollars	Chained dollars[1]
OLD BASIS										
1960	0.6	2.7	1.7	9.9	4.22	3.37	2.89	2.34	3.93	4.10
1961	0.9	2.1	2.5	7.8	4.12	3.30	2.81	2.29	3.84	4.03
1962	0.6	5.5	1.7	20.4	4.14	3.32	2.82	2.34	3.87	4.11
1963	0.5	5.1	1.4	19.0	3.95	3.25	2.78	2.32	3.81	4.07
1964	-1.2	6.0	-3.8	21.8	3.79	3.17	2.75	2.31	3.79	4.07
1965	0.8	8.4	2.5	30.5	3.77	3.09	2.72	2.29	3.71	3.99
1966	-0.5	14.1	-1.4	50.2	3.92	3.26	2.92	2.50	4.01	4.38
1967	0.9	9.0	2.5	31.5	3.90	3.35	2.99	2.59	4.14	4.57
1968	1.4	7.7	4.1	26.5	3.79	3.33	2.90	2.58	4.03	4.56
1969	0.0	9.2	0.0	30.9	3.88	3.40	2.98	2.68	4.18	4.76
1970	-0.8	2.8	-2.4	8.6	3.81	3.39	2.96	2.68	4.23	4.83
1971	1.7	6.6	4.1	20.6	3.76	3.33	2.88	2.64	4.12	4.75
1972	0.3	8.8	0.4	26.7	3.74	3.18	2.77	2.55	3.94	4.53
1973	1.5	14.4	1.8	40.5	4.20	3.22	2.98	2.62	4.22	4.67
1974	-2.8	16.8	-4.4	39.0	4.52	3.46	3.54	2.88	5.11	5.26
1975	3.4	-9.6	5.8	-21.4	4.04	3.26	3.16	2.66	4.59	4.88
1976	-0.8	18.0	-1.6	37.6	3.95	3.23	3.19	2.68	4.68	4.92
1977	4.5	17.8	7.2	35.7	3.89	3.22	3.16	2.67	4.63	4.87
1978	1.4	24.4	2.1	44.9	3.98	3.14	3.15	2.63	4.54	4.73
1979	3.6	14.4	4.2	23.8	4.19	3.16	3.34	2.64	4.85	4.75
1980	-6.1	-0.2	-7.2	-0.4	4.24	3.13	3.44	2.65	5.08	4.82
1981	8.8	21.0	10.1	28.2	4.17	3.28	3.49	2.75	5.20	5.03
1982	5.8	-20.7	7.5	-27.4	3.97	3.23	3.30	2.68	5.10	4.99
1983	-15.4	9.6	-17.4	10.7	3.69	2.98	3.08	2.52	4.77	4.64
1984	5.7	59.7	6.3	72.3	3.72	3.05	3.16	2.60	4.89	4.72
1985	5.8	16.1	7.0	18.4	3.51	2.98	3.01	2.53	4.74	4.65
1986	-1.5	8.0	-2.3	10.4	3.25	2.90	2.82	2.47	4.49	4.53
1987	-6.4	33.6	-9.1	41.1	3.33	2.90	2.90	2.50	4.65	4.62
1988	-11.9	30.4	-13.1	35.4	3.29	2.81	2.86	2.47	4.63	4.55
1989	0.0	27.7	0.0	30.8	3.23	2.80	2.83	2.47	4.63	4.56
1990	2.4	12.2	2.5	14.0	3.22	2.83	2.82	2.49	4.71	4.66
1991	-1.3	0.9	-1.8	0.4	3.06	2.83	2.70	2.50	4.62	4.74
1992	6.3	10.1	7.1	11.0	2.92	2.73	2.56	2.39	4.41	4.53
1993	-6.2	27.0	-7.5	29.8	2.85	2.68	2.51	2.38	4.33	4.47
1994	12.0	51.8	13.7	55.9	2.89	2.72	2.56	2.40	4.39	4.47
1995	-11.1	42.2	-13.0	44.3	2.88	2.69	2.58	2.40	4.45	4.46
1996	8.6	22.1	8.3	23.2	2.76	2.62	2.47	2.33	4.24	4.28
1997	3.3	67.7	3.7	73.6	2.70	2.65	2.42	2.37	4.17	4.32
NEW BASIS										
1998	1.3	62.5	2.8	86.5	2.47	2.92	2.25	2.54	3.69	4.56
1999	-2.7	63.5	-6.3	87.7	2.49	2.90	2.27	2.54	3.75	4.56
2000	-1.4	55.9	-3.0	77.6	2.51	2.90	2.29	2.56	3.82	4.61
2001	0.0	-38.3	0.2	-51.4	2.33	2.81	2.13	2.47	3.55	4.44
2002	-2.5	22.5	-5.2	27.1	2.38	2.84	2.17	2.50	3.71	4.56
2003	0.1	14.0	0.2	19.2	2.33	2.71	2.10	2.39	3.57	4.29
2004	8.8	55.3	13.5	70.3	2.39	2.73	2.17	2.40	3.71	4.31
2005	0.2	57.3	0.4	61.5	2.42	2.71	2.20	2.39	3.80	4.29
2006	-3.6	72.6	-6.3	89.1	2.42	2.72	2.21	2.41	3.83	4.32
2007	0.6	33.3	-1.4	40.6	2.51	2.70	2.28	2.40	4.01	4.32
2008	-0.5	-28.7	-0.6	-31.5	2.50	2.76	2.28	2.46	4.14	4.56
2009	-6.7	-144.1	-10.0	-165.2	2.38	2.59	2.17	2.29	4.00	4.28
2010	-12.2	66.1	-17.8	70.2	2.49	2.58	2.26	2.31	4.20	4.31
2011	-2.1	48.3	-2.2	48.4	2.58	2.57	2.32	2.30	4.29	4.25
2012	-18.7	89.9	-18.7	89.9	2.55	2.56	2.32	2.33	4.26	4.27
2013	11.7	92.8	10.4	98.2	2.52	2.60	2.29	2.36	4.19	4.27
2014	-3.2	87.2	-3.5	90.1	2.47	2.59	2.24	2.36	4.10	4.26
2015	1.5	135.3	1.1	136.5	2.40	2.68	2.21	2.46	4.09	4.45
2016	-5.9	42.2	-6.7	41.2	2.38	2.65	2.22	2.44	4.13	4.39
2017	-5.2	34.6	-6.4	38.6	2.36	2.58	2.20	2.38	4.07	4.25
2018	-7.9	66.7	-9.1	72.7	2.36	2.58	2.22	2.39	4.14	4.27
2019	-15.3	88.9	-17.2	89.0	2.31	2.56	2.18	2.39	4.02	4.21
2020	-6.0	-53.6	-7.7	-35.3	2.38	2.62	2.26	2.45	3.95	4.06
2021	-5.4	-14.4	-22.9	-14.0	2.45	2.44	2.34	2.30	4.08	3.87
2019										
1st quarter	-18.7	137.2	-17.1	145.7	2.39	2.60	2.24	2.41	4.15	4.28
2nd quarter	-16.5	104.9	-17.3	98.7	2.35	2.59	2.22	2.41	4.10	4.26
3rd quarter	-15.1	82.1	-20.1	83.7	2.32	2.58	2.20	2.41	4.06	4.24
4th quarter	-10.8	31.4	-14.3	27.8	2.31	2.56	2.18	2.39	4.02	4.21
2020										
1st quarter	-10.9	-9.7	-16.8	-15.4	2.30	2.60	2.18	2.43	3.95	4.19
2nd quarter	-7.2	-282.7	-8.1	-242.3	2.53	2.84	2.41	2.66	4.12	4.33
3rd quarter	-3.6	18.6	-2.1	26.4	2.35	2.63	2.24	2.46	3.89	4.07
4th quarter	-2.2	59.4	-3.9	90.2	2.38	2.62	2.26	2.45	3.95	4.06
2021										
1st quarter	-3.3	-90.9	-15.7	-74.4	2.39	2.53	2.27	2.36	3.91	3.88
2nd quarter	-4.6	-169.7	-22.7	-147.7	2.38	2.42	2.27	2.27	3.92	3.75
3rd quarter	-5.1	-55.1	-24.3	-46.5	2.39	2.41	2.28	2.26	3.99	3.80
4th quarter	-8.5	257.9	-28.9	212.8	2.45	2.44	2.34	2.30	4.08	3.87

[1]Before 1997, 2005 dollars; 1997 forward, 2012 dollars.

Table 1-8B. Inventory Change and Inventory-Sales Ratios: Historical Data

(Quarterly dollar data are at seasonally adjusted annual rates.)   NIPA Tables 5.7.5B, 5.7.6B, 5.8.5B, 5.8.6B

| Year and quarter | Change in private inventories | | | | Ratio, inventories at end of quarter to monthly rate of sales during the quarter | | | | | |
| | Billions of current dollars | | Billions of chained dollars [1] | | Total private inventories to final sales of domestic business | | Nonfarm inventories to final sales of domestic business | | Nonfarm inventories to final sales of goods and structures | |
	Farm	Nonfarm	Farm	Nonfarm	Current dollars	Chained dollars[1]	Current dollars	Chained dollars[1]	Current dollars	Chained dollars[1]
OLD BASIS										
1929	-0.1	1.7	-0.6	10.6	...	...	...	...	...	...
1930	-0.3	0.0	-1.7	-2.4	...	...	...	...	...	...
1931	0.5	-1.6	3.1	-13.4	...	...	...	...	...	...
1932	0.1	-2.5	0.8	-21.2	...	...	...	...	...	...
1933	-0.1	-1.3	-1.1	-9.4	...	...	...	...	...	...
1934	-0.8	0.2	-5.7	1.0	...	...	...	...	...	...
1935	0.7	0.4	4.0	2.5	...	...	...	...	...	...
1936	-0.9	2.0	-5.4	15.5	...	...	...	...	...	...
1937	0.9	1.7	4.1	7.9	...	...	...	...	...	...
1938	0.4	-1.0	2.8	-6.0	...	...	...	...	...	...
1939	-0.1	0.3	-1.1	2.7	...	...	...	...	...	...
1940	0.5	1.9	2.8	12.4	...	...	...	...	...	...
1941	0.4	3.9	1.9	24.3	...	...	...	...	...	...
1942	1.3	0.6	5.6	3.0	...	...	...	...	...	...
1943	-0.2	-0.5	-1.1	-2.3	...	...	...	...	...	...
1944	-0.3	-0.6	-1.5	-2.5	...	...	...	...	...	...
1945	-0.9	-0.6	-3.3	-3.8	...	...	...	...	...	...
1946	-0.2	6.2	-1.0	31.8	...	...	...	...	...	...
1947	-1.8	1.2	-4.5	4.4	...	...	...	...	...	...
1948	2.7	3.0	6.1	12.4	...	...	...	...	...	...
1949	-0.6	-2.1	-1.9	-8.6	...	...	...	...	...	...
1950	-0.1	5.9	-0.3	22.8	...	...	...	...	...	...
1951	1.0	8.9	2.1	28.4	5.81	3.67	3.04	2.30	3.94	3.97
1952	1.4	2.1	3.1	7.4	5.85	3.76	3.15	2.46	4.07	4.24
1953	0.7	1.2	2.0	4.5	5.24	3.74	3.06	2.45	3.98	4.23
1954	0.2	-2.1	0.5	-7.5	4.74	3.52	2.88	2.28	3.81	3.94
1949										
1st quarter	-0.2	0.6	-1.2	-0.4	5.66	3.90	2.97	2.36	3.88	4.14
2nd quarter	-1.2	-4.0	-3.0	-15.1	5.38	3.82	2.83	2.30	3.70	4.02
3rd quarter	-0.9	-0.4	-2.3	-0.6	5.39	3.81	2.82	2.29	3.69	4.00
4th quarter	-0.2	-4.5	-0.9	-18.4	5.23	3.73	2.77	2.23	3.61	3.87
1950										
1st quarter	-0.1	2.2	-1.0	9.7	5.26	3.69	2.76	2.22	3.61	3.84
2nd quarter	-1.3	4.2	-2.5	16.2	5.27	3.62	2.75	2.20	3.57	3.79
3rd quarter	0.5	3.7	0.6	15.2	5.21	3.47	2.72	2.12	3.50	3.63
4th quarter	0.7	13.4	1.5	50.2	5.81	3.67	3.04	2.30	3.94	3.97
1951										
1st quarter	1.2	9.2	2.6	29.0	5.94	3.68	3.12	2.33	4.01	4.01
2nd quarter	0.9	13.8	2.5	44.3	5.99	3.81	3.25	2.45	4.23	4.28
3rd quarter	0.8	9.0	1.6	29.3	5.89	3.79	3.20	2.47	4.16	4.29
4th quarter	1.1	3.6	1.7	11.0	5.85	3.76	3.15	2.46	4.07	4.24
1952										
1st quarter	1.0	3.8	2.7	12.8	5.77	3.79	3.16	2.49	4.11	4.31
2nd quarter	1.9	-3.4	3.6	-10.5	5.63	3.75	3.08	2.44	4.01	4.24
3rd quarter	2.2	3.4	4.5	11.2	5.63	3.85	3.15	2.51	4.13	4.38
4th quarter	0.5	4.8	1.5	16.2	5.24	3.74	3.06	2.45	3.98	4.23
1953										
1st quarter	0.8	3.1	2.5	10.6	5.06	3.69	3.02	2.42	3.93	4.17
2nd quarter	-0.7	4.3	-0.2	14.1	5.00	3.69	3.06	2.43	3.99	4.20
3rd quarter	0.7	1.6	1.8	5.8	4.99	3.72	3.09	2.45	4.05	4.23
4th quarter	2.1	-4.1	3.8	-12.3	5.04	3.74	3.08	2.45	4.04	4.22
1954										
1st quarter	0.8	-2.8	2.1	-9.2	5.02	3.72	3.04	2.42	4.01	4.20
2nd quarter	-0.2	-3.2	0.5	-10.8	4.91	3.66	2.98	2.38	3.93	4.11
3rd quarter	0.7	-2.8	0.8	-9.1	4.85	3.59	2.93	2.32	3.89	4.04
4th quarter	-0.5	0.2	-1.5	-0.9	4.74	3.52	2.88	2.28	3.81	3.94
1955										
1st quarter	-0.1	3.9	-1.7	14.0	4.68	3.46	2.86	2.25	3.77	3.88
2nd quarter	-1.1	5.7	-2.1	20.0	4.57	3.44	2.87	2.26	3.73	3.83
3rd quarter	-1.3	5.6	-2.0	17.9	4.47	3.42	2.89	2.26	3.77	3.85
4th quarter	0.3	6.9	-1.6	22.7	4.43	3.44	2.95	2.29	3.87	3.94
1956										
1st quarter	0.0	6.4	-2.9	20.8	4.50	3.48	3.00	2.33	3.96	4.02
2nd quarter	-1.5	5.0	-3.4	16.2	4.57	3.48	3.03	2.35	3.99	4.04
3rd quarter	-0.8	4.3	-3.2	13.2	4.50	3.48	3.02	2.36	3.98	4.07
4th quarter	-1.6	3.9	-3.3	12.1	4.47	3.45	3.03	2.35	4.00	4.07
1957										
1st quarter	0.3	1.9	-0.9	5.7	4.44	3.44	3.02	2.35	3.97	4.05
2nd quarter	0.7	2.0	-0.2	6.8	4.48	3.48	3.04	2.38	4.00	4.11
3rd quarter	0.5	2.3	1.8	7.5	4.46	3.47	3.03	2.38	3.99	4.10
4th quarter	-1.0	-3.5	1.1	-10.2	4.46	3.48	3.01	2.37	4.01	4.14
1958										
1st quarter	2.2	-6.3	7.6	-20.4	4.67	3.56	3.04	2.41	4.06	4.20
2nd quarter	1.6	-5.8	6.9	-18.6	4.65	3.56	3.00	2.38	4.00	4.17
3rd quarter	2.2	-0.7	6.2	-2.5	4.58	3.48	2.92	2.32	3.92	4.07
4th quarter	1.8	3.4	2.5	10.6	4.50	3.44	2.90	2.30	3.88	4.00

[1]Before 1997, 2005 dollars; 1997 forward, 2009 dollars.
. . . = Not available.

Table 1-8B. Inventory Change and Inventory-Sales Ratios: Historical Data—*Continued*

(Quarterly dollar data are at seasonally adjusted annual rates.)   **NIPA Tables 5.7.5B, 5.7.6B, 5.8.5B, 5.8.6B**

| Year and quarter | Change in private inventories | | | | Ratio, inventories at end of quarter to monthly rate of sales during the quarter | | | | | |
| | Billions of current dollars | | Billions of chained dollars [1] | | Total private inventories to final sales of domestic business | | Nonfarm inventories to final sales of domestic business | | Nonfarm inventories to final sales of goods and structures | |
	Farm	Nonfarm	Farm	Nonfarm	Current dollars	Chained dollars[1]	Current dollars	Chained dollars[1]	Current dollars	Chained dollars[1]
1959										
1st quarter	-0.3	4.2	-3.5	14.9	4.37	3.35	2.83	2.25	3.79	3.93
2nd quarter	-1.9	9.2	-5.3	33.8	4.33	3.34	2.86	2.27	3.85	3.98
3rd quarter	-2.3	2.6	-5.4	9.6	4.25	3.31	2.84	2.27	3.82	3.96
4th quarter	-1.8	5.9	-4.6	21.1	4.26	3.37	2.90	2.32	3.94	4.08
1960										
1st quarter	0.6	10.6	0.4	39.0	4.29	3.37	2.93	2.35	3.96	4.10
2nd quarter	0.9	2.4	1.9	9.0	4.21	3.36	2.91	2.34	3.95	4.11
3rd quarter	1.0	3.3	3.1	12.1	4.27	3.41	2.95	2.38	3.99	4.15
4th quarter	-0.2	-5.6	1.5	-20.2	4.22	3.37	2.89	2.34	3.93	4.10
1961										
1st quarter	0.6	-3.1	2.5	-11.3	4.19	3.35	2.86	2.32	3.90	4.07
2nd quarter	0.6	1.2	2.2	4.7	4.12	3.33	2.83	2.30	3.89	4.07
3rd quarter	0.9	5.7	2.6	21.0	4.17	3.35	2.85	2.32	3.89	4.08
4th quarter	1.4	4.6	2.8	16.8	4.12	3.30	2.81	2.29	3.84	4.03
1962										
1st quarter	1.5	7.9	2.5	29.0	4.15	3.32	2.82	2.32	3.85	4.07
2nd quarter	0.2	5.2	0.8	19.2	4.09	3.29	2.80	2.31	3.84	4.06
3rd quarter	0.2	5.9	1.4	22.0	4.17	3.32	2.83	2.33	3.87	4.09
4th quarter	0.4	3.0	2.2	11.3	4.14	3.32	2.82	2.34	3.87	4.11
1963										
1st quarter	1.9	4.9	7.5	18.2	4.12	3.34	2.83	2.35	3.87	4.12
2nd quarter	0.1	4.8	0.7	17.4	4.04	3.29	2.79	2.32	3.83	4.08
3rd quarter	-0.6	6.4	-1.7	23.6	4.00	3.27	2.79	2.33	3.81	4.07
4th quarter	0.6	4.5	-0.8	16.7	3.95	3.25	2.78	2.32	3.81	4.07
1964										
1st quarter	-0.6	5.8	-3.9	21.1	3.85	3.19	2.74	2.29	3.75	4.01
2nd quarter	-1.2	5.7	-4.3	20.7	3.79	3.17	2.73	2.29	3.75	4.02
3rd quarter	-1.8	6.5	-4.2	23.8	3.78	3.15	2.73	2.29	3.74	4.00
4th quarter	-1.1	6.1	-3.1	21.7	3.79	3.17	2.75	2.31	3.79	4.07
1965										
1st quarter	0.3	11.2	0.9	40.8	3.81	3.17	2.76	2.33	3.79	4.08
2nd quarter	1.1	7.4	2.9	26.9	3.82	3.15	2.75	2.32	3.79	4.08
3rd quarter	0.8	8.5	3.1	30.5	3.78	3.14	2.76	2.32	3.78	4.06
4th quarter	1.0	6.6	3.2	23.7	3.77	3.09	2.72	2.29	3.71	3.99
1966										
1st quarter	0.6	13.2	1.1	46.8	3.80	3.09	2.73	2.31	3.71	4.00
2nd quarter	-1.7	14.0	-2.7	50.2	3.86	3.16	2.80	2.38	3.83	4.16
3rd quarter	-0.6	12.4	-1.7	43.7	3.91	3.19	2.84	2.42	3.88	4.22
4th quarter	-0.4	16.9	-2.3	59.9	3.92	3.26	2.92	2.50	4.01	4.38
1967										
1st quarter	1.7	13.7	3.4	48.6	3.94	3.32	2.98	2.55	4.11	4.50
2nd quarter	2.1	4.2	7.6	14.7	3.92	3.31	2.95	2.54	4.07	4.46
3rd quarter	0.5	8.7	1.4	29.7	3.92	3.34	2.97	2.57	4.10	4.52
4th quarter	-0.9	9.3	-2.2	33.1	3.90	3.35	2.99	2.59	4.14	4.57
1968										
1st quarter	3.0	5.4	7.3	19.1	3.87	3.32	2.94	2.57	4.08	4.51
2nd quarter	4.3	9.8	13.4	33.9	3.87	3.34	2.93	2.58	4.07	4.55
3rd quarter	0.2	7.5	1.2	25.1	3.81	3.32	2.90	2.56	4.03	4.51
4th quarter	-2.0	8.0	-5.5	27.8	3.79	3.33	2.90	2.58	4.03	4.56
1969										
1st quarter	1.8	9.7	3.9	33.0	3.79	3.32	2.90	2.59	4.02	4.54
2nd quarter	1.4	7.8	4.4	26.6	3.83	3.35	2.91	2.61	4.06	4.61
3rd quarter	-1.2	11.4	-2.5	38.6	3.83	3.38	2.94	2.64	4.10	4.67
4th quarter	-1.9	7.7	-5.8	25.5	3.88	3.40	2.98	2.68	4.18	4.76
1970										
1st quarter	1.6	0.2	3.4	0.0	3.86	3.38	2.96	2.66	4.18	4.74
2nd quarter	0.4	4.7	1.9	14.9	3.85	3.40	2.96	2.68	4.20	4.80
3rd quarter	-1.8	6.9	-4.4	21.9	3.84	3.39	2.97	2.67	4.22	4.79
4th quarter	-3.5	-0.5	-10.3	-2.2	3.81	3.39	2.96	2.68	4.23	4.83
1971										
1st quarter	2.5	9.7	6.6	31.3	3.83	3.38	2.95	2.68	4.21	4.81
2nd quarter	4.2	6.7	10.7	20.6	3.81	3.39	2.94	2.68	4.20	4.81
3rd quarter	2.3	7.9	5.8	25.2	3.80	3.38	2.93	2.68	4.18	4.80
4th quarter	-2.3	2.0	-6.8	5.4	3.76	3.33	2.88	2.64	4.12	4.75
1972										
1st quarter	-0.5	3.7	0.1	11.1	3.72	3.30	2.84	2.62	4.06	4.69
2nd quarter	2.0	10.0	6.8	30.6	3.75	3.27	2.83	2.60	4.03	4.64
3rd quarter	1.0	12.7	1.9	38.5	3.77	3.26	2.83	2.60	4.05	4.66
4th quarter	-1.4	8.9	-7.1	26.5	3.74	3.18	2.77	2.55	3.94	4.53
1973										
1st quarter	-4.2	14.8	-10.7	42.9	3.86	3.11	2.79	2.52	3.92	4.45
2nd quarter	5.0	13.2	12.0	38.3	4.03	3.15	2.86	2.54	4.02	4.51
3rd quarter	2.6	7.2	3.5	20.0	4.11	3.16	2.87	2.56	4.05	4.55
4th quarter	2.8	22.2	2.3	60.9	4.20	3.22	2.98	2.62	4.22	4.67

[1]Before 1997, 2005 dollars; 1997 forward, 2009 dollars.

Table 1-8B. Inventory Change and Inventory-Sales Ratios: Historical Data—*Continued*

(Quarterly dollar data are at seasonally adjusted annual rates.)   **NIPA Tables 5.7.5B, 5.7.6B, 5.8.5B, 5.8.6B**

Year and quarter	Change in private inventories				Ratio, inventories at end of quarter to monthly rate of sales during the quarter					
	Billions of current dollars		Billions of chained dollars¹		Total private inventories to final sales of domestic business		Nonfarm inventories to final sales of domestic business		Nonfarm inventories to final sales of goods and structures	
	Farm	Nonfarm	Farm	Nonfarm	Current dollars	Chained dollars¹	Current dollars	Chained dollars¹	Current dollars	Chained dollars¹
1974										
1st quarter	-3.3	15.9	-5.2	39.7	4.26	3.27	3.13	2.68	4.42	4.76
2nd quarter	1.0	16.4	0.9	39.6	4.29	3.31	3.28	2.72	4.67	4.86
3rd quarter	-0.1	5.7	1.7	11.7	4.45	3.34	3.40	2.75	4.84	4.93
4th quarter	-8.7	29.2	-15.0	64.9	4.52	3.46	3.54	2.88	5.11	5.26
1975										
1st quarter	7.1	-17.1	16.4	-38.3	4.32	3.42	3.41	2.82	4.94	5.16
2nd quarter	3.1	-17.1	5.4	-38.6	4.26	3.35	3.30	2.75	4.81	5.06
3rd quarter	0.8	-2.2	-1.0	-5.0	4.18	3.31	3.24	2.71	4.69	4.95
4th quarter	2.5	-2.1	2.3	-3.7	4.04	3.26	3.16	2.66	4.59	4.88
1976										
1st quarter	-0.5	15.2	0.1	33.2	4.00	3.22	3.14	2.64	4.56	4.83
2nd quarter	-1.8	24.3	-1.9	51.8	4.07	3.26	3.21	2.69	4.67	4.91
3rd quarter	2.0	18.8	5.4	38.9	4.04	3.28	3.23	2.70	4.74	4.96
4th quarter	-3.0	13.6	-9.8	26.5	3.95	3.23	3.19	2.68	4.68	4.92
1977										
1st quarter	-1.3	16.1	-7.0	33.0	3.96	3.22	3.21	2.68	4.72	4.92
2nd quarter	5.3	14.2	11.3	27.8	3.88	3.19	3.16	2.65	4.62	4.84
3rd quarter	4.4	26.5	16.3	53.8	3.86	3.22	3.16	2.67	4.63	4.88
4th quarter	9.8	14.4	8.4	28.1	3.89	3.22	3.16	2.67	4.63	4.87
1978										
1st quarter	-0.6	26.1	-3.6	48.9	4.02	3.26	3.21	2.72	4.78	5.00
2nd quarter	0.4	23.9	0.2	44.2	3.92	3.14	3.12	2.62	4.55	4.75
3rd quarter	7.2	17.8	11.1	32.3	3.95	3.15	3.13	2.62	4.54	4.74
4th quarter	-1.5	30.0	0.5	54.1	3.98	3.14	3.15	2.63	4.54	4.73
1979										
1st quarter	4.2	19.6	6.6	33.0	4.15	3.17	3.22	2.65	4.66	4.78
2nd quarter	3.1	24.3	5.3	40.4	4.19	3.21	3.29	2.69	4.78	4.87
3rd quarter	6.6	5.5	7.0	8.2	4.16	3.16	3.28	2.64	4.74	4.73
4th quarter	0.3	8.3	-1.9	13.4	4.19	3.16	3.34	2.64	4.85	4.75
1980										
1st quarter	-0.6	10.5	-2.6	17.4	4.25	3.17	3.45	2.66	5.02	4.78
2nd quarter	-5.2	13.0	-5.9	19.3	4.40	3.28	3.57	2.76	5.26	5.02
3rd quarter	-12.5	-21.4	-14.2	-32.6	4.34	3.18	3.50	2.68	5.15	4.88
4th quarter	-6.1	-3.0	-6.0	-5.8	4.24	3.13	3.44	2.65	5.08	4.82
1981										
1st quarter	6.8	31.9	10.3	44.6	4.26	3.17	3.48	2.67	5.13	4.84
2nd quarter	9.9	1.8	10.9	1.7	4.24	3.18	3.47	2.67	5.15	4.87
3rd quarter	11.8	32.1	14.5	42.6	4.20	3.22	3.48	2.71	5.16	4.93
4th quarter	6.5	18.3	4.5	23.8	4.17	3.28	3.49	2.75	5.20	5.03
1982										
1st quarter	5.1	-26.5	6.7	-34.3	4.19	3.28	3.46	2.74	5.20	5.03
2nd quarter	4.3	-8.5	6.4	-12.2	4.15	3.28	3.42	2.74	5.17	5.04
3rd quarter	9.0	-3.2	12.0	-5.5	4.12	3.33	3.43	2.77	5.26	5.15
4th quarter	4.6	-44.4	4.9	-57.5	3.97	3.23	3.30	2.68	5.10	4.99
1983										
1st quarter	-7.3	-27.8	-10.4	-37.3	3.89	3.15	3.19	2.62	4.98	4.89
2nd quarter	-13.0	5.3	-12.6	6.5	3.81	3.09	3.14	2.58	4.89	4.80
3rd quarter	-32.4	28.2	-37.7	34.3	3.73	3.03	3.12	2.55	4.86	4.73
4th quarter	-8.8	32.7	-9.0	39.4	3.69	2.98	3.08	2.52	4.77	4.64
1984										
1st quarter	5.5	67.5	7.4	81.9	3.78	3.02	3.15	2.56	4.87	4.71
2nd quarter	5.6	63.7	6.4	77.2	3.76	3.03	3.16	2.57	4.88	4.69
3rd quarter	6.8	64.5	8.1	78.9	3.75	3.06	3.18	2.60	4.93	4.75
4th quarter	5.0	43.0	3.3	51.0	3.72	3.05	3.16	2.60	4.89	4.72
1985										
1st quarter	7.9	8.3	8.4	8.8	3.60	3.00	3.06	2.55	4.77	4.65
2nd quarter	4.2	17.4	4.8	20.3	3.55	2.99	3.04	2.55	4.76	4.66
3rd quarter	6.6	9.7	9.1	12.0	3.47	2.96	2.98	2.51	4.67	4.60
4th quarter	4.3	28.8	5.9	32.7	3.51	2.98	3.01	2.53	4.74	4.65
1986										
1st quarter	2.5	27.8	1.7	33.3	3.42	2.97	2.94	2.52	4.65	4.63
2nd quarter	-3.5	19.1	-5.9	22.3	3.37	2.97	2.92	2.53	4.63	4.65
3rd quarter	-3.1	-3.9	-4.3	-5.5	3.29	2.92	2.85	2.49	4.52	4.55
4th quarter	-1.8	-11.0	-0.6	-8.5	3.25	2.90	2.82	2.47	4.49	4.53
1987										
1st quarter	-7.7	35.6	-9.7	44.5	3.31	2.94	2.86	2.51	4.62	4.66
2nd quarter	-10.7	27.2	-14.5	33.1	3.30	2.90	2.86	2.49	4.60	4.60
3rd quarter	-4.0	5.0	-5.2	4.1	3.25	2.85	2.82	2.45	4.52	4.51
4th quarter	-3.3	66.4	-7.0	82.5	3.33	2.90	2.90	2.50	4.65	4.62
1988										
1st quarter	-4.4	21.4	-7.6	25.1	3.30	2.86	2.86	2.47	4.61	4.56
2nd quarter	-12.2	31.9	-15.2	38.0	3.29	2.83	2.85	2.46	4.60	4.52
3rd quarter	-11.2	29.4	-11.4	32.6	3.30	2.83	2.85	2.47	4.63	4.57
4th quarter	-19.7	38.8	-18.3	45.9	3.29	2.81	2.86	2.47	4.63	4.55

¹Before 1997, 2005 dollars; 1997 forward, 2009 dollars.

Table 1-8B. Inventory Change and Inventory-Sales Ratios: Historical Data—*Continued*

(Quarterly dollar data are at seasonally adjusted annual rates.)   **NIPA Tables 5.7.5B, 5.7.6B, 5.8.5B, 5.8.6B**

| Year and quarter | Change in private inventories | | | | Ratio, inventories at end of quarter to monthly rate of sales during the quarter | | | | | |
| | Billions of current dollars | | Billions of chained dollars [1] | | Total private inventories to final sales of domestic business | | Nonfarm inventories to final sales of domestic business | | Nonfarm inventories to final sales of goods and structures | |
	Farm	Nonfarm	Farm	Nonfarm	Current dollars	Chained dollars[1]	Current dollars	Chained dollars[1]	Current dollars	Chained dollars[1]
1989										
1st quarter	7.2	41.0	7.8	46.6	3.32	2.83	2.89	2.48	4.70	4.58
2nd quarter	2.9	33.2	3.6	37.6	3.28	2.83	2.87	2.48	4.65	4.56
3rd quarter	-5.5	15.5	-5.8	16.9	3.21	2.79	2.82	2.45	4.55	4.49
4th quarter	-4.6	21.2	-5.6	22.3	3.23	2.80	2.83	2.47	4.63	4.56
1990										
1st quarter	1.8	12.1	1.7	13.3	3.18	2.78	2.78	2.45	4.53	4.50
2nd quarter	-1.5	35.3	-2.6	39.9	3.17	2.81	2.78	2.47	4.58	4.60
3rd quarter	4.0	17.9	4.4	20.3	3.20	2.82	2.82	2.48	4.67	4.63
4th quarter	5.2	-16.6	6.7	-17.7	3.22	2.83	2.82	2.49	4.71	4.66
1991										
1st quarter	0.0	-15.6	0.7	-18.1	3.18	2.85	2.78	2.51	4.65	4.71
2nd quarter	-0.7	-17.3	-0.5	-20.6	3.08	2.81	2.70	2.47	4.55	4.66
3rd quarter	-10.9	11.7	-13.8	13.1	3.04	2.81	2.69	2.48	4.54	4.67
4th quarter	6.4	24.7	6.1	27.1	3.06	2.83	2.70	2.50	4.62	4.74
1992										
1st quarter	8.0	-7.8	10.5	-7.5	3.00	2.78	2.63	2.44	4.52	4.64
2nd quarter	9.4	13.8	10.9	13.2	2.99	2.77	2.62	2.43	4.50	4.61
3rd quarter	5.1	15.4	4.7	16.6	2.96	2.75	2.60	2.41	4.47	4.57
4th quarter	2.5	18.9	2.4	21.6	2.92	2.73	2.56	2.39	4.41	4.53
1993										
1st quarter	-5.6	41.6	-6.2	46.5	2.95	2.75	2.58	2.42	4.47	4.60
2nd quarter	-4.9	29.0	-5.3	32.3	2.92	2.74	2.57	2.41	4.44	4.56
3rd quarter	-12.5	19.1	-14.2	20.6	2.89	2.72	2.54	2.40	4.42	4.55
4th quarter	-1.7	18.3	-4.1	19.9	2.85	2.68	2.51	2.38	4.33	4.47
1994										
1st quarter	16.5	28.8	19.4	31.1	2.87	2.69	2.51	2.38	4.33	4.48
2nd quarter	17.1	64.3	21.0	70.0	2.86	2.71	2.53	2.39	4.37	4.49
3rd quarter	10.7	42.5	10.6	46.1	2.86	2.71	2.53	2.39	4.36	4.48
4th quarter	3.7	71.5	3.7	76.3	2.89	2.72	2.56	2.40	4.39	4.47
1995										
1st quarter	-5.8	67.0	-5.9	71.2	2.93	2.75	2.62	2.43	4.49	4.52
2nd quarter	-13.7	47.4	-13.6	50.1	2.94	2.75	2.64	2.44	4.55	4.55
3rd quarter	-20.4	31.7	-26.4	32.8	2.90	2.71	2.60	2.41	4.49	4.50
4th quarter	-4.4	22.8	-6.2	22.9	2.88	2.69	2.58	2.40	4.45	4.46
1996										
1st quarter	1.1	5.8	-2.9	6.2	2.84	2.66	2.55	2.38	4.39	4.42
2nd quarter	11.8	18.6	7.4	19.8	2.81	2.63	2.51	2.35	4.30	4.35
3rd quarter	17.1	34.0	27.4	35.0	2.81	2.65	2.50	2.35	4.29	4.34
4th quarter	4.5	30.2	1.3	31.7	2.76	2.62	2.47	2.33	4.24	4.28
1997										
1st quarter	-0.5	50.3	-10.8	53.3	2.74	2.62	2.45	2.33	4.21	4.28
2nd quarter	0.8	87.6	8.2	95.7	2.73	2.65	2.44	2.36	4.21	4.33
3rd quarter	8.3	59.6	10.1	65.5	2.69	2.63	2.41	2.34	4.14	4.27
4th quarter	4.7	73.1	7.2	79.8	2.70	2.65	2.42	2.37	4.17	4.32
1998										
1st quarter	-0.6	50.3	-13.5	45.4	2.66	2.93	2.37	2.54	3.91	4.62
2nd quarter	0.8	87.6	13.1	130.9	2.64	2.97	2.36	2.57	3.90	4.67
3rd quarter	8.3	59.6	15.1	82.4	2.60	2.94	2.33	2.55	3.83	4.61
4th quarter	4.6	73.0	10.0	93.4	2.60	2.97	2.34	2.57	3.86	4.65
NEW BASIS										
1998										
1st quarter	5.6	99.5	9.4	144.4	2.60	2.99	2.34	2.60	3.87	4.71
2nd quarter	-4.9	42.2	-4.0	57.0	2.55	2.96	2.30	2.57	3.81	4.66
3rd quarter	0.5	51.9	4.5	65.5	2.51	2.95	2.28	2.56	3.75	4.63
4th quarter	3.8	56.2	1.3	79.1	2.47	2.92	2.25	2.54	3.69	4.56
1999										
1st quarter	4.1	79.3	-2.9	114.9	2.48	2.94	2.25	2.56	3.71	4.61
2nd quarter	-0.2	35.3	1.6	46.9	2.46	2.91	2.24	2.54	3.68	4.56
3rd quarter	-9.1	49.6	-18.1	71.1	2.46	2.89	2.25	2.53	3.70	4.55
4th quarter	-5.7	90.0	-5.9	118.0	2.49	2.90	2.27	2.54	3.75	4.56
2000										
1st quarter	-17.7	33.9	-30.9	40.7	2.48	2.86	2.26	2.52	3.75	4.52
2nd quarter	5.9	84.5	10.4	112.1	2.48	2.87	2.27	2.53	3.76	4.55
3rd quarter	-1.1	58.4	-3.5	86.1	2.48	2.89	2.28	2.55	3.79	4.59
4th quarter	7.3	47.0	11.8	71.5	2.51	2.90	2.29	2.56	3.82	4.61
2001										
1st quarter	5.6	-36.2	10.0	-50.7	2.48	2.88	2.26	2.54	3.80	4.57
2nd quarter	-3.0	-8.6	-5.0	0.8	2.44	2.88	2.23	2.53	3.72	4.56
3rd quarter	1.8	-31.9	2.6	-46.8	2.41	2.88	2.20	2.53	3.69	4.56
4th quarter	-4.3	-76.6	-6.9	-108.8	2.33	2.81	2.13	2.47	3.55	4.44
2002										
1st quarter	4.1	-3.8	4.1	-10.2	2.31	2.81	2.11	2.47	3.54	4.46
2nd quarter	-10.3	31.5	-16.4	43.0	2.32	2.82	2.12	2.48	3.60	4.51
3rd quarter	-2.9	28.3	-5.6	31.5	2.35	2.82	2.14	2.48	3.65	4.51
4th quarter	-0.8	33.8	-3.0	44.1	2.38	2.84	2.17	2.50	3.71	4.56

[1] Before 1997, 2005 dollars; 1997 forward, 2009 dollars.

Table 1-8B. Inventory Change and Inventory-Sales Ratios: Historical Data—*Continued*

(Quarterly dollar data are at seasonally adjusted annual rates.)   **NIPA Tables 5.7.5B, 5.7.6B, 5.8.5B, 5.8.6B**

Year and quarter	Change in private inventories				Ratio, inventories at end of quarter to monthly rate of sales during the quarter					
	Billions of current dollars		Billions of chained dollars [1]		Total private inventories to final sales of domestic business		Nonfarm inventories to final sales of domestic business		Nonfarm inventories to final sales of goods and structures	
	Farm	Nonfarm	Farm	Nonfarm	Current dollars	Chained dollars[1]	Current dollars	Chained dollars[1]	Current dollars	Chained dollars[1]
2003										
1st quarter	2.8	23.2	4.9	35.1	2.42	2.83	2.21	2.49	3.78	4.54
2nd quarter	-1.4	-5.1	-1.5	-7.9	2.37	2.79	2.15	2.46	3.70	4.46
3rd quarter	0.9	-0.4	0.3	2.5	2.33	2.73	2.10	2.40	3.58	4.31
4th quarter	-2.1	38.4	-2.9	47.3	2.33	2.71	2.10	2.39	3.57	4.29
2004										
1st quarter	4.4	41.6	8.6	50.7	2.36	2.73	2.13	2.40	3.65	4.32
2nd quarter	18.4	55.5	23.7	77.1	2.39	2.74	2.15	2.41	3.69	4.34
3rd quarter	7.7	56.5	12.6	71.5	2.39	2.73	2.17	2.40	3.71	4.31
4th quarter	4.7	67.4	9.0	82.0	2.39	2.73	2.17	2.40	3.71	4.31
2005										
1st quarter	-6.7	109.2	-7.6	126.7	2.41	2.74	2.19	2.42	3.76	4.33
2nd quarter	0.9	27.9	1.2	23.0	2.37	2.71	2.16	2.39	3.70	4.27
3rd quarter	4.3	8.0	5.0	4.1	2.38	2.68	2.17	2.37	3.70	4.22
4th quarter	2.3	84.1	2.9	92.4	2.42	2.71	2.20	2.39	3.80	4.29
2006										
1st quarter	3.7	74.5	2.6	98.0	2.38	2.70	2.18	2.38	3.73	4.23
2nd quarter	-8.1	83.6	-11.0	97.5	2.42	2.71	2.22	2.40	3.81	4.28
3rd quarter	-6.3	85.1	-9.4	101.2	2.44	2.74	2.23	2.43	3.85	4.35
4th quarter	-3.6	47.1	-7.1	59.7	2.42	2.72	2.21	2.41	3.83	4.32
2007										
1st quarter	7.9	13.4	5.3	22.6	2.44	2.71	2.22	2.41	3.85	4.33
2nd quarter	-4.1	46.4	5.9	50.4	2.46	2.71	2.24	2.41	3.89	4.32
3rd quarter	-1.7	46.6	-15.5	54.3	2.46	2.71	2.24	2.41	3.91	4.33
4th quarter	0.4	26.9	-1.4	35.2	2.51	2.70	2.28	2.40	4.01	4.32
2008										
1st quarter	-8.6	-8.1	-6.1	6.5	2.61	2.72	2.37	2.42	4.21	4.38
2nd quarter	3.8	-26.1	2.1	-26.6	2.71	2.69	2.46	2.39	4.39	4.33
3rd quarter	4.1	-20.0	2.3	-20.7	2.68	2.72	2.44	2.42	4.37	4.39
4th quarter	-1.5	-60.8	-0.8	-85.0	2.50	2.76	2.28	2.46	4.14	4.56
2009										
1st quarter	-4.8	-146.2	-8.6	-168.1	2.43	2.75	2.21	2.44	4.02	4.56
2nd quarter	-6.3	-189.7	-9.5	-215.3	2.40	2.69	2.19	2.38	3.98	4.45
3rd quarter	-10.9	-193.1	-13.5	-228.3	2.35	2.60	2.14	2.30	3.91	4.29
4th quarter	-4.6	-47.4	-8.4	-49.0	2.38	2.59	2.17	2.29	4.00	4.28
2010										
1st quarter	-6.6	5.3	-14.0	6.1	2.42	2.59	2.21	2.29	4.10	4.29
2nd quarter	-11.7	48.4	-16.5	45.2	2.40	2.57	2.19	2.28	4.07	4.26
3rd quarter	-16.5	129.4	-20.6	141.9	2.45	2.60	2.24	2.31	4.18	4.35
4th quarter	-13.9	81.2	-20.0	87.7	2.49	2.58	2.26	2.31	4.20	4.31
2011										
1st quarter	-2.1	34.2	-2.1	34.3	2.60	2.59	2.34	2.31	4.37	4.33
2nd quarter	-5.7	66.8	-4.1	74.4	2.62	2.59	2.37	2.32	4.41	4.33
3rd quarter	-1.2	-10.8	-2.2	-15.4	2.58	2.56	2.33	2.29	4.32	4.26
4th quarter	0.7	103.2	-0.4	100.2	2.58	2.57	2.32	2.30	4.29	4.25
2012										
1st quarter	-6.4	86.7	-10.8	83.7	2.57	2.55	2.32	2.29	4.27	4.22
2nd quarter	-15.4	106.8	-16.4	103.3	2.54	2.56	2.30	2.31	4.22	4.23
3rd quarter	-29.9	114.3	-25.1	122.8	2.57	2.58	2.34	2.34	4.28	4.29
4th quarter	-23.1	51.8	-22.5	49.8	2.55	2.56	2.32	2.33	4.26	4.27
2013										
1st quarter	2.4	79.9	0.1	80.7	2.51	2.56	2.30	2.33	4.21	4.24
2nd quarter	15.0	72.7	12.4	73.7	2.51	2.58	2.30	2.35	4.21	4.27
3rd quarter	17.4	118.8	15.0	132.5	2.52	2.60	2.30	2.36	4.20	4.29
4th quarter	11.9	100.0	14.1	105.9	2.52	2.60	2.29	2.36	4.19	4.27
2014										
1st quarter	-3.5	55.7	-5.1	63.3	2.57	2.62	2.33	2.38	4.28	4.31
2nd quarter	0.0	96.3	-3.1	102.0	2.54	2.60	2.30	2.37	4.21	4.27
3rd quarter	-2.0	101.5	-1.5	108.1	2.51	2.59	2.28	2.36	4.15	4.25
4th quarter	-7.4	95.2	-4.4	87.0	2.47	2.59	2.24	2.36	4.10	4.26
2015										
1st quarter	5.9	169.7	4.8	173.1	2.45	2.63	2.22	2.40	4.10	4.36
2nd quarter	2.2	147.8	2.2	154.7	2.44	2.65	2.23	2.42	4.09	4.38
3rd quarter	-1.9	128.7	-1.5	126.4	2.41	2.67	2.22	2.44	4.07	4.41
4th quarter	-0.1	94.8	-1.2	91.8	2.40	2.68	2.21	2.46	4.09	4.45
2016										
1st quarter	-12.5	67.0	-11.8	69.7	2.39	2.67	2.20	2.45	4.07	4.43
2nd quarter	-3.2	33.6	-4.3	26.7	2.39	2.66	2.22	2.45	4.11	4.41
3rd quarter	-0.6	4.0	-1.7	-4.7	2.36	2.64	2.20	2.42	4.08	4.36
4th quarter	-7.4	64.2	-8.9	73.1	2.38	2.65	2.22	2.44	4.13	4.39
2017										
1st quarter	-5.4	0.8	-6.4	-7.5	2.38	2.61	2.21	2.41	4.11	4.32
2nd quarter	-5.1	26.2	-5.7	23.3	2.38	2.61	2.20	2.40	4.10	4.30
3rd quarter	-5.4	64.5	-6.9	88.2	2.36	2.61	2.21	2.41	4.09	4.30
4th quarter	-4.7	47.1	-6.8	50.5	2.36	2.58	2.20	2.38	4.07	4.25
2018										
1st quarter	-4.9	50.8	-4.9	67.5	2.37	2.58	2.21	2.38	4.11	4.24
2nd quarter	-6.1	30.3	-6.7	17.0	2.35	2.55	2.20	2.35	4.07	4.17
3rd quarter	-9.0	86.2	-10.9	108.5	2.36	2.57	2.22	2.38	4.14	4.24
4th quarter	-11.7	99.4	-14.1	97.8	2.36	2.58	2.22	2.39	4.14	4.27

[1]Before 1997, 2005 dollars; 1997 forward, 2009 dollars.

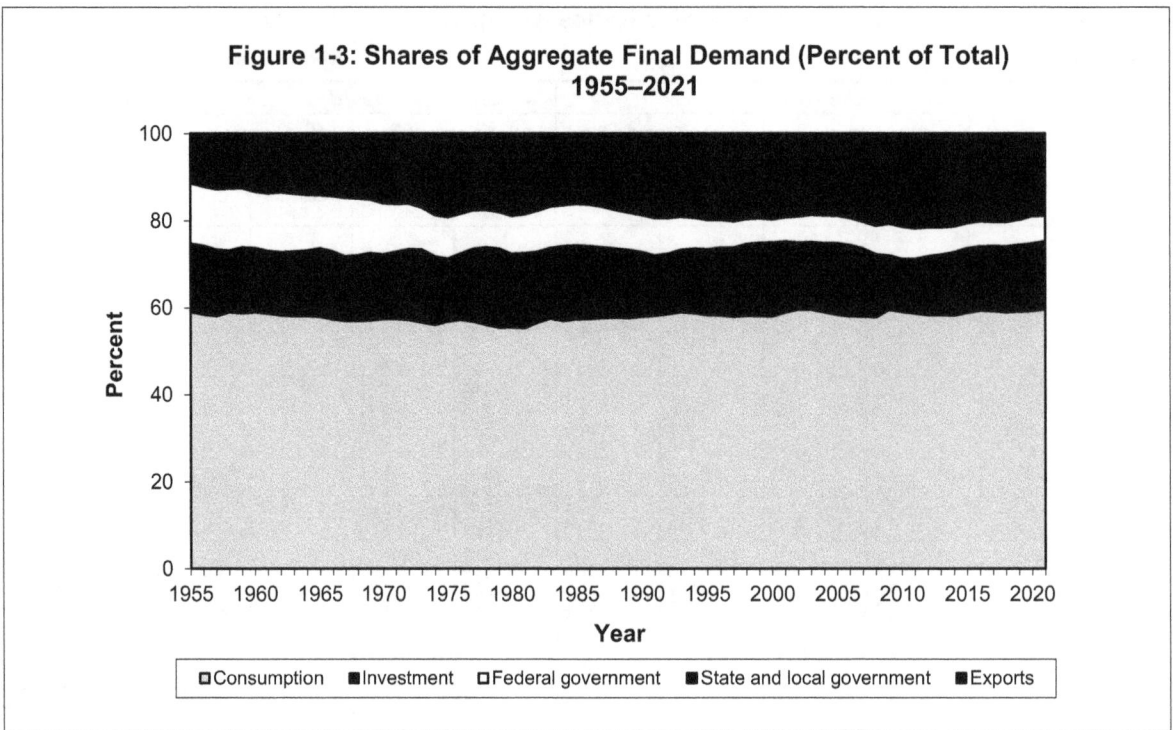

Figure 1-3: Shares of Aggregate Final Demand (Percent of Total) 1955–2021

- People often want to know how various sources of demand, especially consumption spending, affect GDP. Often, it is said that consumption "accounts for" about 70 percent, or sometimes two-thirds, of GDP. That is based on a NIPA table showing the components of GDP as a percent of total GDP. In such a calculation, personal consumption expenditures (PCE) amounted to 68.5 percent of total GDP in 2021, up from a range of 60 to 65 percent earlier in the postwar period and an increase from 2020 when it was 67.2 percent. (Table 1-1A)

- Is "amounted to" the same as "accounted for"? No, because the value of PCE includes imported goods and services—coffee, cocoa, and bananas; crude oil from the Middle East, transformed into gasoline; clothing, cars, and toys manufactured overseas—even the money that U.S. consumers spend when they travel. These imports included in PCE don't account for demand for U.S. GDP, which excludes imports; instead, they account for demand for GDP in China and other countries that export to us.

- It is not possible with NIPA data to precisely estimate and subtract out the import content of PCE, and so there is no way to precisely estimate PCE's contribution to GDP. What we can do is calculate PCE and the other sources of aggregate final demand for U.S. output as shares of total final demand; this is shown in Table 1-10 and Figure 1-3. These shares also approximate their contributions to GDP (excluding inventory change) if each final demand source has, in aggregate, about the same percentage import content as total GDP.

- The share of imports in the total supply of goods and services in the U.S. market rose from around 4 percent in the 1950s to a high of 14.9 percent in 2008. By 2021, the import share decreased to 12.9 percent. Although it was decline from 2008, it was an increase from 11.7 percent in 2020. (Table 1-9)

Table 1-9. Shares of Aggregate Supply

(Billions of dollars, quarterly dollar data are at seasonally adjusted rates, percents.)   **NIPA Table 1.1.5**

Year and quarter	Aggregate supply (billions of dollars)			Shares of aggregate supply (percent)	
	Total	GDP	Imports	Domestic production (GDP)	Imports
1955	442.7	425.5	17.2	96.1	3.9
1956	468.3	449.4	18.9	96.0	4.0
1957	493.9	474.0	19.9	96.0	4.0
1958	501.2	481.2	20.0	96.0	4.0
1959	544.0	521.7	22.3	95.9	4.1
1960	565.2	542.4	22.8	96.0	4.0
1961	584.9	562.2	22.7	96.1	3.9
1962	628.9	603.9	25.0	96.0	4.0
1963	663.6	637.5	26.1	96.1	3.9
1964	712.6	684.5	28.1	96.1	3.9
1965	773.8	742.3	31.5	95.9	4.1
1966	850.5	813.4	37.1	95.6	4.4
1967	899.9	860.0	39.9	95.6	4.4
1968	987.3	940.7	46.6	95.3	4.7
1969	1 068.1	1 017.6	50.5	95.3	4.7
1970	1 129.1	1 073.3	55.8	95.1	4.9
1971	1 227.2	1 164.9	62.3	94.9	5.1
1972	1 353.3	1 279.1	74.2	94.5	5.5
1973	1 516.6	1 425.4	91.2	94.0	6.0
1974	1 672.7	1 545.2	127.5	92.4	7.6
1975	1 807.6	1 684.9	122.7	93.2	6.8
1976	2 024.5	1 873.4	151.1	92.5	7.5
1977	2 264.2	2 081.8	182.4	91.9	8.1
1978	2 563.9	2 351.6	212.3	91.7	8.3
1979	2 880.0	2 627.3	252.7	91.2	8.8
1980	3 151.1	2 857.3	293.8	90.7	9.3
1981	3 524.8	3 207.0	317.8	91.0	9.0
1982	3 647.0	3 343.8	303.2	91.7	8.3
1983	3 962.6	3 634.0	328.6	91.7	8.3
1984	4 442.7	4 037.6	405.1	90.9	9.1
1985	4 756.2	4 339.0	417.2	91.2	8.8
1986	5 032.5	4 579.6	452.9	91.0	9.0
1987	5 363.9	4 855.2	508.7	90.5	9.5
1988	5 790.4	5 236.4	554.0	90.4	9.6
1989	6 232.6	5 641.6	591.0	90.5	9.5
1990	6 592.8	5 963.1	629.7	90.4	9.6
1991	6 781.6	6 158.1	623.5	90.8	9.2
1992	7 188.1	6 520.3	667.8	90.7	9.3
1993	7 578.6	6 858.6	720.0	90.5	9.5
1994	8 100.6	7 287.2	813.4	90.0	10.0
1995	8 542.3	7 639.7	902.6	89.4	10.6
1996	9 037.1	8 073.1	964.0	89.3	10.7
1997	9 633.4	8 577.6	1 055.8	89.0	11.0
1998	10 178.5	9 062.8	1 115.7	89.0	11.0
1999	10 883.7	9 631.2	1 252.5	88.5	11.5
2000	11 728.2	10 251.0	1 477.2	87.4	12.6
2001	11 985.5	10 581.9	1 403.6	88.3	11.7
2002	12 366.8	10 929.1	1 437.7	88.4	11.6
2003	13 013.6	11 456.5	1 557.1	88.0	12.0
2004	14 027.7	12 217.2	1 810.5	87.1	12.9
2005	15 080.7	13 039.2	2 041.5	86.5	13.5
2006	16 072.2	13 815.6	2 256.6	86.0	14.0
2007	16 869.4	14 474.2	2 395.2	85.8	14.2
2008	17 346.1	14 769.9	2 576.2	85.1	14.9
2009	16 480.0	14 478.1	2 001.9	87.9	12.1
2010	17 438.6	15 049.0	2 389.6	86.3	13.7
2011	18 295.2	15 599.7	2 695.5	85.3	14.7
2012	19 023.3	16 254.0	2 769.3	85.4	14.6
2013	19 609.6	16 843.2	2 766.4	85.9	14.1
2014	20 438.1	17 550.7	2 887.4	85.9	14.1
2015	21 000.9	18 206.0	2 794.9	86.7	13.3
2016	21 433.5	18 695.1	2 738.4	87.2	12.8
2017	22 403.3	19 479.6	2 923.7	86.9	13.1
2018	23 656.9	20 527.2	3 129.7	86.8	13.2
2019	24 488.6	21 372.6	3 116.0	87.3	12.7
2020	23 668.3	20 893.7	2 774.6	88.3	11.7
2021	26 392.6	22 996.1	3 396.5	87.1	12.9
2019					
1st quarter	24 132.6	21 001.6	3 131.0	87.0	13.0
2nd quarter	24 455.0	21 289.3	3 165.7	87.1	12.9
3rd quarter	24 631.1	21 505.0	3 126.1	87.3	12.7
4th quarter	24 735.6	21 694.5	3 041.1	87.7	12.3
2020					
1st quarter	24 408.7	21 481.4	2 927.3	88.0	12.0
2nd quarter	21 824.1	19 477.4	2 346.7	89.2	10.8
3rd quarter	23 943.9	21 138.6	2 805.3	88.3	11.7
4th quarter	24 496.7	21 477.6	3 019.1	87.7	12.3
2021					
1st quarter	25 222.7	22 038.2	3 184.5	87.4	12.6
2nd quarter	26 084.2	22 741.0	3 343.2	87.2	12.8
3rd quarter	26 634.6	23 202.3	3 432.3	87.1	12.9
4th quarter	27 628.7	24 002.8	3 625.9	86.9	13.1

Table 1-10. Shares of Aggregate Final Demand

(Billions of dollars, quarterly dollar data are at seasonally adjusted rates, percents.)   NIPA Table 1.1.5

Year and quarter	Aggregate final demand (billions of dollars)							Shares of aggregate final demand (percent)					
	Total	Consumption (PCE)	Nonresidential fixed investment	Residential investment	Exports	Government consumption and gross investment		PCE	Nonresidential investment	Residential investment	Exports	Federal government	State and local government
						Federal	State and local						
1955	437.7	258.3	43.4	25.4	17.7	61.0	31.9	59.0	9.9	5.8	4.0	13.9	7.3
1956	464.3	271.1	49.7	24.0	21.3	63.1	35.1	58.4	10.7	5.2	4.6	13.6	7.6
1957	493.2	286.3	53.1	22.6	24.0	68.5	38.7	58.0	10.8	4.6	4.9	13.9	7.8
1958	501.6	295.6	48.5	22.8	20.6	71.5	42.6	58.9	9.7	4.5	4.1	14.3	8.5
1959	540.0	317.1	53.1	28.6	22.7	73.6	44.9	58.7	9.8	5.3	4.2	13.6	8.3
1960	562.0	331.2	56.4	26.9	27.0	72.9	47.6	58.9	10.0	4.8	4.8	13.0	8.5
1961	582.0	341.5	56.6	27.0	27.6	77.4	51.9	58.7	9.7	4.6	4.7	13.3	8.9
1962	622.8	362.6	61.2	29.6	29.1	85.5	54.8	58.2	9.8	4.8	4.7	13.7	8.8
1963	658.0	382.0	64.8	32.9	31.1	87.9	59.3	58.1	9.8	5.0	4.7	13.4	9.0
1964	707.7	410.6	72.2	35.1	35.0	90.3	64.5	58.0	10.2	5.0	4.9	12.8	9.1
1965	764.6	443.0	85.2	35.2	37.1	93.2	70.9	57.9	11.1	4.6	4.9	12.2	9.3
1966	836.9	479.9	97.2	33.4	40.9	106.6	78.9	57.3	11.6	4.0	4.9	12.7	9.4
1967	890.0	506.7	99.2	33.6	43.5	120.0	87.0	56.9	11.1	3.8	4.9	13.5	9.8
1968	978.3	556.9	107.7	40.2	47.9	128.0	97.6	56.9	11.0	4.1	4.9	13.1	10.0
1969	1 058.9	603.6	120.0	44.4	51.9	131.2	107.8	57.0	11.3	4.2	4.9	12.4	10.2
1970	1 127.0	646.7	124.6	43.4	59.7	132.8	119.8	57.4	11.1	3.9	5.3	11.8	10.6
1971	1 219.0	699.9	130.4	58.2	63.0	134.5	133.0	57.4	10.7	4.8	5.2	11.0	10.9
1972	1 344.1	768.2	146.6	72.4	70.8	141.6	144.5	57.2	10.9	5.4	5.3	10.5	10.8
1973	1 500.7	849.6	172.7	78.3	95.3	146.2	158.6	56.6	11.5	5.2	6.4	9.7	10.6
1974	1 658.8	930.2	191.1	69.5	126.7	158.8	182.5	56.1	11.5	4.2	7.6	9.6	11.0
1975	1 813.8	1 030.5	196.8	66.7	138.7	173.7	207.4	56.8	10.9	3.7	7.6	9.6	11.4
1976	2 007.5	1 147.7	219.3	86.8	149.5	184.8	219.4	57.2	10.9	4.3	7.4	9.2	10.9
1977	2 241.9	1 274.0	259.1	115.2	159.3	200.3	234.0	56.8	11.6	5.1	7.1	8.9	10.4
1978	2 538.1	1 422.3	314.6	138.0	186.9	218.9	257.4	56.0	12.4	5.4	7.4	8.6	10.1
1979	2 861.9	1 585.4	373.8	147.8	230.1	240.6	284.2	55.4	13.1	5.2	8.0	8.4	9.9
1980	3 157.5	1 750.7	406.9	129.5	280.8	274.9	314.7	55.4	12.9	4.1	8.9	8.7	10.0
1981	3 495.0	1 934.0	472.9	128.5	305.2	314.0	340.4	55.3	13.5	3.7	8.7	9.0	9.7
1982	3 661.8	2 071.3	485.1	110.8	283.2	348.3	363.1	56.6	13.2	3.0	7.7	9.5	9.9
1983	3 968.5	2 281.6	482.2	161.1	277.0	382.4	384.2	57.5	12.2	4.1	7.0	9.6	9.7
1984	4 377.3	2 492.3	564.3	190.4	302.4	411.8	416.1	56.9	12.9	4.3	6.9	9.4	9.5
1985	4 734.4	2 712.8	607.8	200.1	303.2	452.9	457.6	57.3	12.8	4.2	6.4	9.6	9.7
1986	5 026.0	2 886.3	607.8	234.8	321.0	481.7	494.4	57.4	12.1	4.7	6.4	9.6	9.8
1987	5 336.7	3 076.3	615.2	249.8	363.9	502.8	528.7	57.6	11.5	4.7	6.8	9.4	9.9
1988	5 771.9	3 330.0	662.3	256.2	444.6	511.4	567.4	57.7	11.5	4.4	7.7	8.9	9.8
1989	6 205.0	3 576.8	716.0	256.0	504.3	534.1	617.8	57.6	11.5	4.1	8.1	8.6	10.0
1990	6 578.4	3 809.0	739.2	239.7	551.9	562.4	676.2	57.9	11.2	3.6	8.4	8.5	10.3
1991	6 782.0	3 943.4	723.6	221.2	594.9	582.9	716.0	58.1	10.7	3.3	8.8	8.6	10.6
1992	7 171.8	4 197.6	741.9	254.7	633.1	588.5	756.0	58.5	10.3	3.6	8.8	8.2	10.5
1993	7 557.8	4 452.0	799.2	286.8	654.8	580.2	784.8	58.9	10.6	3.8	8.7	7.7	10.4
1994	8 036.9	4 721.0	868.9	323.8	720.9	574.7	827.6	58.7	10.8	4.0	9.0	7.2	10.3
1995	8 511.1	4 962.6	962.2	324.1	812.8	576.7	872.7	58.3	11.3	3.8	9.5	6.8	10.3
1996	9 006.4	5 244.6	1 043.2	358.1	867.6	579.2	913.7	58.2	11.6	4.0	9.6	6.4	10.1
1997	9 562.4	5 536.8	1 149.1	375.6	953.8	583.3	963.8	57.9	12.0	3.9	10.0	6.1	10.1
1998	10 114.7	5 877.2	1 254.1	418.8	953.0	585.5	1 026.1	58.1	12.4	4.1	9.4	5.8	10.1
1999	10 822.9	6 283.8	1 364.5	461.8	992.9	610.7	1 109.2	58.1	12.6	4.3	9.2	5.6	10.2
2000	11 673.6	6 767.2	1 498.4	485.4	1 096.1	633.1	1 193.4	58.0	12.8	4.2	9.4	5.4	10.2
2001	12 023.8	7 073.8	1 460.1	513.1	1 026.8	670.2	1 279.8	58.8	12.1	4.3	8.5	5.6	10.6
2002	12 346.8	7 348.9	1 352.8	557.6	998.0	743.1	1 346.4	59.5	11.0	4.5	8.1	6.0	10.9
2003	12 999.5	7 740.7	1 375.9	637.1	1 035.2	826.8	1 383.8	59.5	10.6	4.9	8.0	6.4	10.6
2004	13 967.4	8 232.0	1 467.4	749.8	1 176.4	892.1	1 446.0	59.0	10.5	5.4	8.4	6.4	10.4
2005	15 023.2	8 769.1	1 621.0	856.2	1 301.6	947.8	1 527.5	58.4	10.8	5.7	8.7	6.3	10.2
2006	16 003.3	9 277.2	1 793.8	838.2	1 470.2	1 001.2	1 622.7	58.0	11.2	5.2	9.2	6.3	10.1
2007	16 835.5	9 746.6	1 948.6	690.5	1 659.3	1 051.0	1 739.5	57.9	11.6	4.1	9.9	6.2	10.3
2008	17 375.4	10 050.1	1 990.9	516.0	1 835.3	1 152.0	1 831.1	57.8	11.5	3.0	10.6	6.6	10.5
2009	16 630.8	9 891.2	1 690.4	390.0	1 582.8	1 220.8	1 855.6	59.5	10.2	2.3	9.5	7.3	11.2
2010	17 384.7	10 260.3	1 735.0	376.6	1 857.2	1 300.2	1 855.4	59.0	10.0	2.2	10.7	7.5	10.7
2011	18 249.1	10 698.9	1 907.5	378.8	2 115.9	1 299.8	1 848.2	58.6	10.5	2.1	11.6	7.1	10.1
2012	18 952.1	11 047.4	2 118.5	432.0	2 217.7	1 287.0	1 849.5	58.3	11.2	2.3	11.7	6.8	9.8
2013	19 505.1	11 363.5	2 211.5	510.0	2 287.0	1 227.2	1 905.9	58.3	11.3	2.6	11.7	6.3	9.8
2014	20 354.2	11 847.7	2 400.1	560.2	2 377.4	1 216.0	1 952.8	58.2	11.8	2.8	11.7	6.0	9.6
2015	20 864.2	12 263.5	2 466.6	633.8	2 268.7	1 221.8	2 009.8	58.8	11.8	3.0	10.9	5.9	9.6
2016	21 397.1	12 693.3	2 469.3	699.4	2 232.1	1 234.5	2 068.5	59.3	11.5	3.3	10.4	5.8	9.7
2017	22 373.9	13 239.1	2 591.6	760.3	2 383.8	1 262.8	2 136.3	59.2	11.6	3.4	10.7	5.6	9.5
2018	23 598.1	13 913.5	2 780.6	798.5	2 533.5	1 339.0	2 233.0	59.0	11.8	3.4	10.7	5.7	9.5
2019	24 414.9	14 428.7	2 938.7	813.9	2 519.7	1 414.9	2 299.0	59.1	12.0	3.3	10.3	5.8	9.4
2020	23 728.0	14 047.6	2 799.6	897.8	2 123.4	1 501.8	2 357.8	59.2	11.8	3.8	8.9	6.3	9.9
2021	26 412.4	15 741.6	3 053.7	1 086.1	2 478.3	1 565.0	2 487.7	59.6	11.6	4.1	9.4	5.9	9.4
2019													
1st quarter	24 014.1	14 155.6	2 886.9	796.5	2 524.6	1 387.0	2 263.5	58.9	12.0	3.3	10.5	5.8	9.4
2nd quarter	24 366.6	14 375.7	2 946.1	808.5	2 533.4	1 406.9	2 296.0	59.0	12.1	3.3	10.4	5.8	9.4
3rd quarter	24 564.1	14 529.5	2 969.3	821.9	2 512.1	1 424.1	2 307.2	59.1	12.1	3.3	10.2	5.8	9.4
4th quarter	24 714.9	14 653.9	2 952.6	828.8	2 508.7	1 441.7	2 329.2	59.3	11.9	3.4	10.2	5.8	9.4
2020													
1st quarter	24 429.2	14 439.1	2 900.1	872.9	2 385.5	1 454.7	2 376.9	59.1	11.9	3.6	9.8	6.0	9.7
2nd quarter	22 114.1	12 989.7	2 659.1	797.8	1 807.9	1 525.0	2 334.6	58.7	12.0	3.6	8.2	6.9	10.6
3rd quarter	23 928.8	14 293.8	2 776.6	917.2	2 079.6	1 515.1	2 346.5	59.7	11.6	3.8	8.7	6.3	9.8
4th quarter	24 439.5	14 467.6	2 862.7	1 003.2	2 220.7	1 512.3	2 373.0	59.2	11.7	4.1	9.1	6.2	9.7
2021													
1st quarter	25 316.8	15 005.4	2 956.7	1 065.5	2 311.9	1 568.6	2 408.7	59.3	11.7	4.2	9.1	6.2	9.5
2nd quarter	26 258.5	15 681.7	3 029.2	1 070.2	2 461.5	1 563.3	2 452.6	59.7	11.5	4.1	9.4	6.0	9.3
3rd quarter	26 694.8	15 964.9	3 073.9	1 085.9	2 485.2	1 562.0	2 522.9	59.8	11.5	4.1	9.3	5.9	9.5
4th quarter	27 379.4	16 314.2	3 154.9	1 122.9	2 654.5	1 566.2	2 566.7	59.6	11.5	4.1	9.7	5.7	9.4

SECTION 1B: INCOME AND VALUE ADDED

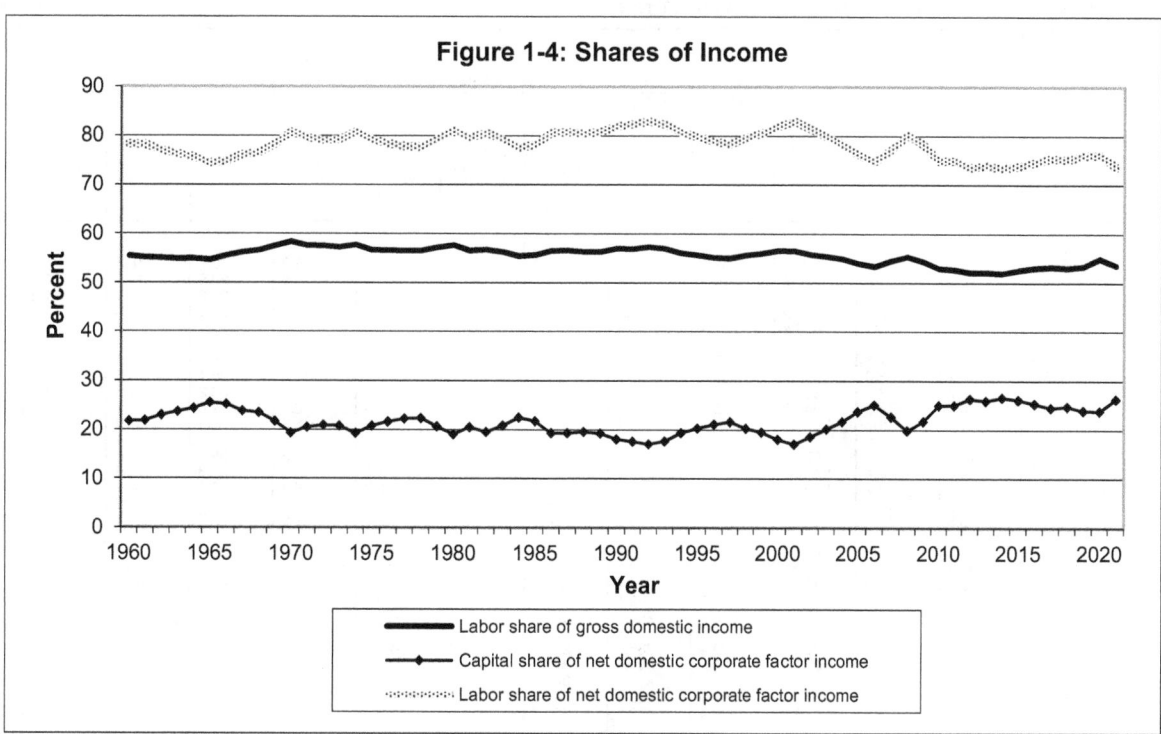

Figure 1-4: Shares of Income

- Employee compensation has fallen since the early 1970s to a record low of 52.0 percent of gross domestic income, in 2014, as shown in the middle line in Figure 1-4. In 2021, the share grew to 53.6 percent. One factor in this decline has been a rising share of output required to replace used-up capital ("consumption of fixed capital"), reflecting increased use of capital per unit of production. In addition, the "net operating surplus" which is largely profits, interest, and proprietor's income, reached its peak in 2014 as a percent of total net factor income but declined to 23.9 percent by 2020. However, it increased to 26.3 percent of net factor income in 2021. (Tables 1-12 and 1-16)

- Narrowing the focus to the corporate business sector, net income shares become clearer. (Proprietor's, i.e. unincorporated business; income includes a labor compensation component of uncertain size.) Total net factor income (that is, net of capital consumption) can be completely attributed to either labor or capital. These shares are also charted in Figure 1-4. Between 1959 and 2004, the shares vary cyclically but seem stable over time, averaging around 78 percent for labor and 22 percent for capital. Since then, they have broken out of that range. (Tables 1-14 and 1-16)

Table 1-11. Relation of Gross Domestic Product, Gross and Net National Product, National Income, and Personal Income

(Billions of dollars, quarterly data are at seasonally adjusted annual rates.)   NIPA Table 1.7.5

Year and quarter	Gross domestic product	Plus: Income receipts from the rest of the world	Less: Income payments to the rest of the world	Equals: Gross national product	Less: Consumption of fixed capital — Total	Private Total	Domestic business Total	Capital consumption allowances	Less: Capital consumption adjustment	House-holds and institutions	Government Total	General government	Government enter-prises	Equals: Net national product
1960	542.4	4.9	1.8	545.5	67.9	48.2	40.0	39.7	-0.3	8.2	19.7	18.6	1.1	477.6
1961	562.2	5.3	1.8	565.7	70.6	49.8	41.3	41.7	0.4	8.5	20.8	19.7	1.1	495.1
1962	603.9	5.9	1.8	608.0	74.1	51.8	42.9	46.6	3.6	8.8	22.3	21.1	1.2	533.9
1963	637.5	6.5	2.1	641.9	78.0	54.2	44.9	49.9	5.0	9.3	23.9	22.6	1.3	563.9
1964	684.5	7.2	2.3	689.4	82.4	57.3	47.4	53.2	5.8	9.9	25.1	23.7	1.4	607.0
1965	742.3	7.9	2.6	747.6	88.0	61.6	50.9	57.0	6.1	10.7	26.4	25.0	1.5	659.6
1966	813.4	8.1	3.0	818.5	95.3	67.2	55.6	61.9	6.2	11.5	28.1	26.5	1.6	723.2
1967	860.0	8.7	3.3	865.4	103.6	73.3	60.9	66.9	6.0	12.4	30.2	28.5	1.8	761.8
1968	940.7	10.1	4.0	946.7	113.4	80.6	67.0	72.5	5.6	13.6	32.8	30.8	2.0	833.4
1969	1 017.6	11.8	5.7	1 023.7	124.9	89.4	74.2	79.7	5.5	15.2	35.5	33.3	2.2	898.8
1970	1 073.3	12.8	6.4	1 079.7	136.8	98.3	81.8	85.9	4.1	16.5	38.6	36.1	2.5	942.9
1971	1 164.9	14.0	6.4	1 172.4	148.9	107.6	89.4	92.3	2.9	18.2	41.3	38.5	2.8	1 023.5
1972	1 279.1	16.3	7.7	1 287.7	161.0	117.5	97.2	102.3	5.2	20.3	43.5	40.4	3.1	1 126.7
1973	1 425.4	23.5	10.9	1 438.0	178.7	131.5	108.2	111.9	3.7	23.3	47.2	43.7	3.5	1 259.3
1974	1 545.2	29.8	14.3	1 560.8	206.9	153.2	126.1	123.9	-2.2	27.0	53.7	49.4	4.3	1 353.9
1975	1 684.9	28.0	15.0	1 697.9	238.5	178.8	147.9	135.9	-12.0	30.9	59.7	54.6	5.1	1 459.4
1976	1 873.4	32.4	15.5	1 890.3	260.2	196.5	162.2	147.4	-14.8	34.3	63.7	58.2	5.5	1 630.0
1977	2 081.8	37.2	16.9	2 102.1	289.8	221.1	181.5	167.0	-14.5	39.6	68.7	62.7	6.0	1 812.3
1978	2 351.6	46.3	24.7	2 373.2	327.2	252.1	205.5	189.4	-16.2	46.6	75.1	68.5	6.6	2 046.0
1979	2 627.3	68.3	36.4	2 659.3	373.9	290.7	236.4	216.1	-20.2	54.4	83.1	75.6	7.5	2 285.4
1980	2 857.3	79.1	44.9	2 891.5	428.4	335.0	272.8	245.8	-26.9	62.2	93.5	84.7	8.7	2 463.1
1981	3 207.0	92.0	59.1	3 240.0	487.2	381.9	313.5	301.2	-12.3	68.5	105.3	95.4	9.9	2 752.7
1982	3 343.8	101.0	64.5	3 380.3	537.0	420.4	347.5	343.1	-4.4	72.9	116.6	105.7	10.8	2 843.3
1983	3 634.0	101.9	64.8	3 671.1	562.6	438.8	362.8	385.6	22.8	76.0	123.8	112.4	11.4	3 108.5
1984	4 037.6	121.9	85.6	4 073.9	598.4	463.5	382.7	435.6	52.9	80.9	134.9	122.8	12.1	3 475.5
1985	4 339.0	112.7	87.3	4 364.3	640.1	496.4	410.3	493.5	83.2	86.2	143.7	130.9	12.8	3 724.2
1986	4 579.6	111.3	94.4	4 596.6	685.3	531.6	438.1	512.0	73.9	93.4	153.7	140.1	13.6	3 911.3
1987	4 855.2	123.3	105.8	4 872.7	730.4	566.3	464.5	533.1	68.6	101.8	164.1	149.6	14.5	4 142.3
1988	5 236.4	152.1	129.5	5 259.1	784.5	607.9	499.2	563.7	64.5	108.8	176.6	161.1	15.5	4 474.6
1989	5 641.6	177.7	152.9	5 666.4	838.3	649.6	532.6	589.5	56.9	117.0	188.6	172.0	16.6	4 828.1
1990	5 963.1	188.8	154.2	5 997.8	888.5	688.4	564.6	596.0	31.4	123.8	200.1	182.3	17.8	5 109.3
1991	6 158.1	168.4	136.8	6 189.7	932.4	721.5	592.3	611.6	19.3	129.2	210.9	192.1	18.8	5 257.3
1992	6 520.3	152.1	121.0	6 551.4	960.2	742.9	608.2	628.4	20.2	134.7	217.4	197.6	19.8	5 591.2
1993	6 858.6	155.6	124.4	6 889.7	1 003.5	778.2	634.2	658.9	24.7	144.0	225.3	204.2	21.1	5 886.2
1994	7 287.2	184.5	161.6	7 310.2	1 055.6	822.5	669.0	701.6	32.6	153.5	233.1	210.9	22.2	6 254.6
1995	7 639.7	229.8	201.9	7 667.7	1 122.4	880.7	717.8	753.9	36.1	162.9	241.7	218.2	23.5	6 545.3
1996	8 073.1	246.4	215.5	8 104.0	1 175.3	929.1	758.5	808.3	49.8	170.6	246.2	221.6	24.6	6 928.7
1997	8 577.6	280.1	256.8	8 600.9	1 239.3	987.8	807.9	877.0	69.2	179.9	251.6	225.9	25.7	7 361.5
1998	9 062.8	286.8	269.4	9 080.2	1 309.7	1 052.2	860.1	941.4	81.3	192.1	257.6	230.8	26.8	7 770.5
1999	9 631.2	324.6	293.7	9 662.1	1 398.9	1 132.2	924.0	1 023.8	99.8	208.2	266.7	238.3	28.4	8 263.1
2000	10 251.0	390.6	352.2	10 289.4	1 511.2	1 231.5	1 004.6	1 096.1	91.5	227.0	279.7	249.4	30.3	8 778.2
2001	10 581.9	339.6	289.3	10 632.3	1 599.5	1 311.7	1 064.9	1 180.1	115.2	246.8	287.8	256.0	31.8	9 032.8
2002	10 929.1	335.8	290.0	10 974.9	1 658.0	1 361.8	1 098.8	1 283.9	185.1	263.0	296.2	262.9	33.2	9 316.9
2003	11 456.5	377.4	318.9	11 514.9	1 719.1	1 411.9	1 125.4	1 303.5	178.1	286.6	307.1	272.2	34.9	9 795.9
2004	12 217.2	464.7	388.0	12 293.9	1 821.8	1 497.1	1 178.8	1 332.0	153.2	318.3	324.7	286.9	37.9	10 472.1
2005	13 039.2	569.2	494.5	13 114.0	1 971.0	1 622.6	1 266.4	1 169.5	-97.0	356.2	348.4	307.0	41.4	11 143.0
2006	13 815.6	702.6	656.2	13 862.0	2 124.1	1 751.8	1 362.6	1 245.1	-117.4	389.2	372.3	327.6	44.7	11 737.9
2007	14 474.2	850.2	754.5	14 569.9	2 252.8	1 852.5	1 446.7	1 326.8	-119.8	405.8	400.3	352.1	48.2	12 317.1
2008	14 769.9	855.2	710.0	14 915.1	2 358.8	1 931.8	1 524.9	1 584.1	59.3	407.0	427.0	375.7	51.3	12 556.2
2009	14 478.1	689.3	539.0	14 628.3	2 371.5	1 928.7	1 531.2	1 562.1	30.9	397.5	442.8	389.8	53.0	12 256.8
2010	15 049.0	760.0	554.3	15 254.6	2 390.9	1 933.8	1 537.1	1 605.9	68.8	396.7	457.2	402.2	55.0	12 863.7
2011	15 599.7	827.9	589.9	15 837.7	2 474.5	1 997.3	1 595.1	1 831.3	236.2	402.2	477.2	419.3	57.8	13 363.2
2012	16 254.0	827.4	594.7	16 486.7	2 576.0	2 082.4	1 670.4	1 665.9	-4.5	412.0	493.6	433.0	60.7	13 910.7
2013	16 843.2	847.2	616.9	17 073.5	2 681.2	2 176.6	1 738.8	1 753.6	14.8	437.8	504.6	441.8	62.9	14 392.3
2014	17 550.7	881.6	646.4	17 785.9	2 815.0	2 298.5	1 831.2	1 866.4	35.2	467.3	516.6	451.4	65.2	14 970.9
2015	18 206.0	860.8	640.4	18 426.4	2 911.4	2 388.5	1 903.1	1 981.9	78.8	485.4	522.9	455.8	67.1	15 515.0
2016	18 695.1	893.5	661.5	18 927.1	2 987.1	2 459.9	1 950.9	2 075.3	124.3	509.0	527.1	458.1	69.0	15 940.0
2017	19 479.6	1 032.7	738.2	19 774.2	3 118.2	2 576.1	2 037.6	2 303.3	265.6	538.4	542.1	470.0	72.1	16 656.0
2018	20 527.2	1 142.1	847.9	20 821.3	3 273.4	2 708.1	2 133.3	2 566.2	433.0	574.8	565.4	489.3	76.1	17 547.9
2019	21 372.6	1 160.3	893.9	21 639.0	3 435.6	2 848.6	2 248.3	2 712.2	463.9	600.3	586.9	506.7	80.3	18 203.4
2020	20 893.7	992.9	770.6	21 116.1	3 575.9	2 969.6	2 338.6	2 754.7	416.1	631.0	606.4	523.5	82.8	17 540.2
2021	22 996.1	1 145.0	892.5	23 248.5	3 847.9	3 202.3	2 495.9	2 889.2	393.3	706.4	645.5	557.0	88.5	19 400.7
2019														
1st quarter	21 001.6	1 140.8	888.1	21 254.3	3 378.0	2 798.1	2 207.4	2 629.4	421.9	590.6	580.0	501.1	78.9	17 876.3
2nd quarter	21 289.3	1 184.4	908.8	21 564.9	3 421.0	2 836.1	2 239.5	2 695.6	456.1	596.5	584.9	504.9	80.0	18 143.9
3rd quarter	21 505.0	1 168.8	893.0	21 780.8	3 457.9	2 867.9	2 264.0	2 745.7	481.7	604.0	589.9	509.1	80.8	18 322.9
4th quarter	21 694.5	1 147.3	885.8	21 956.0	3 485.5	2 892.5	2 282.4	2 778.1	495.8	610.1	593.0	511.6	81.4	18 470.5
2020														
1st quarter	21 481.4	1 048.9	809.0	21 721.3	3 522.3	2 924.5	2 308.7	2 735.2	426.6	615.9	597.8	515.8	82.0	18 198.9
2nd quarter	19 477.4	883.5	711.5	19 649.4	3 550.9	2 949.0	2 327.5	2 744.7	417.2	621.5	601.9	519.8	82.1	16 098.6
3rd quarter	21 138.6	996.1	769.2	21 365.4	3 591.0	2 981.5	2 345.3	2 757.6	412.3	636.2	609.6	526.4	83.2	17 774.4
4th quarter	21 477.6	1 043.2	792.5	21 728.2	3 639.4	3 023.3	2 372.9	2 781.3	408.5	650.4	616.1	532.1	84.0	18 088.8
2021														
1st quarter	22 038.2	1 081.6	846.7	22 273.1	3 696.0	3 071.2	2 401.1	2 844.0	442.9	670.1	624.7	539.8	85.0	18 577.1
2nd quarter	22 741.0	1 112.4	882.0	22 971.4	3 787.9	3 150.1	2 455.6	2 873.5	417.9	694.0	637.8	550.5	87.3	19 183.5
3rd quarter	23 202.3	1 184.1	916.4	23 470.0	3 895.8	3 244.4	2 524.3	2 904.0	379.7	720.0	651.5	561.9	89.6	19 574.2
4th quarter	24 002.8	1 202.0	925.1	24 279.7	4 011.8	3 343.7	2 602.6	2 935.2	332.5	741.0	668.1	576.0	92.1	20 267.9

Table 1-12. Gross Domestic Income by Type of Income

(Billions of dollars, quarterly data are at seasonally adjusted annual rates.)

NIPA Tables 1.10

Year and quarter	Gross domestic income	Compensation of employees			Taxes on production and imports	Less: Subsidies	Net operating surplus					
		Total	Wages and salaries	Supple-ments to wages and salaries			Total	Private enterprises				
								Total	Net interest and miscel-laneous payments, domestic industries	Business current transfer payments, net	Proprietors' income with IVA and CCAdj	Rental income of persons with CCAdj
1960	543.7	301.4	273.0	28.4	44.5	1.1	130.9	130.5	10.1	1.7	50.6	16.5
1961	563.1	310.6	280.7	29.9	47.0	2.0	137.0	136.7	11.7	1.9	53.2	17.2
1962	603.9	332.3	299.5	32.8	50.4	2.3	149.4	149.0	13.4	2.1	55.2	18.0
1963	638.9	350.5	314.9	35.6	53.4	2.2	159.3	158.5	14.4	2.5	56.4	18.7
1964	684.5	376.0	337.8	38.2	57.3	2.7	171.6	170.7	16.5	3.0	59.1	18.8
1965	741.5	405.4	363.8	41.7	60.7	3.0	190.4	189.6	18.6	3.5	63.7	19.3
1966	808.3	449.2	400.3	48.9	63.2	3.9	204.5	204.2	21.3	3.4	67.9	19.9
1967	856.6	481.8	429.0	52.8	67.9	3.8	207.2	206.9	24.3	3.6	69.5	20.3
1968	937.5	530.7	472.0	58.8	76.4	4.2	221.2	220.7	26.5	4.2	73.8	20.1
1969	1 016.0	584.4	518.3	66.1	83.9	4.5	227.4	227.2	33.2	4.8	77.0	20.3
1970	1 068.0	623.3	551.5	71.8	91.4	4.8	221.2	222.2	40.2	4.4	77.8	20.7
1971	1 155.3	665.0	584.5	80.4	100.5	4.7	245.6	247.1	44.4	4.2	83.9	21.8
1972	1 271.9	731.3	638.8	92.5	107.9	6.6	278.3	279.2	49.0	4.8	95.1	22.7
1973	1 419.2	812.7	708.8	103.9	117.2	5.2	315.9	317.8	58.0	5.7	112.5	23.1
1974	1 537.8	887.7	772.3	115.4	124.9	3.3	321.6	324.0	73.6	6.8	112.2	23.2
1975	1 671.6	947.3	814.9	132.4	135.3	4.5	355.0	359.0	85.3	9.0	118.2	22.3
1976	1 852.8	1 048.4	899.8	148.6	146.4	5.1	402.9	405.3	87.1	9.1	131.0	20.3
1977	2 062.4	1 165.9	994.2	171.7	159.7	7.1	454.1	457.1	101.9	8.1	144.5	15.9
1978	2 328.3	1 316.9	1 120.7	196.2	170.9	8.9	522.3	524.6	116.0	10.4	166.0	16.5
1979	2 582.3	1 477.3	1 253.4	223.9	180.1	8.5	559.5	562.2	139.6	12.8	179.4	16.1
1980	2 812.9	1 622.3	1 373.5	248.8	200.3	9.8	571.6	576.0	183.4	14.0	171.6	19.0
1981	3 169.0	1 792.7	1 511.5	281.2	235.6	11.5	664.9	669.6	231.4	16.9	179.7	23.8
1982	3 335.0	1 893.2	1 587.7	305.5	240.9	15.0	678.9	682.3	270.7	19.3	171.2	23.8
1983	3 577.1	2 012.7	1 677.7	335.0	263.3	21.3	759.8	761.7	284.6	21.7	186.3	24.4
1984	3 996.0	2 216.1	1 845.1	371.0	289.8	21.1	912.8	913.7	330.3	29.2	228.2	24.7
1985	4 284.7	2 387.5	1 982.8	404.8	308.1	21.4	970.3	968.4	350.7	34.1	241.1	26.2
1986	4 499.6	2 543.8	2 104.1	439.7	323.4	24.9	972.0	969.4	373.8	36.0	256.5	18.3
1987	4 811.4	2 723.8	2 257.6	466.1	347.5	30.3	1 040.0	1 037.2	382.9	33.3	286.5	16.6
1988	5 233.4	2 948.9	2 440.6	508.2	374.5	29.5	1 155.1	1 149.6	411.3	32.8	325.5	22.5
1989	5 573.6	3 140.9	2 584.3	556.6	398.9	27.4	1 223.0	1 215.8	467.7	38.3	341.1	21.5
1990	5 867.6	3 342.7	2 743.5	599.2	425.0	27.0	1 238.4	1 234.7	472.5	39.2	353.2	28.2
1991	6 065.2	3 453.3	2 817.2	636.0	457.1	27.5	1 249.9	1 241.7	433.9	38.9	354.2	38.6
1992	6 404.4	3 671.2	2 968.5	702.7	483.4	30.1	1 319.6	1 309.2	404.7	39.7	400.2	60.6
1993	6 702.6	3 820.6	3 082.7	737.9	503.1	36.7	1 412.1	1 400.6	395.5	39.4	428.0	90.1
1994	7 147.3	4 010.2	3 240.6	769.6	545.2	32.5	1 568.7	1 556.1	398.3	40.7	456.6	113.7
1995	7 546.7	4 202.2	3 422.1	780.1	557.9	34.8	1 699.1	1 682.6	418.3	45.0	481.2	124.9
1996	8 015.0	4 421.1	3 620.6	800.5	580.8	35.2	1 873.1	1 855.4	428.9	52.6	543.8	142.5
1997	8 566.0	4 713.2	3 881.2	832.0	611.6	33.8	2 035.6	2 017.5	474.3	50.1	584.0	147.1
1998	9 118.1	5 075.7	4 186.2	889.5	639.5	36.4	2 129.5	2 112.6	537.5	64.1	640.2	165.2
1999	9 659.5	5 409.9	4 465.2	944.8	673.6	45.2	2 222.2	2 205.4	549.6	67.7	696.4	178.5
2000	10 345.2	5 854.6	4 832.4	1 022.2	708.6	45.8	2 316.6	2 305.2	641.8	85.2	753.9	183.5
2001	10 695.7	6 046.3	4 961.6	1 084.7	727.7	58.7	2 380.9	2 375.2	652.7	99.2	831.0	202.4
2002	11 006.4	6 143.4	5 004.1	1 139.3	760.0	41.4	2 486.5	2 478.9	564.7	80.8	870.0	208.4
2003	11 476.3	6 362.3	5 147.0	1 215.3	805.6	49.1	2 638.4	2 633.3	535.3	76.0	897.5	227.1
2004	12 240.9	6 729.3	5 430.8	1 298.5	868.1	46.4	2 868.1	2 868.0	485.9	82.2	962.9	242.8
2005	13 091.7	7 077.7	5 703.0	1 374.7	942.4	60.9	3 161.4	3 166.0	611.1	91.7	979.1	221.1
2006	14 019.9	7 491.3	6 068.3	1 422.9	997.0	51.5	3 459.0	3 466.0	746.5	80.9	1 050.9	181.1
2007	14 454.4	7 889.4	6 407.3	1 482.1	1 036.8	54.6	3 330.0	3 344.2	868.5	98.5	995.5	186.3
2008	14 572.9	8 068.7	6 545.9	1 522.7	1 049.7	52.6	3 148.2	3 166.4	906.6	114.3	959.7	290.3
2009	14 276.0	7 767.2	6 257.3	1 509.9	1 026.8	58.3	3 168.9	3 185.0	735.1	126.6	937.6	347.6
2010	14 966.4	7 933.0	6 380.1	1 552.9	1 063.1	55.8	3 635.3	3 655.4	643.6	127.9	1 107.3	433.7
2011	15 612.0	8 234.0	6 634.0	1 600.0	1 103.7	60.0	3 859.9	3 879.3	616.4	131.7	1 227.4	506.5
2012	16 442.8	8 575.4	6 936.1	1 639.2	1 136.1	58.0	4 213.4	4 228.8	658.6	97.3	1 346.4	534.5
2013	16 958.0	8 843.6	7 122.6	1 721.0	1 188.7	59.7	4 304.2	4 320.2	619.2	109.5	1 402.2	577.4
2014	17 807.9	9 259.7	7 485.8	1 773.9	1 240.8	58.1	4 550.4	4 561.4	665.0	132.7	1 445.6	602.7
2015	18 440.5	9 709.5	7 869.6	1 839.9	1 275.2	57.2	4 601.6	4 606.9	755.8	155.6	1 420.8	609.5
2016	18 788.5	9 977.1	8 102.2	1 874.9	1 311.6	61.7	4 574.5	4 578.9	744.3	166.9	1 423.3	626.6
2017	19 598.5	10 436.7	8 485.3	1 951.5	1 366.3	59.9	4 737.2	4 743.9	806.2	149.1	1 505.8	652.7
2018	20 652.6	10 969.8	8 910.8	2 059.0	1 461.7	63.3	5 011.0	5 019.5	815.9	158.0	1 580.4	681.9
2019	21 442.2	11 459.4	9 335.3	2 124.2	1 532.3	73.0	5 087.8	5 101.1	793.5	162.3	1 598.9	692.1
2020	21 064.3	11 580.1	9 452.0	2 128.0	1 534.7	761.4	5 135.0	5 152.5	843.3	158.6	1 650.0	711.6
2021	23 533.4	12 607.9	10 353.1	2 254.9	1 641.1	493.1	5 929.5	5 942.5	915.8	164.0	1 821.9	726.4
2019												
1st quarter	21 195.6	11 347.4	9 237.7	2 109.7	1 504.8	69.0	5 034.4	5 046.6	804.2	170.8	1 585.5	687.0
2nd quarter	21 361.6	11 405.9	9 287.2	2 118.7	1 520.9	58.8	5 072.7	5 086.3	801.9	162.5	1 572.8	691.0
3rd quarter	21 481.9	11 465.8	9 338.7	2 127.1	1 547.4	81.2	5 092.0	5 105.9	776.4	168.2	1 610.6	691.5
4th quarter	21 729.8	11 618.8	9 477.6	2 141.2	1 556.3	82.8	5 152.2	5 165.6	791.3	147.5	1 626.8	699.0
2020												
1st quarter	21 755.9	11 764.8	9 613.3	2 151.4	1 577.1	80.9	4 972.6	4 987.1	796.8	149.4	1 638.3	712.2
2nd quarter	19 620.2	11 036.1	8 985.9	2 050.2	1 460.5	1 124.3	4 696.9	4 716.4	848.7	152.8	1 471.1	709.5
3rd quarter	20 908.5	11 547.2	9 417.8	2 129.4	1 544.0	1 221.2	5 447.5	5 465.1	843.1	165.8	1 760.7	714.5
4th quarter	21 972.6	11 972.3	9 791.1	2 181.1	1 557.0	619.2	5 423.2	5 441.3	884.4	166.3	1 730.0	710.0
2021												
1st quarter	22 547.9	12 097.8	9 888.1	2 209.7	1 580.1	406.3	5 580.3	5 599.6	917.9	165.8	1 714.0	716.9
2nd quarter	23 132.7	12 425.3	10 189.1	2 236.2	1 636.3	705.6	5 988.7	6 004.1	914.7	166.0	1 848.2	716.3
3rd quarter	23 833.2	12 766.5	10 497.2	2 269.3	1 654.7	555.1	6 071.3	6 077.1	913.9	162.5	1 867.0	729.0
4th quarter	24 619.9	13 142.2	10 837.8	2 304.4	1 693.4	305.3	6 077.8	6 089.0	916.7	161.7	1 858.5	743.6

Table 1-13A. National Income by Type of Income: Recent Data

(Billions of dollars, quarterly data are at seasonally adjusted annual rates.)   **NIPA Tables 1.7.5, 1.12**

Year and quarter	National income, total	Compensation of employees							Proprietors' income with IVA and CCAdj			Rental income of persons with CCAdj
		Total	Wages and salaries			Supplements to wages and salaries			Total	Farm	Nonfarm	
			Total	Government	Other	Total	Employer contributions for:					
							Employee pension and insurance funds	Government social insurance				
1965	658.8	405.4	363.8	69.9	293.8	41.7	28.6	13.1	63.7	12.0	51.6	19.3
1966	718.1	449.2	400.3	78.4	321.9	48.9	32.1	16.8	67.9	13.0	54.9	19.9
1967	758.4	481.8	429.0	86.5	342.5	52.8	34.8	18.0	69.5	11.6	57.8	20.3
1968	830.2	530.8	472.0	96.7	375.3	58.8	38.8	20.0	73.8	11.7	62.2	20.1
1969	897.2	584.5	518.3	105.6	412.7	66.1	43.4	22.8	77.0	12.8	64.2	20.3
1970	937.5	623.3	551.6	117.2	434.3	71.8	47.9	23.8	77.8	12.9	64.9	20.7
1971	1 014.0	665.0	584.5	126.8	457.8	80.4	54.0	26.4	83.9	13.4	70.5	21.8
1972	1 119.5	731.3	638.8	137.9	500.9	92.5	61.4	31.2	95.1	17.0	78.1	22.7
1973	1 253.2	812.7	708.8	148.8	560.0	103.9	64.1	39.8	112.5	29.1	83.4	23.1
1974	1 346.4	887.7	772.3	160.5	611.8	115.4	70.7	44.7	112.2	23.5	88.7	23.2
1975	1 446.0	947.2	814.8	176.2	638.6	132.4	85.7	46.7	118.2	22.0	96.2	22.3
1976	1 609.4	1 048.3	899.7	188.9	710.8	148.6	94.2	54.4	131.0	17.2	113.8	20.3
1977	1 792.8	1 165.8	994.2	202.6	791.6	171.7	110.6	61.1	144.5	16.0	128.5	15.9
1978	2 022.7	1 316.8	1 120.6	220.0	900.6	196.2	124.7	71.5	166.0	19.9	146.1	16.5
1979	2 240.3	1 477.2	1 253.3	237.1	1 016.2	223.9	141.3	82.6	179.4	22.2	157.3	16.1
1980	2 418.6	1 622.2	1 373.4	261.5	1 112.0	248.8	159.9	88.9	171.6	11.7	159.9	19.0
1981	2 714.7	1 792.5	1 511.4	285.8	1 225.5	281.2	177.5	103.6	179.7	19.0	160.7	23.8
1982	2 834.5	1 893.0	1 587.5	307.5	1 280.0	305.5	195.7	109.8	171.2	13.3	157.9	23.8
1983	3 051.5	2 012.5	1 677.5	324.8	1 352.7	335.0	215.1	119.9	186.3	6.2	180.1	24.4
1984	3 433.9	2 215.9	1 844.9	348.1	1 496.8	371.0	231.9	139.0	228.2	20.9	207.3	24.7
1985	3 669.9	2 387.3	1 982.6	373.9	1 608.7	404.8	257.0	147.7	241.1	21.0	220.1	26.2
1986	3 831.2	2 542.1	2 102.3	397.2	1 705.1	439.7	281.9	157.9	256.5	22.8	233.7	18.3
1987	4 098.5	2 722.4	2 256.3	423.1	1 833.2	466.1	299.9	166.3	286.5	28.9	257.6	16.6
1988	4 471.6	2 948.0	2 439.8	452.0	1 987.7	508.2	323.6	184.6	325.5	26.8	298.7	22.5
1989	4 760.1	3 139.6	2 583.1	481.1	2 101.9	556.6	362.9	193.7	341.1	33.0	308.1	21.5
1990	5 013.8	3 340.4	2 741.2	519.0	2 222.2	599.2	392.7	206.5	353.2	32.2	321.0	28.2
1991	5 164.4	3 450.5	2 814.5	548.8	2 265.7	636.0	420.9	215.1	354.2	26.8	327.4	38.6
1992	5 475.2	3 668.2	2 965.5	572.0	2 393.5	702.7	474.3	228.4	400.2	34.8	365.4	60.6
1993	5 730.3	3 817.3	3 079.3	589.0	2 490.3	737.9	498.3	239.7	428.0	31.4	396.6	90.1
1994	6 114.6	4 006.2	3 236.6	609.5	2 627.1	769.6	515.5	254.1	456.6	34.7	422.0	113.7
1995	6 452.3	4 198.1	3 418.0	629.0	2 789.0	780.1	515.9	264.1	481.2	22.0	459.2	124.9
1996	6 870.6	4 416.9	3 616.5	648.1	2 968.4	800.5	525.7	274.8	543.8	37.3	506.4	142.5
1997	7 349.9	4 708.8	3 876.8	671.9	3 205.0	832.0	542.4	289.6	584.0	32.4	551.6	147.1
1998	7 825.7	5 071.1	4 181.6	701.3	3 480.3	889.5	582.3	307.2	640.2	28.5	611.7	165.2
1999	8 291.5	5 402.7	4 457.9	733.8	3 724.2	944.8	621.4	323.3	696.4	28.1	668.3	178.5
2000	8 872.4	5 847.1	4 824.9	779.8	4 045.2	1 022.2	677.0	345.2	753.9	31.5	722.4	183.5
2001	9 146.6	6 038.3	4 953.6	822.0	4 131.6	1 084.7	726.7	358.0	831.0	32.1	798.9	202.4
2002	9 394.2	6 135.1	4 995.8	872.9	4 123.0	1 139.3	773.2	366.0	870.0	20.2	849.8	208.4
2003	9 815.6	6 353.6	5 138.3	914.0	4 224.3	1 215.3	832.8	382.5	897.5	37.1	860.4	227.1
2004	10 495.8	6 719.5	5 421.0	952.3	4 468.7	1 298.5	889.7	408.8	962.9	52.4	910.5	242.8
2005	11 195.5	7 066.1	5 691.4	991.3	4 700.1	1 374.7	946.7	428.1	979.1	47.9	931.2	221.1
2006	11 942.3	7 479.7	6 056.7	1 034.5	5 022.2	1 422.9	975.6	447.3	1 050.9	34.3	1 016.6	181.1
2007	12 297.3	7 878.5	6 396.4	1 088.5	5 307.8	1 482.1	1 020.4	461.7	995.5	41.7	953.8	186.3
2008	12 359.3	8 056.8	6 534.1	1 143.9	5 390.2	1 522.7	1 051.3	471.4	959.7	38.9	920.7	290.3
2009	12 054.8	7 759.0	6 249.1	1 175.2	5 073.9	1 509.9	1 051.8	458.1	937.6	27.2	910.5	347.6
2010	12 781.1	7 925.4	6 372.5	1 191.2	5 181.3	1 552.9	1 083.9	469.0	1 107.3	37.6	1 069.7	433.7
2011	13 375.5	8 226.2	6 626.2	1 194.9	5 431.3	1 600.0	1 107.3	492.7	1 227.4	63.0	1 164.4	506.5
2012	14 099.6	8 567.4	6 928.1	1 198.3	5 729.8	1 639.2	1 125.9	513.3	1 346.4	59.9	1 286.4	534.5
2013	14 507.1	8 835.0	7 114.0	1 208.0	5 906.0	1 721.0	1 194.7	526.3	1 402.2	87.0	1 315.3	577.4
2014	15 228.1	9 250.2	7 476.3	1 236.9	6 239.4	1 773.9	1 227.5	546.4	1 445.6	67.7	1 377.9	602.7
2015	15 749.5	9 699.4	7 859.5	1 275.8	6 583.7	1 839.9	1 270.6	569.4	1 420.8	54.1	1 366.7	609.5
2016	16 033.4	9 966.1	8 091.2	1 308.0	6 783.2	1 874.9	1 293.9	580.9	1 423.3	34.1	1 389.2	626.6
2017	16 774.9	10 426.0	8 474.7	1 348.0	7 126.7	1 951.5	1 346.5	604.9	1 505.8	39.5	1 466.4	652.7
2018	17 673.3	10 959.0	8 900.5	1 401.4	7 499.1	2 059.0	1 434.3	624.7	1 580.4	38.9	1 541.5	681.9
2019	18 273.1	11 447.0	9 323.5	1 450.2	7 873.3	2 124.2	1 474.6	649.6	1 598.9	38.4	1 560.5	692.1
2020	17 710.7	11 572.0	9 444.1	1 494.5	7 949.6	2 128.0	1 464.4	663.7	1 650.0	70.2	1 579.9	711.6
2021	19 938.0	12 598.0	10 343.0	1 535.5	8 808.3	2 254.9	1 526.4	728.5	1 821.9	97.8	1 724.1	726.4
2019												
1st quarter	18 070.4	11 336.0	9 226.3	1 423.6	7 802.7	2 109.7	1 466.6	643.2	1 585.5	33.1	1 552.4	687.0
2nd quarter	18 216.3	11 394.0	9 275.4	1 435.0	7 840.4	2 118.7	1 472.5	646.2	1 572.8	23.6	1 549.2	691.0
3rd quarter	18 299.7	11 453.0	9 326.8	1 459.1	7 867.8	2 127.1	1 477.4	649.6	1 610.6	46.4	1 564.1	691.5
4th quarter	18 505.9	11 606.0	9 465.6	1 483.3	7 982.4	2 141.2	1 481.8	659.4	1 626.8	50.6	1 576.1	699.0
2020												
1st quarter	18 473.4	11 755.0	9 604.1	1 515.2	8 088.9	2 151.4	1 483.7	667.7	1 638.3	58.1	1 580.2	712.2
2nd quarter	16 241.3	11 029.0	8 979.0	1 467.7	7 511.3	2 050.2	1 410.5	639.7	1 471.1	44.9	1 426.2	709.5
3rd quarter	17 544.3	11 539.0	9 410.3	1 498.8	7 911.5	2 129.4	1 464.9	664.5	1 760.7	69.2	1 691.5	714.5
4th quarter	18 583.8	11 964.0	9 783.0	1 496.4	8 286.6	2 181.1	1 498.3	682.8	1 730.0	108.5	1 621.5	710.0
2021												
1st quarter	19 086.8	12 088.0	9 879.2	1 502.7	8 376.5	2 209.7	1 510.9	698.9	1 714.0	73.0	1 640.9	716.9
2nd quarter	19 575.1	12 416.0	10 180.0	1 519.1	8 661.3	2 236.2	1 518.3	717.9	1 848.2	119.4	1 728.7	716.3
3rd quarter	20 205.0	12 756.0	10 487.0	1 554.2	8 933.0	2 269.3	1 531.9	737.4	1 867.0	110.6	1 756.3	729.0
4th quarter	20 885.0	13 132.0	10 828.0	1 565.8	9 262.4	2 304.4	1 544.6	759.8	1 858.5	88.0	1 770.5	743.6

Table 1-13A. National Income by Type of Income: Recent Data—*Continued*

(Billions of dollars, quarterly data are at seasonally adjusted annual rates.)

NIPA Tables 1.7.5, 1.12

Year and quarter	Corporate profits with IVA and CCAdj					Net interest and miscellaneous payments	Taxes on production and imports	Less: Subsidies	Business current transfer payments, net			Current surplus of government enterprises	Addendum: Net national factor income
			Profits after tax										
	Total	Taxes on corporate income	Total	Net dividends	Undistributed corporate profits				Total 1	To persons	To government		
1965	89.3	29.8	59.5	21.5	38.0	19.1	60.7	3.0	3.5	2.3	1.2	. . .	596.8
1966	96.1	32.2	63.9	22.3	41.6	21.8	63.2	3.9	3.4	2.1	1.3	. . .	655.1
1967	93.9	31.0	62.9	23.4	39.5	24.9	67.9	3.8	3.6	2.3	1.4	. . .	690.4
1968	101.7	37.2	64.6	26.0	38.6	27.0	76.4	4.2	4.2	2.8	1.4	. . .	753.4
1969	98.4	37.0	61.5	27.3	34.2	32.7	83.9	4.5	4.8	3.3	1.5	. . .	813.0
1970	86.2	31.3	55.0	27.8	27.2	39.5	91.4	4.8	4.4	2.9	1.4	. . .	847.6
1971	100.6	34.8	65.8	28.4	37.5	44.2	100.5	4.7	4.2	2.7	1.5	. . .	915.5
1972	117.2	39.1	78.1	30.1	48.0	48.0	107.9	6.6	4.8	3.1	1.7	. . .	1 014.4
1973	133.4	45.6	87.8	34.2	53.5	55.7	117.2	5.2	5.7	3.9	1.8	. . .	1 137.4
1974	125.7	47.2	78.5	38.8	39.7	71.7	124.9	3.3	6.8	4.7	2.1	. . .	1 220.5
1975	138.9	46.3	92.6	38.3	54.3	83.7	135.3	4.5	9.0	6.8	2.2	. . .	1 310.3
1976	174.3	59.4	114.9	44.9	70.0	87.4	146.4	5.1	9.1	6.7	2.4	. . .	1 461.4
1977	205.8	68.5	137.3	50.7	86.6	103.2	159.7	7.1	8.1	5.1	3.0	. . .	1 635.2
1978	238.6	77.9	160.7	57.8	102.9	114.8	170.9	8.9	10.4	6.5	3.9	. . .	1 852.7
1979	249.0	80.7	168.2	66.8	101.4	137.0	180.1	8.5	12.8	8.2	4.5	. . .	2 058.7
1980	223.6	75.5	148.1	75.8	72.3	182.2	200.3	9.8	14.0	8.6	5.4	. . .	2 218.6
1981	247.5	70.3	177.2	87.8	89.4	234.8	235.6	11.5	16.9	11.2	5.7	. . .	2 478.3
1982	229.9	51.3	178.6	92.9	85.6	274.8	240.9	15.0	19.3	12.4	6.9	. . .	2 592.7
1983	279.8	66.4	213.3	97.7	115.7	286.8	263.3	21.3	21.7	13.8	7.9	. . .	2 789.8
1984	337.9	81.5	256.4	106.9	149.5	330.2	289.8	21.1	29.2	19.7	9.4	. . .	3 136.9
1985	354.5	81.6	272.9	115.3	157.5	338.2	308.1	21.4	34.1	22.3	11.8	. . .	3 347.2
1986	324.4	91.9	232.5	124.0	108.5	353.1	323.4	24.9	36.0	22.9	13.0	. . .	3 494.3
1987	366.0	112.7	253.3	130.1	123.2	353.7	347.5	30.3	33.3	20.2	13.1	. . .	3 745.2
1988	414.5	124.3	290.2	147.3	142.9	377.9	374.5	29.5	32.8	20.6	12.2	. . .	4 088.3
1989	414.3	124.4	289.9	179.6	110.3	426.6	398.9	27.4	38.3	23.2	15.1	. . .	4 343.2
1990	417.7	121.8	295.9	192.7	103.2	433.4	425.0	27.0	39.2	22.2	17.0	. . .	4 572.9
1991	452.6	117.8	334.8	201.3	133.5	391.8	457.1	27.5	38.9	17.6	21.3	. . .	4 687.6
1992	477.2	131.9	345.3	206.3	139.0	365.6	483.4	30.1	39.7	16.3	23.6	-0.1	4 971.8
1993	524.6	155.0	369.5	221.3	148.2	353.1	503.1	36.7	39.4	14.1	25.6	-0.3	5 213.0
1994	624.8	172.7	452.1	256.4	195.7	347.3	545.2	32.5	40.7	13.3	27.9	-0.4	5 548.6
1995	706.2	194.4	511.8	282.3	229.4	357.4	557.9	34.8	45.0	18.7	24.9	1.4	5 867.7
1996	789.5	211.4	578.1	323.6	254.5	361.9	580.8	35.2	52.6	22.9	30.7	-1.0	6 254.7
1997	869.7	224.8	645.0	360.1	284.9	394.4	611.6	33.8	50.1	19.4	29.8	0.8	6 704.0
1998	808.5	221.8	586.6	383.6	203.0	456.7	639.5	36.4	64.1	26.0	34.3	3.8	7 141.7
1999	834.9	227.4	607.5	373.5	234.0	466.0	673.6	45.2	67.7	34.0	36.5	-2.7	7 578.6
2000	786.6	233.4	553.1	410.2	142.9	542.1	708.6	45.8	85.2	42.4	41.9	0.8	8 113.1
2001	758.7	170.1	588.6	397.9	190.7	542.2	727.7	58.7	99.2	46.8	43.9	8.6	8 372.7
2002	911.7	160.7	751.0	424.9	326.2	462.0	760.0	41.4	80.8	34.2	46.2	0.3	8 587.3
2003	1 056.3	213.8	842.5	456.0	386.5	443.6	805.6	49.1	76.0	26.3	48.3	1.5	8 978.0
2004	1 289.3	278.5	1 010.8	582.2	428.6	377.3	868.1	46.4	82.2	16.8	52.4	13.1	9 591.8
2005	1 488.6	379.7	1 108.9	602.0	506.9	471.8	942.4	60.9	91.7	25.8	53.4	12.5	10 226.0
2006	1 646.3	430.1	1 216.1	755.1	461.1	564.8	997.0	51.5	80.9	20.8	57.5	2.6	10 922.0
2007	1 533.2	391.8	1 141.4	853.5	287.9	637.3	1 036.8	54.6	98.5	30.8	60.9	6.9	11 230.0
2008	1 285.8	255.9	1 029.9	840.3	189.6	673.4	1 049.7	52.6	114.3	35.8	69.5	9.0	11 266.0
2009	1 386.8	203.9	1 182.9	622.1	560.8	544.7	1 026.8	58.3	126.6	39.0	86.1	1.5	10 975.0
2010	1 728.7	272.3	1 456.5	643.2	813.3	471.0	1 063.1	55.8	127.9	43.7	84.1	0.0	11 666.0
2011	1 809.8	280.8	1 529.0	779.1	749.9	449.6	1 103.7	60.0	131.7	48.5	86.8	-3.7	12 219.0
2012	1 997.4	334.6	1 662.8	948.7	714.1	494.0	1 136.1	58.0	97.3	40.4	69.0	-12.1	12 939.0
2013	2 010.7	362.6	1 648.1	1 009.0	639.1	459.2	1 188.7	59.7	109.5	38.4	84.7	-13.6	13 284.0
2014	2 120.2	407.1	1 713.1	1 096.1	617.1	504.8	1 240.8	58.1	132.7	42.9	98.1	-8.3	13 923.0
2015	2 060.5	396.3	1 664.2	1 164.9	499.3	591.1	1 275.2	57.2	155.6	50.3	110.5	-5.2	14 381.2
2016	2 037.7	376.2	1 661.5	1 189.4	472.1	567.3	1 311.6	61.7	166.9	59.7	105.3	1.9	14 621.1
2017	2 128.9	312.3	1 816.6	1 264.1	552.5	612.5	1 366.3	55.9	149.1	48.7	99.7	0.7	15 326.0
2018	2 305.0	281.5	2 023.4	1 338.4	685.0	598.7	1 461.7	63.3	158.0	50.2	103.8	4.1	16 125.4
2019	2 367.8	302.2	2 065.6	1 386.4	679.2	558.2	1 532.3	73.0	162.3	56.0	95.7	10.6	16 664.7
2020	2 243.8	275.6	1 968.1	1 394.9	573.3	618.8	1 534.7	761.4	158.6	59.9	97.8	0.9	16 796.3
2021	2 805.8	381.2	2 424.6	1 418.6	1 006.0	686.1	1 641.1	493.1	164.0	67.0	95.3	1.8	18 638.8
2019													
1st quarter	2 297.2	297.4	1 999.8	1 367.5	632.3	570.2	1 504.8	69.0	170.8	54.2	90.3	26.4	16 475.9
2nd quarter	2 387.0	303.8	2 083.2	1 393.7	689.5	560.4	1 520.9	58.8	162.5	55.6	92.9	14.1	16 605.3
3rd quarter	2 381.8	291.5	2 090.3	1 387.0	703.2	541.6	1 547.4	81.2	168.2	56.7	109.2	2.4	16 679.3
4th quarter	2 405.1	316.0	2 089.2	1 397.4	691.8	560.7	1 556.3	82.8	147.5	57.5	90.7	-0.7	16 898.4
2020													
1st quarter	2 169.5	245.4	1 924.0	1 417.7	506.3	566.9	1 577.1	80.9	149.4	58.0	93.3	-1.9	16 842.4
2nd quarter	1 942.6	241.2	1 701.5	1 395.7	305.8	619.3	1 460.5	1 124.3	152.8	63.3	95.1	-5.6	15 771.8
3rd quarter	2 435.4	300.3	2 135.1	1 368.6	766.5	623.0	1 544.0	1 221.2	165.8	58.9	99.7	7.2	17 073.4
4th quarter	2 427.5	315.6	2 111.9	1 397.5	714.4	666.1	1 557.0	619.2	166.3	59.2	103.2	3.9	17 497.8
2021													
1st quarter	2 551.4	343.7	2 207.7	1 359.7	848.0	695.2	1 580.1	406.3	165.8	62.0	98.4	5.4	17 766.4
2nd quarter	2 819.2	378.6	2 440.6	1 411.0	1 029.6	693.6	1 636.3	705.6	166.0	71.2	94.4	0.4	18 493.8
3rd quarter	2 916.1	393.3	2 522.7	1 438.7	1 084.0	680.3	1 654.7	555.1	162.5	67.9	94.0	0.6	18 948.8
4th quarter	2 936.5	409.1	2 527.4	1 465.1	1 062.3	675.1	1 693.4	305.3	161.7	66.7	94.4	0.6	19 346.4

1Includes net transfer payments to the rest of the world, not shown separately.
. . . = Not available.

Table 1-13B. National Income by Type of Income: Historical Data

(Billions of dollars, quarterly data are at seasonally adjusted annual rates.)

NIPA Tables 1.7.5, 1.12

Year and quarter	National income, total	Compensation of employees							Proprietors' income with IVA and CCAdj			Rental income of persons with CCAdj
		Total	Wages and salaries			Supplements to wages and salaries			Total	Farm	Nonfarm	
			Total	Government	Other	Total	Employer contributions for:					
							Employee pension and insurance funds	Government social insurance				
1929	94.2	51.4	50.5	5.0	45.5	0.9	0.9	0.0	14.0	5.7	8.4	6.1
1930	83.1	47.2	46.2	5.2	41.0	1.0	0.9	0.0	10.9	3.9	7.0	5.4
1931	67.7	40.1	39.2	5.3	33.9	0.9	0.9	0.0	8.3	3.0	5.3	4.4
1932	51.3	31.3	30.5	5.0	25.5	0.8	0.8	0.0	5.0	1.8	3.3	3.6
1933	48.9	29.8	29.0	5.2	23.9	0.8	0.8	0.0	5.3	2.2	3.0	2.9
1934	58.3	34.6	33.7	6.1	27.6	0.8	0.8	0.0	7.0	2.6	4.4	2.5
1935	66.3	37.7	36.7	6.5	30.2	0.9	0.9	0.0	10.1	4.9	5.2	2.6
1936	75.1	43.3	42.0	7.9	34.1	1.3	1.1	0.2	10.4	3.9	6.4	2.7
1937	83.7	48.3	46.1	7.5	38.6	2.2	1.1	1.0	12.5	5.6	6.9	3.0
1938	77.0	45.4	43.0	8.3	34.8	2.4	1.2	1.2	10.6	4.0	6.6	3.5
1939	82.4	48.6	46.0	8.2	37.7	2.6	1.3	1.3	11.1	4.0	7.1	3.7
1940	91.5	52.7	49.9	8.5	41.4	2.9	1.5	1.4	12.2	4.1	8.2	3.8
1941	117.3	66.2	62.1	10.2	51.9	4.1	2.4	1.7	16.7	6.0	10.6	4.4
1942	152.4	88.0	82.1	16.0	66.1	5.9	3.9	2.0	23.3	9.7	13.7	5.5
1943	187.2	112.7	105.8	26.6	79.2	6.9	4.6	2.3	28.2	11.5	16.7	6.0
1944	200.9	124.3	116.7	33.0	83.8	7.6	5.0	2.5	29.3	11.4	17.9	6.3
1945	201.3	126.3	117.5	34.9	82.6	8.8	5.3	3.5	30.8	11.8	19.0	6.6
1946	201.3	122.5	112.0	20.7	91.3	10.5	5.4	5.1	35.7	14.2	21.5	6.9
1947	218.7	132.4	123.1	17.5	105.6	9.3	5.3	3.9	34.6	14.3	20.2	6.9
1948	244.8	144.3	135.6	19.0	116.5	8.8	5.8	3.0	39.3	16.7	22.6	7.5
1949	239.7	144.3	134.7	20.8	113.9	9.6	6.3	3.3	34.7	12.0	22.7	7.8
1948												
1st quarter	235.8	140.4	131.7	18.3	113.4	8.7	5.5	3.2	36.4	14.5	21.9	7.3
2nd quarter	244.0	142.1	133.4	18.6	114.7	8.7	5.7	3.0	40.2	18.0	22.3	7.5
3rd quarter	248.8	146.8	138.1	19.3	118.8	8.8	5.8	2.9	40.6	17.9	22.7	7.5
4th quarter	250.7	147.9	139.1	19.9	119.2	8.8	6.0	2.9	39.9	16.4	23.5	7.6
1949												
1st quarter	243.3	146.3	136.7	20.4	116.4	9.5	6.0	3.5	35.4	12.7	22.7	7.5
2nd quarter	239.7	144.7	135.0	20.7	114.3	9.7	6.1	3.5	34.9	12.1	22.8	7.7
3rd quarter	239.9	143.6	134.0	21.1	112.9	9.6	6.3	3.3	34.2	11.6	22.6	7.9
4th quarter	236.0	142.8	133.2	21.2	112.0	9.6	6.5	3.0	34.2	11.5	22.7	8.1
1950												
1st quarter	246.3	147.0	136.9	21.2	115.6	10.1	6.9	3.3	36.2	12.2	24.0	8.5
2nd quarter	258.5	153.6	143.0	21.8	121.2	10.6	7.3	3.3	36.8	12.2	24.6	8.7
3rd quarter	275.6	162.3	151.0	23.0	128.1	11.3	7.9	3.4	38.5	13.1	25.4	8.8
4th quarter	286.1	170.2	158.1	24.5	133.5	12.1	8.5	3.6	38.5	13.9	24.6	9.1
1951												
1st quarter	297.8	178.6	165.3	26.7	138.6	13.2	9.2	4.0	40.9	15.0	25.9	9.3
2nd quarter	305.2	184.9	171.0	28.5	142.5	13.9	9.8	4.1	42.5	15.4	27.1	9.6
3rd quarter	310.6	187.9	173.5	30.2	143.3	14.4	10.3	4.1	43.2	15.1	28.1	9.9
4th quarter	317.0	191.5	176.6	31.5	145.1	14.9	10.7	4.1	43.7	15.7	28.0	10.1
1952												
1st quarter	318.5	196.1	181.0	32.4	148.6	15.1	11.0	4.1	41.7	13.7	28.0	10.4
2nd quarter	320.4	197.4	182.1	33.1	149.0	15.3	11.2	4.1	43.0	14.5	28.4	10.7
3rd quarter	327.0	201.5	186.0	33.8	152.2	15.6	11.4	4.1	44.7	16.0	28.8	10.9
4th quarter	338.5	209.3	193.5	34.2	159.3	15.9	11.6	4.2	42.8	13.0	29.7	11.3
1953												
1st quarter	344.5	213.1	197.1	34.3	162.7	16.1	11.9	4.2	42.9	13.0	29.9	11.6
2nd quarter	347.3	216.2	200.0	34.4	165.7	16.2	12.0	4.2	42.3	12.4	29.9	11.9
3rd quarter	345.6	216.5	200.1	34.3	165.9	16.4	12.1	4.3	41.2	11.7	29.5	12.2
4th quarter	338.0	215.1	198.7	34.4	164.3	16.4	12.2	4.2	41.6	11.5	30.0	12.5
1954												
1st quarter	339.6	213.1	196.4	34.4	162.0	16.7	12.1	4.6	42.7	12.9	29.8	12.8
2nd quarter	339.9	212.7	196.0	34.7	161.2	16.7	12.1	4.6	42.1	11.7	30.4	13.0
3rd quarter	343.3	213.2	196.3	35.1	161.2	16.9	12.3	4.6	42.2	11.8	30.5	13.1
4th quarter	352.2	217.5	200.4	35.4	165.0	17.2	12.5	4.6	42.0	10.7	31.3	13.3
1955												
1st quarter	364.6	221.9	204.1	35.5	168.6	17.8	12.8	5.0	43.7	10.9	32.7	13.3
2nd quarter	374.0	228.1	209.9	36.2	173.6	18.2	13.1	5.1	44.3	11.3	33.0	13.4
3rd quarter	381.4	233.9	215.2	37.4	177.8	18.7	13.4	5.2	44.6	10.7	33.9	13.4
4th quarter	387.7	238.4	219.5	37.3	182.2	18.9	13.7	5.3	44.5	10.0	34.5	13.5
1956												
1st quarter	391.2	242.8	223.3	37.8	185.4	19.5	14.0	5.6	44.9	10.2	34.7	13.6
2nd quarter	397.0	247.5	227.5	38.5	189.0	20.0	14.3	5.7	45.3	10.4	34.9	13.6
3rd quarter	401.9	250.4	230.0	39.2	190.8	20.5	14.8	5.7	46.4	10.9	35.5	13.7
4th quarter	410.1	256.4	235.4	39.7	195.7	21.0	15.2	5.8	46.8	10.9	35.8	13.8
1957												
1st quarter	416.8	260.2	238.3	40.2	198.0	22.0	15.6	6.4	46.9	9.9	37.0	13.9
2nd quarter	418.9	262.1	239.6	40.7	198.9	22.4	16.0	6.4	47.7	10.5	37.2	14.0
3rd quarter	422.6	264.7	241.8	41.5	200.3	22.9	16.5	6.4	48.8	11.0	37.8	14.1
4th quarter	415.8	263.3	240.1	41.6	198.5	23.2	16.9	6.3	47.7	10.7	37.0	14.3
1958												
1st quarter	409.7	259.8	236.7	42.0	194.7	23.0	16.7	6.3	50.3	13.3	36.9	14.6
2nd quarter	411.6	259.4	236.3	43.1	193.2	23.2	16.9	6.3	50.3	13.0	37.3	14.8
3rd quarter	424.5	267.2	243.8	46.1	197.7	23.4	17.0	6.4	50.1	12.1	38.0	14.9
4th quarter	437.2	272.3	248.4	45.3	203.2	23.8	17.4	6.4	49.9	11.2	38.7	15.0

Table 1-13B. National Income by Type of Income: Historical Data—*Continued*

(Billions of dollars, quarterly data are at seasonally adjusted annual rates.)

NIPA Tables 1.7.5, 1.12

Year and quarter	Corporate profits with IVA and CCAdj					Net interest and miscel-laneous payments	Taxes on production and imports	Less: Subsidies	Business current transfer payments, net			Current surplus of govern-ment enterprises	Addendum: Net national factor income
	Total	Taxes on corporate income	Profits after tax						Total ¹	To persons	To govern-ment		
			Total	Net dividends	Undis-tributed corporate profits								
1929	10.8	1.4	9.5	5.8	3.7	4.6	6.8	0.0	0.5	0.4	0.1	. . .	86.9
1930	7.5	0.8	6.7	5.5	1.2	4.8	7.0	0.1	0.5	0.4	0.1	. . .	75.7
1931	3.0	0.5	2.5	4.1	-1.6	4.8	6.7	0.1	0.5	0.4	0.1	. . .	60.6
1932	-0.2	0.4	-0.6	2.5	-3.1	4.5	6.6	0.1	0.6	0.5	0.1	. . .	44.2
1933	-0.2	0.5	-0.7	2.0	-2.7	4.0	6.9	0.2	0.5	0.4	0.1	. . .	41.7
1934	2.5	0.7	1.8	2.6	-0.8	4.0	7.6	0.5	0.5	0.4	0.1	. . .	50.6
1935	4.0	1.0	3.1	2.8	0.2	4.1	8.0	0.6	0.5	0.4	0.1	. . .	58.4
1936	6.2	1.4	4.8	4.5	0.3	3.8	8.5	0.3	0.5	0.4	0.1	. . .	66.4
1937	7.1	1.5	5.6	4.7	0.9	3.7	8.9	0.3	0.5	0.4	0.1	. . .	74.5
1938	5.0	1.0	4.0	3.2	0.8	3.6	8.9	0.5	0.4	0.3	0.2	. . .	68.1
1939	6.6	1.4	5.2	3.8	1.4	3.6	9.1	0.8	0.4	0.3	0.2	. . .	73.6
1940	9.9	2.8	7.0	4.0	3.0	3.3	9.8	0.7	0.5	0.3	0.2	. . .	82.0
1941	15.7	7.6	8.1	4.4	3.7	3.3	11.1	0.5	0.5	0.4	0.2	. . .	106.2
1942	20.8	11.4	9.4	4.3	5.1	3.2	11.5	0.5	0.5	0.3	0.2	. . .	140.8
1943	24.9	14.1	10.8	4.4	6.4	2.9	12.4	0.6	0.6	0.4	0.3	. . .	174.7
1944	25.0	12.9	12.0	4.6	7.4	2.4	13.7	1.0	0.8	0.4	0.4	. . .	187.4
1945	20.5	10.7	9.8	4.6	5.2	2.3	15.1	1.1	0.9	0.5	0.4	. . .	186.5
1946	18.2	9.1	9.1	5.6	3.6	1.8	16.8	1.4	0.7	0.4	0.3	. . .	185.1
1947	24.2	11.2	13.0	6.4	6.6	2.3	18.1	0.4	0.7	0.4	0.3	. . .	200.3
1948	31.4	12.3	19.1	7.2	11.9	2.5	19.7	0.5	0.7	0.4	0.3	. . .	225.0
1949	29.1	10.0	19.0	7.4	11.6	2.8	20.9	0.5	0.7	0.4	0.3	. . .	218.6
1948													
1st quarter	30.0	12.0	18.0	7.2	10.8	2.4	19.0	0.4	0.7	0.4	0.4	. . .	216.5
2nd quarter	31.8	12.6	19.1	6.8	12.3	2.4	19.7	0.3	0.7	0.4	0.3	. . .	224.0
3rd quarter	31.2	12.4	18.8	7.3	11.5	2.5	20.0	0.6	0.7	0.4	0.3	. . .	228.7
4th quarter	32.7	12.0	20.7	7.6	13.1	2.5	20.3	0.9	0.7	0.4	0.3	. . .	230.6
1949													
1st quarter	31.0	10.8	20.2	7.4	12.7	2.7	20.4	0.6	0.7	0.3	0.3	. . .	222.9
2nd quarter	28.7	9.5	19.1	7.4	11.7	2.7	20.8	0.4	0.7	0.3	0.3	. . .	218.7
3rd quarter	29.9	9.9	20.0	7.3	12.7	2.8	21.3	0.5	0.7	0.4	0.3	. . .	218.5
4th quarter	26.6	9.7	16.9	7.6	9.3	2.8	21.2	0.5	0.7	0.4	0.3	. . .	214.5
1950													
1st quarter	30.1	13.4	16.6	8.5	8.1	3.0	21.6	0.7	0.7	0.4	0.3	. . .	224.8
2nd quarter	33.9	16.1	17.8	8.6	9.2	3.1	22.5	0.8	0.8	0.5	0.3	. . .	236.0
3rd quarter	38.4	19.7	18.7	9.4	9.4	3.1	24.4	0.8	0.9	0.6	0.3	. . .	251.1
4th quarter	41.8	21.6	20.2	9.7	10.5	3.1	23.4	1.1	0.9	0.7	0.3	. . .	262.8
1951													
1st quarter	40.7	26.0	14.7	8.6	6.1	3.3	25.1	1.2	1.1	0.8	0.3	. . .	272.8
2nd quarter	40.6	22.0	18.6	8.9	9.7	3.5	24.1	1.1	1.2	0.9	0.3	. . .	281.1
3rd quarter	41.1	19.9	21.2	8.8	12.4	3.7	24.5	0.9	1.2	0.9	0.3	. . .	285.8
4th quarter	42.4	21.3	21.1	9.0	12.2	3.8	25.3	1.0	1.2	0.9	0.3	. . .	291.5
1952													
1st quarter	40.0	19.5	20.5	8.4	12.1	3.8	26.1	0.8	1.2	0.9	0.3	. . .	292.0
2nd quarter	38.1	18.4	19.8	9.0	10.8	3.9	26.9	0.8	1.2	0.9	0.3	. . .	293.1
3rd quarter	38.1	18.3	19.8	8.9	10.9	4.0	27.3	0.8	1.2	0.9	0.3	. . .	299.3
4th quarter	42.4	20.2	22.2	9.1	13.1	4.1	28.1	0.7	1.2	0.9	0.3	. . .	309.9
1953													
1st quarter	43.3	21.3	22.1	8.8	13.3	4.3	28.7	0.7	1.2	0.9	0.3	. . .	315.3
2nd quarter	42.5	21.4	21.1	9.5	11.6	4.4	29.2	0.5	1.2	0.9	0.3	. . .	317.4
3rd quarter	41.3	20.9	20.4	9.4	11.0	4.6	29.3	0.7	1.2	0.8	0.3	. . .	315.8
4th quarter	34.0	16.2	17.8	9.2	8.5	4.8	29.2	0.2	1.1	0.8	0.3	. . .	307.9
1954													
1st quarter	36.5	16.1	20.4	9.7	10.7	5.0	28.7	0.1	1.0	0.6	0.3	. . .	310.1
2nd quarter	37.8	16.6	21.2	9.2	12.1	5.3	28.8	0.7	0.9	0.5	0.3	. . .	310.9
3rd quarter	39.9	17.7	22.2	9.6	12.7	5.5	28.7	0.3	0.9	0.5	0.4	. . .	314.0
4th quarter	43.6	19.0	24.6	9.7	14.8	5.7	29.3	0.2	0.9	0.6	0.4	. . .	322.1
1955													
1st quarter	48.8	21.1	27.7	10.3	17.4	5.8	30.2	0.3	1.1	0.7	0.4	. . .	333.5
2nd quarter	50.1	21.4	28.7	10.4	18.3	6.0	31.2	0.3	1.2	0.9	0.4	. . .	341.8
3rd quarter	50.2	21.9	28.3	11.0	17.2	5.9	31.9	0.0	1.4	1.0	0.4	. . .	348.1
4th quarter	51.6	22.8	28.8	11.2	17.6	5.9	32.5	0.2	1.5	1.1	0.4	. . .	354.0
1956													
1st quarter	49.4	21.7	27.7	11.5	16.2	6.2	33.0	0.3	1.6	1.2	0.4	. . .	356.9
2nd quarter	49.6	22.1	27.5	11.6	16.0	6.4	33.6	0.6	1.6	1.2	0.4	. . .	362.3
3rd quarter	49.3	20.7	28.6	11.6	17.0	6.7	34.6	0.9	1.7	1.3	0.4	. . .	366.5
4th quarter	50.2	21.9	28.4	12.0	16.3	6.7	35.7	1.2	1.7	1.3	0.4	. . .	373.8
1957													
1st quarter	51.7	22.3	29.3	12.1	17.2	7.5	36.1	1.3	1.8	1.4	0.4	. . .	380.2
2nd quarter	50.3	21.4	28.9	12.3	16.6	7.7	36.6	1.2	1.8	1.4	0.4	. . .	381.7
3rd quarter	49.3	20.9	28.5	12.5	16.0	7.8	37.0	1.1	1.8	1.4	0.4	. . .	384.8
4th quarter	45.3	19.0	26.3	12.3	14.0	7.6	36.7	1.0	1.8	1.4	0.4	. . .	378.2
1958													
1st quarter	39.5	16.3	23.1	12.1	11.0	8.1	36.8	1.1	1.8	1.3	0.5	. . .	372.2
2nd quarter	40.6	16.7	23.9	12.2	11.7	8.7	37.3	1.3	1.7	1.3	0.5	. . .	373.8
3rd quarter	44.8	18.9	25.9	12.1	13.7	9.5	37.8	1.5	1.7	1.2	0.5	. . .	386.5
4th quarter	50.6	21.8	28.7	11.8	16.9	10.6	38.9	1.6	1.6	1.2	0.4	. . .	398.3

¹Includes net transfer payments to the rest of the world, not shown separately.

. . . = Not available.

Table 1-13B. National Income by Type of Income: Historical Data—*Continued*

(Billions of dollars, quarterly data are at seasonally adjusted annual rates.)

Year and quarter	National income, total	Compensation of employees							Proprietors' income with IVA and CCAdj			Rental income of persons with CCAdj
		Total	Wages and salaries			Supplements to wages and salaries			Total	Farm	Nonfarm	
			Total	Government	Other	Total	Employer contributions for:					
							Employee pension and insurance funds	Government social insurance				
1959												
1st quarter	448.3	279.7	254.0	45.5	208.6	25.7	18.0	7.8	50.1	10.9	39.2	15.0
2nd quarter	462.4	286.5	260.6	45.8	214.7	25.9	18.0	7.9	50.3	9.9	40.5	15.4
3rd quarter	459.6	286.9	260.9	46.2	214.7	26.0	18.2	7.9	50.4	9.4	41.0	15.8
4th quarter	464.8	290.2	263.9	46.7	217.2	26.3	18.4	7.9	50.6	10.1	40.5	16.0
1960												
1st quarter	478.1	298.7	270.7	47.7	223.0	28.0	18.7	9.3	49.7	9.6	40.1	16.2
2nd quarter	478.8	301.7	273.4	48.6	224.8	28.3	19.1	9.3	50.7	10.6	40.1	16.4
3rd quarter	480.2	302.6	274.0	49.9	224.1	28.6	19.3	9.3	50.9	11.0	39.9	16.5
4th quarter	478.5	302.1	273.3	50.5	222.8	28.8	19.6	9.2	51.0	11.3	39.7	16.7
1961												
1st quarter	480.3	303.1	273.8	51.1	222.7	29.3	19.9	9.5	52.3	11.5	40.8	16.9
2nd quarter	489.9	307.3	277.6	51.8	225.8	29.7	20.1	9.6	52.6	10.9	41.8	17.1
3rd quarter	499.7	312.3	282.3	52.8	229.5	30.1	20.4	9.6	53.3	11.0	42.3	17.3
4th quarter	514.2	318.9	288.4	54.2	234.2	30.5	20.7	9.8	54.5	11.5	43.0	17.5
1962												
1st quarter	523.4	325.5	293.3	55.3	238.0	32.2	21.2	11.0	55.3	11.9	43.5	17.7
2nd quarter	530.5	331.4	298.7	56.0	242.8	32.7	21.5	11.2	55.0	11.1	43.9	18.0
3rd quarter	536.9	334.2	301.2	56.5	244.7	33.1	21.8	11.2	54.9	10.7	44.2	18.2
4th quarter	544.9	337.7	304.2	57.6	246.6	33.4	22.1	11.3	55.8	11.3	44.5	18.3
1963												
1st quarter	551.8	342.7	308.0	58.6	249.3	34.7	22.5	12.2	56.0	11.4	44.6	18.5
2nd quarter	560.9	347.6	312.4	59.4	253.0	35.2	22.9	12.3	55.8	10.8	45.0	18.7
3rd quarter	569.4	352.6	316.8	60.2	256.7	35.8	23.3	12.5	56.2	10.7	45.6	18.8
4th quarter	579.4	358.8	322.2	61.9	260.3	36.5	23.9	12.6	57.6	11.1	46.5	18.8
1964												
1st quarter	591.7	365.2	328.2	63.1	265.1	37.0	24.5	12.4	57.9	9.9	48.0	18.8
2nd quarter	601.8	372.6	334.8	64.2	270.7	37.8	25.2	12.6	58.8	9.5	49.3	18.8
3rd quarter	613.2	380.0	341.4	65.7	275.7	38.6	25.9	12.7	59.3	9.3	50.0	18.9
4th quarter	621.4	386.1	346.7	66.8	279.9	39.4	26.6	12.8	60.5	10.4	50.1	18.8
1965												
1st quarter	640.0	392.9	352.8	67.5	285.4	40.1	27.3	12.8	61.9	11.4	50.5	19.1
2nd quarter	651.2	399.9	358.9	68.5	290.3	41.0	28.1	13.0	63.2	12.0	51.2	19.3
3rd quarter	662.4	408.3	366.2	70.5	295.7	42.1	29.0	13.2	64.0	12.2	51.8	19.5
4th quarter	681.8	420.5	377.1	73.2	304.0	43.3	29.9	13.4	65.6	12.5	53.0	19.5
1966												
1st quarter	702.0	433.1	385.8	74.9	310.8	47.3	30.9	16.5	69.2	14.9	54.4	19.8
2nd quarter	711.8	444.4	395.9	76.9	319.0	48.5	31.8	16.7	67.2	12.7	54.5	19.8
3rd quarter	723.1	455.7	406.1	79.8	326.3	49.5	32.5	17.0	67.2	12.3	54.9	20.0
4th quarter	735.5	463.8	413.5	82.0	331.5	50.3	33.1	17.2	68.1	12.2	55.9	20.0
1967												
1st quarter	741.8	470.0	418.8	83.5	335.4	51.2	33.6	17.6	68.9	11.9	57.0	20.3
2nd quarter	748.4	475.6	423.6	85.0	338.6	52.0	34.3	17.8	68.5	11.1	57.4	20.4
3rd quarter	763.8	485.3	432.0	87.1	344.9	53.3	35.1	18.2	70.5	12.0	58.6	20.4
4th quarter	779.7	496.2	441.6	90.4	351.2	54.7	36.1	18.6	70.0	11.5	58.4	20.3
1968												
1st quarter	800.5	510.9	454.2	92.8	361.5	56.7	37.2	19.4	71.7	11.6	60.1	20.1
2nd quarter	821.5	524.0	465.9	95.2	370.7	58.1	38.3	19.8	73.2	11.2	61.9	20.1
3rd quarter	841.0	537.8	478.3	98.7	379.6	59.5	39.4	20.1	75.0	11.8	63.2	20.2
4th quarter	858.0	550.3	489.4	100.1	389.4	60.9	40.4	20.5	75.5	12.0	63.5	20.0
1969												
1st quarter	874.6	562.8	499.1	101.3	397.8	63.7	41.6	22.1	75.6	11.6	64.1	20.2
2nd quarter	890.1	576.7	511.4	103.1	408.3	65.3	42.8	22.5	77.1	12.5	64.6	20.3
3rd quarter	908.1	593.4	526.4	108.2	418.3	67.0	44.0	23.0	78.0	13.1	64.8	20.4
4th quarter	916.3	604.9	536.5	109.8	426.6	68.5	45.1	23.4	77.3	14.1	63.2	20.4
1970												
1st quarter	921.1	615.0	545.1	114.4	430.7	69.9	46.2	23.7	77.1	13.5	63.5	20.4
2nd quarter	933.2	620.2	549.1	116.5	432.6	71.2	47.3	23.9	76.7	12.4	64.3	20.2
3rd quarter	947.7	628.2	555.7	118.3	437.4	72.5	48.5	23.9	78.5	13.2	65.3	20.9
4th quarter	948.0	630.0	556.4	119.7	436.6	73.7	49.8	23.9	78.9	12.5	66.4	21.2
1971												
1st quarter	984.6	647.9	570.5	123.9	446.6	77.4	51.3	26.1	80.3	13.1	67.2	21.1
2nd quarter	1 004.4	659.8	580.4	125.6	454.8	79.3	52.9	26.4	82.8	13.3	69.6	21.7
3rd quarter	1 022.4	670.1	588.8	128.0	460.8	81.3	54.8	26.5	84.6	13.0	71.6	22.0
4th quarter	1 044.7	682.2	598.4	129.6	468.8	83.7	56.9	26.8	87.9	14.2	73.6	22.5
1972												
1st quarter	1 077.9	708.4	618.5	134.2	484.3	89.9	59.3	30.6	87.9	13.1	74.8	23.1
2nd quarter	1 098.2	722.5	630.4	135.7	494.7	92.1	61.1	31.0	91.3	15.4	75.9	20.2
3rd quarter	1 127.9	735.7	642.3	138.4	503.9	93.4	62.3	31.2	95.5	17.2	78.4	23.9
4th quarter	1 174.0	758.8	664.0	143.3	520.7	94.8	63.0	31.8	105.6	22.4	83.3	23.8
1973												
1st quarter	1 211.0	785.4	683.4	145.0	538.3	102.1	63.3	38.7	104.1	21.8	82.4	23.5
2nd quarter	1 235.7	803.2	700.2	147.2	553.0	103.0	63.7	39.3	109.9	27.6	82.4	23.3
3rd quarter	1 264.0	820.4	716.2	149.6	566.6	104.2	64.3	39.9	113.8	29.5	84.3	22.3
4th quarter	1 301.9	841.7	735.3	153.4	582.0	106.4	65.3	41.1	122.2	37.5	84.7	23.3

Table 1-13B. National Income by Type of Income: Historical Data—*Continued*

(Billions of dollars, quarterly data are at seasonally adjusted annual rates.)

NIPA Tables 1.7.5, 1.12

| Year and quarter | Corporate profits with IVA and CCAdj | | | | | Net interest and miscellaneous payments | Taxes on production and imports | Less: Subsidies | Business current transfer payments, net | | | Current surplus of government enterprises | Addendum: Net national factor income |
| | Total | Taxes on corporate income | Profits after tax | | | | | | Total [1] | To persons | To government | | |
			Total	Net dividends	Undistributed corporate profits								
1959													
1st quarter	54.3	22.8	31.5	12.8	18.7	8.5	39.8	1.1	1.6	1.3	0.3	. . .	407.5
2nd quarter	59.1	25.0	34.1	13.2	20.9	9.5	40.3	0.9	1.7	1.3	0.3	. . .	420.8
3rd quarter	54.2	22.1	32.1	13.8	18.3	9.5	41.7	1.1	1.7	1.3	0.3	. . .	416.8
4th quarter	54.5	21.4	33.1	14.1	19.0	9.8	42.4	1.1	1.7	1.4	0.3	. . .	421.2
1960													
1st quarter	58.6	24.2	34.4	14.1	20.3	9.8	43.7	1.0	1.7	1.3	0.4	. . .	433.1
2nd quarter	54.8	22.1	32.7	14.2	18.5	9.9	44.3	1.3	1.7	1.3	0.4	. . .	433.5
3rd quarter	53.8	21.1	32.7	14.4	18.2	10.5	44.9	1.0	1.7	1.3	0.4	. . .	434.3
4th quarter	51.5	20.1	31.4	14.3	17.1	10.9	45.3	1.2	1.8	1.3	0.5	. . .	432.3
1961													
1st quarter	50.2	20.0	30.3	14.3	16.0	11.3	45.8	1.6	1.9	1.3	0.5	. . .	433.9
2nd quarter	54.5	21.4	33.1	14.3	18.7	11.9	46.5	2.0	1.9	1.3	0.5	. . .	443.4
3rd quarter	57.2	22.7	34.5	14.6	19.9	12.2	47.3	2.2	1.9	1.4	0.5	. . .	452.4
4th quarter	61.8	24.7	37.1	15.2	21.9	12.9	48.4	2.3	2.0	1.4	0.6	. . .	465.7
1962													
1st quarter	62.6	23.1	39.4	15.3	24.1	12.7	49.4	2.3	2.0	1.5	0.6	. . .	473.8
2nd quarter	62.5	22.9	39.7	15.8	23.9	13.7	49.9	2.4	2.1	1.5	0.6	. . .	480.6
3rd quarter	64.2	23.6	40.7	16.0	24.7	14.2	50.9	2.2	2.1	1.6	0.6	. . .	485.7
4th quarter	66.9	23.6	43.2	16.2	27.0	14.6	51.3	2.2	2.2	1.6	0.6	. . .	493.2
1963													
1st quarter	67.2	23.7	43.5	16.6	26.9	14.3	52.0	2.0	2.4	1.8	0.6	. . .	498.7
2nd quarter	70.2	25.4	44.8	16.9	27.9	14.5	52.9	2.2	2.5	1.8	0.7	. . .	506.8
3rd quarter	71.7	26.1	45.5	17.2	28.3	15.0	53.9	2.3	2.5	1.9	0.7	. . .	514.4
4th quarter	73.0	26.7	46.2	17.7	28.5	15.5	54.7	2.4	2.6	2.0	0.7	. . .	523.6
1964													
1st quarter	77.1	26.4	50.7	19.0	31.7	16.2	55.7	2.7	2.7	2.1	0.6	. . .	535.1
2nd quarter	77.3	26.4	50.9	19.6	31.3	16.7	56.7	2.9	2.8	2.2	0.6	. . .	544.3
3rd quarter	78.4	27.0	51.5	20.0	31.4	17.5	57.9	2.6	3.2	2.2	1.0	. . .	554.1
4th quarter	78.0	26.5	51.5	20.5	31.0	17.6	58.8	2.7	3.3	2.3	1.0	. . .	561.1
1965													
1st quarter	85.8	28.3	57.5	20.4	37.1	18.6	60.2	2.9	3.5	2.3	1.2	. . .	578.4
2nd quarter	88.0	29.2	58.8	21.2	37.7	19.0	60.3	3.0	3.5	2.3	1.2	. . .	589.4
3rd quarter	89.3	29.8	59.5	21.9	37.6	19.5	60.5	3.0	3.5	2.2	1.2	. . .	600.6
4th quarter	94.0	31.7	62.3	22.6	39.7	19.5	61.8	3.1	3.4	2.2	1.3	. . .	619.0
1966													
1st quarter	97.4	32.7	64.7	22.7	41.9	20.7	61.4	3.6	3.4	2.2	1.3	. . .	640.2
2nd quarter	96.4	32.6	63.7	22.5	41.3	21.3	62.8	3.9	3.4	2.1	1.3	. . .	649.1
3rd quarter	94.8	32.2	62.7	22.2	40.4	22.1	63.7	4.1	3.4	2.1	1.3	. . .	659.8
4th quarter	95.9	31.4	64.5	21.8	42.6	23.2	64.9	4.2	3.4	2.1	1.3	. . .	671.1
1967													
1st quarter	93.3	30.6	62.7	22.9	39.8	24.0	65.6	4.0	3.5	2.2	1.3	. . .	676.4
2nd quarter	92.2	30.3	61.8	23.5	38.3	24.8	66.8	3.9	3.6	2.2	1.4	. . .	681.5
3rd quarter	93.2	30.6	62.6	23.9	38.7	25.2	68.7	3.7	3.7	2.3	1.4	. . .	694.7
4th quarter	96.8	32.4	64.4	23.2	41.1	25.7	70.6	3.7	3.8	2.4	1.4	. . .	709.0
1968													
1st quarter	98.1	36.5	61.7	24.9	36.8	26.0	73.4	4.0	3.9	2.5	1.4	. . .	726.7
2nd quarter	102.1	37.1	65.1	25.8	39.2	26.3	75.4	4.2	4.1	2.7	1.4	. . .	745.7
3rd quarter	102.6	37.1	65.5	26.5	39.0	27.1	77.7	4.2	4.3	2.9	1.4	. . .	762.8
4th quarter	104.1	38.0	66.1	26.8	39.3	28.4	79.1	4.2	4.4	3.0	1.4	. . .	778.3
1969													
1st quarter	103.5	38.7	64.8	26.7	38.1	31.4	80.6	4.3	4.7	3.3	1.5	. . .	793.5
2nd quarter	100.3	37.5	62.9	27.1	35.8	32.2	82.9	4.5	4.8	3.4	1.5	. . .	806.6
3rd quarter	97.4	36.1	61.4	27.3	34.0	33.3	85.2	4.7	4.8	3.4	1.5	. . .	822.6
4th quarter	92.4	35.6	56.8	27.9	29.0	34.1	86.7	4.7	4.8	3.3	1.5	. . .	829.2
1970													
1st quarter	84.7	31.1	53.6	27.9	25.7	36.2	88.5	4.7	4.6	3.1	1.5	. . .	833.3
2nd quarter	88.5	31.2	57.3	27.8	29.6	38.5	90.5	4.8	4.5	3.0	1.5	. . .	844.2
3rd quarter	88.4	32.1	56.2	27.8	28.4	40.9	92.5	4.7	4.2	2.8	1.4	. . .	856.8
4th quarter	83.5	30.7	52.8	27.7	25.1	42.4	94.1	4.8	4.1	2.8	1.4	. . .	855.9
1971													
1st quarter	96.6	34.4	62.2	28.5	33.8	43.4	97.7	4.8	4.1	2.7	1.5	. . .	889.4
2nd quarter	98.7	35.3	63.4	28.2	35.2	44.3	98.9	4.8	4.1	2.7	1.4	. . .	907.4
3rd quarter	101.4	34.6	66.9	28.5	38.4	44.4	101.7	4.5	4.2	2.7	1.5	. . .	922.6
4th quarter	105.8	35.0	70.8	28.3	42.5	44.5	103.7	4.6	4.2	2.8	1.5	. . .	942.8
1972													
1st quarter	111.5	37.1	74.4	29.3	45.0	45.4	104.6	6.1	4.5	2.9	1.6	. . .	976.3
2nd quarter	113.4	37.5	76.0	29.6	46.3	46.6	106.8	6.2	4.7	3.0	1.7	. . .	994.0
3rd quarter	118.2	38.8	79.4	30.3	49.1	48.9	108.9	7.2	4.9	3.2	1.7	. . .	1 022.2
4th quarter	125.7	43.1	82.7	31.0	51.7	51.1	111.5	7.1	5.0	3.3	1.7	. . .	1 065.0
1973													
1st quarter	133.5	46.0	87.5	32.1	55.4	51.6	114.6	5.9	5.6	3.6	1.9	. . .	1 098.1
2nd quarter	131.2	46.0	85.2	33.5	51.7	53.4	116.2	5.7	5.9	3.9	2.0	. . .	1 121.1
3rd quarter	133.0	44.0	89.0	35.0	54.0	57.3	118.4	4.7	5.6	4.1	1.6	. . .	1 146.8
4th quarter	135.8	46.5	89.3	36.4	52.9	60.5	119.7	4.6	5.8	4.2	1.6	. . .	1 183.5

¹Includes net transfer payments to the rest of the world, not shown separately.
. . . = Not available.

Table 1-13B. National Income by Type of Income: Historical Data—*Continued*

(Billions of dollars, quarterly data are at seasonally adjusted annual rates.)

NIPA Tables 1.7.5, 1.12

Year and quarter	National income, total	Compensation of employees							Proprietors' income with IVA and CCAdj			Rental income of persons with CCAdj
		Total	Wages and salaries			Supplements to wages and salaries			Total	Farm	Nonfarm	
			Total	Government	Other	Total	Employer contributions for:					
							Employee pension and insurance funds	Government social insurance				
1974												
1st quarter	1 313.9	858.3	748.2	155.6	592.5	110.2	66.6	43.6	115.7	28.6	87.1	23.5
2nd quarter	1 334.6	878.5	765.3	158.2	607.1	113.2	68.7	44.5	108.6	20.1	88.5	22.9
3rd quarter	1 360.6	900.2	783.1	161.3	621.8	117.1	71.8	45.3	111.0	21.5	89.5	23.3
4th quarter	1 376.5	913.8	792.5	166.9	625.6	121.3	75.9	45.4	113.5	23.7	89.8	23.0
1975												
1st quarter	1 383.4	918.4	791.9	170.5	621.4	126.5	80.7	45.7	112.7	19.7	93.0	22.7
2nd quarter	1 413.8	931.2	800.4	174.5	625.9	130.8	84.8	46.0	114.3	20.1	94.2	22.4
3rd quarter	1 471.7	956.0	821.3	177.8	643.5	134.7	87.7	47.0	120.7	23.8	96.9	22.2
4th quarter	1 515.3	983.4	845.8	182.2	663.6	137.6	89.4	48.2	125.2	24.3	100.8	21.9
1976												
1st quarter	1 565.6	1 014.7	871.2	184.8	686.4	143.5	90.4	53.1	126.4	19.4	107.0	21.6
2nd quarter	1 591.3	1 035.5	889.4	187.3	702.1	146.1	92.2	53.9	128.6	17.0	111.6	20.5
3rd quarter	1 623.6	1 058.4	908.5	189.5	719.0	149.9	95.1	54.9	132.7	16.1	116.6	20.0
4th quarter	1 656.9	1 084.8	929.9	194.1	735.8	154.9	99.2	55.7	136.2	16.3	119.9	19.1
1977												
1st quarter	1 704.1	1 113.3	950.0	196.7	753.3	163.2	104.2	59.1	138.6	16.0	122.6	16.4
2nd quarter	1 770.3	1 150.3	980.9	199.7	781.2	169.4	108.8	60.6	140.5	14.1	126.4	16.3
3rd quarter	1 825.0	1 182.1	1 007.5	203.7	803.8	174.6	112.9	61.7	142.4	11.8	130.6	15.6
4th quarter	1 871.9	1 217.6	1 038.2	210.3	827.9	179.4	116.4	63.0	156.5	22.0	134.5	15.1
1978												
1st quarter	1 910.5	1 250.9	1 063.8	213.6	850.3	187.1	119.4	67.6	158.5	18.5	140.0	15.9
2nd quarter	2 006.3	1 299.1	1 106.0	217.3	888.8	193.1	122.6	70.4	166.1	20.9	145.2	15.6
3rd quarter	2 054.8	1 336.9	1 138.0	222.4	915.6	198.9	126.3	72.6	168.3	20.8	147.6	17.1
4th quarter	2 119.1	1 380.2	1 174.4	226.8	947.6	205.8	130.3	75.4	170.9	19.5	151.4	17.5
1979												
1st quarter	2 172.6	1 422.5	1 208.6	231.3	977.2	214.0	134.7	79.2	180.1	23.8	156.3	17.3
2nd quarter	2 212.5	1 454.7	1 234.4	233.5	1 000.9	220.4	139.0	81.4	179.2	21.8	157.3	15.6
3rd quarter	2 264.9	1 496.7	1 269.4	239.4	1 030.0	227.3	143.5	83.9	180.7	22.3	158.5	15.4
4th quarter	2 311.3	1 534.9	1 300.9	244.3	1 056.6	234.0	148.1	85.9	177.8	20.8	157.0	16.1
1980												
1st quarter	2 353.0	1 573.6	1 333.8	250.2	1 083.6	239.8	152.9	86.9	167.6	13.3	154.3	15.8
2nd quarter	2 356.2	1 599.2	1 353.9	260.6	1 093.3	245.3	157.7	87.6	160.3	3.1	157.2	17.1
3rd quarter	2 422.8	1 628.6	1 377.3	264.2	1 113.1	251.3	162.2	89.1	173.4	11.7	161.7	19.9
4th quarter	2 542.6	1 687.6	1 428.7	270.8	1 157.9	258.9	166.7	92.2	185.0	18.7	166.3	23.2
1981												
1st quarter	2 630.5	1 739.6	1 467.7	277.3	1 190.3	271.9	171.0	100.9	188.2	17.6	170.6	24.0
2nd quarter	2 676.3	1 774.8	1 496.7	282.6	1 214.1	278.1	175.3	102.7	176.4	18.2	158.2	23.3
3rd quarter	2 769.4	1 815.1	1 530.6	288.6	1 241.9	284.5	179.7	104.8	182.3	23.3	158.9	23.1
4th quarter	2 782.5	1 840.7	1 550.6	294.8	1 255.8	290.1	184.1	106.0	171.8	17.0	154.9	24.7
1982												
1st quarter	2 786.1	1 864.7	1 567.5	300.8	1 266.8	297.1	188.5	108.6	165.2	14.4	150.8	23.5
2nd quarter	2 833.6	1 884.4	1 581.7	305.4	1 276.3	302.6	193.2	109.5	169.4	12.8	156.6	21.1
3rd quarter	2 852.9	1 904.8	1 596.4	309.5	1 286.9	308.3	198.0	110.3	170.7	11.9	158.8	24.4
4th quarter	2 865.4	1 918.1	1 604.4	314.5	1 289.9	313.8	203.1	110.7	179.5	14.2	165.3	26.3
1983												
1st quarter	2 924.4	1 947.2	1 622.4	318.7	1 303.7	324.8	208.4	116.4	183.3	12.9	170.4	25.8
2nd quarter	3 004.2	1 986.3	1 654.7	322.6	1 332.1	331.6	213.2	118.4	182.6	7.9	174.8	24.7
3rd quarter	3 085.1	2 029.6	1 691.4	326.7	1 364.7	338.2	217.5	120.7	183.8	0.2	183.6	23.7
4th quarter	3 192.4	2 086.8	1 741.5	331.2	1 410.4	345.3	221.3	124.0	195.3	3.8	191.5	23.5
1984												
1st quarter	3 320.8	2 143.8	1 784.0	337.8	1 446.2	359.8	224.7	135.1	221.9	19.5	202.4	23.2
2nd quarter	3 408.8	2 195.2	1 828.1	344.8	1 483.4	367.0	228.9	138.1	231.8	21.3	210.5	21.7
3rd quarter	3 474.3	2 241.6	1 867.1	351.9	1 515.2	374.6	234.0	140.5	232.4	20.4	211.9	24.4
4th quarter	3 531.6	2 282.9	1 900.5	358.1	1 542.4	382.4	240.0	142.4	226.9	22.5	204.4	29.3
1985												
1st quarter	3 593.1	2 323.5	1 932.1	363.9	1 568.2	391.4	247.0	144.4	240.7	22.8	217.8	26.9
2nd quarter	3 641.2	2 363.6	1 963.6	370.4	1 593.2	400.0	253.8	146.2	238.5	20.4	218.0	25.3
3rd quarter	3 702.9	2 406.4	1 997.4	378.1	1 619.3	409.0	260.4	148.6	240.7	19.3	221.5	27.1
4th quarter	3 742.5	2 455.7	2 037.0	383.0	1 654.0	418.7	266.9	151.8	244.3	21.4	223.0	25.6
1986												
1st quarter	3 793.2	2 491.1	2 063.5	387.9	1 675.6	427.6	273.1	154.5	245.6	18.3	227.4	22.0
2nd quarter	3 804.1	2 517.2	2 081.8	393.6	1 688.3	435.4	279.1	156.3	251.6	19.6	232.0	21.1
3rd quarter	3 842.3	2 555.2	2 111.5	399.4	1 712.0	443.8	284.9	158.9	264.4	26.6	237.8	16.6
4th quarter	3 885.3	2 604.7	2 152.5	407.9	1 744.6	452.2	290.4	161.8	264.2	26.6	237.6	13.4
1987												
1st quarter	3 953.9	2 647.8	2 192.7	413.5	1 779.1	455.1	292.4	162.7	275.4	27.3	248.2	14.5
2nd quarter	4 053.5	2 692.0	2 229.9	419.9	1 810.0	462.1	297.5	164.6	282.3	29.0	253.3	14.1
3rd quarter	4 146.6	2 740.3	2 270.8	425.1	1 845.7	469.5	302.4	167.1	289.5	28.8	260.7	17.5
4th quarter	4 239.9	2 809.6	2 331.7	433.9	1 897.8	477.8	307.2	170.6	298.6	30.4	268.2	20.3
1988												
1st quarter	4 329.2	2 857.6	2 366.2	441.7	1 924.4	491.4	312.1	179.2	319.2	33.3	285.9	21.1
2nd quarter	4 421.4	2 923.1	2 421.5	448.5	1 973.0	501.6	318.6	183.0	322.5	27.4	295.1	20.3
3rd quarter	4 514.3	2 975.8	2 462.9	454.5	2 008.3	513.0	326.8	186.2	333.6	28.8	304.8	21.2
4th quarter	4 621.4	3 035.4	2 508.6	463.4	2 045.2	526.9	336.8	190.0	326.8	17.7	309.2	27.4

Table 1-13B. National Income by Type of Income: Historical Data—*Continued*

(Billions of dollars, quarterly data are at seasonally adjusted annual rates.)

NIPA Tables 1.7.5, 1.12

Year and quarter	Corporate profits with IVA and CCAdj					Net interest and miscel-laneous payments	Taxes on production and imports	Less: Subsidies	Business current transfer payments, net			Current surplus of govern-ment enterprises	Addendum: Net national factor income
	Total	Taxes on corporate income	Profits after tax						Total [1]	To persons	To govern-ment		
			Total	Net dividends	Undis-tributed corporate profits								
1974													
1st quarter	130.3	44.6	85.7	37.7	48.0	64.9	120.8	3.6	6.3	4.3	2.0	. . .	1 192.8
2nd quarter	128.9	46.7	82.3	38.8	43.5	69.8	124.1	2.9	6.6	4.5	2.1	. . .	1 208.8
3rd quarter	124.3	51.5	72.8	39.4	33.4	73.4	127.1	3.2	7.0	4.9	2.1	. . .	1 232.2
4th quarter	119.3	46.2	73.2	39.2	33.9	78.5	127.7	3.6	7.3	5.2	2.1	. . .	1 248.1
1975													
1st quarter	117.8	38.3	79.4	38.4	41.0	82.6	128.8	4.2	8.4	6.1	2.2	. . .	1 254.1
2nd quarter	128.9	41.4	87.5	38.0	49.5	83.1	133.0	4.3	9.1	6.9	2.2	. . .	1 279.9
3rd quarter	149.8	52.0	97.7	38.0	59.7	84.3	138.2	4.6	9.3	7.1	2.2	. . .	1 333.0
4th quarter	159.0	53.3	105.7	38.9	66.8	84.7	141.1	4.9	9.4	7.2	2.2	. . .	1 374.1
1976													
1st quarter	175.1	60.8	114.3	41.9	72.3	84.1	141.7	5.1	9.5	7.0	2.5	. . .	1 422.0
2nd quarter	173.2	59.4	113.8	43.9	69.9	86.6	144.9	4.8	9.4	7.0	2.4	. . .	1 444.4
3rd quarter	174.7	59.0	115.8	45.8	69.9	88.4	147.7	5.1	9.1	6.7	2.4	. . .	1 474.3
4th quarter	174.3	58.5	115.9	47.9	68.0	90.4	151.3	5.5	8.6	6.1	2.5	. . .	1 504.9
1977													
1st quarter	184.1	62.9	121.2	48.6	72.6	97.1	154.8	5.8	8.2	5.5	2.7	. . .	1 549.6
2nd quarter	204.9	68.4	136.5	49.9	86.6	101.0	158.0	5.9	7.8	5.0	2.8	. . .	1 613.0
3rd quarter	219.6	70.8	148.8	51.5	97.3	105.3	161.5	6.4	8.0	4.9	3.2	. . .	1 665.1
4th quarter	214.5	71.8	142.6	52.8	89.8	109.3	164.3	10.3	8.3	5.0	3.3	. . .	1 713.0
1978													
1st quarter	209.9	66.2	143.7	54.6	89.2	110.8	166.9	8.7	9.4	5.6	3.7	. . .	1 746.1
2nd quarter	239.7	80.0	159.7	56.1	103.7	113.7	173.1	8.4	10.0	6.2	3.9	. . .	1 834.3
3rd quarter	246.2	80.2	166.0	59.0	107.0	115.4	169.7	8.3	10.7	6.7	4.0	. . .	1 884.0
4th quarter	258.4	85.0	173.4	61.6	111.8	119.4	173.9	10.4	11.4	7.3	4.1	. . .	1 946.4
1979													
1st quarter	249.7	81.9	167.8	63.6	104.2	125.0	176.4	8.4	12.3	7.9	4.4	. . .	1 994.5
2nd quarter	252.1	82.1	170.0	65.8	104.3	130.8	178.5	8.8	12.7	8.2	4.5	. . .	2 032.5
3rd quarter	250.1	81.0	169.0	67.6	101.4	138.9	180.9	8.1	13.0	8.4	4.6	. . .	2 081.8
4th quarter	244.0	77.9	166.1	70.2	95.9	153.1	184.6	8.9	13.1	8.5	4.6	. . .	2 126.0
1980													
1st quarter	237.5	85.4	152.1	73.4	78.7	168.6	189.5	9.2	13.2	8.2	5.0	. . .	2 163.1
2nd quarter	207.0	64.9	142.1	76.6	65.5	176.1	196.9	9.6	13.4	8.3	5.1	. . .	2 159.8
3rd quarter	214.6	72.1	142.5	75.7	66.8	182.9	204.3	10.1	13.7	8.7	5.0	. . .	2 219.4
4th quarter	235.1	79.5	155.6	77.4	78.2	201.3	210.6	10.3	15.7	9.3	6.4	. . .	2 332.2
1981													
1st quarter	244.4	78.1	166.2	81.7	84.5	203.8	230.8	10.6	16.4	10.4	6.1	. . .	2 399.9
2nd quarter	240.8	69.1	171.8	86.3	85.5	223.7	235.5	10.7	16.6	11.0	5.6	. . .	2 439.0
3rd quarter	257.8	71.6	186.2	90.4	95.8	252.3	237.5	11.1	17.1	11.5	5.6	. . .	2 530.6
4th quarter	246.9	62.4	184.5	92.8	91.8	259.5	238.8	13.5	17.5	11.9	5.7	. . .	2 543.7
1982													
1st quarter	221.8	50.6	171.2	92.8	78.4	272.2	237.4	14.0	18.6	12.0	6.6	. . .	2 547.5
2nd quarter	236.2	52.7	183.5	92.2	91.2	282.1	238.3	13.6	19.2	12.3	6.9	. . .	2 593.1
3rd quarter	233.7	53.2	180.5	92.5	87.9	274.6	241.8	13.0	19.5	12.5	7.0	. . .	2 608.1
4th quarter	227.7	48.6	179.1	94.1	85.0	270.3	246.3	19.4	20.0	12.7	7.2	. . .	2 621.9
1983													
1st quarter	244.6	50.2	194.3	95.0	99.4	275.1	250.7	19.9	20.3	12.8	7.5	. . .	2 676.0
2nd quarter	274.7	65.3	209.4	96.0	113.4	277.4	261.2	21.6	20.9	13.2	7.7	. . .	2 745.7
3rd quarter	291.2	74.0	217.2	98.6	118.6	291.2	267.5	22.2	21.9	14.0	7.9	. . .	2 819.7
4th quarter	308.6	76.1	232.4	101.2	131.3	303.6	273.7	21.5	23.6	15.3	8.4	. . .	2 917.8
1984													
1st quarter	336.6	88.4	248.2	104.0	144.1	309.8	281.6	21.2	26.7	17.6	9.1	. . .	3 035.4
2nd quarter	338.2	87.1	251.1	106.6	144.5	327.6	287.7	21.0	28.6	19.2	9.4	. . .	3 114.5
3rd quarter	333.6	74.7	258.8	107.4	151.5	341.7	292.2	20.9	30.1	20.6	9.6	. . .	3 173.7
4th quarter	343.1	75.6	267.5	109.4	158.1	341.9	297.5	21.2	31.2	21.5	9.7	. . .	3 224.1
1985													
1st quarter	347.9	80.5	267.4	113.6	153.8	341.3	301.0	21.1	32.2	21.9	10.3	. . .	3 280.2
2nd quarter	351.5	78.8	272.7	115.2	157.6	337.3	305.7	21.0	38.1	22.1	16.0	. . .	3 316.3
3rd quarter	368.9	84.7	284.1	115.8	168.3	334.1	311.9	21.3	32.8	22.3	10.5	. . .	3 377.2
4th quarter	349.7	82.4	267.3	116.8	150.5	340.0	313.9	22.0	33.1	22.6	10.5	. . .	3 415.3
1986													
1st quarter	340.7	87.8	252.9	122.0	130.9	354.9	317.5	23.1	42.1	23.3	18.7	. . .	3 454.3
2nd quarter	326.6	88.4	238.2	124.3	113.9	355.3	319.5	24.2	34.5	23.5	11.1	. . .	3 471.8
3rd quarter	315.6	90.0	225.6	124.8	100.8	354.0	326.2	25.5	33.2	23.0	10.2	. . .	3 505.8
4th quarter	314.7	101.2	213.4	124.9	88.6	348.1	330.4	26.8	34.0	22.0	12.0	. . .	3 545.1
1987													
1st quarter	325.9	101.5	224.3	126.0	98.3	345.6	336.0	28.3	34.0	21.3	12.7	. . .	3 609.1
2nd quarter	362.9	115.1	247.8	127.5	120.2	351.0	344.4	30.4	34.4	20.6	13.8	. . .	3 702.4
3rd quarter	386.4	119.9	266.5	131.3	135.2	356.9	352.4	31.3	32.5	19.7	12.8	. . .	3 790.5
4th quarter	388.8	114.3	274.5	135.3	139.2	361.4	357.4	31.1	32.3	19.3	13.0	. . .	3 878.7
1988													
1st quarter	394.2	112.6	281.6	138.5	143.1	369.1	365.2	30.4	31.1	19.6	11.5	. . .	3 961.1
2nd quarter	408.6	120.0	288.6	143.1	145.5	366.4	372.5	29.8	31.7	20.1	11.6	. . .	4 040.9
3rd quarter	415.2	129.1	286.1	150.3	135.8	380.4	377.5	29.2	33.2	20.8	12.4	. . .	4 126.3
4th quarter	439.8	135.4	304.5	157.3	147.2	395.5	382.6	28.6	35.1	21.9	13.2	. . .	4 225.0

[1] Includes net transfer payments to the rest of the world, not shown separately.
. . . = Not available.

Table 1-13B. National Income by Type of Income: Historical Data—Continued

(Billions of dollars, quarterly data are at seasonally adjusted annual rates.)   **NIPA Tables 1.7.5, 1.12**

Year and quarter	National income, total	Compensation of employees							Proprietors' income with IVA and CCAdj			Rental income of persons with CCAdj
		Total	Wages and salaries			Supplements to wages and salaries			Total	Farm	Nonfarm	
			Total	Government	Other	Total	Employer contributions for:					
							Employee pension and insurance funds	Government social insurance				
1989												
1st quarter	4 697.6	3 079.1	2 540.8	469.5	2 071.3	538.3	348.1	190.1	348.1	36.7	311.4	23.1
2nd quarter	4 732.4	3 114.6	2 563.5	476.9	2 086.6	551.1	358.8	192.3	339.5	32.6	306.9	21.2
3rd quarter	4 785.4	3 155.0	2 592.3	485.1	2 107.1	562.8	368.2	194.6	337.2	30.3	306.9	20.0
4th quarter	4 825.0	3 209.7	2 635.7	493.0	2 142.7	574.1	376.4	197.7	339.7	32.5	307.2	21.8
1990												
1st quarter	4 927.3	3 272.8	2 684.4	503.5	2 180.9	588.3	386.3	202.0	345.6	34.5	311.1	23.1
2nd quarter	5 014.2	3 334.7	2 738.8	518.7	2 220.1	595.9	390.3	205.6	351.1	32.7	318.4	26.7
3rd quarter	5 042.9	3 372.5	2 769.3	523.9	2 245.5	603.2	394.7	208.5	358.9	31.8	327.2	31.6
4th quarter	5 070.6	3 381.5	2 772.2	530.1	2 242.1	609.3	399.6	209.6	357.0	29.7	327.3	31.3
1991												
1st quarter	5 093.1	3 387.5	2 771.7	539.6	2 232.1	615.8	405.2	210.6	347.5	26.2	321.3	33.0
2nd quarter	5 133.7	3 427.6	2 800.1	546.0	2 254.1	627.5	413.6	213.9	353.0	27.9	325.2	35.5
3rd quarter	5 185.5	3 469.9	2 828.1	551.6	2 276.5	641.8	425.1	216.8	353.6	24.5	329.1	39.4
4th quarter	5 245.1	3 517.0	2 858.0	557.8	2 300.2	659.0	439.7	219.3	362.6	28.6	333.9	46.4
1992												
1st quarter	5 369.1	3 595.7	2 912.9	564.2	2 348.7	682.8	456.8	226.0	378.7	32.9	345.8	50.0
2nd quarter	5 451.9	3 651.9	2 952.0	569.8	2 382.2	699.9	471.0	229.0	395.2	35.4	359.8	57.3
3rd quarter	5 492.3	3 688.5	2 976.6	575.2	2 401.4	712.0	481.4	230.6	407.9	36.7	371.1	64.3
4th quarter	5 587.6	3 736.9	3 020.8	578.8	2 442.0	716.1	488.1	228.0	418.8	34.1	384.8	70.7
1993												
1st quarter	5 596.5	3 745.6	3 015.9	582.8	2 433.1	729.6	491.7	238.0	418.9	28.6	390.3	80.7
2nd quarter	5 696.8	3 800.2	3 066.5	586.6	2 479.8	733.8	495.6	238.2	429.6	34.9	394.6	86.9
3rd quarter	5 744.2	3 834.1	3 093.6	591.8	2 501.9	740.5	500.2	240.3	423.4	26.1	397.4	92.5
4th quarter	5 883.6	3 889.3	3 141.4	594.8	2 546.5	747.9	505.7	242.2	440.0	35.8	404.2	100.2
1994												
1st quarter	5 949.8	3 913.4	3 152.7	601.1	2 551.6	760.7	511.4	249.3	450.2	41.8	408.4	109.0
2nd quarter	6 073.8	3 991.5	3 223.3	607.2	2 616.2	768.2	515.4	252.8	454.1	36.7	417.5	113.5
3rd quarter	6 163.9	4 031.8	3 258.7	612.5	2 646.2	773.0	517.6	255.5	456.8	32.1	424.6	116.3
4th quarter	6 271.1	4 088.1	3 311.6	617.2	2 694.4	776.5	517.4	259.0	465.5	28.1	437.4	115.9
1995												
1st quarter	6 331.9	4 134.4	3 358.1	622.4	2 735.7	776.3	515.6	260.8	467.4	20.3	447.1	118.3
2nd quarter	6 397.0	4 172.9	3 395.2	627.5	2 767.7	777.7	514.9	262.8	472.0	18.4	453.6	121.6
3rd quarter	6 497.6	4 219.7	3 438.9	630.9	2 808.0	780.8	515.6	265.3	484.5	21.4	463.1	125.7
4th quarter	6 582.7	4 265.3	3 479.9	635.3	2 844.6	785.4	517.8	267.7	501.0	28.1	472.9	134.0
1996												
1st quarter	6 701.0	4 314.5	3 524.4	640.0	2 884.4	790.1	521.0	269.1	523.3	36.9	486.4	139.5
2nd quarter	6 827.4	4 387.5	3 590.0	645.6	2 944.3	797.6	524.4	273.2	547.5	44.2	503.3	141.6
3rd quarter	6 909.7	4 451.2	3 647.2	650.7	2 996.5	804.0	527.3	276.7	547.5	33.5	514.0	143.7
4th quarter	7 044.3	4 514.5	3 704.3	656.0	3 048.2	810.2	530.0	280.3	556.8	34.7	522.1	145.3
1997												
1st quarter	7 159.1	4 592.4	3 776.4	662.3	3 114.1	816.0	532.7	283.3	575.6	37.8	537.8	144.2
2nd quarter	7 273.8	4 660.0	3 835.6	668.0	3 167.7	824.3	537.4	286.9	575.1	28.1	547.0	144.6
3rd quarter	7 422.5	4 738.9	3 903.0	674.1	3 228.9	835.9	544.7	291.2	588.5	32.4	556.1	147.4
4th quarter	7 544.4	4 844.0	3 992.4	683.2	3 309.2	851.6	554.7	297.0	596.6	31.2	565.4	152.1
1998												
1st quarter	7 641.9	4 942.0	4 074.9	689.8	3 385.1	867.1	566.7	300.4	617.4	27.9	589.5	156.8
2nd quarter	7 767.1	5 028.3	4 145.5	697.4	3 448.1	882.8	578.0	304.9	629.6	26.4	603.2	162.6
3rd quarter	7 898.7	5 114.9	4 217.4	705.6	3 511.8	897.4	587.9	309.5	645.0	26.6	618.4	168.0
4th quarter	7 995.3	5 199.4	4 288.7	712.4	3 576.2	910.7	596.6	314.1	668.7	33.0	635.7	173.4
1999												
1st quarter	8 149.3	5 287.0	4 364.6	718.1	3 646.5	922.3	604.1	318.2	681.9	33.6	648.3	176.1
2nd quarter	8 213.5	5 343.9	4 409.3	727.0	3 682.3	934.6	613.9	320.7	690.1	28.1	661.9	179.6
3rd quarter	8 314.1	5 424.0	4 473.7	738.6	3 735.1	950.3	626.3	324.0	699.8	26.2	673.6	179.4
4th quarter	8 488.9	5 555.9	4 584.1	751.4	3 832.7	971.8	641.4	330.5	713.9	24.5	689.4	178.9
2000												
1st quarter	8 710.9	5 749.2	4 751.5	765.2	3 986.3	997.7	657.1	340.6	720.9	27.1	693.9	179.8
2nd quarter	8 817.3	5 791.7	4 779.1	778.6	4 000.5	1 012.7	671.3	341.4	751.3	33.4	717.9	180.2
3rd quarter	8 946.1	5 903.9	4 871.3	783.8	4 087.5	1 032.7	684.6	348.1	760.8	31.9	728.9	182.9
4th quarter	9 015.4	5 943.7	4 898.0	791.5	4 106.4	1 045.8	694.9	350.8	782.4	33.7	748.7	191.0
2001												
1st quarter	9 157.9	6 050.1	4 979.5	801.8	4 177.7	1 070.7	712.9	357.8	809.8	34.0	775.7	197.1
2nd quarter	9 183.2	6 040.9	4 961.4	814.0	4 147.4	1 079.5	721.6	358.0	827.7	32.5	795.2	202.6
3rd quarter	9 124.8	6 024.6	4 935.9	828.9	4 107.0	1 088.6	731.2	357.4	845.6	32.6	813.0	204.8
4th quarter	9 120.3	6 037.8	4 937.8	843.3	4 094.4	1 100.0	741.3	358.7	840.9	29.2	811.7	205.1
2002												
1st quarter	9 237.4	6 060.7	4 945.9	855.1	4 090.7	1 114.9	753.2	361.6	859.5	17.7	841.8	207.3
2nd quarter	9 345.3	6 129.1	4 998.3	868.2	4 130.2	1 130.8	764.8	366.0	864.5	13.6	850.9	208.9
3rd quarter	9 425.1	6 156.9	5 012.1	879.8	4 132.3	1 144.8	777.3	367.5	872.9	21.8	851.2	207.7
4th quarter	9 569.2	6 193.7	5 027.1	888.4	4 138.7	1 166.6	797.6	369.0	883.3	27.8	855.5	209.9
2003												
1st quarter	9 589.5	6 213.2	5 027.0	901.2	4 125.8	1 186.2	812.2	374.0	876.3	29.9	846.4	218.7
2nd quarter	9 721.0	6 307.3	5 101.4	911.9	4 189.4	1 205.9	826.2	379.8	892.4	37.3	855.1	223.2
3rd quarter	9 889.3	6 393.7	5 168.7	917.8	4 251.0	1 225.0	839.9	385.0	905.3	39.8	865.5	227.5
4th quarter	10 063.2	6 500.2	5 256.0	924.9	4 331.0	1 244.3	852.8	391.4	916.1	41.5	874.5	239.0

Table 1-13B. National Income by Type of Income: Historical Data—*Continued*

(Billions of dollars, quarterly data are at seasonally adjusted annual rates.)   NIPA Tables 1.7.5, 1.12

Year and quarter	Corporate profits with IVA and CCAdj					Net interest and miscellaneous payments	Taxes on production and imports	Less: Subsidies	Business current transfer payments, net			Current surplus of government enterprises	Addendum: Net national factor income
			Profits after tax										
	Total	Taxes on corporate income	Total	Net dividends	Undistributed corporate profits				Total [1]	To persons	To government		
1989													
1st quarter	423.7	137.2	286.5	169.2	117.3	416.3	391.0	28.0	37.2	23.3	14.0	. . .	4 290.2
2nd quarter	415.8	123.0	292.9	177.8	115.1	426.5	397.5	27.4	37.7	23.1	14.5	. . .	4 317.6
3rd quarter	416.6	118.9	297.7	182.5	115.2	433.4	403.9	27.1	39.1	23.2	15.9	. . .	4 362.2
4th quarter	401.0	118.6	282.4	189.0	93.4	430.3	403.0	27.3	39.0	23.1	16.0	. . .	4 402.6
1990													
1st quarter	413.9	116.8	297.1	192.7	104.4	435.0	419.5	27.1	39.4	23.3	16.1	. . .	4 490.3
2nd quarter	433.9	121.7	312.2	193.1	119.1	432.8	419.5	27.0	39.0	22.9	16.0	. . .	4 579.2
3rd quarter	407.7	125.1	282.6	194.7	87.9	430.0	426.8	26.9	38.9	21.9	17.0	. . .	4 600.8
4th quarter	415.4	123.7	291.7	190.1	101.6	435.9	434.2	27.0	39.5	20.7	18.8	. . .	4 621.1
1991													
1st quarter	455.0	120.2	334.8	196.7	138.1	407.7	444.0	27.1	39.8	19.2	20.6	. . .	4 630.6
2nd quarter	452.7	116.0	336.7	200.9	135.7	393.8	451.6	27.2	38.7	17.9	20.7	. . .	4 662.6
3rd quarter	450.7	116.9	333.8	203.6	130.2	390.9	461.3	27.5	38.5	17.0	21.5	. . .	4 704.6
4th quarter	452.0	118.2	333.8	203.9	129.9	374.8	471.5	28.1	38.7	16.4	22.2	. . .	4 752.7
1992													
1st quarter	478.2	130.4	347.8	202.9	144.8	370.3	476.4	28.6	38.6	16.5	22.4	-0.2	4 872.9
2nd quarter	479.6	132.4	347.3	205.5	141.7	367.0	481.2	29.2	38.4	16.5	22.0	-0.1	4 951.0
3rd quarter	465.2	127.8	337.4	207.3	130.1	360.6	486.0	30.4	38.9	16.3	22.7	-0.1	4 986.5
4th quarter	485.7	137.1	348.6	209.4	139.2	364.6	489.9	32.2	43.0	15.9	27.1	0.0	5 076.7
1993													
1st quarter	483.6	141.7	341.9	213.0	128.9	363.5	489.7	35.5	40.2	15.1	25.1	-0.1	5 092.4
2nd quarter	511.9	154.1	357.8	217.1	140.7	357.3	497.6	37.6	39.3	14.4	25.1	-0.2	5 185.8
3rd quarter	526.3	146.4	379.9	223.3	156.5	350.1	504.9	37.7	38.7	13.7	25.4	-0.4	5 226.5
4th quarter	576.5	178.0	398.5	231.8	166.7	341.5	520.3	36.0	39.3	13.1	26.9	-0.6	5 347.4
1994													
1st quarter	584.3	155.9	428.4	244.2	184.2	341.5	531.5	33.6	40.7	12.8	28.7	-0.8	5 398.4
2nd quarter	607.3	164.1	443.2	253.3	189.9	342.9	544.4	32.4	39.7	12.8	27.7	-0.8	5 509.3
3rd quarter	641.4	180.2	461.2	260.9	200.3	345.1	550.5	31.9	41.3	13.2	28.4	-0.4	5 591.3
4th quarter	666.0	190.4	475.6	267.4	208.3	359.6	554.6	32.2	41.2	14.2	26.8	0.2	5 695.2
1995													
1st quarter	667.8	194.7	473.0	270.6	202.4	362.6	555.3	34.0	43.6	16.0	25.9	1.7	5 750.5
2nd quarter	692.4	191.0	501.4	277.0	224.4	358.1	553.6	34.6	44.9	17.8	25.1	1.9	5 816.9
3rd quarter	726.4	198.0	528.4	285.4	243.0	355.1	558.9	35.1	45.8	19.6	24.6	1.6	5 911.4
4th quarter	738.3	194.0	544.3	296.4	247.9	353.7	563.8	35.5	45.5	21.4	23.9	0.2	5 992.2
1996													
1st quarter	772.3	201.7	570.6	306.2	264.4	352.5	570.4	35.5	46.8	22.8	24.7	-0.7	6 102.1
2nd quarter	784.8	213.4	571.4	318.7	252.6	358.2	577.7	35.4	48.2	23.5	25.8	-1.1	6 219.6
3rd quarter	790.0	213.7	576.3	329.9	246.4	363.6	581.8	35.2	48.9	23.2	26.8	-1.2	6 296.0
4th quarter	810.9	216.8	594.1	339.6	254.5	373.4	593.2	34.8	66.7	21.9	45.5	-0.8	6 401.0
1997													
1st quarter	839.0	218.2	620.8	347.7	273.2	381.8	595.7	34.4	46.9	19.7	27.8	-0.6	6 532.9
2nd quarter	861.6	222.5	639.2	356.2	282.9	389.8	610.4	33.6	47.4	18.7	28.5	0.1	6 631.1
3rd quarter	896.6	234.2	662.4	364.4	298.0	396.4	616.6	33.4	53.5	19.0	33.4	1.2	6 767.8
4th quarter	881.6	224.2	657.4	372.2	285.3	409.8	623.8	33.8	52.5	20.4	29.6	2.5	6 884.2
1998													
1st quarter	812.7	222.1	590.5	383.5	207.0	442.0	629.1	33.8	58.9	22.8	31.1	5.0	6 970.9
2nd quarter	809.4	218.9	590.5	386.4	204.1	459.0	635.5	35.0	60.4	25.1	30.4	4.9	7 088.9
3rd quarter	817.6	225.5	592.2	385.2	207.0	467.0	643.0	36.8	62.6	27.1	31.8	3.7	7 212.6
4th quarter	794.1	220.7	573.4	379.4	194.0	458.8	650.3	39.9	74.3	28.9	43.9	1.6	7 294.3
1999													
1st quarter	847.1	226.5	620.6	368.7	251.8	459.0	657.5	42.4	65.4	31.2	35.6	-1.4	7 451.0
2nd quarter	840.2	223.6	616.7	366.6	250.1	453.3	667.1	45.0	67.1	32.8	36.2	-1.9	7 507.0
3rd quarter	823.7	227.6	596.1	372.1	224.1	469.9	679.0	46.4	67.9	34.8	36.2	-3.1	7 596.8
4th quarter	828.7	231.9	596.7	386.6	210.2	482.0	690.7	46.9	70.3	37.1	37.8	-4.5	7 759.4
2000													
1st quarter	808.5	243.3	565.2	400.6	164.6	503.1	698.6	45.1	81.0	39.8	41.0	0.2	7 961.5
2nd quarter	798.1	241.7	556.4	412.0	144.4	536.2	707.3	45.5	84.3	41.5	41.8	1.0	8 057.6
3rd quarter	781.2	222.8	558.4	416.0	142.4	555.5	711.3	45.8	86.3	43.3	42.0	1.0	8 184.2
4th quarter	758.4	226.0	532.4	412.3	120.2	573.6	717.1	47.0	89.0	45.2	42.8	1.1	8 249.0
2001													
1st quarter	748.0	188.6	559.4	404.2	155.2	579.1	724.2	55.2	98.6	47.9	42.8	7.9	8 384.1
2nd quarter	778.0	182.7	595.3	396.5	198.8	567.1	724.1	62.0	100.2	48.3	43.2	8.6	8 416.3
3rd quarter	746.7	162.8	583.9	393.7	190.2	539.3	725.3	71.2	100.5	47.0	44.2	9.3	8 361.0
4th quarter	762.2	146.5	615.7	397.1	218.6	483.4	737.1	46.4	97.7	43.9	45.2	8.5	8 329.3
2002													
1st quarter	852.5	147.4	705.1	412.3	292.8	463.5	744.0	42.6	87.8	39.1	46.5	2.2	8 443.5
2nd quarter	883.2	153.7	729.6	424.3	305.3	461.1	751.3	39.8	81.6	35.2	45.9	0.5	8 546.8
3rd quarter	914.6	161.8	752.8	428.2	324.6	458.0	768.5	41.3	77.5	32.3	45.8	-0.6	8 610.1
4th quarter	996.5	179.9	816.7	434.7	382.0	465.3	776.3	41.9	76.2	30.2	46.8	-0.8	8 748.8
2003													
1st quarter	988.6	199.9	788.7	435.3	353.4	466.3	788.6	47.1	77.8	29.6	47.1	1.1	8 763.1
2nd quarter	1 024.8	196.5	828.3	435.6	392.8	449.2	800.0	57.1	75.6	28.0	47.7	-0.1	8 896.9
3rd quarter	1 075.7	217.7	858.0	457.8	400.3	440.2	813.0	45.9	75.7	25.5	48.6	1.7	9 042.3
4th quarter	1 135.9	241.0	894.9	495.4	399.5	418.6	820.9	46.0	75.0	22.0	49.8	3.2	9 209.8

[1] Includes net transfer payments to the rest of the world, not shown separately.
. . . = Not available.

Table 1-13B. National Income by Type of Income: Historical Data—*Continued*

(Billions of dollars, quarterly data are at seasonally adjusted annual rates.)

NIPA Tables 1.7.5, 1.12

Year and quarter	National income, total	Compensation of employees Total	Wages and salaries Total	Government	Other	Supplements to wages and salaries Total	Employer contributions for: Employee pension and insurance funds	Government social insurance	Proprietors' income with IVA and CCAdj Total	Farm	Nonfarm	Rental income of persons with CCAdj
2004												
1st quarter	10 237.0	6 541.3	5 274.5	936.6	4 337.9	1 266.8	868.0	398.8	946.5	56.3	890.3	243.0
2nd quarter	10 414.2	6 668.5	5 380.7	948.3	4 432.5	1 287.7	881.6	406.1	963.0	55.3	907.8	243.4
3rd quarter	10 617.0	6 803.7	5 492.8	956.6	4 536.1	1 310.9	897.1	413.9	964.2	47.1	917.1	241.8
4th quarter	10 715.1	6 864.5	5 536.1	967.9	4 568.2	1 328.4	912.2	416.2	977.8	50.9	926.8	242.9
2005												
1st quarter	10 920.0	6 926.3	5 574.6	977.8	4 596.8	1 351.6	930.6	421.1	957.1	47.6	909.5	233.7
2nd quarter	11 085.7	7 005.6	5 637.8	986.1	4 651.7	1 367.7	943.1	424.6	964.1	51.2	913.0	231.2
3rd quarter	11 270.1	7 122.6	5 738.3	995.5	4 742.8	1 384.4	953.4	430.9	988.1	49.6	938.5	213.6
4th quarter	11 506.3	7 209.9	5 814.8	1 005.8	4 809.0	1 395.2	959.5	435.6	1 007.2	43.3	963.9	206.0
2006												
1st quarter	11 776.8	7 379.7	5 971.4	1 014.6	4 956.8	1 408.3	964.7	443.6	1 049.1	34.8	1 014.2	194.5
2nd quarter	11 909.7	7 428.0	6 012.6	1 025.8	4 986.8	1 415.4	970.1	445.3	1 052.1	33.9	1 018.2	183.4
3rd quarter	12 014.7	7 487.3	6 061.9	1 041.9	5 019.9	1 425.4	978.5	447.0	1 049.0	33.7	1 015.3	177.8
4th quarter	12 067.8	7 623.6	6 181.1	1 055.8	5 125.3	1 442.6	989.2	453.3	1 053.3	34.8	1 018.5	168.7
2007												
1st quarter	12 163.7	7 806.0	6 343.8	1 071.6	5 272.1	1 462.2	1 002.5	459.7	1 017.5	43.1	974.4	162.5
2nd quarter	12 322.2	7 845.2	6 370.3	1 080.5	5 289.8	1 474.8	1 015.0	459.8	997.9	38.5	959.3	180.3
3rd quarter	12 309.3	7 885.2	6 397.6	1 093.6	5 304.0	1 487.6	1 026.8	460.9	986.8	38.8	947.9	193.6
4th quarter	12 394.0	7 977.5	6 473.9	1 108.5	5 365.5	1 503.6	1 037.3	466.3	979.8	46.3	933.5	208.7
2008												
1st quarter	12 399.1	8 054.9	6 539.4	1 124.8	5 414.6	1 515.5	1 045.8	469.7	964.1	48.0	916.1	249.2
2nd quarter	12 423.7	8 054.9	6 532.7	1 136.0	5 396.7	1 522.2	1 051.9	470.4	967.2	44.2	923.1	280.9
3rd quarter	12 506.0	8 074.4	6 547.2	1 151.2	5 396.0	1 527.2	1 054.4	472.8	956.6	33.8	922.8	305.3
4th quarter	12 108.2	8 043.2	6 517.2	1 163.4	5 353.8	1 526.0	1 053.3	472.7	950.7	29.7	921.0	325.7
2009												
1st quarter	11 889.4	7 730.4	6 225.6	1 162.8	5 062.8	1 504.8	1 048.8	456.0	913.2	22.9	890.3	326.6
2nd quarter	11 933.3	7 762.0	6 254.5	1 176.0	5 078.4	1 507.5	1 048.1	459.4	901.5	23.6	878.0	335.9
3rd quarter	12 076.5	7 746.5	6 237.2	1 179.0	5 058.2	1 509.3	1 051.5	457.8	934.5	26.7	907.9	355.8
4th quarter	12 320.0	7 797.2	6 279.2	1 183.1	5 096.1	1 518.1	1 058.9	459.2	1 001.3	35.5	965.7	372.0
2010												
1st quarter	12 467.7	7 767.6	6 233.2	1 185.8	5 047.5	1 534.4	1 070.3	464.1	1 055.8	30.4	1 025.4	404.9
2nd quarter	12 676.4	7 910.6	6 360.7	1 196.6	5 164.1	1 549.9	1 080.4	469.5	1 102.7	34.0	1 068.7	428.9
3rd quarter	12 929.6	7 982.2	6 422.5	1 191.3	5 231.3	1 559.7	1 088.9	470.8	1 128.0	39.8	1 088.2	442.6
4th quarter	13 050.9	8 041.0	6 473.6	1 191.1	5 282.5	1 567.4	1 095.9	471.5	1 142.7	46.0	1 096.7	458.3
2011												
1st quarter	13 130.8	8 170.1	6 577.3	1 193.1	5 384.2	1 592.8	1 102.0	490.8	1 179.0	64.8	1 114.2	489.1
2nd quarter	13 319.3	8 206.4	6 608.2	1 199.2	5 409.0	1 598.2	1 106.4	491.8	1 210.2	59.2	1 151.0	501.4
3rd quarter	13 447.6	8 287.3	6 681.6	1 197.6	5 484.0	1 605.7	1 109.5	496.2	1 251.6	64.6	1 187.1	510.1
4th quarter	13 604.3	8 240.9	6 637.6	1 189.5	5 448.1	1 603.3	1 111.1	492.2	1 268.9	63.6	1 205.3	525.6
2012												
1st quarter	13 999.2	8 456.4	6 836.3	1 198.7	5 637.6	1 620.1	1 112.1	508.0	1 321.8	59.9	1 261.9	526.7
2nd quarter	14 081.0	8 503.8	6 876.0	1 195.8	5 680.2	1 627.8	1 117.8	510.0	1 355.6	58.1	1 297.5	532.4
3rd quarter	14 016.5	8 546.1	6 906.1	1 196.8	5 709.2	1 640.0	1 128.8	511.2	1 344.9	59.4	1 285.5	536.1
4th quarter	14 301.7	8 763.2	7 094.2	1 202.0	5 892.2	1 669.0	1 145.1	523.9	1 363.2	62.4	1 300.8	542.8
2013												
1st quarter	14 324.1	8 732.6	7 043.9	1 206.4	5 837.5	1 688.7	1 168.4	520.4	1 387.2	93.0	1 294.2	560.8
2nd quarter	14 464.7	8 819.6	7 103.0	1 206.8	5 896.2	1 716.6	1 190.7	525.9	1 410.6	94.1	1 316.5	573.1
3rd quarter	14 536.1	8 845.6	7 112.9	1 204.8	5 908.0	1 732.7	1 205.9	526.8	1 411.0	92.8	1 318.2	585.1
4th quarter	14 703.6	8 942.5	7 196.3	1 214.0	5 982.3	1 746.2	1 214.0	532.1	1 400.0	67.9	1 332.0	590.7
2014												
1st quarter	14 825.9	9 114.2	7 358.6	1 221.9	6 136.8	1 755.6	1 216.1	539.5	1 411.4	66.3	1 345.1	598.1
2nd quarter	15 140.7	9 172.4	7 409.4	1 230.6	6 178.8	1 763.1	1 221.3	541.8	1 450.6	77.0	1 373.6	602.6
3rd quarter	15 412.4	9 280.6	7 503.0	1 241.5	6 261.6	1 777.6	1 229.9	547.7	1 466.2	63.9	1 402.2	604.6
4th quarter	15 533.3	9 433.5	7 634.3	1 253.7	6 380.6	1 799.2	1 242.5	556.7	1 454.4	63.7	1 390.7	605.5
2015												
1st quarter	15 604.6	9 563.8	7 746.2	1 263.2	6 483.0	1 817.7	1 256.2	561.5	1 434.9	54.5	1 380.4	596.2
2nd quarter	15 746.9	9 666.2	7 830.8	1 273.0	6 557.8	1 835.4	1 267.9	567.5	1 411.3	54.5	1 356.8	611.3
3rd quarter	15 807.8	9 751.7	7 903.0	1 280.2	6 622.8	1 848.7	1 276.3	572.4	1 423.2	55.8	1 367.4	614.9
4th quarter	15 838.8	9 816.0	7 958.0	1 286.7	6 671.3	1 858.0	1 281.9	576.1	1 413.8	51.6	1 362.3	615.6
2016												
1st quarter	15 905.1	9 851.7	7 992.7	1 294.4	6 698.3	1 858.9	1 284.4	574.5	1 410.1	38.0	1 372.1	619.8
2nd quarter	15 911.1	9 905.2	8 039.2	1 302.6	6 736.7	1 866.0	1 288.7	577.3	1 409.6	37.6	1 372.0	626.7
3rd quarter	16 056.2	9 998.5	8 119.3	1 314.1	6 805.2	1 879.2	1 296.5	582.7	1 431.0	33.7	1 397.4	627.6
4th quarter	16 261.2	10 109.1	8 213.7	1 321.0	6 892.7	1 895.3	1 306.1	589.2	1 442.5	27.1	1 415.4	632.5
2017												
1st quarter	16 479.9	10 225.4	8 311.4	1 331.5	6 979.9	1 914.0	1 319.2	594.9	1 484.4	44.0	1 440.3	643.9
2nd quarter	16 639.7	10 337.9	8 402.5	1 340.1	7 062.4	1 935.4	1 334.7	600.7	1 498.5	42.2	1 456.3	645.1
3rd quarter	16 841.6	10 480.5	8 518.5	1 352.9	7 165.5	1 962.0	1 354.3	607.7	1 502.9	35.5	1 467.4	654.9
4th quarter	17 138.5	10 660.7	8 666.4	1 367.4	7 298.9	1 994.3	1 377.8	616.5	1 537.5	36.1	1 501.4	667.0
2018												
1st quarter	17 383.2	10 784.1	8 762.3	1 381.3	7 381.0	2 021.8	1 404.6	617.2	1 567.0	37.4	1 529.5	671.8
2nd quarter	17 541.8	10 891.8	8 842.9	1 394.2	7 448.7	2 048.9	1 427.7	621.1	1 572.1	39.5	1 532.6	677.3
3rd quarter	17 799.7	11 044.3	8 969.8	1 411.1	7 558.7	2 074.5	1 445.8	628.7	1 581.3	30.1	1 551.1	689.8
4th quarter	17 968.6	11 118.0	9 027.1	1 419.0	7 608.1	2 090.9	1 459.0	631.9	1 601.4	48.6	1 552.8	688.6

Table 1-13B. National Income by Type of Income: Historical Data—*Continued*

(Billions of dollars, quarterly data are at seasonally adjusted annual rates.)   NIPA Tables 1.7.5, 1.12

| Year and quarter | Corporate profits with IVA and CCAdj | | | | | Net interest and miscellaneous payments | Taxes on production and imports | Less: Subsidies | Business current transfer payments, net | | | Current surplus of government enterprises | Addendum: Net national factor income |
| | Total | Taxes on corporate income | Profits after tax | | | | | | Total ¹ | To persons | To government | | |
			Total	Net dividends	Undistributed corporate profits								
2004													
1st quarter	1 242.4	251.4	991.0	532.7	458.3	378.4	847.3	44.2	80.3	17.5	51.3	11.5	9 351.7
2nd quarter	1 271.7	271.6	1 000.1	560.3	439.7	370.5	859.9	43.7	79.8	15.4	52.5	11.9	9 517.1
3rd quarter	1 330.4	292.7	1 037.7	567.2	470.5	373.0	871.3	45.4	78.8	15.7	53.0	10.1	9 713.1
4th quarter	1 312.9	298.3	1 014.5	668.5	346.0	387.3	893.8	52.3	90.0	18.4	52.6	19.0	9 785.3
2005													
1st quarter	1 442.1	375.7	1 066.3	575.2	491.2	420.4	915.1	56.7	85.0	23.7	52.0	9.3	9 979.6
2nd quarter	1 457.0	364.0	1 093.0	592.1	501.0	457.7	937.3	60.7	97.6	26.7	53.2	17.7	10 115.6
3rd quarter	1 483.0	370.2	1 112.8	598.4	514.3	485.0	952.1	62.0	93.2	27.3	53.5	12.5	10 292.3
4th quarter	1 572.5	409.0	1 163.4	642.3	521.1	524.0	965.3	64.2	91.1	25.6	55.0	10.6	10 519.7
2006													
1st quarter	1 629.6	421.4	1 208.2	714.1	494.2	523.4	981.8	55.7	77.9	21.6	56.0	0.3	10 776.3
2nd quarter	1 643.1	432.6	1 210.5	747.2	463.3	591.3	991.7	51.5	77.4	19.7	57.1	0.6	10 898.0
3rd quarter	1 688.7	451.3	1 237.4	765.6	471.8	582.2	1 004.1	49.9	83.8	19.9	58.0	5.9	10 985.0
4th quarter	1 623.6	415.3	1 208.4	793.4	415.0	562.5	1 010.5	48.7	84.6	22.1	58.9	3.6	11 031.8
2007													
1st quarter	1 528.8	418.6	1 110.2	820.3	289.9	586.6	1 025.9	49.5	99.0	26.5	59.2	13.2	11 101.4
2nd quarter	1 593.0	413.3	1 179.7	858.8	320.9	648.2	1 033.1	58.2	96.3	30.0	59.9	6.5	11 264.5
3rd quarter	1 525.9	376.5	1 149.4	868.1	281.3	651.7	1 035.8	55.9	99.8	32.5	60.8	6.5	11 243.2
4th quarter	1 485.0	358.7	1 126.3	866.8	259.5	662.6	1 052.6	54.7	99.0	34.1	63.7	1.3	11 313.6
2008													
1st quarter	1 388.4	298.0	1 090.4	903.0	187.4	652.9	1 045.7	51.9	113.4	34.7	65.2	13.5	11 309.5
2nd quarter	1 364.6	285.2	1 079.4	866.5	212.9	664.6	1 054.7	51.7	107.0	35.4	66.1	5.5	11 332.3
3rd quarter	1 372.6	270.7	1 101.9	820.8	281.2	702.1	1 058.5	52.0	107.1	36.1	65.3	5.7	11 410.9
4th quarter	1 017.8	169.8	848.0	770.9	77.0	674.1	1 040.0	54.6	129.5	36.9	81.2	11.4	11 011.4
2009													
1st quarter	1 255.1	172.0	1 083.1	702.8	380.3	598.3	1 015.9	55.4	122.5	37.8	82.3	2.4	10 823.5
2nd quarter	1 283.8	195.3	1 088.4	620.7	467.7	561.8	1 017.3	55.5	142.3	38.6	99.1	4.6	10 844.9
3rd quarter	1 456.5	206.4	1 250.1	584.1	666.0	516.8	1 028.8	67.1	119.7	39.4	81.2	-1.0	11 010.2
4th quarter	1 551.9	242.0	1 309.9	580.5	729.3	502.0	1 045.3	55.5	122.1	40.2	81.8	0.0	11 224.4
2010													
1st quarter	1 642.6	256.3	1 386.2	593.9	792.4	497.2	1 044.6	54.8	127.5	41.0	82.4	4.0	11 368.1
2nd quarter	1 640.8	262.2	1 378.5	613.0	765.5	482.5	1 062.1	55.5	124.2	42.4	81.4	0.4	11 565.5
3rd quarter	1 802.8	279.2	1 523.6	661.7	861.9	451.1	1 069.1	56.0	130.9	44.1	86.1	0.7	11 806.7
4th quarter	1 828.8	291.3	1 537.5	704.3	833.2	453.3	1 076.4	56.9	128.8	47.4	86.5	-5.1	11 924.1
2011													
1st quarter	1 670.4	285.1	1 385.2	748.0	637.2	463.6	1 091.5	58.9	147.1	48.8	88.9	9.5	11 972.1
2nd quarter	1 791.8	285.1	1 506.6	761.0	745.6	451.7	1 105.5	59.9	132.0	49.5	87.2	-4.7	12 161.6
3rd quarter	1 818.5	256.4	1 562.1	787.5	774.6	425.9	1 103.9	60.2	129.6	48.9	87.9	-7.2	12 293.4
4th quarter	1 958.5	296.4	1 662.1	819.8	842.2	457.2	1 114.0	61.1	118.0	47.0	83.3	-12.3	12 451.0
2012													
1st quarter	2 025.6	319.9	1 705.7	879.7	826.0	502.7	1 130.9	58.4	109.8	43.5	77.0	-10.7	12 833.0
2nd quarter	2 006.9	334.2	1 672.7	902.1	770.6	523.4	1 133.9	58.1	98.6	41.0	69.9	-12.3	12 922.1
3rd quarter	1 985.4	341.7	1 643.7	906.9	736.9	455.6	1 131.3	56.3	88.3	39.1	63.0	-13.8	12 868.1
4th quarter	1 971.7	342.5	1 629.2	1 106.1	523.2	494.4	1 148.4	59.4	92.5	38.1	66.0	-11.5	13 135.3
2013													
1st quarter	1 983.5	360.7	1 622.8	870.8	751.9	459.5	1 174.6	59.4	100.5	37.8	78.8	-16.1	13 123.6
2nd quarter	2 000.2	357.2	1 643.1	1 127.8	515.3	452.0	1 180.8	60.1	104.8	37.9	80.6	-13.7	13 255.5
3rd quarter	2 011.1	364.8	1 646.4	958.4	688.0	460.2	1 195.0	60.0	104.3	38.5	77.3	-11.6	13 313.1
4th quarter	2 047.9	367.9	1 680.0	1 079.0	601.0	465.1	1 204.1	59.4	128.5	39.5	102.0	-13.1	13 446.1
2014													
1st quarter	1 967.4	403.7	1 563.7	1 052.4	511.3	473.7	1 220.5	58.7	111.8	40.9	81.8	-10.9	13 564.9
2nd quarter	2 138.3	425.8	1 712.5	1 093.2	619.3	494.0	1 237.5	58.5	115.3	42.2	82.3	-9.3	13 857.8
3rd quarter	2 191.0	397.9	1 793.1	1 105.6	687.6	516.3	1 248.4	58.2	174.0	43.6	137.9	-7.5	14 058.7
4th quarter	2 184.2	400.9	1 783.3	1 133.1	650.2	535.3	1 257.0	57.0	130.0	45.0	90.2	-5.3	14 212.8
2015													
1st quarter	2 121.3	414.4	1 706.9	1 149.4	557.5	565.2	1 262.2	56.0	123.8	46.4	85.9	-8.4	14 281.6
2nd quarter	2 108.8	419.6	1 689.2	1 129.5	559.7	603.8	1 273.1	56.4	134.9	48.5	93.4	-7.0	14 401.3
3rd quarter	2 066.3	390.7	1 675.6	1 157.0	518.6	600.9	1 275.5	57.7	137.5	51.3	88.9	-2.7	14 456.9
4th quarter	1 945.5	360.3	1 585.2	1 223.7	361.5	594.3	1 289.9	58.7	226.0	54.8	173.9	-2.8	14 385.2
2016													
1st quarter	2 040.0	375.1	1 664.9	1 176.7	488.2	586.1	1 295.9	60.7	165.1	59.2	105.2	0.7	14 507.6
2nd quarter	2 003.2	378.9	1 624.2	1 178.2	446.0	562.4	1 301.0	62.4	170.2	61.2	110.0	-0.9	14 507.0
3rd quarter	2 035.7	385.7	1 649.9	1 198.7	451.3	558.2	1 320.8	63.0	152.3	60.7	92.2	-0.6	14 651.0
4th quarter	2 072.0	364.9	1 707.0	1 204.1	503.0	562.5	1 328.9	60.9	179.9	57.8	113.7	8.4	14 818.5
2017													
1st quarter	2 073.2	300.5	1 772.6	1 242.3	530.3	617.2	1 339.4	59.3	161.9	52.5	115.9	-6.5	15 044.1
2nd quarter	2 095.9	306.7	1 789.2	1 271.9	517.3	614.7	1 359.4	58.0	152.8	48.9	93.3	10.6	15 192.2
3rd quarter	2 153.0	323.7	1 829.3	1 268.3	561.0	611.2	1 372.1	61.9	135.9	46.9	94.1	-5.1	15 402.4
4th quarter	2 193.4	318.3	1 875.1	1 273.9	601.2	606.8	1 394.4	60.2	145.9	46.6	95.4	3.9	15 665.4
2018													
1st quarter	2 240.1	256.8	1 983.3	1 288.6	694.7	607.7	1 427.2	58.7	150.9	48.0	105.8	-2.9	15 870.7
2nd quarter	2 264.4	282.9	1 981.4	1 314.5	666.9	604.9	1 448.6	58.2	148.7	49.4	98.8	0.5	16 010.4
3rd quarter	2 320.3	287.2	2 033.1	1 355.7	677.3	588.3	1 468.9	57.8	173.6	50.9	117.5	5.2	16 223.9
4th quarter	2 395.0	299.2	2 095.9	1 394.8	701.1	593.8	1 502.2	78.5	158.9	52.5	92.9	13.4	16 396.8

¹Includes net transfer payments to the rest of the world, not shown separately.

Table 1-14. Gross and Net Value Added of Domestic Corporate Business

(Billions of dollars, quarterly data are at seasonally adjusted annual rates.)   NIPA Table 1.14

Year and quarter	Gross value added of corporate business, total	Consumption of fixed capital	Net value added												Gross value added of financial corporate business
			Total	Compensation of employees	Taxes on production and imports less subsidies	Net operating surplus									
						Total	Net interest and miscellaneous payments	Business current transfer payments	Corporate profits with IVA and CCAdj						
									Total	Taxes on corporate income	Profits after tax				
											Total	Net dividends	Undistributed		
1960	299.9	28.5	271.4	190.7	27.8	52.9	-0.2	1.5	51.5	21.9	29.7	12.3	17.4		17.4
1961	308.7	29.5	279.2	195.6	28.9	54.7	0.4	1.7	52.6	22.2	30.4	12.2	18.2		18.3
1962	336.0	30.8	305.1	211.0	31.2	62.9	0.8	1.9	60.3	23.3	37.0	13.2	23.8		19.1
1963	357.4	32.4	324.9	222.7	33.2	69.1	0.4	2.3	66.4	25.5	40.9	14.4	26.5		19.5
1964	386.0	34.4	351.6	239.2	35.6	76.8	0.8	2.7	73.2	26.6	46.7	16.6	30.1		21.5
1965	423.8	37.1	386.6	259.9	37.8	89.0	1.2	3.1	84.6	29.8	54.8	18.2	36.6		23.0
1966	465.1	40.9	424.2	288.5	38.9	96.8	2.3	2.9	91.6	32.2	59.4	19.5	39.9		25.0
1967	491.2	45.1	446.1	308.4	41.4	96.3	4.0	3.1	89.1	31.0	58.1	20.2	37.9		28.0
1968	542.1	50.0	492.1	340.2	47.8	104.1	4.3	3.7	96.1	37.2	58.9	22.6	36.3		31.2
1969	590.7	55.7	534.9	377.5	52.9	104.6	8.5	4.3	91.8	37.0	54.9	23.4	31.4		36.0
1970	612.1	61.8	550.3	398.0	57.0	95.3	12.5	3.7	79.1	31.3	47.9	23.9	24.0		39.2
1971	660.9	67.6	593.3	421.7	62.8	108.8	12.6	3.4	92.8	34.8	58.0	23.7	34.3		42.8
1972	732.9	73.4	659.5	468.2	67.3	124.0	12.4	3.9	107.7	39.1	68.6	25.2	43.4		47.0
1973	820.2	82.0	738.2	526.1	74.1	138.0	14.7	4.8	118.5	45.6	72.9	27.4	45.4		51.4
1974	889.6	96.0	793.5	577.3	78.6	137.6	23.1	6.3	108.2	47.2	61.0	29.0	32.0		59.5
1975	965.5	113.5	852.0	607.8	84.5	159.7	27.2	8.2	124.2	46.3	78.0	31.8	46.2		67.3
1976	1 087.3	125.0	962.3	682.8	91.4	188.1	22.7	7.6	157.8	59.4	98.4	35.9	62.4		72.6
1977	1 232.5	140.5	1 092.1	771.7	100.0	220.3	27.7	6.0	186.7	68.5	118.2	39.6	78.5		85.1
1978	1 406.9	159.3	1 247.6	884.7	108.7	254.2	30.6	7.9	215.7	77.9	137.8	46.6	91.2		103.0
1979	1 564.3	183.4	1 380.9	1 004.4	115.0	261.5	36.3	10.8	214.4	80.7	133.6	50.8	82.9		114.0
1980	1 702.2	212.1	1 490.1	1 102.0	128.6	259.6	59.4	12.0	188.1	75.5	112.6	59.0	53.6		127.9
1981	1 934.8	244.9	1 689.9	1 220.6	154.4	314.9	82.8	14.3	217.8	70.3	147.5	72.3	75.2		146.1
1982	2 018.4	272.5	1 745.9	1 275.1	161.3	309.4	95.5	16.6	197.3	51.3	146.0	76.5	69.4		163.7
1983	2 172.4	285.9	1 886.5	1 353.0	177.4	356.1	91.9	19.5	244.7	66.4	178.3	85.5	92.7		186.6
1984	2 434.6	303.2	2 131.5	1 501.1	195.6	434.8	106.6	26.9	301.3	81.5	219.8	94.6	125.3		208.8
1985	2 601.3	326.9	2 274.4	1 615.9	209.0	449.5	102.2	30.9	316.4	81.6	234.8	103.5	131.3		232.3
1986	2 706.6	349.9	2 356.7	1 723.4	219.6	413.7	99.5	29.3	284.9	91.9	193.0	106.1	86.9		241.9
1987	2 894.9	371.3	2 523.6	1 847.6	233.4	442.6	99.7	24.9	318.0	112.7	205.3	113.3	91.9		253.2
1988	3 142.4	399.9	2 742.5	2 002.3	252.0	488.2	104.4	26.4	357.5	124.3	233.2	115.4	117.8		268.6
1989	3 320.0	427.1	2 892.8	2 119.3	267.5	506.0	125.2	33.6	347.2	124.4	222.7	148.0	74.7		299.9
1990	3 467.1	454.7	3 012.5	2 234.9	284.5	493.1	117.4	34.0	341.6	121.8	219.8	167.7	52.1		306.6
1991	3 554.4	479.6	3 074.8	2 277.8	307.9	489.1	79.3	33.7	376.1	117.8	258.3	177.0	81.3		323.5
1992	3 741.9	494.3	3 247.6	2 420.5	325.9	501.2	63.2	34.0	404.1	131.9	272.2	178.3	93.9		365.9
1993	3 918.3	517.2	3 401.2	2 515.7	343.8	541.7	62.3	31.8	447.6	155.0	292.6	200.7	91.9		383.9
1994	4 209.4	547.6	3 661.8	2 649.0	376.1	636.7	57.7	32.2	546.8	172.7	374.1	218.3	155.9		393.5
1995	4 473.4	590.4	3 882.9	2 787.9	384.8	710.3	60.2	36.9	613.3	194.4	418.8	249.6	169.2		432.7
1996	4 769.1	626.3	4 142.8	2 953.7	398.4	790.7	59.4	43.7	687.5	211.4	476.1	283.2	192.9		473.8
1997	5 141.8	670.1	4 471.8	3 176.6	416.9	878.3	81.7	34.4	762.2	224.8	537.4	312.9	224.5		533.8
1998	5 473.4	715.0	4 758.4	3 447.5	430.8	880.2	121.6	52.8	705.7	221.8	483.9	341.4	142.5		600.1
1999	5 801.1	769.6	5 031.4	3 684.3	454.0	893.1	126.1	53.8	713.2	227.4	485.8	331.8	154.0		635.1
2000	6 214.4	838.6	5 375.8	4 008.9	479.8	887.1	173.8	72.4	640.9	233.4	407.4	380.8	26.7		706.6
2001	6 199.7	888.6	5 311.1	4 013.8	469.4	827.9	153.2	84.8	589.9	170.1	419.8	357.0	62.8		732.7
2002	6 294.3	914.6	5 379.7	3 972.7	497.5	909.4	92.9	61.6	754.9	160.7	594.3	376.8	217.5		756.4
2003	6 520.7	932.5	5 588.1	4 040.9	524.3	1 023.0	75.3	50.3	897.3	213.8	683.6	423.9	259.7		794.4
2004	6 955.9	973.0	5 982.9	4 240.2	569.4	1 173.3	24.3	54.8	1 094.2	278.5	815.7	519.8	295.8		832.1
2005	7 481.9	1 042.0	6 439.9	4 443.0	616.3	1 380.7	61.2	56.5	1 262.9	379.7	883.2	341.1	542.0		920.5
2006	8 024.9	1 119.3	6 905.6	4 681.2	654.5	1 569.9	115.8	47.6	1 406.5	430.1	976.4	677.2	299.2		1 020.3
2007	8 192.8	1 188.9	7 003.9	4 894.2	676.3	1 433.4	168.4	69.6	1 195.4	391.8	803.6	713.1	90.5		970.4
2008	8 105.0	1 256.6	6 848.4	4 940.3	685.0	1 223.1	231.3	96.2	895.7	255.9	639.7	659.8	-20.1		813.6
2009	7 808.9	1 263.8	6 545.1	4 607.5	655.5	1 282.2	146.1	98.0	1 038.0	203.9	834.1	503.9	330.2		940.0
2010	8 226.5	1 271.2	6 955.3	4 700.8	684.9	1 569.6	126.5	100.1	1 343.0	272.3	1 070.7	521.8	548.9		977.5
2011	8 613.4	1 324.6	7 288.8	4 928.0	718.7	1 642.2	136.6	108.3	1 397.2	280.8	1 116.5	624.2	492.3		994.4
2012	9 171.8	1 392.5	7 779.3	5 182.7	743.2	1 853.5	199.3	62.2	1 592.1	334.6	1 257.5	768.8	488.7		1 111.4
2013	9 469.8	1 450.2	8 019.6	5 352.4	793.1	1 874.1	194.8	67.4	1 611.9	362.6	1 249.2	870.6	378.6		1 091.7
2014	10 045.9	1 527.5	8 518.4	5 645.2	828.3	2 044.9	234.4	95.1	1 715.3	407.1	1 308.3	934.4	373.8		1 260.5
2015	10 471.9	1 588.2	8 883.7	5 944.4	838.1	2 101.2	313.0	122.9	1 665.3	396.3	1 269.0	1 002.1	266.9		1 343.4
2016	10 648.6	1 627.4	9 021.2	6 099.6	853.8	2 067.8	309.1	140.9	1 617.8	376.2	1 241.6	1 003.7	237.9		1 410.5
2017	11 089.1	1 700.8	9 388.3	6 420.3	887.1	2 080.8	334.9	116.0	1 630.0	312.3	1 317.7	1 053.7	263.9		1 425.0
2018	11 735.5	1 780.5	9 954.9	6 768.2	959.0	2 227.8	313.8	130.7	1 783.3	281.5	1 501.7	437.4	1 064.3		1 555.6
2019	12 199.6	1 880.2	10 319.4	7 090.3	997.8	2 231.4	240.6	136.3	1 854.4	302.2	1 552.2	920.1	632.1		1 595.6
2020	11 890.6	1 957.0	9 933.7	7 157.6	531.7	2 244.4	322.6	132.7	1 789.0	275.6	1 513.4	1 086.1	427.3		1 721.9
2021	13 579.0	2 081.4	11 497.6	7 890.5	798.5	2 808.6	358.0	136.3	2 314.3	381.2	1 933.1	1 122.8	810.4		1 912.3
2019															
1st quarter	12 046.3	1 844.6	10 201.7	7 030.0	980.7	2 190.9	247.0	144.8	1 799.2	297.4	1 501.8	881.3	620.5		1 593.4
2nd quarter	12 157.1	1 872.7	10 284.3	7 065.2	994.0	2 225.2	230.5	136.6	1 858.1	303.8	1 554.2	881.7	672.6		1 594.1
3rd quarter	12 219.1	1 893.8	10 325.3	7 085.8	1 005.5	2 234.0	232.4	142.3	1 859.3	291.5	1 567.8	911.2	656.5		1 572.6
4th quarter	12 375.8	1 909.6	10 466.2	7 180.1	1 010.8	2 275.3	252.6	121.7	1 901.0	316.0	1 585.0	1 006.1	579.0		1 622.3
2020															
1st quarter	12 298.9	1 932.5	10 366.4	7 247.4	1 013.7	2 105.3	291.4	123.5	1 690.4	245.4	1 445.0	963.1	481.9		1 644.6
2nd quarter	10 940.9	1 948.9	8 992.0	6 789.2	224.1	1 978.7	317.4	127.0	1 534.3	241.2	1 293.2	1 103.2	189.9		1 688.7
3rd quarter	11 794.2	1 962.2	9 831.9	7 134.7	240.8	2 456.4	336.0	139.5	1 981.0	300.3	1 680.7	1 107.1	573.6		1 731.7
4th quarter	12 528.6	1 984.3	10 544.3	7 459.2	648.1	2 437.0	345.8	140.7	1 950.5	315.6	1 634.9	1 171.1	463.7		1 822.5
2021															
1st quarter	12 922.2	2 005.3	10 916.9	7 538.1	800.8	2 577.9	358.5	134.4	2 085.0	343.7	1 741.3	1 007.6	733.7		1 846.7
2nd quarter	13 348.2	2 048.5	11 299.7	7 768.4	675.0	2 856.3	357.4	139.9	2 359.0	378.6	1 980.4	1 157.5	823.0		1 903.3
3rd quarter	13 776.9	2 103.9	11 673.0	7 991.6	783.1	2 898.3	357.4	136.0	2 404.8	393.3	2 011.5	1 086.1	925.3		1 923.9
4th quarter	14 268.7	2 167.8	12 100.9	8 263.8	935.0	2 902.1	358.7	134.9	2 408.5	409.1	1 999.4	1 240.0	759.4		1 975.3

Table 1-15. Gross Value Added of Nonfinancial Domestic Corporate Business in Current and Chained Dollars

(Billions of dollars, quarterly data are at seasonally adjusted annual rates.)   NIPA Table 1.14

Year and quarter	Total	Consumption of fixed capital	Net value added Total	Compensation of employees	Taxes on production and imports less subsidies	Net operating surplus Total	Net interest and miscellaneous payments	Business current transfer payments	Corporate profits with IVA and CCAdj Total	Taxes on corporate income	Profits after tax Total	Net dividends	Undistributed	Gross value added in billions of chained (2009) dollars
1960	282.5	27.6	254.9	180.4	26.6	47.9	3.3	1.3	43.3	19.1	24.2	10.5	13.7	1 288.2
1961	290.4	28.6	261.9	184.5	27.6	49.7	3.8	1.4	44.5	19.4	25.1	10.6	14.5	1 319.1
1962	316.8	29.8	287.0	199.3	29.9	57.9	4.5	1.6	51.8	20.6	31.2	11.6	19.6	1 430.8
1963	337.8	31.3	306.5	210.1	31.7	64.7	4.8	1.6	58.3	22.8	35.5	12.4	23.1	1 519.0
1964	364.5	33.3	331.3	225.7	33.9	71.7	5.3	1.9	64.6	23.9	40.7	14.0	26.7	1 625.5
1965	400.7	35.8	364.9	245.4	36.0	83.5	6.0	2.1	75.4	27.1	48.3	16.2	32.1	1 762.0
1966	440.1	39.4	400.7	272.9	37.0	90.9	7.2	2.6	81.1	29.5	51.6	16.8	34.8	1 892.2
1967	463.2	43.5	419.7	291.1	39.3	89.4	8.6	2.7	78.1	27.8	50.2	17.3	33.0	1 946.4
1968	510.9	48.1	462.9	320.9	45.5	96.4	10.1	2.9	83.4	33.5	49.8	19.0	30.8	2 072.7
1969	554.6	53.5	501.1	356.1	50.2	94.9	13.5	3.0	78.3	33.3	45.0	19.0	25.9	2 155.6
1970	572.9	59.3	513.6	374.5	54.2	84.9	17.9	3.2	63.9	27.3	36.6	18.3	18.3	2 136.8
1971	618.1	64.7	553.4	396.2	59.5	97.7	18.9	3.6	75.2	30.0	45.2	18.1	27.0	2 221.0
1972	685.9	70.2	615.8	439.9	63.7	112.2	20.0	3.9	88.3	33.8	54.5	19.7	34.8	2 389.1
1973	768.8	78.2	690.7	495.1	70.1	125.5	23.7	4.5	97.2	40.4	56.8	20.8	36.1	2 534.8
1974	830.0	91.4	738.7	542.9	74.4	121.3	30.1	3.7	87.4	42.8	44.6	21.5	23.0	2 496.5
1975	898.3	107.7	790.6	569.0	80.2	141.3	32.4	4.7	104.3	41.9	62.4	24.6	37.8	2 461.9
1976	1 014.7	118.3	896.4	640.0	86.7	169.7	30.0	6.7	133.0	53.5	79.6	27.8	51.8	2 663.6
1977	1 147.4	132.6	1 014.8	723.3	94.6	196.9	33.0	8.7	155.1	60.6	94.6	30.9	63.6	2 860.6
1978	1 303.9	150.2	1 153.8	829.5	102.7	221.6	36.6	9.2	175.8	67.6	108.2	35.9	72.3	3 046.3
1979	1 450.3	172.4	1 277.8	942.4	108.8	226.7	43.6	9.0	174.0	70.6	103.4	37.6	65.8	3 144.1
1980	1 574.4	198.9	1 375.5	1 030.7	121.5	223.3	58.0	9.6	155.7	68.2	87.5	44.7	42.8	3 113.9
1981	1 788.7	229.1	1 559.6	1 139.9	146.7	273.1	72.5	10.7	189.9	66.0	123.9	52.5	71.4	3 240.6
1982	1 854.7	253.9	1 600.8	1 183.3	152.9	264.6	83.2	8.1	173.3	48.8	124.5	54.1	70.5	3 170.0
1983	1 985.8	264.6	1 721.2	1 250.1	168.0	303.1	82.6	10.0	210.5	61.7	148.8	63.2	85.6	3 324.9
1984	2 225.9	279.0	1 946.9	1 388.2	185.0	373.7	93.8	10.9	268.9	75.9	193.0	67.2	125.8	3 621.0
1985	2 369.0	299.0	2 070.0	1 490.1	196.6	383.3	96.9	15.4	271.1	71.1	200.0	72.0	128.0	3 787.4
1986	2 464.7	317.9	2 146.8	1 578.2	204.6	364.1	107.0	26.9	230.2	76.2	154.0	72.9	81.1	3 886.1
1987	2 641.7	334.7	2 307.0	1 685.5	216.8	404.7	115.7	29.7	259.4	94.2	165.1	76.3	88.9	4 092.1
1988	2 873.7	358.2	2 515.5	1 825.3	233.8	456.4	135.4	27.0	294.0	104.0	190.0	82.2	107.8	4 343.6
1989	3 020.0	380.2	2 639.9	1 934.8	248.2	456.9	159.4	23.5	274.0	101.2	172.8	105.4	67.5	4 426.2
1990	3 160.5	402.6	2 757.9	2 037.5	263.5	456.8	169.5	24.9	262.5	98.5	164.0	118.3	45.7	4 490.3
1991	3 231.0	423.6	2 807.4	2 071.1	285.7	450.6	156.4	26.1	268.1	88.6	179.5	125.5	54.0	4 467.0
1992	3 376.1	436.3	2 939.8	2 188.7	302.5	448.6	130.9	30.7	287.1	94.4	192.6	134.3	58.4	4 602.9
1993	3 534.4	455.8	3 078.6	2 271.0	319.3	488.2	117.0	29.5	341.7	108.0	233.7	149.2	84.5	4 716.7
1994	3 815.9	482.3	3 333.5	2 398.7	350.7	584.1	116.3	34.7	433.2	132.4	300.8	158.0	142.9	5 007.3
1995	4 040.6	520.8	3 519.8	2 524.6	358.7	636.6	125.6	30.2	480.8	140.3	340.5	178.0	162.5	5 249.1
1996	4 295.3	554.2	3 741.1	2 667.7	371.7	701.7	118.9	37.3	545.5	152.9	392.6	197.6	195.1	5 556.6
1997	4 608.0	594.6	4 013.4	2 862.6	388.9	762.0	126.6	38.5	596.9	161.4	435.5	215.9	219.6	5 928.1
1998	4 873.3	634.1	4 239.2	3 093.8	402.9	742.5	146.4	34.1	562.0	158.7	403.3	241.0	162.3	6 250.7
1999	5 166.0	679.1	4 486.9	3 310.0	424.6	752.3	156.0	45.6	550.7	166.5	384.3	224.7	159.6	6 565.3
2000	5 507.8	737.5	4 770.4	3 597.3	449.9	723.2	193.3	45.4	484.5	165.1	319.4	251.3	68.1	6 880.2
2001	5 467.0	781.5	4 685.5	3 582.3	441.5	661.7	220.7	55.2	385.8	106.2	279.6	245.4	34.2	6 715.0
2002	5 537.9	802.9	4 735.0	3 540.5	467.0	727.5	198.4	52.0	477.1	91.1	386.0	254.8	131.2	6 781.0
2003	5 726.3	816.1	4 910.1	3 594.3	491.1	824.7	173.4	61.6	589.6	126.5	463.2	293.4	169.8	6 933.3
2004	6 123.7	849.7	5 274.0	3 761.3	531.7	980.9	163.3	62.4	755.3	179.2	576.1	364.5	211.6	7 274.0
2005	6 561.5	911.0	5 650.5	3 928.7	575.7	1 146.1	178.3	79.1	888.7	262.5	626.2	170.8	455.4	7 539.0
2006	7 004.5	981.5	6 023.0	4 127.5	611.8	1 283.7	189.0	68.3	1 026.4	296.1	730.4	471.1	259.3	7 828.0
2007	7 222.4	1 044.0	6 178.5	4 307.1	631.3	1 240.1	252.8	58.8	928.5	277.4	651.1	484.6	166.5	7 899.1
2008	7 291.4	1 105.0	6 186.4	4 364.3	637.4	1 184.7	314.6	46.1	824.0	207.8	616.2	474.2	142.0	7 814.2
2009	6 868.9	1 110.7	5 758.2	4 094.9	608.5	1 054.8	288.3	60.3	706.2	162.1	544.1	351.4	192.7	7 259.7
2010	7 248.9	1 119.8	6 129.2	4 166.6	638.2	1 324.4	288.8	71.6	964.0	203.8	760.2	375.5	384.7	7 574.0
2011	7 619.0	1 169.3	6 449.7	4 372.7	670.8	1 406.1	286.5	79.7	1 039.9	209.0	830.9	441.0	389.9	7 777.8
2012	8 060.4	1 230.6	6 829.8	4 608.3	695.1	1 526.3	292.1	82.1	1 152.1	245.4	906.7	517.9	388.7	8 060.4
2013	8 378.0	1 279.7	7 098.3	4 768.1	742.0	1 588.2	283.8	84.2	1 220.2	263.5	956.7	531.9	424.8	8 265.4
2014	8 785.5	1 349.2	7 436.2	5 026.2	767.6	1 642.4	293.2	79.4	1 269.8	290.7	979.1	597.5	381.5	8 522.2
2015	9 128.5	1 401.7	7 726.8	5 292.6	772.8	1 661.4	304.5	99.3	1 257.7	283.2	974.5	641.1	333.4	8 775.8
2016	9 238.2	1 430.2	7 808.0	5 430.6	785.7	1 591.6	324.1	74.9	1 192.6	261.9	930.8	690.7	240.1	8 819.5
2017	9 664.1	1 492.8	8 171.3	5 705.4	827.0	1 638.9	330.7	95.3	1 212.9	224.9	988.0	720.7	267.3	9 066.4
2018	10 179.9	1 561.2	8 618.7	6 023.8	882.8	1 712.1	279.9	98.5	1 333.7	200.5	1 133.1	226.0	907.1	9 355.0
2019	10 604.0	1 644.8	8 959.1	6 315.2	931.3	1 712.6	273.5	91.6	1 347.5	203.6	1 143.9	695.7	448.2	9 567.6
2020	10 168.8	1 707.6	8 461.2	6 327.5	463.3	1 670.4	254.2	94.1	1 322.0	189.6	1 132.4	796.2	336.2	9 164.2
2021	11 666.7	1 811.1	9 855.6	6 990.8	715.6	2 149.2	267.8	98.4	1 783.0	269.6	1 513.4	841.0	672.4	10 051.6
2019														
1st quarter	10 452.9	1 615.5	8 837.4	6 254.1	915.5	1 667.8	274.4	95.9	1 297.4	202.7	1 094.7	663.8	430.9	9 512.9
2nd quarter	10 563.0	1 638.9	8 924.0	6 293.9	928.1	1 702.1	275.6	82.7	1 343.8	205.6	1 138.2	645.6	492.6	9 550.7
3rd quarter	10 646.5	1 655.9	8 990.6	6 318.9	938.4	1 733.2	274.1	102.9	1 356.2	192.5	1 163.7	731.3	432.4	9 577.2
4th quarter	10 753.5	1 669.0	9 084.5	6 393.9	943.3	1 747.3	269.8	84.9	1 392.6	213.4	1 179.2	742.3	436.9	9 629.6
2020														
1st quarter	10 654.3	1 688.0	8 966.3	6 443.0	928.9	1 594.3	262.9	93.1	1 238.4	162.8	1 075.6	756.5	319.1	9 549.8
2nd quarter	9 252.3	1 701.2	7 551.1	5 965.9	165.4	1 419.9	254.7	96.5	1 068.7	158.7	910.0	789.5	120.4	8 440.6
3rd quarter	10 062.5	1 711.6	8 350.9	6 311.2	181.0	1 858.8	250.5	94.0	1 514.3	214.1	1 300.2	766.3	533.9	9 041.9
4th quarter	10 706.1	1 729.6	8 976.5	6 589.9	578.0	1 808.6	248.9	92.9	1 466.8	222.7	1 244.0	872.5	371.5	9 624.3
2021														
1st quarter	11 075.5	1 748.4	9 327.1	6 650.1	719.6	1 957.4	258.0	99.5	1 600.0	244.8	1 355.2	759.1	596.1	9 832.4
2nd quarter	11 444.9	1 783.7	9 661.2	6 868.0	592.1	2 201.1	277.3	102.5	1 821.3	276.1	1 545.2	874.8	670.4	9 969.8
3rd quarter	11 853.0	1 829.1	10 024.0	7 103.5	703.0	2 217.5	267.5	97.1	1 852.9	276.4	1 576.5	808.5	768.0	10 133.1
4th quarter	12 293.4	1 883.2	10 410.2	7 341.6	847.6	2 221.0	268.6	94.5	1 857.9	281.0	1 576.9	921.8	655.1	10 256.4

Table 1-16. Shares of Income

(Billions of dollars, percent, quarterly data are at seasonally adjusted annual rates.)   **NIPA Tables 1.10, 1.14**

Year and quarter	Gross domestic income, total economy									Net factor income, domestic corporate business				
	Billions of dollars					Percent of total				Billions of dollars			Percent of total	
	Total	Compensation of employees	Taxes on production and imports less subsidies	Net operating surplus	Consumption of fixed capital	Compensation of employees	Taxes on production and imports less subsidies	Net operating surplus	Consumption of fixed capital	Total	Compensation of employees	Net operating surplus	Compensation	Net operating surplus
1959	521.5	285.9	40.0	130.1	65.4	54.8	7.7	24.9	12.5	234.3	180.3	54.0	77.0	23.0
1960	543.7	301.4	43.4	130.9	67.9	55.4	8.0	24.1	12.5	243.6	190.7	52.9	78.3	21.7
1961	563.1	310.6	45.0	137.0	70.6	55.2	8.0	24.3	12.5	250.3	195.6	54.7	78.1	21.9
1962	603.9	332.3	48.1	149.4	74.1	55.0	8.0	24.7	12.3	273.9	211.0	62.9	77.0	23.0
1963	638.9	350.5	51.2	159.3	78.0	54.9	8.0	24.9	12.2	291.8	222.7	69.1	76.3	23.7
1964	684.5	376.0	54.6	171.6	82.4	54.9	8.0	25.1	12.0	316.0	239.2	76.8	75.7	24.3
1965	741.5	405.4	57.7	190.4	88.0	54.7	7.8	25.7	11.9	348.9	259.9	89.0	74.5	25.5
1966	808.3	449.2	59.3	204.5	95.3	55.6	7.3	25.3	11.8	385.3	288.5	96.8	74.9	25.1
1967	856.6	481.8	64.1	207.2	103.6	56.2	7.5	24.2	12.1	404.7	308.4	96.3	76.2	23.8
1968	937.5	530.7	72.2	221.2	113.4	56.6	7.7	23.6	12.1	444.3	340.2	104.1	76.6	23.4
1969	1 016.0	584.4	79.4	227.4	124.9	57.5	7.8	22.4	12.3	482.1	377.5	104.6	78.3	21.7
1970	1 068.0	623.3	86.6	221.2	136.8	58.4	8.1	20.7	12.8	493.3	398.0	95.3	80.7	19.3
1971	1 155.3	665.0	95.8	245.6	148.9	57.6	8.3	21.3	12.9	530.5	421.7	108.8	79.5	20.5
1972	1 271.9	731.3	101.3	278.3	161.0	57.5	8.0	21.9	12.7	592.2	468.2	124.0	79.1	20.9
1973	1 419.2	812.7	112.0	315.9	178.7	57.3	7.9	22.3	12.6	664.1	526.1	138.0	79.2	20.8
1974	1 537.8	887.7	121.6	321.6	206.9	57.7	7.9	20.9	13.5	714.9	577.3	137.6	80.8	19.2
1975	1 671.6	947.3	130.8	355.0	238.5	56.7	7.8	21.2	14.3	767.5	607.8	159.7	79.2	20.8
1976	1 852.8	1 048.4	141.3	402.9	260.2	56.6	7.6	21.7	14.0	870.9	682.8	188.1	78.4	21.6
1977	2 062.4	1 165.9	152.6	454.1	289.8	56.5	7.4	22.0	14.1	992.0	771.7	220.3	77.8	22.2
1978	2 328.3	1 316.9	162.0	522.3	327.2	56.6	7.0	22.4	14.1	1 138.9	884.7	254.2	77.7	22.3
1979	2 582.3	1 477.3	171.6	559.5	373.9	57.2	6.6	21.7	14.5	1 265.9	1 004.4	261.5	79.3	20.7
1980	2 812.9	1 622.3	190.5	571.6	428.4	57.7	6.8	20.3	15.2	1 361.6	1 102.0	259.6	80.9	19.1
1981	3 169.0	1 792.7	224.1	664.9	487.2	56.6	7.1	21.0	15.4	1 535.5	1 220.6	314.9	79.5	20.5
1982	3 335.0	1 893.2	225.9	678.9	537.0	56.8	6.8	20.4	16.1	1 584.5	1 275.1	309.4	80.5	19.5
1983	3 577.1	2 012.7	242.0	759.8	562.6	56.3	6.8	21.2	15.7	1 709.1	1 353.0	356.1	79.2	20.8
1984	3 996.0	2 216.1	268.7	912.8	598.4	55.5	6.7	22.8	15.0	1 935.9	1 501.1	434.8	77.5	22.5
1985	4 284.7	2 387.5	286.7	970.3	640.1	55.7	6.7	22.6	14.9	2 065.4	1 615.9	449.5	78.2	21.8
1986	4 499.6	2 543.8	298.5	972.0	685.3	56.5	6.6	21.6	15.2	2 137.1	1 723.4	413.7	80.6	19.4
1987	4 811.4	2 723.8	317.2	1 040.0	730.4	56.6	6.6	21.6	15.2	2 290.2	1 847.6	442.6	80.7	19.3
1988	5 233.4	2 948.9	345.0	1 155.1	784.5	56.3	6.6	22.1	15.0	2 490.5	2 002.3	488.2	80.4	19.6
1989	5 573.6	3 140.9	371.5	1 223.0	838.3	56.4	6.7	21.9	15.0	2 625.3	2 119.3	506.0	80.7	19.3
1990	5 867.6	3 342.7	398.0	1 238.4	888.5	57.0	6.8	21.1	15.1	2 728.0	2 234.9	493.1	81.9	18.1
1991	6 065.2	3 453.3	429.6	1 249.9	932.4	56.9	7.1	20.6	15.4	2 766.9	2 277.8	489.1	82.3	17.7
1992	6 404.4	3 671.2	453.3	1 319.6	960.2	57.3	7.1	20.6	15.0	2 921.7	2 420.5	501.2	82.8	17.2
1993	6 702.6	3 820.6	466.4	1 412.1	1 003.5	57.0	7.0	21.1	15.0	3 057.4	2 515.7	541.7	82.3	17.7
1994	7 147.3	4 010.2	512.7	1 568.7	1 055.6	56.1	7.2	21.9	14.8	3 285.7	2 649.0	636.7	80.6	19.4
1995	7 546.7	4 202.2	523.1	1 699.1	1 122.4	55.7	6.9	22.5	14.9	3 498.2	2 787.9	710.3	79.7	20.3
1996	8 015.0	4 421.1	545.6	1 873.1	1 175.3	55.2	6.8	23.4	14.7	3 744.4	2 953.7	790.7	78.9	21.1
1997	8 566.0	4 713.2	577.8	2 035.6	1 239.3	55.0	6.7	23.8	14.5	4 054.9	3 176.6	878.3	78.3	21.7
1998	9 118.1	5 075.7	603.1	2 129.5	1 309.7	55.7	6.6	23.4	14.4	4 327.7	3 447.5	880.2	79.7	20.3
1999	9 659.5	5 409.9	628.4	2 222.2	1 398.9	56.0	6.5	23.0	14.5	4 577.4	3 684.3	893.1	80.5	19.5
2000	10 345.2	5 854.6	662.8	2 316.6	1 511.2	56.6	6.4	22.4	14.6	4 896.0	4 008.9	887.1	81.9	18.1
2001	10 695.7	6 046.3	669.0	2 380.9	1 599.5	56.5	6.3	22.3	15.0	4 841.7	4 013.8	827.9	82.9	17.1
2002	11 006.4	6 143.4	718.6	2 486.5	1 658.0	55.8	6.5	22.6	15.1	4 882.1	3 972.7	909.4	81.4	18.6
2003	11 476.3	6 362.3	756.5	2 638.4	1 719.1	55.4	6.6	23.0	15.0	5 063.9	4 040.9	1 023.0	79.8	20.2
2004	12 240.9	6 729.3	821.7	2 868.1	1 821.8	55.0	6.7	23.4	14.9	5 413.5	4 240.2	1 173.3	78.3	21.7
2005	13 091.7	7 077.7	881.5	3 161.4	1 971.0	54.1	6.7	24.1	15.1	5 823.7	4 443.0	1 380.7	76.3	23.7
2006	14 019.9	7 491.3	945.5	3 459.0	2 124.1	53.4	6.7	24.7	15.2	6 251.1	4 681.2	1 569.9	74.9	25.1
2007	14 454.4	7 889.4	982.2	3 330.0	2 252.8	54.6	6.8	23.0	15.6	6 327.6	4 894.2	1 433.4	77.3	22.7
2008	14 572.9	8 068.7	997.1	3 148.2	2 358.8	55.4	6.8	21.6	16.2	6 163.4	4 940.3	1 223.1	80.2	19.8
2009	14 276.0	7 767.2	968.5	3 168.9	2 371.5	54.4	6.8	22.2	16.6	5 889.7	4 607.5	1 282.2	78.2	21.8
2010	14 966.4	7 933.0	1 007.3	3 635.3	2 390.9	53.0	6.7	24.3	16.0	6 270.4	4 700.8	1 569.6	75.0	25.0
2011	15 612.0	8 234.0	1 043.7	3 859.9	2 474.5	52.7	6.7	24.7	15.8	6 570.2	4 928.0	1 642.2	75.0	25.0
2012	16 442.8	8 575.4	1 078.1	4 213.4	2 576.0	52.2	6.6	25.6	15.7	7 036.2	5 182.7	1 853.5	73.7	26.3
2013	16 958.0	8 843.6	1 129.0	4 304.2	2 681.2	52.2	6.7	25.4	15.8	7 226.5	5 352.4	1 874.1	74.1	25.9
2014	17 807.9	9 259.7	1 182.7	4 550.4	2 815.0	52.0	6.6	25.6	15.8	7 690.1	5 645.2	2 044.9	73.4	26.6
2015	18 440.5	9 709.5	1 218.0	4 601.6	2 911.4	52.7	6.6	25.0	15.8	8 045.6	5 944.4	2 101.2	73.9	26.1
2016	18 788.5	9 977.1	1 249.9	4 574.5	2 987.1	53.1	6.7	24.3	15.9	8 167.4	6 099.6	2 067.8	74.7	25.3
2017	19 598.5	10 436.7	1 306.4	4 737.2	3 118.2	53.3	6.7	24.2	15.9	8 501.1	6 420.3	2 080.8	75.5	24.5
2018	20 652.6	10 969.8	1 398.4	5 011.0	3 273.4	53.1	6.8	24.3	15.8	8 996.0	6 768.2	2 227.8	75.2	24.8
2019	21 442.2	11 459.4	1 459.3	5 087.8	3 435.6	53.4	6.8	23.7	16.0	9 321.7	7 090.3	2 231.4	76.1	23.9
2020	21 064.3	11 580.1	773.3	5 135.0	3 575.9	55.0	3.7	24.4	17.0	9 402.0	7 157.6	2 244.4	76.1	23.9
2021	23 533.4	12 607.9	1 148.0	5 929.5	3 847.9	53.6	4.9	25.2	16.4	10 699.1	7 890.5	2 808.6	73.7	26.3
2019														
1st quarter	21 195.6	11 347.4	1 435.8	5 034.4	3 378.0	53.5	6.8	23.8	15.9	9 220.9	7 030.0	2 190.9	76.2	23.8
2nd quarter	21 361.6	11 405.9	1 462.1	5 072.7	3 421.0	53.4	6.8	23.7	16.0	9 290.4	7 065.2	2 225.2	76.0	24.0
3rd quarter	21 481.9	11 465.8	1 466.2	5 092.0	3 457.9	53.4	6.8	23.7	16.1	9 319.8	7 085.8	2 234.0	76.0	24.0
4th quarter	21 729.8	11 618.8	1 473.5	5 152.2	3 485.5	53.5	6.8	23.7	16.0	9 455.4	7 180.1	2 275.3	75.9	24.1
2020														
1st quarter	21 755.9	11 764.8	1 496.2	4 972.6	3 522.3	54.1	6.9	22.9	16.2	9 352.7	7 247.4	2 105.3	77.5	22.5
2nd quarter	19 620.2	11 036.1	336.2	4 696.9	3 550.9	56.2	1.7	23.9	18.1	8 767.9	6 789.2	1 978.7	77.4	22.6
3rd quarter	20 908.5	11 547.2	322.8	5 447.5	3 591.0	55.2	1.5	26.1	17.2	9 591.1	7 134.7	2 456.4	74.4	25.6
4th quarter	21 972.6	11 972.3	937.8	5 423.2	3 639.4	54.5	4.3	24.7	16.6	9 896.2	7 459.2	2 437.0	75.4	24.6
2021														
1st quarter	22 547.9	12 097.8	1 173.8	5 580.3	3 696.0	53.7	5.2	24.7	16.4	10 116.0	7 538.1	2 577.9	74.5	25.5
2nd quarter	23 132.7	12 425.3	930.7	5 988.7	3 787.9	53.7	4.0	25.9	16.4	10 624.7	7 768.4	2 856.3	73.1	26.9
3rd quarter	23 833.2	12 766.5	1 099.6	6 071.3	3 895.8	53.6	4.6	25.5	16.3	10 889.9	7 991.6	2 898.3	73.4	26.6
4th quarter	24 619.9	13 142.2	1 388.1	6 077.8	4 011.8	53.4	5.6	24.7	16.3	11 165.9	8 263.8	2 902.1	74.0	26.0

NOTES AND DEFINITIONS, CHAPTER 1

Tables 1-1 through 1-16

National Income and Product

SOURCE: U.S. DEPARTMENT OF COMMERCE, BUREAU OF ECONOMIC ANALYSIS (BEA)

The mission of the Bureau of Economic Analysis (BEA) of the Department of Commerce is to promote a better understanding of the U.S. economy by providing timely, relevant, and accurate economic accounts. As such BEA quarterly and annually collect and produce data on how the U.S. economy is functioning. Featured in the NIPAs is gross domestic product (GDP), which measures the value of the goods and services produced by the U.S. economy in a given time period. GDP is one of the most comprehensive and closely watched economic statistics.

The National Income and Product Accounts (NIPA) are a set of economic accounts that provide information on the value and composition of output produced in the United States during a given period and on the types and uses of the income generated by that production. NIPA was created during the Great Depression to try to understand why the U.S. economy was in freefall and how to stop it.

U.S. input – output (I-O) accounts are a primary component of the U.S. economic accounts. I-O analysis is an economic tool that measures the relationships between various industries in the economy. These tables provides a detailed snapshot of the economy. More specifically, I-O tables show the commodity inputs that are used by each industry to produce its outputs; the commodities produced by each industry and the use of commodities by consumers.

NIPA is a snapshot of the economy at a certain time period. Over the past eight decades, new products have been created that use different inputs. To incorporate these changes, BEA conducts comprehensive revisions, called benchmarks, every five years. These comprehensive updates seek to introduce major improvements to maintain and improve the NIPA data.

Information on COVID-19 and how it impacts data from the BEA can be found at https://www.bea.gov.

The 2018 comprehensive benchmark revision in July 2018 incorporated three major types of revisions: 1) statistical changes to introduce new and improved technologies and newly available source data; 2) changes in definitions to more accurately portray the evolving U.S. economy to more accurately portray the evolving U.S. economy and to provide consistent comparisons with data for other national economies; and 3) changes in presentations to reflect the definitional and statistical changes, where necessary, or to provide additional data or perspective for users. Also

output and price measures will be expressed with 2012 equal to 100. The estimates for most tables showing real, or chained-dollar, estimates will begin with 2002.

Major statistical changes to the NIPA data include the 2012 benchmark input-output (I-O) accounts which incorporated the quinquennial economic census. The I-O accounts tracks the flows of detailed inputs and outputs throughout the economy. Another change is the incorporation of the improved methodology for seasonal adjustments over historical time spans and extending back improvements in previous annual updates. Other changes incorporated the handling of issues such as

- fixed investment in software, medical equipment, and communications equipment

- savings institutions and credit unions

- state and local defined benefit pension plans

Major changes in definitions in this comprehensive update are as follows:

- reclassifications of research and development (R & D) for software originals

- recognition of capital services

- reclassification of payments by Federal Reserve banks to the U.S. government

- reclassification of 'other' state and local personal taxes

The above revisions will be incorporated into the presentations produced by BEA.

Currently, BEA has adopted an expansion of the basic concept of production embodied in the accounts and changed the method of accounting for an important category of pension plans. Also, the constant-dollar or "real" estimates were restated to 2012 dollars, so that the levels shown are different even if the indicated rates of change are the same.

Fixed investment, one of the basic building blocks of the estimation of gross domestic product, was expanded in this revision by recognizing expenditures for research and development by business, government, and nonprofit institutions serving households (NPISHs) as investment.

The workers and capital that produce this R&D have always been reported in the labor and capital tabulations, but were treated as if they were costs of producing this year's output only. In the national income accounting as in conventional business accounting, the full costs of the R&D were subtracted from current-year business receipts in calculating business profit.

Now, in the NIPAs, the estimated value of the research over the whole life of the product—for example, from the estimated future sales of a new drug—is added to the value produced this year. However, this R&D will lose value over time and, as with a piece of machinery, its use and obsolescence, called consumption of fixed capital (CFC), is estimated and charged against GDP in each year that this capital is in use. For that reason, this change adds more to gross national product than to net national product and income.

The basic concept of the NIPAs requires equivalence (except for measurement error) between the value of output and the income and other charges against that value. The higher values of production are balanced on the income side of the accounts by the higher capital consumption allowances and by addition, to profits and other operating surplus (nonlabor income) components, of the net R&D investment—the difference between gross investment value and current year's CFC. (This does not change the tax accounting treatment. The firm still gets to charge off the entire expenditure in the year it is made, which is the most favorable treatment possible.)

Similarly, BEA is now capitalizing private spending for certain entertainment, literary, and other artistic originals as fixed investment. This includes movies, books, music, and long-lived TV programs such as situation comedies and drama (but not news, sports, games, or reality shows).

In a third expansion of the GDP investment definition, all ownership transfer costs for residential and nonresidential structures are capitalized (instead of only broker's commissions as in the previous treatment).

The other important conceptual change introduced in this revision was the adoption of accrual instead of cash accounting for defined benefit pension plans. This does not increase income and saving (or dis-saving) overall, but relocates it. Pension benefits are credited to the labor income and saving of employees when earned instead of when paid—matched by an equal and opposite change in the surplus or deficit of the employing government or business.

All the quarterly NIPA data published here, including indexes of quantity and price, are seasonally adjusted; this is not specifically noted on each table. All of the quarterly level values in current and constant dollars are also expressed at annual rates, which means that seasonally adjusted quarterly levels have been multiplied by 4 so that their scale will be comparable with the annual values shown, and this is noted on the pertinent *Business Statistics* tables. Where quarterly percent changes are shown, they are expressed as seasonally adjusted annual rates, which means that the quarter-to-quarter change in the level of GDP is calculated and then raised to the 4th power in order to express what that rate

of change would be if continued over an entire year; this is noted in the column headings. For further information on these concepts see "General Notes" at the front of this volume.

Each table is notated, just above the table at the right-hand side, with the numbers of the NIPA tables from which the data are drawn.

All data and references are available on the BEA website, <https://www.bea.gov>.

DEFINITIONS AND NOTES ON THE DATA:

Basic concepts of total output and income (Tables 1-1, 1-11, 1-12, and 1-13)

The NIPAs depict the U.S. economy in several different dimensions. The basic concept, and the measure that is now most frequently cited, is gross domestic product (GDP), which is the market value of all goods and services produced by labor and property located in the United States.

In principle, GDP can be measured by summing the values created by each industry in the economy. However, it can also, and more readily, be measured by summing all the final demands for the economy's output. This final-demand approach also has the advantage of depicting the origins of demand for economic production, whether from consumers, businesses, or government.

Since production for the market necessarily generates incomes equal to its value, there is also an income total that corresponds to the production value total. This income can be measured and its distribution among labor, capital, and other income recipients can be depicted.

The relationships of several of these major concepts are illustrated in Table 1-11. The definitions of these concepts are as follows:

Gross domestic product (GDP), the featured measure of the value of U.S. output, is the market value of the goods and services produced by labor and property located in the United States. Market values represent output valued at the prices paid by the final customer, and therefore include taxes on production and imports, such as sales taxes, customs duties, and taxes on property.

The term "gross" in gross domestic product and gross national product is used to indicate that capital consumption allowances (economic depreciation) have not been deducted.

GDP is primarily measured by summing the values of all of the final demands in the economy, net of the demands met by imports; this is shown in Table 1-1. Specifically, GDP is the sum of personal consumption expenditures (PCE), gross private domestic investment (including change in private inventories and before deduction of charges for consumption of fixed capital), net exports of goods and services, and government consumption expenditures and gross investment. GDP measured in this way excludes duplication involving "intermediate" purchases of goods and services (goods and services purchased by industries and used in production), the value of which is already included in the value of the final products. Production of any intermediate goods that are not used in further production in the current period is captured in the measurement of inventory change.

In concept, GDP is equal to the sum of the economic value added by (also referred to as "gross product originating in") all industries in the United States. This, in turn, also makes it the conceptual equivalent of *gross domestic income (GDI),* a new concept introduced in the 2003 revision. GDI is the sum of the incomes earned in each domestic industry, plus the taxes on production and imports and less the subsidies that account for the difference between output value and factor input value. This derivation is shown in Table 1-12. Since the incomes and taxes can be measured directly, they can be summed to a total that is equivalent to GDP in concept but differs due to imperfections in measurement. The difference between the two is known as the *statistical discrepancy.* It is defined as GDP minus GDI, and is shown in Tables 1-11 and 1-12.

Gross national product (GNP) refers to all goods and services produced by labor and property supplied by U.S. residents—whether located in the United States or abroad—expressed at market prices. It is equal to GDP, plus *income receipts from the rest of the world,* less *income payments to the rest of the world. Domestic* production and income refer to the location of the factors of production, with only factors located in the United States included; *national* production and income refer to the ownership of the factors of production, with only factors owned by United States residents included.

Before the comprehensive NIPA revisions that were made in 1991, GNP was the commonly used measure of U.S. production. However, GDP is clearly preferable to GNP when used in conjunction with indicators such as employment, hours worked, and capital utilized—for example, in the calculation of labor and capital productivity—because it is confined to production taking place within the borders of the United States.

The income-side aggregate corresponding to GNP is *gross national income (GNI),* shown as an addendum to Table 1-11. It consists of gross domestic income plus income receipts from the rest of the world, less income payments to the rest of the world. It is used as the denominator for a national saving-income ratio, presented in Chapter 5. National income is the preferred measure for calculating and comparing saving, since it is the income aggregate from which that saving arises. As with GDP and gross domestic income, the statistical discrepancy indicates the difference between the product-side and income-side measurement of the same concept.

Net national product is the market value, net of depreciation, of goods and services attributable to the labor and property supplied by U.S. residents. It is equal to GNP minus the *consumption of fixed capital (CFC).* CFC relates only to fixed capital located in the United States. (Investment in that capital is measured by private fixed investment and government gross investment.) As of the 2009 comprehensive revision, CFC represents only the normal using-up of capital in the process of production, and no longer includes extraordinary disaster losses such as those caused by Hurricane Katrina and the 9/11 attacks. These losses are still estimated and used to write down the estimates of the capital stock, but they no longer have negative effects on our calculation of current income from production.

National income has been redefined and now includes all net incomes (net of the consumption of fixed capital) earned by U.S. residents, and also includes not only "factor incomes"—net incomes received by labor and capital as a result of their participation in the production process, but also "nonfactor charges"—taxes on production and imports, business transfer payments, and the current surplus of government enterprises, less subsidies. This change has been made to conform with the international guidelines for national accounts, *System of National Accounts (SNA) 1993.* According to *SNA 1993,* these charges cannot be eliminated from the input and output prices.

Since national income now includes the nonfactor charges, it is conceptually equivalent to *net national product* and differs only by the amount of the statistical discrepancy.

The concept formerly known as "national income," which excludes the nonfactor charges, is still included in the accounts as an addendum item, now called "net national factor income." It is shown in Table 1-13. *Net national factor income* consists of compensation of employees, proprietors' income with inventory valuation and capital consumption adjustments (IVA and CCadj, respectively), rental income of persons with capital consumption adjustment, corporate profits with inventory valuation and capital consumption adjustments, and net interest.

By definition, national income and its components exclude all income from capital gains (increases in the value of owned assets). Such increases have no counterpart on the production side of the accounts. This exclusion is partly accomplished by means of the inventory valuation and capital consumption adjustments, which will be described in the definitions of the components of product and income.

DEFINITIONS AND NOTES ON THE DATA:

Imputation

The term *imputation* will appear from time to time in the definitions of product and income components. Imputed values are values estimated by BEA statisticians for certain important product and income components that are not explicitly valued in the source data, usually because a market transaction in money terms is not involved. Imputed values appear on both the product and income side of the accounts; they add equal amounts to income and spending, so that no imputed saving is created.

One important example is the imputed rent on owner-occupied housing. The building of such housing is counted as investment, yet in the monetary accounts of the household sector, there is no income from that investment nor any rental paid for it. In the NIPAs, the rent that each such dwelling would earn if rented is estimated and added to both national and personal income (as part of rental income receipts) and to personal consumption expenditures (as part of expenditures on housing services).

Another important example is imputed interest. For example, many individuals keep monetary balances in a bank or other financial institution, receiving either no interest or below-market interest, but receiving the institution's services, such as clearing checks and otherwise facilitating payments, with little or no charge. In this case, where is the product generated by the institution's workers and capital? In the NIPAs, the depositor is imputed a market-rate-based interest return on his or her balance, which is then imputed as a service charge received by the institution, and therefore included in the value of the institution's output.

DEFINITIONS AND NOTES ON THE DATA:

Components of product (Tables 1-1 through 1-6)

Personal consumption expenditures (PCE) is goods and services purchased by persons residing in the United States. PCE consists mainly of purchases of new goods and services by individuals from businesses. It includes purchases that are financed by insurance, such as government-provided and private medical insurance. In addition, PCE includes purchases of new goods and services by nonprofit institutions, net purchases of used goods ("net" here indicates purchases of used goods from business less sales of used goods to business) by individuals and nonprofit institutions, and purchases abroad of goods and services by U.S. residents traveling or working in foreign countries. PCE also includes purchases for certain goods and services provided by government agencies. (See the notes and definitions for Chapter 4 for additional information.) In the 2009 revision, new detail was provided on the allocation of PCE between the household and nonprofit sectors.

Gross private domestic investment consists of gross private fixed investment and change in private inventories.

Private fixed investment consists of both nonresidential and residential fixed investment. The term "residential" refers to the construction and equipping of living quarters for permanent occupancy. Hotels and motels are included in *nonresidential fixed investment*, as described subsequently in this section.

Private fixed investment consists of purchases of fixed assets, which are commodities that will be used in a production process for more than one year, including replacements and additions to the capital stock, and now also including research and development and other intellectual property. It is measured "gross," before a deduction for consumption of existing fixed capital. It covers all investment by private businesses and nonprofit institutions in the United States, regardless of whether the investment is owned by U.S. residents. The residential component includes investment in owner-occupied housing; the homeowner is treated equivalently to a business in these investment accounts. (However, when GDP by sector is calculated, owner-occupied housing is no longer included in the business sector. It is allocated to the households and institutions sector.) Private fixed investment does not include purchases of the same types of equipment and structures by government agencies, which are included in government gross investment, nor does it include investment by U.S. residents in other countries.

Nonresidential fixed investment is the total of nonresidential structures, nonresidential equipment, and intellectual property.

Nonresidential structures consists of new construction, brokers' commissions and other ownership transfer costs on sales of structures, and net purchases of used structures by private business and by nonprofit institutions from government agencies (that is, purchases of used structures from government minus sales of used structures to government). New construction also includes hotels and motels and mining exploration, shafts, and wells.

Nonresidential equipment consists of private business purchases on capital account of new machinery, equipment, and vehicles; dealers' margins on sales of used equipment; and net purchases of used equipment from government agencies, persons, and the rest of the world (that is, purchases of such equipment minus sales of such equipment). It does not include the estimated personal-use portion of equipment purchased for both business and personal use, which is allocated to PCE.

Intellectual property consists of purchases and in-house production of software; research and development; and private expenditures for specified entertainment, literary, and artistic originals. (See above for further description.)

Residential private fixed investment consists of both residential structures and residential producers' durable equipment (including such equipment as appliances owned by landlords and rented to tenants). Investment in structures consists of new units, improvements to existing units, purchases of manufactured homes, brokers' commissions and other ownership transfer costs on the sale of residential property, and net purchases of used residential structures from government agencies (that is, purchases of such structures from government minus sales of such structures to government). As noted above, it includes investment in owner-occupied housing.

Change in private inventories is the change in the physical volume of inventories held by businesses, with that change being valued at the average price of the period. It differs from the change in the book value of inventories reported by most businesses; an *inventory valuation adjustment (IVA)* converts book value change using historical cost valuations to the change in physical volume, valued at average replacement cost.

Net exports of goods and services is *exports of goods and services* less *imports of goods and services*. It does not include income payments or receipts or transfer payments to and from the rest of the world.

Government consumption expenditures is the estimated value of the services produced by governments (federal, state, and local) for current consumption. Since these are generally not sold, there is no market valuation and they are priced at the cost of inputs. The input costs consist of the compensation of general government employees; the estimated consumption of general government fixed capital including software and R&D (CFC, or economic depreciation); and the cost of goods and services purchased by government less the value of sales to other sectors. The value of investment in equipment and structures produced by government workers and capital is also subtracted, and is instead included in government investment. Government sales to other sectors consist primarily of receipts of tuition payments for higher education and receipts of charges for medical care.

This definition of government consumption expenditures differs in concept—but not in the amount contributed to GDP—from the treatment in existence before the 2003 revision of the NIPAs. In the current definition, goods and services purchased by government are considered to be intermediate output. In the previous definition, they were considered to be final sales. Since their value is added to the other components to yield total government consumption expenditures, the dollar total contributed to GDP is the same. The only practical difference is that the goods purchased disappear from the goods account and appear in the services account instead. In the industry sector accounts, the value added by government is also unchanged. It continues to be measured as the sum of compensation and CFC, or equivalently as gross government output less the value of goods and services purchased.

Gross government investment consists of general government and government enterprise expenditures for fixed assets (structures, equipment, software, and R&D). Government inventory investment is included in government consumption expenditures.

DEFINITIONS AND NOTES ON THE DATA:

Real values, quantity and price indexes (Tables 1-2 through 1-7)

Real, or chained (2012) dollar, estimates are estimates from which the effect of price change has been removed. Prior to the 1996 comprehensive revision, constant-dollar measures were obtained by combining real output measures for different goods and services using the relative prices of a single year as weights for the entire time span of the series. In the recent environment of rapid technological change, which has caused the prices of computers and electronic components to decline rapidly relative to other prices, this method distorts the measurement of economic growth and causes excessive revisions of growth rates at each benchmark revision. The current, chained-dollar measure changes the relative price weights each year, as relative prices shift over time. As a result, recent changes in relative prices do not change historical growth rates.

Chained-dollar estimates, although expressed for continuity's sake as if they had occurred according to the prices of a single year (currently 2009), are usually not additive. This means that because of the changes in price weights each year, the chained (2009) dollar components in any given table for any year other than 2009 usually do not add to the chained (2009) dollar total. The amount of the difference for the major components of GDP is called the *residual* and is shown in Table 1-2. It is specific to each individual BEA tabulation, corresponding to the sum of the lowest level of aggregation on that tabulation. In time periods close to the base year, residuals are usually quite small; over longer periods, the differences become much larger. For this reason, BEA no longer publishes chained-dollar estimates prior to 1999, except for selected aggregate series. For the more detailed components of GDP, historical trends and fluctuations in real volumes are represented by *chain-type quantity indexes,* which are presented in Tables 1-5, 4-3, 5-4, 5-6, 6-6, 6-7, 6-11, 6-16, 7-2, 7-5, and 14-2.

Chain-weighting leads to complexity in estimating the contribution of economic sectors to an overall change in output: it becomes difficult, for someone without access to the complicated statistical methods that BEA uses, to find the correct answers to questions such as "How much are government spending cuts contributing to the drag on GDP growth?" Because of this, BEA is now calculating and publishing estimates of the arithmetic contribution of each major component to the total change in real GDP. *Business Statistics* reproduces these calculations in Table 1-4. (As will be explained later, users of these calculations should, however, bear in mind that imports are treated as a negative contribution to GDP instead of being subtracted from the demand components that give rise to them.) For further information, see J. Steven Landefeld, Brent R. Moulton, and Cindy M. Vojtech, "Chained-Dollar Indexes: Issues, Tips on Their Use, and Upcoming Changes," *Survey of Current Business* (November 2003); and J. Steven Landefeld and Robert P. Parker, "BEA's Chain Indexes, Time Series, and Measures of Long-Term Economic Growth," *Survey of Current Business* (May 1997).

GDP price indexes measure price changes between any two adjacent years (or quarters) for a fixed "market basket" of goods and services consisting of the average quantities purchased in those two years (or quarters). The annual measures are chained together to form an index with prices in 2009 set to equal 100. Using average quantities as weights while changing weights each period eliminates the substitution bias that arises in more conventional indexes, in which weights are taken from a single base period that usually takes place early in the period under measurement. Generally, using a single, early base period leads to an overstatement of price increase. The CPI-U and the CPI-W are examples of such conventional indexes, technically known as "Laspeyres" indexes. See the "General Notes" at the beginning of this volume and the notes and definitions for Chapter 8 for further explanation.

The chain-type formula guarantees that a GDP price index change will differ only trivially from the change in the implicit deflator (ratio of current-dollar to real value, expressed as a percent). Therefore, *Business Statistics* is no longer publishing a separate table of implicit deflators.

DEFINITIONS AND NOTES ON THE DATA:

BEA Aggregates of sales and purchases (Tables 1-1 and 1-5 through 1-7)

Final sales of domestic product is GDP minus change in private inventories. It is the sum of personal consumption expenditures, gross private domestic fixed investment, government consumption expenditures and gross investment, and net exports of goods and services.

Gross domestic purchases is the market value of goods and services purchased by U.S. residents, regardless of where those goods and services were produced. It is GDP minus net exports (that is, minus exports plus imports) of goods and services; equivalently, it is the sum of personal consumption expenditures, gross private domestic investment, and government consumption expenditures and gross investment. The price index for gross domestic purchases is therefore a measure of price change for goods and services purchased by (rather than produced by) U.S. residents.

Final sales to domestic purchasers is gross domestic purchases minus change in private inventories.

DEFINITIONS AND NOTES ON THE DATA:

U.S. Population and per capita product and income estimates (Table 1-3)

In Table 1-3, annual and quarterly measures of product, income, and consumption spending are expressed in per capita terms—the aggregate dollar amount divided by the U.S. population. Population data from 1991 forward reflect the results of the 2000 and 2010 Censuses.

DEFINITIONS AND NOTES ON THE DATA:

Inventory-sales ratios (Table 1-8)

Inventories to sales ratios. The ratios shown in Table 1-8 are based on the inventory estimates underlying the measurement of inventory change in the NIPAs. They include data and estimates for not only the inventories held in manufacturing and trade (which are shown in Chapter 16), but also stocks held by all other businesses in the U.S. economy.

For the current-dollar ratios, inventories at the end of each quarter are valued in the prices that prevailed at the end of that quarter. For the constant-dollar ratios, they are valued in chained (2009) dollars. In both cases, the inventory-sales ratio is the value of the inventories at the end of the quarter divided by quarterly total sales at monthly rates (quarterly totals divided by 3). In other words, they represent how many months' supply businesses had on hand at the end of the period. This makes them comparable in concept and order of magnitude to the ratios shown in Chapter 16. Annual ratios are those for the fourth quarter.

Inventory data consistent with the 2013 revision are only available from 1997 to date. Tables 1-8A and B show the old estimates for earlier years with an overlap period.

DEFINITIONS AND NOTES ON THE DATA:

Shares of aggregate supply and demand (Tables 1-9 and 1-10)

These tables, developed by the editor of *Business Statistics*, are not official NIPA calculations. They are components of current-dollar GDP rearranged in order to highlight relationships that are not always apparent in the official presentation of the NIPAs.

Aggregate supply combines domestic production (GDP) and imports, the two sources that, between them, supply the goods and services demanded by consumers, businesses, and governments in the U.S. economy. In this table the user can observe the growing share of imports that satisfy demands in the U.S. marketplace.

Aggregate final demand is the sum of all final (that is, excluding inventory change) demands for goods and services in the U.S. market—consumption spending, fixed investment, exports, and government consumption and investment. It is different from *final sales of domestic product* (Tables 1-1 and 1-7) because imports are not subtracted; in this table, imports are considered a source of supply, not a negative element of demand. It is different from *gross domestic purchases* (Tables 1-5 and 1-6) because it includes exports, since they are a source of demand for U.S. output, but excludes inventory change. It is like *final sales to domestic purchasers* (Table 1-7) in excluding inventory change, but different because it also includes exports.

Table 1-10 provides alternative data on the question of the relative importance of consumption spending and other final demands to the U.S. economy. NIPA statistics on PCE as a percent of GDP are frequently cited, but there is a problem with this, since PCE includes the value of imports while GDP does not.

DEFINITIONS AND NOTES ON THE DATA:

Components of income (Tables 1-11, 1-12 and 1-13)

There are now two different presentations of aggregate income for the United States: *gross domestic income* (Table 1-12) and *national income* (Table 1-13). As noted above, domestic income refers to income generated from production within the United States, while national income refers to income received by residents of the United States. This means that some of the income components differ between the two tables. Domestic income payments include payments to the rest of the world from domestic industries. National income payments exclude payments to the rest of the world but include payments received by U.S. residents from the rest of the world. These differences are seen in employee compensation, interest, and corporate profits. Taxes on production and imports, taxes on corporate income, business transfer payments, subsidies, proprietors' income, rental income, and the current surplus of government enterprises are the same in both accounts.

All income entries are now calculated on an accrual basis, associating the income with the period in which it was earned rather than when it was paid.

A third important income aggregate is *personal income.* The derivation of this well-known statistic from national income is shown in Table 1-11. See Chapter 4 and its notes and definitions for data and more information.

Compensation of employees is the income accruing to employees as remuneration for their work. It is the sum of wage and salary accruals and supplements to wages and salaries. In the domestic income account, it refers to all payments generated by domestic production, including those to workers residing in the "rest of the world." In the national and personal income accounts, there is a slightly different "compensation of employees," including that received by U.S. residents from the rest of the world but excluding that paid from the domestic production account to workers residing elsewhere.

Wages and salaries consists of the monetary remuneration of employees, including the compensation of corporate officers; corporate directors' fees paid to directors who are also employees of the corporation; commissions, tips, and bonuses; voluntary employee contributions to certain deferred compensation plans, such as 401(k) plans; and receipts-in-kind that represent income. As of the 2003 revision, it also includes judicial fees to jurors and witnesses, compensation of prison inmates, and marriage fees to justices of the peace, all of which were formerly included in "other labor income."

In concept, wages and salaries include the value of the exercise by employees of "nonqualified stock options," in which an employee is allowed to buy stock for less than its current market price. (Actual measurement of these values involves a number of problems, particularly in the short run. Such stock options are not included in the monthly wage data from the Bureau of Labor Statistics, which are the main source for current extrapolations of wages and salaries, and are not consistently reported in corporate financial statements. They are, however, generally included in the unemployment insurance wage data that are used to correct the preliminary wage and salary estimates.) Another form of stock option, the "incentive stock option," leads to a capital gain only and is thus not included in the definition of wages and salaries.

Supplements to wages and salaries consists of *employer contributions for employee pension and insurance funds* and *employer contributions for government social insurance.*

Employer contributions for employee pension and insurance funds consists of employer payments (including payments-in-kind) to private pension and profit-sharing plans, private group health and life insurance plans, privately administered workers' compensation plans, government employee retirement plans, and supplemental unemployment benefit plans. They are now measured in the period in which the employee earns the obligation rather than when the employer makes the cash payment into the fund. This includes the major part of what was once called "other labor income." The remainder of "other labor income" has been reclassified as wages and salaries, as noted above.

Employer contributions for government social insurance consists of employer payments under the following federal, state, and local government programs: old-age, survivors, and disability insurance (Social Security); hospital insurance (Medicare); unemployment insurance; railroad retirement; pension benefit guaranty; veterans' life insurance; publicly administered workers' compensation; military medical insurance; and temporary disability insurance.

Taxes on production and imports is included in the gross domestic income account to make it comparable in concept to gross domestic product. It consists of federal excise taxes and customs duties and of state and local sales taxes, property taxes (including residential real estate taxes), motor vehicle license taxes, severance taxes, special assessments, and other taxes. It is equal to the former "indirect business taxes and nontax liabilities" less most of the nontax liabilities, which have now been reclassified as "business transfer payments."

Subsidies (payments by government to business other than purchases of goods and services) are now presented separately from the current surplus of government enterprises, which is presented as a component of net operating surplus. However, for data representing the years before 1959, subsidies continue to be presented as net of the current surplus of government enterprises, since detailed data to separate the series for this period are not available.

Net operating surplus is a new aggregate introduced in the 2003 NIPA revision—a grouping of the business income components of the gross domestic income account. It represents the net income accruing to business capital. It is equal to gross domestic income minus compensation of employees, taxes on production and imports less subsidies (that is, the taxes are taken out of income and the subsidies are put in), and consumption of fixed capital (CFC). Net operating surplus consists of the surplus for private enterprises and the current surplus of government enterprises. The net operating surplus of private enterprises comprises net interest and miscellaneous payments, business current transfer payments, proprietors' income, rental income of persons, and corporate profits.

Net interest and miscellaneous payments, domestic industries consists of interest paid by domestic private enterprises and of rents and royalties paid by private enterprises to government, less interest received by domestic private enterprises. Interest received does not include interest received by noninsured pension plans, which are recorded as being directly received by persons in personal income. Both interest categories include monetary and imputed interest. In the *national* account, interest paid to the rest of the world is subtracted from the interest paid by domestic industries and interest received from the rest of the world is added. Interest payments on mortgage and home improvement loans and on home equity loans are included as net interest in the private enterprises account.

It should be noted that net interest does not include interest paid by federal, state, or local governments. In fact, government interest does not enter into the national and domestic income accounts, though it does appear as a component of personal income. The NIPAs draw a distinction between interest paid by government and that paid by business.

The reasoning behind this distinction is that interest paid by business is one of the income counterparts of the production side of the account. The value of business production (as measured by its output of goods and services) includes the value added by business capital, and interest paid by business to its lenders is part of the total return to business capital.

However, there is no product flow in the accounts that is a counterpart to the payment of interest by government. The output of government does not have a market value. For purposes of GDP measurement, BEA estimates the government contribution to GDP as the sum of government's compensation of employees, purchases of goods and services, and consumption of government fixed capital. (See above, and also the notes and definitions to Chapter 6.) This implies an estimate (described as "conservative" by BEA) that the net return to government capital is zero—that is, that the gross return is just sufficient to pay down the depreciation. Consequently, this assumption generates no income, imputed or actual, that might correspond to the government's interest payment.

Supporting the distinction between business and government interest payments, it may be noted that most federal government debt was not incurred to finance investment, but rather to finance wars, to avoid tax increases and spending cuts during recessions, or to stimulate the economy. Furthermore, some of the largest and most productive government investments—highways—are typically financed by taxes on a pay-as-you-go basis and not by borrowing.

Business current transfer payments, net consists of payments to persons, government, and the rest of the world by private business for which no current services are performed. Net insurance settlements—actual insured losses (or claims payable) less a normal level of losses—are treated as transfer payments. Payments to government consist of federal deposit insurance premiums, fines, regulatory and inspection fees, tobacco settlements, and other miscellaneous payments previously classified as "nontaxes." Taxes paid by domestic corporations to foreign governments, formerly classified as transfer payments, are now counted as taxes on corporate income.

In the NIPAs, capital income other than interest—corporate profits, proprietors' income, and rental income—is converted from the basis usually shown in the books of business, and reported to the Internal Revenue Service, to a basis that more closely represents income from current production. In the business accounts that provide the source data, depreciation of structures and equipment typically reflects a historical cost basis and a possibly arbitrary service life allowed by law to be used for tax purposes. BEA adjusts these values to reflect the average actual life of the capital goods and the cost of replacing them in the current period's prices. This conversion is done for all three forms of capital income. In addition, corporate and proprietors' incomes also require an adjustment for inventory valuation to exclude any profits or losses that might appear in the books, should the cost of inventory acquisition not be valued in the current period's prices. These two adjustments are called the *capital consumption adjustment (CCAdj)* and the *inventory valuation adjustment (IVA)*. They are described in more detail below.

Proprietors' income with inventory valuation and capital consumption adjustments is the current-production income (including income-in-kind) of sole proprietorships and partnerships and of tax-exempt cooperatives. The imputed net rental income of owner-occupants of farm dwellings is included, but the imputed net rental income of owner-occupants of nonfarm dwellings is included in rental income of persons. Fees paid to outside directors of corporations are included. Proprietors' income excludes dividends and monetary interest received by nonfinancial business and rental incomes received by persons not primarily engaged in the real estate business; these incomes are included in dividends, net interest, and rental income of persons, respectively.

Rental income of persons with capital consumption adjustment is the net current-production income of persons from the rental of real property (except for the income of persons primarily engaged in the real estate business), the imputed net rental income of owner-occupants of nonfarm dwellings, and the royalties received by persons from patents, copyrights, and rights to natural resources. Consistent with the classification of investment in owner-occupied housing as business investment, the homeowner is considered to be paying himself or herself the rental value of the house (classified as PCE for services) and receiving as net income the amount of the rental that remains after paying interest and other costs.

Corporate profits with inventory valuation and capital consumption adjustments, often referred to as "economic profits," is the current-production income, net of economic depreciation, of organizations treated as corporations in the NIPAs. These organizations consist of all entities required to file federal corporate tax returns, including mutual financial institutions and cooperatives subject to federal income tax; private noninsured pension funds; nonprofit institutions that primarily serve business; Federal Reserve Banks, which accrue income stemming from the conduct of monetary policy; and federally sponsored credit agencies. This income is measured as receipts less expenses as defined in federal tax law, except for the following differences: receipts exclude capital gains and dividends received; expenses exclude depletion and capital losses and losses resulting from bad debts; inventory withdrawals are valued at replacement cost; and depreciation is on a consistent accounting basis and is valued at replacement cost.

Since *national* income is defined as the income of U.S. residents, its profits component includes income earned abroad by U.S. corporations and excludes income earned by the rest of the world within the United States.

Taxes on corporate income consists of taxes on corporate income paid to government and to the rest of the world.

Taxes on corporate income paid to government is the sum of federal, state, and local income taxes on all income subject to taxes. This income includes capital gains and other income excluded from profits before tax. These taxes are measured on an accrual basis, net of applicable tax credits.

Taxes on corporate income paid to the rest of the world consists of nonresident taxes, which are those paid by domestic corporations to foreign governments. These taxes were formerly classified as "business transfer payments to the rest of the world."

Profits after tax is total corporate profits with IVA and CCAdj less taxes on corporate income. It consists of dividends and undistributed corporate profits.

Dividends is payments in cash or other assets, excluding those made using corporations' own stock, that are made by corporations to stockholders. In the domestic account, these are payments by domestic industries to stockholders in the United States and abroad; in the national account, these are dividends received by U.S. residents from domestic and foreign industries. The payments are measured net of dividends received by U.S. corporations. Dividends paid to state and local government social insurance funds and general government are included.

Undistributed profits is corporate profits after tax with IVA and CCAdj less dividends.

The *inventory valuation adjustment (IVA)* is the difference between the cost of inventory withdrawals valued at replacement cost and the cost as valued in the source data used to determine profits before tax, which in many cases charge inventories at acquisition cost. It is calculated separately for corporate profits and for nonfarm proprietors' income. Its behavior is determined by price changes, especially for materials. When prices are rising, which has been typical of much of the postwar period, the business-reported value of inventory change will include a capital gains component, which needs to be removed from reported inventory change on the product side in order to correctly measure the change in the volume of inventories, and from reported profits on the income side of the accounts in order to remove the capital gains element. At such times, the IVA will be a negative figure, which is added to reported profits to yield economic profits. Occasionally, falling prices—especially for petroleum and products—will result in a positive IVA. No adjustment is needed for farm proprietors' income, as farm inventories are measured on a current-market-cost basis.

Consumption of fixed capital (CFC) is a charge for the using-up of private and government fixed capital located in the United States. It is not based on the depreciation schedules allowed in tax law, but instead on studies of prices of used equipment and structures in resale markets and other service life information.

For general government and for nonprofit institutions that primarily serve individuals, CFC on their capital assets is recorded in government consumption expenditures and in personal consumption expenditures, respectively. It is considered to be the value of the current services of the fixed capital assets owned and used by these entities.

Private capital consumption allowances consists of tax-return-based depreciation charges for corporations and nonfarm proprietorships; BEA estimates for R&D and other intellectual property; and historical cost depreciation (calculated by BEA using a geometric pattern of price declines) for farm proprietorships, rental income of persons, and nonprofit institutions.

The *private capital consumption adjustment (CCAdj)* is the difference between private capital consumption allowances and private consumption of fixed capital. The CCAdj has two parts:

- The first component of CCAdj converts tax-return-based depreciation to consistent historical cost accounting based on actual service lives of capital. In the postwar period, this has usually been a large positive number, that is, a net addition to profits and subtraction from reported depreciation. This is the case because U.S. tax law typically allows depreciation periods shorter than actual service lives. Tax depreciation was accelerated even further for 2001 through 2004. This component is a reallocation of gross business saving from depreciation to profits; gross saving is unchanged, with exactly offsetting changes in capital consumption and net saving.

- The second component is analogous to the IVA: it converts reported business capital consumption allowances from the historical cost basis to a replacement cost basis. It is determined by the price behavior of capital goods. These prices have had an upward drift in the postwar period, which has been much more stable than the changes in materials prices. Hence, this component is consistently negative (serving to reduce economic profits relative to the reported data) but less volatile than the IVA.

In 1982 through 2004, positive values for the first component outweighed negative values for the second, resulting in a net positive CCAdj, an addition to profits. However, when the accelerated depreciation expired in 2005, there was a sharp decline in the consistent-accounting adjustment and it was outweighed by the price adjustment. This led to negative CCAdjs in 2005 through 2007, reducing profits from the reported numbers.

DEFINITIONS AND NOTES ON THE DATA:

Gross value added of domestic corporate business (Tables 1-14 and 1-15)

Gross value added is the term now used for what was formerly called "gross domestic product originating." It represents the share of the GDP that is produced in the specified sector or industry. Tables 1-14 and 1-15 show the current-dollar value of gross value added for all domestic corporate business and its financial and nonfinancial components. For the total and for nonfinancial corporations, consumption of fixed capital and net value added are shown, as is the allocation of net value added among employee compensation, taxes and transfer payments, and capital income. Constant-dollar values are also shown for nonfinancial corporations.

The data for nonfinancial corporations are often considered to be somewhat sturdier than data for the other sectors of the economy, since they exclude sectors whose outputs are difficult to evaluate—households, institutions, general government, and financial business—as well as excluding all noncorporate business, in which the separate contributions of labor and capital are not readily measured.

Data availability and revisions

Annual data are available beginning with 1929. Quarterly data begin with 1946 for current-dollar values and 1947 for quantity and price measures such as real GDP and the GDP price index. Not all data are available for all time periods.

New data are normally released toward the end of each month. The "advance" estimate of GDP for each calendar quarter is released at the end of the month after the quarter's end. The "second" estimate, including more complete product data and the first estimates of corporate profits, is released at the end of the second month after the quarter's end, and a "third" estimate including still more complete data at the end of the third month. Wage and salary and related income-side components may be revised for previous quarters as well.

At the end of each July, there is an "annual" revision, incorporating more complete data and other improvements, affecting at least the previous 3 years. Every five years, there is a "comprehensive" revision, such as the 2013 revision incorporated in this volume, corresponding with updated statistics from the quinquennial benchmark input-output accounts and incorporating a revision of the base year for constant-price and index numbers.

The most recent data are published each month in the *Survey of Current Business*. Current and historical data may be obtained from the BEA Web site at <https://www.bea.gov> and the STAT-USA subscription Web site at <https://www.stat-usa.gov>.

REFERENCES

Other documentation available on the BEA Web site at <https://www.bea.gov> includes the following: "NIPA Handbook: Concepts and Methods of the U.S. National Income and Product Accounts, October 2009"; separate chapters from the Handbook on Personal Consumption Expenditures, Private Fixed Investment, and Change in Private Inventories; "Measuring the Economy: A Primer on GDP and the National Income and Product

Accounts"; "An Introduction to the National Income and Product Accounts"; and "Taking the Pulse of the Economy: Measuring GDP," *Journal of Economic Perspectives*, Spring 2008.

The treatment of employee stock options is discussed in Carol Moylan, "Treatment of Employee Stock Options in the U.S. National Economic Accounts," available on the BEA Web site at <https://www.bea.gov>.

The data for 1929 through 1946 published here have been calculated after the fact and differ from the national income data that were currently available during the 1930s and 1940s. For an article on what was available at that time and the history of the NIPAs during that period, see Rosemary D. Marcuss and Richard E. Kane, "U.S. National Income and Product Statistics: Born of the Great Depression and World War II," *Survey of Current Business*, February 2007, pp. 32-46.

CHAPTER 2: INDUSTRIAL PRODUCTION AND CAPACITY UTILIZATION

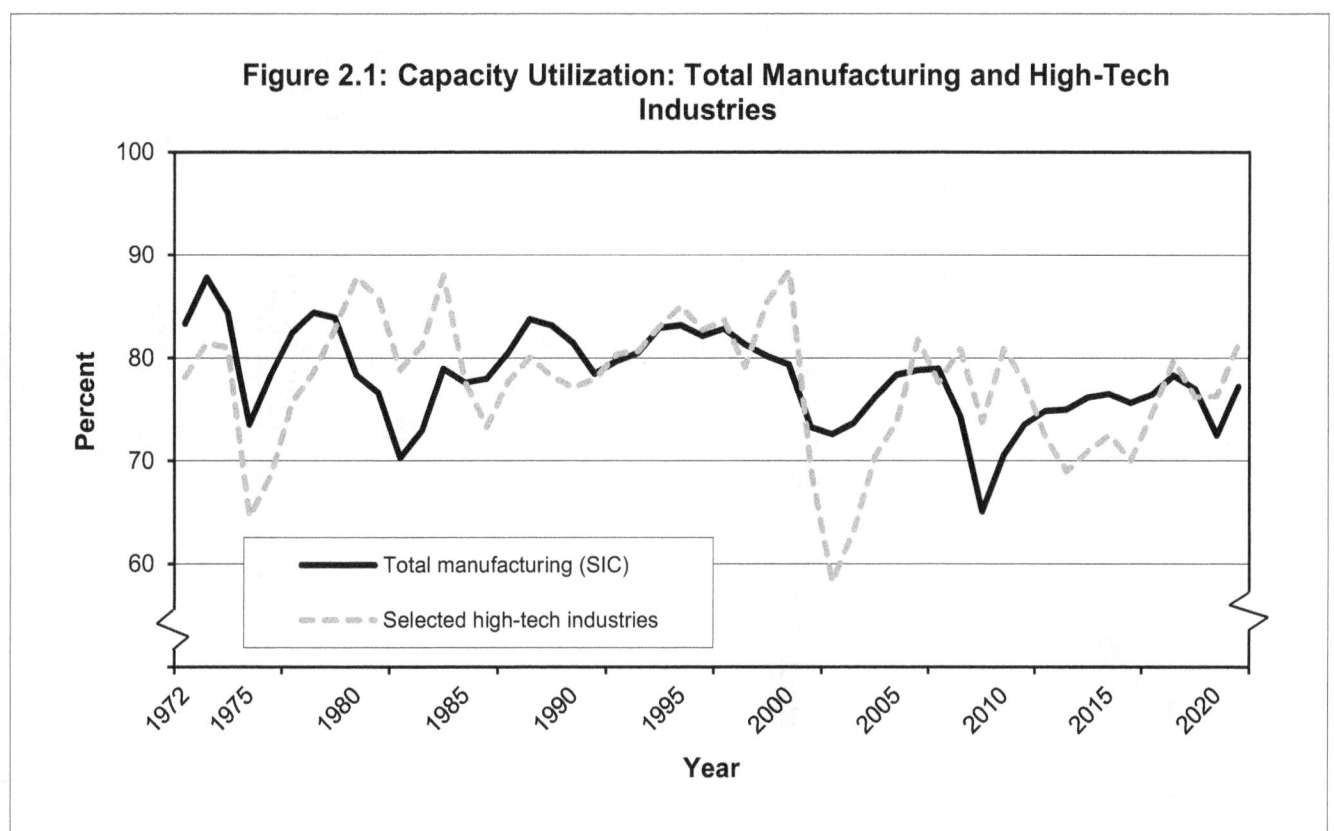

Figure 2.1: Capacity Utilization: Total Manufacturing and High-Tech Industries

- Manufacturing capacity utilization is a key statistic for the U.S. economy, despite being limited to a sector that by some measures has diminished in importance. The Federal Reserve also provides measures of capacity utilization for "total industry"—manufacturing, mining, and utilities. However, mining and utilities are less significant in the context of business cycle analysis, and much of the variation in capacity use by utilities is a result of transitory weather variations, not economic factors. Manufacturing utilization is an important indicator of inflationary pressure and also measures an important element in the demand for new capital goods. (Tables 2-3 and 2-4A)

- In 2021, industrial production increased for almost all categories listed in Table 2-2 after decreasing in 2020. Food, beverage, and tobacco products was one of the few categories that experienced an increase in 2020. Total industrial production increased significantly from 95.3 to 100.0. (Table 2-2)

- Manufacturing capacity utilization plunged in 2008 and 2009 following the Great Recession. In April 2007, capacity utilization reached 79.4 but by June 2009, it collapsed to 63.4. Manufacturing capacity has fluctuated monthly in the years since and it reached a high of 78.6 in December 2021, but it never recovered to its high in 2007. (Table 2-4A)

- Capacity utilization in the high-tech industries (computers and office equipment, communications equipment, and semiconductors and related electronic components) peaked in 2000, before the Tech Bubble, at 88.5 but fell 34.2 percent by 2002. Capacity utilization has recovered but not to its 2000 level as seen in Figure 2-1. (Tables 2-3 and 2-4A)

Table 2-1. Industrial Production Indexes by Market Groups

(Seasonally adjusted, 2017 = 100.)

Year and month	Total industrial production	Final products and nonindustrial supplies — Total	Consumer goods — Total	Durable consumer goods — Total	Automotive products	Home electronics	Appliances, furniture, and carpeting	Miscellaneous durable goods	Nondurable consumer goods — Total
1970	37.5	39.6	51.5	33.7	26.7	1.0	69.8	61.0	60.0
1971	38.1	40.1	54.4	38.2	34.1	1.1	73.7	64.3	61.8
1972	41.7	43.8	58.8	42.7	36.8	1.2	86.5	72.2	65.7
1973	45.2	47.1	61.5	46.0	40.1	1.4	93.6	75.5	67.6
1974	45.0	47.0	59.7	41.9	34.7	1.3	85.3	72.8	67.7
1975	41.0	43.7	57.3	38.0	33.3	1.1	73.4	64.2	66.5
1976	44.2	46.8	62.0	42.9	37.9	1.3	82.7	71.6	70.7
1977	47.6	50.6	65.9	48.3	43.0	1.6	92.9	79.4	73.3
1978	50.3	53.6	67.9	49.5	42.7	1.7	97.9	82.2	75.8
1979	51.8	55.4	66.9	47.6	38.4	1.7	98.4	82.9	75.3
1980	50.4	54.6	64.3	41.4	29.5	1.8	91.7	76.1	75.3
1981	51.1	55.7	64.7	42.0	30.5	1.9	90.5	77.1	75.6
1982	48.4	54.3	64.5	39.6	29.6	1.7	81.8	72.7	76.9
1983	49.8	55.8	66.9	44.0	34.4	2.3	90.3	74.9	77.8
1984	54.2	60.5	70.0	49.2	38.5	2.9	100.4	82.9	79.3
1985	54.9	62.0	70.6	49.2	38.3	3.1	99.9	83.1	80.4
1986	55.4	63.2	73.0	52.2	41.2	3.8	104.7	85.8	82.2
1987	58.3	66.4	76.1	55.4	44.2	3.7	110.5	91.1	85.2
1988	61.3	69.6	79.0	58.1	46.3	4.6	112.5	95.2	88.0
1989	61.9	70.4	79.3	59.4	47.8	5.2	113.4	95.7	87.7
1990	62.5	71.2	79.6	57.7	45.1	5.6	110.6	94.7	89.2
1991	61.5	70.1	79.5	55.0	42.3	6.4	103.0	91.3	90.5
1992	63.3	72.0	82.0	60.3	48.9	7.4	108.9	94.4	91.4
1993	65.4	74.3	84.5	65.2	53.8	9.3	115.1	98.5	92.6
1994	68.9	77.6	88.1	71.2	59.2	12.4	123.2	104.2	94.8
1995	72.1	80.7	90.5	73.8	60.3	18.0	122.7	107.4	97.1
1996	75.3	83.9	92.1	76.1	61.3	21.6	123.9	111.1	98.4
1997	80.7	89.5	95.6	81.3	66.2	30.3	129.6	113.2	100.8
1998	85.5	94.7	99.1	87.2	71.0	39.9	138.2	117.1	103.1
1999	89.2	97.5	101.2	94.0	78.9	50.4	142.6	120.1	103.1
2000	92.7	100.6	103.1	96.8	80.2	58.2	146.6	123.6	104.6
2001	89.8	98.0	102.1	92.3	77.0	60.1	140.3	114.7	105.1
2002	90.1	97.5	104.2	98.3	85.3	61.5	143.6	118.1	105.4
2003	91.2	98.7	105.6	101.2	89.3	68.2	143.8	118.2	106.1
2004	93.6	100.9	106.7	102.7	88.7	79.7	148.2	120.5	107.1
2005	96.8	105.0	109.5	103.1	86.1	90.9	151.1	124.1	110.8
2006	99.0	107.6	110.2	102.6	83.2	109.9	146.5	126.2	111.8
2007	101.5	109.5	110.2	102.3	85.6	118.1	137.4	122.2	112.0
2008	98.0	104.9	104.4	90.1	70.9	132.6	119.6	113.2	108.5
2009	86.8	92.6	96.6	72.5	56.5	113.6	91.0	93.7	104.2
2010	91.6	95.6	97.8	80.0	68.4	77.4	89.9	100.3	103.2
2011	94.5	97.6	98.9	83.0	73.0	81.6	89.5	101.1	103.6
2012	97.4	99.3	97.6	85.0	76.0	89.9	92.1	99.9	101.3
2013	99.3	100.0	98.2	89.7	82.4	95.7	94.1	102.1	100.7
2014	102.3	101.2	99.0	94.2	89.8	92.8	95.7	102.8	100.5
2015	100.8	100.5	100.5	98.0	95.6	99.5	99.9	102.3	101.2
2016	98.7	99.2	101.1	100.3	98.5	100.5	101.4	103.9	101.3
2017	100.0	100.0	100.0	100.0	100.0	100.0	100.0	100.0	100.0
2018	103.2	102.0	100.8	103.2	104.3	116.5	99.1	102.1	100.1
2019	102.5	100.4	100.5	102.2	103.6	128.9	95.1	100.9	100.0
2020	95.3	94.9	97.9	98.7	99.6	139.0	91.5	97.7	97.7
2021	100.0	100.1	102.3	108.7	109.7	158.8	100.7	107.1	100.4
2020									
January	101.3	100.0	102.2	103.0	104.3	133.1	96.8	101.2	102.0
February	102.0	101.0	103.9	113.2	121.0	135.4	99.9	102.5	101.2
March	98.1	96.4	98.0	95.7	92.0	138.7	97.7	98.7	98.8
April	82.9	80.5	82.3	58.2	35.8	130.2	84.0	84.0	89.3
May	85.2	84.6	86.2	68.8	52.4	128.5	86.3	87.8	91.3
June	93.1	93.1	97.2	98.7	99.9	134.4	93.1	96.4	96.8
July	95.3	95.2	99.2	101.8	105.1	134.8	93.7	96.7	98.4
August	98.3	98.9	104.0	112.3	123.6	139.2	91.4	98.8	101.6
September	95.9	96.1	100.0	108.4	118.3	141.0	85.9	98.4	97.5
October	96.7	97.2	100.2	112.8	122.6	147.1	92.8	101.2	96.5
November	96.5	96.5	99.3	107.9	114.5	151.1	87.9	102.5	96.7
December	98.1	98.8	102.6	103.6	105.5	154.6	89.0	104.4	102.3
2021									
January	99.6	100.4	105.8	111.3	113.9	149.7	110.5	102.9	104.2
February	96.7	98.6	104.3	112.0	116.2	149.0	110.0	101.1	102.0
March	99.2	100.3	104.3	115.5	121.6	151.7	107.4	104.7	101.1
April	97.6	97.3	99.2	108.4	107.6	155.6	108.3	106.2	96.6
May	98.6	98.1	99.4	108.3	108.7	159.1	103.7	105.7	96.8
June	101.4	100.6	102.6	110.3	110.5	162.1	106.9	107.6	100.4
July	100.8	100.0	100.6	102.0	97.6	155.0	101.8	106.9	100.1
August	102.5	102.3	104.0	109.1	111.7	158.7	94.3	108.5	102.5
September	99.5	99.8	100.7	103.2	103.2	157.8	88.0	108.0	99.9
October	101.0	100.9	101.5	111.8	116.3	165.9	93.0	109.8	98.6
November	101.5	101.2	102.0	109.2	111.1	169.7	89.9	112.1	99.9
December	101.6	101.7	102.9	103.2	98.3	171.7	95.2	112.2	102.7

Table 2-1. Industrial Production Indexes by Market Groups—Continued

(Seasonally adjusted, 2017 = 100.)

Year and month	Nondurable non-energy consumer goods Total	Foods and tobacco	Clothing	Chemical products	Paper products	Consumer energy products	Business equipment Total	Transit	Information processing	Industrial and other	Defense and space equipment	Construction supplies	Business supplies
1970	64.3	58.1	639.4	36.4	96.2	46.5	16.1	41.3	1.0	54.2	53.1	57.4	38.9
1971	65.9	59.8	635.7	38.5	98.2	48.7	15.3	40.0	0.9	51.8	47.7	59.2	40.1
1972	70.2	63.2	691.8	42.1	99.0	51.4	17.4	43.6	1.1	59.0	46.4	67.2	44.1
1973	72.5	64.7	705.0	45.3	102.3	52.0	20.1	51.9	1.3	67.1	50.9	73.0	46.8
1974	72.2	65.3	661.1	47.7	100.6	53.5	21.3	50.6	1.6	69.9	52.6	71.3	46.6
1975	70.3	64.0	643.5	46.0	94.8	54.7	19.0	44.6	1.5	61.2	53.0	60.3	42.9
1976	74.9	68.2	677.5	50.0	98.6	57.6	20.3	46.1	1.8	63.6	51.5	64.9	45.7
1977	77.6	69.6	710.7	52.1	107.8	59.8	23.4	54.7	2.4	69.3	46.1	70.6	49.5
1978	80.6	72.1	727.8	55.3	113.1	60.7	26.4	63.3	3.0	74.2	47.1	74.5	52.2
1979	79.4	71.5	687.0	55.5	114.3	62.3	29.7	74.1	3.7	78.8	50.2	76.5	54.0
1980	80.3	72.6	698.9	55.3	115.7	59.6	30.4	69.8	4.7	76.2	59.6	70.8	52.7
1981	80.9	72.8	698.9	56.1	118.6	59.2	31.3	65.4	5.6	76.0	64.6	69.7	53.9
1982	82.5	75.3	697.0	56.3	121.7	59.5	28.7	50.0	6.3	65.8	77.3	63.2	53.2
1983	83.6	75.4	717.0	56.9	127.1	59.8	28.9	49.3	7.3	60.9	77.6	67.7	55.7
1984	85.0	76.3	719.6	58.2	133.5	61.7	33.1	50.8	8.9	69.5	89.0	73.5	60.6
1985	86.4	78.6	689.4	58.8	140.3	61.5	34.4	52.7	9.6	70.3	99.6	75.3	62.1
1986	88.5	79.9	689.6	63.4	142.2	62.5	33.9	48.2	9.8	70.0	105.8	77.7	64.1
1987	91.7	81.7	696.4	68.3	150.3	64.8	36.2	48.8	11.2	72.5	108.0	82.7	67.9
1988	94.4	84.1	686.2	72.4	154.3	68.2	39.9	54.5	12.5	78.7	108.9	84.6	70.4
1989	93.9	83.5	655.3	73.9	155.0	68.5	41.3	57.3	12.9	81.3	109.1	84.2	71.3
1990	96.1	85.8	643.8	76.7	158.0	67.9	42.8	61.2	14.0	80.7	105.2	83.6	73.0
1991	97.1	86.3	641.7	79.4	158.8	66.9	42.3	63.7	14.2	76.5	97.5	79.1	71.9
1992	98.5	87.7	656.7	79.2	160.7	69.0	44.1	62.3	16.1	77.8	90.5	82.4	73.6
1993	99.3	87.1	668.9	81.3	164.4	72.0	46.3	58.2	17.7	83.0	85.6	86.1	75.9
1994	101.9	90.5	681.1	83.1	162.7	72.8	49.5	56.3	20.1	88.6	80.4	92.3	78.8
1995	104.3	92.8	677.9	86.7	163.7	74.7	54.1	55.8	24.3	94.2	77.7	94.5	81.9
1996	105.0	92.5	660.0	90.9	163.0	78.0	59.6	59.0	29.8	97.5	75.7	98.8	85.1
1997	108.3	94.1	658.3	96.0	177.5	77.4	68.5	69.3	37.9	103.5	74.7	103.5	91.1
1998	111.4	96.7	625.4	100.8	185.8	77.1	76.4	81.4	45.5	106.8	78.0	109.0	96.2
1999	110.6	94.8	599.5	102.5	189.5	79.9	80.6	79.6	55.2	104.3	75.7	111.7	100.1
2000	112.1	96.2	579.9	106.4	188.7	81.5	86.8	70.6	67.3	110.6	67.2	114.1	104.0
2001	112.5	96.2	517.6	112.3	183.4	82.5	81.3	68.1	65.1	100.0	73.9	108.8	100.2
2002	112.0	94.4	396.7	121.7	180.7	86.1	75.7	61.6	56.7	98.4	74.8	108.7	100.3
2003	112.8	95.4	373.7	124.6	174.1	86.4	75.9	58.3	59.7	97.9	79.6	108.5	102.0
2004	113.7	96.7	316.1	127.7	175.1	88.0	80.0	61.6	65.7	100.6	78.1	111.1	104.5
2005	117.5	99.9	303.6	134.4	173.2	91.1	86.0	67.5	72.0	106.0	85.6	116.5	108.3
2006	118.8	100.1	294.4	139.2	172.6	91.5	94.1	78.5	82.5	110.3	85.3	119.4	110.1
2007	117.5	100.0	236.5	140.2	165.4	95.2	99.8	81.2	92.2	114.6	101.5	118.4	111.3
2008	113.0	96.7	191.0	135.3	154.7	94.8	97.6	73.3	95.4	112.2	109.6	107.6	106.5
2009	107.2	95.3	139.8	124.8	136.5	95.2	80.9	59.6	85.8	89.6	105.2	82.8	94.4
2010	105.4	95.6	138.2	119.0	129.0	97.2	86.8	66.4	87.6	97.0	113.1	85.6	97.4
2011	105.7	95.6	135.1	121.0	125.4	98.0	92.0	68.7	87.8	106.5	109.8	87.6	98.3
2012	103.5	95.8	128.4	114.2	121.6	95.2	101.2	83.3	95.1	113.7	111.8	91.3	98.9
2013	100.8	97.2	118.4	103.5	114.3	100.3	101.2	88.5	95.6	110.5	108.2	94.2	100.3
2014	100.5	96.8	113.2	104.4	112.4	100.2	103.1	96.9	93.6	110.8	104.3	97.1	101.1
2015	102.0	98.5	107.6	106.8	108.5	98.4	100.8	101.5	94.9	103.2	101.3	97.8	99.8
2016	101.5	99.3	102.7	104.6	104.8	100.6	95.5	93.1	94.8	97.1	97.7	98.8	99.9
2017	100.0	100.0	100.0	100.0	100.0	100.0	100.0	100.0	100.0	100.0	100.0	100.0	100.0
2018	98.8	99.2	96.4	98.3	96.8	103.9	103.9	101.8	105.2	104.6	102.3	101.7	102.0
2019	99.1	99.0	97.0	100.4	92.3	103.0	95.8	77.9	107.8	101.6	115.6	100.4	100.1
2020	98.5	99.1	82.5	100.8	83.8	94.5	83.3	54.0	106.7	91.4	113.1	96.5	94.3
2021	101.1	100.4	90.2	106.2	81.9	97.7	91.4	66.8	110.5	98.4	125.0	101.0	97.8
2020													
January	97.9	97.4	90.6	100.8	87.5	117.3	90.9	63.6	110.2	99.4	117.1	95.5	100.4
February	99.5	100.4	92.6	100.9	83.2	107.8	92.4	65.3	111.6	100.6	118.3	96.1	99.2
March	100.1	99.9	87.0	105.0	78.9	93.4	86.4	52.7	110.4	96.8	117.2	96.3	95.6
April	91.6	91.1	62.0	98.2	72.6	80.1	64.6	17.3	104.0	77.0	100.6	88.4	82.5
May	94.5	95.2	72.6	98.1	76.9	78.4	71.4	29.2	102.8	83.8	109.3	94.1	85.0
June	99.2	102.0	80.7	98.5	82.9	87.1	80.4	48.7	108.5	88.1	110.4	97.6	91.0
July	97.4	97.6	77.1	99.8	87.2	103.2	82.1	52.3	107.8	89.6	109.7	98.3	95.2
August	102.3	104.4	84.3	101.5	91.5	99.4	86.0	61.5	110.2	91.1	112.8	99.3	97.0
September	100.6	102.1	81.9	100.8	90.6	85.4	84.3	62.7	101.8	90.2	112.5	97.4	95.3
October	100.5	102.1	87.1	100.7	86.9	80.6	86.4	65.9	102.6	92.2	115.0	100.3	96.8
November	99.2	99.9	85.5	101.2	84.6	86.8	86.7	64.4	105.1	92.7	117.6	98.1	95.5
December	98.9	97.7	88.2	104.1	83.0	114.9	88.0	64.4	105.9	94.8	117.3	96.7	98.0
2021													
January	99.8	100.1	87.1	103.1	80.7	120.7	89.7	70.7	104.9	94.8	121.1	94.0	96.8
February	98.7	98.7	86.8	102.8	78.7	114.1	88.7	71.6	102.7	93.3	121.0	91.5	93.3
March	101.3	102.1	88.6	104.4	78.3	100.5	91.5	72.4	106.3	96.9	124.7	98.1	95.4
April	100.0	99.7	88.8	104.7	79.0	84.5	89.0	64.2	106.5	96.7	122.7	100.7	94.1
May	100.6	99.5	91.3	106.8	79.7	83.2	90.9	65.4	110.7	98.1	121.3	101.7	95.7
June	102.6	102.7	91.7	107.0	80.8	91.9	91.2	65.4	111.9	98.2	125.9	103.5	98.6
July	100.1	98.9	89.9	104.9	85.6	99.2	91.2	62.0	112.6	99.9	127.0	103.7	100.4
August	103.0	102.4	91.8	107.0	88.9	99.8	92.7	66.1	113.8	100.1	127.0	104.0	101.5
September	102.7	101.4	91.0	108.4	86.6	90.0	91.3	64.0	111.2	99.5	124.5	103.7	98.9
October	102.7	102.2	92.5	107.7	83.3	84.3	93.3	68.7	113.5	99.7	127.4	105.0	99.2
November	101.0	99.6	92.1	107.4	81.1	95.2	93.4	67.3	114.9	100.5	128.4	104.6	99.6
December	100.5	97.3	90.3	110.4	79.9	108.5	94.4	63.9	116.6	103.5	128.4	101.8	100.4

Table 2-1. Industrial Production Indexes by Market Groups—*Continued*

(Seasonally adjusted, 2017 = 100.)

Year and month		Materials										Energy materials
			Non-energy materials									
				Durable				Nondurable				
	Total	Total	Total	Consumer parts	Equipment parts	Other	Total	Textile	Paper	Chemicals		
1970	34.7	30.1	19.8	43.2	3.3	63.7	61.8	166.5	70.6	45.1		60.5
1971	35.3	30.6	19.8	47.9	3.3	61.4	64.4	174.4	73.7	47.8		61.0
1972	38.8	34.3	22.4	53.2	3.8	69.4	71.0	183.6	78.6	55.6		63.3
1973	42.3	38.0	25.6	61.7	4.5	77.0	74.6	179.0	84.8	61.3		65.2
1974	42.2	37.9	25.3	54.6	4.8	76.8	75.7	167.0	89.2	63.0		65.0
1975	37.6	32.5	21.2	43.9	4.1	64.0	67.7	163.5	77.6	52.8		64.6
1976	40.9	36.2	23.6	56.2	4.4	68.8	75.1	182.6	85.3	60.5		66.1
1977	43.8	39.2	25.8	61.6	5.0	72.9	80.5	194.7	89.1	67.2		68.4
1978	46.0	41.8	27.8	65.2	5.6	77.8	83.5	192.4	93.4	71.3		69.3
1979	47.2	42.9	28.7	61.5	6.1	79.7	85.1	190.9	97.2	74.2		71.1
1980	45.4	40.3	26.6	47.3	6.3	73.7	82.3	186.4	98.0	68.7		71.7
1981	45.7	40.5	26.6	44.9	6.5	73.8	82.9	182.2	99.9	69.2		72.5
1982	42.2	36.4	23.2	38.2	5.9	62.1	78.6	166.6	100.7	62.1		69.5
1983	43.3	38.9	24.7	46.3	6.0	65.1	84.1	186.7	107.0	68.6		67.4
1984	47.4	43.4	28.7	55.1	7.3	72.1	87.8	186.1	113.6	72.9		71.6
1985	47.4	43.4	28.8	57.4	7.3	71.5	87.0	176.1	112.9	71.7		71.4
1986	47.3	44.2	29.2	56.9	7.4	72.9	89.7	183.1	117.6	75.2		68.8
1987	49.9	47.2	31.3	58.5	8.1	78.1	95.1	204.3	123.2	81.7		70.6
1988	52.7	50.1	33.8	63.1	8.8	83.7	98.6	202.4	127.3	86.6		73.3
1989	53.1	50.4	33.9	60.0	9.1	84.0	99.4	206.5	127.2	87.8		74.1
1990	53.5	50.5	34.0	55.8	9.4	84.4	99.7	196.3	127.7	88.7		75.7
1991	52.7	49.5	33.0	52.6	9.4	80.8	98.6	196.3	124.9	87.4		75.9
1992	54.4	51.9	35.2	59.2	10.0	85.2	101.1	207.9	128.0	89.6		75.2
1993	56.3	54.2	37.5	67.0	10.6	88.5	102.2	216.6	128.0	90.1		75.6
1994	59.9	58.5	41.7	77.3	12.0	95.0	105.3	229.6	132.8	92.9		76.8
1995	63.1	62.4	45.9	80.4	14.5	98.6	106.3	225.5	136.2	93.6		78.1
1996	66.4	66.3	50.8	82.4	18.0	101.5	105.3	219.1	131.9	94.1		79.3
1997	71.6	73.3	57.8	88.8	22.7	106.6	110.3	229.2	133.3	100.9		79.2
1998	75.8	78.7	64.0	92.0	27.9	109.5	111.7	227.2	134.6	101.0		79.7
1999	80.6	85.0	71.6	101.1	34.5	111.2	113.0	223.3	136.5	103.8		79.7
2000	84.5	89.9	78.2	101.5	42.5	112.2	112.4	214.4	134.3	104.2		81.1
2001	81.2	85.4	74.9	90.3	43.4	104.3	105.1	189.6	127.3	96.4		80.3
2002	82.3	87.2	76.5	95.1	44.5	104.5	107.1	192.5	127.5	100.0		80.1
2003	83.4	88.8	79.2	94.6	49.5	103.7	106.2	182.7	123.4	100.5		80.0
2004	86.2	93.1	84.4	95.7	56.2	107.6	108.3	174.4	124.8	105.8		80.1
2005	88.3	96.8	89.3	98.0	63.3	110.1	109.6	178.5	124.3	107.0		79.5
2006	90.1	99.2	92.8	97.9	68.8	112.4	109.7	161.8	123.2	108.9		80.4
2007	93.2	103.4	96.8	98.3	77.8	112.2	114.5	148.0	123.2	119.2		82.1
2008	90.9	98.6	93.8	85.5	81.4	107.0	106.1	128.3	117.8	105.7		82.8
2009	80.8	82.0	73.8	61.0	67.1	83.8	95.9	105.2	103.6	93.4		80.6
2010	87.7	91.2	85.0	77.5	77.6	93.1	101.6	116.9	105.7	103.6		84.2
2011	91.5	95.5	92.2	84.4	88.4	97.6	100.8	112.2	105.4	102.5		87.6
2012	95.6	98.2	96.7	94.0	94.3	99.1	100.7	109.8	106.0	101.8		93.2
2013	98.8	100.1	99.1	97.7	96.0	101.6	101.7	114.8	106.2	102.5		98.1
2014	103.7	102.2	103.3	102.6	102.0	104.2	100.5	113.2	104.5	100.0		106.2
2015	101.3	100.5	101.2	104.3	98.6	101.7	99.3	106.2	103.0	97.5		102.8
2016	98.0	99.5	99.2	102.0	96.2	100.1	99.9	103.2	101.6	98.4		95.2
2017	100.0	100.0	100.0	100.0	100.0	100.0	100.0	100.0	100.0	100.0		100.0
2018	104.7	101.4	102.6	100.6	103.3	102.8	99.7	98.8	97.4	99.3		110.3
2019	105.1	99.0	99.8	94.4	102.8	100.0	97.7	94.4	97.3	95.6		115.6
2020	95.7	91.3	89.4	76.3	92.9	92.0	94.3	87.4	90.2	91.3		103.0
2021	99.8	96.1	94.5	85.1	99.0	95.3	98.5	92.3	91.4	97.0		105.6
2020												
January	102.8	96.0	95.2	86.9	97.0	97.0	97.4	95.3	100.0	93.3		114.7
February	103.2	97.3	97.4	93.7	98.3	98.1	97.2	96.2	100.1	92.3		113.1
March	100.3	95.0	93.2	77.7	97.8	95.9	97.9	94.3	97.1	94.1		109.3
April	86.1	80.8	75.5	36.9	85.4	83.2	89.3	68.4	89.3	87.5		95.5
May	85.9	83.1	79.2	46.4	88.0	85.5	89.4	77.1	83.9	87.9		89.6
June	92.9	88.8	87.0	75.5	91.0	88.8	91.4	82.2	84.7	88.4		99.5
July	95.3	88.5	86.6	72.4	89.1	90.0	91.5	83.0	84.8	89.5		108.1
August	97.4	92.2	91.4	87.7	91.3	92.7	93.4	89.1	85.4	90.1		106.4
September	95.5	91.9	90.6	84.6	92.9	91.5	93.9	91.9	86.4	90.6		101.2
October	95.8	94.4	92.7	88.0	93.1	94.2	96.9	91.8	89.4	93.4		96.6
November	96.4	94.1	92.4	85.6	94.2	93.7	96.9	88.6	90.4	94.3		99.1
December	97.2	93.4	91.7	79.8	96.1	93.3	96.2	91.3	90.7	93.8		103.1
2021												
January	98.4	94.4	92.5	88.4	94.7	92.8	97.3	88.7	92.8	94.5		104.6
February	94.2	91.2	92.3	88.5	94.0	92.6	89.4	88.4	87.9	81.4		98.6
March	97.8	95.5	95.5	91.8	99.3	94.7	95.5	91.6	90.9	90.2		101.0
April	97.8	95.7	93.8	85.9	95.9	95.3	98.9	93.5	90.7	97.8		100.4
May	99.2	96.5	94.2	84.9	98.3	95.2	100.2	93.1	91.3	101.0		103.0
June	102.2	97.9	95.7	86.0	100.4	96.5	101.5	93.1	90.3	102.9		108.9
July	101.6	95.8	92.8	75.2	99.1	95.5	100.4	90.4	91.9	102.6		111.2
August	102.8	97.4	95.6	86.3	99.2	96.9	100.3	91.4	93.3	100.1		111.6
September	99.2	95.4	93.9	79.9	100.4	95.2	97.8	93.4	92.1	95.5		105.4
October	101.1	98.1	96.6	88.6	101.1	96.9	100.6	93.5	91.7	99.0		105.9
November	101.8	97.8	96.2	86.0	101.8	96.8	100.4	94.8	91.3	99.7		108.1
December	101.4	97.0	95.2	80.3	104.1	95.7	99.9	95.4	93.1	99.4		108.5

Table 2-1. Industrial Production Indexes by Market Groups—Continued

(Seasonally adjusted, 2017 = 100.)

Year and month	Energy — Total	Consumer energy products	Commercial energy products	Oil and gas well drilling	Converted fuels	Primary energy	Non-energy — Total	Selected high-tech — Total	Computers and peripheral equipment	Communications equipment	Semiconductors and related components	Total non-energy, excluding high-tech
1970	54.3	46.5	33.6	. . .	61.9	64.8	35.6	0.1	. . .	. . .	. . .	57.5
1971	55.4	48.7	35.3	. . .	63.5	64.3	36.1	0.1	. . .	. . .	. . .	58.6
1972	57.9	51.4	37.2	100.3	67.5	65.4	39.9	0.1	0.0	1.7	0.0	64.4
1973	59.4	52.0	39.0	94.4	70.2	66.6	43.5	0.1	0.1	1.9	0.0	69.9
1974	59.8	53.5	39.1	109.7	69.0	67.2	43.3	0.1	0.1	2.1	0.0	69.1
1975	60.1	54.7	40.5	123.8	66.7	68.2	38.7	0.1	0.1	2.0	0.0	61.6
1976	62.1	57.6	42.5	139.4	70.4	68.2	42.1	0.1	0.1	2.1	0.0	66.8
1977	64.6	59.8	43.9	177.0	73.2	70.4	45.7	0.1	0.2	2.6	0.1	71.9
1978	65.6	60.7	45.0	197.2	72.6	72.3	48.6	0.2	0.3	2.8	0.1	75.8
1979	67.6	62.3	47.4	210.3	75.2	73.8	50.0	0.2	0.4	3.4	0.1	77.2
1980	67.8	59.6	46.4	248.7	74.1	75.3	48.4	0.3	0.5	4.0	0.1	73.6
1981	68.9	59.2	47.2	298.8	73.1	76.9	48.9	0.3	0.7	4.3	0.1	73.7
1982	66.4	59.5	47.9	262.9	67.3	74.9	46.1	0.4	0.8	4.6	0.1	68.7
1983	64.4	59.8	48.6	203.7	67.2	71.8	48.4	0.4	1.2	4.9	0.1	71.2
1984	68.2	61.7	51.4	221.9	71.3	76.3	53.2	0.6	1.7	5.2	0.2	77.4
1985	68.1	61.5	53.0	203.2	71.2	76.1	54.1	0.6	2.0	5.0	0.2	78.5
1986	65.7	62.5	54.3	99.0	68.8	73.1	55.3	0.6	2.1	4.8	0.2	80.2
1987	67.7	64.8	57.2	95.5	72.3	74.0	58.5	0.8	2.8	5.3	0.2	84.0
1988	70.5	68.2	59.2	114.6	75.6	76.5	61.6	0.9	3.4	6.2	0.2	87.8
1989	71.3	68.5	61.2	99.8	78.3	76.2	62.2	0.9	3.6	6.5	0.3	88.2
1990	72.5	67.9	62.9	105.6	78.9	78.4	62.7	1.1	3.8	7.7	0.3	88.3
1991	72.9	69.9	63.6	82.3	78.9	78.8	61.5	1.1	4.0	8.3	0.3	86.0
1992	72.0	69.0	63.3	65.4	80.3	76.8	63.8	1.4	5.0	9.8	0.4	88.3
1993	73.2	72.0	64.9	82.7	82.1	76.3	66.1	1.6	6.2	11.6	0.5	90.6
1994	74.6	72.8	67.6	83.1	83.3	77.7	70.1	2.1	7.7	14.5	0.6	94.6
1995	76.1	74.7	69.9	81.0	84.5	79.2	73.7	2.9	10.7	17.9	0.9	97.0
1996	78.0	78.0	72.1	92.2	86.0	80.2	77.3	4.1	15.3	22.8	1.3	98.5
1997	78.3	77.4	75.0	108.7	87.5	79.2	83.9	6.1	22.0	31.8	2.0	103.4
1998	78.6	77.1	76.1	99.9	89.0	79.3	89.6	8.4	30.6	38.5	2.9	107.2
1999	79.3	79.9	78.9	81.3	90.8	78.2	94.0	12.2	40.6	48.8	4.7	108.5
2000	81.2	81.5	81.8	97.9	93.1	79.3	97.9	16.9	48.6	65.9	7.0	109.3
2001	81.2	82.5	83.0	116.2	91.0	79.0	94.2	17.7	50.3	60.2	7.9	104.1
2002	81.4	86.1	84.2	85.4	92.6	77.8	94.5	17.8	51.6	44.1	9.4	104.4
2003	82.1	86.4	88.6	99.8	92.8	77.7	95.8	21.6	57.0	47.2	12.4	104.4
2004	82.9	88.0	91.5	110.2	95.1	76.9	98.7	25.8	59.4	54.1	16.0	106.4
2005	83.4	91.1	94.0	122.1	96.7	75.5	102.8	30.7	72.4	56.2	19.9	109.8
2006	84.5	91.5	94.8	140.1	96.3	76.8	105.4	36.8	92.8	70.3	22.8	111.4
2007	86.7	95.2	96.8	146.2	100.9	77.7	108.1	44.0	110.4	72.8	29.0	113.0
2008	87.3	94.8	96.8	157.4	98.9	79.1	102.8	50.7	134.4	73.1	34.8	106.2
2009	84.6	95.2	94.5	101.4	93.3	77.7	88.2	44.8	120.1	63.8	30.6	90.9
2010	87.9	97.2	95.6	114.2	98.8	80.8	93.6	55.0	98.9	67.4	45.3	95.6
2011	91.1	98.0	96.6	141.3	97.6	85.4	96.4	62.0	85.4	73.7	54.4	98.0
2012	95.0	95.2	95.4	160.3	101.3	91.5	98.8	68.1	105.6	73.4	60.1	100.2
2013	99.6	100.3	97.5	160.4	101.1	97.6	99.6	75.4	105.9	86.0	66.7	100.6
2014	105.9	100.2	98.6	173.2	102.0	107.5	101.0	83.7	108.4	80.8	80.7	101.7
2015	101.9	98.4	98.1	121.2	102.5	102.7	100.5	86.4	118.1	86.9	80.9	101.0
2016	96.0	100.6	98.4	69.8	101.1	92.5	99.5	91.4	118.0	90.2	87.6	99.7
2017	100.0	100.0	100.0	100.0	100.0	100.0	100.0	100.0	100.0	100.0	100.0	100.0
2018	108.6	103.9	103.4	128.8	106.3	112.0	101.4	109.0	115.0	114.0	106.3	101.2
2019	111.9	103.0	103.9	128.1	105.8	119.7	99.4	113.8	132.6	125.6	107.1	99.0
2020	99.7	94.5	95.4	75.7	100.0	103.9	93.7	118.3	146.4	130.5	110.0	93.0
2021	103.0	97.7	101.5	89.2	103.9	105.9	98.8	132.6	172.6	146.6	122.2	97.8
2020												
January	114.9	117.3	109.0	123.2	102.3	120.7	97.1	112.2	137.4	133.0	102.0	96.6
February	111.2	107.8	102.0	126.9	99.1	120.1	99.0	112.6	137.8	131.1	103.1	98.6
March	105.0	93.4	96.5	125.7	93.4	117.4	95.8	119.7	144.1	131.8	112.1	95.1
April	90.5	80.1	81.1	93.2	81.5	102.7	80.5	109.7	137.8	128.8	99.7	79.7
May	85.5	78.4	80.7	61.0	83.9	92.4	84.7	110.4	137.5	129.0	100.6	83.9
June	94.6	87.1	90.5	50.4	102.3	97.3	92.2	117.9	144.4	127.0	110.7	91.5
July	105.0	103.2	102.3	48.2	122.1	99.4	92.4	114.3	143.3	123.5	106.9	91.8
August	102.9	99.4	101.2	48.3	120.0	98.1	96.7	117.0	146.9	123.7	110.1	96.1
September	95.8	85.4	94.6	50.9	103.6	99.1	95.5	124.0	150.4	124.7	119.1	94.7
October	91.9	80.6	93.7	54.8	97.1	95.6	97.5	124.4	157.3	132.1	116.8	96.7
November	94.6	86.8	91.6	59.5	92.7	101.6	96.6	125.8	159.7	137.1	117.1	95.7
December	104.5	114.9	102.2	66.3	102.3	102.8	96.0	131.0	160.3	143.6	122.3	95.0
2021												
January	107.1	120.7	104.9	72.5	103.3	104.7	97.0	123.2	152.0	141.6	113.1	96.3
February	101.1	114.1	98.4	77.0	102.3	96.4	95.1	120.4	150.3	140.4	109.9	94.3
March	99.8	100.5	97.1	77.7	91.0	104.9	98.7	132.9	156.5	143.9	125.3	97.8
April	95.7	84.5	91.4	81.5	90.5	104.4	97.8	126.8	165.0	144.7	115.8	97.0
May	97.5	83.2	94.1	85.2	94.5	106.3	98.6	130.7	172.4	147.5	119.5	97.7
June	104.1	91.9	102.3	87.1	112.7	107.1	100.2	135.3	178.2	146.4	125.4	99.2
July	107.8	99.2	108.1	91.7	121.0	107.0	98.2	129.0	169.9	142.0	118.8	97.4
August	108.5	99.8	110.9	93.4	122.2	107.0	100.3	131.4	175.2	140.1	122.1	99.5
September	101.6	90.0	103.1	91.9	106.9	104.4	98.6	137.9	178.1	142.4	129.9	97.6
October	100.6	84.3	100.4	99.6	101.2	107.2	100.9	137.7	187.5	152.0	126.1	99.9
November	104.5	95.2	101.4	104.4	100.5	110.5	100.3	140.1	193.0	157.4	127.4	99.2
December	107.7	108.5	105.9	108.1	101.0	110.9	99.2	145.3	193.4	161.2	133.3	98.0

. . . = Not available.

Table 2-2. Industrial Production Indexes by NAICS Industry Groups

(Seasonally adjusted, 2017 = 100.)

Year and month	Total industrial production	Manu-facturing (SIC)	Manufacturing (NAICS)										
			Total	Durable goods manufacturing									
				Total	Wood products	Nonmetallic mineral products	Primary metals	Fabricated metal products	Machinery	Computer and electronic products	Electrical equipment, appliances, and components	Motor vehicles and parts	Aerospace and miscellaneous transport equipment
1970	37.5	35.5	. . .	. . .	. . .	. . .	. . .	. . .	. . .	. . .	. . .	. . .	. . .
1971	38.1	36.0	. . .	. . .	. . .	. . .	. . .	. . .	. . .	. . .	. . .	. . .	. . .
1972	41.7	39.8	37.5	24.7	84.5	85.6	126.0	70.7	64.0	0.4	80.3	37.1	51.2
1973	45.2	43.4	40.9	27.8	81.9	91.9	146.7	78.1	73.9	0.5	90.3	42.4	58.4
1974	45.0	43.3	40.8	27.6	74.3	90.9	150.2	76.8	77.5	0.6	88.2	36.5	59.3
1975	41.0	38.7	36.5	24.0	68.5	81.4	116.5	66.3	67.5	0.5	70.9	31.8	56.4
1976	44.2	42.2	39.8	26.2	77.2	85.9	123.6	71.1	70.4	0.6	79.9	40.6	52.7
1977	47.6	45.8	43.2	28.8	83.2	91.4	125.1	77.1	76.8	0.8	88.2	46.2	53.2
1978	50.3	48.6	45.9	31.1	84.3	97.5	133.1	80.9	82.7	1.0	93.5	48.2	58.6
1979	51.8	50.1	47.3	32.6	81.2	97.3	136.1	84.5	87.3	1.2	97.4	44.0	68.3
1980	50.4	48.3	45.5	31.1	75.3	87.7	119.3	79.7	83.0	1.5	91.6	32.4	73.5
1981	51.1	48.8	46.0	31.5	73.6	84.0	119.4	79.1	82.2	1.7	90.5	31.6	69.9
1982	48.4	46.2	43.3	28.8	66.1	74.4	83.9	70.9	68.7	1.9	81.5	28.5	65.5
1983	49.8	48.4	45.5	30.2	76.5	79.9	86.3	71.4	62.0	2.2	84.2	36.3	62.5
1984	54.2	53.1	50.0	34.5	82.0	86.3	94.8	77.7	72.3	2.7	94.8	43.5	66.7
1985	54.9	54.0	50.8	35.2	82.9	87.9	87.4	78.8	72.5	2.9	93.3	45.2	71.3
1986	55.4	55.1	51.9	35.8	90.0	91.5	85.5	78.2	71.4	3.0	95.0	45.2	75.0
1987	58.3	58.3	54.8	37.9	98.0	96.5	92.3	79.8	72.8	3.4	96.3	46.9	77.8
1988	61.3	61.4	57.9	40.7	97.8	98.5	103.2	83.8	80.2	3.8	101.1	50.1	81.8
1989	61.9	61.9	58.4	41.2	96.2	97.7	100.8	83.1	83.2	3.9	99.3	49.5	86.8
1990	62.5	62.3	59.0	41.3	95.1	96.2	99.6	82.2	81.2	4.2	96.8	46.6	87.1
1991	61.5	61.2	57.9	40.1	88.9	88.6	93.6	78.5	76.1	4.4	91.7	44.5	84.0
1992	63.3	63.4	60.2	42.2	93.9	92.5	96.2	80.9	75.9	5.0	97.2	50.7	77.7
1993	65.4	65.7	62.5	44.5	95.0	94.4	100.9	83.9	81.6	5.5	103.3	56.0	72.5
1994	68.9	69.6	66.4	48.4	100.7	99.8	108.5	91.3	89.4	6.5	110.8	64.4	65.0
1995	72.1	73.1	69.9	52.4	103.2	102.7	109.7	96.9	95.7	8.3	113.5	66.3	61.8
1996	75.3	76.7	73.6	57.1	106.6	109.3	112.2	100.3	99.0	10.9	116.9	66.8	64.2
1997	80.7	83.1	79.8	63.9	109.4	113.0	116.9	104.9	104.5	14.5	121.3	72.1	71.7
1998	85.5	88.7	85.1	70.7	114.2	118.7	118.9	108.3	107.3	18.6	125.8	75.8	83.1
1999	89.2	93.2	89.5	76.7	118.5	119.8	118.7	109.1	105.0	24.6	127.7	84.0	79.9
2000	92.7	97.0	93.4	82.2	116.9	119.9	114.6	113.4	110.5	31.9	134.2	83.6	70.2
2001	89.8	93.4	90.1	78.8	109.6	115.4	103.8	105.2	97.8	33.0	120.8	76.4	74.6
2002	90.1	93.8	90.7	79.1	114.3	115.5	104.3	102.9	94.2	32.6	111.4	84.0	70.6
2003	91.2	95.1	92.1	81.2	114.1	116.5	102.3	101.7	93.7	37.3	108.6	87.1	67.5
2004	93.6	98.0	95.1	85.0	117.0	120.1	111.2	102.2	97.6	43.9	110.5	87.5	66.4
2005	96.8	102.0	99.3	90.1	124.8	125.2	108.2	106.9	103.6	49.9	112.4	88.0	74.0
2006	99.0	104.6	102.0	94.3	125.8	127.5	111.2	112.8	108.5	56.8	113.1	86.7	78.6
2007	101.5	107.5	105.3	99.0	117.7	126.1	113.5	117.6	113.2	65.5	117.8	86.0	92.3
2008	98.0	102.4	100.5	95.6	100.6	111.4	113.7	113.3	110.1	70.8	113.1	68.8	94.0
2009	86.8	88.3	86.8	77.8	76.8	84.0	84.6	87.2	85.7	63.2	89.1	50.4	85.6
2010	91.6	93.5	92.5	86.2	79.6	86.6	103.8	92.9	95.7	72.2	92.6	66.9	86.8
2011	94.5	96.3	95.5	91.5	79.7	88.0	111.4	99.4	107.8	78.1	97.2	73.2	86.6
2012	97.4	98.7	98.2	96.6	84.5	90.3	109.2	102.4	116.5	84.3	99.5	80.9	95.8
2013	99.3	99.6	99.3	98.7	89.4	95.0	112.7	104.2	111.2	87.1	99.4	86.8	98.6
2014	102.3	100.7	100.5	101.6	91.6	98.5	113.5	106.1	112.7	90.7	101.2	94.7	102.2
2015	100.8	100.2	100.1	100.5	95.3	99.2	105.7	102.6	103.7	91.2	100.8	99.7	102.3
2016	98.7	99.4	99.3	98.4	98.8	100.5	101.0	98.8	95.8	93.2	100.6	101.0	95.3
2017	100.0	100.0	100.0	100.0	100.0	100.0	100.0	100.0	100.0	100.0	100.0	100.0	100.0
2018	103.2	101.3	101.5	103.1	100.4	100.4	103.2	104.5	104.6	104.9	101.6	104.1	99.8
2019	102.5	99.4	99.6	100.2	95.7	100.8	97.3	102.4	101.5	106.3	101.3	102.3	91.3
2020	95.3	93.1	93.3	91.5	96.0	97.1	86.2	93.2	90.2	106.1	96.9	88.4	77.0
2021	100.0	98.4	98.8	98.7	101.2	97.5	96.6	95.8	98.7	112.2	103.3	96.4	90.7
2020													
January	101.3	97.1	97.3	97.0	96.8	95.2	98.0	99.6	97.3	106.5	100.2	103.2	82.8
February	102.0	99.0	99.4	100.0	97.9	95.7	98.3	100.4	101.1	107.9	102.0	113.8	79.9
March	98.1	95.4	96.0	94.0	95.9	94.9	94.6	97.6	98.9	109.5	99.2	110.2	77.8
April	82.9	79.7	80.0	72.8	86.6	85.2	74.1	86.1	79.6	101.2	91.6	95.5	58.3
May	85.2	83.8	84.1	78.7	90.4	93.5	71.3	89.8	83.4	100.3	91.8	99.9	67.9
June	93.1	91.6	91.9	89.8	96.1	99.9	76.2	91.7	88.7	107.1	93.6	101.0	70.9
July	95.3	91.7	91.8	90.4	97.0	100.2	78.8	90.3	88.2	105.1	93.7	102.7	73.3
August	98.3	95.9	95.9	95.2	98.5	101.5	84.2	92.0	88.7	107.4	95.1	109.4	78.6
September	95.9	94.7	94.7	93.7	96.1	98.6	87.1	91.3	88.1	105.7	94.2	104.9	80.0
October	96.7	96.7	96.8	96.2	101.1	102.7	88.9	92.5	89.4	105.6	100.9	127.5	83.0
November	96.5	95.9	96.0	95.5	97.7	99.9	91.8	93.2	88.5	107.3	100.8	114.2	85.3
December	98.1	95.4	95.7	95.0	97.6	97.3	91.2	94.2	90.8	109.4	99.3	98.9	86.6
2021													
January	99.6	96.6	97.0	97.0	99.8	91.7	93.5	93.8	96.3	106.1	101.9	127.9	92.0
February	96.7	94.5	94.9	96.3	98.1	88.2	94.8	91.4	97.6	103.7	100.6	125.1	92.2
March	99.2	98.3	98.9	100.1	102.9	94.6	95.4	95.6	100.6	110.4	103.1	124.6	93.3
April	97.6	97.4	97.9	97.7	103.9	98.1	98.8	94.5	100.3	107.7	103.1	128.4	89.7
May	98.6	98.2	98.7	98.2	103.0	97.0	96.2	95.3	100.1	111.6	102.9	124.9	88.0
June	101.4	99.8	100.2	99.6	103.5	100.1	97.9	96.3	101.0	114.3	101.9	114.9	90.7
July	100.8	97.9	98.2	97.2	100.3	99.9	97.0	95.7	100.1	112.7	102.5	111.8	91.2
August	102.5	99.9	100.2	99.9	102.0	101.7	97.9	96.7	97.3	114.6	103.3	115.3	90.5
September	99.5	98.1	98.3	97.7	100.7	100.8	96.7	94.8	96.5	114.7	103.0	116.7	89.3
October	101.0	100.5	100.8	100.9	104.0	101.1	97.8	97.4	97.0	115.3	106.5	128.2	90.2
November	101.5	100.0	100.5	100.6	99.5	100.6	97.8	99.0	96.4	116.5	106.6	119.6	91.0
December	101.6	99.0	99.5	99.4	97.3	96.8	95.9	99.3	101.4	119.4	104.0	106.5	90.7

. . . = Not available.

Table 2-2. Industrial Production Indexes by NAICS Industry Groups—*Continued*

(Seasonally adjusted, 2017 = 100.)

Year and month	Durable goods manufacturing—*Continued*		Manufacturing (NAICS)—*Continued* Nondurable goods manufacturing									Other manu-facturing (non-NAICS)
	Furniture and related products	Miscel-laneous manu-facturing	Total	Food, beverage, and tobacco products	Textile and product mills	Apparel and leather	Paper	Printing and support	Petroleum and coal products	Chemicals	Plastics and rubber products	
1970	. . .	. . .	. . .	. . .	. . .	. . .	. . .	. . .	. . .	. . .	. . .	. . .
1971	. . .	. . .	. . .	. . .	. . .	. . .	. . .	. . .	. . .	. . .	. . .	. . .
1972	73.4	41.4	64.3	60.8	171.1	632.8	78.9	67.0	63.5	51.8	37.4	138.5
1973	76.9	42.7	67.3	61.4	169.7	643.1	85.3	70.5	62.4	56.6	42.2	142.9
1974	71.1	41.8	67.6	62.5	156.0	605.1	89.1	68.3	67.3	58.9	40.7	143.7
1975	61.0	38.9	62.6	61.2	150.8	590.6	77.2	63.8	66.4	51.7	34.4	136.6
1976	68.0	42.4	68.3	65.4	168.1	621.0	85.1	68.4	73.5	57.9	38.0	140.9
1977	77.9	46.2	73.0	66.7	183.6	651.1	88.9	74.1	78.7	63.0	44.9	154.4
1978	84.0	47.2	75.6	69.1	183.2	665.4	92.9	78.5	79.5	66.2	46.8	159.8
1979	83.8	47.5	76.1	68.7	182.7	624.3	94.3	80.8	84.9	67.7	46.2	163.1
1980	80.9	45.0	73.7	69.8	175.3	636.2	94.0	81.4	75.2	63.9	41.3	168.8
1981	80.2	46.7	74.4	70.4	171.5	636.1	95.3	83.5	71.7	65.0	43.8	172.8
1982	75.6	47.2	73.3	72.6	159.4	632.3	93.7	89.8	68.6	60.8	43.1	174.8
1983	82.9	47.2	76.7	72.7	179.1	650.2	99.8	96.5	69.7	65.0	46.8	179.8
1984	92.8	51.1	80.3	73.7	183.4	649.6	104.7	105.1	71.2	68.9	54.1	188.1
1985	93.8	51.8	80.7	76.0	177.0	621.8	102.5	109.4	70.2	68.3	56.2	195.5
1986	98.0	53.1	83.0	77.0	183.8	619.9	106.6	114.9	69.8	71.4	58.6	199.5
1987	105.0	57.1	87.5	78.6	201.7	627.3	110.0	123.3	73.1	77.0	64.9	210.9
1988	104.0	62.4	90.4	80.7	199.8	616.8	114.3	127.3	75.4	81.4	67.8	210.0
1989	103.6	63.3	91.0	80.4	202.8	590.1	115.5	127.8	74.6	82.9	70.1	207.1
1990	101.5	66.3	92.4	82.6	194.7	578.1	115.4	132.6	74.7	84.8	72.0	204.6
1991	93.8	67.6	92.1	83.2	192.0	574.5	115.7	128.5	73.6	84.6	71.2	196.2
1992	101.2	70.5	94.6	84.5	202.6	590.9	118.5	135.5	73.3	85.9	76.7	192.2
1993	105.5	74.6	95.9	84.3	210.4	602.8	119.9	135.9	73.8	86.9	82.2	193.6
1994	109.0	75.0	99.2	87.0	221.6	610.1	125.0	137.3	75.8	89.1	89.0	191.9
1995	110.7	77.9	100.9	89.4	219.2	605.6	126.8	139.4	77.2	90.6	91.2	191.9
1996	111.7	81.7	101.3	88.8	214.0	591.7	122.9	140.4	79.0	92.5	94.3	190.0
1997	123.7	84.0	105.0	90.8	225.9	591.2	125.4	143.2	81.6	97.9	100.1	206.1
1998	132.5	88.9	106.7	93.7	224.1	562.7	126.5	145.0	80.1	99.5	103.7	218.3
1999	136.8	90.9	107.3	91.9	224.9	536.0	127.4	144.4	83.2	101.6	109.2	224.6
2000	139.2	96.0	107.8	93.2	220.4	516.8	124.1	145.7	82.5	103.0	110.3	224.0
2001	130.5	95.0	104.8	93.1	197.4	454.2	117.1	140.9	82.0	101.3	103.9	209.5
2002	135.0	100.4	106.0	92.1	198.3	357.6	118.5	137.7	86.4	107.1	107.6	202.4
2003	132.9	103.5	106.2	93.8	190.4	333.0	115.7	132.3	85.1	108.9	107.7	196.7
2004	136.7	103.5	107.8	94.1	188.1	292.3	116.6	132.6	90.1	113.2	109.0	197.6
2005	141.7	110.3	110.6	97.5	190.8	285.8	116.2	132.4	92.6	117.0	110.2	196.9
2006	139.7	113.8	111.2	97.7	173.0	279.5	114.9	130.9	94.2	119.9	110.9	194.6
2007	134.4	110.9	112.5	97.9	153.0	227.8	115.4	133.6	96.8	125.8	107.8	183.6
2008	121.4	112.8	105.8	95.1	134.5	183.5	110.5	125.0	92.6	116.4	97.7	167.5
2009	88.0	104.5	97.7	94.5	106.6	135.3	98.6	104.7	91.4	105.1	81.7	140.1
2010	86.9	108.3	99.8	94.8	113.8	136.5	100.6	104.6	90.5	108.6	89.0	129.5
2011	89.8	107.7	100.0	94.6	111.4	134.3	100.6	102.9	92.6	108.6	90.3	123.5
2012	94.6	104.7	100.0	95.0	108.0	126.7	103.3	101.1	92.4	107.1	94.5	116.4
2013	95.3	108.1	100.0	96.5	112.0	117.4	103.6	101.4	96.1	103.5	95.7	110.0
2014	95.8	104.8	99.3	96.5	114.2	112.5	102.6	99.6	92.6	102.4	98.2	108.3
2015	100.6	105.2	99.7	98.5	109.0	107.3	101.9	98.6	90.6	102.0	99.9	103.9
2016	100.8	105.5	100.5	99.7	106.9	102.5	100.9	100.3	96.5	101.5	101.2	101.0
2017	100.0	100.0	100.0	100.0	100.0	100.0	100.0	100.0	100.0	100.0	100.0	100.0
2018	101.1	103.5	99.7	99.8	98.6	96.4	99.1	100.4	99.9	98.6	103.0	96.7
2019	94.5	100.1	98.8	99.9	95.6	96.7	99.1	96.5	99.9	97.2	101.1	92.6
2020	85.4	93.7	95.2	100.3	88.5	82.4	94.0	88.2	80.3	95.4	95.5	85.2
2021	88.1	103.5	98.8	101.5	94.2	90.6	95.5	89.1	92.0	99.8	99.7	85.0
2020												
January	93.2	98.8	97.7	99.2	94.7	90.3	100.6	98.4	90.0	96.8	101.8	89.3
February	92.5	98.9	98.8	101.9	94.7	92.1	100.4	100.8	87.8	96.8	104.0	84.6
March	89.1	95.2	98.2	101.5	93.2	86.9	100.2	94.3	85.1	98.9	97.5	78.1
April	68.3	77.7	87.8	92.4	71.7	62.9	94.4	71.6	71.4	92.0	78.1	69.5
May	79.5	81.6	90.1	96.0	79.5	72.9	88.2	79.8	73.2	92.8	83.1	73.1
June	85.0	90.3	94.1	102.7	86.2	80.7	89.8	83.1	76.8	92.8	93.2	80.8
July	87.4	95.0	93.2	98.5	86.6	77.2	88.6	85.4	80.9	93.9	93.1	88.0
August	87.8	96.4	96.6	104.6	89.7	83.9	90.5	86.4	80.2	95.2	99.2	94.1
September	84.2	92.8	95.8	102.9	91.7	81.6	91.4	87.5	77.6	94.8	98.2	94.1
October	85.9	96.8	97.3	103.4	94.1	86.6	95.0	90.8	79.7	96.5	100.0	94.4
November	84.8	99.3	96.5	101.5	90.1	85.3	95.1	89.4	79.4	96.9	98.9	89.8
December	87.7	101.3	96.3	99.5	89.4	87.9	93.7	91.0	81.0	97.8	99.4	86.8
2021												
January	87.4	100.9	96.9	101.6	90.1	87.5	96.7	86.4	80.8	97.3	100.1	82.6
February	84.1	99.1	93.4	100.2	89.5	87.0	93.2	84.1	75.5	90.7	99.8	80.4
March	85.7	102.0	97.4	103.5	93.9	89.1	96.3	86.5	87.3	95.6	98.5	79.9
April	84.9	101.4	98.1	101.0	96.9	89.5	96.1	86.2	92.4	98.9	97.4	81.1
May	87.7	102.8	99.3	100.5	94.0	92.0	95.7	88.1	95.5	102.0	97.8	81.3
June	88.8	103.6	100.9	103.3	96.3	92.2	95.1	89.3	98.0	102.6	99.8	84.8
July	90.0	104.7	99.1	99.5	95.0	90.7	95.0	88.9	98.2	102.0	97.9	89.5
August	90.1	105.2	100.4	102.8	94.0	92.5	97.5	89.1	97.8	101.2	100.8	92.8
September	87.4	103.2	99.0	102.1	94.5	91.4	95.4	90.8	94.3	99.3	99.8	91.2
October	89.7	104.2	100.7	103.5	96.9	92.7	96.2	92.8	95.0	101.8	101.0	89.6
November	89.7	107.5	100.4	101.3	95.4	92.3	94.5	93.3	95.9	102.6	102.3	85.2
December	91.1	107.0	99.7	99.2	94.0	90.5	94.7	93.7	93.0	103.9	101.0	82.0

. . . = Not available.

Table 2-3. Capacity Utilization by NAICS Industry Groups

(Output as a percent of capacity, seasonally adjusted.)

Year and month	Total industry	Total manufacturing (SIC)	Manufacturing (NAICS)											
			Total	Durable goods manufacturing										
				Total	Wood products	Nonmetallic mineral products	Primary metals	Fabricated metal products	Machinery	Computer and electronic products	Electrical equipment, appliances, and components	Motor vehicles and parts	Aerospace and miscellaneous transportation equipment
1970	81.3	79.5	. . .	77.7	. . .	73.5	79.4	78.4	79.7	. . .	. . .	66.4	75.4
1971	79.6	78.0	. . .	75.5	. . .	75.0	73.0	78.4	73.7	. . .	. . .	79.2	67.0
1972	84.7	83.4	83.4	82.0	92.2	79.1	82.9	85.1	83.2	80.8	89.8	84.3	65.7
1973	88.3	87.7	87.8	88.6	87.9	84.0	94.7	90.9	92.4	85.2	97.7	91.7	73.6
1974	85.1	84.4	84.4	84.6	77.9	81.6	96.5	86.2	91.9	83.1	91.5	76.7	73.6
1975	75.7	73.7	73.5	71.7	70.0	72.7	75.2	72.3	77.7	68.7	70.8	66.0	70.4
1976	79.8	78.4	78.4	76.5	79.5	77.4	78.6	75.8	79.9	72.2	78.8	81.7	66.2
1977	83.5	82.5	82.5	81.2	86.0	82.4	79.3	79.9	85.5	78.0	85.6	89.8	66.2
1978	85.2	84.5	84.5	83.9	84.8	86.3	84.2	80.7	88.6	80.7	87.7	90.8	72.6
1979	85.0	84.0	84.0	84.0	79.8	84.4	86.1	81.6	90.2	83.7	88.7	81.0	80.9
1980	80.7	78.7	78.4	77.5	72.4	75.0	76.0	75.2	83.6	86.9	81.7	59.8	83.4
1981	79.5	76.9	76.6	75.1	70.6	72.3	77.1	72.8	80.5	84.7	78.7	57.3	76.8
1982	73.6	70.9	70.4	66.5	63.8	64.7	56.5	64.7	66.6	81.3	69.5	50.8	69.8
1983	74.9	73.5	73.0	68.8	75.2	70.2	59.8	66.7	60.5	82.2	72.7	67.4	66.4
1984	80.5	79.4	79.0	77.0	81.1	75.3	69.6	73.7	70.9	87.9	82.3	81.7	69.8
1985	79.3	78.2	77.7	75.9	79.7	75.6	67.9	74.2	70.5	80.7	79.0	83.5	72.5
1986	78.6	78.5	78.0	75.5	83.7	78.0	69.8	73.9	70.0	77.9	80.1	79.2	74.0
1987	81.2	81.0	80.6	77.7	85.7	80.6	78.2	75.5	71.8	80.2	82.4	78.0	75.4
1988	84.3	84.0	83.8	82.1	84.2	81.5	89.3	80.2	80.1	81.6	87.3	82.6	79.7
1989	83.8	83.3	83.2	81.8	82.1	80.7	86.2	79.8	83.8	79.2	86.2	80.9	85.3
1990	82.4	81.6	81.5	79.4	80.2	79.3	84.7	77.6	81.4	79.0	83.8	71.9	84.6
1991	80.0	78.6	78.5	75.5	76.0	73.2	80.1	73.9	76.3	78.6	79.0	64.0	84.6
1992	80.7	79.7	79.7	77.3	78.7	76.9	82.0	76.0	75.1	79.2	82.2	72.4	80.0
1993	81.6	80.6	80.5	78.8	78.8	78.6	85.3	76.9	78.6	78.6	86.6	78.7	75.0
1994	83.6	82.9	82.9	81.7	82.8	81.3	90.7	81.1	83.3	80.5	91.8	86.1	68.4
1995	84.0	83.2	83.2	82.2	80.9	81.5	89.3	83.0	85.5	83.2	91.3	83.4	65.5
1996	83.4	82.2	82.2	81.6	81.2	85.0	88.9	82.4	84.6	81.5	89.8	80.5	67.9
1997	84.1	83.1	83.0	82.4	80.9	84.0	89.9	81.4	85.0	82.0	88.3	81.8	74.1
1998	82.9	81.7	81.4	80.9	81.0	84.5	87.4	79.7	82.0	78.0	85.7	79.2	82.8
1999	81.9	80.6	80.3	80.4	81.4	82.4	86.4	77.8	76.5	81.6	83.1	83.4	77.4
2000	81.6	79.9	79.5	79.9	78.2	79.9	83.1	79.0	77.8	84.4	85.9	81.7	67.0
2001	76.2	73.9	73.4	71.6	72.3	75.1	73.6	73.0	68.3	69.8	76.9	72.8	71.0
2002	75.0	73.1	72.7	70.2	75.0	74.4	76.9	72.1	67.0	60.7	73.4	78.8	67.1
2003	76.0	74.1	73.7	71.3	76.1	74.3	76.0	73.5	68.6	64.3	74.5	78.7	64.0
2004	78.2	76.5	76.2	74.2	79.1	74.8	83.7	75.8	72.6	71.3	77.1	77.2	63.1
2005	80.2	78.6	78.4	76.7	80.7	75.4	81.4	79.6	76.6	73.4	80.9	77.4	69.8
2006	80.5	78.8	78.8	77.8	77.9	73.7	80.7	84.5	79.7	77.7	82.8	72.2	73.1
2007	80.6	78.8	78.9	78.5	73.0	69.0	79.6	86.9	82.4	76.6	87.7	71.7	84.7
2008	77.7	74.5	74.4	74.5	63.3	59.6	77.1	82.0	79.8	77.6	85.6	57.8	84.0
2009	68.4	65.3	65.2	61.3	50.5	45.8	55.1	64.7	62.4	71.2	69.0	43.9	73.8
2010	73.4	70.4	70.7	68.7	56.2	49.3	69.5	71.7	69.8	77.1	74.3	59.3	73.3
2011	76.1	73.3	73.7	72.5	60.5	52.1	75.5	77.6	77.1	77.0	79.5	64.7	71.3
2012	76.9	74.5	75.0	75.0	67.1	54.7	74.6	77.9	82.4	75.8	80.8	70.8	77.1
2013	77.2	74.6	75.0	74.9	71.8	59.1	74.8	78.4	78.2	72.7	80.0	72.5	77.6
2014	78.6	75.7	76.1	76.4	71.8	63.2	72.8	80.3	78.9	72.1	80.9	77.5	82.0
2015	77.0	76.0	76.4	75.9	74.3	66.1	67.8	78.5	73.2	70.8	78.1	81.2	82.7
2016	75.2	75.2	75.5	74.2	77.3	67.3	65.9	76.2	69.6	68.8	76.5	80.7	76.8
2017	76.5	76.2	76.4	75.4	79.3	67.0	67.0	77.1	74.3	73.3	76.9	77.8	79.1
2018	79.2	77.7	77.9	77.5	81.7	68.7	70.6	80.2	78.7	76.2	76.6	78.1	77.0
2019	77.4	75.8	76.0	75.3	78.2	68.6	69.2	78.5	76.8	72.4	75.8	75.0	75.3
2020	71.6	71.1	71.4	69.2	76.1	68.9	61.7	73.3	72.8	72.6	72.7	62.8	61.4
2021	78.7	76.8	77.0	76.4	79.6	69.6	70.1	80.5	79.4	73.8	75.6	75.1	75.3
2020													
January	78.1	76.4	76.5	76.0	77.8	67.2	69.2	79.6	78.6	73.5	76.1	75.6	75.6
February	78.1	76.3	76.5	75.9	76.6	67.6	69.6	79.4	78.6	72.9	76.4	76.1	75.5
March	77.5	75.7	75.8	75.3	77.3	68.2	70.2	78.7	76.4	72.5	75.5	75.3	74.2
April	77.6	75.7	75.9	75.3	77.8	68.3	69.5	78.2	77.5	72.0	77.1	76.7	72.7
May	77.4	75.9	76.0	75.3	77.7	68.6	68.3	78.2	76.7	72.1	76.6	77.9	73.6
June	77.1	75.6	75.7	75.1	78.0	68.3	68.6	77.7	75.8	71.9	77.2	76.9	74.4
July	77.5	76.0	76.1	75.4	77.8	69.1	69.8	78.3	77.0	71.6	76.9	76.8	74.9
August	77.2	75.5	75.6	74.8	78.5	69.5	69.4	78.1	75.3	72.0	75.5	72.9	76.0
September	76.5	75.0	75.1	73.8	79.1	68.8	68.2	77.9	75.0	71.3	73.7	68.5	77.1
October	76.8	75.6	75.8	75.2	78.9	68.4	68.3	77.8	75.5	71.9	74.7	75.9	77.4
November	76.5	75.6	75.8	75.0	79.1	69.7	69.7	77.7	76.0	72.7	74.4	72.7	76.7
December	76.1	75.5	75.6	74.4	80.3	72.2	70.3	78.1	76.4	73.0	75.2	73.5	68.1
2021													
January	76.3	75.5	75.7	74.4	79.4	72.5	68.7	78.7	77.5	73.8	76.3	75.2	64.6
February	73.4	72.2	72.4	69.5	76.9	68.9	66.8	75.9	75.3	73.1	74.2	54.9	62.1
March	63.4	60.8	61.0	54.7	67.9	58.8	52.3	67.8	61.7	70.0	69.3	16.0	46.0
April	64.7	63.7	63.9	59.0	70.6	64.3	50.7	69.7	65.1	69.2	68.6	29.0	53.5
May	68.7	68.3	68.6	65.9	73.3	67.4	54.3	71.0	68.5	72.3	69.5	59.9	56.1
June	71.5	71.2	71.5	70.5	76.4	68.9	57.4	71.0	71.8	73.2	72.1	77.4	60.1
July	72.3	72.3	72.6	71.3	75.6	69.1	60.3	72.0	74.3	74.1	71.4	74.2	63.2
August	72.1	72.4	72.6	71.5	75.9	68.5	62.9	73.7	74.9	72.6	71.7	72.8	64.1
September	72.9	73.5	73.7	72.5	77.4	70.6	64.5	73.6	76.6	73.0	74.2	72.4	65.9
October	73.3	74.0	74.2	73.2	78.1	71.7	66.3	74.3	75.7	73.8	74.2	74.4	66.5
November	74.1	74.4	74.7	73.5	80.9	74.1	65.5	74.3	76.3	73.7	75.1	74.1	66.1

. . . = Not available.

Table 2-3. Capacity Utilization by NAICS Industry Groups—*Continued*

(Output as a percent of capacity, seasonally adjusted.)

Year and month	Durable goods manufacturing—*Continued*		Manufacturing (NAICS)—*Continued*									Other manufacturing (non-NAICS)
			Nondurable goods manufacturing									
	Furniture and related products	Miscellaneous manufacturing	Total	Food, beverage, and tobacco products	Textile and product mills	Apparel and leather	Paper	Printing and support	Petroleum and coal products	Chemicals	Plastics and rubber products	
1970	83.6	. . .	82.2	84.1	. . .	. . .	86.2	. . .	95.9	76.3	79.3	. . .
1971	84.3	. . .	81.8	84.1	. . .	. . .	86.9	. . .	94.6	75.6	79.8	. . .
1972	93.6	80.3	85.3	85.2	88.8	81.6	91.4	92.3	93.1	80.3	88.6	85.5
1973	94.6	79.5	86.6	84.7	86.2	82.2	94.9	94.0	90.3	83.8	92.5	84.8
1974	83.5	74.6	84.2	83.9	76.4	76.3	94.9	88.0	92.5	83.9	84.2	82.7
1975	69.6	67.6	76.1	80.1	72.7	74.6	80.5	79.6	83.7	71.7	70.1	77.2
1976	76.3	72.4	81.2	83.2	81.6	78.3	87.6	82.3	86.0	77.9	77.3	77.6
1977	84.6	77.6	84.4	82.9	89.0	81.6	90.2	86.0	87.7	81.4	88.4	83.1
1978	86.1	78.8	85.3	83.6	88.2	84.5	92.2	87.4	86.5	82.6	88.7	85.0
1979	81.0	78.4	83.9	81.2	87.7	79.7	90.7	86.0	88.5	83.0	83.7	85.5
1980	75.0	73.4	79.8	80.9	83.7	80.5	88.1	83.7	76.4	76.7	74.1	86.7
1981	71.8	75.7	78.9	80.3	80.7	79.3	87.0	81.2	73.1	76.1	77.6	87.4
1982	66.3	73.7	76.4	81.3	74.4	78.3	83.9	82.4	71.2	69.3	74.5	87.3
1983	72.2	70.8	79.4	80.8	84.0	81.6	88.6	84.3	74.3	72.9	81.5	87.8
1984	79.0	75.9	82.1	81.3	85.8	81.7	91.0	87.0	78.4	76.0	91.2	89.4
1985	77.2	73.9	80.5	82.6	81.5	78.3	87.8	84.7	80.0	73.5	87.0	90.1
1986	78.9	73.9	81.8	82.8	84.2	80.2	90.1	85.4	81.8	76.0	85.3	88.7
1987	82.7	77.1	84.8	83.8	91.3	82.5	90.2	89.0	82.4	81.0	89.5	90.3
1988	80.4	81.7	86.2	85.3	88.7	82.6	91.2	90.2	83.3	84.5	89.0	88.4
1989	79.0	79.7	85.0	83.7	88.3	80.7	90.5	88.9	84.3	83.3	87.1	85.5
1990	76.1	79.5	84.2	84.0	83.4	79.5	89.6	88.8	84.7	82.9	83.8	83.6
1991	70.6	78.2	82.4	83.0	81.5	80.7	88.1	84.1	82.6	81.1	78.7	80.7
1992	76.5	77.1	82.8	82.6	85.5	83.3	88.9	86.3	85.3	79.7	82.0	80.1
1993	79.1	77.4	82.8	81.1	87.9	84.3	89.3	84.8	89.0	79.1	86.6	81.3
1994	80.6	77.1	84.6	83.3	90.1	85.4	90.8	84.0	89.0	80.5	91.3	81.4
1995	80.0	79.6	84.5	84.3	86.2	85.0	89.3	83.3	89.6	80.8	89.6	82.2
1996	78.8	81.0	83.2	82.4	82.3	83.7	85.3	83.0	91.7	80.4	88.4	80.5
1997	83.4	79.2	83.8	82.4	84.4	83.5	87.2	81.4	95.3	81.3	89.1	85.5
1998	83.0	79.6	82.2	82.8	81.8	77.8	87.0	79.8	93.0	78.6	87.7	86.7
1999	80.7	77.2	80.1	78.4	81.6	76.4	86.6	77.7	90.7	77.2	86.3	87.1
2000	77.5	76.8	78.9	77.4	79.3	79.3	84.6	77.0	89.4	76.4	82.4	87.4
2001	70.8	73.4	75.7	76.2	71.4	75.6	80.3	74.8	88.5	72.2	76.6	82.8
2002	72.6	74.2	76.0	75.4	73.6	67.3	82.1	74.8	88.9	73.8	78.8	81.5
2003	71.6	75.0	76.8	77.0	72.8	70.0	82.0	75.4	89.9	73.9	79.3	81.5
2004	76.9	75.7	78.8	77.2	74.8	70.7	83.6	77.5	92.9	76.6	83.2	82.4
2005	80.3	78.6	80.4	79.3	78.1	75.8	84.3	77.5	92.1	77.2	84.1	82.0
2006	79.2	77.8	79.9	78.9	75.5	75.9	84.2	77.4	89.2	77.5	82.1	79.6
2007	75.4	73.8	79.4	78.6	73.3	75.8	84.2	76.9	87.3	78.1	78.6	76.6
2008	71.0	74.2	74.2	76.3	69.6	79.0	82.4	69.5	81.3	71.4	69.8	78.0
2009	57.4	69.9	69.7	75.9	57.0	62.8	76.7	59.9	78.3	66.5	59.7	67.4
2010	61.0	75.6	73.1	76.6	63.2	67.4	80.9	62.8	80.4	70.6	68.0	63.5
2011	66.7	77.2	75.0	78.0	65.2	70.6	80.8	63.4	84.6	72.6	69.1	64.0
2012	71.5	75.3	74.9	77.9	66.1	68.7	83.0	63.8	82.9	71.0	74.6	62.7
2013	73.2	77.3	75.2	78.3	70.8	64.4	83.2	66.5	84.2	69.3	79.0	62.4
2014	75.7	76.1	75.7	76.9	73.5	64.0	84.0	68.0	82.0	71.8	81.6	64.7
2015	80.0	79.5	77.0	77.7	70.9	64.1	85.5	70.0	81.9	73.1	84.5	65.5
2016	79.1	82.5	77.1	77.2	71.3	63.5	87.2	73.6	79.1	73.8	84.4	66.7
2017	78.7	79.9	77.6	77.9	69.4	65.9	87.7	75.5	81.4	74.2	82.4	69.6
2018	82.4	83.0	78.4	78.0	70.9	68.0	87.8	75.6	83.8	74.5	85.7	70.4
2019	79.8	80.0	76.8	76.4	70.2	71.6	86.8	75.0	80.3	73.2	83.4	70.6
2020	78.0	73.5	73.9	75.2	63.7	68.8	83.1	68.7	69.3	72.3	77.9	63.9
2021	80.7	81.7	77.7	76.9	70.8	67.8	88.5	74.8	83.5	73.5	85.8	70.8
2020												
January	79.6	82.1	77.1	76.6	71.0	67.0	87.7	73.6	80.1	73.6	85.1	71.6
February	78.7	81.7	77.0	76.6	72.1	68.8	87.1	73.6	80.7	73.4	84.3	71.5
March	79.0	81.5	76.5	75.8	71.5	71.2	87.0	74.0	80.2	73.1	82.8	71.5
April	79.4	80.8	76.6	76.3	70.9	71.8	86.7	74.7	80.4	72.6	83.7	70.8
May	78.8	79.8	76.8	77.4	70.9	73.0	84.4	74.6	80.6	72.5	84.2	71.5
June	79.2	79.8	76.4	75.6	69.4	73.2	86.0	75.2	81.1	73.1	82.3	71.0
July	78.9	79.6	76.9	75.7	69.9	73.3	87.3	75.7	81.2	73.8	83.3	70.8
August	79.6	78.8	76.7	75.8	69.2	74.0	87.1	76.0	80.4	73.6	82.2	70.7
September	80.1	77.5	76.6	76.5	68.7	73.4	86.8	76.1	78.8	73.4	81.9	69.7
October	81.5	78.5	76.4	76.3	69.2	72.8	86.5	76.6	78.2	73.1	82.6	68.4
November	82.3	78.2	76.7	77.5	69.3	73.1	86.6	75.5	78.4	72.9	82.4	69.1
December	83.4	78.4	77.1	76.9	70.8	72.0	87.4	77.1	80.2	73.3	83.7	70.3
2021												
January	84.5	77.9	77.1	76.9	70.6	73.4	87.2	78.7	79.2	73.3	84.5	69.6
February	80.4	74.4	75.9	75.9	67.8	69.5	87.9	72.4	74.4	74.2	79.0	64.6
March	62.6	60.7	68.3	70.3	50.9	51.2	83.9	55.2	60.5	69.5	64.0	55.7
April	72.4	63.1	69.6	72.6	57.2	60.0	78.9	60.9	61.0	69.8	67.1	56.9
May	76.8	69.8	71.8	75.0	60.1	66.7	79.3	63.7	63.7	70.2	74.5	58.9
June	78.3	74.7	72.7	74.4	61.6	65.7	79.4	66.4	67.4	71.4	77.2	59.9
July	79.3	75.9	74.0	76.0	63.3	71.9	79.7	67.2	67.5	72.3	80.2	64.0
August	79.7	74.7	73.8	74.9	66.0	71.4	81.3	68.7	67.5	72.3	80.5	66.5
September	79.6	76.4	75.0	75.6	65.5	74.9	83.7	71.5	69.2	73.6	81.6	68.1
October	78.9	77.7	75.3	76.6	64.3	73.9	84.4	71.2	69.3	73.7	80.9	66.6
November	80.2	78.2	76.1	77.3	66.0	74.9	84.0	71.8	71.6	74.3	81.6	65.4

. . . = Not available.

Table 2-3. Capacity Utilization by NAICS Industry Groups—*Continued*

(Output as a percent of capacity, seasonally adjusted.)

Year and month	Mining	Utilities	Selected high-tech industries				Measures excluding selected high-tech industries		Stage-of-process groups		
			Total	Computers and peripheral equipment	Communications equipment	Semiconductors and related electronic components	Total industry	Manufacturing	Crude	Primary and semi-finished	Finished
1970	89.5	96.4	83.0	. . .	. . .	. . .	81.0	79.3	84.6	81.4	78.1
1971	88.1	94.9	73.8	. . .	. . .	. . .	80.0	78.3	83.6	81.5	75.6
1972	90.8	94.9	78.2	81.6	73.4	81.5	84.9	83.6	88.4	88.1	79.6
1973	91.6	92.8	81.4	82.1	75.2	88.5	88.5	88.0	90.0	92.0	83.2
1974	91.1	86.5	81.0	88.4	73.3	83.4	85.2	84.5	90.9	87.2	80.3
1975	89.4	84.9	64.6	69.1	62.2	63.3	76.2	74.1	83.9	75.2	73.7
1976	89.6	85.5	68.6	77.2	62.0	68.6	80.2	78.8	87.0	80.1	76.9
1977	89.5	86.7	75.7	78.1	72.5	76.7	83.7	82.8	89.1	84.5	79.9
1978	89.6	86.9	78.6	78.0	77.5	80.3	85.4	84.7	88.6	86.2	82.3
1979	91.1	86.9	82.8	78.4	85.8	85.1	85.0	84.0	89.9	85.8	81.7
1980	91.3	85.2	87.9	87.4	92.1	84.6	80.4	78.2	89.3	78.8	79.3
1981	90.9	84.1	85.9	85.8	89.7	83.0	79.2	76.5	89.3	77.2	77.5
1982	84.1	79.7	78.9	70.8	88.1	82.0	73.3	70.4	82.3	70.4	73.1
1983	79.9	79.0	81.2	76.3	86.3	82.7	74.6	73.0	80.0	74.5	73.0
1984	86.1	81.6	88.0	85.9	86.2	91.2	80.1	78.8	86.0	81.1	77.2
1985	84.7	81.5	77.7	76.6	80.1	77.1	79.3	78.2	84.1	79.8	76.6
1986	76.5	80.7	73.3	72.9	76.9	71.3	78.8	78.8	78.5	79.7	77.1
1987	80.3	83.3	77.8	74.0	80.4	80.0	81.4	81.2	82.9	82.8	78.7
1988	84.0	86.6	80.1	76.4	83.7	81.5	84.5	84.3	86.4	85.9	81.7
1989	85.1	86.6	78.3	75.0	80.3	79.8	84.1	83.7	86.8	84.7	81.7
1990	87.0	86.3	77.2	71.5	81.9	79.4	82.8	81.9	88.0	82.6	80.6
1991	85.4	87.7	78.0	73.7	78.2	80.9	80.1	78.7	85.6	79.9	78.4
1992	85.2	86.2	80.4	78.2	79.4	82.1	80.7	79.7	85.9	81.5	78.4
1993	85.7	88.0	80.7	79.9	82.2	80.1	81.6	80.6	85.9	83.3	78.5
1994	86.7	88.1	83.1	74.4	85.2	86.5	83.6	82.8	87.9	86.3	79.3
1995	87.6	89.1	85.0	78.3	79.9	90.6	83.8	83.0	89.0	86.3	79.8
1996	90.5	90.5	82.8	87.0	76.2	84.0	83.3	82.0	89.0	85.4	79.3
1997	91.8	89.9	83.7	83.4	80.2	85.5	84.1	82.9	90.4	85.8	80.5
1998	89.2	92.4	79.1	79.3	85.2	76.1	83.1	81.9	87.0	84.0	80.4
1999	86.2	94.0	85.5	84.6	88.0	84.5	81.5	80.0	86.1	84.2	78.1
2000	90.5	94.1	88.5	81.4	92.3	89.3	80.9	78.9	88.6	83.8	77.1
2001	89.8	90.0	69.2	70.8	70.2	68.1	76.7	74.2	85.5	77.3	72.6
2002	85.9	87.5	58.2	68.7	43.4	63.4	76.3	74.4	83.2	77.4	70.6
2003	87.7	85.6	63.3	72.6	44.8	71.6	76.9	74.9	85.0	78.2	71.4
2004	88.2	84.4	70.5	77.3	53.2	78.1	78.7	77.0	86.6	80.3	73.4
2005	88.5	85.0	73.7	75.8	58.7	80.6	80.6	78.9	86.7	81.9	75.8
2006	90.1	83.6	81.8	78.3	77.7	85.7	80.5	78.7	88.1	81.4	76.5
2007	89.4	85.7	77.7	76.2	76.7	77.7	80.9	79.0	88.7	81.0	77.2
2008	90.0	84.1	80.8	79.0	81.9	81.4	77.6	74.2	87.7	76.7	73.9
2009	80.8	80.5	73.8	89.8	81.2	65.5	68.2	64.8	78.4	65.4	67.9
2010	84.2	82.8	80.9	99.2	82.1	76.9	73.1	69.8	83.6	71.3	70.9
2011	86.4	81.3	77.7	76.0	81.8	76.9	75.9	73.0	85.1	74.0	73.4
2012	87.8	78.3	72.5	68.9	76.7	72.3	77.0	74.4	85.9	74.4	74.6
2013	86.8	79.8	69.0	63.0	81.5	66.3	77.4	74.7	85.8	75.5	73.8
2014	89.4	80.7	71.0	70.0	68.5	72.1	78.9	75.9	87.6	77.2	75.0
2015	80.6	79.7	72.5	77.3	69.0	72.9	77.2	76.3	79.7	77.1	75.9
2016	71.5	78.6	70.1	76.4	67.6	69.7	75.4	75.5	74.2	76.3	74.6
2017	77.8	76.9	74.6	73.1	66.8	78.4	76.6	76.3	78.6	77.0	75.1
2018	87.3	80.2	79.8	76.5	66.2	86.7	79.5	78.0	86.1	79.8	76.2
2019	87.3	78.8	76.2	71.3	68.6	80.4	78.4	76.9	86.0	78.4	75.2
2020	71.9	74.8	76.3	73.5	65.8	81.2	72.5	72.3	73.6	72.9	71.9
2021	81.4	74.4	81.4	86.2	65.6	87.2	77.3	77.0	81.0	76.6	76.7
2020											
January	83.1	74.2	76.5	72.2	69.0	80.3	77.0	76.5	82.5	77.1	74.9
February	82.0	76.3	75.5	72.7	69.6	78.4	77.3	76.8	82.1	77.5	75.3
March	81.8	73.5	75.8	74.4	69.0	78.9	74.3	73.4	82.0	74.1	72.1
April	70.8	74.8	74.0	70.2	67.7	77.3	64.3	61.9	71.8	66.1	60.5
May	61.7	73.2	73.1	67.7	66.2	76.9	65.4	64.7	65.2	67.1	64.1
June	63.5	74.8	74.3	70.5	64.8	78.9	69.7	69.7	66.7	70.4	70.1
July	67.3	77.7	75.8	72.3	63.9	81.3	72.4	72.3	69.3	72.8	73.2
August	67.9	75.7	75.9	73.7	63.5	81.5	73.2	73.5	70.1	73.1	74.4
September	69.3	74.2	77.3	75.8	63.5	83.3	73.2	73.6	71.5	73.5	73.8
October	69.2	74.6	78.9	76.4	63.9	85.5	73.9	74.5	72.3	74.4	74.2
November	72.4	71.6	79.3	77.6	64.3	85.9	74.3	74.9	74.8	73.9	74.8
December	73.6	76.6	79.4	78.1	64.7	85.8	75.3	75.2	75.5	75.4	75.2
2021											
January	76.1	74.3	79.8	78.0	65.1	86.3	76.3	76.5	76.9	75.7	76.8
February	70.1	79.0	80.2	78.3	65.6	86.7	74.0	73.8	69.2	75.2	74.7
March	78.9	72.8	81.5	80.3	66.3	88.1	76.2	76.2	77.7	75.5	76.6
April	80.0	74.2	82.4	83.3	66.8	88.7	76.5	76.1	79.7	76.0	75.9
May	81.7	73.7	82.9	84.7	66.8	89.3	77.1	76.8	82.3	76.1	76.4
June	82.7	76.6	81.8	86.6	66.4	87.5	77.6	76.8	83.2	76.8	76.3
July	83.6	74.8	81.3	85.6	65.7	87.1	78.2	77.7	83.8	77.0	77.3
August	83.9	75.9	81.0	88.1	64.5	86.7	78.2	77.6	83.3	77.4	77.1
September	82.7	74.3	81.2	89.9	65.0	86.5	77.4	76.9	81.5	76.9	76.5
October	85.7	72.1	81.7	91.9	65.7	86.7	78.5	78.2	84.7	77.4	77.3
November	85.9	73.0	82.0	94.2	65.6	86.8	78.9	78.6	85.0	78.0	77.6
December	85.8	71.8	81.3	93.9	64.1	86.4	78.7	78.5	84.7	77.5	77.7

. . . = Not available.

Table 2-4A. Industrial Production and Capacity Utilization, Historical Data, 1955–2021

(Seasonally adjusted.)

Year and month	Production indexes, 2007 = 100										Capacity utilization (output as percent of capacity)	
	Total industry	Manufac-turing (SIC)	Market groups								Total industry	Manufac-turing (SIC)
			Consumer goods			Business equipment	Defense and space equipment	Construction supplies	Business supplies	Materials		
			Total	Durable	Nondurable							
1956	21.4	20.4	29.0	18.2	34.4	8.8	31.7	38.6	20.1	20.1	. . .	86.1
1957	21.8	20.7	29.7	18.3	35.5	9.2	33.1	38.1	20.4	20.1	. . .	83.6
1958	20.3	19.2	29.4	16.1	36.5	7.8	33.3	36.7	20.2	18.1	. . .	75.0
1959	22.8	21.6	32.3	19.2	39.1	8.7	35.1	41.2	22.0	20.8	. . .	81.6
1960	23.3	22.1	33.5	20.3	40.3	8.9	36.0	40.2	22.8	21.1	. . .	80.1
1961	23.4	22.2	34.2	20.0	41.6	8.7	36.6	40.5	23.4	21.1	. . .	77.3
1962	25.4	24.1	36.5	22.6	43.6	9.4	42.4	43.0	24.9	23.0	. . .	81.4
1963	27.0	25.6	38.6	24.5	45.6	9.9	45.8	45.0	26.5	24.5	. . .	83.5
1964	28.8	27.4	40.8	26.4	47.8	11.1	44.3	47.8	28.4	26.5	. . .	85.6
1965	31.6	30.3	44.0	30.8	49.9	12.7	49.0	50.7	30.3	29.5	. . .	89.5
1966	34.4	33.1	46.2	32.6	52.3	14.7	57.6	52.9	32.6	32.2	. . .	91.1
1967	35.2	33.7	47.4	31.4	55.0	15.0	65.7	54.2	34.3	31.9	87.0	87.2
1968	37.1	35.6	50.2	35.0	57.1	15.7	65.9	57.1	36.4	34.0	87.3	87.1
1969	38.8	37.2	52.1	36.5	59.1	16.7	62.7	59.5	38.8	36.0	87.4	86.7
1970	37.6	35.5	51.5	33.7	60.1	16.1	53.1	57.4	38.9	34.7	81.2	79.5
1971	38.1	36.0	54.4	38.1	61.8	15.3	47.7	59.2	40.1	35.3	79.6	77.9
1972	41.7	39.8	58.8	42.7	65.7	17.4	46.4	67.2	44.1	38.8	84.7	83.4
1973	45.2	43.4	61.5	46.0	67.6	20.1	50.9	73.0	46.8	42.3	88.3	87.7
1974	45.0	43.3	59.7	41.9	67.7	21.3	52.6	71.3	46.6	42.2	85.0	84.4
1975	41.0	38.7	57.3	38.0	66.5	19.0	53.0	60.3	42.9	37.6	75.7	73.7
1976	44.2	42.2	62.0	42.9	70.7	20.3	51.5	64.9	45.7	40.9	79.8	78.4
1977	47.6	45.8	65.9	48.3	73.3	23.4	46.1	70.6	49.5	43.8	83.4	82.5
1978	50.3	48.6	67.9	49.5	75.8	26.4	47.1	74.5	52.2	46.0	85.1	84.4
1979	51.8	50.1	66.9	47.6	75.3	29.7	50.2	76.5	54.0	47.2	84.9	84.0
1980	50.4	48.3	64.3	41.4	75.3	30.4	59.6	70.8	52.7	45.4	80.7	78.7
1981	51.1	48.8	64.7	42.0	75.6	31.3	64.6	69.7	53.9	45.7	79.5	77.0
1982	48.4	46.2	64.5	39.6	76.9	28.7	77.3	63.2	53.2	42.2	73.6	70.9
1983	49.8	48.4	66.9	44.0	77.8	28.9	77.6	67.7	55.7	43.3	74.9	73.5
1984	54.2	53.1	70.0	49.2	79.3	33.1	89.0	73.5	60.6	47.4	80.5	79.4
1985	54.9	54.0	70.6	49.2	80.4	34.4	99.6	75.3	62.1	47.4	79.3	78.1
1986	55.4	55.1	73.0	52.2	82.2	33.9	105.8	77.7	64.1	47.3	78.5	78.5
1987	58.3	58.3	76.1	55.4	85.2	36.2	108.0	82.7	67.9	49.9	81.2	81.0
1988	61.3	61.4	79.0	58.1	88.0	39.9	108.9	84.6	70.4	52.7	84.3	84.0
1989	61.9	61.9	79.3	59.4	87.7	41.3	109.1	84.2	71.3	53.1	83.7	83.3
1990	62.5	62.3	79.6	57.7	89.2	42.8	105.2	83.6	73.0	53.5	82.4	81.6
1991	61.5	61.2	79.5	55.0	90.5	42.3	97.5	79.1	71.9	52.7	80.0	78.6
1992	63.3	63.4	82.0	60.3	91.4	44.1	90.5	82.4	73.6	54.4	80.7	79.7
1993	65.4	65.7	84.5	65.2	92.6	46.3	85.6	86.1	75.9	56.3	81.6	80.6
1994	68.9	69.6	88.1	71.2	94.8	49.5	80.4	92.3	78.8	59.9	83.6	82.8
1995	72.1	73.1	90.5	73.8	97.1	54.1	77.7	94.5	81.9	63.1	83.9	83.1
1996	75.3	76.7	92.1	76.1	98.4	59.6	75.7	98.8	85.1	66.4	83.3	82.1
1997	80.7	83.1	95.6	81.3	100.8	68.5	74.7	103.5	91.1	71.6	84.0	83.0
1998	85.5	88.7	99.1	87.2	103.1	76.4	78.0	109.0	96.2	75.8	82.8	81.6
1999	89.2	93.2	101.2	94.0	103.1	80.6	75.7	111.7	100.1	80.6	81.8	80.5
2000	92.7	97.0	103.1	96.8	104.6	86.8	67.2	114.1	104.0	84.5	81.5	79.8
2001	89.8	93.4	102.1	92.3	105.1	81.3	73.9	108.8	100.2	81.2	76.1	73.8
2002	90.1	93.8	104.2	98.3	105.4	75.7	74.8	108.7	100.3	82.3	75.0	73.0
2003	91.2	95.1	105.6	101.2	106.1	75.9	79.6	108.5	102.0	83.4	76.0	74.1
2004	93.6	98.0	106.7	102.7	107.1	80.0	78.1	111.1	104.5	86.2	78.2	76.5
2005	96.8	102.0	109.5	103.1	110.8	86.0	85.6	116.5	108.3	88.3	80.2	78.6
2006	99.0	104.6	110.2	102.6	111.8	94.1	85.3	119.4	110.1	90.1	80.5	78.8
2007	101.5	107.5	110.2	102.3	112.0	99.8	101.5	118.4	111.3	93.2	80.7	78.9
2008	98.0	102.4	104.4	90.1	108.5	97.6	109.6	107.6	106.5	90.9	77.7	74.6
2009	86.8	88.3	96.6	72.5	104.2	80.9	105.2	82.8	94.4	80.8	68.4	65.2
2010	91.6	93.5	97.8	80.0	103.2	86.8	113.1	85.6	97.4	87.7	73.3	70.3
2011	94.5	96.3	98.9	83.0	103.6	92.0	109.8	87.6	98.3	91.5	76.0	73.1
2012	97.4	98.7	97.6	85.0	101.3	101.2	111.8	91.3	98.9	95.6	76.8	74.3
2013	99.3	99.6	98.2	89.7	100.7	101.2	108.2	94.2	100.3	98.8	77.1	74.5
2014	102.3	100.7	99.0	94.2	100.5	103.1	104.3	97.1	101.1	103.7	78.7	75.8
2015	100.8	100.2	100.5	98.0	101.2	100.8	101.3	97.8	99.8	101.3	77.1	76.1
2016	98.7	99.4	101.1	100.3	101.3	95.5	97.7	98.8	99.9	98.0	75.3	75.4
2017	100.0	100.0	100.0	100.0	100.0	100.0	100.0	100.0	100.0	100.0	76.5	76.2
2018	103.2	101.3	100.8	103.2	100.1	103.9	102.3	101.7	102.0	104.7	79.5	78.1
2019	102.5	99.4	100.5	102.2	100.0	95.8	115.6	100.4	100.1	105.1	78.3	76.9
2020	95.3	93.1	97.9	98.7	97.7	83.3	113.1	96.5	94.3	95.7	72.6	72.4
2021	100.0	98.4	102.3	108.7	100.4	91.4	125.0	101.0	97.8	99.8	77.4	77.1
1955												
January	19.3	18.5	26.9	17.8	31.3	7.0	32.9	35.2	18.0	18.0	. . .	83.5
February	19.6	18.7	27.0	18.0	31.3	7.1	32.9	35.7	18.2	18.4	. . .	84.1
March	20.0	19.1	27.5	18.5	31.8	7.2	32.8	36.9	18.7	18.9	. . .	85.8
April	20.3	19.4	27.7	18.8	32.0	7.4	32.7	37.1	18.6	19.3	. . .	86.7
May	20.6	19.7	28.1	19.3	32.2	7.6	32.7	37.3	18.9	19.6	. . .	87.9
June	20.6	19.7	27.9	18.9	32.1	7.6	32.4	37.9	19.1	19.7	. . .	87.6
July	20.8	19.8	28.0	19.2	32.1	7.7	32.4	38.0	19.1	19.9	. . .	87.7
August	20.7	19.8	28.0	19.1	32.1	7.7	32.1	38.0	18.9	19.9	. . .	87.3
September	20.9	19.9	28.2	19.2	32.4	7.8	32.2	38.2	19.3	20.1	. . .	87.5
October	21.2	20.2	28.7	19.3	33.2	8.1	32.1	38.2	19.5	20.4	. . .	88.4
November	21.3	20.3	28.8	19.1	33.5	8.2	32.0	38.7	19.8	20.3	. . .	88.3
December	21.4	20.5	29.0	19.1	33.8	8.3	32.1	38.9	19.7	20.4	. . .	89.0

. . . = Not available.

Table 2-4A. Industrial Production and Capacity Utilization, Historical Data, 1955–2021—*Continued*

(Seasonally adjusted.)

Year and month	Production indexes, 2007 = 100										Capacity utilization (output as percent of capacity)	
	Total industry	Manufac-turing (SIC)	Market groups								Total industry	Manufac-turing (SIC)
			Consumer goods			Business equipment	Defense and space equipment	Construction supplies	Business supplies	Materials		
			Total	Durable	Nondurable							
1956												
January	21.5	20.4	29.0	18.9	34.0	8.4	31.8	39.5	19.8	20.5	. . .	88.2
February	21.3	20.3	28.9	18.5	34.0	8.5	31.4	39.4	19.9	20.1	. . .	87.4
March	21.3	20.3	28.9	18.6	34.0	8.6	30.8	39.3	20.0	20.0	. . .	87.0
April	21.5	20.6	29.0	18.8	34.0	8.8	31.0	39.1	20.2	20.2	. . .	87.8
May	21.3	20.3	28.8	18.4	34.1	8.8	31.1	38.6	20.1	19.8	. . .	86.3
June	21.1	20.2	28.8	18.0	34.2	8.8	31.1	38.1	20.0	19.5	. . .	85.3
July	20.5	19.3	28.8	18.0	34.4	8.8	31.1	36.1	20.1	18.0	. . .	81.5
August	21.3	20.2	29.0	18.0	34.6	8.9	31.4	38.0	20.2	19.6	. . .	84.9
September	21.8	20.6	29.0	17.7	34.6	9.0	31.8	39.0	20.1	20.7	. . .	86.0
October	22.0	20.8	29.2	17.9	34.9	9.0	32.6	38.7	20.3	21.0	. . .	86.5
November	21.8	20.7	29.0	17.7	34.8	9.2	33.1	38.4	20.3	20.5	. . .	85.8
December	22.1	21.0	29.3	18.4	34.7	9.3	33.8	39.1	20.4	20.9	. . .	86.8
1957												
January	22.0	20.9	29.5	18.5	34.9	9.4	34.0	38.5	20.5	20.5	. . .	86.2
February	22.2	21.2	29.8	18.8	35.2	9.6	34.1	39.7	20.5	20.6	. . .	87.0
March	22.2	21.1	29.9	18.7	35.5	9.6	34.1	39.1	20.4	20.5	. . .	86.4
April	21.9	20.8	29.6	18.2	35.3	9.4	34.2	38.2	20.4	20.3	. . .	85.0
May	21.8	20.7	29.7	18.1	35.4	9.2	33.7	38.0	20.6	20.2	. . .	84.2
June	21.9	20.9	29.8	18.4	35.5	9.3	33.9	38.3	20.4	20.3	. . .	84.6
July	22.0	20.9	29.9	18.2	35.8	9.3	33.5	38.4	20.5	20.4	. . .	84.3
August	22.0	20.9	30.0	18.7	35.7	9.3	33.5	38.1	20.5	20.5	. . .	84.2
September	21.8	20.7	30.0	18.6	35.8	9.2	32.9	37.8	20.5	20.2	. . .	83.2
October	21.5	20.3	29.6	18.0	35.5	8.9	32.1	37.4	20.3	19.9	. . .	81.4
November	21.0	19.9	29.5	17.9	35.3	8.7	31.0	36.9	20.1	19.2	. . .	79.4
December	20.6	19.5	29.3	17.1	35.6	8.4	30.8	36.4	20.0	18.5	. . .	77.5
1958												
January	20.2	19.1	28.9	16.4	35.6	8.3	31.1	35.9	19.9	18.0	. . .	75.7
February	19.8	18.6	28.7	15.8	35.6	8.0	31.3	34.7	19.9	17.4	. . .	73.8
March	19.5	18.4	28.5	15.3	35.6	7.8	32.0	34.6	19.9	16.9	. . .	72.7
April	19.2	18.1	28.2	14.7	35.6	7.6	32.5	34.1	19.8	16.5	. . .	71.3
May	19.4	18.3	28.6	15.3	35.9	7.4	32.9	35.3	19.7	16.7	. . .	71.9
June	19.9	18.9	29.2	15.7	36.5	7.4	33.8	36.7	19.9	17.4	. . .	73.9
July	20.2	19.1	29.6	15.9	36.9	7.5	33.8	36.4	20.0	17.9	. . .	74.3
August	20.6	19.5	29.7	16.2	37.0	7.6	34.1	38.1	20.2	18.4	. . .	75.7
September	20.8	19.6	29.4	15.1	37.1	7.7	34.4	38.2	20.5	18.9	. . .	76.2
October	21.0	19.7	29.7	15.8	37.2	7.8	34.3	38.1	20.8	19.2	. . .	76.4
November	21.7	20.5	31.1	18.6	37.6	7.9	34.6	39.6	21.0	19.7	. . .	79.1
December	21.7	20.5	31.2	18.6	37.6	8.0	34.6	39.1	20.8	19.8	. . .	79.0
1959												
January	22.0	20.9	31.6	18.7	38.2	8.1	34.8	39.9	21.4	20.1	. . .	80.2
February	22.4	21.3	31.8	18.8	38.5	8.3	34.5	41.0	21.6	20.8	. . .	81.4
March	22.8	21.6	31.8	19.2	38.3	8.3	34.6	42.0	21.7	21.3	. . .	82.5
April	23.3	22.1	32.3	19.3	39.0	8.6	34.8	43.2	21.7	21.9	. . .	84.0
May	23.6	22.4	32.5	19.7	39.0	8.8	35.1	43.6	21.8	22.5	. . .	84.9
June	23.6	22.4	32.3	19.8	38.7	9.1	35.2	43.4	22.0	22.3	. . .	84.8
July	23.1	22.0	32.7	20.2	39.0	9.1	35.3	41.7	22.2	21.0	. . .	83.0
August	22.3	21.1	32.8	19.6	39.5	9.0	35.1	39.1	22.2	19.4	. . .	79.5
September	22.3	21.1	32.7	19.1	39.7	8.9	35.3	38.6	22.3	19.4	. . .	79.0
October	22.1	20.9	32.5	19.5	39.2	8.9	35.3	38.7	22.3	19.2	. . .	78.2
November	22.2	21.0	31.8	17.1	39.7	8.7	35.2	40.1	22.2	19.9	. . .	78.5
December	23.6	22.5	32.9	19.3	39.9	8.8	35.5	43.2	22.4	22.1	. . .	83.6
1960												
January	24.2	23.1	33.9	21.4	40.1	9.2	35.8	42.9	22.7	22.7	. . .	85.6
February	24.0	22.9	33.5	21.1	39.7	9.2	36.0	42.4	22.7	22.4	. . .	84.6
March	23.8	22.6	33.6	20.7	40.0	9.2	36.2	41.1	22.7	22.0	. . .	83.2
April	23.6	22.5	33.8	20.6	40.4	9.1	35.9	41.1	23.0	21.5	. . .	82.3
May	23.6	22.3	34.0	20.8	40.6	9.2	36.3	40.7	23.2	21.3	. . .	81.5
June	23.3	22.1	33.7	20.6	40.3	9.1	35.4	40.0	22.9	21.0	. . .	80.2
July	23.2	22.0	33.4	19.8	40.4	9.0	36.3	40.4	22.9	21.0	. . .	79.7
August	23.2	21.9	33.5	20.1	40.4	8.8	36.5	39.4	22.7	20.9	. . .	79.1
September	22.9	21.7	33.4	19.8	40.3	8.8	36.4	39.0	22.6	20.6	. . .	77.9
October	22.9	21.7	33.7	20.0	40.7	8.7	36.0	39.1	22.7	20.5	. . .	77.5
November	22.6	21.3	33.1	19.4	40.3	8.7	36.2	38.7	22.7	20.0	. . .	75.8
December	22.1	20.9	32.9	18.7	40.2	8.5	35.6	38.2	22.3	19.4	. . .	74.3
1961												
January	22.2	20.9	32.6	18.0	40.4	8.5	36.0	37.8	22.7	19.6	. . .	74.1
February	22.1	20.8	32.8	17.9	40.7	8.4	35.7	37.8	22.7	19.4	. . .	73.5
March	22.3	21.0	32.8	17.9	40.7	8.4	35.6	38.6	22.9	19.6	. . .	73.9
April	22.7	21.5	33.6	19.2	41.0	8.5	35.7	39.6	23.0	20.2	. . .	75.4
May	23.1	21.8	33.9	19.8	41.3	8.5	35.7	39.7	23.2	20.8	. . .	76.4
June	23.4	22.1	34.3	20.5	41.5	8.6	35.7	40.6	23.3	21.1	. . .	77.3
July	23.7	22.4	34.6	20.9	41.7	8.7	36.0	41.2	23.6	21.4	. . .	78.1
August	23.9	22.7	34.9	20.9	42.0	8.7	36.2	41.7	23.7	21.8	. . .	79.0
September	23.9	22.5	34.3	19.7	41.8	8.8	36.9	42.1	23.6	21.9	. . .	78.2
October	24.3	23.0	35.2	20.8	42.5	8.8	37.8	42.4	24.0	22.3	. . .	79.6
November	24.7	23.4	35.8	21.8	42.9	9.1	38.7	42.1	24.2	22.6	. . .	80.8
December	24.9	23.7	35.9	22.2	42.9	9.1	39.4	42.4	24.4	22.9	. . .	81.6

. . . = Not available.

Table 2-4A. Industrial Production and Capacity Utilization, Historical Data, 1955–2021—*Continued*

(Seasonally adjusted.)

Year and month	Production indexes, 2007 = 100										Capacity utilization (output as percent of capacity)	
	Total industry	Manufac-turing (SIC)	Market groups								Total industry	Manufac-turing (SIC)
			Consumer goods			Business equipment	Defense and space equipment	Construction supplies	Business supplies	Materials		
			Total	Durable	Nondurable							
1962												
January	24.7	23.4	35.6	21.7	42.8	9.1	39.8	40.4	24.4	22.7	. . .	80.2
February	25.1	23.8	35.9	21.8	43.0	9.2	40.5	42.8	24.6	23.1	. . .	81.4
March	25.2	24.0	36.1	22.1	43.3	9.3	41.0	43.3	24.5	23.1	. . .	81.9
April	25.3	24.0	36.4	22.6	43.3	9.4	41.4	42.7	24.5	23.1	. . .	81.7
May	25.3	24.0	36.6	22.8	43.6	9.4	41.7	42.7	25.0	22.8	. . .	81.3
June	25.2	23.9	36.4	22.4	43.5	9.4	42.1	43.0	24.9	22.7	. . .	80.9
July	25.5	24.1	37.0	22.9	44.0	9.5	42.9	42.8	24.9	22.9	. . .	81.5
August	25.5	24.2	36.6	22.6	43.6	9.6	43.5	43.6	25.0	23.0	. . .	81.4
September	25.7	24.4	36.8	22.9	43.9	9.6	43.6	44.1	25.3	23.1	. . .	81.8
October	25.7	24.3	36.8	23.0	43.7	9.7	43.7	43.3	25.2	23.1	. . .	81.4
November	25.8	24.5	37.0	23.0	43.9	9.7	44.2	43.5	25.4	23.3	. . .	81.8
December	25.8	24.6	37.1	23.2	44.1	9.6	44.4	43.9	25.2	23.2	. . .	81.7
1963												
January	26.0	24.7	37.6	23.4	44.7	9.6	46.4	42.8	25.4	23.3	. . .	81.9
February	26.3	24.9	38.0	23.7	45.2	9.7	46.1	42.9	25.7	23.7	. . .	82.4
March	26.4	25.1	38.2	23.7	45.4	9.6	45.9	43.4	25.4	24.0	. . .	82.6
April	26.7	25.4	38.3	23.9	45.6	9.7	45.8	44.9	26.3	24.2	. . .	83.5
May	27.0	25.6	38.4	24.3	45.4	9.7	45.8	45.9	26.5	24.8	. . .	84.0
June	27.1	25.7	38.7	24.7	45.5	9.7	45.8	45.7	26.4	24.9	. . .	83.9
July	27.0	25.6	38.5	24.7	45.3	9.9	45.3	45.5	26.6	24.6	. . .	83.3
August	27.0	25.7	38.8	24.7	45.8	10.1	45.5	45.6	26.7	24.4	. . .	83.5
September	27.3	25.9	39.0	25.2	45.7	10.1	45.7	45.3	27.0	24.9	. . .	83.8
October	27.5	26.1	39.2	25.2	46.0	10.3	45.7	46.0	27.2	25.1	. . .	84.3
November	27.6	26.2	39.3	25.5	46.0	10.3	45.5	46.5	27.5	25.2	. . .	84.3
December	27.6	26.2	39.5	25.5	46.4	10.3	45.6	45.9	27.3	25.1	. . .	84.0
1964												
January	27.8	26.5	39.9	25.6	46.9	10.6	45.2	46.1	27.6	25.3	. . .	84.5
February	28.0	26.6	39.8	25.7	46.7	10.5	44.8	47.4	27.7	25.6	. . .	84.7
March	28.0	26.6	39.6	25.5	46.5	10.7	44.7	47.5	27.9	25.6	. . .	84.4
April	28.5	27.1	40.6	26.2	47.6	10.9	44.6	47.7	28.3	25.9	. . .	85.6
May	28.6	27.2	40.9	26.4	48.1	11.0	43.8	47.9	28.6	26.2	. . .	85.6
June	28.7	27.2	40.9	26.6	47.8	11.1	43.5	47.6	28.6	26.3	. . .	85.4
July	28.9	27.5	41.4	27.1	48.4	11.2	43.4	48.5	28.6	26.4	. . .	85.9
August	29.1	27.7	41.4	27.3	48.1	11.2	43.7	48.0	28.5	26.9	. . .	86.1
September	29.2	27.8	40.9	26.6	47.8	11.3	43.9	47.6	28.5	27.3	. . .	86.2
October	28.8	27.4	40.1	23.9	48.5	11.2	44.3	47.8	28.6	26.8	. . .	84.6
November	29.7	28.2	41.6	27.1	48.6	11.6	44.7	48.9	28.8	27.7	. . .	86.8
December	30.0	28.7	42.4	28.7	48.9	11.8	45.0	48.3	29.1	28.0	. . .	88.0
1965												
January	30.3	29.0	43.1	29.2	49.5	11.8	45.5	48.7	29.3	28.3	. . .	88.6
February	30.5	29.2	43.2	29.6	49.5	12.0	46.0	49.9	29.4	28.4	. . .	88.7
March	30.9	29.6	43.6	30.4	49.5	12.1	46.9	50.3	29.8	28.9	. . .	89.3
April	31.1	29.8	43.4	30.4	49.4	12.3	47.5	49.6	29.8	29.2	. . .	89.3
May	31.3	30.0	43.7	30.6	49.6	12.4	48.5	50.1	30.1	29.3	. . .	89.4
June	31.6	30.2	43.8	30.8	49.7	12.6	49.1	50.1	30.2	29.6	. . .	89.5
July	31.9	30.6	43.8	31.1	49.5	12.8	49.8	51.5	30.2	29.9	. . .	90.3
August	32.0	30.7	43.8	30.8	49.7	12.8	50.2	51.0	30.5	30.2	. . .	89.9
September	32.1	30.7	44.4	31.3	50.3	13.1	50.3	50.6	30.5	29.9	. . .	89.6
October	32.4	31.0	44.7	31.6	50.5	13.3	51.0	51.4	30.8	30.3	. . .	89.8
November	32.5	31.1	44.9	31.8	50.8	13.5	51.4	52.1	31.0	30.1	. . .	89.6
December	32.9	31.6	45.2	32.5	50.7	13.8	51.9	53.2	31.5	30.5	. . .	90.5
1966												
January	33.3	31.9	45.4	32.6	51.0	14.1	53.0	53.1	31.5	30.9	. . .	90.9
February	33.5	32.1	45.5	32.5	51.3	14.0	53.9	52.6	31.9	31.2	. . .	90.9
March	33.9	32.5	45.9	32.8	51.6	14.3	54.3	53.7	32.2	31.8	. . .	91.6
April	34.0	32.7	46.0	33.4	51.6	14.4	55.5	53.7	31.9	31.7	. . .	91.5
May	34.3	33.0	46.0	32.9	51.9	14.6	56.5	53.9	32.4	32.1	. . .	91.6
June	34.5	33.1	46.2	32.9	52.1	14.8	57.3	53.2	32.8	32.3	. . .	91.5
July	34.7	33.3	46.1	32.2	52.5	15.0	58.1	53.7	33.1	32.4	. . .	91.4
August	34.7	33.3	46.0	31.7	52.6	15.0	58.8	52.1	33.0	32.6	. . .	91.1
September	35.0	33.6	46.1	31.9	52.7	15.2	59.6	52.1	33.2	33.0	. . .	91.2
October	35.2	33.9	47.1	33.6	53.1	15.2	60.5	52.1	33.2	33.1	. . .	91.6
November	35.0	33.6	46.9	32.6	53.4	14.9	61.6	52.2	33.3	32.6	. . .	90.1
December	35.1	33.7	46.8	32.2	53.5	15.2	62.3	52.1	33.3	32.6	. . .	90.0
1967												
January	35.2	33.8	47.2	31.4	54.7	15.0	63.3	53.5	34.0	32.5	89.4	89.8
February	34.8	33.4	46.5	30.5	54.3	15.1	64.1	53.0	33.8	31.9	88.0	88.4
March	34.7	33.3	46.7	30.8	54.3	15.0	64.8	53.1	33.8	31.3	87.1	87.5
April	35.0	33.5	47.5	31.1	55.4	15.0	65.4	52.9	34.1	31.6	87.5	87.7
May	34.7	33.3	46.6	30.6	54.2	15.1	65.8	53.8	33.6	31.2	86.4	86.6
June	34.7	33.2	46.7	30.3	54.7	15.0	65.7	54.1	33.8	31.2	86.0	86.1
July	34.6	33.1	46.6	30.7	54.3	14.7	66.1	54.3	33.9	31.1	85.4	85.3
August	35.3	33.7	47.1	31.1	54.8	15.0	66.2	54.9	34.8	32.1	86.6	86.5
September	35.2	33.7	47.2	31.0	55.0	14.9	66.4	55.4	34.9	31.9	86.1	86.1
October	35.5	34.0	47.8	31.5	55.6	14.8	66.9	55.1	35.1	32.3	86.4	86.4
November	36.0	34.6	48.8	33.3	56.1	15.2	67.0	55.4	35.2	32.6	87.3	87.5
December	36.4	34.9	49.6	34.6	56.5	15.3	67.0	55.4	35.2	33.1	87.8	88.0

. . . = Not available.

Table 2-4A. Industrial Production and Capacity Utilization, Historical Data, 1955–2021—*Continued*

(Seasonally adjusted.)

Year and month	Production indexes, 2007 = 100										Capacity utilization (output as percent of capacity)	
			Market groups									
	Total industry	Manufac-turing (SIC)	Consumer goods			Business equipment	Defense and space equipment	Construction supplies	Business supplies	Materials	Total industry	Manufac-turing (SIC)
			Total	Durable	Nondurable							
1968												
January	36.3	34.9	49.0	33.6	56.1	15.4	66.7	55.8	35.3	33.2	87.4	87.4
February	36.5	35.0	49.2	34.1	56.2	15.4	67.5	56.3	35.6	33.2	87.3	87.4
March	36.6	35.1	49.5	34.1	56.7	15.5	66.2	56.4	35.6	33.3	87.3	87.2
April	36.6	35.1	49.4	34.1	56.6	15.5	64.9	56.7	35.9	33.6	87.1	86.9
May	37.0	35.6	49.7	34.5	56.7	15.7	65.8	57.0	36.2	34.1	87.7	87.6
June	37.2	35.6	50.0	34.9	57.0	15.6	66.1	57.0	36.4	34.2	87.7	87.4
July	37.1	35.5	49.9	34.6	57.0	15.5	66.1	57.0	36.4	34.3	87.2	86.7
August	37.2	35.7	50.5	35.0	57.6	15.6	66.3	57.3	36.8	34.0	87.1	86.8
September	37.4	35.7	50.7	35.4	57.7	15.8	66.2	56.9	36.9	34.1	87.1	86.5
October	37.4	35.9	51.0	35.8	57.9	15.9	64.5	56.8	37.1	34.2	86.9	86.6
November	37.9	36.4	51.7	36.7	58.4	16.0	65.2	58.2	37.5	34.7	87.7	87.5
December	38.0	36.5	51.4	37.0	57.7	16.1	64.8	59.2	37.7	34.9	87.6	87.1
1969												
January	38.3	36.7	51.7	36.9	58.2	16.3	64.9	59.6	37.9	35.1	87.9	87.3
February	38.5	37.0	52.1	36.9	58.8	16.3	64.5	60.2	37.8	35.5	88.1	87.7
March	38.8	37.2	52.5	37.1	59.3	16.5	64.7	60.4	39.0	35.6	88.5	88.0
April	38.7	37.1	51.7	36.1	58.7	16.7	64.2	59.8	38.4	35.7	87.8	87.3
May	38.5	36.9	51.3	35.6	58.4	16.6	64.0	59.4	38.8	35.6	87.2	86.6
June	38.9	37.2	51.9	36.8	58.5	16.7	63.2	59.8	39.1	36.1	87.7	86.8
July	39.1	37.4	52.8	36.8	60.0	16.9	62.9	59.2	38.9	36.1	87.9	87.1
August	39.2	37.5	52.7	37.2	59.6	16.8	62.0	59.2	39.0	36.5	87.8	86.9
September	39.2	37.4	52.3	36.9	59.2	17.0	61.7	59.2	38.9	36.6	87.4	86.5
October	39.2	37.5	52.3	37.1	59.1	17.0	61.1	59.4	39.1	36.6	87.2	86.2
November	38.8	37.1	51.9	35.5	59.4	16.7	60.0	59.0	38.8	36.4	86.0	85.0
December	38.7	36.9	51.9	35.3	59.6	16.6	59.2	58.7	39.3	36.2	85.5	84.3
1970												
January	38.0	36.1	51.1	33.5	59.5	16.4	58.4	56.9	39.3	35.4	83.6	82.1
February	38.0	36.1	51.6	34.0	60.0	16.4	57.4	56.7	39.0	35.2	83.3	81.9
March	37.9	36.0	51.5	34.3	59.7	16.5	56.2	57.2	39.2	35.1	83.0	81.4
April	37.8	35.9	51.7	34.3	60.0	16.5	54.9	57.7	39.0	34.8	82.5	80.9
May	37.8	35.8	52.0	34.3	60.4	16.4	53.7	57.8	38.9	34.7	82.1	80.5
June	37.7	35.7	52.1	35.0	60.2	16.3	52.8	57.6	38.8	34.6	81.6	80.0
July	37.8	35.8	52.3	35.0	60.4	16.3	51.9	58.2	39.0	34.7	81.6	80.0
August	37.7	35.6	51.4	34.0	59.7	16.3	51.5	58.0	38.7	35.2	81.2	79.2
September	37.4	35.3	51.2	33.1	60.0	15.9	51.0	57.8	38.9	34.9	80.4	78.3
October	36.7	34.5	50.5	31.1	60.3	15.4	50.3	57.2	38.8	34.0	78.5	76.3
November	36.5	34.3	50.2	31.2	59.7	15.3	49.9	56.5	38.9	33.8	77.8	75.6
December	37.3	35.2	52.4	34.8	60.7	15.5	49.3	57.2	38.9	34.6	79.3	77.3
1971												
January	37.6	35.5	53.1	36.2	61.0	15.2	49.7	57.2	39.1	35.0	79.7	77.8
February	37.5	35.5	53.1	37.0	60.4	15.2	48.5	57.6	39.5	34.8	79.4	77.6
March	37.5	35.4	53.3	37.1	60.6	15.1	48.1	57.4	39.1	34.9	79.1	77.2
April	37.7	35.6	53.7	37.3	61.2	15.0	48.1	57.9	39.5	35.1	79.3	77.5
May	37.9	35.8	53.7	37.9	60.8	14.9	48.7	58.2	39.6	35.5	79.5	77.8
June	38.1	35.9	54.1	38.2	61.3	15.0	48.0	58.8	39.4	35.7	79.7	77.8
July	37.9	36.0	55.0	38.9	62.1	15.0	47.6	59.3	40.5	34.8	79.2	77.7
August	37.7	35.6	54.4	38.5	61.4	15.2	47.6	58.3	40.0	34.6	78.6	76.6
September	38.3	36.3	54.9	38.4	62.2	15.6	47.1	60.5	40.6	35.3	79.6	78.0
October	38.6	36.8	55.6	39.1	63.0	15.7	46.8	61.3	40.9	35.4	80.0	78.9
November	38.8	36.9	56.0	39.5	63.4	15.8	46.5	61.5	41.3	35.5	80.2	79.0
December	39.2	37.3	56.4	39.7	63.9	15.9	45.8	62.6	41.5	36.2	80.9	79.5
1972												
January	40.2	38.2	57.3	40.9	64.5	16.4	45.8	64.3	42.2	37.3	82.6	81.4
February	40.6	38.6	57.6	41.1	64.9	16.7	45.9	64.6	43.0	37.7	83.3	81.8
March	40.9	38.8	57.6	40.8	65.1	16.9	46.3	65.0	43.4	38.1	83.7	82.2
April	41.3	39.3	58.3	42.0	65.3	17.1	46.5	65.7	43.4	38.5	84.3	82.9
May	41.3	39.3	58.0	41.6	65.2	17.1	46.1	66.1	43.6	38.5	84.1	82.8
June	41.4	39.5	58.0	41.6	65.2	17.2	45.9	66.7	44.1	38.6	84.1	82.9
July	41.3	39.4	58.5	42.5	65.3	17.2	46.0	67.6	44.0	38.3	83.8	82.6
August	41.9	40.0	59.1	42.9	66.0	17.6	45.9	68.0	44.6	38.9	84.7	83.5
September	42.2	40.3	59.4	43.4	66.2	17.7	46.3	68.7	44.6	39.3	85.1	83.9
October	42.8	40.9	60.3	44.3	66.9	18.1	46.3	69.7	45.3	39.7	86.0	84.9
November	43.3	41.4	60.7	45.4	66.8	18.4	47.6	70.2	45.4	40.3	86.7	85.7
December	43.8	41.9	61.2	46.3	67.0	18.6	48.3	69.9	45.6	40.9	87.4	86.6
1973												
January	44.1	42.2	61.1	46.2	66.9	18.9	49.0	70.8	45.9	41.3	87.8	87.0
February	44.7	42.9	61.9	47.0	67.6	19.3	50.1	72.1	46.4	41.9	88.8	88.1
March	44.7	43.0	62.0	47.1	67.8	19.5	49.9	72.5	46.4	41.8	88.5	88.0
April	44.7	42.9	61.4	46.3	67.3	19.6	49.5	72.4	46.4	41.8	88.1	87.5
May	45.0	43.2	61.8	46.2	68.0	19.8	49.9	72.7	46.7	42.1	88.4	87.8
June	45.0	43.2	61.4	46.2	67.3	20.0	50.5	72.9	46.8	42.2	88.2	87.5
July	45.2	43.4	61.2	46.1	67.1	20.3	51.5	73.5	47.0	42.4	88.2	87.6
August	45.1	43.3	60.6	44.7	67.2	20.3	51.5	73.5	47.0	42.4	87.8	87.1
September	45.5	43.6	61.6	46.2	67.6	20.7	51.5	73.4	46.9	42.6	88.2	87.4
October	45.9	44.0	61.8	45.9	68.3	21.0	52.8	73.4	47.4	43.0	88.6	88.0
November	46.1	44.3	62.0	45.9	68.7	21.1	52.2	73.9	47.5	43.2	88.7	88.3
December	45.9	44.4	60.9	44.9	67.5	21.2	51.9	74.5	47.1	43.4	88.2	88.1

Table 2-4A. Industrial Production and Capacity Utilization, Historical Data, 1955–2021—*Continued*

(Seasonally adjusted.)

Year and month	Production indexes, 2007 = 100										Capacity utilization (output as percent of capacity)	
	Total industry	Manufac-turing (SIC)	Market groups									
			Consumer goods			Business equipment	Defense and space equipment	Construction supplies	Business supplies	Materials	Total industry	Manufac-turing (SIC)
			Total	Durable	Nondurable							
1974												
January	45.6	44.0	60.1	42.6	67.9	21.2	51.7	74.6	47.2	43.1	87.4	87.1
February	45.5	43.8	59.9	42.5	67.6	21.1	52.2	73.7	47.0	43.0	86.8	86.5
March	45.5	43.8	60.0	42.5	67.8	21.3	52.2	73.9	47.0	42.8	86.6	86.1
April	45.4	43.6	59.8	42.2	67.7	21.0	52.0	73.2	47.1	42.8	86.1	85.5
May	45.7	43.9	60.4	42.4	68.5	21.4	52.2	73.6	47.3	43.1	86.6	85.9
June	45.6	44.0	60.6	43.0	68.4	21.4	51.4	73.1	47.4	42.8	86.2	85.7
July	45.7	43.9	60.6	42.9	68.5	21.5	52.1	71.8	47.2	43.1	86.2	85.4
August	45.2	43.5	60.5	42.8	68.4	21.4	53.1	70.8	46.8	42.3	85.1	84.5
September	45.2	43.5	60.0	42.7	67.6	21.8	53.0	70.4	46.6	42.4	84.9	84.3
October	45.1	43.2	60.0	42.2	68.0	21.8	54.0	69.1	46.5	42.2	84.5	83.5
November	43.6	42.0	58.3	40.2	66.6	21.5	53.7	66.9	45.2	40.4	81.6	80.9
December	42.1	40.1	56.4	36.8	65.9	20.6	53.0	63.8	44.3	38.8	78.5	77.1
1975												
January	41.5	39.2	55.1	35.3	64.8	20.1	53.4	63.4	43.7	38.5	77.3	75.3
February	40.5	38.2	54.4	34.3	64.3	19.4	50.8	61.6	42.8	37.6	75.4	73.1
March	40.1	37.6	54.5	34.7	64.3	19.1	51.2	59.2	42.2	37.0	74.4	72.0
April	40.2	37.6	55.7	36.1	65.2	19.0	51.0	58.8	42.3	36.8	74.5	71.9
May	40.0	37.6	55.9	36.9	65.0	18.8	53.4	58.7	42.1	36.6	74.1	71.7
June	40.3	37.9	56.7	37.3	66.0	18.6	54.0	58.5	42.3	36.8	74.5	72.2
July	40.7	38.4	58.1	39.2	67.0	18.7	53.3	59.2	42.7	37.0	75.1	73.1
August	41.1	38.8	58.5	39.7	67.2	18.6	53.2	59.9	43.0	37.6	75.7	73.7
September	41.6	39.5	59.3	40.5	68.0	18.9	54.7	60.6	43.2	38.1	76.6	74.8
October	41.8	39.7	59.4	40.4	68.3	18.9	54.7	60.9	43.4	38.3	76.8	75.0
November	41.9	39.7	59.6	40.4	68.6	18.9	52.5	61.2	43.5	38.4	76.7	75.0
December	42.4	40.3	60.2	41.1	69.0	19.3	54.1	61.2	44.0	39.0	77.6	76.0
1976												
January	43.0	40.8	60.9	41.8	69.7	19.4	54.0	62.6	44.4	39.6	78.5	76.7
February	43.5	41.4	61.2	42.3	69.7	19.6	54.0	63.8	44.6	40.2	79.2	77.7
March	43.5	41.5	61.1	42.3	69.6	19.7	54.1	62.8	44.8	40.3	79.1	77.7
April	43.8	41.8	61.2	42.2	69.9	19.9	52.9	63.6	45.0	40.6	79.4	78.0
May	43.9	42.0	61.7	42.3	70.6	20.0	52.4	64.3	45.2	40.7	79.5	78.2
June	44.0	42.0	61.5	42.2	70.4	20.1	51.8	64.8	44.9	40.8	79.5	78.1
July	44.2	42.3	61.9	42.4	70.9	20.2	50.3	66.2	45.6	40.9	79.7	78.5
August	44.5	42.6	62.0	43.0	70.6	20.6	50.3	65.6	45.7	41.4	80.1	78.8
September	44.7	42.7	62.0	42.7	70.9	20.5	49.9	66.0	46.7	41.5	80.1	78.8
October	44.7	42.7	62.5	43.3	71.3	20.6	49.9	65.9	47.0	41.2	79.9	78.5
November	45.4	43.2	63.6	44.7	72.1	21.2	49.5	66.2	47.2	41.8	81.0	79.4
December	45.8	43.7	64.3	45.8	72.4	21.6	48.7	66.7	47.7	42.3	81.6	80.0
1977												
January	45.5	43.5	64.0	45.6	72.1	21.6	48.0	65.5	47.4	41.9	80.9	79.5
February	46.3	44.3	64.9	46.2	73.1	22.2	47.8	67.1	48.0	42.5	82.0	80.8
March	46.8	45.0	65.0	47.4	72.4	22.5	46.8	68.5	48.3	43.3	82.8	81.7
April	47.3	45.5	65.5	47.8	72.9	22.8	47.1	70.1	48.9	43.7	83.4	82.4
May	47.7	45.8	65.5	48.0	72.7	23.3	46.9	71.1	49.3	44.0	83.8	82.8
June	48.0	46.2	65.9	48.9	72.9	23.8	46.9	71.6	49.7	44.2	84.2	83.3
July	48.1	46.2	66.1	49.0	73.1	24.0	46.8	71.7	49.9	44.2	84.1	83.1
August	48.1	46.5	66.2	49.0	73.2	24.0	46.5	72.3	50.2	44.1	84.0	83.3
September	48.3	46.5	66.3	49.2	73.3	24.1	46.5	72.0	50.4	44.4	84.1	83.1
October	48.4	46.6	66.8	49.2	74.1	24.0	42.5	71.9	50.4	44.6	84.0	83.0
November	48.5	46.7	66.9	49.2	74.2	24.0	42.1	72.3	50.6	44.7	83.9	83.0
December	48.6	47.2	67.5	49.5	75.0	24.4	45.1	73.0	50.7	44.3	83.8	83.6
1978												
January	47.9	46.5	65.7	46.9	73.9	23.9	45.5	71.6	50.4	43.9	82.3	82.1
February	48.1	46.7	66.8	48.1	74.9	24.5	43.3	71.4	50.6	43.8	82.6	82.2
March	49.1	47.5	68.1	49.5	76.0	25.2	47.2	72.7	51.5	44.5	83.9	83.5
April	50.0	48.3	68.6	50.5	76.1	25.7	46.9	74.3	51.9	45.7	85.3	84.5
May	50.3	48.5	68.2	49.8	76.0	25.9	47.2	74.3	52.2	46.2	85.5	84.6
June	50.6	48.8	68.6	50.0	76.4	26.3	47.7	74.9	52.6	46.4	85.8	85.0
July	50.5	48.8	68.2	50.0	75.8	26.5	47.7	74.8	52.5	46.4	85.5	84.6
August	50.8	49.0	68.1	49.8	75.8	27.0	48.2	74.9	52.5	46.5	85.6	84.8
September	50.9	49.3	68.2	49.5	76.1	27.3	48.1	75.2	52.6	46.6	85.6	84.9
October	51.3	49.6	68.1	49.7	75.9	27.8	47.6	75.9	53.0	47.1	86.0	85.2
November	51.7	50.1	68.3	49.8	76.1	28.3	47.3	76.4	53.2	47.5	86.4	85.7
December	51.9	50.4	68.4	49.9	76.2	28.6	47.9	77.7	53.6	47.7	86.6	86.1
1979												
January	51.7	50.1	68.3	50.3	75.8	28.9	48.3	75.8	53.6	47.1	85.9	85.2
February	51.9	50.2	67.8	49.7	75.4	29.2	49.2	76.3	54.1	47.5	86.1	85.2
March	52.1	50.5	68.1	49.6	75.9	29.5	48.8	77.2	54.3	47.5	86.2	85.4
April	51.5	49.6	66.8	47.1	75.5	28.9	47.4	75.9	54.0	47.2	84.9	83.7
May	51.9	50.3	67.3	48.5	75.3	29.7	48.4	76.5	54.2	47.5	85.5	84.6
June	51.9	50.4	67.0	48.0	75.3	29.8	48.8	76.8	54.0	47.5	85.2	84.5
July	51.8	50.4	66.5	47.4	74.9	30.1	49.6	76.8	54.0	47.4	84.9	84.3
August	51.5	49.8	65.8	45.4	75.0	29.7	50.4	76.1	54.2	47.1	84.2	83.1
September	51.5	49.9	66.1	46.9	74.5	30.5	50.7	76.2	53.5	46.8	84.0	83.0
October	51.8	50.1	66.3	46.7	75.1	30.2	52.6	76.8	54.1	47.3	84.4	83.2
November	51.8	50.0	66.2	45.9	75.3	30.1	53.7	76.7	54.3	47.1	84.1	82.7
December	51.8	50.1	66.2	45.8	75.4	30.3	54.9	76.9	54.3	47.1	83.9	82.8

Table 2-4A. Industrial Production and Capacity Utilization, Historical Data, 1955–2021—Continued

(Seasonally adjusted.)

Year and month	Production indexes, 2007 = 100										Capacity utilization (output as percent of capacity)	
	Total industry	Manufac-turing (SIC)	Market groups								Total industry	Manufac-turing (SIC)
			Consumer goods			Business equipment	Defense and space equipment	Construction supplies	Business supplies	Materials		
			Total	Durable	Nondurable							
1980												
January	52.1	50.3	66.0	44.9	75.7	30.9	55.6	76.7	54.0	47.4	84.2	83.0
February	52.1	50.3	66.1	44.6	76.2	31.0	57.8	75.6	54.1	47.3	84.1	82.7
March	51.9	49.9	65.6	43.8	75.9	30.8	58.4	74.6	53.8	47.3	83.6	81.8
April	50.8	48.9	64.6	41.9	75.5	30.5	58.9	71.2	53.0	46.1	81.8	80.0
May	49.6	47.4	63.2	39.3	75.1	30.0	59.2	68.3	51.9	44.8	79.6	77.5
June	49.0	46.7	62.9	38.6	74.9	29.6	59.6	66.9	51.3	44.0	78.4	76.1
July	48.6	46.2	62.9	38.6	75.0	29.6	60.1	66.3	51.5	43.3	77.7	75.1
August	48.8	46.5	63.1	38.9	75.1	29.6	60.4	67.3	51.7	43.5	77.8	75.5
September	49.6	47.3	63.7	40.7	74.9	30.2	60.2	69.0	52.4	44.3	78.9	76.6
October	50.2	48.2	64.2	41.4	75.1	30.7	61.3	70.4	52.5	45.0	79.8	77.7
November	51.0	49.0	64.5	42.4	74.9	31.2	62.1	71.8	53.1	46.0	80.9	78.9
December	51.4	49.2	64.5	41.9	75.3	31.3	62.3	71.9	53.8	46.4	81.3	79.0
1981												
January	51.1	49.0	64.5	41.7	75.5	31.4	61.9	71.6	53.8	45.9	80.6	78.4
February	50.9	48.8	64.4	41.6	75.3	31.0	61.8	71.0	53.3	45.8	80.0	77.8
March	51.1	48.9	64.3	42.1	74.9	31.3	61.8	71.3	53.3	46.0	80.2	77.8
April	50.9	49.2	64.5	42.7	74.8	31.7	61.9	71.3	53.2	45.4	79.7	78.0
May	51.2	49.4	65.1	43.3	75.4	31.7	62.5	71.3	53.9	45.7	79.9	78.2
June	51.4	49.2	64.7	43.0	74.9	31.5	62.9	70.2	54.3	46.3	80.2	77.6
July	51.8	49.3	65.1	43.2	75.5	31.6	63.7	70.4	54.7	46.6	80.5	77.5
August	51.7	49.3	65.1	42.9	75.7	31.5	64.8	70.1	54.4	46.5	80.2	77.3
September	51.5	49.1	64.7	41.9	75.6	31.6	65.9	69.8	54.5	46.2	79.6	76.8
October	51.1	48.6	65.0	41.7	76.2	31.5	67.7	67.6	54.0	45.5	78.8	75.9
November	50.5	48.0	64.9	41.0	76.6	30.9	69.3	66.5	53.8	44.7	77.7	74.7
December	49.9	47.2	64.2	39.2	76.7	30.5	71.2	65.3	53.7	44.1	76.7	73.3
1982												
January	48.9	46.0	63.0	38.2	75.5	29.3	70.5	63.0	52.8	43.4	74.9	71.4
February	49.9	47.3	64.8	39.6	77.4	30.4	74.4	65.3	54.0	43.9	76.3	73.2
March	49.6	47.0	64.5	39.4	76.9	30.0	75.6	63.9	53.8	43.6	75.6	72.5
April	49.1	46.6	64.4	40.2	76.4	29.5	76.4	63.4	53.5	43.0	74.8	71.8
May	48.8	46.5	64.4	40.2	76.4	29.3	77.7	63.8	53.2	42.5	74.2	71.6
June	48.7	46.5	64.9	40.5	76.9	28.8	77.9	63.3	53.2	42.4	73.9	71.4
July	48.5	46.4	65.0	40.7	77.0	28.7	79.0	63.1	53.1	42.1	73.5	71.2
August	48.1	46.0	64.9	40.1	77.1	28.0	78.7	63.2	53.1	41.7	72.8	70.4
September	47.9	45.9	64.8	39.5	77.5	27.9	79.5	63.3	53.3	41.5	72.5	70.2
October	47.5	45.4	64.9	39.0	77.9	27.3	79.1	62.4	53.1	41.0	71.7	69.3
November	47.3	45.1	64.7	38.9	77.7	27.2	79.5	62.1	53.0	40.8	71.5	68.8
December	47.0	45.0	63.9	38.9	76.4	27.4	78.9	61.6	52.8	40.5	70.9	68.6
1983												
January	47.9	46.0	65.3	40.6	77.5	27.5	78.3	63.8	53.4	41.4	72.2	70.1
February	47.6	46.0	64.5	40.4	76.2	27.4	77.0	63.5	53.4	41.2	71.7	70.1
March	48.0	46.4	64.7	41.0	76.3	27.7	77.1	64.2	54.1	41.6	72.3	70.7
April	48.6	47.0	66.0	41.9	77.7	27.7	76.5	65.1	54.8	42.1	73.2	71.5
May	48.9	47.5	66.2	42.7	77.6	28.1	76.2	66.3	54.9	42.4	73.6	72.3
June	49.2	47.9	66.5	43.5	77.5	28.3	75.8	67.5	55.1	42.7	74.0	72.9
July	49.9	48.6	67.3	44.5	78.2	28.9	76.7	68.9	55.8	43.4	75.1	73.9
August	50.5	49.0	67.9	45.3	78.6	29.2	77.2	69.2	56.4	44.0	76.0	74.5
September	51.2	49.9	68.8	46.1	79.4	29.9	77.8	70.0	57.4	44.6	77.1	75.8
October	51.6	50.4	68.4	46.7	78.4	30.3	79.0	71.2	57.6	45.2	77.6	76.5
November	51.8	50.7	68.5	46.8	78.5	30.6	79.6	71.0	57.9	45.4	77.9	76.9
December	52.1	50.8	68.6	47.9	78.0	30.9	80.4	71.2	58.0	45.6	78.2	77.0
1984												
January	53.1	51.7	70.0	49.0	79.4	31.6	82.5	71.6	59.1	46.6	79.7	78.3
February	53.4	52.3	69.8	49.2	79.1	31.8	84.3	73.2	59.3	46.8	79.9	79.0
March	53.6	52.5	70.1	49.3	79.4	32.2	84.8	72.8	59.8	47.0	80.2	79.2
April	53.9	52.8	70.3	49.2	79.8	32.4	86.7	73.3	59.8	47.3	80.5	79.5
May	54.2	53.0	70.0	48.8	79.7	32.6	87.7	73.4	60.7	47.7	80.8	79.5
June	54.4	53.2	70.0	48.9	79.5	32.9	89.0	74.0	61.0	47.8	81.0	79.7
July	54.6	53.4	70.0	49.4	79.2	33.4	88.0	73.7	61.3	47.9	81.0	79.9
August	54.7	53.5	69.7	49.8	78.4	33.7	90.9	74.0	61.4	47.9	81.0	79.8
September	54.5	53.3	69.4	49.0	78.5	33.8	92.7	74.2	61.2	47.7	80.5	79.3
October	54.5	53.6	70.0	48.7	79.7	34.0	93.7	74.0	61.4	47.3	80.3	79.5
November	54.7	53.8	70.2	49.4	79.6	34.3	93.0	73.8	61.7	47.4	80.4	79.5
December	54.7	53.9	70.6	50.0	79.8	34.5	94.7	74.5	61.3	47.3	80.3	79.5
1985												
January	54.7	53.8	70.2	49.4	79.5	34.5	95.2	73.3	61.3	47.4	80.0	79.1
February	54.8	53.6	70.6	48.9	80.4	34.2	96.1	73.3	61.9	47.6	80.0	78.5
March	54.9	54.0	70.5	49.4	80.0	34.6	97.5	75.3	61.9	47.5	79.9	78.9
April	54.8	53.8	70.1	48.7	79.8	34.3	97.8	75.3	62.2	47.4	79.6	78.4
May	54.9	53.9	70.3	48.8	80.0	34.4	98.4	75.6	62.3	47.5	79.5	78.3
June	54.8	53.9	70.5	48.7	80.4	34.4	99.6	76.0	61.9	47.3	79.3	78.1
July	54.6	53.7	70.2	48.7	80.0	34.3	99.1	75.7	61.6	47.1	78.7	77.6
August	54.7	54.0	70.6	49.2	80.2	34.3	100.6	75.8	62.1	47.1	78.8	77.8
September	54.9	54.0	70.9	49.2	80.8	34.2	100.8	75.7	62.5	47.4	78.9	77.7
October	54.8	53.9	70.8	48.9	80.8	34.2	102.3	75.9	62.1	47.1	78.5	77.4
November	54.9	54.3	71.2	50.1	80.7	34.5	103.7	75.8	62.3	47.1	78.6	77.8
December	55.5	54.5	71.9	50.2	81.7	34.4	104.3	75.6	63.2	47.8	79.3	78.0

Table 2-4A. Industrial Production and Capacity Utilization, Historical Data, 1955–2021—*Continued*

(Seasonally adjusted.)

Year and month	Production indexes, 2007 = 100										Capacity utilization (output as percent of capacity)	
	Total industry	Manufac-turing (SIC)	Market groups								Total industry	Manufac-turing (SIC)
			Consumer goods			Business equipment	Defense and space equipment	Construction supplies	Business supplies	Materials		
			Total	Durable	Nondurable							
1986												
January	55.8	55.1	72.7	51.5	82.3	34.5	105.2	77.2	63.6	47.9	79.5	78.8
February	55.4	54.8	72.1	51.1	81.5	34.1	103.7	76.4	63.1	47.7	78.9	78.3
March	55.0	54.6	71.9	51.1	81.1	34.1	104.7	76.6	62.7	47.2	78.2	77.9
April	55.1	54.8	72.3	51.0	81.9	33.9	104.9	77.3	63.3	47.1	78.2	78.2
May	55.2	54.9	72.7	51.1	82.5	33.8	105.3	77.8	63.7	47.1	78.3	78.3
June	55.0	54.7	72.7	51.7	82.1	33.5	105.4	77.0	64.1	46.8	77.9	77.9
July	55.3	55.0	73.2	52.3	82.4	33.7	106.4	77.4	64.2	47.2	78.3	78.3
August	55.2	55.1	73.1	52.6	82.2	33.7	106.5	78.2	64.3	47.0	78.1	78.4
September	55.4	55.3	73.2	53.0	82.1	33.8	106.0	78.3	64.4	47.2	78.3	78.5
October	55.6	55.5	73.5	53.0	82.5	33.7	106.6	78.3	64.8	47.4	78.5	78.6
November	55.8	55.7	74.0	53.8	82.9	33.7	107.2	78.5	64.8	47.6	78.7	78.8
December	56.3	56.2	74.8	54.8	83.5	34.1	107.3	79.0	65.7	48.0	79.3	79.4
1987												
January	56.1	56.0	74.0	54.3	82.4	34.1	107.7	79.8	65.2	47.9	78.9	78.9
February	56.9	56.9	75.0	55.3	83.4	34.9	108.2	81.4	65.8	48.5	79.8	79.9
March	57.0	56.9	75.1	55.0	83.8	34.9	107.9	81.0	66.2	48.6	79.8	79.8
April	57.3	57.2	75.0	54.7	83.8	35.2	108.1	81.4	66.9	49.1	80.2	80.0
May	57.7	57.6	75.6	55.1	84.5	35.5	107.8	82.1	67.6	49.3	80.5	80.4
June	58.0	57.9	75.8	54.6	85.2	35.7	107.3	82.3	68.0	49.7	80.8	80.5
July	58.4	58.3	76.3	54.5	86.0	36.0	106.9	82.7	68.5	50.0	81.2	80.9
August	58.8	58.6	76.7	55.0	86.3	36.5	108.1	83.3	68.7	50.4	81.6	81.1
September	59.0	59.0	76.5	55.5	85.7	37.1	108.3	83.7	69.0	50.6	81.8	81.5
October	59.8	59.9	77.8	57.2	86.7	37.8	108.1	84.7	69.5	51.2	82.8	82.5
November	60.1	60.2	77.8	57.2	86.8	38.1	108.4	84.7	69.4	51.7	83.1	82.9
December	60.5	60.6	78.0	56.7	87.3	38.5	109.4	85.5	69.6	52.0	83.4	83.3
1988												
January	60.5	60.5	78.3	56.5	87.9	38.6	111.8	84.0	69.9	51.8	83.3	83.0
February	60.8	60.7	78.7	56.4	88.5	38.9	110.1	84.8	70.4	52.1	83.7	83.2
March	60.9	60.8	78.6	56.8	88.1	39.3	109.4	85.1	70.3	52.2	83.8	83.4
April	61.2	61.4	79.2	58.1	88.3	39.7	108.5	84.9	70.4	52.6	84.3	84.1
May	61.1	61.2	78.8	58.1	87.7	39.9	108.0	85.0	69.8	52.5	84.1	83.9
June	61.3	61.3	78.8	58.4	87.5	40.2	107.4	84.3	70.0	52.8	84.3	84.0
July	61.3	61.3	78.7	57.1	88.2	39.9	108.6	84.4	70.3	52.8	84.3	83.9
August	61.6	61.4	79.2	57.5	88.7	40.0	108.3	83.9	70.9	53.1	84.6	84.0
September	61.4	61.6	78.8	58.5	87.4	40.4	108.3	84.2	70.4	52.9	84.3	84.2
October	61.7	61.8	79.4	59.1	88.0	40.7	108.7	84.5	70.7	53.0	84.6	84.5
November	61.8	62.1	79.5	59.9	87.8	40.8	108.6	84.9	70.8	53.2	84.8	84.8
December	62.1	62.3	79.9	60.5	88.0	40.9	109.2	84.8	71.0	53.4	85.1	85.1
1989												
January	62.3	62.8	80.0	61.9	87.3	41.3	109.0	86.4	71.0	53.6	85.2	85.6
February	62.0	62.2	80.0	61.3	87.7	41.2	109.1	84.3	71.2	53.2	84.7	84.7
March	62.2	62.2	80.1	60.4	88.4	41.0	108.3	84.5	71.9	53.4	84.8	84.4
April	62.2	62.3	80.0	60.8	87.9	41.6	109.9	84.5	71.3	53.3	84.6	84.4
May	61.8	61.8	79.2	59.6	87.5	41.0	110.5	83.8	71.1	53.2	84.0	83.6
June	61.8	61.9	79.3	58.9	88.0	41.6	110.2	84.0	71.3	52.9	83.8	83.5
July	61.2	61.1	77.5	56.9	86.4	41.0	110.8	84.0	70.6	52.7	82.8	82.3
August	61.8	61.7	78.9	59.1	87.3	41.6	111.3	83.9	71.0	53.1	83.5	82.8
September	61.6	61.6	78.6	59.0	86.8	41.4	110.6	83.7	71.3	52.8	83.0	82.4
October	61.6	61.4	78.8	58.0	87.7	40.9	106.4	84.1	71.3	52.9	82.7	82.0
November	61.8	61.6	79.1	58.4	88.0	41.2	105.1	84.1	71.7	53.1	82.8	82.0
December	62.1	61.6	80.3	59.0	89.6	41.7	107.3	83.1	72.0	53.0	83.0	81.8
1990												
January	61.8	61.5	78.6	55.7	88.8	41.4	108.0	84.9	72.7	52.9	82.4	81.5
February	62.3	62.4	79.6	59.1	88.4	42.1	107.6	85.2	72.5	53.4	83.0	82.4
March	62.6	62.7	80.1	60.2	88.5	42.8	107.1	85.1	73.0	53.5	83.2	82.6
April	62.5	62.5	79.8	58.9	88.8	42.6	106.1	84.3	72.9	53.5	82.8	82.1
May	62.7	62.6	79.7	59.4	88.4	43.2	105.4	83.8	73.3	53.7	82.9	82.1
June	62.9	62.8	80.6	60.2	89.2	43.2	105.2	84.1	73.3	53.7	83.0	82.2
July	62.8	62.7	79.9	58.4	89.2	43.4	105.6	83.4	73.4	53.7	82.7	81.9
August	63.0	62.9	80.2	58.4	89.6	43.6	104.1	83.3	73.4	54.1	82.9	82.0
September	63.0	62.8	80.7	58.6	90.4	43.6	103.6	83.0	73.3	53.9	82.8	81.7
October	62.6	62.4	79.6	56.7	89.7	43.5	104.1	82.2	73.2	53.7	82.2	81.0
November	61.9	61.7	78.7	53.6	90.1	42.5	102.2	82.1	72.9	53.0	81.0	80.0
December	61.4	61.2	78.1	52.7	89.7	42.1	103.4	81.6	72.4	52.6	80.4	79.2
1991												
January	61.2	60.8	78.5	52.8	90.2	42.0	102.3	78.6	72.2	52.4	80.0	78.6
February	60.8	60.4	77.8	51.6	89.8	41.7	101.2	78.3	71.6	52.1	79.3	78.0
March	60.4	59.9	77.8	51.8	89.7	41.6	100.6	77.3	70.7	51.6	78.8	77.3
April	60.6	60.2	77.8	53.0	89.1	41.6	97.9	78.0	71.1	51.9	79.0	77.6
May	61.2	60.6	79.2	53.9	90.6	41.9	96.1	78.1	71.7	52.4	79.7	78.0
June	61.7	61.1	80.1	55.3	91.3	42.4	96.5	79.4	72.1	52.7	80.2	78.7
July	61.9	61.4	79.9	56.3	90.4	42.6	95.9	79.2	71.7	53.1	80.4	79.0
August	61.9	61.5	79.9	55.4	90.9	42.4	96.5	80.0	72.2	53.1	80.3	79.0
September	62.4	62.2	81.1	57.7	91.4	43.0	95.8	80.3	72.5	53.4	80.9	79.7
October	62.3	62.1	80.9	57.5	91.3	42.8	96.4	79.5	72.4	53.5	80.7	79.5
November	62.2	62.0	81.0	57.6	91.3	42.7	95.8	80.2	72.5	53.2	80.5	79.2
December	62.0	61.8	80.0	57.1	90.1	42.7	94.8	80.2	72.4	53.2	80.0	78.9

Table 2-4A. Industrial Production and Capacity Utilization, Historical Data, 1955–2021—*Continued*

(Seasonally adjusted.)

Year and month	Production indexes, 2007 = 100										Capacity utilization (output as percent of capacity)	
	Total industry	Manufac-turing (SIC)	Market groups								Total industry	Manufac-turing (SIC)
			Consumer goods			Business equipment	Defense and space equipment	Construction supplies	Business supplies	Materials		
			Total	Durable	Nondurable							
1992												
January	61.6	61.5	79.2	54.7	90.3	42.0	93.6	80.3	72.3	53.2	79.4	78.3
February	62.1	62.0	80.1	57.0	90.2	42.8	93.2	80.9	72.3	53.4	79.8	78.8
March	62.6	62.7	80.8	58.2	90.7	43.3	92.5	81.5	72.8	53.8	80.3	79.5
April	63.1	63.0	81.5	59.3	91.2	43.7	91.0	82.1	73.3	54.3	80.8	79.7
May	63.3	63.4	82.1	61.1	91.0	44.1	90.6	82.9	73.5	54.3	80.9	80.0
June	63.3	63.6	81.7	60.3	90.9	44.2	90.4	82.6	73.5	54.5	80.7	80.0
July	63.9	64.1	82.7	61.8	91.7	44.6	89.5	83.1	74.0	54.9	81.3	80.5
August	63.5	63.8	82.8	61.3	92.0	44.4	89.3	83.3	73.8	54.3	80.7	79.9
September	63.7	63.9	82.4	61.1	91.5	44.6	89.2	83.2	74.2	54.7	80.7	79.8
October	64.2	64.3	83.5	62.4	92.5	44.7	89.0	83.2	74.3	55.1	81.1	80.1
November	64.4	64.5	83.7	63.0	92.5	45.1	88.8	82.9	74.5	55.4	81.3	80.2
December	64.5	64.5	83.7	63.6	92.1	45.5	88.8	83.3	74.9	55.3	81.3	80.0
1993												
January	64.8	65.1	84.2	64.6	92.3	45.7	88.1	83.5	75.0	55.5	81.5	80.6
February	65.1	65.3	84.3	64.3	92.6	45.7	87.6	85.1	75.4	55.9	81.7	80.7
March	65.0	65.2	84.3	64.7	92.5	45.8	86.7	84.4	75.9	55.8	81.5	80.4
April	65.2	65.5	84.4	65.0	92.5	46.1	86.7	84.6	75.9	56.0	81.6	80.6
May	64.9	65.4	83.8	65.1	91.5	46.2	85.7	85.6	75.5	55.8	81.2	80.4
June	65.1	65.3	83.9	64.5	92.0	45.8	85.2	85.5	75.7	56.1	81.3	80.2
July	65.3	65.4	84.6	64.4	93.1	45.8	86.1	86.0	75.7	56.0	81.3	80.2
August	65.2	65.3	84.5	63.7	93.3	45.4	84.4	86.3	75.8	56.1	81.1	79.9
September	65.5	65.8	84.7	65.0	93.0	46.2	85.0	86.7	76.1	56.3	81.4	80.3
October	66.0	66.3	85.2	66.7	92.8	47.2	84.1	87.5	76.2	56.8	81.9	80.9
November	66.3	66.6	85.3	67.2	92.6	47.5	84.1	88.2	76.3	57.2	82.1	81.1
December	66.7	67.0	85.5	67.6	92.8	47.8	83.3	89.4	76.8	57.6	82.4	81.4
1994												
January	66.9	67.1	86.1	68.6	93.1	48.0	82.4	89.0	77.2	57.7	82.5	81.3
February	67.0	67.2	86.2	68.5	93.4	47.6	81.0	88.4	77.4	57.9	82.3	81.2
March	67.6	68.1	87.0	69.1	94.2	48.1	82.0	90.0	78.0	58.5	82.9	82.0
April	68.0	68.7	87.2	70.0	94.1	48.5	82.2	91.5	78.2	58.9	83.2	82.5
May	68.4	69.1	87.7	70.2	94.7	48.6	80.9	92.2	78.4	59.3	83.4	82.8
June	68.8	69.3	88.3	70.9	95.3	48.9	80.0	92.3	79.0	59.8	83.7	82.7
July	68.9	69.5	87.9	71.0	94.6	49.5	79.5	93.2	78.8	60.0	83.5	82.8
August	69.3	70.1	89.0	72.2	95.7	49.6	78.4	93.2	78.9	60.4	83.8	83.2
September	69.6	70.4	88.5	72.5	94.8	50.1	79.1	94.0	79.3	60.7	83.8	83.2
October	70.1	71.1	89.4	73.4	95.7	51.0	78.9	94.4	79.8	61.1	84.2	83.7
November	70.6	71.7	89.5	73.3	95.8	51.6	79.9	94.6	80.1	61.6	84.5	84.1
December	71.3	72.4	90.2	74.0	96.5	52.1	80.2	95.3	80.6	62.4	85.0	84.7
1995												
January	71.4	72.6	90.0	74.4	96.1	52.4	80.0	95.6	80.9	62.6	84.9	84.5
February	71.3	72.4	90.2	73.9	96.6	52.5	78.7	94.3	80.9	62.4	84.5	84.0
March	71.4	72.6	90.2	73.8	96.6	52.9	78.8	94.3	81.1	62.5	84.3	83.9
April	71.3	72.4	89.7	73.6	96.1	52.9	78.3	93.6	80.9	62.6	83.9	83.2
May	71.7	72.6	90.1	73.0	96.8	53.5	78.4	93.2	81.4	62.8	84.0	83.2
June	71.9	73.0	90.4	73.4	97.2	54.2	78.8	93.4	81.8	62.8	83.9	83.2
July	71.6	72.5	89.9	71.9	97.2	53.9	78.1	93.1	81.7	62.6	83.3	82.3
August	72.5	73.3	91.3	74.1	98.1	54.9	77.8	94.0	82.6	63.3	84.0	82.9
September	72.8	74.0	91.5	74.9	98.0	55.4	77.4	95.5	82.7	63.6	84.0	83.2
October	72.7	73.9	90.7	74.1	97.2	55.4	76.3	95.4	82.9	63.7	83.6	82.7
November	72.9	73.9	91.0	74.2	97.6	55.6	74.8	95.4	83.2	63.9	83.4	82.4
December	73.1	74.2	91.3	74.6	97.8	56.0	74.7	95.8	83.1	64.1	83.3	82.2
1996												
January	72.7	73.7	90.2	72.7	97.2	55.4	74.0	94.5	82.8	64.1	82.5	81.3
February	73.8	74.8	91.6	74.6	98.3	56.8	76.0	95.5	83.7	64.9	83.3	82.0
March	73.7	74.6	91.0	72.3	98.6	56.6	76.2	96.7	83.8	64.8	82.8	81.4
April	74.4	75.5	91.9	75.6	98.2	58.0	76.1	97.2	83.8	65.5	83.3	81.9
May	75.0	76.1	92.0	76.0	98.2	58.8	76.2	98.2	84.7	66.0	83.5	82.1
June	75.5	76.8	92.7	77.6	98.4	59.7	75.5	99.8	84.9	66.5	83.7	82.4
July	75.5	77.1	92.2	77.9	97.6	60.5	76.2	99.4	85.0	66.5	83.3	82.3
August	75.9	77.5	91.9	76.9	97.6	60.7	76.1	100.2	85.8	67.1	83.4	82.3
September	76.4	78.1	92.8	77.7	98.5	61.4	75.8	100.5	86.2	67.4	83.5	82.5
October	76.4	78.0	92.3	76.1	98.6	61.3	75.8	100.7	86.4	67.5	83.1	81.9
November	77.1	78.7	93.4	77.1	99.7	62.2	75.3	101.4	87.1	68.0	83.4	82.2
December	77.6	79.4	93.6	78.3	99.5	63.3	75.2	101.0	87.6	68.5	83.6	82.5
1997												
January	77.7	79.5	93.4	77.8	99.4	63.7	74.2	100.0	88.2	68.7	83.3	82.1
February	78.6	80.6	93.9	79.1	99.5	64.7	74.7	102.0	89.1	69.7	83.9	82.8
March	79.1	81.4	94.6	80.1	100.0	65.7	74.5	102.9	89.3	70.0	84.0	83.1
April	79.2	81.3	93.6	78.0	99.6	66.2	74.6	102.7	89.7	70.3	83.6	82.5
May	79.6	81.9	94.3	78.9	100.2	67.0	74.4	103.2	90.1	70.5	83.7	82.6
June	80.0	82.4	94.3	80.5	99.3	68.1	74.1	103.1	90.4	71.0	83.6	82.6
July	80.6	83.0	95.2	80.5	100.6	68.5	74.6	103.1	91.1	71.6	83.8	82.7
August	81.5	84.0	96.0	82.2	101.0	70.0	74.9	103.9	91.3	72.3	84.2	83.2
September	82.2	84.8	96.7	82.8	101.8	70.6	74.7	104.4	92.4	73.1	84.4	83.4
October	82.9	85.6	98.2	83.9	103.4	71.6	75.1	105.0	93.4	73.4	84.6	83.5
November	83.6	86.4	98.4	86.0	102.7	72.9	74.7	105.3	93.6	74.2	84.8	83.7
December	84.0	86.9	98.1	85.8	102.4	73.4	75.8	106.7	94.1	74.7	84.6	83.6

Table 2-4A. Industrial Production and Capacity Utilization, Historical Data, 1955–2021—*Continued*

(Seasonally adjusted.)

Year and month	Total industry	Manufac-turing (SIC)	Consumer goods Total	Durable	Nondurable	Business equipment	Defense and space equipment	Construction supplies	Business supplies	Materials	Total industry	Manufac-turing (SIC)
1998												
January	84.3	87.5	98.6	86.2	102.8	74.4	76.3	107.3	94.0	74.9	84.4	83.6
February	84.5	87.7	98.4	86.0	102.7	74.7	76.7	108.0	94.3	75.0	84.0	83.1
March	84.5	87.5	98.5	86.2	102.7	75.1	76.3	107.2	94.8	74.9	83.5	82.4
April	84.8	88.0	99.1	86.5	103.5	75.3	76.4	107.7	95.1	75.1	83.3	82.2
May	85.4	88.4	99.5	87.2	103.7	75.7	77.2	109.0	95.9	75.6	83.3	82.0
June	84.8	87.8	98.5	83.2	104.1	75.8	77.5	108.5	96.0	75.1	82.3	80.8
July	84.5	87.4	97.6	79.8	104.4	75.3	78.7	109.2	96.6	74.7	81.5	80.0
August	86.2	89.5	100.3	89.1	104.1	77.6	79.1	109.5	97.1	76.2	82.7	81.4
September	86.2	89.4	99.6	89.2	103.0	77.6	78.5	109.3	97.3	76.4	82.2	80.9
October	86.8	90.2	100.0	90.8	102.8	78.5	80.2	110.2	97.4	77.0	82.4	81.1
November	86.7	90.3	99.3	90.5	101.9	78.5	79.8	110.4	97.7	77.2	81.9	80.8
December	87.1	90.8	99.4	91.2	101.7	78.7	79.3	111.8	97.7	77.8	81.9	80.9
1999												
January	87.4	91.1	100.4	91.3	103.1	78.6	78.8	111.1	98.5	78.0	81.9	80.7
February	87.9	91.9	100.8	92.1	103.4	79.3	79.3	111.3	98.8	78.5	82.0	81.0
March	88.1	91.9	100.6	91.8	103.2	79.2	79.2	110.1	99.1	79.1	81.8	80.6
April	88.3	92.2	100.5	92.8	102.5	79.7	78.2	110.5	99.3	79.4	81.7	80.5
May	88.8	92.9	101.4	93.7	103.5	80.5	77.3	110.7	99.6	79.8	81.9	80.8
June	88.8	92.7	100.4	93.2	102.3	80.3	76.3	110.8	99.8	80.3	81.5	80.2
July	89.3	93.1	100.1	93.5	101.7	80.8	75.9	111.6	100.3	81.2	81.7	80.2
August	89.7	93.7	101.3	95.6	102.6	81.4	75.4	111.6	100.4	81.3	81.8	80.4
September	89.3	93.3	100.6	94.1	102.1	81.0	73.5	111.6	100.4	81.0	81.1	79.7
October	90.5	94.7	102.5	97.2	103.5	81.7	72.8	113.0	101.2	82.0	81.9	80.6
November	91.0	95.3	102.4	96.5	103.7	81.8	71.3	113.6	101.8	82.9	82.0	80.8
December	91.7	96.0	103.6	96.6	105.3	82.5	70.3	114.8	102.6	83.4	82.4	81.0
2000												
January	91.6	96.0	102.2	98.4	102.6	83.7	70.3	115.1	102.7	83.6	82.1	80.7
February	92.0	96.2	103.0	98.0	103.8	84.4	68.6	115.4	102.9	83.8	82.1	80.6
March	92.3	96.9	102.6	97.7	103.5	85.5	68.0	115.5	103.6	84.3	82.1	80.8
April	92.9	97.5	103.5	99.0	104.1	86.5	66.6	116.0	104.6	84.6	82.3	80.9
May	93.2	97.5	103.6	98.6	104.6	87.3	65.9	114.3	104.7	85.0	82.3	80.6
June	93.2	97.6	103.7	98.2	104.8	87.4	66.4	113.8	104.6	85.1	82.1	80.4
July	93.0	97.7	103.3	96.8	104.8	87.9	67.8	114.3	104.5	84.7	81.7	80.2
August	92.8	97.1	102.8	96.5	104.3	87.5	66.0	113.5	104.3	84.7	81.2	79.3
September	93.2	97.5	103.8	96.7	105.5	88.2	63.8	113.6	104.2	84.9	81.2	79.4
October	92.8	97.1	102.7	95.6	104.4	88.3	66.2	113.2	103.9	84.8	80.7	78.8
November	92.8	96.9	103.0	93.7	105.7	88.0	68.3	112.9	104.1	84.6	80.4	78.3
December	92.5	96.3	103.6	92.3	107.1	87.4	68.9	111.2	103.6	84.1	79.9	77.5
2001												
January	92.0	95.8	102.7	90.7	106.5	87.3	70.9	111.9	103.7	83.3	79.2	76.9
February	91.4	95.2	102.0	90.3	105.7	86.7	70.7	110.5	102.1	82.9	78.4	76.1
March	91.2	94.9	102.0	92.5	104.8	86.1	72.7	110.6	101.4	82.6	78.0	75.6
April	90.9	94.6	102.4	92.6	105.2	84.2	73.3	110.4	100.7	82.4	77.5	75.1
May	90.4	94.0	102.4	93.3	104.9	82.8	73.8	109.7	100.2	81.9	76.9	74.5
June	89.9	93.5	102.4	92.8	105.2	81.7	75.0	109.0	99.9	81.1	76.2	73.8
July	89.3	93.0	101.9	93.1	104.3	80.9	75.9	109.0	99.7	80.4	75.6	73.3
August	89.2	92.6	102.1	92.5	104.9	79.4	74.9	107.7	99.4	80.8	75.3	72.8
September	88.7	92.2	101.5	91.6	104.5	78.1	75.3	107.5	99.3	80.4	74.7	72.4
October	88.5	91.8	102.1	90.9	105.5	77.0	75.3	106.5	99.0	80.0	74.3	71.9
November	88.0	91.5	101.9	92.4	104.7	76.3	74.4	106.1	98.2	79.5	73.8	71.6
December	87.9	91.7	102.5	94.5	104.6	75.6	74.5	106.9	98.3	79.2	73.6	71.6
2002												
January	88.5	92.3	103.5	94.9	105.9	75.4	73.8	106.8	98.1	80.1	74.0	72.0
February	88.5	92.3	102.9	95.2	104.9	75.2	73.4	107.0	98.2	80.5	73.9	71.9
March	89.2	92.9	103.7	96.2	105.7	75.5	73.2	108.7	99.0	81.2	74.3	72.4
April	89.6	93.2	103.6	97.6	104.9	75.2	73.3	108.7	99.7	82.1	74.6	72.6
May	90.0	93.7	104.0	98.0	105.2	75.5	73.2	109.1	100.2	82.5	74.9	72.9
June	90.8	94.6	105.0	99.1	106.3	76.0	74.0	109.9	100.6	83.2	75.5	73.6
July	90.7	94.5	105.1	100.3	105.8	75.8	74.4	108.6	100.8	83.2	75.4	73.5
August	90.6	94.5	104.4	99.4	105.2	76.2	74.7	108.9	100.7	83.2	75.3	73.6
September	90.7	94.6	104.5	99.4	105.4	76.2	75.8	109.9	101.3	83.1	75.4	73.6
October	90.5	94.3	104.4	98.9	105.5	75.9	76.6	109.4	101.8	82.7	75.2	73.4
November	91.0	94.8	105.2	101.2	105.5	76.2	76.2	109.4	101.6	83.3	75.6	73.7
December	90.5	94.2	104.2	99.5	104.9	75.4	79.0	108.6	101.5	83.0	75.3	73.3
2003												
January	91.2	95.0	105.5	101.2	106.0	75.6	78.9	109.0	102.5	83.5	75.9	73.9
February	91.3	94.9	105.9	99.6	107.3	75.6	80.0	108.2	102.6	83.5	76.0	73.8
March	91.1	94.9	105.9	99.9	107.1	75.7	80.0	107.7	102.4	83.0	75.8	73.9
April	90.5	94.2	105.1	99.0	106.4	75.0	79.5	106.6	101.5	82.7	75.4	73.3
May	90.5	94.3	104.8	99.0	105.9	74.9	80.1	108.0	101.7	82.6	75.4	73.4
June	90.6	94.7	105.0	100.0	105.8	75.2	80.1	108.4	101.2	82.7	75.5	73.7
July	91.1	95.0	106.0	102.5	106.2	75.6	79.6	107.9	101.8	83.0	75.9	74.0
August	90.8	94.5	105.1	100.5	105.8	75.7	79.9	108.6	101.5	83.0	75.8	73.7
September	91.4	95.3	106.0	103.1	106.0	76.5	80.1	108.3	101.6	83.6	76.3	74.3
October	91.6	95.4	105.3	102.4	105.3	76.4	79.9	108.9	102.1	84.1	76.4	74.4
November	92.2	96.3	106.0	103.6	105.7	77.6	79.3	110.1	102.6	84.6	76.9	75.1
December	92.3	96.2	106.2	103.6	106.0	77.6	77.4	110.2	102.4	84.7	77.0	75.1

Table 2-4A. Industrial Production and Capacity Utilization, Historical Data, 1955–2021—*Continued*

(Seasonally adjusted.)

Year and month	Production indexes, 2007 = 100										Capacity utilization (output as percent of capacity)	
			Market groups									
	Total industry	Manufac-turing (SIC)	Consumer goods			Business equipment	Defense and space equipment	Construction supplies	Business supplies	Materials	Total industry	Manufac-turing (SIC)
			Total	Durable	Nondurable							
2004												
January	92.4	96.1	106.5	104.7	106.0	77.7	75.2	110.0	102.9	84.9	77.1	75.0
February	93.0	96.9	107.1	104.5	106.9	78.7	76.6	110.0	103.7	85.3	77.6	75.6
March	92.6	96.8	106.0	103.6	105.8	78.6	76.9	110.1	103.0	85.2	77.3	75.6
April	93.0	97.2	106.7	103.6	106.7	78.8	76.9	109.8	103.7	85.5	77.7	75.9
May	93.6	97.8	107.1	102.8	107.7	79.5	77.4	111.1	104.3	86.2	78.2	76.5
June	92.9	97.2	105.7	100.5	106.5	79.4	76.5	110.3	104.3	85.6	77.6	76.0
July	93.6	98.1	106.0	101.0	106.8	81.0	77.8	111.6	104.9	86.2	78.2	76.7
August	93.7	98.5	106.4	101.8	107.1	80.7	78.4	111.8	104.9	86.2	78.3	77.0
September	93.8	98.5	106.4	101.1	107.3	81.0	79.8	110.9	104.7	86.4	78.4	77.0
October	94.6	99.4	107.4	103.3	107.9	81.6	79.8	112.7	105.2	87.2	79.0	77.6
November	94.8	99.4	107.3	101.9	108.2	81.3	80.6	112.3	105.6	87.7	79.2	77.5
December	95.6	100.2	108.0	103.0	108.9	82.1	81.5	112.4	106.4	88.4	79.8	78.0
2005												
January	95.9	100.8	108.3	102.1	109.5	83.4	81.4	113.6	107.3	88.4	80.0	78.4
February	96.6	101.7	109.0	104.4	109.6	84.3	84.3	114.5	107.4	89.1	80.5	79.0
March	96.5	101.2	108.5	102.5	109.6	84.3	85.9	113.3	107.4	89.1	80.3	78.5
April	96.7	101.6	108.4	101.5	109.9	85.3	87.4	115.4	108.1	88.9	80.4	78.7
May	96.8	101.9	109.0	101.5	110.7	86.1	86.7	115.5	108.1	88.7	80.4	78.8
June	97.2	102.1	110.0	102.1	111.7	85.9	87.4	114.5	108.5	89.0	80.6	78.7
July	96.9	101.8	109.6	100.2	111.8	85.4	86.8	115.4	108.2	88.8	80.3	78.3
August	97.2	102.3	110.1	103.1	111.5	86.5	87.6	115.9	108.5	88.8	80.4	78.6
September	95.3	101.2	110.2	105.3	110.9	83.9	84.2	117.6	108.5	85.3	78.8	77.6
October	96.5	102.6	110.1	106.3	110.5	88.4	84.9	120.0	108.9	86.4	79.6	78.5
November	97.6	103.5	110.0	104.9	110.9	89.6	85.3	120.9	109.4	88.2	80.4	79.0
December	98.0	103.6	110.8	103.7	112.3	88.9	85.7	120.8	109.7	88.9	80.6	79.0
2006												
January	98.2	104.5	109.9	105.0	110.6	90.5	83.7	122.3	110.0	89.2	80.7	79.5
February	98.2	104.2	109.4	103.2	110.6	90.9	84.6	121.1	109.9	89.6	80.6	79.1
March	98.5	104.2	110.0	104.1	111.1	91.7	82.5	120.9	110.3	89.6	80.7	79.0
April	98.8	104.6	110.3	103.9	111.5	93.2	83.0	120.3	110.3	89.7	80.8	79.2
May	98.8	104.3	110.1	103.3	111.5	93.2	82.6	119.4	110.2	89.9	80.7	78.8
June	99.1	104.6	110.6	104.0	112.0	94.0	83.4	118.9	110.2	90.2	80.8	78.9
July	99.0	104.2	109.7	100.2	112.0	94.7	85.0	119.3	110.1	90.3	80.6	78.5
August	99.5	104.9	110.7	103.0	112.4	95.5	85.0	118.4	109.9	90.6	80.8	78.9
September	99.3	105.0	110.2	101.3	112.3	95.6	86.1	118.2	109.8	90.4	80.4	78.8
October	99.2	104.5	110.0	99.9	112.6	95.8	87.5	117.0	110.0	90.2	80.1	78.2
November	99.1	104.6	110.2	100.4	112.6	96.2	89.3	116.7	109.6	90.0	79.9	78.1
December	100.1	106.1	110.8	102.8	112.6	97.7	91.1	119.8	110.5	90.9	80.5	79.1
2007												
January	99.7	105.7	110.1	100.1	112.6	96.0	93.5	117.9	110.6	90.9	80.0	78.6
February	100.7	106.1	111.4	101.3	113.9	96.8	94.3	118.1	111.5	91.8	80.6	78.7
March	100.9	107.0	110.5	101.9	112.5	98.6	93.4	119.5	111.8	92.1	80.6	79.1
April	101.6	107.7	111.1	103.7	112.6	99.6	95.9	119.0	112.7	92.8	81.0	79.4
May	101.6	107.6	110.7	103.1	112.3	99.7	98.1	118.7	112.2	93.2	80.9	79.2
June	101.7	108.0	110.8	104.4	112.0	99.7	101.5	119.3	111.5	93.1	80.8	79.2
July	101.6	108.0	110.5	103.3	112.0	99.8	102.8	118.8	110.6	93.2	80.6	79.0
August	101.8	107.7	110.2	103.0	111.8	100.0	104.6	118.3	110.7	93.7	80.7	78.6
September	102.0	108.0	110.1	101.6	112.1	101.5	107.2	118.4	111.2	93.8	80.8	78.7
October	101.7	107.8	109.1	101.3	110.9	101.1	107.4	117.7	111.0	93.9	80.5	78.5
November	102.3	108.4	109.1	101.7	110.7	101.9	109.5	117.7	111.4	94.8	81.0	78.8
December	102.3	108.5	108.8	101.7	110.3	102.9	110.2	117.8	110.9	94.8	81.0	78.8
2008												
January	102.2	108.2	108.5	99.2	110.8	103.3	111.0	117.8	110.9	94.5	81.0	78.6
February	101.8	107.5	108.3	98.7	110.8	103.3	110.7	115.4	110.8	94.1	80.7	78.0
March	101.4	106.9	106.8	96.0	109.6	104.1	111.1	113.9	110.2	94.1	80.5	77.6
April	100.7	105.9	106.1	93.7	109.5	102.2	110.9	111.8	109.3	93.8	80.0	76.9
May	100.1	105.3	105.5	92.7	109.0	102.5	110.5	110.6	108.5	93.1	79.5	76.5
June	99.9	104.6	105.3	93.4	108.5	101.8	111.7	109.4	107.6	93.1	79.4	76.1
July	99.5	103.5	104.6	91.3	108.3	99.9	110.4	109.2	106.9	93.1	79.0	75.3
August	97.9	102.2	102.7	87.3	107.2	98.0	110.2	106.9	106.2	91.5	77.7	74.5
September	93.7	98.7	102.0	86.5	106.5	90.2	107.8	104.1	104.6	85.5	74.3	72.0
October	94.6	98.0	102.3	84.4	107.6	87.7	107.7	102.4	103.7	88.0	74.9	71.6
November	93.3	95.6	101.4	81.1	107.6	88.9	107.1	97.3	101.4	86.6	73.9	69.9
December	90.7	92.4	99.4	77.4	106.2	89.7	106.5	91.9	97.9	83.4	71.7	67.7
2009												
January	88.5	89.4	97.0	68.7	106.1	84.7	106.0	87.8	96.3	81.9	69.8	65.6
February	87.9	89.3	97.1	70.3	105.7	84.3	105.2	86.3	95.2	81.4	69.3	65.6
March	86.6	87.7	96.6	70.1	105.0	82.5	103.5	83.4	94.1	79.9	68.1	64.5
April	85.9	87.1	96.3	70.3	104.6	80.9	103.0	81.9	93.7	79.3	67.5	64.1
May	85.0	86.2	95.0	67.3	104.0	78.6	102.9	81.6	93.2	78.8	66.8	63.5
June	84.7	86.0	94.6	66.6	103.7	78.0	103.3	81.6	93.4	78.6	66.6	63.4
July	85.7	87.3	95.9	73.4	102.9	78.9	104.8	81.9	93.2	79.7	67.3	64.5
August	86.6	88.2	96.7	74.3	103.7	79.8	105.7	82.5	93.7	80.9	68.1	65.3
September	87.4	89.1	97.5	77.6	103.6	80.3	107.0	82.3	94.1	81.7	68.7	66.0
October	87.5	89.2	97.8	76.3	104.4	80.6	106.5	80.8	94.7	81.9	69.0	66.1
November	87.9	90.1	97.2	77.7	103.1	80.5	106.9	82.5	95.0	82.8	69.3	66.9
December	88.2	90.0	97.1	77.2	103.2	81.9	107.3	80.6	95.9	83.1	69.7	66.9

Table 2-4A. Industrial Production and Capacity Utilization, Historical Data, 1955–2021—*Continued*

(Seasonally adjusted.)

Year and month	Production indexes, 2007 = 100										Capacity utilization (output as percent of capacity)	
	Total industry	Manufac-turing (SIC)	Market groups								Total industry	Manufac-turing (SIC)
			Consumer goods			Business equipment	Defense and space equipment	Construction supplies	Business supplies	Materials		
			Total	Durable	Nondurable							
2010												
January	89.2	90.9	97.7	78.1	103.7	83.1	109.7	82.2	96.3	84.2	70.6	67.7
February	89.5	90.8	96.9	76.8	103.1	82.7	110.5	82.3	96.3	85.3	71.0	67.7
March	90.1	92.0	97.2	77.9	103.2	84.3	113.4	83.7	96.4	85.7	71.7	68.7
April	90.5	92.7	96.4	78.1	102.0	85.3	114.5	86.2	97.1	86.2	72.1	69.4
May	91.7	93.9	98.2	81.0	103.4	86.8	114.4	86.5	97.8	87.4	73.2	70.4
June	91.9	93.9	98.0	80.3	103.3	87.3	114.1	86.4	97.9	87.9	73.5	70.5
July	92.3	94.4	98.6	83.5	103.1	88.1	115.8	86.0	97.8	88.1	74.0	71.0
August	92.6	94.5	98.4	81.1	103.6	88.2	115.9	86.5	97.7	88.9	74.4	71.2
September	92.9	94.6	98.0	81.1	103.1	88.6	114.1	86.6	97.8	89.5	74.7	71.4
October	92.6	94.6	98.0	81.5	103.0	88.8	112.3	86.7	97.2	89.1	74.6	71.5
November	92.7	94.7	97.5	80.2	102.7	88.8	111.9	87.4	98.2	89.3	74.7	71.7
December	93.6	95.2	98.6	80.0	104.2	89.5	111.2	86.3	98.7	90.4	75.5	72.1
2011												
January	93.4	95.2	98.6	80.8	104.0	90.2	110.8	85.9	98.2	90.0	75.3	72.3
February	93.0	95.4	98.4	82.8	103.1	90.4	110.0	85.5	98.1	89.4	75.0	72.5
March	94.0	96.0	98.7	84.3	103.0	90.1	109.3	86.3	98.4	91.1	75.8	73.0
April	93.7	95.5	98.5	80.9	103.8	89.5	108.9	86.3	98.3	90.7	75.5	72.6
May	93.8	95.5	98.7	81.9	103.7	90.2	108.8	87.4	98.2	90.6	75.6	72.6
June	94.0	95.6	98.6	81.5	103.7	90.3	108.1	87.6	98.0	91.2	75.7	72.7
July	94.5	96.1	99.3	82.8	104.2	91.5	108.7	88.5	98.3	91.3	76.0	73.1
August	95.1	96.6	99.9	83.7	104.7	92.6	109.4	88.3	98.7	92.0	76.4	73.5
September	95.1	96.9	99.3	83.7	103.9	93.1	109.2	88.5	99.0	91.9	76.3	73.6
October	95.7	97.4	99.5	85.3	103.8	94.4	110.4	88.7	98.6	92.9	76.7	74.0
November	95.7	97.2	98.6	83.9	103.0	95.2	112.2	88.8	97.7	93.3	76.5	73.8
December	96.2	97.8	98.5	84.4	102.7	96.7	111.8	89.4	98.2	93.9	76.8	74.2
2012												
January	96.8	98.7	98.4	86.6	101.9	98.3	112.1	90.7	98.6	94.6	77.1	74.7
February	97.1	99.1	98.3	86.1	101.9	99.0	113.2	91.5	99.0	94.9	77.2	74.9
March	96.6	98.5	96.7	85.1	100.2	99.9	113.2	91.2	98.2	94.7	76.6	74.4
April	97.3	99.0	97.5	85.5	101.0	100.8	111.8	92.6	99.1	95.3	77.1	74.7
May	97.5	98.7	98.0	84.8	102.0	101.5	110.5	91.6	99.2	95.4	77.1	74.4
June	97.5	98.9	97.7	85.0	101.5	102.8	109.6	90.9	99.3	95.3	76.9	74.5
July	97.7	98.7	97.8	84.9	101.7	101.7	112.0	90.5	99.2	96.0	77.0	74.3
August	97.3	98.6	97.3	83.9	101.3	102.4	112.0	91.0	98.9	95.3	76.5	74.1
September	97.2	98.4	97.0	82.9	101.2	102.1	111.6	90.8	98.6	95.5	76.4	73.8
October	97.6	98.2	97.0	83.8	101.0	101.1	111.8	90.5	98.6	96.3	76.5	73.6
November	98.0	98.8	97.5	84.9	101.2	102.3	112.1	91.8	99.0	96.5	76.7	74.0
December	98.2	99.5	97.4	86.7	100.6	103.1	111.8	92.2	99.1	96.9	76.8	74.5
2013												
January	98.2	99.2	97.4	86.1	100.8	101.1	110.9	92.7	99.2	97.2	76.7	74.3
February	98.7	99.7	97.9	88.1	100.8	102.0	110.7	94.1	99.4	97.6	76.9	74.5
March	99.1	99.6	98.5	89.0	101.3	102.4	109.9	93.7	99.6	98.0	77.2	74.4
April	99.0	99.3	98.2	88.6	101.0	101.8	109.4	93.3	99.8	98.1	77.0	74.2
May	99.1	99.6	98.1	89.1	100.7	101.3	108.2	93.2	100.5	98.4	77.0	74.4
June	99.2	99.7	98.4	90.3	100.8	101.2	108.3	94.0	100.4	98.4	77.0	74.5
July	98.9	98.9	97.4	88.0	100.2	99.4	107.2	93.9	100.3	98.7	76.7	73.9
August	99.5	99.8	97.9	90.6	100.1	100.9	107.6	94.4	100.8	99.2	77.1	74.6
September	100.0	99.9	98.2	91.0	100.3	101.7	107.3	95.4	100.9	99.9	77.5	74.7
October	99.9	100.0	98.5	91.2	100.7	101.3	107.6	95.3	101.0	99.6	77.3	74.8
November	100.1	100.0	98.5	92.2	100.4	101.0	105.9	96.0	100.8	100.2	77.5	74.8
December	100.4	99.8	99.2	92.2	101.4	100.2	105.0	94.4	101.3	100.5	77.6	74.7
2014												
January	100.0	98.8	97.6	89.4	100.1	100.4	103.8	94.1	100.7	100.7	77.3	73.9
February	100.7	99.7	98.8	92.5	100.7	101.8	103.9	94.6	101.1	101.3	77.8	74.7
March	101.7	100.5	99.4	93.4	101.2	102.9	104.9	95.9	101.5	102.5	78.5	75.4
April	101.8	100.5	99.0	92.6	100.9	102.7	104.4	95.3	101.3	102.9	78.5	75.4
May	102.2	100.8	98.9	94.4	100.2	103.3	104.4	96.9	101.6	103.5	78.7	75.7
June	102.6	101.1	98.9	94.8	100.1	102.9	104.1	97.6	101.4	104.2	79.0	76.0
July	102.8	101.6	99.0	97.2	99.6	104.2	104.9	98.5	101.3	104.4	79.1	76.4
August	102.6	101.0	98.5	94.4	99.7	103.3	103.8	98.4	100.9	104.5	78.9	76.0
September	103.0	101.0	98.9	94.2	100.3	102.8	104.5	98.8	101.0	104.9	79.0	76.1
October	103.0	100.9	98.6	93.8	100.0	104.0	104.6	98.2	100.8	104.9	79.0	76.1
November	103.6	101.6	100.4	96.8	101.5	105.1	104.0	98.1	101.3	104.9	79.4	76.7
December	103.6	101.4	100.1	96.3	101.3	104.0	103.9	98.9	100.6	105.4	79.3	76.6
2015												
January	102.8	100.8	100.2	96.1	101.5	103.4	102.3	97.9	100.5	104.1	78.6	76.3
February	102.2	100.0	99.9	93.7	101.7	102.7	103.9	96.8	100.1	103.6	78.1	75.8
March	101.8	100.4	101.0	96.6	102.3	102.7	103.1	96.2	99.7	102.7	77.8	76.1
April	101.2	100.4	100.1	97.4	100.9	101.9	102.4	96.9	100.0	102.2	77.3	76.2
May	100.8	100.4	100.0	99.7	100.1	102.1	101.8	97.4	99.5	101.4	77.0	76.3
June	100.5	100.0	99.9	97.1	100.7	101.6	101.5	97.8	99.3	101.0	76.7	76.0
July	101.1	100.8	101.4	102.0	101.3	101.3	101.0	97.7	99.4	101.5	77.2	76.6
August	100.9	100.4	101.4	99.5	101.9	101.0	101.1	98.3	99.7	100.9	77.1	76.4
September	100.6	100.1	101.1	99.0	101.7	100.0	100.2	97.6	99.7	100.9	76.9	76.2
October	100.2	100.0	100.7	99.0	101.2	99.1	99.7	98.6	100.0	100.2	76.5	76.1
November	99.4	99.7	100.3	98.2	100.9	97.7	99.1	98.7	100.1	99.1	75.9	75.9
December	98.9	99.4	99.6	98.2	100.1	96.7	99.8	99.1	99.6	98.6	75.5	75.6

Table 2-4A. Industrial Production and Capacity Utilization, Historical Data, 1955–2021—Continued

(Seasonally adjusted.)

Year and month	Production indexes, 2007 = 100										Capacity utilization (output as percent of capacity)	
	Total industry	Manufac-turing (SIC)	Market groups								Total industry	Manufac-turing (SIC)
			Consumer goods			Business equipment	Defense and space equipment	Construction supplies	Business supplies	Materials		
			Total	Durable	Nondurable							
2016												
January	99.4	99.8	101.1	99.4	101.6	96.7	98.3	99.0	100.1	99.0	76.0	75.9
February	98.9	99.5	100.9	99.2	101.4	96.2	97.3	99.0	99.9	98.3	75.6	75.6
March	98.1	99.4	100.1	99.1	100.4	95.6	96.8	98.8	99.2	97.5	75.0	75.5
April	98.4	99.3	101.1	100.3	101.4	95.4	96.6	99.1	99.4	97.6	75.2	75.3
May	98.2	99.2	100.8	99.0	101.3	95.2	97.8	98.5	99.5	97.4	75.0	75.2
June	98.7	99.4	101.7	101.1	101.9	95.3	96.9	98.2	99.8	97.9	75.3	75.3
July	98.8	99.5	101.5	101.4	101.6	95.3	96.8	99.0	100.4	98.1	75.4	75.4
August	98.7	99.1	101.7	100.9	102.0	95.1	97.4	98.2	100.2	97.9	75.3	75.1
September	98.6	99.3	101.5	101.2	101.6	94.6	97.5	98.6	100.4	97.7	75.2	75.2
October	98.7	99.5	101.0	101.9	100.8	95.1	98.3	99.1	99.9	98.1	75.3	75.3
November	98.3	99.4	99.9	100.2	99.9	95.0	99.2	99.6	99.7	97.8	74.9	75.2
December	98.9	99.3	101.4	100.5	101.7	96.1	99.5	97.9	99.8	98.1	75.4	75.2
2017												
January	98.7	99.5	100.1	100.8	99.9	96.2	99.7	99.7	99.2	98.3	75.3	75.4
February	98.4	99.5	98.8	100.5	98.3	96.2	98.9	100.0	99.1	98.4	75.0	75.5
March	99.1	99.2	99.5	99.5	99.5	97.0	98.9	99.2	99.6	99.2	75.6	75.3
April	100.1	100.3	100.3	102.0	99.8	100.0	100.2	99.9	99.9	100.0	76.4	76.2
May	100.1	100.1	100.8	100.9	100.8	99.9	100.6	99.8	99.8	99.9	76.5	76.2
June	100.3	100.2	100.3	100.3	100.3	99.9	100.3	99.8	100.0	100.5	76.7	76.3
July	100.1	99.9	100.0	97.8	100.6	99.8	100.3	99.7	100.1	100.3	76.6	76.2
August	99.7	99.6	99.8	98.5	100.1	100.1	100.9	98.9	99.8	99.5	76.3	76.1
September	99.8	99.7	99.7	99.7	99.7	101.6	100.5	100.6	99.6	99.3	76.5	76.2
October	101.0	100.8	100.5	100.5	100.5	102.9	100.2	101.0	100.5	101.1	77.5	77.2
November	101.2	100.8	99.9	99.4	100.1	103.3	100.3	101.0	100.9	101.7	77.8	77.2
December	101.4	100.5	100.3	100.0	100.4	103.2	99.4	100.6	101.3	101.8	78.0	77.1
2018												
January	101.3	100.1	100.7	100.1	100.9	103.8	99.1	98.8	101.0	101.5	78.0	76.9
February	101.7	101.1	100.1	102.2	99.6	104.4	98.7	101.7	101.5	102.1	78.3	77.7
March	102.3	101.1	100.5	104.5	99.4	104.6	98.3	100.9	101.8	103.1	78.8	77.8
April	103.4	101.8	102.2	104.9	101.5	105.7	99.8	101.9	102.6	104.0	79.7	78.4
May	102.5	101.0	99.5	100.6	99.2	103.6	99.4	102.5	102.0	104.0	79.0	77.8
June	103.3	101.5	100.4	103.4	99.6	105.0	100.8	102.3	102.3	104.7	79.6	78.3
July	103.5	101.7	100.3	101.5	100.0	104.5	101.3	102.2	102.5	105.3	79.8	78.4
August	104.2	102.0	101.2	103.9	100.4	104.7	103.2	102.5	102.5	106.2	80.3	78.6
September	104.2	101.9	101.1	105.2	100.0	104.2	104.7	101.8	102.5	106.3	80.3	78.6
October	104.0	101.5	101.2	103.9	100.4	103.3	105.7	101.8	102.3	106.2	80.1	78.3
November	104.0	101.1	101.2	103.3	100.6	101.8	106.3	101.4	101.6	106.5	80.0	78.0
December	103.9	101.2	101.0	105.4	99.7	100.9	109.9	102.2	101.0	106.5	79.9	78.1
2019												
January	103.3	100.4	100.2	100.3	100.2	99.5	110.8	101.9	101.1	105.9	79.4	77.5
February	102.8	100.0	100.6	101.5	100.3	98.6	111.2	100.1	100.4	105.3	78.9	77.2
March	102.9	99.9	101.1	101.5	100.9	98.3	112.2	100.1	100.1	105.3	78.9	77.2
April	102.4	99.3	99.7	101.6	99.2	96.2	113.5	99.7	99.8	105.5	78.5	76.7
May	102.6	99.3	100.3	102.7	99.6	95.7	113.9	100.4	100.1	105.6	78.5	76.8
June	102.6	99.7	100.9	103.9	100.1	95.8	116.0	101.3	99.5	105.1	78.5	77.1
July	102.2	99.1	100.6	102.8	100.0	94.4	116.3	100.6	99.7	104.7	78.1	76.6
August	102.9	99.7	101.0	103.9	100.1	95.3	116.8	100.9	100.2	105.7	78.5	77.2
September	102.6	99.0	100.2	101.9	99.7	93.7	117.8	100.6	100.3	105.8	78.2	76.6
October	101.8	98.2	100.0	98.5	100.4	93.1	118.6	99.7	99.8	104.5	77.5	76.1
November	102.1	98.9	101.3	104.5	100.4	94.5	119.2	99.2	100.0	104.1	77.7	76.6
December	101.8	98.8	100.4	102.9	99.8	94.2	120.7	100.1	100.1	103.8	77.4	76.5
2020												
January	101.3	98.7	100.1	104.6	98.8	91.7	116.8	102.4	100.7	103.3	77.0	76.5
February	101.7	99.0	101.2	107.3	99.4	91.5	118.1	102.4	101.3	103.3	77.3	76.8
March	97.9	94.7	96.3	91.0	97.9	85.3	116.2	99.0	96.8	100.7	74.3	73.5
April	85.0	80.2	85.2	56.6	93.6	65.4	102.7	88.2	85.5	88.0	64.5	62.3
May	86.3	83.7	88.9	67.8	95.1	71.2	109.7	91.6	86.5	86.6	65.6	65.0
June	91.8	89.9	96.6	95.5	96.9	79.4	109.9	92.9	89.9	91.3	69.8	69.8
July	95.2	93.1	101.1	111.2	98.1	83.6	110.6	94.4	92.9	94.5	72.5	72.4
August	96.1	94.6	101.8	110.5	99.2	85.7	112.7	95.6	94.1	95.0	73.3	73.6
September	96.1	94.7	100.3	108.8	97.9	85.5	113.2	96.0	94.8	95.6	73.3	73.7
October	96.8	95.7	100.7	109.2	98.2	86.0	115.5	98.1	96.4	96.2	74.0	74.6
November	97.1	96.2	100.7	111.0	97.7	86.8	116.8	98.1	95.9	96.7	74.4	75.1
December	98.1	96.5	102.2	111.0	99.7	87.6	115.6	99.4	96.7	97.6	75.3	75.4
2021												
January	99.3	98.0	103.3	113.4	100.3	90.3	120.6	100.4	96.7	98.5	76.4	76.6
February	96.2	94.6	101.0	106.2	99.4	88.1	120.6	97.0	95.1	94.3	74.2	74.0
March	98.9	97.5	102.2	109.0	100.2	90.4	123.6	100.7	96.7	98.0	76.3	76.4
April	99.0	97.3	101.7	106.4	100.3	89.2	122.9	99.8	97.0	99.0	76.6	76.3
May	99.8	98.2	102.2	108.0	100.6	90.9	122.1	99.5	97.4	99.9	77.3	77.0
June	100.2	98.1	102.1	107.1	100.7	90.2	125.5	99.1	97.6	100.9	77.7	77.0
July	100.9	99.2	102.7	110.3	100.5	92.7	128.3	100.2	98.2	101.1	78.2	77.8
August	100.8	98.9	102.5	108.6	100.8	92.7	127.1	100.6	98.8	100.9	78.2	77.7
September	99.8	98.2	101.6	104.7	100.7	92.2	126.1	101.9	98.3	99.4	77.4	77.1
October	101.4	99.8	102.4	109.7	100.3	92.9	127.6	103.3	99.1	101.6	78.6	78.3
November	102.0	100.4	103.0	110.8	100.8	93.4	128.1	104.8	99.9	102.1	79.0	78.7
December	101.8	100.3	102.6	110.2	100.5	94.2	127.0	105.0	99.1	101.9	78.7	78.6

Table 2-4B. Industrial Production: Historical Data, 1919–1947

(Seasonally adjusted, 2012 = 100.)

Year and month	January	February	March	April	May	June	July	August	September	October	November	December	Annual averages
1919													
Industrial production, total ...	4.88	4.66	4.53	4.61	4.63	4.93	5.23	5.31	5.20	5.15	5.07	5.15	4.94
Manufacturing	4.89	4.79	4.61	4.71	4.69	5.02	5.30	5.43	5.22	5.12	5.30	5.20	5.02
1920													
Industrial production, total ..	5.63	5.63	5.52	5.23	5.36	5.42	5.28	5.31	5.12	4.90	4.50	4.23	5.18
Manufacturing	5.74	5.74	5.61	5.28	5.45	5.45	5.25	5.28	5.15	4.87	4.35	4.05	5.18
1921													
Industrial production, total ..	3.99	3.91	3.80	3.80	3.91	3.88	3.85	3.99	4.02	4.26	4.20	4.18	3.98
Manufacturing	3.84	3.84	3.74	3.74	3.87	3.84	3.84	3.99	4.05	4.23	4.28	4.23	3.96
1922													
Industrial production, total ..	4.34	4.53	4.77	4.61	4.85	5.09	5.09	4.99	5.25	5.55	5.79	5.96	5.07
Manufacturing	4.33	4.43	4.64	4.84	5.10	5.33	5.38	5.17	5.33	5.56	5.76	5.94	5.15
1923													
Industrial production, total ..	5.82	5.90	6.09	6.22	6.31	6.25	6.20	6.09	5.96	5.93	5.93	5.79	6.04
Manufacturing	5.84	5.89	6.15	6.22	6.35	6.27	6.17	6.02	5.99	5.89	5.89	5.81	6.04
1924													
Industrial production, total ...	5.93	6.04	5.93	5.74	5.50	5.25	5.17	5.36	5.55	5.69	5.79	5.96	5.66
Manufacturing	5.92	6.04	5.94	5.79	5.51	5.22	5.15	5.33	5.53	5.69	5.81	6.02	5.66
1925													
Industrial production, total ..	6.14	6.14	6.14	6.20	6.17	6.12	6.28	6.17	6.09	6.33	6.47	6.55	6.23
Manufacturing	6.20	6.22	6.25	6.25	6.20	6.17	6.30	6.20	6.22	6.48	6.66	6.81	6.33
1926													
Industrial production, total ..	6.44	6.44	6.52	6.52	6.47	6.55	6.57	6.66	6.76	6.76	6.74	6.71	6.60
Manufacturing	6.66	6.61	6.58	6.58	6.53	6.61	6.61	6.68	6.81	6.76	6.71	6.68	6.65
1927													
Industrial production, total ..	6.68	6.74	6.82	6.66	6.71	6.68	6.60	6.60	6.49	6.36	6.36	6.39	6.59
Manufacturing	6.63	6.68	6.73	6.71	6.73	6.73	6.68	6.63	6.53	6.43	6.40	6.48	6.62
1928													
Industrial production, total ..	6.52	6.57	6.63	6.60	6.68	6.74	6.82	6.95	7.01	7.14	7.28	7.41	6.86
Manufacturing	6.61	6.68	6.71	6.68	6.79	6.86	6.97	7.12	7.14	7.27	7.43	7.55	6.98
1929													
Industrial production, total ..	7.52	7.49	7.52	7.65	7.79	7.84	7.95	7.87	7.81	7.68	7.30	6.98	7.62
Manufacturing	7.61	7.58	7.66	7.76	7.91	8.02	8.09	8.04	7.89	7.81	7.38	6.94	7.72
1930													
Industrial production, total ..	6.98	6.95	6.84	6.79	6.68	6.49	6.20	6.06	5.96	5.79	5.66	5.52	6.33
Manufacturing	7.02	6.97	6.73	6.84	6.71	6.53	6.22	5.99	5.94	5.74	5.58	5.45	6.31
1931													
Industrial production, total ..	5.50	5.52	5.63	5.66	5.58	5.44	5.36	5.17	4.93	4.74	4.69	4.66	5.24
Manufacturing	5.45	5.51	5.61	5.61	5.56	5.35	5.28	5.10	4.87	4.64	4.56	4.53	5.17
1932													
Industrial production, total ..	4.53	4.42	4.37	4.07	3.93	3.80	3.69	3.80	4.04	4.18	4.18	4.10	4.09
Manufacturing	4.48	4.35	4.20	3.94	3.84	3.71	3.59	3.69	3.94	4.05	4.07	3.99	3.99
1933													
Industrial production, total ..	4.02	4.04	3.80	4.07	4.74	5.47	5.98	5.74	5.42	5.15	4.85	4.88	4.85
Manufacturing	3.94	3.84	3.61	3.99	4.69	5.45	6.02	5.66	5.38	5.07	4.74	4.79	4.77
1934													
Industrial production, total ..	5.04	5.28	5.52	5.52	5.63	5.52	5.15	5.09	4.80	5.01	5.07	5.39	5.25
Manufacturing	4.94	5.22	5.43	5.53	5.61	5.48	5.04	5.02	4.74	4.92	4.99	5.35	5.19
1935													
Industrial production, total ..	5.82	5.93	5.90	5.79	5.79	5.87	5.87	6.09	6.25	6.44	6.57	6.66	6.08
Manufacturing	5.84	5.94	5.86	5.81	5.79	5.76	5.94	6.17	6.33	6.50	6.66	6.73	6.11
1936													
Industrial production, total ..	6.55	6.39	6.47	6.87	7.01	7.14	7.28	7.38	7.52	7.63	7.84	8.08	7.18
Manufacturing	6.61	6.40	6.53	6.94	7.12	7.27	7.40	7.53	7.66	7.78	7.99	8.25	7.29
1937													
Industrial production, total ..	8.06	8.16	8.35	8.35	8.38	8.27	8.33	8.27	8.00	7.41	6.68	6.09	7.86
Manufacturing	8.25	8.37	8.43	8.55	8.60	8.45	8.50	8.40	8.09	7.43	6.56	5.86	7.96
1938													
Industrial production, total ..	5.96	5.90	5.90	5.79	5.66	5.71	6.04	6.36	6.55	6.71	6.98	7.06	6.22
Manufacturing	5.76	5.74	5.76	5.58	5.56	5.56	5.89	6.27	6.48	6.68	6.99	7.04	6.11

Table 2-4B. Industrial Production: Historical Data, 1919–1947—*Continued*

(Seasonally adjusted, 2012 = 100.)

Year and month	January	February	March	April	May	June	July	August	September	October	November	December	Annual averages
1939													
Industrial production, total	7.06	7.11	7.14	7.11	7.09	7.25	7.46	7.57	8.03	8.43	8.65	8.65	7.63
Products	7.69	7.72	7.81	7.81	7.87	7.95	8.10	8.18	8.44	8.67	8.84	8.90	8.17
Consumer goods	11.78	11.78	11.97	11.97	12.01	12.12	12.28	12.32	12.51	12.63	12.74	12.78	12.24
Materials	6.18	6.28	6.28	6.08	6.06	6.35	6.62	6.69	7.45	8.17	8.31	8.31	6.90
Manufacturing	6.71	6.76	6.76	6.68	6.68	6.84	7.04	7.25	7.66	8.09	8.25	8.35	7.26
1940													
Industrial production, total	8.54	8.27	8.08	8.25	8.49	8.76	8.87	8.92	9.11	9.24	9.46	9.78	8.81
Products	8.81	8.73	8.64	8.73	8.84	9.04	9.04	9.16	9.42	9.59	9.76	10.11	9.16
Consumer goods	12.74	12.70	12.55	12.63	12.70	12.82	12.78	12.78	13.13	13.36	13.63	14.05	12.99
Materials	8.09	7.65	7.36	7.58	7.92	8.34	8.56	8.63	8.73	8.83	9.00	9.32	8.33
Manufacturing	8.22	7.96	7.78	7.86	8.19	8.55	8.66	8.78	8.96	9.09	9.24	9.58	8.57
1941													
Industrial production, total	10.02	10.32	10.64	10.67	11.16	11.24	11.37	11.51	11.51	11.61	11.67	11.86	11.13
Products	10.42	10.74	11.02	11.25	11.63	11.74	11.83	11.97	12.00	12.12	12.17	12.35	11.60
Consumer goods	14.33	14.75	15.14	15.41	15.87	15.91	15.91	15.95	15.87	15.87	15.91	15.91	15.57
Materials	9.44	9.71	10.05	9.83	10.45	10.59	10.74	10.81	10.81	10.86	10.94	11.16	10.45
Manufacturing	9.76	10.12	10.37	10.65	11.01	11.14	11.27	11.34	11.32	11.42	11.45	11.60	10.95
1942													
Industrial production, total	12.10	12.31	12.45	12.10	12.13	12.15	12.45	12.83	13.12	13.55	13.88	14.20	12.77
Products	12.72	13.03	13.18	12.35	12.37	12.43	12.78	13.15	13.61	14.10	14.56	15.02	13.27
Consumer goods	16.22	16.02	16.02	13.82	13.67	13.44	13.63	13.75	13.78	14.02	14.09	14.40	14.41
Materials	11.18	11.35	11.45	11.75	11.72	11.75	11.97	12.31	12.46	12.80	13.00	13.14	12.07
Manufacturing	11.86	12.14	12.32	11.96	12.01	12.09	12.47	12.88	13.27	13.75	14.14	14.52	12.78
1943													
Industrial production, total	14.34	14.71	14.82	15.01	15.12	15.04	15.49	15.82	16.22	16.46	16.68	16.46	15.51
Products	15.07	15.42	15.59	15.79	15.93	16.11	16.54	16.82	17.28	17.54	17.80	17.43	16.44
Consumer goods	13.98	14.09	14.13	14.29	14.52	14.75	14.98	15.06	15.17	15.06	15.02	14.71	14.65
Materials	13.34	13.68	13.83	13.95	13.93	13.58	14.10	14.37	14.74	14.98	15.10	15.10	14.23
Manufacturing	14.72	15.03	15.16	15.34	15.44	15.49	15.85	16.18	16.62	16.98	17.21	16.93	15.91
1944													
Industrial production, total	16.65	16.79	16.76	16.76	16.65	16.60	16.57	16.79	16.68	16.73	16.60	16.55	12.54
Products	17.66	17.83	17.83	17.89	17.86	17.91	18.06	18.26	18.12	18.14	17.91	17.77	12.62
Consumer goods	14.87	14.94	15.14	15.21	15.33	15.41	15.48	15.83	15.48	15.52	15.48	15.48	12.70
Materials	15.25	15.37	15.30	15.25	15.03	14.81	14.59	14.76	14.74	14.79	14.81	14.88	12.79
Manufacturing	17.18	17.31	17.29	17.26	17.13	17.11	17.11	17.34	17.23	17.29	17.13	17.13	12.87
1945													
Industrial production, total	16.38	16.33	16.22	15.93	15.49	15.14	14.79	13.26	12.07	11.59	12.02	12.07	13.11
Products	17.63	17.43	17.17	16.85	16.39	16.08	15.82	14.10	12.63	12.32	12.49	12.52	13.19
Consumer goods	15.72	15.60	15.56	15.68	15.72	15.83	15.79	15.10	15.83	16.06	16.53	16.72	13.27
Materials	14.71	14.86	14.88	14.66	14.27	13.90	13.39	12.14	11.23	10.62	11.35	11.48	13.35
Manufacturing	16.90	16.82	16.65	16.29	15.77	15.34	14.98	13.16	11.70	11.24	11.55	11.68	13.44
1946													
Industrial production, total	11.40	10.83	11.96	11.75	11.32	12.02	12.42	12.88	13.12	13.37	13.45	13.53	13.68
Products	12.37	12.26	12.55	12.75	12.60	12.75	13.03	13.46	13.84	14.07	14.21	14.35	13.76
Consumer goods	17.45	18.15	18.03	18.22	18.30	18.34	18.77	19.38	19.77	20.00	20.27	20.39	13.84
Materials	10.05	8.85	11.13	10.40	9.61	10.96	11.60	12.04	12.11	12.38	12.36	12.43	13.92
Manufacturing	10.88	10.19	11.47	11.50	10.96	11.57	11.96	12.50	12.75	13.03	13.19	13.24	14.00
1947													
Industrial production, total	13.69	13.77	13.85	13.74	13.80	13.80	13.72	13.80	13.90	14.04	14.23	14.28	14.25
Products	14.50	14.56	14.61	14.61	14.64	14.61	14.58	14.67	14.81	15.02	15.22	15.30	14.33
Consumer goods	19.96	19.89	19.96	19.89	19.73	19.77	19.85	20.00	20.19	20.50	20.81	20.85	14.41
Materials	12.43	12.53	12.95	12.63	12.68	12.55	12.43	12.41	12.58	12.68	12.97	12.82	14.49
Manufacturing	13.19	13.24	13.29	13.32	13.21	13.21	13.14	13.21	13.27	13.44	13.65	13.67	14.57

NOTES AND DEFINITIONS, CHAPTER 2

Tables 2-1 through 2-4

SOURCE: BOARD OF GOVERNORS OF THE FEDERAL RESERVE SYSTEM

Ever since the Federal Reserve was founded in 1913, understanding current business conditions has been a central focus in pursuing its mission of a stable and secure financial system. The index of industrial production is one of the oldest continuous statistical series maintained by the Federal government, and one of the few economic indicators for which monthly data are available before the post-World-War-II period.

The Federal Reserve's monthly index of industrial production and the related capacity indexes and capacity utilization rates cover manufacturing, mining, and electric and gas utilities. The industrial sector, together with construction, accounts for the bulk of the variation in national output over the course of the business cycle. The industrial detail provided by these measures helps illuminate structural developments in the economy.

Around the 15th day of each month, the Federal Reserve issues estimates of industrial production and capacity utilization for the previous month. The production estimates are in the form of index numbers (2012 = 100) that reflect the monthly levels of total output of the nation's factories, mines, and gas and electric utilities expressed as a percent of the monthly average in the 2012 base year. Capacity estimates are expressed as index numbers, 2012 output (not 2012 capacity) = 100, and capacity utilization is measured by the production index as a percent of the capacity index. Since, for each component industry, the bases of those two indexes are the same, this procedure yields production as a percent of capacity. Monthly estimates are subject to revision in subsequent months, as well as to annual and comprehensive revisions in subsequent years.

Definitions and notes on the data

The *industrial production index* measures changes in the physical volume or quantity of output of manufacturing, mining, and electric and gas utilities. *Capacity utilization* is calculated by dividing a seasonally adjusted industrial production index for an industry or group of industries by a related index of productive capacity.

The index of industrial production measures a large portion of the goods output of the national economy on a monthly basis. This portion, together with construction, has also accounted for the bulk of the variation in output over the course of many historical business cycles. The substantial industrial detail included in the index illuminates structural developments in the economy.

The total industrial production index and the indexes for its major components are constructed from individual industry series (312 series for data from 1997 forward) based on the 2012 North American Industry Classification System (NAICS). See the Preface to this volume for information on NAICS.

The Federal Reserve has been able to provide a longer continuous historical series on the NAICS basis than some other government agencies. In a major research effort, the Fed and the Census Bureau's Center for Economic Studies re-coded data from seven Censuses of Manufactures, beginning in 1963, to establish benchmark NAICS data for output, value added, and capacity utilization. The resulting indexes are shown annually for the last 48 years (52 years for aggregate levels) in Tables 2-1 through 2-4.

The Fed's featured indexes for total industry and total manufacturing are on the Standard Industrial Classification (SIC) basis and do <u>not</u> observe the reclassifications under NAICS of the logging industry to the Agriculture sector and the publishing industry to the Information sector. (The reason cited by the Fed was to avoid "changing the scope or historical continuity of these statistics.") One advantage of the SIC index for capacity utilization is that it is a continuous series back to 1949 (shown in Table 2-4A). On the new NAICS basis, production and capacity utilization are shown back to 1970 in Tables 2-2 and 2-3.

The individual series components of the indexes are grouped in two ways: market groups and industry groups.

Market groups. For analyzing market trends and product flows, the individual series are grouped into two major divisions: *final products and nonindustrial supplies* and *materials*. *Final products* consists of products purchased by consumers, businesses, or government for final use. *Nonindustrial supplies* are expected to become inputs in nonindustrial sectors: the two major subgroups are *construction supplies* and *business supplies*. *Materials* comprises industrial output that requires further processing within the industrial sector. This twofold division distinguishes between products that are ready to ship outside the industrial sector and those that will stay within the sector for further processing.

Final products are divided into *consumer goods* and *equipment*, and *equipment* is divided into *business equipment* and *defense and space equipment*. Further subdivisions of each market group are based on type of product and the market destination for the product.

Industry groups are typically groupings by 3-digit NAICS industries and major aggregates of these industries—for example, *durable goods* and *nondurable goods manufacturing, mining,* and *utilities*. Indexes are also calculated for *stage-of-process* industry groups—*crude, primary and semifinished,* and *finished* processing. The stage-of-process grouping was a new feature in the 2002 revision, replacing the two narrower and less well-defined "primary processing manufacturing" and "advanced processing manufacturing" groups that were previously published. *Crude processing* consists of logging, much of mining, and certain basic manufacturing activities in the chemical, paper, and metals industries. *Primary and semifinished processing* represents industries that produce materials and parts used as inputs by other industries. *Finished processing* includes industries that produce goods in their finished form for use by consumers, business investment, or government.

The indexes of industrial production are constructed using data from a variety of sources. Current monthly estimates of production are based on measures of physical output where possible and appropriate. For a few high-tech industries, the estimated value of nominal output is deflated by a corresponding price index. For industries in which such direct measurement is not possible on a monthly basis, output is inferred from production-worker hours, adjusted for trends in worker productivity derived from annual and benchmark revisions. (Between the 1960s and 1997, electric power consumption was used as a monthly output indicator for some industries instead of hours. However, the coverage of the electric power consumption survey deteriorated, and in the 2005 revision, the decision was made to resume the use of hours in those industries, beginning with the data for 1997.)

In annual and benchmark revisions, the individual indexes are revised using data from the quinquennial Economic Census which includes Manufactures and Mineral Industries, the Annual Survey of Manufactures, and the quarterly Survey of Plant Capacity, prepared by the Census Bureau; deflators from the Producer Price Indexes and other sources; the *Minerals Yearbook*, prepared by the Department of the Interior; publications from the Department of Energy; and other sources.

The weights used in compiling the indexes are based on Census value added—the difference between the value of production and the cost of materials and supplies consumed. Census value added differs in some respects from the economic concept of industry value added used in the national income and product accounts (NIPAs). Industry value added as defined in the NIPAs is not available in sufficient detail for the industrial production indexes. See Chapter 14 for data and a description of NIPA value added (equivalently, gross domestic product) by major industry group.

Before 1972, a linked-Laspeyres formula (base period prices) is used to compute the weighted individual indexes. Beginning with 1972, the index uses a version of the Fisher-ideal index formula—a chain-weighting (continually updated average price) system similar to that in the NIPAs. See the "General Notes" article at the front of this book and the notes and definitions for Chapter 1 for more information. Chain-weighting keeps the index from being distorted by the use of obsolete relative prices.

For the purpose of these value-added weights, value added per unit of output is based on data from the Censuses of Manufacturing and Mineral Industries, the Census Bureau's Annual Survey of Manufactures, and revenue and expense data reported by the Department of Energy and the American Gas Association, which are projected into recent years by using changes in relevant Producer Price Indexes.

To separate seasonal movements from cyclical patterns and underlying trends, each component of the index is seasonally adjusted by the Census X-12-ARIMA method.

The index does not cover production on farms, in the construction industry, in transportation, or in various trade and service industries. A number of groups and subgroups include data for individual series not published separately.

Capacity utilization is calculated for the manufacturing, mining, and electric and gas utilities industries. Output is measured by seasonally adjusted indexes of industrial production. The capacity indexes attempt to capture the concept of sustainable maximum output, which is defined as the greatest level of output that a plant can maintain within the framework of a realistic work schedule, taking account of normal downtime and assuming sufficient availability of inputs to operate the machinery and equipment in place. The 89 individual industry capacity indexes are based on a variety of data, including capacity data measured in physical units compiled by government agencies and trade associations, Census Bureau surveys of utilization rates and investment, and estimates of growth of the capital stock.

In the "Explanatory Note" to its monthly release, the statistics cover output, capacity, and capacity utilization in the U.S. industrial sector, which is defined by the Federal Reserve to comprise manufacturing, mining, and electric and gas utilities. Mining is defined as all industries in sector 21 of the North American Industry Classification System (NAICS); electric and gas utilities are those in NAICS sectors 2211 and 2212. Manufacturing comprises NAICS manufacturing industries (sector 31-33) plus the logging industry and the newspaper, periodical, book, and directory publishing industries. Logging and publishing are classified elsewhere in NAICS (under agriculture and information respectively), but historically they were considered to be manufacturing and were included in the industrial sector under the Standard Industrial Classification (SIC) system. In December 2002 the Federal Reserve reclassified all its industrial output data from the SIC system to NAICS.

Revisions

Revisions normally occur annual with the latest release on June 28, 2022. This revision incorporated newly available annual data on both output and prices. As noted earlier, the updated IP indexes incorporated new data for manufacturing from the U.S. Census Bureau's 2020 ASM. The monthly estimates of production have been updated to include late-arriving or revised quarterly or monthly indicator data, including information from the BLS's benchmark revisions to the Current Employment Statistics. The monthly IP estimates also reflect updated seasonal factors.

Data availability

Data are available monthly in Federal Reserve release G.17. Current and historical data and background information are available on the Federal Reserve Web site at <https://www.federalreserve.gov>.

Chain-weighting makes it difficult for the user to analyze in detail the sources of aggregate output change. An "Explanatory Note," included in each month's index release, provides some assistance for the user, including a reference to a an Internet location with the exact contribution of a monthly change in a component index to the monthly change in the total index.

References

The G.17 release each month contains extensive explanatory material, as well as references for further detail.

An earlier detailed description of the industrial production index, together with a history of the index, a glossary of terms, and a bibliography is presented in *Industrial Production—1986 Edition*, available from Publication Services, Mail Stop 127, Board of Governors of the Federal Reserve System, Washington, DC 20551.

CHAPTER 3: INCOME DISTRIBUTION AND POVERTY

SECTION 3A: HOUSEHOLD AND FAMILY INCOME

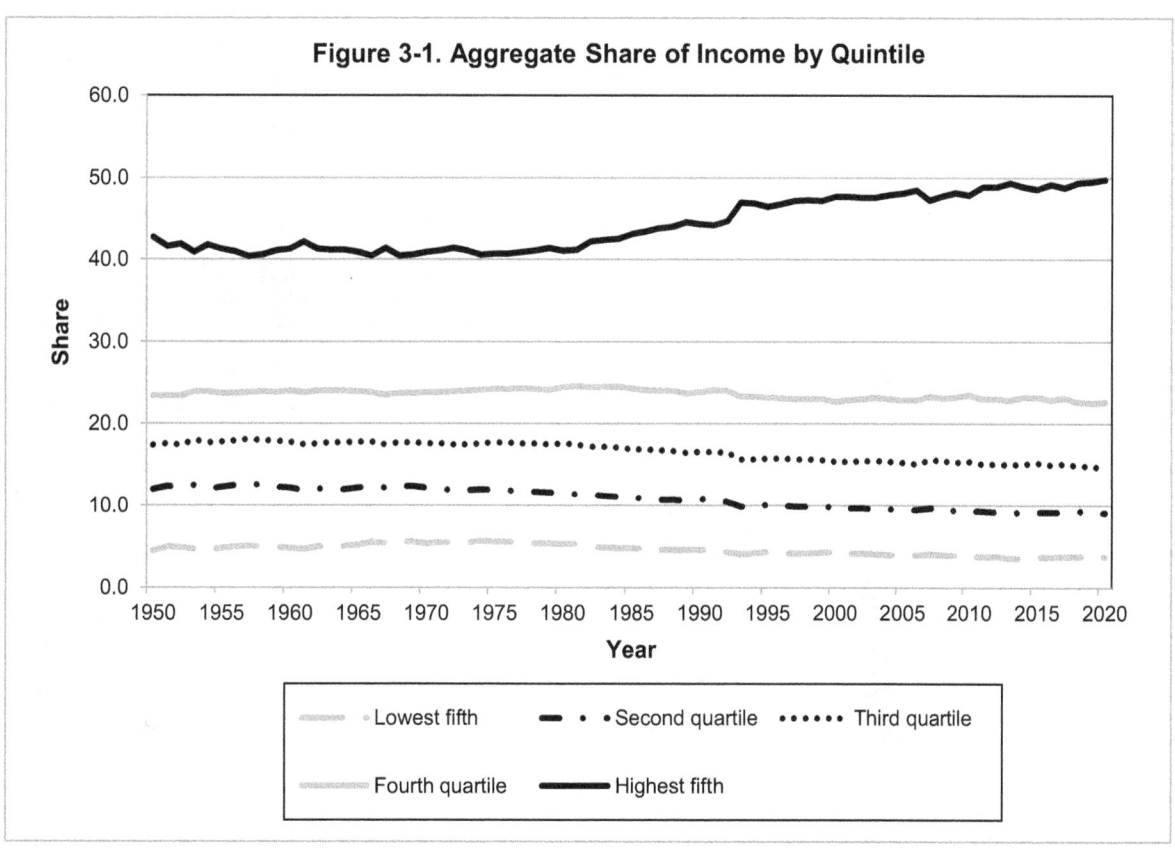

Figure 3-1. Aggregate Share of Income by Quintile

- The Census Bureau collects data on income and poverty in the United States based on information collected in the 2021 Current Population Survey Annual Social and Economic Supplements (CPS ASEC). The 2021 report provides estimates for calendar 2020—the first year of the economic downturn after the great recession. See the Notes Definition section at the end of Chapter 3 for how the pandemic disrupted the collection of this data.

- Tables 3-1 to 3-5 illustrates the impact of COVID-19. The American people experienced declining income regardless of gender, race, and ethnicity. In 2020, median household income was $67,521, a decrease of 2.9 percent from the 2019 median of $69,560. This is the first statistically significant decline in median household income since 2011.

- Asian Americans suffered the largest decline in median household income at 4.5 percent. In comparison, non-Hispanic Whites experienced a decline of 2.7 percent, Hispanics experienced a decline of 2.6 percent, and Blacks experienced a decline of 0.3 percent.

- Income inequality is the disparity of shares of aggregate income distributions across five quintiles. Table 3-3 depicts how the gap in U.S. income has widen for the bottom four-fifths of population, with the largest decline in the second quintile, a loss of nearly 30 percent between 1947 to 2020. The Gini Coefficient measures income distribution acres a population. It serves as a gage of income inequality. In 2020, income inequality worsened from 0.465 in 2019 to 0.469 in 2020. See Figure 3-1.

Table 3-1. Median and Mean Household Income and Median Earnings

(2020 dollars.)

Year	Number of households (thousands)	Average size of household (number of people)	Median household income						Mean household income, all races	Median earnings of year-round, full-time workers (2019 dollars)		
			All races	White		Black	Asian [1]	Hispanic (any race)		Male workers	Female workers	Ratio, female to male
				Total	Not Hispanic							
1980	82 368	2.73	53 116	56 037	57 030	32 284	. . .	40 942	63 172	55 821	33 582	0.602
1981	83 527	2.72	52 272	55 229	56 026	30 992	. . .	41 929	62 447	55 522	32 888	0.592
1982	83 918	2.73	52 130	54 575	55 490	30 930	. . .	39 226	62 824	54 472	33 633	0.617
1983	85 407	2.71	51 764	54 285	. . .	30 806	. . .	39 424	62 957	54 233	34 489	0.636
1984	86 789	2.69	53 337	56 269	57 437	32 055	. . .	40 433	65 351	55 248	35 169	0.637
1985	88 458	2.67	54 334	57 302	58 590	34 092	. . .	40 179	66 868	55 662	35 944	0.646
1986	89 479	2.66	56 291	59 181	60 526	34 095	. . .	41 493	69 545	57 103	36 700	0.643
1987	91 124	2.64	56 964	60 017	61 667	34 256	70 439	42 264	70 841	56 712	36 964	0.652
1988	92 830	2.62	57 433	60 716	62 389	34 612	68 070	42 949	71 761	56 233	37 141	0.660
1989	93 347	2.63	58 425	61 457	62 779	36 550	72 970	44 307	73 815	55 242	37 936	0.687
1990	94 312	2.63	57 677	60 158	61 533	35 974	74 063	43 013	72 047	53 314	38 182	0.716
1991	95 669	2.62	55 992	58 674	60 076	34 955	67 744	42 174	70 482	54 682	38 200	0.699
1992	96 426	2.66	55 559	58 411	60 372	34 012	68 553	40 980	70 437	54 763	38 764	0.708
1993	97 107	2.67	55 263	58 303	60 449	34 552	67 832	40 483	73 282	53 787	38 468	0.715
1994	98 990	2.65	55 905	58 961	60 864	36 434	70 144	40 582	74 738	53 462	38 475	0.720
1995	99 627	2.65	57 655	60 515	62 904	37 888	68 718	38 678	76 034	53 290	38 064	0.714
1996	101 018	2.64	58 494	61 244	63 924	38 700	71 322	41 047	77 662	52 976	39 076	0.738
1997	102 528	2.62	59 697	62 870	65 459	40 411	72 996	42 956	80 163	54 323	40 287	0.742
1998	103 874	2.61	61 891	65 118	67 548	40 350	74 230	45 091	82 535	56 257	41 163	0.732
1999	106 434	2.60	63 423	65 962	68 817	43 497	79 419	47 916	85 306	56 714	41 013	0.723
2000	108 209	2.58	63 292	66 195	68 768	44 718	84 043	49 995	86 120	56 151	41 394	0.737
2001	109 297	2.58	61 889	65 244	67 864	43 191	78 607	49 193	85 309	56 095	42 817	0.763
2002	111 278	2.57	61 190	. . .	. . .	. . .	. . .	47 763	83 472	56 890	43 578	0.766
2003	112 000	2.57	61 113	. . .	. . .	. . .	. . .	46 552	83 332	57 375	43 346	0.755
2004	113 343	2.57	60 901	. . .	. . .	. . .	. . .	47 078	83 062	56 041	42 914	0.766
2005	114 384	2.57	61 553	. . .	. . .	. . .	. . .	47 789	84 164	54 989	42 329	0.770
2006	116 011	2.56	62 033	. . .	. . .	. . .	. . .	48 623	85 673	54 389	41 846	0.769
2007	116 783	2.56	62 865	. . .	. . .	. . .	. . .	48 406	84 611	56 458	43 929	0.778
2008	117 181	2.57	60 624	. . .	. . .	. . .	. . .	45 692	82 464	55 881	43 079	0.771
2009	117 538	2.59	60 200	. . .	. . .	. . .	. . .	46 004	82 210	56 995	43 874	0.770
2010	119 927	2.56	58 627	. . .	. . .	. . .	. . .	44 772	80 180	57 050	43 888	0.769
2011	121 084	2.55	57 732	. . .	. . .	. . .	. . .	44 549	80 366	55 596	42 812	0.770
2012	122 459	2.54	57 623	. . .	. . .	. . .	. . .	44 055	80 503	55 794	42 684	0.765
2013	122 952	2.55	57 808	. . .	. . .	. . .	. . .	45 592	80 849	55 686	43 581	0.783
2014	124 587	2.54	58 725	. . .	. . .	. . .	. . .	46 505	82 892	55 142	43 364	0.786
2015	125 819	2.53	61 748	. . .	. . .	. . .	. . .	49 328	86 601	55 953	44 514	0.796
2016	126 224	2.54	63 683	. . .	. . .	. . .	. . .	51 425	89 683	55 702	44 823	0.805
2017	127 586	2.53	64 806	. . .	. . .	. . .	. . .	53 311	91 044	55 106	45 004	0.805
2018	128 579	2.52	65 127	. . .	. . .	. . .	. . .	53 036	92 796	56 995	46 487	0.816
2019	128 451	2.53	69 560	. . .	. . .	. . .	. . .	56 814	99 312	58 173	47 889	0.823
2020	129 931	2.51	67 521	. . .	. . .	. . .	. . .	55 321	97 026	61 417	50 982	0.830
By race												
Race alone												
2005	. . .	. . .	. . .	64 513	67 476	41 001	81 175	. . .	. . .	. . .	. . .	. . .
2006	. . .	. . .	. . .	65 215	67 467	41 143	82 672	. . .	. . .	. . .	. . .	. . .
2007	. . .	. . .	. . .	65 221	68 731	42 445	82 726	. . .	. . .	. . .	. . .	. . .
2008	. . .	. . .	. . .	63 046	66 924	41 239	79 105	. . .	. . .	. . .	. . .	. . .
2009	. . .	. . .	. . .	62 720	65 865	39 407	79 178	. . .	. . .	. . .	. . .	. . .
2010	. . .	. . .	. . .	61 521	64 794	38 220	76 453	. . .	. . .	. . .	. . .	. . .
2011	. . .	. . .	. . .	60 224	63 912	37 173	75 120	. . .	. . .	. . .	. . .	. . .
2012	. . .	. . .	. . .	60 660	64 391	37 635	77 523	. . .	. . .	. . .	. . .	. . .
2013	. . .	. . .	. . .	61 501	64 854	38 507	74 643	. . .	. . .	. . .	. . .	. . .
2014	. . .	. . .	. . .	62 237	65 948	38 742	81 315	. . .	. . .	. . .	. . .	. . .
2015	. . .	. . .	. . .	65 674	68 778	40 314	84 310	. . .	. . .	. . .	. . .	. . .
2016	. . .	. . .	. . .	66 724	70 157	42 596	87 837	. . .	. . .	. . .	. . .	. . .
2017	. . .	. . .	. . .	68 925	71 958	42 511	85 946	. . .	. . .	. . .	. . .	. . .
2018	. . .	. . .	. . .	69 007	72 820	42 636	89 882	. . .	. . .	. . .	. . .	. . .
2019	. . .	. . .	. . .	73 105	77 007	46 005	99 400	. . .	. . .	. . .	. . .	. . .
2020	. . .	. . .	. . .	71 231	74 912	45 870	94 903	. . .	. . .	. . .	. . .	. . .
Race alone or in combination												
2005	. . .	. . .	. . .	. . .	. . .	41 128	81 114	. . .	. . .	. . .	. . .	. . .
2006	. . .	. . .	. . .	. . .	. . .	41 353	82 237	. . .	. . .	. . .	. . .	. . .
2007	. . .	. . .	. . .	. . .	. . .	42 664	82 442	. . .	. . .	. . .	. . .	. . .
2008	. . .	. . .	. . .	. . .	. . .	41 392	79 020	. . .	. . .	. . .	. . .	. . .
2009	. . .	. . .	. . .	. . .	. . .	39 608	78 699	. . .	. . .	. . .	. . .	. . .
2010	. . .	. . .	. . .	. . .	. . .	38 258	75 582	. . .	. . .	. . .	. . .	. . .
2011	. . .	. . .	. . .	. . .	. . .	37 331	74 965	. . .	. . .	. . .	. . .	. . .
2012	. . .	. . .	. . .	. . .	. . .	38 084	77 010	. . .	. . .	. . .	. . .	. . .
2013	. . .	. . .	. . .	. . .	. . .	38 704	74 978	. . .	. . .	. . .	. . .	. . .
2014	. . .	. . .	. . .	. . .	. . .	39 021	81 897	. . .	. . .	. . .	. . .	. . .
2015	. . .	. . .	. . .	. . .	. . .	40 656	83 867	. . .	. . .	. . .	. . .	. . .
2016	. . .	. . .	. . .	. . .	. . .	43 217	87 180	. . .	. . .	. . .	. . .	. . .
2017	. . .	. . .	. . .	. . .	. . .	42 865	85 491	. . .	. . .	. . .	. . .	. . .
2018	. . .	. . .	. . .	. . .	. . .	42 977	89 491	. . .	. . .	. . .	. . .	. . .
2019	. . .	. . .	. . .	. . .	. . .	46 648	98 363	. . .	. . .	. . .	. . .	. . .
2020	. . .	. . .	. . .	. . .	. . .	46 600	94 718	. . .	. . .	. . .	. . .	. . .

[1] For 1987 through 2001, Asian and Pacific Islander.
. . . = Not available.

Table 3-2. Median Family Income by Type of Family

(2020 dollars, except as noted.)

Year	All families	Married couples			Male householder [1]	Female householder [1]	4-person families	Average size of family (number of people)
		Total	Wife in paid labor force	Wife not in paid labor force				
1950	31 240	32 435	35 681	29 549	29 319	18 091	34 590	3.54
1951	32 354	33 471	38 256	30 020	30 112	19 365	35 957	3.54
1952	33 323	34 788	39 751	30 924	30 967	19 146	37 460	3.53
1953	36 095	37 193	43 554	33 175	34 997	20 889	. . .	3.59
1954	35 143	36 543	42 617	32 354	33 853	19 347	. . .	3.59
1955	37 425	38 959	45 101	34 704	35 494	20 932	41 669	3.58
1956	39 872	41 482	47 056	36 692	34 758	22 972	44 368	3.60
1957	40 107	41 649	46 968	36 964	36 997	22 315	44 323	3.64
1958	39 983	41 775	46 253	37 090	33 483	21 544	44 683	3.65
1959	42 228	44 138	49 499	39 252	35 961	21 547	47 319	3.67
1960	43 106	45 046	50 119	40 095	37 276	22 765	48 283	3.70
1961	43 549	45 843	51 691	40 213	38 492	22 728	48 880	3.67
1962	44 782	47 090	53 125	41 041	42 940	23 541	50 797	3.68
1963	46 345	48 896	54 705	42 414	42 347	23 814	52 938	3.70
1964	48 063	50 719	56 610	43 916	42 378	25 301	54 787	3.70
1965	50 132	52 352	58 668	44 985	44 303	25 452	56 207	3.69
1966	52 779	54 924	61 357	47 302	45 071	28 099	58 448	3.67
1967	53 905	57 357	64 066	48 976	46 301	29 178	61 114	3.63
1968	56 441	59 789	66 169	50 868	47 869	29 273	64 301	3.60
1969	59 045	62 601	68 934	52 632	52 204	30 183	66 494	3.58
1970	58 862	62 734	69 353	52 563	53 762	30 383	66 618	3.57
1971	58 780	62 809	69 564	52 737	49 847	29 227	66 444	3.53
1972	61 680	66 047	73 025	55 469	57 180	29 641	71 069	3.48
1973	62 929	68 031	75 350	56 464	56 094	30 271	71 592	3.44
1974	61 248	66 095	72 924	54 986	55 343	30 800	71 061	3.42
1975	60 180	65 216	71 606	52 974	57 005	30 022	69 520	3.39
1976	62 046	67 210	73 579	54 724	53 343	29 911	71 822	3.37
1977	62 463	68 733	74 890	55 658	56 645	30 297	73 052	3.33
1978	64 410	70 617	76 450	55 865	58 297	31 171	74 590	3.31
1979	65 324	71 467	78 520	55 922	56 056	32 951	75 079	3.29
1980	63 052	69 405	76 344	53 886	52 543	31 216	72 977	3.27
1981	61 354	68 690	75 903	52 749	54 505	30 036	72 003	3.25
1982	60 560	67 244	74 261	52 128	52 050	29 679	71 379	3.26
1983	60 923	67 630	75 362	51 380	54 144	29 220	72 334	3.24
1984	62 898	70 463	78 122	53 140	55 502	30 465	73 996	3.23
1985	63 806	71 547	79 370	53 499	52 043	31 425	75 405	3.21
1986	66 604	74 171	82 105	55 248	56 438	30 855	78 492	3.19
1987	67 694	76 238	84 353	55 144	55 099	32 094	81 062	3.17
1988	67 909	76 765	85 323	54 380	56 594	32 374	82 381	3.16
1989	69 152	77 912	86 644	55 025	56 285	33 233	82 391	3.17
1990	68 098	76 847	85 328	55 208	55 949	32 615	79 844	3.18
1991	66 796	76 194	84 783	52 936	52 693	31 024	80 024	3.17
1992	66 326	75 968	85 484	51 821	50 009	30 875	80 250	3.19
1993	65 377	76 072	85 776	50 620	46 818	30 855	79 886	3.20
1994	67 199	77 902	87 475	51 157	48 085	31 598	81 459	3.19
1995	68 712	79 627	89 446	51 875	51 365	33 317	84 069	3.20
1996	69 714	81 921	91 118	52 672	52 079	32 815	84 906	3.19
1997	71 897	83 227	92 685	55 039	53 171	33 914	86 064	3.18
1998	74 389	86 236	96 092	56 013	56 792	35 276	89 229	3.18
1999	76 101	88 055	98 113	56 792	58 191	37 032	93 126	3.15
2000	76 469	89 081	98 829	57 072	56 866	38 762	94 463	3.14
2001	75 342	88 426	98 312	56 602	53 626	37 732	92 740	3.15
2002	74 566	88 201	99 481	54 795	54 452	38 124	90 513	3.13
2003	74 321	87 866	100 431	54 941	53 656	37 457	91 834	3.13
2004	74 263	87 403	99 979	54 918	55 444	37 047	90 695	3.13
2005	74 664	87 568	99 096	55 939	54 624	36 199	93 423	3.13
2006	76 784	89 321	100 900	55 767	53 852	37 102	94 483	3.13
2007	75 168	90 843	102 439	56 092	55 513	37 915	94 706	3.15
2008	72 670	87 669	98 862	55 356	52 511	36 311	92 160	3.15
2009	74 144	86 625	98 437	54 573	50 191	36 004	89 986	3.16
2010	71 667	85 950	98 472	54 908	51 405	34 688	88 935	3.14
2011	70 328	85 110	97 232	55 066	49 676	34 901	87 163	3.13
2012	70 300	85 315	98 170	54 424	47 843	34 659	90 017	3.12
2013	71 026	84 965	99 393	54 639	49 500	34 649	89 436	3.14
2014	72 926	88 448	103 629	56 776	52 093	34 771	91 292	3.14
2015	77 242	92 130	107 295	57 952	54 380	37 285	96 302	3.14
2016	78 426	93 640	108 363	59 956	55 625	39 542	97 884	3.14
2017	81 070	95 192	110 893	61 901	55 913	39 174	100 104	3.13
2018	80 395	96 206	. . .	. . .	56 011	41 473	100 641	3.14
2019	87 085	103 306	. . .	. . .	62 475	43 900	107 897	3.15
2020	84 008	101 240	. . .	. . .	60 216	43 895	107 416	3.13

[1]No spouse present.
. . . = Not available.

Table 3-3. Shares of Aggregate Income Received by Each Fifth and Top 5 Percent of Households

Year	Money income							Equivalence-adjusted income					
	Share of aggregate income (percent)						Gini coefficient	Share of aggregate income (percent)					Gini coefficient
	Lowest fifth	Second fifth	Third fifth	Fourth fifth	Highest fifth	Top 5 percent		Lowest fifth	Second fifth	Third fifth	Fourth fifth	Highest fifth	
1970	4.1	10.8	17.4	24.5	43.3	16.6	0.394	5.7	12.1	17.3	23.4	41.5	0.357
1971	4.1	10.6	17.3	24.5	43.5	16.7	0.396	5.7	12.0	17.2	23.4	41.7	0.359
1972	4.1	10.4	17.0	24.5	43.9	17.0	0.401	5.6	11.9	17.2	23.4	41.9	0.362
1973	4.2	10.4	17.0	24.5	43.9	16.9	0.400	5.6	12.0	17.2	23.5	41.7	0.360
1974	4.3	10.6	17.0	24.6	43.5	16.5	0.395	5.8	12.1	17.3	23.6	41.2	0.354
1975	4.3	10.4	17.0	24.7	43.6	16.5	0.397	5.6	11.9	17.3	23.6	41.6	0.359
1976	4.3	10.3	17.0	24.7	43.7	16.6	0.398	5.6	11.8	17.4	23.8	41.5	0.359
1977	4.2	10.2	16.9	24.7	44.0	16.8	0.402	5.5	11.7	17.3	23.7	41.7	0.362
1978	4.2	10.2	16.8	24.7	44.1	16.8	0.402	5.4	11.8	17.3	23.7	41.8	0.363
1979	4.1	10.2	16.8	24.6	44.2	16.9	0.404	5.3	11.7	17.2	23.8	41.9	0.366
1980	4.2	10.2	16.8	24.7	44.1	16.5	0.403	5.2	11.6	17.3	24.0	41.9	0.367
1981	4.1	10.1	16.7	24.8	44.3	16.5	0.406	5.0	11.4	17.2	24.0	42.4	0.373
1982	4.0	10.0	16.5	24.5	45.0	17.0	0.412	4.7	11.1	17.0	23.9	43.2	0.384
1983	4.0	9.9	16.4	24.6	45.1	17.0	0.414	4.6	11.0	16.9	24.0	43.5	0.389
1984	4.0	9.9	16.3	24.6	45.2	17.1	0.415	4.6	11.0	16.8	24.0	43.6	0.389
1985	3.9	9.8	16.2	24.4	45.6	17.6	0.419	4.6	10.9	16.7	23.7	44.1	0.394
1986	3.8	9.7	16.2	24.3	46.1	18.0	0.425	4.5	10.8	16.6	23.8	44.3	0.397
1987	3.8	9.6	16.1	24.3	46.2	18.2	0.426	4.4	10.8	16.7	23.8	44.4	0.399
1988	3.8	9.6	16.0	24.2	46.3	18.3	0.426	4.4	10.7	16.5	23.7	44.7	0.402
1989	3.8	9.5	15.8	24.0	46.8	18.9	0.431	4.4	10.5	16.3	23.4	45.3	0.408
1990	3.8	9.6	15.9	24.0	46.6	18.5	0.428	4.4	10.6	16.3	23.5	45.1	0.406
1991	3.8	9.6	15.9	24.2	46.5	18.1	0.428	4.3	10.6	16.5	23.6	45.0	0.406
1992	3.8	9.4	15.8	24.2	46.9	18.6	0.433	4.2	10.4	16.3	23.7	45.5	0.412
1993	3.6	9.0	15.1	23.5	48.9	21.0	0.454	3.9	9.8	15.6	23.0	47.7	0.436
1994	3.6	8.9	15.0	23.4	49.1	21.2	0.456	4.0	9.8	15.6	22.8	47.8	0.436
1995	3.7	9.1	15.2	23.3	48.7	21.0	0.450	4.1	9.9	15.6	22.8	47.6	0.433
1996	3.6	9.0	15.1	23.3	49.0	21.4	0.455	4.0	9.8	15.5	22.7	47.9	0.437
1997	3.6	8.9	15.0	23.2	49.4	21.7	0.459	4.0	9.8	15.4	22.6	48.3	0.440
1998	3.6	9.0	15.0	23.2	49.2	21.4	0.456	4.0	9.8	15.4	22.7	48.1	0.439
1999	3.6	8.9	14.9	23.2	49.4	21.5	0.458	4.0	9.7	15.3	22.6	48.4	0.441
2000	3.6	8.9	14.8	23.0	49.8	22.1	0.462	4.1	9.8	15.2	22.3	48.6	0.442
2001	3.5	8.7	14.6	23.0	50.1	22.4	0.466	4.0	9.6	15.2	22.4	48.8	0.446
2002	3.5	8.8	14.8	23.3	49.7	21.7	0.462	4.0	9.6	15.2	22.7	48.4	0.443
2003	3.4	8.7	14.8	23.4	49.8	21.4	0.464	3.9	9.5	15.2	22.8	48.6	0.445
2004	3.4	8.7	14.7	23.2	50.1	21.8	0.466	3.8	9.6	15.2	22.7	48.7	0.447
2005	3.4	8.6	14.6	23.0	50.4	22.2	0.469	3.8	9.5	15.1	22.6	49.1	0.450
2006	3.4	8.6	14.5	22.9	50.5	22.3	0.470	3.8	9.4	14.9	22.5	49.3	0.452
2007	3.4	8.7	14.8	23.4	49.7	21.2	0.463	3.8	9.5	15.3	22.9	48.5	0.444
2008	3.4	8.6	14.7	23.3	50.0	21.5	0.466	3.7	9.4	15.1	22.8	48.9	0.450
2009	3.4	8.6	14.6	23.2	50.3	21.7	0.468	3.6	9.3	15.0	22.9	49.4	0.456
2010	3.3	8.5	14.6	23.4	50.3	21.3	0.470	3.4	9.2	15.0	23.1	49.2	0.456
2011	3.2	8.4	14.3	23.0	51.1	22.3	0.477	3.4	9.0	14.8	22.8	50.0	0.463
2012	3.2	8.3	14.4	23.0	51.0	22.3	0.477	3.4	9.0	14.8	22.9	49.9	0.463
2013	3.2	8.4	14.4	23.0	51.0	22.2	0.476	3.4	8.8	14.7	22.8	50.3	0.459
2014	3.1	8.2	14.3	23.2	51.2	21.9	0.480	3.3	9.0	14.8	22.9	50.0	0.464
2015	3.1	8.2	14.3	23.2	51.1	22.1	0.479	3.4	9.0	14.8	22.9	49.8	0.462
2016	3.1	8.3	14.2	22.9	51.5	22.6	0.481	3.5	9.1	14.7	22.5	50.2	0.464
2017	3.0	8.1	14.0	22.6	52.3	23.2	0.489	3.5	9.0	14.7	22.7	50.1	0.471
2018	3.1	8.3	14.1	22.6	52.0	23.1	0.486	3.5	9.1	14.7	22.4	50.3	0.464
2019	3.1	8.3	14.1	22.7	51.9	23.0	0.484	3.6	9.0	14.6	22.3	50.5	0.465
2020	3.0	8.1	14.0	22.6	52.2	23.0	0.489	3.4	8.9	14.5	22.4	50.8	0.469

. . . = Not available.

Table 3-4. Shares of Aggregate Income Received by Each Fifth and Top 5 Percent of Families

| Year | Number of families (thousands) | Share of aggregate income (percent) | | | | | | Mean family income (2019 dollars) | | | | | | Gini coefficient |
		Lowest fifth	Second fifth	Third fifth	Fourth fifth	Highest fifth	Top 5 percent	Lowest fifth	Second fifth	Third fifth	Fourth fifth	Highest fifth	Top 5 percent	
1950	39 929	4.5	12.0	17.4	23.4	42.7	17.3	. . .	. . .	. . .	. . .	. . .	. . .	0.379
1951	40 578	5.0	12.4	17.6	23.4	41.6	16.8	. . .	. . .	. . .	. . .	. . .	. . .	0.363
1952	40 832	4.9	12.3	17.4	23.4	41.9	17.4	. . .	. . .	. . .	. . .	. . .	. . .	0.368
1953	41 202	4.7	12.5	18.0	23.9	40.9	15.7	. . .	. . .	. . .	. . .	. . .	. . .	0.359
1954	41 951	4.5	12.1	17.7	23.9	41.8	16.3	. . .	. . .	. . .	. . .	. . .	. . .	0.371
1955	42 889	4.8	12.3	17.8	23.7	41.3	16.4	. . .	. . .	. . .	. . .	. . .	. . .	0.363
1956	43 497	5.0	12.5	17.9	23.7	41.0	16.1	. . .	. . .	. . .	. . .	. . .	. . .	0.358
1957	43 696	5.1	12.7	18.1	23.8	40.4	15.6	. . .	. . .	. . .	. . .	. . .	. . .	0.351
1958	44 232	5.0	12.5	18.0	23.9	40.6	15.4	. . .	. . .	. . .	. . .	. . .	. . .	0.354
1959	45 111	4.9	12.3	17.9	23.8	41.1	15.9	. . .	. . .	. . .	. . .	. . .	. . .	0.361
1960	45 539	4.8	12.2	17.8	24.0	41.3	15.9	. . .	. . .	. . .	. . .	. . .	. . .	0.364
1961	46 418	4.7	11.9	17.5	23.8	42.2	16.6	. . .	. . .	. . .	. . .	. . .	. . .	0.374
1962	47 059	5.0	12.1	17.6	24.0	41.3	15.7	. . .	. . .	. . .	. . .	. . .	. . .	0.362
1963	47 540	5.0	12.1	17.7	24.0	41.2	15.8	. . .	. . .	. . .	. . .	. . .	. . .	0.362
1964	47 956	5.1	12.0	17.7	24.0	41.2	15.9	. . .	. . .	. . .	. . .	. . .	. . .	0.361
1965	48 509	5.2	12.2	17.8	23.9	40.9	15.5	. . .	. . .	. . .	. . .	. . .	. . .	0.356
1966	49 214	5.6	12.4	17.8	23.8	40.5	15.6	16 432	36 480	52 198	69 877	119 258	183 123	0.349
1967	50 111	5.4	12.2	17.5	23.5	41.4	16.4	16 689	37 318	53 640	71 939	127 026	200 976	0.358
1968	50 823	5.6	12.4	17.7	23.7	40.5	15.6	17 988	39 232	56 049	74 958	128 085	197 446	0.348
1969	51 586	5.6	12.4	17.7	23.7	40.6	15.6	18 559	40 987	58 651	78 569	134 559	206 674	0.349
1970	52 227	5.4	12.2	17.6	23.8	40.9	15.6	18 279	40 417	58 439	78 829	135 556	206 415	0.353
1971	53 296	5.5	12.0	17.6	23.8	41.1	15.7	18 294	39 823	58 266	78 909	135 912	207 231	0.355
1972	54 373	5.5	11.9	17.5	23.9	41.4	15.9	19 093	41 660	61 192	83 564	144 928	222 184	0.359
1973	55 053	5.5	11.9	17.5	24.0	41.1	15.5	19 593	42 439	62 355	85 216	146 208	220 652	0.356
1974	55 698	5.7	12.0	17.6	24.1	40.6	14.8	19 938	42 089	61 448	84 187	141 856	206 911	0.355
1975	56 245	5.6	11.9	17.7	24.2	40.7	14.9	19 157	40 498	60 216	82 447	138 938	203 813	0.357
1976	56 710	5.6	11.9	17.7	24.2	40.7	14.9	19 620	41 521	61 938	84 627	142 434	208 465	0.358
1977	57 215	5.5	11.7	17.6	24.3	40.9	14.9	19 536	41 760	62 806	86 638	145 956	212 781	0.363
1978	57 804	5.4	11.7	17.6	24.2	41.1	15.1	19 812	42 965	64 516	88 888	150 833	221 030	0.363
1979	59 550	5.4	11.6	17.5	24.1	41.4	15.3	20 004	43 249	65 224	89 797	154 021	227 986	0.365
1980	60 309	5.3	11.6	17.6	24.4	41.1	14.6	19 228	41 857	63 232	87 727	147 705	209 975	0.365
1981	61 019	5.3	11.4	17.5	24.6	41.2	14.4	18 643	40 543	62 009	87 059	146 076	204 116	0.369
1982	61 393	5.0	11.3	17.2	24.4	42.2	15.3	17 587	39 903	60 930	86 435	149 355	213 689	0.380
1983	62 015	4.9	11.2	17.2	24.5	42.4	15.3	17 318	39 845	61 304	87 371	151 494	218 424	0.382
1984	62 706	4.8	11.1	17.1	24.5	42.5	15.4	17 896	40 975	63 219	90 403	157 118	227 164	0.383
1985	63 558	4.8	11.0	16.9	24.3	43.1	16.1	18 103	41 541	64 137	91 934	163 382	244 159	0.389
1986	64 491	4.7	10.9	16.9	24.1	43.4	16.5	18 626	43 006	66 626	95 198	171 468	260 385	0.392
1987	65 204	4.6	10.7	16.8	24.0	43.8	17.2	18 594	43 521	67 580	96 721	176 760	276 707	0.393
1988	65 837	4.6	10.7	16.7	24.0	44.0	17.2	18 765	43 698	68 000	97 659	179 187	279 974	0.395
1989	66 090	4.6	10.6	16.5	23.7	44.6	17.9	19 129	44 503	69 137	99 470	187 291	300 024	0.401
1990	66 322	4.6	10.8	16.6	23.8	44.3	17.4	18 941	44 178	68 038	97 846	181 843	285 320	0.396
1991	67 173	4.5	10.7	16.6	24.1	44.2	17.1	18 092	42 943	66 633	96 642	177 553	274 733	0.397
1992	68 216	4.3	10.5	16.5	24.0	44.7	17.6	17 384	41 930	66 242	96 287	179 179	282 104	0.404
1993	68 506	4.1	9.9	15.7	23.3	47.0	20.3	17 227	41 375	65 566	97 195	196 379	338 944	0.429
1994	69 313	4.2	10.0	15.7	23.3	46.9	20.1	17 998	42 582	67 244	99 400	200 317	343 662	0.426
1995	69 597	4.4	10.1	15.8	23.2	46.5	20.0	19 060	43 915	68 756	100 599	202 110	346 621	0.421
1996	70 241	4.2	10.0	15.8	23.1	46.8	20.3	18 768	44 246	69 989	102 266	207 043	358 218	0.425
1997	70 884	4.2	9.9	15.7	23.0	47.2	20.7	19 450	45 576	71 909	105 444	216 629	379 137	0.429
1998	71 551	4.2	9.9	15.7	23.0	47.3	20.7	19 937	46 925	74 270	108 917	224 177	392 373	0.430
1999	73 206	4.3	9.9	15.6	23.0	47.2	20.3	20 740	48 209	76 095	112 314	230 188	396 886	0.429
2000	73 778	4.3	9.8	15.4	22.7	47.7	21.1	21 286	48 670	76 492	112 734	236 526	419 129	0.433
2001	74 340	4.2	9.7	15.4	22.9	47.7	21.0	20 549	47 582	75 534	112 332	233 973	410 823	0.435
2002	75 616	4.2	9.7	15.5	23.0	47.6	20.8	20 224	46 923	74 839	111 308	229 843	402 251	0.434
2003	76 232	4.1	9.6	15.5	23.2	47.6	20.5	19 569	46 410	74 795	112 460	230 416	397 096	0.436
2004	76 866	4.0	9.6	15.4	23.0	47.9	20.9	19 505	46 427	74 513	111 326	231 691	403 642	0.438
2005	77 418	4.0	9.6	15.3	22.9	48.1	21.1	19 621	46 686	74 708	111 736	234 237	410 080	0.440
2006	77 908	4.0	9.5	15.1	22.9	48.5	21.5	19 998	47 321	75 268	113 760	241 164	426 890	0.444
2007	78 454	4.1	9.7	15.6	23.3	47.3	20.1	20 109	47 937	76 896	114 987	233 437	396 240	0.432
2008	78 867	4.0	9.6	15.5	23.1	47.8	20.5	19 170	45 948	74 218	111 070	229 467	394 009	0.438
2009	78 874	3.9	9.4	15.3	23.2	48.2	20.7	18 490	44 802	72 451	110 009	229 163	393 080	0.443
2010	79 559	3.8	9.4	15.4	23.5	47.9	20.0	17 755	43 915	71 577	109 204	222 628	372 248	0.440
2011	80 529	3.8	9.3	15.1	23.0	48.9	21.3	17 626	43 317	70 395	107 534	228 296	397 383	0.450
2012	80 944	3.8	9.2	15.1	23.0	48.9	21.3	17 545	43 128	70 552	107 836	228 787	397 959	0.451
2013	81 217	3.8	9.3	15.1	23.0	48.8	21.2	17 929	43 979	71 138	108 191	230 041	399 255	0.455
2014	81 730	3.6	9.2	15.1	23.2	48.9	20.8	17 632	44 524	73 218	112 855	237 521	405 043	0.452
2015	82 199	3.7	9.2	15.2	23.2	48.6	20.9	18 975	46 653	77 027	117 471	246 135	422 640	0.448
2016	82 854	3.7	9.2	15.0	22.9	49.2	21.4	19 634	48 478	78 639	120 000	258 325	449 900	0.452
2017	83 103	3.8	9.2	15.1	23.1	48.8	20.7	20 004	48 939	80 084	122 316	258 750	439 952	0.458
2018	83 508	3.8	9.3	14.9	22.6	49.4	21.6	21 006	50 731	81 400	123 600	269 831	471 283	0.452
2019	83 698	3.9	9.2	14.8	22.5	49.5	21.9	23 125	54 495	87 338	133 253	292 751	517 670	0.454
2020	83 918	3.7	9.1	14.7	22.6	49.8	21.6	21 260	52 332	84 681	130 147	286 391	497 661	0.458

. . . = Not available.

SECTION 3B: POVERTY

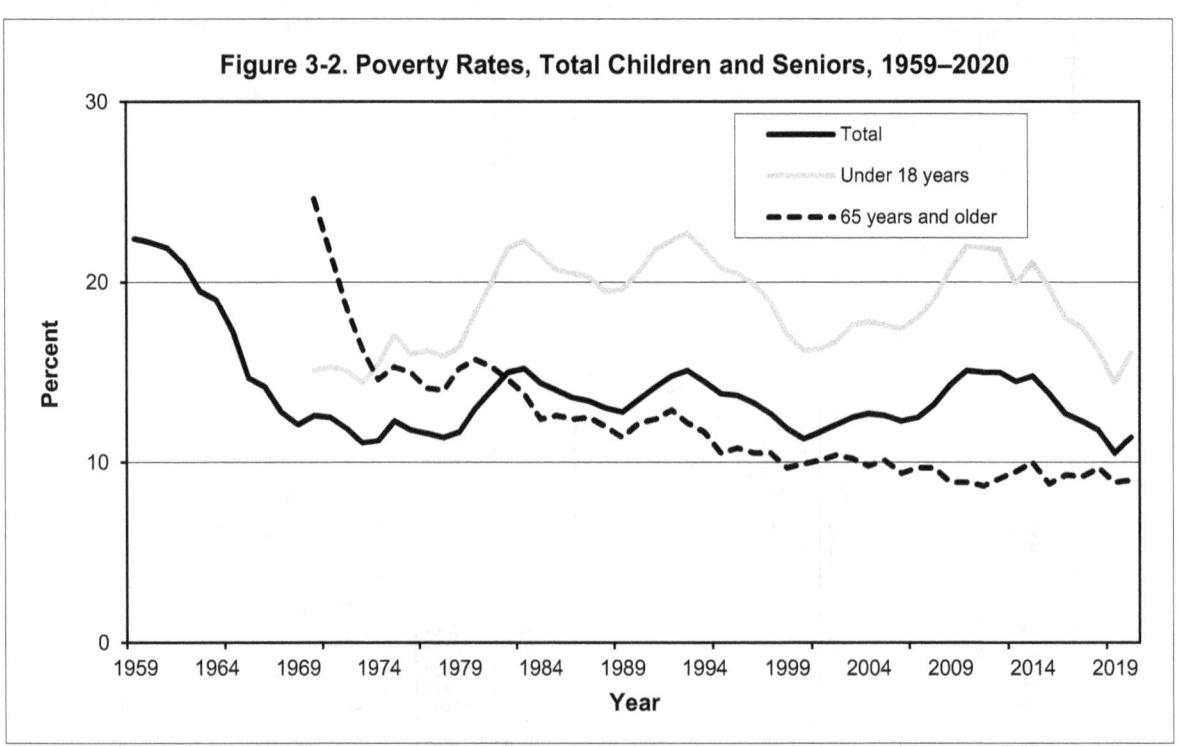

Figure 3-2. Poverty Rates, Total Children and Seniors, 1959–2020

- Poverty measures the ability of families and individuals who cannot earn an income to cover the cost of a minimum standard of living. There is not one poverty amount but rather a range of income depending on age and types and sizes of families. In 2020, an individual aged 65 and under is considered in poverty with an income of $13,465. For a family of three, their poverty level income is $20,591. (Table 3-5)

- Figure 3-2 illustrates the growing percentage of employed persons who are classified as working poor. In 2020, 29.6 percent of the civilian labor force were identified as working poor. Full time workers are less likely to be working poor but women, Blacks, and Hispanics, as well as those without a high school diploma are all more likely to be working poor. (Table 3-9)

- The official poverty rate in 2020 was 11.4 percent, up nearly 1.0 percentage points from 10.5 percent in 2019. This is the first increase in poverty after declining for five consecutive years. There were 37.2 million people in poverty in 2020 nearly 3.3 million more than in 2019. Stimulus payments in 2020 moved 11.7 individuals out of poverty and protected millions more from falling into poverty. (Table 3-6)

- Beginning in 2011, the U.S. Census Bureau began publishing the Supplemental Poverty Measure (SPM), including programs not in the official poverty measure. These programs include Supplemental Nutrition Assistance Program (SNAP), Women and Infant and Children (WIC) and Medicare. In 2020, the overall SPM rate was 9.1 percent down significantly from 11.8 in 2019. (Table 3-10)

Table 3-5. Weighted Average Poverty Thresholds by Family Size

(Dollars.)

Year	Unrelated individuals			Families of 2 people			Families, all ages							CPI-U, all items (1982–1984 = 100)
	All ages	Under 65 years	65 years and older	All ages	House-holder under 65 years	House-holder 65 years and older	3 people	4 people	5 people	6 people	7 people	8 people	9 people or more	
1959	1 467	1 503	1 397	1 894	1 952	1 761	2 324	2 973	3 506	3 944	. . .	. . .	. . .	29.2
1960	1 490	1 526	1 418	1 924	1 982	1 788	2 359	3 022	3 560	4 002	. . .	. . .	. . .	29.6
1961	1 506	1 545	1 433	1 942	2 005	1 808	2 383	3 054	3 597	4 041	. . .	. . .	. . .	29.9
1962	1 519	1 562	1 451	1 962	2 027	1 828	2 412	3 089	3 639	4 088	. . .	. . .	. . .	30.3
1963	1 539	1 581	1 470	1 988	2 052	1 850	2 442	3 128	3 685	4 135	. . .	. . .	. . .	30.6
1964	1 558	1 601	1 488	2 015	2 079	1 875	2 473	3 169	3 732	4 193	. . .	. . .	. . .	31.0
1965	1 582	1 626	1 512	2 048	2 114	1 906	2 514	3 223	3 797	4 264	. . .	. . .	. . .	31.5
1966	1 628	1 674	1 556	2 107	2 175	1 961	2 588	3 317	3 908	4 388	. . .	. . .	. . .	32.5
1967	1 675	1 722	1 600	2 168	2 238	2 017	2 661	3 410	4 019	4 516	. . .	. . .	. . .	33.4
1968	1 748	1 797	1 667	2 262	2 333	2 102	2 774	3 553	4 188	4 706	. . .	. . .	. . .	34.8
1969	1 840	1 893	1 757	2 383	2 458	2 215	2 924	3 743	4 415	4 958	. . .	. . .	. . .	36.7
1970	1 954	2 010	1 861	2 525	2 604	2 348	3 099	3 968	4 680	5 260	. . .	. . .	. . .	38.8
1971	2 040	2 098	1 940	2 633	2 716	2 448	3 229	4 137	4 880	5 489	. . .	. . .	. . .	40.5
1972	2 109	2 168	2 005	2 724	2 808	2 530	3 339	4 275	5 044	5 673	. . .	. . .	. . .	41.8
1973	2 247	2 307	2 130	2 895	2 984	2 688	3 548	4 540	5 358	6 028	. . .	. . .	. . .	44.4
1974	2 495	2 562	2 364	3 211	3 312	2 982	3 936	5 038	5 950	6 699	. . .	. . .	. . .	49.3
1975	2 724	2 797	2 581	3 506	3 617	3 257	4 293	5 500	6 499	7 316	. . .	. . .	. . .	53.8
1976	2 884	2 959	2 730	3 711	3 826	3 445	4 540	5 815	6 876	7 760	. . .	. . .	. . .	56.9
1977	3 075	3 152	2 906	3 951	4 072	3 666	4 833	6 191	7 320	8 261	. . .	. . .	. . .	60.6
1978	3 311	3 392	3 127	4 249	4 383	3 944	5 201	6 662	7 880	8 891	. . .	. . .	. . .	65.2
1979	3 689	3 778	3 479	4 725	4 878	4 390	5 784	7 412	8 775	9 914	. . .	. . .	. . .	72.6
1980	4 190	4 290	3 949	5 363	5 537	4 983	6 565	8 414	9 966	11 269	12 761	14 199	16 896	82.4
1981	4 620	4 729	4 359	5 917	6 111	5 498	7 250	9 287	11 007	12 449	14 110	15 655	18 572	90.9
1982	4 901	5 019	4 626	6 281	6 487	5 836	7 693	9 862	11 684	13 207	15 036	16 719	19 698	96.5
1983	5 061	5 180	4 775	6 483	6 697	6 023	7 938	10 178	12 049	13 630	15 500	17 170	20 310	99.6
1984	5 278	5 400	4 979	6 762	6 983	6 282	8 277	10 609	12 566	14 207	16 096	17 961	21 247	103.9
1985	5 469	5 593	5 156	6 998	7 231	6 503	8 573	10 989	13 007	14 696	16 656	18 512	22 083	107.6
1986	5 572	5 701	5 255	7 138	7 372	6 630	8 737	11 203	13 259	14 986	17 049	18 791	22 497	109.6
1987	5 778	5 909	5 447	7 397	7 641	6 872	9 056	11 611	13 737	15 509	17 649	19 515	23 105	113.6
1988	6 022	6 155	5 674	7 704	7 958	7 157	9 435	12 092	14 304	16 146	18 232	20 253	24 129	118.3
1989	6 310	6 451	5 947	8 076	8 343	7 501	9 885	12 674	14 990	16 921	19 162	21 328	25 480	124.0
1990	6 652	6 800	6 268	8 509	8 794	7 905	10 419	13 359	15 792	17 839	20 241	22 582	26 848	130.7
1991	6 932	7 086	6 532	8 865	9 165	8 241	10 860	13 924	16 456	18 587	21 058	23 582	27 942	136.2
1992	7 143	7 299	6 729	9 137	9 443	8 487	11 186	14 335	16 952	19 137	21 594	24 053	28 745	140.3
1993	7 363	7 518	6 930	9 414	9 728	8 740	11 522	14 763	17 449	19 718	22 383	24 838	29 529	144.5
1994	7 547	7 710	7 108	9 661	9 976	8 967	11 821	15 141	17 900	20 235	22 923	25 427	30 300	148.2
1995	7 763	7 929	7 309	9 933	10 259	9 219	12 158	15 569	18 408	20 804	23 552	26 237	31 280	152.4
1996	7 995	8 163	7 525	10 233	10 564	9 491	12 516	16 036	18 952	21 389	24 268	27 091	31 971	156.9
1997	8 183	8 350	7 698	10 473	10 805	9 712	12 802	16 400	19 380	21 886	24 802	27 593	32 566	160.5
1998	8 316	8 480	7 818	10 634	10 972	9 862	13 003	16 660	19 680	22 228	25 257	28 166	33 339	163.0
1999	8 499	8 667	7 990	10 864	11 213	10 075	13 289	17 030	20 128	22 730	25 918	28 970	34 436	166.6
2000	8 791	8 959	8 259	11 235	11 589	10 418	13 740	17 604	20 815	23 533	26 750	29 701	35 150	172.2
2001	9 039	9 214	8 494	11 569	11 920	10 715	14 128	18 104	21 405	24 195	27 517	30 627	36 286	177.1
2002	9 183	9 359	8 628	11 756	12 110	10 885	14 348	18 392	21 744	24 576	28 001	30 907	37 062	179.9
2003	9 393	9 573	8 825	12 015	12 384	11 133	14 680	18 810	22 245	25 122	28 544	31 589	37 656	184.0
2004	9 646	9 827	9 060	12 335	12 714	11 430	15 066	19 307	22 830	25 787	29 233	32 641	39 062	188.9
2005	9 973	10 160	9 367	12 755	13 145	11 815	15 577	19 971	23 613	26 683	30 249	33 610	40 288	195.3
2006	10 294	10 488	9 669	13 167	13 569	12 201	16 079	20 614	24 382	27 560	31 205	34 774	41 499	201.6
2007	10 590	10 787	9 944	13 540	13 954	12 550	16 530	21 203	25 080	28 323	32 233	35 816	42 739	207.3
2008	10 991	11 201	10 326	14 051	14 489	13 030	17 163	22 025	26 049	29 456	33 529	37 220	44 346	215.3
2009	10 956	11 161	10 289	13 991	14 439	12 982	17 098	21 954	25 991	29 405	33 372	37 252	44 366	214.5
2010	11 137	11 344	10 458	14 216	14 676	13 194	17 373	22 315	26 442	29 904	34 019	37 953	45 224	218.1
2011	11 484	11 702	10 788	14 657	15 139	13 609	17 916	23 021	27 251	30 847	35 085	39 064	46 572	224.9
2012	11 720	11 945	11 011	14 937	15 450	13 892	18 284	23 492	27 827	31 471	35 743	39 688	47 297	229.6
2013	11 888	12 119	11 173	15 142	15 679	14 095	18 552	23 834	28 265	31 925	36 384	40 484	48 065	233.0
2014	12 071	12 316	11 354	15 379	15 934	14 326	18 850	24 230	28 695	32 473	36 927	40 968	49 021	236.7
2015	12 082	12 331	11 367	15 391	15 952	14 342	18 871	24 257	28 741	32 542	36 998	41 029	49 177	237.0
2016	12 228	12 486	11 511	15 569	16 151	14 522	19 105	24 563	29 111	32 928	37 458	41 781	49 721	240.0
2017	12 488	12 752	11 756	15 877	16 493	14 828	19 515	25 094	29 714	33 618	38 173	42 684	50 681	245.1
2018	12 784	13 064	12 043	16 247	16 889	15 193	19 985	25 701	30 454	34 533	39 194	43 602	51 393	251.1
2019	13 011	13 300	12 261	16 521	17 196	15 468	20 335	26 172	31 021	35 129	40 016	44 461	52 875	255.7
2020	13 171	13 465	12 413	16 733	17 413	15 659	20 591	26 496	31 417	35 499	40 406	44 755	53 905	258.8

. . . = Not available.

Table 3-6. Poverty Status of People by Race and Hispanic Origin

(Thousands of people, percent of population.)

Year	Number of people, all races	All races		White		White, not Hispanic		Black		Asian [1]		Hispanic (any race)	
		Number	Poverty rate (percent)	Number	Poverty rate (percent)	Number	Poverty rate (percent)	Number	Poverty rate (percent)	Number	Poverty rate (percent)	Number	Poverty rate (percent)
						Below poverty level							
1975	210 864	25 877	12.3	17 770	9.7	14 883	8.6	7 545	31.3	. . .	. . .	2 991	26.9
1976	212 303	24 975	11.8	16 713	9.1	14 025	8.1	7 595	31.1	. . .	. . .	2 783	24.7
1977	213 867	24 720	11.6	16 416	8.9	13 802	8.0	7 726	31.3	. . .	. . .	2 700	22.4
1978	215 656	24 497	11.4	16 259	8.7	13 755	7.9	7 625	30.6	. . .	. . .	2 607	21.6
1979	222 903	26 072	11.7	17 214	9.0	14 419	8.1	8 050	31.0	. . .	. . .	2 921	21.8
1980	225 027	29 272	13.0	19 699	10.2	16 365	9.1	8 579	32.5	. . .	. . .	3 491	25.7
1981	227 157	31 822	14.0	21 553	11.1	17 987	9.9	9 173	34.2	. . .	. . .	3 713	26.5
1982	229 412	34 398	15.0	23 517	12.0	19 362	10.6	9 697	35.6	. . .	. . .	4 301	29.9
1983	231 700	35 303	15.2	23 984	12.1	19 538	10.8	9 882	35.7	. . .	. . .	4 633	28.0
1984	233 816	33 700	14.4	22 955	11.5	18 300	10.0	9 490	33.8	. . .	. . .	4 806	28.4
1985	236 594	33 064	14.0	22 860	11.4	17 839	9.7	8 926	31.3	. . .	. . .	5 236	29.0
1986	238 554	32 370	13.6	22 183	11.0	17 244	9.4	8 983	31.1	. . .	. . .	5 117	27.3
1987	240 982	32 221	13.4	21 195	10.4	16 029	8.7	9 520	32.4	1 021	16.1	5 422	28.0
1988	243 530	31 745	13.0	20 715	10.1	15 565	8.4	9 356	31.3	1 117	17.3	5 357	26.7
1989	245 992	31 528	12.8	20 785	10.0	15 599	8.3	9 302	30.7	939	14.1	5 430	26.2
1990	248 644	33 585	13.5	22 326	10.7	16 622	8.8	9 837	31.9	858	12.2	6 006	28.1
1991	251 192	35 708	14.2	23 747	11.3	17 741	9.4	10 242	32.7	996	13.8	6 339	28.7
1992	256 549	38 014	14.8	25 259	11.9	18 202	9.6	10 827	33.4	985	12.7	7 592	29.6
1993	259 278	39 265	15.1	26 226	12.2	18 882	9.9	10 877	33.1	1 134	15.3	8 126	30.6
1994	261 616	38 059	14.5	25 379	11.7	18 110	9.4	10 196	30.6	974	14.6	8 416	30.7
1995	263 733	36 425	13.8	24 423	11.2	16 267	8.5	9 872	29.3	1 411	14.6	8 574	30.3
1996	266 218	36 529	13.7	24 650	11.2	16 462	8.6	9 694	28.4	1 454	14.5	8 697	29.4
1997	268 480	35 574	13.3	24 396	11.0	16 491	8.6	9 116	26.5	1 468	14.0	8 308	27.1
1998	271 059	34 476	12.7	23 454	10.5	15 799	8.2	9 091	26.1	1 360	12.5	8 070	25.6
1999	276 208	32 791	11.9	22 169	9.8	14 735	7.7	8 441	23.6	1 285	10.7	7 876	22.7
2000	278 944	31 581	11.3	21 645	9.5	14 366	7.4	7 982	22.5	1 258	9.9	7 747	21.5
2001	281 475	32 907	11.7	22 739	9.9	15 271	7.8	8 136	22.7	1 275	10.2	7 997	21.4
2002	285 317	34 570	12.1	. . .	. . .	. . .	. . .	. . .	. . .	. . .	. . .	8 555	21.8
2003	287 699	35 861	12.5	. . .	. . .	. . .	. . .	. . .	. . .	. . .	. . .	9 051	22.5
2004	290 617	37 040	12.7	. . .	. . .	. . .	. . .	. . .	. . .	. . .	. . .	9 122	21.9
2005	293 135	36 950	12.6	. . .	. . .	. . .	. . .	. . .	. . .	. . .	. . .	9 368	21.8
2006	296 450	36 460	12.3	. . .	. . .	. . .	. . .	. . .	. . .	. . .	. . .	9 243	20.6
2007	298 699	37 276	12.5	. . .	. . .	. . .	. . .	. . .	. . .	. . .	. . .	9 890	21.5
2008	301 041	39 829	13.2	. . .	. . .	. . .	. . .	. . .	. . .	. . .	. . .	10 987	23.2
2009	303 820	43 569	14.3	. . .	. . .	. . .	. . .	. . .	. . .	. . .	. . .	12 350	25.3
2010	306 130	46 343	15.1	. . .	. . .	. . .	. . .	. . .	. . .	. . .	. . .	13 522	26.5
2011	308 456	46 247	15.0	. . .	. . .	. . .	. . .	. . .	. . .	. . .	. . .	13 244	25.3
2012	310 648	46 496	15.0	. . .	. . .	. . .	. . .	. . .	. . .	. . .	. . .	13 616	25.6
2013	312 965	45 318	14.5	. . .	. . .	. . .	. . .	. . .	. . .	. . .	. . .	12 744	23.5
2014	315 804	46 657	14.8	. . .	. . .	. . .	. . .	. . .	. . .	. . .	. . .	13 104	23.6
2015	318 454	43 123	13.5	. . .	. . .	. . .	. . .	. . .	. . .	. . .	. . .	12 133	21.4
2016	319 911	40 616	12.7	. . .	. . .	. . .	. . .	. . .	. . .	. . .	. . .	11 137	19.4
2017	322 549	39 698	12.3	. . .	. . .	. . .	. . .	. . .	. . .	. . .	. . .	10 790	18.3
2018	323 847	38 146	11.8	. . .	. . .	. . .	. . .	. . .	. . .	. . .	. . .	10 526	17.6
2019	324 754	33 984	10.5	. . .	. . .	. . .	. . .	. . .	. . .	. . .	. . .	9 545	15.7
2020	325 713	37 247	11.4	. . .	. . .	. . .	. . .	. . .	. . .	. . .	. . .	10 409	17.0
By race													
Race alone													
2005	. . .	. . .	. . .	24 872	10.6	16 227	8.3	9 168	24.9	. . .	. . .	. . .	. . .
2006	. . .	. . .	. . .	24 416	10.3	16 013	8.2	9 048	24.3	. . .	. . .	. . .	. . .
2007	. . .	. . .	. . .	25 120	10.5	16 032	8.2	9 237	24.5	. . .	. . .	. . .	. . .
2008	. . .	. . .	. . .	26 990	11.2	17 024	8.6	9 379	24.7	. . .	. . .	. . .	. . .
2009	. . .	. . .	. . .	29 830	12.3	18 530	9.4	9 944	25.8	. . .	. . .	. . .	. . .
2010	. . .	. . .	. . .	31 083	13.0	19 251	9.9	10 746	27.4	. . .	. . .	. . .	. . .
2011	. . .	. . .	. . .	30 849	12.8	19 171	9.8	10 929	27.6	. . .	. . .	. . .	. . .
2012	. . .	. . .	. . .	30 816	12.7	18 940	9.7	10 911	27.2	. . .	. . .	. . .	. . .
2013	. . .	. . .	. . .	31 287	12.9	19 552	10.0	10 186	25.2	. . .	. . .	. . .	. . .
2014	. . .	. . .	. . .	31 089	12.7	19 652	10.1	10 755	26.2	. . .	. . .	. . .	. . .
2015	. . .	. . .	. . .	28 566	11.6	17 786	9.1	10 020	24.1	. . .	. . .	. . .	. . .
2016	. . .	. . .	. . .	27 113	11.0	17 263	8.8	9 234	22.0	. . .	. . .	. . .	. . .
2017	. . .	. . .	. . .	26 026	10.5	16 619	8.5	8 993	21.2	. . .	. . .	. . .	. . .
2018	. . .	. . .	. . .	24 945	10.1	15 725	8.1	8 884	20.8	. . .	. . .	. . .	. . .
2019	. . .	. . .	. . .	22 512	9.1	14 152	7.3	8 073	18.8	. . .	. . .	. . .	. . .
2020	. . .	. . .	. . .	25 007	10.1	15 942	8.2	8 472	19.5	. . .	. . .	. . .	. . .
Race alone or in combination													
2010	. . .	. . .	. . .	. . .	. . .	. . .	. . .	. . .	. . .	2 064	12.0	. . .	. . .
2011	. . .	. . .	. . .	. . .	. . .	. . .	. . .	. . .	. . .	2 189	12.3	. . .	. . .
2012	. . .	. . .	. . .	. . .	. . .	. . .	. . .	. . .	. . .	2 072	11.4	. . .	. . .
2013	. . .	. . .	. . .	. . .	. . .	. . .	. . .	. . .	. . .	2 398	12.5	. . .	. . .
2014	. . .	. . .	. . .	. . .	. . .	. . .	. . .	. . .	. . .	2 268	11.5	. . .	. . .
2015	. . .	. . .	. . .	. . .	. . .	. . .	. . .	. . .	. . .	2 234	11.1	. . .	. . .
2016	. . .	. . .	. . .	. . .	. . .	. . .	. . .	. . .	. . .	2 062	9.9	. . .	. . .
2017	. . .	. . .	. . .	. . .	. . .	. . .	. . .	. . .	. . .	2 104	9.8	. . .	. . .
2018	. . .	. . .	. . .	. . .	. . .	. . .	. . .	. . .	. . .	2 166	9.8	. . .	. . .
2019	. . .	. . .	. . .	. . .	. . .	. . .	. . .	. . .	. . .	1 588	7.1	. . .	. . .
2020	. . .	. . .	. . .	. . .	. . .	. . .	. . .	. . .	. . .	1 808	8.0	. . .	. . .

[1] For 1987 through 2001, Asian and Pacific Islander.
. . . = Not available.

Table 3-7. Poverty Status of Families by Type of Family

(Thousands of families, percent.)

Year	Married couple families				Families with no spouse present						Unrelated individuals	
	Number of families		Poverty rate (percent)		Male householder			Female householder				
						Poverty rate (percent)			Poverty rate (percent)		Below poverty level	Poverty rate
	Total	Total below poverty level	Total	With children under 18 years	Familes below poverty level	Total	With children under 18 years	Familes below poverty level	Total	With children under 18 years		
1959	39 335	. . .	. . .	. . .	. . .	. . .	. . .	1 916	42.6	59.9	4 928	46.1
1960	39 624	. . .	. . .	. . .	. . .	. . .	. . .	1 955	42.4	56.3	4 926	45.2
1961	40 405	. . .	. . .	. . .	. . .	. . .	. . .	1 954	42.1	56.0	5 119	45.9
1962	40 923	. . .	. . .	. . .	. . .	. . .	. . .	2 034	42.9	59.7	5 002	45.4
1963	41 311	. . .	. . .	. . .	. . .	. . .	. . .	1 972	40.4	55.7	4 938	44.2
1964	41 648	. . .	. . .	. . .	. . .	. . .	. . .	1 822	36.4	49.7	5 143	42.7
1965	42 107	. . .	. . .	. . .	. . .	. . .	. . .	1 916	38.4	52.2	4 827	39.8
1966	42 553	. . .	. . .	. . .	. . .	. . .	. . .	1 721	33.1	47.1	4 701	38.3
1967	43 292	. . .	. . .	. . .	. . .	. . .	. . .	1 774	33.3	44.5	4 998	38.1
1968	43 842	. . .	. . .	. . .	. . .	. . .	. . .	1 755	32.3	44.6	4 694	34.0
1969	44 436	. . .	. . .	. . .	. . .	. . .	. . .	1 827	32.7	44.9	4 972	34.0
1970	44 739	. . .	. . .	. . .	. . .	. . .	. . .	1 952	32.5	43.8	5 090	32.9
1971	45 752	. . .	. . .	. . .	. . .	. . .	. . .	2 100	33.9	44.9	5 154	31.6
1972	46 314	. . .	. . .	. . .	. . .	. . .	. . .	2 158	32.7	44.5	4 883	29.0
1973	46 812	2 482	5.3	. . .	154	10.7	. . .	2 193	32.2	43.2	4 674	25.6
1974	47 069	2 474	5.3	6.0	125	8.9	15.4	2 324	32.1	43.7	4 553	24.1
1975	47 318	2 904	6.1	7.2	116	8.0	11.7	2 430	32.5	44.0	5 088	25.1
1976	47 497	2 606	5.5	6.4	162	10.8	15.4	2 543	33.0	44.1	5 344	24.9
1977	47 385	2 524	5.3	6.3	177	11.1	14.8	2 610	31.7	41.8	5 216	22.6
1978	47 692	2 474	5.2	5.9	152	9.2	14.7	2 654	31.4	42.2	5 435	22.1
1979	49 112	2 640	5.4	6.1	176	10.2	15.5	2 645	30.4	39.6	5 743	21.9
1980	49 294	3 032	6.2	7.7	213	11.0	18.0	2 972	32.7	42.9	6 227	22.9
1981	49 630	3 394	6.8	8.7	205	10.3	14.0	3 252	34.6	44.3	6 490	23.4
1982	49 908	3 789	7.6	9.8	290	14.4	20.6	3 434	36.3	47.8	6 458	23.1
1983	50 081	3 815	7.6	10.1	268	13.2	20.2	3 564	36.0	47.1	6 740	23.1
1984	50 350	3 488	6.9	9.4	292	13.1	18.1	3 498	34.5	45.7	6 609	21.8
1985	50 933	3 438	6.7	8.9	311	12.9	17.1	3 474	34.0	45.4	6 725	21.5
1986	51 537	3 123	6.1	8.0	287	11.4	17.8	3 613	34.6	46.0	6 846	21.6
1987	51 675	3 011	5.8	7.7	340	12.0	16.8	3 654	34.2	45.5	6 857	20.8
1988	52 100	2 897	5.6	7.2	336	11.8	18.0	3 642	33.4	44.7	7 070	20.6
1989	52 317	2 931	5.6	7.3	348	12.1	18.1	3 504	32.2	42.8	6 760	19.2
1990	52 147	2 981	5.7	7.8	349	12.0	18.8	3 768	33.4	44.5	7 446	20.7
1991	52 457	3 158	6.0	8.3	392	13.0	19.6	4 161	35.6	47.1	7 773	21.1
1992	53 090	3 385	6.4	8.6	484	15.8	22.5	4 275	35.4	46.2	8 075	21.9
1993	53 181	3 481	6.5	9.0	488	16.8	22.5	4 424	35.6	46.1	8 388	22.1
1994	53 865	3 272	6.1	8.3	549	17.0	22.6	4 232	34.6	44.0	8 287	21.5
1995	53 570	2 982	5.6	7.5	493	14.0	19.7	4 057	32.4	41.5	8 247	20.9
1996	53 604	3 010	5.6	7.5	531	13.8	20.0	4 167	32.6	41.9	8 452	20.8
1997	54 321	2 821	5.2	7.1	507	13.0	18.7	3 995	31.6	41.0	8 687	20.8
1998	54 778	2 879	5.3	6.9	476	12.0	16.6	3 831	29.9	38.7	8 478	19.9
1999	56 290	2 748	4.9	6.4	485	11.8	16.3	3 559	27.8	35.7	8 400	19.1
2000	56 598	2 637	4.7	6.0	485	11.3	15.3	3 278	25.4	33.0	8 653	19.0
2001	56 755	2 760	4.9	6.1	583	13.1	17.7	3 470	26.4	33.6	9 226	19.9
2002	57 327	3 052	5.3	6.8	564	12.1	16.6	3 613	26.5	33.7	9 618	20.4
2003	57 725	3 115	5.4	7.0	636	13.5	19.1	3 856	28.0	35.5	9 713	20.4
2004	57 983	3 216	5.5	7.0	657	13.4	17.1	3 962	28.3	35.9	9 926	20.4
2005	58 189	2 944	5.1	6.5	669	13.0	17.6	4 044	28.7	36.2	10 425	21.1
2006	58 964	2 910	4.9	6.4	671	13.2	17.9	4 087	28.3	36.5	9 977	20.0
2007	58 395	2 849	4.9	6.7	696	13.6	17.5	4 078	28.3	37.0	10 189	19.7
2008	59 137	3 261	5.5	7.5	723	13.8	17.6	4 163	28.7	37.2	10 710	20.8
2009	58 428	3 409	5.8	8.3	942	16.9	23.7	4 441	29.9	38.5	11 678	22.0
2010	58 667	3 681	6.3	9.0	892	15.8	24.1	4 827	31.7	40.9	12 449	22.9
2011	58 963	3 652	6.2	8.8	950	16.1	21.9	4 894	31.2	40.9	12 416	22.8
2012	59 224	3 705	6.3	8.9	1 023	16.4	22.6	4 793	30.9	40.9	12 558	22.4
2013	59 692	3 476	5.8	7.6	1 008	15.9	19.7	4 646	30.6	39.6	13 181	23.3
2014	60 015	3 735	6.2	8.2	969	15.7	22.0	4 764	30.6	39.8	13 374	23.1
2015	60 258	3 245	5.4	7.5	939	14.9	22.1	4 404	28.2	36.5	12 671	21.5
2016	60 821	3 096	5.1	6.6	847	13.1	17.3	4 138	26.6	35.6	12 336	21.0
2017	61 254	3 005	4.9	6.4	793	12.4	16.2	3 959	25.7	34.4	12 465	20.8
2018	61 971	2 938	4.7	5.8	824	12.7	16.6	3 742	24.9	33.8	12 287	20.2
2019	62 355	2 507	4.0	5.1	746	11.5	15.3	3 300	22.2	30.7	11 300	18.8
2020	61 463	2 866	4.7	5.9	796	11.4	14.0	3 633	23.4	32.1	11 916	19.1

. . . = Not available.

Table 3-8. Poverty Status of People by Sex and Age

(Thousands of people, percent of population.)

Year	Poverty status of people by sex				Poverty status of people by age					
	Males below poverty level		Females below poverty level		Children under 18 years below poverty level		People 18 to 64 years below poverty level		People 65 years and older below poverty level	
	Number (thousands)	Poverty rate (percent)	Number (thousands)	Poverty rate (percent)	Number (thousands)	Poverty rate (percent)	Number (thousands)	Poverty rate (percent)	Number (thousands)	Poverty rate (percent)
1966	12 225	13.0	16 265	16.3	12 389	17.6	11 007	10.5	5 114	28.5
1967	11 813	12.5	15 951	15.8	11 656	16.6	10 725	10.0	5 388	29.5
1968	10 793	11.3	14 578	14.3	10 954	15.6	9 803	9.0	4 632	25.0
1969	10 292	10.6	13 978	13.6	9 691	14.0	9 669	8.7	4 787	25.3
1970	10 879	11.1	14 632	14.0	10 440	15.1	10 187	9.0	4 793	24.6
1971	10 708	10.8	14 841	14.1	10 551	15.3	10 735	9.3	4 273	21.6
1972	10 190	10.2	14 258	13.4	10 284	15.1	10 438	8.8	3 738	18.6
1973	9 642	9.6	13 316	12.5	9 642	14.4	9 977	8.3	3 354	16.3
1974	9 945	9.8	13 429	12.5	10 156	15.4	10 132	8.3	3 085	14.6
1975	10 908	10.7	14 970	13.8	11 104	17.1	11 456	9.2	3 317	15.3
1976	10 373	10.1	14 603	13.4	10 273	16.0	11 389	9.0	3 313	15.0
1977	10 340	10.0	14 381	13.0	10 288	16.2	11 316	8.8	3 177	14.1
1978	10 017	9.6	14 480	13.0	9 931	15.9	11 332	8.7	3 233	14.0
1979	10 861	10.1	15 211	13.2	10 377	16.4	12 014	8.9	3 682	15.2
1980	12 207	11.2	17 065	14.7	11 543	18.3	13 858	10.1	3 871	15.7
1981	13 360	12.1	18 462	15.8	12 505	20.0	15 464	11.1	3 853	15.3
1982	14 842	13.4	19 556	16.5	13 647	21.9	17 000	12.0	3 751	14.6
1983	15 296	13.6	20 006	16.8	13 911	22.3	17 767	12.4	3 625	13.8
1984	14 537	12.8	19 163	15.9	13 420	21.5	16 952	11.7	3 330	12.4
1985	14 140	12.3	18 923	15.6	13 010	20.7	16 598	11.3	3 456	12.6
1986	13 721	11.8	18 649	15.2	12 876	20.5	16 017	10.8	3 477	12.4
1987	13 781	11.8	18 439	14.9	12 843	20.3	15 815	10.6	3 563	12.5
1988	13 599	11.5	18 146	14.5	12 455	19.5	15 809	10.5	3 481	12.0
1989	13 366	11.2	18 162	14.4	12 590	19.6	15 575	10.2	3 363	11.4
1990	14 211	11.7	19 373	15.2	13 431	20.6	16 496	10.7	3 658	12.2
1991	15 082	12.3	20 626	16.0	14 341	21.8	17 586	11.4	3 781	12.4
1992	16 222	12.9	21 792	16.6	15 294	22.3	18 793	11.9	3 928	12.9
1993	16 900	13.3	22 365	16.9	15 727	22.7	19 781	12.4	3 755	12.2
1994	16 316	12.8	21 744	16.3	15 289	21.8	19 107	11.9	3 663	11.7
1995	15 683	12.2	20 742	15.4	14 665	20.8	18 442	11.4	3 318	10.5
1996	15 611	12.0	20 918	15.4	14 463	20.5	18 638	11.4	3 428	10.8
1997	15 187	11.6	20 387	14.9	14 113	19.9	18 085	10.9	3 376	10.5
1998	14 712	11.1	19 764	14.3	13 467	18.9	17 623	10.5	3 386	10.5
1999	14 079	10.4	18 712	13.2	12 280	17.1	17 289	10.1	3 222	9.7
2000	13 536	9.9	18 045	12.6	11 587	16.2	16 671	9.6	3 323	9.9
2001	14 327	10.4	18 580	12.9	11 733	16.3	17 760	10.1	3 414	10.1
2002	15 162	10.9	19 408	13.3	12 133	16.7	18 861	10.6	3 576	10.4
2003	15 783	11.2	20 078	13.7	12 866	17.6	19 443	10.8	3 552	10.2
2004	16 399	11.5	20 641	13.9	13 041	17.8	20 545	11.3	3 453	9.8
2005	15 950	11.1	21 000	14.1	12 896	17.6	20 450	11.1	3 603	10.1
2006	16 000	11.0	20 460	13.6	12 827	17.4	20 239	10.8	3 394	9.4
2007	16 302	11.1	20 973	13.8	13 324	18.0	20 396	10.9	3 556	9.7
2008	17 698	12.0	22 131	14.4	14 068	19.0	22 105	11.7	3 656	9.7
2009	19 475	13.0	24 094	15.6	15 451	20.7	24 684	12.9	3 433	8.9
2010	20 893	14.0	25 451	16.3	16 286	22.0	26 499	13.8	3 558	8.9
2011	20 501	13.6	25 746	16.3	16 134	21.9	26 492	13.7	3 620	8.7
2012	20 656	13.6	25 840	16.3	16 073	21.8	26 497	13.7	3 926	9.1
2013	20 119	13.1	25 199	15.8	14 659	19.9	26 429	13.6	4 231	9.5
2014	20 708	13.4	25 949	16.1	15 540	21.1	26 527	13.5	4 590	10.0
2015	19 037	12.2	24 086	14.8	14 509	19.7	24 414	12.4	4 201	8.8
2016	17 685	11.3	22 931	14.0	13 253	18.0	22 795	11.6	4 568	9.3
2017	17 365	11.0	22 333	13.6	12 808	17.5	22 209	11.2	4 681	9.2
2018	16 782	10.6	21 363	12.9	11 869	16.2	21 130	10.7	5 146	9.7
2019	14 976	9.4	19 008	11.5	10 466	14.4	18 660	9.4	4 858	8.9
2020	16 334	10.2	20 912	12.6	11 607	16.1	20 640	10.4	5 000	9.0

. . . = Not available.

Table 3-9. Working-Age Poor People by Work Experience

(Thousands of people, percent of population [poverty rate], percent of total poor people.)

| Year | Total number of working-age poor people | Worked | | | | | | | | | Did not work | | |
| | | Number | Percent of total poor | Worked year-round, full-time | | | Worked less than year-round or full-time | | | Number | Poverty rate (percent) | Percent of total poor |
				Number	Poverty rate (percent)	Percent of total poor	Number	Poverty rate (percent)	Percent of total poor			
16 Years and Over												
1978	16 914	6 599	39.0	1 309	. . .	7.7	. . .	. . .	31.3	. . .	. . .	61.0
1979	16 803	6 601	39.3	1 394	. . .	8.3	. . .	. . .	31.0	. . .	. . .	60.7
1980	18 892	7 674	40.6	1 644	. . .	8.7	. . .	. . .	31.9	. . .	. . .	59.4
1981	20 571	8 524	41.4	1 881	. . .	9.1	. . .	. . .	32.3	. . .	. . .	58.6
1982	22 100	9 013	40.8	1 999	. . .	9.0	. . .	. . .	31.7	. . .	. . .	59.2
1983	22 741	9 329	41.0	2 064	. . .	9.1	. . .	. . .	31.9	. . .	. . .	59.0
1984	21 541	8 999	41.8	2 076	. . .	9.6	. . .	. . .	32.1	. . .	. . .	58.2
1985	21 243	9 008	42.4	1 972	. . .	9.3	. . .	. . .	33.1	. . .	. . .	57.6
1986	20 688	8 743	42.3	2 007	. . .	9.7	. . .	. . .	32.6	. . .	. . .	57.7
1987	20 546	8 258	40.2	1 821	2.4	8.9	6 436	12.5	31.3	12 288	21.6	59.8
1988	20 323	8 363	41.2	1 929	2.4	9.5	6 434	12.7	31.7	11 959	21.2	58.8
1989	19 952	8 376	42.0	1 908	2.4	9.6	6 468	12.5	32.4	11 576	20.8	58.0
1990	21 242	8 716	41.0	2 076	2.6	9.8	6 639	12.6	31.3	12 526	22.1	59.0
1991	22 530	9 208	40.9	2 103	2.6	9.3	7 105	13.4	31.5	13 323	22.8	59.1
1992	23 951	9 739	40.6	2 211	2.7	9.2	7 529	14.1	31.4	14 212	23.7	59.3
1993	24 832	10 144	40.8	2 408	2.9	9.7	7 737	14.6	31.2	14 688	24.2	59.1
1994	24 108	9 829	40.8	2 520	2.9	10.5	7 309	13.9	30.3	14 279	23.6	59.2
1995	23 077	9 484	41.1	2 418	2.7	10.5	7 066	13.7	30.6	13 593	22.3	58.9
1996	23 472	9 586	40.8	2 263	2.5	9.6	7 322	14.1	31.2	13 886	22.7	59.2
1997	22 753	9 444	41.5	2 345	2.5	10.3	7 098	13.8	31.2	13 310	21.7	58.5
1998	22 256	9 133	41.0	2 804	2.9	12.6	6 330	12.7	28.4	13 122	21.1	59.0
1999	21 762	9 251	42.5	2 559	2.6	11.8	6 692	13.2	30.8	12 511	19.9	57.5
2000	21 080	8 511	40.4	2 439	2.4	11.6	6 072	12.1	28.8	12 569	19.8	59.6
2001	22 245	8 530	38.3	2 567	2.6	11.5	5 964	11.8	26.8	13 715	20.6	61.7
2002	23 601	8 954	37.9	2 635	2.6	11.2	6 318	12.4	26.8	14 647	21.0	62.1
2003	24 266	8 820	36.3	2 636	2.6	10.9	6 183	12.2	25.5	15 446	21.5	63.7
2004	25 256	9 384	37.2	2 891	2.8	11.4	6 493	12.8	25.7	15 871	21.7	62.8
2005	25 381	9 340	36.8	2 894	2.8	11.4	6 446	12.8	25.4	16 041	21.8	63.2
2006	24 896	9 181	36.9	2 906	2.7	11.7	6 275	12.6	25.2	15 715	21.1	63.1
2007	25 297	9 089	35.9	2 768	2.5	10.9	6 320	12.7	25.0	16 208	21.5	64.1
2008	27 216	10 085	37.1	2 754	2.6	10.1	7 331	13.5	26.9	17 131	22.0	62.9
2009	29 625	10 680	36.1	2 641	2.7	8.9	8 039	14.5	27.1	18 944	22.7	63.9
2010	31 731	10 742	33.9	2 640	2.7	8.3	8 102	15.0	25.5	20 989	23.9	66.1
2011	31 630	10 588	33.5	2 770	2.7	8.8	7 818	14.9	24.7	21 042	23.6	66.5
2012	31 933	10 977	34.4	2 904	2.8	9.1	8 073	15.0	25.3	20 956	23.6	65.6
2013	32 011	11 025	34.4	2 812	2.7	8.8	8 213	15.8	25.7	20 986	23.2	65.6
2014	32 508	10 469	32.2	3 142	2.9	9.7	7 327	14.3	22.5	22 039	24.2	67.8
2015	30 123	9 795	32.5	2 576	2.3	8.6	7 220	13.9	24.0	20 328	22.5	67.5
2016	28 696	9 109	31.7	2 448	2.2	8.5	6 661	13.0	21.6	19 587	21.6	68.3
2017	28 167	8 503	30.2	2 468	2.1	8.8	6 035	12.0	21.4	19 664	21.4	69.7
2018	27 496	8 213	29.9	2 591	2.2	9.4	5 621	11.4	20.4	19 283	20.9	70.1
2019	24 502	7 632	31.1	2 356	2.0	9.6	5 277	10.5	21.5	16 870	18.5	68.9
2020	26 791	7 929	29.6	1 640	1.6	6.1	6 289	10.3	23.5	18 862	19.8	70.4

. . . = Not available.

Table 3-10. Number and Percent of People in Poverty Using the Supplemental Poverty Measure, 2018–2020, and Comparison With Official Measures in 2020

(Numbers in thousands; percent of population.)

Characteristic	SPM 2018		SPM 2019		SPM 2020		Official 2020[1]	
	Number	Percent	Number	Percent	Number	Percent	Number	Percent
All People	41 420	12.8	38 300	11.8	29 805	9.1	37 314	11.4
Sex								
Male	19 269	12.1	17 666	11.1	13 837	8.6	16 370	10.2
Female	22 151	13.4	20 634	12.4	15 968	9.6	20 944	12.6
Age								
Under 18 years	10 096	13.7	9 253	12.6	7 079	9.7	11 674	16.0
18 to 64 years	24 151	12.2	22 073	11.2	17 433	8.8	20 640	10.4
65 years and older	7 174	13.6	6 975	12.8	5 293	9.5	5 000	9.0
Type of Unit								
In married-couple unit	15 043	7.7	13 479	6.8	9 728	5.0	10 193	5.3
In female householder unit	3 659	13.9	3 147	12.1	2 466	8.5	6 661	23.1
In male householder unit	10 390	25.0	9 732	23.8	7 668	18.2	10 073	23.1
Cohabitating	2 197	15.1	2 141	14.2	1 818	11.7	1 636	10.5
Unrelated individuals	10 132	21.9	9 801	21.6	8 125	17.5	8 752	18.9
Race and Hispanic Origin								
White	27 820	11.2	26 029	10.5	20 156	8.1	25 052	10.1
White, not Hispanic	16 932	8.7	15 921	8.2	12 646	6.5	15 974	8.2
Black	8 727	20.4	8 144	18.9	6 369	14.6	8 493	19.5
Asian	2 749	13.9	2 257	11.3	1 770	8.8	1 629	8.1
Hispanic, any race	12 216	20.3	11 437	18.8	8 570	14.0	10 422	17.0
Nativity								
Native born	26 158	11.8	24 312	10.9	18 866	8.4	21 443	9.5
Foreign born	6 320	28.8	5 600	27.7	4 068	20.3	4 953	24.7
Naturalized citizen	9 272	14.9	8 588	13.9	6 929	11.1	8 273	13.2
Not a citizen	5 599	9.7	5 449	9.5	4 177	7.3	4 781	8.4
Educational Attainment								
Total, age 25 and over	4 967	6.2	4 674	5.6	3 692	4.3	3 436	4.0
No high school diploma	32 540	11.7	30 460	10.9	23 657	8.4	31 292	11.1
High school, no college	8 880	19.4	7 840	17.5	6 148	13.1	6 022	13.4
Some college	3 297	14.8	3 076	13.5	2 335	10.3	2 080	9.2
Bachelor's degree or higher	5 584	23.7	4 764	21.5	3 813	17.2	3 942	17.8
Tenure								
Owner/ mortgage	7 831	5.9	7 035	5.1	5 283	3.9	5 570	4.1
Owner/no-mortgage/rent-free	10 146	11.8	9 726	10.9	7 313	8.2	9 707	10.8
Renter	23 443	22.4	21 540	22.1	17 210	17.1	22 036	21.9
Residence								
Inside metropolitan statistical areas	31 978	12.9	33 359	11.8	26 286	9.3	31 337	11.0
Inside principal cities	15 309	16.0	15 654	14.9	12 573	11.9	15 128	14.3
Outside principal cities	16 669	11.0	17 705	10.0	13 712	7.7	16 209	9.1
Outside metropolitan statistical areas	6 222	12.2	4 941	11.6	3 519	8.3	5 977	14.1
Region								
Northeast	5 689	12.2	6 341	11.5	4 686	8.5	5 558	10.1
Midwest	7 008	9.2	6 081	9.0	4 498	6.7	6 840	10.1
South	16 786	13.9	15 662	12.6	12 704	10.1	16 651	13.3
West	8 716	14.4	10 216	13.1	7 918	10.1	8 265	10.6
Health Insurance Coverage								
With private insurance	8 376	5.9	11 933	5.4	8 976	4.1	8 642	4.0
With public, no private insurance	23 520	27.8	19 993	25.8	15 290	18.8	22 182	27.3
Not insured	6 305	24.4	6 375	23.8	5 538	19.4	6 490	22.8
Work Experience								
Total, 18 to 64 years	21 130	12.2	22 073	11.2	17 433	8.8	20 640	10.4
All workers	7 781	7.2	10 491	6.8	7 056	4.6	7 595	5.0
Full-time, year-round	2 544	4.3	4 371	3.9	1 864	1.9	1 609	1.6
Less than full-time, year-round	5 237	14.9	6 120	14.6	5 192	9.8	5 984	11.3
Did not work at least 1 week	13 349	29.4	11 582	27.0	10 377	22.9	13 047	28.8
Disability Status								
Total, 18 to 64 years	24 151	12.2	22 073	11.2	17 433	8.8	20 640	10.4
With a disability	3 609	24.3	3 203	22.2	2 562	17.6	3 643	25.0
With no disability	20 500	11.3	18 804	10.3	14 842	8.2	16 966	9.3

[1]Differs from published official rates because these figures include unrelated individuals under 15 years of age as does the SPM.

SECTION 3C: HEALTH INSURANCE COVERAGE

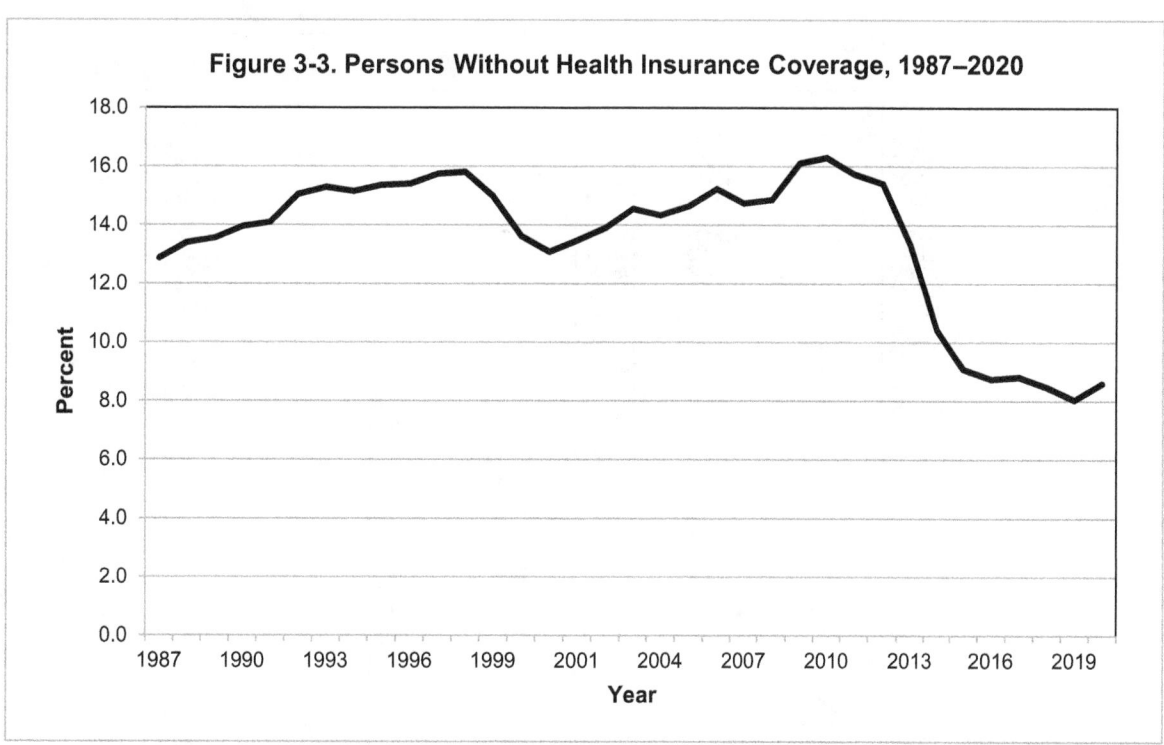

Figure 3-3. Persons Without Health Insurance Coverage, 1987–2020

- Health insurance is a means for financing a person's health care expenses. Over time, changes in the percentage of people covered may reflect economic trends, policy changes, or shifts in demographics. For example, Baby Boomers are retiring and thus switching from private insurance to public insurance. Access to health insurance expanded in 2010 with the passage of Patient Protection and Affordable Care Act (ACA). During the COVID-19 pandemic, the numbers of those without insurance rose as unemployment increased.

- From 2019 to 2020, the percentage of people covered by private insurance declined from 68.0 percent to 66.5 percent. This was driven by a decline in the employment-based coverage. In contrast, public health insurance coverage increased from 34.1 percent to 34.8 percent. These public programs include Medicare Medicaid TRICARE (Military) and Department of Veterans Affairs (CHAMPVA) coverage (0.9 percent).

- The percentage of those without insurance has declined from 15.7 percent in 2011 to 8.0 percent in 2019. However, in 2020 during the global pandemic, the percentage of those without insurance rose to 8.6 percent. As unemployment increased, people lost their employment-based insurance. (Table 3-12)

Table 3-11.　Health Insurance Coverage

(Number in thousands. People as of March of the following year.)

| Year | Total | Total covered | Private health insurance | | | Government health insurance | | | | Not covered |
			Total	Employment	Direct purchase	Total	Medicaid	Medicare	Military	
NUMBER										
1987	241 187	210 161	182 160	149 739	. . .	56 282	20 211	30 458	10 542	31 026
1988	243 685	211 005	182 019	150 940	. . .	56 850	20 728	30 925	10 105	32 680
1989	246 191	212 807	183 610	151 644	. . .	57 382	21 185	31 495	9 870	33 384
1990	248 886	214 167	182 135	150 215	. . .	60 965	24 261	32 260	9 922	34 719
1991	251 447	216 003	181 375	150 077	. . .	63 882	26 880	32 907	9 820	35 444
1992	256 830	218 189	181 466	148 796	. . .	66 244	29 416	33 230	9 510	38 641
1993	259 753	220 040	182 351	148 318	. . .	68 554	31 749	33 097	9 560	39 713
1994	262 105	222 387	184 318	159 634	31 349	70 163	31 645	33 901	11 165	39 718
1995	264 314	223 733	185 881	161 453	30 188	69 776	31 877	34 655	9 375	40 581
1996	266 792	225 699	188 224	164 096	28 419	69 000	31 451	35 227	8 712	41 093
1997	269 094	226 735	189 955	166 419	27 431	66 685	28 956	35 590	8 527	42 359
1998	271 743	228 800	192 507	170 105	26 165	66 087	27 854	35 887	8 747	42 943
1999	550 891	472 175	398 557	349 227	56 608	133 279	55 243	73 056	17 056	78 716
2000	279 517	242 932	205 575	181 862	28 432	68 183	28 062	37 787	8 937	36 585
2001	282 082	244 059	204 142	179 984	28 398	70 330	30 166	37 870	9 580	38 023
2002	285 933	246 157	204 163	179 563	29 287	72 825	31 934	38 359	9 892	39 776
2003	288 280	246 332	201 989	177 362	28 826	76 119	34 326	39 284	10 124	41 948
2004	291 166	249 414	203 014	177 924	29 161	79 480	38 055	39 757	10 584	41 752
2005	293 834	250 799	203 205	178 391	28 980	80 283	38 191	40 167	11 164	43 035
2006	296 824	251 610	203 942	178 880	29 033	80 343	38 370	40 336	10 543	45 214
2007	299 106	255 018	203 903	178 971	28 500	83 147	39 685	41 387	10 955	44 088
2008	301 483	256 702	202 626	177 543	28 513	87 586	42 831	43 031	11 562	44 781
2009	304 280	255 295	196 245	170 762	29 098	93 245	47 847	43 434	12 414	48 985
2010	306 553	256 603	196 147	169 372	30 347	95 525	48 533	44 906	12 927	49 950
2011	308 827	260 214	197 323	170 102	30 244	99 497	50 835	46 922	13 712	48 613
2012	311 116	263 165	198 812	170 877	30 622	101 493	50 903	48 884	13 702	47 951
2013	313 401	271 606	201 038	174 418	35 755	108 287	54 919	49 020	14 016	41 795
2014	316 168	283 200	208 600	175 027	46 165	115 470	61 650	50 546	14 143	32 968
2015	318 868	289 903	214 238	177 540	52 057	118 395	62 384	51 865	14 849	28 966
2016	320 372	292 320	216 203	178 455	51 961	119 361	62 303	53 372	14 638	28 052
2017	323 156	294 613	217 007	181 036	51 821	121 965	62 492	55 623	15 532	28 543
2018	323 668	296 206	217 780	178 350	34 846	111 330	57 819	57 720	11 754	27 462
2019	324 550	298 438	220 848	183 005	33 170	110 687	55 851	581 779	11 755	26 111
2020	325 638	297 680	216 532	177 175	34 041	113 337	57 921	59 844	2 979	27 957

. . . = Not available.

Table 3-12.   Percentage of People by Type of Health Insurance by Selected Demographics, 2019–2020

(Number in thousands. Percent. People as of March of the following year.)

Characteristic	Any health insurance		Private health insurance		Government health insurance		Uninsured	
	2019	2020	2019	2020	2019	2020	2019	2020
Total	92.0	91.4	68.0	66.5	34.1	34.8	8.0	8.6
Age								
Under age 19	94.8	94.4	63.8	62.2	34.3	35.1	5.2	5.6
Aged 19 to 64	88.9	88.1	74.4	73.0	17.2	17.7	11.1	11.9
Aged 65 and older	98.9	99.0	51.6	49.6	93.8	93.6	1.1	1.0
Marital Status								
Married	92.4	91.5	83.4	82.1	12.2	12.3	7.6	8.5
Widowed	86.5	87.9	56.5	60.1	33.5	32.6	13.5	12.1
Divorced	88.0	86.8	67.4	65.0	23.6	24.9	12.0	13.2
Separated	81.0	79.8	51.8	53.0	31.4	29.7	19.0	20.2
Never married	84.3	84.0	65.1	63.9	21.3	22.1	15.7	16.0
Disability Status								
With a disability	91.6	91.0	47.3	45.5	52.4	52.9	8.4	9.0
With no disability	89.1	88.2	75.8	74.4	15.6	16.2	10.9	11.8
Work Experience								
All workers	89.9	89.0	80.8	79.8	11.2	11.4	10.2	11.0
Worked full-time, year-round	91.1	91.6	85.8	87.0	7.0	6.1	8.9	8.4
Worked less than full-time, year-round	86.6	84.3	68.2	66.7	21.6	20.9	13.4	15.7
Did not work at least one week	87.8	87.1	53.2	52.2	39.1	39.1	12.2	12.9
Educational Attainment								
Total, 26 to 64 years old	89.4	88.5	75.1	73.7	17.2	17.6	10.6	11.5
No high school diploma	71.5	68.1	38.9	35.4	35.9	35.4	28.5	31.9
High school graduate (includes equivalency)	85.1	83.9	64.2	61.5	24.2	25.8	14.9	16.1
Some college, no degree	89.8	89.3	73.7	72.6	19.7	20.4	10.2	10.7
Associate degree	91.6	91.0	79.3	77.7	15.8	16.5	8.4	9.0
Bachelor's degree	94.7	94.1	87.6	87.5	9.1	8.8	5.3	5.9
Graduate or profesional degree	96.8	96.5	93.2	92.3	5.4	5.8	3.2	3.5
Family Status								
In families	92.6	91.9	69.4	67.8	32.9	33.3	7.4	8.1
Householder	93.1	92.4	72.4	71.1	34.9	34.9	6.9	7.6
Related children under 18	95.0	94.6	63.8	62.6	34.3	35.0	5.0	5.4
Related children under 6	95.2	94.7	61.7	60.6	36.6	37.0	4.8	5.3
In unrelated subfamilies	90.6	86.5	58.5	51.3	38.2	38.2	9.4	13.5
Unrelated individuals	89.2	89.5	62.4	61.2	39.9	41.1	10.8	10.5
Residence								
Inside metropolitan statistical areas	92.1	91.5	68.9	67.2	32.8	35.4	7.9	8.5
Inside principal cities	90.4	89.7	63.9	62.1	34.7	30.9	9.6	10.3
Outside principal cities	93.1	92.5	71.8	70.3	31.7	36.8	6.9	7.5
Outside metropolitan statistical areas	91.2	91.0	62.4	61.5	42.6	24.9	8.8	9.0
Race and Hispanic Origin								
White	92.2	91.7	70.1	68.6	33.5	34.3	7.8	8.3
White, not Hispanic	94.8	94.6	75.2	73.9	33.0	33.8	5.2	5.4
Black	90.4	89.6	55.2	54.6	41.8	41.4	9.6	10.4
Asian	93.8	94.1	74.4	72.4	25.2	27.0	6.2	5.9
Hispanic (any race)	83.3	87.7	51.6	49.9	35.8	35.9	16.7	18.3
Nativity								
Native born	93.5	93.1	69.7	68.2	34.6	35.4	6.5	6.9
Foreign born	82.2	80.7	57.7	55.8	30.8	30.9	17.8	19.3
Naturalized citizen	91.3	91.7	64.0	63.8	36.6	36.8	8.7	8.3
Not a citizen	72.9	69.4	51.3	47.5	24.9	24.9	21.7	30.6

. . . = Not available.

NOTES AND DEFINITIONS, CHAPTER 3

Tables 3-1 through 3-12

Income Distribution and Poverty

SOURCE: U.S. DEPARTMENT OF COMMERCE, BUREAU OF THE CENSUS

All data in this chapter are derived from the Current Population Survey (CPS), which is also the source of the data on labor force, employment, and unemployment used in Chapter 10. (See the notes and definitions for Tables 10-1 through 10-5.) In March of each year (with some data also collected in February and April), the households in this monthly survey are asked additional questions concerning earnings and other income in the previous year. This additional information, informally known as the "March Supplement," is now formally known as the Current Population Survey Annual Social and Economic Supplement (CPS-ASEC). It was previously called the Annual Demographic Supplement.

Collected annually, CPS-ASEC is one of the most widely used socioeconomic surveys, and provides detailed information on income, work experience, poverty, health insurance coverage, and living arrangements in the U.S. For the past several years, the Census Bureau has engaged in implementing improvements to the CPS-ASEC, especially to improve data quality, using redesigned income questions. More information on these changes in the section *Notes on the Data.*

The U.S. Census Bureau administers the CPS ASEC each year between February and April by telephone and in-person interviews, with the majority of data collected in March. In 2020, data collection faced extraordinary circumstances due to the onset of the COVID-19 pandemic as the Census Bureau suspended in-person interviews and closed both telephone contact centers. The response rate for the CPS basic household survey was 73 percent in March 2020, about 10 percentage points lower than preceding months and the same period in 2019, which were regularly above 80 percent.

During collection of the 2021 CPS ASEC, for the safety of both interviewers and respondents, in-person interviews were only conducted when telephone interviews could not be done. In March 2021, the response rate for the CPS basic household survey improved to about 76 percent, though not quite returning to the pre-pandemic trend. While the response rate improved, it is important to examine how respondents differ from nonrespondents, as this difference could affect income and poverty estimates. Using administrative data, Census Bureau researchers have documented that the nonrespondents in both 2020 and 2021 are less similar to respondents than in earlier years. Of particular interest for the estimates in this report, are the differences in median income and educational attainment, indicating that respondents in 2020 and 2021 had relatively higher income and were more educated than nonrespondents.

Researchers should use caution when comparing results over time. Due to the changes, comparison of variables between 2013 and 2018 are not comparable. The 2014 CPS ASEC included redesigned questions for income and health insurance coverage. All of the approximately 98,000 addresses were eligible to receive the redesigned set of health insurance coverage questions. The redesigned income questions were implemented to a subsample of these 98,000 addresses using a probability split panel design.

The population represented by the income and poverty survey is the civilian noninstitutional population of the United States and members of the armed forces in the United States living off post or with their families on post, but excluding all other members of the armed forces. This is slightly different from the population base for the civilian employment and unemployment data, which excludes those armed forces households. As it is a survey of households, homeless persons are not included.

Tables 3-1 through 3-10

Definitions: Racial classification and Hispanic origin

In 2002 and all earlier years, the CPS required respondents to report identification with only one race group. Since 2003, the CPS has allowed respondents to choose more than one race group. Income data for 2002 were collected in early 2003; thus, in the data for 2002 and all subsequent years, an individual could report identification with more than one race group. In the 2010 census, about 2.9 percent of people reported identification with more than one race.

Therefore, data from 2002 onward that are classified by race are not strictly comparable with race-classified data for 2001 and earlier years. As alternative approaches to dealing with this problem, the Census Bureau has tabulated two different race concepts for each racial category in a number of cases. In the case of Blacks, for example, this means there is one income measure for "Black alone," consisting of persons who report Black and no other race, and one for "Black alone or in combination," which includes all the "Black alone" reporters plus those who report Black in combination with any other race. The tables in this volume show both the "alone" and the "alone or in combination" values where available.

The race classifications now used in the CPS are *White, Black, Asian, American Indian and Alaska Native,* and *Native Hawaiian and Other Pacific Islander.* (Native Hawaiians and other Pacific Islanders were included in the "Asian" category in the data for 1987 through 2001.) The last two of these five racial groups are too small to provide reliable data for a single year, but in new Census Bureau tables available on the website, household income and poverty data for all five groups are presented in 2- and 3-year averages. Table 3-1 displays some of these data.

Hispanic origin is a separate question in the survey—not a racial classification—and Hispanics may be of any race. A subgroup of *White non-Hispanic* is shown in some tables. According to the Census 2010 population results, "Being Hispanic was reported by 11.6 percent of White householders who reported only one race, 4.5 percent of Black householders who reported only one race, and 3.5 percent of Asian householders who reported only one race. Data users should exercise caution when interpreting aggregate results for the Hispanic population or for race groups because these populations consist of many distinct groups that differ in socioeconomic characteristics, culture, and recent immigration status." ("Income, and Poverty in the United States: 2017", footnote 2, p. 3 and "Health Insurance Coverage in the United States: 2017" footnote 2, p. 3.

Definitions: General

A *household* consists of all persons who occupy a housing unit. A household includes the related family members and all the unrelated persons, if any (such as lodgers, foster children, wards, or employees), who share the housing unit. A person living alone in a housing unit or a group of unrelated persons sharing a housing unit as partners is also counted as a household. The count of households excludes group quarters.

Earnings includes all income from work, including wages, salaries, armed forces pay, commissions, tips, piece-rate payments, and cash bonuses, before deductions such as taxes, bonds, pensions, and union dues. This category also includes net income from nonfarm self-employment and farm self-employment. Wage and salary supplements that are paid directly by the employer, such as the employer share of Social Security taxes and the cost of employer-provided health insurance, are not included.

Income, in the official definition used in the survey, is money income, including *earnings* from work as defined above; unemployment compensation; workers' compensation; Social Security; Supplemental Security Income; cash public assistance (welfare payments); veterans' payments; survivor benefits; disability benefits; pension or retirement income; interest income; dividends (but not capital gains); rents, royalties, and payments from estates or trusts; educational assistance, such as scholarships or grants; child support; alimony; financial assistance from outside of the household; and other cash income regularly received, such as foster child payments, military family allotments, and foreign government pensions. Receipts not counted as income include capital gains or losses, withdrawals of bank deposits, money borrowed, tax refunds, gifts, and lump-sum inheritances or insurance payments.

A *year-round, full-time worker* is a person who worked 35 or more hours per week and 50 or more weeks during the previous calendar year.

A *family* is a group of two or more persons related by birth, marriage, or adoption who reside together.

Unrelated individuals are persons 15 years old and over who are not living with any relatives. In the official poverty measure, the poverty status of unrelated individuals is determined independently of and is not affected by the incomes of other persons with whom they may share a household.

Median income is the amount of income that divides a ranked income distribution into two equal groups, with half having incomes above the median, and half having incomes below the median. The median income for persons is based on persons 15 years old and over with income. Since median income is updated annually to inflation adjusted current dollars, comparison between editions is not possible.

Mean income is the amount obtained by dividing the total aggregate income of a group by the number of units in that group. In this survey, as in most surveys of incomes, means are higher than medians because of the skewed nature of the income distribution; see the section "Whose standard of living?" in the article at the beginning of this book.

Historical income figures are shown in constant *2018 dollars*. All constant-dollar figures are converted from current-dollar values using the *CPI-U-RS* (the Consumer Price Index, All Urban, Research Series), which measures changes in prices for past periods using the methodologies of the current CPI, and is similar in concept and behavior to the deflators used in the NIPAs for consumer income and spending. See Chapter 8 for CPI-U-RS data and the corresponding notes and definitions.

Definitions: Income distribution

Income distribution is portrayed by dividing the total ranked distribution of families or households into *fifths*, also known as *quintiles,* and also by separately tabulating the top 5 percent (which is included in the highest fifth). The households or families are arrayed from those with the lowest income to those with the highest income, then divided into five groups, with each group containing one-fifth of the total number of households. Within each quintile, incomes are summed and calculated as a share of total income for all quintiles, and are averaged to show the average (mean) income within that quintile.

A statistical measure that summarizes the dispersion of income across the entire income distribution is the *Gini coefficient* (also known as Gini ratio, Gini index, or index of income concentration), wirh values ranging from 0 to 1. A Gini value of 1 indicates "perfect" inequality; that is, one household has all the income and the rest have none. A value of 0 indicates "perfect" equality, a situation in which each household has the same income. Rising quotient values signal increasing inequality.

A new "equivalence-adjusted" measure of household income inequality was introduced recently and is displayed in Table 3-3. For a Census-defined household, a given level of money income can have different implications for that household's well-being, depending on the size of the household and how many children, if any, are in the household. Since there have been substantial changes over past decades in the average size and composition of households, some have questioned the pertinence of standard income distribution tables. In response, the Census Bureau now also reports measures of income inequality for households using "equivalence-adjusted" income.

The equivalence adjustment is based on a three-parameter scale reflecting the size of the household and the facts that children consume less than adults; that as family size increases, expenses do not increase at the same rate; and that the increase in expenses is larger for the first child of a single-parent family than the first child of a two-adult family. The same equivalence concept is used in the poverty thresholds for the NAS-based alternative poverty estimates shown in Tables 3-11 and described later in these Notes.

As can be seen in Table 3-3, the equivalence-adjusted measures generally show somewhat less inequality than the raw money income measures, but they show a greater rise in inequality over the period 1967-2018.

Definitions: Poverty

The *number of people below poverty level,* or the number of poor people, is the number of people with family or individual incomes below a specified level that is intended to measure the cost of a minimum standard of living. These minimum levels vary by size and composition of family and are known as *poverty thresholds.*

The official poverty thresholds are based on a definition developed in 1964 by Mollie Orshansky of the Social Security Administration. She calculated food budgets for families of various sizes and compositions, using an "economy food plan" developed by the U.S. Department of Agriculture (the cheapest of four plans developed). Reflecting a 1955 Department of Agriculture survey that found that families of three or more persons spent about one-third of their after-tax incomes on food, Orshansky multiplied the costs of the food plan by 3 to arrive at a set of thresholds for poverty income for families of three or larger. For 2-person families, the multiplier was 3.7; for 1-person families, the threshold was 80 percent of the two-person threshold.

These poverty thresholds have been adjusted each year for price increases, using the percent change in the Consumer Price Index for All Urban Consumers (CPI-U). See Chapter 8 for additional information on the Consumer Price Index.

For more information on the Orshansky thresholds (the description of which has been simplified here), see Gordon Fisher, "The Development of the Orshansky Thresholds and Their Subsequent History as the Official U.S. Poverty Measure" (May 1992), available on the Census Bureau Web site at https://www.census.gov/library/working-papers/1997/demo/fisher-02.html.

The *poverty rate* for a demographic group is the number of poor people or poor families in that group expressed as a percentage of the total number of people or families in the group.

Average poverty thresholds. There are 48 different threshold values depending on size of household, number of children, and whether the householder is 65 years old or over (with lower thresholds for the older householders). To give a general sense of the "poverty line," the Census Bureau also publishes the average threshold for each size family, based on the actual mix of family types in that year. These are the values shown in Table 3-5 to represent the history of poverty thresholds.

A person with *work experience* (Table 3-9) is one who, during the preceding calendar year and on a part-time or full-time basis, did any work for pay or profit or worked without pay on a family-operated farm or business at any time during the year). A *year-round* worker is one who worked for 50 weeks or more during the preceding calendar year. A person is classified as having worked *full time* if he or she worked 35 hours or more per week during a majority of the weeks worked. A *year-round, full-time worker* is a person who worked 35 or more hours per week and 50 or more weeks during the previous calendar year.

Working poor: Those workers employed full- or -part time whose income still falls below the poverty thresholds of their family size.

Toward better measures of income and poverty

The definition of the official poverty rate is established by the Office of Management of Budget in the Executive Office of the President and has not been substantially changed since 1969. Criticisms of the current definition are legion. In response to these criticisms, the Census Bureau has published extensive research work illustrating the effects of various ways of modifying income definitions and poverty thresholds. Some of the results of this work are published here in Tables 3-10 and 3-11 and explained in the notes and definitions below.

Improving the Income Concept

One type of criticism accepted the general concept of the Orshansky threshold but recommended making the income definition more realistic by including some or all of the following: capital gains; taxes and tax credits; noncash food, housing, and health benefits provided by government and employers; and the value of homeownership. There is debate about whether it is appropriate to use income data augmented in this way in conjunction with the official thresholds. The original 1964 thresholds made no allowance for health insurance or other health expenses—in effect, they assumed that the poor would get free medical care, or at least that the poverty calculation was not required to allow for medical needs—and because of the imprecision of Orshansky's multiplier it is not clear to what extent they include housing expenses in a way that is comparable with the inclusion of a homeownership component in income. Nevertheless, the Census Bureau has calculated and published income and poverty figures based on broadened income definitions and either the official thresholds or thresholds that are closely related to the official ones. Some of these calculations are presented in Table 3-10 and 3-11 and described below.

Still accepting the validity of the basic Orshansky threshold concept, some critics have also argued that use of the CPI-U in the official measure to update the thresholds each year has overstated the price increase, and that an inflator such as the CPI-U-RS should be used instead. (See the notes and definitions for Chapter 8.) Use of the CPI-U-RS leads to lower poverty thresholds beginning in the late 1970s, when the CPI began to be distorted by housing and other biases subsequently corrected by new methods; these newer methods were not carried backward to revise the official CPI-U. Use of the CPI-U-RS, which does carry current methods back and thereby revises the CPI time series, eliminates a presumed upward bias in the poverty rate relative to the poverty rates estimated before the bias emerged. This is a bias in the behavior of the time series given the concept of the Orshansky threshold, not necessarily a bias in the current level of poverty, since all the other criticisms of the Orshansky thresholds need to be considered when assessing the general adequacy of today's poverty measurements.

Improving the concepts of income and poverty together

Another type of criticism argues that the official thresholds are also no longer relevant to today's needs, and that the concepts of income (or "resources") and of the threshold level that depicts a minimum adequate standard of living need to be rethought together. These critics cite the availability of more up-to-date and detailed information about consumer spending at various income levels. The Consumer Expenditure Survey (CEX), originally designed to provide the weights for the Consumer Price Index, is now conducted quarterly and provides extensive data on consumer spending patterns. To give just one example of the information available now that was not available to Mollie Orshansky, the CEX indicates that food now accounts for one-sixth, not one-third, of total family expenditures, even among low-income families. (For data from, and notes on, the Consumer Expenditure Survey, see Bernan Press, *Handbook of U.S. Labor Statistics.*)

A special panel of the National Academy of Sciences (NAS) undertook a study that reconsidered both resources and thresholds. The Census Bureau has calculated and published experimental poverty rates for 1999 through 2015, developed following

NAS recommendations, which are presented in Table 3-10. Beginning in November 2011 the Bureau has issued "The Research Supplemental Poverty Measure" or SPM for the most recent two years, a further refinement of the NAS recommendations; SPM measures are presented in Tables 3-10.

Supplemental Poverty Measure—Tables 3-10

In March of 2010, an Interagency Technical Working Group produced suggestions for a Supplemental Poverty Measure (SPM), which were first implemented in the "Research Supplemental Poverty Measure: 2010" issued by the Census Bureau in November 2011. The SPM goes beyond the experimental measures just described, and takes advantage of new data from questions introduced in the CPS-ASEC in recent years. In the new SPM:

- The measurement unit now covers not just the family but "all related individuals who live at the same address, including any co-resident unrelated children who are cared for by the family (such as foster children) and any co-habitors and their children." This redefinition adds unrelated individuals under the age of 15 to the universe measured by the official rate. The "official" measures shown in Table 3-10 have been adjusted to include these individuals, and are therefore slightly higher than the regular published official rates shown in Tables 3-6 through 3-9.

- The SPM thresholds are calculated separately for three housing status groups: owners with mortgages, owners without mortgages, and renters. For each of these three groups the basic threshold represents the 33rd percentile of expenditures on food, clothing, shelter, and utilities (FCSU), averaged over a five-year period, by consumer units with two children, multiplied by 1.2 to allow for other needs. (Before averaging, the expenditures are converted to their dollar values in the prices of the threshold year using the CPI-U.) The consumer units selected for calculating the threshold include not only two-adult two-child families but also other types with two children, such as single-parent families. But they are adjusted to a four-person basis, using the equivalence scales, before averaging them to determine the basic threshold appropriate to a two-adult two-child household. Then that threshold is used as the basis for calculating thresholds for other size measurement units, again using the three-parameter equivalence scales for family size and composition, and for geographic differences.

- The thresholds are updated each year, using an updated five-year moving average of FCSU at the 33rd percentile, expressed in the prices of the new threshold year. Thus the thresholds are adjusted for inflation, but in addition, the "real" (constant-dollar) purchasing power of the poverty threshold will change (gradually) over time as the real standard of FCSU spending in the 33rd percentile changes. The real value of the threshold will likely change more slowly and gradually than in the "experimental" measures described above, because of using five instead of three years in the average.

- Family resources include cash income, plus in-kind benefits that families can use to meet their FCSU needs (for example, the Supplemental Nutrition Assistance Program [SNAP] formerly known as food stamps), minus income and payroll taxes, plus tax credits, minus childcare and other work-related expenses, minus child support payments to another household, and minus out-of-pocket medical expenses.

The SPM is not intended to replace the official poverty measure and is not to be used in calculations affecting program eligibility and funding distribution. According to the report referenced above, it is "designed to provide information on aggregate levels of economic need at a national level or within large subpopulations or areas...providing further understanding of economic conditions and trends." Census Bureau presentation of the SPM has focused on the different distribution of the poverty population indicated by the new measures, as shown in Table 3-10.

Notes on the data

The following are the principal changes that may affect year-to-year comparability of all income and poverty data from the CPS.

- Beginning in 1952, the estimates are based on 1950 census population controls. Earlier figures were based on 1940 census population controls.

- Beginning in 1962, 1960 census–based sample design and population controls are fully implemented.

- With 1971 and 1972 data, 1970 census–based sample design and population controls were introduced.

- With 1983–1985 data, 1980 census–based sample design was introduced; 1980 population controls were introduced; and these were extended back to 1979 data.

- With 1993 data, there was a major redesign of the CPS, including the introduction of computer-assisted interviewing. The limits used to "code" reported income amounts were changed, resulting in reporting of higher income values for the highest-income families and, consequently, an exaggerated year-to-year increase in income inequality. (It is possible that this jump actually reflects in one year an increase that had emerged more gradually, so that the distribution measures for 1993 and later years may be properly comparable with data for decades earlier even if they should not be directly compared with 1992.) In addition, 1990 census–based population

controls were introduced, and these were extended back to the 1992 data.

- With 1995 data, the 1990 census–based sample design was implemented and the sample was reduced by 7,000 households.

- Data for 2001 implemented population controls based on the 2000 census, which were carried back to 2000 and 1999 data as well. Data from 2000 forward also incorporate results from a 28,000-household sample expansion.

- Beginning with the data for 2010 presented here, population controls based on the 2010 census were implemented. (This resulted in some revision of CPS data initially published for 2010.)

- In 2014, the Census Bureau introduced redesigned income and health insurance questions in the CPS-ASEC. The second phase of the implementation in 2019, updated the processing system that imputes missing data, determines family relationships and constructs key health insurance measures.

For more information on these and other changes that could affect comparability, see "Current Population Survey Technical Paper 63RV: Design and Methodology" (March 2002) and footnotes to CPS historical income tables, both available on the Census Bureau Web site at www.census.gov/hhes/income.

Data availability

Data embodying the official definitions of income and poverty are published annually in late summer or early fall by the Census Bureau, as part of a series with the general title *Current Population Reports: Consumer Income, P60*. Most of the data up to 2012 in this chapter were derived from report P60-245, "Income, Poverty, and Health Insurance Coverage in the United States: 2012" (September 2013), and from the "Historical Income Tables" and "Historical Poverty Tables" on the Census Web site (see below for the address). In 2013, the Census Bureau split the previous report in two. Health insurance coverage is now published separately from income and poverty. The historical tables can be found in the "CPS-ASEC" section under the "Data" category.

The SPM data in Tables 3-10 are from reports entitled "The Research Supplemental Poverty Measure." Reports for 2012, 2011, and 2010 respectively are numbered P60-247, P60-244, and P60-241, and are available on the Census Web site.

All these reports and related data, including historical tabulations, used in *Business Statistics* are available on the Census Bureau Web site at <https://www.census.gov>, under the general headings of "Income" and "Poverty."

References

Definitions and descriptions of the concepts and data of all series are provided in the source documents listed above and in the references contained therein.

Tables 3-11 and 3-12

Health Insurance Coverage

SOURCE: U.S. DEPARTMENT COMMERCE, BUREAU OF THE CENSUS

The Current Population Survey Annual Social and Economic Supplement (CPS ASEC) and the American Community Survey (ACS) is used to produce official estimates of income and poverty, and it serves as the most widely-cited source of estimates on health insurance coverage.

Due to questions of the validity of the health insurance data in previous reports, the Census Bureau implemented changes in 2014 to CPS ACS, including a complete redesign of the health insurance questions that replaced the existing questions in the CPS ASEC. Due the differences in measurement, health insurance estimates from calendar year 2013 are different from estimates in previous years.

Health insurance coverage in the CPS ASEC refers to comprehensive coverage during the calendar year. The American Community Survey (ACS) health insurance coverage status is at the time the individual is interviewed. Therefore, two uninsured measures are reported.

Since the passage of the Patient Protection and Affordable Care Act (ACA) in 2010, several provisions of the ACA have gone into effect at different times. For example, in 2010, the Young Adult Provision enabled adults under age 26 to remain as dependents on their parents' health insurance plans. In 2014 policy changes associated with the ACA provide the option for states to expand Medicaid to people whose income-to-poverty ratio full under a particular threshold. The decreases in the uninsured rates in 2013 and 2014 are consistent with what some of the provisions of the ACA intended.

Definitions

Health insurance coverage refers to comprehensive coverage during the calendar year for the civilian, noninstitutionalized population.

Private coverage is a plan provided through market forces.

Employment-based provided by an employer or union.

Direct-purchase: Coverage purchased directly from an insurance company or a federal or state marketplace or exchange.

TRICARE: Coverage through TRICARE, formerly known as Civilian Health and Medical Program of the Uniformed Services (e.g. healthcare.gov).

Government health insurance: Coverage provided by the federal government.

Medicare: Federal program that helps to pay health care costs for people aged 65 years and older and for certain people under age 65 with long-term disabilities.

Medicaid: Medicaid, the Children's Health Insurance Program (CHIP), and individual state health plans.

CHAMPVA or *VA*: Civilian Health and Medical Program of the Department of Veterans Affairs, as well as care provided by the Department of Veterans Affairs and the military.

Uninsured are people if, for an entire year, they were not covered by any type of health insurance. Additionally, people were considered uninsured if they only had coverage through the Indian Health Service (IHS).

Data availability

Detailed health insurance questions have been asked in the CPS since 1988 as part of a mandate to collect data on non-cash basis. However, as noted, comparing older results with newer ones is uncertain due to the changes in questions in 2013, 2014, and 2018.

CHAPTER 4: CONSUMER INCOME AND SPENDING

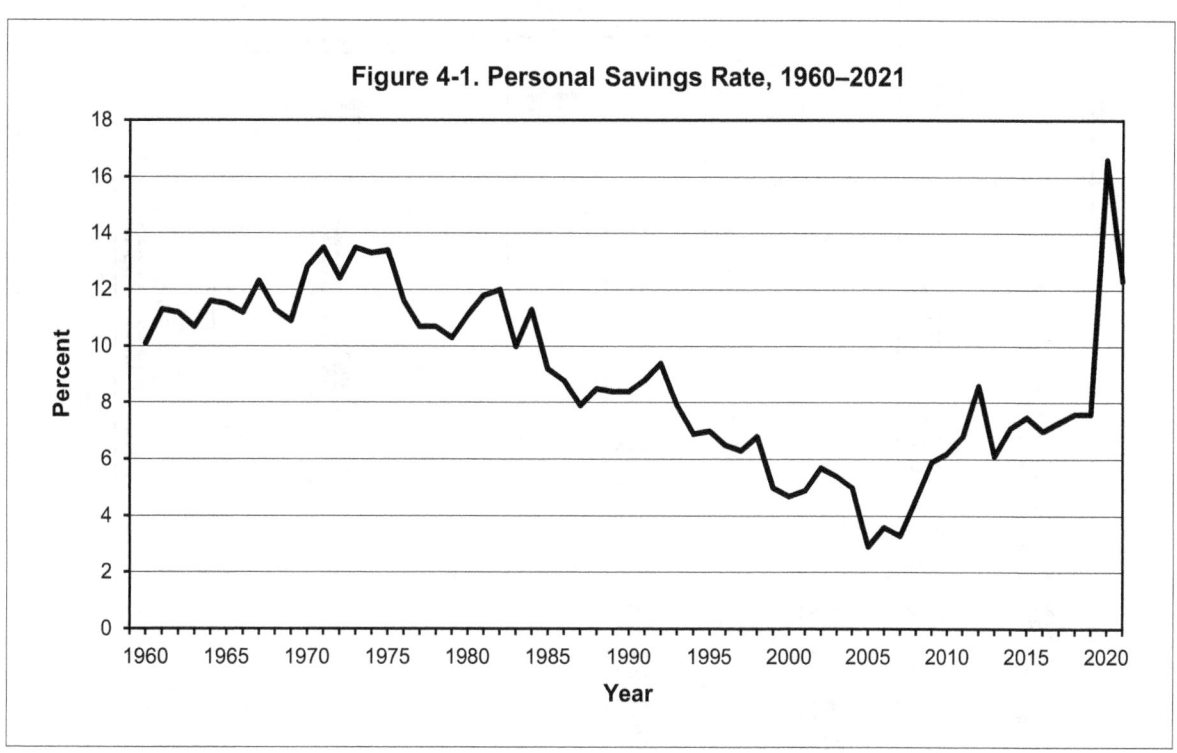

Figure 4-1. Personal Savings Rate, 1960–2021

- The personal saving rate—now defined to include saving in individual pension plans as the earned benefits rather than the employer contributions—got as high as 13.5 percent in the 1970s. (Benefits from social insurance systems such as Social Security, unlike those in private and government employee retirement plans, do not figure in personal saving; any excess of receipts over payments is counted as government saving.) Since then, the personal saving rate entered a downtrend for many years, and hit the lowest rates since the Great Depression in the real estate bubble years 2005 through 2007, saving as a percent of disposable personal income has increased. In 2020, however, the personal savings rate skyrocketed to a high of 16.6 percent, more than double the 7.6 percent in 2019. Although it fell to 12.3 percent in 2021, it was still much lower than in prior years. (Tables 4-1A and B)

- It should be noted that personal income does not, by definition, include any capital gains. Despite that, taxes on realized capital gains are deducted (along with all other income taxes) from personal income to get after-tax income. Capital gains, both realized and unrealized, can be a source of spending power in addition to current disposable income; during the housing price bubble they were converted into cash by asset sales, refinancing, and home equity loans, all of which were reflected in low saving rates. (Table 12-7)

- Government social benefits were 5.8 percent of personal income in 1960, rising to 14.1 percent in the high-employment year 2007. In the recession they rose further, to 18.1 percent in 2010, and increased to 21.3 percent in 2020 and 21.5 percent in 2021 due in large part to government related COVID-19 assistance specifically unemployment insurance. It should be understood that this category counts as income all spending financed by government health insurance programs such as Medicare and Medicaid, simultaneously counting that spending as personal consumption expenditures rather than direct government spending in the NIPAs. (Table 4-1)

Table 4-1A. Personal Income and Its Disposition: Recent Data

(Billions of current dollars, except as noted; quarterly data are at seasonally adjusted annual rates.)   **NIPA Table 2.1**

Year and quarter	Personal income											
					Personal income receipts on assets		Personal current transfer receipts					
							Government social benefits to persons					
	Total	Compensation of employees	Proprietors' income with IVA and CCAdj	Rental income of persons with CCAdj	Personal interest income	Personal dividend income	Total	Social Security and Medicare	Government unemployment insurance	Veterans	Medicaid	Other government benefits to persons
1960	422.1	301.3	50.6	16.5	31.1	13.4	24.4	11.1	3.1	4.5	. . .	5.7
1961	440.6	310.4	53.2	17.2	33.4	13.9	28.1	12.6	4.4	4.9	. . .	6.2
1962	468.8	332.2	55.2	18.0	37.1	15.0	28.8	14.3	3.2	4.6	. . .	6.8
1963	492.8	350.4	56.4	18.7	40.5	16.2	30.3	15.2	3.1	4.8	. . .	7.3
1964	528.2	376.0	59.1	18.8	44.9	18.2	31.3	16.0	2.8	4.6	. . .	7.9
1965	570.7	405.4	63.7	19.3	49.3	20.2	33.9	18.1	2.4	4.8	. . .	8.6
1966	620.3	449.2	67.9	19.9	54.3	20.7	37.5	20.8	1.9	4.8	1.9	8.1
1967	665.7	481.8	69.5	20.3	59.5	21.5	45.8	25.8	2.2	5.5	2.7	9.4
1968	730.9	530.8	73.8	20.1	65.3	23.5	53.3	30.5	2.2	5.9	4.0	10.8
1969	800.3	584.5	77.0	20.3	76.1	24.2	59.0	33.1	2.3	6.6	4.6	12.4
1970	865.0	623.3	77.8	20.7	90.6	24.3	71.7	38.7	4.2	7.5	5.5	16.0
1971	932.8	665.0	83.9	21.8	100.1	25.0	85.4	44.6	6.2	8.4	6.7	19.4
1972	1 024.5	731.3	95.1	22.7	109.8	26.8	94.8	49.7	6.0	9.4	8.2	21.4
1973	1 140.8	812.7	112.5	23.1	125.5	29.9	108.6	60.9	4.6	10.2	9.6	23.3
1974	1 251.8	887.7	112.2	23.2	147.4	33.2	128.6	70.3	7.0	11.6	11.2	28.4
1975	1 369.4	947.2	118.2	22.3	168.0	32.9	163.1	81.5	18.1	14.0	13.9	35.7
1976	1 502.6	1 048.3	131.0	20.3	181.0	39.0	177.6	93.3	16.4	13.8	15.5	38.7
1977	1 659.2	1 165.8	144.5	15.9	206.9	44.7	189.5	105.3	13.1	13.3	16.7	40.9
1978	1 863.7	1 316.8	166.0	16.5	235.1	50.7	203.4	116.9	9.4	13.6	18.6	44.9
1979	2 082.1	1 477.2	179.4	16.1	269.7	57.4	227.3	132.5	9.7	14.2	21.1	49.9
1980	2 323.6	1 622.2	171.6	19.0	332.9	64.0	271.5	154.8	16.1	14.7	23.9	62.1
1981	2 605.1	1 792.5	179.7	23.8	412.2	73.6	307.8	182.1	15.9	15.8	27.7	66.3
1982	2 791.6	1 893.0	171.2	23.8	479.5	77.6	343.1	204.6	25.2	16.3	30.2	66.8
1983	2 981.1	2 012.5	186.3	24.4	516.3	83.3	370.5	222.2	26.4	16.4	33.9	71.5
1984	3 292.7	2 215.9	228.2	24.7	590.1	90.6	380.9	237.7	16.0	16.3	36.6	74.3
1985	3 524.9	2 387.3	241.1	26.2	628.9	97.4	403.1	253.0	15.9	16.6	39.7	78.0
1986	3 733.1	2 542.1	256.5	18.3	662.1	106.0	428.6	268.9	16.5	16.6	43.6	83.0
1987	3 961.6	2 722.4	286.5	16.6	679.0	112.2	447.9	282.6	14.6	16.5	47.8	86.4
1988	4 283.4	2 948.0	325.5	22.5	721.7	129.7	476.9	300.2	13.3	16.7	53.0	93.6
1989	4 625.6	3 139.6	341.1	21.5	806.5	157.8	521.1	325.6	14.4	17.2	60.8	103.1
1990	4 913.8	3 340.4	353.2	28.2	836.5	168.8	574.7	351.7	18.2	17.7	73.1	113.9
1991	5 084.9	3 450.5	354.2	38.6	823.5	180.2	650.5	381.7	26.8	18.1	96.9	127.0
1992	5 420.9	3 668.2	400.2	60.6	809.8	189.1	731.8	414.4	39.6	18.6	116.2	142.9
1993	5 657.9	3 817.3	428.0	90.1	802.3	204.7	778.9	444.7	34.8	19.3	130.1	150.0
1994	5 947.1	4 006.2	456.6	113.7	814.6	235.2	815.7	476.6	23.9	19.7	139.4	156.1
1995	6 291.4	4 198.1	481.2	124.9	878.6	258.0	864.7	508.9	21.7	20.5	149.6	164.0
1996	6 678.5	4 416.9	543.8	142.5	899.0	302.2	906.3	536.9	22.3	21.4	158.2	167.6
1997	7 092.5	4 708.8	584.0	147.1	947.1	337.9	935.4	563.5	20.1	22.3	163.1	166.4
1998	7 606.7	5 071.1	640.2	165.2	1 015.5	355.4	957.9	574.8	19.7	23.3	170.2	170.0
1999	8 006.8	5 402.7	696.4	178.5	1 017.7	346.6	992.2	588.6	20.5	24.1	184.6	174.4
2000	8 655.9	5 847.1	753.9	183.5	1 106.5	383.5	1 044.9	620.5	20.7	25.0	199.5	179.1
2001	9 012.8	6 038.3	831.0	202.4	1 112.3	369.3	1 145.8	667.7	31.9	26.6	227.3	192.4
2002	9 160.9	6 135.1	870.0	208.4	1 014.8	398.8	1 251.0	706.6	53.5	29.5	250.0	211.3
2003	9 498.5	6 353.6	897.5	227.1	1 020.2	432.1	1 321.0	740.2	53.2	31.8	264.5	231.2
2004	10 044.3	6 719.5	962.9	242.8	965.4	561.7	1 404.5	789.9	36.4	34.1	289.8	254.3
2005	10 604.9	7 066.1	979.1	221.1	1 117.4	577.8	1 490.9	844.8	31.8	36.4	304.4	273.5
2006	11 384.7	7 479.7	1 050.9	181.1	1 258.9	722.8	1 593.0	943.2	30.4	38.9	299.1	281.5
2007	12 021.4	7 878.5	995.5	186.3	1 379.2	815.3	1 697.3	1 003.9	32.7	41.7	324.2	294.9
2008	12 477.6	8 056.8	959.7	290.3	1 399.4	804.6	1 919.3	1 067.1	51.1	45.0	338.3	417.7
2009	12 080.4	7 759.0	937.6	347.6	1 300.7	553.0	2 107.7	1 157.5	131.2	51.5	369.6	398.0
2010	12 594.5	7 925.4	1 107.3	433.7	1 242.9	543.9	2 281.4	1 203.6	138.9	58.0	396.9	484.2
2011	13 339.3	8 226.2	1 227.4	506.5	1 255.6	681.5	2 310.1	1 248.9	107.2	63.3	406.0	484.8
2012	14 014.3	8 567.4	1 346.4	534.5	1 318.6	835.1	2 322.6	1 316.8	83.6	70.1	417.5	434.4
2013	14 193.6	8 835.0	1 402.2	577.4	1 265.6	793.3	2 385.9	1 371.8	62.5	79.1	440.0	432.5
2014	14 976.6	9 250.2	1 445.6	602.7	1 336.8	953.2	2 498.6	1 434.6	35.5	84.2	490.9	453.5
2015	15 685.2	9 699.4	1 420.8	609.5	1 441.8	1 033.1	2 635.1	1 506.7	32.5	92.6	535.9	467.4
2016	16 096.9	9 966.1	1 423.3	626.6	1 465.2	1 077.4	2 717.3	1 558.6	32.0	96.8	562.8	467.1
2017	16 850.2	10 426.1	1 505.8	652.7	1 553.4	1 154.5	2 807.6	1 618.6	30.2	111.4	573.8	473.6
2018	17 706.0	10 959.5	1 580.4	681.9	1 615.0	1 253.3	2 926.1	1 707.3	27.7	119.7	589.8	481.5
2019	18 424.4	11 447.7	1 598.9	692.1	1 652.0	1 316.0	3 083.1	1 816.4	27.6	130.9	614.0	494.2
2020	19 627.6	11 572.2	1 650.0	711.6	1 614.4	1 297.8	4 181.3	1 897.1	536.6	145.5	657.3	944.7
2021	21 092.8	12 598.7	1 821.9	726.4	1 640.7	1 300.7	4 530.9	1 941.0	339.1	160.1	746.1	1 344.6
2019												
1st quarter	18 238.9	11 336.1	1 585.5	687.0	1 647.4	1 296.9	3 039.6	1 787.7	28.4	125.6	598.8	499.0
2nd quarter	18 345.4	11 394.1	1 572.8	691.0	1 660.5	1 312.0	3 074.1	1 807.5	27.8	128.9	614.5	495.4
3rd quarter	18 464.7	11 453.9	1 610.6	691.5	1 646.2	1 327.0	3 101.0	1 826.3	27.4	132.5	622.4	492.4
4th quarter	18 648.5	11 606.8	1 626.8	699.0	1 654.0	1 328.0	3 117.9	1 844.2	26.8	136.6	620.5	489.8
2020												
1st quarter	18 842.2	11 755.5	1 638.3	712.2	1 638.2	1 338.1	3 173.8	1 876.4	39.5	140.8	606.2	511.0
2nd quarter	20 348.7	11 029.2	1 471.1	709.5	1 611.3	1 299.6	5 570.5	1 896.4	1 039.4	144.4	654.2	1 836.1
3rd quarter	19 777.4	11 539.7	1 760.7	714.5	1 597.6	1 254.2	4 310.5	1 906.0	767.8	147.4	690.4	799.0
4th quarter	19 542.0	11 964.2	1 730.0	710.0	1 610.3	1 299.2	3 670.2	1 909.8	299.9	149.5	678.3	632.7
2021												
1st quarter	21 867.3	12 088.9	1 714.0	716.9	1 630.2	1 268.7	5 920.6	1 920.4	565.8	152.4	695.9	2 586.0
2nd quarter	20 669.9	12 416.6	1 848.2	716.3	1 639.4	1 292.8	4 257.8	1 925.0	480.4	156.5	730.5	965.4
3rd quarter	20 823.8	12 756.5	1 867.0	729.0	1 636.3	1 308.8	4 069.6	1 943.7	272.3	162.3	775.0	916.2
4th quarter	21 010.0	13 132.6	1 858.5	743.6	1 656.8	1 332.4	3 875.5	1 974.8	37.7	169.2	782.9	911.0

. . . = Not available.

Table 4-1A. Personal Income and Its Disposition: Recent Data—*Continued*

(Billions of current dollars, except as noted; quarterly data are at seasonally adjusted annual rates.)   NIPA Table 2.1

Year and quarter	Personal income—Continued		Less: Personal current taxes	Equals: Disposable personal income	Less: Personal outlays						Equals: Personal saving		Billions of chained (2009) dollars	
	Personal current transfer receipts—Continued: From business, net	Less: Contributions for government social insurance, domestic			Total	Personal consumption expenditures	Personal interest payments	Personal current transfer payments			Billions of dollars	Percent of disposable personal income	Percent income excluding current transfers	Disposable personal income
								Total	To government	To the rest of the world, net				
1960	1.3	16.4	46.1	376.1	338.2	331.2	6.2	0.8	0.3	0.5	37.9	10.1	2 411.0	2 287.4
1961	1.4	17.0	47.3	393.3	348.9	341.5	6.5	1.0	0.5	0.5	44.4	11.3	2 474.9	2 367.8
1962	1.5	19.1	51.6	417.3	370.6	362.6	6.9	1.1	0.5	0.6	46.7	11.2	2 608.8	2 482.9
1963	1.9	21.7	54.6	438.2	391.1	382.0	7.9	1.2	0.5	0.7	47.1	10.7	2 708.0	2 576.7
1964	2.2	22.4	52.1	476.1	420.8	410.6	8.9	1.3	0.6	0.7	55.3	11.6	2 867.2	2 759.6
1965	2.3	23.4	57.7	513.0	454.2	443.0	9.9	1.4	0.6	0.8	58.8	11.5	3 053.8	2 931.0
1966	2.1	31.3	66.4	554.0	492.1	479.9	10.6	1.6	0.8	0.8	61.9	11.2	3 236.2	3 087.1
1967	2.3	34.9	73.0	592.8	519.8	506.7	11.1	2.0	1.0	1.0	73.0	12.3	3 358.0	3 222.4
1968	2.8	38.7	87.0	643.9	571.0	556.9	12.1	2.0	1.0	1.0	72.9	11.3	3 530.3	3 368.7
1969	3.3	44.1	104.5	695.8	619.8	603.6	13.9	2.2	1.1	1.1	76.1	10.9	3 694.6	3 483.3
1970	2.9	46.4	103.1	762.0	664.4	646.7	15.1	2.6	1.3	1.3	97.6	12.8	3 779.9	3 644.1
1971	2.7	51.2	101.7	831.1	719.2	699.9	16.4	2.8	1.5	1.4	111.9	13.5	3 875.0	3 812.6
1972	3.1	59.2	123.6	900.8	789.3	768.2	18.0	3.2	1.8	1.4	111.5	12.4	4 110.3	3 996.2
1973	3.9	75.5	132.4	1 008.4	872.6	849.6	19.6	3.4	1.8	1.6	135.8	13.5	4 328.3	4 244.8
1974	4.7	85.2	151.0	1 100.8	954.5	930.2	20.9	3.4	2.1	1.4	146.3	13.3	4 264.5	4 196.8
1975	6.8	89.3	147.6	1 221.8	1 057.8	1 030.5	23.4	3.8	2.5	1.3	164.0	13.4	4 221.1	4 299.8
1976	6.7	101.3	172.7	1 330.0	1 175.6	1 147.7	23.5	4.4	3.0	1.4	154.4	11.6	4 398.2	4 437.1
1977	5.1	113.1	197.9	1 461.4	1 305.4	1 274.0	26.6	4.8	3.5	1.4	155.9	10.7	4 588.1	4 577.7
1978	6.5	131.3	229.6	1 634.1	1 459.0	1 422.3	31.3	5.4	3.9	1.6	175.1	10.7	4 843.6	4 785.8
1979	8.2	152.7	268.9	1 813.8	1 627.0	1 585.4	35.5	6.0	4.3	1.7	186.8	10.3	4 968.3	4 878.6
1980	8.6	166.2	299.5	2 024.1	1 800.1	1 750.7	42.5	6.9	5.0	2.0	224.1	11.1	4 962.2	4 915.1
1981	11.2	195.7	345.8	2 259.3	1 993.9	1 934.0	48.4	11.5	6.0	5.6	265.5	11.8	5 094.9	5 035.2
1982	12.4	208.9	354.7	2 436.9	2 143.5	2 071.3	58.5	13.8	7.1	6.7	293.3	12.0	5 143.5	5 145.0
1983	13.8	226.0	352.9	2 628.2	2 364.2	2 281.6	67.4	15.1	8.1	7.0	264.0	10.0	5 258.9	5 322.6
1984	19.7	257.5	377.9	2 914.8	2 584.5	2 492.3	75.0	17.1	9.2	7.9	330.3	11.3	5 643.9	5 688.2
1985	22.3	281.4	417.8	3 107.1	2 822.1	2 712.8	90.6	18.8	10.4	8.3	284.9	9.2	5 844.8	5 859.0
1986	22.9	303.4	437.8	3 295.3	3 004.7	2 886.3	97.3	21.1	12.0	9.1	290.6	8.8	6 056.2	6 081.6
1987	20.2	323.1	489.6	3 472.0	3 196.6	3 076.3	97.1	23.2	13.2	10.0	275.4	7.9	6 254.5	6 216.1
1988	20.6	361.5	505.9	3 777.5	3 457.0	3 330.0	101.3	25.6	14.8	10.8	320.5	8.5	6 523.2	6 508.6
1989	23.2	385.2	567.7	4 057.8	3 717.9	3 576.8	113.1	28.0	16.5	11.6	340.0	8.4	6 738.0	6 699.2
1990	22.2	410.1	594.7	4 319.1	3 958.0	3 809.0	118.4	30.6	18.4	12.2	361.1	8.4	6 827.2	6 830.7
1991	17.6	430.2	588.9	4 496.0	4 100.0	3 943.4	119.9	36.7	22.6	14.1	396.0	8.8	6 759.1	6 880.4
1992	16.3	455.0	612.8	4 808.1	4 354.2	4 197.6	116.1	40.5	26.0	14.5	453.9	9.4	6 965.3	7 166.9
1993	14.1	477.4	648.8	5 009.2	4 611.5	4 452.0	113.9	45.6	28.6	17.1	397.7	7.9	7 075.4	7 285.2
1994	13.3	508.2	693.1	5 254.0	4 890.6	4 721.0	119.9	49.8	30.9	18.9	363.4	6.9	7 291.5	7 485.1
1995	18.7	532.8	748.4	5 543.0	5 155.9	4 962.6	140.4	52.9	32.6	20.3	387.1	7.0	7 545.5	7 733.9
1996	22.9	555.1	837.1	5 841.4	5 459.2	5 244.6	157.0	57.6	34.9	22.6	382.3	6.5	7 853.9	7 979.5
1997	19.4	587.2	931.8	6 160.7	5 770.4	5 536.8	169.7	63.9	38.2	25.7	390.3	6.3	8 240.9	8 271.8
1998	26.0	624.7	1 032.4	6 574.2	6 127.7	5 877.2	180.9	69.5	39.9	29.7	446.5	6.8	8 822.1	8 757.4
1999	34.0	661.3	1 111.9	6 894.9	6 550.9	6 283.8	190.8	76.3	44.1	32.3	344.0	5.0	9 165.2	9 052.7
2000	42.4	705.8	1 236.3	7 419.6	7 068.1	6 767.2	217.7	83.2	48.8	34.5	351.4	4.7	9 692.1	9 501.3
2001	46.8	733.2	1 239.0	7 773.8	7 390.9	7 073.8	225.6	91.5	52.9	38.6	382.8	4.9	9 817.5	9 759.2
2002	34.2	751.5	1 052.2	8 108.8	7 646.3	7 348.9	200.6	96.7	56.4	40.4	462.5	5.7	9 759.0	10 047.8
2003	26.3	779.3	1 003.5	8 495.0	8 038.3	7 740.7	196.5	101.1	60.5	40.6	456.7	5.4	9 892.6	10 309.7
2004	16.8	829.2	1 048.7	8 995.5	8 550.1	8 232.0	207.3	110.9	66.9	44.0	445.4	5.0	10 211.7	10 652.8
2005	25.8	873.3	1 212.5	9 392.5	9 124.5	8 769.1	237.3	118.1	71.6	46.5	268.0	2.9	10 461.1	10 811.4
2006	20.8	922.5	1 357.0	10 027.7	9 669.1	9 277.2	266.9	124.9	75.3	49.6	358.7	3.6	10 938.9	11 226.5
2007	30.8	961.4	1 492.5	10 528.9	10 176.2	9 746.6	291.2	138.4	79.2	59.2	352.7	3.3	11 235.4	11 492.6
2008	35.8	988.4	1 507.5	10 970.1	10 466.7	10 050.1	272.0	144.6	81.0	63.7	503.4	4.6	11 155.5	11 630.0
2009	39.0	964.3	1 152.4	10 928.0	10 288.4	9 891.2	252.8	144.3	80.1	64.3	639.7	5.9	10 560.7	11 617.9
2010	43.7	983.7	1 237.6	11 356.9	10 647.6	10 260.3	242.3	145.0	79.4	65.6	709.3	6.2	10 725.5	11 861.4
2011	48.5	916.7	1 453.7	11 885.6	11 079.6	10 698.9	229.9	150.8	82.2	68.6	806.0	6.8	11 185.3	12 107.2
2012	40.4	950.5	1 509.5	12 504.8	11 431.8	11 047.4	229.6	154.8	86.3	68.5	1 073.1	8.6	11 651.3	12 504.8
2013	38.4	1 104.3	1 676.4	12 517.3	11 751.3	11 363.5	229.5	158.3	87.5	70.8	766.0	6.1	11 612.1	12 350.0
2014	42.9	1 153.6	1 784.6	13 192.0	12 261.1	11 847.7	243.7	169.6	93.4	76.3	930.9	7.1	12 086.1	12 821.9
2015	50.3	1 204.7	1 939.9	13 745.3	12 710.4	12 263.5	263.5	183.5	100.9	82.5	1 034.9	7.5	12 607.0	13 330.0
2016	59.7	1 238.8	1 958.2	14 138.7	13 150.8	12 693.3	272.8	184.8	103.4	81.4	987.8	7.0	12 789.3	13 575.5
2017	48.7	1 298.8	2 049.0	14 801.2	13 724.8	13 239.1	291.6	194.1	107.5	86.7	1 076.4	7.3	13 195.3	13 956.6
2018	50.2	1 360.5	2 076.3	15 629.7	14 438.8	13 913.5	321.0	204.3	113.9	90.3	1 190.9	7.6	13 598.5	14 429.4
2019	56.0	1 421.4	2 205.1	16 219.3	14 981.5	14 428.7	340.4	212.4	118.6	93.9	1 237.8	7.6	13 905.6	14 755.2
2020	59.9	1 459.5	2 195.6	17 432.0	14 544.5	14 047.6	285.4	211.5	114.6	96.9	2 887.5	16.6	13 833.7	15 672.8
2021	67.0	1 593.4	2 585.2	18 507.6	16 226.3	15 741.6	266.5	218.3	116.4	101.9	2 281.3	12.3	14 276.8	16 018.8
2019														
1st quarter	54.2	1 407.6	2 169.3	16 069.6	14 692.9	14 155.6	330.6	206.8	117.6	89.1	1 376.7	8.6	13 882.2	14 729.6
2nd quarter	55.6	1 414.6	2 222.8	16 122.6	14 928.3	14 375.7	339.3	213.2	118.7	94.5	1 194.4	7.4	13 853.6	14 679.3
3rd quarter	56.7	1 422.0	2 205.2	16 259.6	15 087.9	14 529.5	346.6	211.8	119.1	92.7	1 171.7	7.2	13 898.3	14 763.1
4th quarter	57.5	1 441.4	2 223.2	16 425.3	15 216.9	14 653.9	345.0	217.9	118.8	99.1	1 208.4	7.4	13 989.7	14 850.5
2020														
1st quarter	58.0	1 472.0	2 241.6	16 600.6	14 989.2	14 439.1	337.8	212.3	114.9	97.5	1 611.4	9.7	14 070.2	14 962.7
2nd quarter	63.3	1 405.9	2 099.0	18 249.6	13 477.7	12 989.7	273.6	214.4	114.4	100.0	4 772.0	26.1	13 317.7	16 516.9
3rd quarter	58.9	1 458.7	2 181.8	17 595.7	14 774.3	14 293.8	274.4	206.1	114.3	91.8	2 821.3	16.0	13 820.2	15 782.4
4th quarter	59.2	1 501.3	2 259.8	17 282.2	14 936.8	14 467.6	255.9	213.2	114.8	98.4	2 345.5	13.6	14 129.7	15 443.0
2021														
1st quarter	62.0	1 533.8	2 412.1	19 455.3	15 475.6	15 005.4	255.3	214.8	115.3	99.5	3 979.7	20.5	14 061.1	17 221.6
2nd quarter	71.2	1 572.2	2 532.5	18 137.4	16 165.0	15 681.7	267.4	215.9	116.0	99.9	1 972.4	10.9	14 240.1	15 805.6
3rd quarter	67.9	1 611.3	2 641.1	18 182.7	16 456.2	15 964.9	271.7	219.6	116.8	102.8	1 726.4	9.5	14 352.9	15 640.0
4th quarter	66.7	1 656.1	2 754.9	18 255.1	16 808.4	16 314.2	271.6	222.6	117.5	105.2	1 446.7	7.9	14 456.6	15 462.3

Table 4-1B. Personal Income and Its Disposition: Historical Data

(Billions of current dollars, except as noted; quarterly data are at seasonally adjusted annual rates.)　　　　　　NIPA Table 2.1

Year and quarter	Personal income Total	Compensation of employees	Proprietors' income with IVA and CCAdj	Rental income of persons with CCAdj	Personal income receipts on assets	Personal current transfer receipts	Less: Contributions for government social insurance, domestic	Less: Personal current taxes	Equals: Disposable personal income	Less: Personal outlays	Equals: Personal saving — Billions of dollars	Equals: Personal saving — Percent of disposable personal income	Billions of chained (2009) dollars — Personal income excluding current transfers	Billions of chained (2009) dollars — Disposable personal income
1929	85.3	51.4	14.0	6.1	12.7	1.2	0.1	1.7	83.6	79.6	4.0	4.7	904.7	898.9
1930	76.5	47.2	10.9	5.4	12.0	1.2	0.1	1.6	75.0	71.6	3.3	4.5	846.0	842.1
1931	65.7	40.1	8.3	4.4	10.6	2.3	0.1	1.0	64.7	61.8	2.8	4.4	796.6	813.5
1932	50.3	31.3	5.0	3.6	8.7	1.7	0.1	0.7	49.6	49.7	-0.1	-0.2	692.5	707.1
1933	47.2	29.8	5.3	2.9	7.7	1.7	0.1	0.8	46.4	46.8	-0.3	-0.7	673.6	686.6
1934	54.1	34.6	7.0	2.5	8.3	1.8	0.1	0.9	53.2	52.3	0.9	1.7	740.5	752.6
1935	60.8	37.7	10.1	2.6	8.6	2.0	0.1	1.1	59.8	56.8	3.0	5.1	812.9	825.4
1936	69.2	43.3	10.4	2.7	10.1	3.1	0.3	1.3	67.9	63.1	4.8	7.1	905.0	929.4
1937	74.7	48.3	12.5	3.0	10.4	2.0	1.5	1.9	72.8	67.9	4.9	6.7	960.2	960.9
1938	69.1	45.4	10.6	3.5	8.8	2.4	1.6	1.9	67.2	65.3	2.0	2.9	900.9	908.2
1939	73.6	48.6	11.1	3.7	9.5	2.5	1.8	1.5	72.1	68.2	3.9	5.4	970.1	984.2
1940	79.4	52.7	12.2	3.8	9.8	2.7	1.9	1.7	77.7	72.4	5.3	6.8	1 037.9	1 051.3
1941	97.9	66.2	16.7	4.4	10.3	2.7	2.3	2.3	95.6	82.3	13.3	13.9	1 212.7	1 217.1
1942	126.7	88.0	23.3	5.5	10.1	2.7	2.9	4.9	121.8	90.0	31.9	26.2	1 405.0	1 379.8
1943	156.2	112.7	28.2	6.0	10.5	2.5	3.8	16.7	139.5	100.8	38.6	27.7	1 594.0	1 446.2
1944	169.7	124.3	29.3	6.3	11.0	3.1	4.3	17.7	152.1	109.7	42.4	27.9	1 634.0	1 491.2
1945	175.8	126.3	30.8	6.6	11.8	5.6	5.3	19.4	156.3	121.2	35.2	22.5	1 604.5	1 474.4
1946	182.5	122.5	35.7	6.9	13.5	10.5	6.6	17.2	165.3	145.8	19.6	11.8	1 516.3	1 457.6
1947	194.5	132.4	34.6	6.9	15.4	10.8	5.6	19.8	174.7	163.7	11.0	6.3	1 470.2	1 398.4
1948	213.5	144.3	39.3	7.5	16.8	10.3	4.6	19.2	194.3	177.1	17.2	8.8	1 539.8	1 472.0
1949	211.1	144.3	34.7	7.8	17.9	11.2	4.9	16.7	194.3	180.7	13.6	7.0	1 526.1	1 483.9
1950	233.7	158.3	37.5	8.8	20.7	14.0	5.5	18.9	214.8	194.8	20.0	9.3	1 658.3	1 621.1
1951	264.2	185.7	42.6	9.7	21.4	11.4	6.6	27.1	237.2	211.3	25.9	10.9	1 786.2	1 675.6
1952	282.5	201.1	43.0	10.8	22.6	11.9	6.9	32.0	250.5	222.6	27.8	11.1	1 873.2	1 733.9
1953	299.2	215.2	42.0	12.0	24.5	12.5	7.1	33.2	266.0	236.8	29.2	11.0	1 959.1	1 817.5
1954	302.2	214.1	42.3	13.1	26.5	14.3	8.1	30.2	272.1	243.9	28.1	10.3	1 950.8	1 843.5
1955														
1st quarter	313.5	221.9	43.7	13.3	28.2	15.3	8.9	31.4	282.1	255.9	26.2	9.3	2 019.8	1 910.6
2nd quarter ...	321.1	228.1	44.3	13.4	28.7	15.6	9.0	32.4	288.6	261.2	27.5	9.5	2 066.7	1 952.9
3rd quarter	328.5	233.9	44.6	13.4	29.8	15.9	9.2	33.4	295.1	265.6	29.5	10.0	2 106.8	1 988.9
4th quarter	333.6	238.4	44.5	13.5	30.4	16.0	9.3	34.2	299.4	269.8	29.6	9.9	2 134.9	2 012.1
1956														
1st quarter	339.0	242.8	44.9	13.6	31.2	16.3	9.9	35.4	303.6	271.6	32.1	10.6	2 159.8	2 032.4
2nd quarter ...	344.8	247.5	45.3	13.6	31.8	16.6	10.0	36.2	308.6	274.3	34.2	11.1	2 182.4	2 051.7
3rd quarter	350.1	250.4	46.4	13.7	32.5	17.1	10.0	36.9	313.2	277.6	35.5	11.3	2 192.9	2 062.3
4th quarter	357.8	256.4	46.8	13.8	33.6	17.3	10.1	37.9	319.9	283.1	36.8	11.5	2 228.6	2 094.2
1957														
1st quarter	362.4	260.2	46.9	13.9	34.5	18.2	11.4	38.6	323.8	287.7	36.1	11.1	2 233.0	2 100.8
2nd quarter ...	367.1	262.1	47.7	14.0	35.4	19.4	11.4	39.0	328.1	290.1	38.1	11.6	2 241.5	2 115.6
3rd quarter	371.7	264.7	48.8	14.1	35.9	19.6	11.5	39.2	332.5	294.7	37.8	11.4	2 251.4	2 126.3
4th quarter	370.8	263.3	47.7	14.3	36.0	20.8	11.3	38.8	332.0	296.4	35.6	10.7	2 226.5	2 112.1
1958														
1st quarter	371.3	259.8	50.3	14.6	35.9	22.1	11.3	38.2	333.1	295.9	37.2	11.2	2 194.4	2 093.4
2nd quarter ...	373.7	259.4	50.3	14.8	36.6	23.9	11.3	37.7	336.0	298.8	37.2	11.1	2 194.5	2 108.0
3rd quarter	382.6	267.2	50.1	14.9	37.6	24.2	11.4	38.9	343.7	303.8	39.9	11.6	2 246.8	2 154.3
4th quarter	388.2	272.3	49.9	15.0	38.9	23.7	11.5	39.4	348.8	307.8	41.0	11.8	2 286.0	2 187.4
1959														
1st quarter	394.0	279.7	50.1	15.0	38.8	24.0	13.7	40.8	353.2	315.4	37.9	10.7	2 304.4	2 200.1
2nd quarter ...	402.4	286.5	50.3	15.4	40.1	23.9	13.9	42.0	360.4	321.6	38.8	10.8	2 347.5	2 235.6
3rd quarter	404.7	286.9	50.4	15.8	41.4	24.2	13.9	42.7	362.1	327.1	35.0	9.7	2 346.6	2 232.5
4th quarter	410.4	290.2	50.6	16.0	42.6	24.8	13.9	43.7	366.6	329.4	37.2	10.2	2 364.3	2 248.4
1960														
1st quarter	416.7	298.7	49.7	16.2	43.7	24.6	16.4	45.3	371.4	333.1	38.3	10.3	2 400.9	2 274.4
2nd quarter ...	421.7	301.7	50.7	16.4	44.1	25.3	16.5	46.0	375.7	339.2	36.5	9.7	2 415.5	2 289.1
3rd quarter	424.4	302.6	50.9	16.5	44.9	26.0	16.5	46.5	377.8	339.3	38.6	10.2	2 417.8	2 293.5
4th quarter	425.8	302.1	51.0	16.7	45.3	27.0	16.4	46.4	379.4	341.3	38.0	10.0	2 409.8	2 292.5
1961														
1st quarter	430.2	303.1	52.3	16.9	45.7	28.8	16.7	46.5	383.7	341.9	41.7	10.9	2 420.8	2 314.2
2nd quarter ...	436.4	307.3	52.6	17.1	46.6	29.7	16.9	46.9	389.4	346.8	42.6	10.9	2 453.4	2 349.5
3rd quarter	443.4	312.3	53.3	17.3	47.7	29.9	17.1	47.4	396.0	349.8	46.2	11.7	2 485.9	2 380.6
4th quarter	452.3	318.9	54.5	17.5	49.3	29.4	17.3	48.1	404.2	357.2	47.0	11.6	2 539.5	2 427.0
1962														
1st quarter	459.3	325.5	55.3	17.7	49.7	30.0	18.9	49.4	409.9	362.5	47.4	11.6	2 566.9	2 450.9
2nd quarter ...	466.8	331.4	55.0	18.0	51.5	30.0	19.1	50.9	415.8	368.4	47.5	11.4	2 602.1	2 477.4
3rd quarter	471.5	334.2	54.9	18.2	53.0	30.4	19.2	52.3	419.2	372.5	46.7	11.1	2 620.8	2 490.7
4th quarter	477.8	337.7	55.8	18.3	54.1	31.2	19.3	53.6	424.2	379.0	45.2	10.7	2 645.6	2 512.8
1963														
1st quarter	483.2	342.7	56.0	18.5	54.7	32.6	21.3	54.1	429.1	382.9	46.2	10.8	2 661.4	2 534.6
2nd quarter ...	488.1	347.6	55.8	18.7	55.9	31.7	21.5	54.3	433.7	387.3	46.4	10.7	2 691.4	2 558.0
3rd quarter	495.2	352.6	56.2	18.8	57.3	32.0	21.8	54.6	440.6	394.7	45.9	10.4	2 718.8	2 586.0
4th quarter	504.6	358.8	57.6	18.8	58.9	32.5	22.0	55.2	449.4	399.6	49.8	11.1	2 760.6	2 628.1

Table 4-1B. Personal Income and Its Disposition: Historical Data—*Continued*

(Billions of current dollars, except as noted; quarterly data are at seasonally adjusted annual rates.)   **NIPA Table 2.1**

Year and quarter	Total	Compensation of employees	Proprietors' income with IVA and CCAdj	Rental income of persons with CCAdj	Personal income receipts on assets	Personal current transfer receipts	Less: Contributions for government social insurance, domestic	Less: Personal current taxes	Equals: Disposable personal income	Less: Personal outlays	Equals: Personal saving — Billions of dollars	Percent of disposable personal income	Personal income excluding current transfers	Disposable personal income
1964														
1st quarter	514.1	365.2	57.9	18.8	60.7	33.6	22.0	53.8	460.4	409.3	51.1	11.1	2 797.0	2 679.5
2nd quarter ...	523.6	372.6	58.8	18.8	62.4	33.2	22.3	49.7	473.8	417.6	56.3	11.9	2 847.6	2 751.7
3rd quarter	533.2	380.0	59.3	18.9	64.0	33.5	22.5	51.6	481.6	426.8	54.7	11.4	2 892.2	2 787.6
4th quarter	541.9	386.1	60.5	18.8	65.4	33.7	22.7	53.2	488.7	429.6	59.0	12.1	2 931.8	2 819.3
1965														
1st quarter	553.0	392.9	61.9	19.1	66.9	35.0	22.9	57.0	496.0	440.5	55.5	11.2	2 978.7	2 852.5
2nd quarter ...	562.6	399.9	63.2	19.3	68.7	34.6	23.2	58.4	504.1	447.9	56.3	11.2	3 020.8	2 884.7
3rd quarter	576.9	408.3	64.0	19.5	70.5	38.1	23.6	57.0	519.9	457.3	62.6	12.0	3 071.1	2 963.6
4th quarter	590.2	420.5	65.6	19.5	71.8	36.9	24.0	58.3	532.0	471.4	60.6	11.4	3 144.7	3 023.3
1966														
1st quarter	602.9	433.1	69.2	19.8	73.3	37.8	30.4	61.5	541.4	481.9	59.5	11.0	3 186.7	3 053.2
2nd quarter ...	612.8	444.4	67.2	19.8	74.4	37.9	30.8	65.6	547.2	487.3	59.9	11.0	3 216.1	3 061.3
3rd quarter	626.0	455.7	67.2	20.0	75.5	39.6	31.9	67.9	558.2	496.6	61.6	11.0	3 255.5	3 098.7
4th quarter	639.6	463.8	68.1	20.0	76.7	43.1	32.2	70.6	569.1	502.6	66.5	11.7	3 286.0	3 135.0
1967														
1st quarter	650.5	470.0	68.9	20.3	78.9	46.1	33.6	71.2	579.3	507.1	72.2	12.5	3 320.1	3 182.2
2nd quarter ...	657.6	475.6	68.5	20.4	80.5	47.2	34.6	70.9	586.7	516.8	69.9	11.9	3 337.2	3 207.5
3rd quarter	671.6	485.3	70.5	20.4	81.9	48.7	35.2	73.8	597.8	523.8	74.0	12.4	3 374.1	3 238.0
4th quarter	683.2	496.2	70.0	20.3	82.6	50.0	36.0	75.9	607.3	531.4	75.9	12.5	3 400.5	3 261.6
1968														
1st quarter	702.5	510.9	71.7	20.1	85.1	52.4	37.6	78.6	624.0	549.8	74.2	11.9	3 454.9	3 316.0
2nd quarter ...	722.4	524.0	73.2	20.1	87.6	55.9	38.4	81.7	640.7	563.9	76.8	12.0	3 506.0	3 370.6
3rd quarter	741.3	537.8	75.0	20.2	90.0	57.3	39.1	91.9	649.4	580.6	68.8	10.6	3 561.1	3 381.4
4th quarter	757.5	550.3	75.5	20.0	92.7	58.7	39.7	95.9	661.7	589.8	71.9	10.9	3 598.9	3 407.5
1969														
1st quarter	772.4	562.8	75.6	20.2	96.2	60.4	42.9	102.6	669.8	602.3	67.4	10.1	3 631.0	3 416.0
2nd quarter ...	790.6	576.7	77.1	20.3	98.7	61.5	43.7	105.7	685.0	614.3	70.6	10.3	3 671.6	3 449.4
3rd quarter	811.6	593.4	78.0	20.4	101.5	62.9	44.6	104.1	707.5	625.0	82.5	11.7	3 724.9	3 519.7
4th quarter	826.8	604.9	77.3	20.4	105.0	64.3	45.3	105.6	721.1	637.4	83.7	11.6	3 749.7	3 546.6
1970														
1st quarter	841.7	615.0	77.1	20.4	109.2	66.1	46.0	104.6	737.2	648.9	88.3	12.0	3 770.9	3 583.9
2nd quarter ...	860.0	620.2	76.7	20.2	113.1	76.1	46.3	105.5	754.5	659.1	95.4	12.6	3 769.6	3 628.1
3rd quarter	874.7	628.2	78.5	20.9	117.5	76.3	46.7	100.7	774.0	671.3	102.7	13.3	3 801.8	3 686.1
4th quarter	883.7	630.0	78.9	21.2	120.0	80.1	46.5	101.5	782.2	678.2	103.9	13.3	3 777.9	3 677.2
1971														
1st quarter	903.7	647.9	80.3	21.1	122.8	82.0	50.5	98.3	805.3	697.6	107.7	13.4	3 826.6	3 750.6
2nd quarter ...	927.1	659.8	82.8	21.7	124.2	89.6	51.0	100.7	826.4	712.1	114.2	13.8	3 856.5	3 805.2
3rd quarter	941.1	670.1	84.6	22.0	126.1	89.6	51.3	102.3	838.8	725.1	113.7	13.6	3 883.2	3 825.1
4th quarter	959.3	682.2	87.9	22.5	127.4	91.3	51.9	105.5	853.8	741.8	112.1	13.1	3 934.1	3 869.7
1972														
1st quarter	986.5	708.4	87.9	23.1	131.0	94.3	58.1	119.8	866.8	759.4	107.4	12.4	4 001.5	3 887.4
2nd quarter ...	1 004.2	722.5	91.3	20.2	134.1	94.9	58.8	123.4	880.8	778.4	102.4	11.6	4 054.8	3 927.8
3rd quarter	1 030.1	735.7	95.5	23.9	138.4	96.0	59.5	124.3	905.8	797.2	108.7	12.0	4 129.0	4 004.2
4th quarter	1 077.0	758.8	105.6	23.8	142.8	106.4	60.4	127.1	949.9	822.2	127.6	13.4	4 255.6	4 164.7
1973														
1st quarter	1 095.1	785.4	104.1	23.5	146.6	109.1	73.6	126.4	968.7	847.0	121.7	12.6	4 271.4	4 196.3
2nd quarter ...	1 124.9	803.2	109.9	23.3	151.6	111.5	74.7	129.2	995.7	863.0	132.7	13.3	4 307.1	4 231.7
3rd quarter	1 152.5	820.4	113.8	22.3	158.8	113.3	76.1	134.1	1 018.4	881.8	136.6	13.4	4 337.6	4 250.8
4th quarter	1 190.7	841.7	122.2	23.3	164.6	116.5	77.6	140.0	1 050.7	898.4	152.3	14.5	4 393.4	4 297.4
1974														
1st quarter	1 206.8	858.3	115.7	23.5	170.5	121.9	83.1	142.8	1 064.0	915.3	148.7	14.0	4 309.1	4 226.0
2nd quarter ...	1 232.9	878.5	108.6	22.9	177.6	129.9	84.7	148.9	1 084.0	944.4	139.6	12.9	4 260.1	4 186.7
3rd quarter	1 269.1	900.2	111.0	23.3	183.9	137.1	86.4	154.9	1 114.2	973.9	140.2	12.6	4 257.4	4 190.5
4th quarter	1 298.5	913.8	113.5	23.0	190.4	144.3	86.6	157.6	1 140.9	984.3	156.5	13.7	4 233.7	4 184.9
1975														
1st quarter	1 318.4	918.4	112.7	22.7	196.4	155.9	87.6	158.0	1 160.4	1 011.8	148.6	12.8	4 186.1	4 178.6
2nd quarter ...	1 350.0	931.2	114.3	22.4	198.5	171.5	88.0	121.1	1 228.9	1 040.4	188.5	15.3	4 192.3	4 371.9
3rd quarter	1 386.5	956.0	120.7	22.2	202.5	174.8	89.8	152.8	1 233.6	1 074.8	158.9	12.9	4 231.5	4 308.3
4th quarter	1 422.7	983.4	125.2	21.9	206.5	177.6	91.8	158.5	1 264.2	1 104.0	160.1	12.7	4 276.4	4 342.0
1976														
1st quarter	1 456.1	1 014.7	126.4	21.6	210.5	181.8	98.9	162.5	1 293.6	1 137.3	156.3	12.1	4 329.0	4 394.4
2nd quarter ...	1 481.2	1 035.5	128.6	20.5	217.1	180.0	100.4	169.3	1 311.9	1 157.1	154.8	11.8	4 383.4	4 419.4
3rd quarter	1 518.4	1 058.4	132.7	20.0	222.8	186.7	102.2	176.1	1 342.3	1 186.9	155.4	11.6	4 418.7	4 453.9
4th quarter	1 554.9	1 084.8	136.2	19.1	229.7	188.8	103.8	182.7	1 372.1	1 221.1	151.0	11.0	4 462.2	4 482.1
1977														
1st quarter	1 588.8	1 113.3	138.6	16.4	238.8	191.0	109.3	188.8	1 400.0	1 258.2	141.9	10.1	4 485.3	4 492.2
2nd quarter ...	1 633.0	1 150.3	140.5	16.3	246.6	191.4	112.1	195.7	1 437.3	1 287.0	150.4	10.5	4 547.9	4 534.4
3rd quarter	1 677.7	1 182.1	142.4	15.6	255.4	196.6	114.3	198.6	1 479.2	1 318.8	160.4	10.8	4 603.6	4 597.4
4th quarter	1 737.4	1 217.6	156.5	15.1	265.5	199.3	116.7	208.5	1 528.9	1 357.8	171.1	11.2	4 713.3	4 685.3

Table 4-1B. Personal Income and Its Disposition: Historical Data—*Continued*

(Billions of current dollars, except as noted; quarterly data are at seasonally adjusted annual rates.)   **NIPA Table 2.1**

| Year and quarter | Personal income | | | | | | | Less: Personal current taxes | Equals: Disposable personal income | Less: Personal outlays | Equals: Personal saving | | Billions of chained (2009) dollars | |
	Total	Compensation of employees	Proprietors' income with IVA and CCAdj	Rental income of persons with CCAdj	Personal income receipts on assets	Personal current transfer receipts	Less: Contributions for government social insurance, domestic				Billions of dollars	Percent of disposable personal income	Personal income excluding current transfers	Disposable personal income
1978														
1st quarter	1 778.1	1 250.9	158.5	15.9	273.3	203.3	123.9	212.0	1 566.1	1 388.5	177.6	11.3	4 748.1	4 722.1
2nd quarter ...	1 838.2	1 299.1	166.1	15.6	281.3	205.1	129.0	223.1	1 615.1	1 447.5	167.6	10.4	4 825.1	4 772.0
3rd quarter	1 892.6	1 336.9	168.3	17.1	289.8	213.9	133.4	236.3	1 656.3	1 479.8	176.5	10.7	4 874.2	4 809.1
4th quarter	1 946.0	1 380.2	170.9	17.5	298.9	217.2	138.8	247.2	1 698.7	1 520.2	178.5	10.5	4 926.3	4 840.8
1979														
1st quarter	2 005.4	1 422.5	180.1	17.3	308.8	222.7	146.0	253.6	1 751.8	1 556.7	195.0	11.1	4 985.8	4 899.4
2nd quarter ...	2 045.4	1 454.7	179.2	15.6	318.8	227.4	150.3	262.0	1 783.4	1 598.3	185.1	10.4	4 949.3	4 855.1
3rd quarter	2 110.9	1 496.7	180.7	15.4	330.4	243.0	155.4	274.8	1 836.0	1 653.9	182.1	9.9	4 961.7	4 877.1
4th quarter	2 169.0	1 534.9	177.8	16.1	350.4	249.1	159.4	285.2	1 883.8	1 698.9	184.9	9.8	4 979.2	4 885.7
1980														
1st quarter	2 231.9	1 573.6	167.6	15.8	377.5	259.4	161.9	284.8	1 947.1	1 751.3	195.8	10.1	4 966.6	4 902.6
2nd quarter ...	2 269.4	1 599.2	160.3	17.1	391.2	264.6	162.9	292.2	1 977.3	1 753.6	223.6	11.3	4 927.4	4 859.5
3rd quarter	2 348.5	1 628.6	173.4	19.9	397.0	296.6	167.0	302.2	2 046.3	1 812.2	234.1	11.4	4 927.6	4 914.1
4th quarter	2 444.7	1 687.6	185.0	23.2	421.9	300.0	173.0	318.9	2 125.8	1 883.0	242.9	11.4	5 026.0	4 981.8
1981														
1st quarter	2 508.9	1 739.6	188.2	24.0	440.5	306.5	189.9	330.9	2 178.0	1 941.4	236.6	10.9	5 030.6	4 974.8
2nd quarter ...	2 559.8	1 774.8	176.4	23.3	469.0	309.9	193.6	342.7	2 217.1	1 975.7	241.4	10.9	5 054.1	4 980.6
3rd quarter	2 659.1	1 815.1	182.3	23.1	508.5	328.5	198.4	356.9	2 302.2	2 019.6	282.6	12.3	5 150.8	5 088.0
4th quarter	2 692.7	1 840.7	171.8	24.7	525.4	331.1	201.0	352.7	2 340.0	2 038.8	301.2	12.9	5 140.6	5 093.6
1982														
1st quarter	2 727.8	1 864.7	165.2	23.5	544.1	336.3	206.0	352.5	2 375.3	2 082.1	293.2	12.3	5 140.7	5 105.9
2nd quarter ...	2 772.3	1 884.4	169.4	21.1	559.9	345.5	208.0	359.7	2 412.5	2 110.9	301.6	12.5	5 166.9	5 136.7
3rd quarter	2 812.5	1 904.8	170.7	24.4	560.8	362.1	210.3	350.1	2 462.3	2 159.3	303.0	12.3	5 136.2	5 161.3
4th quarter	2 853.8	1 918.1	179.5	26.3	563.2	377.9	211.2	356.6	2 497.2	2 221.7	275.5	11.0	5 133.3	5 177.5
1983														
1st quarter	2 892.4	1 947.2	183.3	25.8	574.3	380.7	218.9	350.9	2 541.5	2 263.2	278.4	11.0	5 165.0	5 226.4
2nd quarter ...	2 942.1	1 986.3	182.6	24.7	584.4	386.9	222.9	359.6	2 582.5	2 330.6	251.9	9.8	5 206.9	5 262.6
3rd quarter	3 001.2	2 029.6	183.8	23.7	609.2	382.5	227.7	345.4	2 655.8	2 403.9	251.8	9.5	5 267.1	5 341.6
4th quarter	3 088.6	2 086.8	195.3	23.5	630.2	387.0	234.3	355.7	2 732.9	2 458.9	274.0	10.0	5 397.8	5 460.6
1984														
1st quarter	3 178.9	2 143.8	221.9	23.2	645.6	393.9	249.5	361.2	2 817.8	2 506.0	311.8	11.1	5 505.0	5 569.6
2nd quarter ...	3 262.9	2 195.2	231.8	21.7	671.4	398.3	255.5	370.4	2 892.4	2 566.5	325.9	11.3	5 607.7	5 662.2
3rd quarter	3 337.4	2 241.6	232.4	24.4	698.4	401.0	260.5	384.1	2 953.3	2 607.2	346.1	11.7	5 704.1	5 736.9
4th quarter	3 391.7	2 282.9	226.9	29.3	707.7	409.4	264.5	395.9	2 995.7	2 658.1	337.6	11.3	5 757.8	5 783.7
1985														
1st quarter	3 455.4	2 323.5	240.7	26.9	718.6	420.0	274.3	432.3	3 023.1	2 740.5	282.7	9.3	5 792.0	5 768.6
2nd quarter ...	3 495.5	2 363.6	238.5	25.3	723.8	422.6	278.3	388.5	3 107.0	2 789.6	317.3	10.2	5 816.4	5 881.0
3rd quarter	3 543.1	2 406.4	240.7	27.1	724.1	427.9	283.2	421.5	3 121.5	2 865.2	256.4	8.2	5 850.5	5 862.6
4th quarter	3 605.5	2 455.7	244.3	25.6	738.7	430.9	289.6	428.9	3 176.6	2 893.3	283.3	8.9	5 920.9	5 924.6
1986														
1st quarter	3 667.6	2 491.1	245.6	22.0	762.3	443.2	296.7	426.3	3 241.3	2 940.1	301.2	9.3	5 971.1	6 002.5
2nd quarter ...	3 708.8	2 517.2	251.6	21.1	770.2	449.1	300.4	429.4	3 279.4	2 969.3	310.0	9.5	6 042.8	6 079.3
3rd quarter	3 757.1	2 555.2	264.4	16.6	770.3	456.1	305.5	439.5	3 317.7	3 036.0	281.7	8.5	6 087.4	6 118.0
4th quarter	3 798.8	2 604.7	264.2	13.4	769.8	457.8	311.1	456.0	3 342.8	3 073.2	269.5	8.1	6 124.0	6 127.3
1987														
1st quarter	3 856.0	2 647.8	275.4	14.5	771.1	463.1	315.9	450.7	3 405.3	3 102.2	303.0	8.9	6 161.2	6 183.8
2nd quarter ...	3 917.5	2 692.0	282.3	14.1	781.0	468.1	320.0	511.7	3 405.8	3 172.7	233.2	6.8	6 204.3	6 125.9
3rd quarter	3 988.5	2 740.3	289.5	17.5	796.9	469.2	324.8	489.0	3 499.6	3 238.6	260.9	7.5	6 270.8	6 235.5
4th quarter	4 084.3	2 809.6	298.6	20.3	815.4	472.2	331.7	507.0	3 577.4	3 273.0	304.4	8.5	6 381.1	6 319.6
1988														
1st quarter	4 160.6	2 857.6	319.2	21.1	824.0	489.9	351.1	502.1	3 658.5	3 355.5	303.0	8.3	6 433.6	6 412.3
2nd quarter ...	4 234.8	2 923.1	322.5	20.3	833.7	493.5	358.3	497.8	3 737.0	3 417.4	319.6	8.6	6 485.8	6 478.3
3rd quarter	4 326.3	2 975.8	333.6	21.2	860.5	499.6	364.5	506.7	3 819.6	3 489.6	330.0	8.6	6 553.1	6 541.0
4th quarter	4 411.9	3 035.4	326.8	27.4	887.5	506.8	372.0	517.2	3 894.7	3 565.3	329.4	8.5	6 620.4	6 602.7
1989														
1st quarter	4 537.2	3 079.1	348.1	23.1	933.6	531.4	378.0	552.9	3 984.4	3 626.3	358.0	9.0	6 713.8	6 677.8
2nd quarter ...	4 592.9	3 114.6	339.5	21.2	961.5	538.8	382.6	566.7	4 026.2	3 693.9	332.3	8.3	6 704.3	6 658.2
3rd quarter	4 648.5	3 155.0	337.2	20.0	975.6	547.9	387.2	571.6	4 076.9	3 751.7	325.2	8.0	6 741.4	6 702.4
4th quarter	4 723.7	3 209.7	339.7	21.8	986.6	558.8	393.1	579.8	4 143.9	3 799.5	344.4	8.3	6 793.3	6 759.1
1990														
1st quarter	4 818.9	3 272.8	345.6	23.1	999.5	579.5	401.6	582.5	4 236.3	3 884.5	351.9	8.3	6 815.9	6 811.0
2nd quarter ...	4 899.2	3 334.7	351.1	26.7	1 003.1	590.5	406.9	594.6	4 304.6	3 930.6	374.0	8.7	6 865.0	6 858.4
3rd quarter	4 958.5	3 372.5	358.9	31.6	1 010.0	600.0	414.6	600.7	4 357.8	3 997.1	360.7	8.3	6 857.1	6 856.0
4th quarter	4 978.6	3 381.5	357.0	31.3	1 008.7	617.5	417.4	600.8	4 377.8	4 019.8	357.9	8.2	6 771.6	6 797.5
1991														
1st quarter	4 992.5	3 387.5	347.5	33.0	1 003.9	641.6	421.0	580.8	4 411.7	4 028.3	383.4	8.7	6 720.5	6 814.5
2nd quarter ...	5 054.1	3 427.6	353.0	35.5	1 004.2	661.4	427.7	585.9	4 468.2	4 083.2	384.9	8.6	6 748.4	6 864.4
3rd quarter	5 107.1	3 469.9	353.6	39.4	1 006.8	670.8	433.5	590.2	4 516.8	4 130.5	386.3	8.6	6 769.5	6 892.4
4th quarter	5 186.0	3 517.0	362.6	46.4	999.9	698.8	438.6	598.7	4 587.4	4 158.2	429.1	9.4	6 798.1	6 949.7

Table 4-1B. Personal Income and Its Disposition: Historical Data—*Continued*

(Billions of current dollars, except as noted; quarterly data are at seasonally adjusted annual rates.)   NIPA Table 2.1

| Year and quarter | Personal income | | | | | | | Less: Personal current taxes | Equals: Disposable personal income | Less: Personal outlays | Equals: Personal saving | | Billions of chained (2009) dollars | |
	Total	Compensation of employees	Proprietors' income with IVA and CCAdj	Rental income of persons with CCAdj	Personal income receipts on assets	Personal current transfer receipts	Less: Contributions for government social insurance, domestic				Billions of dollars	Percent of disposable personal income	Personal income excluding current transfers	Disposable personal income
1992														
1st quarter	5 297.8	3 595.7	378.7	50.0	996.8	727.0	450.4	588.9	4 708.9	4 255.1	453.8	9.6	6 881.6	7 089.6
2nd quarter ...	5 394.4	3 651.9	395.2	57.3	1 000.4	745.6	456.0	607.2	4 787.2	4 311.2	476.0	9.9	6 952.8	7 159.9
3rd quarter ...	5 456.3	3 688.5	407.9	64.3	997.1	757.6	459.1	616.2	4 840.1	4 388.0	452.1	9.3	6 982.9	7 193.1
4th quarter ...	5 535.0	3 736.9	418.8	70.7	1 000.9	762.0	454.4	638.9	4 896.1	4 462.5	433.5	8.9	7 044.3	7 225.8
1993														
1st quarter	5 560.7	3 745.6	418.9	80.7	1 007.7	781.6	473.8	617.0	4 943.7	4 508.3	435.4	8.8	7 011.4	7 252.9
2nd quarter ...	5 635.8	3 800.2	429.6	86.9	1 007.4	786.0	474.2	643.5	4 992.3	4 578.0	414.3	8.3	7 067.6	7 275.3
3rd quarter ...	5 677.6	3 834.1	423.4	92.5	1 006.4	799.9	478.8	659.2	5 018.4	4 646.1	372.3	7.4	7 077.4	7 281.7
4th quarter ...	5 757.7	3 889.3	440.0	100.2	1 006.7	804.3	482.9	675.3	5 082.4	4 713.7	368.7	7.3	7 146.1	7 332.3
1994														
1st quarter	5 807.9	3 913.4	450.2	109.0	1 015.2	818.1	498.0	673.7	5 134.3	4 783.9	350.4	6.8	7 173.0	7 380.7
2nd quarter ...	5 912.7	3 991.5	454.1	113.5	1 035.9	822.9	505.1	697.8	5 214.9	4 850.1	364.8	7.0	7 276.3	7 455.0
3rd quarter ...	5 978.4	4 031.8	456.8	116.3	1 057.7	826.9	511.0	695.4	5 283.0	4 925.8	357.2	6.8	7 311.8	7 498.5
4th quarter ...	6 089.4	4 088.1	465.5	115.9	1 090.4	848.0	518.5	705.4	5 384.0	5 002.8	381.2	7.1	7 404.7	7 606.1
1995														
1st quarter	6 181.2	4 134.4	467.4	118.3	1 112.7	874.0	525.5	724.6	5 456.6	5 042.6	414.0	7.6	7 461.1	7 671.1
2nd quarter ...	6 250.7	4 172.9	472.0	121.6	1 130.9	883.5	530.0	746.8	5 503.9	5 124.1	379.9	6.9	7 501.8	7 692.8
3rd quarter ...	6 329.3	4 219.7	484.5	125.7	1 144.3	890.4	535.4	752.2	5 577.0	5 195.4	381.6	6.8	7 571.0	7 763.3
4th quarter ...	6 404.3	4 265.3	501.0	134.0	1 158.4	886.0	540.3	770.0	5 634.3	5 261.6	372.7	6.6	7 647.9	7 808.7
1996														
1st quarter	6 521.0	4 314.5	523.3	139.5	1 170.8	916.0	543.2	801.7	5 719.2	5 337.7	381.5	6.7	7 725.1	7 882.6
2nd quarter ...	6 649.8	4 387.5	547.5	141.6	1 188.5	936.4	551.6	839.6	5 810.3	5 432.5	377.8	6.5	7 822.4	7 954.9
3rd quarter ...	6 725.9	4 451.2	547.5	143.7	1 210.7	931.8	559.0	843.5	5 882.3	5 492.0	390.4	6.6	7 899.0	8 019.3
4th quarter ...	6 817.5	4 514.5	556.8	145.3	1 234.7	932.6	566.5	863.5	5 954.0	5 574.5	379.4	6.4	7 968.5	8 062.0
1997														
1st quarter	6 939.4	4 592.4	575.6	144.2	1 251.4	950.2	574.4	902.1	6 037.2	5 658.1	379.1	6.3	8 074.0	8 138.8
2nd quarter ...	7 022.3	4 660.0	575.1	144.6	1 274.5	950.0	581.9	916.2	6 106.0	5 702.5	403.6	6.6	8 165.6	8 211.0
3rd quarter ...	7 135.3	4 738.9	588.5	147.4	1 294.9	956.2	590.5	941.1	6 194.2	5 815.8	378.4	6.1	8 287.4	8 307.6
4th quarter ...	7 273.0	4 844.0	596.6	152.1	1 319.4	963.1	602.2	967.8	6 305.2	5 905.2	400.0	6.3	8 436.3	8 429.9
1998														
1st quarter	7 434.6	4 942.0	617.4	156.8	1 353.9	974.7	610.3	996.1	6 438.4	5 961.5	476.9	7.4	8 636.1	8 607.4
2nd quarter ...	7 561.1	5 028.3	629.6	162.6	1 379.1	981.1	619.7	1 022.4	6 538.7	6 082.6	456.1	7.0	8 780.8	8 725.8
3rd quarter ...	7 668.1	5 114.9	645.0	168.0	1 385.2	984.5	629.5	1 043.2	6 624.9	6 181.1	443.8	6.7	8 891.8	8 813.7
4th quarter ...	7 762.9	5 199.4	668.7	173.4	1 365.3	995.4	639.2	1 068.0	6 694.9	6 285.6	409.3	6.1	8 979.8	8 883.4
1999														
1st quarter	7 859.1	5 287.0	681.9	176.1	1 349.7	1 014.6	650.2	1 077.9	6 781.2	6 358.1	423.1	6.2	9 064.4	8 980.4
2nd quarter ...	7 922.9	5 343.9	690.1	179.6	1 347.3	1 017.8	655.7	1 095.2	6 827.8	6 496.9	330.8	4.8	9 092.9	8 991.1
3rd quarter ...	8 038.3	5 424.0	699.8	179.4	1 367.2	1 030.9	663.0	1 120.6	6 917.7	6 604.6	313.1	4.5	9 177.2	9 059.7
4th quarter ...	8 206.9	5 555.9	713.9	178.9	1 393.0	1 041.4	676.2	1 154.0	7 052.9	6 743.8	309.1	4.4	9 327.5	9 181.0
2000														
1st quarter	8 443.3	5 749.2	720.9	179.8	1 432.6	1 056.7	696.0	1 208.8	7 234.6	6 902.9	331.7	4.6	9 537.8	9 341.5
2nd quarter ..	8 586.0	5 791.7	751.3	180.2	1 477.5	1 083.7	698.4	1 230.2	7 355.9	7 004.5	351.4	4.8	9 641.2	9 453.0
3rd quarter ...	8 746.9	5 903.9	760.8	182.9	1 512.9	1 098.0	711.6	1 247.7	7 499.2	7 127.7	371.5	5.0	9 766.5	9 575.4
4th quarter ...	8 847.4	5 943.7	782.4	191.0	1 536.8	1 110.8	717.3	1 258.7	7 588.7	7 237.5	351.2	4.6	9 822.7	9 634.9
2001														
1st quarter	9 009.2	6 050.1	809.8	197.1	1 528.9	1 155.6	732.3	1 301.9	7 707.3	7 315.0	392.3	5.1	9 897.7	9 713.4
2nd quarter ...	9 032.4	6 040.9	827.7	202.6	1 507.0	1 187.4	733.1	1 308.9	7 723.6	7 361.9	361.7	4.7	9 840.8	9 688.4
3rd quarter ...	9 009.7	6 024.6	845.6	204.8	1 474.9	1 192.0	732.4	1 113.6	7 896.1	7 389.1	507.0	6.4	9 801.2	9 899.7
4th quarter ...	8 999.9	6 037.8	840.9	205.1	1 416.0	1 235.2	735.0	1 231.8	7 768.1	7 497.9	270.2	3.5	9 731.1	9 735.3
2002														
1st quarter	9 041.5	6 060.7	859.5	207.3	1 397.0	1 260.0	743.1	1 075.2	7 966.4	7 520.6	445.7	5.6	9 732.7	9 963.9
2nd quarter ...	9 141.3	6 129.1	864.5	208.9	1 408.1	1 282.3	751.5	1 051.0	8 090.3	7 606.2	484.2	6.0	9 757.4	10 044.6
3rd quarter ...	9 188.4	6 156.9	872.9	207.7	1 413.1	1 292.1	754.3	1 044.1	8 144.2	7 691.0	453.2	5.6	9 753.2	10 059.5
4th quarter ...	9 272.6	6 193.7	883.3	209.9	1 436.3	1 306.4	757.0	1 038.4	8 234.2	7 767.3	466.8	5.7	9 793.9	10 123.4
2003														
1st quarter	9 313.6	6 213.2	876.3	218.7	1 444.5	1 324.2	763.3	1 021.3	8 292.3	7 859.7	432.6	5.2	9 748.0	10 117.5
2nd quarter ...	9 425.6	6 307.3	892.4	223.2	1 436.1	1 340.6	773.9	1 020.8	8 404.8	7 957.7	447.1	5.3	9 854.8	10 244.6
3rd quarter ...	9 559.0	6 393.7	905.3	227.5	1 455.3	1 361.0	783.8	950.7	8 608.3	8 117.1	491.2	5.7	9 927.1	10 424.0
4th quarter ...	9 695.8	6 500.2	916.1	239.0	1 473.4	1 363.2	796.1	1 021.3	8 674.5	8 218.8	455.7	5.3	10 040.8	10 452.8
2004														
1st quarter	9 792.4	6 541.3	946.5	243.0	1 473.6	1 397.1	809.2	1 012.3	8 780.1	8 356.6	423.5	4.8	10 039.0	10 499.2
2nd quarter ...	9 957.8	6 668.5	963.0	243.4	1 490.5	1 416.0	823.6	1 026.8	8 931.0	8 460.5	470.5	5.3	10 146.0	10 608.3
3rd quarter ...	10 103.6	6 803.7	964.2	241.8	1 507.5	1 425.5	839.2	1 064.4	9 039.2	8 603.8	435.4	4.8	10 257.4	10 684.3
4th quarter ...	10 323.3	6 864.5	977.8	242.9	1 636.7	1 446.3	844.9	1 091.6	9 231.7	8 779.3	452.4	4.9	10 403.6	10 819.3
2005														
1st quarter	10 345.2	6 926.3	957.1	233.7	1 598.1	1 488.1	858.1	1 172.3	9 172.9	8 891.0	281.9	3.1	10 320.2	10 688.3
2nd quarter ...	10 516.8	7 005.6	964.1	231.2	1 669.6	1 512.6	866.3	1 196.3	9 320.5	9 054.8	265.6	2.9	10 425.7	10 792.0
3rd quarter ...	10 686.1	7 122.6	988.1	213.6	1 713.0	1 528.3	879.5	1 225.5	9 460.6	9 229.1	231.4	2.4	10 490.4	10 837.2
4th quarter ...	10 871.7	7 209.9	1 007.2	206.0	1 800.1	1 537.9	889.5	1 255.8	9 615.9	9 322.9	293.0	3.0	10 607.4	10 928.0

Table 4-1B. Personal Income and Its Disposition: Historical Data—*Continued*

(Billions of current dollars, except as noted; quarterly data are at seasonally adjusted annual rates.)   NIPA Table 2.1

Year and quarter	Personal income — Total	Compensation of employees	Proprietors' income with IVA and CCAdj	Rental income of persons with CCAdj	Personal income receipts on assets	Personal current transfer receipts	Less: Contributions for government social insurance, domestic	Less: Personal current taxes	Equals: Disposable personal income	Less: Personal outlays	Equals: Personal saving — Billions of dollars	Percent of disposable personal income	Billions of chained (2009) dollars — Personal income excluding current transfers	Disposable personal income
2006														
1st quarter	11 181.1	7 379.7	1 049.1	194.5	1 882.7	1 588.3	913.2	1 320.5	9 860.6	9 474.0	386.6	3.9	10 845.1	11 147.9
2nd quarter ...	11 336.3	7 428.0	1 052.1	183.4	1 988.0	1 602.8	918.1	1 351.3	9 985.0	9 612.8	372.3	3.7	10 908.4	11 190.4
3rd quarter	11 435.7	7 487.3	1 049.0	177.8	2 015.8	1 628.3	922.6	1 358.6	10 077.1	9 750.4	326.6	3.2	10 912.7	11 212.8
4th quarter	11 585.7	7 623.6	1 053.3	168.7	2 040.4	1 635.9	936.2	1 397.5	10 188.3	9 839.1	349.1	3.4	11 089.6	11 355.3
2007														
1st quarter	11 824.1	7 806.0	1 017.5	162.5	2 087.1	1 706.7	955.7	1 466.5	10 357.5	9 988.2	369.3	3.6	11 174.3	11 439.5
2nd quarter ...	11 988.7	7 845.2	997.9	180.3	2 212.3	1 710.4	957.3	1 495.9	10 492.8	10 109.8	383.0	3.6	11 256.5	11 491.3
3rd quarter	12 069.2	7 885.2	986.8	193.6	2 231.6	1 732.7	960.6	1 498.9	10 570.4	10 232.7	337.6	3.2	11 256.6	11 511.2
4th quarter	12 203.4	7 977.5	979.8	208.7	2 246.9	1 762.7	972.1	1 508.6	10 694.8	10 374.1	320.7	3.0	11 255.5	11 529.3
2008														
1st quarter	12 335.3	8 054.9	964.1	249.2	2 248.2	1 802.9	984.0	1 535.1	10 800.2	10 433.3	366.9	3.4	11 262.4	11 548.8
2nd quarter ...	12 669.4	8 054.9	967.2	280.9	2 204.2	2 148.4	986.2	1 552.5	11 117.0	10 549.4	567.5	5.1	11 141.6	11 772.7
3rd quarter	12 508.6	8 074.4	956.6	305.3	2 222.5	1 941.4	991.5	1 497.5	11 011.1	10 578.1	433.0	3.9	11 072.3	11 537.5
4th quarter	12 396.9	8 043.2	950.7	325.7	2 141.3	1 927.8	991.7	1 444.9	10 951.9	10 306.0	646.0	5.9	11 147.5	11 661.6
2009														
1st quarter	12 057.0	7 730.4	913.2	326.6	2 006.9	2 039.7	959.8	1 202.4	10 854.7	10 214.0	640.7	5.9	10 739.0	11 636.7
2nd quarter ...	12 087.3	7 762.0	901.5	335.9	1 875.6	2 178.6	966.3	1 131.1	10 956.2	10 203.1	753.2	6.9	10 580.6	11 699.1
3rd quarter	12 033.3	7 746.5	934.5	355.8	1 783.9	2 176.3	963.8	1 135.3	10 898.0	10 335.7	562.2	5.2	10 453.3	11 557.3
4th quarter	12 144.0	7 797.2	1 001.3	372.0	1 748.4	2 192.3	967.2	1 140.7	11 003.3	10 400.7	602.6	5.5	10 473.1	11 579.7
2010														
1st quarter	12 321.2	7 767.6	1 055.8	404.9	1 763.3	2 303.2	973.6	1 191.8	11 129.4	10 495.1	634.3	5.7	10 502.3	11 667.4
2nd quarter ...	12 544.7	7 910.6	1 102.7	428.9	1 775.8	2 311.1	984.5	1 213.2	11 331.4	10 596.1	735.4	6.5	10 711.7	11 860.9
3rd quarter	12 682.0	7 982.2	1 128.0	442.6	1 780.5	2 336.1	987.4	1 256.3	11 425.7	10 685.3	740.5	6.5	10 808.5	11 936.6
4th quarter	12 830.2	8 041.0	1 142.7	458.3	1 827.5	2 350.1	989.5	1 289.1	11 541.1	10 813.9	727.2	6.3	10 879.0	11 980.4
2011														
1st quarter	13 175.9	8 170.1	1 179.0	489.1	1 887.8	2 361.8	911.8	1 426.6	11 749.3	10 937.9	811.4	6.9	11 132.1	12 094.8
2nd quarter ...	13 280.6	8 206.4	1 210.2	501.4	1 915.4	2 361.6	914.5	1 445.9	11 834.7	11 054.1	780.7	6.6	11 130.6	12 064.1
3rd quarter	13 413.8	8 287.3	1 251.6	510.1	1 935.6	2 352.1	922.9	1 471.4	11 942.3	11 135.2	807.1	6.8	11 224.2	12 117.7
4th quarter	13 486.9	8 240.9	1 268.9	525.6	2 009.8	2 359.3	917.4	1 470.9	12 016.0	11 191.2	824.8	6.9	11 253.9	12 152.3
2012														
1st quarter	13 786.3	8 456.4	1 321.8	526.7	2 081.4	2 340.4	940.3	1 468.3	12 317.9	11 342.4	975.5	7.9	11 499.6	12 375.7
2nd quarter ...	13 945.9	8 503.8	1 355.6	532.4	2 136.0	2 362.8	944.7	1 487.7	12 458.2	11 390.1	1 068.1	8.6	11 609.3	12 486.5
3rd quarter	13 922.7	8 546.1	1 344.9	536.1	2 078.6	2 364.7	947.6	1 510.0	12 412.6	11 441.9	970.7	7.8	11 550.6	12 404.8
4th quarter	14 402.6	8 763.2	1 363.2	542.8	2 318.7	2 384.2	969.4	1 572.0	12 830.5	11 552.6	1 278.0	10.0	11 943.8	12 750.9
2013														
1st quarter	14 019.5	8 732.6	1 387.2	560.8	2 026.1	2 403.5	1 090.6	1 650.0	12 369.5	11 651.9	717.6	5.8	11 502.5	12 248.6
2nd quarter ...	14 153.0	8 819.6	1 410.6	573.1	2 036.5	2 416.2	1 103.1	1 682.5	12 470.5	11 678.0	792.5	6.4	11 613.8	12 339.8
3rd quarter	14 244.1	8 845.6	1 411.0	585.1	2 074.2	2 434.5	1 106.3	1 674.9	12 569.2	11 766.6	802.6	6.4	11 638.6	12 387.2
4th quarter	14 358.0	8 942.5	1 400.0	590.7	2 099.0	2 443.2	1 117.2	1 698.1	12 659.9	11 908.6	751.3	5.9	11 693.4	12 424.6
2014														
1st quarter	14 625.1	9 114.2	1 411.4	598.1	2 167.0	2 474.1	1 139.8	1 744.8	12 880.3	12 019.9	860.4	6.7	11 868.1	12 580.4
2nd quarter ...	14 874.6	9 172.4	1 450.6	602.6	2 266.7	2 526.8	1 144.5	1 758.4	13 116.2	12 192.4	923.8	7.0	12 000.3	12 747.1
3rd quarter	15 099.5	9 280.6	1 466.2	604.6	2 336.0	2 568.2	1 156.1	1 798.6	13 300.9	12 350.2	950.7	7.1	12 144.2	12 890.1
4th quarter	15 307.1	9 433.5	1 454.4	605.5	2 390.4	2 597.1	1 173.8	1 836.5	13 470.6	12 481.9	988.7	7.3	12 331.6	13 069.5
2015														
1st quarter	15 497.7	9 563.8	1 434.9	596.2	2 447.6	2 644.1	1 188.9	1 904.6	13 593.2	12 518.3	1 074.9	7.9	12 522.9	13 243.4
2nd quarter ...	15 639.9	9 666.2	1 411.3	611.3	2 469.7	2 682.3	1 200.9	1 943.0	13 696.9	12 669.2	1 027.7	7.5	12 563.2	13 280.1
3rd quarter	15 757.0	9 751.7	1 423.2	614.9	2 478.9	2 699.1	1 210.9	1 947.3	13 809.6	12 799.7	1 009.9	7.3	12 629.8	13 357.0
4th quarter	15 846.4	9 816.0	1 413.8	615.6	2 503.2	2 716.1	1 218.3	1 964.9	13 881.4	12 854.5	1 027.0	7.4	12 712.6	13 439.8
2016														
1st quarter	15 918.6	9 851.7	1 410.1	619.8	2 517.0	2 745.4	1 225.3	1 924.6	13 994.0	12 947.8	1 046.2	7.5	12 747.4	13 541.6
2nd quarter ...	16 002.1	9 905.2	1 409.6	626.7	2 524.3	2 767.7	1 231.4	1 943.4	14 058.7	13 089.1	969.6	6.9	12 726.7	13 519.5
3rd quarter	16 151.6	9 998.5	1 431.0	627.6	2 549.9	2 787.1	1 242.5	1 972.0	14 179.6	13 218.4	961.2	6.8	12 803.9	13 584.8
4th quarter	16 315.3	10 109.1	1 442.5	632.5	2 579.4	2 807.9	1 256.0	1 992.9	14 322.4	13 348.0	974.3	6.8	12 879.8	13 656.9
2017														
1st quarter	16 552.0	10 225.4	1 484.4	643.9	2 643.2	2 832.1	1 277.0	2 005.0	14 547.0	13 515.0	1 032.0	7.1	13 010.9	13 795.2
2nd quarter ...	16 739.7	10 337.9	1 498.5	645.1	2 708.8	2 838.9	1 289.6	2 007.2	14 732.5	13 627.2	1 105.3	7.5	13 145.3	13 931.9
3rd quarter	16 932.4	10 480.5	1 502.9	654.9	2 728.2	2 870.8	1 304.8	2 056.1	14 876.2	13 758.5	1 117.7	7.5	13 248.0	14 015.4
4th quarter	17 176.7	10 660.7	1 537.5	667.0	2 751.6	2 883.6	1 323.7	2 127.6	15 049.1	13 998.4	1 050.7	7.0	13 376.6	14 084.1
2018														
1st quarter	17 406.1	10 784.1	1 567.0	671.8	2 786.0	2 940.6	1 343.4	2 076.2	15 329.8	14 176.5	1 153.0	7.5	13 449.7	14 253.3
2nd quarter ...	17 598.5	10 891.8	1 572.1	677.3	2 842.4	2 967.9	1 352.9	2 049.8	15 548.7	14 383.7	1 165.0	7.5	13 524.3	14 373.0
3rd quarter	17 821.1	11 044.3	1 581.3	689.8	2 884.4	2 990.3	1 369.0	2 091.3	15 729.7	14 536.1	1 193.7	7.6	13 663.6	14 491.8
4th quarter	17 998.3	11 118.0	1 601.4	688.6	2 960.5	3 006.5	1 376.6	2 087.7	15 910.6	14 658.8	1 251.8	7.9	13 756.1	14 599.1
2019														
1st quarter	18 238.9	11 336.1	1 585.5	687.0	2 944.3	3 093.8	1 407.6	2 169.3	16 069.6	14 692.9	1 376.7	8.6	13 882.2	14 729.6
2nd quarter ...	18 345.4	11 394.1	1 572.8	691.0	2 972.5	3 129.6	1 414.6	2 222.8	16 122.6	14 928.3	1 194.4	7.4	13 853.6	14 679.3
3rd quarter	18 464.7	11 453.9	1 610.6	691.5	2 973.2	3 157.7	1 422.0	2 205.2	16 259.6	15 087.9	1 171.7	7.2	13 898.3	14 763.1
4th quarter	18 648.5	11 606.8	1 626.8	699.0	2 982.1	3 175.3	1 441.4	2 223.2	16 425.3	15 216.9	1 208.4	7.4	13 989.7	14 850.5

Table 4-2. Personal Consumption Expenditures by Major Type of Product

(Billions of dollars, quarterly data are at seasonally adjusted rates.) NIPA Table 2.3.5

Year and quarter	Personal consumption expend-itures, total	Total goods	Durable goods, total	Motor vehicles and parts	Furnishings and household equipment	Recreational goods and vehicles	Other durable goods	Nondurable goods, total	Food and beverages off-premises	Clothing and footwear	Gasoline and other energy goods	Other nondurable goods
1960	331.2	177.0	45.6	19.6	15.4	6.4	4.3	131.4	62.6	25.9	15.8	27.1
1961	341.5	178.8	44.2	17.7	15.6	6.6	4.3	134.6	63.7	26.6	15.7	28.6
1962	362.6	189.0	49.5	21.4	16.4	6.9	4.7	139.5	64.7	27.9	16.3	30.7
1963	382.0	198.2	54.2	24.2	17.5	7.6	4.9	143.9	65.9	28.6	16.9	32.5
1964	410.6	212.3	59.6	25.8	19.5	8.8	5.5	152.7	69.5	31.1	17.7	34.5
1965	443.0	229.7	66.4	29.6	20.7	10.1	6.0	163.3	74.4	32.7	19.1	37.1
1966	479.9	249.6	71.7	29.9	22.6	12.3	6.9	177.9	80.6	35.8	20.7	40.8
1967	506.7	259.0	74.0	29.6	23.7	13.6	7.1	185.0	82.6	37.5	21.9	43.0
1968	556.9	284.6	84.8	35.4	26.1	15.3	8.0	199.8	88.8	41.3	23.2	46.5
1969	603.6	304.7	90.5	37.4	27.6	16.7	8.7	214.2	95.4	44.3	25.0	49.5
1970	646.7	318.8	90.0	34.5	28.2	17.9	9.4	228.8	103.5	45.5	26.3	53.6
1971	699.9	342.1	102.4	43.2	29.9	19.2	10.1	239.7	107.1	49.0	27.6	55.9
1972	768.2	373.8	116.4	49.4	33.5	22.6	11.0	257.4	114.5	53.5	29.4	60.0
1973	849.6	416.6	130.5	54.4	38.0	25.3	12.9	286.1	126.7	59.2	34.3	65.8
1974	930.2	451.5	130.2	48.2	40.9	26.6	14.5	321.4	143.0	62.4	43.8	72.1
1975	1 030.5	491.3	142.2	52.6	42.6	30.4	16.5	349.2	156.6	66.9	48.0	77.7
1976	1 147.7	546.3	168.6	68.2	47.2	34.2	19.1	377.7	167.3	72.2	53.0	85.2
1977	1 274.0	600.4	192.0	79.8	53.4	37.7	21.1	408.4	179.8	79.3	57.8	91.5
1978	1 422.3	663.6	213.3	89.2	59.0	41.7	23.5	450.2	196.1	89.3	61.5	103.3
1979	1 585.4	737.9	226.3	90.2	65.3	45.8	25.1	511.6	218.4	96.4	80.4	116.5
1980	1 750.7	799.8	226.4	84.4	67.8	46.5	27.6	573.4	239.2	103.0	101.9	129.3
1981	1 934.0	869.4	243.9	93.0	71.5	49.9	29.6	625.4	255.3	113.2	113.4	143.5
1982	2 071.3	899.3	253.0	100.0	71.8	51.3	29.9	646.3	267.1	116.7	108.4	154.0
1983	2 281.6	973.8	295.0	122.9	79.8	58.7	33.7	678.8	277.0	126.4	106.5	168.8
1984	2 492.3	1 063.7	342.2	147.2	88.8	67.8	38.3	721.5	291.1	137.6	108.2	184.6
1985	2 712.8	1 137.6	380.4	170.1	94.6	74.1	41.6	757.2	303.0	146.8	110.5	196.9
1986	2 886.3	1 195.6	421.4	187.5	103.5	83.0	47.5	774.2	316.4	157.2	91.2	209.4
1987	3 076.3	1 256.3	442.0	188.2	109.5	91.8	52.5	814.3	324.3	167.7	96.4	225.9
1988	3 330.0	1 337.3	475.1	202.2	115.2	99.9	57.8	862.3	342.8	178.2	99.9	241.4
1989	3 576.8	1 423.8	494.3	207.8	121.4	103.9	61.3	929.5	365.4	190.4	110.4	263.3
1990	3 809.0	1 491.3	497.1	205.1	120.9	105.6	65.5	994.2	391.2	195.2	124.2	283.6
1991	3 943.4	1 497.4	477.2	185.7	118.8	107.7	64.9	1 020.3	403.0	199.1	121.1	297.1
1992	4 197.6	1 563.3	508.1	204.8	124.3	111.0	68.0	1 055.2	404.5	211.2	125.0	314.5
1993	4 452.0	1 642.3	551.5	224.7	131.4	123.5	72.0	1 090.8	413.5	219.1	126.9	331.4
1994	4 721.0	1 746.6	607.2	249.8	140.5	140.3	76.5	1 139.4	432.1	227.4	129.2	350.6
1995	4 962.6	1 815.5	635.7	255.7	146.7	153.7	79.6	1 179.8	443.7	231.2	133.4	371.4
1996	5 244.6	1 917.7	676.3	273.5	153.5	164.9	84.3	1 241.4	461.9	239.5	144.7	395.2
1997	5 536.8	2 006.5	715.5	293.1	160.5	174.6	87.3	1 291.0	474.8	247.5	147.7	421.0
1998	5 877.2	2 108.4	779.3	320.2	173.6	191.4	94.2	1 329.1	487.4	257.8	132.4	451.5
1999	6 283.8	2 287.1	855.6	350.7	191.2	210.9	102.7	1 431.5	515.5	271.1	146.5	498.3
2000	6 767.2	2 453.2	912.6	363.2	208.1	230.9	110.4	1 540.6	540.6	280.8	184.5	534.7
2001	7 073.8	2 525.6	941.5	383.3	214.9	234.9	108.4	1 584.1	564.0	277.9	178.0	564.2
2002	7 348.9	2 598.8	985.4	401.3	225.9	244.8	113.4	1 613.4	575.1	278.8	167.9	591.7
2003	7 740.7	2 722.6	1 017.8	401.5	235.2	259.5	121.7	1 704.8	599.6	285.3	196.4	623.5
2004	8 232.0	2 902.0	1 080.6	409.3	254.3	284.8	132.1	1 821.4	632.6	297.4	232.7	658.7
2005	8 769.1	3 082.9	1 128.6	410.0	271.3	306.4	141.0	1 954.3	668.2	310.5	283.8	691.8
2006	9 277.2	3 239.7	1 158.3	394.9	283.6	326.3	153.5	2 081.3	700.3	320.0	319.7	741.4
2007	9 746.6	3 367.0	1 188.0	400.6	283.5	339.2	164.8	2 179.0	737.3	323.5	345.5	772.6
2008	10 050.1	3 363.2	1 098.8	343.3	264.3	328.1	163.0	2 264.5	769.1	317.4	391.1	786.9
2009	9 891.2	3 180.0	1 012.1	318.6	238.3	297.5	157.7	2 167.9	772.9	304.0	287.0	803.9
2010	10 260.3	3 317.8	1 049.0	344.5	240.9	298.6	165.0	2 268.9	786.9	316.6	336.7	828.7
2011	10 698.9	3 518.1	1 093.5	365.2	246.9	305.4	176.1	2 424.6	819.5	332.6	413.8	858.7
2012	11 047.4	3 637.7	1 144.2	396.6	253.9	311.8	181.9	2 493.5	846.2	345.2	421.9	880.2
2013	11 363.5	3 730.0	1 189.4	417.5	263.6	321.6	186.7	2 540.6	864.0	350.5	418.2	907.8
2014	11 847.7	3 863.0	1 242.1	442.0	276.2	329.9	194.0	2 620.9	896.9	360.8	403.3	959.9
2015	12 263.5	3 923.0	1 307.6	475.3	294.2	336.5	201.6	2 615.4	921.0	368.7	309.4	1 016.3
2016	12 693.3	3 991.8	1 345.2	484.3	308.5	349.4	203.0	2 646.7	940.6	375.7	275.7	1 054.6
2017	13 239.1	4 158.6	1 396.6	501.3	322.7	366.4	206.2	2 761.9	973.1	381.0	309.9	1 097.9
2018	13 913.5	4 353.7	1 469.2	519.5	345.5	391.1	213.1	2 884.5	1 000.3	392.0	350.4	1 141.8
2019	14 428.7	4 478.9	1 513.3	514.5	360.2	420.9	217.6	2 965.6	1 030.9	398.2	337.6	1 198.9
2020	14 047.6	4 653.8	1 616.4	541.3	390.4	476.2	208.5	3 037.4	1 146.7	362.4	246.8	1 281.5
2021	15 741.6	5 481.4	2 026.2	700.1	469.7	577.3	279.2	3 455.2	1 234.8	468.7	359.4	1 392.3
2019												
1st quarter	14 155.6	4 382.8	1 473.3	500.1	351.8	406.8	214.6	2 909.5	1 013.4	393.4	323.9	1 178.9
2nd quarter	14 375.7	4 479.4	1 509.2	512.6	360.0	419.5	217.2	2 970.1	1 027.4	398.3	350.1	1 194.4
3rd quarter	14 529.5	4 512.7	1 531.4	519.0	364.5	428.6	219.4	2 981.3	1 041.3	400.0	332.8	1 207.1
4th quarter	14 653.9	4 540.8	1 539.2	526.6	364.5	428.8	219.3	3 001.6	1 041.5	401.0	343.7	1 215.4
2020												
1st quarter	14 439.1	4 530.9	1 484.9	482.0	365.7	428.7	208.5	3 046.0	1 125.1	366.3	305.2	1 249.5
2nd quarter	12 989.7	4 349.9	1 468.3	485.2	361.2	458.0	163.9	2 881.7	1 152.1	293.6	188.5	1 247.4
3rd quarter	14 293.8	4 867.2	1 753.3	595.8	419.3	509.5	228.8	3 113.9	1 159.5	394.2	245.4	1 314.7
4th quarter	14 467.6	4 867.3	1 759.2	602.1	415.4	508.7	233.1	3 108.1	1 150.0	395.6	247.9	1 314.6
2021												
1st quarter	15 005.4	5 245.0	1 957.8	674.9	461.9	559.4	261.7	3 287.2	1 201.5	436.8	300.3	1 348.5
2nd quarter	15 681.7	5 529.8	2 092.2	758.1	473.7	580.8	279.6	3 437.6	1 223.4	477.0	345.5	1 391.9
3rd quarter	15 964.9	5 500.1	1 995.2	667.9	468.7	575.0	283.6	3 505.0	1 245.3	479.7	376.2	1 403.7
4th quarter	16 314.2	5 650.8	2 059.7	699.4	474.4	594.1	291.8	3 591.1	1 268.8	481.4	415.8	1 425.0

Table 4-2. Personal Consumption Expenditures by Major Type of Product—*Continued*

(Billions of dollars, quarterly data are at seasonally adjusted rates.)

NIPA Table 2.3.5

Year and quarter	Services	Household services, total	Housing and utilities	Health care	Transportation services	Recreation services	Food services and accommodations	Financial services and insurance	Other services	Final consumption expenditures	Gross output	Less: receipts from sales of goods and services
1960	154.2	149.1	56.7	16.0	9.2	6.5	20.5	13.2	27.1	5.1	14.8	9.8
1961	162.7	157.4	60.3	17.1	9.6	6.9	21.0	14.3	28.3	5.2	15.8	10.5
1962	173.6	168.1	64.5	19.1	10.1	7.5	22.3	14.8	29.9	5.5	16.9	11.5
1963	183.9	178.1	68.2	21.0	10.6	7.9	23.3	15.5	31.6	5.8	18.3	12.6
1964	198.4	191.9	72.1	24.1	11.4	8.5	24.9	17.2	33.8	6.4	20.3	13.8
1965	213.3	206.3	76.6	26.0	12.1	9.0	27.2	18.8	36.6	7.0	22.1	15.1
1966	230.3	222.8	81.2	28.7	13.1	9.8	29.6	20.6	39.9	7.5	24.3	16.9
1967	247.7	239.6	86.3	31.9	14.3	10.5	31.0	22.1	43.6	8.1	27.0	18.9
1968	272.2	263.4	92.7	36.6	15.9	11.7	34.6	25.2	46.8	8.8	30.3	21.6
1969	299.0	289.5	101.0	42.1	18.0	12.9	37.5	27.7	50.5	9.4	34.0	24.6
1970	327.9	317.5	109.4	47.7	20.0	14.0	41.6	30.1	54.6	10.5	38.1	27.6
1971	357.8	346.1	120.0	53.7	22.4	15.1	43.8	33.1	58.1	11.7	42.8	31.1
1972	394.3	381.5	131.2	59.8	24.5	16.3	48.9	37.1	63.7	12.8	47.4	34.5
1973	432.9	419.2	143.5	67.2	26.1	18.3	54.8	39.9	69.3	13.8	51.8	38.1
1974	478.6	463.1	158.6	76.1	28.5	20.9	60.6	44.1	74.4	15.5	58.8	43.3
1975	539.2	522.2	176.5	89.0	32.0	23.7	68.8	51.8	80.3	17.0	67.2	50.2
1976	601.4	582.4	194.7	101.8	36.2	26.5	77.8	56.8	88.6	19.0	76.3	57.3
1977	673.6	653.0	217.8	115.7	41.4	29.6	85.7	65.1	97.7	20.6	85.2	64.5
1978	758.7	735.7	244.3	131.2	45.2	32.9	97.1	76.7	108.3	23.0	96.7	73.6
1979	847.5	821.4	273.4	148.8	50.7	36.7	110.9	83.6	117.2	26.1	109.4	83.2
1980	950.9	920.8	312.5	171.7	55.4	40.8	121.7	91.7	127.1	30.0	126.1	96.1
1981	1 064.6	1 030.4	352.1	201.9	59.8	47.1	133.9	98.5	137.2	34.1	145.7	111.5
1982	1 172.0	1 134.0	387.5	225.2	61.7	52.5	142.5	113.7	150.9	38.0	163.8	125.8
1983	1 307.8	1 267.1	421.2	253.1	68.9	59.4	153.6	141.0	169.9	40.8	179.2	138.5
1984	1 428.6	1 383.3	457.5	276.5	80.0	66.1	164.9	150.8	187.5	45.4	194.4	149.0
1985	1 575.2	1 527.3	500.6	302.2	90.1	74.0	174.3	178.2	207.9	47.9	209.3	161.4
1986	1 690.7	1 638.0	537.0	330.2	95.0	80.4	186.7	187.7	221.2	52.6	227.3	174.7
1987	1 820.0	1 764.3	571.6	366.0	103.1	87.3	204.4	189.5	242.4	55.7	246.9	191.2
1988	1 992.7	1 929.4	614.4	410.1	114.2	99.2	225.8	202.9	262.8	63.3	275.5	212.2
1989	2 153.0	2 084.9	655.2	451.2	121.8	110.7	242.6	222.3	281.1	68.0	301.2	233.2
1990	2 317.7	2 241.8	696.5	506.2	126.4	121.8	262.7	230.8	297.5	75.9	334.4	258.6
1991	2 446.0	2 365.9	735.2	555.8	123.7	127.2	273.4	250.1	300.5	80.1	362.9	282.8
1992	2 634.3	2 546.4	771.1	612.8	133.6	139.8	286.3	277.0	325.7	87.9	396.4	308.5
1993	2 809.6	2 719.6	814.9	648.8	145.7	153.4	298.4	314.0	344.3	90.1	418.7	328.7
1994	2 974.4	2 876.6	863.3	680.5	161.0	164.7	308.3	327.9	371.0	97.8	440.1	342.3
1995	3 147.1	3 044.7	913.7	719.9	176.4	181.1	316.1	347.0	390.6	102.3	458.5	356.2
1996	3 326.9	3 216.9	962.4	752.1	192.7	195.6	326.6	372.1	415.5	110.0	483.1	373.1
1997	3 530.3	3 424.7	1 009.8	790.9	211.8	208.3	343.4	408.9	451.5	105.6	502.6	397.0
1998	3 768.8	3 645.0	1 065.5	832.0	225.2	220.2	361.8	446.1	494.2	123.8	542.5	418.7
1999	3 996.7	3 858.5	1 123.1	863.6	241.3	238.1	380.3	484.6	527.4	138.2	576.3	438.1
2000	4 314.0	4 156.0	1 198.6	918.4	261.3	254.4	408.8	541.9	572.6	158.0	621.6	463.6
2001	4 548.2	4 369.1	1 287.5	996.6	259.8	262.3	419.7	529.3	614.0	179.1	676.4	497.4
2002	4 750.1	4 551.8	1 329.5	1 082.9	251.9	271.4	436.3	539.0	640.8	198.3	737.1	538.7
2003	5 018.2	4 812.6	1 391.1	1 154.0	259.6	288.9	462.7	574.2	682.1	205.5	774.6	569.1
2004	5 329.9	5 123.6	1 466.6	1 238.9	271.2	311.5	498.2	619.3	717.9	206.4	819.0	612.6
2005	5 686.1	5 475.9	1 580.1	1 320.5	283.9	328.1	533.6	676.8	752.8	210.3	868.5	658.2
2006	6 037.6	5 798.4	1 665.7	1 391.9	297.1	351.3	570.6	719.5	802.3	239.2	932.2	693.0
2007	6 379.6	6 130.8	1 759.6	1 478.2	307.6	375.6	601.5	762.7	845.7	248.8	983.1	734.4
2008	6 686.9	6 399.6	1 872.7	1 555.3	312.7	389.1	620.2	777.5	872.1	287.3	1 047.4	760.1
2009	6 711.2	6 422.0	1 900.0	1 632.7	297.4	388.4	612.7	720.5	870.3	289.2	1 088.3	799.1
2010	6 942.4	6 648.0	1 947.9	1 699.6	305.2	403.7	635.7	768.0	887.9	294.4	1 128.6	834.2
2011	7 180.7	6 868.9	1 983.3	1 757.1	328.4	409.0	669.5	811.1	910.6	311.9	1 173.5	861.7
2012	7 409.6	7 068.1	2 014.7	1 821.3	341.1	430.8	704.9	830.9	924.4	341.5	1 236.5	895.0
2013	7 633.6	7 281.0	2 083.5	1 858.2	359.9	447.1	732.3	869.3	930.7	352.6	1 271.7	919.1
2014	7 984.8	7 619.2	2 151.4	1 940.5	383.0	466.6	776.9	922.9	977.7	365.6	1 322.4	956.8
2015	8 340.5	7 968.9	2 206.6	2 057.3	398.7	491.7	832.9	974.4	1 007.3	371.6	1 383.3	1 011.7
2016	8 701.4	8 300.0	2 280.8	2 159.4	419.7	518.6	873.2	996.1	1 052.1	401.4	1 460.1	1 058.7
2017	9 080.6	8 662.6	2 363.2	2 238.8	440.9	542.3	913.5	1 069.0	1 095.0	417.9	1 510.2	1 092.3
2018	9 559.8	9 115.1	2 472.1	2 339.6	469.4	564.7	960.8	1 151.9	1 156.7	444.7	1 587.8	1 143.1
2019	9 949.8	9 509.9	2 571.5	2 458.2	495.3	583.3	1 008.3	1 171.6	1 221.8	439.9	1 643.6	1 203.7
2020	9 393.7	8 872.9	2 668.1	2 308.4	363.4	416.5	801.5	1 196.3	1 118.5	520.9	1 644.8	1 123.9
2021	10 260.0	9 777.2	2 776.7	2 545.3	430.1	502.7	1 027.0	1 270.8	1 224.6	482.9	1 722.7	1 239.8
2019												
1st quarter	9 772.7	9 336.7	2 534.7	2 408.7	479.6	573.7	986.9	1 156.3	1 196.7	436.1	1 625.1	1 189.0
2nd quarter	9 896.3	9 459.1	2 554.1	2 449.7	492.2	582.5	1 006.8	1 166.6	1 207.2	437.3	1 637.8	1 200.5
3rd quarter	10 016.0	9 571.5	2 585.3	2 469.9	502.2	582.8	1 019.4	1 177.0	1 234.9	445.3	1 650.4	1 205.1
4th quarter	10 113.0	9 672.3	2 611.8	2 504.3	507.3	594.0	1 020.0	1 186.5	1 248.4	440.9	1 661.1	1 220.2
2020												
1st quarter	9 908.2	9 387.7	2 622.6	2 406.9	467.3	541.7	933.6	1 193.9	1 221.7	520.5	1 668.1	1 147.6
2nd quarter	8 639.8	8 062.8	2 667.7	2 000.3	291.2	303.7	616.8	1 168.7	1 014.4	577.0	1 585.3	1 008.3
3rd quarter	9 426.6	8 932.1	2 682.6	2 369.2	342.5	405.7	829.8	1 200.5	1 102.0	494.6	1 640.2	1 145.6
4th quarter	9 600.4	9 109.0	2 699.7	2 457.2	352.8	415.0	826.1	1 222.0	1 136.1	491.4	1 685.5	1 194.1
2021												
1st quarter	9 760.4	9 281.7	2 727.2	2 464.2	356.8	442.5	888.3	1 244.9	1 157.8	478.7	1 672.7	1 194.0
2nd quarter	10 151.0	9 684.8	2 753.4	2 534.4	417.3	490.5	1 028.7	1 256.4	1 204.0	467.1	1 708.5	1 241.5
3rd quarter	10 464.0	9 984.4	2 792.6	2 574.5	467.8	525.9	1 083.1	1 276.3	1 264.1	480.4	1 733.1	1 252.7
4th quarter	10 663.0	10 157.0	2 833.4	2 608.2	478.6	551.9	1 107.7	1 305.7	1 272.4	505.5	1 776.4	1 271.0

Table 4-3. Chain-Type Quantity Indexes for Personal Consumption Expenditures by Major Type of Product

(Index numbers, 2012 = 100.)   NIPA Table 2.3.3

Year and quarter	Personal consumption expenditures, total	Total goods	Goods									
			Durable goods					Nondurable goods				
			Durable goods, total	Motor vehicles and parts	Furnishings and household equipment	Recreational goods and vehicles	Other durable goods	Nondurable goods, total	Food and beverages off-premises	Clothing and footwear	Gasoline and other energy goods	Other nondurable goods
1960	18.2	18.3	7.0	16.7	12.2	0.8	7.9	29.2	44.7	14.5	53.2	18.5
1961	18.6	18.4	6.8	15.0	12.2	0.8	8.0	29.8	45.4	14.8	52.9	19.5
1962	19.5	19.3	7.5	17.8	12.9	0.9	8.8	30.7	45.7	15.5	54.6	20.9
1963	20.3	20.1	8.2	20.1	13.8	0.9	9.1	31.3	46.0	15.7	56.5	21.8
1964	21.5	21.3	9.0	21.2	15.3	1.1	9.9	32.8	47.6	16.9	59.5	22.8
1965	22.9	22.8	10.1	24.5	16.3	1.3	10.9	34.5	50.0	17.6	62.3	24.2
1966	24.2	24.3	11.0	24.9	17.7	1.6	12.6	36.4	51.9	18.8	65.7	26.1
1967	24.9	24.7	11.1	24.3	18.1	1.7	12.7	37.2	53.1	19.0	67.4	26.8
1968	26.4	26.3	12.4	28.1	19.2	1.9	13.9	38.7	55.5	19.7	70.2	27.9
1969	27.4	27.1	12.8	29.2	19.6	2.0	14.4	39.8	57.0	20.1	73.3	28.7
1970	28.0	27.3	12.5	26.1	19.6	2.2	15.1	40.7	58.6	19.9	76.1	29.7
1971	29.1	28.4	13.7	31.2	20.5	2.2	15.8	41.4	59.3	20.7	78.7	29.8
1972	30.8	30.3	15.5	35.5	22.6	2.6	16.7	43.1	60.5	22.2	82.7	31.2
1973	32.4	31.9	17.1	38.9	25.0	2.9	19.0	44.4	59.4	23.8	87.5	33.3
1974	32.1	30.7	16.0	32.5	24.9	2.9	19.9	43.3	58.2	23.3	80.4	33.2
1975	32.8	30.9	16.0	32.3	23.6	3.1	21.1	43.7	59.3	23.9	82.2	32.1
1976	34.7	33.1	18.0	38.9	25.1	3.4	23.2	45.7	62.2	25.0	86.6	33.5
1977	36.1	34.5	19.6	43.0	27.4	3.6	24.5	46.8	63.1	26.4	88.2	34.0
1978	37.7	35.9	20.7	44.9	28.8	3.9	25.8	48.5	62.8	29.1	89.6	36.4
1979	38.6	36.5	20.5	42.2	30.0	4.1	25.5	49.7	63.7	30.8	87.0	38.5
1980	38.5	35.6	18.9	36.8	28.8	3.9	23.3	49.6	64.4	31.8	79.3	39.2
1981	39.0	36.0	19.1	37.7	28.3	4.0	23.7	50.3	64.1	33.8	78.3	40.1
1982	39.6	36.2	19.1	38.7	27.0	4.0	23.7	50.8	65.4	34.4	78.4	40.0
1983	41.8	38.6	21.8	46.1	29.3	4.7	25.9	52.4	67.0	36.7	80.2	41.0
1984	44.0	41.3	24.9	53.6	32.3	5.5	28.8	54.6	68.4	39.8	82.3	43.2
1985	46.3	43.5	27.4	60.6	34.0	6.1	31.0	56.2	70.4	41.5	83.9	44.4
1986	48.2	45.9	30.0	65.0	36.8	7.0	34.5	58.2	71.8	44.6	88.2	45.4
1987	49.9	46.8	30.6	62.4	38.3	7.9	35.7	59.2	71.4	46.3	89.9	47.1
1988	51.9	48.5	32.4	66.0	39.7	8.6	36.9	60.8	73.3	47.7	92.4	48.1
1989	53.5	49.7	33.1	65.9	41.8	9.0	37.4	62.4	74.2	50.2	93.9	49.7
1990	54.5	50.0	32.9	64.8	41.2	9.2	37.6	63.2	75.7	49.8	92.2	51.0
1991	54.6	49.0	31.2	57.1	40.2	9.5	36.0	63.0	75.6	49.9	91.5	50.7
1992	56.6	50.6	32.9	61.8	41.6	10.1	36.7	64.2	75.3	52.5	95.1	51.8
1993	58.6	52.7	35.4	65.2	43.7	11.7	38.5	65.8	75.9	54.8	97.5	53.6
1994	60.9	55.5	38.2	69.3	46.1	13.6	40.3	68.4	78.1	57.8	99.1	56.3
1995	62.7	57.1	39.7	68.2	48.2	15.5	41.2	70.1	78.5	60.2	100.9	58.7
1996	64.9	59.7	42.7	71.5	50.3	17.9	44.0	72.1	79.2	63.1	102.5	61.3
1997	67.3	62.5	46.2	76.3	52.6	20.7	46.2	74.2	79.9	65.2	104.6	64.6
1998	70.9	66.7	51.8	84.3	57.0	24.8	50.7	77.0	81.0	69.2	107.5	68.0
1999	74.7	72.0	58.4	92.1	63.6	29.9	56.8	80.9	84.3	73.7	110.0	72.2
2000	78.4	75.7	63.4	95.0	69.7	34.9	61.8	83.5	86.4	77.3	107.1	75.8
2001	80.4	78.0	66.8	99.9	73.3	38.2	60.5	85.0	87.6	78.0	107.0	78.2
2002	82.4	81.0	71.7	105.1	78.6	42.5	64.4	86.5	88.0	80.4	107.9	80.5
2003	85.0	85.0	76.8	108.2	84.2	48.1	70.7	89.6	90.0	84.4	108.0	84.6
2004	88.2	89.3	83.2	111.2	92.2	55.5	77.1	92.5	92.1	88.2	108.9	88.3
2005	91.4	93.0	87.8	109.7	98.3	63.2	83.1	95.6	95.6	92.9	108.4	91.4
2006	94.0	96.5	91.7	105.6	103.3	71.6	89.7	98.7	98.6	96.2	108.1	95.9
2007	96.3	99.2	96.1	107.7	104.1	79.9	94.5	100.4	99.9	98.1	107.9	98.5
2008	96.4	96.2	90.6	94.1	97.8	81.3	91.2	98.8	98.2	97.0	103.7	98.0
2009	95.2	93.2	85.0	87.4	88.5	78.3	88.0	97.2	97.5	92.2	104.3	95.8
2010	97.0	95.8	89.8	90.8	93.4	84.5	92.4	98.7	99.0	96.6	103.8	97.0
2011	98.7	97.9	94.4	93.3	97.2	92.4	96.1	99.6	99.1	99.8	101.4	99.0
2012	100.0	100.0	100.0	100.0	100.0	100.0	100.0	100.0	100.0	100.0	100.0	100.0
2013	101.5	103.1	106.1	104.7	105.8	108.9	104.9	101.8	101.1	100.5	101.9	103.0
2014	104.2	107.4	113.8	110.8	114.8	116.9	113.5	104.5	103.0	103.2	101.9	107.6
2015	107.7	112.5	122.4	119.2	125.4	124.2	122.3	108.0	104.6	106.7	106.6	112.6
2016	110.3	116.3	129.0	122.8	135.0	135.5	124.1	110.7	107.9	109.1	107.4	115.4
2017	113.0	120.8	137.1	128.7	145.2	147.9	127.7	113.7	111.8	111.3	106.8	118.8
2018	116.3	125.6	146.7	133.9	157.2	164.1	134.5	116.4	114.3	114.4	106.2	122.8
2019	118.8	129.8	152.9	132.3	162.7	184.1	140.5	119.8	116.6	117.8	106.1	128.5
2020	114.3	135.9	164.7	136.6	175.0	217.6	138.5	123.5	125.5	113.0	91.6	135.9
2021	123.3	152.4	194.5	157.1	200.1	259.3	183.2	134.7	131.0	143.2	100.4	146.8
2019												
1st quarter	117.5	127.3	148.0	129.0	158.2	174.0	139.0	118.3	114.7	115.5	106.4	126.9
2nd quarter	118.5	129.5	151.8	131.6	162.2	182.4	138.9	119.7	116.4	117.6	106.8	128.2
3rd quarter	119.4	131.0	155.0	133.3	164.4	188.9	141.8	120.6	117.9	117.8	106.2	129.4
4th quarter	119.9	131.6	156.8	135.5	166.1	191.2	142.3	120.7	117.6	120.2	105.0	129.3
2020												
1st quarter	117.8	131.7	151.9	124.3	165.6	193.6	136.4	122.8	126.1	109.4	98.1	132.7
2nd quarter	106.4	128.3	151.3	125.7	163.5	210.2	108.3	118.3	124.8	93.5	81.0	132.3
3rd quarter	116.1	141.8	177.5	147.9	186.8	233.1	152.1	126.7	126.1	124.1	95.1	139.0
4th quarter	117.0	141.7	178.0	148.7	184.1	233.4	157.1	126.4	125.0	125.1	92.0	139.6
2021												
1st quarter	120.2	150.6	196.9	166.7	203.6	254.1	174.3	131.1	130.4	135.0	93.3	143.1
2nd quarter	123.7	155.2	202.4	173.0	203.6	261.3	182.9	135.4	131.4	146.3	100.8	147.1
3rd quarter	124.3	151.7	188.6	145.2	197.8	257.1	185.1	136.1	131.3	146.1	103.6	148.1
4th quarter	125.1	152.1	189.8	143.6	195.5	264.8	190.7	136.2	131.0	145.2	103.9	148.9

Table 4-3. Chain-Type Quantity Indexes for Personal Consumption Expenditures by Major Type of Product—*Continued*

(Index numbers, 2012 = 100.)

NIPA Table 2.3.3

		Services											
Year and quarter	Services	Household consumption expenditures for services									Nonprofit institutions serving households (NPISHs)		
		Household services, total	Housing and utilities	Health care	Transportation services	Recreation services	Food services and accommodations	Financial services and insurance	Other services	Final consumption expenditures	Gross output	Less: receipts from sales of goods and services
1960	17.6	18.8	20.8	14.0	20.6	10.3	26.4	12.1	25.0	2.9	12.6	19.3
1961	18.3	19.5	21.8	14.7	20.9	10.7	26.5	12.8	25.8	2.9	13.1	20.4
1962	19.2	20.5	23.1	16.0	21.7	11.3	27.5	12.7	26.8	3.0	13.8	21.7
1963	20.0	21.3	24.2	17.0	22.6	11.7	28.2	13.2	27.8	3.1	14.6	23.1
1964	21.2	22.6	25.3	19.0	23.8	12.2	29.6	14.1	29.1	3.5	15.7	24.6
1965	22.3	23.8	26.7	19.8	25.1	12.7	31.7	15.1	30.7	3.7	16.7	26.1
1966	23.4	25.0	27.9	20.9	26.5	13.4	33.3	15.6	32.5	3.8	17.8	28.2
1967	24.4	26.0	29.2	21.9	27.9	13.9	33.0	16.4	34.4	4.0	18.8	30.1
1968	25.7	27.4	30.6	23.6	29.7	14.7	35.0	17.3	35.4	4.2	20.1	32.4
1969	26.8	28.7	32.3	25.3	31.7	15.6	35.8	17.5	36.4	4.2	21.2	34.6
1970	27.9	29.8	33.5	26.7	32.8	16.2	37.0	18.1	37.6	4.5	22.2	36.2
1971	28.9	30.8	35.0	28.6	34.2	16.7	37.0	18.8	37.7	4.8	23.8	39.0
1972	30.5	32.6	36.9	30.6	36.1	17.6	39.8	19.9	39.4	5.0	25.2	41.3
1973	32.0	34.1	38.6	32.8	36.8	19.1	41.8	21.0	40.5	5.0	25.9	42.8
1974	32.6	34.8	40.4	33.9	37.0	20.4	41.4	21.5	39.2	5.0	26.2	43.8
1975	33.8	36.2	41.7	35.7	37.5	21.5	43.1	23.6	39.5	5.0	27.2	45.9
1976	35.2	37.7	42.9	37.2	39.3	22.9	45.7	24.8	41.0	5.3	28.7	48.3
1977	36.7	39.3	44.1	39.0	42.1	24.4	46.9	26.4	43.0	5.4	29.8	50.5
1978	38.4	41.1	46.2	40.8	43.1	25.6	48.9	27.6	45.3	5.6	31.4	53.4
1979	39.6	42.4	47.8	42.2	44.4	26.8	50.4	28.5	45.7	5.8	32.3	54.8
1980	40.2	43.0	49.5	43.4	41.8	27.7	50.5	28.9	45.5	6.1	33.3	56.1
1981	40.8	43.6	50.2	45.5	40.3	30.1	51.0	28.7	44.5	6.6	34.7	57.7
1982	41.7	44.3	50.6	45.6	39.4	31.8	51.3	31.2	45.4	7.8	36.2	58.1
1983	43.8	46.4	51.6	47.0	42.3	34.5	53.0	35.5	48.4	9.0	37.6	58.4
1984	45.5	48.0	53.4	47.7	47.3	36.8	54.4	35.7	50.8	10.5	38.9	58.3
1985	47.8	50.4	55.5	49.2	52.3	39.4	55.2	39.2	54.4	11.4	40.2	59.6
1986	49.3	51.8	56.8	50.7	54.5	41.2	56.8	40.6	55.0	12.9	42.2	61.1
1987	51.5	54.1	58.4	52.8	56.8	43.1	59.7	43.0	58.8	13.9	43.9	62.8
1988	53.9	56.4	60.4	54.9	60.1	47.2	63.3	43.8	61.2	16.0	46.3	64.6
1989	55.6	58.0	61.9	55.5	61.4	50.2	65.0	46.3	63.1	18.4	47.9	64.9
1990	57.2	59.3	63.0	57.4	61.3	52.3	67.4	47.0	64.1	22.4	50.8	66.1
1991	58.1	60.0	64.4	58.5	58.4	52.0	67.4	50.9	61.8	25.6	52.7	66.6
1992	60.4	62.1	65.7	60.3	61.4	55.4	69.1	54.3	64.3	30.9	55.5	67.6
1993	62.3	63.9	67.5	60.6	64.7	58.9	70.6	58.4	65.7	33.4	56.9	68.2
1994	64.2	65.8	69.7	61.0	70.7	61.9	71.7	59.8	68.2	36.4	58.1	68.5
1995	66.1	67.6	71.8	62.3	75.8	66.6	71.9	61.7	69.5	38.1	58.9	68.8
1996	68.0	69.5	73.5	63.6	82.0	69.6	72.3	63.8	71.9	40.3	60.4	69.9
1997	70.2	72.0	75.1	65.6	88.0	71.8	73.8	67.2	76.0	37.1	61.3	72.9
1998	73.3	75.2	77.4	67.7	92.0	74.1	75.7	73.1	81.5	40.7	64.2	75.4
1999	76.3	78.1	79.7	68.8	97.3	77.6	77.6	80.1	84.9	43.9	66.4	76.9
2000	80.0	81.9	82.1	71.1	102.2	79.8	81.1	88.5	90.5	47.5	68.9	78.7
2001	81.8	83.4	84.3	74.7	101.1	79.7	81.0	86.0	94.0	51.5	72.2	81.6
2002	83.3	84.7	84.7	79.1	98.1	80.2	82.2	85.5	94.3	56.7	76.5	85.2
2003	85.1	86.4	85.9	81.2	99.0	82.8	85.4	85.6	96.5	60.9	78.3	85.6
2004	87.7	89.0	88.1	84.1	102.1	87.0	89.0	88.6	98.1	61.9	80.3	88.1
2005	90.5	92.0	91.6	86.9	103.1	89.1	92.3	93.3	99.4	61.7	82.3	91.0
2006	92.8	94.0	92.7	88.9	103.5	92.3	95.5	95.1	102.3	69.3	85.4	92.0
2007	94.8	96.0	94.6	91.0	104.9	96.0	96.9	97.4	104.4	71.3	87.4	94.0
2008	96.6	97.3	97.3	93.2	101.0	96.5	96.2	99.8	103.2	81.7	90.7	94.3
2009	96.2	96.7	97.6	95.3	93.8	95.2	92.9	98.8	100.6	84.7	93.0	96.2
2010	97.6	98.1	99.8	96.7	94.1	98.0	95.1	98.7	100.1	87.5	94.9	97.7
2011	99.0	99.4	100.2	98.2	98.2	97.6	97.7	101.3	100.7	91.7	96.7	98.6
2012	100.0	100.0	100.0	100.0	100.0	100.0	100.0	100.0	100.0	100.0	100.0	100.0
2013	100.7	100.7	100.0	100.6	104.5	102.0	101.7	99.4	98.4	101.2	100.7	100.5
2014	102.7	102.8	101.2	103.9	109.8	104.6	105.2	99.7	102.0	101.1	102.4	102.9
2015	105.4	105.7	101.2	109.5	113.8	108.5	109.7	102.2	104.3	99.1	105.0	107.3
2016	107.5	107.7	101.7	113.7	119.1	111.7	112.1	100.0	107.8	103.6	108.6	110.6
2017	109.5	109.7	101.9	116.1	123.6	113.6	114.9	101.9	111.7	104.0	109.6	111.8
2018	112.1	112.3	103.4	119.1	128.8	115.9	118.1	103.4	115.7	108.2	112.6	114.2
2019	114.0	114.5	104.3	123.0	133.2	117.4	120.5	102.2	120.5	103.7	113.7	117.7
2020	105.4	104.6	105.4	112.7	98.8	82.1	94.1	102.5	108.6	120.4	110.7	106.6
2021	111.5	111.8	106.6	120.7	111.0	95.7	115.6	105.6	116.6	104.2	111.4	114.3
2019												
1st quarter	113.1	113.5	104.0	121.4	130.0	116.3	119.2	102.6	118.5	104.9	113.7	117.2
2nd quarter	113.6	114.1	104.0	122.9	132.4	117.5	120.4	101.9	119.5	103.5	113.6	117.7
3rd quarter	114.3	114.9	104.5	123.4	135.0	117.3	121.3	101.9	121.6	103.6	113.6	117.6
4th quarter	114.8	115.4	104.8	124.3	135.4	118.4	121.2	102.4	122.5	102.6	113.7	118.2
2020												
1st quarter	111.8	111.3	104.5	118.9	125.8	107.5	110.4	102.0	119.1	120.5	113.4	110.4
2nd quarter	97.4	95.5	105.7	97.9	79.9	59.9	73.0	101.3	98.8	134.9	107.3	95.9
3rd quarter	105.5	105.0	105.8	115.0	94.2	79.9	97.1	102.6	106.7	114.1	109.9	108.0
4th quarter	106.8	106.6	105.8	118.8	95.5	81.0	95.9	104.1	109.9	112.2	112.3	112.1
2021												
1st quarter	107.9	107.8	106.3	117.5	96.8	86.1	103.0	105.3	111.6	108.4	110.2	110.9
2nd quarter	110.9	111.2	106.4	120.4	107.5	93.9	117.2	104.5	115.1	103.1	111.4	114.5
3rd quarter	113.1	113.6	106.8	121.9	118.8	99.6	120.8	105.5	119.8	102.2	111.5	115.2
4th quarter	114.0	114.5	106.9	123.0	120.8	103.2	121.5	107.3	119.9	103.2	112.6	116.4

Table 4-4.   Chain-Type Price Indexes for Personal Consumption Expenditures by Major Type of Product

(Index numbers, 2012 =1000.)   NIPA Table 2.3.4

Year and quarter	Personal consumption expenditures, total	Total goods	Goods									
			Durable goods					Nondurable goods				
			Durable goods, total	Motor vehicles and parts	Furnishings and household equipment	Recreational goods and vehicles	Other durable goods	Nondurable goods, total	Food and beverages off-premises	Clothing and footwear	Gasoline and other energy goods	Other nondurable goods
1960	16.4	26.6	56.9	29.6	50.0	266.2	29.7	18.1	16.5	51.7	7.0	16.6
1961	16.6	26.7	57.0	29.8	50.2	264.8	29.6	18.1	16.6	52.0	7.1	16.6
1962	16.8	26.9	57.3	30.2	50.1	261.9	29.5	18.2	16.7	52.2	7.1	16.7
1963	17.0	27.1	57.5	30.5	50.1	261.3	29.6	18.4	16.9	52.6	7.1	16.9
1964	17.3	27.4	57.8	30.7	50.2	258.2	30.4	18.7	17.3	53.1	7.0	17.2
1965	17.5	27.7	57.3	30.5	49.8	254.6	30.2	19.0	17.6	53.6	7.3	17.4
1966	17.9	28.3	57.2	30.3	50.3	251.8	30.2	19.6	18.3	55.1	7.5	17.8
1967	18.4	28.8	58.1	30.7	51.4	253.3	30.9	20.0	18.4	57.4	7.7	18.2
1968	19.1	29.8	59.9	31.7	53.4	258.3	31.6	20.7	18.9	60.6	7.8	18.9
1969	20.0	30.9	61.6	32.4	55.3	264.2	33.2	21.6	19.8	63.9	8.1	19.6
1970	20.9	32.1	63.0	33.4	56.5	264.6	34.0	22.6	20.9	66.3	8.2	20.5
1971	21.8	33.1	65.1	35.0	57.5	274.0	35.0	23.2	21.4	68.6	8.3	21.3
1972	22.5	33.9	65.9	35.1	58.4	278.0	36.1	23.9	22.4	69.9	8.4	21.8
1973	23.8	35.9	66.8	35.2	59.7	282.2	37.3	25.9	25.2	72.2	9.3	22.4
1974	26.2	40.4	71.2	37.4	64.6	294.7	40.2	29.8	29.0	77.5	12.9	24.6
1975	28.4	43.7	77.6	41.1	71.0	314.2	43.2	32.1	31.2	81.0	13.8	27.5
1976	30.0	45.4	81.8	44.2	74.1	325.1	45.3	33.1	31.8	83.6	14.5	28.9
1977	31.9	47.8	85.5	46.8	76.8	334.4	47.3	35.0	33.7	87.2	15.5	30.6
1978	34.1	50.8	90.3	50.1	80.7	346.4	49.9	37.3	36.9	88.8	16.3	32.2
1979	37.2	55.6	96.3	53.8	85.7	361.8	54.1	41.3	40.5	90.6	21.9	34.3
1980	41.2	61.8	104.6	57.8	92.7	381.9	65.1	46.3	43.9	93.9	30.4	37.5
1981	44.9	66.4	111.6	62.3	99.6	399.0	68.7	49.9	47.1	97.0	34.3	40.6
1982	47.4	68.2	116.0	65.2	104.7	408.2	69.4	51.0	48.3	98.4	32.7	43.8
1983	49.4	69.4	118.3	67.3	107.1	403.3	71.6	51.9	48.8	99.7	31.5	46.8
1984	51.2	70.7	120.1	69.2	108.4	397.6	73.1	53.0	50.3	100.3	31.1	48.5
1985	53.0	71.9	121.4	70.8	109.6	390.6	73.9	54.0	50.9	102.4	31.2	50.4
1986	54.2	71.5	122.7	72.7	110.8	378.3	75.7	53.3	52.1	102.0	24.5	52.4
1987	55.9	73.8	126.2	76.1	112.5	373.5	80.8	55.1	53.7	104.9	25.4	54.5
1988	58.0	75.8	128.3	77.3	114.1	371.1	86.1	56.9	55.3	108.3	25.6	57.0
1989	60.6	78.7	130.6	79.6	114.5	370.1	90.1	59.7	58.2	109.9	27.9	60.1
1990	63.2	81.9	131.9	79.8	115.6	367.1	95.8	63.1	61.1	113.5	31.9	63.2
1991	65.3	83.9	133.9	82.1	116.3	362.4	99.3	65.0	63.0	115.6	31.4	66.5
1992	67.1	84.9	134.8	83.6	117.7	351.3	101.9	65.9	63.5	116.5	31.1	69.0
1993	68.8	85.7	136.1	86.9	118.3	338.7	102.7	66.4	64.3	115.9	30.8	70.2
1994	70.2	86.6	138.8	90.9	120.1	331.6	104.4	66.8	65.4	113.9	30.9	70.7
1995	71.7	87.4	139.8	94.5	119.9	317.7	106.1	67.5	66.8	111.3	31.3	71.9
1996	73.2	88.3	138.4	96.4	120.3	295.2	105.5	69.0	68.9	109.9	33.5	73.3
1997	74.5	88.2	135.4	96.8	120.1	270.5	104.0	69.7	70.2	110.0	33.5	74.1
1998	75.1	86.9	131.5	95.7	120.0	247.6	102.1	69.2	71.1	108.0	29.2	75.5
1999	76.2	87.3	128.0	96.0	118.4	226.1	99.5	70.9	72.2	106.5	31.6	78.4
2000	78.1	89.1	125.7	96.4	117.6	211.9	98.2	74.0	73.9	105.3	40.8	80.1
2001	79.7	89.0	123.3	96.8	115.5	197.5	98.5	74.8	76.1	103.2	39.4	82.0
2002	80.7	88.2	120.1	96.3	113.2	184.7	96.9	74.8	77.2	100.5	36.9	83.5
2003	82.4	88.1	115.8	93.5	110.0	173.0	94.7	76.3	78.7	98.0	43.1	83.7
2004	84.4	89.3	113.5	92.8	108.6	164.5	94.2	79.0	81.2	97.6	50.7	84.7
2005	86.9	91.1	112.3	94.2	108.6	155.6	93.3	82.0	82.6	96.8	62.0	86.0
2006	89.3	92.3	110.4	94.3	108.1	146.2	94.1	84.6	84.0	96.4	70.1	87.8
2007	91.6	93.3	108.0	93.8	107.2	136.2	95.9	87.0	87.2	95.5	75.9	89.1
2008	94.3	96.1	106.0	92.0	106.5	129.4	98.3	91.9	92.6	94.7	89.4	91.2
2009	94.1	93.8	104.0	91.9	106.1	121.8	98.6	89.5	93.7	95.6	65.2	95.3
2010	95.7	95.2	102.1	95.7	101.5	113.4	98.2	92.2	93.9	94.9	76.9	97.0
2011	98.2	98.8	101.3	98.7	100.0	106.0	100.8	97.7	97.7	96.5	96.7	98.5
2012	100.0	100.0	100.0	100.0	100.0	100.0	100.0	100.0	100.0	100.0	100.0	100.0
2013	101.4	99.4	98.0	100.5	98.1	94.7	97.9	100.1	101.0	101.0	97.3	100.2
2014	102.9	98.9	95.4	100.6	94.7	90.5	94.0	100.6	102.9	101.3	93.8	101.3
2015	103.1	95.9	93.4	100.5	92.4	86.9	90.6	97.1	104.1	100.1	68.8	102.5
2016	104.1	94.3	91.1	99.4	90.0	82.7	89.9	95.9	103.0	99.8	60.9	103.8
2017	106.1	94.6	89.1	98.2	87.5	79.4	88.7	97.5	102.9	99.2	68.8	105.0
2018	108.3	95.3	87.5	97.8	86.6	76.4	87.1	99.3	103.4	99.3	78.2	105.6
2019	109.9	94.8	86.5	98.0	87.2	73.3	85.2	99.2	104.4	97.9	75.4	106.0
2020	111.2	94.2	85.8	99.9	87.8	70.2	82.8	98.6	108.0	92.9	63.9	107.1
2021	115.5	98.9	91.2	113.1	92.5	71.4	83.7	102.8	111.4	94.8	85.3	107.7
2019												
1st quarter	109.1	94.6	87.0	97.7	87.6	74.9	84.9	98.7	104.4	98.6	72.1	105.5
2nd quarter	109.8	95.1	86.8	98.2	87.4	73.7	86.0	99.5	104.3	98.1	77.6	105.8
3rd quarter	110.1	94.7	86.4	98.2	87.3	72.7	85.1	99.1	104.4	98.4	74.3	106.0
4th quarter	110.6	94.9	85.8	98.0	86.4	71.9	84.7	99.7	104.7	96.6	77.7	106.8
2020												
1st quarter	111.0	94.6	85.5	97.9	87.0	71.0	84.0	99.5	105.5	97.0	74.0	107.0
2nd quarter	110.5	93.2	84.8	97.5	87.0	69.8	83.2	97.7	109.1	91.0	55.5	107.1
3rd quarter	111.5	94.4	86.4	101.8	88.5	70.1	82.6	98.6	108.7	92.0	61.6	107.4
4th quarter	111.9	94.4	86.5	102.3	88.9	69.9	81.5	98.6	108.7	91.6	64.4	107.0
2021												
1st quarter	113.0	95.8	86.9	102.3	89.4	70.6	82.5	100.6	108.9	93.7	76.9	107.1
2nd quarter	114.8	97.9	90.4	110.7	91.7	71.3	84.0	101.8	110.0	94.4	81.8	107.5
3rd quarter	116.3	99.7	92.5	116.2	93.4	71.7	84.1	103.3	112.1	95.1	86.8	107.7
4th quarter	118.1	102.1	94.9	123.0	95.6	71.9	84.1	105.7	114.4	96.0	95.7	108.7

Table 4-4. Chain-Type Price Indexes for Personal Consumption Expenditures by Major Type of Product—Continued

(Index numbers, 2012 =1000.)

NIPA Table 2.3.4

Year and quarter	Services	Household consumption expenditures for services								Nonprofit institutions serving households (NPISHs)		
		Household services, total	Housing and utilities	Health care	Transportation services	Recreation services	Food services and accommodations	Financial services and insurance	Other services	Final consumption expenditures	Gross output	Less: receipts from sales of goods and services
1960	11.8	11.2	13.5	6.3	13.0	14.6	11.0	13.1	11.7	51.5	9.6	5.7
1961	12.0	11.4	13.7	6.4	13.4	15.0	11.2	13.5	11.8	52.1	9.7	5.8
1962	12.2	11.6	13.9	6.6	13.7	15.4	11.5	14.0	12.0	52.8	9.9	5.9
1963	12.4	11.8	14.0	6.8	13.8	15.7	11.7	14.1	12.3	53.7	10.2	6.1
1964	12.7	12.0	14.1	7.0	14.0	16.1	11.9	14.7	12.6	53.9	10.4	6.3
1965	12.9	12.3	14.3	7.2	14.2	16.5	12.2	15.0	12.9	55.4	10.7	6.5
1966	13.3	12.6	14.4	7.5	14.5	16.9	12.6	15.9	13.3	57.4	11.1	6.7
1967	13.7	13.0	14.7	8.0	15.0	17.5	13.3	16.2	13.7	59.3	11.6	7.0
1968	14.3	13.6	15.0	8.5	15.7	18.4	14.0	17.5	14.3	61.5	12.2	7.4
1969	15.0	14.3	15.5	9.1	16.6	19.2	14.9	19.0	15.0	65.4	13.0	7.9
1970	15.9	15.1	16.2	9.8	17.9	20.1	16.0	20.0	15.7	68.3	13.9	8.5
1971	16.7	15.9	17.0	10.3	19.2	21.0	16.8	21.2	16.6	72.1	14.5	8.9
1972	17.4	16.6	17.7	10.7	19.9	21.5	17.4	22.4	17.5	75.1	15.2	9.4
1973	18.3	17.4	18.5	11.3	20.8	22.3	18.6	22.9	18.5	79.9	16.2	10.0
1974	19.8	18.8	19.5	12.3	22.6	23.8	20.8	24.7	20.5	91.5	18.1	11.1
1975	21.5	20.4	21.0	13.7	25.1	25.6	22.6	26.5	22.0	99.9	19.9	12.2
1976	23.0	21.8	22.5	15.0	26.9	26.9	24.1	27.5	23.4	105.1	21.5	13.3
1977	24.8	23.5	24.5	16.3	28.8	28.1	25.9	29.7	24.6	112.2	23.1	14.3
1978	26.7	25.3	26.3	17.7	30.7	29.8	28.2	33.4	25.9	119.6	24.9	15.4
1979	28.9	27.4	28.4	19.4	33.5	31.8	31.2	35.3	27.7	131.3	27.4	17.0
1980	31.9	30.3	31.4	21.7	38.8	34.2	34.2	38.2	30.3	143.5	30.6	19.1
1981	35.2	33.5	34.8	24.4	43.5	36.4	37.3	41.2	33.4	150.6	34.0	21.6
1982	37.9	36.2	38.0	27.1	46.0	38.4	39.4	43.9	36.0	142.8	36.6	24.2
1983	40.3	38.6	40.5	29.6	47.7	40.0	41.1	47.8	38.0	132.1	38.6	26.5
1984	42.4	40.8	42.5	31.8	49.6	41.8	43.0	50.8	39.9	126.3	40.5	28.6
1985	44.5	42.9	44.8	33.7	50.6	43.6	44.8	54.7	41.4	123.5	42.1	30.3
1986	46.3	44.7	46.9	35.7	51.1	45.2	46.7	55.6	43.5	119.5	43.6	32.0
1987	47.7	46.1	48.6	38.0	53.2	47.0	48.5	53.0	44.6	117.2	45.5	34.0
1988	49.9	48.4	50.5	41.0	55.7	48.8	50.6	55.7	46.5	115.8	48.2	36.7
1989	52.3	50.9	52.6	44.6	58.2	51.2	52.9	57.8	48.2	108.3	50.8	40.2
1990	54.7	53.5	54.8	48.4	60.4	54.0	55.3	59.1	50.2	99.2	53.2	43.7
1991	56.8	55.8	56.7	52.2	62.1	56.8	57.5	59.2	52.6	91.7	55.7	47.4
1992	58.9	58.0	58.2	55.8	63.8	58.6	58.8	61.4	54.8	83.3	57.7	51.0
1993	60.9	60.2	59.9	58.8	66.1	60.5	59.9	64.7	56.7	78.9	59.5	53.8
1994	62.5	61.9	61.5	61.2	66.8	61.8	61.0	66.0	58.8	78.7	61.2	55.8
1995	64.3	63.7	63.1	63.4	68.2	63.1	62.4	67.7	60.8	78.7	62.9	57.9
1996	66.1	65.4	65.0	64.9	68.9	65.2	64.1	70.2	62.5	80.0	64.7	59.6
1997	67.9	67.3	66.8	66.2	70.5	67.3	66.0	73.2	64.3	83.4	66.3	60.9
1998	69.4	68.6	68.3	67.5	71.8	69.0	67.8	73.5	65.6	89.1	68.3	62.1
1999	70.7	69.9	70.0	69.0	72.7	71.2	69.5	72.8	67.2	92.3	70.2	63.6
2000	72.7	71.8	72.4	70.9	75.0	74.0	71.5	73.7	68.4	97.4	72.9	65.8
2001	75.1	74.1	75.8	73.3	75.4	76.4	73.5	74.1	70.7	101.9	75.7	68.1
2002	77.0	76.1	78.0	75.2	75.3	78.6	75.3	75.9	73.5	102.3	77.9	70.7
2003	79.6	78.8	80.4	78.0	76.9	81.0	76.9	80.7	76.5	98.7	80.0	74.3
2004	82.0	81.4	82.7	80.9	77.8	83.1	79.4	84.1	79.1	97.6	82.5	77.7
2005	84.8	84.2	85.6	83.5	80.7	85.5	82.0	87.3	81.9	99.7	85.4	80.8
2006	87.8	87.3	89.2	86.0	84.1	88.4	84.8	91.0	84.8	101.0	88.3	84.1
2007	90.8	90.3	92.3	89.2	86.0	90.8	88.0	94.2	87.6	102.2	91.0	87.2
2008	93.5	93.1	95.6	91.6	90.8	93.6	91.5	93.7	91.4	102.9	93.3	90.1
2009	94.2	93.9	96.6	94.1	93.0	94.7	93.5	87.7	93.6	99.9	94.6	92.8
2010	96.0	95.9	96.8	96.5	95.1	95.7	94.8	93.7	95.9	98.5	96.2	95.4
2011	97.9	97.8	98.2	98.2	98.1	97.3	97.2	96.4	97.8	99.6	98.1	97.6
2012	100.0	100.0	100.0	100.0	100.0	100.0	100.0	100.0	100.0	100.0	100.0	100.0
2013	102.3	102.3	102.5	101.4	101.0	101.7	102.1	105.2	102.3	102.0	102.1	102.2
2014	104.9	104.8	105.5	102.5	102.3	103.6	104.8	111.4	103.7	105.9	104.4	103.9
2015	106.8	106.7	108.2	103.1	102.7	105.2	107.7	114.8	104.5	109.8	106.5	105.3
2016	109.2	109.0	111.3	104.3	103.3	107.8	110.5	119.9	105.5	113.5	108.7	107.0
2017	112.0	111.7	115.1	105.9	104.6	110.8	112.8	126.3	106.0	117.7	111.4	109.1
2018	115.1	114.9	118.7	107.8	106.9	113.1	115.4	134.1	108.2	120.3	114.1	111.8
2019	117.8	117.5	122.3	109.7	109.0	115.3	118.7	138.0	109.6	124.3	116.9	114.3
2020	120.3	120.0	125.6	112.5	107.8	117.8	120.9	140.5	111.4	126.6	120.1	117.8
2021	124.2	123.7	129.3	115.8	113.5	121.7	125.9	144.8	113.6	135.7	125.0	121.2
2019												
1st quarter	116.7	116.4	120.9	108.9	108.1	114.5	117.5	135.6	109.2	121.8	115.6	113.4
2nd quarter	117.5	117.3	121.9	109.4	109.0	115.1	118.7	137.8	109.2	123.7	116.6	114.0
3rd quarter	118.3	117.9	122.8	109.9	109.1	115.3	119.2	139.0	109.9	125.8	117.5	114.5
4th quarter	118.9	118.6	123.7	110.7	109.9	116.4	119.4	139.4	110.2	125.8	118.1	115.4
2020												
1st quarter	119.6	119.3	124.6	111.1	109.0	117.0	120.0	140.9	111.0	126.4	118.9	116.1
2nd quarter	119.7	119.5	125.3	112.2	107.0	117.7	119.9	138.8	111.1	125.2	119.5	117.5
3rd quarter	120.6	120.3	125.9	113.1	106.8	117.8	121.3	140.8	111.7	126.8	120.7	118.5
4th quarter	121.3	120.9	126.6	113.5	108.5	118.8	122.2	141.3	111.9	128.2	121.4	119.0
2021												
1st quarter	122.1	121.8	127.3	115.1	108.2	119.2	122.4	142.3	112.2	129.3	122.7	120.4
2nd quarter	123.6	123.2	128.4	115.5	114.0	121.2	124.5	144.8	113.1	132.5	124.0	121.0
3rd quarter	124.9	124.3	129.7	116.0	115.6	122.5	127.2	145.6	114.2	137.5	125.7	121.5
4th quarter	126.3	125.5	131.6	116.4	116.3	124.1	129.3	146.5	114.8	143.3	127.6	122.0

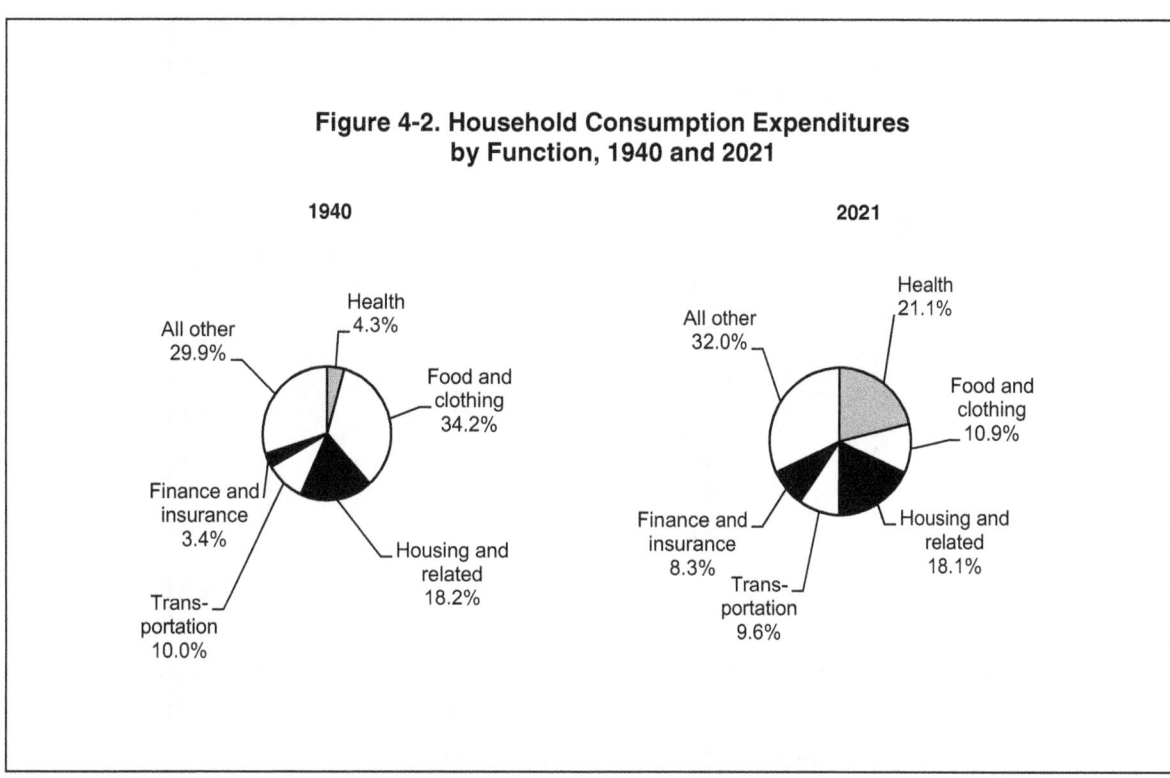

Figure 4-2. Household Consumption Expenditures by Function, 1940 and 2021

- Figure 4-2 compares the composition of household consumer spending (excluding the net spending of nonprofit institutions) in 1940 and 2021, the latest available data at the time this edition of *Business Statistics* was compiled. (Table 4-5)

- Household spending on health in 2021 made up 21.1 percent of all household consumption spending—nearly five times the percentage in 1940. It is important to recognize that household consumption spending, as presented in these data, includes (in health spending and in the total) medical care payments made by government and private insurance on behalf of individuals as well as out-of-pocket consumer payments. (Table 4-5)

- In 2021, a much smaller share was required for food and clothing than in 1940, (10.9 percent vs 34.2 percent respectively) as seen in Figure 4-2. The shares of housing-related spending and transportation were similar in the two years. The share of finance and insurance spending more than doubled, and households also spent a larger share on the remaining category, here labeled "all other," which includes communication, recreation, education, food services, accommodations, and other miscellaneous goods and services. (Table 4-5)

Table 4-5. Household Consumption Expenditures by Function

(Billions of dollars.)   NIPA Table 2.5.5

Year	Household consumption expenditures, total	Food and beverages off-premises	Clothing, footwear, and related services	Housing, utilities, and fuels	Furnishings, household equipment, and maintenance	Health	Transportation	Communication	Recreation	Education	Food services and accommodations	Financial services and insurance	Other goods and services	Foreign travel and expenditures, net
1940	70.2	15.9	8.1	12.8	6.0	3.0	7.0	0.7	3.9	0.6	4.4	2.4	5.3	0.1
1941	80.0	18.2	9.5	13.7	7.1	3.2	8.3	0.8	4.5	0.6	5.3	2.5	6.0	0.1
1942	87.7	21.6	11.8	14.8	7.4	3.6	5.4	1.0	4.9	0.7	6.9	2.6	6.8	0.2
1943	98.4	24.3	14.4	15.5	7.4	4.0	5.4	1.2	5.3	0.8	9.1	2.8	8.0	0.3
1944	107.0	26.0	15.7	16.2	8.0	4.5	5.7	1.3	5.8	0.9	10.9	3.0	8.5	0.6
1945	118.2	28.2	17.6	16.9	8.9	4.8	6.6	1.4	6.5	0.9	12.7	3.2	9.3	1.2
1946	142.2	34.9	19.7	18.8	12.7	5.9	12.1	1.6	9.0	1.0	12.7	3.7	10.3	-0.1
1947	159.7	40.2	20.4	21.2	15.5	6.6	15.4	1.7	9.8	1.2	12.5	4.1	11.1	0.0
1948	172.6	41.8	21.8	23.9	16.8	7.6	18.0	1.9	10.3	1.3	12.6	4.6	11.7	0.3
1949	176.0	40.4	21.1	25.6	16.3	7.9	21.2	2.1	10.6	1.4	12.4	4.8	11.8	0.6
1950	189.6	41.4	21.4	28.4	18.7	8.5	24.6	2.3	11.7	1.5	12.7	5.4	12.2	0.7
1951	205.7	46.0	23.1	31.6	19.7	9.3	24.2	2.6	12.3	1.6	15.0	6.2	13.3	0.9
1952	216.4	48.4	23.9	34.6	19.3	10.1	24.4	2.9	13.0	1.7	16.0	6.6	14.3	1.1
1953	229.7	49.3	24.2	37.9	20.0	11.0	28.0	3.2	13.8	1.8	16.5	7.5	15.0	1.5
1954	236.4	50.6	24.3	40.9	19.9	11.9	27.4	3.3	14.3	1.9	16.6	8.3	15.4	1.5
1955	254.9	52.0	25.4	43.8	22.3	12.8	33.4	3.6	15.4	2.1	17.0	9.2	16.3	1.6
1956	267.3	54.2	26.5	46.8	23.6	14.1	32.7	3.9	16.4	2.4	17.7	10.0	17.5	1.7
1957	282.3	57.1	26.8	50.0	23.9	15.5	35.7	4.3	16.8	2.6	18.5	10.6	18.8	1.7
1958	291.3	59.8	27.1	53.3	24.1	17.1	33.7	4.5	17.3	2.9	18.7	11.2	19.9	1.9
1959	312.3	61.6	28.6	56.9	25.6	18.8	38.8	4.8	18.8	3.1	19.7	12.1	21.4	2.0
1960	326.1	62.6	29.3	60.5	26.2	20.4	40.8	5.2	19.7	3.4	20.5	13.2	22.4	2.1
1961	336.2	63.7	29.9	64.0	26.8	21.8	39.3	5.6	20.5	3.6	21.0	14.3	23.7	2.0
1962	357.1	64.7	31.3	68.2	28.3	24.3	44.1	5.9	22.1	4.0	22.3	14.8	24.9	2.3
1963	376.3	65.9	32.1	72.2	29.8	26.4	47.8	6.4	23.9	4.3	23.3	15.5	26.2	2.5
1964	404.2	69.5	34.7	76.2	32.7	29.8	50.7	6.9	26.3	4.8	24.9	17.2	27.8	2.6
1965	436.0	74.4	36.5	81.0	34.7	32.0	56.5	7.5	28.9	5.5	27.2	18.8	30.2	2.9
1966	472.5	80.6	39.8	85.8	37.8	35.0	59.0	8.1	33.4	6.2	29.6	20.6	33.3	3.1
1967	498.6	82.6	41.7	91.1	39.7	38.4	61.0	8.9	35.8	6.9	31.0	22.1	35.8	3.8
1968	548.1	88.8	45.6	97.4	43.2	43.8	69.8	9.7	39.9	7.7	34.6	25.2	38.6	3.7
1969	594.2	95.4	48.8	105.5	45.4	50.0	75.9	10.7	43.7	8.7	37.5	27.7	41.0	4.0
1970	636.3	103.5	49.9	113.8	46.6	56.8	76.5	11.6	47.0	9.9	41.6	30.1	44.3	4.5
1971	688.2	107.1	53.4	124.5	48.8	63.4	88.7	12.8	50.1	10.9	43.8	33.1	47.0	4.8
1972	755.3	114.5	58.0	136.2	53.5	70.4	98.3	14.4	56.2	11.7	48.9	37.1	51.0	5.2
1973	835.8	126.7	63.7	149.7	59.9	78.7	108.6	16.1	63.0	13.0	54.8	39.9	56.9	4.7
1974	914.7	143.0	66.9	166.3	64.6	88.7	112.8	17.7	68.9	14.2	60.6	44.1	62.2	4.7
1975	1 013.5	156.6	71.4	184.8	67.8	102.7	124.4	20.0	77.1	15.9	68.8	51.8	67.8	4.4
1976	1 128.7	167.3	76.9	204.6	75.0	116.8	147.4	22.4	86.2	17.4	77.8	56.8	76.3	3.8
1977	1 253.3	179.8	84.3	228.7	84.0	131.6	168.1	24.3	94.9	18.8	85.7	65.1	83.8	4.3
1978	1 399.2	196.1	94.6	255.6	93.6	149.4	184.5	27.0	106.3	20.9	97.1	76.7	93.2	4.3
1979	1 559.3	218.4	101.9	287.5	104.3	169.9	207.1	29.4	118.9	22.9	110.9	83.6	100.4	4.1
1980	1 720.6	239.2	108.8	327.7	110.7	195.5	226.5	31.8	127.4	25.4	121.7	91.7	110.7	3.5
1981	1 899.8	255.3	119.1	367.6	118.3	228.9	250.7	36.0	141.6	28.3	133.9	98.5	121.2	0.4
1982	2 033.3	267.1	122.7	401.7	121.0	254.9	255.9	41.1	151.4	31.0	142.5	113.7	127.8	2.5
1983	2 240.8	277.0	132.9	434.6	132.3	287.1	284.9	44.8	169.3	34.3	153.6	141.0	143.4	5.4
1984	2 447.0	291.1	144.7	471.1	147.1	315.2	321.8	48.4	190.0	37.7	164.9	150.8	157.7	6.6
1985	2 664.9	303.0	154.3	513.9	156.0	345.3	357.4	53.1	207.2	41.2	174.3	178.2	173.3	7.7
1986	2 833.7	316.4	165.1	548.1	168.7	378.4	362.6	56.9	225.4	44.5	186.7	187.7	190.0	3.3
1987	3 020.6	324.3	176.4	582.6	176.9	419.9	376.6	60.0	247.0	48.8	204.4	189.5	208.2	6.1
1988	3 266.7	342.8	188.1	625.9	186.6	470.7	404.8	63.1	273.4	54.4	225.8	202.9	225.4	2.8
1989	3 508.7	365.4	201.2	666.9	197.5	519.0	428.3	67.3	295.7	60.6	242.6	222.3	245.7	-3.7
1990	3 733.1	391.2	206.5	709.3	200.6	583.7	442.9	70.1	314.7	66.0	262.7	230.8	262.3	-7.7
1991	3 863.3	403.0	210.1	747.5	199.1	638.4	418.3	73.9	326.3	70.6	273.4	250.1	268.0	-15.2
1992	4 109.6	404.5	223.0	783.3	209.4	700.4	451.3	81.1	346.8	76.4	286.3	277.0	290.1	-20.0
1993	4 361.9	413.5	231.1	827.3	221.9	741.7	485.0	85.8	378.4	81.1	298.4	314.0	304.5	-20.7
1994	4 623.2	432.1	240.1	876.1	238.6	779.9	527.3	93.3	414.0	86.4	308.3	327.9	316.9	-17.6
1995	4 860.3	443.7	244.7	926.7	251.7	826.0	552.5	98.9	449.8	92.3	316.1	347.0	332.7	-21.9
1996	5 134.6	461.9	253.5	976.7	263.7	868.3	596.7	108.3	481.5	99.6	326.6	372.1	350.8	-25.2
1997	5 431.2	474.8	262.0	1 023.1	277.3	919.9	639.3	120.1	509.5	107.1	343.4	408.9	368.4	-22.5
1998	5 753.4	487.4	273.1	1 077.0	297.3	979.7	666.2	128.8	543.3	115.2	361.8	446.1	393.7	-17.3
1999	6 145.5	515.5	287.2	1 135.5	320.6	1 033.3	726.3	140.2	589.9	123.9	380.3	484.6	429.4	-21.2
2000	6 609.1	540.6	297.5	1 214.5	344.0	1 109.6	793.1	153.8	633.7	134.3	408.8	541.9	458.5	-21.1
2001	6 894.7	564.0	294.6	1 303.0	353.2	1 209.4	805.6	159.1	647.0	143.6	419.7	529.3	477.9	-11.6
2002	7 150.6	575.1	295.2	1 343.8	366.3	1 317.1	806.8	161.1	669.3	149.5	436.3	539.0	496.8	-5.8
2003	7 535.2	599.6	301.4	1 408.5	381.1	1 410.7	840.1	165.1	704.3	159.5	462.7	574.2	526.5	1.5
2004	8 025.6	632.6	313.4	1 486.0	406.6	1 514.9	893.8	171.2	758.8	169.0	498.2	619.3	559.1	2.6
2005	8 558.8	668.2	326.4	1 602.4	430.1	1 612.3	955.3	177.3	805.2	180.5	533.6	676.8	589.5	1.1
2006	9 038.1	700.3	336.2	1 689.4	448.7	1 715.0	987.9	190.5	855.7	193.1	570.6	719.5	624.5	6.7
2007	9 497.8	737.3	339.5	1 785.2	455.0	1 823.2	1 028.0	203.0	897.0	206.0	601.5	762.7	657.6	1.7
2008	9 762.8	769.1	333.1	1 902.8	438.7	1 909.3	1 017.0	214.0	900.0	216.4	620.2	777.5	667.9	-3.2
2009	9 602.0	772.9	319.1	1 923.2	405.9	1 999.3	879.7	212.8	863.4	226.1	612.7	720.5	666.4	0.0
2010	9 965.8	786.9	331.7	1 972.5	410.7	2 078.1	961.8	220.7	884.4	240.3	635.7	768.0	687.2	-12.1
2011	10 387.0	819.5	347.1	2 010.3	423.7	2 153.2	1 080.3	228.1	901.6	248.2	669.5	811.1	712.1	-17.7
2012	10 705.8	846.2	359.5	2 038.9	438.6	2 230.7	1 135.5	232.5	934.4	250.6	704.9	830.9	725.4	-22.2
2013	11 010.9	864.0	365.3	2 108.7	454.3	2 288.3	1 170.5	237.5	967.4	256.7	732.3	869.3	740.1	-43.3
2014	11 482.1	896.9	376.0	2 177.7	476.6	2 409.1	1 202.0	254.0	1 004.5	263.3	776.9	922.9	766.2	-44.1
2015	11 891.9	921.0	384.1	2 226.4	500.1	2 564.8	1 163.7	259.6	1 045.6	271.9	832.9	974.4	797.9	-50.7
2016	12 291.8	940.6	391.3	2 297.4	519.1	2 690.1	1 163.1	268.1	1 094.1	281.7	873.2	996.1	822.1	-45.2
2017	12 819.2	972.9	396.4	2 382.5	540.2	2 794.9	1 234.6	266.4	1 143.0	289.2	915.6	1 064.8	855.8	-37.2
2018	13 463.5	999.7	407.8	2 495.2	576.0	2 918.3	1 319.1	273.3	1 197.9	298.0	964.0	1 145.5	890.9	-22.1
2019	13 953.8	1 030.8	414.6	2 593.6	600.5	3 078.9	1 328.2	276.2	1 254.1	305.6	1 009.6	1 142.3	924.5	-5.2
2020	13 613.0	1 126.1	371.8	2 684.1	668.4	2 986.3	1 132.0	273.5	1 226.2	295.8	813.5	1 170.6	875.6	-11.0
2021	15 437.0	1 205.0	475.8	2 797.2	774.9	3 254.7	1 480.4	295.8	1 481.2	305.9	1 060.9	1 275.0	1 003.2	27.1

NOTES AND DEFINITIONS, CHAPTER 4

Tables 4-1 Through Table 4-5

SOURCE: U.S. DEPARTMENT OF COMMERCE, BUREAU OF ECONOMIC ANALYSIS (BEA)

All personal income and personal consumption expenditure series are from the national income and product accounts (NIPAs). All quarterly series are shown at seasonally adjusted annual rates. Current and constant dollar values are in billions of dollars. Indexes of price and quantity are based on the average for the year 2009, which equals 100.

Tables 4-1 through 4-4 cover all income and spending by the personal sector, which includes nonprofit institutions serving households (NPISHs). In a new feature introduced in the 2009 comprehensive revision of the NIPAs, Tables 4-2, 4-3, and 4-4 show the services component of personal consumption expenditures broken down into separate aggregates for "household consumption expenditures for services" and "final consumption expenditures" by NPISHs.

The last table gives further details of the separate accounts for households and NPISHs that are only available annually. Table 4-5 shows a more detailed functional breakdown of household consumption expenditures, not including NPISHs.

In several cases, the notes and definitions below will refer to *imputations* or *imputed values*. See the notes and definitions to Chapter 1 for an explanation of imputation and the role it plays in national and personal income measurement.

Tables 4-1 through 4-4

SOURCES AND DISPOSITION OF PERSONAL INCOME; PERSONAL CONSUMPTION EXPENDITURES BY MAJOR TYPE OF PRODUCT

Definitions

Personal income is the income received by persons residing in the United States from participation in production, from government and business transfer payments, and from government interest, which is treated similarly to a transfer payment rather than as income from participation in production. *Persons* denotes the total for individuals, *nonprofit institutions that primarily serve households (NPISHs),* private noninsured welfare funds, and private trust funds. Personal income, outlays, and saving excluding NPISHs are referred to as *household* income, outlays, and saving. All proprietors' income is treated as received by individuals. Life insurance carriers and private noninsured pension funds are not counted as persons, but their saving is credited to persons.

Income from the sale of illegal goods and services is excluded by definition from national and personal income, and the value of purchases of illegal goods and services is not included in personal consumption expenditures.

Personal income is the sum of compensation received by employees, proprietors' income with inventory valuation and capital consumption adjustments (IVA and CCAdj), rental income of persons with capital consumption adjustment, personal receipts on assets, and personal current transfer receipts, less contributions for social insurance.

Personal income differs from national income in that it includes current transfer payments and interest received by persons, regardless of source, while it excludes the following national income components: employee and employer contributions for social insurance; business transfer payments, interest payments, and other payments on assets other than to persons; taxes on production and imports less subsidies; the current surplus of government enterprises; and undistributed corporate profits with IVA and CCAdj. The relationships of GDP, gross and net national product, national income, and personal income are displayed in Table 1-11.

Compensation of employees is the sum of wages and salaries and supplements to wages and salaries, as defined in the *national* income account (see Table 1-13 and the notes and definitions to Chapter 1).

As in *national* income, the *compensation of employees* component of personal income refers to compensation received by residents of the United States, including compensation from the rest of the world, but excludes compensation from domestic industries to workers residing in the rest of the world.

Wages and salaries consists of the monetary remuneration of employees, including wages and salaries as conventionally defined; the compensation of corporate officers; corporate directors' fees paid to directors who are also employees of the corporation; the value of employee exercise of "nonqualified stock options"; commissions, tips, and bonuses; voluntary employee contributions to certain deferred-compensation plans, such as 401(k) plans; and receipts in kind that represent income. This category also now includes judicial fees to jurors and witnesses, compensation of prison inmates, and marriage fees to justices of the peace, which earlier were classified as "other labor income". As of the 2013 revision, wages and salaries are now measured on an accrual basis, that is to say when earned rather than when paid, consistent with the treatment in the gross domestic income and national income tables.

Supplements to wages and salaries consists of employer contributions to employee pension and insurance funds and to government social insurance funds. In a substantial change introduced in the 2013 revision, defined benefit pension plan transactions are now recorded on an accrual basis instead of a cash transactions basis: employees are now credited with defined pension benefits, based on actuarial estimates of pension costs, at the time they earn them. (This was already the case with defined contribution plans.)

The following two categories, *proprietors' income* and *rental income,* are both measured net of depreciation of the capital (structures, equipment, and intellectual property products) involved. BEA calculates normal depreciation, based on the estimated life of the capital, and subtracts it from the estimated value of receipts to yield net income.

Proprietors' income with inventory valuation and capital consumption adjustments is the currentproduction income (including income-in-kind) of sole proprietors and partnerships and of taxexempt cooperatives. The imputed net rental income of owneroccupants of farm dwellings is included. Dividends and monetary interest received by proprietors of nonfinancial business and rental incomes received by persons not primarily engaged in the real estate business are excluded. These incomes are included in personal income receipts on assets and rental income of persons, respectively. Fees paid to outside directors of corporations are included. The two valuation adjustments are designed to obtain income measures that exclude any element of capital gains: inventory withdrawals are valued at replacement cost, rather than historical cost, and charges for depreciation are on an economically consistent accounting basis and are valued at replacement cost.

Rental income of persons with capital consumption adjustment consists of the net currentproduction income of persons from the rental of real property (other than the incomes of persons primarily engaged in the real estate business), the imputed net rental income of owneroccupants of nonfarm dwellings, and the royalties received by persons from patents, copyrights, and rights to natural resources. The capital consumption adjustment converts charges for depreciation to an economically consistent accounting basis valued at replacement cost. Rental income is net of interest and other expenses, and hence is affected by changing indebtedness and interest payments on owner-occupied and other housing.

Personal income receipts on assets consists of personal interest income and personal dividend income.

Personal interest income is the interest income (monetary and imputed) of persons from all sources, including interest paid by government to government employee retirement plans as well as government interest paid directly to persons.

Personal dividend income is the dividend income of persons from all sources, excluding capital gains distributions. It equals net dividends paid by corporations (dividends paid by corporations minus dividends received by corporations) less a small amount of corporate dividends received by general government. Dividends received by government employee retirement systems are included in personal dividend income.

Personal current transfer receipts is income payments to persons for which no current services are performed. It consists of government social benefits to persons and net receipts from business.

Government social benefits to persons consists of benefits from the following categories of programs:

- *Social Security and Medicare*, consisting of federal oldage, survivors, disability, and health insurance benefits distributed from the Social Security and Medicare trust funds;

- *Medicaid,* the federal-state means-tested program covering medical expenses for lower-income children and adults as well as nursing care expenses;

- *Unemployment insurance*;

- *Veterans' benefits;*

- *Other government benefits to persons*, which includes pension benefit guaranty; workers' compensation; military medical insurance; temporary disability insurance; food stamps; Black Lung benefits; supplemental security income; family assistance, which consists of aid to families with dependent children and (beginning in 1996) assistance programs operating under the Personal Responsibility and Work Opportunity Reconciliation Act of 1996; educational assistance; and the earned income credit. Government payments to nonprofit institutions, other than for work under research and development contracts, also are included. Payments from government employee retirement plans are not included.

Note that the value of Medicare and Medicaid spending, though in practice it is usually paid directly from the government to the health care provider, is treated as if it were cash income to the consumer which is then expended in personal consumption expenditures; this value is not treated in the national accounts as a government purchase of medical services but as a government benefit paid to persons, which then finances personal consumption spending.

Contributions for government social insurance, domestic, which is subtracted to arrive at personal income, includes payments by U.S. employers, employees, selfemployed, and other individuals who participate in the following programs: oldage, survivors, and disability insurance (Social Security); hospital insurance and supplementary medical insurance (Medicare); unemployment insurance; railroad retirement; veterans' life insurance; and temporary disability insurance. Contributions to government employee retirement plans are not included in this item.

In the 2009 comprehensive revision, most transactions between the U.S. government and economic agents in Guam, the U.S. Virgin Islands, American Samoa, Puerto Rico, and the Northern Mariana Islands are treated as government transactions with the rest of the world. Since the NIPAs only cover the 50 states and the District of Columbia, the *domestic* contributions to government social insurance funds are the only ones that need to be subtracted from NIPA payroll data to calculate personal income. The social insurance receipts of governments, shown in Chapter 6, will be somewhat larger than this personal income entry because they will include contributions from residents of those territories and commonwealths.

Personal current taxes is tax payments (net of refunds) by persons residing in the United States that are not chargeable to business expenses, including taxes on income, on realized net capital gains, and on personal property. As of the 1999 revisions, estate and gift taxes are classified as capital transfers and are not included in personal current taxes.

Disposable personal income is personal income minus personal current taxes. It is the income from current production that is available to persons for spending or saving. However, it is not the cash flow available, since it excludes realized capital gains. Disposable personal income in chained (2009) dollars represents the inflation-adjusted value of disposable personal income, using the implicit price deflator for personal consumption expenditures.

Personal income excluding current transfer receipts, also shown in chained (2009) dollars using the implicit price deflator for personal consumption expenditures, is an important business cycle indicator, to which particular attention is paid because it is calculated monthly as well as quarterly and annually, and thus can help establish monthly cycle turning point dates. As a pre-income-tax measure which excludes transfer payments, it is a better measure of income generated by the economy than alternative monthly income indicators such as total or disposable personal income, which are more oriented toward purchasing power.

Personal outlays is the sum of *personal consumption expenditures* (defined below), *personal interest payments,* and *personal current transfer payments.*

Personal interest payments is nonmortgage interest paid by households. As noted above in the definition of rental income, mortgage interest has been subtracted from gross rental or imputed rental receipts of persons to yield a net rental income estimate; hence, it is not included as an interest outlay in this category.

Personal current transfer payments to government includes donations, fees, and fines paid to federal, state, and local governments.

Personal current transfer payments to the rest of the world (net) is personal remittances in cash and in kind to the rest of the world less such remittances from the rest of the world.

Personal saving is derived by subtracting personal outlays from disposable personal income. It is the current net saving of individuals (including proprietors), nonprofit institutions that primarily serve individuals, life insurance carriers, retirement funds (including those of government employees), private noninsured welfare funds, and private trust funds. Conceptually, personal saving may also be viewed as the sum of the net acquisition of financial assets and the change in physical assets less the sum of net borrowing and consumption of fixed capital. In either case, it is defined to exclude both realized and unrealized capital gains.

Note that in the context of national income accounting, the term just defined is *saving,* not "savings." *Saving* refers to a flow of income during a particular time span (such as a year or a quarter) that is not consumed. It is therefore available to finance a commensurate flow of investment during that time span. Strictly defined, "savings" denotes an accumulated stock of monetary funds—possibly the cumulative effects of successive periods of *saving*—available to the owner in asset form, such as in a bank savings account.

Personal consumption expenditures (PCE) is goods and services purchased by persons residing in the United States. Persons are defined as individuals and nonprofit institutions that primarily serve individuals. PCE mostly consists of purchases of new goods and services by individuals from business, including purchases financed by insurance (such as both private and government medical insurance). In addition, PCE includes purchases of new goods and services by nonprofit institutions, net purchases of used goods by individuals and nonprofit institutions, and purchases abroad of goods and services by U.S. residents traveling or working in foreign countries. PCE also includes purchases for certain goods and services provided by the government, primarily tuition payments for higher education, charges for medical care, and charges for water and sanitary services. Finally, PCE includes imputed purchases that keep PCE invariant to changes in the way that certain activities are carried out. For example, to take account of the value of the services provided by owner-occupied housing, PCE includes an imputation equal to what (estimated) rent homeowners would pay if they rented their houses from themselves. (See the discussion of imputation in the notes and definitions to Chapter 1.) Actual purchases of residential structures by individuals are classified as gross private domestic investment.

In the 2009 comprehensive revision, the classification system used for breakdowns of PCE was revised, and new calculations were introduced separating the consumption spending of the household sector proper from that of nonprofit institutions serving households.

Goods is the sum of *Durable* and *Nondurable goods.*

The PCE category *Durable goods* is subdivided into *Motor vehicles and parts, Furnishings and household equipment* (which includes appliances), *Recreational goods and vehicles* (which includes video, audio, photographic, and information processing equipment and media), and *Other durable goods.*

Nondurable goods encompasses *Food and beverages off-prem-ises, Clothing and footwear, Gasoline and other energy goods,* and *Other nondurable goods.* This food and beverages category no longer includes meals and beverages purchased for consumption on the premises, which are now included in services, since they have a high service component and since their prices are much more stable than those of off-premises food and beverages.

Services, total is subdivided into *Household services* and *Final consumption expenditures of nonprofit institutions serving households (NPISHs).* The latter is the difference between the *gross output* of NPISHs and the amounts that they receive from sales of goods and services to households—for example, payments for services of a nonprofit hospital. Such sales of goods and services appear in the appropriate category of household expenditures—for example, *Health* in the case of the hospital services.

The components of *Household services* are *Housing and utili-ties, Health care, Transportation services, Recreation services, Food services and accommodations* (which includes meals and beverages purchased for consumption on premises, as well as payments for hotels and similar accommodations), *Financial services and insurance,* and *Other services.*

These are the categories used in the quarterly data presented in Tables 4-2, 4-3, and 4-4. This classification system is not par-ticularly helpful with respect to the objective of spending. For example, the *Health care* component of services does not include drugs and medicines, which are included instead in nondurable goods. For a more precise classification of consumption spending by objective, see Table 4-5, Household Consumption Expendi-tures by Function, described in more detail below. This classi-fication by type of expenditure is only available on an annual basis, and later than the principal quarterly NIPA data.

Data availability

Monthly data on personal income and spending are made avail-able in a BEA press release, usually distributed the first busi-ness day following the monthly release of the latest quarterly national income and product account (NIPA) estimates. Monthly and quarterly data are subsequently published each month in the BEA's *Survey of Current Business.* Current and historical data are available on the BEA Web site at <https://www.bea.gov>, and may also be obtained from the STAT-USA subscription Web site at <https://www.stat-usa.gov>.

References

References can be found in the notes and definitions to Chapter 1. A discussion of monthly estimates of personal income and its disposition appears in the November 1979 edition of the *Sur-vey of Current Business.* Additional and more recent information can be found in the articles listed in the notes and definitions for Chapter 1.

Table 4-5

Household Consumption Expenditures by Function

SOURCE: BUREAU OF ECONOMIC ANALYSIS (BEA)

In this table, also derived from the NIPAs, annual estimates of the current-dollar value of PCE by households—excluding the "final" consumption expenditures of nonprofit institutions serv-ing households (NPISHs); see definition above--are presented by function.

Definitions

Food and beverages includes food and beverages (including alcoholic beverages) purchased for home consumption and food produced and consumed on farms.

Clothing, footwear, and related services includes purchases, rental, cleaning, and repair of clothing and footwear.

Housing, utilities, and fuels includes rents paid for rental hous-ing, imputed rent of owner-occupied dwellings, and purchase of fuels and utility services.

Furnishings, household equipment, and routine household maintenance includes furniture, floor coverings, household tex-tiles, appliances, tableware etc., tools, and other supplies and services.

Health includes drugs, other medical products and equipment, and outpatient, hospital, and nursing home services.

Transportation includes the purchase and operation of motor vehicles and public transportation services.

Communication includes telephone equipment, postal and deliv-ery services, telecommunication services, and Internet access.

Recreation includes video and audio equipment, computers, and related services; sports vehicles and other sports goods and services; memberships and admissions; magazines, newspa-pers, books, and stationery; pets and related goods and services; photo goods and services; tour services; and legal gambling. (As noted earlier, purchases of goods and services that are illegal and the incomes from such purchases are outside the scope of the national income and product accounts.)

Education includes educational services and books.

Food services and accommodations includes meals and bever-ages purchased for consumption on the premises, food furnished to employees, and hotel and other accommodations including housing at schools.

Financial services and insurance consists of financial services and life, household, medical care, motor vehicle, and other insurance.

Other goods and services includes personal goods (such as cosmetics, jewelry, and luggage) and services, social services and religious activities, professional and other services, and tobacco.

Foreign travel and expenditures, net consists of foreign travel spending and other expenditures abroad by U.S. residents <u>minus</u> expenditures in the United States by nonresidents. A negative figure indicates that foreigners spent more here than U.S. residents spent abroad. Positive values for this foreign travel category, indicating that U.S. residents spent more abroad than foreigners spent here, appear in the 1980s when the dollar was strong against other major currencies. (The international value of the dollar is shown in Table 13-2.) Negative values in subsequent years have resulted in part from the weakening of the dollar, which discouraged U.S. residents' travel abroad and encouraged tourism by foreigners in the United States. The negative sign does not indicate a drain on GDP—these effects of a weaker dollar are in fact positive for real GDP—but rather reflects the fact that the goods and services purchased by foreigners in the United States must be subtracted from the total consumer purchases recorded in the other columns of this table in order to be added to other exports and classified in the category of exports rather than in the consumption spending of U.S. residents.

Data availability and revisions

Data are updated once a year, after the general midyear revision of the NIPAs, and are available on the BEA Web site at <https://www.bea.gov>.

CHAPTER 5: SAVING AND INVESTMENT

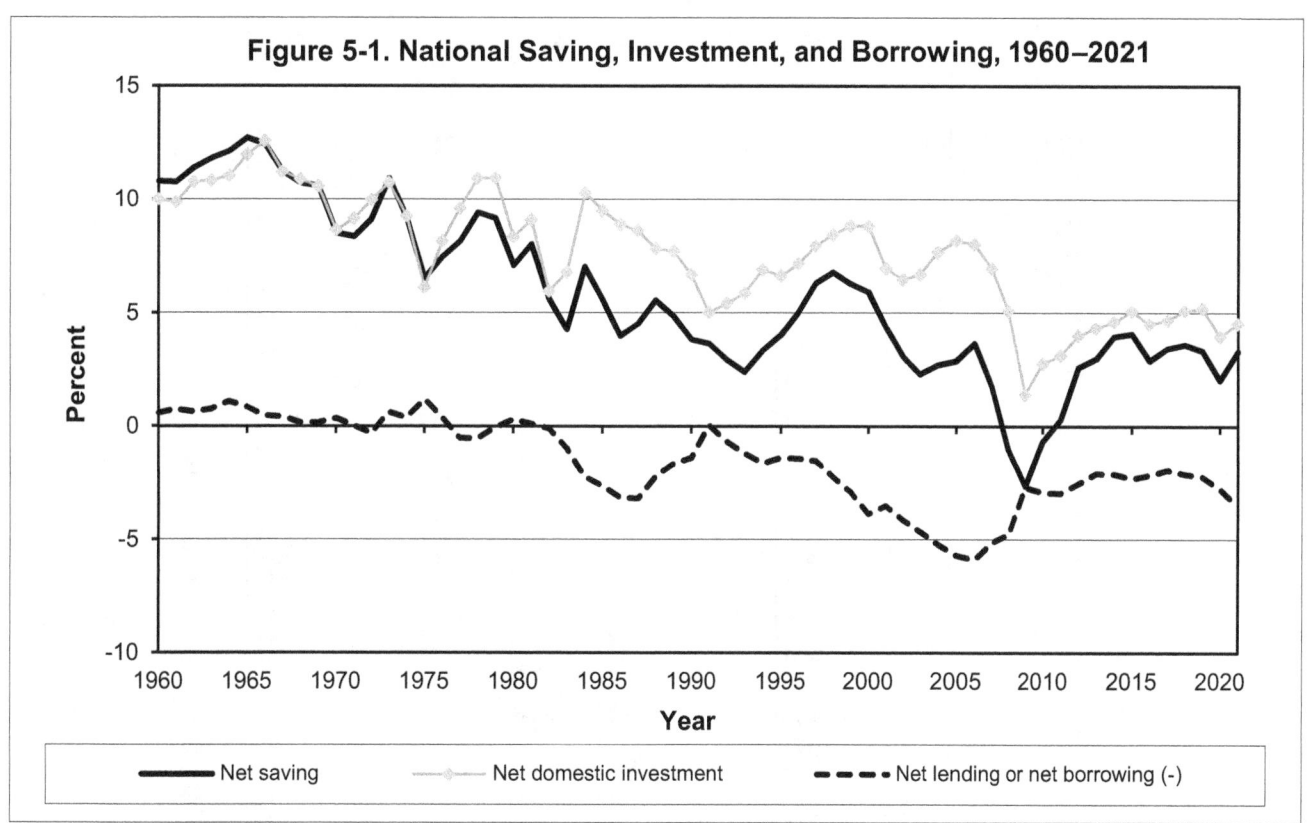

Figure 5-1. National Saving, Investment, and Borrowing, 1960–2021

- Net national saving—the middle line in Figure 5-1—averaged a much lower rate of gross national income (GNI) in the years 1984 through 2000, than in the rates seen in the 1950s and 1960s. Net saving is gross saving by U.S. persons, businesses, and governments, less the consumption of fixed capital. Thus, it represents saving available for investment over and above the replacement of the existing capital stock. (Tables 5-1A and B)

- In the recession that began at the end of 2007, net national saving fell into negative territory, for the first time since the depression years 1931 through 1934. Government deficits soared as the Great Recession cut deeply into tax revenues and called forth both automatic and discretionary anti-recession spending such as unemployment compensation, food stamps (Supplemental Nutrition Assistance Program – SNAP, and temporary assistance for needy families - TANF. In one year, 2008 to 2009, the budget deficit more than doubled. In 2020, the deficit more than tripled from 2019, due in large part to the global pandemic. However, it fell 11.4 percent. (Tables 5-1A and B and Table 6-14B)

- Net saving is currently much lower than it was in the 1960s and 1970s. In 1965, net saving got as high as 12.7 percent. It gradually declined through the 1980 and 1990s. It declined significantly in 2020 but bounced back quicky to 3.3 in 2021. (Table 5-1A)

Table 5-1A. Saving and Investment: Recent Data

(Billions of dollars, except as noted; quarterly data are at seasonally adjusted annual rates.)   NIPA Tables 1.7.5, 5.1

Year and quarter	Gross saving Total	Net saving Total	Private Total	Private Personal saving	Private Domestic corporate business	Government Federal	Government State and local	Consumption of fixed capital Total	Private Total	Private Domestic business	Private Households and institutions	Government Federal	Government State and local
1960	127.0	59.1	56.4	37.9	18.5	0.2	2.5	67.9	48.2	40.0	8.2	15.2	4.5
1961	131.6	61.0	63.5	44.4	19.2	-4.7	2.2	70.6	49.8	41.3	8.5	16.0	4.8
1962	143.4	69.3	71.6	46.7	24.9	-5.4	3.1	74.1	51.8	42.9	8.8	17.2	5.1
1963	154.1	76.1	75.0	47.1	27.9	-2.2	3.3	78.0	54.2	44.9	9.3	18.4	5.5
1964	166.1	83.7	86.6	55.3	31.4	-6.9	3.9	82.4	57.3	47.4	9.9	19.2	5.9
1965	182.9	94.9	96.8	58.8	38.0	-5.5	3.7	88.0	61.6	50.9	10.7	20.0	6.4
1966	196.5	101.2	103.4	61.9	41.6	-7.0	4.7	95.3	67.2	55.6	11.5	21.0	7.1
1967	200.5	96.9	112.5	73.0	39.5	-19.5	4.0	103.6	73.3	60.9	12.4	22.5	7.8
1968	214.6	101.2	111.5	72.9	38.6	-13.8	3.5	113.4	80.6	67.0	13.6	24.2	8.6
1969	233.1	108.2	110.3	76.1	34.2	-5.1	3.1	124.9	89.4	74.2	15.2	25.8	9.6
1970	228.2	91.4	124.8	97.6	27.2	-34.8	1.4	136.8	98.3	81.8	16.5	27.6	10.9
1971	246.1	97.2	149.4	111.9	37.5	-50.9	-1.3	148.9	107.6	89.4	18.2	29.1	12.2
1972	277.6	116.6	159.6	111.5	48.0	-49.0	6.1	161.0	117.5	97.2	20.3	30.2	13.3
1973	335.3	156.6	189.3	135.8	53.5	-38.3	5.6	178.7	131.5	108.2	23.3	32.4	14.8
1974	349.2	142.3	186.0	146.3	39.7	-41.3	-2.3	206.9	153.2	126.1	27.0	35.4	18.4
1975	348.1	109.6	218.3	164.0	54.3	-97.9	-10.7	238.5	178.8	147.9	30.9	38.7	21.0
1976	399.3	139.1	224.4	154.4	70.0	-80.9	-4.4	260.2	196.5	162.2	34.3	41.7	22.0
1977	459.4	169.6	242.5	155.9	86.6	-73.4	0.5	289.8	221.1	181.5	39.6	45.3	23.4
1978	548.0	220.8	278.0	175.1	102.9	-62.0	4.9	327.2	252.1	205.5	46.6	49.7	25.4
1979	613.5	239.6	288.2	186.8	101.4	-47.4	-1.2	373.9	290.7	236.4	54.4	54.6	28.6
1980	630.1	201.7	296.4	224.1	72.3	-88.8	-5.9	428.4	335.0	272.8	62.2	60.4	33.1
1981	743.9	256.6	354.9	265.5	89.4	-88.1	-10.2	487.2	381.9	313.5	68.5	67.5	37.8
1982	725.8	188.9	379.0	293.3	85.6	-167.4	-22.8	537.0	420.4	347.5	72.9	75.4	41.2
1983	716.7	154.1	379.7	264.0	115.7	-207.2	-18.4	562.6	438.8	362.8	76.0	81.1	42.7
1984	881.6	283.2	479.9	330.3	149.5	-196.5	-0.2	598.4	463.5	382.7	80.9	90.6	44.3
1985	881.0	240.8	442.5	284.9	157.5	-199.2	-2.4	640.1	496.4	410.3	86.2	97.0	46.8
1986	864.5	179.2	399.1	290.6	108.5	-215.9	-4.0	685.3	531.6	438.1	93.4	103.6	50.1
1987	948.9	218.5	398.6	275.4	123.2	-165.7	-14.4	730.4	566.3	464.5	101.8	110.1	54.0
1988	1 076.6	292.1	463.4	320.5	142.9	-160.0	-11.3	784.5	607.9	499.2	108.8	118.9	57.7
1989	1 109.8	271.5	450.2	340.0	110.3	-159.4	-19.3	838.3	649.6	532.6	117.0	126.9	61.8
1990	1 113.4	224.8	464.4	361.1	103.2	-203.3	-36.2	888.5	688.4	564.6	123.8	133.5	66.6
1991	1 153.4	221.0	529.5	396.0	133.5	-248.4	-60.1	932.4	721.5	592.3	129.2	140.1	70.8
1992	1 147.6	187.4	592.8	453.9	139.0	-334.5	-71.0	960.2	742.9	608.2	134.7	143.3	74.1
1993	1 163.4	159.9	545.9	397.7	148.2	-313.5	-72.5	1 003.5	778.2	634.2	144.0	147.0	78.3
1994	1 295.1	239.5	559.0	363.4	195.7	-255.6	-63.9	1 055.6	822.5	669.0	153.5	150.3	82.8
1995	1 426.3	303.9	616.5	387.1	229.4	-242.1	-70.4	1 122.4	880.7	717.8	162.9	153.5	88.1
1996	1 578.9	403.6	636.8	382.3	254.5	-179.4	-53.8	1 175.3	929.1	758.5	170.6	153.7	92.5
1997	1 780.5	541.2	675.1	390.3	284.9	-92.0	-42.0	1 239.3	987.8	807.9	179.9	154.3	97.3
1998	1 930.6	620.8	649.5	446.5	203.0	1.4	-30.1	1 309.7	1 052.4	860.1	192.1	155.4	102.2
1999	2 007.2	608.3	578.1	344.0	234.0	69.1	-38.9	1 398.9	1 132.2	924.0	208.2	158.2	108.6
2000	2 124.6	613.4	494.3	351.4	142.9	159.7	-40.6	1 511.2	1 231.5	1 004.6	227.0	163.1	116.6
2001	2 069.1	469.6	573.5	382.8	190.7	15.0	-119.0	1 599.5	1 311.7	1 064.9	246.8	164.4	123.4
2002	1 996.0	338.0	788.7	462.5	326.2	-267.8	-182.9	1 658.0	1 361.8	1 098.8	263.0	166.8	129.3
2003	1 983.5	264.5	843.1	456.7	386.5	-397.4	-181.3	1 719.1	1 411.9	1 125.4	286.6	172.2	134.9
2004	2 153.4	331.6	874.1	445.4	428.6	-393.5	-149.0	1 821.8	1 497.1	1 178.8	318.3	180.5	144.2
2005	2 349.4	378.3	774.9	268.0	506.9	-293.8	-102.8	1 971.0	1 622.6	1 266.4	356.2	190.5	157.9
2006	2 636.9	512.8	819.7	358.7	461.1	-221.9	-85.0	2 124.1	1 751.8	1 362.6	389.2	201.3	171.0
2007	2 504.4	251.6	640.5	352.7	287.9	-259.7	-129.3	2 252.8	1 852.5	1 446.7	405.8	212.8	187.5
2008	2 206.0	-152.8	693.0	503.4	189.6	-624.9	-220.9	2 358.8	1 931.8	1 524.9	407.0	225.9	201.2
2009	1 987.4	-384.1	1 200.5	639.7	560.8	-1 243.2	-341.3	2 371.5	1 928.7	1 531.2	397.5	233.6	209.1
2010	2 287.7	-103.3	1 522.6	709.3	813.3	-1 318.4	-307.5	2 390.9	1 933.8	1 537.1	396.7	243.7	213.4
2011	2 521.2	46.7	1 555.9	806.0	749.9	-1 234.1	-275.1	2 474.5	1 997.3	1 595.1	402.2	254.9	222.2
2012	3 007.7	431.7	1 787.2	1 073.1	714.1	-1 072.7	-282.8	2 576.0	2 082.4	1 670.4	412.0	261.6	232.0
2013	3 189.2	507.9	1 405.0	766.0	639.1	-631.8	-265.3	2 681.2	2 176.6	1 738.8	437.8	265.9	238.8
2014	3 527.8	712.7	1 548.0	930.9	617.1	-597.4	-237.9	2 815.0	2 298.5	1 831.2	467.3	270.2	246.3
2015	3 669.6	758.2	1 534.2	1 034.9	499.3	-560.2	-215.8	2 911.4	2 388.5	1 903.1	485.4	271.5	251.4
2016	3 534.7	547.7	1 460.0	987.8	472.1	-667.6	-244.7	2 987.1	2 459.9	1 950.9	509.0	270.7	256.4
2017	3 795.8	677.6	1 628.9	1 076.4	552.5	-720.7	-230.6	3 118.2	2 576.1	2 037.6	538.4	275.9	266.2
2018	4 025.6	752.1	1 876.0	1 190.9	685.0	-928.1	-195.8	3 273.4	2 708.1	2 133.3	574.8	284.9	280.5
2019	4 156.1	720.5	1 917.0	1 237.8	679.2	-1 047.5	-149.0	3 435.6	2 848.6	2 248.3	600.3	293.3	293.7
2020	4 002.9	426.9	3 460.8	2 887.5	573.3	-3 110.0	76.1	3 575.9	2 969.6	2 338.6	631.0	303.5	302.8
2021	4 628.4	780.6	3 287.3	2 281.3	1 006.0	-2 783.8	277.1	3 847.9	3 202.3	2 495.9	706.4	320.3	325.2
2019													
1st quarter	4 203.4	825.4	2 009.0	1 376.7	632.3	-1 015.4	-168.2	3 378.0	2 798.1	2 207.4	590.6	291.3	288.7
2nd quarter	4 147.3	726.3	1 883.9	1 194.4	689.5	-1 033.2	-124.4	3 421.0	2 836.1	2 239.5	596.5	291.9	293.1
3rd quarter	4 101.4	643.5	1 874.9	1 171.7	703.2	-1 080.9	-150.5	3 457.9	2 867.9	2 264.0	604.0	294.2	295.7
4th quarter	4 172.2	686.8	1 900.2	1 208.4	691.8	-1 060.4	-153.0	3 485.5	2 892.5	2 282.4	610.1	295.8	297.2
2020													
1st quarter	4 347.5	825.2	2 117.7	1 611.4	506.3	-1 158.0	-134.6	3 522.3	2 924.5	2 308.7	615.9	298.2	299.6
2nd quarter	3 556.7	5.8	5 077.8	4 772.0	305.8	-5 625.6	553.6	3 550.9	2 949.0	2 327.5	621.5	301.6	300.3
3rd quarter	3 596.3	5.2	3 587.9	2 821.3	766.5	-3 516.3	-66.3	3 591.0	2 981.5	2 345.3	636.2	305.1	304.5
4th quarter	4 511.0	871.6	3 059.8	2 345.5	714.4	-2 140.1	-48.2	3 639.4	3 023.3	2 372.9	650.4	309.2	306.9
2021													
1st quarter	4 423.0	727.0	4 827.7	3 979.7	848.0	-4 088.9	-11.8	3 696.0	3 071.2	2 401.1	670.1	312.7	312.0
2nd quarter	4 305.8	518.0	3 001.9	1 972.4	1 029.6	-3 312.7	828.7	3 787.9	3 150.1	2 455.6	694.4	317.1	320.7
3rd quarter	4 676.3	780.5	2 810.5	1 726.4	1 084.0	-2 235.6	205.6	3 895.8	3 244.4	2 524.3	720.0	322.6	328.9
4th quarter	5 108.5	1 096.7	2 508.9	1 446.7	1 062.3	-1 498.1	85.9	4 011.8	3 343.7	2 602.6	741.0	328.8	339.4

Table 5-1A. Saving and Investment: Recent Data—*Continued*

(Billions of dollars, except as noted; quarterly data are at seasonally adjusted annual rates.)   **NIPA Tables 1.7.5, 5.1**

Year and quarter	Gross domestic investment, capital account transactions, and net lending, NIPAs										
		Gross domestic investment			Capital account transactions, net	Net lending or net borrowing (-), NIPAs	Statistical discrepancy	Net domestic investment	Gross national income	Gross saving as a percent of gross national income	Net saving as a percent of gross national income
	Total	Total	Private	Government							
1960	125.7	122.5	86.5	36.0	. . .	3.2	-1.3	54.6	546.8	23.2	10.8
1961	130.7	126.5	86.6	39.9	. . .	4.2	-0.9	55.9	566.6	23.2	10.8
1962	143.4	139.6	97.0	42.6	. . .	3.8	0.0	65.5	608.0	23.6	11.4
1963	152.7	147.7	103.3	44.4	. . .	4.9	-1.5	69.7	643.4	24.0	11.8
1964	166.0	158.5	112.2	46.4	. . .	7.5	0.0	76.2	689.4	24.1	12.1
1965	183.7	177.5	129.6	47.9	. . .	6.2	0.7	89.5	746.8	24.5	12.7
1966	201.6	197.8	144.2	53.6	. . .	3.8	5.1	102.4	813.4	24.2	12.4
1967	203.9	200.4	142.7	57.7	. . .	3.5	3.4	96.8	862.0	23.3	11.2
1968	217.7	216.2	156.9	59.2	. . .	1.5	3.1	102.8	943.6	22.7	10.7
1969	234.7	233.1	173.6	59.5	0.0	1.6	1.6	108.2	1 022.1	22.8	10.6
1970	233.6	229.8	170.0	59.8	0.0	3.7	5.3	93.0	1 074.4	21.2	8.5
1971	255.6	255.3	196.8	58.5	0.0	0.3	9.5	106.4	1 162.9	21.2	8.4
1972	284.8	288.8	228.1	60.7	0.0	-4.1	7.2	127.8	1 280.5	21.7	9.1
1973	341.4	332.6	266.9	65.6	0.0	8.8	6.1	153.9	1 431.8	23.4	10.9
1974	356.6	350.7	274.5	76.2	0.0	5.9	7.4	143.8	1 553.3	22.5	9.2
1975	361.5	341.7	257.3	84.4	0.1	19.8	13.3	103.1	1 684.6	20.7	6.5
1976	420.0	412.9	323.2	89.6	0.1	7.0	20.7	152.6	1 869.6	21.4	7.4
1977	478.9	489.8	396.6	93.2	0.1	-11.0	19.4	199.9	2 082.7	22.1	8.1
1978	571.3	583.9	478.4	105.6	0.1	-12.7	23.3	256.7	2 349.9	23.3	9.4
1979	658.6	659.8	539.7	120.1	0.1	-1.3	45.1	285.9	2 614.2	23.5	9.2
1980	674.6	666.0	530.1	135.9	0.1	8.4	44.4	237.6	2 847.1	22.1	7.1
1981	781.9	778.6	631.2	147.3	0.1	3.3	38.1	291.3	3 201.9	23.2	8.0
1982	734.7	738.0	581.0	156.9	0.1	-3.4	8.8	201.0	3 371.4	21.5	5.6
1983	773.6	808.7	637.5	171.2	0.1	-35.2	57.0	246.1	3 614.2	19.8	4.3
1984	923.2	1 013.3	820.1	193.2	0.1	-90.2	41.6	414.9	4 032.3	21.9	7.0
1985	935.2	1 049.5	829.7	219.9	0.1	-114.5	54.3	409.4	4 310.1	20.4	5.6
1986	944.6	1 087.2	849.1	238.1	0.1	-142.8	80.1	401.9	4 516.5	19.1	4.0
1987	992.7	1 146.8	892.2	254.6	0.1	-154.2	43.8	416.4	4 828.9	19.7	4.5
1988	1 079.6	1 195.4	937.0	258.4	0.1	-115.9	3.0	410.9	5 256.1	20.5	5.6
1989	1 177.8	1 270.1	999.7	270.4	0.3	-92.7	68.0	431.9	5 598.4	19.8	4.9
1990	1 208.9	1 283.8	993.4	290.4	7.4	-82.3	95.5	395.3	5 902.3	18.9	3.8
1991	1 246.3	1 238.4	944.3	294.1	5.3	2.6	93.0	306.0	6 096.8	18.9	3.6
1992	1 263.6	1 309.1	1 013.0	296.1	-1.3	-44.3	115.9	348.9	6 435.5	17.8	2.9
1993	1 319.3	1 398.7	1 106.8	291.9	0.9	-80.2	156.0	395.2	6 733.8	17.3	2.4
1994	1 435.1	1 550.7	1 256.5	294.2	1.3	-116.9	140.0	495.0	7 170.3	18.1	3.3
1995	1 519.3	1 625.2	1 317.5	307.7	0.4	-106.3	93.0	502.8	7 574.7	18.8	4.0
1996	1 637.0	1 752.0	1 432.1	320.0	0.2	-115.2	58.1	576.7	8 045.9	19.6	5.0
1997	1 792.1	1 922.2	1 595.6	326.6	0.5	-130.6	11.6	682.9	8 589.3	20.7	6.3
1998	1 875.3	2 080.7	1 736.7	344.0	0.2	-205.6	-55.2	770.9	9 135.5	21.1	6.8
1999	1 978.9	2 255.5	1 887.1	368.5	6.7	-283.3	-28.3	856.6	9 690.4	20.7	6.3
2000	2 030.4	2 427.3	2 038.4	388.9	4.6	-401.4	-94.2	916.0	10 383.7	20.5	5.9
2001	1 955.3	2 346.7	1 934.8	411.9	-11.9	-379.5	-113.8	747.2	10 746.1	19.3	4.4
2002	1 918.7	2 374.1	1 930.4	443.7	4.2	-459.6	-77.3	716.1	11 052.2	18.1	3.1
2003	1 963.6	2 491.3	2 027.1	464.2	8.8	-536.4	-19.9	772.2	11 534.8	17.2	2.3
2004	2 129.7	2 767.5	2 281.3	486.2	4.6	-642.4	-23.7	945.6	12 317.6	17.5	2.7
2005	2 296.8	3 048.0	2 534.7	513.3	-0.7	-750.5	-52.5	1 077.0	13 166.5	17.8	2.9
2006	2 432.5	3 251.8	2 701.0	550.9	7.7	-827.0	-204.3	1 127.7	14 066.4	18.7	3.6
2007	2 524.2	3 265.0	2 673.0	592.0	6.4	-747.2	19.8	1 012.2	14 550.1	17.2	1.7
2008	2 403.0	3 107.2	2 477.6	629.6	0.8	-705.0	197.0	748.4	14 718.1	15.0	-1.0
2009	2 189.5	2 572.6	1 929.7	642.9	6.3	-389.4	202.0	201.1	14 426.3	13.8	-2.7
2010	2 370.2	2 810.0	2 165.5	644.5	7.4	-447.2	82.5	419.1	15 172.1	15.1	-0.7
2011	2 508.8	2 969.2	2 332.6	636.6	9.5	-469.8	-12.3	494.7	15 850.0	15.9	0.3
2012	2 818.8	3 242.8	2 621.8	621.0	-0.5	-423.4	-188.9	666.8	16 675.6	18.0	2.6
2013	3 074.3	3 426.4	2 826.0	600.4	7.0	-359.0	-114.8	745.2	17 188.3	18.6	3.0
2014	3 270.6	3 646.7	3 044.2	602.6	6.9	-383.0	-257.2	831.7	18 043.1	19.6	4.0
2015	3 435.1	3 859.8	3 237.2	622.6	8.3	-433.0	-234.5	948.4	18 660.9	19.7	4.1
2016	3 441.3	3 845.0	3 205.0	639.9	7.0	-410.7	-93.4	857.9	19 020.5	18.6	2.9
2017	3 676.9	4 049.8	3 381.4	668.4	16.0	-388.9	-118.9	931.6	19 893.1	19.1	3.4
2018	3 900.1	4 340.4	3 637.8	702.6	4.7	-445.0	-125.5	1 067.0	20 946.8	19.2	3.6
2019	4 086.4	4 566.3	3 826.3	740.0	6.9	-486.7	-69.7	1 130.7	21 708.7	19.1	3.3
2020	3 832.3	4 419.4	3 637.8	781.5	5.9	-593.0	-170.6	843.5	21 286.6	18.8	2.0
2021	4 091.1	4 922.3	4 120.0	802.3	3.7	-834.8	-537.3	1 074.4	23 785.9	19.5	3.3
2019											
1st quarter	4 009.4	4 526.8	3 801.9	724.8	11.4	-528.7	-194.0	1 148.7	21 448.4	19.6	3.8
2nd quarter	4 075.0	4 581.1	3 843.0	738.1	3.9	-510.0	-72.3	1 160.0	21 637.3	19.2	3.4
3rd quarter	4 124.5	4 601.2	3 858.2	743.0	4.0	-480.7	23.1	1 143.3	21 757.6	18.9	3.0
4th quarter	4 136.8	4 556.0	3 801.9	754.1	8.2	-427.4	-35.4	1 070.6	21 991.4	19.0	3.1
2020											
1st quarter	4 073.0	4 525.1	3 752.4	772.7	11.9	-463.9	-274.5	1 002.7	21 995.8	19.8	3.8
2nd quarter	3 413.9	3 941.7	3 167.0	774.7	4.2	-532.0	-142.8	390.8	19 792.2	18.0	0.0
3rd quarter	3 826.3	4 491.1	3 708.8	782.3	2.7	-667.4	230.0	900.0	21 135.4	17.0	0.0
4th quarter	4 016.0	4 719.7	3 923.2	796.5	4.9	-708.7	-495.0	1 080.3	22 223.2	20.3	3.9
2021											
1st quarter	3 913.3	4 718.8	3 928.0	790.8	14.6	-820.1	-509.7	1 022.9	22 782.7	19.4	3.2
2nd quarter	3 914.2	4 717.6	3 925.1	792.5	3.9	-807.3	-391.7	929.7	23 363.0	18.4	2.2
3rd quarter	4 045.5	4 907.7	4 099.6	808.1	-11.6	-850.6	-630.9	1 011.9	24 100.9	19.4	3.2
4th quarter	4 491.5	5 345.1	4 527.2	817.9	7.8	-861.4	-617.0	1 333.3	24 896.8	20.5	4.4

. . . = Not available.

Table 5-1B. Saving and Investment: Historical Data

(Billions of dollars, except as noted; quarterly data are at seasonally adjusted annual rates.)   NIPA Tables 1.7.5, 5.1

Year and quarter	Gross saving Total	Net saving Private	Net saving Government Federal	Net saving Government State and local	Consumption of fixed capital Total	Consumption of fixed capital Private	Consumption of fixed capital Government Federal	Consumption of fixed capital Government State and local	Gross domestic investment Total	Gross domestic investment Private	Gross domestic investment Government	Net lending or net borrowing (-), NIPAs	Net domestic investment	Gross national income	Net saving as a percentage of gross national income
1929	20.1	7.6	0.8	1.3	10.4	9.4	0.2	0.8	20.1	17.2	2.9	0.8	9.7	104.6	. . .
1930	15.8	4.5	0.0	1.1	10.2	9.2	0.2	0.8	14.7	11.4	3.3	0.7	4.5	93.3	. . .
1931	9.1	1.2	-2.4	0.7	9.5	8.6	0.2	0.7	9.6	6.5	3.1	0.2	0.1	77.2	. . .
1932	4.0	-3.2	-1.6	0.4	8.3	7.5	0.2	0.7	4.1	1.8	2.3	0.2	-4.3	59.6	. . .
1933	3.9	-3.1	-1.2	0.2	8.0	7.0	0.2	0.7	4.3	2.3	2.0	0.2	-3.7	56.9	. . .
1934	7.0	0.1	-2.6	1.0	8.4	7.3	0.3	0.9	7.0	4.3	2.7	0.4	-1.5	66.7	. . .
1935	10.4	3.2	-2.3	1.0	8.5	7.3	0.3	0.9	10.2	7.4	2.9	-0.1	1.7	74.8	. . .
1936	12.3	5.1	-3.6	2.1	8.8	7.5	0.4	0.9	13.6	9.4	4.2	-0.1	4.8	83.9	. . .
1937	17.1	5.8	-0.2	1.8	9.8	8.4	0.4	1.0	16.9	13.0	3.9	0.2	7.1	93.4	. . .
1938	12.7	2.8	-1.8	1.7	10.0	8.6	0.4	1.0	12.2	7.9	4.3	1.2	2.2	87.1	. . .
1939	14.6	5.3	-2.6	1.7	10.1	8.6	0.5	1.1	14.8	10.2	4.6	1.0	4.7	92.5	. . .
1940	19.5	8.3	-1.0	1.6	10.6	9.0	0.5	1.1	19.0	14.6	4.4	1.5	8.4	102.1	. . .
1941	31.1	16.9	0.6	1.5	12.1	10.0	0.9	1.2	30.2	19.4	10.8	1.3	18.1	129.4	. . .
1942	41.6	37.0	-11.4	1.1	14.9	11.2	2.2	1.4	40.7	11.8	29.0	-0.1	25.8	167.3	. . .
1943	47.0	45.0	-17.1	1.0	18.0	11.5	5.0	1.5	47.3	7.4	39.9	-2.1	29.3	205.2	. . .
1944	42.8	49.8	-29.4	1.1	21.3	12.0	7.8	1.5	47.3	9.2	38.2	-2.0	26.0	222.2	. . .
1945	32.6	40.4	-32.0	1.1	23.1	12.5	9.2	1.4	37.7	12.4	25.3	-1.3	14.6	224.4	. . .
1946	41.5	23.1	-8.1	0.8	25.7	14.2	9.9	1.6	37.8	33.1	4.7	4.9	12.1	227.0	. . .
1947	49.2	17.6	2.5	0.1	29.1	17.7	9.5	1.9	42.8	37.1	5.7	9.3	13.7	247.9	. . .
1948	61.5	29.1	1.0	0.1	31.3	20.8	8.4	2.1	58.8	50.3	8.5	2.4	27.5	276.2	. . .
1949	49.6	25.2	-8.5	0.5	32.3	22.6	7.5	2.2	50.4	39.1	11.3	0.9	18.1	272.0	. . .
1950	64.9	29.3	1.9	0.3	33.4	24.3	6.9	2.2	68.0	56.5	11.5	-1.8	34.6	300.0	. . .
1951	79.8	35.9	4.5	1.6	37.7	27.7	7.4	2.6	82.3	62.8	19.6	0.9	44.6	345.4	. . .
1952	79.9	39.5	-2.1	1.9	40.6	29.5	8.3	2.8	81.9	57.3	24.6	0.6	41.3	366.7	. . .
1953	82.0	40.3	-4.2	2.3	43.5	31.3	9.3	2.9	87.1	60.4	26.7	-1.3	43.6	387.3	. . .
1954	80.7	40.7	-8.0	2.0	46.0	33.0	10.1	3.0	83.5	58.1	25.4	0.2	37.5	389.7	. . .
1948															
1st quarter	59.0	23.6	5.1	-0.3	30.6	19.9	8.7	2.0	54.7	47.2	7.5	4.9	24.1	266.5	10.6
2nd quarter	62.7	29.0	2.6	0.1	31.1	20.6	8.4	2.1	58.6	50.3	8.2	3.0	27.5	275.1	11.5
3rd quarter	62.0	31.4	-1.1	0.1	31.7	21.2	8.3	2.2	61.3	52.5	8.8	0.9	29.6	280.4	10.8
4th quarter	62.4	32.6	-2.7	0.5	32.0	21.7	8.1	2.2	60.7	51.3	9.4	0.8	28.7	282.7	10.8
1949															
1st quarter	54.7	27.9	-6.0	0.6	32.2	22.1	8.0	2.2	53.4	43.1	10.3	2.2	21.1	275.6	8.2
2nd quarter	48.6	24.9	-9.1	0.4	32.3	22.4	7.6	2.2	47.5	36.2	11.3	1.7	15.3	272.0	6.0
3rd quarter	50.1	26.6	-9.4	0.6	32.3	22.8	7.3	2.2	51.5	39.5	11.9	0.6	19.2	272.1	6.6
4th quarter	44.8	21.5	-9.4	0.3	32.4	23.1	7.1	2.2	49.3	37.5	11.8	-1.0	16.9	268.4	4.6
1950															
1st quarter	53.2	32.3	-11.5	0.0	32.4	23.4	6.9	2.1	57.4	46.7	10.7	-1.0	25.0	278.7	7.4
2nd quarter	61.7	29.8	-0.6	-0.3	32.8	23.9	6.8	2.1	63.4	52.3	11.1	-1.2	30.6	291.3	9.9
3rd quarter	67.1	23.1	9.6	0.8	33.6	24.6	6.8	2.2	70.4	58.6	11.7	-2.7	36.8	309.1	10.8
4th quarter	77.6	32.0	10.0	0.8	34.8	25.5	7.0	2.3	80.8	68.4	12.3	-2.5	45.9	320.9	13.3
1951															
1st quarter	74.3	23.6	12.7	1.7	36.3	26.6	7.2	2.5	79.5	64.6	14.9	-1.7	43.2	334.1	11.4
2nd quarter	82.5	38.5	5.1	1.5	37.3	27.5	7.2	2.6	85.6	67.4	18.2	0.4	48.3	342.5	13.2
3rd quarter	80.7	41.6	-0.5	1.4	38.3	28.2	7.4	2.7	83.1	62.0	21.1	2.2	44.9	348.8	12.2
4th quarter	81.5	40.1	0.7	1.7	39.0	28.7	7.6	2.7	81.2	57.1	24.1	2.7	42.1	356.0	11.9
1952															
1st quarter	82.0	39.4	1.2	1.8	39.5	29.0	7.9	2.7	82.2	58.1	24.1	3.5	42.7	358.1	11.9
2nd quarter	76.0	36.9	-2.4	1.3	40.2	29.3	8.1	2.8	77.3	53.0	24.3	1.1	37.1	360.6	9.9
3rd quarter	79.3	40.9	-4.8	2.1	41.0	29.7	8.4	2.9	82.1	57.2	24.8	-1.1	41.1	368.0	10.4
4th quarter	82.3	40.8	-2.5	2.3	41.7	30.2	8.7	2.8	86.0	60.7	25.3	-1.2	44.3	380.2	10.7
1953															
1st quarter	84.0	41.2	-1.5	1.7	42.5	30.7	8.9	2.9	88.2	61.7	26.5	-1.3	45.7	387.0	10.7
2nd quarter	84.2	41.4	-3.3	2.8	43.3	31.1	9.2	2.9	89.3	62.1	27.2	-1.8	46.0	390.6	10.5
3rd quarter	83.7	40.2	-2.6	2.3	43.8	31.6	9.3	2.9	88.5	61.4	27.0	-1.2	44.6	389.4	10.2
4th quarter	76.0	38.4	-9.2	2.4	44.4	32.0	9.5	2.9	82.4	56.4	25.9	-0.9	38.0	382.4	8.3
1954															
1st quarter	78.9	41.2	-9.7	2.4	44.9	32.4	9.7	2.8	82.1	55.7	26.4	-0.5	37.2	384.6	8.8
2nd quarter	79.2	39.8	-8.4	2.1	45.7	32.8	10.0	3.0	81.4	55.4	25.9	0.3	35.7	385.6	8.7
3rd quarter	80.2	39.7	-7.6	1.8	46.3	33.2	10.2	3.0	83.7	59.0	24.7	-0.1	37.4	389.6	8.7
4th quarter	84.7	42.1	-6.3	1.9	47.0	33.5	10.4	3.0	86.6	62.1	24.5	0.9	39.6	399.2	9.4
1955															
1st quarter	89.9	43.7	-2.9	1.7	47.5	34.0	10.5	3.0	92.8	68.7	24.1	0.5	45.4	412.1	10.3
2nd quarter	95.4	45.8	-0.5	2.0	48.2	34.5	10.6	3.1	97.4	72.7	24.8	-0.2	49.3	422.1	11.2
3rd quarter	97.8	46.8	-0.7	2.5	49.3	35.3	10.8	3.2	99.0	74.7	24.3	0.8	49.7	430.7	11.3
4th quarter	102.3	47.2	1.9	2.6	50.6	36.2	11.1	3.3	103.2	78.9	24.3	0.4	52.5	438.3	11.8
1956															
1st quarter	105.6	48.3	2.3	2.9	52.1	37.3	11.4	3.5	103.9	78.3	25.6	0.9	51.7	443.4	12.1
2nd quarter	107.5	50.2	0.7	3.1	53.5	38.4	11.6	3.6	103.6	77.0	26.6	2.2	50.1	450.5	12.0
3rd quarter	111.6	52.5	1.2	3.1	54.8	39.3	11.8	3.7	106.0	78.3	27.8	3.0	51.2	456.7	12.4
4th quarter	113.4	53.1	1.4	2.9	56.0	40.2	12.0	3.8	105.8	77.1	28.7	4.5	49.8	466.1	12.3
1957															
1st quarter	114.3	53.3	0.4	3.4	57.3	41.1	12.4	3.8	107.5	77.7	29.8	5.6	50.2	474.2	12.0
2nd quarter	114.4	54.7	-1.6	2.8	58.4	41.9	12.6	4.0	107.6	77.9	29.7	4.8	49.2	477.3	11.7
3rd quarter	114.2	53.8	-1.6	2.5	59.5	42.7	12.8	4.0	109.9	79.3	30.6	4.9	50.5	482.1	11.3
4th quarter	104.3	49.6	-7.7	1.9	60.4	43.4	13.1	4.0	101.9	71.0	30.8	3.6	41.4	476.2	9.2

. . . = Not available.

Table 5-1B. Saving and Investment: Historical Data—*Continued*

(Billions of dollars, except as noted; quarterly data are at seasonally adjusted annual rates.)   **NIPA Tables 1.7.5, 5.1**

Year and quarter	Gross saving	Net saving			Consumption of fixed capital				Gross domestic investment and net lending, NIPAs				Net domestic invest- ment	Gross national income	Net saving as a percent- age of gross national income
			Government				Government		Gross domestic investment			Net lending or net borrow- ing (-), NIPAs			
	Total	Private	Federal	State and local	Total	Private	Federal	State and local	Total	Private	Govern- ment				
1958															
1st quarter	100.1	48.2	-10.2	1.0	61.1	44.0	13.1	4.0	98.0	66.7	31.3	1.5	36.9	470.8	8.3
2nd quarter	96.8	48.9	-15.0	0.9	62.0	44.7	13.3	4.1	97.0	65.1	32.0	0.8	35.0	473.6	7.3
3rd quarter	105.0	53.6	-12.5	0.9	62.9	45.2	13.5	4.2	104.9	72.0	32.9	1.0	42.0	487.4	8.6
4th quarter	113.1	57.9	-10.6	1.9	63.8	45.7	13.8	4.2	114.3	80.0	34.3	-0.1	50.5	501.0	9.8
1959															
1st quarter	117.8	56.6	-4.6	1.3	64.5	46.2	14.0	4.3	119.4	83.2	36.2	-1.4	54.9	512.7	10.4
2nd quarter	124.9	59.7	-1.8	2.0	65.1	46.6	14.2	4.3	125.5	89.4	36.2	-2.9	60.4	527.5	11.3
3rd quarter	117.3	53.3	-4.3	2.5	65.8	47.0	14.4	4.3	119.7	83.6	36.1	0.0	54.0	525.4	9.8
4th quarter	120.3	56.2	-5.0	2.6	66.4	47.4	14.6	4.4	121.5	86.5	34.9	-0.8	55.1	531.2	10.1
1960															
1st quarter	132.9	58.6	4.7	2.6	67.0	47.7	14.9	4.4	131.6	96.5	35.1	1.9	64.6	545.1	12.1
2nd quarter	126.3	55.0	1.2	2.5	67.6	48.0	15.1	4.5	122.3	87.1	35.2	1.7	54.7	546.4	10.8
3rd quarter	127.1	56.8	-0.4	2.5	68.2	48.4	15.3	4.6	123.2	86.4	36.8	4.2	55.0	548.5	10.7
4th quarter	121.5	55.1	-4.9	2.5	68.8	48.7	15.5	4.6	112.8	76.0	36.9	4.9	44.0	547.3	9.6
1961															
1st quarter	124.6	57.8	-4.7	2.1	69.5	49.1	15.7	4.7	118.0	78.4	39.6	5.4	48.5	549.8	10.0
2nd quarter	127.0	61.3	-6.4	1.9	70.2	49.5	15.9	4.8	122.6	84.1	38.5	3.2	52.4	560.1	10.1
3rd quarter	134.6	66.1	-4.9	2.4	71.0	50.0	16.2	4.8	130.8	90.9	39.9	4.3	59.8	570.7	11.1
4th quarter	140.2	68.9	-2.9	2.5	71.8	50.5	16.4	4.9	134.5	92.9	41.6	3.9	62.8	586.0	11.7
1962															
1st quarter	141.6	71.5	-5.4	2.8	72.7	51.0	16.7	5.0	140.0	98.1	42.0	3.1	67.3	596.1	11.6
2nd quarter	142.0	71.3	-5.7	2.8	73.5	51.5	16.9	5.1	138.6	96.7	41.9	3.7	65.0	604.1	11.3
3rd quarter	144.4	71.4	-4.9	3.4	74.5	52.1	17.3	5.2	141.3	98.2	43.1	4.8	66.7	611.5	11.4
4th quarter	145.5	72.3	-5.5	3.2	75.6	52.6	17.7	5.3	138.4	95.0	43.5	3.6	62.8	620.5	11.3
1963															
1st quarter	149.1	73.1	-3.5	3.0	76.5	53.2	18.0	5.4	142.9	99.7	43.3	4.0	66.4	628.4	11.5
2nd quarter	153.8	74.3	-1.1	3.1	77.5	53.8	18.3	5.5	145.2	101.7	43.6	4.3	67.7	638.4	12.0
3rd quarter	154.7	74.3	-1.7	3.6	78.5	54.5	18.5	5.5	150.4	104.6	45.8	5.2	71.9	647.9	11.8
4th quarter	158.9	78.4	-2.4	3.4	79.5	55.2	18.7	5.7	152.3	107.2	45.1	6.3	72.8	658.9	12.1
1964															
1st quarter	161.9	82.8	-5.5	4.1	80.6	55.9	18.9	5.8	156.3	110.5	45.8	8.2	75.6	672.4	12.1
2nd quarter	163.0	87.6	-10.2	3.9	81.8	56.8	19.1	5.9	157.0	110.5	46.5	6.0	75.3	683.6	11.9
3rd quarter	166.4	86.2	-6.7	4.0	82.9	57.7	19.3	6.0	159.2	112.6	46.6	8.1	76.3	696.1	12.0
4th quarter	172.9	90.0	-5.1	3.7	84.2	58.7	19.5	6.1	161.7	115.0	46.7	7.6	77.5	705.6	12.6
1965															
1st quarter	180.8	92.6	-1.0	3.5	85.6	59.7	19.7	6.2	172.7	126.5	46.2	5.7	87.1	725.6	13.1
2nd quarter	182.7	93.9	-2.0	3.7	87.1	60.9	19.9	6.4	174.0	127.1	46.9	6.3	86.8	738.3	12.9
3rd quarter	183.3	100.2	-9.4	3.7	88.8	62.1	20.1	6.5	180.1	131.2	48.9	6.6	91.3	751.2	12.6
4th quarter	185.0	100.3	-9.6	3.8	90.5	63.5	20.4	6.6	183.2	133.8	49.5	6.1	92.7	772.2	12.2
1966															
1st quarter	194.3	101.4	-4.1	4.7	92.3	65.0	20.6	6.8	196.1	144.2	51.9	4.6	103.8	794.3	12.8
2nd quarter	194.9	101.2	-5.7	5.0	94.3	66.4	20.9	7.0	195.4	143.5	51.9	3.3	101.1	806.1	12.5
3rd quarter	195.3	102.0	-7.9	4.9	96.3	67.9	21.2	7.2	197.4	143.2	54.2	3.2	101.1	819.4	12.1
4th quarter	201.4	109.1	-10.3	4.3	98.3	69.4	21.5	7.4	202.1	145.9	56.2	4.1	103.8	833.8	12.4
1967															
1st quarter	197.6	112.0	-19.3	4.6	100.3	70.9	21.8	7.5	200.7	142.8	57.9	4.3	100.4	842.0	11.6
2nd quarter	194.0	108.2	-20.5	4.0	102.4	72.5	22.2	7.6	194.1	137.5	56.6	3.3	91.7	850.8	10.8
3rd quarter	201.9	112.6	-18.8	3.5	104.6	74.1	22.7	7.9	200.8	142.8	57.9	3.6	96.1	868.5	11.2
4th quarter	208.5	117.0	-19.5	4.0	107.0	75.8	23.1	8.1	206.0	147.7	58.3	2.8	99.0	886.7	11.4
1968															
1st quarter	207.0	111.0	-17.0	3.5	109.5	77.6	23.6	8.3	210.6	152.3	58.4	1.6	101.1	909.9	10.7
2nd quarter	213.6	116.0	-18.7	4.3	111.9	79.5	23.9	8.5	218.5	158.9	59.5	2.0	106.5	933.5	10.9
3rd quarter	215.5	107.8	-10.1	3.2	114.5	81.6	24.3	8.6	215.2	155.7	59.5	1.8	100.7	955.5	10.6
4th quarter	222.1	111.2	-9.3	2.8	117.5	83.7	24.8	8.9	220.3	160.8	59.6	0.7	102.9	975.5	10.7
1969															
1st quarter	231.0	105.5	2.2	2.8	120.5	86.1	25.2	9.2	233.9	172.4	61.5	1.7	113.4	995.1	11.1
2nd quarter	231.3	106.4	-1.6	3.0	123.5	88.3	25.6	9.5	232.4	172.7	59.7	0.5	108.9	1 013.6	10.6
3rd quarter	237.7	116.5	-8.7	3.6	126.3	90.6	26.0	9.8	237.5	177.6	59.9	1.7	111.2	1 034.4	10.8
4th quarter	232.5	112.7	-12.6	3.2	129.3	92.8	26.4	10.1	228.6	171.6	57.0	2.5	99.3	1 045.6	9.9
1970															
1st quarter	226.9	113.9	-22.3	3.0	132.2	94.9	27.0	10.4	227.1	168.1	59.0	3.9	94.9	1 053.4	9.0
2nd quarter	229.8	125.0	-32.7	2.3	135.3	97.1	27.4	10.8	230.3	171.5	58.8	5.0	95.0	1 068.5	8.8
3rd quarter	231.3	131.2	-39.6	1.4	138.3	99.4	27.9	11.1	234.1	173.9	60.2	3.7	95.8	1 086.1	8.6
4th quarter	224.9	129.0	-44.7	-0.9	141.5	101.7	28.3	11.5	227.9	166.8	61.1	2.2	86.3	1 089.5	7.7
1971															
1st quarter	238.7	141.4	-45.6	-1.8	144.6	104.1	28.7	11.8	247.5	189.5	58.1	4.5	102.9	1 129.3	8.3
2nd quarter	243.2	149.4	-52.5	-1.3	147.6	106.5	29.0	12.1	255.7	197.3	58.3	-0.2	108.1	1 152.0	8.3
3rd quarter	249.0	152.1	-51.8	-1.7	150.4	108.8	29.2	12.3	261.2	202.1	59.2	0.0	110.9	1 172.7	8.4
4th quarter	253.6	154.6	-53.7	-0.4	153.1	111.1	29.3	12.7	256.9	198.4	58.5	-3.1	103.8	1 197.8	8.4
1972															
1st quarter	263.0	152.4	-45.8	0.4	155.9	113.4	29.6	12.9	273.0	213.0	60.0	-5.1	117.0	1 233.8	8.7
2nd quarter	265.7	148.8	-51.1	9.1	159.0	116.0	29.9	13.1	287.7	226.8	60.9	-4.8	128.8	1 257.2	8.5
3rd quarter	279.8	157.8	-40.9	0.2	162.7	118.8	30.5	13.4	292.3	233.1	59.2	-3.6	129.6	1 290.6	9.1
4th quarter	302.1	179.3	-58.3	14.7	166.4	121.8	30.8	13.8	302.3	239.7	62.6	-2.8	135.9	1 340.5	10.1

Table 5-1B. Saving and Investment: Historical Data—*Continued*

(Billions of dollars, except as noted; quarterly data are at seasonally adjusted annual rates.)

NIPA Tables 1.7.5, 5.1

Year and quarter	Gross saving Total	Net saving Private	Net saving Government Federal	Net saving Government State and local	Consumption of fixed capital Total	Consumption of fixed capital Private	Consumption of fixed capital Government Federal	Consumption of fixed capital Government State and local	Gross domestic investment Total	Gross domestic investment Private	Gross domestic investment Government	Net lending or net borrow-ing (-), NIPAs	Net domestic invest-ment	Gross national income	Net saving as a percent-age of gross national income
1973															
1st quarter	316.0	177.1	-40.5	9.0	170.5	125.2	31.2	14.2	320.5	254.3	66.2	2.2	150.0	1 381.5	10.5
2nd quarter	324.8	184.4	-40.8	5.8	175.4	129.0	31.8	14.6	333.7	268.2	65.5	5.4	158.3	1 411.1	10.6
3rd quarter	339.0	190.7	-37.3	4.4	181.2	133.4	32.8	15.0	329.0	264.3	64.6	12.4	147.7	1 445.2	10.9
4th quarter	361.4	205.2	-34.5	3.1	187.6	138.3	33.7	15.6	347.1	280.9	66.2	15.3	159.5	1 489.5	11.7
1974															
1st quarter	355.8	196.7	-36.1	0.9	194.3	143.8	34.0	16.5	339.3	268.4	71.0	16.5	145.0	1 508.2	10.7
2nd quarter	346.4	183.1	-38.1	-0.7	202.1	149.7	34.6	17.8	353.4	277.4	76.0	2.6	151.3	1 536.8	9.4
3rd quarter	345.9	173.6	-37.0	-1.9	211.2	156.1	36.0	19.1	349.2	271.0	78.2	0.3	138.0	1 571.7	8.6
4th quarter	348.7	190.5	-54.2	-7.6	220.0	163.0	36.9	20.0	360.8	281.3	79.5	4.4	140.9	1 596.5	8.1
1975															
1st quarter	329.8	189.7	-76.2	-12.3	228.7	170.3	37.8	20.6	327.3	244.3	83.0	17.8	98.6	1 612.1	6.3
2nd quarter	330.0	237.9	-132.9	-10.8	235.8	176.6	38.3	20.9	322.4	243.3	79.2	21.4	86.7	1 649.6	5.7
3rd quarter	360.1	218.6	-90.9	-9.7	242.1	182.0	39.1	21.1	350.7	265.2	85.5	18.3	108.6	1 713.8	6.9
4th quarter	372.6	226.9	-91.7	-10.0	247.4	186.3	39.8	21.4	366.1	276.2	89.9	21.6	118.7	1 762.7	7.1
1976															
1st quarter	392.0	228.6	-81.9	-6.6	251.9	189.6	40.7	21.7	397.5	304.6	92.9	13.1	145.6	1 817.5	7.7
2nd quarter	399.3	224.7	-76.8	-5.3	256.7	193.7	41.1	22.0	411.3	322.3	89.0	8.9	154.6	1 848.0	7.7
3rd quarter	402.1	225.3	-80.8	-5.2	262.7	198.6	42.0	22.1	417.0	328.3	88.7	2.4	154.3	1 886.3	7.4
4th quarter	403.8	219.1	-84.2	-0.7	269.6	204.2	42.9	22.4	425.6	337.7	88.0	3.8	156.1	1 926.5	7.0
1977															
1st quarter	416.0	214.5	-73.5	-2.5	277.5	210.7	44.0	22.8	451.7	360.3	91.4	-8.1	174.2	1 981.7	7.0
2nd quarter	454.4	237.0	-67.6	-0.7	285.7	217.5	45.0	23.2	483.9	389.7	94.2	-8.9	198.3	2 056.0	8.2
3rd quarter	479.3	257.7	-75.1	2.9	293.8	224.5	45.6	23.6	507.8	414.1	93.6	-7.9	214.0	2 118.8	8.8
4th quarter	488.0	260.9	-77.7	2.4	302.4	231.8	46.5	24.0	515.7	422.3	93.4	-19.0	213.3	2 174.3	8.5
1978															
1st quarter	500.5	266.8	-81.6	3.7	311.6	239.4	47.7	24.5	528.3	434.8	93.5	-25.1	216.7	2 222.1	8.5
2nd quarter	540.6	271.3	-62.3	9.6	322.0	247.5	49.4	25.1	575.5	470.6	105.0	-12.9	253.5	2 328.3	9.4
3rd quarter	561.5	283.5	-56.0	2.0	332.0	256.2	50.1	25.7	602.0	492.4	109.7	-11.5	270.1	2 386.7	9.6
4th quarter	589.4	290.3	-48.3	4.1	343.2	265.4	51.4	26.3	629.9	515.8	114.1	-1.4	286.7	2 462.3	10.0
1979															
1st quarter	608.8	299.2	-45.1	-0.1	354.8	275.2	52.5	27.1	635.5	525.8	109.7	-1.9	280.8	2 527.4	10.1
2nd quarter	612.5	289.4	-42.6	-1.6	367.2	285.3	53.9	28.0	656.2	539.3	116.9	-2.8	289.0	2 579.7	9.5
3rd quarter	615.0	283.5	-48.5	-0.3	380.3	295.8	55.5	29.0	671.0	545.6	125.4	2.3	290.7	2 645.2	8.9
4th quarter	617.8	280.8	-53.3	-2.9	393.2	306.6	56.6	30.1	676.2	547.9	128.4	-2.7	283.0	2 704.5	8.3
1980															
1st quarter	611.5	274.4	-66.2	-3.5	406.8	317.7	57.9	31.2	690.3	554.6	135.7	-10.8	283.5	2 759.7	7.4
2nd quarter	607.9	289.2	-93.3	-9.0	421.0	329.0	59.6	32.4	654.0	519.3	134.7	9.7	233.0	2 777.2	6.7
3rd quarter	624.8	300.8	-104.1	-7.3	435.4	340.7	61.0	33.7	629.4	495.1	134.4	28.0	194.1	2 858.1	6.6
4th quarter	676.3	321.1	-91.5	-3.9	450.6	352.5	63.1	35.0	690.5	551.5	139.0	6.6	239.9	2 993.2	7.5
1981															
1st quarter	707.9	321.1	-74.3	-4.5	465.5	364.7	64.7	36.2	765.8	619.4	146.4	1.5	300.2	3 096.0	7.8
2nd quarter	719.4	326.9	-78.7	-9.2	480.4	376.4	66.7	37.3	755.1	609.8	145.3	0.1	274.7	3 156.7	7.6
3rd quarter	775.7	378.4	-86.8	-10.5	494.5	387.8	68.4	38.3	798.0	652.3	145.7	7.0	303.5	3 263.9	8.6
4th quarter	772.5	393.0	-112.4	-16.5	508.4	398.8	70.4	39.3	795.4	643.4	152.0	4.5	287.0	3 291.0	8.0
1982															
1st quarter	736.9	371.6	-136.7	-20.0	521.9	409.4	72.5	40.1	738.6	588.3	150.2	0.5	216.6	3 308.0	6.5
2nd quarter	762.0	392.9	-143.3	-21.5	533.9	418.0	74.9	41.0	750.0	593.6	156.4	17.3	216.1	3 367.5	6.8
3rd quarter	730.6	390.9	-179.3	-23.7	542.7	424.7	76.4	41.7	750.4	593.0	157.4	-14.1	207.6	3 395.7	5.5
4th quarter	673.7	360.5	-210.2	-25.9	549.3	429.5	77.8	42.0	713.0	549.2	163.8	-17.4	163.7	3 414.7	3.6
1983															
1st quarter	691.6	377.7	-208.6	-29.8	552.3	432.3	77.7	42.3	730.2	565.5	164.7	-8.0	177.9	3 476.1	4.0
2nd quarter	700.9	365.3	-203.2	-20.2	559.1	436.0	80.5	42.5	780.8	613.8	167.1	-27.7	221.8	3 563.3	4.0
3rd quarter	703.1	370.5	-219.8	-13.7	566.2	440.6	82.7	42.8	826.8	652.3	174.5	-48.0	260.6	3 651.3	3.8
4th quarter	771.1	405.3	-197.1	-10.1	572.9	446.2	83.6	43.1	896.9	718.5	178.4	-56.9	324.0	3 765.3	5.3
1984															
1st quarter	854.4	455.9	-182.3	-1.5	582.2	452.6	86.1	43.5	975.0	790.9	184.1	-78.6	392.7	3 903.1	7.0
2nd quarter	873.6	470.4	-191.0	2.7	591.5	459.5	87.9	44.0	1 008.4	818.9	189.5	-88.0	416.9	4 000.3	7.1
3rd quarter	898.1	497.5	-199.6	-3.0	603.2	467.0	91.6	44.6	1 032.6	838.9	193.8	-90.5	429.4	4 077.5	7.2
4th quarter	900.3	495.7	-213.1	1.0	616.7	474.9	96.7	45.0	1 037.1	831.7	205.4	-103.5	420.5	4 148.3	6.8
1985															
1st quarter	889.6	436.4	-171.0	0.6	623.6	483.4	94.5	45.8	1 018.1	809.9	208.3	-89.5	394.5	4 216.8	6.3
2nd quarter	887.3	474.9	-221.4	-0.7	634.6	492.0	96.2	46.4	1 045.4	827.0	218.4	-111.5	410.9	4 275.8	5.9
3rd quarter	865.9	424.7	-200.6	-3.3	645.2	500.7	97.4	47.1	1 048.4	822.2	226.3	-121.4	403.2	4 348.0	5.1
4th quarter	880.9	433.9	-203.9	-6.2	657.2	509.6	99.7	47.8	1 086.1	859.5	226.6	-135.3	428.9	4 399.7	5.1
1986															
1st quarter	895.5	432.0	-206.5	1.8	668.2	518.6	100.9	48.6	1 092.5	863.5	229.0	-128.4	424.3	4 461.4	5.1
2nd quarter	871.0	423.9	-228.0	-4.8	679.9	527.4	102.9	49.6	1 089.7	855.2	234.4	-142.0	409.8	4 484.0	4.3
3rd quarter	838.6	382.5	-232.3	-2.4	691.0	536.0	104.4	50.6	1 081.5	835.8	245.7	-150.3	390.6	4 533.2	3.3
4th quarter	852.8	358.1	-196.9	-10.4	702.1	544.3	106.1	51.7	1 085.3	842.1	243.2	-150.4	383.2	4 587.5	3.3
1987															
1st quarter	897.9	401.3	-197.6	-18.4	712.6	552.3	107.7	52.6	1 118.8	871.2	247.7	-151.1	406.2	4 666.5	4.0
2nd quarter	926.6	353.4	-144.0	-6.6	723.8	561.2	109.1	53.5	1 128.0	874.6	253.5	-154.5	404.3	4 777.3	4.2
3rd quarter	961.2	396.1	-155.6	-15.4	736.1	570.7	110.9	54.5	1 134.8	876.5	258.3	-154.2	398.7	4 882.7	4.6
4th quarter	1 009.8	443.6	-165.8	-17.1	749.1	581.0	112.8	55.3	1 205.6	946.5	259.1	-157.2	456.5	4 989.0	5.2

Table 5-1B. Saving and Investment: Historical Data—*Continued*

(Billions of dollars, except as noted; quarterly data are at seasonally adjusted annual rates.)   **NIPA Tables 1.7.5, 5.1**

Year and quarter	Gross saving Total	Net saving Private	Net saving Government Federal	Net saving Government State and local	Consumption of fixed capital Total	Consumption of fixed capital Private	Consumption of fixed capital Government Federal	Consumption of fixed capital Government State and local	Gross domestic investment Total	Gross domestic investment Private	Gross domestic investment Government	Net lending or net borrowing (-), NIPAs	Net domestic investment	Gross national income	Net saving as a percentage of gross national income
1988															
1st quarter	1 029.9	446.1	-166.6	-13.4	763.8	591.9	115.6	56.3	1 162.1	908.6	253.5	-127.0	398.3	5 093.1	5.2
2nd quarter	1 069.0	465.1	-158.7	-15.1	777.7	602.6	117.9	57.2	1 192.7	934.5	258.2	-110.1	415.0	5 199.1	5.6
3rd quarter	1 096.4	465.8	-153.3	-7.5	791.4	613.3	119.9	58.1	1 200.1	942.0	258.1	-106.6	408.7	5 305.7	5.7
4th quarter	1 111.3	476.6	-161.3	-9.1	805.1	623.9	122.2	59.1	1 226.5	962.7	263.8	-119.7	421.4	5 426.5	5.6
1989															
1st quarter	1 145.0	475.4	-140.1	-8.7	818.4	634.4	124.0	60.1	1 269.3	1 005.5	263.8	-106.8	450.9	5 516.1	5.9
2nd quarter	1 104.7	447.4	-161.5	-12.9	831.7	644.7	125.8	61.2	1 268.3	1 001.0	267.2	-93.7	436.6	5 564.1	4.9
3rd quarter	1 100.5	440.3	-165.6	-19.1	844.9	654.8	127.8	62.3	1 271.5	996.5	275.0	-81.8	426.6	5 630.3	4.5
4th quarter	1 089.0	437.8	-170.3	-36.6	858.0	664.6	129.9	63.5	1 271.5	995.8	275.6	-88.5	413.4	5 683.0	4.1
1990															
1st quarter	1 102.7	456.3	-198.6	-24.9	870.0	674.3	131.0	64.7	1 297.7	1 010.8	286.8	-90.9	427.7	5 797.3	4.0
2nd quarter	1 134.9	493.1	-208.0	-32.4	882.2	683.8	132.4	66.0	1 303.0	1 014.7	288.3	-73.0	420.8	5 896.4	4.3
3rd quarter	1 105.6	448.6	-199.6	-38.4	895.0	693.1	134.4	67.4	1 292.4	1 000.8	291.6	-82.5	397.3	5 937.9	3.5
4th quarter	1 110.2	459.5	-206.9	-49.3	906.9	702.3	136.1	68.4	1 242.2	947.5	294.7	-82.7	335.3	5 977.5	3.4
1991															
1st quarter	1 199.7	521.6	-185.8	-55.0	919.0	711.4	138.2	69.4	1 215.7	924.6	291.1	42.1	296.7	6 012.1	4.7
2nd quarter	1 144.5	520.7	-244.6	-60.4	928.9	719.0	139.5	70.5	1 222.6	926.5	296.0	14.2	293.6	6 062.6	3.6
3rd quarter	1 122.7	516.5	-273.3	-58.3	937.8	725.3	141.1	71.4	1 243.5	947.5	296.0	-29.0	305.7	6 123.3	3.0
4th quarter	1 146.4	559.1	-290.0	-66.6	943.9	730.2	141.6	72.1	1 272.0	978.8	293.2	-17.0	328.1	6 189.0	3.3
1992															
1st quarter	1 156.0	598.7	-325.6	-65.2	948.2	733.7	141.8	72.7	1 256.3	956.8	299.5	-22.0	308.2	6 317.3	3.3
2nd quarter	1 175.0	617.7	-328.7	-69.2	955.2	738.8	142.7	73.7	1 310.2	1 013.1	297.1	-39.8	355.0	6 407.0	3.4
3rd quarter	1 125.4	582.3	-344.2	-76.0	963.4	745.4	143.4	74.5	1 318.3	1 024.2	294.1	-46.8	354.9	6 455.7	2.5
4th quarter	1 134.0	572.7	-339.5	-73.4	974.3	753.6	145.1	75.5	1 351.7	1 058.0	293.7	-68.6	377.4	6 561.9	2.4
1993															
1st quarter	1 131.0	564.3	-337.5	-82.0	986.2	763.4	146.1	76.8	1 372.3	1 083.8	288.5	-60.0	386.2	6 582.6	2.2
2nd quarter	1 168.0	555.1	-308.8	-75.8	997.5	773.2	146.5	77.9	1 387.7	1 094.5	293.2	-74.7	390.1	6 694.4	2.5
3rd quarter	1 143.8	528.8	-318.9	-74.8	1 008.7	783.1	146.9	78.7	1 386.5	1 095.9	290.7	-77.9	377.8	6 752.9	2.0
4th quarter	1 210.9	535.4	-289.0	-57.1	1 021.6	793.2	148.7	79.7	1 448.3	1 153.1	295.2	-108.5	426.7	6 905.2	2.7
1994															
1st quarter	1 232.5	534.6	-269.1	-66.3	1 033.3	803.3	149.0	81.0	1 485.4	1 201.7	283.7	-93.1	452.1	6 983.1	2.9
2nd quarter	1 297.0	554.7	-238.6	-66.1	1 047.0	815.0	149.9	82.0	1 555.2	1 264.9	290.3	-112.8	508.3	7 120.7	3.5
3rd quarter	1 305.9	557.5	-256.8	-57.1	1 062.3	828.4	150.5	83.4	1 553.8	1 251.7	302.1	-122.8	491.5	7 226.2	3.4
4th quarter	1 345.0	589.4	-258.0	-66.3	1 079.9	843.3	151.9	84.7	1 608.2	1 307.6	300.6	-138.8	528.3	7 351.0	3.6
1995															
1st quarter	1 394.2	616.4	-254.4	-66.9	1 099.2	859.8	153.1	86.2	1 634.6	1 327.6	307.0	-119.5	535.4	7 431.0	4.0
2nd quarter	1 394.1	604.2	-243.0	-82.9	1 115.8	874.8	153.4	87.6	1 614.4	1 304.0	310.4	-119.1	498.6	7 512.7	3.7
3rd quarter	1 437.0	624.6	-247.0	-71.3	1 130.8	888.2	153.8	88.8	1 610.4	1 303.2	307.1	-101.8	479.6	7 628.4	4.0
4th quarter	1 479.9	620.6	-224.0	-60.6	1 143.9	900.1	153.8	90.0	1 641.4	1 335.1	306.3	-84.8	497.5	7 726.6	4.3
1996															
1st quarter	1 520.1	645.9	-224.8	-56.6	1 155.6	910.4	154.0	91.1	1 672.2	1 355.4	316.8	-103.1	516.6	7 856.6	4.6
2nd quarter	1 559.9	630.4	-180.2	-57.9	1 167.6	922.0	153.6	91.9	1 736.1	1 418.4	317.8	-109.5	568.6	7 995.0	4.9
3rd quarter	1 596.2	636.8	-170.6	-51.9	1 181.9	934.9	153.9	93.0	1 795.4	1 474.4	321.0	-133.7	613.5	8 091.5	5.1
4th quarter	1 639.4	633.9	-141.9	-48.8	1 196.2	949.0	153.1	94.1	1 804.4	1 480.1	324.2	-114.5	608.2	8 240.5	5.4
1997															
1st quarter	1 696.4	652.3	-121.5	-47.8	1 213.3	964.4	153.6	95.3	1 841.7	1 522.4	319.3	-132.2	628.4	8 372.4	5.8
2nd quarter	1 767.8	686.5	-104.0	-45.9	1 231.2	979.9	154.6	96.7	1 914.2	1 590.2	324.0	-102.5	683.0	8 505.0	6.3
3rd quarter	1 818.3	676.4	-68.5	-37.4	1 247.8	995.5	154.5	97.8	1 956.7	1 625.3	331.5	-123.5	708.9	8 670.3	6.6
4th quarter	1 839.6	685.3	-73.8	-36.8	1 265.0	1 011.2	154.6	99.2	1 976.2	1 644.5	331.7	-161.4	711.2	8 809.4	6.5
1998															
1st quarter	1 910.1	683.9	-24.5	-30.7	1 281.3	1 027.0	154.2	100.2	2 043.6	1 712.3	331.2	-165.1	762.2	8 923.2	7.0
2nd quarter	1 915.7	660.1	-10.4	-34.1	1 300.0	1 043.3	155.5	101.2	2 036.8	1 695.8	341.1	-196.3	736.8	9 067.1	6.8
3rd quarter	1 958.0	650.8	19.9	-31.5	1 318.8	1 060.4	155.6	102.8	2 095.8	1 741.6	354.2	-224.9	777.0	9 217.4	6.9
4th quarter	1 938.5	603.3	20.6	-24.2	1 338.8	1 078.0	156.4	104.4	2 146.5	1 797.0	349.5	-236.0	807.7	9 334.1	6.4
1999															
1st quarter	2 046.3	674.9	48.0	-35.3	1 358.7	1 096.3	156.6	105.9	2 210.1	1 853.1	357.1	-235.6	851.4	9 508.0	7.2
2nd quarter	1 988.2	580.9	68.2	-44.2	1 383.2	1 117.9	157.5	107.7	2 210.9	1 848.3	362.5	-263.9	827.6	9 596.7	6.3
3rd quarter	1 979.9	537.1	71.7	-39.6	1 410.7	1 143.1	158.3	109.3	2 263.8	1 893.7	370.0	-295.0	853.1	9 724.7	5.9
4th quarter	2 014.5	519.3	88.6	-36.6	1 443.2	1 171.6	160.2	111.4	2 337.4	1 953.1	384.3	-338.8	894.2	9 932.1	5.8
2000															
1st quarter	2 123.9	496.3	175.5	-26.9	1 479.0	1 203.5	162.0	113.4	2 339.8	1 950.7	389.2	-372.9	860.8	10 189.8	6.3
2nd quarter	2 122.2	495.8	147.6	-27.4	1 506.1	1 227.5	162.8	115.8	2 461.6	2 075.8	385.8	-381.3	955.5	10 323.5	6.0
3rd quarter	2 151.8	513.9	157.7	-44.7	1 525.0	1 243.5	163.7	117.7	2 446.2	2 060.0	386.2	-420.4	921.2	10 471.1	6.0
4th quarter	2 100.6	471.3	158.0	-63.6	1 534.8	1 251.5	163.9	119.5	2 461.5	2 067.2	394.2	-431.1	926.6	10 550.3	5.4
2001															
1st quarter	2 162.6	547.5	128.4	-79.8	1 566.4	1 281.2	164.0	121.2	2 372.2	1 971.3	400.9	-424.2	805.8	10 724.3	5.6
2nd quarter	2 142.6	560.5	94.8	-106.7	1 594.0	1 307.1	164.3	122.7	2 392.0	1 973.0	418.9	-379.8	797.9	10 777.2	5.1
3rd quarter	2 049.6	697.2	-130.0	-129.2	1 611.6	1 322.8	164.8	124.0	2 348.4	1 944.9	403.5	-361.0	736.8	10 736.4	4.1
4th quarter	1 921.5	488.8	-33.0	-160.3	1 626.0	1 335.7	164.8	125.5	2 274.3	1 850.1	424.3	-353.0	648.4	10 746.3	2.7
2002															
1st quarter	1 983.5	738.6	-225.8	-165.6	1 636.3	1 343.8	165.5	127.1	2 347.4	1 912.7	434.7	-413.4	711.1	10 873.7	3.2
2nd quarter	1 991.1	789.4	-262.2	-185.1	1 648.9	1 354.0	166.2	128.7	2 371.7	1 933.3	438.4	-458.2	722.9	10 994.2	3.1
3rd quarter	1 981.4	777.8	-278.7	-183.0	1 665.2	1 367.8	167.2	130.1	2 380.3	1 933.2	447.1	-463.5	715.0	11 090.3	2.9
4th quarter	2 027.9	848.8	-304.6	-197.8	1 681.5	1 381.7	168.4	131.4	2 397.0	1 942.5	454.5	-503.4	715.5	11 250.7	3.1

Table 5-1B. Saving and Investment: Historical Data—*Continued*

(Billions of dollars, except as noted; quarterly data are at seasonally adjusted annual rates.)   NIPA Tables 1.7.5, 5.1

Year and quarter	Gross saving										Gross domestic investment and net lending, NIPAs				Net domestic investment	Gross national income	Net saving as a percentage of gross national income
	Total	Net saving			Consumption of fixed capital				Gross domestic investment			Net lending or net borrowing (-), NIPAs			
		Private	Government		Total	Private	Government		Total	Private	Government				
			Federal	State and local			Federal	State and local							
2003															
1st quarter	1 938.2	786.0	-330.4	-212.8	1 695.5	1 392.7	169.7	133.0	2 417.3	1 960.2	457.1	-554.3	721.9	11 285.0	2.2
2nd quarter	1 965.0	839.9	-387.3	-196.1	1 708.5	1 403.1	171.2	134.2	2 430.7	1 972.4	458.3	-538.0	722.2	11 429.5	2.2
3rd quarter	1 981.0	891.5	-469.4	-167.2	1 726.1	1 417.5	173.0	135.5	2 513.4	2 044.3	469.1	-536.6	787.3	11 615.4	2.2
4th quarter	2 050.0	855.2	-402.4	-149.1	1 746.3	1 434.4	175.1	136.8	2 603.7	2 131.3	472.4	-516.9	857.4	11 809.5	2.6
2004															
1st quarter	2 069.1	881.8	-429.0	-157.8	1 774.1	1 458.2	177.3	138.5	2 628.4	2 154.1	474.3	-560.7	854.3	12 011.1	2.5
2nd quarter	2 153.4	910.2	-396.9	-163.4	1 803.5	1 482.3	179.4	141.8	2 745.9	2 262.6	483.3	-629.2	942.4	12 217.7	2.9
3rd quarter	2 225.0	905.9	-366.0	-150.7	1 835.8	1 508.4	181.2	146.2	2 808.4	2 318.3	490.1	-642.4	972.6	12 452.8	3.1
4th quarter	2 166.2	798.4	-382.1	-124.0	1 873.9	1 539.5	184.0	150.4	2 887.2	2 390.1	497.1	-737.1	1 013.3	12 589.0	2.3
2005															
1st quarter	2 276.0	773.0	-305.2	-103.3	1 911.5	1 572.4	186.7	152.5	2 987.6	2 486.1	501.6	-713.5	1 076.1	12 831.5	2.8
2nd quarter	2 301.7	766.6	-306.7	-106.7	1 948.5	1 603.4	189.1	156.0	2 986.7	2 476.5	510.2	-730.2	1 038.2	13 034.2	2.7
3rd quarter	2 328.0	745.8	-300.6	-107.1	1 989.9	1 638.1	191.7	160.1	3 048.4	2 531.1	517.3	-703.0	1 058.6	13 259.9	2.5
4th quarter	2 491.7	814.1	-262.5	-94.1	2 034.2	1 676.6	194.7	163.0	3 169.3	2 645.3	524.0	-855.2	1 135.1	13 540.5	3.4
2006															
1st quarter	2 640.2	880.8	-245.3	-66.0	2 070.7	1 708.4	197.4	164.9	3 249.4	2 709.7	539.7	-812.1	1 178.7	13 847.5	4.1
2nd quarter	2 646.4	835.6	-230.6	-65.9	2 107.2	1 737.9	200.0	169.3	3 261.1	2 709.3	551.8	-836.4	1 153.8	14 016.9	3.8
3rd quarter	2 632.6	798.4	-212.9	-93.8	2 140.9	1 765.7	202.7	172.5	3 259.5	2 709.4	550.1	-881.8	1 118.6	14 155.6	3.5
4th quarter	2 628.3	764.1	-199.1	-114.4	2 177.7	1 795.2	205.1	177.4	3 237.4	2 675.4	562.0	-777.8	1 059.7	14 245.5	3.2
2007															
1st quarter	2 553.1	659.2	-209.8	-111.2	2 214.9	1 823.9	208.4	182.6	3 238.6	2 664.3	574.3	-818.1	1 023.7	14 378.6	2.4
2nd quarter	2 610.4	703.8	-231.0	-103.8	2 241.3	1 844.2	211.2	185.9	3 288.9	2 699.2	589.6	-780.3	1 047.5	14 563.5	2.5
3rd quarter	2 465.6	619.0	-279.0	-139.4	2 265.0	1 861.7	214.3	189.0	3 281.9	2 686.0	596.0	-713.0	1 016.9	14 574.3	1.4
4th quarter	2 388.5	580.2	-318.9	-162.8	2 290.0	1 880.2	217.3	192.6	3 250.8	2 642.6	608.2	-677.5	960.8	14 684.0	0.7
2008															
1st quarter	2 301.5	554.3	-404.6	-168.2	2 319.9	1 903.0	221.0	196.0	3 175.3	2 563.7	611.6	-747.4	855.4	14 719.1	-0.1
2nd quarter	2 184.7	780.4	-776.4	-166.5	2 347.3	1 923.9	224.5	198.9	3 168.2	2 540.6	627.6	-735.2	820.9	14 771.0	-1.1
3rd quarter	2 223.3	714.2	-619.5	-247.4	2 376.0	1 945.7	227.7	202.6	3 136.0	2 498.2	637.7	-698.8	759.9	14 882.0	-1.0
4th quarter	2 114.5	723.0	-699.2	-301.4	2 392.1	1 954.7	230.3	207.1	2 949.3	2 307.9	641.4	-638.6	557.2	14 500.3	-1.9
2009															
1st quarter	1 976.2	1 020.9	-1 100.3	-331.1	2 386.7	1 946.0	231.3	209.3	2 654.9	2 014.9	640.0	-407.4	268.3	14 276.0	-2.9
2nd quarter	1 954.4	1 220.8	-1 300.8	-335.0	2 369.5	1 927.9	232.5	209.0	2 510.2	1 863.7	646.5	-364.1	140.7	14 302.7	-2.9
3rd quarter	1 924.0	1 228.2	-1 307.4	-355.8	2 359.1	1 916.4	234.0	208.7	2 486.4	1 841.4	644.9	-372.5	127.3	14 435.6	-3.0
4th quarter	2 095.1	1 331.9	-1 264.1	-343.5	2 370.7	1 924.5	236.7	209.5	2 638.8	1 998.7	640.1	-413.6	268.1	14 690.7	-1.9
2010															
1st quarter	2 124.1	1 426.7	-1 344.4	-333.7	2 375.6	1 925.3	239.3	211.0	2 671.3	2 038.2	633.2	-434.7	295.8	14 843.2	-1.7
2nd quarter	2 225.1	1 500.9	-1 325.0	-333.8	2 383.1	1 927.8	242.5	212.7	2 796.8	2 148.8	648.0	-449.0	413.7	15 059.5	-1.0
3rd quarter	2 395.7	1 602.4	-1 309.1	-290.1	2 392.6	1 933.5	244.9	214.2	2 885.9	2 236.5	649.4	-477.9	493.3	15 322.2	0.0
4th quarter	2 405.7	1 560.3	-1 294.8	-272.3	2 412.5	1 948.5	248.2	215.8	2 885.8	2 238.4	647.4	-427.2	473.4	15 463.4	0.0
2011															
1st quarter	2 361.5	1 448.7	-1 244.4	-279.1	2 436.4	1 966.7	251.8	217.9	2 845.3	2 206.0	639.4	-483.9	408.9	15 567.2	-0.5
2nd quarter	2 457.2	1 526.3	-1 274.4	-256.8	2 462.2	1 987.2	254.2	220.7	2 933.6	2 297.4	636.3	-494.8	471.4	15 781.5	0.0
3rd quarter	2 563.6	1 581.7	-1 218.5	-287.6	2 487.9	2 007.7	256.4	223.8	2 958.0	2 322.8	635.1	-443.0	470.0	15 935.5	0.5
4th quarter	2 702.3	1 667.0	-1 199.3	-276.8	2 511.4	2 027.6	257.3	226.5	3 139.8	2 504.1	635.7	-457.6	628.5	16 115.7	1.2
2012															
1st quarter	2 948.1	1 801.5	-1 110.4	-279.6	2 536.5	2 047.9	259.7	228.9	3 194.6	2 567.8	626.8	-475.8	658.1	16 535.8	2.5
2nd quarter	3 028.5	1 838.6	-1 093.1	-281.5	2 564.4	2 071.8	261.2	231.4	3 264.0	2 636.9	627.1	-453.3	699.5	16 645.5	2.8
3rd quarter	2 924.4	1 707.6	-1 086.7	-287.5	2 591.0	2 095.2	262.6	233.2	3 263.5	2 644.1	619.4	-404.4	672.5	16 607.5	2.0
4th quarter	3 130.0	1 801.1	-1 000.5	-282.7	2 612.0	2 114.6	263.0	234.4	3 249.0	2 638.3	610.8	-360.2	637.0	16 913.7	3.1
2013															
1st quarter	3 069.0	1 469.6	-774.0	-261.6	2 635.0	2 135.5	263.6	235.9	3 336.9	2 738.2	598.7	-389.1	701.9	16 959.1	2.6
2nd quarter	3 196.4	1 307.8	-528.5	-247.1	2 664.2	2 161.3	265.1	237.7	3 373.7	2 775.3	598.5	-385.6	709.5	17 128.9	3.1
3rd quarter	3 208.6	1 490.6	-699.2	-277.0	2 694.2	2 188.4	266.2	239.6	3 483.2	2 880.0	603.2	-359.6	789.0	17 230.3	3.0
4th quarter	3 282.7	1 352.3	-525.3	-275.6	2 731.4	2 221.0	268.5	241.9	3 511.8	2 910.5	601.3	-301.9	780.4	17 435.0	3.2
2014															
1st quarter	3 330.0	1 371.7	-558.9	-253.5	2 770.8	2 257.1	269.8	243.9	3 488.0	2 899.2	588.7	-382.5	717.2	17 596.6	3.2
2nd quarter	3 533.6	1 543.1	-582.4	-224.4	2 797.3	2 281.9	269.9	245.6	3 633.1	3 030.4	602.7	-351.8	835.8	17 938.0	4.1
3rd quarter	3 607.1	1 638.3	-631.3	-232.8	2 832.9	2 315.1	270.4	247.4	3 714.1	3 107.6	606.5	-362.3	881.2	18 245.3	4.2
4th quarter	3 640.3	1 638.9	-616.8	-240.9	2 859.1	2 339.9	270.7	248.5	3 751.8	3 139.5	612.3	-435.5	892.7	18 392.5	4.2
2015															
1st quarter	3 717.0	1 632.4	-582.5	-225.7	2 892.8	2 371.8	271.8	249.2	3 853.0	3 245.1	608.0	-431.6	960.3	18 497.4	4.5
2nd quarter	3 711.7	1 587.3	-546.9	-231.7	2 903.0	2 380.7	271.3	251.0	3 872.2	3 245.8	626.4	-409.9	969.2	18 649.9	4.3
3rd quarter	3 630.9	1 528.5	-568.3	-249.5	2 920.2	2 396.0	271.8	252.5	3 882.2	3 251.7	630.5	-468.0	961.9	18 728.0	3.8
4th quarter	3 618.6	1 388.5	-543.2	-156.2	2 929.5	2 405.5	271.1	253.0	3 831.6	3 206.1	625.5	-422.6	902.1	18 768.4	3.7
2016															
1st quarter	3 588.7	1 534.4	-642.5	-243.2	2 940.0	2 417.9	269.0	253.1	3 814.3	3 174.4	639.9	-439.5	874.3	18 845.1	3.4
2nd quarter	3 475.0	1 415.6	-653.4	-262.2	2 975.0	2 448.7	270.3	256.0	3 815.7	3 178.5	637.2	-403.6	840.7	18 886.1	2.6
3rd quarter	3 486.9	1 412.5	-682.1	-243.2	2 999.8	2 471.5	271.1	257.2	3 822.8	3 185.7	637.0	-401.9	823.0	19 056.0	2.6
4th quarter	3 588.3	1 477.3	-692.4	-230.1	3 033.5	2 501.6	272.6	259.3	3 927.1	3 281.5	645.6	-397.7	893.6	19 294.7	2.9
2017															
1st quarter	3 700.5	1 562.2	-683.8	-243.5	3 065.5	2 530.1	273.4	262.1	3 940.4	3 283.5	656.9	-366.7	874.9	19 545.4	3.2
2nd quarter	3 746.0	1 622.6	-708.0	-271.6	3 103.0	2 563.4	275.0	264.5	4 022.1	3 357.4	664.8	-442.0	919.2	19 742.7	3.3
3rd quarter	3 850.3	1 678.7	-729.4	-236.3	3 137.3	2 593.0	276.6	267.8	4 080.1	3 413.3	666.8	-384.2	942.7	19 978.9	3.6
4th quarter	3 886.3	1 651.9	-761.5	-170.9	3 166.8	2 617.9	278.6	270.4	4 156.4	3 471.4	685.0	-362.7	989.6	20 305.3	3.5
2018															
1st quarter	3 980.7	1 848.1	-909.7	-167.4	3 209.7	2 654.6	281.0	274.1	4 241.9	3 550.8	691.0	-399.6	1 032.1	20 593.0	3.7
2nd quarter	3 938.5	1 831.9	-928.8	-221.0	3 256.3	2 693.0	284.2	279.1	4 308.8	3 603.2	705.6	-387.4	1 052.5	20 798.1	3.3
3rd quarter	4 065.6	1 871.0	-901.4	-199.7	3 295.7	2 726.9	286.3	282.4	4 388.0	3 679.6	708.4	-489.3	1 092.3	21 095.4	3.6
4th quarter	4 117.5	1 952.9	-972.5	-195.0	3 332.0	2 757.7	288.1	286.2	4 422.9	3 717.5	705.4	-503.6	1 090.9	21 300.7	3.7

Table 5-2. Gross Private Fixed Investment by Type

(Billions of dollars, quarterly data are at seasonally adjusted annual rates.)   NIPA Table 5.3.5

Year and quarter	Total gross private fixed investment	Nonresidential Total	Structures Total	Commercial and health care	Manufacturing	Power and communication	Mining exploration, shafts, and wells	Other non-residential structures	Equipment Total	Information processing equipment Total	Computers and peripheral equipment	Other information processing	Industrial equipment
1960	83.2	56.4	19.6	4.8	2.9	4.4	2.3	5.2	29.7	4.7	0.2	4.6	9.4
1961	83.6	56.6	19.7	5.5	2.8	4.1	2.3	5.0	28.9	5.1	0.3	4.8	8.8
1962	90.9	61.2	20.8	6.2	2.8	4.1	2.5	5.2	32.1	5.5	0.3	5.1	9.3
1963	97.7	64.8	21.2	6.1	2.9	4.4	2.3	5.6	34.4	6.1	0.7	5.4	10.0
1964	107.3	72.2	23.7	6.8	3.6	4.8	2.4	6.2	38.7	6.8	0.9	5.9	11.4
1965	120.4	85.2	28.3	8.2	5.1	5.4	2.4	7.2	45.8	7.8	1.2	6.7	13.7
1966	130.6	97.2	31.3	8.3	6.6	6.3	2.5	7.8	53.0	9.7	1.7	8.0	16.2
1967	132.8	99.2	31.5	8.2	6.0	7.1	2.4	7.8	53.7	10.1	1.9	8.2	16.9
1968	147.9	107.7	33.6	9.4	6.0	8.3	2.6	7.3	58.5	10.6	1.9	8.7	17.3
1969	164.4	120.0	37.7	11.7	6.8	8.7	2.8	7.8	65.2	12.8	2.4	10.4	19.1
1970	168.0	124.6	40.3	12.5	7.0	10.2	2.8	7.8	66.4	14.3	2.7	11.6	20.3
1971	188.6	130.4	42.7	14.9	6.3	11.0	2.7	7.9	69.1	14.9	2.8	12.2	19.5
1972	219.0	146.6	47.2	17.6	5.9	12.1	3.1	8.6	78.9	16.7	3.5	13.2	21.4
1973	251.0	172.7	55.0	19.8	7.9	13.8	3.5	9.9	95.1	19.9	3.5	16.3	26.0
1974	260.5	191.1	61.2	20.6	10.0	15.1	5.2	10.3	104.3	23.1	3.9	19.2	30.7
1975	263.5	196.8	61.4	17.7	10.6	15.7	7.4	10.1	107.6	23.8	3.6	20.2	31.3
1976	306.1	219.3	65.9	18.1	10.1	18.2	8.6	11.0	121.2	27.5	4.4	23.1	34.1
1977	374.3	259.1	74.6	20.3	11.1	19.3	11.5	12.5	148.7	33.7	5.7	28.0	39.4
1978	452.6	314.6	93.6	25.3	16.2	21.4	15.4	15.2	180.6	42.3	7.6	34.8	47.7
1979	521.7	373.8	117.7	33.5	22.0	24.6	19.0	18.5	208.1	50.3	10.2	40.2	56.2
1980	536.4	406.9	136.2	41.0	20.5	27.3	27.4	20.0	216.4	58.9	12.5	46.4	60.7
1981	601.4	472.9	167.3	48.3	25.4	30.0	42.5	21.2	240.9	69.6	17.1	52.5	65.5
1982	595.9	485.1	177.6	55.8	26.1	29.6	44.8	21.3	234.9	74.2	18.9	55.3	62.7
1983	643.3	482.2	154.3	55.8	19.5	25.8	30.0	23.3	246.5	83.7	23.9	59.8	58.9
1984	754.7	564.3	177.4	70.6	20.9	26.5	31.3	28.1	291.9	101.2	31.6	69.6	68.1
1985	807.8	607.8	194.5	84.1	24.1	26.5	27.9	31.8	307.9	106.6	33.7	72.9	72.5
1986	842.6	607.8	176.5	80.9	21.0	28.3	15.7	30.7	317.7	111.1	33.4	77.7	75.4
1987	865.0	615.2	174.2	80.8	21.2	25.4	13.1	33.7	320.9	112.2	35.8	76.4	76.7
1988	918.5	662.3	182.8	86.3	23.2	25.0	15.7	32.5	346.8	120.8	38.0	82.8	84.2
1989	972.0	716.0	193.7	88.3	28.8	27.5	14.9	34.3	372.2	130.7	43.1	87.6	93.3
1990	978.9	739.2	202.9	87.5	33.6	26.3	17.9	37.6	371.9	129.6	38.6	90.9	92.1
1991	944.7	723.6	183.6	68.9	31.4	31.6	18.5	33.2	360.8	129.2	37.7	91.5	89.3
1992	996.7	741.9	172.6	64.5	29.0	33.9	14.2	31.0	381.7	142.1	44.0	98.1	93.0
1993	1 086.0	799.2	177.2	69.4	23.6	33.2	16.6	34.5	425.1	153.3	47.9	105.4	102.2
1994	1 192.7	868.9	186.8	75.4	28.9	31.2	16.4	34.9	476.4	167.0	52.4	114.6	113.6
1995	1 286.3	962.2	207.3	83.1	35.5	33.1	15.0	40.6	528.1	188.4	66.1	122.3	129.0
1996	1 401.3	1 043.2	224.6	91.5	38.2	29.2	16.8	48.9	565.3	204.7	72.8	131.9	136.5
1997	1 524.7	1 149.1	250.3	104.3	37.6	28.8	22.4	57.2	610.9	222.8	81.4	141.4	140.4
1998	1 673.0	1 254.1	276.0	116.0	40.5	34.2	22.3	63.1	660.0	240.1	87.9	152.2	147.4
1999	1 826.2	1 364.5	285.7	125.4	35.1	40.4	18.3	66.4	713.6	259.8	97.2	162.5	149.1
2000	1 983.9	1 498.4	321.0	139.3	37.6	48.1	23.7	72.2	766.1	293.8	103.2	190.6	162.9
2001	1 973.1	1 460.1	333.5	137.3	37.8	51.1	34.6	72.7	711.5	265.9	87.6	178.4	151.9
2002	1 910.4	1 352.8	287.0	119.4	22.7	51.0	30.2	63.6	659.6	236.7	79.7	157.0	141.7
2003	2 013.0	1 375.9	286.6	115.0	21.4	48.1	38.5	63.6	670.6	242.7	79.9	162.8	143.4
2004	2 217.2	1 467.4	307.7	125.3	23.2	43.1	47.3	68.8	721.9	255.8	84.2	171.6	144.2
2005	2 477.2	1 621.0	353.0	135.9	28.4	48.1	69.4	71.2	794.9	267.0	84.2	182.8	162.4
2006	2 632.0	1 793.8	425.2	156.3	32.3	55.8	96.0	84.7	862.3	288.5	92.6	195.9	181.6
2007	2 639.1	1 948.6	510.3	181.8	40.2	81.6	102.2	104.5	893.4	310.9	95.4	215.5	194.1
2008	2 506.9	1 990.9	571.1	181.9	53.0	95.6	120.3	120.3	845.4	306.3	93.9	212.4	194.3
2009	2 080.4	1 690.4	455.8	126.8	56.8	95.8	79.2	97.3	670.3	275.6	88.9	186.7	153.7
2010	2 111.6	1 735.0	379.8	92.1	40.3	83.8	93.5	70.1	777.0	307.5	99.6	207.9	155.2
2011	2 286.3	1 907.5	404.5	93.4	39.6	81.8	124.7	65.0	881.3	313.3	95.6	217.7	191.5
2012	2 550.5	2 118.5	479.4	103.8	46.8	102.4	152.9	73.6	983.4	331.2	103.5	227.7	211.2
2013	2 721.5	2 211.5	492.5	109.8	49.9	98.9	155.6	78.3	1 027.0	341.7	102.1	239.6	209.3
2014	2 960.2	2 400.1	577.6	127.4	58.1	115.3	188.3	88.4	1 091.9	346.0	101.9	244.1	218.8
2015	3 100.4	2 466.6	584.4	145.4	79.6	121.1	137.1	101.1	1 119.5	352.8	101.3	251.5	218.2
2016	3 168.8	2 469.3	560.4	172.1	76.3	124.3	75.8	111.9	1 087.8	353.0	99.4	253.6	213.9
2017	3 351.9	2 591.6	599.3	181.6	67.6	121.3	108.5	120.2	1 117.4	369.2	104.7	264.5	225.0
2018	3 579.1	2 780.6	633.3	191.2	69.6	118.6	126.6	127.3	1 190.5	390.2	119.3	270.9	242.7
2019	3 752.6	2 938.7	672.6	203.2	77.9	132.5	127.3	131.8	1 231.3	393.9	119.1	274.8	251.9
2020	3 697.4	2 799.6	597.2	204.7	69.4	130.3	75.6	117.2	1 123.9	413.9	128.1	285.8	241.7
2021	4 139.8	3 053.7	580.2	201.9	72.2	118.8	85.3	102.0	1 274.9	471.9	146.3	325.6	287.6
2019													
1st quarter	3 683.4	2 886.9	639.9	194.5	77.8	110.2	126.7	130.7	1 240.2	396.6	120.0	276.6	249.5
2nd quarter	3 754.5	2 946.1	669.4	197.7	78.6	129.3	133.2	130.5	1 247.4	397.6	121.8	275.8	254.2
3rd quarter	3 791.2	2 969.3	696.0	208.3	77.8	142.4	133.9	133.5	1 227.4	391.0	115.6	275.4	256.0
4th quarter	3 781.4	2 952.6	685.3	212.2	77.1	148.1	115.3	132.6	1 210.3	390.2	118.9	271.3	247.8
2020													
1st quarter	3 773.0	2 900.1	687.1	218.7	74.1	145.3	119.4	129.6	1 141.9	379.1	113.5	265.6	242.8
2nd quarter	3 456.9	2 659.1	585.9	208.0	69.0	129.5	60.6	118.8	1 020.6	397.0	126.0	270.9	229.1
3rd quarter	3 693.8	2 776.6	563.5	198.9	69.0	126.0	56.8	112.8	1 135.5	432.2	133.9	298.3	241.5
4th quarter	3 865.9	2 862.7	552.3	193.0	65.6	120.3	65.7	107.6	1 197.5	447.3	138.9	308.5	253.4
2021													
1st quarter	4 022.2	2 956.7	565.0	194.9	68.7	119.9	76.9	104.5	1 244.5	472.1	152.8	319.2	260.8
2nd quarter	4 099.4	3 029.2	572.8	198.9	71.3	118.5	83.9	100.2	1 270.4	461.9	137.4	324.5	284.7
3rd quarter	4 159.8	3 073.9	581.9	204.3	71.8	118.9	87.2	99.7	1 277.2	461.4	143.2	318.2	294.9
4th quarter	4 277.8	3 154.9	601.2	209.6	76.9	118.0	93.3	103.5	1 307.7	492.1	151.8	340.4	310.1

Table 5-2. Gross Private Fixed Investment by Type—*Continued*

(Billions of dollars, quarterly data are at seasonally adjusted annual rates.)

NIPA Table 5.3.5

	Nonresidential—*Continued*						Residential						
	Equipment—*Continued*		Intellectual property					Residential structures					
									Permanent site				
Year and quarter	Transportation equipment	Other nonresidential equipment	Total	Software [1]	Research and development [2]	Entertainment, literary, and artistic originals	Total	Total	Total	Single family	Multifamily	Other residential structures	Residential equipment
1960	8.5	7.1	7.1	0.1	4.9	2.1	26.9	26.3	17.5	14.9	2.6	8.8	0.5
1961	8.0	7.0	8.0	0.2	5.2	2.7	27.0	26.5	17.4	14.1	3.3	9.1	0.5
1962	9.8	7.5	8.4	0.2	5.6	2.6	29.6	29.1	19.9	15.1	4.8	9.2	0.5
1963	9.4	8.8	9.2	0.4	6.0	2.8	32.9	32.3	22.4	16.0	6.4	9.8	0.6
1964	10.6	9.9	9.8	0.5	6.5	2.8	35.1	34.5	24.1	17.6	6.4	10.4	0.6
1965	13.2	11.0	11.1	0.7	7.2	3.2	35.2	34.5	23.8	17.8	6.0	10.6	0.7
1966	14.5	12.7	12.8	1.0	8.1	3.7	33.4	32.7	21.8	16.6	5.2	10.9	0.7
1967	14.3	12.4	14.0	1.2	9.0	3.8	33.6	32.9	21.5	16.8	4.7	11.4	0.7
1968	17.6	13.0	15.6	1.3	9.9	4.3	40.2	39.3	26.7	19.5	7.2	12.6	0.9
1969	18.9	14.4	17.2	1.8	11.0	4.4	44.4	43.4	29.2	19.7	9.5	14.1	1.0
1970	16.2	15.6	17.9	2.3	11.5	4.1	43.4	42.3	27.1	17.5	9.5	15.2	1.1
1971	18.4	16.3	18.7	2.4	11.9	4.4	58.2	56.9	38.7	25.8	12.9	18.2	1.3
1972	21.8	19.0	20.6	2.8	12.9	4.9	72.4	70.9	50.1	32.8	17.2	20.8	1.5
1973	26.6	22.6	22.7	3.2	14.6	4.9	78.3	76.6	54.6	35.2	19.4	22.0	1.7
1974	26.3	24.3	25.5	3.9	16.4	5.2	69.5	67.6	43.4	29.7	13.7	24.2	1.9
1975	25.2	27.4	27.8	4.8	17.5	5.5	66.7	64.8	36.3	29.6	6.7	28.5	1.9
1976	30.0	29.6	32.2	5.2	19.6	7.4	86.8	84.6	50.8	43.9	6.9	33.9	2.1
1977	39.3	36.3	35.8	5.5	21.8	8.6	115.2	112.8	72.2	62.2	10.0	40.6	2.4
1978	47.3	43.2	40.4	6.3	24.9	9.1	138.0	135.3	85.6	72.8	12.8	49.7	2.7
1979	53.6	47.9	48.1	8.1	29.1	10.9	147.8	144.7	89.3	72.3	17.0	55.4	3.2
1980	48.4	48.3	54.4	9.8	34.2	10.3	129.5	126.1	69.6	52.9	16.7	56.5	3.4
1981	50.6	55.2	64.8	11.8	39.7	13.2	128.5	124.9	69.4	52.0	17.5	55.4	3.6
1982	46.8	51.2	72.7	14.0	44.8	13.9	110.8	107.2	57.0	41.5	15.5	50.2	3.7
1983	53.5	50.4	81.3	16.4	49.6	15.3	161.1	156.9	95.0	72.5	22.4	61.9	4.2
1984	64.4	58.2	95.0	20.4	56.9	17.8	190.4	185.6	114.6	86.4	28.2	71.0	4.7
1985	69.0	59.9	105.3	23.8	63.0	18.6	200.1	195.0	115.9	87.4	28.5	79.1	5.1
1986	70.5	60.7	113.5	25.6	66.5	21.4	234.8	229.3	135.2	104.1	31.0	94.1	5.5
1987	68.1	64.0	120.1	29.0	69.2	21.9	249.8	244.0	142.7	117.2	25.5	101.3	5.8
1988	72.9	69.0	132.7	33.3	76.4	23.0	256.2	250.1	142.4	120.1	22.3	107.7	6.1
1989	67.9	80.2	150.1	40.6	84.1	25.4	256.0	249.9	143.2	120.9	22.3	106.6	6.1
1990	70.0	80.2	164.4	45.4	91.5	27.5	239.7	233.7	132.1	112.9	19.3	101.5	6.0
1991	71.5	70.8	179.1	48.7	101.0	29.4	221.2	215.4	114.6	99.4	15.1	100.8	5.7
1992	74.7	72.0	187.7	51.1	105.4	31.2	254.7	248.8	135.1	122.0	13.1	113.8	5.9
1993	89.4	80.2	196.9	57.2	106.3	33.4	286.8	280.7	150.9	140.1	10.8	129.8	6.1
1994	107.7	88.1	205.7	60.4	109.2	36.1	323.8	317.6	176.4	162.3	14.1	141.2	6.2
1995	116.1	94.7	226.8	65.5	121.2	40.2	324.1	317.7	171.4	153.5	17.9	146.3	6.3
1996	123.2	101.0	253.3	74.5	134.5	44.3	358.1	351.7	191.1	170.8	20.3	160.6	6.3
1997	135.5	112.1	288.0	93.8	148.1	46.1	375.6	369.3	198.1	175.2	22.9	171.3	6.3
1998	147.1	125.4	318.1	109.2	160.6	48.3	418.8	412.1	224.0	199.4	24.6	188.2	6.7
1999	174.4	130.4	365.1	136.6	177.5	51.0	461.8	454.5	251.3	223.8	27.4	203.2	7.3
2000	170.8	138.6	411.3	156.8	199.0	55.6	485.4	477.7	265.0	236.8	28.3	212.7	7.7
2001	154.2	139.5	415.0	157.7	202.7	54.7	513.1	505.2	279.4	249.1	30.3	225.8	7.8
2002	141.6	139.6	406.2	152.5	196.1	57.6	557.6	549.6	298.8	265.9	33.0	250.7	8.0
2003	134.1	150.5	418.7	155.0	201.0	62.7	637.1	628.8	345.7	310.6	35.1	283.1	8.3
2004	159.2	162.7	437.8	166.3	207.4	64.1	749.8	740.8	417.5	377.6	39.9	323.3	9.0
2005	179.6	186.0	473.1	178.6	224.7	69.8	856.2	846.6	480.8	433.5	47.3	365.8	9.6
2006	194.3	198.0	506.3	189.5	245.6	71.2	838.2	828.1	468.8	416.0	52.8	359.3	10.0
2007	188.8	199.6	544.8	206.4	268.0	70.4	690.5	680.6	354.1	305.2	49.0	326.5	9.9
2008	148.7	196.1	574.4	223.8	284.2	66.4	516.0	506.4	230.1	185.8	44.3	276.3	9.6
2009	74.9	166.1	564.4	226.0	274.6	63.7	390.0	381.2	133.9	105.3	28.5	247.3	8.8
2010	135.8	178.5	578.2	226.4	282.4	69.4	376.6	367.4	127.3	112.6	14.7	240.2	9.2
2011	177.8	198.7	621.7	249.8	303.4	68.6	378.8	369.1	123.2	108.2	15.0	245.9	9.8
2012	215.3	225.7	655.7	272.1	313.4	70.2	432.0	421.5	154.5	132.0	22.5	267.0	10.5
2013	242.5	233.6	691.9	283.7	337.9	70.3	510.0	499.0	202.3	170.8	31.5	296.7	11.0
2014	272.8	254.4	730.5	297.5	359.5	73.4	560.2	548.8	235.2	193.6	41.6	313.7	11.3
2015	306.3	242.2	762.7	307.1	378.3	77.3	633.8	622.1	273.6	221.1	52.5	348.5	11.8
2016	292.3	228.5	821.2	334.8	404.4	82.0	699.4	687.3	304.4	242.5	61.9	383.0	12.1
2017	294.0	229.1	875.0	365.7	423.5	85.8	760.3	747.9	332.6	270.2	62.5	415.3	12.4
2018	309.5	248.1	956.7	401.3	465.6	89.8	798.5	785.6	355.0	289.6	65.5	430.6	12.9
2019	320.3	265.3	1 034.8	427.7	514.4	92.7	813.9	800.8	349.4	280.0	69.4	451.4	13.1
2020	206.0	262.3	1 078.5	453.4	537.7	87.4	897.8	883.4	381.9	309.4	72.5	501.5	14.3
2021	221.2	294.3	1 198.5	503.9	600.9	93.7	1 086.1	1 069.0	491.7	408.4	83.3	577.3	17.1
2019													
1st quarter	333.0	261.1	1 006.7	415.5	499.7	91.6	796.5	783.6	343.2	271.8	71.3	440.4	13.0
2nd quarter	328.3	267.3	1 029.3	423.5	513.4	92.4	808.5	795.3	346.6	276.5	70.1	448.7	13.2
3rd quarter	312.5	267.8	1 046.0	432.7	520.2	93.1	821.9	808.6	351.4	283.0	68.5	457.2	13.3
4th quarter	307.4	264.8	1 057.0	439.1	524.3	93.6	828.8	815.7	356.3	288.6	67.7	459.4	13.1
2020													
1st quarter	260.2	259.8	1 071.1	449.2	529.8	92.2	872.9	859.7	376.2	306.3	70.0	483.4	13.2
2nd quarter	155.5	239.1	1 052.6	444.9	519.9	87.9	797.8	784.1	347.1	279.4	67.7	437.0	13.7
3rd quarter	191.2	270.7	1 077.6	453.6	539.9	84.1	901.8	888.3	373.6	298.9	74.7	528.2	15.4
4th quarter	217.1	279.7	1 112.9	466.0	561.3	85.6	1 003.2	988.2	430.7	353.0	77.7	557.4	15.0
2021													
1st quarter	225.4	286.3	1 147.2	484.2	576.3	86.7	1 065.5	1 048.7	470.4	388.9	81.4	578.3	16.9
2nd quarter	231.2	292.6	1 186.0	501.3	594.5	90.2	1 070.2	1 052.9	488.9	405.0	83.9	563.9	17.4
3rd quarter	222.3	298.6	1 214.9	511.7	607.2	95.9	1 085.9	1 068.7	498.8	415.1	83.7	569.9	17.1
4th quarter	205.8	299.6	1 246.0	518.3	625.6	102.1	1 122.9	1 105.9	508.8	424.6	84.2	597.2	17.0

[1] Excludes software "embedded," or bundled, in computers and other equipment. Includes software development expenditures.
[2] Excludes software development.

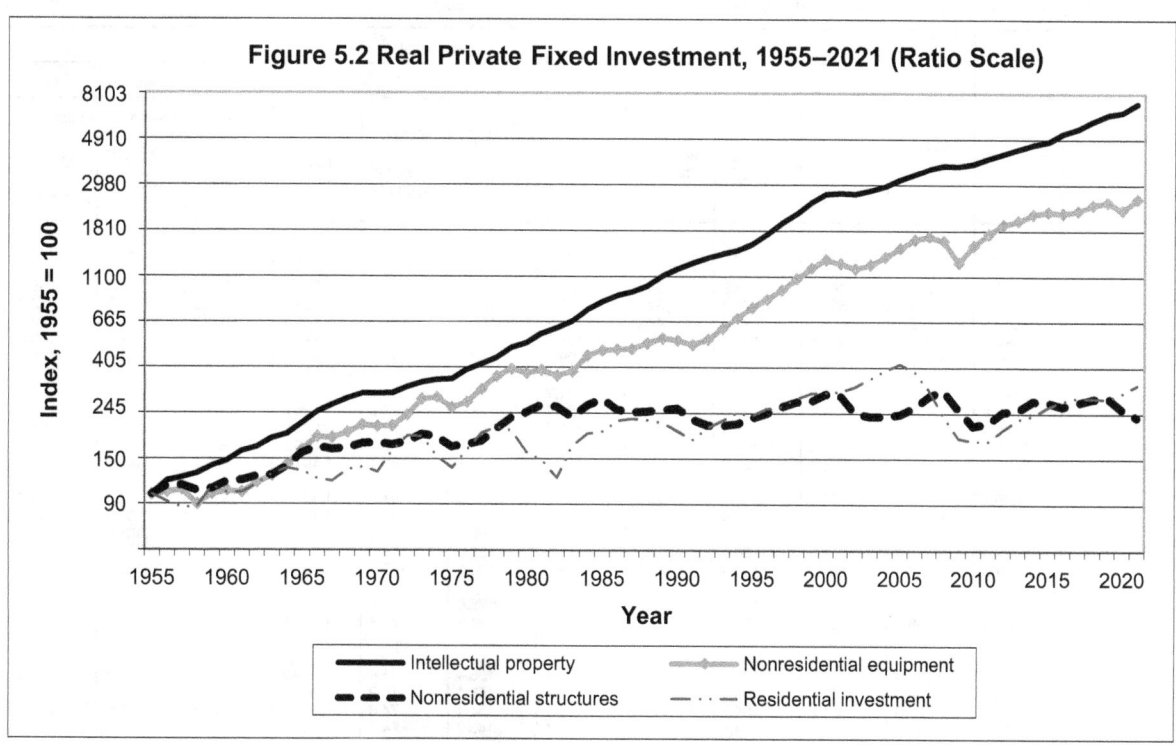

Figure 5.2 Real Private Fixed Investment, 1955–2021 (Ratio Scale)

- Between 1955 and 2006, which was the recent high point for total real (constant-dollar) investment, the quantity of real gross private fixed investment increased eightfold, with an average annual growth rate of 4.2 percent. Every major type of investment grew in real terms between those two years, but as Figure 5-2 indicates, by far the fastest-growing major category has been "intellectual property products." Computer software is the main driver of growth in this category, but it also includes research and development and "entertainment, literary, and artistic originals." (Table 5-3)

- Between 2008 and 2009, overall total gross private fixed investment fell 16.0 percent in real terms—a collapse unprecedented in the postwar period. (Table 5-3) By 2021, gross investment surpassed the 2006 level by 33.6 percent, achieving a new all-time high after declining in 2020. (Table 5-4)

- Intellectual property investment barely hesitated in 2009 and went on to new record peaks in each year through 2021. Equipment purchases continued to increase and went on to a new record in 2021 after declining in 2020. On the other hand, residential investment dropped 40.6 percent between 2007 and 2009. Residential investment increased steadily from 2012 to 2017 declined in 2018 and 2019 and increased again in 2020 and 2021. (Table 5-4)

Table 5-3. Real Gross Private Fixed Investment by Type

(Billions of chained [2012] dollars, quarterly data are at seasonally adjusted annual rates.)   NIPA Table 5.3.6

Year and quarter	Total gross private fixed investment	Nonresidential											
			Structures						Equipment				
										Information processing equipment			
		Total	Total	Commercial and health care	Manufacturing	Power and communication	Mining exploration, shafts, and wells	Other nonresidential structures	Total	Total	Computers and peripheral equipment[1]	Other information processing	Industrial equipment
2004	2 440.7	1 594.0	456.3	165.7	30.7	64.0	103.6	82.0	688.6	169.4	45.7	124.7	178.8
2005	2 618.7	1 716.4	466.1	164.3	34.9	66.4	113.4	79.7	760.0	187.6	51.8	136.5	194.2
2006	2 686.8	1 854.2	501.7	174.2	37.2	70.4	122.5	89.1	832.6	217.0	64.7	152.4	210.6
2007	2 653.5	1 982.1	568.6	191.6	44.0	98.1	120.5	105.0	865.8	247.2	73.9	173.3	217.3
2008	2 499.4	1 994.2	605.4	184.6	55.1	107.8	129.4	118.9	824.4	260.6	79.7	180.9	208.3
2009	2 099.8	1 704.3	492.2	128.0	57.9	109.3	92.4	98.1	649.7	247.5	81.1	166.5	162.7
2010	2 164.2	1 781.0	412.8	96.2	42.2	91.7	108.3	72.6	781.2	289.1	94.1	195.1	162.5
2011	2 317.8	1 935.4	424.1	95.8	40.6	84.6	136.7	66.5	886.2	303.2	93.9	209.3	194.9
2012	2 550.5	2 118.5	479.4	103.8	46.8	102.4	152.9	73.6	983.4	331.2	103.5	227.7	211.2
2013	2 692.1	2 206.0	485.5	107.5	48.7	97.8	155.4	76.1	1 029.2	351.8	103.0	248.8	208.4
2014	2 869.2	2 365.3	538.8	121.3	55.0	112.5	167.8	82.4	1 101.1	370.2	102.9	267.7	216.5
2015	2 979.0	2 420.3	534.1	136.0	74.0	116.4	119.9	91.0	1 134.6	393.3	103.4	291.0	216.7
2016	3 041.0	2 442.0	511.0	158.8	70.4	118.9	69.7	97.5	1 114.6	410.5	103.0	309.3	213.4
2017	3 164.3	2 541.4	532.5	163.8	61.0	113.5	96.9	101.4	1 145.5	438.6	108.9	331.9	222.5
2018	3 316.2	2 704.4	553.6	166.0	59.9	107.0	123.0	102.8	1 218.8	472.0	123.7	349.2	235.4
2019	3 421.3	2 822.0	565.0	168.5	63.2	114.9	121.0	102.3	1 258.8	489.6	127.6	363.0	240.6
2020	3 329.4	2 671.1	494.2	166.2	54.7	109.5	75.6	88.2	1 154.0	523.0	140.7	382.5	228.8
2021	3 587.8	2 868.5	454.7	153.7	54.1	93.9	84.2	72.8	1 304.8	599.6	158.9	441.5	260.8
2012													
1st quarter	2 499.4	2 081.3	476.0	101.7	44.5	102.0	156.4	71.4	959.6	327.3	105.3	222.0	210.3
2nd quarter	2 549.8	2 128.0	487.4	104.0	46.6	104.8	158.1	73.9	986.7	333.5	104.6	228.9	215.0
3rd quarter	2 553.6	2 120.9	481.8	105.2	47.4	103.2	151.1	74.8	983.8	327.3	100.6	226.7	207.5
4th quarter	2 599.4	2 144.0	472.5	104.1	48.6	99.4	145.9	74.4	1 003.4	336.8	103.6	233.2	212.1
2013													
1st quarter	2 643.9	2 171.6	462.1	106.3	47.0	81.9	153.3	73.4	1 021.1	349.9	105.9	244.0	210.1
2nd quarter	2 665.3	2 177.5	475.8	103.4	46.2	91.3	159.3	75.4	1 019.0	348.6	100.2	248.5	207.7
3rd quarter	2 711.3	2 214.7	499.8	106.9	51.0	104.2	159.9	77.7	1 019.0	352.1	101.2	251.0	209.2
4th quarter	2 748.0	2 260.0	504.2	113.2	50.7	113.9	148.9	77.7	1 057.9	356.5	104.8	251.8	206.4
2014													
1st quarter	2 775.6	2 291.7	521.9	113.1	49.6	126.1	155.5	78.5	1 066.9	358.9	101.3	257.9	211.4
2nd quarter	2 852.8	2 353.3	540.3	119.2	50.4	119.0	170.9	81.2	1 093.6	372.1	103.5	269.0	217.1
3rd quarter	2 907.3	2 400.8	542.2	124.2	54.6	109.4	171.7	82.4	1 127.0	370.6	102.3	268.7	222.0
4th quarter	2 941.2	2 415.5	551.0	128.8	65.6	95.5	173.1	87.4	1 116.9	379.3	104.7	275.1	215.3
2015													
1st quarter	2 949.5	2 412.6	545.1	129.4	72.4	106.6	152.1	85.8	1 126.0	381.8	103.0	279.5	215.8
2nd quarter	2 974.9	2 423.6	549.1	138.1	76.8	122.9	122.7	92.1	1 130.3	388.4	103.5	285.7	217.6
3rd quarter	2 999.8	2 432.4	531.8	137.1	74.7	121.3	108.1	94.5	1 148.3	399.2	105.6	294.5	216.0
4th quarter	2 991.8	2 412.8	510.6	139.6	72.1	114.6	96.6	91.5	1 133.6	403.8	101.3	304.3	217.4
2016													
1st quarter	3 009.2	2 410.4	491.9	148.7	70.3	110.4	74.4	92.1	1 127.6	406.5	104.7	303.2	212.7
2nd quarter	3 025.5	2 426.1	501.5	154.5	72.8	114.5	64.7	99.0	1 113.4	406.9	103.5	305.0	215.1
3rd quarter	3 052.8	2 457.8	521.4	164.4	71.1	121.8	69.2	99.4	1 108.3	411.5	101.0	312.7	212.1
4th quarter	3 076.5	2 473.6	529.0	167.3	67.5	128.8	70.5	99.7	1 109.0	417.2	102.9	316.4	213.8
2017													
1st quarter	3 124.7	2 505.1	538.3	165.5	63.2	124.9	89.1	100.4	1 115.7	423.0	103.4	322.0	216.2
2nd quarter	3 154.2	2 531.0	538.6	165.5	62.8	115.2	97.0	102.2	1 138.6	437.0	107.5	331.8	222.4
3rd quarter	3 158.1	2 538.7	523.8	161.4	58.7	108.3	97.5	101.5	1 147.4	439.0	112.6	327.9	223.3
4th quarter	3 220.3	2 590.5	529.3	162.9	59.1	105.5	104.0	101.4	1 180.4	455.4	112.0	345.9	227.9
2018													
1st quarter	3 273.2	2 654.0	554.2	168.9	59.4	112.2	113.9	104.0	1 196.6	467.2	121.1	347.2	231.6
2nd quarter	3 321.2	2 698.0	563.7	168.3	59.4	112.9	124.2	104.1	1 205.4	468.4	124.5	344.4	233.3
3rd quarter	3 327.9	2 716.7	557.7	166.4	60.7	103.7	130.1	102.6	1 221.3	475.5	125.3	350.9	235.6
4th quarter	3 342.6	2 749.0	538.9	160.4	59.9	99.3	123.8	100.7	1 251.7	477.1	123.9	354.4	241.0
2019													
1st quarter	3 372.8	2 780.7	544.7	164.2	64.5	96.8	120.8	102.8	1 265.2	487.0	125.7	362.8	239.2
2nd quarter	3 423.2	2 826.0	563.2	164.5	63.9	112.8	125.4	102.0	1 273.1	492.6	129.9	363.5	243.1
3rd quarter	3 449.3	2 846.5	582.0	171.5	62.8	123.2	127.4	103.1	1 256.4	487.8	124.7	364.8	244.1
4th quarter	3 439.9	2 834.7	570.0	173.8	61.8	126.8	110.4	101.4	1 240.6	490.8	130.3	361.1	235.8
2020													
1st quarter	3 419.6	2 775.5	568.8	177.9	59.0	123.1	115.9	98.2	1 168.3	478.0	125.1	353.8	230.2
2nd quarter	3 123.0	2 535.7	485.8	169.0	54.5	109.1	61.0	89.6	1 044.0	501.7	138.1	363.0	217.4
3rd quarter	3 318.5	2 646.9	466.0	161.4	54.0	105.6	57.9	84.6	1 166.6	545.9	146.6	399.5	228.5
4th quarter	3 456.6	2 726.2	456.1	156.6	51.5	100.1	67.6	80.4	1 237.1	566.5	152.9	413.7	238.8
2021													
1st quarter	3 564.1	2 810.4	462.1	156.9	53.7	98.4	78.5	77.1	1 278.5	600.1	167.8	431.1	243.0
2nd quarter	3 593.0	2 873.1	458.6	155.5	55.4	95.2	83.6	72.7	1 315.7	588.1	150.2	440.0	260.9
3rd quarter	3 585.0	2 884.8	453.8	155.5	54.0	92.9	85.3	70.5	1 307.9	586.1	154.6	432.4	265.1
4th quarter	3 609.1	2 905.5	444.1	146.8	53.3	89.2	89.2	71.1	1 317.0	624.2	163.0	462.6	274.0

[1]See notes and definitions.

Table 5-3. Real Gross Private Fixed Investment by Type—*Continued*

(Billions of chained [2012] dollars, quarterly data are at seasonally adjusted annual rates.)

Year and quarter	Nonresidential—*Continued*						Residential							
	Equipment—*Continued*		Intellectual property				Total	Residential structures						Residential equipment
								Total	Permanent site				Other residential structures	
	Transportation equipment	Other nonresidential equipment	Total	Software [2]	Research and development [3]	Entertainment, literary, and artistic originals			Total	Total	Single family	Multifamily		
2004	171.2	193.3	459.2	149.3	248.1	65.6	830.9	822.1	464.3	405.4	53.4	355.4	9.1
2005	192.1	211.9	493.1	163.4	261.6	71.0	885.4	876.3	497.0	432.8	58.7	376.7	9.5
2006	206.4	220.7	521.5	173.5	279.6	71.8	818.9	809.5	453.6	390.4	59.1	353.5	9.7
2007	197.7	218.0	554.3	191.1	296.1	70.0	665.8	656.6	337.7	283.5	52.3	317.7	9.4
2008	155.0	207.4	575.3	206.7	304.8	66.0	504.6	495.7	224.2	178.1	46.0	270.9	9.1
2009	72.5	165.3	572.4	212.9	297.4	63.4	395.3	386.9	134.5	105.3	29.3	252.3	8.4
2010	141.5	186.2	588.1	220.9	298.5	69.5	383.0	373.8	129.1	114.3	14.7	244.7	9.3
2011	181.8	206.2	624.8	245.2	311.0	68.9	382.5	372.4	124.5	109.1	15.4	247.9	10.0
2012	215.3	225.7	655.7	272.1	313.4	70.2	432.0	421.5	154.5	132.0	22.5	267.0	10.5
2013	238.5	230.6	691.4	287.2	333.8	70.3	485.5	474.1	192.4	161.8	30.6	281.7	11.4
2014	265.0	248.9	724.8	305.3	346.9	72.7	504.1	491.8	210.4	171.8	38.8	281.4	12.4
2015	292.8	232.4	752.4	320.2	357.1	75.5	555.4	542.0	235.2	191.5	44.0	306.8	13.4
2016	276.3	218.9	818.8	354.0	387.1	78.5	592.1	577.7	250.5	201.3	49.3	327.1	14.5
2017	273.5	219.0	865.2	392.6	394.7	81.0	615.9	600.6	261.6	214.8	47.2	338.9	15.5
2018	287.0	234.0	935.5	437.1	419.9	83.7	612.3	596.9	266.4	220.7	46.2	330.2	15.7
2019	295.0	244.1	1 002.9	467.8	454.8	85.5	606.7	591.3	254.7	206.8	48.2	336.5	15.8
2020	191.3	240.2	1 031.3	502.3	458.8	79.6	648.0	631.6	269.7	219.7	50.2	361.9	16.9
2021	219.2	260.6	1 135.0	569.2	496.9	82.9	707.7	689.8	317.2	260.0	57.6	372.4	18.5
2012													
1st quarter	205.6	216.5	645.7	263.1	312.3	70.3	418.3	407.8	139.3	120.5	18.8	268.5	10.4
2nd quarter	215.6	222.7	653.9	272.1	311.5	70.2	421.9	411.5	147.6	126.2	21.4	263.9	10.4
3rd quarter	216.1	232.9	655.2	272.8	312.4	70.1	432.7	422.1	158.1	134.5	23.6	264.1	10.6
4th quarter	223.9	230.6	668.0	280.2	317.6	70.2	455.2	444.5	173.1	146.9	26.2	271.4	10.7
2013													
1st quarter	232.2	229.0	688.6	288.3	330.1	70.2	471.8	460.7	184.3	156.0	28.2	276.4	11.1
2nd quarter	236.6	226.2	682.9	280.2	331.9	70.8	486.8	475.5	192.6	163.0	29.5	282.9	11.3
3rd quarter	237.2	220.7	695.8	288.3	337.1	70.3	495.5	483.9	196.5	165.7	30.8	287.4	11.6
4th quarter	248.2	246.4	698.1	292.1	336.1	70.0	487.7	476.2	196.3	162.6	33.8	279.9	11.5
2014													
1st quarter	252.4	243.8	702.5	296.2	335.3	71.2	484.3	472.6	199.9	165.0	35.0	272.8	11.7
2nd quarter	260.5	243.8	718.5	303.3	343.3	72.1	499.8	487.5	207.6	169.5	38.3	279.9	12.4
3rd quarter	275.6	257.5	731.4	309.8	348.7	73.2	507.1	494.7	209.9	169.9	40.3	284.8	12.6
4th quarter	271.6	250.5	746.6	311.9	360.2	74.4	525.2	512.4	224.1	182.8	41.6	288.3	12.8
2015													
1st quarter	286.6	241.4	741.1	315.2	351.5	74.7	535.5	522.5	227.4	185.4	42.3	295.0	13.0
2nd quarter	292.4	232.1	743.6	318.2	350.9	75.0	548.9	535.6	229.6	187.3	42.5	306.0	13.4
3rd quarter	302.8	230.9	753.6	320.3	357.8	75.8	563.7	550.1	239.0	194.4	44.8	311.1	13.6
4th quarter	289.4	225.2	771.3	327.1	368.1	76.3	573.6	559.9	244.8	198.7	46.3	315.0	13.7
2016													
1st quarter	286.8	224.4	795.1	339.6	378.8	77.2	591.2	577.0	252.6	203.7	49.1	324.3	14.3
2nd quarter	274.6	220.9	814.3	348.9	388.6	77.4	592.0	577.7	252.4	202.9	49.6	325.2	14.3
3rd quarter	272.7	216.9	829.4	359.2	391.8	79.3	588.9	574.4	246.4	196.8	49.8	328.1	14.7
4th quarter	270.9	213.2	836.3	368.2	389.4	80.2	596.3	581.6	250.6	201.9	48.9	331.0	14.8
2017													
1st quarter	267.3	216.1	851.2	378.1	394.5	80.5	611.8	596.7	254.1	206.7	47.6	342.8	15.2
2nd quarter	269.0	218.4	854.7	387.0	390.0	80.6	615.7	600.5	261.2	214.0	47.6	339.2	15.3
3rd quarter	275.1	218.0	870.4	398.2	394.8	80.9	612.7	597.4	264.0	218.0	46.4	333.2	15.5
4th quarter	282.6	223.4	884.6	406.9	399.7	81.8	623.2	607.6	267.0	220.4	47.0	340.5	15.9
2018													
1st quarter	281.9	226.1	905.2	420.1	407.1	82.5	616.5	600.9	267.9	222.7	45.8	332.7	16.0
2nd quarter	279.2	234.5	930.3	434.5	417.6	83.2	621.5	605.8	271.8	226.7	45.8	333.7	15.9
3rd quarter	285.6	235.0	940.8	441.4	421.0	83.8	612.2	596.8	267.7	222.7	45.5	328.9	15.6
4th quarter	301.3	240.5	965.8	452.2	433.8	85.1	599.0	584.0	258.1	210.8	47.7	325.7	15.2
2019													
1st quarter	307.7	240.7	978.5	454.8	443.4	85.1	599.1	584.0	251.3	201.9	49.5	332.6	15.4
2nd quarter	301.2	246.3	995.7	461.4	453.8	85.1	605.2	589.8	253.9	205.5	48.6	335.9	15.7
3rd quarter	288.5	246.2	1 010.5	471.2	458.7	85.7	610.6	595.0	255.9	208.6	47.6	339.0	16.0
4th quarter	282.7	243.1	1 027.1	483.8	463.4	86.0	612.2	596.4	257.8	211.1	47.1	338.5	16.2
2020													
1st quarter	237.1	238.2	1 036.6	497.4	463.0	84.2	641.2	625.2	269.9	221.8	48.5	355.1	16.3
2nd quarter	140.9	218.7	1 008.0	492.2	446.1	79.2	584.9	569.2	247.8	201.1	46.9	321.3	16.6
3rd quarter	178.5	247.7	1 027.7	503.5	457.1	77.0	657.8	640.6	262.0	210.5	51.7	378.9	17.8
4th quarter	208.7	256.1	1 053.0	516.1	469.0	78.0	708.2	691.3	299.0	245.6	53.7	392.2	16.8
2021													
1st quarter	212.6	260.8	1 091.9	547.1	480.1	78.0	730.6	712.2	318.6	262.4	56.5	393.4	18.9
2nd quarter	236.1	262.9	1 124.6	565.5	493.0	80.3	708.2	689.9	321.3	263.4	58.2	368.5	19.1
3rd quarter	225.8	262.5	1 149.3	578.2	501.6	84.2	694.2	676.5	316.6	259.0	58.0	359.7	18.2
4th quarter	202.3	256.0	1 174.0	586.0	513.1	88.9	697.9	680.5	312.4	255.1	57.7	368.0	17.8

[2]Excludes software "embedded," or bundled, in computers and other equipment.
[3]Excludes software development.

Table 5-4. Chain-Type Quantity Indexes for Private Fixed Investment by Type

(Index numbers, 2012 = 100, quarterly data are seasonally adjusted.)   NIPA Table 5.3.3

Year and quarter	Total gross private fixed investment	Nonresidential Total	Structures Total	Commercial and health care	Manufacturing	Power and communication	Mining exploration, shafts, and wells	Other nonresidential structures	Equipment Total	Information processing equipment Total	Computers and peripheral equipment[1]	Other information processing	Industrial equipment
1960	13.9	8.8	46.3	47.3	60.9	36.1	42.0	62.1	5.4	0.2	0.0	2.3	28.7
1961	13.9	8.8	46.9	54.0	59.6	33.8	42.8	60.6	5.3	0.2	0.0	2.5	27.2
1962	15.1	9.5	49.1	60.2	60.2	34.0	44.9	61.9	5.9	0.3	0.0	2.7	28.6
1963	16.3	10.1	49.7	58.3	60.4	36.3	42.1	65.5	6.4	0.3	0.0	2.8	30.9
1964	17.8	11.2	54.8	63.4	72.6	39.5	45.1	71.8	7.2	0.3	0.0	3.0	34.9
1965	19.7	13.0	63.6	74.3	100.4	43.7	44.6	80.7	8.5	0.4	0.0	3.4	41.1
1966	20.9	14.6	67.9	72.5	124.8	49.8	42.2	83.8	9.8	0.5	0.0	4.0	47.3
1967	20.7	14.6	66.2	69.7	109.8	54.5	40.4	82.0	9.7	0.6	0.0	4.0	47.5
1968	22.1	15.3	67.1	76.3	105.7	60.6	40.6	72.4	10.3	0.6	0.0	4.1	46.5
1969	23.4	16.4	70.7	88.0	111.2	60.6	42.3	71.8	11.1	0.7	0.0	4.8	49.6
1970	23.0	16.2	70.9	89.2	107.3	66.3	39.8	67.5	10.9	0.8	0.0	5.2	50.3
1971	24.5	16.2	69.8	97.5	88.6	66.9	36.9	63.3	11.0	0.8	0.0	5.2	46.2
1972	27.3	17.6	72.0	106.5	77.4	69.7	39.5	64.0	12.4	1.0	0.0	5.5	49.9
1973	29.7	19.9	77.8	111.2	95.9	74.2	42.2	69.0	14.7	1.1	0.0	6.7	58.9
1974	28.0	20.1	76.2	104.3	109.3	69.5	50.2	63.1	15.0	1.3	0.0	7.4	63.5
1975	25.3	18.3	68.2	81.3	104.8	64.0	58.6	55.6	13.4	1.3	0.0	7.1	53.8
1976	27.8	19.3	69.8	80.2	96.8	69.8	63.2	58.4	14.3	1.4	0.0	7.8	54.1
1977	31.5	21.4	72.7	84.4	99.4	68.7	71.4	61.6	16.5	1.8	0.0	9.4	57.3
1978	35.2	24.4	83.2	96.2	132.6	72.0	81.4	70.0	19.0	2.3	0.1	11.2	63.8
1979	37.2	26.8	93.7	114.7	162.9	74.7	86.7	76.9	20.5	2.8	0.1	12.6	68.3
1980	35.0	26.8	99.2	126.1	136.2	75.4	121.9	74.7	19.6	3.3	0.1	13.5	65.4
1981	35.9	28.5	107.2	136.5	154.7	77.4	141.7	72.3	20.3	3.8	0.2	14.3	64.4
1982	33.7	27.6	105.4	148.7	149.3	73.1	131.0	68.2	19.0	4.0	0.3	14.4	58.8
1983	36.3	27.5	94.0	144.3	108.0	62.8	108.4	72.0	19.9	4.6	0.4	15.1	54.1
1984	42.1	32.1	107.1	175.6	111.8	64.2	123.3	84.4	23.8	5.9	0.7	17.2	61.9
1985	44.4	34.2	114.7	202.8	125.0	63.5	109.8	92.8	25.1	6.5	0.9	17.8	64.8
1986	45.2	33.6	102.4	188.4	105.0	67.8	64.4	87.2	25.4	7.0	1.0	18.5	64.5
1987	45.5	33.6	99.2	181.5	102.4	60.3	62.9	92.4	25.5	7.3	1.3	17.7	62.9
1988	47.0	35.3	99.9	187.0	108.0	56.8	69.0	86.2	27.2	7.9	1.4	19.0	66.1
1989	48.5	37.3	101.9	184.6	129.4	59.0	62.4	87.9	28.6	8.7	1.7	19.8	70.7
1990	47.8	37.7	103.4	177.3	146.6	54.9	72.1	93.3	28.0	8.8	1.7	20.3	66.6
1991	45.3	36.2	91.9	137.7	135.0	65.2	70.5	81.0	26.7	9.0	1.9	20.2	62.3
1992	47.8	37.3	86.3	128.0	124.0	69.2	58.4	75.0	28.3	10.3	2.6	21.4	63.4
1993	51.5	40.1	86.1	133.2	97.4	66.0	67.8	81.0	31.9	11.7	3.3	23.1	68.8
1994	55.7	43.2	87.7	139.4	115.3	59.8	65.9	79.2	35.8	13.3	4.1	25.2	75.0
1995	59.1	47.4	93.2	147.6	135.9	61.0	56.0	88.7	40.1	16.1	6.1	27.1	82.3
1996	64.3	51.7	98.5	159.0	142.9	52.5	59.6	104.3	44.0	19.4	8.9	29.7	85.3
1997	69.8	57.3	105.8	175.7	136.5	50.6	70.2	118.3	48.9	23.4	12.9	32.3	87.2
1998	77.0	63.5	111.5	186.7	141.1	59.4	61.4	126.5	55.3	28.9	18.7	36.3	91.0
1999	84.0	69.8	112.0	193.5	117.7	70.1	51.9	128.4	62.1	35.3	26.5	40.5	91.5
2000	89.9	76.3	121.1	206.4	121.4	80.8	64.8	134.1	68.2	42.6	32.2	48.8	99.4
2001	88.7	74.6	119.6	196.4	118.0	83.4	76.4	129.5	65.3	42.1	33.0	47.3	92.1
2002	85.6	69.5	98.8	166.4	68.9	81.3	55.9	110.9	61.8	40.3	34.6	43.2	85.9
2003	89.4	71.2	95.2	155.8	63.8	74.9	63.9	108.2	64.5	45.4	38.9	44.8	86.3
2004	95.7	75.2	95.2	159.7	65.7	62.6	67.8	111.4	70.0	51.2	44.1	54.8	84.7
2005	102.7	81.0	97.2	158.3	74.6	64.8	74.2	108.3	77.3	56.6	50.0	60.0	91.9
2006	105.3	87.5	104.6	167.9	79.6	68.8	80.1	121.0	84.7	65.5	62.5	66.9	99.7
2007	104.0	93.6	118.6	184.6	94.1	95.8	78.8	142.6	88.0	74.6	71.4	76.1	102.9
2008	98.0	94.1	126.3	177.9	117.9	105.4	84.6	161.4	83.8	78.7	77.0	79.4	98.6
2009	82.3	80.5	102.7	123.3	123.9	106.8	60.4	133.2	66.1	74.7	78.3	73.1	77.0
2010	84.9	84.1	86.1	92.7	90.2	89.6	70.8	98.6	79.4	87.3	90.9	85.7	76.9
2011	90.9	91.4	88.5	92.3	86.8	82.6	89.4	90.4	90.1	91.5	90.7	91.9	92.3
2012	100.0	100.0	100.0	100.0	100.0	100.0	100.0	100.0	100.0	100.0	100.0	100.0	100.0
2013	105.6	104.1	101.3	103.6	104.2	95.6	101.6	103.3	104.7	106.2	99.5	109.3	98.6
2014	112.5	111.6	112.4	116.9	117.7	109.9	109.7	111.9	112.0	111.8	99.4	117.6	102.5
2015	116.8	114.2	111.4	131.1	158.2	113.7	78.4	123.6	115.4	118.7	99.8	127.8	102.6
2016	119.2	115.3	106.6	153.0	150.6	116.1	45.6	132.5	113.3	123.9	99.5	135.8	101.0
2017	124.1	120.0	111.1	157.9	130.3	110.8	63.4	137.7	116.5	132.4	105.2	145.7	105.3
2018	130.0	127.7	115.5	160.0	128.0	104.5	80.4	139.7	123.9	142.5	119.5	153.4	111.4
2019	134.1	133.2	117.8	162.4	135.2	112.3	79.1	139.0	128.0	147.8	123.3	159.4	113.9
2020	130.5	126.1	103.1	160.2	117.0	107.0	49.4	119.8	117.3	157.9	135.9	168.0	108.3
2021	140.7	135.4	94.8	148.1	115.7	91.8	55.0	98.9	132.7	181.0	153.5	193.9	123.5
2019													
1st quarter	132.2	131.3	113.6	158.2	137.8	94.6	79.0	139.7	128.7	147.0	121.4	159.3	113.2
2nd quarter	134.2	133.4	117.5	158.5	136.6	110.2	82.0	138.5	129.5	148.7	125.4	159.6	115.1
3rd quarter	135.2	134.4	121.4	165.3	134.2	120.4	83.3	140.0	127.8	147.3	120.4	160.2	115.6
4th quarter	134.9	133.8	118.9	167.5	132.1	123.9	72.2	137.8	126.2	148.2	125.8	158.6	111.7
2020													
1st quarter	134.1	131.0	118.6	171.4	126.0	120.3	75.8	133.4	118.8	144.3	120.8	155.4	109.0
2nd quarter	122.4	119.7	101.3	162.9	116.4	106.6	39.9	121.7	106.2	151.5	133.4	159.4	102.9
3rd quarter	130.1	124.9	97.2	155.5	115.5	103.2	37.9	114.9	118.6	164.8	141.6	175.5	108.2
4th quarter	135.5	128.7	95.1	150.9	110.1	97.8	44.2	109.3	125.8	171.0	147.7	181.7	113.1
2021													
1st quarter	139.7	132.7	96.4	151.2	114.9	96.1	51.3	104.7	130.0	181.2	162.1	189.3	115.1
2nd quarter	140.9	135.6	95.7	149.8	118.3	93.0	54.7	98.8	133.8	177.5	145.1	193.2	123.5
3rd quarter	140.6	136.2	94.7	149.8	115.5	90.8	55.8	95.8	133.0	176.9	149.3	189.9	125.5
4th quarter	141.5	137.1	92.6	141.5	114.0	87.2	58.3	96.5	133.9	188.4	157.4	203.2	129.7

[1]See notes and definitions.

Table 5-4. Chain-Type Quantity Indexes for Private Fixed Investment by Type—*Continued*

(Index numbers, 2012 = 100, quarterly data are seasonally adjusted.)   NIPA Table 5.3.3

Year and quarter	Equipment—*Continued*		Intellectual property				Residential							
									Residential structures					
										Permanent site				
	Transportation equipment	Other nonresidential equipment	Total	Software 2	Research and development 3	Entertainment, literary, and artistic originals	Total	Total	Total	Total	Single family	Multifamily	Other residential structures	Residential equipment
1960	16.5	18.9	3.5	0.0	8.0	17.5	49.9	51.7	97.3	92.6	114.5	25.8	8.6
1961	15.6	18.7	3.9	0.0	8.5	21.1	50.1	51.9	96.8	87.7	144.3	26.4	8.6
1962	19.2	20.0	4.0	0.0	9.2	20.2	54.9	56.9	110.4	93.5	209.8	26.7	9.1
1963	18.6	23.2	4.4	0.1	9.9	21.7	61.3	63.6	125.2	99.9	281.6	28.8	10.2
1964	21.0	25.8	4.6	0.1	10.6	20.6	65.0	67.4	133.7	109.6	279.7	30.0	10.9
1965	26.3	28.6	5.2	0.1	11.9	22.9	63.4	65.5	127.8	107.1	251.4	30.3	12.2
1966	29.0	32.2	5.9	0.2	13.3	25.0	58.0	59.9	112.1	95.4	210.8	30.2	12.5
1967	28.0	30.4	6.4	0.3	14.7	24.8	56.5	58.3	106.9	93.5	183.1	30.6	12.8
1968	33.7	30.8	6.9	0.3	15.9	25.9	64.2	66.1	125.6	102.7	264.5	32.3	15.3
1969	35.0	32.8	7.2	0.4	16.9	24.5	66.2	68.0	129.2	97.6	329.1	33.3	17.4
1970	28.7	34.3	7.2	0.5	17.0	21.4	62.7	64.2	116.9	84.8	322.1	34.1	18.9
1971	31.0	34.2	7.2	0.6	16.9	21.1	79.4	81.6	157.5	117.7	409.9	38.6	21.3
1972	36.1	38.7	7.8	0.7	17.7	22.8	93.2	95.7	190.6	139.9	513.2	42.3	25.5
1973	43.4	45.2	8.1	0.7	18.9	21.8	92.6	94.8	189.7	136.8	527.6	41.4	28.6
1974	39.2	44.7	8.4	0.9	19.0	22.1	74.5	75.8	137.3	105.0	339.7	40.8	29.2
1975	33.8	41.3	8.5	1.0	18.7	21.4	65.5	66.5	105.1	95.9	151.5	44.1	27.2
1976	37.6	41.7	9.4	1.1	19.9	27.2	80.0	81.6	138.1	133.5	146.8	49.1	28.6
1977	45.7	46.9	10.0	1.1	20.9	30.3	96.4	98.5	178.2	171.5	194.6	53.2	31.3
1978	50.5	51.7	10.7	1.4	22.6	29.8	102.8	105.0	186.4	177.1	219.2	58.7	34.0
1979	52.7	52.7	11.9	1.7	24.2	34.2	98.9	100.8	174.4	157.0	267.8	58.7	37.3
1980	43.0	47.3	12.5	2.0	25.9	31.0	78.2	79.3	122.5	103.2	239.7	54.1	37.3
1981	41.8	48.6	13.9	2.3	27.5	37.4	71.8	72.6	113.0	93.9	230.6	49.1	37.3
1982	37.1	42.1	14.8	2.7	29.0	37.7	58.8	59.1	88.1	72.0	187.9	42.2	35.8
1983	41.8	40.5	15.9	3.2	30.6	39.7	83.5	84.6	143.9	125.0	257.3	50.6	40.0
1984	49.7	45.9	18.1	4.0	33.7	44.3	95.8	97.1	169.1	145.1	314.5	56.1	44.3
1985	51.7	46.3	19.7	4.7	36.6	44.1	98.0	99.2	166.9	143.8	306.4	60.4	47.8
1986	49.7	45.5	21.1	5.3	38.1	48.7	110.1	111.6	186.3	164.6	315.4	68.7	51.7
1987	47.3	46.8	21.9	6.1	38.8	47.9	112.3	113.8	188.8	177.9	248.9	70.6	53.8
1988	50.0	49.0	23.5	7.0	40.9	48.4	111.3	112.7	182.1	175.7	212.4	72.5	55.7
1989	45.1	54.7	26.2	9.0	43.7	50.6	107.7	108.9	177.6	170.7	211.8	69.3	56.0
1990	44.5	52.7	28.4	10.5	46.5	52.4	98.6	99.5	160.4	155.1	184.8	64.3	54.3
1991	43.3	45.0	30.3	11.3	49.9	52.9	89.8	90.5	138.1	135.9	142.4	62.5	52.2
1992	44.3	44.8	32.0	13.0	50.8	55.5	102.2	103.3	161.0	165.1	121.0	69.5	53.8
1993	52.8	49.0	33.4	14.7	50.6	58.5	110.5	111.8	171.9	180.8	97.6	76.6	54.8
1994	61.8	53.0	34.7	16.1	50.9	61.6	120.4	122.1	192.4	200.1	126.1	81.1	55.2
1995	66.5	55.8	37.1	17.6	53.7	66.7	116.3	117.8	179.7	181.6	156.3	81.5	55.9
1996	68.7	57.9	41.3	20.6	58.8	71.5	125.9	127.7	196.6	198.4	172.8	87.2	55.6
1997	73.7	63.5	46.7	26.9	62.8	73.6	128.9	130.8	197.7	197.8	186.1	91.4	55.2
1998	79.7	70.0	51.8	32.6	67.1	77.1	140.0	142.2	216.5	219.4	184.1	98.5	59.1
1999	94.0	71.9	58.6	40.6	72.4	79.4	148.8	151.0	232.5	235.6	198.7	103.2	65.3
2000	92.1	75.9	64.1	45.8	78.3	84.1	149.8	151.9	234.4	238.2	195.3	103.4	69.4
2001	83.4	75.3	64.8	46.3	79.9	81.5	151.2	153.2	235.8	238.5	203.8	104.7	70.7
2002	75.4	74.7	64.3	46.1	77.9	85.6	160.3	162.6	245.3	247.8	214.5	113.8	72.8
2003	69.8	79.8	66.8	49.1	78.5	92.0	174.9	177.4	269.3	274.2	220.2	123.3	77.3
2004	79.5	85.6	70.0	54.9	79.2	93.4	192.3	195.1	300.5	307.1	237.3	133.1	86.2
2005	89.2	93.9	75.2	60.1	83.5	101.2	204.9	207.9	321.5	327.8	260.9	141.1	90.0
2006	95.9	97.8	79.5	63.8	89.2	102.3	189.5	192.1	293.6	295.8	262.6	132.4	91.7
2007	91.8	96.6	84.5	70.2	94.5	99.8	154.1	155.8	218.5	214.7	232.6	119.0	89.1
2008	72.0	91.9	87.7	76.0	97.2	94.1	116.8	117.6	145.1	134.9	204.5	101.5	86.3
2009	33.7	73.3	87.3	78.2	94.9	90.4	91.5	91.8	87.0	79.7	130.1	94.5	80.1
2010	65.7	82.5	89.7	81.2	95.2	99.0	88.7	88.7	83.5	86.6	65.3	91.7	87.9
2011	84.5	91.4	95.3	90.1	99.2	98.2	88.5	88.4	80.6	82.6	68.2	92.9	95.4
2012	100.0	100.0	100.0	100.0	100.0	100.0	100.0	100.0	100.0	100.0	100.0	100.0	100.0
2013	110.8	102.2	105.4	105.6	106.5	100.2	112.4	112.5	124.5	122.6	136.0	105.5	107.9
2014	123.1	110.3	110.5	112.2	110.7	103.6	116.7	116.7	136.1	130.1	172.3	105.4	117.3
2015	136.0	103.0	114.7	117.7	113.9	107.5	128.6	128.6	152.2	145.0	195.4	114.9	127.5
2016	128.3	97.0	124.9	130.1	123.5	111.9	137.1	137.1	162.1	152.5	219.2	122.5	137.9
2017	127.1	97.0	132.0	144.3	125.9	115.4	142.6	142.5	169.3	162.7	209.5	127.0	147.0
2018	133.3	103.7	142.7	160.7	134.0	119.2	141.7	141.6	172.4	167.2	205.3	123.7	149.2
2019	137.0	108.2	153.0	171.9	145.1	121.8	140.4	140.3	164.9	156.6	214.0	126.1	150.4
2020	88.9	106.4	157.3	184.6	146.4	113.4	150.0	149.8	174.5	166.4	223.1	135.6	160.4
2021	101.8	115.5	173.1	209.2	158.5	118.1	163.8	163.7	205.3	196.9	256.0	139.5	175.6
2019													
1st quarter	142.9	106.7	149.2	167.2	141.5	121.3	138.7	138.6	162.7	153.0	219.8	124.6	146.1
2nd quarter	139.9	109.1	151.9	169.6	144.8	121.2	140.1	139.9	164.3	155.7	215.8	125.8	149.2
3rd quarter	134.0	109.1	154.1	173.2	146.3	122.1	141.3	141.2	165.6	158.0	211.4	127.0	152.3
4th quarter	131.3	107.7	156.6	177.8	147.8	122.6	141.7	141.5	166.9	159.9	209.1	126.8	154.0
2020													
1st quarter	110.1	105.6	158.1	182.8	147.7	120.0	148.4	148.3	174.7	168.0	215.5	133.0	154.5
2nd quarter	65.4	96.9	153.7	180.9	142.3	112.8	135.4	135.1	160.3	152.3	208.4	120.4	157.9
3rd quarter	82.9	109.8	156.7	185.1	145.8	109.7	152.3	152.0	169.6	159.4	229.8	141.9	169.3
4th quarter	97.0	113.5	160.6	189.7	149.6	111.2	163.9	164.0	193.5	186.0	238.7	146.9	159.7
2021													
1st quarter	98.7	115.6	166.5	201.1	153.2	111.2	169.1	169.0	206.2	198.8	251.2	147.4	179.5
2nd quarter	109.7	116.5	171.5	207.9	157.3	114.4	163.9	163.7	207.9	199.5	258.7	138.0	181.2
3rd quarter	104.9	116.3	175.3	212.5	160.0	120.0	160.7	160.5	204.9	196.2	257.6	134.8	172.9
4th quarter	94.0	113.5	179.1	215.4	163.7	126.7	161.6	161.5	202.1	193.2	256.5	137.9	168.6

2Excludes software "embedded," or bundled, in computers and other equipment.
3Excludes software development.

Table 5-5A. Current-Cost Net Stock of Fixed Assets: Recent Data

(Billions of dollars, year-end estimates.)

Year	Total	Private						Government							
		Total	Nonresidential				Resi-dential	Total	Nonresidential				Resi-dential	Federal	State and local
			Total	Equip-ment	Struc-tures	Intellec-tual property products			Total	Equip-ment	Struc-tures	Intellect-ual property products			
1955	1 197.2	888.8	457.0	141.2	296.3	19.6	431.7	308.4	301.1	68.3	219.5	13.3	7.3	158.3	150.0
1956	1 301.6	958.5	505.5	158.6	324.9	22.1	452.9	343.1	334.5	72.4	246.2	15.9	8.6	173.1	170.0
1957	1 369.5	1 008.9	540.6	172.9	343.3	24.4	468.3	360.6	351.6	74.7	257.9	19.0	9.0	182.4	178.2
1958	1 415.1	1 034.0	551.3	178.0	346.9	26.4	482.6	381.1	371.3	76.2	273.0	22.1	9.8	191.4	189.7
1959	1 471.2	1 078.1	573.9	186.6	358.4	29.0	504.1	393.1	382.4	80.5	277.0	25.0	10.7	198.0	195.1
1960	1 520.5	1 111.0	586.9	192.7	363.0	31.1	524.1	409.6	398.2	83.5	286.7	28.1	11.3	205.2	204.4
1961	1 580.2	1 147.6	604.3	196.1	374.6	33.7	543.3	432.6	420.5	87.5	301.4	31.6	12.1	215.7	216.8
1962	1 652.8	1 190.4	626.8	203.7	387.2	35.9	563.6	462.4	449.5	94.6	319.6	35.3	12.9	230.3	232.2
1963	1 717.5	1 228.7	650.6	212.3	399.5	38.9	578.1	488.8	475.6	96.7	338.3	40.6	13.2	240.7	248.1
1964	1 829.7	1 314.0	689.3	224.9	422.5	41.9	624.6	515.7	501.8	98.9	356.6	46.3	14.0	251.0	264.8
1965	1 954.3	1 402.9	738.8	242.5	450.6	45.8	664.0	551.5	536.8	100.6	384.0	52.2	14.7	263.0	288.5
1966	2 119.9	1 522.1	804.3	270.0	483.7	50.5	717.8	597.8	582.0	104.3	418.6	59.1	15.7	278.9	318.9
1967	2 285.4	1 636.6	871.2	296.2	518.7	56.3	765.3	648.8	632.3	110.2	455.6	66.6	16.5	299.8	349.0
1968	2 511.4	1 804.7	957.9	326.5	568.5	62.8	846.9	706.6	688.1	114.1	499.0	75.1	18.5	319.6	387.1
1969	2 744.0	1 962.9	1 055.8	360.1	625.2	70.5	907.1	781.1	760.5	117.7	558.0	84.8	20.6	343.0	438.0
1970	2 990.8	2 121.0	1 161.7	394.8	689.4	77.5	959.3	869.8	847.8	123.2	629.9	94.7	21.9	370.2	499.6
1971	3 294.5	2 352.7	1 275.1	422.5	770.1	82.5	1 077.6	941.9	917.3	123.3	691.3	102.6	24.6	391.2	550.7
1972	3 621.8	2 594.0	1 385.7	455.1	841.9	88.7	1 208.2	1 027.9	1 000.3	127.7	761.8	110.8	27.5	424.7	603.1
1973	4 110.6	2 946.9	1 560.5	507.1	955.0	98.4	1 386.4	1 163.7	1 132.6	135.9	872.9	123.8	31.1	470.8	692.9
1974	4 887.7	3 468.3	1 893.8	625.5	1 156.4	111.9	1 574.5	1 419.4	1 384.7	149.1	1 096.7	138.9	34.7	539.7	879.7
1975	5 277.3	3 786.4	2 083.8	716.2	1 246.2	121.5	1 702.6	1 490.9	1 452.8	165.0	1 138.2	149.6	38.0	572.1	918.8
1976	5 747.3	4 168.9	2 280.1	792.5	1 354.7	132.9	1 888.7	1 578.5	1 536.0	180.7	1 194.5	160.8	42.5	619.5	958.9
1977	6 415.5	4 735.7	2 532.5	891.6	1 495.1	145.8	2 203.2	1 679.7	1 630.9	198.3	1 258.6	174.1	48.9	656.0	1 023.7
1978	7 261.1	5 412.9	2 870.3	1 018.0	1 689.2	163.2	2 542.5	1 848.2	1 791.7	222.5	1 378.7	190.6	56.5	722.1	1 126.1
1979	8 360.7	6 264.5	3 313.9	1 181.9	1 945.2	186.8	2 950.5	2 096.2	2 028.9	236.7	1 578.9	213.3	67.3	800.2	1 296.0
1980	9 512.5	7 118.0	3 800.4	1 369.9	2 216.6	213.8	3 317.6	2 394.5	2 320.8	260.3	1 819.6	240.9	73.7	888.6	1 505.9
1981	10 490.4	7 860.3	4 300.0	1 528.5	2 526.7	244.9	3 560.2	2 630.1	2 549.3	286.7	1 992.5	270.1	80.8	960.0	1 670.1
1982	11 083.9	8 297.0	4 588.9	1 619.9	2 694.9	274.1	3 708.0	2 787.0	2 701.3	315.1	2 092.4	293.8	85.7	1 024.5	1 762.5
1983	11 468.9	8 599.6	4 744.7	1 670.5	2 770.2	304.1	3 854.8	2 869.3	2 773.3	345.2	2 110.8	317.3	96.0	1 084.6	1 784.7
1984	12 140.1	9 112.5	5 041.0	1 758.8	2 943.8	338.5	4 071.5	3 027.5	2 928.0	404.3	2 182.7	341.0	99.5	1 182.2	1 845.4
1985	12 759.0	9 619.0	5 332.4	1 858.0	3 101.8	372.6	4 286.6	3 140.0	3 039.6	400.2	2 274.6	364.7	100.4	1 210.4	1 929.6
1986	13 548.2	10 230.6	5 603.6	1 964.7	3 232.5	406.4	4 627.0	3 317.6	3 213.7	413.1	2 415.0	385.6	103.9	1 260.1	2 057.5
1987	14 342.5	10 843.5	5 919.1	2 055.3	3 415.1	448.7	4 924.4	3 499.0	3 385.6	431.0	2 538.2	416.3	113.4	1 318.2	2 180.8
1988	15 228.3	11 536.2	6 311.3	2 178.1	3 641.8	491.5	5 224.9	3 692.1	3 563.5	466.3	2 648.8	448.4	128.6	1 405.8	2 286.3
1989	16 093.7	12 203.1	6 699.8	2 300.6	3 858.7	540.5	5 503.2	3 890.7	3 753.2	498.4	2 780.9	474.0	137.4	1 477.7	2 413.0
1990	16 856.4	12 773.6	7 071.3	2 423.7	4 055.4	592.3	5 702.3	4 082.8	3 940.9	534.7	2 907.9	498.2	141.9	1 541.0	2 541.8
1991	17 273.0	13 058.9	7 242.6	2 482.2	4 116.7	643.6	5 816.3	4 214.1	4 071.3	559.1	2 994.6	517.6	142.8	1 592.5	2 621.5
1992	17 999.5	13 608.9	7 487.0	2 544.3	4 251.0	691.7	6 121.9	4 390.6	4 239.5	585.5	3 120.0	534.0	151.1	1 652.1	2 738.4
1993	18 900.8	14 321.2	7 837.6	2 642.4	4 458.5	736.6	6 483.7	4 579.6	4 417.8	608.9	3 262.5	546.4	161.8	1 704.8	2 874.8
1994	20 027.3	15 202.7	8 272.9	2 784.9	4 696.8	791.2	6 929.8	4 824.5	4 652.0	634.4	3 452.8	564.8	172.6	1 770.4	3 054.1
1995	20 999.8	15 951.3	8 723.3	2 959.2	4 913.2	851.0	7 228.0	5 048.5	4 869.7	641.7	3 648.7	579.2	178.8	1 811.0	3 237.5
1996	22 001.5	16 767.8	9 152.3	3 104.1	5 136.2	912.1	7 615.4	5 233.7	5 047.1	633.9	3 826.7	586.4	186.6	1 833.8	3 399.9
1997	23 170.1	17 703.7	9 674.8	3 235.2	5 445.7	993.8	8 029.0	5 466.3	5 271.2	629.5	4 043.3	598.5	195.1	1 864.3	3 602.0
1998	24 472.3	18 775.2	10 226.6	3 384.7	5 759.2	1 082.7	8 548.6	5 697.1	5 492.1	639.3	4 240.2	612.6	205.0	1 902.5	3 794.6
1999	26 042.8	20 027.0	10 849.4	3 578.7	6 063.8	1 206.8	9 177.6	6 015.7	5 798.0	660.8	4 503.0	634.2	217.8	1 967.3	4 048.4
2000	27 759.9	21 418.9	11 608.8	3 805.2	6 468.4	1 335.1	9 810.2	6 341.0	6 111.4	655.2	4 799.9	656.3	229.6	2 003.8	4 337.2
2001	29 310.4	22 706.4	12 189.4	3 913.4	6 880.7	1 395.2	10 517.0	6 604.0	6 359.8	650.9	5 040.4	668.5	244.2	2 026.4	4 577.6
2002	30 737.0	23 838.3	12 615.9	3 959.5	7 212.5	1 444.0	11 222.4	6 898.7	6 641.1	666.8	5 285.2	689.1	257.6	2 077.6	4 821.1
2003	32 394.9	25 197.2	13 036.2	4 000.4	7 514.3	1 521.6	12 161.0	7 197.7	6 922.0	685.7	5 510.1	726.2	275.7	2 149.8	5 047.9
2004	35 711.1	27 734.8	14 150.5	4 225.9	8 334.0	1 590.6	13 584.3	7 976.3	7 673.3	711.2	6 199.5	762.6	303.0	2 289.1	5 687.2
2005	39 293.0	30 580.2	15 429.8	4 423.0	9 311.4	1 695.4	15 150.4	8 712.8	8 380.8	735.3	6 842.1	803.4	332.0	2 432.9	6 279.9
2006	42 509.6	32 900.5	16 707.3	4 729.2	10 180.9	1 797.2	16 193.2	9 609.2	9 262.1	768.0	7 654.8	839.3	347.0	2 579.5	7 029.7
2007	44 415.9	34 061.0	17 653.8	4 952.1	10 772.1	1 929.6	16 407.2	10 354.9	10 010.1	803.6	8 316.4	890.1	344.8	2 709.8	7 645.1
2008	45 920.8	34 882.8	18 787.1	5 200.2	11 557.2	2 029.7	16 095.7	11 038.0	10 702.1	855.2	8 919.1	927.8	335.9	2 828.7	8 209.3
2009	45 085.8	33 995.6	18 237.6	5 120.2	11 029.7	2 087.7	15 758.0	11 090.2	10 760.4	885.7	8 918.4	956.4	329.8	2 838.4	8 251.8
2010	45 984.7	34 467.5	18 684.5	5 224.0	11 286.3	2 174.2	15 783.0	11 517.2	11 184.7	923.4	9 249.1	1 012.2	332.5	2 955.8	8 561.4
2011	47 576.5	35 444.0	19 551.3	5 459.7	11 799.6	2 292.0	15 892.7	12 132.5	11 795.5	954.8	9 800.5	1 040.2	337.0	3 061.3	9 071.2
2012	49 092.1	36 569.3	20 216.9	5 699.6	12 126.7	2 390.6	16 352.4	12 522.8	12 175.1	969.0	10 142.0	1 064.1	347.6	3 126.7	9 396.0
2013	51 510.7	38 567.6	21 073.3	5 897.2	12 641.7	2 534.5	17 494.3	12 943.2	12 572.0	979.9	10 492.1	1 100.0	371.1	3 204.8	9 738.4
2014	53 585.1	40 346.1	22 037.1	6 138.8	13 245.0	2 653.3	18 309.0	13 238.9	12 854.9	992.4	10 747.2	1 115.3	384.0	3 248.7	9 990.2
2015	54 879.1	41 443.7	22 487.0	6 307.0	13 442.6	2 737.3	18 956.7	13 435.5	13 044.2	990.7	10 935.0	1 118.5	391.3	3 250.9	10 184.5
2016	57 158.8	43 342.2	23 130.4	6 460.2	13 765.2	2 905.0	20 211.9	13 816.6	13 401.0	995.6	11 266.3	1 139.2	415.5	3 305.2	10 511.3
2017	59 521.3	45 154.9	24 000.4	6 650.9	14 249.5	3 100.0	21 154.5	14 366.5	13 939.2	1 014.1	11 743.1	1 181.9	427.3	3 396.7	10 969.8
2018	62 690.5	47 599.6	25 252.2	6 955.9	14 982.4	3 313.9	22 347.4	15 090.9	14 644.4	1 050.2	12 361.1	1 233.0	446.5	3 521.3	11 569.6
2019	65 150.4	49 540.9	26 411.1	7 197.4	15 683.4	3 530.4	23 129.8	15 609.5	15 149.4	1 079.8	12 805.1	1 264.6	460.0	3 603.7	12 005.7
2020	67 866.4	51 719.6	27 014.3	7 335.6	15 865.5	3 813.1	24 705.4	16 146.7	15 657.1	1 126.3	13 197.7	1 333.1	489.7	3 734.0	12 412.8

Table 5-5B. Current-Cost Net Stock of Fixed Assets: Historical Data

(Billions of dollars, year-end estimates.)

Year	Total	Private						Government							
		Total	Nonresidential				Residential	Total	Nonresidential				Residential	Federal	State and local
			Total	Equipment	Structures	Intellectual property products			Total	Equipment	Structures	Intellectual property products			
1925	261.7	223.4	127.0	31.1	94.0	1.9	96.4	38.3	38.3	2.6	35.6	0.1	0.0	8.9	29.4
1926	270.5	231.6	131.5	32.8	96.7	2.0	100.0	38.9	38.9	2.6	36.2	0.1	0.0	8.8	30.1
1927	277.2	236.9	134.2	33.5	98.5	2.1	102.7	40.3	40.3	2.6	37.7	0.1	0.0	8.6	31.7
1928	289.2	248.6	137.8	34.2	101.3	2.3	110.8	40.7	40.7	2.5	38.0	0.1	0.0	8.3	32.4
1929	294.4	251.7	137.1	34.3	100.3	2.5	114.6	42.7	42.7	2.5	40.0	0.2	0.0	8.9	33.8
1930	281.7	239.4	130.2	32.7	95.0	2.5	109.2	42.3	42.3	2.4	39.7	0.2	0.0	8.4	33.9
1931	245.5	205.4	116.2	29.7	84.0	2.5	89.2	40.0	40.0	2.4	37.4	0.3	0.0	7.8	32.3
1932	222.3	187.6	107.6	26.7	78.6	2.4	79.9	34.7	34.7	2.3	32.1	0.3	0.0	7.5	27.2
1933	236.3	196.5	109.3	26.4	80.5	2.4	87.2	39.8	39.8	2.3	37.1	0.4	0.0	8.5	31.3
1934	246.0	198.6	110.6	26.5	81.6	2.6	87.9	47.4	47.4	2.5	44.5	0.4	0.0	9.4	38.0
1935	247.3	199.5	110.3	25.9	81.6	2.8	89.2	47.7	47.7	2.6	44.6	0.4	0.0	10.5	37.2
1936	275.1	220.4	121.4	27.8	90.4	3.1	99.1	54.7	54.5	2.7	51.3	0.5	0.1	12.1	42.5
1937	289.9	231.7	126.5	29.9	93.1	3.4	105.2	58.1	57.9	3.0	54.4	0.5	0.3	13.4	44.7
1938	292.7	232.0	125.2	29.9	91.6	3.7	106.8	60.7	60.4	3.1	56.7	0.6	0.3	14.2	46.5
1939	298.2	235.6	125.5	30.5	91.0	4.0	110.1	62.6	62.2	3.3	58.3	0.6	0.4	14.8	47.7
1940	320.5	254.4	133.6	32.8	96.5	4.3	120.8	66.1	65.6	3.7	61.3	0.6	0.6	16.8	49.3
1941	365.5	282.8	151.0	37.6	108.2	5.1	131.9	82.7	81.6	7.1	73.6	0.9	1.1	27.1	55.6
1942	424.9	302.3	160.5	38.5	115.9	6.0	141.8	122.5	120.6	21.0	98.3	1.3	1.9	57.5	65.0
1943	478.7	317.1	163.3	38.9	117.6	6.8	153.8	161.6	158.6	46.5	109.9	2.2	3.0	92.5	69.1
1944	513.4	329.3	165.2	38.8	119.0	7.5	164.1	184.0	180.7	67.4	109.8	3.5	3.3	117.0	67.1
1945	554.9	353.0	180.2	44.2	127.9	8.1	172.8	201.9	198.3	78.5	115.5	4.3	3.6	135.7	66.2
1946	639.7	434.0	221.0	53.3	158.6	9.1	213.0	205.7	201.4	70.7	125.7	5.0	4.3	132.7	73.0
1947	734.2	516.6	265.7	65.5	189.6	10.6	250.9	217.6	212.0	60.0	146.4	5.5	5.6	124.2	93.3
1948	780.0	562.2	291.6	80.3	199.9	11.3	270.6	217.9	212.9	50.2	156.6	6.2	5.0	116.2	101.7
1949	785.1	581.1	296.7	84.6	200.4	11.7	284.4	204.0	198.9	42.4	149.7	6.8	5.1	106.7	97.2

Table 5-6A. Chain-Type Quantity Indexes for Net Stock of Fixed Assets: Recent Data

(Index numbers, 2012 = 100.)

Year	Total	Private						Government							
		Total	Nonresidential				Resi-dential	Total	Nonresidential				Resi-dential	Federal	State and local
			Total	Equip-ment	Struc-tures	Intellect-ual property products			Total	Equip-ment	Struc-tures	Intellect-ual property products			
1950	17.3	16.4	14.5	8.3	24.0	3.1	18.9	20.5	20.6	28.2	22.3	4.7	17.1	34.7	14.5
1951	18.0	17.0	15.0	8.8	24.6	3.2	19.6	21.4	21.4	30.3	23.0	5.0	18.3	36.2	15.1
1952	18.7	17.5	15.5	9.2	25.1	3.4	20.4	22.5	22.6	34.2	23.8	5.4	19.7	38.9	15.6
1953	19.4	18.2	16.0	9.7	25.8	3.7	21.1	23.8	23.9	38.4	24.7	5.9	20.9	41.7	16.2
1954	20.2	18.8	16.5	10.0	26.5	4.0	21.9	24.9	25.0	40.5	25.7	6.4	21.5	43.5	17.0
1955	21.0	19.6	17.1	10.5	27.2	4.3	22.9	25.8	25.9	41.3	26.8	7.1	21.9	44.5	17.9
1956	21.8	20.3	17.8	11.0	28.1	4.6	23.8	26.8	26.9	41.8	27.8	8.3	22.5	45.7	18.8
1957	22.5	21.0	18.4	11.4	28.9	5.0	24.5	27.8	27.9	42.5	28.8	9.6	23.5	46.9	19.7
1958	23.2	21.6	18.8	11.6	29.6	5.3	25.3	29.0	29.1	43.2	30.0	10.8	25.4	48.4	20.8
1959	24.1	22.3	19.3	11.9	30.4	5.6	26.3	30.3	30.4	45.0	31.2	12.1	27.5	50.3	21.9
1960	24.9	23.0	19.9	12.2	31.2	6.0	27.3	31.5	31.6	46.3	32.4	13.5	29.1	52.0	23.0
1961	25.8	23.7	20.5	12.5	32.0	6.4	28.2	33.0	33.1	48.3	33.7	15.0	31.0	54.1	24.1
1962	26.7	24.5	21.1	12.9	32.9	6.8	29.2	34.5	34.6	50.4	35.0	16.8	33.1	56.5	25.3
1963	27.8	25.4	21.8	13.4	33.8	7.2	30.3	36.1	36.1	51.6	36.4	19.2	34.2	58.5	26.7
1964	28.9	26.4	22.7	14.1	34.9	7.6	31.6	37.6	37.7	52.4	37.9	21.8	35.3	60.4	28.1
1965	30.1	27.5	23.8	15.1	36.2	8.2	32.7	39.2	39.2	52.5	39.4	24.4	36.6	62.0	29.6
1966	31.5	28.7	25.2	16.4	37.6	8.8	33.7	40.9	41.0	53.2	41.1	27.5	37.9	64.1	31.3
1967	32.7	29.8	26.4	17.4	39.0	9.5	34.6	42.8	42.8	54.4	42.8	30.5	39.4	66.1	33.0
1968	34.0	31.0	27.6	18.6	40.3	10.1	35.7	44.4	44.5	54.4	44.5	33.4	40.9	67.4	34.8
1969	35.3	32.3	28.9	19.8	41.7	10.8	36.8	45.8	45.9	53.9	46.0	36.0	42.7	68.3	36.5
1970	36.4	33.4	30.0	20.8	43.1	11.3	37.8	47.0	47.0	53.2	47.3	37.8	44.6	68.7	38.0
1971	37.5	34.5	31.1	21.6	44.4	11.6	39.3	47.9	47.9	51.0	48.6	39.3	46.4	68.3	39.3
1972	38.8	36.0	32.3	22.8	45.7	12.0	41.0	48.7	48.7	49.2	49.7	40.8	48.0	68.1	40.6
1973	40.2	37.5	33.7	24.4	47.2	12.5	42.7	49.5	49.5	47.7	50.8	42.1	49.5	68.0	41.8
1974	41.3	38.8	35.1	25.9	48.6	12.9	43.8	50.4	50.3	47.2	51.9	42.9	50.9	68.0	43.0
1975	42.2	39.7	36.0	26.8	49.6	13.2	44.7	51.2	51.1	46.8	52.8	43.7	52.6	68.0	44.1
1976	43.2	40.8	36.9	27.7	50.7	13.8	45.9	52.0	52.0	46.7	53.8	44.6	53.9	68.3	45.2
1977	44.5	42.2	38.2	29.1	51.8	14.4	47.6	52.8	52.7	46.7	54.6	45.7	55.1	68.6	46.2
1978	46.0	43.8	39.8	31.0	53.2	15.1	49.3	53.7	53.6	46.5	55.6	47.0	56.2	69.0	47.3
1979	47.6	45.6	41.6	33.0	54.9	16.1	50.9	54.7	54.6	46.9	56.7	48.4	57.2	69.6	48.5
1980	48.9	46.9	43.2	34.4	56.8	17.0	51.9	55.7	55.6	47.4	57.7	49.9	58.4	70.3	49.6
1981	50.1	48.3	44.9	35.8	59.0	18.2	52.7	56.6	56.5	48.2	58.5	51.5	59.9	71.2	50.5
1982	51.1	49.3	46.3	36.5	61.0	19.4	53.2	57.5	57.3	49.3	59.2	53.0	61.3	72.3	51.3
1983	52.2	50.4	47.5	37.2	62.5	20.6	54.3	58.4	58.3	51.1	59.8	54.7	63.0	73.7	52.0
1984	53.7	52.1	49.3	38.7	64.5	22.3	55.8	59.6	59.4	53.2	60.6	56.8	64.4	75.3	53.0
1985	55.4	53.8	51.2	40.2	66.8	24.1	57.2	61.0	60.9	56.0	61.6	59.5	66.2	77.4	54.2
1986	57.0	55.5	52.8	41.3	68.6	25.8	58.9	62.6	62.5	59.6	62.6	62.1	68.0	79.9	55.4
1987	58.6	57.0	54.2	42.2	70.3	27.5	60.7	64.3	64.1	63.3	63.8	64.9	70.0	82.5	56.7
1988	60.2	58.7	55.8	43.3	71.9	28.9	62.4	65.8	65.6	65.9	64.9	67.1	71.7	84.2	58.1
1989	61.7	60.2	57.4	44.5	73.5	31.0	63.8	67.2	67.0	68.7	66.0	68.8	73.3	85.6	59.5
1990	63.1	61.6	58.9	45.4	75.3	33.1	65.1	68.7	68.5	71.6	67.2	70.4	74.9	87.0	61.1
1991	64.2	62.6	59.9	45.9	76.5	35.2	66.0	70.1	69.9	73.7	68.5	71.3	76.4	87.9	62.7
1992	65.3	63.6	60.9	46.5	77.3	37.3	67.2	71.4	71.1	75.4	69.8	72.0	77.9	88.5	64.2
1993	66.6	65.0	62.2	47.9	78.2	39.2	68.6	72.4	72.2	76.1	71.1	72.3	79.3	88.7	65.7
1994	68.0	66.5	63.7	49.8	79.1	41.0	70.3	73.3	73.1	76.0	72.3	72.4	80.4	88.4	67.1
1995	69.6	68.3	65.5	52.1	80.2	43.0	71.8	74.4	74.1	76.0	73.6	72.4	81.8	88.2	68.7
1996	71.4	70.3	67.7	54.8	81.6	45.7	73.6	75.5	75.3	76.0	75.1	72.5	83.2	88.4	70.3
1997	73.3	72.5	70.2	57.8	83.2	49.0	75.4	76.6	76.3	75.5	76.6	72.8	84.6	87.9	72.0
1998	75.5	74.9	73.0	61.4	84.9	52.7	77.5	77.8	77.5	75.4	78.1	73.3	85.9	87.5	73.9
1999	77.9	77.6	76.0	65.5	86.6	57.1	79.7	79.2	78.9	75.8	79.7	73.9	87.1	87.3	75.9
2000	80.4	80.4	79.3	69.8	88.6	61.8	81.9	80.6	80.3	76.1	81.3	74.7	88.2	87.1	78.0
2001	82.5	82.7	81.7	72.6	90.3	65.3	84.0	82.1	81.8	76.4	83.1	76.0	89.3	87.0	80.2
2002	84.4	84.6	83.3	74.4	91.3	67.9	86.3	83.9	83.7	77.6	85.0	77.9	90.6	87.6	82.5
2003	86.4	86.6	84.7	76.3	92.2	70.5	89.0	85.8	85.6	78.7	86.9	80.2	91.7	88.5	84.8
2004	88.5	88.8	86.3	78.8	92.9	73.2	91.8	87.6	87.4	80.3	88.7	82.7	92.9	89.6	86.9
2005	90.6	91.1	88.1	82.0	93.6	76.4	94.6	89.2	89.0	82.3	90.1	85.4	93.8	90.7	88.6
2006	92.9	93.6	90.4	86.0	94.7	79.9	97.3	90.9	90.8	84.8	91.7	88.1	94.7	92.0	90.6
2007	95.0	95.7	93.0	90.0	96.3	83.9	99.1	92.7	92.6	87.8	93.3	90.6	95.5	93.3	92.5
2008	96.5	97.2	95.2	92.6	98.0	87.6	99.7	94.5	94.4	91.4	94.9	92.9	96.6	94.8	94.4
2009	97.2	97.6	95.8	91.9	98.8	90.4	99.8	96.2	96.1	94.5	96.4	95.0	97.6	96.4	96.1
2010	98.0	98.1	96.7	93.3	99.0	93.1	99.8	97.8	97.7	97.1	97.9	97.0	98.8	98.1	97.7
2011	98.9	98.9	98.1	96.1	99.4	96.5	99.8	99.1	99.1	98.8	99.1	98.7	99.7	99.3	99.0
2012	100.0	100.0	100.0	100.0	100.0	100.0	100.0	100.0	100.0	100.0	100.0	100.0	100.0	100.0	100.0
2013	101.2	101.4	102.0	104.0	100.8	103.9	100.7	100.7	100.8	100.2	100.8	101.0	100.0	100.0	101.0
2014	102.6	103.1	104.4	108.5	101.9	107.8	101.4	101.4	101.4	100.2	101.5	101.5	100.0	99.8	101.9
2015	104.1	104.8	106.7	112.8	103.0	111.9	102.5	102.1	102.2	100.0	102.4	102.1	100.0	99.6	103.0
2016	105.6	106.4	108.7	116.1	103.9	117.1	103.7	103.0	103.1	100.4	103.3	103.1	99.9	99.5	104.1
2017	106.9	108.0	110.8	119.3	104.8	122.5	104.7	103.9	104.0	101.4	104.3	104.5	99.9	99.8	105.3
2018	108.6	109.8	113.3	123.4	106.0	128.7	105.8	104.9	105.0	102.9	105.1	106.1	100.1	100.1	106.4
2019	110.3	111.8	115.9	127.6	107.2	135.6	107.1	105.9	106.1	105.3	106.0	107.5	100.4	100.8	107.6
2020	111.7	113.3	117.5	129.4	107.9	141.6	108.5	107.1	107.3	107.8	107.0	109.5	101.0	101.8	108.8

Table 5-6B. Chain-Type Quantity Indexes for Net Stock of Fixed Assets: Historical Data

(Index numbers, 2012 = 100.)

Year	Total	Private						Government							
		Total	Nonresidential				Resi-dential	Total	Nonresidential				Resi-dential	Federal	State and local
			Total	Equip-ment	Struc-tures	Intellect-ual property products			Total	Equip-ment	Struc-tures	Intellect-ual property products			
1925	10.6	11.5	10.6	4.8	19.8	0.7	13.1	5.5	5.7	2.5	8.0	0.10	0.00	4.5	6.7
1926	11.0	12.0	10.9	5.0	20.4	0.7	13.7	5.8	6.0	2.4	8.3	0.10	0.00	4.4	7.0
1927	11.4	12.4	11.2	5.1	21.0	0.8	14.2	6.0	6.2	2.4	8.7	0.10	0.00	4.3	7.5
1928	11.8	12.8	11.5	5.2	21.6	0.8	14.7	6.3	6.5	2.4	9.2	0.10	0.00	4.3	7.9
1929	12.1	13.2	11.9	5.4	22.2	0.9	15.0	6.6	6.8	2.5	9.6	0.10	0.00	4.3	8.4
1930	12.4	13.3	12.1	5.4	22.7	1.0	15.0	7.0	7.2	2.4	10.2	0.20	0.00	4.3	9.0
1931	12.5	13.3	12.0	5.2	22.8	1.1	15.1	7.3	7.6	2.5	10.7	0.30	0.10	4.4	9.6
1932	12.4	13.2	11.8	4.9	22.6	1.1	15.0	7.6	7.9	2.4	11.2	0.30	0.10	4.6	10.0
1933	12.4	13.0	11.6	4.7	22.4	1.2	14.9	7.9	8.1	2.4	11.5	0.40	0.10	4.8	10.2
1934	12.4	12.9	11.4	4.5	22.2	1.2	14.8	8.1	8.4	2.4	11.9	0.40	0.10	5.1	10.4
1935	12.4	12.9	11.3	4.5	22.0	1.3	14.8	8.4	8.7	2.6	12.3	0.40	0.20	5.6	10.7
1936	12.6	12.9	11.4	4.6	22.0	1.4	14.8	8.9	9.2	2.6	13.1	0.50	0.70	6.1	11.2
1937	12.8	13.0	11.6	4.8	22.1	1.5	14.9	9.3	9.6	2.7	13.6	0.50	1.30	6.5	11.6
1938	12.9	13.1	11.6	4.7	22.0	1.7	15.0	9.8	10.0	2.9	14.3	0.50	1.50	6.9	12.1
1939	13.2	13.2	11.6	4.8	22.0	1.8	15.2	10.3	10.5	3.1	15.0	0.60	1.90	7.3	12.8
1940	13.4	13.3	11.8	5.0	22.1	1.9	15.4	10.8	11.0	3.2	15.7	0.60	2.80	7.9	13.2
1941	13.9	13.6	12.0	5.2	22.2	2.1	15.7	12.3	12.5	6.1	17.0	0.90	5.20	11.9	13.5
1942	14.6	13.5	11.9	5.2	22.0	2.2	15.7	16.3	16.5	19.2	19.8	1.20	8.10	24.0	13.5
1943	15.2	13.4	11.8	5.1	21.8	2.3	15.6	20.8	21.0	45.0	20.9	1.70	12.00	38.7	13.4
1944	15.8	13.4	11.8	5.1	21.6	2.4	15.6	24.4	24.8	70.1	21.2	2.40	13.00	51.0	13.2
1945	16.1	13.5	12.0	5.4	21.6	2.5	15.5	25.8	26.2	79.2	21.4	3.00	13.40	55.8	13.1
1946	16.1	13.9	12.4	5.9	22.1	2.6	15.9	23.9	24.2	64.6	21.2	3.40	14.90	49.7	13.1
1947	16.2	14.5	13.0	6.7	22.5	2.8	16.5	22.3	22.5	50.9	21.1	3.70	15.30	43.8	13.3
1948	16.5	15.1	13.6	7.4	23.0	2.9	17.3	21.1	21.3	39.7	21.3	4.00	15.50	39.2	13.5
1949	16.8	15.7	14.0	7.8	23.4	3.0	17.9	20.8	20.9	33.9	21.8	4.30	16.40	36.9	14.0

Table 5-7. Capital Expenditures

(Millions of dollars, except totals are shown in billions.)

Capital expenditures	All companies												
	2008	2009	2010	2011	2012	2013	2014	2015	2016	2017	2018	2019	2020
TOTAL (billions)	1 374.2	1 090.7	1 105.7	1 243.0	1 424.2	1 491.3	1 597.9	1 642.0	1 574.8	1 678.8	. . .	1 919.2	1 706.4
Structures	562 381	449 545	428 713	471 779	570 489	581 836	643 590	642 859	599 707	665 642	. . .	770	675
New	522 999	422 780	394 517	442 745	534 696	549 359	606 980	589 689	543 758	616 850	. . .	703	624
Used	39 382	26 765	34 196	29 034	35 793	32 477	36 610	53 171	55 948	48 792	. . .	67	51
Equipment	811 779	641 149	676 989	771 177	853 661	909 477	954 261	999 122	975 138	101 318	. . .	1 150	1 031
New	765 279	606 576	639 214	730 033	800 519	856 012	898 581	941 297	924 954	956 582	. . .	1 077	968
Used	46 501	34 572	37 775	41 144	53 142	53 466	55 680	57 825	50 184	56 607	. . .	73	63

Capital expenditures	Companies with employees												
	2008	2009	2010	2011	2012	2013	2014	2015	2016	2017	2018	2019	2020
TOTAL (billions)	1 294.5	1 015.3	1 036.2	1 169.6	1 334.9	1 400.9	1 506.6	1 548.1	1 479.4	1 577.8	1 699.1	1 805.7	1 597.4
Structures	529 393	414 051	395 531	440 893	533 115	546 056	608 698	600 766	552 637	612 025	648	711	616
New	500 474	395 022	366 853	414 958	501 420	518 430	577 743	557 641	508 523	576 460	613	658	578
Used	28 919	19 030	28 678	25 935	31 695	27 625	30 955	43 126	44 114	35 565	36	53	38
Equipment	765 098	601 270	640 631	728 710	801 820	854 827	897 885	947 291	926 802	965 760	1 051	1 095	981
New	728 322	577 051	612 441	697 766	759 632	813 972	853 888	900 519	887 884	920 780	998	1 037	927
Used	36 776	24 219	28 190	30 944	42 189	40 855	43 996	46 772	38 918	44 981	53	58	55

Capital expenditures	Companies without employees												
	2008	2009	2010	2011	2012	2013	2014	205	2016	2017	2018	2019	2020
TOTAL (billions)	79.7	75.4	69.5	73.4	89.2	90.4	91.3	93.9	95.4	101.0	. . .	111.4	109.0
Structures	32 988	35 493	33 182	30 886	37 374	35 780	34 892	42 093	47 070	53 617	. . .	59	59
New	22 525	27 758	27 664	27 787	33 276	30 929	29 237	32 048	35 236	40 390	. . .	45	46
Used	10 463	7 735	5 518	3 099	4 098	4 851	5 655	10 045	11 834	13 227	. . .	14	13
Equipment	46 681	39 878	36 357	42 467	51 840	54 650	56 376	51 831	48 336	47 429	. . .	52	50
New	36 957	29 525	26 773	32 267	40 887	42 040	44 693	40 778	37 070	35 802	. . .	37	41
Used	9 724	10 353	9 585	10 200	10 953	12 610	11 684	11 053	11 266	11 627	. . .	15	8

. . . = Not available.

Table 5-8. Capital Expenditures for Structures and Equipment for Companies with Employees by Major Industry Sector

(Millions of dollars.)

Year and type of expenditure	Total	Forestry, fishing, and agricultural services (113–115)	Mining (21)	Utilities (22)	Construction (23)	Manufacturing (31–33)			Wholesale trade (42)	Retail trade (44–45)	Transportation and warehousing (48–49)	Information (51)
						Total	Durable goods industries (321, 327, 33)	Nondurable goods industries (31, 322–326)				
2011												
Total expenditures	1 169 604	3 063	165 693	98 047	21 778	192 441	110 151	82 290	35 745	68 131	72 722	100 057
Structures, total	440 893	529	124 508	46 729	2 867	36 339	17 394	18 946	7 988	27 332	29 026	20 152
Equipment, total	728 710	2 534	41 185	51 319	18 910	156 102	92 758	63 344	27 757	40 799	43 696	79 905
2012												
Total expenditures	1 334 421	3 149	196 653	124 958	23 555	203 119	113 299	89 820	40 852	77 567	81 792	106 537
Structures, total	533 042	496	150 653	70 940	1 975	43 080	20 181	22 900	9 367	33 443	32 397	23 263
Equipment, total	801 378	2 653	46 000	54 017	21 580	160 039	93 118	66 921	31 485	44 124	49 395	83 274
2013												
Total expenditures	1 400 883	2 965	202 213	111 310	27 562	221 345	121 494	99 850	37 505	77 520	92 616	123 881
Structures, total	546 056	492	152 441	58 051	2 545	46 594	20 303	26 291	9 659	33 865	37 645	33 297
Equipment, total	854 827	2 473	49 773	53 260	25 018	174 751	101 191	73 560	27 846	43 655	54 971	90 584
2014												
Total expenditures	1 506 582	3 985	230 776	118 895	30 277	231 089	124 797	106 292	44 758	82 402	111 010	132 049
Structures, total	608 698	952	187 348	63 844	3 815	50 481	19 520	30 962	12 288	35 564	40 557	33 315
Equipment, total	897 885	3 033	43 428	55 052	26 462	180 608	105 277	75 331	32 470	46 838	70 453	98 734
2015												
Total expenditures	1 548 057	3 322	174 069	130 514	33 276	245 123	127 714	117 409	42 378	85 963	116 633	132 671
Structures, total	600 766	598	135 552	71 277	2 600	54 716	22 845	31 871	12 624	37 005	42 490	30 161
Equipment, total	947 291	2 724	38 517	59 237	30 676	190 407	104 869	85 537	29 754	48 959	74 144	102 510
2016												
Total expenditures	1 479 439	4 561	92 641	133 455	35 979	243 595	122 898	120 698	43 768	86 931	109 650	142 911
Structures, total	552 637	559	75 865	73 533	4 302	57 171	22 759	34 412	13 290	39 098	35 717	32 303
Equipment, total	926 802	4 002	16 776	59 922	31 676	186 425	100 139	86 286	30 478	47 833	73 933	110 608
2017												
Total expenditures	1 577 785	4 497	134 380	133 888	34 989	247 013	129 121	117 891	43 977	90 493	108 538	158 888
Structures, total	612 025	750	108 370	66 586	3 251	57 732	24 206	33 526	14 000	38 739	40 439	34 432
Equipment, total	965 760	3 747	26 011	67 302	31 738	189 281	104 915	84 366	29 977	51 754	68 098	124 456
2018												
Total expenditures	1 699 123	4 653	153 370	151 043	38 979	258 073	137 785	120 288	42 799	89 233	122 356	175 084
Structures, total	648 379	716	114 089	78 323	4 045	58 915	26 336	32 579	12 762	38 864	44 618	43 490
Equipment, total	1 050 744	3 937	39 281	72 720	34 935	199 159	111 449	87 710	30 036	50 368	77 738	131 594
2019												
Total expenditures	1 805 748	4 057	160 757	172 889	50 765	272 737	142 092	130 645	40 241	98 808	130 765	176 766
Structures, total	711 093	840	116 459	90 820	8 084	65 813	27 619	38 194	10 125	42 835	54 949	51 422
Equipment, total	1 094 655	3 216	44 298	82 069	42 682	206 924	114 473	92 450	30 116	55 972	75 816	125 343
2020												
Total expenditures	1 597 437	3 246	97 076	182 207	53 199	258 059	130 072	127 987	36 016	105 535	98 262	169 654
Structures, total	616 011	551	66 101	96 534	10 805	68 741	27 666	41 075	9 576	43 617	39 213	47 783
Equipment, total	981 426	2 694	30 975	85 673	42 394	189 318	102 405	86 912	26 440	61 918	59 049	121 871

Table 5-8. Capital Expenditures for Structures and Equipment for Companies with Employees by Major Industry Sector—*Continued*

(Millions of dollars.)

Year and type of expenditure	Finance and insurance (52)	Real estate and rental and leasing (53)	Professional, scientific, and technical services (54)	Management of companies and enterprises (55)	Administrative and support and waste management (56)	Educational services (61)	Health care and social assistance (62)	Arts, entertainment, and recreation (71)	Accommodation and food services (72)	Other services, except public administration (81)	Structure and equipment expenditures serving multiple industries
2011											
Total expenditures	109 229	91 124	28 109	5 449	18 423	21 019	83 114	11 430	24 833	16 064	3 133
Structures, total	14 405	33 540	6 733	1 368	3 536	15 037	42 910	6 589	12 021	8 675	608
Equipment, total	94 823	57 583	21 376	4 081	14 887	5 982	40 204	4 841	12 811	7 389	2 524
2012											
Total expenditures	130 168	115 652	31 605	6 916	18 811	21 629	88 860	13 296	28 802	16 789	3 711
Structures, total	17 749	42 034	7 536	2 555	3 578	15 721	45 981	8 055	14 154	9 078	988
Equipment, total	112 419	73 618	24 069	4 361	15 233	5 908	42 879	5 241	14 649	7 711	2 722
2013											
Total expenditures	137 824	114 181	35 655	6 147	21 760	22 619	94 181	14 981	34 532	18 615	3 472
Structures, total	15 458	39 359	8 571	1 577	4 123	16 583	49 364	8 263	16 304	10 999	868
Equipment, total	122 366	74 821	27 084	4 570	17 637	6 036	44 817	6 718	18 228	7 616	2 604
2014											
Total expenditures	153 260	121 919	30 383	5 366	22 568	25 823	89 011	19 550	29 836	20 304	3 321
Structures, total	17 843	44 677	7 228	1 237	4 112	19 710	47 481	12 153	14 181	11 075	837
Equipment, total	135 417	77 241	23 156	4 128	18 456	6 114	41 531	7 397	15 654	9 230	2 484
2015											
Total expenditures	164 594	151 875	33 327	5 180	26 183	33 176	93 755	16 142	33 066	23 195	3 613
Structures, total	19 787	62 188	8 393	1 047	6 547	25 906	49 234	8 822	17 331	13 092	1 395
Equipment, total	144 807	89 688	24 933	4 133	19 636	7 270	44 521	7 321	15 734	10 103	2 218
2016											
Total expenditures	161 653	150 686	31 728	6 161	27 672	30 424	93 588	22 544	29 855	27 249	4 389
Structures, total	19 485	62 906	8 736	1 618	6 867	23 999	48 238	13 534	16 795	16 794	1 827
Equipment, total	142 168	87 779	22 992	4 543	20 805	6 425	45 350	9 010	13 059	10 456	2 562
2017											
Total expenditures	163 038	161 396	37 213	6 918	26 505	36 951	104 628	22 448	35 828	21 667	4 530
Structures, total	22 742	73 028	11 569	1 674	4 948	30 171	56 711	13 972	18 295	13 178	1 439
Equipment, total	140 297	88 368	25 643	5 244	21 557	6 781	47 917	8 476	17 533	8 489	3 091
2018											
Total expenditures	181 508	173 879	41 995	6 879	29 386	35 496	108 552	24 740	35 396	22 210	3 493
Structures, total	25 555	70 473	13 579	1 749	6 960	29 118	59 881	14 760	17 385	12 374	722
Equipment, total	155 953	103 406	28 416	5 130	22 426	6 378	48 671	9 979	18 011	9 836	2 770
2019											
Total expenditures	195 205	180 249	43 640	7 302	31 207	31 610	114 396	24 544	41 438	25 279	3 093
Structures, total	31 893	71 525	13 306	1 731	7 323	24 870	66 860	15 225	21 242	15 206	564
Equipment, total	163 312	108 723	30 334	5 571	23 885	6 740	47 536	9 318	20 196	10 073	2 529
2020											
Total expenditures	173 597	134 248	40 438	7 073	28 722	32 844	104 740	17 780	30 009	22 544	2 190
Structures, total	26 854	63 988	11 160	1 695	5 705	26 099	59 312	11 319	14 015	12 429	513
Equipment, total	146 743	70 260	29 278	5 378	23 017	6 745	45 428	6 460	15 993	10 115	1 677

NOTES AND DEFINITIONS, CHAPTER 5

Tables 5-1 through 5-4

Gross Saving and Investment Accounts

SOURCE: U.S. DEPARTMENT OF COMMERCE, BUREAU OF ECONOMIC ANALYSIS (BEA)

An explanation of NIPA data is described in the Notes and Definitions to Chapter 1. All quarterly series are shown at seasonally adjusted annual rates. Current and constant dollar values are in billions of dollars. Constant dollar values are in 2009 dollars. Indexes of quantity are based on the average for the year 2009, set to equal 100.

The 2013 revision included a major expansion of the investment accounts. Expenditures for research and development are now recognized as fixed investment. Before 2013, they were treated as if they were costs of producing this year's output. R&D spending by business, government, and nonprofit institutions serving households (NPISHs) is now counted as fixed investment. It is depreciated (with the estimated depreciation added to capital consumption allowances), so that there can be either positive or negative net investment in R&D. A similar treatment is now given to expenditures by private enterprises for the creation of entertainment, literary, and artistic originals. Finally, an expanded set of ownership transfer costs for residential fixed assets is recognized as fixed investment.

Results from the 2017 Annual Update of NIPA slightly revised the average growth rates of GDP between 2013 and 2016. Other revisions were incorporated include the Census Bureau's annual retail sales, construction, manufacturing plus others.

Definitions: Table 5-1

Gross saving is saving before the deduction of allowances for the consumption of fixed capital. It represents the amount of saving available to finance gross investment. *Net saving* is gross saving less allowances for fixed capital consumption. It represents the amount of saving available for financing expansion of the capital stock, and comprises net private saving (the sum of personal saving, undistributed corporate profits, and wage accruals less disbursements) and the net saving of federal, state, and local governments.

Personal saving is derived by subtracting personal outlays from disposable personal income. (See Chapter 4 for more information.) It is the current net saving of individuals (including proprietors of unincorporated businesses), nonprofit institutions that primarily serve individuals, life insurance carriers, retirement funds, private noninsured welfare funds, and private trust funds. Conceptually, personal saving may also be viewed as the sum for all persons (including institutions as previously

defined) of the net acquisition of financial assets and the change in physical assets, less the sum of net borrowing and consumption of fixed capital. In either case, it is defined to exclude capital gains. That is, it excludes profits on the increase in the value of homes, securities, and other property—whether realized or unrealized—and therefore includes the noncorporate inventory valuation adjustment and the capital consumption adjustment (IVA and CCAdj, respectively). (See notes and definitions to Chapter 1.)

The net saving of *Domestic corporate business* is corporate profits after tax less dividends plus the corporate IVA and corporate CCAdj. (See notes and definitions for Chapter 1.)

Government net saving was formerly called "current surplus or deficit (-) of general government." (See Chapter 6 for further detail from the government accounts.) Where current receipts of government exceed current expenditures, government has a current surplus (indicated by a positive value) and saving is made available to finance investment by government or other sectors—for example, by the repayment of debt, which can free up funds for private investment. Where current expenditures exceed current receipts, there is a government deficit (indicated by a negative value) and government must borrow, drawing on funds that would otherwise be available for private investment. In these accounts, current expenditures are defined to include a charge for the consumption of fixed capital.

Consumption of fixed capital is an accounting charge for the using-up of private and government fixed capital, including software, located in the United States. It is based on studies of prices of used equipment and structures in resale markets. As of the 2013 revision, it also includes estimated charges for the using-up of the research and development and other intellectual property capital now defined as investment spending.

For general government and nonprofit institutions that primarily serve individuals, consumption of fixed capital is recorded in government consumption expenditures and in personal consumption expenditures (PCE), respectively, and taken to be the value of the current services of the fixed capital assets owned and used by these entities and the estimated using-up of R&D and other intellectual property.

Private consumption of fixed capital consists of tax-return-based depreciation charges for corporations and nonfarm proprietorships and historical-cost depreciation (calculated by the Bureau of Economic Analysis [BEA] using a geometric pattern of price declines) for farm proprietorships, rental income of persons, and nonprofit institutions, minus the capital consumption adjustments. (In other words, in the NIPA treatment of saving, the amount of the CCAdj is taken out of book depreciation and added to income and profits—a reallocation from one form of gross saving to another.) It also includes the charges for the using-up of private R&D and other intellectual property, as described above.

Gross private domestic investment consists of gross private fixed investment and change in private inventories. (See the notes and definitions for Chapter 1.)

Gross government investment consists of federal, state, and local general government and government enterprise expenditures for fixed assets (structures, equipment, and intellectual property). Government inventory investment is included in government consumption expenditures. For further detail, see Chapter 6.

Capital account transactions, net are the net cash or in-kind transfers between the United States and the rest of the world that are linked to the acquisition or disposition of assets rather than the purchase or sale of currently-produced goods and services. When positive, it represents a net transfer from the United States to the rest of the world; when negative, it represents a net transfer to the United States from the rest of the world. This is a definitional category that was introduced in the 1999 revision of the NIPAs. Estimates are available only from 1982 forward. With the new treatment of disaster losses and disaster insurance introduced in the 2009 revision, this line will include disaster-related insurance payouts to the rest of the world less what is received from the rest of the world.

Net lending or net borrowing (-), NIPAs is equal to the international balance on current account as measured in the NIPAs (see Chapter 7) less capital account transactions, net. When positive, this represents net investment by the United States in the rest of the world; when negative, it represents net borrowing by the United States from the rest of the world. For data before 1982, net lending or net borrowing equals the NIPA balance on current account, because estimates of capital account transactions are not available.

By definition, gross national saving must equal the sum of gross domestic investment, capital account transactions, and net international lending (where net international borrowing appears as negative lending). In practice, due to differences in measurement, these two aggregates differ by the *statistical discrepancy* calculated in the product and income accounts. (See Chapter 1.) Gross saving is therefore equal to the sum of gross domestic investment, capital account transactions, and net international lending minus the statistical discrepancy. Where the statistical discrepancy is negative, it means that the sum of measured investment, capital transactions, and net international lending has fallen short of measured saving.

Net domestic investment is gross domestic investment minus consumption of fixed capital, calculated by the editors from the data shown in the table.

Gross national income is national income plus the consumption of fixed capital. (See Chapter 1 for further information.) This is a new concept introduced in the 2003 revision. It is conceptually equal to gross national product, but differs by the statistical discrepancy. Gross national income is an appropriate denominator for the national saving ratios. Saving was previously shown as a percentage of gross national product; in the revision, it is instead shown as a percentage of the income-side equivalent of gross national product. Since saving is measured as a residual from income, it is appropriate to involve consistent measurements—and consistent imperfections in those measurements—in both the numerator and the denominator of the fraction.

Definitions: Tables 5-2 through 5-4

Gross private fixed investment comprises both nonresidential and residential fixed investment. It consists of purchases of fixed assets, which are commodities that will be used in a production process for more than one year, including replacements and additions to the capital stock, and intellectual property, including software, research and development, and entertainment, literary, and artistic originals. It is "gross" in the sense that it is measured before a deduction for consumption of fixed capital. It covers investment by private businesses and nonprofit institutions in the United States, regardless of whether the investment is owned by U.S. residents. It does not include purchases of the same types of equipment, structures, or intellectual property by government agencies, which are included in government gross investment. It also does not include investment by U.S. residents in other countries.

Gross nonresidential fixed investment consists of structures, equipment, and intellectual property that are not related to personal residences.

Nonresidential structures consists of new construction, brokers' commissions on sales of structures, and net purchases (purchases less sales) of used structures by private business and by nonprofit institutions from government agencies. New construction includes hotels, motels, and mining exploration, shafts, and wells.

Other nonresidential structures consists primarily of religious, educational, vocational, lodging, railroads, farm, and amusement and recreational structures, net purchases of used structures, and brokers' commissions on the sale of structures.

Nonresidential equipment consists of private business purchases—on capital account—of new machinery, equipment, and vehicles; dealers' margins on sales of used equipment; and net purchases (purchases less sales) of used equipment from government agencies, persons, and the rest of the world. (However, it does not include the personal-use portion of equipment purchased for both business and personal use. This is included in PCE.)

Computers have displayed phenomenal growth in numbers and power not easily represented by index numbers or constant-dollar estimates at the scale shown in these tables. Zero entries shown in the quantity indexes for early years actually represent very small quantities. Because of rapid growth in computing power and declines in its price, constant-dollar measures are deemed not meaningful and are not calculated by BEA.

Other information processing includes communication equipment, nonmedical instruments, medical equipment and instruments, photocopy and related equipment, and office and accounting equipment.

Other nonresidential equipment consists primarily of furniture and fixtures, agricultural machinery, construction machinery, mining and oilfield machinery, service industry machinery, and electrical equipment not elsewhere classified.

Intellectual property comprises information processing software, research and development, and entertainment, literary, and artistic originals.

Software excludes the value of software "embedded," or bundled, in computers and other equipment, which is instead included in the value of that equipment.

Research and development consists of expenditures for both purchased and own-account R&D by businesses, NPISHs, and general governments. Government R&D expenditures are treated as investment regardless of whether the R&D is protected or made freely available to the public. Investment is measured as the sum of production costs.

Entertainment, literary, and other artistic originals include theatrical movies, long-lived television programs, books, music, and other miscellaneous entertainment.

Residential private fixed investment consists of both *structures* and residential producers' durable *equipment*—that is, equipment owned by landlords and rented to tenants. Investment in *structures* consists of new units, improvements to existing units, manufactured homes, brokers' commissions and other ownership transfer costs on the sale of residential property, and net purchases (purchases less sales) of used structures from government agencies.

Other residential structures consists primarily of manufactured homes, improvements, dormitories, net purchases of used structures, and brokers' commissions on the sale of residential structures.

Real gross private investment (Table 5-3) and *chain-type quantity indexes for private fixed investment* (Table 5-4) are defined and explained in the notes and definitions to Chapter 1. The chained-dollar (2012) estimates in Table 5-3 are constructed by applying the changes in the chain-type quantity indexes, as shown in Table 5-4, to the 2012 current-dollar values. Thus, they do not contain any information about time trends that is not already present in the quantity indexes.

In Table 5-4, the user may wish to distinguish between the use of the "not available" symbol (…) and the publication of zero values (0.0). The "not available" values shown for computers and software mean that BEA has no separate estimates of their values; they are included in total "information processing equipment and software." The zeroes indicate quantities so small relative to the 2009 base that they round to zero, but they do exist and are included in the higher-level aggregates.

As the quantity indexes are chain-weighted at the basic level of aggregation, chained constant-dollar components generally do not add to the chained constant-dollar totals. For this reason, BEA only makes available year-2009-dollar estimates back to 1999 (except for the very highest levels of aggregation of gross domestic product [GDP]), since the addition problem is less severe for years close to the base year. However, the addition problem is so severe for computers that BEA does not even publish recent year-2012-dollar values for this component. BEA notes that "The quantity index for computers can be used to accurately measure the real growth rate of this component. However, because computers exhibit rapid changes in prices relative to other prices in the economy, the chained-dollar estimates should not be used to measure the component's relative importance or its contribution to the growth rate of more aggregate series." (Footnote to BEA Table 5.3.6, *Survey of Current Business*, available on the BEA Web site at <https://www.bea.gov>.) Accurate estimates of these contributions are shown in BEA Table 5.3.2, which is published in the *Survey of Current Business* and can be found on the BEA Web site.

Data availability, revisions, and references

See the information on the NIPAs at the end of the notes and definitions to Chapter 1. All current and historical data are available on the BEA Web site at <https://www.bea.gov> or the STAT-USA subscription Web site at <https://www.stat-usa.gov>.

Tables 5-5 and 5-6

Current-Cost Net Stock of Fixed Assets; Chain-Type Quantity Indexes for Net Stock of Fixed Assets

SOURCE: U.S. DEPARTMENT OF COMMERCE, BUREAU OF ECONOMIC ANALYSIS (BEA)

The Bureau of Economic Analysis (BEA) calculates annual, end-of-year measurements, integrated with the national income and product accounts (NIPAs), of the level of the stock of fixed assets in the U.S. economy, or what is commonly called the "capital stock." (The fixed investment component of the GDP is a flow, or the increment of new capital goods into the capital stock.) Data on consumer stocks of durable goods are also included in the accounts, but are not shown here. Historical data are available back to 1901, with detailed estimates of net stocks, depreciation, and investment by type and by NAICS (North American Industry Classification System) industry. From this data system, *Business Statistics* presents time series data on the net stock of fixed assets valued in current dollars and also as constant-dollar quantity indexes.

The expanded definition of investment introduced in the 2013 comprehensive revision of the NIPAs, explained at the beginning of the Notes and Definitions to this chapter, was not incorporated in the fixed assets accounts until October 2013, so this edition of *Business Statistics* now publishes for the first time fixed assets data including the new NIPA categories.

Definitions and methods

The definitions of capital stock categories are now the same as the fixed investment categories listed earlier in these Notes and Definitions.

The values of fixed capital and depreciation typically reported by businesses are inadequate for economic analysis and are not typically used in these measures. In business reports, capital is generally valued at historical costs—each year's capital acquisition in the prices of the year acquired—and the totals thus represent a mixture of pricing bases. Reported depreciation is generally based on historical cost and on depreciation rates allowable by federal income tax law, rather than on a realistic rate of economic depreciation.

In these data, the *net stock of fixed assets* is measured by a perpetual inventory method. In other words, net stock at any given time is the cumulative value of past gross investment less the cumulative value of past depreciation (measured by "consumption of fixed capital," the component of the NIPAs that is subtracted from GDP in order to yield net domestic product) and also less damages from disasters and war losses that exceed normal depreciation (such as Hurricane Katrina and the terrorist attacks of September 11, 2001).

The initial calculations using this perpetual inventory method are performed in real terms for each type of asset. They are then aggregated to higher levels using an annual-weighted Fisher-type index. (See the definition of *real or chained-dollar estimates* in the notes and definitions for Chapter 1.) This provides the *chain-type quantity indexes* shown in Table 5-6. Growth rates in these indexes measure real growth in the capital stock.

The real values are then converted to a *current-cost* basis to yield the values shown in Table 5-5. They are converted by multiplying the real values by the appropriate price index for the period under consideration. A major use of the current-cost net stock figures is comparison with the value of output in that year; for example, the current-cost net stock of fixed assets for the total economy divided by the current-dollar value of GDP yields a capital-output ratio for the entire economy. Growth rates in current-cost values will reflect both the real growth measured by the quantity indexes and the increase in the value at current prices of the existing stock.

Data availability and references

The 2017 Capital Spending Report: U.S.: Capital Spending Patterns, 2006 – 2015 was released on May 3, 2017. Full historical data are available on the BEA website at www.bea.gov (select Surveys and Programs.

Tables 5-7 and 5-8

Annual Capital Expenditures

SOURCE: U.S. DEPARTMENT OF COMMERCE, CENSUS BUREAU

These data are from the Census Bureau's Annual Capital Expenditures Survey (ACES). The survey provides detailed information on capital investment in new and used structures and equipment by nonfarm businesses.

The survey is based on a stratified random sample of approximately 45,000 companies with employees and 30,000 non-employer businesses (businesses with an owner but no employees). For companies with employees, the Census Bureau reports data for 132 separate industry categories from the North American Industry Classification System (NAICS). Major exclusions are foreign operations of U.S. businesses, businesses in U.S. territories, government operations (including the U.S. Postal Service, agricultural production companies and private households.

Table 5-8 shows these data for the major NAICS sectors. Total capital expenditures, with no industry detail, are reported for the nonemployer businesses and are shown in Table 5-7, where they can be compared with the totals for companies with employees. The 1999 ACES was the first to use NAICS, providing data for the years 1998 forward on that basis.

Definitions

Capital expenditures include all capitalized costs during the year for both new and used structures and equipment, including software, that were chargeable to fixed asset accounts for which depreciation or amortization accounts are ordinarily maintained. For projects lasting longer than one year, this definition includes gross additions to construction-in-progress accounts, even if the asset was not in use and not yet depreciated. For *capital leases*, the company using the asset (lessee) is asked to include the cost or present value of the leased assets in the year in which the lease was entered. Also included in capital expenditures are capitalized leasehold improvements and capitalized interest charges on loans used to finance capital projects.

Structures consist of the capitalized costs of buildings and other structures and all necessary expenditures to acquire, construct, and prepare the structures. The costs of any machinery and equipment that is integral to or built-in features of the structures are classified as structures. Also included are major additions and alterations to existing structures and capitalized repairs and improvements to buildings.

New structures include new buildings and other structures not previously owned, as well as buildings and other structures that have been previously owned but not used or occupied.

Used structures are buildings and other structures that have been previously owned and occupied.

Equipment includes machinery, furniture and fixtures, computers, and vehicles used in the production and distribution of goods and services. Expenditures for machinery and equipment that is housed in structures and can be removed or replaced without significantly altering the structure are classified as equipment.

New equipment consists of machinery and equipment purchased new, as well as equipment produced in the company for the company's own use.

Used equipment is secondhand machinery and equipment.

Capital leases consist of new assets acquired under capital lease arrangements entered into during the year. Capital leases are defined by the criteria in the Financial Accounting Standards (FASB) Number 13.

Capitalized computer software consists of costs of materials and services directly related to the development or acquisition of software; payroll and payroll-related costs for employees directly associated with software development; and interest cost incurred while developing the software. Capitalized computer software is defined by the criteria in Statement of Position 98-1, Accounting for the Costs of Computer Software Developed or Obtained for Internal Use.

Prepackaged software is purchased off-the-shelf through retailers or other mass-market outlets for internal use by the company and includes the cost of licensing fees and service/maintenance agreements.

Vendor-customized software is externally developed by vendors and customized for the company's use.

Internally-developed software is developed by the company's employees for internal use and includes loaded payroll (salaries, wages, benefits, and bonuses related to all software development activities).

Data availability and references

Current and historical data and references are available on the Census Bureau Web site at https://www.census.gov/programs-surveys/aces.html.

CHAPTER 6: GOVERNMENT

SECTION 6A: FEDERAL GOVERNMENT IN THE NATIONAL INCOME AND PRODUCT ACCOUNTS

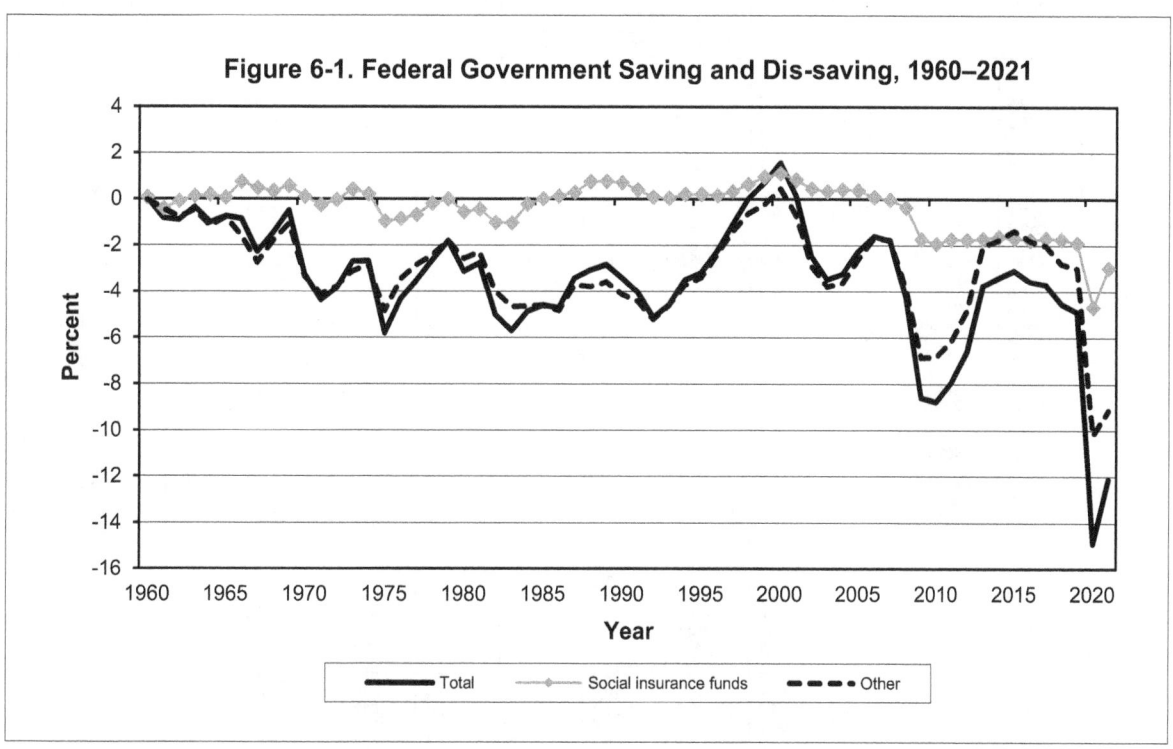

Figure 6-1. Federal Government Saving and Dis-saving, 1960–2021

- With the onset of the most severe recession of the postwar period beginning in December 2007, deficits grew rapidly, due both to the "automatic stabilizers"; such as unemployment insurance, built into the budget structure and to anti-recession programs, such as the American Recovery and Reinvestment Act of 2009. (Table 6-1)

- In calendar 2009, the NIPA budget deficit peaked up until that point 10.7 percent of GDP, including a $251.7 billion deficit in social insurance funds. This was not as great as World War II deficits but exceeded in scale the deficits of the 1930s. By 2015, the deficit shrank to less than a third from its peak and was 2.6 percent of GDP, the smallest since 2007. From 2015 to 2020, the deficit increased each year and ballooned to 15.0 percent of GDP in 2020 in response to the pandemic. However, in 2021, it decreased to 12.2 percent. (Tables 6-1, 1-1, and 6-14B)

- The main contributors to the rise in the deficit from 2007 to 2010 were increasing social benefits to persons, such as Social Security and unemployment insurance, and a drop in non-social-insurance tax receipts. Federal consumption spending and grants to state and local governments also rose. The deficit shrinkage from 2010 to 2015 was powered mainly by a resurgence in non-social-insurance tax receipts while the increase in the deficit in 2018 and 2019 was due to tax cuts. The deficit, as a percent of GDP, more than tripled in 2020 as a result of COVID-19. In 2021, it declined but remained higher than it was before the pandemic. (Table 6-1)

- Total federal government current expenditures have increased from 17.2 percent of gross domestic product (GDP) in 1960 to 24.1 percent in 2009, decreasing again to 21.8 percent in 2017 and then increasing to 32.5 percent in 2020 but falling to 30.5 in 2021. The composition of current expenditures changed significantly over the last several decades. As a percent of GDP, "Consumption" spending on defense and nondefense programs fell significantly while benefits to persons, such as Social Security and Medicare, increased significantly. (Tables 6-1, 1-1 and 6-3)

Table 6-1. Federal Government Current Receipts and Expenditures

(National income and product accounts, calendar years, billions of dollars, quarterly data are at seasonally adjusted annual rates.)

NIPA Table 3.2

Year and quarter	Total current receipts	Total tax receipts [1]	Personal current taxes	Taxes on production and imports — Excise taxes	Taxes on production and imports — Customs duties	Taxes on corporate income — Federal Reserve banks	Taxes on corporate income — Other corporate taxes	Taxes from the rest of the world	Contributions for government social insurance	Interest receipts	Non-federal reserve bank dividends	Rents and royalties	Current transfer receipts	Current surplus of government enterprises
1965	120.4	94.3	51.1	13.8	1.6	1.3	27.6	0.2	22.7	1.8	...	0.2	0.9	-0.9
1966	137.4	103.1	58.6	12.6	1.9	1.6	29.8	0.2	30.6	2.0	...	0.2	1.0	-1.2
1967	146.3	107.9	64.4	13.3	1.9	1.9	28.1	0.2	34.1	2.3	...	0.3	1.0	-1.3
1968	170.6	127.2	76.4	14.6	2.3	2.5	33.6	0.3	37.9	2.7	...	0.3	1.0	-1.0
1969	191.8	143.0	91.7	15.4	2.4	3.0	33.0	0.4	43.3	2.5	...	0.3	1.0	-1.3
1970	185.1	134.4	88.9	15.6	2.5	3.5	27.1	0.4	45.5	2.8	...	0.4	1.0	-2.5
1971	190.7	135.3	85.8	15.9	3.1	3.4	30.1	0.4	50.3	3.1	...	0.5	0.9	-2.8
1972	219.0	155.0	102.8	15.5	3.0	3.2	33.4	0.4	58.3	3.3	...	0.5	1.1	-2.4
1973	249.2	168.7	109.6	16.5	3.3	4.3	38.9	0.4	74.5	3.4	...	0.7	1.0	-3.4
1974	278.5	186.5	126.5	16.4	3.7	5.6	39.6	0.4	84.1	3.6	...	0.9	1.1	-3.2
1975	276.8	181.5	120.7	16.2	5.9	5.4	38.2	0.5	88.1	4.3	...	1.0	1.1	-4.4
1976	322.6	212.4	141.6	16.8	4.6	5.9	48.7	0.7	99.8	5.2	...	1.1	1.2	-2.9
1977	363.9	241.6	162.5	17.3	5.4	5.9	55.7	0.7	111.1	5.8	...	1.3	1.6	-3.4
1978	423.8	279.8	189.2	18.2	7.1	7.0	64.4	1.0	128.7	7.4	...	1.5	2.2	-2.9
1979	487.0	316.9	224.9	18.2	7.5	9.3	65.1	1.1	149.8	9.2	...	2.1	2.5	-2.7
1980	533.7	344.5	250.6	26.5	7.2	11.7	58.6	1.6	163.6	11.3	...	3.0	3.1	-3.6
1981	621.1	394.3	291.2	41.3	8.6	14.0	51.7	1.5	193.0	14.8	...	4.4	3.1	-2.6
1982	618.7	371.8	295.6	32.3	8.6	15.2	33.8	1.4	206.0	18.3	...	5.1	4.4	-2.1
1983	644.8	379.5	286.8	35.3	9.1	14.2	47.1	1.2	223.1	20.4	...	4.3	5.2	-1.9
1984	711.2	409.7	301.9	35.4	11.9	16.1	59.2	1.3	254.1	22.8	...	4.9	6.3	-2.7
1985	775.7	442.9	336.5	33.9	12.2	17.8	58.5	1.9	277.9	25.6	...	4.6	8.6	-1.6
1986	817.9	462.0	350.6	30.0	13.7	17.8	66.0	1.7	298.9	28.8	...	3.3	7.6	-0.6
1987	899.5	526.4	393.0	30.4	15.5	17.7	85.4	2.0	317.4	25.1	...	3.1	10.2	-0.5
1988	962.4	549.8	403.8	33.4	16.4	17.4	93.8	2.4	354.8	27.4	...	2.8	9.6	0.7
1989	1 042.5	601.1	453.1	32.3	17.5	21.6	95.6	2.7	378.0	25.9	...	3.0	11.8	1.1
1990	1 087.6	620.6	472.1	33.4	17.5	23.6	94.5	3.0	402.0	26.9	...	3.5	13.3	-2.3
1991	1 107.8	617.1	463.6	44.9	16.8	20.8	89.2	2.6	420.6	26.2	...	3.8	17.2	2.1
1992	1 154.4	645.4	477.5	45.0	18.3	16.8	102.0	2.6	444.0	22.2	...	3.5	18.4	4.1
1993	1 231.0	699.3	507.7	46.5	19.8	16.0	122.5	2.7	465.5	22.9	...	3.8	20.2	3.5
1994	1 329.3	763.5	545.1	57.5	21.4	20.5	136.3	3.1	496.2	20.1	...	3.6	21.6	4.0
1995	1 417.4	825.7	590.3	55.7	19.8	23.4	155.9	3.9	521.9	20.9	...	3.0	17.5	5.0
1996	1 536.3	917.0	668.4	53.6	19.2	20.1	170.5	5.2	545.4	22.6	...	4.1	22.7	4.5
1997	1 667.4	1 015.1	749.8	58.2	19.6	20.7	182.3	5.1	579.4	21.0	...	4.5	20.1	6.6
1998	1 789.8	1 095.3	831.2	60.2	19.6	26.6	177.7	5.7	617.4	17.4	...	4.2	21.5	7.6
1999	1 906.0	1 174.5	897.4	63.3	19.2	25.4	187.6	6.1	654.8	16.5	...	4.0	23.4	7.2
2000	2 067.8	1 288.5	999.6	65.1	21.1	25.3	194.1	7.6	698.6	18.8	...	6.3	24.9	5.3
2001	2 032.4	1 226.8	996.0	63.7	20.6	27.1	137.6	7.9	723.3	18.3	...	8.4	25.7	2.8
2002	1 870.9	1 053.2	832.3	65.9	19.9	24.5	126.0	8.1	739.4	15.5	...	6.5	25.0	6.8
2003	1 896.1	1 053.9	778.6	67.7	21.5	22.0	175.8	9.2	763.3	17.1	...	7.0	26.2	6.6
2004	2 028.1	1 140.6	803.0	70.9	23.3	18.1	232.2	10.1	809.0	17.0	0.1	8.7	29.8	4.8
2005	2 304.7	1 367.8	937.2	72.7	25.3	21.5	319.5	11.7	853.4	17.5	0.2	9.7	33.7	0.9
2006	2 538.8	1 534.8	1 055.8	71.5	26.7	29.1	366.0	13.7	905.7	19.1	0.3	9.9	38.1	1.9
2007	2 668.3	1 607.7	1 170.9	64.8	28.8	34.6	328.2	13.9	947.3	22.6	0.2	11.1	42.7	2.1
2008	2 582.1	1 489.5	1 176.6	63.7	29.2	31.7	202.0	16.9	974.5	21.2	0.6	13.8	49.7	1.1
2009	2 242.1	1 123.7	866.6	67.3	23.1	47.4	153.0	12.8	950.7	26.4	18.7	7.0	67.2	0.9
2010	2 446.3	1 273.6	943.6	67.2	28.6	79.3	219.4	13.9	970.9	31.7	17.0	8.0	68.1	-2.4
2011	2 573.6	1 478.4	1 130.8	75.7	31.9	75.4	224.0	15.1	903.2	27.1	18.8	9.9	67.1	-6.3
2012	2 700.8	1 573.0	1 166.4	80.6	33.5	88.4	274.7	16.7	938.0	21.8	21.1	10.2	56.1	-7.8
2013	3 139.6	1 744.9	1 302.9	89.0	35.5	79.6	298.4	18.1	1 091.8	23.5	131.3	9.3	69.3	-10.1
2014	3 293.0	1 900.1	1 403.7	97.8	37.4	96.9	339.6	20.4	1 140.1	24.8	40.7	10.3	87.3	-7.1
2015	3 449.0	2 024.2	1 532.6	101.0	38.1	110.4	329.1	22.2	1 190.8	28.0	16.0	6.7	76.2	-3.2
2016	3 463.8	2 020.4	1 547.9	97.8	37.5	91.5	311.9	24.1	1 224.4	29.7	14.8	4.8	79.7	-1.4
2017	3 525.2	2 015.5	1 613.6	91.9	38.5	80.6	245.4	24.9	1 284.2	29.8	23.2	6.1	85.0	1.0
2018	3 569.0	2 014.6	1 616.5	109.1	53.3	65.3	208.8	25.7	1 345.4	36.4	13.7	7.8	86.3	-0.6
2019	3 713.7	2 127.6	1 708.6	95.7	77.8	54.9	217.0	27.2	1 406.2	37.7	8.9	8.4	72.5	-2.6
2020	3 684.5	2 057.8	1 679.6	88.1	68.6	90.7	192.7	27.4	1 444.6	23.5	0.1	5.5	62.9	-0.6
2021	4 237.6	2 466.0	1 990.0	85.8	86.7	111.4	272.1	30.1	1 576.8	20.9	0.1	5.5	58.1	-1.2
2019														
1st quarter	3 676.4	2 107.7	1 696.4	96.3	75.9	44.9	211.3	26.6	1 392.4	37.1	19.1	8.4	69.3	-2.4
2nd quarter	3 706.0	2 120.4	1 701.9	97.3	73.6	58.8	218.9	27.4	1 399.3	37.3	16.3	8.5	68.4	-2.9
3rd quarter	3 708.9	2 117.1	1 707.8	95.1	79.0	53.4	206.5	27.5	1 406.9	38.0	0.2	8.4	87.8	-2.8
4th quarter	3 763.4	2 165.3	1 728.6	94.2	82.5	62.4	231.4	27.4	1 426.4	38.5	0.2	8.3	64.5	-2.2
2020														
1st quarter	3 751.2	2 119.0	1 737.9	103.9	80.7	73.1	166.7	28.6	1 457.1	35.0	0.2	8.2	59.5	-0.9
2nd quarter	3 481.1	1 913.3	1 581.5	78.3	58.7	89.7	167.4	26.1	1 391.6	19.1	0.2	5.1	62.7	-0.6
3rd quarter	3 690.5	2 051.8	1 662.2	85.1	65.0	108.4	211.7	26.6	1 443.8	19.5	0.1	4.3	62.6	-0.2
4th quarter	3 815.1	2 147.0	1 736.9	85.2	70.1	91.5	225.1	28.3	1 486.0	20.3	0.1	4.4	66.6	-0.8
2021														
1st quarter	3 982.6	2 294.0	1 851.9	84.6	80.4	84.1	246.4	29.4	1 517.9	20.5	0.1	4.8	62.8	-1.6
2nd quarter	4 177.8	2 428.3	1 946.1	86.9	89.6	111.8	275.1	29.3	1 555.7	21.9	0.1	5.2	56.7	-1.9
3rd quarter	4 324.8	2 525.0	2 036.0	85.9	85.7	123.5	285.9	30.3	1 594.4	20.6	0.1	5.9	55.6	-0.3
4th quarter	4 465.4	2 616.7	2 125.9	85.9	91.1	126.0	281.2	31.4	1 639.0	20.8	0.1	6.2	57.5	-1.0

[1]Does not include "contributions for government social insurance" (the taxes that fund Social Security, Medicare, and unemployment insurance), which are shown separately in column 9.
. . . = Not available.

Table 6-1. Federal Government Current Receipts and Expenditures—*Continued*

(National income and product accounts, calendar years, billions of dollars, quarterly data are at seasonally adjusted annual rates.)

NIPA Table 3.2

Year and quarter	Total current expenditures	Consumption expenditures	Government social benefits — Benefits to persons	Government social benefits — Benefits to the rest of the world	Other current transfer payments — Grants-in-aid to state and local governments	Other current transfer payments — Payments to the rest of the world (net)	Interest payments — Total	Interest payments — To persons and business	Interest payments — To the rest of the world	Subsidies	Net federal government saving, NIPA (surplus + / deficit -) — Total	Net federal government saving, NIPA — Social insurance funds	Net federal government saving, NIPA — Other
1965	125.9	66.5	27.3	0.5	6.6	3.6	18.6	18.1	0.5	3.0	-5.5	0.4	-5.9
1966	144.4	76.5	29.9	0.5	9.4	4.0	20.3	19.7	0.5	3.9	-7.0	6.0	-13.0
1967	165.8	88.1	36.5	0.6	10.9	4.0	21.9	21.3	0.6	3.8	-19.5	4.1	-23.6
1968	184.3	96.8	41.9	0.6	11.8	4.5	24.6	23.9	0.7	4.1	-13.8	3.2	-16.9
1969	197.0	100.5	45.8	0.6	13.7	4.5	27.5	26.7	0.8	4.5	-5.1	5.7	-10.8
1970	219.9	102.3	55.6	0.7	18.3	4.8	33.3	32.4	0.9	4.8	-34.8	1.0	-35.8
1971	241.6	106.7	66.1	0.8	22.1	6.0	35.2	33.5	1.8	4.6	-50.9	-3.0	-47.9
1972	268.0	112.3	72.9	1.0	30.5	7.2	37.6	35.1	2.6	6.6	-49.0	-0.6	-48.4
1973	287.6	114.5	84.5	1.2	33.5	5.4	43.3	39.6	3.7	5.1	-38.3	5.9	-44.2
1974	319.8	123.2	103.3	1.3	34.9	6.0	48.0	43.9	4.0	3.2	-41.3	3.2	-44.5
1975	374.8	133.9	132.3	2.0	43.6	6.1	52.5	48.1	4.3	4.3	-97.9	-16.3	-81.6
1976	403.5	140.0	143.5	2.5	49.1	4.5	58.9	54.6	4.3	4.9	-80.9	-16.0	-64.9
1977	437.3	151.1	152.4	2.6	54.8	4.2	65.3	60.0	5.2	6.9	-73.4	-14.1	-59.4
1978	485.9	164.2	162.7	2.7	63.5	5.0	79.1	70.9	8.2	8.7	-62.0	-4.7	-57.3
1979	534.4	178.8	183.0	3.0	64.0	5.8	91.5	80.9	10.6	8.2	-47.4	-0.1	-47.3
1980	622.5	204.6	220.3	3.5	69.7	7.3	107.5	95.7	11.9	9.4	-88.8	-15.8	-73.0
1981	709.1	233.6	250.7	4.3	69.4	6.7	133.4	117.2	16.3	11.1	-88.1	-14.3	-73.8
1982	786.0	258.4	281.9	4.1	66.3	8.1	152.7	134.7	18.0	14.6	-167.4	-34.4	-132.9
1983	851.9	280.0	303.6	3.6	67.9	8.9	167.0	148.9	18.1	20.9	-207.2	-37.9	-169.3
1984	907.7	296.2	309.7	3.7	72.3	11.2	193.8	173.7	20.2	20.7	-196.5	-9.4	-187.1
1985	975.0	320.4	325.9	4.0	76.2	13.8	213.7	191.6	22.2	21.0	-199.2	0.8	-200.1
1986	1 033.8	339.8	344.3	4.4	82.4	14.2	224.2	200.9	23.3	24.6	-215.9	5.6	-221.5
1987	1 065.2	350.3	357.2	4.3	78.4	12.7	232.3	208.2	24.1	30.0	-165.7	14.4	-180.2
1988	1 122.4	363.5	378.4	4.6	85.7	13.2	247.9	219.2	28.8	29.2	-160.0	39.0	-198.9
1989	1 201.8	382.9	411.7	5.1	91.8	13.5	269.7	235.1	34.5	27.1	-159.4	42.6	-201.9
1990	1 290.9	404.2	447.0	6.2	104.4	13.5	289.0	253.0	36.1	26.6	-203.3	42.3	-245.6
1991	1 356.2	426.1	494.0	6.3	124.0	-25.6	304.4	268.3	36.1	27.1	-248.4	24.6	-273.0
1992	1 488.9	432.1	551.8	6.2	141.7	20.6	306.9	272.6	34.3	29.7	-334.5	5.3	-339.8
1993	1 544.6	429.5	583.7	6.2	155.7	21.7	311.4	277.3	34.2	36.3	-313.5	2.8	-316.3
1994	1 585.0	429.3	609.0	6.8	166.8	19.9	320.8	284.5	36.4	32.2	-255.6	15.3	-270.9
1995	1 659.5	429.0	647.1	6.8	174.5	15.4	352.3	305.2	47.1	34.5	-242.1	15.5	-257.6
1996	1 715.7	429.4	682.1	7.6	181.5	20.4	360.0	303.2	56.8	34.9	-179.4	12.8	-192.2
1997	1 759.4	439.6	707.9	7.9	188.1	17.0	365.6	295.9	69.7	33.4	-92.0	28.8	-120.8
1998	1 788.4	437.8	722.1	8.2	200.8	18.0	365.6	293.5	72.1	35.9	1.4	58.2	-56.8
1999	1 836.8	455.9	739.9	8.7	219.2	16.3	352.2	285.1	67.1	44.8	69.1	92.2	-23.1
2000	1 908.1	475.7	773.4	8.9	233.1	17.9	353.7	288.6	65.1	45.3	159.7	114.0	45.7
2001	2 017.3	506.4	840.8	9.8	261.3	16.9	331.2	273.6	57.6	51.1	15.0	87.7	-72.6
2002	2 138.7	560.9	918.0	9.9	288.7	19.4	301.3	251.3	50.0	40.5	-267.8	48.8	-316.6
2003	2 293.5	631.6	967.5	10.4	321.7	21.7	291.7	243.5	48.2	49.0	-397.4	37.5	-434.9
2004	2 421.6	683.7	1 019.5	11.0	332.3	23.0	306.0	249.4	56.7	46.0	-393.5	50.8	-444.3
2005	2 598.5	725.8	1 084.4	11.6	343.5	28.3	344.4	272.6	71.8	60.5	-293.8	48.0	-341.7
2006	2 760.7	765.5	1 189.1	12.4	341.0	29.3	372.2	285.0	87.2	51.1	-221.9	11.8	-233.7
2007	2 928.0	801.0	1 263.3	13.3	359.1	35.9	408.0	305.0	102.9	47.5	-259.7	-3.2	-256.5
2008	3 207.0	880.3	1 463.2	15.4	371.2	38.9	388.4	286.3	102.1	49.6	-624.9	-53.6	-571.3
2009	3 485.2	938.2	1 614.5	16.0	458.1	46.9	354.5	265.9	88.7	56.9	-1 243.2	-251.7	-991.5
2010	3 764.6	1 002.9	1 757.5	16.5	505.2	46.8	381.5	286.9	94.6	54.2	-1 318.4	-290.6	-1 027.8
2011	3 807.8	1 004.1	1 779.5	17.0	472.5	49.8	425.4	320.7	104.7	59.5	-1 234.1	-271.5	-962.7
2012	3 773.5	999.7	1 781.8	18.0	444.4	49.3	422.6	320.6	102.0	57.6	-1 072.7	-287.7	-785.0
2013	3 771.3	957.5	1 821.5	18.9	450.1	47.7	416.3	316.4	100.0	59.2	-631.8	-288.6	-343.1
2014	3 890.4	952.2	1 881.1	19.5	495.0	45.8	439.1	338.5	100.6	57.6	-597.4	-287.2	-310.1
2015	4 009.2	955.1	1 969.9	20.4	533.1	44.8	429.3	334.3	95.0	56.7	-560.2	-310.9	-249.4
2016	4 131.4	965.7	2 024.2	20.9	556.7	48.2	454.3	348.8	105.5	61.2	-667.6	-330.4	-337.2
2017	4 245.9	982.7	2 098.6	21.8	560.5	46.0	476.8	360.2	116.6	59.3	-720.7	-330.3	-390.4
2018	4 497.1	1 039.4	2 196.4	22.8	582.5	51.5	541.8	404.4	137.4	62.7	-928.1	-357.9	-570.1
2019	4 761.1	1 097.4	2 324.4	24.0	609.2	50.3	583.5	438.1	145.4	72.4	-1 047.5	-409.5	-638.0
2020	6 794.5	1 161.4	3 373.0	33.1	880.5	51.4	534.2	411.9	122.3	760.8	-3 110.0	-977.2	-2 132.8
2021	7 021.4	1 205.0	3 628.9	30.6	1 093.8	58.5	514.8	384.5	130.3	490.0	-2 783.8	-683.0	-2 100.8
2019													
1st quarter	4 691.8	1 075.5	2 298.1	23.5	593.8	52.1	580.5	433.8	146.7	68.4	-1 015.4	-392.2	-623.2
2nd quarter	4 739.1	1 095.7	2 315.5	23.7	610.5	46.3	589.2	441.1	148.1	58.2	-1 033.2	-405.4	-627.8
3rd quarter	4 789.8	1 105.1	2 333.2	24.3	610.4	50.7	585.6	439.2	146.4	80.6	-1 080.9	-419.2	-661.7
4th quarter	4 823.8	1 113.3	2 350.8	24.5	622.4	51.9	578.7	438.2	140.5	82.2	-1 060.4	-421.2	-639.2
2020													
1st quarter	4 909.2	1 124.7	2 417.9	25.2	640.6	54.2	566.4	434.2	132.2	80.3	-1 158.0	-440.6	-717.4
2nd quarter	9 106.7	1 187.6	4 766.7	44.1	1 400.0	47.3	537.3	416.4	120.9	1 123.6	-5 625.6	-1 542.1	-4 083.5
3rd quarter	7 206.8	1 169.4	3 468.3	35.0	738.5	53.6	521.5	403.8	117.6	1 220.5	-3 516.3	-1 222.0	-2 294.3
4th quarter	5 955.2	1 164.1	2 839.1	28.2	743.0	50.5	511.7	393.1	118.5	618.6	-2 140.1	-704.0	-1 436.1
2021													
1st quarter	8 071.4	1 219.9	5 070.6	36.8	781.5	56.4	502.5	380.4	122.0	403.8	-4 088.9	-948.1	-3 140.0
2nd quarter	7 490.5	1 208.1	3 372.3	29.4	1 632.2	47.7	503.8	380.7	123.1	697.0	-3 312.7	-829.1	-2 483.6
3rd quarter	6 560.4	1 196.1	3 136.3	28.4	1 057.1	76.4	511.6	380.4	131.1	554.5	-2 235.6	-600.7	-1 634.9
4th quarter	5 963.5	1 195.6	2 936.3	27.7	904.2	53.5	541.5	396.4	145.1	304.7	-1 498.1	-353.2	-1 144.9

Table 6-2. Federal Government Consumption Expenditures and Gross Investment

(National income and product accounts, calendar years, billions of dollars, quarterly data are at seasonally adjusted annual rates.)

NIPA Tables 3.9.5, 3.10.5

Year and quarter	Total	Consumption expenditures Total	Compensation of general government employees	Consumption of general government fixed capital	Intermediate goods and services purchased [1]	Less: Own-account investment and sales to other sectors	Gross investment Total	National defense Structures	National defense Equipment	National defense Intellectual property	Nondefense Structures	Nondefense Equipment	Nondefense Intellectual property
1965	93.2	66.5	34.8	19.8	16.0	4.2	26.7	1.1	8.9	6.7	2.8	0.5	6.8
1966	106.6	76.5	39.8	20.8	20.6	4.7	30.1	1.3	10.4	7.0	2.8	0.6	7.9
1967	120.0	88.1	43.8	22.2	26.5	4.5	31.9	1.2	12.2	7.9	2.2	0.6	7.8
1968	128.0	96.8	48.3	23.9	29.3	4.6	31.1	1.2	10.8	7.9	2.1	0.5	8.6
1969	131.2	100.5	51.4	25.5	28.7	5.1	30.7	1.5	9.7	8.2	1.9	0.6	8.8
1970	132.8	102.3	55.2	27.3	25.3	5.4	30.5	1.3	9.6	8.1	2.1	0.7	8.8
1971	134.5	106.7	58.8	28.7	25.0	5.8	27.8	1.8	5.5	8.4	2.5	0.8	8.9
1972	141.6	112.3	62.6	29.7	26.9	6.9	29.3	1.8	6.3	9.2	2.7	1.1	9.2
1973	146.2	114.5	64.6	31.8	25.8	7.7	31.7	2.1	6.0	9.7	3.1	1.1	9.6
1974	158.8	123.2	67.8	34.7	29.2	8.6	35.7	2.2	8.2	10.0	3.4	1.5	10.4
1975	173.7	133.9	72.5	38.0	31.8	8.4	39.9	2.3	9.9	10.5	4.1	1.7	11.5
1976	184.8	140.0	76.5	40.8	31.3	8.5	44.8	2.1	12.1	11.3	4.6	1.8	12.7
1977	200.3	151.1	80.9	44.3	35.6	9.7	49.2	2.4	13.3	12.3	5.0	2.3	14.0
1978	218.9	164.2	87.1	48.6	39.3	10.8	54.7	2.5	14.3	13.3	6.1	2.7	15.9
1979	240.6	178.8	92.0	53.4	45.8	12.4	61.7	2.5	17.5	14.9	6.3	2.7	17.9
1980	274.9	204.6	100.8	59.1	58.4	13.6	70.2	3.2	19.8	17.2	7.1	3.2	19.8
1981	314.0	233.6	112.2	66.0	69.6	14.3	80.4	3.2	24.1	20.9	7.7	3.3	21.2
1982	348.3	258.4	122.0	73.7	77.6	14.9	90.0	4.0	29.1	25.2	6.8	3.9	21.1
1983	382.4	280.0	127.7	79.4	88.8	15.9	102.3	4.8	35.2	29.8	6.7	4.3	21.6
1984	411.8	296.2	136.5	88.7	88.3	17.4	115.6	4.9	41.1	35.0	7.0	4.7	22.8
1985	452.9	320.4	145.0	95.0	99.1	18.7	132.5	6.2	47.9	41.3	7.3	5.1	24.6
1986	481.7	339.8	149.1	101.5	108.7	19.6	141.9	6.8	52.7	43.9	8.0	4.8	25.7
1987	502.8	350.3	153.1	108.0	110.2	20.9	152.4	7.7	55.0	48.1	9.0	5.2	27.4
1988	511.4	363.5	161.9	116.6	107.4	22.5	148.0	7.4	49.6	48.5	6.8	6.1	29.6
1989	534.1	382.9	168.5	124.3	114.0	23.9	151.2	6.4	51.5	47.3	6.9	7.2	31.9
1990	562.4	404.2	176.0	130.7	123.1	25.6	158.2	6.1	54.6	46.6	8.0	8.1	34.8
1991	582.9	426.1	186.5	137.0	129.4	26.8	156.8	4.6	53.4	43.3	9.2	8.9	37.4
1992	588.5	432.1	189.6	140.0	129.4	26.9	156.4	5.2	50.7	41.3	10.3	10.0	38.9
1993	580.2	429.5	188.0	143.4	125.1	27.2	150.7	5.3	44.7	39.2	11.2	9.9	40.4
1994	574.7	429.3	186.1	146.6	126.1	29.3	145.4	5.8	41.9	38.1	10.2	7.5	41.9
1995	576.7	429.0	183.3	149.6	123.2	27.3	147.7	6.7	39.8	38.4	10.8	8.6	43.4
1996	579.2	429.4	182.2	149.6	125.2	27.6	149.8	6.3	39.9	38.9	11.3	9.7	43.8
1997	583.3	439.6	183.5	150.1	131.6	25.6	143.7	6.1	33.6	39.2	9.9	10.0	44.9
1998	585.5	437.8	185.8	150.9	127.7	26.6	147.7	5.8	34.1	39.4	10.8	10.2	47.5
1999	610.7	455.9	191.7	153.3	136.4	25.6	154.9	5.4	36.8	39.3	10.7	11.9	50.7
2000	633.1	475.7	202.4	157.9	143.6	28.2	157.4	5.4	37.8	40.2	8.4	10.8	54.8
2001	670.2	506.4	211.2	159.1	165.7	29.6	163.8	5.3	39.9	42.5	8.1	10.0	58.1
2002	743.1	560.9	236.3	161.5	194.5	31.5	182.2	6.1	46.4	47.9	10.0	11.9	59.8
2003	826.8	631.6	267.7	167.0	230.4	33.5	195.2	7.1	50.0	53.0	10.3	12.3	62.5
2004	892.1	683.7	284.3	175.1	259.0	34.6	208.4	6.9	55.7	58.3	9.6	13.3	64.5
2005	947.8	725.8	303.5	184.9	276.6	39.2	222.0	7.2	61.4	62.9	8.1	15.2	67.3
2006	1 001.2	765.5	314.5	195.4	295.7	40.0	235.6	7.8	66.0	65.7	9.4	17.4	69.2
2007	1 051.0	801.0	329.1	206.7	305.4	40.1	250.0	10.0	71.8	69.4	11.4	16.1	71.4
2008	1 152.0	880.3	349.6	219.5	353.6	42.3	271.7	13.7	82.6	70.8	11.4	17.5	75.7
2009	1 220.8	938.2	375.8	227.2	378.8	43.6	282.6	17.1	86.6	69.6	12.0	17.8	79.5
2010	1 300.2	1 002.9	402.8	237.2	409.4	46.5	297.2	16.7	89.3	70.2	16.0	19.2	85.9
2011	1 299.8	1 004.1	411.6	248.1	395.2	50.9	295.7	13.3	87.3	71.3	16.7	18.4	88.5
2012	1 287.0	999.7	409.1	254.6	383.0	47.0	287.3	8.1	85.2	70.5	14.5	18.7	90.2
2013	1 227.2	957.5	399.8	258.6	346.0	46.9	269.6	6.5	78.8	67.7	11.6	16.2	88.8
2014	1 216.0	952.2	404.2	262.7	334.4	49.0	263.8	5.3	74.7	64.8	12.0	17.4	89.6
2015	1 221.8	955.1	409.9	263.7	330.9	49.4	266.6	5.0	72.6	65.3	12.7	18.8	92.2
2016	1 234.5	965.7	421.1	262.8	333.3	51.5	268.8	4.8	72.3	61.8	12.3	18.9	98.6
2017	1 262.8	982.7	431.7	267.5	335.7	52.2	280.0	5.6	77.4	61.7	10.2	19.0	106.2
2018	1 339.0	1 039.4	449.9	276.1	367.3	53.8	299.6	6.0	84.2	64.8	12.1	19.7	112.7
2019	1 414.9	1 097.4	465.5	284.0	404.7	56.8	317.5	7.4	93.6	66.0	15.3	20.0	115.2
2020	1 501.8	1 161.4	488.6	293.9	436.5	57.6	340.3	10.0	97.2	73.7	17.6	20.6	121.3
2021	1 565.0	1 205.0	507.6	310.3	453.0	66.0	360.0	11.0	101.9	83.6	15.3	23.6	124.7
2019													
1st quarter	1 387.0	1 075.5	459.6	282.1	388.0	54.3	311.5	7.4	90.9	64.7	15.2	19.3	114.0
2nd quarter	1 406.9	1 095.7	463.1	282.6	406.7	56.8	311.2	7.3	88.8	65.2	15.0	20.2	114.8
3rd quarter	1 424.1	1 105.1	467.7	284.8	409.3	56.7	319.0	7.0	94.6	66.3	15.3	20.2	115.6
4th quarter	1 441.7	1 113.3	471.5	286.3	414.9	59.4	328.4	8.0	100.0	67.9	15.8	20.3	116.3
2020													
1st quarter	1 454.7	1 124.7	476.9	288.7	416.4	57.3	330.0	8.8	95.2	70.3	17.8	20.3	117.5
2nd quarter	1 525.0	1 187.6	484.7	292.0	467.3	56.5	337.4	9.6	99.0	72.3	18.8	20.5	117.2
3rd quarter	1 515.1	1 169.4	496.7	295.4	434.8	57.5	345.7	10.7	95.3	74.8	18.4	20.4	126.1
4th quarter	1 512.3	1 164.1	496.0	299.5	427.6	59.1	348.2	10.7	99.2	77.3	15.3	21.1	124.5
2021													
1st quarter	1 568.6	1 219.9	500.1	302.9	477.5	60.5	348.7	10.4	99.1	80.2	15.5	22.3	121.3
2nd quarter	1 563.3	1 208.1	505.7	307.2	461.1	65.9	355.1	10.6	100.7	82.8	14.4	23.0	123.6
3rd quarter	1 562.0	1 196.1	509.9	312.5	438.8	65.0	365.9	11.2	104.5	84.8	15.0	24.5	125.8
4th quarter	1 566.2	1 195.6	514.9	318.5	434.8	72.5	370.5	11.6	103.5	86.3	16.3	24.7	128.1

[1] Includes general government intermediate inputs for goods and services sold to other sectors and for own-account investment.

Table 6-3. Federal Government Defense and Nondefense Consumption Expenditures by Type

(National income and product accounts, calendar years, billions of dollars, quarterly data are at seasonally adjusted annual rates.)

NIPA Table 3.10.5

Year and quarter	Defense consumption expenditures [1]						Nondefense consumption expenditures [1]					
	Total	Compensation of general government employees	Consumption of general government fixed capital	Intermediate goods and services purchased [2]			Total	Compensation of general government employees	Consumption of general government fixed capital	Intermediate goods and services purchased [2]		
				Durable goods	Nondurable goods	Services				Durable goods	Nondurable goods	Services
1965	53.9	26.4	17.1	4.2	3.2	5.1	12.6	8.3	2.8	0.1	0.4	3.1
1966	63.8	30.8	17.5	6.1	4.7	7.0	12.7	9.0	3.3	0.1	-0.7	3.3
1967	73.7	34.2	18.4	6.2	7.3	9.7	14.3	9.7	3.9	0.1	0.1	3.1
1968	81.4	37.6	19.4	7.4	8.4	10.5	15.4	10.7	4.5	0.1	0.8	2.0
1969	82.6	40.0	20.3	6.4	7.6	10.5	17.9	11.5	5.2	0.1	1.4	2.6
1970	81.8	41.9	21.3	6.1	5.4	9.6	20.6	13.3	6.0	0.1	0.5	3.6
1971	82.3	43.4	21.9	4.6	4.4	10.6	24.3	15.5	6.7	0.1	0.9	4.4
1972	84.4	45.6	22.4	5.5	4.7	9.5	27.9	17.0	7.4	0.2	1.2	5.8
1973	84.9	46.1	23.6	5.3	4.3	9.3	29.7	18.4	8.2	0.2	1.0	5.8
1974	89.5	47.7	25.3	5.0	5.2	10.7	33.6	20.1	9.4	0.3	1.4	6.7
1975	95.3	50.2	27.3	5.8	5.1	10.9	38.5	22.3	10.6	0.3	2.1	7.6
1976	99.3	51.8	29.2	5.7	4.4	11.7	40.7	24.7	11.6	0.3	2.1	7.1
1977	106.5	53.9	31.5	7.6	4.5	12.7	44.7	27.0	12.8	0.4	2.5	7.8
1978	115.1	57.6	34.4	9.0	4.9	13.3	49.0	29.5	14.3	0.5	3.2	8.4
1979	125.7	60.9	37.3	10.8	6.2	14.9	53.1	31.1	16.1	0.6	3.3	10.0
1980	143.2	66.7	40.6	12.3	10.0	18.7	61.4	34.0	18.5	0.8	5.5	11.2
1981	165.1	76.3	45.0	15.7	11.8	22.0	68.4	35.9	21.1	0.8	8.7	10.5
1982	187.2	84.8	50.4	19.1	11.5	28.1	71.2	37.2	23.3	0.8	7.5	10.7
1983	202.3	89.3	55.2	24.6	11.3	28.9	77.7	38.4	24.2	0.8	10.1	13.1
1984	217.7	95.9	62.3	26.6	10.4	30.7	78.5	40.7	26.4	0.9	5.8	13.9
1985	234.1	102.4	67.2	29.0	9.9	34.7	86.3	42.6	27.8	0.9	8.9	15.7
1986	249.0	106.2	72.6	31.7	10.2	38.3	90.8	42.9	28.9	0.9	11.7	16.1
1987	261.6	109.5	77.7	33.6	10.2	40.9	88.7	43.6	30.2	1.0	6.2	18.3
1988	276.6	113.8	84.4	33.4	10.6	45.4	86.8	48.1	32.2	1.1	-0.8	17.7
1989	286.1	117.9	90.1	32.0	10.8	46.5	96.8	50.6	34.2	1.2	5.1	18.2
1990	297.7	121.2	94.5	31.6	11.0	51.8	106.5	54.8	36.2	1.4	5.0	22.2
1991	312.7	126.8	98.5	31.0	10.7	58.1	113.4	59.7	38.6	1.5	5.9	22.3
1992	309.3	126.8	99.8	28.4	9.4	57.6	122.8	62.8	40.2	1.6	6.5	25.9
1993	302.4	121.0	101.3	26.4	8.5	58.1	127.1	67.1	42.1	1.6	7.6	23.0
1994	296.3	117.4	102.7	22.9	7.6	60.2	133.0	68.7	43.9	1.5	6.1	27.7
1995	292.2	114.1	103.3	20.9	6.3	59.8	136.8	69.2	46.4	1.4	7.5	27.3
1996	292.3	112.0	101.7	20.8	7.6	62.5	137.1	70.2	47.9	1.5	6.6	26.0
1997	293.0	111.4	100.4	20.9	7.6	64.6	146.6	72.0	49.7	1.6	8.5	28.5
1998	289.5	110.8	99.7	20.9	7.0	62.6	148.3	75.1	51.3	1.5	9.4	26.3
1999	301.8	112.7	99.4	22.2	8.2	70.9	154.1	79.0	53.9	1.7	7.2	26.3
2000	309.2	116.9	100.7	22.1	10.4	71.4	166.5	85.5	57.2	1.8	9.3	28.5
2001	325.5	123.2	99.8	22.3	10.3	84.2	180.9	88.0	59.3	1.9	12.2	34.8
2002	358.5	139.3	100.4	23.4	11.4	100.0	202.4	97.0	61.1	2.2	12.6	44.8
2003	411.2	160.8	103.5	26.0	13.5	124.6	220.4	106.9	63.5	2.2	15.4	48.7
2004	448.9	172.2	108.8	28.5	17.1	139.8	234.8	112.1	66.3	2.5	17.1	54.0
2005	478.0	186.0	115.2	29.8	21.0	145.3	247.8	117.5	69.7	2.7	19.0	58.9
2006	501.3	193.0	122.1	32.8	22.3	152.5	264.3	121.5	73.3	3.0	20.3	64.9
2007	528.1	201.5	129.6	37.0	24.0	157.9	272.9	127.6	77.1	3.0	20.2	63.3
2008	583.2	214.3	138.3	43.2	30.3	180.0	297.1	135.2	81.2	3.3	23.6	73.3
2009	614.3	229.2	143.5	47.1	24.5	193.0	323.9	146.6	83.7	3.5	26.6	84.0
2010	651.8	244.0	149.5	47.4	26.8	207.8	351.1	158.8	87.7	3.9	28.4	94.9
2011	662.0	250.8	156.3	46.2	33.0	201.8	342.1	160.8	91.8	3.7	24.8	85.8
2012	650.3	248.0	159.6	45.2	31.9	191.6	349.4	161.1	95.0	3.7	24.0	86.7
2013	611.2	239.6	160.5	39.9	28.2	169.4	346.3	160.2	98.1	3.5	22.6	82.5
2014	598.7	239.1	160.9	36.5	26.0	162.8	353.5	165.0	101.8	3.6	22.0	83.5
2015	586.8	238.7	159.7	35.7	21.0	158.2	368.3	171.3	104.0	3.8	23.0	89.2
2016	588.9	242.2	157.0	36.2	20.5	158.9	376.8	179.0	105.8	3.9	22.7	91.1
2017	601.8	246.6	157.3	38.5	22.9	161.8	380.9	185.1	110.2	3.7	22.2	86.5
2018	637.8	257.9	160.0	41.5	26.0	178.9	401.7	192.0	116.1	3.9	24.3	92.7
2019	680.5	268.2	162.7	45.3	24.7	207.4	416.9	197.2	121.3	4.1	26.1	97.0
2020	700.5	280.1	167.5	47.9	22.1	212.3	461.0	208.5	126.4	8.5	25.9	119.9
2021	708.8	291.9	176.6	46.7	27.1	198.4	496.1	215.7	133.7	5.4	40.6	134.8
2019												
1st quarter	666.3	264.3	162.1	43.1	24.9	199.3	409.1	195.3	120.0	3.9	24.9	91.9
2nd quarter	679.1	266.7	162.0	43.7	25.1	209.3	416.6	196.4	120.6	4.1	27.0	97.5
3rd quarter	684.5	269.5	162.9	45.2	24.5	210.5	420.6	198.2	121.9	4.1	26.5	98.4
4th quarter	692.0	272.5	163.7	49.4	24.4	210.4	421.3	199.1	122.6	4.2	26.2	100.3
2020												
1st quarter	693.9	274.6	164.9	45.5	24.0	213.7	430.8	202.3	123.8	6.2	25.6	101.4
2nd quarter	691.5	279.6	166.4	50.0	20.0	204.7	496.1	205.1	125.7	10.7	25.6	156.4
3rd quarter	703.0	282.1	168.2	48.5	22.0	212.0	466.4	214.7	127.3	10.7	25.8	115.9
4th quarter	713.5	284.3	170.5	47.6	22.5	218.8	450.6	211.8	128.9	6.3	26.5	105.9
2021												
1st quarter	707.4	288.5	172.6	46.8	25.1	205.4	512.6	211.5	130.4	5.6	40.2	154.4
2nd quarter	710.0	291.3	175.0	45.0	26.2	204.2	498.1	214.5	132.2	5.2	42.1	138.4
3rd quarter	710.3	292.8	177.9	46.0	27.6	198.1	485.8	217.1	134.6	5.5	38.2	123.3
4th quarter	707.6	295.0	181.1	48.8	29.4	185.9	488.1	219.9	137.4	5.5	42.1	123.0

[1]Excludes government sales to other sectors and government own-account investment (construction and software).
[2]Includes general government intermediate inputs for goods and services sold to other sectors and for own-account investment.

Table 6-4. National Defense Consumption Expenditures and Gross Investment: Selected Detail

(National income and product accounts, calendar years, billions of dollars, quarterly data are at seasonally adjusted annual rates.)

NIPA Table 3.11.5

Year and quarter	Defense consumption expenditures								Defense gross investment				
	Compensation of general government employees		Intermediate goods and services purchased [1]						Aircraft	Missiles	Ships	Software	Research and development
			Durable goods	Nondurable goods		Services							
	Military	Civilian	Aircraft	Petroleum products	Ammunition	Installation support	Weapons support	Personnel support					
1980	41.5	25.2	5.6	6.8	1.4	8.3	3.9	2.3	6.1	2.3	4.1	1.0	16.2
1981	48.8	27.6	7.7	7.7	1.6	9.6	4.8	2.9	7.5	2.8	5.1	1.3	19.6
1982	54.9	29.9	10.2	6.8	2.1	12.6	6.3	3.6	8.4	3.4	6.2	1.4	23.7
1983	57.8	31.5	13.6	6.4	2.5	12.4	7.0	3.9	10.1	4.6	7.1	1.7	28.1
1984	62.0	33.9	14.0	5.9	2.2	13.8	7.2	3.7	10.9	5.7	8.0	2.2	32.8
1985	66.2	36.1	15.4	5.8	1.3	15.1	8.4	5.0	13.4	6.6	9.0	2.7	38.6
1986	69.4	36.8	17.2	3.6	3.6	16.0	9.4	6.2	17.9	7.9	8.9	3.2	40.7
1987	72.2	37.3	18.2	3.9	2.8	17.7	9.2	6.8	17.6	8.7	8.8	3.6	44.5
1988	74.8	39.0	17.9	3.5	3.5	18.3	10.3	9.5	13.5	7.8	8.6	4.3	44.3
1989	76.5	41.4	16.4	4.2	3.1	18.0	10.5	10.2	12.2	8.8	10.0	4.8	42.5
1990	78.5	42.7	14.8	5.3	2.8	21.4	11.6	10.1	12.0	11.2	10.8	5.2	41.4
1991	82.4	44.4	13.6	4.7	2.7	22.9	10.0	9.5	9.2	10.8	10.2	5.4	37.9
1992	80.9	45.9	12.2	3.5	2.6	23.1	9.4	13.7	8.3	10.6	10.1	5.6	35.6
1993	75.1	45.9	10.7	3.2	2.5	25.2	8.8	14.7	9.3	7.9	8.7	5.4	33.7
1994	71.7	45.7	9.2	3.0	1.8	26.2	9.4	16.3	10.5	5.7	8.1	5.3	32.8
1995	69.5	44.6	8.9	2.8	1.2	24.9	9.5	17.0	9.0	4.7	8.0	5.3	33.1
1996	67.7	44.3	8.8	3.4	1.4	25.6	9.0	19.3	9.2	4.1	6.8	5.5	33.4
1997	67.8	43.6	9.4	2.9	1.7	24.7	10.5	21.3	5.8	2.9	6.1	5.6	33.6
1998	68.0	42.8	9.9	2.1	1.9	23.5	10.0	20.6	5.8	3.3	6.4	5.9	33.5
1999	69.8	42.9	10.5	2.6	1.9	24.5	11.3	26.0	7.0	2.9	6.7	5.9	33.3
2000	72.9	44.1	9.8	4.1	1.8	24.7	11.7	26.1	7.8	2.7	6.6	6.0	34.2
2001	78.4	44.8	9.8	4.2	2.1	27.1	14.8	32.4	8.5	3.3	7.2	5.8	36.7
2002	89.7	49.6	9.8	4.6	2.4	30.6	18.0	41.3	9.6	3.3	8.4	5.6	42.3
2003	107.4	53.4	11.4	5.3	2.7	35.8	22.6	49.5	9.2	3.5	9.3	5.7	47.3
2004	113.9	58.3	12.0	7.0	3.6	36.8	23.8	62.4	11.1	4.0	9.8	5.8	52.5
2005	123.3	62.7	10.8	10.1	4.0	36.0	26.5	66.9	13.5	4.0	9.6	6.1	56.8
2006	128.1	64.9	11.1	11.4	4.1	38.3	27.8	71.4	13.6	4.5	10.5	6.4	59.3
2007	133.4	68.1	11.5	12.2	4.2	38.4	29.0	70.7	12.9	4.3	10.3	6.8	62.5
2008	143.0	71.3	12.9	17.6	4.3	41.6	31.3	86.5	13.5	4.3	11.0	7.4	63.4
2009	152.5	76.8	14.9	10.5	4.2	44.2	32.8	93.4	13.8	5.1	11.1	7.5	62.1
2010	159.1	84.9	16.2	13.7	4.2	46.5	37.4	99.3	16.7	5.6	11.8	8.1	62.1
2011	160.9	89.9	18.0	19.2	4.2	44.5	35.6	97.1	20.2	5.1	11.7	8.7	62.6
2012	159.1	88.9	19.3	18.3	4.3	41.9	33.6	97.3	20.2	6.9	12.0	9.0	61.5
2013	153.2	86.3	17.9	15.0	3.6	35.5	28.9	89.9	21.7	6.4	12.5	9.1	58.5
2014	150.0	89.1	16.3	13.3	3.1	39.2	31.1	78.0	19.2	6.6	13.3	9.4	55.4
2015	147.5	91.2	15.8	8.4	2.8	36.5	32.3	75.8	17.6	6.6	13.5	9.4	55.9
2016	148.2	94.0	15.8	6.7	3.1	37.9	33.5	73.3	16.4	4.8	14.4	10.3	51.6
2017	149.0	97.5	16.8	7.9	3.7	39.3	35.7	72.3	18.7	4.7	14.1	11.1	50.6
2018	155.8	102.1	17.1	10.3	4.7	40.4	39.4	83.9	19.7	4.6	15.5	12.3	52.5
2019	162.7	105.6	17.9	8.8	5.5	40.5	44.3	106.5	23.3	5.1	17.2	13.0	53.0
2020	169.6	110.5	18.8	6.0	5.4	45.0	46.3	108.5	21.8	6.8	18.6	13.4	60.3
2021	176.3	115.6	19.0	10.1	5.7	44.7	45.6	94.4	28.1	7.3	18.6	14.6	68.9
2015													
1st quarter	147.5	90.6	16.0	9.1	2.8	37.3	31.7	77.4	15.6	6.5	13.8	9.4	56.3
2nd quarter	147.2	90.8	15.3	8.9	2.8	37.0	32.8	76.8	19.2	6.3	13.1	9.4	56.5
3rd quarter	147.4	91.4	15.7	8.1	2.8	35.5	32.1	74.5	18.1	5.8	13.6	9.4	56.0
4th quarter	147.9	92.0	16.2	7.4	2.9	36.2	32.8	74.3	17.6	7.7	13.6	9.5	54.9
2016													
1st quarter	148.2	92.5	16.3	6.1	2.9	37.2	33.2	73.5	18.7	5.1	14.4	9.9	53.2
2nd quarter	148.3	93.5	14.6	6.5	3.0	37.3	32.5	69.2	16.6	5.6	13.8	10.1	51.9
3rd quarter	148.3	94.5	15.7	7.0	3.1	38.1	34.2	75.4	15.2	5.0	14.7	10.4	50.9
4th quarter	147.9	95.4	16.5	7.2	3.2	38.9	34.1	75.2	15.3	3.7	14.6	10.6	50.4
2017													
1st quarter	148.1	96.4	16.7	8.1	3.4	38.3	33.3	67.5	17.6	5.1	12.3	10.8	50.2
2nd quarter	148.1	96.8	18.2	7.2	3.6	39.2	35.3	75.0	18.4	4.8	14.4	11.1	50.3
3rd quarter	149.2	97.9	15.6	7.6	3.8	39.8	36.8	72.4	18.1	4.7	14.4	11.3	50.6
4th quarter	150.7	99.1	16.8	8.7	4.0	40.0	37.3	74.3	20.5	4.2	15.3	11.5	51.2
2018													
1st quarter	153.0	100.3	15.5	10.3	4.3	39.9	37.3	74.6	17.8	4.7	15.4	11.8	52.1
2nd quarter	154.7	101.7	17.4	10.3	4.5	40.9	39.7	83.3	17.4	4.1	15.7	12.2	52.6
3rd quarter	157.0	102.9	19.3	10.5	4.8	40.3	39.6	84.9	19.7	4.2	15.2	12.4	52.8
4th quarter	158.7	103.6	16.3	10.0	5.1	40.5	41.0	92.7	24.1	5.3	15.8	12.6	52.6
2019													
1st quarter	160.2	104.1	16.9	9.1	5.4	39.8	42.4	101.2	23.7	4.8	16.1	12.7	52.1
2nd quarter	161.6	105.1	17.1	9.2	5.5	40.0	44.1	109.1	20.9	4.0	16.7	12.9	52.3
3rd quarter	163.7	105.8	17.6	8.5	5.6	40.6	44.9	108.9	22.8	4.9	17.9	13.2	53.1
4th quarter	165.2	107.3	20.0	8.5	5.5	41.6	45.7	107.0	25.8	6.7	18.0	13.3	54.6
2020													
1st quarter	165.7	108.9	17.1	8.0	5.5	43.6	46.0	109.3	20.2	6.1	18.5	13.5	56.8
2nd quarter	170.0	109.6	20.3	3.9	5.4	43.9	45.3	104.9	22.8	7.4	18.5	13.2	59.1
3rd quarter	170.8	111.3	19.1	5.8	5.3	45.8	46.4	107.4	20.1	7.0	18.3	13.4	61.4
4th quarter	171.9	112.3	18.7	6.3	5.2	46.6	47.4	112.3	24.1	6.8	18.8	13.6	63.8
2021													
1st quarter	174.8	113.7	19.3	8.8	5.2	45.1	45.2	101.3	24.2	7.7	18.9	14.0	66.2
2nd quarter	176.2	115.1	18.1	9.5	5.4	45.0	45.8	98.5	28.2	6.0	18.8	14.6	68.2
3rd quarter	176.5	116.3	18.6	10.5	5.8	44.8	45.7	94.6	30.4	7.6	18.6	14.9	70.0
4th quarter	177.8	117.2	20.3	11.7	6.4	44.1	45.5	83.4	29.5	7.9	17.9	15.0	71.3

[1] Includes general government intermediate inputs for goods and services sold to other sectors and for own-account investment.

Table 6-5. Federal Government Output, Lending and Borrowing, and Net Investment

(National income and product accounts, calendar years, billions of dollars, quarterly data are at seasonally adjusted annual rates.)

NIPA Tables 3.2, 3.10.5

Year and quarter	Output						Net lending (net borrowing -)							Net investment
	Gross		Value added		Intermediate goods and services purchased [1]		Net saving, current (surplus +, deficit -)	Plus: capital transfer receipts	Minus			Plus: Consumption of fixed capital	Equals: Net lending (borrowing -)	
	Defense	Non-defense	Defense	Non-defense	Defense	Non-defense			Gross investment	Capital transfer payments	Net purchases of non-produced assets			
1965	55.9	14.7	43.5	11.1	12.4	3.6	-5.5	2.8	26.7	4.0	0.5	20.0	-13.9	6.7
1966	66.1	15.1	48.3	12.4	17.9	2.7	-7.0	3.0	30.1	4.4	0.6	21.0	-18.0	9.1
1967	75.7	16.8	52.5	13.5	23.2	3.3	-19.5	3.1	31.9	4.3	-0.2	22.5	-30.0	9.4
1968	83.4	18.0	57.0	15.1	26.4	2.9	-13.8	3.1	31.1	6.0	-0.9	24.2	-22.7	6.9
1969	84.9	20.7	60.3	16.6	24.6	4.1	-5.1	3.6	30.7	5.9	0.1	25.8	-12.5	4.9
1970	84.2	23.5	63.2	19.3	21.0	4.3	-34.8	3.7	30.5	5.3	-0.3	27.6	-39.0	2.9
1971	84.9	27.6	65.3	22.2	19.6	5.4	-50.9	4.6	27.8	5.9	-0.4	29.1	-50.6	-1.3
1972	87.6	31.6	68.0	24.4	19.7	7.2	-49.0	5.4	29.3	6.1	-0.7	30.2	-48.1	-0.9
1973	88.6	33.6	69.7	26.6	18.9	6.9	-38.3	5.1	31.7	6.0	-3.2	32.4	-35.3	-0.7
1974	93.8	37.8	73.0	29.5	20.8	8.3	-41.3	4.8	35.7	7.9	-5.7	35.4	-39.1	0.3
1975	99.4	42.9	77.6	32.9	21.8	10.0	-97.9	4.9	39.9	9.7	-0.4	38.7	-103.4	1.2
1976	102.8	45.8	81.0	36.2	21.8	9.5	-80.9	5.6	44.8	10.6	-2.4	41.7	-86.6	3.1
1977	110.3	50.5	85.4	39.8	24.8	10.8	-73.4	7.2	49.2	11.2	-1.4	45.3	-80.0	3.9
1978	119.2	55.8	92.0	43.8	27.2	12.1	-62.0	5.2	54.7	12.0	-0.6	49.7	-73.2	5.0
1979	130.1	61.1	98.2	47.2	31.9	13.9	-47.4	5.5	61.7	14.5	-2.8	54.6	-60.7	7.1
1980	148.2	70.0	107.3	52.5	40.9	17.5	-88.8	6.5	70.2	16.7	-4.1	60.4	-104.8	9.8
1981	170.9	77.0	121.3	57.0	49.6	20.1	-88.1	6.9	80.4	15.7	-5.5	67.5	-104.3	12.9
1982	193.9	79.5	135.2	60.5	58.7	19.0	-167.4	7.5	90.0	14.7	-3.7	75.4	-185.4	14.6
1983	209.3	86.6	144.4	62.6	64.8	24.0	-207.2	5.8	102.3	15.6	-4.9	81.1	-233.3	21.2
1984	225.9	87.6	158.2	67.1	67.7	20.5	-196.5	6.0	115.6	17.8	-4.0	90.6	-229.4	25.0
1985	243.2	95.8	169.6	70.4	73.6	25.4	-199.2	6.4	132.5	19.6	-1.2	97.0	-246.8	35.5
1986	258.9	100.4	178.8	71.8	80.1	28.6	-215.9	7.0	141.9	20.1	-3.0	103.6	-264.3	38.3
1987	272.0	99.3	187.2	73.8	84.8	25.5	-165.7	7.2	152.4	19.1	-0.4	110.1	-219.5	42.3
1988	287.6	98.3	198.2	80.3	89.4	18.0	-160.0	7.6	148.0	19.8	-0.2	118.9	-201.0	29.1
1989	297.4	109.3	208.0	84.8	89.4	24.5	-159.4	8.9	151.2	20.2	-0.7	126.9	-194.3	24.3
1990	310.1	119.6	215.7	91.0	94.5	28.6	-203.3	11.6	158.2	28.2	-0.8	133.5	-243.8	24.7
1991	324.9	128.0	225.2	98.3	99.7	29.7	-248.4	11.0	156.8	26.5	0.1	140.1	-280.8	16.7
1992	322.0	137.0	226.6	103.0	95.4	34.0	-334.5	11.3	156.4	22.6	0.2	143.3	-359.2	13.1
1993	315.3	141.3	222.3	109.2	92.9	32.2	-313.5	12.9	150.7	24.3	0.2	147.0	-328.7	3.7
1994	310.8	147.9	220.0	112.6	90.7	35.3	-255.6	15.1	145.4	26.0	0.1	150.3	-261.7	-4.9
1995	304.4	151.8	217.4	115.6	87.0	36.2	-242.1	14.9	147.7	27.9	-7.9	153.5	-241.3	-5.8
1996	304.7	152.2	213.7	118.1	91.0	34.2	-179.4	17.5	149.8	28.4	-4.8	153.7	-181.7	-3.9
1997	304.9	160.3	211.8	121.7	93.0	38.6	-92.0	20.6	143.7	29.2	-8.8	154.3	-81.2	-10.6
1998	301.0	163.5	210.4	126.4	90.5	37.2	1.4	25.2	147.7	28.9	-6.0	155.4	11.4	-7.7
1999	313.3	168.1	212.0	133.0	101.3	35.2	69.1	28.8	154.9	38.8	-1.2	158.2	63.6	-3.3
2000	321.6	182.4	217.6	142.7	104.0	39.6	159.7	28.1	157.4	41.2	-0.6	163.1	152.9	-5.7
2001	339.8	196.2	223.0	147.3	116.8	48.9	15.0	28.0	163.8	43.6	-1.5	164.4	1.5	-0.6
2002	374.6	217.8	239.7	158.1	134.9	59.7	-267.8	25.3	182.2	53.4	-0.3	166.8	-310.9	15.4
2003	428.3	236.8	264.3	170.4	164.1	66.4	-397.4	22.0	195.2	69.8	-0.8	172.2	-467.2	23.0
2004	466.3	252.0	281.0	178.4	185.4	73.6	-393.5	24.6	208.4	71.4	-0.6	180.5	-467.5	27.9
2005	497.2	267.8	301.2	187.2	196.0	80.7	-293.8	25.0	222.0	97.5	-1.8	190.5	-396.0	31.5
2006	522.6	283.0	315.1	194.8	207.5	88.2	-221.9	27.8	235.6	76.7	-14.2	201.3	-290.9	34.3
2007	550.0	291.1	331.1	204.6	218.9	86.5	-259.7	26.5	250.0	85.9	-3.3	212.8	-353.0	37.2
2008	606.1	316.5	352.6	216.4	253.5	100.1	-624.9	28.3	271.7	152.1	-20.4	225.9	-774.2	45.8
2009	637.3	344.4	372.7	230.3	264.6	114.1	-1 243.2	20.6	282.6	212.6	-8.9	233.6	-1 475.3	49.0
2010	675.6	373.8	393.5	246.5	282.1	127.3	-1 318.4	15.1	297.2	148.1	-1.0	243.7	-1 504.0	53.5
2011	688.1	366.9	407.1	252.6	281.0	114.2	-1 234.1	9.6	295.7	131.2	-0.9	254.9	-1 395.6	40.8
2012	676.3	370.4	407.6	256.1	268.7	114.3	-1 072.7	14.1	287.3	105.0	-2.0	261.6	-1 187.3	25.7
2013	637.6	366.8	400.1	258.3	237.5	108.5	-631.8	20.9	269.6	85.1	-2.5	265.9	-697.3	3.7
2014	625.3	375.9	400.0	266.8	225.3	109.1	-597.4	18.8	263.8	83.7	-2.6	270.2	-653.2	-6.4
2015	613.3	391.3	398.4	275.3	214.9	116.0	-560.2	20.2	266.6	80.1	-30.9	271.5	-584.4	-4.9
2016	614.7	402.5	399.1	284.8	215.6	117.7	-667.6	20.1	268.8	80.6	-8.9	270.7	-717.3	-1.9
2017	627.2	407.8	403.9	295.3	223.3	112.4	-720.7	273.2	280.0	91.2	-2.2	275.9	-540.7	4.1
2018	664.3	429.0	418.0	308.0	246.3	121.0	-928.1	22.7	299.6	82.2	-0.8	284.9	-1 001.5	14.7
2019	708.4	445.8	430.9	318.5	277.5	127.3	-1 047.5	16.2	317.5	93.9	-2.6	293.3	-1 146.9	24.2
2020	729.9	489.1	447.6	334.9	282.3	154.2	-3 110.0	19.1	340.3	91.8	-2.9	303.5	-3 216.5	36.8
2021	740.6	530.3	468.5	349.4	272.1	180.9	-2 783.8	22.5	360.0	144.9	-9.2	320.3	-2 936.8	39.7
2019														
1st quarter	693.7	436.0	426.4	315.3	267.3	120.7	-1 015.4	17.7	311.5	84.5	-6.3	291.3	-1 096.1	20.2
2nd quarter	706.8	445.6	428.8	316.9	278.1	128.6	-1 033.2	15.5	311.2	77.9	-1.8	291.9	-1 113.1	19.3
3rd quarter	712.6	449.2	432.4	320.2	280.2	129.0	-1 080.9	15.5	319.0	81.0	-1.7	294.2	-1 169.5	24.8
4th quarter	720.4	452.3	436.2	321.7	284.2	130.7	-1 060.4	16.0	328.4	132.3	-0.4	295.8	-1 208.9	32.6
2020														
1st quarter	722.7	459.3	439.5	326.1	283.2	133.2	-1 158.0	17.8	330.0	92.5	-0.3	298.2	-1 264.1	31.8
2nd quarter	720.7	523.4	446.0	330.8	274.7	192.7	-5 625.6	19.3	337.4	92.0	-0.1	301.6	-5 733.9	35.8
3rd quarter	732.7	494.3	450.2	341.9	282.4	152.4	-3 516.3	19.7	345.7	92.1	-11.1	305.1	-3 618.2	40.6
4th quarter	743.7	479.5	454.8	340.7	288.9	138.7	-2 140.1	19.6	348.2	90.4	-0.2	309.2	-2 249.7	39.0
2021														
1st quarter	738.3	542.1	461.1	341.9	277.3	200.2	-4 088.9	20.5	348.7	297.7	-18.3	312.7	-4 383.7	36.0
2nd quarter	741.6	532.4	466.2	346.7	275.4	185.7	-3 312.7	21.0	355.1	89.9	-0.3	317.1	-3 419.2	38.0
3rd quarter	742.4	518.7	470.7	351.7	271.8	167.0	-2 235.6	23.3	365.9	100.6	-18.2	322.6	-2 337.9	43.3
4th quarter	740.2	527.9	476.1	357.3	264.1	170.7	-1 498.1	25.0	370.5	91.4	0.0	328.8	-1 606.2	41.7

[1] Includes general government intermediate inputs for goods and services sold to other sectors and for own-account investment.

Table 6-6. Chain-Type Quantity Indexes for Federal Government Defense and Nondefense Consumption Expenditures and Gross Investment

(Seasonally adjusted, 2012 = 100.)   NIPA Tables 3.9.3, 3.10.3

Year and quarter	Defense consumption expenditures [1]						Defense gross investment	Nondefense consumption expenditures [1]						Non-defense gross investment
	Total	Compensation of general government employees	Consumption of general government fixed capital	Intermediate goods and services purchased [2]				Total	Compensation of general government employees	Consumption of general government fixed capital	Intermediate goods and services purchased [2]			
				Durable goods	Non-durable goods	Services					Durable goods	Non-durable goods excluding CCC inventory change	Services	
1965	67.1	124.2	59.0	35.1	123.2	20.9	40.4	26.1	57.5	13.4	4.7	16.8	21.7	33.8
1966	76.2	136.9	59.8	51.0	175.7	26.8	44.9	25.3	59.8	15.9	5.0	17.0	22.4	37.8
1967	85.7	149.0	61.4	50.4	269.3	34.2	50.4	28.0	62.8	18.2	4.9	19.0	20.4	34.8
1968	89.6	151.0	63.0	58.3	309.3	35.4	46.0	28.2	64.2	20.5	3.2	12.6	12.5	35.5
1969	86.5	151.2	63.3	48.6	274.6	33.1	42.9	30.9	64.8	22.6	3.2	13.1	15.2	34.2
1970	79.4	140.2	62.9	43.5	191.2	30.7	39.2	32.1	65.7	24.4	3.9	16.5	20.9	32.8
1971	73.5	129.5	61.2	31.4	156.4	31.2	30.7	34.9	67.8	26.0	4.8	20.3	24.3	32.7
1972	68.8	119.7	59.0	38.3	159.1	26.8	27.6	38.1	69.8	27.3	7.9	24.8	32.0	33.8
1973	64.1	113.6	57.2	35.0	118.3	24.7	28.8	38.1	70.0	28.7	7.2	23.8	30.4	34.0
1974	62.3	111.9	55.9	30.4	102.4	26.0	31.0	40.6	73.5	30.0	7.7	25.1	31.4	34.1
1975	60.9	110.4	54.9	32.2	84.8	23.9	32.3	42.4	74.8	31.2	8.1	22.8	31.8	35.1
1976	59.5	108.2	54.3	29.1	67.5	23.9	34.4	42.2	78.5	32.6	8.5	22.6	26.6	37.4
1977	59.8	107.2	54.1	36.5	64.5	23.8	35.4	43.9	80.2	34.1	11.1	22.3	29.0	39.5
1978	60.2	108.0	53.9	40.1	65.4	23.0	35.7	45.6	82.3	35.9	12.8	32.9	29.8	43.6
1979	60.6	107.1	53.9	43.7	67.4	23.5	39.1	46.4	82.2	37.8	15.0	32.3	32.5	44.1
1980	62.1	107.7	54.4	46.0	73.7	26.0	41.9	49.6	84.4	39.7	16.9	31.4	33.2	45.2
1981	65.1	111.1	55.5	54.1	78.4	28.1	46.5	50.8	81.9	41.4	15.8	58.7	28.2	44.5
1982	68.6	113.6	57.3	59.4	78.1	33.7	52.5	49.8	80.4	42.8	14.6	43.8	26.7	41.3
1983	71.5	115.4	60.1	70.9	81.4	34.0	60.5	53.3	81.6	44.1	15.6	54.8	32.2	41.2
1984	73.2	117.0	63.7	72.0	77.0	35.5	68.1	51.6	81.6	45.4	16.9	57.0	33.1	42.4
1985	76.8	119.2	68.5	77.7	75.4	39.1	80.4	54.6	81.8	46.6	17.4	49.6	35.9	44.7
1986	80.8	119.6	73.9	83.7	95.8	41.7	89.5	56.4	80.5	47.9	17.2	42.3	35.7	45.8
1987	83.6	120.7	79.3	88.9	93.9	42.6	97.0	54.9	82.0	49.3	19.6	49.0	40.2	48.8
1988	85.3	119.2	83.8	91.2	91.2	44.8	90.6	51.8	84.1	50.7	20.7	48.8	37.9	48.2
1989	85.8	119.2	86.9	87.7	88.2	44.8	88.3	56.1	84.5	52.2	23.4	43.6	37.5	50.6
1990	86.1	118.5	89.1	84.5	78.3	47.5	88.3	60.1	88.7	53.8	26.7	46.4	44.5	54.5
1991	87.4	118.0	90.1	81.1	79.4	51.2	81.7	60.4	88.5	55.7	28.4	40.6	44.1	58.1
1992	83.6	111.3	90.0	72.8	73.6	49.5	77.0	64.0	90.1	57.3	30.9	50.5	49.7	61.6
1993	80.8	106.5	88.9	65.9	67.6	48.9	68.9	63.4	90.0	58.9	30.1	55.0	42.5	62.7
1994	77.2	101.0	87.1	56.5	61.5	49.4	64.4	64.1	87.5	60.3	28.3	46.2	50.0	59.7
1995	74.1	95.5	85.0	51.5	50.3	47.6	61.8	63.5	84.0	61.7	27.6	52.1	48.2	61.0
1996	72.7	91.4	83.0	51.1	55.5	48.7	61.3	62.2	81.8	63.3	31.4	45.0	45.5	62.9
1997	71.6	88.1	81.2	51.3	56.0	49.4	57.0	64.9	81.3	65.0	33.8	54.9	48.4	62.4
1998	69.7	85.3	79.4	51.7	57.8	47.0	57.1	64.5	82.2	66.8	34.0	59.7	44.3	65.9
1999	70.7	83.2	77.9	55.0	64.2	52.1	57.7	65.1	82.4	69.1	38.1	44.4	43.9	69.9
2000	69.7	82.6	76.7	54.4	67.3	51.1	58.3	67.7	84.9	71.5	41.9	50.5	46.1	69.0
2001	71.6	83.1	75.7	54.7	69.6	58.0	61.6	71.9	84.9	73.5	45.1	67.1	54.2	70.6
2002	75.5	85.3	75.7	57.3	80.0	67.4	70.8	77.1	86.4	75.6	54.9	73.3	67.8	75.8
2003	81.7	88.2	76.9	62.9	87.3	81.0	76.6	80.4	88.6	77.5	56.5	88.0	71.9	78.3
2004	85.7	89.9	78.9	68.3	97.9	88.0	83.0	82.2	87.8	79.5	62.6	98.5	77.2	79.2
2005	86.7	90.2	81.5	70.0	99.0	88.8	88.5	83.5	87.7	81.7	68.9	99.7	81.4	80.4
2006	87.4	88.9	84.5	75.4	96.3	90.3	92.6	86.3	87.8	84.4	77.2	98.4	86.8	84.2
2007	89.0	88.6	87.6	84.8	98.3	90.8	98.6	86.3	88.4	87.1	79.0	95.6	81.9	85.4
2008	94.8	91.9	91.2	97.9	100.1	100.2	106.6	91.4	91.7	89.6	88.6	106.3	91.6	88.5
2009	100.8	97.8	94.5	106.1	105.9	107.1	110.4	98.8	96.5	92.3	96.7	123.2	105.1	92.6
2010	104.4	101.0	97.3	106.7	102.3	113.4	111.1	103.8	100.7	94.8	106.5	129.8	115.1	100.6
2011	102.9	102.0	99.2	103.0	104.3	106.7	105.9	98.6	99.5	97.5	99.8	106.9	100.5	101.0
2012	100.0	100.0	100.0	100.0	100.0	100.0	100.0	100.0	100.0	100.0	100.0	100.0	100.0	100.0
2013	93.4	96.5	99.7	87.6	88.9	87.2	93.0	97.5	97.1	102.3	94.7	92.3	94.0	93.7
2014	90.1	94.5	98.5	79.7	83.3	82.4	86.9	97.3	97.0	104.3	97.9	90.2	93.4	94.1
2015	88.0	92.2	97.0	77.5	84.6	80.0	85.8	100.2	98.1	106.2	102.7	95.9	100.1	97.9
2016	88.0	92.1	95.6	78.7	90.4	79.6	83.6	101.4	100.1	108.3	104.4	96.3	101.2	102.6
2017	88.3	92.2	94.6	83.6	93.0	79.5	86.4	99.8	99.9	111.1	100.2	91.8	94.0	105.5
2018	90.8	93.1	94.2	89.4	94.7	85.8	91.2	101.6	99.2	114.2	104.4	95.5	98.2	110.1
2019	95.3	94.6	94.5	96.9	93.0	97.5	97.1	103.1	99.1	117.2	106.2	101.7	100.4	112.6
2020	97.1	96.8	95.5	101.8	94.9	98.8	103.8	112.8	104.0	120.1	217.2	101.0	122.8	117.4
2021	94.5	97.3	97.3	97.2	95.7	89.5	109.8	117.4	103.3	123.0	135.0	151.0	134.5	116.7
2019														
1st quarter	93.8	94.1	94.3	92.3	93.7	94.3	94.9	99.3	93.8	116.1	101.5	97.0	96.0	111.1
2nd quarter	95.2	94.3	94.4	93.4	93.0	98.6	94.0	104.0	100.6	116.8	107.2	104.2	101.2	112.7
3rd quarter	95.7	94.8	94.5	96.5	92.7	98.9	97.6	104.7	101.3	117.6	107.8	103.9	101.5	112.9
4th quarter	96.4	95.4	94.7	105.4	92.3	98.3	102.0	104.3	100.9	118.3	108.5	101.9	102.9	113.9
2020														
1st quarter	96.4	95.8	95.0	96.8	93.6	99.5	100.8	106.2	101.8	119.0	159.9	100.2	103.9	115.9
2nd quarter	96.5	97.2	95.3	106.4	94.1	95.7	104.3	121.8	102.7	119.7	273.9	101.5	160.5	115.5
3rd quarter	97.2	97.0	95.7	102.9	95.2	98.6	103.7	113.9	107.0	120.5	272.7	98.3	118.6	121.1
4th quarter	98.1	97.2	96.1	101.1	96.6	101.4	106.6	109.4	104.4	121.2	162.3	103.9	108.0	117.3
2021														
1st quarter	96.0	97.8	96.6	98.9	95.6	94.1	107.5	123.4	103.1	121.9	142.7	153.7	156.5	115.2
2nd quarter	95.3	97.8	97.0	94.4	94.9	92.6	109.0	118.7	103.5	122.7	129.1	158.2	138.9	115.7
3rd quarter	94.2	97.0	97.5	95.6	95.3	88.9	111.8	114.2	103.4	123.4	135.0	140.9	122.2	117.4
4th quarter	92.5	96.5	98.1	100.0	97.0	82.4	110.8	113.2	103.3	124.1	133.1	151.2	120.4	118.3

[1] Excludes government sales to other sectors and government own-account investment (construction and software).
[2] Includes general government intermediate inputs for goods and services sold to other sectors and for own-account investment.

Table 6-7. Chain-Type Quantity Indexes for National Defense Consumption Expenditures and Gross Investment: Selected Detail

(Seasonally adjusted, 2012 = 100.)   NIPA Table 3.11.3

Year and quarter	Defense consumption expenditures								Defense gross investment				
	Compensation of general government employees		Intermediate goods and services purchased [1]						Aircraft	Missiles	Ships	Software	Research and develop-ment
			Durable goods	Nondurable goods		Services							
	Military	Civilian	Aircraft	Petroleum products	Ammu-nition	Installation support	Weapons support	Personnel support					
1980	103.8	113.6	49.9	118.3	65.8	51.4	30.8	8.6	31.9	32.0	84.7	11.7	61.4
1981	107.2	116.8	64.3	116.3	74.3	55.8	33.6	9.6	36.9	37.1	96.5	14.0	68.2
1982	109.1	120.6	75.0	109.6	91.6	68.1	41.4	11.3	37.1	47.9	112.6	15.3	76.8
1983	111.0	122.1	91.4	117.2	107.4	65.1	43.3	12.4	42.1	60.6	125.1	17.8	87.1
1984	112.3	124.2	86.5	116.9	90.9	70.5	43.9	11.5	45.3	72.9	132.5	23.5	97.5
1985	114.0	127.5	92.9	119.1	54.2	74.7	49.5	14.9	61.8	83.1	145.6	28.7	112.3
1986	115.0	126.8	102.7	119.6	145.9	74.7	54.5	17.5	94.2	105.3	140.5	34.1	116.6
1987	116.4	127.2	109.9	122.0	110.7	79.4	52.6	17.7	108.1	119.8	136.5	38.1	125.4
1988	115.5	124.4	113.7	103.4	127.8	79.0	56.6	21.0	88.9	109.1	129.5	44.2	119.5
1989	115.0	125.6	107.2	113.2	106.9	77.0	55.3	21.3	81.3	124.9	143.7	50.6	111.1
1990	115.3	122.7	94.2	111.9	96.4	87.4	59.3	19.6	75.0	162.2	151.6	54.8	105.8
1991	116.6	118.8	84.2	110.6	90.9	92.0	48.7	17.5	53.9	163.1	136.0	56.3	93.8
1992	106.7	118.2	73.4	92.4	86.3	90.5	43.7	24.0	47.2	161.3	131.4	60.8	86.2
1993	101.2	115.0	63.7	89.0	85.7	98.1	39.3	25.0	50.8	117.2	110.9	58.0	80.1
1994	96.4	108.3	54.0	91.6	59.0	99.0	41.0	26.8	50.8	86.0	99.8	57.1	76.1
1995	91.4	101.9	51.5	83.0	37.8	91.1	40.7	27.0	41.1	72.5	93.9	56.0	73.6
1996	88.1	96.5	51.1	83.7	44.2	92.7	37.8	29.5	40.0	64.9	79.3	58.9	73.1
1997	85.7	91.6	54.6	75.4	54.3	89.1	42.7	32.0	27.8	48.0	70.4	60.5	71.9
1998	83.8	87.4	57.9	73.5	61.5	83.7	40.5	30.2	28.0	54.1	74.4	64.6	70.7
1999	82.3	84.3	61.2	79.7	62.6	85.8	44.7	36.9	29.1	49.0	78.8	64.4	68.9
2000	83.0	81.5	57.0	73.5	59.5	85.3	44.9	35.5	33.9	46.2	75.0	63.6	68.6
2001	84.7	80.2	56.2	87.0	68.0	90.7	55.5	42.4	39.6	58.0	82.2	60.2	73.4
2002	87.8	80.7	56.6	103.2	80.5	100.3	66.9	52.5	47.3	58.0	95.1	58.7	84.3
2003	92.6	80.5	64.3	99.5	87.4	112.2	82.3	61.2	45.0	59.8	103.3	60.4	92.8
2004	93.7	83.2	66.2	103.0	110.7	110.3	84.4	75.3	55.4	67.9	105.0	62.6	100.8
2005	93.1	85.0	58.5	100.5	117.7	103.1	91.3	78.8	69.5	65.8	100.0	65.8	106.5
2006	91.0	85.2	58.9	99.2	112.9	105.7	93.6	81.9	70.7	74.1	105.7	68.9	109.0
2007	90.2	85.7	61.0	98.3	111.0	102.0	95.7	78.3	67.4	70.3	99.4	73.3	112.1
2008	94.2	87.8	68.0	99.0	105.1	106.6	100.7	94.1	68.2	68.1	102.3	78.6	110.6
2009	101.5	91.3	78.2	99.8	107.2	114.2	103.5	100.2	69.1	79.1	101.1	80.3	108.5
2010	103.1	97.2	85.0	102.0	105.3	116.7	116.3	105.2	82.7	85.6	104.6	88.6	106.1
2011	102.7	100.7	94.2	104.8	99.7	106.9	108.0	101.2	97.5	75.4	98.7	95.5	103.6
2012	100.0	100.0	100.0	100.0	100.0	100.0	100.0	100.0	100.0	100.0	100.0	100.0	100.0
2013	97.5	94.7	92.6	83.8	82.7	83.5	84.8	91.2	110.1	92.8	104.7	101.6	94.3
2014	94.4	94.6	83.8	77.5	70.7	90.2	89.8	78.0	97.5	96.5	108.7	104.9	87.3
2015	91.0	94.2	80.8	80.4	64.9	85.6	91.9	74.8	93.5	95.5	110.8	106.7	87.3
2016	90.4	94.8	80.7	82.2	71.4	88.4	94.0	71.3	87.2	71.0	117.9	117.2	80.8
2017	90.5	94.9	85.9	77.1	85.5	89.6	98.7	68.9	100.7	70.8	114.6	128.4	77.6
2018	91.6	95.6	87.1	75.9	108.8	89.4	106.9	78.2	106.9	69.3	125.0	142.8	78.1
2019	93.0	97.3	90.6	71.7	127.2	87.9	118.1	97.5	126.3	76.9	137.3	151.5	77.0
2020	95.3	99.3	94.6	75.1	124.2	95.9	121.5	97.8	118.0	105.4	147.1	158.0	84.4
2021	95.7	99.9	94.7	78.3	123.3	91.7	116.9	82.8	150.7	113.9	142.8	174.4	93.3
2015													
1st quarter	91.6	94.5	81.8	82.0	64.5	87.6	90.1	76.9	80.7	94.5	113.3	106.2	87.8
2nd quarter	90.9	94.1	78.0	77.1	63.6	86.7	93.3	76.0	102.9	91.9	107.5	106.2	87.8
3rd quarter	90.7	94.1	80.6	79.5	64.7	83.2	91.3	73.4	96.2	85.8	111.3	106.4	87.3
4th quarter	90.7	94.2	82.9	82.8	66.8	85.0	92.9	73.1	94.3	110.0	111.2	108.1	86.1
2016													
1st quarter	90.7	94.4	83.4	85.9	68.4	87.5	93.7	72.0	99.5	75.9	118.2	112.7	84.1
2nd quarter	90.5	94.7	74.5	80.9	70.0	87.3	91.4	67.4	88.8	80.4	113.3	115.6	81.4
3rd quarter	90.4	95.0	80.4	82.0	72.0	88.6	95.8	73.1	79.9	72.6	120.3	118.9	79.7
4th quarter	90.2	95.1	84.3	79.8	74.9	90.0	95.2	72.7	80.7	54.9	119.8	121.7	78.1
2017													
1st quarter	90.1	95.1	85.4	78.2	78.5	88.3	92.8	64.7	94.3	76.1	99.8	124.1	77.7
2nd quarter	90.1	94.8	92.4	76.9	82.7	89.6	97.8	71.7	99.7	72.3	117.6	126.8	77.4
3rd quarter	90.6	94.9	79.8	76.3	87.6	90.3	101.7	69.0	98.2	71.8	117.0	129.7	77.5
4th quarter	91.2	94.9	85.9	76.9	93.0	90.0	102.5	70.3	110.4	63.1	124.2	133.1	77.9
2018													
1st quarter	91.2	94.7	78.8	79.7	99.0	89.0	102.1	70.1	97.5	70.8	124.5	137.2	78.4
2nd quarter	91.4	95.7	88.7	75.0	105.2	90.7	108.0	77.9	94.8	60.2	126.9	142.0	78.3
3rd quarter	91.8	96.1	98.2	75.1	111.9	89.0	107.2	79.0	106.6	64.9	121.6	144.3	78.2
4th quarter	92.0	96.0	82.8	73.7	119.1	89.0	110.5	85.9	128.6	81.4	126.9	147.6	77.6
2019													
1st quarter	92.6	96.6	85.9	73.8	124.2	86.9	113.7	93.1	126.6	72.2	129.4	147.2	76.3
2nd quarter	92.6	97.1	86.6	71.9	127.6	87.1	118.0	100.0	113.6	62.2	134.2	150.2	76.1
3rd quarter	93.1	97.5	89.1	70.9	128.9	88.0	119.5	99.5	125.2	72.9	142.5	153.0	76.7
4th quarter	93.8	98.1	101.0	70.3	128.3	89.7	121.2	97.3	139.6	100.4	143.0	155.8	78.7
2020													
1st quarter	93.9	98.8	86.1	72.3	127.3	93.6	121.7	98.7	110.4	91.3	147.2	158.5	81.0
2nd quarter	96.2	98.9	102.7	73.5	125.6	94.1	119.2	95.0	126.7	108.7	147.2	155.9	83.1
3rd quarter	95.5	99.6	95.7	75.2	123.5	97.5	121.4	96.9	108.4	111.2	145.1	157.8	85.6
4th quarter	95.7	99.8	94.0	79.5	120.6	98.5	123.6	100.7	126.5	110.3	148.9	160.0	88.0
2021													
1st quarter	96.4	100.1	96.5	78.4	117.9	94.7	117.2	89.5	128.2	123.9	147.5	167.5	90.8
2nd quarter	96.3	100.2	90.1	78.2	118.6	93.1	118.2	86.6	149.5	97.7	146.4	173.7	92.9
3rd quarter	95.2	100.0	92.1	77.9	124.0	90.9	116.9	82.7	165.6	115.7	142.7	177.5	94.3
4th quarter	94.8	99.3	100.1	78.5	132.7	88.1	115.4	72.4	159.4	118.4	134.5	179.1	95.2

[1] Includes general government intermediate inputs for goods and services sold to other sectors and for own-account investment.

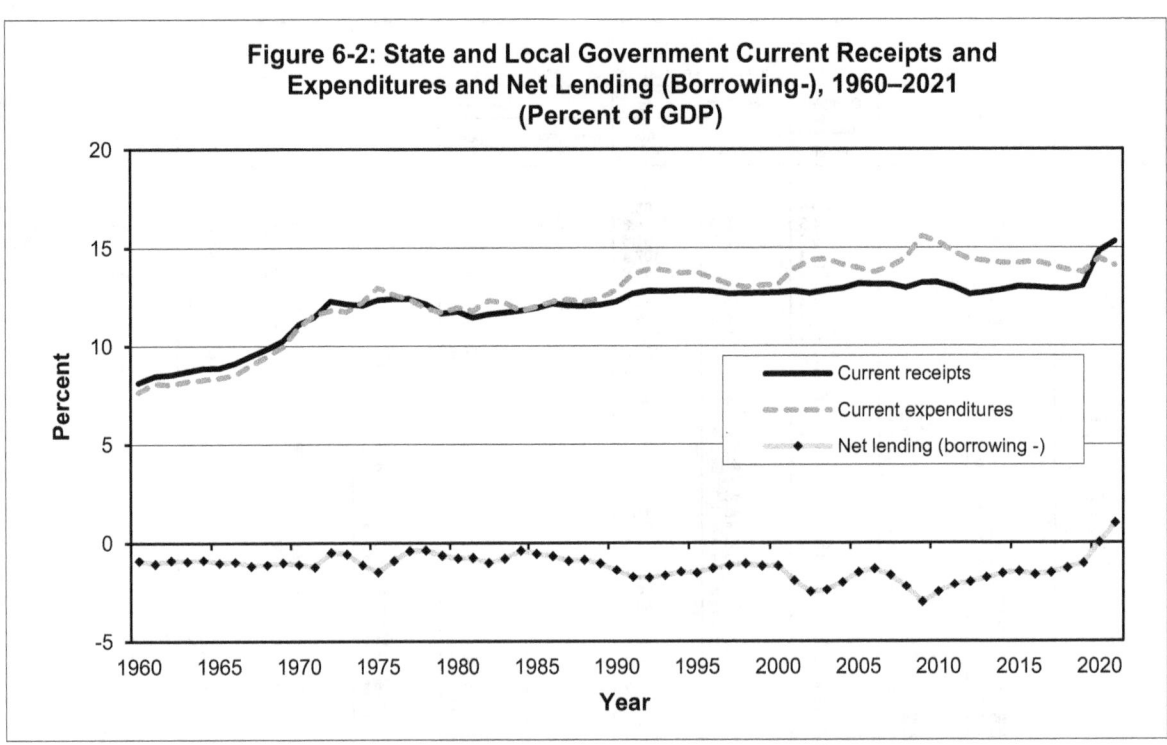

Figure 6-2: State and Local Government Current Receipts and Expenditures and Net Lending (Borrowing-), 1960–2021 (Percent of GDP)

SECTION 6B: STATE AND LOCAL GOVERNMENT IN THE NATIONAL INCOME AND PRODUCT ACCOUNTS

- Both current receipts and current spending of state and local governments have increased as a share of gross domestic product (GDP) over the postwar period, but the growth slowed markedly after the early 1970s. (Tables 6-8 and 1-1)

- State and local governments have consistently been net borrowers in capital markets, as can be seen by the negative values in Figure 6-2. Although they are usually constrained to balance their statutory budgets, they have consistently made net investments and been able to borrow for that purpose. In addition, as revealed by the accrual accounting adopted in the NIPA accounts last year, they have often incurred hidden deficits by failing to fund commitments for public employee retirement benefits. (Table 6-10)

- A larger gap between current expenditures and current receipts appeared during the slow-growth years 2001–2003, and a still-greater one during the Great Recession beginning in late 2007. Generally, in both of those periods of rising deficits, receipts barely kept pace with the economy, while general ("consumption") expenditures, social benefits, and interest payments all fueled higher spending. (Table 6-8)

- Net lending by state and local government reached a high of $-437 billion in 2009 but declined to $-220.7 billion in 2019. By 2020, it was a positive $3.1 billion and in 2021, it increased to $226.5. (Table 6-10)

Table 6-8. State and Local Government Current Receipts

(National income and product accounts, calendar years, billions of dollars, quarterly data are at seasonally adjusted annual rates.)

NIPA Table 3.3

Year and quarter	Total current receipts	Current tax receipts							Contributions for government social insurance	Income receipts on assets		
		Total tax receipts	Personal current taxes		Taxes on production and imports			Taxes on corporate income		Interest receipts	Dividends	Rents and royalties
			Income taxes	Other personal taxes	Sales taxes	Property taxes	Other taxes on prod. and imports					
1965	65.9	53.9	4.4	2.2	8.6	23.2	3.9	2.0	0.8	1.8	. . .	0.4
1966	74.2	58.8	5.4	2.4	9.8	24.5	4.3	2.2	0.8	2.1	. . .	0.5
1967	81.7	64.0	6.1	2.5	10.7	27.0	4.4	2.6	0.9	2.4	. . .	0.6
1968	92.6	73.4	7.8	2.7	13.1	29.9	4.6	3.3	0.9	2.8	. . .	0.7
1969	104.5	82.5	9.8	3.0	15.1	32.8	4.7	3.6	1.0	3.6	. . .	0.8
1970	119.1	91.3	10.9	3.3	17.0	36.7	5.0	3.7	1.1	4.3	. . .	0.8
1971	133.7	101.7	12.4	3.5	19.1	40.4	5.7	4.3	1.2	4.6	. . .	0.9
1972	157.1	115.6	17.2	3.7	21.8	43.2	6.4	5.3	1.3	4.9	. . .	1.0
1973	173.0	126.3	18.9	4.0	24.5	46.4	7.0	6.0	1.5	6.6	0.0	1.1
1974	186.6	136.0	20.4	4.2	28.0	49.0	7.7	6.7	1.7	8.9	0.0	1.3
1975	208.0	147.4	22.5	4.4	30.3	53.4	8.1	7.3	1.8	9.8	0.0	1.3
1976	232.2	165.7	26.3	4.8	34.4	58.2	9.0	9.6	2.2	9.0	0.0	1.3
1977	258.3	183.7	30.4	5.0	39.0	63.2	9.7	11.4	2.8	10.4	0.0	1.3
1978	285.8	198.2	35.0	5.5	44.2	63.7	10.9	12.1	3.4	13.3	0.1	1.3
1979	306.3	212.0	38.2	5.8	49.5	64.4	12.7	13.6	3.9	18.1	0.1	1.9
1980	335.9	230.0	42.6	6.3	53.6	68.8	15.0	14.5	3.6	23.1	0.1	3.1
1981	367.5	255.8	47.9	6.7	58.8	77.1	17.9	15.4	3.9	28.5	0.1	3.3
1982	388.5	273.2	51.9	7.3	62.0	85.3	18.5	14.0	4.0	33.1	0.2	3.5
1983	425.3	300.9	58.3	7.8	70.4	91.9	19.4	15.9	4.1	37.0	0.2	4.3
1984	476.1	337.3	67.5	8.6	80.6	99.7	21.8	18.8	4.7	42.6	0.2	4.9
1985	517.5	363.7	72.1	9.2	87.9	107.5	23.5	20.2	4.9	50.1	0.2	5.4
1986	557.4	389.5	77.4	9.8	93.7	116.2	23.7	22.7	6.0	52.6	0.2	6.2
1987	585.5	422.1	86.0	10.6	100.9	126.4	24.9	23.9	7.2	53.0	0.2	5.3
1988	630.4	452.8	90.6	11.5	110.0	136.5	25.7	26.0	8.4	56.6	0.2	4.4
1989	681.4	488.0	102.3	12.4	117.4	149.9	26.9	24.2	9.0	62.3	0.2	4.1
1990	730.1	519.1	109.6	13.0	125.6	161.5	28.2	22.5	10.0	64.1	0.2	4.2
1991	779.9	544.3	111.7	13.6	128.0	176.1	28.6	23.6	11.6	62.4	0.3	4.5
1992	836.1	579.8	120.4	14.9	136.0	184.7	31.1	24.4	13.1	58.8	0.5	4.8
1993	878.0	604.7	126.2	14.8	143.7	187.3	33.1	26.9	14.1	56.2	0.6	4.5
1994	935.1	644.2	132.2	15.8	155.4	199.4	35.4	30.0	14.5	58.4	0.8	4.5
1995	981.0	672.1	141.7	16.4	164.4	202.6	37.0	31.7	13.6	63.8	1.0	4.5
1996	1 033.7	709.6	152.3	16.3	174.4	212.4	39.3	33.0	12.5	68.0	1.4	4.6
1997	1 086.7	749.9	164.7	17.3	184.2	223.5	41.6	34.1	10.8	72.0	1.5	4.8
1998	1 149.6	794.9	183.0	18.2	194.9	231.0	43.9	34.9	10.4	75.2	1.6	4.6
1999	1 222.9	840.4	195.5	19.0	208.6	242.8	45.8	35.8	9.8	79.0	1.5	5.1
2000	1 304.3	893.2	217.4	19.4	221.4	254.7	49.8	35.2	10.8	86.8	1.4	6.3
2001	1 354.1	914.3	223.3	19.7	223.1	268.0	52.6	28.9	13.7	82.2	1.4	6.5
2002	1 386.9	923.9	199.3	20.6	222.5	289.2	56.3	30.9	15.8	71.4	1.6	6.6
2003	1 470.9	974.3	202.8	22.1	233.3	306.9	63.0	34.0	19.9	63.7	1.8	7.6
2004	1 579.2	1 060.3	221.4	24.3	252.0	326.1	77.4	41.7	24.7	65.7	2.3	8.5
2005	1 717.5	1 173.2	249.1	26.2	272.8	351.2	91.7	54.9	24.6	76.3	2.5	9.8
2006	1 815.3	1 258.2	274.2	26.9	293.9	375.2	92.1	59.2	21.5	94.2	3.0	10.5
2007	1 901.4	1 321.7	294.3	27.3	301.4	403.7	92.9	57.9	18.8	103.9	3.4	11.7
2008	1 915.3	1 334.1	304.1	26.8	301.1	415.7	94.7	47.4	18.7	91.1	3.4	12.2
2009	1 915.5	1 265.8	258.9	26.9	279.6	439.6	72.3	44.5	18.6	73.8	2.9	11.2
2010	1 993.1	1 306.4	265.8	28.3	295.1	438.6	77.8	46.1	17.8	67.8	3.0	11.4
2011	2 029.1	1 366.4	294.1	28.8	311.3	439.2	83.9	48.4	17.9	65.9	3.4	12.2
2012	2 055.2	1 414.7	313.1	30.0	324.4	444.3	86.7	50.7	17.2	64.3	4.1	12.5
2013	2 144.9	1 490.6	343.1	30.4	343.9	456.8	91.6	53.9	17.7	64.3	4.7	12.5
2014	2 256.4	1 541.9	349.4	31.5	361.7	475.0	93.0	56.5	18.7	65.3	5.3	12.7
2015	2 372.6	1 598.4	374.5	32.9	374.2	490.4	89.0	56.2	19.2	64.9	5.4	11.2
2016	2 429.1	1 638.8	375.9	34.4	384.8	511.6	91.8	53.4	20.0	66.6	5.7	10.8
2017	2 517.6	1 724.7	399.8	35.6	405.6	536.0	97.1	54.6	19.8	71.4	5.9	10.9
2018	2 650.6	1 818.4	421.8	38.0	426.9	555.1	107.4	60.5	20.4	77.4	6.1	10.9
2019	2 793.1	1 927.0	457.1	39.4	443.9	599.6	108.9	72.9	20.4	78.2	6.6	12.0
2020	3 096.6	1 963.6	476.1	39.8	448.9	615.3	109.8	71.0	19.9	76.8	6.3	13.3
2021	3 519.4	2 159.6	554.2	41.0	499.5	632.8	119.9	97.0	22.1	78.4	6.5	13.6
2019												
1st quarter	2 725.8	1 877.5	434.1	38.9	434.2	585.2	106.9	73.2	20.6	78.6	6.7	11.5
2nd quarter	2 811.4	1 942.4	481.7	39.2	437.8	597.1	108.6	72.8	20.5	78.3	6.6	11.8
3rd quarter	2 810.2	1 942.6	457.8	39.6	452.7	605.6	109.1	73.1	20.3	78.0	6.4	12.2
4th quarter	2 824.8	1 945.5	454.9	39.8	451.0	610.5	111.1	72.4	20.2	77.7	6.8	12.6
2020												
1st quarter	2 856.3	1 961.6	463.9	39.9	457.0	612.0	115.0	66.5	20.1	76.8	6.3	13.0
2nd quarter	3 550.7	1 901.6	480.2	37.3	419.3	613.9	101.0	61.9	19.1	76.8	6.2	13.2
3rd quarter	2 979.2	1 989.1	478.7	40.9	457.2	616.3	111.0	76.8	19.9	76.7	5.9	13.4
4th quarter	3 000.2	2 002.0	481.8	41.1	462.0	619.1	112.2	78.8	20.5	77.1	6.7	13.5
2021												
1st quarter	3 100.7	2 059.5	519.7	40.5	471.0	622.7	115.5	85.5	21.2	77.5	6.7	13.5
2nd quarter	4 031.4	2 136.8	545.6	40.9	499.8	628.3	117.6	91.9	21.9	78.1	6.4	13.6
3rd quarter	3 511.7	2 182.3	564.3	40.9	506.0	636.5	119.8	95.3	22.5	78.8	6.3	13.6
4th quarter	3 433.8	2 259.6	587.4	41.6	521.3	643.8	126.7	115.4	22.8	79.3	6.6	13.7

. . . = Not available.

Table 6-9. State and Local Government Consumption Expenditures and Gross Investment

(National income and product accounts, calendar years, billions of dollars, quarterly data are at seasonally adjusted annual rates.)

NIPA Tables 3.9.5, 3.10.5

Year and quarter	State and local government consumption expenditures and gross investment										Gross investment			
	Total	Consumption expenditures [1]					Less							
								Sales to other sectors						
		Total	Compensation of general government employees	Consumption of general government fixed capital	Intermediate goods and services purchased [2]	Own-account investment	Total [3]	Tuition and related educational charges	Health and hospital charges	Total	Structures	Equipment	Intellectual property
1965	70.9	49.7	39.8	5.1	13.4	1.4	7.2	1.0	1.8	21.2	19.0	1.8	0.4
1966	78.9	55.4	44.6	5.7	14.9	1.5	8.2	1.2	2.1	23.5	21.0	2.0	0.4
1967	87.0	61.3	49.5	6.2	16.4	1.6	9.3	1.4	2.5	25.7	23.0	2.2	0.5
1968	97.6	69.4	56.3	6.9	18.6	1.8	10.7	1.6	3.1	28.1	25.2	2.3	0.6
1969	107.8	79.0	63.2	7.8	21.8	1.9	11.8	1.9	3.5	28.8	25.6	2.6	0.7
1970	119.8	90.4	71.5	8.8	25.3	2.1	13.1	2.4	3.8	29.3	25.8	2.8	0.8
1971	133.0	102.3	80.5	9.8	29.1	2.2	14.9	2.9	4.6	30.7	27.0	2.9	0.8
1972	144.5	113.2	89.5	10.7	32.0	2.3	16.7	3.2	5.6	31.3	27.1	3.3	0.9
1973	158.6	124.6	98.5	11.9	35.3	2.4	18.7	3.7	6.6	34.0	29.1	3.8	1.0
1974	182.5	142.0	108.1	14.7	42.6	2.8	20.5	4.0	7.4	40.5	34.7	4.6	1.2
1975	207.4	162.8	121.3	16.7	50.5	3.0	22.6	4.3	8.5	44.6	38.1	5.1	1.3
1976	219.4	174.5	130.6	17.4	55.0	3.0	25.6	4.7	9.9	44.9	38.1	5.3	1.5
1977	234.0	190.0	142.1	18.4	60.8	3.1	28.3	5.2	10.9	44.0	36.9	5.4	1.6
1978	257.4	206.6	155.7	19.9	66.6	3.5	32.0	5.8	12.7	50.8	42.8	6.1	1.9
1979	284.2	225.9	170.6	22.2	73.9	4.3	36.6	6.4	15.2	58.4	49.0	7.1	2.2
1980	314.7	249.0	187.9	25.7	81.6	4.9	41.2	7.2	17.3	65.7	55.1	8.1	2.6
1981	340.4	273.5	205.9	29.3	91.2	5.3	47.6	8.3	21.0	66.9	55.4	8.5	3.0
1982	363.1	296.1	223.6	32.0	100.0	5.7	53.8	9.4	24.5	67.0	54.2	9.4	3.4
1983	384.2	315.4	239.6	33.0	109.0	6.1	60.1	10.6	27.8	68.8	54.2	10.8	3.8
1984	416.1	338.5	257.8	34.1	118.4	7.0	64.7	11.7	29.4	77.6	60.5	12.7	4.4
1985	457.6	370.3	281.7	35.9	131.4	7.9	70.8	12.7	32.0	87.3	67.6	14.8	5.0
1986	494.4	398.2	304.2	38.6	141.7	8.8	77.4	13.8	34.8	96.2	74.2	16.4	5.6
1987	528.7	426.6	327.8	41.6	150.0	9.5	83.4	15.0	37.0	102.2	78.8	17.2	6.2
1988	567.4	457.0	354.4	44.5	159.8	10.4	91.2	16.6	40.3	110.4	84.8	18.6	7.0
1989	617.8	498.5	388.4	47.7	175.8	11.9	101.4	18.4	45.0	119.2	88.7	21.9	8.6
1990	676.2	544.0	426.5	51.6	190.5	13.1	111.6	20.3	50.0	132.2	98.5	23.9	9.7
1991	716.0	578.7	457.2	55.1	204.7	14.1	124.1	22.6	57.0	137.3	103.2	23.5	10.6
1992	756.0	616.3	492.6	57.6	218.9	14.4	138.4	25.4	65.3	139.7	104.2	24.0	11.4
1993	784.8	643.6	516.1	60.8	234.0	14.8	152.5	27.4	73.1	141.2	104.5	24.9	11.9
1994	827.6	678.8	541.9	64.3	251.5	15.4	163.5	29.3	78.8	148.8	108.7	28.1	12.0
1995	872.7	712.8	565.4	68.6	270.6	16.1	175.6	31.1	85.0	160.0	117.3	30.5	12.3
1996	913.7	743.5	586.6	72.0	285.8	16.8	184.0	32.9	86.6	170.2	126.8	30.5	12.8
1997	963.8	781.0	613.5	75.8	304.2	18.3	194.3	35.4	89.9	182.9	136.6	32.0	14.3
1998	1 026.1	829.8	646.3	79.9	326.7	19.4	203.7	37.9	93.4	196.3	146.1	34.7	15.5
1999	1 109.2	895.6	688.1	85.1	357.5	20.7	214.4	40.5	96.7	213.6	159.7	37.4	16.5
2000	1 193.4	961.9	732.5	91.5	392.3	22.6	231.8	43.6	104.0	231.5	174.6	38.8	18.1
2001	1 279.8	1 031.8	785.4	96.9	425.8	25.0	251.4	46.1	116.2	248.0	190.6	38.4	19.1
2002	1 346.4	1 084.9	829.1	101.4	444.9	26.0	264.6	49.3	120.7	261.5	204.1	38.0	19.4
2003	1 383.8	1 114.8	864.9	105.2	449.9	26.7	278.6	53.4	124.8	269.1	211.1	37.6	20.4
2004	1 446.0	1 168.2	907.6	111.8	471.2	27.8	294.4	56.7	130.9	277.8	219.1	37.2	21.5
2005	1 527.5	1 236.3	944.9	122.1	506.7	29.7	307.8	60.9	132.3	291.3	231.5	37.1	22.7
2006	1 622.7	1 307.4	989.8	132.2	541.7	32.2	324.2	64.0	141.0	315.3	251.4	39.1	24.7
2007	1 739.5	1 397.5	1 045.8	145.4	577.5	34.3	336.9	65.9	149.3	342.0	271.4	44.0	26.6
2008	1 831.1	1 473.2	1 095.9	156.2	605.0	36.1	347.8	67.8	158.4	357.9	284.5	45.1	28.3
2009	1 855.6	1 495.3	1 117.9	162.6	610.7	36.3	359.7	69.7	168.7	360.3	288.9	43.1	28.3
2010	1 855.4	1 508.1	1 141.1	165.0	610.8	35.6	373.1	71.6	176.1	347.3	279.8	39.6	27.9
2011	1 848.2	1 507.2	1 141.9	171.2	615.6	35.9	385.6	73.6	182.4	341.0	273.4	38.6	29.0
2012	1 849.5	1 515.7	1 147.1	178.4	621.6	35.8	395.5	76.1	188.5	333.7	265.0	39.2	29.6
2013	1 905.9	1 575.1	1 197.8	183.2	638.9	36.4	408.4	78.9	197.6	330.8	259.3	39.9	31.5
2014	1 952.8	1 614.1	1 232.5	188.7	656.0	37.3	425.8	81.3	209.0	338.8	266.1	39.9	32.8
2015	2 009.8	1 653.8	1 275.3	192.0	673.5	39.2	447.7	85.8	220.1	356.0	281.4	40.3	34.2
2016	2 068.5	1 697.4	1 303.3	195.3	706.2	40.8	466.6	90.0	229.1	371.1	292.5	42.8	35.9
2017	2 136.3	1 748.0	1 338.7	202.4	736.6	42.8	487.0	92.4	240.9	388.3	304.1	45.8	38.5
2018	2 233.0	1 830.0	1 392.9	213.2	778.7	45.0	509.8	94.8	254.0	403.0	314.1	47.7	41.3
2019	2 299.0	1 876.5	1 433.3	222.7	791.7	46.0	525.3	97.7	261.4	422.5	330.9	48.8	42.7
2020	2 357.8	1 916.5	1 459.8	229.6	768.8	47.7	493.9	97.4	250.9	441.2	345.5	50.4	45.4
2021	2 487.7	2 045.4	1 496.0	246.7	873.3	50.6	520.1	99.7	268.2	442.3	340.3	51.8	50.2
2019													
1st quarter	2 263.5	1 850.2	1 412.5	219.0	787.0	45.4	522.8	97.1	258.5	413.3	322.0	49.3	42.0
2nd quarter	2 296.0	1 869.1	1 420.8	222.4	797.4	45.7	525.8	97.8	260.2	426.9	335.1	49.5	42.3
3rd quarter	2 307.2	1 883.2	1 440.5	224.3	790.7	46.1	526.1	97.9	261.8	424.0	332.8	48.2	43.0
4th quarter	2 329.2	1 903.5	1 459.6	225.3	791.8	46.7	526.3	98.1	265.0	425.7	333.7	48.3	43.7
2020													
1st quarter	2 376.9	1 934.3	1 486.0	227.1	784.7	47.3	516.2	97.5	260.5	442.7	349.1	48.6	45.0
2nd quarter	2 334.6	1 897.3	1 438.4	227.7	733.2	46.6	455.5	97.5	222.8	437.3	346.2	47.7	43.4
3rd quarter	2 346.5	1 909.9	1 458.6	231.0	767.6	48.1	499.1	97.3	257.7	436.6	338.7	52.1	45.8
4th quarter	2 373.0	1 924.7	1 456.0	232.7	789.7	48.8	504.9	97.3	262.7	448.3	348.0	53.1	47.3
2021													
1st quarter	2 408.7	1 966.5	1 459.5	236.8	829.3	49.5	509.6	98.2	264.2	442.2	340.9	52.7	48.5
2nd quarter	2 452.6	2 015.3	1 477.9	243.3	859.4	50.0	515.4	99.1	266.8	437.3	336.6	51.1	49.7
3rd quarter	2 522.9	2 080.6	1 518.8	249.4	885.2	51.1	521.7	100.2	267.9	442.3	340.7	50.8	50.8
4th quarter	2 566.7	2 119.3	1 527.8	257.5	919.4	51.9	533.5	101.4	273.9	447.4	342.9	52.6	51.9

[1]Excludes government sales to other sectors and government own-account investment (construction and software).
[2]Includes general government intermediate inputs for goods and services sold to other sectors and for own-account investment.
[3]Includes components not shown separately.

Table 6-10. State and Local Government Output, Lending and Borrowing, and Net Investment

(National income and product accounts, calendar years, billions of dollars, quarterly data are at seasonally adjusted annual rates.)

NIPA Tables 3.3, 3.10.5

Year and quarter	Output			Net lending (net borrowing -)							Net investment
	Gross	Value added	Intermediate goods and services purchased [1]	Net saving, current (surplus +, deficit -)	Plus: Capital transfer receipts	Minus			Plus: consumption of fixed capital	Equals: Net lending (borrowing -)	
						Gross investment	Capital transfer payments	Net purchases of nonproduced assets			
1965	58.3	44.9	13.4	3.7	4.7	21.2	. . .	1.3	6.4	-7.6	14.8
1966	65.1	50.2	14.9	4.7	5.1	23.5	. . .	1.4	7.1	-7.9	16.4
1967	72.2	55.8	16.4	4.0	5.1	25.7	. . .	1.4	7.8	-10.2	17.9
1968	81.9	63.3	18.6	3.5	6.8	28.1	. . .	1.4	8.6	-10.6	19.5
1969	92.7	70.9	21.8	3.1	6.8	28.8	. . .	1.0	9.6	-10.2	19.2
1970	105.6	80.3	25.3	1.4	6.2	29.3	. . .	1.1	10.9	-11.8	18.4
1971	119.4	90.3	29.1	-1.3	7.0	30.7	. . .	1.6	12.2	-14.4	18.5
1972	132.2	100.2	32.0	6.1	7.3	31.3	. . .	1.7	13.3	-6.3	18.0
1973	145.7	110.4	35.3	5.6	7.3	34.0	. . .	1.7	14.8	-8.0	19.2
1974	165.3	122.8	42.6	-2.3	9.2	40.5	. . .	1.9	18.4	-17.2	22.1
1975	188.5	138.0	50.5	-10.7	11.0	44.6	. . .	1.9	21.0	-25.3	23.6
1976	203.0	148.0	55.0	-4.4	12.0	44.9	. . .	1.7	22.0	-17.0	22.9
1977	221.4	160.6	60.8	0.5	13.1	44.0	. . .	1.6	23.4	-8.5	20.6
1978	242.1	175.5	66.6	4.9	13.7	50.8	. . .	1.8	25.4	-8.6	25.4
1979	266.7	192.8	73.9	-1.2	16.2	58.4	. . .	2.0	28.6	-16.8	29.8
1980	295.1	213.5	81.6	-5.9	18.6	65.7	. . .	2.2	33.1	-22.1	32.6
1981	326.4	235.2	91.2	-10.2	17.8	66.9	. . .	2.2	37.8	-23.8	29.1
1982	355.6	255.6	100.0	-22.8	16.9	67.0	. . .	2.2	41.2	-33.8	25.8
1983	381.6	272.6	109.0	-18.4	18.0	68.8	. . .	2.2	42.7	-28.8	26.1
1984	410.2	291.9	118.4	-0.2	20.1	77.6	. . .	2.6	44.3	-16.0	33.3
1985	449.0	317.6	131.4	-2.4	22.0	87.3	. . .	3.1	46.8	-24.1	40.5
1986	484.4	342.7	141.7	-4.0	23.0	96.2	. . .	3.7	50.1	-30.7	46.1
1987	519.5	369.4	150.0	-14.4	22.3	102.2	. . .	4.2	54.0	-44.4	48.2
1988	558.6	398.8	159.8	-11.3	23.1	110.4	. . .	4.3	57.7	-45.3	52.7
1989	611.8	436.1	175.8	-19.3	23.4	119.2	0.0	4.9	61.8	-58.3	57.4
1990	668.7	478.2	190.5	-36.2	25.0	132.2	0.0	5.7	66.6	-82.5	65.6
1991	716.9	512.2	204.7	-60.1	25.8	137.3	0.0	5.8	70.8	-106.6	66.5
1992	769.2	550.2	218.9	-71.0	26.9	139.7	0.0	5.9	74.1	-115.5	65.6
1993	810.9	576.9	234.0	-72.5	28.2	141.2	0.0	5.9	78.3	-113.1	62.9
1994	857.7	606.2	251.5	-63.9	29.9	148.8	0.0	6.2	82.8	-106.3	66.0
1995	904.5	633.9	270.6	-70.4	32.4	160.0	0.0	6.6	88.1	-116.5	71.9
1996	944.4	658.6	285.8	-53.8	33.8	170.2	0.0	6.0	92.5	-103.6	77.7
1997	993.5	689.3	304.2	-42.0	35.2	182.9	0.0	5.8	97.3	-98.2	85.6
1998	1 052.9	726.2	326.7	-30.1	35.9	196.3	0.0	7.6	102.2	-95.9	94.1
1999	1 130.6	773.1	357.5	-38.9	40.0	213.6	0.0	8.6	108.6	-112.6	105.0
2000	1 216.3	824.0	392.3	-40.6	44.2	231.5	0.0	8.6	116.6	-119.9	114.9
2001	1 308.1	882.3	425.8	-119.0	51.7	248.0	0.0	10.1	123.4	-202.1	124.6
2002	1 375.5	930.6	444.9	-182.9	52.9	261.5	0.0	11.2	129.3	-273.3	132.2
2003	1 420.0	970.1	449.9	-181.3	52.3	269.1	0.0	11.4	134.9	-274.6	134.2
2004	1 490.5	1 019.3	471.2	-149.0	52.5	277.8	4.5	11.3	144.2	-245.8	133.6
2005	1 573.8	1 067.0	506.7	-102.8	56.9	291.3	6.4	10.0	157.9	-195.7	133.4
2006	1 663.8	1 122.1	541.7	-85.0	57.9	315.3	0.0	11.2	171.0	-182.5	144.3
2007	1 768.7	1 191.2	577.5	-129.3	59.8	342.0	0.0	13.9	187.5	-237.9	154.5
2008	1 857.1	1 252.1	605.0	-220.9	63.1	357.9	0.0	13.3	201.2	-327.8	156.7
2009	1 891.3	1 280.5	610.7	-341.3	68.0	360.3	0.0	12.6	209.1	-437.1	151.2
2010	1 916.9	1 306.1	610.8	-307.5	76.9	347.3	0.0	12.0	213.4	-376.4	133.9
2011	1 928.7	1 313.1	615.6	-275.1	74.1	341.0	0.0	11.5	222.2	-331.2	118.8
2012	1 947.1	1 325.5	621.6	-282.8	74.4	333.7	0.0	10.9	232.0	-321.1	101.7
2013	2 019.9	1 380.9	638.9	-265.3	71.6	330.8	0.0	10.4	238.8	-296.0	92.0
2014	2 077.1	1 421.1	656.0	-237.9	70.6	338.8	0.0	10.6	246.3	-270.3	92.5
2015	2 140.8	1 467.3	673.5	-215.8	69.8	356.0	0.0	11.9	251.4	-262.4	104.6
2016	2 204.9	1 498.6	706.2	-244.7	72.6	371.1	0.0	12.9	256.4	-299.7	114.7
2017	2 277.8	1 541.2	736.6	-230.6	73.2	388.3	1.2	14.3	266.2	-295.0	122.1
2018	2 384.8	1 606.1	778.7	-195.8	72.2	403.0	0.0	16.1	280.5	-262.2	122.5
2019	2 447.8	1 656.1	791.7	-149.0	73.9	422.5	0.0	16.8	293.7	-220.7	128.8
2020	2 458.2	1 689.4	768.8	76.1	82.7	441.2	0.0	17.3	302.8	3.1	138.4
2021	2 616.1	1 742.8	873.3	277.1	84.8	442.3	0.0	18.4	325.2	226.5	117.1
2019											
1st quarter	2 418.4	1 631.4	787.0	-167.4	69.6	400.0	0.0	15.5	274.1	-239.3	125.9
2nd quarter	2 440.6	1 643.2	797.4	-221.0	70.6	410.0	0.0	16.0	279.1	-297.3	130.9
3rd quarter	2 455.5	1 664.8	790.7	-199.7	78.2	406.6	0.0	16.3	282.4	-262.0	124.2
4th quarter	2 476.6	1 684.8	791.8	-195.0	70.4	395.5	0.0	16.5	286.2	-250.4	109.3
2020											
1st quarter	2 497.8	1 713.1	784.7	-168.2	71.6	413.3	0.0	16.6	288.7	-237.9	124.6
2nd quarter	2 399.3	1 666.2	733.2	-124.4	72.4	426.9	0.0	16.7	293.1	-202.5	133.8
3rd quarter	2 457.2	1 689.6	767.6	-150.5	75.2	424.0	0.0	16.8	295.7	-220.4	128.3
4th quarter	2 478.4	1 688.7	789.7	-153.0	76.5	425.7	0.0	16.9	297.2	-222.0	128.5
2021											
1st quarter	2 525.7	1 696.4	829.3	-134.6	78.4	442.7	0.0	17.0	299.6	-216.2	143.1
2nd quarter	2 580.6	1 721.2	859.4	553.6	85.0	437.3	0.0	17.2	300.3	484.4	137.0
3rd quarter	2 653.4	1 768.2	885.2	-66.3	84.5	436.6	0.0	17.4	304.5	-131.3	132.1
4th quarter	2 704.7	1 785.3	919.4	-48.2	82.8	448.3	0.0	17.7	306.9	-124.5	141.4

[1]Includes general government intermediate inputs for goods and services sold to other sectors and for own-account investment.
. . . = Not available.

Table 6-11. Chain-Type Quantity Indexes for State and Local Government Consumption Expenditures and Gross Investment

(Seasonally adjusted, 2012 = 100.)

NIPA Tables 3.9.3, 3.10.3

Year and quarter	State and local government consumption expenditures and gross investment												
	Total	Consumption expenditures [1]								Gross investment			
		Total	Compensation of general government employees	Consumption of general government fixed capital	Intermediate goods and services purchased [2]	Less				Total	Structures	Equipment	Intellectual property
						Own-account investment	Sales to other sectors						
							Total [3]	Tuition and related educational charges	Health and hospital charges				
1965	36.5	33.2	43.8	18.5	16.6	29.2	23.0	32.3	15.4	47.3	72.0	9.0	4.4
1966	38.7	35.2	46.4	19.7	17.9	31.2	25.1	36.6	17.6	50.4	76.5	9.8	5.2
1967	40.7	36.8	48.2	21.0	19.4	31.4	27.7	40.8	20.0	53.6	81.3	10.2	5.8
1968	43.1	39.2	51.1	22.3	21.3	33.2	30.1	45.9	23.3	56.0	85.0	10.6	6.2
1969	44.6	41.7	53.3	23.6	23.7	33.7	31.3	50.5	24.1	53.8	80.5	11.4	6.9
1970	45.9	44.3	55.7	24.8	26.1	34.6	32.6	58.8	24.6	50.5	74.4	11.8	7.6
1971	47.3	46.5	57.9	25.9	28.5	35.1	35.4	66.2	28.6	49.1	72.0	11.9	7.9
1972	48.4	48.2	59.9	26.8	30.3	34.7	37.9	70.3	32.8	47.6	68.5	13.3	8.3
1973	49.7	49.9	62.0	27.8	31.2	34.6	39.5	75.8	36.4	47.9	67.9	14.9	8.8
1974	51.5	52.1	64.3	28.8	32.6	36.2	39.3	75.6	37.5	48.2	67.6	16.2	9.1
1975	53.4	54.7	66.2	29.8	35.3	35.1	39.9	75.7	38.6	47.9	67.1	15.7	9.8
1976	53.9	55.5	67.0	30.7	36.4	32.9	42.2	78.1	41.0	47.2	66.1	15.4	10.4
1977	54.1	56.6	67.9	31.4	37.7	31.5	43.6	81.3	41.7	44.5	61.7	15.0	10.8
1978	55.9	57.7	69.5	32.2	38.7	33.9	45.8	85.8	44.6	48.6	67.7	15.7	12.0
1979	56.7	58.0	70.7	33.0	38.7	38.0	48.0	88.2	48.4	51.0	70.6	17.0	13.2
1980	56.6	57.8	71.6	33.9	37.3	39.6	48.8	91.1	48.8	51.2	70.2	18.1	14.0
1981	55.4	57.6	71.3	34.7	37.5	38.7	50.7	93.1	51.9	47.0	63.2	17.7	14.9
1982	55.5	58.5	71.7	35.4	39.1	39.4	51.9	92.9	53.4	44.2	58.0	18.6	15.9
1983	56.2	59.2	71.2	36.1	41.8	39.8	53.8	95.7	54.8	44.9	57.4	21.2	17.3
1984	58.4	60.5	71.4	37.1	44.0	43.3	53.9	95.6	53.5	50.3	63.9	24.8	19.1
1985	61.7	63.2	73.4	38.4	47.7	47.1	55.8	95.5	54.8	55.8	70.1	28.7	21.5
1986	64.8	66.1	75.5	40.0	51.6	51.4	57.8	96.3	56.2	59.7	74.4	31.5	23.8
1987	66.2	67.4	76.7	41.6	52.8	53.5	59.0	96.9	56.2	61.3	76.0	32.7	25.6
1988	68.7	69.8	79.3	43.4	54.4	56.0	60.2	99.9	56.2	64.5	79.3	34.9	28.4
1989	71.4	72.3	81.6	45.6	57.0	60.9	61.9	102.9	56.7	67.9	80.9	40.3	33.7
1990	74.4	74.7	83.8	48.1	58.9	63.9	63.2	105.2	57.3	73.1	86.9	43.3	37.5
1991	76.0	76.3	84.5	50.4	61.9	66.4	65.3	106.9	59.7	74.8	89.7	41.8	40.3
1992	77.6	78.0	85.7	52.6	64.9	65.8	68.2	108.9	63.2	75.8	90.1	42.6	43.8
1993	78.6	79.4	86.6	54.7	67.8	65.7	71.4	107.6	66.9	75.2	88.1	44.0	44.8
1994	80.8	81.6	87.9	56.7	71.6	66.7	73.8	107.7	69.6	77.5	89.1	49.6	45.2
1995	83.0	83.5	89.5	58.7	74.5	67.5	76.3	108.1	72.7	80.8	92.1	54.4	45.0
1996	84.9	85.1	90.6	60.9	76.5	69.3	77.8	108.4	72.4	84.3	96.5	55.7	47.4
1997	87.6	87.4	92.2	63.4	80.3	74.1	80.4	110.9	74.1	89.0	100.3	60.9	53.0
1998	91.5	90.9	93.9	66.3	86.6	77.7	82.8	114.0	76.3	94.3	104.1	69.4	58.1
1999	95.3	94.1	95.1	69.5	92.9	80.6	85.0	117.4	77.6	100.4	109.6	77.8	61.6
2000	97.8	96.1	96.8	72.8	96.6	84.9	89.3	121.4	81.4	105.4	114.7	82.2	65.9
2001	101.4	99.4	98.8	76.0	103.4	91.7	94.1	122.1	88.2	110.6	121.1	83.9	68.8
2002	104.3	102.0	100.6	78.9	107.4	93.9	96.2	122.2	88.6	114.7	126.1	85.6	70.2
2003	103.8	101.1	100.9	81.2	104.1	94.2	96.8	122.1	87.3	116.3	127.5	86.4	74.1
2004	103.7	101.2	101.0	83.6	104.2	95.2	97.6	118.3	87.6	115.0	125.1	86.3	78.3
2005	103.7	101.8	101.4	86.0	104.6	98.3	98.1	118.3	85.6	112.2	120.4	87.7	82.2
2006	104.9	102.8	102.1	88.4	106.2	103.6	99.2	116.6	87.7	114.2	120.5	95.5	88.6
2007	106.7	104.7	103.3	91.2	107.8	106.9	99.0	112.9	89.9	115.5	118.9	109.5	94.1
2008	106.9	105.0	104.4	93.9	105.0	108.4	98.1	109.3	92.7	115.9	118.3	113.3	97.7
2009	109.0	107.7	104.5	96.0	111.5	108.2	98.7	106.1	96.0	114.7	117.5	109.0	98.0
2010	106.0	105.0	103.2	97.6	106.8	104.0	99.5	103.6	97.5	110.4	113.4	101.4	96.1
2011	102.2	101.5	101.7	98.9	101.1	102.5	100.1	101.3	99.0	105.5	107.1	99.5	98.7
2012	100.0	100.0	100.0	100.0	100.0	100.0	100.0	100.0	100.0	100.0	100.0	100.0	100.0
2013	99.7	100.3	99.7	101.1	101.4	99.3	100.8	99.5	102.8	97.3	95.7	101.7	105.6
2014	99.9	100.4	99.6	102.1	103.0	99.7	103.0	98.9	107.4	97.5	95.8	100.3	109.3
2015	102.9	103.1	100.3	103.2	111.4	105.0	106.9	100.8	112.1	101.5	100.1	101.0	115.6
2016	105.8	105.9	101.4	104.6	118.3	108.5	109.9	102.9	115.3	105.1	103.0	107.4	121.3
2017	106.4	106.2	102.3	106.2	118.7	111.4	112.6	103.6	119.2	107.5	104.2	114.4	129.1
2018	106.9	106.7	103.0	108.0	119.8	113.5	115.1	104.0	122.8	107.8	103.2	118.1	137.0
2019	108.2	107.9	104.0	109.8	121.1	113.9	116.0	104.2	123.9	109.7	104.8	120.7	140.7
2020	109.2	108.4	102.0	111.8	119.4	116.3	106.5	102.5	115.3	113.1	107.7	124.9	148.5
2021	109.6	110.2	103.1	113.8	123.3	118.1	109.0	104.0	119.7	107.2	99.4	124.6	161.5
2019													
1st quarter	107.3	107.1	103.1	109.1	121.2	112.9	116.3	104.2	123.5	108.5	103.6	121.1	138.3
2nd quarter	108.1	107.5	103.4	109.6	121.4	113.4	116.4	104.3	123.7	110.8	106.2	122.2	139.1
3rd quarter	108.4	108.1	104.2	110.1	121.1	114.1	116.1	104.3	124.0	109.5	104.8	119.4	141.0
4th quarter	109.1	108.9	105.3	110.5	120.4	115.4	115.4	104.0	124.4	109.8	104.8	120.2	144.3
2020													
1st quarter	110.3	109.5	105.1	111.0	120.4	116.5	112.5	102.8	121.6	113.9	109.1	121.2	148.7
2nd quarter	108.7	107.8	99.8	111.5	116.9	114.0	98.3	102.4	102.7	112.8	108.8	118.2	142.3
3rd quarter	108.8	108.1	102.1	112.0	119.2	117.1	107.1	102.3	117.6	111.5	105.3	128.7	149.8
4th quarter	109.1	108.0	101.2	112.5	121.1	117.6	108.0	102.5	119.4	114.1	107.7	131.5	153.3
2021													
1st quarter	109.1	108.6	101.5	113.1	122.0	117.9	107.9	103.1	118.6	110.9	103.6	130.0	158.0
2nd quarter	109.1	109.5	102.3	113.6	122.8	117.7	108.4	103.7	119.2	107.3	99.7	124.3	160.5
3rd quarter	110.4	111.3	104.3	114.1	123.8	118.5	109.1	104.3	119.3	106.3	98.6	120.8	163.0
4th quarter	110.0	111.2	104.2	114.6	124.7	118.2	110.8	105.0	121.7	104.4	95.9	123.2	164.7

[1] Excludes government sales to other sectors and government own-account investment (construction and software).
[2] Includes general government intermediate inputs for goods and services sold to other sectors and for own-account investment.
[3] Includes components not shown separately.

Table 6-12. State Government Current Receipts and Expenditures

(National income and product accounts, calendar years, billions of dollars.)

NIPA Table 3.20

Year	Current receipts Total [1]	Current tax receipts Total	Personal current taxes Total [1]	Personal current taxes Income taxes	Taxes on production and imports Total	Taxes on production and imports Sales taxes	Taxes on production and imports Property taxes	Taxes on production and imports Other	Taxes on corporate income	Contributions for government social insurance	Income receipts on assets Total [1]	Income receipts on assets Interest receipts	Income receipts on assets Rents and royalties
1959	21.6	16.7	3.1	2.0	12.5	10.0	0.5	2.0	1.1	0.4	0.5	0.3	0.2
1960	23.3	18.1	3.4	2.3	13.5	10.8	0.5	2.2	1.2	0.5	0.5	0.4	0.2
1961	25.0	19.3	3.7	2.5	14.4	11.6	0.5	2.3	1.3	0.5	0.6	0.4	0.2
1962	27.1	21.0	4.0	2.8	15.4	12.6	0.6	2.3	1.5	0.5	0.6	0.4	0.2
1963	29.1	22.4	4.3	3.1	16.4	13.4	0.6	2.4	1.6	0.6	0.6	0.4	0.2
1964	31.8	24.5	4.9	3.6	17.7	14.5	0.6	2.6	1.8	0.7	0.7	0.4	0.2
1965	35.1	26.9	5.4	3.9	19.6	16.1	0.7	2.8	1.9	0.8	0.8	0.5	0.3
1966	41.5	30.2	6.4	4.8	21.7	18.0	0.7	3.0	2.2	0.8	0.9	0.6	0.3
1967	45.6	32.7	7.0	5.3	23.3	19.4	0.7	3.1	2.5	0.9	1.1	0.8	0.3
1968	53.8	38.6	8.8	6.9	26.7	22.8	0.8	3.2	3.1	0.9	1.7	1.4	0.3
1969	61.6	44.0	10.8	8.6	29.9	25.7	0.9	3.3	3.4	1.0	2.1	1.8	0.3
1970	69.1	48.1	12.0	9.6	32.7	28.2	0.9	3.6	3.5	1.1	2.5	2.2	0.3
1971	78.2	53.8	13.4	11.0	36.3	31.4	1.0	3.9	4.0	1.2	2.7	2.3	0.4
1972	95.0	63.5	17.9	15.2	40.7	35.2	1.1	4.4	5.0	1.3	2.9	2.5	0.4
1973	103.1	70.2	19.8	16.8	44.7	38.8	1.2	4.7	5.7	1.5	3.9	3.3	0.5
1974	112.1	75.9	21.1	18.0	48.4	42.0	1.1	5.3	6.3	1.7	5.0	4.4	0.6
1975	125.8	81.9	23.2	19.9	51.8	44.7	1.4	5.6	6.9	1.8	5.6	5.0	0.6
1976	141.7	93.8	27.0	23.4	57.7	49.9	1.5	6.3	9.1	2.2	5.3	4.7	0.6
1977	158.1	105.1	30.9	27.2	63.4	55.0	1.5	6.9	10.8	2.8	6.1	5.4	0.6
1978	177.2	117.4	35.6	31.6	70.3	60.8	1.9	7.6	11.5	3.4	7.4	6.7	0.6
1979	194.8	128.9	38.9	34.6	77.1	65.7	2.3	9.0	12.9	3.9	10.3	9.2	1.1
1980	216.0	140.9	43.7	39.1	83.4	70.0	2.6	10.8	13.7	3.6	13.4	11.2	2.0
1981	236.4	155.6	48.5	43.6	92.7	76.5	2.7	13.6	14.5	3.9	15.6	13.2	2.2
1982	244.7	162.3	52.3	47.0	97.0	80.3	2.8	13.9	13.1	4.0	17.5	15.3	2.1
1983	269.3	180.5	58.9	53.2	106.8	90.0	3.0	13.8	14.9	4.1	19.5	17.2	2.2
1984	303.7	205.4	68.2	61.9	119.7	100.9	3.4	15.5	17.4	4.7	22.4	19.8	2.5
1985	328.6	220.9	73.2	66.1	129.0	109.0	3.5	16.5	18.7	4.9	26.1	23.4	2.6
1986	354.0	234.0	78.3	70.7	134.9	115.8	3.6	15.6	20.7	6.0	27.5	24.6	2.7
1987	375.0	253.7	87.5	79.1	144.3	124.6	3.7	16.0	21.8	7.2	28.4	25.6	2.6
1988	403.1	269.4	90.4	81.5	155.2	135.1	3.8	16.3	23.8	8.4	30.8	28.0	2.7
1989	435.2	288.4	102.4	92.9	163.5	142.3	4.3	17.0	22.4	9.0	32.8	30.2	2.4
1990	469.2	305.6	109.6	99.6	175.4	152.5	4.6	18.3	20.5	10.0	33.9	31.4	2.3
1991	504.1	314.2	111.8	101.4	180.8	157.5	4.9	18.3	21.6	11.6	34.1	31.2	2.6
1992	551.4	338.8	120.6	109.0	195.9	169.7	6.1	20.1	22.2	13.1	33.6	30.4	2.7
1993	584.8	357.1	126.3	114.9	206.3	179.4	5.9	21.0	24.5	14.1	32.4	29.4	2.5
1994	621.6	380.4	132.1	120.2	220.8	191.7	7.0	22.1	27.5	14.5	33.9	30.6	2.5
1995	653.2	401.5	140.9	128.4	231.3	200.5	7.2	23.6	29.2	13.6	36.9	33.4	2.6
1996	686.2	425.9	150.9	138.6	245.0	211.8	8.2	25.0	29.9	12.5	39.4	35.3	2.7
1997	719.6	449.1	162.7	149.7	255.4	221.3	8.1	26.0	31.0	10.8	41.8	37.5	2.7
1998	764.1	480.7	180.4	166.8	268.8	233.3	8.5	27.0	31.6	10.4	43.3	39.2	2.4
1999	812.5	507.9	192.6	178.4	283.0	245.9	9.1	27.9	32.3	9.8	46.6	42.5	2.6
2000	867.7	540.1	213.5	199.2	294.8	255.5	7.8	31.6	31.7	10.8	49.3	44.3	3.6
2001	904.5	546.8	220.1	205.7	300.8	259.9	8.1	32.8	25.9	13.7	46.5	41.4	3.7
2002	917.8	533.7	199.1	184.3	309.6	268.0	7.7	33.9	25.0	15.8	42.4	37.2	3.7
2003	970.5	558.8	202.4	186.4	328.9	282.0	9.1	37.8	27.5	19.9	42.0	35.9	4.4
2004	1 048.7	606.4	220.3	203.4	352.3	300.5	8.3	43.5	33.8	24.7	44.4	37.4	5.1
2005	1 136.5	676.3	246.5	229.0	385.3	325.6	9.1	50.6	44.5	24.6	50.6	42.7	6.0
2006	1 193.9	728.1	271.0	252.5	409.1	346.6	9.7	52.7	48.0	21.5	59.2	50.7	6.5
2007	1 247.9	759.7	288.9	269.8	424.0	359.0	9.8	55.2	46.9	18.9	65.0	55.3	7.5
2008	1 264.0	763.6	299.8	280.9	425.4	354.3	9.7	61.3	38.4	18.7	60.1	49.6	7.9
2009	1 267.1	688.2	256.6	236.3	393.2	335.6	10.4	47.2	38.4	18.6	52.2	43.0	7.0
2010	1 336.1	720.0	264.7	242.2	415.5	354.7	10.7	50.1	39.8	18.1	51.3	42.4	6.6
2011	1 357.8	773.2	293.2	270.5	437.6	369.9	9.8	57.9	42.4	18.3	50.7	41.8	6.7
2012	1 372.3	804.9	313.8	290.4	448.3	379.2	9.7	59.3	42.9	17.5	50.1	40.8	6.9

[1] Includes components not shown separately.

Table 6-12. State Government Current Receipts and Expenditures—*Continued*

(National income and product accounts, calendar years, billions of dollars.)   **NIPA Table 3.20**

Year	Current receipts—*Continued* — Current transfer receipts					Current expenditures					Net state government saving, NIPA (surplus + / deficit -)		
	Total	Federal grants-in-aid	Local grants-in-aid	From business, net	From persons	Total [1]	Consumption expenditures	Government social benefits to persons	Grants-in-aid to local governments	Interest payments	Total	Social insurance funds	Other
1959	3.6	3.2	0.2	0.0	0.1	20.9	8.2	3.6	7.8	1.2	0.7	0.0	0.7
1960	3.7	3.3	0.2	0.0	0.1	22.9	8.9	3.8	8.8	1.3	0.4	0.0	0.4
1961	4.2	3.7	0.3	0.0	0.1	25.0	9.6	4.1	9.8	1.5	0.0	0.0	0.0
1962	4.6	4.1	0.3	0.1	0.2	27.0	10.2	4.4	10.8	1.6	0.1	0.0	0.1
1963	5.0	4.5	0.3	0.1	0.2	29.4	11.0	4.7	11.9	1.7	-0.3	0.0	-0.3
1964	5.5	4.9	0.3	0.1	0.2	31.9	11.8	5.1	13.0	1.8	-0.1	0.0	-0.1
1965	6.1	5.5	0.3	0.1	0.3	35.6	13.0	5.5	15.0	2.0	-0.4	0.1	-0.5
1966	8.9	8.2	0.4	0.1	0.3	40.7	14.6	6.4	17.4	2.2	0.8	0.1	0.6
1967	10.3	9.4	0.5	0.1	0.3	46.8	16.7	7.7	19.9	2.3	-1.2	0.1	-1.3
1968	11.8	10.7	0.6	0.1	0.3	54.6	19.2	9.5	23.0	2.7	-0.8	0.1	-1.0
1969	13.7	12.4	0.8	0.1	0.4	62.8	22.4	10.8	26.4	2.9	-1.2	0.2	-1.3
1970	16.6	15.2	0.9	0.1	0.4	72.8	25.8	12.9	30.4	3.4	-3.7	0.2	-3.9
1971	19.9	18.4	1.0	0.1	0.4	82.9	28.8	15.3	34.3	4.2	-4.7	0.2	-5.0
1972	26.4	24.6	1.1	0.2	0.5	92.9	31.5	17.5	38.5	5.0	2.2	0.3	1.9
1973	26.6	24.5	1.2	0.2	0.7	103.3	35.3	19.4	42.6	5.4	-0.1	0.3	-0.4
1974	28.6	26.3	1.3	0.2	0.8	116.5	42.1	19.9	47.3	6.4	-4.4	0.4	-4.8
1975	35.4	32.4	1.7	0.2	1.0	134.8	49.1	24.2	52.8	7.5	-9.0	0.5	-9.5
1976	39.1	35.4	2.3	0.3	1.2	145.6	52.8	26.9	57.0	7.7	-4.0	0.6	-4.6
1977	42.8	38.8	2.4	0.3	1.4	158.0	57.5	29.1	61.6	8.5	0.1	1.0	-0.9
1978	47.4	43.1	2.5	0.3	1.5	174.2	63.1	32.0	68.2	9.3	3.0	1.5	1.5
1979	50.1	45.9	2.2	0.4	1.6	193.8	70.0	35.4	76.3	10.3	1.0	1.8	-0.8
1980	56.5	52.1	2.3	0.4	1.7	217.8	78.8	41.3	84.6	11.1	-1.8	1.3	-3.2
1981	59.7	54.6	2.7	0.5	2.0	239.8	86.9	46.7	91.3	12.6	-3.4	1.3	-4.7
1982	58.7	52.7	3.1	0.6	2.3	257.0	93.7	51.0	95.3	14.6	-12.4	1.2	-13.6
1983	62.4	55.0	4.2	0.6	2.6	274.7	99.5	55.9	99.9	16.7	-5.5	1.2	-6.7
1984	67.7	59.0	5.0	0.8	3.0	297.5	106.9	59.8	109.8	17.9	6.2	1.4	4.8
1985	72.2	62.6	5.2	0.9	3.6	327.9	117.4	65.2	121.2	20.8	0.6	1.3	-0.7
1986	81.5	69.3	5.3	2.8	4.1	352.3	124.9	71.4	130.1	22.2	1.7	1.9	-0.1
1987	80.3	69.4	5.5	0.9	4.5	374.8	132.7	77.4	139.5	20.9	0.2	2.2	-2.0
1988	88.0	76.2	5.6	1.1	5.2	402.7	142.4	84.4	149.8	21.2	0.4	2.5	-2.1
1989	98.1	85.1	5.8	1.3	5.9	440.8	153.9	94.4	162.6	24.7	-5.6	2.3	-7.9
1990	112.4	97.6	6.2	1.6	6.9	480.7	167.2	111.0	173.1	23.8	-11.5	2.0	-13.4
1991	136.7	117.1	7.6	2.0	10.0	532.2	175.4	137.6	186.1	27.3	-28.1	2.4	-30.5
1992	158.0	134.3	9.0	2.6	12.1	580.8	183.9	159.5	201.0	30.4	-29.4	3.1	-32.6
1993	172.7	147.6	10.1	2.9	12.1	614.6	193.1	173.6	212.9	29.1	-29.8	4.2	-34.0
1994	183.7	156.9	11.0	3.4	12.4	649.8	204.5	184.4	226.2	28.4	-28.1	4.6	-32.8
1995	191.3	164.0	11.1	4.1	12.2	685.0	213.6	194.8	239.0	30.8	-31.8	4.0	-35.8
1996	197.9	168.9	12.0	5.0	12.0	708.1	219.7	202.5	250.3	27.9	-21.8	2.8	-24.7
1997	207.2	174.1	13.5	6.6	13.0	735.5	231.4	206.8	263.0	25.7	-15.9	1.2	-17.1
1998	219.3	182.9	13.3	9.8	13.2	774.0	248.3	214.6	282.4	19.8	-9.9	1.7	-11.6
1999	238.2	199.1	12.9	11.4	14.9	836.1	272.6	230.3	306.6	17.1	-23.6	1.7	-25.3
2000	258.8	212.6	14.0	15.0	17.2	896.0	292.8	248.4	331.0	13.5	-28.4	2.0	-30.3
2001	289.7	238.9	14.9	16.1	19.8	984.0	314.4	281.0	350.7	20.2	-79.5	2.6	-82.1
2002	317.7	263.5	15.5	17.2	21.5	1 037.5	320.3	307.2	367.5	31.5	-119.7	1.4	-121.1
2003	340.5	285.1	16.4	16.6	22.3	1 086.6	319.2	326.2	383.5	47.5	-116.1	3.2	-119.4
2004	363.4	303.4	17.6	17.7	24.6	1 139.7	327.1	355.8	401.6	44.5	-91.0	7.3	-98.3
2005	374.1	312.2	16.6	18.4	26.9	1 195.2	347.4	375.2	413.9	46.8	-58.7	7.2	-65.9
2006	375.4	314.2	15.6	18.2	28.0	1 239.7	361.2	371.3	441.7	52.3	-45.8	4.6	-50.5
2007	397.4	332.2	17.7	19.0	29.0	1 324.9	384.6	398.5	469.2	51.8	-77.0	2.7	-79.7
2008	415.6	346.6	17.7	21.1	30.7	1 383.9	407.7	418.6	486.1	54.1	-119.9	1.7	-121.6
2009	501.2	432.8	16.5	21.7	30.7	1 455.0	411.7	453.0	486.3	87.3	-187.9	2.2	-190.1
2010	539.5	473.3	16.6	20.1	30.1	1 487.1	411.2	481.5	488.8	88.4	-151.0	3.2	-154.2
2011	507.6	441.0	16.6	19.7	31.3	1 515.1	425.5	489.9	494.6	88.4	-157.2	4.2	-161.4
2012	491.2	424.0	16.8	18.8	32.4	1 579.2	459.7	501.9	502.8	97.8	-206.9	3.9	-210.9

[1] Includes components not shown separately.

Table 6-13. Local Government Current Receipts and Expenditures

(National income and product accounts, calendar years, billions of dollars.) NIPA Table 3.21

Year	Current receipts Total [1]	Current tax receipts Total	Personal current taxes Total [1]	Personal current taxes Income taxes	Taxes on production and imports Total	Taxes on production and imports Sales taxes	Taxes on production and imports Property taxes	Taxes on production and imports Other	Taxes on corporate income	Contributions for government social insurance	Income receipts on assets Total [1]	Income receipts on assets Interest receipts	Income receipts on assets Rents and royalties
1959	27.0	17.1	0.8	0.2	16.4	1.2	14.3	0.9	0.0	. . .	0.7	0.5	0.1
1960	30.0	18.8	0.8	0.3	18.0	1.3	15.7	0.9	0.0	. . .	0.8	0.7	0.1
1961	32.9	20.3	0.9	0.3	19.4	1.4	17.0	1.0	0.0	. . .	0.9	0.7	0.2
1962	35.6	21.8	1.0	0.3	20.8	1.5	18.4	1.0	0.0	. . .	1.0	0.8	0.2
1963	38.7	23.4	1.1	0.4	22.3	1.6	19.7	1.0	0.0	. . .	1.0	0.9	0.2
1964	42.3	25.3	1.2	0.5	24.1	1.9	21.1	1.1	0.0	. . .	1.3	1.1	0.2
1965	46.1	27.0	1.2	0.5	25.7	2.1	22.5	1.1	0.0	. . .	1.4	1.2	0.2
1966	50.5	28.5	1.4	0.6	27.1	2.0	23.8	1.3	0.0	. . .	1.7	1.4	0.3
1967	56.5	31.3	1.6	0.8	29.5	1.9	26.2	1.3	0.2	. . .	2.0	1.6	0.3
1968	62.6	34.8	1.7	0.9	32.8	2.3	29.1	1.4	0.3	. . .	1.7	1.4	0.4
1969	70.1	38.4	2.0	1.1	36.1	2.9	31.9	1.4	0.3	. . .	2.2	1.8	0.4
1970	81.4	43.2	2.3	1.3	40.6	3.5	35.7	1.5	0.2	. . .	2.6	2.2	0.5
1971	90.9	47.9	2.5	1.5	45.2	4.0	39.5	1.8	0.3	. . .	2.8	2.3	0.5
1972	101.9	52.0	3.0	2.0	48.8	4.6	42.2	2.0	0.3	. . .	3.0	2.4	0.6
1973	114.0	56.1	3.0	2.0	52.7	5.2	45.2	2.3	0.3	. . .	3.9	3.3	0.6
1974	123.8	60.2	3.4	2.3	56.4	6.1	47.9	2.4	0.3	. . .	5.2	4.5	0.7
1975	137.7	65.5	3.7	2.5	61.4	7.0	51.9	2.5	0.4	. . .	5.6	4.9	0.7
1976	150.8	71.9	4.1	2.8	67.3	7.9	56.7	2.7	0.5	. . .	5.1	4.4	0.7
1977	165.3	78.6	4.5	3.2	73.6	9.0	61.7	2.9	0.6	. . .	5.6	4.9	0.7
1978	180.5	80.8	4.9	3.4	75.3	10.2	61.8	3.3	0.6	. . .	7.2	6.5	0.7
1979	191.3	83.1	5.1	3.6	77.3	11.5	62.1	3.7	0.6	. . .	9.8	8.9	0.9
1980	208.3	89.1	5.1	3.5	83.3	12.8	66.2	4.2	0.7	. . .	12.9	11.8	1.1
1981	226.9	100.2	6.2	4.3	93.0	14.3	74.4	4.3	1.0	. . .	16.4	15.3	1.1
1982	244.4	110.8	6.9	4.9	103.0	15.9	82.5	4.6	1.0	. . .	19.2	17.8	1.4
1983	262.5	120.4	7.2	5.1	112.1	17.7	88.9	5.5	1.0	. . .	21.9	19.8	2.1
1984	289.9	131.9	7.8	5.6	122.7	20.1	96.3	6.3	1.4	. . .	25.2	22.8	2.4
1985	318.4	142.8	8.2	6.0	133.1	22.1	104.0	7.0	1.5	. . .	29.5	26.7	2.7
1986	342.5	155.6	8.9	6.8	144.7	24.1	112.6	8.1	2.0	. . .	31.4	27.9	3.5
1987	360.1	168.5	9.1	6.8	157.3	25.7	122.7	8.9	2.1	. . .	30.1	27.4	2.7
1988	387.9	183.3	11.7	9.1	169.4	27.2	132.7	9.4	2.3	. . .	30.4	28.6	1.7
1989	420.0	199.6	12.3	9.4	185.6	30.1	145.6	10.0	1.8	. . .	33.8	32.1	1.7
1990	446.2	213.6	12.9	10.0	198.7	31.8	157.0	9.9	2.0	. . .	34.5	32.7	1.8
1991	475.9	230.1	13.5	10.3	214.5	33.2	171.1	10.2	2.1	. . .	33.2	31.2	1.9
1992	501.1	241.0	14.7	11.4	224.2	34.6	178.6	11.0	2.1	. . .	30.4	28.4	2.0
1993	522.2	247.7	14.8	11.3	230.5	37.0	181.3	12.1	2.4	. . .	28.7	26.6	2.1
1994	556.9	263.8	15.9	12.0	245.4	39.7	192.4	13.3	2.5	. . .	29.6	27.6	2.0
1995	584.6	270.7	17.2	13.3	251.0	42.2	195.3	13.4	2.5	. . .	32.2	30.3	2.0
1996	617.4	283.7	17.8	13.7	262.9	44.4	204.2	14.4	3.1	. . .	34.3	32.4	2.0
1997	652.4	300.8	19.3	14.9	278.4	47.4	215.5	15.6	3.1	. . .	36.3	34.3	2.1
1998	690.4	314.2	20.9	16.2	290.0	50.6	222.5	16.9	3.4	. . .	38.0	35.8	2.2
1999	739.5	332.5	21.9	17.1	307.1	55.6	233.7	17.8	3.5	. . .	38.6	36.1	2.5
2000	791.8	353.1	23.2	18.1	326.5	61.3	246.9	18.3	3.5	. . .	44.6	42.0	2.7
2001	825.4	367.5	22.9	17.6	341.6	61.9	260.0	19.8	3.0	. . .	42.6	39.8	2.8
2002	865.1	394.8	22.7	17.1	366.2	63.1	281.6	21.5	5.9	. . .	36.2	33.2	2.9
2003	915.7	419.8	24.4	18.3	389.0	66.8	297.9	24.2	6.5	. . .	31.9	28.6	3.2
2004	957.8	451.5	27.1	20.3	416.4	70.5	317.9	28.0	7.9	. . .	32.4	29.0	3.4
2005	1 016.4	490.2	30.0	22.5	449.8	76.8	342.3	30.7	10.4	. . .	38.0	34.2	3.8
2006	1 089.2	526.4	31.5	23.6	483.6	85.2	365.3	33.1	11.3	. . .	48.0	44.0	3.9
2007	1 154.8	561.6	34.6	26.5	516.0	90.0	394.1	32.0	11.0	. . .	52.9	48.9	4.0
2008	1 164.4	565.3	33.8	26.1	522.6	90.4	404.0	28.1	9.0	. . .	45.6	41.4	4.2
2009	1 171.2	580.0	31.2	23.3	541.6	88.3	424.7	28.6	7.2	. . .	35.7	31.4	4.2
2010	1 184.5	585.7	33.0	25.0	544.9	91.2	424.4	29.3	7.8	. . .	31.3	26.7	4.6
2011	1 200.4	593.1	33.8	25.7	550.9	93.8	427.1	30.1	8.4	. . .	29.3	24.5	4.8
2012	1 204.4	600.3	35.1	26.9	556.7	95.7	430.3	30.7	8.5	. . .	28.4	23.4	5.0

[1]Includes components not shown separately.
. . . = Not available.

Table 6-13. Local Government Current Receipts and Expenditures—*Continued*

(National income and product accounts, calendar years, billions of dollars.)   **NIPA Table 3.21**

| Year | Current receipts—*Continued* | | | | | Current expenditures | | | | | Net local government saving, NIPA (surplus + / deficit -) | | |
| | Current transfer receipts | | | | | Total [1] | Consumption expenditures | Government social benefits to persons | Grants-in-aid to state governments | Interest payments | Total | Social insurance funds | Other |
	Total	Federal grants-in-aid	State grants-in-aid	From business, net	From persons								
1959	8.4	0.4	7.8	0.1	0.1	25.5	23.0	0.7	0.2	1.5	1.5	...	1.5
1960	9.6	0.5	8.8	0.1	0.2	27.9	25.2	0.8	0.2	1.7	2.2	...	2.2
1961	10.8	0.6	9.8	0.2	0.3	30.7	27.7	0.9	0.3	1.8	2.2	...	2.2
1962	11.9	0.6	10.8	0.2	0.3	32.3	29.1	0.9	0.3	1.9	3.3	...	3.3
1963	13.1	0.8	11.9	0.2	0.3	34.7	31.3	1.0	0.3	2.1	4.0	...	4.0
1964	14.6	1.1	13.0	0.2	0.3	37.9	34.2	1.0	0.3	2.3	4.4	...	4.4
1965	16.6	1.1	15.0	0.3	0.3	41.6	37.6	1.1	0.3	2.5	4.5	...	4.5
1966	19.3	1.2	17.4	0.2	0.4	46.1	41.7	1.3	0.4	2.7	4.4	...	4.4
1967	22.4	1.5	19.9	0.4	0.6	50.6	45.6	1.6	0.5	2.9	5.9	...	5.9
1968	25.2	1.1	23.0	0.4	0.7	57.5	51.5	2.0	0.6	3.3	5.1	...	5.1
1969	28.8	1.3	26.4	0.4	0.7	64.9	58.1	2.4	0.8	3.6	5.3	...	5.3
1970	34.8	3.2	30.4	0.4	0.8	74.7	66.3	3.2	0.9	4.3	6.7	...	6.7
1971	39.5	3.8	34.3	0.5	0.9	85.6	75.4	4.0	1.0	5.2	5.3	...	5.3
1972	46.0	5.9	38.5	0.5	1.1	95.6	83.9	4.5	1.1	6.1	6.3	...	6.3
1973	53.2	8.9	42.6	0.7	1.0	104.3	91.5	4.7	1.2	6.8	9.8	...	9.8
1974	57.9	8.7	47.3	0.9	1.1	117.0	102.4	5.4	1.3	7.9	6.8	...	6.8
1975	66.4	11.2	52.8	1.0	1.4	134.3	116.5	6.6	1.7	9.2	3.5	...	3.5
1976	73.5	13.6	57.0	1.1	1.7	144.0	124.4	7.3	2.3	9.8	6.8	...	6.8
1977	80.9	16.0	61.6	1.3	1.9	156.9	135.5	8.0	2.4	10.7	8.4	...	8.4
1978	92.3	20.4	68.2	1.5	2.2	170.1	146.8	8.7	2.5	11.7	10.4	...	10.4
1979	98.8	18.1	76.3	1.8	2.6	184.0	159.4	8.9	2.2	13.2	7.2	...	7.2
1980	107.3	17.6	84.6	2.0	3.0	201.1	174.0	9.9	2.3	14.5	7.2	...	7.2
1981	112.2	14.8	91.3	2.4	3.7	219.4	189.2	10.4	2.7	16.7	7.5	...	7.5
1982	115.6	13.5	95.3	2.7	4.1	237.1	203.7	10.2	3.1	19.6	7.3	...	7.3
1983	120.4	13.0	99.9	3.0	4.5	255.8	217.2	11.0	4.2	22.8	6.7	...	6.7
1984	131.7	13.3	109.8	3.4	5.2	275.2	233.0	11.4	5.0	25.3	14.7	...	14.7
1985	144.0	13.6	121.2	3.5	5.7	298.8	254.4	12.1	5.2	26.4	19.6	...	19.6
1986	153.7	13.2	130.1	3.9	6.5	323.8	275.0	12.9	5.3	29.6	18.7	...	18.7
1987	159.2	9.0	139.5	4.0	6.7	348.3	295.6	13.4	5.5	32.6	11.9	...	11.9
1988	170.5	9.5	149.8	4.3	6.9	371.3	316.5	14.1	5.6	33.8	16.6	...	16.6
1989	181.9	6.8	162.6	5.1	7.5	407.0	347.4	15.0	5.8	37.6	13.0	...	13.0
1990	193.4	6.7	173.1	5.5	8.0	441.2	379.0	16.6	6.2	38.0	5.0	...	5.0
1991	207.7	7.0	186.1	5.9	8.7	472.9	404.7	18.9	7.6	40.3	3.0	...	3.0
1992	224.8	7.4	201.0	6.7	9.8	509.2	435.2	20.5	9.0	43.2	-8.1	...	-8.1
1993	240.0	8.1	212.9	7.7	11.4	529.6	453.4	21.6	10.1	43.1	-7.4	...	-7.4
1994	257.6	9.9	226.2	8.6	12.9	555.8	477.7	22.4	11.0	43.3	1.2	...	1.2
1995	273.2	10.5	239.0	9.4	14.3	584.3	503.2	22.9	11.1	45.8	0.3	...	0.3
1996	288.7	12.6	250.3	10.2	15.7	608.0	528.4	21.8	12.0	44.5	9.4	...	9.4
1997	305.4	14.0	263.0	11.1	17.3	634.8	554.5	20.8	13.5	44.5	17.6	...	17.6
1998	330.0	17.9	282.4	11.8	17.9	665.1	587.4	21.1	13.3	41.7	25.3	...	25.3
1999	358.7	20.1	306.6	12.7	19.3	706.6	629.4	22.1	12.9	40.7	32.9	...	32.9
2000	385.8	20.5	331.0	13.5	20.8	753.6	676.3	23.0	14.0	38.6	38.3	...	38.3
2001	409.1	22.4	350.7	13.7	22.3	811.2	725.4	24.0	14.9	45.3	14.2	...	14.2
2002	430.7	23.7	367.5	15.4	24.1	866.4	770.8	25.8	15.5	52.8	-1.2	...	-1.2
2003	464.4	36.6	383.5	17.2	27.1	921.0	808.0	27.3	16.4	67.7	-5.3	...	-5.3
2004	478.3	28.8	401.6	18.8	29.1	975.2	860.5	29.2	17.6	65.9	-17.4	...	-17.4
2005	492.8	31.1	413.9	18.1	29.6	1 024.3	909.2	31.4	16.6	65.0	-7.9	...	-7.9
2006	520.8	26.6	441.7	20.6	31.3	1 082.8	964.8	32.6	15.6	67.8	6.4	...	6.4
2007	550.4	26.8	469.2	21.5	32.5	1 150.6	1 026.8	34.8	17.7	69.7	4.3	...	4.3
2008	566.0	24.4	486.1	22.4	32.6	1 209.6	1 081.0	36.8	17.7	73.0	-45.2	...	-45.2
2009	567.7	25.3	486.3	22.3	33.3	1 255.2	1 096.7	39.6	16.5	101.4	-84.0	...	-84.0
2010	577.8	31.9	488.8	23.3	33.1	1 270.8	1 107.1	42.3	16.6	103.7	-86.3	...	-86.3
2011	585.4	31.4	494.6	24.4	33.9	1 256.2	1 092.0	42.1	16.6	104.5	-55.9	...	-55.9
2012	581.0	19.2	502.8	23.1	35.1	1 250.2	1 076.7	42.4	16.8	113.2	-45.8	...	-45.8

[1]Includes components not shown separately.
. . . = Not available.

SECTION 6C: FEDERAL GOVERNMENT BUDGET ACCOUNTS

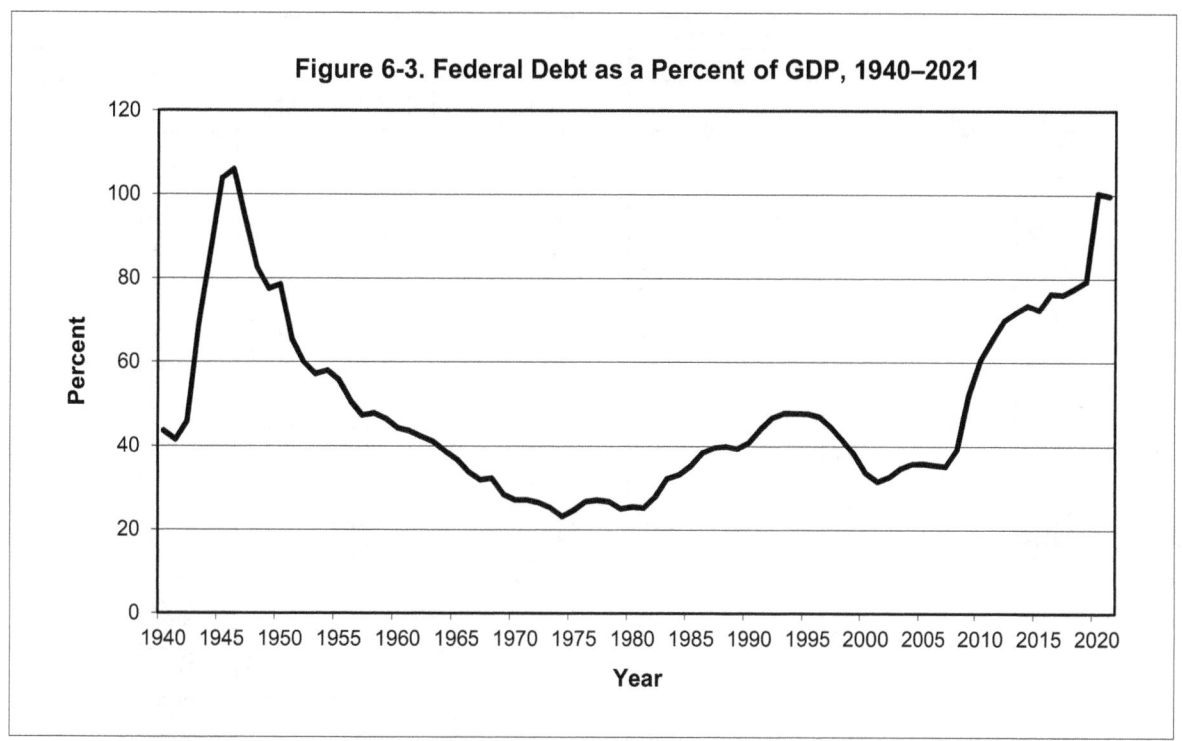

Figure 6-3. Federal Debt as a Percent of GDP, 1940–2021

- The "debt held by the public" is generally thought to be a more significant measure of the burden of the federal debt on credit markets than the gross debt, because it nets out the intragovernmental debt of the Social Security and other U.S. government trust funds. The ratio of debt held by the public to GDP was reduced in the late 1990s, began to creep back upward after 2001, and then rose rapidly beginning in 2008, as the recession reduced revenues and increased spending, and taxes were reduced further. The spending increases were a result of both automatic stabilizer programs, such as unemployment insurance, and an unprecedented level of spending for stimulus and financial rescue programs. At the end of fiscal year 2020, the debt/GDP ratio was over 100 percent. for the first time since 1946. In 2021, it decreased slightly to 99.7 percent. (Tables 6-14 and 6-15)

- At the end of 2021, foreign residents—including central banks—held nearly $7.6 trillion of Treasury debt, 34 percent of the $22.2 trillion total debt held by the public. (Table 6-15)

Table 6-14A. Federal Government Receipts and Outlays by Fiscal Year [1]

(Budget accounts, millions of dollars.)

Year	Total receipts, net	Total outlays, net	Budget surplus or deficit (-) — Total	On-budget	Off-budget	Sources of financing, total — Borrowing from the public	Other financing	Individual income taxes	Corporate income taxes	Social insurance taxes and contributions — Employment taxes and contributions	Unemployment insurance	Other retirement contributions
1945	45 159	92 712	-47 553	-48 720	1 167	50 386	-2 833	18 372	15 988	1 592	1 568	291
1946	39 296	55 232	-15 936	-16 964	1 028	6 679	9 257	16 098	11 883	1 517	1 316	282
1947	38 514	34 496	4 018	2 861	1 157	-17 522	13 504	17 935	8 615	1 835	1 329	259
1948	41 560	29 764	11 796	10 548	1 248	-8 069	-3 727	19 315	9 678	2 168	1 343	239
1949	39 415	38 835	580	-684	1 263	-1 948	1 368	15 552	11 192	2 246	1 205	330
1950	39 443	42 562	-3 119	-4 702	1 583	4 701	-1 582	15 755	10 449	2 648	1 332	358
1951	51 616	45 514	6 102	4 259	1 843	-4 697	-1 405	21 616	14 101	3 688	1 609	377
1952	66 167	67 686	-1 519	-3 383	1 864	432	1 087	27 934	21 226	4 315	1 712	418
1953	69 608	76 101	-6 493	-8 259	1 766	3 625	2 868	29 816	21 238	4 722	1 675	423
1954	69 701	70 855	-1 154	-2 831	1 677	6 116	-4 962	29 542	21 101	5 192	1 561	455
1955	65 451	68 444	-2 993	-4 091	1 098	2 117	876	28 747	17 861	5 981	1 449	431
1956	74 587	70 640	3 947	2 494	1 452	-4 460	513	32 188	20 880	7 059	1 690	571
1957	79 990	76 578	3 412	2 639	773	-2 836	-576	35 620	21 167	7 405	1 950	642
1958	79 636	82 405	-2 769	-3 315	546	7 016	-4 247	34 724	20 074	8 624	1 933	682
1959	79 249	92 098	-12 849	-12 149	-700	8 365	4 484	36 719	17 309	8 821	2 131	770
1960	92 492	92 191	301	510	-209	2 139	-2 440	40 715	21 494	11 248	2 667	768
1961	94 388	97 723	-3 335	-3 766	431	1 517	1 818	41 338	20 954	12 679	2 903	857
1962	99 676	106 821	-7 146	-5 881	-1 265	9 653	-2 507	45 571	20 523	12 835	3 337	875
1963	106 560	111 316	-4 756	-3 966	-789	5 968	-1 212	47 588	21 579	14 746	4 112	946
1964	112 613	118 528	-5 915	-6 546	632	2 871	3 044	48 697	23 493	16 959	3 997	1 007
1965	116 817	118 228	-1 411	-1 605	194	3 929	-2 518	48 792	25 461	17 358	3 803	1 081
1966	130 835	134 532	-3 698	-3 068	-630	2 936	762	55 446	30 073	20 662	3 755	1 129
1967	148 822	157 464	-8 643	-12 620	3 978	2 912	5 731	61 526	33 971	27 823	3 575	1 221
1968	152 973	178 134	-25 161	-27 742	2 581	22 919	2 242	68 726	28 665	29 224	3 346	1 354
1969	186 882	183 640	3 242	-507	3 749	-11 437	8 195	87 249	36 678	34 236	3 328	1 451
1970	192 807	195 649	-2 842	-8 694	5 852	5 090	-2 248	90 412	32 829	39 133	3 464	1 765
1971	187 139	210 172	-23 033	-26 052	3 019	19 839	3 194	86 230	26 785	41 699	3 674	1 952
1972	207 309	230 681	-23 373	-26 068	2 695	19 340	4 033	94 737	32 166	46 120	4 357	2 097
1973	230 799	245 707	-14 908	-15 246	338	18 533	-3 625	103 246	36 153	54 876	6 051	2 187
1974	263 224	269 359	-6 135	-7 198	1 063	2 789	3 346	118 952	38 620	65 888	6 837	2 347
1975	279 090	332 332	-53 242	-54 148	906	51 001	2 241	122 386	40 621	75 199	6 771	2 565
1976	298 060	371 792	-73 732	-69 427	-4 306	82 704	-8 972	131 603	41 409	79 901	8 054	2 814
1977	355 559	409 218	-53 659	-49 933	-3 726	71 700	-18 041	157 626	54 892	92 199	11 312	2 974
1978	399 561	458 746	-59 185	-55 416	-3 770	58 022	1 163	180 988	59 952	103 88	13 850	3 237
1979	463 302	504 028	-40 726	-39 633	-1 093	33 180	7 546	217 841	65 677	12 005	15 387	3 494
1980	517 112	590 941	-73 830	-73 141	-689	71 617	2 213	244 069	64 600	13 874	15 336	3 719
1981	599 272	678 241	-78 968	-73 859	-5 109	77 487	1 481	285 917	61 137	16 297	15 763	3 984
1982	617 766	745 743	-127 977	-120 593	-7 384	135 165	-7 188	297 744	49 207	18 068	16 600	4 212
1983	600 562	808 364	-207 802	-207 692	-110	212 693	-4 891	288 938	37 022	18 576	18 799	4 429
1984	666 438	851 805	-185 367	-185 269	-98	169 707	15 660	298 415	56 893	20 965	25 138	4 580
1985	734 037	946 344	-212 308	-221 529	9 222	200 285	12 023	334 531	61 331	23 464	25 758	4 759
1986	769 155	990 382	-221 227	-237 915	16 688	233 363	-12 136	348 959	63 143	25 506	24 098	4 742
1987	854 287	1 004 017	-149 730	-168 357	18 627	149 130	600	392 557	83 926	27 302	25 575	4 715
1988	909 238	1 064 416	-155 178	-192 265	37 087	161 863	-6 685	401 181	94 508	30 509	24 584	4 658
1989	991 104	1 143 743	-152 639	-205 393	52 754	139 100	13 539	445 690	10 329	33 285	22 011	4 546
1990	1 031 958	1 252 993	-221 036	-277 626	56 590	220 842	194	466 884	93 507	35 389	21 635	4 522
1991	1 054 988	1 324 226	-269 238	-321 435	52 198	277 441	-8 203	467 827	98 086	37 052	20 922	4 568
1992	1 091 208	1 381 529	-290 321	-340 408	50 087	310 738	-20 417	475 964	10 027	38 549	23 410	4 788
1993	1 154 334	1 409 386	-255 051	-300 398	45 347	248 659	6 392	509 680	11 752	39 693	26 556	4 805
1994	1 258 566	1 461 752	-203 186	-258 840	55 654	184 669	18 517	543 055	14 038	42 881	28 004	4 661
1995	1 351 790	1 515 742	-163 952	-226 367	62 415	171 313	-7 361	590 244	15 700	45 104	28 878	4 550
1996	1 453 053	1 560 484	-107 431	-174 019	66 588	129 695	-22 264	656 417	17 182	47 636	28 584	4 469
1997	1 579 232	1 601 116	-21 884	-103 248	81 364	38 271	-16 387	737 466	18 229	50 675	28 202	4 418
1998	1 721 728	1 652 458	69 270	-29 925	99 195	-51 245	-18 025	828 586	18 867	54 001	27 484	4 333
1999	1 827 452	1 701 842	125 610	1 920	123 690	-88 736	-36 874	879 480	18 468	58 088	26 480	4 473
2000	2 025 191	1 788 950	236 241	86 422	149 819	-222 559	-13 682	100 446	20 728	62 045	27 640	4 761
2001	1 991 082	1 862 846	128 236	-32 445	160 681	-90 189	-38 047	994 339	15 107	66 144	27 812	4 713
2002	1 853 136	2 010 894	-157 758	-317 417	159 659	220 812	-63 054	858 345	14 804	66 854	27 619	4 594
2003	1 782 314	2 159 899	-377 585	-538 418	160 833	373 016	4 569	793 699	13 177	67 498	33 366	4 631
2004	1 880 114	2 292 841	-412 727	-567 961	155 234	382 101	30 626	808 959	18 937	68 936	39 453	4 594
2005	2 153 611	2 471 957	-318 346	-493 611	175 265	296 668	21 678	927 222	27 828	74 766	42 002	4 459
2006	2 406 869	2 655 050	-248 181	-434 494	186 313	236 760	11 421	104 390	35 391	79 004	43 420	4 358
2007	2 567 985	2 728 686	-160 701	-342 153	181 452	206 157	-45 456	116 347	37 024	82 425	41 091	4 258
2008	2 523 991	2 982 544	-458 553	-641 848	183 295	767 921	-309 368	114 574	30 434	85 645	39 527	4 169
2009	2 104 989	3 517 677	-1 412 688	-1 549 681	136 993	1 741 657	-328 969	915 308	138 229	848 885	37 889	4 143
2010	2 162 706	3 457 079	-1 294 373	-1 371 378	77 005	1 474 175	-179 802	898 549	191 437	815 894	44 823	4 097
2011	2 303 466	3 603 065	-1 299 599	-1 366 781	67 182	1 109 305	190 294	1 091 473	181 085	758 516	56 241	4 035
2012	2 449 990	3 526 563	-1 076 573	-1 138 486	61 913	1 152 944	-76 371	1 132 206	242 289	774 927	66 647	3 740
2013	2 775 106	3 454 881	-679 775	-719 238	39 463	701 582	-21 807	1 316 405	273 506	887 445	56 811	3 564
2014	3 021 491	3 506 284	-484 793	-514 305	29 512	797 186	-312 393	1 394 568	320 731	965 029	54 957	3 472
2015	3 249 890	3 691 850	-441 960	-469 255	27 295	336 793	105 167	1 540 802	343 797	101 042	51 178	3 652
2016	3 267 965	3 852 615	-584 650	-620 157	35 507	1 050 932	-466 282	1 546 075	299 571	106 230	48 856	3 904
2017	3 316 184	3 981 630	-665 446	-714 863	49 417	497 815	167 631	1 587 120	297 048	111 189	45 808	4 192
2018	3 329 907	4 109 045	-779 138	-785 313	6 175	1 084 128	-304 990	1 683 538	204 733	112 115	45 042	4 504
2019	3 463 364	4 446 956	-983 592	-991 278	7 686	1 051 133	-67 541	1 717 857	230 245	119 739	40 934	4 786
2020	3 421 164	6 553 603	-3 132 439	-3 142 285	9 846	4 215 969	-1 083 530	1 608 663	211 845	126 165	43 104	5 200
2021	4 047 112	6 822 449	-2 775 337	-2 723 813	-51 524	1 267 357	1 507 980	2 044 377	371 831	125 185	56 602	5 628

[1]Fiscal years through 1976 are from July 1 through June 30. Beginning with October 1976 (fiscal year 1977), fiscal years are from October 1 through September 30. The period from July 1 through September 30, 1976, is a separate fiscal period known as the transition quarter (TQ) and is not included in any fiscal year.
. . . = Not available.

Table 6-14A. Federal Government Receipts and Outlays by Fiscal Year [1]—Continued

(Budget accounts, millions of dollars.)

Year	Receipts by source—Continued					Outlays by function						
				Miscellaneous receipts								
	Excise taxes	Estate and gift taxes	Customs duties and fees	Federal reserve deposits	All other	National defense	International affairs	General science, space, and technology	Energy	Natural resources and environment	Agriculture	Commerce and housing credit
1945	6 265	637	341	. . .	105	82 965	1 913	111	25	455	1 635	-2 630
1946	6 998	668	424	. . .	109	42 681	1 935	34	41	482	610	-1 857
1947	7 211	771	477	15	84	12 808	5 791	5	18	700	814	-923
1948	7 356	890	403	100	168	9 105	4 566	1	292	780	69	306
1949	7 502	780	367	187	241	13 150	6 052	48	341	1 080	1 924	800
1950	7 550	698	407	192	247	13 724	4 673	55	327	1 308	2 049	1 035
1951	8 648	708	609	189	261	23 566	3 647	51	383	1 310	-323	1 228
1952	8 852	818	533	278	359	46 089	2 691	49	474	1 233	176	1 278
1953	9 877	881	596	298	379	52 802	2 119	49	425	1 289	2 253	910
1954	9 945	934	542	341	429	49 266	1 596	46	432	1 007	1 817	-184
1955	9 131	924	585	251	341	42 729	2 223	74	325	940	3 514	92
1956	9 929	1 161	682	287	427	42 523	2 414	79	174	870	3 486	506
1957	9 055	1 365	735	434	573	45 430	3 147	122	240	1 098	2 288	1 424
1958	8 612	1 393	782	664	787	46 815	3 364	141	348	1 407	2 411	930
1959	8 504	1 333	925	491	663	49 015	3 144	294	382	1 632	4 509	1 933
1960	9 137	1 606	1 105	1 093	1 212	48 130	2 988	599	464	1 559	2 623	1 618
1961	9 063	1 896	982	788	918	49 601	3 184	1 042	510	1 779	2 641	1 203
1962	9 585	2 016	1 142	718	843	52 345	5 639	1 723	604	2 044	3 562	1 424
1963	9 915	2 167	1 205	828	1 023	53 400	5 308	3 051	530	2 251	4 384	62
1964	10 211	2 394	1 252	947	1 085	54 757	4 945	4 897	572	2 364	4 609	418
1965	10 911	2 716	1 442	1 372	1 594	50 620	5 273	5 823	699	2 531	3 954	1 157
1966	9 145	3 066	1 767	1 713	1 875	58 111	5 580	6 717	612	2 719	2 447	3 245
1967	9 278	2 978	1 901	1 805	2 108	71 417	5 566	6 233	782	2 869	2 990	3 979
1968	9 700	3 051	2 038	2 091	2 491	81 926	5 301	5 524	1 037	2 988	4 544	4 280
1969	10 585	3 491	2 319	2 662	2 908	82 497	4 600	5 020	1 010	2 900	5 826	-119
1970	10 352	3 644	2 430	3 266	3 424	81 692	4 330	4 511	997	3 065	5 166	2 112
1971	10 510	3 735	2 591	3 533	3 858	78 872	4 159	4 182	1 035	3 915	4 290	2 366
1972	9 506	5 436	3 287	3 252	3 633	79 174	4 781	4 175	1 296	4 241	5 227	2 222
1973	9 836	4 917	3 188	3 495	3 921	76 681	4 149	4 032	1 237	4 775	4 821	931
1974	9 743	5 035	3 334	4 845	5 369	79 347	5 710	3 980	1 303	5 697	2 194	4 705
1975	9 400	4 611	3 676	5 777	6 711	86 509	7 097	3 991	2 916	7 346	2 997	9 947
1976	10 612	5 216	4 074	5 451	8 026	89 619	6 433	4 373	4 204	8 184	3 109	7 619
1977	9 648	7 327	5 150	5 908	6 531	97 241	6 353	4 736	5 770	10 032	6 734	3 093
1978	10 054	5 285	6 573	6 641	7 420	10 449	7 482	4 926	7 991	10 983	11 301	6 254
1979	9 808	5 411	7 439	8 327	9 252	11 634	7 459	5 234	9 179	12 135	11 176	4 686
1980	15 563	6 389	7 174	11 767	12 748	13 399	12 714	5 831	10 156	13 858	8 774	9 390
1981	34 128	6 787	8 083	12 834	13 790	15 751	13 104	6 468	15 166	13 568	11 241	8 206
1982	28 670	7 991	8 854	15 186	16 161	18 530	12 300	7 199	13 527	12 998	15 866	6 256
1983	24 086	6 053	8 655	14 492	15 601	20 990	11 848	7 934	9 353	12 672	22 807	6 681
1984	22 279	6 010	11 370	15 684	17 012	22 741	15 869	8 311	7 073	12 586	13 477	6 959
1985	19 097	6 422	12 079	17 059	18 519	25 274	16 169	8 622	5 608	13 345	25 427	4 337
1986	16 053	6 958	13 327	18 374	19 948	27 337	14 146	8 962	4 690	13 628	31 319	5 058
1987	14 844	7 493	15 085	16 817	19 452	28 199	11 645	9 200	4 072	13 355	26 466	6 434
1988	16 185	7 594	16 198	17 163	20 194	29 036	10 466	10 820	2 296	14 601	17 088	19 163
1989	13 147	8 745	16 334	19 604	23 243	30 355	9 583	12 821	2 705	16 169	16 698	29 709
1990	15 591	11 500	16 707	24 319	27 967	29 932	13 758	14 426	3 341	17 055	11 637	67 599
1991	18 275	11 138	15 949	19 158	23 570	27 328	15 846	16 092	2 436	18 544	14 886	76 270
1992	21 836	11 143	17 359	22 920	27 214	29 834	16 090	16 389	4 499	20 001	14 922	10 918
1993	24 522	12 577	18 802	14 908	19 399	29 108	17 218	17 006	4 319	20 224	20 081	-2 185
1994	31 226	15 225	20 099	18 023	23 103	28 164	17 067	16 189	5 218	21 000	14 795	-4 228
1995	26 941	14 763	19 301	23 378	28 521	27 206	16 429	16 692	4 936	21 889	9 671	-1 780
1996	25 447	17 189	18 670	20 477	25 525	26 574	13 487	16 684	2 839	21 503	9 035	-1 047
1997	27 831	19 845	17 928	19 636	25 405	27 050	15 173	17 136	1 475	21 201	8 889	-1 464
1998	21 665	24 076	18 297	24 540	32 588	26 819	13 054	18 172	1 270	22 278	12 077	1 007
1999	19 293	27 782	18 336	25 917	34 927	27 476	15 239	18 084	911	23 943	22 879	2 641
2000	22 692	29 010	19 914	32 293	42 799	29 436	17 213	18 594	-761	25 003	36 458	3 207
2001	24 286	28 400	19 369	26 124	37 700	30 473	16 485	19 753	9	25 532	26 252	5 731
2002	24 017	26 507	18 602	23 683	33 889	34 845	22 315	20 734	475	29 426	21 965	-407
2003	23 804	21 959	19 862	21 878	34 514	40 473	21 199	20 831	-725	29 667	22 496	727
2004	24 566	24 831	21 083	19 652	32 608	45 581	26 870	23 029	-147	30 694	15 439	5 265
2005	22 547	24 764	23 379	19 297	32 745	495 294	34 565	23 597	440	27 983	26 565	7 566
2006	22 460	27 877	24 810	29 945	44 577	521 820	29 499	23 584	785	33 025	25 969	6 187
2007	11 076	26 044	26 010	32 043	47 540	551 258	28 482	24 407	-852	31 721	17 662	487
2008	15 726	28 844	27 568	33 598	49 997	616 066	28 857	26 773	631	31 820	18 387	27 870
2009	13 854	23 482	22 453	34 318	52 117	661 012	37 529	28 417	4 755	35 573	22 237	291 535
2010	18 256	18 885	25 298	75 845	96 814	693 485	45 195	30 100	11 618	43 667	21 356	-82 316
2011	18 904	7 399	29 519	82 546	102 817	705 554	45 685	29 466	12 174	45 473	20 662	-12 564
2012	20 359	13 973	30 307	81 957	106 840	677 852	36 802	29 060	14 858	41 631	17 791	40 647
2013	28 330	18 912	31 815	75 767	102 641	633 446	46 464	28 908	11 042	38 145	29 678	-83 198
2014	34 240	19 300	33 926	99 235	136 140	603 457	46 879	28 570	5 270	36 171	24 386	-94 861
2015	37 759	19 232	35 041	96 468	147 482	589 659	52 040	29 412	6 841	36 033	18 500	-37 905
2016	33 991	21 354	34 838	115 672	156 036	593 372	45 306	30 174	3 721	39 081	18 344	-34 077
2017	21 191	22 768	34 574	81 287	128 954	598 723	46 308	30 394	3 856	37 896	18 872	-26 685
2018	30 067	22 983	41 299	70 750	111 667	631 130	48 996	31 534	2 169	39 141	21 789	-9 470
2019	34 829	16 672	70 784	52 793	85 779	686 003	52 739	32 410	5 041	37 844	38 257	-25 715
2020	29 579	17 624	68 551	81 880	117 746	724 645	67 666	34 004	7 083	42 450	47 298	572 071
2021	18 387	27 140	79 985	100 054	134 417	753 901	46 947	35 512	5 977	44 160	47 398	307 847

[1]Fiscal years through 1976 are from July 1 through June 30. Beginning with October 1976 (fiscal year 1977), fiscal years are from October 1 through September 30. The period from July 1 through September 30, 1976, is a separate fiscal period known as the transition quarter (TQ) and is not included in any fiscal year.
. . . = Not available.

Table 6-14A. Federal Government Receipts and Outlays by Fiscal Year [1]—Continued

(Budget accounts, millions of dollars.)

Year	Transportation	Community and regional development	Education, employment, and social services	Health	Medicare	Income security	Social Security	Veterans benefits and services	Administration of justice	General government	Net interest
						Outlays by function—Continued					
1945	3 654	243	134	211	. . .	1 137	267	110	178	581	3 112
1946	1 970	200	85	201	. . .	2 384	358	2 465	176	825	4 111
1947	1 130	302	102	177	. . .	2 820	466	6 344	176	1 114	4 204
1948	787	78	191	162	. . .	2 499	558	6 457	170	1 045	4 341
1949	916	-33	178	197	. . .	3 174	657	6 599	184	824	4 523
1950	967	30	241	268	. . .	4 097	781	8 834	193	986	4 812
1951	956	47	235	323	. . .	3 352	1 565	5 526	218	1 097	4 665
1952	1 124	73	339	347	. . .	3 655	2 063	5 341	267	1 163	4 701
1953	1 264	117	441	336	. . .	3 823	2 717	4 519	243	1 209	5 156
1954	1 229	100	370	307	. . .	4 434	3 352	4 613	257	799	4 811
1955	1 246	129	445	291	. . .	5 071	4 427	4 675	256	651	4 850
1956	1 450	92	591	359	. . .	4 734	5 478	4 891	302	1 201	5 079
1957	1 662	135	590	479	. . .	5 427	6 661	5 005	303	1 360	5 354
1958	2 334	169	643	541	. . .	7 535	8 219	5 350	325	655	5 604
1959	3 655	211	789	685	. . .	8 239	9 737	5 443	356	926	5 762
1960	4 126	224	968	795	. . .	7 378	11 602	5 441	366	1 184	6 947
1961	3 987	275	1 063	913	. . .	9 683	12 474	5 705	400	1 354	6 716
1962	4 290	469	1 241	1 198	. . .	9 198	14 365	5 628	429	1 049	6 889
1963	4 596	574	1 458	1 451	. . .	9 304	15 788	5 521	465	1 230	7 740
1964	5 242	933	1 555	1 788	. . .	9 650	16 620	5 682	489	1 518	8 199
1965	5 763	1 114	2 140	1 791	. . .	9 462	17 460	5 723	536	1 499	8 591
1966	5 730	1 105	4 363	2 543	64	9 671	20 694	5 923	564	1 603	9 386
1967	5 936	1 108	6 453	3 351	2 748	10 253	21 725	6 743	618	1 719	10 268
1968	6 316	1 382	7 634	4 390	4 649	11 806	23 854	7 042	659	1 757	11 090
1969	6 526	1 552	7 548	5 162	5 695	13 066	27 298	7 642	766	1 939	12 699
1970	7 008	2 392	8 634	5 907	6 213	15 645	30 270	8 679	959	2 320	14 380
1971	8 052	2 917	9 849	6 843	6 622	22 936	35 872	9 778	1 307	2 442	14 841
1972	8 392	3 423	12 529	8 674	7 479	27 608	40 157	10 732	1 684	2 960	15 478
1973	9 066	4 605	12 744	9 356	8 052	28 265	49 090	12 015	2 174	9 774	17 349
1974	9 172	4 229	12 455	10 733	9 639	33 700	55 867	13 388	2 505	10 032	21 449
1975	10 918	4 322	16 022	12 930	12 875	50 161	64 658	16 599	3 028	10 374	23 244
1976	13 739	5 442	18 910	15 734	15 834	60 784	73 899	18 433	3 430	9 706	26 727
1977	14 829	7 021	21 104	17 302	19 345	61 045	85 061	18 038	3 701	12 791	29 901
1978	15 521	11 841	26 706	18 524	22 768	61 492	93 861	18 978	3 923	11 961	35 458
1979	18 079	10 480	30 218	20 494	26 495	66 364	10 407	19 931	4 286	12 241	42 633
1980	21 329	11 252	31 835	23 169	32 090	86 548	11 854	21 185	4 702	12 975	52 533
1981	23 379	10 568	33 146	26 866	39 149	10 028	13 958	22 991	4 908	11 373	68 766
1982	20 625	8 347	26 609	27 445	46 567	10 813	15 596	23 958	4 842	10 861	85 032
1983	21 334	7 564	26 192	28 643	52 588	12 301	17 072	24 846	5 246	11 181	89 808
1984	23 669	7 673	26 913	30 420	57 540	11 337	17 822	25 601	5 811	11 746	11 110
1985	25 838	7 676	28 584	33 546	65 822	12 900	18 862	26 281	6 426	11 515	12 947
1986	28 113	7 233	29 771	35 935	70 164	12 065	19 875	26 343	6 735	12 491	13 601
1987	26 222	5 049	28 915	39 967	75 120	12 410	20 735	26 761	7 715	7 487	13 861
1988	27 272	5 293	30 939	44 471	78 878	13 038	21 934	29 409	9 397	9 399	15 180
1989	27 608	5 362	35 314	48 390	84 964	13 755	23 254	30 038	9 644	9 317	16 898
1990	29 485	8 531	37 167	57 700	98 102	14 878	24 862	29 088	10 185	10 462	18 434
1991	31 099	6 810	41 260	71 139	10 448	17 258	26 901	31 319	12 486	11 568	19 444
1992	33 332	6 836	42 807	89 415	11 902	19 965	28 758	34 112	14 650	12 883	19 934
1993	35 004	9 146	47 455	99 321	13 055	21 008	30 458	35 690	15 193	12 944	19 871
1994	38 066	10 620	43 337	10 705	14 474	21 723	31 956	37 617	15 516	11 159	20 293
1995	39 350	10 746	51 067	11 535	15 985	22 375	33 584	37 910	16 508	13 799	23 213
1996	39 565	10 741	48 334	11 934	17 422	22 969	34 967	37 003	17 898	11 755	24 105
1997	40 767	11 049	49 014	12 379	19 001	23 498	36 525	39 332	20 617	12 547	24 398
1998	40 343	9 771	50 534	13 140	19 282	23 769	37 921	41 793	23 359	15 544	24 111
1999	42 532	11 865	50 608	14 104	19 044	24 241	39 003	43 216	26 536	15 363	22 975
2000	46 853	10 623	53 766	15 450	19 711	25 367	40 942	47 040	28 499	13 013	22 294
2001	54 447	11 773	57 089	17 223	21 738	26 972	43 295	45 024	30 201	14 358	20 616
2002	61 833	12 981	70 592	19 647	23 085	31 267	45 598	50 979	35 061	16 951	17 094
2003	67 069	18 850	82 733	219 605	249 433	334 574	474 680	56 832	35 340	23 164	15 307
2004	64 627	15 820	87 997	240 148	269 360	333 027	495 548	59 729	45 576	22 338	16 024
2005	67 894	26 262	97 553	250 605	298 638	345 800	523 305	70 112	40 019	16 997	18 398
2006	70 244	54 465	118 473	252 779	329 868	352 425	548 549	69 832	41 016	18 177	22 660
2007	72 905	29 567	91 647	266 425	375 407	365 931	586 153	72 828	42 362	17 425	23 710
2008	77 616	23 952	91 304	280 626	390 758	431 211	617 027	84 711	48 097	20 323	25 275
2009	84 289	27 676	79 744	334 368	430 093	533 080	682 963	95 545	52 581	22 017	18 690
2010	91 972	23 894	128 595	369 081	451 636	622 106	706 737	108 478	54 383	23 014	19 619
2011	92 966	23 883	101 256	372 481	485 653	597 269	730 811	127 269	56 056	27 476	22 996
2012	93 019	25 132	90 822	346 755	471 793	541 248	773 290	124 679	56 277	28 035	22 040
2013	91 673	32 335	72 860	358 264	497 826	536 411	813 551	139 038	52 601	27 737	22 088
2014	91 915	20 670	90 610	409 497	511 688	513 596	850 533	149 621	50 457	26 913	22 895
2015	89 533	20 669	122 035	482 257	546 202	508 800	887 753	159 781	51 906	20 956	22 318
2016	92 566	20 140	109 709	511 325	594 536	514 098	916 067	174 557	55 768	23 146	24 003
2017	93 552	24 907	143 953	533 152	597 307	503 443	944 878	176 584	57 944	23 821	26 255
2018	92 785	42 159	95 503	551 219	588 706	495 289	987 791	178 895	60 418	23 885	324 975
2019	95 756	26 784	136 700	584 816	650 996	514 787	104 440	199 843	65 832	23 488	375 158
2020	145 623	81 878	237 754	747 582	776 225	126 363	109 581	218 655	71 997	180 109	345 470
2021	154 291	44 655	298 406	796 450	696 458	164 773	113 458	234 282	71 430	273 941	352 338

[1]Fiscal years through 1976 are from July 1 through June 30. Beginning with October 1976 (fiscal year 1977), fiscal years are from October 1 through September 30. The period from July 1 through September 30, 1976, is a separate fiscal period known as the transition quarter (TQ) and is not included in any fiscal year.
. . . = Not available.

Table 6-14B. The Federal Budget and GDP

(Billions of dollars; percent.)

Year	Fiscal year GDP	Billions of dollars						Percent of GDP					
		Receipts			Outlays		Total budget surplus or deficit	Receipts			Outlays		Total budget surplus or deficit
		Total	Individual income taxes	Corporate income taxes	Total	National defense		Total	Individual income taxes	Corporate income taxes	Total	National defense	
1955	406.3	65.5	28.7	17.9	68.4	42.7	-3.0	16.1	7.1	4.4	15.9	10.5	-1.0
1956	438.3	74.6	32.2	20.9	70.6	42.5	3.9	17.0	7.3	4.8	15.0	9.7	0.6
1957	463.4	80.0	35.6	21.2	76.6	45.4	3.4	17.3	7.7	4.6	15.2	9.8	0.6
1958	473.5	79.6	34.7	20.1	82.4	46.8	-2.8	16.8	7.3	4.2	15.8	9.9	-0.7
1959	504.6	79.2	36.7	17.3	92.1	49.0	-12.8	15.7	7.3	3.4	16.5	9.7	-2.4
1960	534.3	92.5	40.7	21.5	92.2	48.1	0.3	17.3	7.6	4.0	15.2	9.0	0.1
1961	546.6	94.4	41.3	21.0	97.7	49.6	-3.3	17.3	7.6	3.8	15.7	9.1	-0.7
1962	585.7	99.7	45.6	20.5	106.8	52.3	-7.1	17.0	7.8	3.5	15.9	8.9	-1.0
1963	618.2	106.6	47.6	21.6	111.3	53.4	-4.8	17.2	7.7	3.5	15.6	8.6	-0.6
1964	661.7	112.6	48.7	23.5	118.5	54.8	-5.9	17.0	7.4	3.6	15.5	8.3	-1.0
1965	709.3	116.8	48.8	25.5	118.2	50.6	-1.4	16.5	6.9	3.6	14.3	7.1	-0.2
1966	780.5	130.8	55.4	30.1	134.5	58.1	-3.7	16.8	7.1	3.9	14.7	7.4	-0.4
1967	836.5	148.8	61.5	34.0	157.5	71.4	-8.6	17.8	7.4	4.1	16.4	8.5	-1.5
1968	897.6	153.0	68.7	28.7	178.1	81.9	-25.2	17.0	7.7	3.2	17.4	9.1	-3.1
1969	980.3	186.9	87.2	36.7	183.6	82.5	3.2	19.1	8.9	3.7	16.2	8.4	-0.1
1970	1 046.7	192.8	90.4	32.8	195.6	81.7	-2.8	18.4	8.6	3.1	16.1	7.8	-0.8
1971	1 116.6	187.1	86.2	26.8	210.2	78.9	-23.0	16.8	7.7	2.4	15.9	7.1	-2.3
1972	1 216.3	207.3	94.7	32.2	230.7	79.2	-23.4	17.0	7.8	2.6	15.9	6.5	-2.1
1973	1 352.7	230.8	103.2	36.2	245.7	76.7	-14.9	17.1	7.6	2.7	14.8	5.7	-1.1
1974	1 482.9	263.2	119.0	38.6	269.4	79.3	-6.1	17.8	8.0	2.6	14.6	5.4	-0.5
1975	1 606.9	279.1	122.4	40.6	332.3	86.5	-53.2	17.4	7.6	2.5	16.9	5.4	-3.4
1976	1 786.1	298.1	131.6	41.4	371.8	89.6	-73.7	16.7	7.4	2.3	16.9	5.0	-3.9
1977	2 024.3	355.6	157.6	54.9	409.2	97.2	-53.7	17.6	7.8	2.7	16.2	4.8	-2.5
1978	2 273.5	399.6	181.0	60.0	458.7	104.5	-59.2	17.6	8.0	2.6	16.3	4.6	-2.4
1979	2 565.6	463.3	217.8	65.7	504.0	116.3	-40.7	18.1	8.5	2.6	15.8	4.5	-1.5
1980	2 791.9	517.1	244.1	64.6	590.9	134.0	-73.8	18.5	8.7	2.3	17.1	4.8	-2.6
1981	3 133.2	599.3	285.9	61.1	678.2	157.5	-79.0	19.1	9.1	2.0	17.3	5.0	-2.4
1982	3 313.4	617.8	297.7	49.2	745.7	185.3	-128.0	18.6	9.0	1.5	18.0	5.6	-3.6
1983	3 536.0	600.6	288.9	37.0	808.4	209.9	-207.8	17.0	8.2	1.0	18.7	5.9	-5.9
1984	3 949.2	666.4	298.4	56.9	851.8	227.4	-185.4	16.9	7.6	1.4	17.4	5.8	-4.7
1985	4 265.1	734.0	334.5	61.3	946.3	252.7	-212.3	17.2	7.8	1.4	18.0	5.9	-5.2
1986	4 526.3	769.2	349.0	63.1	990.4	273.4	-221.2	17.0	7.7	1.4	17.8	6.0	-5.3
1987	4 767.7	854.3	392.6	83.9	1 004.0	282.0	-149.7	17.9	8.2	1.8	17.0	5.9	-3.5
1988	5 138.6	909.2	401.2	94.5	1 064.4	290.4	-155.2	17.7	7.8	1.8	16.7	5.7	-3.7
1989	5 554.7	991.1	445.7	103.3	1 143.7	303.6	-152.6	17.8	8.0	1.9	16.8	5.5	-3.7
1990	5 898.8	1 032.0	466.9	93.5	1 253.0	299.3	-221.0	17.5	7.9	1.6	17.4	5.1	-4.7
1991	6 093.2	1 055.0	467.8	98.1	1 324.2	273.3	-269.2	17.3	7.7	1.6	17.8	4.5	-5.3
1992	6 416.3	1 091.2	476.0	100.3	1 381.5	298.3	-290.3	17.0	7.4	1.6	17.6	4.6	-5.3
1993	6 775.3	1 154.3	509.7	117.5	1 409.4	291.1	-255.1	17.0	7.5	1.7	16.9	4.3	-4.4
1994	7 176.9	1 258.6	543.1	140.4	1 461.8	281.6	-203.2	17.5	7.6	2.0	16.5	3.9	-3.6
1995	7 560.4	1 351.8	590.2	157.0	1 515.7	272.1	-164.0	17.9	7.8	2.1	16.2	3.6	-3.0
1996	7 951.3	1 453.1	656.4	171.8	1 560.5	265.7	-107.4	18.3	8.3	2.2	15.8	3.3	-2.2
1997	8 451.0	1 579.2	737.5	182.3	1 601.1	270.5	-21.9	18.7	8.7	2.2	15.3	3.2	-1.2
1998	8 930.8	1 721.7	828.6	188.7	1 652.5	268.2	69.3	19.3	9.3	2.1	15.0	3.0	-0.3
1999	9 479.6	1 827.5	879.5	184.7	1 701.8	274.8	125.6	19.3	9.3	1.9	14.6	2.9	. . .
2000	10 117.1	2 025.2	1 004.5	207.3	1 789.0	294.4	236.2	20.0	9.9	2.0	14.4	2.9	0.9
2001	10 525.7	1 991.1	994.3	151.1	1 862.8	304.7	128.2	18.9	9.4	1.4	14.4	2.9	-0.3
2002	10 828.9	1 853.1	858.3	148.0	2 010.9	348.5	-157.8	17.1	7.9	1.4	15.3	3.2	-2.9
2003	11 278.8	1 782.3	793.7	131.8	2 159.9	404.7	-377.6	15.8	7.0	1.2	15.9	3.6	-4.8
2004	12 028.4	1 880.1	809.0	189.4	2 292.8	455.8	-412.7	15.6	6.7	1.6	15.9	3.8	-4.7
2005	12 840.0	2 153.6	927.2	278.3	2 472.0	495.3	-318.3	16.8	7.2	2.2	16.1	3.9	-3.8
2006	13 636.8	2 406.9	1 043.9	353.9	2 655.1	521.8	-248.2	17.6	7.7	2.6	16.4	3.8	-3.2
2007	14 305.4	2 568.0	1 163.5	370.2	2 728.7	551.3	-160.7	18.0	8.1	2.6	15.9	3.9	-2.4
2008	14 796.6	2 524.0	1 145.7	304.3	2 982.5	616.1	-458.6	17.1	7.7	2.1	16.9	4.2	-4.3
2009	14 467.3	2 105.0	915.3	138.2	3 517.7	661.0	-1 412.7	14.5	6.3	1.0	20.7	4.6	-10.7
2010	14 884.4	2 162.7	898.5	191.4	3 457.1	693.5	-1 294.4	14.5	6.0	1.3	19.5	4.7	-9.2
2011	15 466.5	2 303.5	1 091.5	181.1	3 603.1	705.6	-1 299.6	14.9	7.1	1.2	20.1	4.6	-8.8
2012	16 109.4	2 450.0	1 132.2	242.3	3 526.6	677.9	-1 076.6	15.2	7.0	1.5	18.7	4.2	-7.1
2013	16 665.1	2 775.1	1 316.4	273.5	3 454.9	633.4	-679.8	16.7	7.9	1.6	16.9	3.8	-4.3
2014	17 370.8	3 021.5	1 394.6	320.7	3 506.3	603.5	-484.8	17.4	8.0	1.8	16.1	3.5	-3.0
2015	18 086.1	3 249.9	1 540.8	343.8	3 691.9	589.7	-442.0	18.0	8.5	1.9	16.3	3.3	-2.6
2016	18 536.1	3 268.0	1 546.1	299.6	3 852.6	593.4	-584.7	17.6	8.3	1.6	16.6	3.2	-3.3
2017	19 250.9	3 316.2	1 587.1	297.0	3 981.6	598.7	-665.4	17.2	8.2	1.5	16.5	3.1	-3.7
2018	20 294.6	3 329.9	1 683.5	204.7	4 109.0	631.1	-779.1	16.4	8.3	1.0	16.1	3.1	-3.9
2019	21 152.3	3 463.4	1 717.9	230.2	4 447.0	686.0	-983.6	16.4	8.1	1.1	16.7	3.2	-4.7
2020	20 948.0	3 421.2	1 608.7	211.8	6 553.6	724.6	-3 132.4	16.3	7.7	1.0	26.7	3.5	-15.0
2021	22 357.6	4 047.1	2 044.4	371.8	6 822.4	753.9	-2 775.3	18.1	9.1	1.7	26.0	3.4	-12.2

. . . = Not available.

Table 6-15. Federal Government Debt by Fiscal Year

(Billions of dollars, except as noted.)

Year	Federal government debt held by the public at end of fiscal year		Gross federal debt at end of fiscal year held by:						
							Private investors		
	Debt held by the public	Debt/GDP ratio (percent)	Total	Social Security funds [1]	Other U.S. government accounts	Federal Reserve System	Total	Foreign residents	Domestic investors
1940	43	43.6	51	2	6	2	40	. . .	. . .
1941	48	41.5	58	2	7	2	46	. . .	. . .
1942	68	45.9	79	3	8	3	65	. . .	. . .
1943	128	69.2	143	4	11	7	121	. . .	. . .
1944	185	86.4	204	5	14	15	170	. . .	. . .
1945	235	103.9	260	7	18	22	213	. . .	. . .
1946	242	106.1	271	8	21	24	218	. . .	. . .
1947	224	93.9	257	9	24	22	202	. . .	. . .
1948	216	82.6	252	10	26	21	195	. . .	. . .
1949	214	77.5	253	11	27	19	195	. . .	. . .
1950	219	78.6	257	13	25	18	201	. . .	. . .
1951	214	65.5	255	15	26	23	191	. . .	. . .
1952	215	60.1	259	17	28	23	192	. . .	. . .
1953	218	57.2	266	18	29	25	194	. . .	. . .
1954	224	58.0	271	20	26	25	199	. . .	. . .
1955	227	55.8	274	21	27	24	203	. . .	. . .
1956	222	50.7	273	23	28	24	198	. . .	. . .
1957	219	47.3	272	23	30	23	196	. . .	. . .
1958	226	47.8	280	23	31	25	201	. . .	. . .
1959	235	46.5	287	22	31	26	209	. . .	. . .
1960	237	44.3	291	21	33	27	210	. . .	. . .
1961	238	43.6	293	21	33	27	211	. . .	. . .
1962	248	42.3	303	20	35	30	218	. . .	. . .
1963	254	41.1	310	19	37	32	222	. . .	. . .
1964	257	38.8	316	20	39	35	222	. . .	. . .
1965	261	36.8	322	20	41	39	222	12	209
1966	264	33.8	328	20	45	42	222	12	210
1967	267	31.9	340	24	50	47	220	11	209
1968	290	32.3	369	26	54	52	237	11	226
1969	278	28.4	366	28	59	54	224	10	214
1970	283	27.1	381	33	65	58	225	14	211
1971	303	27.1	408	34	71	66	238	32	206
1972	322	26.5	436	36	77	71	251	49	202
1973	341	25.2	466	36	89	75	266	59	207
1974	344	23.2	484	38	102	81	263	57	206
1975	395	24.6	542	40	107	85	310	66	244
1976	477	26.7	629	38	114	95	383	70	313
1977	549	27.1	706	35	122	105	444	96	348
1978	607	26.7	777	31	138	115	492	121	371
1979	640	25.0	829	28	161	116	525	120	405
1980	712	25.5	909	25	173	121	591	122	469
1981	789	25.2	995	24	182	124	665	131	534
1982	925	27.9	1 137	13	200	134	790	141	649
1983	1 137	32.2	1 372	27	208	156	982	160	822
1984	1 307	33.1	1 565	28	230	155	1 152	176	976
1985	1 507	35.3	1 817	34	276	170	1 337	223	1 114
1986	1 741	38.5	2 121	38	342	191	1 550	266	1 284
1987	1 890	39.6	2 346	58	398	212	1 678	280	1 398
1988	2 052	39.9	2 601	97	453	229	1 822	346	1 476
1989	2 191	39.4	2 868	148	529	220	1 971	395	1 576
1990	2 412	40.9	3 206	203	591	234	2 177	464	1 713
1991	2 689	44.1	3 598	255	654	259	2 430	506	1 924
1992	3 000	46.8	4 002	306	696	296	2 703	563	2 140
1993	3 248	47.9	4 351	356	747	326	2 923	619	2 304
1994	3 433	47.8	4 643	416	794	355	3 078	682	2 396
1995	3 604	47.7	4 921	448	868	374	3 230	820	2 410
1996	3 734	47.0	5 181	499	948	391	3 343	993	2 350
1997	3 772	44.6	5 369	567	1 029	425	3 348	1 231	2 117
1998	3 721	41.7	5 478	653	1 104	458	3 263	1 224	2 039
1999	3 632	38.3	5 606	762	1 211	497	3 136	1 281	1 855
2000	3 410	33.7	5 629	893	1 326	511	2 898	1 039	1 859
2001	3 320	31.5	5 770	1 034	1 416	534	2 785	1 006	1 779
2002	3 540	32.7	6 198	1 174	1 484	604	2 936	1 201	1 735
2003	3 913	34.7	6 760	1 313	1 533	656	3 257	1 454	1 803
2004	4 296	35.7	7 355	1 453	1 606	700	3 595	1 799	1 796
2005	4 592	35.8	7 905	1 616	1 697	736	3 856	1 930	1 926
2006	4 829	35.4	8 451	1 792	1 830	769	4 060	2 025	2 035
2007	5 035	35.2	8 951	1 967	1 948	780	4 255	2 235	2 020
2008	5 803	39.2	9 986	2 150	2 033	491	5 312	2 802	2 510
2009	7 545	52.2	11 876	2 296	2 035	769	6 776	3 571	3 205
2010	9 019	60.6	13 529	2 399	2 111	812	8 207	4 324	3 883
2011	10 128	65.5	14 764	2 492	2 144	1 665	8 464	4 912	3 551
2012	11 281	70.0	16 051	2 586	2 184	1 645	9 636	5 476	4 160
2013	11 983	71.9	16 719	2 655	2 081	2 072	9 910	5 653	4 258
2014	12 780	73.6	17 794	2 713	2 302	2 452	10 328	6 069	4 259
2015	13 117	72.5	18 120	2 767	2 237	2 462	10 655	6 106	4 549
2016	14 168	76.4	19 539	2 797	2 575	2 463	11 704	6 156	5 548
2017	14 665	76.2	20 206	2 820	2 720	2 465	12 200	6 302	5 898
2018	15 750	77.6	21 462	2 801	2 912	2 313	13 436	6 226	7 210
2019	16 801	79.4	22 669	2 804	3 064	2 113	14 687	6 924	7 764
2020	21 017	100.3	26 902	2 811	3 075	4 445	16 571	7 069	9 502
2021	22 284	99.7	28 386	2 756	3 346	5 433	16 851	7 571	9 280

[1] Sum of old age and survivors insurance fund and disability insurance trust fund.
. . . = Not available.

SECTION 6D: GOVERNMENT OUTPUT AND EMPLOYMENT

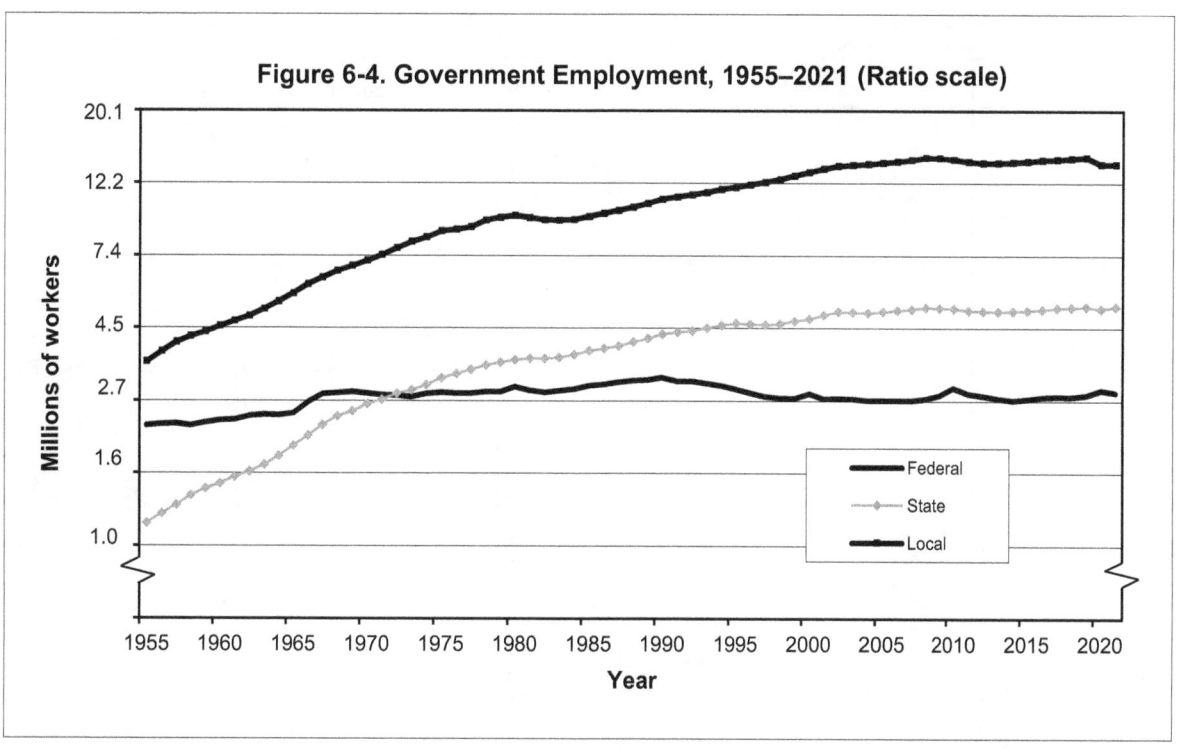

Figure 6-4. Government Employment, 1955–2021 (Ratio scale)

- From 1955 to 2021, total reported employment of civilians by all levels of government has increased 213 percent. Federal employment rose 25.8 percent; state government employment rose 345.8 percent, with 55.1 percent of this increase due to an increase in state education employment. However, budget cuts hit all levels of government employment. For example, the Department of Defense lost 24 percent of its employees between 1955 and 2021. (Tables 6-17)

- Contracting and outsourcing of federal government spending can be seen in comparisons between government purchases and government value added. From 1965 to 2021, the volume (measured by the quantity index) of "intermediate" goods and services purchased for nondefense purposes rose 858 percent, compared with the 216 percent rise in nondefense value added by government itself in such activities. (Real value added comprises the input of government employees and government-owned capital, valued in constant dollars). For defense, government value added rose 5.8 percent over that period, while purchases of goods and services rose 180 percent. (Table 6-16)

- A similar process has occurred at state and local governments, where real value added increased 163.2 from 1965 to 2021 percent while goods and services purchased rose 642.8 percent. (Table 6-16)

Table 6-16. Chain-Type Quantity Indexes for Government Output

(Seasonally adjusted, 2012 = 100.)

NIPA Table 3.10.3

Year and quarter	Federal government									State and local government		
	Gross output of general government			Value added			Intermediate goods and services purchased [1]			Gross output of general government	Value added	Intermediate goods and services purchased [1]
	Total	Defense	Nondefense	Total	Defense	Nondefense	Total	Defense	Nondefense			
1965	51.9	66.0	28.3	69.3	92.0	34.9	26.3	32.6	14.4	31.3	39.7	16.6
1966	57.4	74.9	27.9	74.0	98.2	37.5	32.3	44.8	10.4	33.3	42.0	17.9
1967	63.8	83.5	30.7	79.1	104.7	40.4	40.0	55.8	12.4	35.0	43.8	19.4
1968	66.2	87.2	30.9	81.0	106.5	42.4	42.8	61.6	10.3	37.4	46.5	21.3
1969	65.4	84.4	33.5	81.8	106.8	44.0	40.1	54.9	13.8	39.7	48.6	23.7
1970	61.7	77.6	34.6	79.2	101.4	45.5	34.9	46.5	14.0	42.0	50.7	26.1
1971	59.1	71.9	37.2	76.3	95.3	47.4	32.9	41.0	17.3	44.2	52.8	28.5
1972	58.0	68.0	40.6	73.4	89.3	49.1	34.6	40.1	23.0	46.0	54.7	30.3
1973	55.3	63.8	40.5	71.4	85.4	49.9	30.7	35.1	21.4	47.6	56.6	31.2
1974	55.2	62.3	42.9	71.4	83.9	52.3	30.5	33.5	23.7	49.5	58.7	32.6
1975	54.8	60.5	44.6	71.1	82.6	53.6	29.7	31.1	25.6	51.6	60.4	35.3
1976	53.7	58.8	44.7	71.3	81.2	56.2	26.9	28.9	22.1	52.5	61.2	36.4
1977	54.6	59.1	46.7	71.6	80.6	57.9	28.7	30.4	24.2	53.6	62.2	37.7
1978	55.6	59.5	48.7	72.6	80.9	59.9	29.7	30.9	26.0	54.9	63.7	38.7
1979	56.3	59.9	50.0	72.7	80.5	60.9	31.2	32.3	27.6	55.7	64.8	38.7
1980	58.3	61.5	52.6	73.9	81.1	63.0	34.1	35.1	30.7	55.7	65.7	37.3
1981	60.5	64.5	53.2	75.1	83.3	62.8	37.3	38.8	32.6	55.7	65.7	37.5
1982	62.3	67.9	52.0	76.5	85.5	62.8	39.5	43.5	29.5	56.7	66.2	39.1
1983	65.3	70.8	55.5	78.4	87.8	64.1	43.8	46.8	35.9	57.6	65.9	41.8
1984	66.1	72.7	53.9	80.5	90.7	64.8	42.7	47.5	30.9	58.7	66.3	44.0
1985	69.5	76.4	56.8	83.0	94.3	65.6	47.1	51.1	36.9	61.3	68.2	47.7
1986	72.7	80.4	58.8	85.0	97.4	65.7	51.9	55.9	41.5	64.1	70.2	51.6
1987	74.2	83.2	57.8	87.7	100.9	67.2	51.7	57.8	36.7	65.4	71.6	52.8
1988	74.4	84.9	55.1	89.4	102.5	69.0	49.8	59.6	27.0	67.6	74.1	54.4
1989	76.2	85.3	59.4	90.8	104.1	70.0	52.0	58.5	36.9	70.0	76.3	57.0
1990	77.8	85.9	63.2	92.4	104.8	73.0	53.7	58.7	41.9	72.1	78.6	58.9
1991	78.8	86.8	64.1	92.9	105.2	73.9	55.3	60.5	42.8	73.8	79.7	61.9
1992	77.5	83.3	67.0	91.4	101.7	75.5	54.3	57.0	48.1	75.8	81.0	64.9
1993	75.4	80.5	66.1	89.8	98.7	76.3	51.4	54.5	44.1	77.5	82.1	67.8
1994	73.6	77.4	66.9	87.4	95.1	75.6	50.8	52.2	47.4	79.7	83.6	71.6
1995	71.0	73.8	66.1	84.6	91.2	74.5	48.6	49.0	47.6	81.7	85.2	74.5
1996	69.7	72.5	64.8	82.5	88.2	74.1	48.4	50.1	44.4	83.3	86.5	76.5
1997	69.6	71.2	66.6	81.2	85.6	74.6	50.1	50.6	48.9	85.7	88.2	80.3
1998	68.4	69.3	66.9	80.3	83.2	75.9	48.5	49.2	47.0	89.0	90.1	86.6
1999	69.0	70.2	66.7	79.7	81.4	77.1	51.0	54.0	43.9	92.0	91.6	92.9
2000	69.5	69.4	69.7	80.1	80.5	79.6	51.7	53.3	47.8	94.5	93.6	96.6
2001	72.2	71.5	73.3	80.3	80.3	80.4	58.3	58.6	57.4	98.1	95.8	103.4
2002	76.5	75.6	78.0	81.8	81.5	82.2	67.3	66.7	68.7	100.7	97.7	107.4
2003	81.5	81.6	81.3	83.9	83.7	84.3	77.2	78.4	74.5	100.1	98.3	104.1
2004	84.6	85.5	83.2	85.1	85.5	84.6	83.8	85.4	79.9	100.4	98.6	104.2
2005	86.1	86.6	85.0	86.2	86.7	85.4	85.7	86.4	84.2	101.0	99.4	104.6
2006	87.4	87.6	87.2	86.9	87.1	86.5	88.4	88.2	88.8	102.1	100.2	106.2
2007	88.3	89.1	86.9	88.1	88.2	87.9	88.7	90.5	84.6	103.6	101.6	107.8
2008	93.8	94.8	91.9	91.4	91.6	91.0	98.1	99.7	94.2	103.6	103.0	105.0
2009	100.1	100.6	99.1	95.9	96.5	94.9	107.3	106.7	108.7	105.9	103.4	111.5
2010	104.2	104.1	104.4	99.2	99.6	98.5	113.0	111.0	117.8	103.9	102.5	106.8
2011	101.7	102.9	99.7	100.1	100.9	98.8	104.6	105.8	101.8	101.2	101.3	101.1
2012	100.0	100.0	100.0	100.0	100.0	100.0	100.0	100.0	100.0	100.0	100.0	100.0
2013	95.0	93.7	97.4	98.2	97.8	99.0	89.4	87.5	93.8	100.4	99.9	101.4
2014	93.0	90.5	97.6	97.5	96.1	99.7	85.3	82.1	92.8	100.9	99.9	103.0
2015	92.8	88.5	100.5	96.8	94.1	101.1	85.8	80.0	99.4	103.9	100.7	111.4
2016	93.3	88.3	102.2	97.3	93.5	103.1	86.4	80.5	100.2	106.8	101.8	118.3
2017	92.9	88.5	100.9	97.4	93.1	104.0	85.1	81.5	93.7	107.6	102.8	118.7
2018	95.1	91.0	102.5	97.9	93.6	104.6	90.4	87.3	97.9	108.5	103.7	119.8
2019	98.5	95.4	104.1	98.9	94.6	105.6	98.1	97.0	100.8	109.7	104.8	121.1
2020	102.9	97.2	113.0	101.6	96.4	109.8	105.6	98.9	121.0	108.1	103.3	119.4
2021	103.3	94.9	118.3	102.4	97.3	110.3	105.5	91.3	137.9	110.1	104.5	123.3
2019												
1st quarter	96.0	93.9	100.0	97.1	94.2	101.6	94.6	94.0	96.4	109.1	103.9	121.2
2nd quarter	98.8	95.3	105.1	99.1	94.4	106.4	98.6	97.3	102.0	109.4	104.2	121.4
3rd quarter	99.3	95.8	105.6	99.6	94.7	107.2	99.1	97.9	102.0	109.8	105.0	121.1
4th quarter	99.8	96.5	105.8	99.9	95.2	107.1	100.0	98.9	102.8	110.4	106.0	120.4
2020												
1st quarter	100.2	96.5	106.9	100.4	95.5	108.0	100.3	98.6	104.7	110.2	105.8	120.4
2nd quarter	105.6	96.7	121.3	101.3	96.5	108.8	113.9	97.3	151.6	106.0	101.3	116.9
3rd quarter	103.3	97.3	113.9	102.6	96.6	111.9	105.0	99.0	119.0	108.1	103.3	119.2
4th quarter	102.4	98.2	109.8	102.2	96.8	110.4	103.2	100.9	108.8	108.2	102.7	121.1
2021												
1st quarter	106.0	96.3	123.1	102.2	97.4	109.8	113.4	95.0	155.5	108.7	103.0	122.0
2nd quarter	104.3	95.7	119.7	102.5	97.5	110.3	108.1	93.1	142.6	109.4	103.8	122.8
3rd quarter	101.9	94.6	115.0	102.5	97.3	110.5	101.4	90.5	126.3	111.0	105.6	123.8
4th quarter	101.1	93.0	115.4	102.4	97.1	110.7	99.0	86.7	127.2	111.3	105.5	124.7

[1] Includes general government intermediate inputs for goods and services sold to other sectors and for own-account investment.

Table 6-17. Government Employment

(Calendar years, payroll employment in thousands.)

Year and month	Total government employment	Federal			State			Local		
		Total	Department of Defense	Postal Service	Total	Education	State government hospitals	Total	Education	Local government hospitals
1950	6 120	2 023	533	516	...	...	...	...	...	...
1951	6 502	2 415	797	521	...	...	...	...	...	...
1952	6 727	2 539	868	542	...	...	...	...	...	...
1953	6 758	2 418	818	530	...	...	...	...	...	...
1954	6 858	2 295	744	533	...	...	...	...	...	...
1955	7 021	2 295	744	534	1 168	308	...	3 558	1 751	...
1956	7 386	2 318	749	539	1 249	334	...	3 819	1 884	...
1957	7 724	2 326	729	555	1 328	363	...	4 071	2 026	...
1958	7 946	2 298	695	567	1 415	389	...	4 232	2 115	...
1959	8 192	2 342	699	578	1 484	420	...	4 366	2 198	...
1960	8 464	2 381	681	591	1 536	448	...	4 547	2 314	...
1961	8 706	2 391	683	601	1 607	474	...	4 708	2 411	...
1962	9 004	2 455	697	601	1 669	511	...	4 881	2 522	...
1963	9 341	2 473	687	603	1 747	557	...	5 121	2 674	...
1964	9 711	2 463	676	604	1 856	609	...	5 392	2 839	...
1965	10 191	2 495	679	619	1 996	679	...	5 700	3 031	...
1966	10 910	2 690	741	686	2 141	775	...	6 080	3 297	...
1967	11 525	2 852	802	719	2 302	873	...	6 371	3 490	...
1968	11 972	2 871	801	729	2 442	958	...	6 660	3 649	...
1969	12 330	2 893	815	737	2 533	1 042	...	6 904	3 785	...
1970	12 687	2 865	756	741	2 664	1 104	...	7 158	3 912	...
1971	13 012	2 828	731	731	2 747	1 149	...	7 437	4 091	...
1972	13 465	2 815	720	703	2 859	1 188	459	7 790	4 262	467
1973	13 862	2 794	696	698	2 923	1 205	472	8 146	4 433	477
1974	14 303	2 858	698	710	3 039	1 267	483	8 407	4 584	483
1975	14 820	2 882	704	699	3 179	1 323	503	8 758	4 722	489
1976	15 001	2 863	693	676	3 273	1 371	518	8 865	4 786	492
1977	15 258	2 859	676	657	3 377	1 385	538	9 023	4 859	494
1978	15 812	2 893	661	660	3 474	1 367	541	9 446	4 958	535
1979	16 068	2 894	649	673	3 541	1 378	538	9 633	4 989	571
1980	16 375	3 000	645	673	3 610	1 398	530	9 765	5 090	604
1981	16 180	2 922	655	675	3 640	1 420	515	9 619	5 095	622
1982	15 982	2 884	690	684	3 640	1 433	494	9 458	5 049	635
1983	16 011	2 915	699	685	3 662	1 450	471	9 434	5 020	644
1984	16 159	2 943	716	706	3 734	1 488	459	9 482	5 076	623
1985	16 533	3 014	738	750	3 832	1 540	449	9 687	5 221	608
1986	16 838	3 044	736	792	3 893	1 561	438	9 901	5 358	601
1987	17 156	3 089	736	815	3 967	1 586	439	10 100	5 469	606
1988	17 540	3 124	719	835	4 076	1 621	446	10 339	5 590	619
1989	17 927	3 136	735	838	4 182	1 668	442	10 609	5 740	632
1990	18 415	3 196	722	825	4 305	1 730	426	10 914	5 902	646
1991	18 545	3 110	702	813	4 355	1 768	417	11 081	5 994	653
1992	18 787	3 111	702	800	4 408	1 799	419	11 267	6 076	665
1993	18 989	3 063	670	793	4 488	1 834	414	11 438	6 206	673
1994	19 275	3 018	657	821	4 576	1 882	407	11 682	6 329	673
1995	19 432	2 949	627	850	4 635	1 919	395	11 849	6 453	669
1996	19 539	2 877	597	867	4 606	1 911	376	12 056	6 592	648
1997	19 664	2 806	588	866	4 582	1 904	360	12 276	6 759	632
1998	19 909	2 772	550	881	4 612	1 922	346	12 525	6 921	630
1999	20 307	2 769	525	890	4 709	1 983	344	12 829	7 120	626
2000	20 790	2 865	510	880	4 786	2 031	343	13 139	7 294	622
2001	21 118	2 764	504	873	4 905	2 113	345	13 449	7 479	628
2002	21 513	2 766	499	842	5 029	2 243	349	13 718	7 654	642
2003	21 583	2 761	486	809	5 002	2 255	348	13 820	7 709	651
2004	21 621	2 730	473	782	4 982	2 238	348	13 909	7 765	656
2005	21 804	2 732	488	774	5 032	2 260	350	14 041	7 856	655
2006	21 974	2 732	493	770	5 075	2 293	357	14 167	7 913	647
2007	22 218	2 734	491	769	5 122	2 318	360	14 362	7 987	654
2008	22 509	2 762	496	747	5 177	2 354	361	14 571	8 084	659
2009	22 555	2 832	519	703	5 169	2 360	359	14 554	8 079	661
2010	22 490	2 977	545	659	5 137	2 373	354	14 376	8 013	650
2011	22 086	2 859	559	631	5 078	2 374	348	14 150	7 873	648
2012	21 920	2 820	552	611	5 055	2 389	349	14 045	7 778	647
2013	21 853	2 769	537	595	5 046	2 393	350	14 037	7 777	646
2014	21 882	2 733	524	593	5 050	2 389	347	14 098	7 815	642
2015	22 029	2 757	526	597	5 077	2 401	354	14 195	7 871	648
2016	22 224	2 795	529	609	5 110	2 429	367	14 319	7 905	658
2017	22 350	2 805	527	615	5 165	2 479	376	14 379	7 922	667
2018	22 455	2 800	531	609	5 173	2 487	381	14 481	7 963	674
2019	22 613	2 831	544	607	5 206	2 515	387	14 576	8 001	682
2020	21 986	2 930	560	602	5 135	2 436	400	13 921	7 581	679
2021	22 005	2 886	564	606	5 207	2 534	408	13 912	7 586	675

. . . = Not available.

NOTES AND DEFINITIONS, CHAPTER 6

Tables 6-1 through 6-11 and 6-16

Federal, State, and Local Government in the National Income and Product Accounts

SOURCE: U.S. DEPARTMENT OF COMMERCE, BUREAU OF ECONOMIC ANALYSIS (BEA)

These data are from the national income and product accounts (NIPAs), as redefined in the 2018 comprehensive NIPA revision and updated annually.

The framework for the government accounts

In an earlier major revision in 2003, a new framework was introduced for government consumption expenditures—federal, state, and local—that explicitly recognizes the services produced by general government. Governments serve several functions in the economy. Three of these functions are recognized in the NIPAs: the production of nonmarket services; the consumption of these services, as the value of services provided to the general public is treated as government consumption expenditures; and the provision of transfer payments. These functions are financed through taxation, through contributions to social insurance funds, and by borrowing in the world's capital markets.

In this framework, the value of the government services produced and consumed (most of which are not sold in the market) is measured as the sum of the costs of the three major inputs: compensation of government employees, consumption of fixed capital (CFC), and intermediate goods and services purchased. The purchase from the private sector of goods and services by government, classified as final sales to government before the 2003 revision, was reclassified as intermediate purchases.

The value of government final purchases of consumption expenditures and gross investment, which constitutes the contribution of government demand to the gross domestic product (GDP), was not changed by this reclassification, since the previous definition of that contribution was the sum of compensation, CFC, and goods and services purchased. However, the distribution of GDP by type of product was changed—final sales of goods were reduced by the amount of goods purchased by government, and final sales of services were increased by the same amount.

In addition to this change in the conceptual framework, a number of the categories of government receipts and expenditures were redefined to make more precise distinctions. For example, items that used to be called "nontax payments" and included with taxes are now classified as transfer or fee payments and not included in taxes.

Finally, the concept previously known as "current surplus or deficit (-), national income and product accounts" was renamed "net government saving." This recognizes, in part, the role of government in the capital markets. When government runs a current surplus, net government saving is positive and funds are made available (for example, by retiring outstanding government debt) to finance investment—both private-sector capital spending and government investment. By the same token, when government runs a current deficit, or "dis-saves," it must borrow funds that would otherwise be available to finance investment.

However, this definition of net government saving does not give a complete picture of governments' role in capital markets, because it is based on current receipts and expenditures alone and does not include government investment activity.

In the NIPAs, the capital spending of all levels of government is treated the same way as the accounts treat private investment spending. A depreciation, or more precisely "consumption of fixed capital" (CFC), entry for existing capital is calculated, using estimated replacement costs and realistic depreciation rates. In the government accounts this CFC value is entered as one element of current expenditures and output. Capital spending is excluded from government current expenditures but appears in the account for "net lending or borrowing (-)."

The basic concept expressed in the net lending section of the NIPAs is that when CFC exceeds actual investment expenditures, governments have a positive net cash flow and can lend (or repay debt); if gross investment exceeds CFC, government must borrow to finance the difference, indicating negative net cash flow and requiring borrowing. (As will be seen below in the definitions, capital transfer and purchase accounts also enter into the calculation of net lending.)

The federal *budget* accounts (see Tables 6-1 and 6-2) do not draw a distinction between current and capital spending. The budget accounts of individual state and local governments typically separate capital from current spending and allow capital spending to be financed by borrowing—even when deficit financing of current spending is constitutionally forbidden. However, neither federal nor state and local government budget accounts typically show depreciation as a current expense in the way that is standard to private-sector accounting or in the way adopted in the NIPAs.

Notes on the data

Government receipts and expenditures data are derived from the U.S. government accounts and from Census Bureau censuses and surveys of the finances of state and local governments. However, BEA makes a number of adjustments to the data to convert them from fiscal year to calendar year and quarter bases and to agree with the concepts of national income accounting. Data are converted from the cash basis usually found in financial statements to the timing bases required for the NIPAs. In the NIPAs, receipts from businesses are generally on an accrual basis, purchases of goods and services are recorded when delivered, and receipts from and transfer payments to persons are on a cash basis. The federal receipts and expenditure data from the NIPAs in Table 6-1 therefore differ from the federal receipts and outlay data in Table 6-14. Among other differences, the latter are by fiscal year and are on a modified cash basis.

The NIPA data on government receipts and expenditures record transactions of governments (federal, state, and local) with other U.S. residents and foreigners. Each entry in the government receipts and expenditures account has a corresponding entry elsewhere in the NIPAs. Thus, for example, the sum of personal current taxes received by federal and state and local governments (Tables 6-1 and 6-8) is equal to personal current taxes paid, as shown in personal income (Table 4-1).

Definitions: general

In the 2003 revision of the NIPAs, several items appear separately that were previously treated as "negative expenditures" and netted against other items on the expenditures side. This grossing-up of the accounts raises both receipts and outlays and has no effect on net saving. Grossing-up has been applied to taxes from the rest of the world, interest receipts (back to 1960 for the federal government and back to 1946 for state and local governments), dividends, and subsidies and the current surplus of government enterprises (back to 1959).

Definitions: current receipts

Current tax receipts includes personal current taxes, taxes on production and imports, taxes on corporate income and (for the federal government only) taxes from the rest of the world. The category *total tax receipts* does not include *contributions for government social insurance,* which are the taxes levied to finance Social Security, unemployment insurance, and Medicare, and are included in *receipts* in the budget accounts (Table 6-14). Analysts using NIPA data to analyze tax burdens as they are usually understood should add *contributions for government social insurance* to *tax receipts* for this purpose.

Personal current taxes is personal tax payments from residents of the United States that are not chargeable to business expense. Personal taxes consist of taxes on income, including on realized net capital gains, and on personal property. Personal contributions for social insurance are not included in this category. As of the 1999 revisions, estate and gift taxes are classified as capital transfers and are no longer included in personal current taxes.

However, estate and gift taxes continue to be included in federal government receipts in Table 6-14.

Taxes on production and imports in the case of the federal government consists of *excise taxes* and *customs duties.* In the case of state and local governments, these taxes include *sales taxes, property taxes* (including residential real estate taxes), and *Other* taxes such as motor vehicle licenses, severance taxes, and special assessments. Before the 2003 revision, all of these taxes were components of "indirect business tax and nontax liabilities."

Taxes on corporate income covers federal, state, and local government taxes on all corporate income subject to taxes. This taxable income includes capital gains and other income excluded from NIPA profits. The taxes are measured on an accrual basis, net of applicable tax credits. Federal corporate income tax receipts in the NIPAs include, but show separately, receipts from *Federal Reserve Banks* that represent the return of the surplus earnings of the Federal Reserve system. (In the budget accounts in Table 6-14, these are classified not as corporate taxes but as the major component of "Miscellaneous receipts.")

Contributions for social insurance includes employer and personal contributions for Social Security, Medicare, unemployment insurance, and other government social insurance programs. As of the 1999 revisions, contributions to government employee retirement plans are no longer included in this category; these plans are now treated the same as private pension plans.

Income receipts on assets consists of *interest, dividends* and *rents and royalties.*

Interest receipts (1960 to the present for federal government; 1946 to the present for state and local governments) consists of monetary and imputed interest received on loans and investments. In the NIPAs, this no longer includes interest received by government employee retirement plans, which is now credited to personal income. However, such interest received is still deducted from interest paid in the budget accounts that are shown in Table 6-14. Before the indicated years, receipts are deducted from aggregate interest payments in the NIPAs. Hence, they are not shown as receipts, and net interest is presented on the expenditure side. In the federal budget accounts in Table 6-14, net interest (total interest expenditures minus interest receipts) is the interest "expenditure" concept used throughout the period covered.

Current transfer receipts include receipts in categories other than those specified above from persons and business. In the case of state and local government accounts (Table 6-8), it also includes *federal grants-in-aid,* a component of federal expenditures. Receipts from *business* and *persons* were previously included with income taxes in "tax and nontax payments." They consist of federal deposit insurance premiums and other nontaxes (largely fines and regulatory and inspection fees), state and local fines and other nontaxes (largely donations and tobacco settlements), and net insurance settlements paid to governments as policy holders.

The *current surplus of government enterprises* is the current operating revenue and subsidies received from other levels of government by such enterprises less their current expenses. No deduction is made for depreciation charges or net interest paid. Before 1959, this category of receipts is treated as a deduction from subsidies. In the <u>federal</u> NIPA accounts before 1959, there is no entry shown for the current surplus on the receipts side, and on the expenditure side, there is an entry for subsidies, which is net of the current surplus. (Subsidies are usually a larger amount than the enterprise surplus in the federal accounts.) In the <u>state and local</u> NIPA accounts before 1959, there is an entry for the surplus on the receipts side, which is net of subsidies. (Subsidies are typically smaller than the enterprise surplus in state and local finance.)

Definitions: consumption expenditures, saving, and gross investment

Government consumption expenditures is expenditures by governments (federal or state and local) on services for current consumption. It includes *compensation of general government employees* (including employer contributions to government employee retirement plans, as of the 1999 revision); an allowance for *consumption of general government fixed capital (CFC)*, including R&D and software (depreciation); and *intermediate goods and services purchased*. (See the general discussion above for an explanation.) The estimated value of *own-account investment*—investment goods, including R&D and software, produced by government resources and purchased inputs—is subtracted here, and added to *government gross investment*. *Sales to other sectors*—primarily tuition payments received from individuals for higher education and charges for medical care to individuals—are also deducted, since these are counted elsewhere in the accounts, as (for example) personal consumption expenditures for those categories.

Government social benefits consists of payments to individuals for which the individuals do not render current services. Examples are Social Security benefits, Medicare, Medicaid, unemployment benefits, and public assistance. Retirement payments to retired government employees from their pension plans are no longer included in this category.

Government social benefits to persons consists of payments to persons residing in the United States (with a corresponding entry of an equal amount in the personal income receipts accounts). Government social benefits to the *rest of the world* appear only in the federal government account, and are transfers, mainly retirement benefits, to former residents of the United States.

Other current transfer payments (federal account only) includes *grants-in-aid to state and local governments* and *grants to the rest of the world*—military and nonmilitary grants to foreign governments.

Federal grants-in-aid comprises net payments from federal to state and local governments that are made to help finance programs such as health (Medicaid), public assistance (the old Aid to Families with Dependent Children and the new Temporary Assistance for Needy Families), and education. Investment grants to state and local governments for highways, transit, air transportation, and water treatment plants are now classified as capital transfers and are no longer included in this category. However, such investment grants continue to be included as federal government outlays in Table 6-14.

Interest payments is monetary interest paid to U.S. and foreign persons and businesses and to foreign governments for public debt and other financial obligations. As noted above, from 1960 forward for the federal government and from 1946 forward for state and local governments, this represents gross total (not net) interest payments. Before those dates in the NIPAs, and throughout the federal budget accounts presented in Table 6-14, net instead of aggregate interest is shown; that is, gross total interest paid less interest received.

Subsidies are monetary grants paid by government to business, including to government enterprises at another level of government. Subsidies no longer include federal maritime construction subsidies, which are now classified as a capital transfer. For years prior to 1959, subsidies continue to be presented net of the *current surplus of government enterprises*, because detailed data to separate the series are not available for this period. See the entry for *current surplus of government enterprises*, described above, for explanation of the pre-1959 treatment of this item in the federal accounts in *Business Statistics*, which differs from the treatment in the state and local accounts.

Net saving, NIPA (surplus+/deficit-), is the sum of current receipts less the sum of current expenditures. This is shown separately for *social insurance funds* (which, in the case of the federal government, include Social Security and other trust funds) and *other* (all other government).

Gross government investment consists of general government and government enterprise expenditures for fixed assets—*structures*, *equipment*, and *intellectual property* (R&D and software). The expenditures include the compensation of government employees producing the assets and the purchase of goods and services as intermediate inputs to be incorporated in the assets. Government inventory investment is included in government consumption expenditures.

Capital consumption. Consumption of fixed capital (CFC; economic depreciation) is included in government consumption expenditures as a partial measure of the value of the services of general government fixed assets, including structures, equipment, R&D, and software.

Definitions: output, lending and borrowing, and net investment

In Tables 6-5 and 6-10, current-dollar values of gross output and value added of government are presented, as described in the general discussion above. *Gross output* of government is the sum of the *intermediate goods and services purchased* by government and the value added by government as a producing industry. *Value added* consists of compensation of general government employees and consumption of general government fixed capital. Since this depreciation allowance is the only entry on the product side of the accounts measuring the output associated with such capital, a zero <u>net</u> return on these assets is implicitly assumed.

Gross output minus own-account investment and sales to other sectors (see the previous description) yields *government consumption expenditures*, which represents the contribution of government consumption spending to final demands in GDP.

Net lending (net borrowing -) consists of current *net saving* as defined above, plus the *consumption of fixed capital* (CFC, from the current expenditure account), minus *gross investment*, plus *capital transfer receipts*, and minus *capital transfer payments* and *net purchases of non-produced assets*. (If this definition sounds somehow counter-intuitive, it should be remembered that "subtraction" in this context means "increasing the deficit [negative value] which must be financed.)

Capital transfer receipts and *payments* include grants between levels of government, or between government and the private sector, associated with acquisition or disposal of assets rather than with current consumption expenditures. Examples are federal grants to state and local government for highways, transit, air transportation, and water treatment plants; federal shipbuilding subsidies and other subsidies to businesses; and lump-sum payments to amortize the unfunded liability of the Uniformed Services Retiree Health Care Fund. Government capital transfer receipts include estate and gift taxes, which are no longer included in personal tax receipts. (Federal estate and gift taxes are shown in Table 6-14, where they are reported on a fiscal year basis, and are similar in order of magnitude to the calendar year values for federal capital transfer receipts in Table 6-5.)

Non-produced assets are land and radio spectrum. Unusually large negative entries for net purchases of non-produced assets in some recent years result from the negative purchase–that is, the sale–of spectrum.

The values of *net investment* shown in these tables are calculated by the editor, as gross investment minus the consumption of fixed capital.

Definitions: chain-type quantity indexes

Chain-type quantity indexes represent changes over time in real values, removing the effects of inflation. Indexes for key categories in the government expenditure accounts, as well as for government gross output, value added, and intermediate goods and services purchased, use the chain formula described in the notes and definitions for Chapter 1 and are expressed as index numbers, with the average for the year 2012 equal to 100.

Data availability

The most recent data are published each month in the *Survey of Current Business.* Current and historical data may be obtained from the BEA Web site at <https://www.bea.gov> and the STAT-USA subscription Web site at <https://www.stat-usa.gov>.

References

See the references regarding the 2018 comprehensive revision of the NIPAs in the notes and definitions for Chapter 1. NIPA concepts and their differences from the budget estimates are discussed in "NIPA Estimates of the Federal Sector and the Federal Budget Estimates," *Survey of Current Business,* March 2007, p. 11.

For information about the classification of government expenditures into current consumption and gross investment, first undertaken in the 1996 comprehensive revisions, see the *Survey of Current Business* article, "Preview of the Comprehensive Revision of the National Income and Product Accounts: Recognition of Government Investment and Incorporation of a New Methodology for Calculating Depreciation" September 1995. Other sources of information about the NIPAs are listed in the notes and definitions for Chapter 1.

Tables 6-12 and 6-13

State Government Current Receipts and Expenditures; Local Government Current Receipts and Expenditures

SOURCE: BUREAU OF ECONOMIC ANALYSIS (BEA)

In the standard presentation of the state and local sector of the national income and product accounts (NIPAs) such as in Tables 6-8 through 6-11 above, state and local governments are combined. Annual measures for aggregate state governments and aggregate local governments are also available on the BEA Web site. These measures are shown in Tables 6-12 and 6-13. The definitions are the same as in the other NIPA tables described above.

The data shown here now reflect the 2013 comprehensive revision, affecting some concepts, that has been incorporated in the quarterly and annual data elsewhere in this chapter and this volume.

Two categories not shown in Table 6-8 appear in each table, detailing inter-governmental flows that are consolidated in Table 6-8. State government receipts include not only *federal grants-in-aid* but also *local grants-in-aid*, and state government expenditures include *grants-in-aid to local governments*. Local government receipts include not only *federal grants-in-aid* but also *state grants-in-aid*, and local government expenditures include *grants-in-aid to state governments*. To make room for these columns, the components *current surplus of government enterprises* and *subsidies* are not shown, though they are included in total current receipts and total current expenditures respectively.

These measures are described in "Receipts and Expenditures of State Governments and of Local Governments," *Survey of Current Business*, October 2005. Data back to 1959 are available on the BEA Web site at <https://www.bea.gov>.

Tables 6-14A and 6-14B

Federal Government Receipts and Outlays by Fiscal Year; The Federal Budget and GDP

SOURCE: U.S. OFFICE OF MANAGEMENT AND BUDGET

These data on federal government receipts and outlays are on a modified cash basis and are from the *Budget of the United States Government: Historical Tables*. The data are by federal fiscal years, which are defined as July 1 through June 30 through 1976 and October 1 through September 30 for 1977 and subsequent years. They are identified by the year of the final fiscal quarter—i.e., the year from July 1, 1975, through June 30, 1976, is identified as Fiscal 1976, and the year from October 1, 1976, through June 30, 1977, is identified as Fiscal Year 1977. The period July 1 through September 30, 1976, is a separate fiscal period known as the transition quarter (TQ) and is not included in any fiscal year.

There are numerous differences in both timing and definition between these estimates and the NIPA estimates in Tables 6-1 through 6-7. See the notes and definitions for those tables for the definitional differences that were introduced with the 1999 comprehensive revision of the NIPAs.

Definitions

The definitions for these tables are not affected by the 2013, 2003, or 1999 changes in the government sectors of the NIPAs.

Table references will be given indicating the source of each item in the *Historical Tables*; for example, "HT Table 1.1."

Receipts consist of gifts and of taxes or other compulsory payments to the government. Other types of payments to the government are netted against outlays. (HT Table 1.1)

Outlays occur when the federal government liquidates an obligation through a cash payment or when interest accrues on public debt issues. Beginning with the data for 1992, outlays include the subsidy cost of direct and guaranteed loans made. Before 1992, the costs and repayments associated with such loans are recorded on a cash basis. As noted previously, various types of nontax receipts are netted against cash outlays. These accounts do not distinguish between investment outlays and current consumption and do not include allowances for depreciation. (HT Table 1.1)

The *total budget surplus (deficit-)* is receipts minus outlays. It is sometimes presented, including in Table 6-14, as composed of two components, *on-budget and off-budget*. By law, two government programs that are included in the federal receipts and outlays totals are "off-budget"—old-age, survivors, and disability insurance (Social Security) and the Postal Service. The former accounts for nearly all of the off-budget activity. The *surplus (deficit-)* not accounted for by these two programs is the on-budget surplus or deficit. The *on-budget deficit* is based on an arbitrary distinction and is not customarily referred to as the *budget deficit*, a term reserved in customary use for the total deficit. (HT Table 1.1)

Sources of financing is the means by which the total deficit is financed or the surplus is distributed. By definition, sources of financing sum to the total deficit or surplus with the sign reversed. The principal source is *borrowing from the public*, shown as a positive number, that is, the increase in the debt held by the public. (This entry is calculated by the editors as the change in the debt held by the public as shown in HT Table 7.1.) When there is a budget surplus, as in fiscal years 1998 to 2001, this provides resources for debt reduction, which is indicated by a minus sign in this column. *Other financing* includes drawdown (or buildup, shown here with a minus sign) in Treasury cash balances, seigniorage on coins, direct and guaranteed loan account cash transactions, and miscellaneous other transactions. Large negative "other financing" in 2008 through 2010 resulted from direct loans and asset purchases under TARP and other emergency financial procedures; in other words, the government borrowed from the public to undertake these loans and asset purchases, but they are not included in budget expenditures or the budget deficit. *Other financing* is calculated by the editors, by reversing the sign of the surplus/deficit—so that the deficit becomes a positive number—and subtracting the value of borrowing from the public.

Some of the categories of *receipts by source* are self-explanatory. *Employment taxes and contributions* includes taxes for old-age, survivors, and disability insurance (Social Security), hospital insurance (Medicare), and railroad retirement funds. *Other retirement contributions* includes the employee share of payments for retirement pensions, mainly those for federal employees. *Excise taxes* includes federal taxes on alcohol, tobacco, telephone service, and transportation fuels, as well as taxes funding smaller programs such as black lung disability and vaccine injury compensation. *Miscellaneous receipts* includes deposits of earnings by the Federal Reserve system and all other receipts. (HT Tables 2.1, 2.4, and 2.5)

Outlays by function presents outlays according to the major purpose of the spending. Functional classifications cut across departmental and agency lines. Most categories of offsetting receipts are netted against cash outlays in the appropriate function, which explains how recorded outlays in *energy* and *commerce and housing credit* (which, as its name suggests, includes loan programs) can be negative. There is also a category of "undistributed offsetting receipts" (not shown), always with a negative sign, that includes proceeds from the sale or lease of assets and payments from federal agencies to federal retirement funds and to the Social Security and Medicare trust funds. Note that *Social Security* is recorded separately from other *income security* outlays, and *Medicare* separately from other *health* outlays. (HT Table 3.1) For further explanation, consult the *Budget of the United States Government.*

In order to provide authoritative comparisons of these budget values with the overall size of the economy, a special calculation of gross domestic product by fiscal year is supplied to the Office of Management and Budget by the BEA, and is shown in Table 6-14B. That table also displays selected budget aggregates in dollar values and as a percent of GDP. (HT Tables 1.2, 1.3, 2.3, and 3.1)

Data availability and references

Definitions, budget concepts, and historical data are from *Budget of the United States Government for Fiscal Year 2015: Historical Tables*, available on the Office of Management and Budget Web site at <https://www.whitehouse.gov/omb/Budget/historicals>

Similarly defined data for the latest month, the year-ago month, and the current and year-ago fiscal year to date are published in the *Monthly Treasury Statement* prepared by the Financial Management Service, U.S. Department of the Treasury. For those who need up-to-date budget information, this publication is available on the Financial Management Service Web site at

<https://www.fms.treas.gov>. As these monthly figures are never revised to agree with the final annual data, they are not published in this volume.

Table 6-15

Federal Government Debt by Fiscal Year

SOURCE: U.S. OFFICE OF MANAGEMENT AND BUDGET

Debt outstanding at the end of each fiscal year is from the *Budget of the United States Government.* Most securities are recorded at sales price plus amortized discount or less amortized premium.

Definitions

Federal government debt held by the public consists of all federal debt held outside the federal government accounts—by individuals, financial institutions (including the Federal Reserve Banks), and foreign individuals, businesses, and central banks. It does not include federal debt held by federal government trust funds such as the Social Security trust fund. The level and change of the ratio of this debt to the value of gross domestic product (GDP) provide proportional measures of the impact of federal borrowing on credit markets. (HT Table 7.1) This measure of debt held by the public is very similar in concept and scope to the total federal government credit market debt outstanding in the flow-of-funds accounts, shown in *Business Statistics* in Table 12-5; however, it is not identical, being priced somewhat differently, and is shown here in Chapter 6 on a fiscal year rather than calendar year basis.

Gross federal debt—total. This is the total debt owed by the U.S. Treasury. It includes a small amount of matured debt. (HT Table 7.1)

Debt held by Social Security funds is the sum of the end-year trust fund balances for old age and survivors insurance and disability insurance. The separate disability trust fund begins in 1957. (HT Table 13.1)

Debt held by other U.S. government accounts is calculated by the editors by subtracting the Social Security debt holdings from the total debt held by federal government accounts, which is shown in HT Table 7.1. It includes the balances in all the other trust funds, including the Medicare funds, federal employee retirement funds, and the highway trust fund.

Debt held by the Federal Reserve System is the total value of Treasury securities held by the 12 Federal Reserve Banks, which are acquired in open market operations that carry out monetary policy. (HT Table 7.1)

Debt held by private investors is calculated by subtracting the Federal Reserve debt from the total debt held by the public, and is shown as "Debt Held by the Public: Other" in HT Table 7.1.

Debt held by foreign residents is based on surveys by the Treasury Department. (Table 5-7, *Budget of the United States for Fiscal Year 2015: Analytical Perspectives*.)

Debt held by domestic investors is calculated by the editors by subtracting the foreign-held debt from the total debt held by private investors.

The "debt subject to statutory limitation," not shown here, is close to the gross federal debt in concept and size, but there are some relatively minor definitional differences specified by law. The debt limit can only be changed by an Act of Congress. For information about the debt subject to limit and other debt subjects, see the latest *Budget of the United States Government: Historical Statistics* and *Analytical Perspectives*.

Data availability and references

For the end-of-fiscal-year data, see *Historical Tables* and *Analytical Perspectives* in the *Budget of the United States Government*, which is available on the OMB Web site at <https://www.whitehouse.gov/omb/Budget>. In the *Analytical Perspectives,* debt analysis and data are included in the "Economic and Budget Analysis" section.

Recent quarterly data, measured on a somewhat different basis, are found in the *Treasury Bulletin* in the chapter on "Ownership of Federal Securities (OFS)," in Tables OFS-1 and OFS-2. The *Treasury Bulletin* can be accessed on the Internet at <https://www.fms.treas.gov/bulletin>. Holdings by Social Security funds are also available in the *Bulletin* in the chapter on "Federal Debt," Table FD-3. The Disability Fund is listed separately from the Old-Age and Survivors Fund.

Table 6-17

Government Employment

SOURCE: U.S. DEPARTMENT OF LABOR, BUREAU OF LABOR STATISTICS (SEE NOTES AND DEFINITIONS FOR TABLE 10-8).

Government payroll employment includes federal, state, and local activities such as legislative, executive, and judicial functions, as well as all governmen-towned and government-operated business enterprises, establishments, and institutions (arsenals, navy yards, hospitals, etc.), and government force account construction. The figures relate to civilian employment only. The Bureau of Labor Statistics (BLS) considers regular fulltime teachers (private and governmental) to be employed during the summer vacation period, regardless of whether they are specifically paid in those months.

Employment in federal government establishments reflects employee counts as of the pay period containing the 12th of the month. Federal government employment excludes employees of the Central Intelligence Agency and the National Security Agency.

CHAPTER 7: U.S. FOREIGN TRADE AND FINANCE

SECTION 7A: FOREIGN TRANSACTIONS IN THE NATIONAL INCOME AND PRODUCT ACCOUNTS

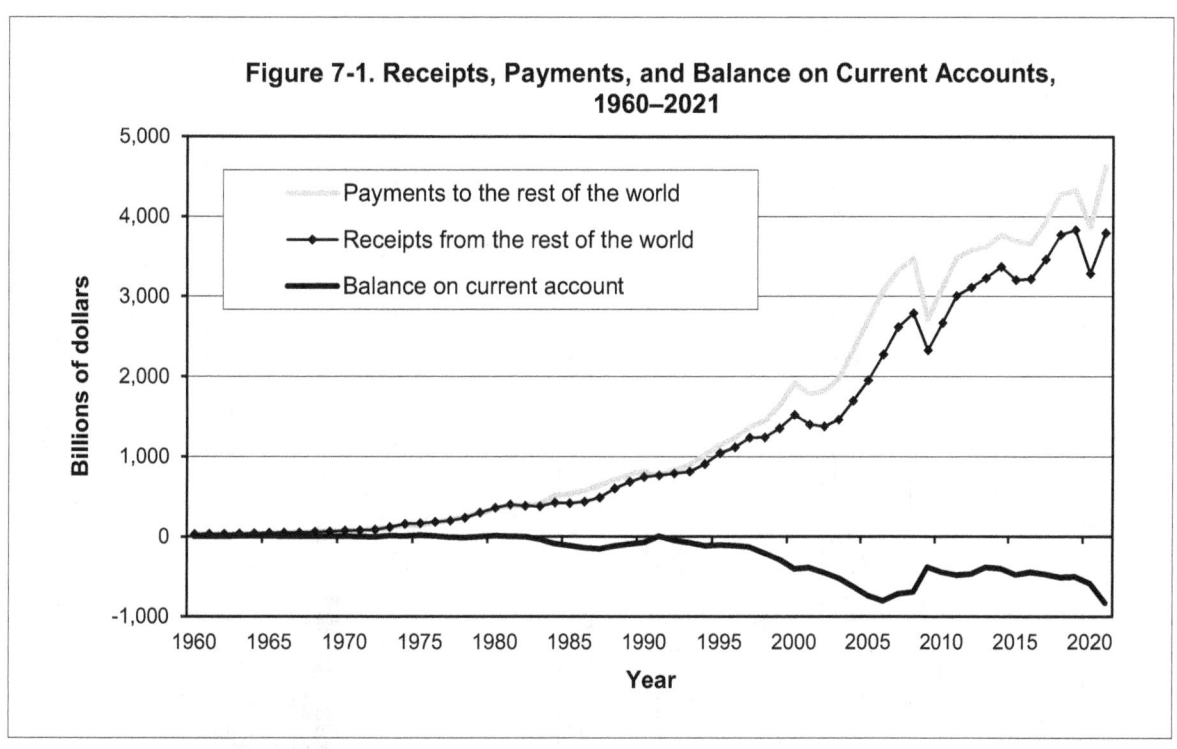

Figure 7-1. Receipts, Payments, and Balance on Current Accounts, 1960–2021

- All major categories of current-account transactions increased in the fourth quarter of 2021, the sixth consecutive quarter of broad-based growth following notable COVID-19 related declines in the second quarter of 2020. The full impact of the COVID-19 pandemic cannot be quantified in the statistics, because the impacts are generally embedded in source data. (Table 7-1)

- Beginning in 1983, chronic current-account deficits in U.S. transactions with the rest of the world have emerged and increased, requiring increasing net capital inflows from abroad to finance them. The only current-account surplus since then occurred in 1991, when payments from other countries financed most of the cost of the first Gulf War. In 2006, the NIPA deficit reached $802 billion, 5.8 percent of GDP which was a record at the time. It declined by more than half by 2013. However, it rose again substantially in 2020 and 2021 due to the global pandemic. By 2021, the balance on current account, reached a record −$831.1 billion. (Tables 7-1 and 1-1A)

- In 2021, the largest exports were industrial goods followed by capital goods. Exports of travel services declined dramatically during the pandemic, dropping more than 62 percent in one year from 2019 to 2020. It fell further in 2021, although at a much slower rate at 4.8 percent. (Table 7-4)

- The term "services" refers to an expanding range of economic activities, such as audiovisual, construction, computer and related services, express delivery, telecommunications, e-commerce, financial, professional, etc. Because measures of service trade are not anchored in any observation of physical movement, they are dependent on definitions of residence. (Table 7-4, 7-12, and 7-13.)

Table 7-1. Foreign Transactions in the National Income and Product Accounts

(Billions of dollars, quarterly data are at seasonally adjusted annual rates.)   **NIPA Table 4.1**

Year and quarter	Current receipts from the rest of the world					Current payments to the rest of the world						Balance on current account, NIPAs	Net lending or net borrowing (-), NIPAs
	Total	Exports of goods and services			Income receipts	Total	Imports of goods and services			Income payments	Current taxes and transfer payments, net		
		Goods ¹		Services ¹			Goods ¹		Services ¹				
		Durable	Nondurable				Durable	Nondurable					
1960	31.9	11.3	9.2	6.6	4.9	28.8	6.4	8.9	7.6	1.8	4.1	3.2	3.2
1961	32.9	11.5	9.4	6.7	5.3	28.7	6.0	9.0	7.6	1.8	4.2	4.2	4.2
1962	35.0	12.0	9.7	7.4	5.9	31.2	6.9	9.9	8.1	1.8	4.4	3.8	3.8
1963	37.6	12.7	10.7	7.7	6.5	32.7	7.4	10.3	8.4	2.1	4.5	4.9	4.9
1964	42.3	14.7	12.1	8.3	7.2	34.8	8.4	11.0	8.7	2.3	4.4	7.5	7.5
1965	45.0	15.8	12.1	9.2	7.9	38.9	10.4	11.8	9.3	2.6	4.7	6.2	6.2
1966	49.0	17.7	13.4	9.8	8.1	45.2	13.3	13.1	10.7	3.0	5.1	3.8	3.8
1967	52.1	18.6	13.9	10.9	8.7	48.7	14.5	13.2	12.2	3.3	5.5	3.5	3.5
1968	58.0	21.2	14.5	12.2	10.1	56.5	18.8	15.1	12.6	4.0	5.9	1.5	1.5
1969	63.7	23.9	14.8	13.2	11.8	62.1	20.8	16.1	13.7	5.7	5.9	1.6	1.6
1970	72.5	27.4	17.7	14.7	12.8	68.8	22.8	18.1	14.9	6.4	6.6	3.7	3.7
1971	77.0	27.9	18.3	16.8	14.0	76.7	26.6	19.9	15.8	6.4	7.9	0.3	0.3
1972	87.1	31.4	21.2	18.3	16.3	91.2	33.3	23.6	17.3	7.7	9.2	-4.0	-4.1
1973	118.8	42.3	33.5	19.5	23.5	109.9	40.8	31.0	19.3	10.9	7.9	8.9	8.8
1974	156.5	57.7	45.8	23.2	29.8	150.5	50.3	54.2	22.9	14.3	8.7	6.0	5.9
1975	166.7	65.2	47.3	26.2	28.0	146.9	45.6	53.4	23.7	15.0	9.1	19.8	19.8
1976	181.9	70.9	50.6	28.0	32.4	174.8	56.8	67.8	26.5	15.5	8.1	7.1	7.0
1977	196.6	74.4	54.0	30.9	37.2	207.5	69.2	83.4	29.8	16.9	8.1	-10.9	-11.0
1978	233.1	87.5	62.4	37.0	46.3	245.8	89.0	88.4	34.8	24.7	8.8	-12.6	-12.7
1979	298.5	109.6	77.6	42.9	68.3	299.6	100.4	112.3	39.9	36.4	10.6	-1.2	-1.3
1980	359.9	135.7	94.8	50.3	79.1	351.4	111.9	136.6	45.3	44.9	12.6	8.5	8.4
1981	397.3	143.2	102.0	60.0	92.0	393.9	126.0	141.8	49.9	59.1	17.0	3.4	3.3
1982	384.2	128.5	94.1	60.7	101.0	387.5	125.1	125.4	52.6	64.5	19.8	-3.3	-3.4
1983	378.9	123.8	90.3	62.9	101.9	413.9	147.3	125.4	56.0	64.8	20.5	-35.1	-35.2
1984	424.2	135.2	96.1	71.1	121.9	514.3	192.4	143.9	68.8	85.6	23.6	-90.1	-90.2
1985	415.9	139.9	87.6	75.7	112.7	530.2	204.2	139.1	73.9	87.3	25.7	-114.3	-114.4
1986	432.3	145.3	86.1	89.6	111.3	575.0	238.8	131.2	82.9	94.4	27.8	-142.7	-142.8
1987	487.2	166.9	98.6	98.4	123.3	641.3	264.2	150.6	93.9	105.8	26.8	-154.1	-154.2
1988	596.7	211.9	120.1	112.5	152.1	712.4	294.8	157.3	101.9	129.5	29.0	-115.7	-115.9
1989	682.0	242.5	132.2	129.5	177.7	774.3	310.3	174.5	106.2	152.9	30.4	-92.4	-92.7
1990	740.7	265.3	138.0	148.6	188.8	815.6	314.5	193.5	121.7	154.2	31.7	-74.9	-82.3
1991	763.3	285.6	144.6	164.8	168.4	755.4	315.5	185.2	122.8	136.8	-4.9	7.9	2.6
1992	785.1	304.2	151.1	177.7	152.1	830.7	346.7	198.2	122.9	121.0	41.9	-45.6	-44.3
1993	810.4	317.9	149.9	187.1	155.6	888.9	386.4	206.4	127.2	123.6	45.4	-78.5	-79.4
1994	905.5	353.8	164.6	202.6	184.5	1 020.2	454.0	222.8	136.6	160.7	46.1	-114.7	-116.0
1995	1 042.6	398.6	193.8	220.4	229.8	1 147.7	510.8	246.7	145.1	201.1	44.1	-105.1	-105.5
1996	1 114.0	426.4	202.4	238.8	246.4	1 228.1	533.4	274.1	156.5	214.6	49.5	-114.1	-114.3
1997	1 233.9	488.4	211.5	253.9	280.1	1 363.2	588.5	297.1	170.1	256.0	51.4	-129.3	-129.8
1998	1 239.8	492.4	200.2	260.4	286.8	1 444.3	637.7	293.0	184.9	268.5	60.0	-204.5	-204.7
1999	1 350.0	508.7	203.0	280.3	321.4	1 636.6	715.8	335.4	197.4	294.3	93.7	-286.6	-291.1
2000	1 520.4	573.4	223.9	299.6	382.7	1 924.1	822.9	428.6	221.2	345.7	105.8	-403.7	-404.1
2001	1 396.8	525.3	218.6	282.9	325.3	1 785.6	757.7	419.0	218.7	273.5	116.7	-388.8	-375.8
2002	1 374.6	492.8	220.4	289.3	315.8	1 825.4	774.2	425.1	229.6	267.2	129.2	-450.8	-451.3
2003	1 462.2	501.8	239.6	298.9	356.1	1 977.9	806.3	489.9	247.7	289.0	144.9	-515.7	-517.8
2004	1 697.2	565.7	268.7	347.1	451.4	2 324.2	936.5	575.0	289.1	362.3	161.3	-627.0	-624.2
2005	1 954.3	629.8	296.8	382.3	575.8	2 692.0	1 025.7	693.7	310.7	483.2	178.7	-737.7	-724.8
2006	2 276.3	715.0	334.6	426.7	724.2	3 078.5	1 131.2	768.5	347.6	656.6	174.6	-802.2	-804.2
2007	2 616.3	782.9	383.5	498.2	875.7	3 334.4	1 176.2	827.5	379.4	750.1	201.2	-718.1	-718.0
2008	2 790.3	829.2	469.6	543.1	856.9	3 482.0	1 163.0	986.4	415.6	684.9	232.0	-691.6	-686.2
2009	2 330.1	671.6	393.5	522.6	648.9	2 712.0	893.8	696.5	392.9	497.8	231.0	-381.9	-382.5
2010	2 669.6	801.4	478.2	572.7	720.0	3 115.5	1 106.9	842.9	415.2	514.1	236.4	-445.9	-446.6
2011	3 004.2	894.0	572.9	639.5	792.6	3 485.8	1 238.7	1 006.0	441.6	546.0	253.4	-481.5	-483.2
2012	3 113.9	939.9	586.1	672.2	801.5	3 582.1	1 328.5	977.3	458.0	563.9	254.3	-468.2	-461.7
2013	3 234.0	957.1	605.5	713.9	825.5	3 620.1	1 360.2	941.3	467.1	581.3	270.2	-386.1	-386.9
2014	3 372.9	994.9	623.2	757.2	852.1	3 774.6	1 454.2	942.2	487.6	604.0	286.5	-401.7	-402.2
2015	3 211.2	955.9	542.5	765.9	813.1	3 688.6	1 491.4	799.6	495.2	607.4	294.9	-477.4	-477.9
2016	3 219.6	924.8	517.8	774.9	859.1	3 665.4	1 465.1	755.9	517.2	643.8	283.5	-445.8	-446.3
2017	3 466.5	958.5	577.4	814.3	957.1	3 939.0	1 566.9	811.7	550.0	713.4	297.0	-472.5	-476.2
2018	3 772.0	1 005.8	655.5	848.9	1 106.2	4 281.3	1 664.3	906.3	577.9	838.3	294.5	-509.5	-506.7
2019	3 831.8	980.0	656.8	878.0	1 169.8	4 334.5	1 634.6	891.0	599.6	900.2	309.1	-502.8	-509.5
2020	3 287.7	825.7	590.9	706.8	992.9	3 874.8	1 506.2	803.0	465.4	770.6	329.6	-587.1	-593.0
2021	3 797.9	964.1	776.4	737.8	1 145.0	4 629.1	1 846.5	1 003.9	546.1	892.5	340.1	-831.1	831.2
2019													
1st quarter	3 816.9	1 007.5	653.1	862.9	1 148.0	4 348.9	1 666.2	884.7	588.1	901.5	308.4	-532.0	-542.7
2nd quarter	3 844.1	973.8	657.3	883.5	1 184.3	4 379.9	1 642.0	914.3	603.0	913.2	307.3	-535.8	-539.6
3rd quarter	3 841.5	970.9	655.2	879.2	1 181.2	4 349.3	1 640.9	893.7	602.4	901.4	310.8	-507.8	-511.5
4th quarter	3 824.5	967.6	661.5	886.5	1 165.9	4 260.1	1 589.3	871.3	604.8	884.8	309.9	-435.6	-444.2
2020													
1st quarter	3 606.6	936.6	649.6	799.3	1 048.9	4 058.6	1 529.7	855.3	542.2	809.0	322.3	-452.0	-463.9
2nd quarter	2 858.7	639.1	507.3	661.5	883.5	3 386.5	1 211.4	730.7	404.6	711.5	328.3	-527.8	-532.0
3rd quarter	3 252.4	836.3	576.7	666.6	996.1	3 917.1	1 570.5	798.2	436.5	769.2	342.6	-664.8	-667.4
4th quarter	3 433.3	891.0	629.8	699.9	1 043.2	4 137.0	1 713.0	827.8	478.3	792.5	325.4	-703.7	-708.7
2021													
1st quarter	3 569.4	920.6	686.9	704.4	1 081.6	4 374.9	1 791.1	907.0	486.4	846.7	343.7	-805.5	-820.1
2nd quarter	3 746.4	967.3	759.5	734.8	1 112.4	4 549.8	1 844.5	974.5	524.2	882.0	324.5	-803.4	-807.3
3rd quarter	3 842.3	964.3	786.3	734.6	1 184.1	4 704.5	1 826.5	1 031.0	574.8	916.4	355.9	-862.2	-850.6
4th quarter	4 033.5	1 004.3	872.7	777.4	1 202.0	4 887.1	1 924.1	1 103.0	598.8	925.1	336.2	-853.6	-861.4

¹Exports and imports of certain goods, primarily military equipment purchased and sold by the federal government, are included in services. Beginning with 1986, repairs and alterations of equipment are reclassified from goods to services.

Table 7-2. Chain-Type Quantity Indexes for Exports and Imports of Goods and Services

(Index numbers, 2012 = 100; quarterly indexes are seasonally adjusted.)   NIPA Table 4.2.3

Year and quarter	Exports of goods and services					Imports of goods and services				
	Total	Goods [1]			Services [1]	Total	Goods [1]			Services [1]
		Total	Durable	Nondurable			Total	Durable	Nondurable	
1975	12.65	12.74	9.79	21.80	12.30	10.78	9.88	4.85	24.69	15.91
1976	13.20	13.40	9.97	23.97	12.43	12.89	12.11	5.94	30.30	17.00
1977	13.52	13.65	10.00	24.97	12.99	14.30	13.59	6.72	33.74	17.85
1978	14.94	15.07	11.08	27.42	14.45	15.54	14.81	7.76	34.84	19.13
1979	16.42	16.67	12.49	29.51	15.48	15.80	15.06	7.94	35.25	19.39
1980	18.19	18.71	13.97	33.33	16.12	14.75	13.94	8.00	30.34	18.96
1981	18.41	18.59	13.53	34.35	17.69	15.13	14.23	8.67	29.43	20.05
1982	17.00	17.02	11.83	33.48	16.91	14.94	13.87	8.76	27.71	21.11
1983	16.56	16.46	11.54	32.01	16.88	16.83	15.75	10.56	29.51	22.82
1984	17.91	17.63	12.70	33.01	18.87	20.92	19.56	14.05	33.61	28.54
1985	18.51	18.25	13.69	32.15	19.40	22.28	20.79	15.46	34.02	30.71
1986	19.93	19.23	14.51	33.55	22.18	24.18	22.91	16.89	38.03	31.06
1987	22.11	21.58	16.70	36.08	23.86	25.62	23.98	17.64	39.95	34.72
1988	25.70	25.41	20.55	39.39	26.70	26.62	24.96	18.38	41.47	35.89
1989	28.67	28.32	23.36	42.35	29.90	27.79	26.03	19.19	43.16	37.63
1990	31.20	30.75	25.88	44.26	32.75	28.79	26.79	19.70	44.62	40.09
1991	33.26	32.81	27.77	46.72	34.83	28.74	26.91	19.81	44.75	39.05
1992	35.57	35.28	29.99	49.82	36.70	30.76	29.45	21.88	48.16	37.99
1993	36.73	36.43	31.54	49.51	37.92	33.42	32.39	24.48	51.41	39.01
1994	39.97	39.91	35.31	51.80	40.57	37.41	36.72	28.52	55.23	41.08
1995	44.08	44.56	40.32	55.15	43.32	40.40	40.03	31.79	57.49	42.32
1996	47.69	48.52	44.96	57.13	46.03	43.91	43.78	35.20	61.34	44.53
1997	53.37	55.55	53.10	61.06	48.45	49.83	50.09	41.00	67.72	48.41
1998	54.61	56.76	54.79	60.95	49.80	55.65	56.02	46.41	73.91	53.67
1999	57.33	59.14	57.35	62.79	53.30	62.10	63.20	53.10	80.86	56.66
2000	62.10	64.94	64.27	65.50	55.73	70.17	71.45	61.16	88.09	63.84
2001	58.63	60.76	58.80	64.80	53.87	68.45	69.11	57.31	90.39	65.12
2002	57.48	58.66	55.57	65.75	54.89	70.96	71.68	59.74	92.90	67.35
2003	58.69	60.35	57.41	67.02	55.01	74.59	76.05	63.30	98.76	67.59
2004	64.35	65.77	64.02	69.58	61.19	82.79	84.58	72.30	105.16	74.23
2005	68.81	70.78	70.30	71.73	64.46	88.16	90.52	78.82	109.37	77.02
2006	75.33	77.89	78.43	76.67	69.66	93.82	96.02	86.18	110.93	83.41
2007	81.93	83.34	84.52	80.79	78.78	96.23	97.87	88.59	111.70	88.35
2008	86.66	88.22	88.60	87.13	83.19	94.16	94.67	85.77	107.90	91.66
2009	79.47	77.75	73.70	84.93	83.22	82.29	80.02	68.38	98.02	92.71
2010	89.71	89.53	86.92	93.90	90.12	93.13	92.33	84.49	103.46	96.94
2011	96.14	96.20	95.24	97.75	96.01	97.61	97.42	92.47	104.22	98.54
2012	100.00	100.00	100.00	100.00	100.00	100.00	100.00	100.00	100.00	100.00
2013	102.97	102.94	102.21	104.11	103.04	101.21	102.01	104.70	98.34	97.46
2014	106.97	107.53	106.45	109.26	105.79	106.44	107.69	113.99	99.15	100.60
2015	107.26	107.15	104.10	112.35	107.43	111.96	113.92	121.58	103.44	103.06
2016	107.70	107.82	102.97	116.56	107.40	113.58	115.18	123.06	104.38	106.13
2017	112.29	112.28	106.26	123.27	112.26	118.70	120.33	131.70	104.08	111.06
2018	115.44	117.01	109.98	129.86	112.49	123.69	126.43	139.07	108.32	111.64
2019	115.98	117.12	107.40	134.93	113.80	125.11	127.05	139.40	109.36	116.14
2020	100.63	105.24	90.20	133.66	92.40	113.90	119.68	129.08	106.37	90.61
2021	106.72	113.03	100.73	136.45	95.47	130.00	137.05	152.31	115.26	101.71
2015										
1st quarter	107.54	107.30	104.46	112.15	107.94	110.80	112.99	120.28	103.12	100.97
2nd quarter	107.82	108.04	104.98	113.26	107.35	111.62	113.78	121.30	103.54	101.90
3rd quarter	106.92	106.92	104.02	111.86	106.87	112.58	114.61	122.57	103.67	103.42
4th quarter	106.76	106.32	102.94	112.15	107.56	112.82	114.28	122.18	103.43	105.96
2016										
1st quarter	106.45	106.84	101.87	115.89	105.67	112.66	114.23	121.53	104.38	105.36
2nd quarter	107.26	106.83	102.57	114.38	107.98	112.78	114.31	121.90	103.99	105.59
3rd quarter	108.92	108.76	103.35	118.58	109.15	113.60	114.90	123.13	103.52	107.32
4th quarter	108.16	108.85	104.10	117.38	106.81	115.28	117.27	125.66	105.64	106.25
2017										
1st quarter	110.96	111.24	104.19	124.21	110.39	117.06	118.72	128.42	105.03	109.33
2nd quarter	111.33	110.94	104.88	122.01	111.99	118.20	119.64	131.13	103.19	111.33
3rd quarter	111.98	111.42	106.74	119.85	112.97	118.11	119.26	131.09	102.27	112.36
4th quarter	114.89	115.51	109.22	127.01	113.70	121.44	123.71	136.17	105.83	111.22
2018										
1st quarter	115.65	116.15	111.01	125.55	114.65	122.46	125.18	137.64	107.32	110.48
2nd quarter	116.27	118.74	110.88	133.12	111.65	122.60	125.16	137.22	107.91	111.25
3rd quarter	114.74	116.18	108.51	130.20	112.03	124.26	127.32	140.01	109.14	110.92
4th quarter	115.09	116.95	109.51	130.58	111.62	125.46	128.06	141.42	108.93	113.92
2019										
1st quarter	116.44	118.53	110.41	133.37	112.56	125.88	128.19	141.34	109.33	115.50
2nd quarter	115.76	116.32	106.88	133.62	114.64	126.09	128.06	140.39	110.39	117.01
3rd quarter	115.75	116.86	106.33	136.14	113.65	125.53	127.53	139.78	109.99	116.33
4th quarter	115.97	116.80	105.98	136.59	114.35	122.94	124.41	136.10	107.73	115.74
2020										
1st quarter	111.26	115.74	102.86	139.46	103.19	119.00	121.93	131.41	108.51	106.27
2nd quarter	87.99	88.27	70.22	123.70	87.17	98.17	102.87	104.42	101.61	79.12
3rd quarter	98.89	105.39	91.07	132.06	87.47	114.98	122.89	134.43	106.20	83.78
4th quarter	104.39	111.54	96.66	139.41	91.77	123.46	131.04	146.07	109.18	93.27
2021										
1st quarter	104.50	111.34	98.76	135.08	92.35	125.74	134.48	149.86	112.31	91.14
2nd quarter	105.75	112.29	101.39	133.32	94.07	128.15	135.79	151.30	113.60	97.67
3rd quarter	105.46	111.24	100.01	132.96	95.15	130.22	135.87	150.15	115.50	107.24
4th quarter	111.18	117.26	102.78	144.46	100.32	135.89	142.08	157.91	119.61	110.80

[1]Exports and imports of certain goods, primarily military equipment purchased and sold by the federal government, are included in services. Beginning with 1986, repairs and alterations of equipment are reclassified from goods to services.

Table 7-3. Chain-Type Price Indexes for Exports and Imports of Goods and Services

(Index numbers, 2012 = 100; quarterly indexes are seasonally adjusted.)   NIPA Table 4.2.4

| Year and quarter | Exports of goods and services | | | | | Imports of goods and services | | | | |
| | Total | Goods [1] | | | Services [1] | Total | Goods [1] | | | Services [1] |
		Total	Durable	Nondurable			Total	Durable	Nondurable	
1975	49.39	57.70	31.30	28.79	30.88	41.23	43.88	30.16	15.43	31.29
1976	51.01	59.27	31.27	28.75	32.67	42.47	45.05	29.82	16.12	32.71
1977	53.09	61.47	32.55	29.94	34.50	46.21	49.18	32.56	17.46	35.03
1978	56.32	65.00	34.05	31.33	37.08	49.47	52.45	34.98	17.77	38.22
1979	63.10	73.43	41.28	37.94	40.13	57.93	61.85	41.76	23.94	43.16
1980	69.50	80.46	46.38	42.62	45.24	72.17	78.06	50.46	36.47	50.09
1981	74.65	86.18	48.09	44.20	49.18	76.07	82.43	51.15	40.08	52.26
1982	75.01	85.47	46.62	42.87	51.97	73.51	79.11	49.25	37.26	52.30
1983	75.31	84.98	45.31	41.64	54.04	70.75	75.80	46.63	34.01	51.44
1984	76.02	85.74	46.72	42.94	54.60	70.14	75.28	46.12	33.82	50.56
1985	73.75	81.46	44.85	40.84	56.57	67.84	72.32	43.75	31.76	50.50
1986	72.52	78.67	45.60	37.81	58.50	67.83	70.70	44.98	21.80	55.97
1987	74.12	80.43	49.70	42.55	59.75	71.94	75.73	48.64	24.68	56.76
1988	77.92	85.38	55.83	46.82	61.08	75.38	79.34	57.70	23.42	59.53
1989	79.21	86.48	57.30	47.50	62.77	77.02	81.56	60.98	26.25	59.22
1990	79.66	85.71	57.02	48.31	65.75	79.23	83.06	58.40	29.35	63.66
1991	80.55	85.67	56.51	46.73	68.56	78.57	81.49	56.70	26.37	65.98
1992	80.15	84.34	57.43	44.34	70.17	78.64	81.04	56.77	25.48	67.84
1993	80.28	83.91	60.97	43.24	71.46	78.03	80.13	56.81	24.06	68.41
1994	81.21	84.87	63.22	46.82	72.32	78.77	80.72	58.83	23.49	69.75
1995	83.03	86.89	67.71	54.68	73.68	80.92	82.87	63.38	25.98	71.93
1996	81.92	84.68	65.37	51.82	75.14	79.51	80.77	62.48	28.29	73.73
1997	80.48	82.34	64.78	51.75	75.90	76.75	77.43	63.60	27.22	73.72
1998	78.57	79.74	62.12	48.62	75.74	72.62	72.76	60.61	21.76	72.28
1999	77.97	78.66	60.50	48.31	76.33	73.02	72.80	60.73	24.61	74.54
2000	79.47	80.02	61.99	53.72	78.16	76.22	76.64	64.11	34.93	74.26
2001	78.84	79.56	60.96	51.82	77.11	74.22	74.46	61.96	31.85	73.21
2002	78.20	78.73	61.12	50.18	76.95	73.24	73.10	59.65	30.87	74.27
2003	79.40	79.51	63.82	54.57	79.17	75.45	74.69	61.17	36.57	79.87
2004	82.28	82.32	72.10	60.65	82.24	79.06	78.23	71.96	43.29	83.82
2005	85.13	84.93	78.57	68.84	85.63	83.70	83.18	75.90	55.60	86.72
2006	87.84	87.59	88.36	74.56	88.49	86.91	86.53	83.18	64.09	89.13
2007	91.14	91.00	94.11	80.56	91.50	89.92	89.43	89.50	70.07	92.77
2008	95.41	95.71	97.00	92.74	94.75	98.96	99.23	98.81	95.73	97.80
2009	89.69	88.92	82.75	73.38	91.39	87.99	86.63	83.50	62.43	94.51
2010	93.35	92.97	92.26	85.13	94.20	92.78	92.05	95.39	77.82	96.42
2011	99.24	99.79	102.08	102.30	98.00	99.83	99.91	104.84	98.81	99.39
2012	100.00	100.00	100.00	100.00	100.00	100.00	100.00	100.00	100.00	100.00
2013	100.17	99.31	96.95	98.35	102.10	98.64	98.05	97.83	96.30	101.58
2014	100.17	98.32	95.52	96.50	104.34	97.78	96.72	97.33	93.46	103.20
2015	95.15	91.28	89.75	76.78	103.84	89.73	87.46	88.74	60.91	101.50
2016	93.25	87.82	86.35	68.31	105.40	86.53	83.77	84.71	50.61	100.92
2017	95.92	90.49	89.76	75.95	108.08	88.51	85.76	92.34	58.90	102.84
2018	99.10	93.19	93.02	84.92	112.39	91.18	88.15	98.98	69.56	107.03
2019	98.75	91.82	92.10	79.33	114.39	89.99	86.39	96.95	64.91	108.77
2020	96.19	88.16	93.46	66.48	114.52	88.08	83.96	102.75	52.37	109.82
2021	107.55	100.91	108.74	94.44	121.42	94.61	90.54	130.38	75.20	115.53
2015										
1st quarter	96.17	92.84	92.25	79.25	103.67	91.68	89.71	93.62	66.54	101.87
2nd quarter	95.97	92.37	91.03	80.52	104.07	90.48	88.26	90.06	63.21	101.98
3rd quarter	94.97	90.90	88.80	76.44	104.11	89.36	87.05	86.89	60.64	101.37
4th quarter	93.48	89.00	86.93	70.93	103.50	87.40	84.83	84.39	53.24	100.77
2016										
1st quarter	92.12	86.57	85.28	63.76	104.50	85.90	83.06	82.47	47.01	100.73
2nd quarter	93.07	87.76	86.04	67.43	104.97	86.22	83.36	84.11	48.89	101.07
3rd quarter	93.61	88.26	86.59	69.63	105.59	86.88	84.18	86.11	52.28	100.95
4th quarter	94.19	88.69	87.47	72.42	106.52	87.12	84.47	86.13	54.27	100.93
2017										
1st quarter	95.07	89.72	89.27	74.38	107.05	88.10	85.58	89.54	59.95	101.21
2nd quarter	95.14	89.61	89.15	73.47	107.50	88.09	85.40	91.21	57.49	102.12
3rd quarter	96.03	90.68	89.45	76.40	108.00	88.31	85.40	92.85	56.33	103.46
4th quarter	97.46	91.94	91.18	79.55	109.79	89.55	86.67	95.76	61.82	104.55
2018										
1st quarter	98.13	92.24	92.85	81.88	111.35	91.12	88.21	98.35	68.87	106.36
2nd quarter	99.36	93.58	94.29	85.22	112.32	91.25	88.25	100.17	69.16	106.94
3rd quarter	99.64	93.80	92.81	87.50	112.75	91.38	88.34	99.27	70.88	107.29
4th quarter	99.28	93.13	92.12	85.07	113.14	90.97	87.82	98.14	69.34	107.51
2019										
1st quarter	98.55	92.00	93.53	92.00	113.32	90.29	86.82	97.33	64.80	108.41
2nd quarter	99.34	92.55	93.87	92.83	114.65	90.49	86.99	96.02	67.37	108.77
3rd quarter	98.76	91.56	94.07	93.45	115.02	89.75	86.09	96.73	63.67	108.87
4th quarter	98.35	91.18	93.66	93.36	114.55	89.43	85.68	97.73	63.78	109.03
2020										
1st quarter	97.78	90.22	92.11	73.10	114.98	89.19	85.27	99.85	60.35	109.75
2nd quarter	93.18	84.82	90.41	58.50	112.38	86.42	82.25	96.10	45.22	108.61
3rd quarter	96.16	88.06	94.55	66.08	114.69	88.10	83.98	104.55	51.16	109.80
4th quarter	97.62	89.55	96.75	68.22	116.02	88.59	84.35	110.51	52.75	111.11
2021										
1st quarter	102.38	95.00	102.11	80.80	118.61	91.39	87.34	122.80	64.06	112.38
2nd quarter	107.03	100.48	108.55	92.89	120.69	94.31	90.29	137.32	73.00	114.88
3rd quarter	109.54	103.19	111.04	99.95	122.50	95.72	91.60	131.30	78.93	116.85
4th quarter	111.25	104.98	113.27	104.11	123.89	97.03	92.92	130.12	84.81	118.03

[1]Exports and imports of certain goods, primarily military equipment purchased and sold by the federal government, are included in services. Beginning with 1986, repairs and alterations of equipment are reclassified from goods to services.

Table 7-4. Exports and Imports of Selected NIPA Types of Product

(Billions of dollars, quarterly data are at seasonally adjusted annual rates.)   NIPA Table 4.2.5

Year and quarter	Exports — Goods					Exports — Services		Imports — Goods						Imports — Services	
	Foods, feeds, and beverages	Industrial supplies and materials	Capital goods, except auto-motive	Auto-motive vehicles, engines, and parts	Consumer goods, except food and auto-motive	Travel	Other business services	Foods, feeds, and beverages	Industrial supplies and materials, except petroleum and products	Petroleum and products	Capital goods, except auto-motive	Auto-motive vehicles, engines, and parts	Consumer goods, except food and auto-motive	Travel	Other business services
1975	19.2	29.3	36.6	10.8	6.6	4.7	3.7	11.5	63.1	27.0	10.2	12.1	13.2	6.4	2.3
1976	19.8	31.6	39.1	12.2	8.0	5.7	4.5	14.0	78.4	34.6	12.3	16.8	17.2	6.9	2.9
1977	19.7	33.2	39.8	13.5	8.9	6.2	4.9	15.8	81.9	45.0	14.0	19.4	21.8	7.5	3.2
1978	25.7	38.4	47.5	15.2	11.4	7.2	6.2	18.0	105.4	42.6	19.3	25.0	29.4	8.5	3.9
1979	30.5	53.3	60.2	17.9	14.0	8.4	7.3	18.6	126.9	60.4	24.6	26.6	31.3	9.4	4.6
1980	36.3	68.0	76.3	17.4	17.8	10.6	8.6	18.6	130.4	79.5	31.6	28.3	34.3	10.4	5.1
1981	38.8	65.7	84.2	19.7	17.7	15.6	10.5	17.5	107.3	78.4	37.1	31.0	38.4	11.8	6.0
1982	32.2	61.8	76.5	17.2	16.1	15.5	13.8	18.8	106.2	62.0	38.4	34.3	39.7	12.8	7.0
1983	32.1	57.1	71.7	18.5	14.9	14.5	14.1	21.9	120.7	55.1	43.7	43.0	47.3	13.6	6.8
1984	32.2	61.9	77.0	22.4	15.1	21.3	14.5	21.8	110.6	58.1	60.4	56.5	61.1	23.4	7.7
1985	24.6	59.4	79.3	24.9	14.6	22.4	14.8	24.4	96.7	51.4	61.3	64.9	66.3	25.1	8.8
1986	23.5	59.0	82.8	25.1	16.7	25.5	23.3	24.8	109.0	34.3	72.0	78.1	79.4	26.5	13.3
1987	25.2	67.4	92.7	27.6	20.3	29.0	24.2	24.9	116.3	42.9	85.1	85.2	88.8	29.9	16.7
1988	33.8	84.2	119.1	33.4	27.0	35.2	25.7	24.9	129.7	39.6	102.2	87.9	96.4	32.8	17.8
1989	36.3	95.4	136.9	35.1	35.9	43.0	30.3	26.4	140.5	50.9	112.3	87.4	103.6	34.2	19.2
1990	35.1	101.9	153.0	36.2	43.5	50.9	32.7	26.2	127.4	62.3	116.4	88.2	105.0	38.2	22.4
1991	35.7	106.2	166.6	39.9	46.6	56.7	39.9	27.6	134.0	51.7	121.1	85.5	107.7	36.2	25.9
1992	40.3	105.2	176.4	46.9	51.2	64.0	41.1	27.9	140.2	51.6	134.8	91.5	122.4	39.6	24.3
1993	40.5	102.9	182.7	51.6	54.5	67.9	43.5	31.0	156.2	51.5	153.2	102.1	133.7	41.9	26.6
1994	42.4	115.4	205.7	57.5	59.7	69.4	49.9	33.2	175.6	51.3	185.0	118.1	145.9	45.1	30.3
1995	50.8	141.0	234.4	61.4	64.2	74.9	53.6	35.7	197.3	56.0	222.1	123.7	159.7	46.4	33.7
1996	56.0	141.3	254.0	64.4	69.3	81.8	61.3	39.7	206.5	72.7	228.4	128.7	172.5	49.7	38.1
1997	52.0	153.0	295.8	73.4	77.0	86.2	71.2	41.3	193.1	71.8	253.6	139.4	195.2	53.8	41.4
1998	46.8	143.3	299.8	72.5	79.4	85.1	78.1	44.1	221.9	50.9	269.8	148.6	218.5	58.5	45.6
1999	46.0	145.7	311.2	75.3	80.9	92.3	79.8	46.5	301.3	72.1	296.1	178.2	243.7	59.6	56.2
2000	47.9	171.1	357.0	80.4	89.3	100.2	83.5	47.2	276.8	126.1	347.7	195.0	284.6	65.8	61.6
2001	49.4	159.5	321.7	75.4	88.3	86.7	88.2	50.3	270.6	109.4	299.2	188.7	287.1	60.7	66.9
2002	49.6	157.3	290.4	78.9	84.3	81.9	95.4	56.5	317.8	109.3	284.9	202.8	311.3	59.9	74.1
2003	55.0	173.3	293.7	80.6	89.9	80.3	102.3	63.0	418.3	140.4	297.6	209.2	338.4	61.9	79.6
2004	56.6	206.3	327.5	89.2	103.2	92.4	118.8	69.1	531.4	189.9	346.1	227.3	378.1	74.0	89.9
2005	59.0	236.8	358.4	98.4	115.2	101.5	128.9	76.1	610.1	263.2	382.8	238.7	412.7	80.0	95.8
2006	66.0	279.1	404.0	107.3	129.0	105.1	151.4	83.0	644.5	316.7	422.6	256.0	447.6	84.2	126.6
2007	84.3	316.3	433.0	121.3	145.9	119.0	184.8	90.4	794.6	346.7	449.1	258.5	479.8	89.2	149.3
2008	108.3	386.9	457.7	121.5	161.2	133.8	202.9	82.9	464.4	476.1	458.7	233.2	485.7	92.5	174.0
2009	93.9	293.5	391.5	81.7	149.3	119.9	211.7	92.5	603.2	267.7	374.1	159.2	429.9	81.4	178.5
2010	107.7	388.6	447.8	112.0	164.9	137.0	227.4	108.3	755.0	353.6	450.4	225.6	485.1	86.6	183.6
2011	126.2	485.3	494.2	133.0	174.7	150.9	251.6	111.1	723.2	462.1	513.4	255.2	515.9	89.7	197.3
2012	133.0	483.2	527.5	146.2	181.0	161.6	263.6	116.0	679.0	434.3	551.8	298.5	518.8	100.3	200.2
2013	136.2	492.4	534.8	152.7	188.1	177.5	286.3	126.8	669.9	387.8	559.0	309.6	532.9	98.1	208.1
2014	143.7	500.7	551.8	159.8	198.4	191.9	309.0	128.8	488.0	353.6	598.8	329.5	558.7	105.7	214.7
2015	127.7	418.1	539.8	151.9	197.3	206.9	315.8	131.0	437.4	197.2	607.2	350.0	596.4	114.5	218.3
2016	130.5	387.4	519.9	150.3	193.3	206.9	323.8	138.8	505.9	159.6	593.9	351.1	585.2	123.6	221.2
2017	132.7	456.2	533.6	157.6	197.1	210.7	350.7	138.8	505.9	199.6	643.6	359.8	603.9	135.0	232.4
2018	133.2	534.6	563.2	158.8	205.5	214.7	369.5	148.4	577.3	240.4	695.9	373.1	649.1	144.5	235.6
2019	131.1	526.8	548.1	162.5	205.0	193.3	432.1	151.6	519.4	207.1	681.1	376.8	655.9	134.6	272.4
2020	139.3	450.4	460.5	127.9	174.0	72.8	440.7	155.4	424.4	125.2	648.5	311.3	641.1	35.8	284.5
2021	160.8	616.2	519.5	144.5	223.0	69.3	471.0	183.5	636.1	214.4	766.3	348.5	771.7	57.4	303.1
2016															
1st quarter	117.4	364.0	521.0	148.6	191.8	207.7	313.1	130.3	403.1	137.7	583.6	350.3	588.4	121.9	221.5
2nd quarter	122.9	386.4	520.8	151.5	191.0	204.5	321.2	129.3	422.9	151.6	595.5	346.3	579.9	121.2	219.8
3rd quarter	149.6	395.9	515.4	152.5	195.9	207.8	328.8	130.4	453.3	170.0	594.8	351.1	582.1	123.2	220.2
4th quarter	132.1	403.1	522.3	148.5	194.3	207.6	332.0	134.1	470.1	178.9	601.5	356.5	590.3	128.0	223.5
2017															
1st quarter	130.7	439.0	521.5	159.0	197.0	207.8	342.4	134.9	509.4	216.7	613.1	361.0	595.1	131.1	225.0
2nd quarter	135.0	441.4	523.5	156.2	196.8	209.6	344.2	137.9	496.6	192.1	631.8	358.2	597.5	134.1	229.5
3rd quarter	136.8	447.3	539.9	156.3	195.5	211.9	354.1	140.3	488.3	181.8	652.9	357.8	592.8	135.3	237.7
4th quarter	128.4	497.1	549.4	159.0	199.2	213.7	361.9	142.2	529.3	207.7	676.7	362.4	630.4	139.6	237.3
2018															
1st quarter	128.3	505.6	556.0	167.0	204.7	217.6	365.0	147.3	565.1	235.8	681.7	369.4	652.6	142.1	233.2
2nd quarter	149.1	544.7	566.5	161.6	205.1	215.9	363.9	148.4	579.3	244.3	696.3	363.1	631.3	141.7	232.4
3rd quarter	135.3	544.0	561.3	155.5	204.5	212.1	373.8	148.4	594.3	256.8	705.3	375.9	646.3	144.6	237.1
4th quarter	120.0	544.3	568.9	151.3	207.7	213.2	375.2	149.4	570.6	224.8	700.4	384.1	666.2	149.5	239.7
2019															
1st quarter	129.5	528.5	568.3	163.8	210.3	194.1	417.8	149.9	528.9	200.4	691.8	382.2	665.7	132.2	260.4
2nd quarter	133.6	528.6	542.0	161.8	204.8	195.4	435.5	153.4	534.8	225.1	681.8	384.8	660.4	138.7	272.4
3rd quarter	132.7	519.1	540.0	165.3	205.9	190.9	436.8	153.3	513.9	203.6	678.0	381.4	668.1	132.6	277.8
4th quarter	128.6	531.2	542.1	159.0	199.2	192.9	438.2	149.6	500.2	199.1	672.5	358.8	629.5	134.9	278.9
2020															
1st quarter	133.4	518.5	525.8	151.1	187.4	145.6	437.3	154.6	479.7	180.0	649.6	353.3	612.2	88.7	282.5
2nd quarter	129.3	370.2	398.3	61.3	134.1	55.7	432.9	147.8	356.7	82.5	588.6	165.0	570.5	9.5	276.1
3rd quarter	139.0	434.9	448.0	145.8	179.3	42.1	437.7	158.9	408.9	113.3	661.1	340.6	670.4	14.7	283.8
4th quarter	155.7	477.9	469.8	153.5	195.1	47.9	454.8	160.4	452.5	125.0	694.6	386.4	711.1	30.2	295.9
2021															
1st quarter	162.7	539.0	489.3	149.6	193.0	53.7	458.8	165.1	541.0	170.1	735.1	362.6	763.7	31.8	293.8
2nd quarter	161.8	611.3	527.2	139.4	211.4	65.3	469.4	185.1	622.4	208.2	762.2	348.9	761.2	47.5	298.3
3rd quarter	148.1	635.2	523.4	137.5	230.4	66.3	475.7	190.1	670.8	230.1	771.1	334.5	747.9	70.2	306.8
4th quarter	170.8	679.3	538.0	151.5	256.9	91.7	480.3	193.7	710.2	249.3	796.6	348.3	814.1	80.2	313.7

Table 7-5. Chain-Type Quantity Indexes for Exports and Imports of Selected NIPA Types of Product

(Index numbers, 2012 = 100; quarterly indexes are seasonally adjusted.)   NIPA Table 4.2.3

| Year and quarter | Exports | | | | | | | Imports | | | | | | | |
| | Goods | | | | | Services | | Goods | | | | | | Services | |
	Foods, feeds, and beverages	Industrial supplies and materials	Capital goods, except automotive	Automotive vehicles, engines, and parts	Consumer goods, except food and automotive	Travel	Other business services	Foods, feeds, and beverages	Industrial supplies and materials, except petroleum and products	Petroleum and products	Capital goods, except automotive	Automotive vehicles, engines, and parts	Consumer goods, except food and automotive	Travel	Other business services
1975	33.04	20.42	5.71	24.41	8.73	14.12	3.14	26.37	38.82	53.59	0.86	14.20	4.67	17.59	2.24
1976	37.49	22.05	5.63	25.52	9.85	16.08	3.63	30.01	47.02	64.61	1.05	18.81	6.02	18.70	2.69
1977	37.46	22.24	5.54	25.70	10.65	16.12	3.74	29.71	53.87	77.73	1.12	19.93	7.27	19.27	2.82
1978	46.28	24.58	6.32	26.39	12.30	17.31	4.43	33.36	54.44	73.49	1.44	21.56	8.93	19.91	3.29
1979	49.09	28.14	7.59	26.55	12.93	18.56	4.94	34.24	53.80	74.34	1.77	20.85	9.00	19.42	3.73
1980	55.34	31.94	8.86	22.36	15.67	20.73	5.28	29.80	44.81	60.04	2.08	20.66	9.07	19.40	3.81
1981	56.50	29.79	8.90	22.11	15.02	27.59	6.03	31.01	42.66	52.60	2.45	19.99	9.93	21.14	4.23
1982	53.09	28.89	7.87	18.12	13.52	25.46	7.47	31.61	37.47	45.24	2.67	21.40	10.38	25.08	4.78
1983	50.75	27.49	7.59	18.74	12.37	22.61	7.26	34.30	40.27	44.78	3.23	26.19	12.49	28.41	4.43
1984	49.38	28.89	8.40	22.12	12.30	31.42	7.24	38.86	46.09	47.30	4.82	33.65	15.77	51.35	4.95
1985	42.73	29.06	9.24	24.07	11.94	31.45	7.12	40.54	44.88	44.41	5.43	37.71	17.21	56.65	5.53
1986	44.08	30.36	10.08	23.67	13.21	34.69	10.89	41.50	50.46	54.91	6.17	40.82	19.07	52.72	8.05
1987	47.18	31.11	11.64	25.51	15.54	37.63	10.90	42.54	51.02	57.35	7.04	41.89	19.69	62.40	9.23
1988	51.85	35.08	14.79	30.28	19.85	43.89	11.54	40.85	53.31	63.44	8.12	40.84	19.98	64.19	9.84
1989	53.93	39.01	17.16	31.13	25.45	51.86	13.47	41.77	54.07	68.60	9.18	39.80	20.91	66.21	11.51
1990	55.64	41.31	19.85	31.17	29.86	58.22	14.02	43.37	54.80	69.33	9.92	39.85	20.54	70.73	12.49
1991	56.70	44.12	21.72	33.43	30.93	60.95	16.48	41.40	54.13	69.08	10.66	37.16	20.89	64.24	13.94
1992	64.27	44.94	23.79	38.54	33.32	67.09	16.66	43.71	58.33	72.20	12.35	39.07	23.07	66.25	12.98
1993	63.95	43.75	25.35	42.02	35.01	70.21	17.42	44.23	63.52	79.09	14.41	42.93	24.98	69.55	13.76
1994	64.61	46.02	29.25	46.44	38.25	71.06	19.84	45.24	71.13	84.44	17.67	48.14	27.07	72.08	15.54
1995	71.38	49.64	34.86	48.95	40.54	75.52	20.94	46.38	72.95	82.91	21.75	48.97	29.20	72.86	17.11
1996	70.24	52.16	40.40	50.76	43.24	80.41	23.59	51.01	77.78	89.90	25.56	50.63	31.44	75.76	18.76
1997	70.68	56.71	49.52	57.46	47.69	82.71	27.14	56.17	83.04	93.62	32.08	54.73	36.01	82.34	20.10
1998	69.96	56.08	51.63	56.67	49.14	80.46	29.96	60.29	91.15	100.07	36.90	58.26	40.87	93.17	22.42
1999	72.00	57.85	54.48	58.46	50.24	85.03	31.51	66.60	96.94	107.56	42.35	69.39	45.90	93.93	27.67
2000	75.60	62.97	62.68	61.74	55.25	88.07	33.71	70.95	102.23	111.48	50.88	75.06	54.04	107.08	31.55
2001	77.63	60.41	56.46	57.70	54.82	75.56	38.00	74.14	101.22	114.76	45.10	72.60	54.92	98.64	36.55
2002	76.26	60.79	51.87	60.10	52.62	71.19	42.25	78.05	102.32	112.09	44.42	77.79	60.21	93.33	40.82
2003	77.57	62.43	54.51	60.95	55.77	67.77	44.97	84.10	105.76	119.57	48.60	79.81	65.88	86.11	43.31
2004	72.50	66.50	61.35	66.91	63.44	74.63	51.18	89.09	117.79	127.47	57.57	85.29	73.49	94.41	48.23
2005	76.76	68.21	67.34	72.98	70.06	78.18	53.87	92.32	122.99	130.04	64.35	88.62	80.03	97.54	50.55
2006	82.83	73.24	76.12	78.59	77.46	77.71	61.73	98.02	124.14	127.59	72.12	94.66	87.15	98.67	66.03
2007	90.10	77.21	81.21	87.83	85.76	84.29	73.32	99.29	120.43	124.57	77.01	94.64	92.96	96.36	76.79
2008	95.64	85.26	85.93	86.90	92.77	90.34	79.35	97.91	114.04	120.29	78.95	83.26	92.48	92.04	88.35
2009	91.84	79.71	73.86	58.17	85.76	83.02	85.57	92.50	96.93	110.55	66.16	56.41	82.93	84.47	92.10
2010	101.26	92.13	85.10	79.30	93.71	91.70	90.14	94.59	102.84	111.09	81.19	79.41	94.51	88.22	94.56
2011	100.79	98.23	93.82	92.63	97.97	96.05	96.73	96.41	104.38	108.99	92.74	87.15	99.34	89.09	99.61
2012	100.00	100.00	100.00	100.00	100.00	100.00	100.00	100.00	100.00	100.00	100.00	100.00	100.00	100.00	100.00
2013	102.11	104.03	101.31	103.88	105.07	108.45	105.63	103.93	97.16	94.12	102.76	104.12	105.19	96.37	102.51
2014	110.23	107.68	104.89	108.12	112.28	114.97	111.28	109.31	98.19	90.49	111.50	111.49	112.75	103.00	104.63
2015	112.39	107.67	103.69	102.88	114.08	124.95	112.87	113.69	99.63	91.58	116.17	120.85	123.89	116.07	106.33
2016	118.73	109.46	101.25	102.61	114.26	123.89	112.37	115.34	102.52	96.56	116.72	122.12	124.53	127.59	106.18
2017	119.45	118.27	102.44	107.35	118.15	123.78	118.13	117.94	104.25	96.18	127.39	125.68	130.14	137.76	109.42
2018	119.24	126.54	108.89	107.34	121.99	123.26	117.81	127.12	104.10	91.41	139.63	130.29	139.00	146.97	105.85
2019	117.80	131.41	105.46	109.59	121.24	118.30	116.54	130.55	98.39	85.20	138.40	132.26	143.39	148.33	112.07
2020	123.61	127.64	88.40	86.34	102.63	43.46	113.87	134.89	90.28	74.60	133.09	108.68	142.85	39.90	113.07
2021	112.52	130.50	98.48	96.43	130.60	39.84	114.06	147.89	99.29	78.72	155.49	119.72	170.63	65.05	115.87
2016															
1st quarter	108.69	108.29	101.19	101.19	113.31	125.59	109.78	117.70	100.13	94.54	114.03	122.06	123.94	125.52	106.75
2nd quarter	110.58	110.30	101.19	103.36	112.91	122.79	111.84	116.95	101.70	95.86	116.77	120.36	122.92	124.23	105.51
3rd quarter	134.60	110.30	100.52	104.28	115.40	124.19	113.53	112.24	103.51	98.53	117.10	122.25	124.46	127.15	105.44
4th quarter	121.03	108.94	102.10	101.61	115.44	123.01	114.34	114.45	104.74	97.32	118.98	123.82	126.80	133.47	107.02
2017															
1st quarter	118.03	115.75	100.61	108.39	119.07	122.55	117.20	116.69	104.84	100.94	121.95	126.07	128.10	137.02	107.26
2nd quarter	122.38	117.47	100.75	106.37	118.24	123.59	116.78	117.28	104.42	96.96	125.29	124.91	128.60	137.26	108.90
3rd quarter	122.90	115.66	103.61	106.36	116.62	124.77	119.07	117.91	103.37	93.58	128.95	124.95	127.75	135.91	111.78
4th quarter	114.51	124.20	104.77	108.29	118.69	124.21	119.45	119.87	104.37	93.25	133.38	126.79	136.12	140.86	133.23
2018															
1st quarter	113.85	123.04	108.08	113.11	121.53	126.22	117.62	123.88	102.83	90.54	136.47	128.66	139.32	141.91	105.59
2nd quarter	130.80	128.17	109.52	109.06	121.59	123.79	116.39	126.91	104.45	93.00	139.40	126.79	134.95	142.20	104.60
3rd quarter	123.89	125.98	108.24	104.95	121.36	121.26	118.64	129.84	105.72	94.39	141.60	131.42	138.03	145.14	106.16
4th quarter	108.43	128.98	109.73	102.23	123.47	121.74	118.58	127.83	103.39	87.71	141.04	134.29	143.69	150.61	107.03
2019															
1st quarter	116.45	130.79	109.18	110.27	125.13	110.51	133.16	128.93	100.51	85.16	139.42	133.90	144.57	132.92	116.42
2nd quarter	120.96	128.71	104.18	108.51	121.12	109.86	136.73	128.90	99.53	87.21	138.27	135.30	144.23	139.00	120.60
3rd quarter	119.17	130.95	103.72	111.27	121.22	107.25	136.45	132.35	99.02	85.50	138.03	134.34	146.05	133.15	122.43
4th quarter	114.41	135.61	104.20	107.50	117.62	108.35	138.06	131.93	95.92	84.36	137.70	126.41	139.11	135.00	123.21
2020															
1st quarter	118.72	137.82	100.92	101.86	110.56	86.04	112.55	133.57	94.77	83.20	133.67	123.79	135.79	98.19	112.26
2nd quarter	119.62	116.57	76.40	41.36	79.57	33.60	114.56	128.24	85.24	67.47	120.71	57.50	127.11	11.25	110.96
3rd quarter	125.53	123.91	85.86	98.65	105.53	25.37	112.86	137.21	87.83	72.39	135.46	118.76	149.20	16.83	112.64
4th quarter	130.57	132.27	90.41	103.50	114.86	28.84	115.50	140.54	93.29	75.32	142.52	134.68	159.29	33.32	116.41
2021															
1st quarter	122.60	130.13	93.89	100.38	114.05	32.14	113.50	141.01	95.37	74.91	150.40	125.71	170.42	35.39	114.20
2nd quarter	111.32	131.14	100.38	93.33	123.66	38.00	114.23	150.26	97.03	78.63	155.23	120.45	169.09	53.44	114.60
3rd quarter	100.36	128.32	98.90	91.64	134.92	37.80	114.22	150.17	101.56	80.88	155.96	114.34	164.60	79.54	116.56
4th quarter	115.80	132.42	100.77	100.37	149.77	51.41	114.31	150.13	103.20	80.45	160.36	118.36	178.42	91.82	118.14

SECTION 7B: U.S. INTERNATIONAL TRANSACTIONS ACCOUNTS

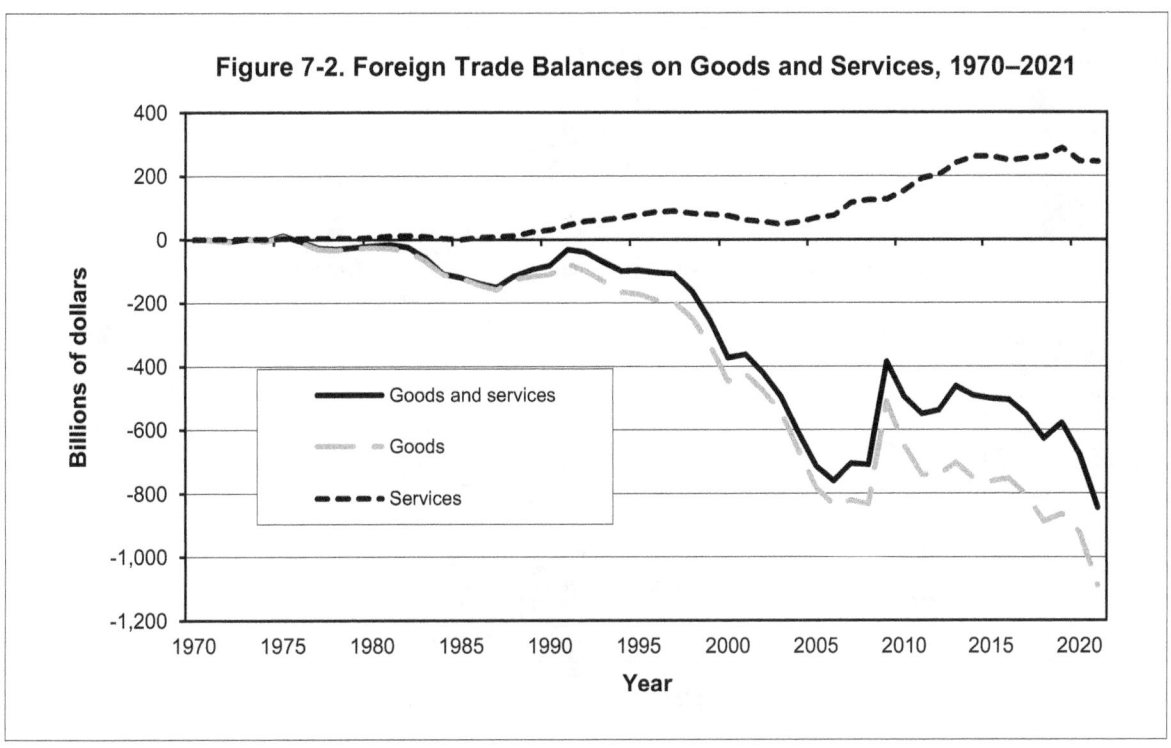

Figure 7-2. Foreign Trade Balances on Goods and Services, 1970–2021

- Supply chain refers to the network of organizations, people, activities, information, and resources involved in delivering a product or service to a consumer. COVID-19 closures, the war in Ukraine, and portage congestion all led to supply chain disturbances. These factors have led to less supply of raw materials and other inputs, thereby hampering the production of such products such as automobiles. For example, computer chips were in short supply during the pandemic. Without these chips, cars cannot be built.

- Beginning in the early 1990s, two new principal end-use categories were emphasized by separating them out: Petroleum and products. and advanced technology products. Imports and exports both fell in 2020 due to the global pandemic but increased again in 2021. Through the early 1980s, the United States was still a net creditor with the world, meaning that the value of stock of U.S. owed assets abroad exceeded the value of U.S. liabilities to the rest of the word. Since then, persistent borrowing to finance current-account deficits has accumulated, resulting in a growing net debtor status. (See Figure 7-2)

- Imports of petroleum and petroleum products soared between 1990 and 2019. Largely due to COVID-19, imports fell substantially before increasing again in 2021. In early December 2018, the United States became a net exporter of oil thus breaking nearly 75 continuous years of dependence on foreign oil. Crude oil is refined into various petroleum products such as gasoline, diesel and jet fuel, waxes, and asphalt. (Tables 7-7, 7-8 and Table 11-3)

Table 7-6. U.S. Exports and Imports of Goods and Services

(Balance of payments basis; millions of dollars, seasonally adjusted.)

Year and month	Goods and services			Goods			Services		
	Exports	Imports	Balance	Exports	Imports	Balance	Exports	Imports	Balance
1975	132 585	120 181	12 404	107 088	98 185	8 903	25 497	21 996	3 501
1976	142 716	148 798	-6 082	114 745	124 228	-9 483	27 971	24 570	3 401
1977	152 301	179 547	-27 246	120 816	151 907	-31 091	31 485	27 640	3 845
1978	178 428	208 191	-29 763	142 075	176 002	-33 927	36 353	32 189	4 164
1979	224 131	248 696	-24 565	184 439	212 007	-27 568	39 692	36 689	3 003
1980	271 834	291 241	-19 407	224 250	249 750	-25 500	47 584	41 491	6 093
1981	294 398	310 570	-16 172	237 044	265 067	-28 023	57 354	45 503	11 851
1982	275 236	299 391	-24 156	211 157	247 642	-36 485	64 079	51 749	12 329
1983	266 106	323 874	-57 767	201 799	268 901	-67 102	64 307	54 973	9 335
1984	291 094	400 166	-109 072	219 926	332 418	-112 492	71 168	67 748	3 420
1985	289 070	410 950	-121 880	215 915	338 088	-122 173	73 155	72 862	294
1986	310 033	448 572	-138 538	223 344	368 425	-145 081	86 689	80 147	6 543
1987	348 869	500 552	-151 684	250 208	409 765	-159 557	98 661	90 787	7 874
1988	431 149	545 715	-114 566	320 230	447 189	-126 959	110 919	98 526	12 393
1989	487 003	580 144	-93 141	359 916	477 665	-117 749	127 087	102 479	24 607
1990	535 233	616 097	-80 864	387 401	498 438	-111 037	147 832	117 659	30 173
1991	578 344	609 479	-31 135	414 083	491 020	-76 937	164 261	118 459	45 802
1992	616 882	656 094	-39 212	439 631	536 528	-96 897	177 251	119 566	57 685
1993	642 863	713 174	-70 311	456 943	589 394	-132 451	185 920	123 780	62 141
1994	703 254	801 747	-98 493	502 859	668 690	-165 831	200 395	133 057	67 338
1995	794 387	890 771	-96 384	575 204	749 374	-174 170	219 183	141 397	77 786
1996	851 602	955 667	-104 065	612 113	803 113	-191 000	239 489	152 554	86 935
1997	934 453	1 042 726	-108 273	678 366	876 794	-198 428	256 087	165 932	90 155
1998	933 174	1 099 314	-166 140	670 416	918 637	-248 221	262 758	180 677	82 081
1999	969 867	1 228 485	-258 617	698 524	1 035 592	-337 068	271 343	192 893	78 450
2000	1 075 321	1 447 837	-372 517	784 940	1 231 722	-446 783	290 381	216 115	74 266
2001	1 005 654	1 367 165	-361 511	731 331	1 153 701	-422 370	274 323	213 465	60 858
2002	978 706	1 397 660	-418 955	698 036	1 173 281	-475 245	280 670	224 379	56 290
2003	1 020 418	1 514 308	-493 890	730 446	1 272 089	-541 643	289 972	242 219	47 754
2004	1 161 549	1 771 433	-609 883	823 584	1 488 349	-664 766	337 966	283 083	54 882
2005	1 286 022	2 000 267	-714 245	913 016	1 695 820	-782 804	373 006	304 448	68 558
2006	1 457 642	2 219 358	-761 716	1 040 905	1 878 194	-837 289	416 738	341 165	75 573
2007	1 653 548	2 358 922	-705 375	1 165 151	1 986 347	-821 196	488 396	372 575	115 821
2008	1 841 612	2 550 339	-708 726	1 308 795	2 141 287	-832 492	532 817	409 052	123 765
2009	1 583 053	1 966 827	-383 774	1 070 331	1 580 025	-509 694	512 722	386 801	125 920
2010	1 853 606	2 348 263	-494 658	1 290 273	1 938 950	-648 678	563 333	409 313	154 020
2011	2 127 021	2 675 646	-548 625	1 499 240	2 239 886	-740 646	627 781	435 761	192 020
2012	2 218 989	2 755 762	-536 773	1 562 578	2 303 749	-741 171	656 411	452 013	204 398
2013	2 293 457	2 755 334	-461 876	1 592 002	2 294 247	-702 244	701 455	461 087	240 368
2014	2 375 905	2 866 241	-490 336	1 633 986	2 385 480	-751 494	741 919	480 761	261 157
2015	2 263 907	2 764 352	-500 445	1 510 757	2 272 612	-761 855	753 150	491 740	261 410
2016	2 208 072	2 712 866	-504 794	1 455 704	2 208 211	-752 507	752 368	504 654	247 714
2017	2 352 546	2 902 669	-550 123	1 553 589	2 358 789	-805 200	798 957	543 880	255 077
2018	2 501 310	3 128 989	-627 679	1 674 330	2 561 667	-887 337	826 980	567 322	259 658
2019	2 528 262	3 105 127	-576 865	1 652 437	2 516 767	-864 331	875 825	588 359	287 466
2020	2 134 441	2 811 125	-676 684	1 428 798	2 350 825	-922 026	705 643	460 301	245 342
2021	2 556 637	3 401 686	-845 049	1 761 363	2 851 661	-1 090 298	795 274	550 025	245 249
2020									
January	205 091	250 543	-45 452	135 567	203 406	-67 839	69 524	47 137	22 387
February	204 819	246 458	-41 639	135 701	199 403	-63 702	69 118	47 055	22 063
March	187 490	234 647	-47 157	126 875	195 594	-68 718	60 615	39 053	21 561
April	150 074	203 033	-52 959	95 025	169 641	-74 616	55 049	33 392	21 657
May	146 108	201 023	-54 915	91 051	167 703	-76 652	55 056	33 320	21 736
June	158 805	209 480	-50 675	103 702	175 706	-72 004	55 103	33 774	21 329
July	170 908	231 651	-60 743	115 880	196 672	-80 792	55 028	34 979	20 049
August	174 287	238 020	-63 733	118 981	201 947	-82 966	55 306	36 073	19 233
September	178 063	240 689	-62 625	121 965	203 577	-81 613	56 099	37 111	18 987
October	182 732	246 410	-63 678	125 761	207 888	-82 127	56 971	38 522	18 450
November	185 186	252 494	-67 307	126 789	213 017	-86 227	58 397	39 477	18 920
December	190 877	256 678	-65 802	131 500	216 270	-84 770	59 377	40 408	18 969
2021									
January	197 546	261 373	-63 827	135 206	221 584	-86 378	62 340	39 789	22 551
February	193 412	258 707	-65 295	131 166	219 465	-88 299	62 246	39 242	23 004
March	207 372	275 441	-68 069	144 023	234 614	-90 591	63 349	40 827	22 522
April	207 642	273 367	-65 725	143 927	231 416	-87 489	63 715	41 951	21 764
May	210 278	276 912	-66 634	145 343	233 376	-88 033	64 935	43 536	21 399
June	212 326	283 684	-71 358	146 285	238 194	-91 909	66 041	45 490	20 551
July	214 122	283 504	-69 382	147 928	235 635	-87 707	66 194	47 869	18 325
August	215 841	287 267	-71 426	149 480	238 190	-88 710	66 361	49 077	17 284
September	211 618	289 953	-78 335	144 484	240 647	-96 163	67 134	49 306	17 828
October	225 898	294 053	-68 155	157 621	243 854	-86 233	68 277	50 199	18 078
November	228 145	306 121	-77 976	156 528	254 791	-98 263	71 617	51 330	20 287
December	232 437	311 304	-78 867	159 372	259 895	-100 523	73 065	51 409	21 656

Table 7-7. U.S. Exports of Goods by End-Use and Advanced Technology Categories

(Census basis, except as noted; billions of dollars; seasonally adjusted, except as noted.)

Year and month	Total exports of goods			Principal end-use category							Advanced technology products [1]
	Total, balance of payments basis	Net adjustments	Total, Census basis	Foods, feeds, and beverages	Industrial supplies and materials		Capital goods, except automotive	Automotive vehicles, engines, and parts	Consumer goods, except automotive	Other goods	
					Total	Petroleum and products					
1980	224.25	3.55	220.70	36.28	72.09	3.57	76.28	17.44	17.75	. . .	. . .
1981	237.04	3.31	233.74	38.84	70.19	4.56	84.17	19.69	17.70	. . .	. . .
1982	211.16	-1.12	212.28	32.20	64.05	6.87	76.50	17.23	16.13	. . .	. . .
1983	201.80	0.09	201.71	32.09	58.94	5.59	71.66	18.46	14.93	. . .	. . .
1984	219.93	1.18	218.74	32.20	64.12	5.43	77.01	22.42	15.09	. . .	. . .
1985	215.92	3.29	212.62	24.57	61.16	5.71	79.32	24.95	14.59	. . .	. . .
1986	223.34	-3.13	226.47	23.52	64.72	4.43	82.82	25.10	16.73	. . .	. . .
1987	250.21	-3.70	253.90	25.23	70.05	4.63	92.71	27.58	20.31	. . .	. . .
1988	320.23	-3.11	323.34	33.77	90.02	4.48	119.10	33.40	26.98	. . .	. . .
1989	359.92	-3.08	363.00	36.34	98.36	6.46	136.94	35.05	36.01	. . .	. . .
1990	387.40	-5.57	392.97	35.18	105.55	8.36	153.07	36.07	43.60	20.73	. . .
1991	414.08	-7.77	421.85	35.79	109.69	8.40	166.72	39.72	46.65	23.66	. . .
1992	439.63	-8.54	448.16	40.27	109.14	7.62	175.92	47.03	51.42	24.39	. . .
1993	456.94	-7.92	465.09	40.63	111.81	7.50	181.70	52.40	54.66	23.89	. . .
1994	502.86	-9.77	512.63	41.96	121.40	6.97	205.02	57.78	59.98	26.50	. . .
1995	575.20	-9.54	584.74	50.47	146.25	8.10	233.05	61.83	64.43	28.72	. . .
1996	612.11	-12.96	625.08	55.53	147.65	9.63	252.98	65.02	70.06	33.84	. . .
1997	678.37	-10.82	689.18	51.51	158.23	10.42	294.55	74.03	77.37	33.51	. . .
1998	670.42	-11.72	682.14	46.40	148.27	8.08	299.35	72.39	80.29	35.44	. . .
1999	698.52	-11.83	695.80	45.98	147.52	8.62	310.79	75.26	80.92	35.32	. . .
2000	784.94	-9.92	781.92	47.87	172.62	12.01	356.93	80.36	89.38	34.77	227.39
2001	731.33	-10.39	729.10	49.41	160.10	10.64	321.71	75.44	88.33	34.11	199.63
2002	698.04	-10.68	693.10	49.62	156.81	10.34	290.44	78.94	84.36	32.94	178.57
2003	730.45	-11.36	724.77	55.03	173.04	12.69	293.67	80.63	89.91	32.49	180.21
2004	823.58	-11.26	814.88	56.57	203.91	17.08	327.54	89.21	103.24	34.40	201.42
2005	913.02	-11.35	901.08	58.96	233.05	22.66	358.43	98.41	115.29	36.96	216.06
2006	1 040.91	-10.16	1 025.97	65.96	276.05	31.57	404.03	107.26	129.08	43.59	252.71
2007	1 165.15	-9.82	1 148.20	84.26	316.38	37.76	433.02	121.26	145.98	47.30	264.88
2008	1 308.80	20.06	1 287.44	108.35	388.03	67.18	457.66	121.45	161.28	50.67	270.13
2009	1 070.33	13.69	1 056.04	93.91	296.51	49.18	391.24	81.72	149.46	43.22	244.71
2010	1 290.28	10.30	1 278.50	107.72	391.66	70.83	447.54	112.01	165.23	54.34	273.31
2011	1 498.89	15.56	1 482.51	126.25	501.08	113.71	493.96	133.04	175.30	52.89	287.72
2012	1 562.63	15.99	1 545.82	133.05	501.18	123.46	527.18	146.16	181.68	56.58	305.01
2013	1 593.71	13.19	1 578.52	136.16	508.21	137.42	534.41	152.66	188.82	58.25	319.79
2014	1 635.56	29.12	1 621.87	143.72	505.81	145.24	551.49	159.81	199.00	62.04	336.48
2015	1 511.38	24.43	1 503.33	127.72	427.02	98.09	539.54	151.89	197.75	59.40	343.13
2016	1 457.39	20.41	1 451.46	130.52	397.27	88.85	519.74	150.40	193.66	59.88	345.52
2017	1 557.00	16.75	1 547.20	132.76	465.16	125.64	533.42	157.87	197.71	60.27	353.80
2018	1 676.91	11.13	1 665.79	133.14	541.24	174.78	563.20	158.83	206.02	63.35	368.58
2019	1 655.10	9.16	1 645.94	130.99	529.48	179.29	547.71	162.75	205.63	66.27	364.01
2020	1 432.22	3.70	1 428.52	139.28	466.16	130.84	520.60	127.92	174.77	56.70	303.17
2021	1 761.36	7.06	1 754.30	164.75	636.85	196.35	279.40	144.07	222.25	65.80	357.29
2019											
January	138.58	0.68	137.90	10.71	44.04	14.23	46.60	13.63	17.54	5.39	28.37
February	139.50	0.79	138.71	10.66	43.21	14.29	48.06	13.81	17.75	5.21	28.85
March	141.05	0.86	140.19	10.95	44.37	15.01	47.97	13.94	17.53	5.44	34.39
April	136.84	0.94	135.90	11.15	44.42	15.40	45.08	13.33	16.94	4.98	27.95
May	139.81	0.84	138.98	10.88	44.31	15.14	46.33	13.98	17.95	5.52	30.25
June	136.85	0.83	136.02	11.40	44.04	14.58	44.88	13.66	16.62	5.43	30.95
July	137.93	0.78	137.16	11.47	43.04	13.94	45.81	13.73	17.59	5.52	29.93
August	137.64	0.78	136.86	11.69	43.93	14.58	44.56	14.10	16.82	5.76	29.86
September	136.61	0.75	135.86	10.48	44.00	14.76	45.27	13.48	17.08	5.55	30.96
October	136.38	0.64	135.74	10.48	44.89	15.78	44.87	13.16	16.50	5.84	32.06
November	136.71	0.61	136.10	10.57	44.06	15.06	45.54	13.53	16.94	5.46	30.03
December	137.19	0.66	136.53	10.58	45.18	16.51	45.53	12.72	16.37	6.15	33.23
2020											
January	136.50	0.81	135.69	11.00	45.04	16.26	44.50	13.39	16.49	5.27	27.70
February	137.17	0.65	136.52	11.31	44.54	15.38	45.21	13.61	16.16	5.70	27.87
March	126.76	0.38	126.38	10.89	41.53	13.02	43.02	11.32	14.53	5.09	29.68
April	94.63	0.08	94.55	10.95	32.76	8.17	32.45	3.73	10.35	4.31	21.46
May	90.32	0.05	90.27	10.37	30.06	6.41	31.75	3.45	10.94	3.71	20.44
June	104.02	0.21	103.81	10.39	32.72	8.11	35.59	8.46	12.50	4.14	23.66
July	115.64	0.24	115.40	10.78	35.31	10.00	37.65	12.01	14.89	4.77	24.57
August	119.06	0.28	118.78	11.82	38.77	10.41	36.51	12.25	14.91	4.51	23.32
September	122.96	0.23	122.73	12.79	39.43	10.46	37.95	12.56	15.34	4.66	24.52
October	125.78	0.26	125.52	12.64	40.78	10.32	39.07	12.53	15.81	4.69	27.08
November	127.25	0.21	127.04	12.66	41.67	10.00	38.98	12.57	16.35	4.81	25.23
December	132.15	0.30	131.85	13.69	43.55	12.30	40.02	12.96	16.52	5.10	27.67
2021											
January	135.21	0.30	134.91	14.04	45.25	12.99	41.62	12.63	16.14	5.24	26.04
February	131.17	0.37	130.79	13.75	45.63	11.66	39.28	11.98	15.26	4.90	23.04
March	144.02	0.46	143.56	13.68	52.01	14.17	42.48	12.84	16.92	5.64	29.55
April	143.93	0.51	143.41	13.69	51.42	15.14	44.39	11.89	16.70	5.33	28.27
May	145.34	0.54	144.80	13.92	52.44	15.67	43.75	11.50	17.78	5.41	27.99
June	146.29	0.62	145.67	13.17	53.47	17.67	43.57	11.70	18.24	5.51	31.86
July	147.93	0.66	147.26	13.30	53.09	16.48	44.38	12.09	18.83	5.58	30.62
August	149.48	0.63	148.85	12.57	57.07	17.83	43.71	11.31	18.91	5.28	29.55
September	144.48	0.60	143.88	12.57	52.32	15.92	42.67	11.00	20.06	5.27	30.83
October	157.62	0.74	156.89	14.81	57.60	18.60	45.13	12.32	20.82	6.20	34.21
November	156.53	0.87	155.66	14.98	57.64	20.28	44.39	12.08	20.68	5.89	30.84
December	159.37	0.76	158.61	14.30	58.90	19.94	45.22	12.73	21.91	5.56	34.50

[1] Not seasonally adjusted.
. . . = Not available.

Table 7-8. U.S. Imports of Goods by End-Use and Advanced Technology Categories

(Census basis, except as noted; billions of dollars; seasonally adjusted, except as noted.)

Year and month	Total imports of goods			Principal end-use category							Advanced technology products [1]
	Total, balance of payments basis	Net adjustments	Total, Census basis	Foods, feeds, and beverages	Industrial supplies and materials		Capital goods, except automotive	Automotive vehicles, engines, and parts	Consumer goods, except automotive	Other goods	
					Total	Petroleum and products					
1980	249.75	4.23	245.52	18.55	124.96	...	30.72	28.13	34.22	...	...
1981	265.07	3.76	261.31	18.53	131.10	...	36.86	30.80	38.30	...	...
1982	247.64	3.70	243.94	17.47	107.82	...	38.22	34.26	39.66	...	...
1983	268.90	7.18	261.72	18.56	105.63	...	42.61	42.04	46.59	...	...
1984	332.42	1.91	330.51	21.92	122.72	...	60.15	56.77	61.19	...	...
1985	338.09	1.71	336.38	21.89	112.48	...	60.81	65.21	66.43	...	...
1986	368.43	2.75	365.67	24.40	101.37	...	71.86	78.25	79.43	...	...
1987	409.77	3.48	406.28	24.81	110.67	...	84.77	85.17	88.82	...	...
1988	447.19	5.26	441.93	24.93	118.06	...	101.79	87.95	96.42	...	...
1989	477.37	3.72	473.65	25.08	132.40	...	112.45	87.38	102.26	...	...
1990	498.34	2.36	495.98	26.65	143.41	62.16	116.04	87.69	105.29	16.09	...
1991	490.98	2.53	488.45	26.21	131.38	51.78	120.80	84.94	107.78	15.94	...
1992	536.53	3.80	532.66	27.61	138.64	51.60	134.25	91.79	122.66	17.71	...
1993	589.39	8.78	580.66	27.87	145.61	51.50	152.37	102.42	134.02	18.39	...
1994	668.69	5.33	663.26	30.96	162.11	51.28	184.37	118.27	146.27	21.27	...
1995	749.37	6.03	743.54	33.18	181.85	56.16	221.43	123.80	159.91	23.39	...
1996	803.11	8.04	795.29	35.71	204.48	72.75	228.07	128.94	171.98	26.10	...
1997	876.79	6.66	869.70	39.69	213.77	71.77	253.28	139.81	193.81	29.34	...
1998	918.64	5.28	911.90	41.24	200.14	50.90	269.45	148.68	217.00	35.39	...
1999	1 035.59	5.37	1 024.62	43.60	221.39	67.81	295.72	178.96	241.91	43.04	...
2000	1 231.72	6.40	1 218.02	45.98	298.98	120.28	347.03	195.88	281.83	48.33	222.08
2001	1 153.70	4.90	1 141.00	46.64	273.87	103.59	297.99	189.78	284.29	48.42	195.18
2002	1 173.28	3.35	1 161.37	49.69	267.69	103.51	283.32	203.74	307.84	49.08	195.15
2003	1 272.09	3.60	1 257.12	55.83	313.82	133.10	295.87	210.14	333.88	47.59	207.03
2004	1 488.35	7.39	1 469.70	62.14	412.77	180.46	343.58	228.16	372.94	50.11	238.28
2005	1 695.82	8.33	1 673.46	68.09	523.77	251.86	379.33	239.45	407.24	55.57	290.76
2006	1 878.19	7.44	1 853.94	74.94	601.99	302.43	418.26	256.63	442.64	59.49	290.76
2007	1 986.35	12.41	1 956.96	81.68	634.75	330.98	444.51	256.67	474.55	64.81	326.81
2008	2 141.29	33.97	2 103.64	89.00	779.48	453.28	453.74	231.24	481.64	68.54	331.18
2009	1 580.03	15.87	1 559.63	81.62	462.38	253.69	370.48	157.65	427.33	60.17	300.89
2010	1 938.95	25.09	1 913.86	91.75	603.10	336.11	449.39	225.10	483.23	61.30	354.25
2011	2 239.89	31.93	2 207.95	107.48	755.78	439.34	510.80	254.62	514.11	65.17	386.44
2012	2 303.75	27.48	2 276.27	110.27	730.64	415.17	548.71	297.78	516.92	71.95	396.23
2013	2 294.25	26.13	2 267.99	115.13	681.53	369.68	555.65	308.80	531.67	75.20	401.08
2014	2 385.48	29.12	2 356.36	125.88	667.02	334.00	594.14	328.64	557.09	83.59	422.10
2015	2 273.25	24.44	2 248.81	127.80	485.97	181.98	602.45	349.16	594.18	89.25	434.99
2016	2 207.19	20.41	2 186.79	130.01	443.27	146.61	589.68	349.92	583.10	90.80	464.47
2017	2 356.35	18.92	2 339.59	137.83	507.00	186.50	639.83	358.23	601.42	95.28	496.01
2018	2 555.66	19.52	2 536.15	147.26	574.63	225.28	690.91	371.11	645.37	106.87	496.06
2019	2 513.59	19.85	2 493.74	150.51	520.84	179.29	675.58	375.15	653.22	118.44	495.99
2020	2 346.10	15.27	2 330.84	154.33	478.77	130.84	643.53	309.16	638.75	106.30	491.30
2021	2 851.66	20.55	2 831.11	182.13	649.79	204.81	520.60	144.07	222.25	65.80	553.24
2019											
January	210.83	1.54	209.29	12.36	43.43	14.23	56.98	31.98	55.58	8.97	38.61
February	210.32	1.67	208.64	12.05	42.79	14.29	57.14	31.61	55.57	9.48	34.74
March	214.15	1.66	212.49	12.97	45.11	15.01	57.65	31.89	55.49	9.38	41.04
April	210.57	1.80	208.77	12.89	44.78	15.40	56.04	31.00	55.18	8.89	38.88
May	215.80	1.90	213.90	12.66	46.12	15.14	56.82	32.75	55.71	9.83	41.31
June	211.14	1.71	209.44	12.60	42.88	14.58	56.72	32.27	54.41	10.56	41.08
July	211.37	1.81	209.57	12.59	44.13	13.94	55.74	32.01	55.20	9.90	41.04
August	210.92	1.97	208.95	12.56	42.62	14.58	56.61	31.58	55.96	9.62	43.03
September	206.65	1.68	204.97	12.55	41.97	14.76	55.32	30.78	53.91	10.44	43.18
October	203.97	1.77	202.19	12.47	41.83	15.78	55.53	29.07	52.44	10.86	47.16
November	201.01	1.55	199.45	12.30	40.92	15.06	55.08	30.01	51.29	9.85	42.56
December	205.64	1.59	204.05	12.50	43.99	16.51	55.14	29.52	52.27	10.64	42.86
2020											
January	203.72	1.54	202.19	12.96	43.43	16.26	56.98	31.98	55.58	8.97	39.10
February	199.78	1.94	197.83	12.68	42.79	15.38	57.14	31.61	55.57	9.48	32.77
March	194.25	1.36	192.90	12.97	45.11	13.02	57.65	31.89	55.49	9.38	39.90
April	169.40	1.10	168.30	12.26	44.78	8.17	56.04	31.00	55.18	8.89	35.00
May	167.05	0.80	166.25	12.03	46.12	6.41	56.82	32.75	55.71	9.83	37.14
June	175.27	1.08	174.19	12.30	42.88	8.11	56.72	32.27	54.41	10.56	42.32
July	196.15	1.12	195.02	12.62	44.13	10.00	55.74	32.01	55.20	9.90	41.46
August	201.47	1.12	200.36	13.33	42.62	10.41	56.61	31.58	55.96	9.62	42.14
September	203.10	1.61	201.50	13.32	41.97	10.46	55.32	30.78	53.91	10.44	42.92
October	207.94	1.29	206.66	13.31	41.83	10.32	55.53	29.07	52.44	10.86	46.23
November	212.63	1.07	211.57	13.39	40.92	10.00	55.08	30.01	51.29	9.85	46.85
December	215.35	1.26	214.09	13.18	43.99	12.30	55.14	29.52	52.27	10.64	45.47
2022											
January	221.58	1.33	220.26	13.76	43.02	12.25	41.62	12.63	16.14	5.24	41.16
February	219.47	1.49	217.98	13.35	46.59	13.20	39.28	11.98	15.26	4.90	35.81
March	234.61	1.58	233.03	14.23	50.33	15.33	42.48	12.84	16.92	5.64	44.31
April	231.42	1.68	229.74	14.70	49.75	15.12	44.39	11.89	16.70	5.33	43.17
May	233.38	1.76	231.62	15.21	51.93	16.58	43.75	11.50	17.78	5.41	43.02
June	238.19	1.90	236.30	15.82	56.27	17.15	43.57	11.70	18.24	5.51	46.72
July	235.64	1.65	233.98	15.75	54.76	17.81	44.38	12.09	18.83	5.58	44.83
August	238.19	1.98	236.21	15.58	56.44	18.03	43.71	11.31	18.91	5.28	45.55
September	240.65	1.69	238.96	15.57	57.91	18.88	42.67	11.00	20.06	5.27	50.49
October	243.85	1.70	242.16	15.92	58.08	19.51	45.13	12.32	20.82	6.20	51.45
November	254.79	1.97	252.83	16.40	63.66	21.08	44.39	12.08	20.68	5.89	52.50
December	259.90	1.84	258.05	15.85	61.05	19.87	45.22	12.73	21.91	5.56	54.23

[1] Not seasonally adjusted.
. . . = Not available.

SECTION 7C: EXPORTS AND IMPORTS

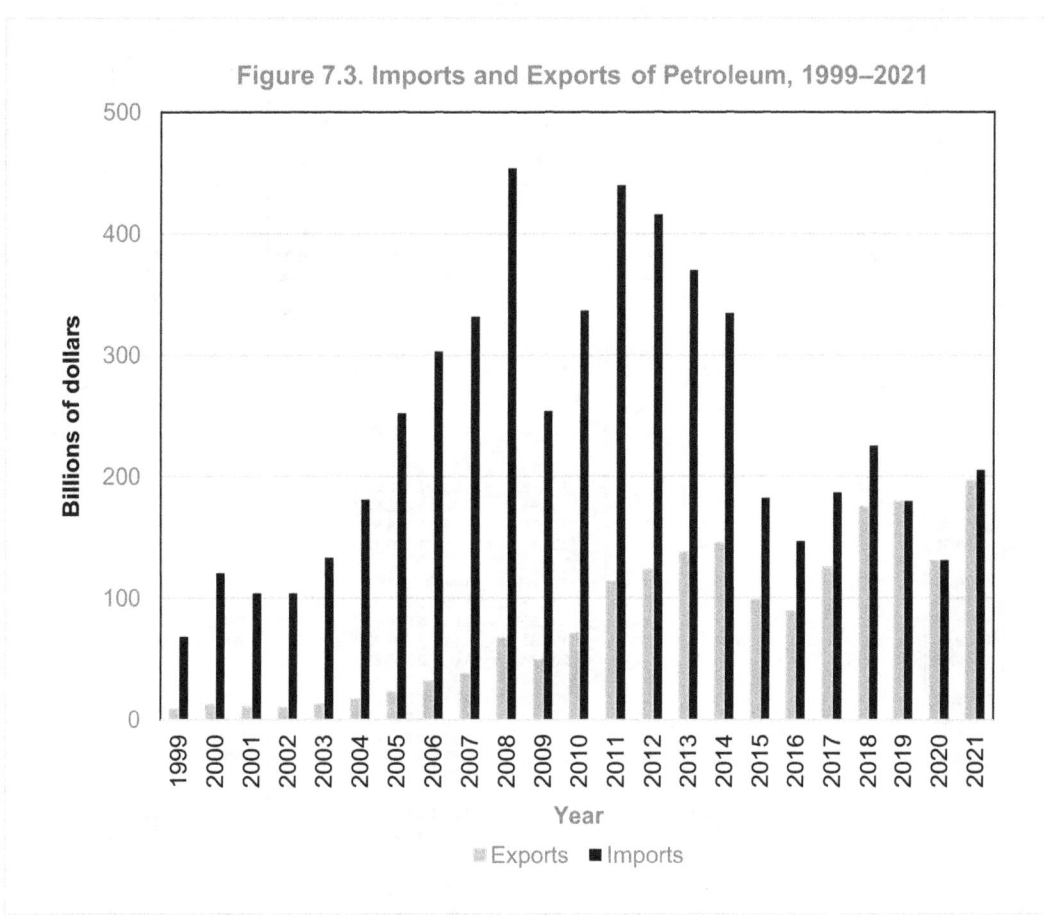

Figure 7.3. Imports and Exports of Petroleum, 1999–2021

- The United States maintains a trade deficit with China. This is largely due to cheaper labor in China and high demand in the United States for goods produced in China. The United States also has a trade deficit with Japan, Germany, Canada, and Mexico.

- Canada and Mexico are the principal trading partners of the United States, with relations governed by the North American Free Trade Agreement (NAFTA). NAFTA was signed in 1994. In July 2020, a new agreement was signed under the name of United States-Mexico-Canada Agreement (USMCA). In 2021, U.S. goods exports to those two countries brought in $584 billion, compared with $271 billion in exports to the European Union and $151 billion in exports to China. (Table 7-10)

- In 2021, U.S. goods imports from Canada and Mexico amounted to $742 billion, while imports to China equaled $504. (Table 7-11)

- Exports of total services increased 9.5 percent in 2021 after declining 18.5 percent in 2020. The disruption to the travel industry due to COVID-19 resulted in a decline of 63.6 percent in the export of travel services and an even greater decline in the import of travel services in 2020. (Table 7-12A)

Table 7-9. U.S. Exports and Imports of Goods by Principal End-Use Category in Constant Dollars

(Census basis; billions of 2012 chain-weighted dollars, except as noted; seasonally adjusted.)

Year and month	Exports							Imports						
	Total	Foods, feeds, and beverages	Industrial supplies and materials	Capital goods, except auto-motive	Auto-motive vehicles, engines, and parts	Consumer goods, except automotive	Other goods	Total	Foods, feeds, and beverages	Industrial supplies and materials	Capital goods, except auto-motive	Auto-motive vehicles, engines, and parts	Consumer goods, except automotive	Other goods
1995	712.38	101.87	253.24	196.62	70.95	76.73	42.73	928.46	50.57	551.80	132.86	144.68	166.43	28.41
1996	787.89	98.62	268.78	233.39	73.84	82.35	49.89	1 025.33	55.99	585.42	160.26	149.62	178.25	31.71
1997	893.07	98.34	290.85	285.92	83.32	90.44	49.54	1 167.72	61.36	625.78	200.68	161.75	202.94	35.87
1998	914.15	97.73	289.74	298.56	81.32	93.97	53.65	1 305.30	66.02	685.91	230.18	171.86	230.06	44.21
1999	943.54	101.08	291.84	314.72	84.21	94.63	53.61	1 462.44	72.10	696.85	264.02	205.26	258.33	53.94
2000	1 047.54	106.71	321.11	364.20	89.05	103.87	51.60	1 656.42	76.78	740.31	316.80	223.15	303.86	59.66
2001	982.79	109.54	306.65	328.47	83.25	102.71	50.69	1 601.50	79.75	736.67	279.63	216.30	308.87	60.23
2002	909.96	107.07	301.64	280.75	86.77	98.41	47.18	1 631.30	85.02	737.94	258.51	231.54	337.43	60.92
2003	933.89	108.87	314.83	286.68	88.18	103.78	45.28	1 718.52	92.87	767.45	274.39	237.52	366.47	58.04
2004	1 016.04	100.50	336.09	322.28	96.86	118.15	45.95	1 921.28	98.59	862.16	323.53	254.00	406.44	59.42
2005	1 088.65	105.18	346.06	352.41	105.73	130.19	47.33	2 058.36	102.24	906.53	360.64	263.89	439.58	63.74
2006	1 198.66	112.76	372.59	396.62	114.04	143.15	53.39	2 182.04	108.21	910.77	403.10	281.53	474.87	66.65
2007	1 293.52	119.92	397.85	426.95	127.59	157.91	55.12	2 223.92	109.13	883.13	429.06	278.75	501.57	70.64
2008	1 385.46	126.88	445.88	453.35	126.38	170.78	55.79	2 158.81	106.70	842.41	438.11	245.30	495.69	70.96
2009	1 198.93	123.67	396.47	388.40	84.63	157.41	50.08	1 820.18	99.87	705.51	363.71	166.20	441.07	64.98
2010	1 379.61	135.65	454.60	445.18	115.49	170.24	59.44	2 091.57	103.66	746.18	447.24	235.88	498.29	64.38
2011	1 486.80	132.97	494.94	493.40	135.10	177.18	53.20	2 221.30	106.79	758.64	508.41	259.44	521.70	65.37
2012	1 545.82	133.05	501.18	527.18	146.16	181.68	56.58	2 276.27	110.27	730.64	548.71	297.78	516.92	71.95
2013	1 589.07	132.72	523.08	533.01	151.88	190.81	58.61	2 301.79	113.99	706.16	563.42	309.75	532.57	75.79
2014	1 648.18	141.79	532.96	550.08	158.11	204.04	63.01	2 405.58	119.39	707.26	607.30	331.35	555.61	84.03
2015	1 638.51	144.92	531.77	541.31	150.43	207.29	64.84	2 519.22	123.48	709.91	630.14	358.82	597.23	92.50
2016	1 638.23	157.31	531.52	528.56	150.04	207.17	67.58	2 540.21	125.21	736.47	633.73	362.60	588.52	95.65
2017	1 708.37	158.87	578.80	540.09	157.01	213.96	66.37	2 643.65	128.09	744.30	688.84	373.07	607.15	99.30
2018	1 780.90	158.89	618.19	566.67	156.97	220.46	67.23	2 786.64	137.50	748.94	740.72	386.76	649.98	109.12
2019	1 781.96	155.74	636.91	549.46	159.99	218.34	71.19	2 781.59	140.31	711.34	732.95	393.15	659.42	122.24
2020	1 611.99	164.44	633.90	461.28	129.27	184.35	63.59	2 655.52	145.26	720.55	698.29	322.41	646.81	109.29
2021	1 754.30	164.75	636.85	520.60	144.07	222.25	65.80	2 831.11	182.13	649.79	761.14	347.09	766.32	124.65
2019														
January	150.68	12.91	53.87	46.77	13.29	18.78	5.86	234.59	11.59	62.19	61.07	33.14	56.08	9.19
February	149.76	12.57	51.85	48.00	13.44	18.77	5.60	231.70	11.09	58.71	61.48	32.99	55.80	9.70
March	150.64	12.93	52.28	47.78	13.57	18.86	5.78	234.15	12.01	59.84	62.17	33.21	55.19	9.83
April	145.46	13.36	51.44	44.93	12.98	18.26	5.28	229.75	11.44	59.13	60.19	32.46	55.38	9.36
May	148.93	13.58	51.54	46.09	13.49	19.06	5.84	235.42	11.45	60.79	61.34	34.17	55.90	10.05
June	146.24	13.10	52.79	45.00	13.25	17.18	5.78	232.62	11.60	57.93	61.47	33.72	54.87	10.86
July	147.82	12.96	51.56	45.79	13.62	18.59	5.91	234.47	11.74	60.39	60.24	33.93	56.03	10.32
August	148.64	13.75	53.44	44.45	13.84	17.91	6.21	235.02	11.73	59.19	61.76	33.28	56.88	10.07
September	147.77	12.71	53.71	45.01	13.24	18.01	6.00	231.03	12.11	57.90	60.84	32.44	54.95	10.59
October	148.45	12.50	54.84	44.97	13.08	17.76	6.33	226.88	11.93	57.75	61.07	30.65	52.73	10.90
November	148.33	12.59	54.12	45.53	13.35	17.74	5.90	225.51	11.87	56.97	60.40	31.60	52.40	10.32
December	149.25	12.77	55.48	45.16	12.85	17.42	6.70	230.46	11.76	60.56	60.91	31.55	53.21	11.05
2020														
January	146.11	12.64	54.33	44.28	13.03	17.32	5.57	225.77	12.27	57.08	60.18	30.65	53.50	10.05
February	148.83	13.38	56.36	44.25	13.12	16.89	6.18	221.30	11.62	56.84	56.90	31.88	52.11	10.14
March	141.21	13.31	54.75	42.49	11.11	15.57	5.63	220.80	12.11	61.52	58.68	29.28	48.65	10.22
April	112.17	13.81	50.06	32.39	3.66	11.01	5.11	196.25	11.63	68.76	52.65	14.02	45.77	7.84
May	107.83	13.30	46.44	31.83	3.31	11.69	4.39	194.66	11.30	73.58	51.99	9.36	47.19	7.62
June	119.93	12.78	47.27	35.46	8.17	13.12	4.75	201.75	11.50	57.89	54.02	19.31	51.35	7.43
July	132.47	12.88	49.64	37.82	11.85	15.69	5.46	224.41	11.93	62.32	58.71	27.06	54.61	8.89
August	135.53	14.09	53.82	36.60	11.89	15.80	5.15	227.78	12.51	56.76	58.86	28.88	57.87	9.77
September	138.16	14.73	53.86	37.73	12.30	15.92	5.25	227.76	12.42	53.76	59.66	32.10	56.71	9.18
October	142.16	14.38	55.65	39.30	12.44	16.77	5.27	233.67	12.34	56.20	61.29	33.20	58.08	8.89
November	142.44	14.16	56.05	39.07	12.36	17.24	5.29	239.65	12.91	57.17	62.41	32.43	61.12	9.64
December	145.16	14.97	55.67	40.06	13.02	17.35	5.54	241.74	12.73	58.68	62.95	34.25	59.85	9.62
2021														
January	134.91	14.04	45.25	41.62	12.63	16.14	5.24	220.26	13.76	43.02	59.85	32.03	62.93	8.67
February	130.79	13.75	45.63	39.28	11.98	15.26	4.90	217.98	13.35	46.59	59.93	28.15	60.51	9.44
March	143.56	13.68	52.01	42.48	12.84	16.92	5.64	233.03	14.23	50.33	62.63	30.20	65.65	10.00
April	143.41	13.69	51.42	44.39	11.89	16.70	5.33	229.74	14.70	49.75	63.44	29.10	63.28	9.48
May	144.80	13.92	52.44	43.75	11.50	17.78	5.41	231.62	15.21	51.93	62.28	29.12	63.28	9.79
June	145.67	13.17	53.47	43.57	11.70	18.24	5.51	236.30	15.82	56.27	63.16	28.67	62.24	10.14
July	147.26	13.30	53.09	44.38	12.09	18.83	5.58	233.98	15.75	54.76	63.03	29.42	60.73	10.31
August	148.85	12.57	57.07	43.71	11.31	18.91	5.28	236.21	15.58	56.44	63.16	28.06	62.85	10.12
September	143.88	12.57	52.32	42.67	11.00	20.06	5.27	238.96	15.57	57.91	65.31	26.11	62.80	11.26
October	156.89	14.81	57.60	45.13	12.32	20.82	6.20	242.16	15.92	58.08	65.04	27.44	64.06	11.63
November	155.66	14.98	57.64	44.39	12.08	20.68	5.89	252.83	16.40	63.66	65.89	28.46	66.31	12.10
December	158.61	14.30	58.90	45.22	12.73	21.91	5.56	258.05	15.85	61.05	67.43	30.33	71.68	11.71

Table 7-10. U.S. Exports of Goods by Selected Regions and Countries

(Census f.a.s. basis; millions of dollars, not seasonally adjusted.)

| Year and month | Total, all countries | Selected regions [1] | | | Selected countries | | | | |
		European Union, 15 countries	European Union, 28 countries	OPEC	Brazil	Canada	China	Japan	Mexico
1985	. . .	48 994	. . .	12 478	3 140	47 251	3 856	22 631	13 635
1986	. . .	53 154	. . .	10 844	3 885	45 333	3 106	26 882	12 392
1987	254 122	60 575	. . .	11 057	4 040	59 814	3 497	28 249	14 582
1988	322 426	75 755	. . .	13 994	4 266	71 622	5 022	37 725	20 629
1989	363 812	86 331	. . .	13 196	4 804	78 809	5 755	44 494	24 982
1990	393 592	98 027	. . .	13 703	5 048	83 674	4 806	48 580	28 279
1991	421 730	103 123	. . .	19 054	6 148	85 150	6 278	48 125	33 277
1992	448 165	102 958	. . .	21 960	5 751	90 594	7 419	47 813	40 592
1993	465 090	96 973	. . .	19 500	6 058	100 444	8 763	47 892	41 581
1994	512 625	102 818	. . .	17 868	8 102	114 439	9 282	53 488	50 844
1995	584 740	123 671	. . .	19 533	11 439	127 226	11 754	64 343	46 292
1996	625 073	127 710	. . .	22 275	12 718	134 210	11 993	67 607	56 792
1997	689 180	140 773	143 931	25 525	15 915	151 767	12 862	65 549	71 389
1998	682 139	149 035	151 967	25 154	15 142	156 604	14 241	57 831	78 773
1999	695 797	151 814	154 825	20 166	13 203	166 600	13 111	57 466	86 909
2000	781 918	165 065	168 181	19 078	15 321	178 941	16 185	64 924	111 349
2001	729 101	158 768	161 931	20 052	15 879	163 424	19 182	57 452	101 297
2002	693 101	143 691	146 621	18 812	12 376	160 923	22 128	51 449	97 470
2003	724 771	151 731	155 170	17 279	11 211	169 924	28 368	52 004	97 412
2004	814 875	168 572	171 230	22 256	13 886	189 880	34 428	53 569	110 731
2005	901 082	. . .	185 166	31 641	15 372	211 899	41 192	54 681	120 248
2006	1 025 967	. . .	211 887	38 658	18 887	230 656	53 673	58 459	133 722
2007	1 148 199	. . .	244 166	48 485	24 172	248 888	62 937	61 160	135 918
2008	1 287 442	. . .	271 810	64 880	32 299	261 150	69 733	65 142	151 220
2009	1 056 043	. . .	220 599	49 857	26 095	204 658	69 497	51 134	128 892
2010	1 278 495	. . .	239 591	54 226	35 418	249 256	91 911	60 472	163 665
2011	1 482 508	. . .	269 069	64 809	43 019	281 292	104 122	65 800	198 289
2012	1 545 821	. . .	265 373	81 727	43 771	292 651	110 517	69 976	215 875
2013	1 578 517	. . .	262 095	84 730	44 106	300 755	121 746	65 237	225 954
2014	1 621 874	. . .	276 274	82 533	42 432	312 817	123 657	66 892	241 007
2015	1 503 328	. . .	271 911	72 878	31 641	280 855	115 873	62 388	236 460
2016	1 451 460	. . .	269 650	71 053	30 193	266 734	115 595	63 247	230 229
2017	1 547 195	. . .	283 291	59 337	37 331	282 774	129 997	67 603	243 609
2018	1 665 787	. . .	318 490	59 282	39 400	299 732	120 281	75 164	265 968
2019	1 645 940	. . .	337 273	51 318	42 863	292 820	106 481	74 480	256 676
2020	1 428 518	. . .	232 686	. . .	34 580	256 212	124 544	64 018	211 441
2021	1 754 300	. . .	271 700	. . .	46 935	307 758	151 442	74 565	276 491
2019									
January	137 903	. . .	27 768	. . .	3 351	22 683	7 105	6 386	21 996
February	138 708	. . .	28 497	. . .	2 964	23 191	8 084	5 420	20 264
March	140 193	. . .	30 615	. . .	3 672	26 448	10 574	6 426	21 758
April	135 895	. . .	27 310	. . .	3 270	25 334	7 900	5 631	22 319
May	138 977	. . .	28 303	. . .	3 537	26 158	9 071	6 652	22 683
June	136 018	. . .	27 516	. . .	3 882	24 887	9 168	6 136	20 726
July	137 155	. . .	25 841	. . .	3 589	23 465	8 701	6 596	22 248
August	136 863	. . .	27 983	. . .	3 715	25 309	9 414	6 157	21 976
September	135 855	. . .	27 840	. . .	3 525	24 307	8 605	5 821	20 638
October	135 742	. . .	30 246	. . .	3 851	25 267	8 855	6 492	22 280
November	136 097	. . .	28 353	. . .	4 048	23 430	10 103	5 977	20 819
December	136 534	. . .	27 001	. . .	3 459	22 340	8 901	6 786	18 969
2020									
January	135 688	. . .	21 542	. . .	3 549	22 614	7 156	5 508	20 725
February	136 518	. . .	22 714	. . .	3 165	23 284	6 827	6 094	19 175
March	126 375	. . .	23 776	. . .	3 426	23 657	7 931	6 492	19 667
April	94 548	. . .	15 882	. . .	2 288	14 735	8 631	5 460	12 377
May	90 269	. . .	15 532	. . .	2 198	14 842	9 693	4 879	10 379
June	103 805	. . .	16 427	. . .	2 171	20 166	9 237	4 775	15 691
July	115 402	. . .	18 546	. . .	2 596	21 320	9 088	4 797	18 440
August	118 778	. . .	18 678	. . .	2 770	22 924	10 963	5 237	16 986
September	122 732	. . .	19 840	. . .	2 879	23 406	11 501	4 805	18 710
October	125 519	. . .	20 767	. . .	3 114	23 664	14 803	5 346	20 497
November	127 039	. . .	19 560	. . .	3 051	22 544	14 207	5 008	19 298
December	131 847	. . .	19 424	. . .	3 375	23 056	14 508	5 619	19 496
2021									
January	134 910	. . .	19 420	. . .	3 076	21 460	13 016	5 935	19 525
February	130 792	. . .	20 107	. . .	2 955	22 218	9 261	5 303	21 355
March	143 561	. . .	22 326	. . .	3 278	28 077	12 809	6 158	23 436
April	143 413	. . .	22 358	. . .	3 216	25 177	11 906	6 318	22 371
May	144 803	. . .	22 418	. . .	3 622	25 456	12 405	6 382	22 961
June	145 670	. . .	23 180	. . .	4 170	26 709	12 140	6 466	24 121
July	147 264	. . .	21 465	. . .	4 356	25 738	11 752	5 837	23 612
August	148 850	. . .	22 709	. . .	4 901	25 767	11 239	6 219	24 121
September	143 884	. . .	23 215	. . .	4 557	24 664	11 028	5 908	22 790
October	156 885	. . .	26 043	. . .	4 670	27 293	16 679	6 952	24 351
November	155 658	. . .	23 883	. . .	3 838	27 599	15 865	6 598	24 004
December	158 610	. . .	24 576	. . .	4 296	27 600	13 344	6 489	23 844

[1]See notes and definitions for definitions of regions.
. . . = Not available.

Table 7-11. U.S. Imports of Goods by Selected Regions and Countries

(Census Customs basis; millions of dollars, not seasonally adjusted.)

Year and month	Total, all countries	Selected regions [1]			Selected countries				
		European Union, 15 countries	European Union, 28 countries	OPEC	Brazil	Canada	China	Japan	Mexico
1985	. . .	67 822	. . .	22 801	7 526	69 006	3 862	68 783	19 132
1986	. . .	75 736	. . .	19 751	6 813	68 253	4 771	81 911	17 302
1987	406 241	81 188	. . .	23 952	7 865	71 085	6 294	84 575	20 271
1988	440 952	84 939	. . .	22 962	9 294	81 398	8 511	89 519	23 260
1989	473 211	85 153	. . .	30 611	8 410	87 953	11 990	93 553	27 162
1990	495 311	91 868	. . .	38 052	7 898	91 380	15 237	89 684	30 157
1991	488 453	86 481	. . .	32 644	6 717	91 064	18 969	91 511	31 130
1992	532 662	93 993	. . .	33 200	7 609	98 630	25 728	97 414	35 211
1993	580 656	97 941	. . .	31 739	7 479	111 216	31 540	107 246	39 918
1994	663 252	110 875	. . .	31 685	8 683	128 406	38 787	119 156	49 494
1995	743 545	131 871	. . .	35 606	8 833	144 370	45 543	123 479	62 100
1996	795 287	142 947	. . .	44 285	8 773	155 893	51 513	115 187	74 297
1997	869 703	157 528	160 896	44 025	9 625	167 234	62 558	121 663	85 938
1998	911 897	176 380	180 550	33 925	10 102	173 256	71 169	121 845	94 629
1999	1 024 616	195 227	200 053	41 977	11 314	198 711	81 788	130 864	109 721
2000	1 218 023	220 019	226 901	67 090	13 853	230 838	100 018	146 479	135 926
2001	1 140 998	220 057	226 568	59 754	14 466	216 268	102 278	126 473	131 338
2002	1 161 366	225 771	232 313	53 245	15 781	209 088	125 193	121 429	134 616
2003	1 257 121	244 826	253 042	68 344	17 910	221 595	152 436	118 037	138 060
2004	1 469 705	272 439	281 959	92 099	21 160	256 360	196 682	129 805	155 902
2005	1 673 454	298 879	309 628	127 169	24 436	290 384	243 470	138 004	170 109
2006	1 853 938	319 590	330 482	150 758	26 367	302 438	287 774	148 181	198 253
2007	1 956 961	. . .	354 409	165 651	25 644	317 057	321 443	145 463	210 714
2008	2 103 641	. . .	367 617	242 579	30 453	339 491	337 773	139 262	215 942
2009	1 559 625	. . .	281 801	111 602	20 070	226 248	296 374	95 804	176 654
2010	1 913 857	. . .	319 264	149 893	23 958	277 637	364 953	120 552	229 986
2011	2 207 954	. . .	368 464	191 470	31 737	315 325	399 371	128 928	262 874
2012	2 276 267	. . .	381 755	180 752	32 123	324 263	425 619	146 432	277 594
2013	2 267 987	. . .	387 510	152 688	27 541	332 504	440 430	138 575	280 556
2014	2 356 356	. . .	420 609	132 370	30 021	349 286	468 475	134 505	295 730
2015	2 248 811	. . .	427 810	66 241	27 474	296 305	483 202	131 445	296 433
2016	2 186 786	. . .	416 331	77 551	26 043	277 720	462 420	132 000	293 501
2017	2 339 591	. . .	434 866	72 165	29 462	299 065	505 165	136 411	312 667
2018	2 536 145	. . .	486 895	80 237	31 203	318 575	538 514	142 228	343 681
2019	2 491 700	. . .	514 996	45 640	30 934	318 589	449 111	143 591	356 094
2020	2 330 836	. . .	415 112	. . .	23 364	270 025	432 683	119 505	323 520
2021	2 831 111	. . .	490 444	. . .	31 264	357 788	504 935	134 860	384 649
2019									
January	209 287	. . .	39 369	. . .	2 546	23 348	41 303	11 536	27 558
February	208 642	. . .	37 748	. . .	2 289	22 815	33 028	11 428	27 485
March	212 490	. . .	44 745	. . .	2 579	27 549	31 079	13 058	31 112
April	208 773	. . .	45 223	. . .	2 477	26 732	34 499	12 980	30 229
May	213 895	. . .	45 456	. . .	3 097	29 196	39 024	11 998	31 908
June	209 435	. . .	41 403	. . .	2 611	27 644	38 733	11 913	30 193
July	209 567	. . .	45 921	. . .	3 096	26 761	41 237	12 883	29 954
August	208 949	. . .	43 171	. . .	2 410	26 634	40 956	12 422	30 887
September	204 965	. . .	41 544	. . .	2 439	26 852	39 867	10 822	29 274
October	202 192	. . .	46 710	. . .	2 390	28 534	39 795	11 575	30 933
November	199 452	. . .	41 211	. . .	2 400	25 240	36 173	11 448	29 061
December	204 052	. . .	42 496	. . .	2 600	27 284	33 418	11 527	27 500
2020									
January	202 185	. . .	35 071	. . .	2 092	25 287	32 952	10 458	28 207
February	197 834	. . .	32 780	. . .	1 554	24 339	22 582	10 665	28 910
March	192 895	. . .	41 354	. . .	2 121	25 081	19 641	12 173	29 887
April	168 299	. . .	31 663	. . .	1 662	14 937	30 740	9 846	15 774
May	166 247	. . .	27 196	. . .	1 761	15 843	36 324	7 383	14 859
June	174 192	. . .	30 228	. . .	1 909	20 315	37 293	6 641	25 673
July	195 023	. . .	33 930	. . .	1 925	22 329	40 482	8 271	28 882
August	200 355	. . .	34 356	. . .	1 702	23 748	40 613	9 698	29 558
September	201 496	. . .	35 645	. . .	1 797	24 595	41 017	9 941	29 792
October	206 655	. . .	36 824	. . .	2 301	24 853	44 672	11 254	32 789
November	211 566	. . .	36 646	. . .	1 942	24 065	44 732	11 687	29 826
December	214 090	. . .	39 420	. . .	2 598	24 632	41 634	11 486	29 364
2021									
January	220 255	. . .	35 743	. . .	1 768	24 743	38 870	10 394	29 147
February	217 978	. . .	35 763	. . .	1 713	25 233	33 871	9 240	27 337
March	233 032	. . .	40 485	. . .	2 168	29 838	39 988	12 152	33 451
April	229 739	. . .	40 448	. . .	2 339	27 504	37 409	12 436	32 153
May	231 615	. . .	39 923	. . .	2 427	29 062	38 508	11 458	31 354
June	236 299	. . .	43 065	. . .	2 824	32 181	39 819	11 314	33 011
July	233 984	. . .	42 211	. . .	3 050	29 834	40 316	12 243	31 904
August	236 211	. . .	42 263	. . .	2 781	30 967	42 896	12 376	32 075
September	238 961	. . .	41 114	. . .	3 300	29 944	47 385	10 544	32 037
October	242 159	. . .	42 548	. . .	3 003	31 605	47 987	10 455	34 324
November	252 826	. . .	44 366	. . .	2 845	33 829	48 361	10 743	34 605
December	258 051	. . .	42 514	. . .	3 046	33 049	49 525	11 506	33 252

[1]See notes and definitions for definitions of regions.
. . . = Not available.

Table 7-12A. U.S. Exports of Services: Recent Data

(Balance of payments basis, millions of dollars, seasonally adjusted.)

Year and month	Total services	Maintenance and repair services, n.i.e.	Transport	Travel for all purposes including education	Construction services	Insurance services	Financial services	Charges for the use of intellectual property n.i.e	Telecommunications, computer and information services	Other business services	Personal, cultural, and recreational services	Government goods and services, n.i.e.
1999	278 001	3 656	46 302	89 146	3 974	3 052	25 998	39 913	12 320	36 415	9 007	8 218
2000	298 023	4 423	49 462	96 872	1 993	3 631	29 192	43 476	12 250	38 217	9 351	9 156
2001	284 035	5 191	45 965	86 408	2 608	3 424	27 500	41 005	12 862	41 250	9 631	8 191
2002	288 059	5 368	45 954	79 625	3 128	4 415	29 903	44 815	12 487	44 625	10 089	7 653
2003	297 740	5 073	46 701	76 983	2 377	5 974	33 499	47 308	14 099	46 171	10 522	9 033
2004	344 536	5 181	54 419	85 648	2 253	7 314	42 767	56 943	15 009	51 609	11 409	11 985
2005	378 487	6 652	58 377	93 423	1 489	7 566	47 405	64 466	15 568	56 846	11 114	15 582
2006	423 086	7 106	64 026	96 148	1 856	9 445	56 522	70 999	17 242	65 990	14 532	19 222
2007	495 664	8 899	70 837	106 918	2 774	10 867	73 980	84 498	20 339	79 366	16 265	20 921
2008	540 791	9 362	78 237	117 030	4 072	13 491	79 897	89 672	23 892	89 975	16 080	19 084
2009	522 461	11 573	65 806	110 757	4 260	14 594	73 844	85 730	24 925	93 508	16 926	20 538
2010	582 041	13 111	76 357	130 315	2 951	14 854	86 512	94 968	26 556	99 595	17 612	19 210
2011	644 665	14 739	82 930	142 197	3 187	14 673	101 077	107 053	29 376	108 423	19 538	21 470
2012	684 823	14 944	88 238	153 921	3 234	15 978	105 419	107 869	33 522	118 451	21 098	22 148
2013	719 529	15 720	89 999	170 979	2 213	15 768	109 794	113 824	36 325	122 166	20 888	21 852
2014	756 705	17 978	90 687	180 265	2 070	16 277	119 933	116 380	38 629	132 240	22 551	19 693
2015	768 362	19 847	84 434	192 602	2 759	15 464	114 951	111 151	41 427	141 421	24 220	20 087
2016	780 530	21 587	81 779	192 868	1 690	16 249	114 762	112 981	43 122	153 089	23 626	18 777
2017	830 388	23 239	86 342	193 834	2 053	18 223	128 035	118 147	47 657	167 270	25 664	19 924
2018	862 433	27 948	93 251	196 465	2 948	17 904	132 420	118 875	49 653	177 261	23 759	21 949
2019	891 177	27 671	91 058	198 982	3 161	18 579	142 546	122 533	55 742	186 178	22 192	22 535
2020	726 433	13 196	57 168	72 481	2 395	20 277	151 033	115 558	56 456	195 046	20 820	22 003
2021	795 273	12 526	65 777	70 214	3 129	22 741	171 740	124 613	59 797	217 426	23 915	23 394
2019												
January	71 905	2 308	7 734	16 299	290	1 531	11 548	9 411	4 226	14 966	1 822	1 768
February	72 674	2 239	7 709	16 720	286	1 512	11 777	9 648	4 310	14 862	1 804	1 807
March	73 627	2 270	7 665	16 895	274	1 487	11 975	9 967	4 436	15 024	1 831	1 802
April	74 375	2 140	7 735	16 652	255	1 453	12 005	10 369	4 605	15 452	1 905	1 804
May	75 413	2 230	7 545	17 057	249	1 460	12 031	10 621	4 721	15 709	1 937	1 853
June	75 382	2 282	7 531	16 761	258	1 507	11 886	10 723	4 782	15 796	1 929	1 926
July	74 585	2 292	7 451	16 265	282	1 593	11 621	10 677	4 790	15 713	1 880	2 022
August	74 595	2 354	7 543	16 265	288	1 636	11 572	10 580	4 790	15 674	1 846	2 045
September	74 438	2 404	7 513	16 216	278	1 636	11 672	10 433	4 781	15 680	1 829	1 996
October	75 015	2 559	7 531	16 602	251	1 592	12 047	10 236	4 764	15 731	1 828	1 874
November	74 782	2 467	7 514	16 606	231	1 578	12 192	10 036	4 762	15 771	1 809	1 816
December	74 386	2 125	7 586	16 642	218	1 594	12 221	9 832	4 775	15 798	1 773	1 822
2020												
January	70 897	1 643	7 555	13 909	211	1 640	12 083	9 624	4 803	15 814	1 719	1 896
February	70 479	1 332	7 362	14 094	208	1 651	12 128	9 466	4 775	15 849	1 684	1 929
March	62 174	1 204	5 431	8 287	207	1 629	12 335	9 130	4 690	15 903	1 510	1 847
April	56 144	1 155	3 747	4 861	209	1 572	12 160	8 841	4 550	15 976	1 353	1 720
May	55 926	1 163	3 526	4 724	210	1 561	12 247	8 862	4 468	16 085	1 365	1 714
June	56 157	1 116	3 724	4 351	210	1 596	12 379	8 966	4 445	16 231	1 387	1 751
July	56 546	967	3 910	3 756	208	1 677	12 304	9 217	4 482	16 412	1 765	1 848
August	57 212	871	4 058	3 371	202	1 739	12 448	9 551	4 575	16 508	1 999	1 891
September	58 334	911	4 179	3 328	190	1 780	12 756	9 974	4 724	16 519	2 086	1 886
October	59 595	900	4 321	3 613	174	1 802	13 055	10 494	4 931	16 445	2 023	1 837
November	61 095	954	4 602	3 984	175	1 814	13 473	10 738	5 020	16 530	1 978	1 827
December	61 874	980	4 752	4 203	191	1 815	13 664	10 696	4 994	16 772	1 950	1 856
2021												
January	62 340	995	4 833	4 340	224	1 806	13 911	10 353	4 851	17 173	1 938	1 917
February	62 246	969	4 627	4 312	243	1 797	14 029	10 099	4 781	17 514	1 928	1 948
March	63 349	983	4 951	4 675	248	1 789	14 196	10 009	4 784	17 795	1 964	1 954
April	63 715	1 028	5 064	4 670	240	1 781	13 999	10 084	4 859	18 017	2 046	1 928
May	64 935	1 041	5 294	5 264	240	1 801	14 093	10 146	4 894	18 162	2 083	1 916
June	66 041	1 063	5 532	5 685	248	1 849	14 357	10 196	4 889	18 229	2 074	1 919
July	66 194	1 092	5 497	5 850	265	1 925	14 351	10 234	4 843	18 219	2 019	1 898
August	66 361	1 094	5 516	5 661	277	1 976	14 481	10 338	4 873	18 259	1 984	1 902
September	67 134	1 116	5 495	5 902	284	2 004	14 610	10 507	4 979	18 350	1 967	1 921
October	68 277	1 088	5 697	6 310	286	2 007	14 574	10 743	5 159	18 491	1 969	1 954
November	71 617	1 021	6 387	8 475	287	2 005	14 614	10 906	5 346	18 585	1 971	2 019
December	73 065	1 037	6 886	9 071	287	2 000	14 526	10 998	5 539	18 632	1 972	2 118

n.i.e = Not included elsewhere.

Table 7-12B. U.S. Exports of Services: Historical Data

(Balance of payments basis, millions of dollars, seasonally adjusted.)

Year	Total	Travel	Passenger fares	Other transportation	Royalties and license fees	Other private services (financial, professional, etc.)	Transfers under U.S. military sales contracts [1]	U.S. government miscellaneous services
1960	6 290	919	175	1 607	837	570	2 030	153
1961	6 295	947	183	1 620	906	607	1 867	164
1962	6 941	957	191	1 764	1 056	585	2 193	195
1963	7 348	1 015	205	1 898	1 162	613	2 219	236
1964	7 840	1 207	241	2 076	1 314	651	2 086	265
1965	8 824	1 380	271	2 175	1 534	714	2 465	285
1966	9 616	1 590	317	2 333	1 516	814	2 721	326
1967	10 667	1 646	371	2 426	1 747	951	3 191	336
1968	11 917	1 775	411	2 548	1 867	1 024	3 939	353
1969	12 806	2 043	450	2 652	2 019	1 160	4 138	343
1970	14 171	2 331	544	3 125	2 331	1 294	4 214	332
1971	16 358	2 534	615	3 299	2 545	1 546	5 472	347
1972	17 841	2 817	699	3 579	2 770	1 764	5 856	357
1973	19 832	3 412	975	4 465	3 225	1 985	5 369	401
1974	22 591	4 032	1 104	5 697	3 821	2 321	5 197	419
1975	25 497	4 697	1 039	5 840	4 300	2 920	6 256	446
1976	27 971	5 742	1 229	6 747	4 353	3 584	5 826	489
1977	31 485	6 150	1 366	7 090	4 920	3 848	7 554	557
1978	36 353	7 183	1 603	8 136	5 885	4 717	8 209	620
1979	39 692	8 441	2 156	9 971	6 184	5 439	6 981	520
1980	47 584	10 588	2 591	11 618	7 085	6 276	9 029	398
1981	57 354	12 913	3 111	12 560	7 284	10 250	10 720	517
1982	64 079	12 393	3 174	12 317	5 603	17 444	12 572	576
1983	64 307	10 947	3 610	12 590	5 778	18 192	12 524	666
1984	71 168	17 177	4 067	13 809	6 177	19 255	9 969	714
1985	73 155	17 762	4 411	14 674	6 678	20 035	8 718	878
1986	86 689	20 385	5 582	15 438	8 113	28 027	8 549	595
1987	98 661	23 563	7 003	17 027	10 174	29 263	11 106	526
1988	110 919	29 434	8 976	19 311	12 139	31 111	9 284	664
1989	127 087	36 205	10 657	20 526	13 818	36 729	8 564	587
1990	147 832	43 007	15 298	22 042	16 634	40 251	9 932	668
1991	164 261	48 385	15 854	22 631	17 819	47 748	11 135	690
1992	177 252	54 742	16 618	21 531	20 841	50 292	12 387	841
1993	185 920	57 875	16 528	21 958	21 695	53 510	13 471	883
1994	200 395	58 417	16 997	23 754	26 712	60 841	12 787	887
1995	219 183	63 395	18 909	26 081	30 289	65 048	14 643	818
1996	239 489	69 809	20 422	26 074	32 470	73 340	16 446	928
1997	256 087	73 426	20 868	27 006	33 228	83 929	16 675	955
1998	262 758	71 325	20 098	25 604	35 626	91 774	17 405	926
1999	268 790	75 161	19 425	23 792	47 731	96 812	5 211	657

Note: The category "Royalties and license fees" is the earlier terminology for the category called "Charges for the use of intellectual property n.i.e" in the revised and updated data shown in Tables 7-15A/7-16A. Other categories differ in both title and content; see the Notes and Definitions.

[1] Contains goods that cannot be separately identified.

Table 7-13A. U.S. Imports of Services: Recent Data

(Balance of payments basis, millions of dollars, seasonally adjusted.)

Year and month	Total services	Maintenance and repair services, n.i.e.	Transport	Travel for all purposes including education	Construction services	Insurance services	Financial services	Charges for the use of intellectual property n.i.e	Telecommunications, computer and information services	Other business services	Personal, cultural, and recreational services	Government goods and services, n.i.e.
1999	196 742	1 193	49 892	58 864	1 524	9 389	12 489	12 845	14 664	19 999	1 670	14 212
2000	220 927	2 316	58 526	64 174	1 447	11 284	16 445	16 139	14 128	20 306	1 645	14 516
2001	222 039	1 821	56 571	60 525	1 870	16 706	15 982	16 207	14 012	21 204	1 820	15 322
2002	233 480	2 016	55 398	59 017	2 616	21 927	15 214	18 981	13 214	24 027	1 719	19 353
2003	252 340	2 043	61 084	61 244	1 974	25 233	15 766	18 653	14 928	25 748	2 049	23 619
2004	290 609	2 181	71 954	70 332	2 303	29 089	19 043	22 818	16 382	28 026	2 183	26 296
2005	312 225	2 730	78 796	74 112	1 295	28 710	21 971	24 127	18 404	32 076	2 550	27 454
2006	349 329	4 091	82 348	78 375	1 650	39 382	27 005	23 076	20 850	41 378	3 822	27 353
2007	385 464	4 590	86 097	82 606	2 570	47 166	33 768	24 615	23 660	48 455	3 678	28 260
2008	420 650	5 128	92 837	84 317	3 526	58 444	29 519	27 764	26 138	59 675	4 421	28 880
2009	407 538	5 257	75 784	82 512	3 667	63 965	24 900	29 421	26 038	59 517	5 016	31 460
2010	436 456	5 857	88 394	85 166	2 578	63 452	27 215	31 116	29 421	65 903	5 393	31 960
2011	458 188	7 168	95 027	86 623	3 025	58 277	30 312	32 911	32 832	74 082	6 636	31 293
2012	469 610	7 078	99 323	90 340	3 340	58 747	28 736	35 061	33 285	78 678	7 160	27 861
2013	465 819	6 674	94 434	91 119	2 583	52 993	29 284	35 295	35 868	84 024	8 205	25 341
2014	490 932	6 732	99 810	96 248	2 314	52 760	32 770	37 562	38 461	90 716	9 323	24 236
2015	497 755	8 084	99 557	102 664	3 012	49 842	32 594	35 178	38 815	95 119	11 358	21 531
2016	511 898	7 595	92 391	109 155	1 768	52 070	32 672	41 974	39 720	100 505	12 544	21 503
2017	544 836	6 796	96 515	117 972	1 950	50 889	36 649	44 405	43 091	106 991	17 530	22 047
2018	562 069	7 133	106 303	126 008	3 151	43 735	39 249	43 933	42 558	107 834	19 190	22 975
2019	588 359	7 823	107 458	134 594	1 327	51 547	40 350	42 733	43 720	113 584	21 140	24 083
2020	466 537	6 203	72 763	34 159	1 131	57 673	45 314	47 708	39 728	112 979	24 325	24 553
2021	550 025	7 982	105 255	56 851	1 495	59 377	49 529	43 342	43 142	129 601	28 304	25 147
2019												
January	48 020	626	9 305	10 877	164	3 716	3 351	3 743	3 517	9 134	1 685	1 901
February	47 887	632	9 007	11 056	103	3 726	3 246	3 700	3 530	9 178	1 711	1 997
March	48 360	712	9 017	11 124	82	3 867	3 380	3 625	3 574	9 242	1 734	2 004
April	48 743	648	8 858	11 406	100	4 139	3 369	3 517	3 648	9 326	1 755	1 977
May	49 057	646	9 059	11 144	111	4 323	3 443	3 465	3 688	9 430	1 764	1 985
June	50 164	670	8 975	12 118	115	4 418	3 393	3 466	3 694	9 555	1 759	2 000
July	49 432	663	8 983	11 186	112	4 426	3 409	3 521	3 666	9 700	1 741	2 024
August	49 339	636	8 874	11 116	110	4 459	3 402	3 552	3 655	9 754	1 743	2 038
September	49 017	642	8 811	10 849	108	4 518	3 345	3 558	3 661	9 717	1 764	2 043
October	49 449	636	8 861	11 278	107	4 604	3 307	3 539	3 683	9 588	1 805	2 040
November	49 345	653	8 758	11 247	107	4 661	3 322	3 527	3 699	9 502	1 832	2 037
December	49 546	660	8 950	11 191	107	4 689	3 381	3 521	3 706	9 459	1 846	2 036
2020												
January	48 031	555	8 824	9 018	116	4 614	3 782	4 498	3 426	9 288	1 889	2 020
February	48 373	529	9 323	8 452	115	4 691	3 784	4 933	3 336	9 271	1 915	2 024
March	39 525	478	6 227	3 536	107	4 697	3 999	4 041	3 273	9 210	1 926	2 031
April	33 618	441	4 585	733	94	4 635	3 750	3 011	3 240	9 163	1 923	2 043
May	33 570	459	4 495	759	83	4 656	3 759	3 003	3 213	9 157	1 934	2 051
June	33 876	471	4 727	768	74	4 761	3 737	3 003	3 194	9 135	1 956	2 050
July	34 855	514	5 009	1 037	67	4 950	3 630	3 280	3 182	9 115	2 030	2 042
August	35 915	522	5 366	1 160	69	5 043	3 562	3 629	3 212	9 224	2 087	2 041
September	37 292	522	5 632	1 328	79	5 040	3 689	4 081	3 284	9 461	2 129	2 048
October	39 541	538	5 901	2 110	98	4 940	3 844	4 667	3 399	9 827	2 155	2 061
November	40 697	565	6 180	2 387	111	4 856	3 934	4 906	3 470	10 038	2 179	2 070
December	41 245	610	6 493	2 871	120	4 789	3 843	4 657	3 498	10 090	2 201	2 073
2021												
January	39 789	658	6 386	2 580	123	4 737	3 791	3 764	3 481	9 980	2 220	2 070
February	39 242	715	6 668	2 394	124	4 705	3 761	3 114	3 478	9 959	2 253	2 073
March	40 827	677	7 568	2 968	124	4 692	3 891	2 973	3 506	10 048	2 300	2 082
April	41 951	640	7 878	3 173	121	4 698	3 849	3 340	3 547	10 246	2 361	2 097
May	43 536	650	8 003	3 998	117	4 752	3 903	3 564	3 550	10 499	2 392	2 107
June	45 490	631	8 740	4 611	111	4 852	4 055	3 645	3 534	10 807	2 392	2 112
July	47 869	648	9 086	5 465	104	5 001	4 132	4 298	3 492	11 169	2 361	2 112
August	49 077	681	9 745	5 742	106	5 111	4 242	4 085	3 515	11 387	2 354	2 109
September	49 306	662	9 778	6 079	117	5 182	4 358	3 593	3 601	11 460	2 371	2 104
October	50 199	681	9 917	6 488	138	5 216	4 444	3 668	3 752	11 389	2 411	2 096
November	51 330	676	10 497	6 818	152	5 224	4 580	3 677	3 835	11 341	2 438	2 093
December	51 409	663	10 989	6 534	158	5 206	4 522	3 621	3 851	11 317	2 451	2 095

n.i.e = Not included elsewhere.

Table 7-13B. U.S. Imports of Services: Historical Data

(Balance of payments basis, millions of dollars, seasonally adjusted.)

Year	Total	Travel	Passenger fares	Other transportation	Royalties and license fees	Other private services (financial, professional, etc.)	Direct defense expenditures [1]	U.S. government miscellaneous services
1960	7 674	1 750	513	1 402	74	593	3 087	254
1961	7 671	1 785	506	1 437	89	588	2 998	268
1962	8 092	1 939	567	1 558	100	528	3 105	296
1963	8 362	2 114	612	1 701	112	493	2 961	370
1964	8 619	2 211	642	1 817	127	527	2 880	415
1965	9 111	2 438	717	1 951	135	461	2 952	457
1966	10 494	2 657	753	2 161	140	506	3 764	513
1967	11 863	3 207	829	2 157	166	565	4 378	561
1968	12 302	3 030	885	2 367	186	668	4 535	631
1969	13 322	3 373	1 080	2 455	221	751	4 856	586
1970	14 520	3 980	1 215	2 843	224	827	4 855	576
1971	15 400	4 373	1 290	3 130	241	956	4 819	592
1972	16 868	5 042	1 596	3 520	294	1 043	4 784	589
1973	18 843	5 526	1 790	4 694	385	1 180	4 629	640
1974	21 379	5 980	2 095	5 942	346	1 262	5 032	722
1975	21 996	6 417	2 263	5 708	472	1 551	4 795	789
1976	24 570	6 856	2 568	6 852	482	2 006	4 895	911
1977	27 640	7 451	2 748	7 972	504	2 190	5 823	951
1978	32 189	8 475	2 896	9 124	671	2 573	7 352	1 099
1979	36 689	9 413	3 184	10 906	831	2 822	8 294	1 239
1980	41 491	10 397	3 607	11 790	724	2 909	10 851	1 214
1981	45 503	11 479	4 487	12 474	650	3 562	11 564	1 287
1982	51 749	12 394	4 772	11 710	795	8 159	12 460	1 460
1983	54 973	13 149	6 003	12 222	943	8 001	13 087	1 568
1984	67 748	22 913	5 735	14 843	1 168	9 040	12 516	1 534
1985	72 862	24 558	6 444	15 643	1 170	10 203	13 108	1 735
1986	80 147	25 913	6 505	17 766	1 401	13 146	13 730	1 686
1987	90 787	29 310	7 283	19 010	1 857	16 485	14 950	1 893
1988	98 526	32 114	7 729	20 891	2 601	17 667	15 604	1 921
1989	102 479	33 416	8 249	22 172	2 528	18 930	15 313	1 871
1990	117 659	37 349	10 531	24 966	3 135	22 229	17 531	1 919
1991	118 459	35 322	10 012	24 975	4 035	25 590	16 409	2 116
1992	119 566	38 552	10 603	23 767	5 161	25 386	13 835	2 263
1993	123 779	40 713	11 410	24 524	5 032	27 760	12 086	2 255
1994	133 057	43 782	13 062	26 019	5 852	31 565	10 217	2 560
1995	141 397	44 916	14 663	27 034	6 919	35 199	10 043	2 623
1996	152 554	48 078	15 809	27 403	7 837	39 679	11 061	2 687
1997	165 932	52 051	18 138	28 959	9 161	43 154	11 707	2 762
1998	180 677	56 483	19 971	30 363	11 235	47 591	12 185	2 849
1999	195 172	59 332	20 946	31 494	13 302	55 885	11 849	2 364

Note: The category "Royalties and license fees" is the earlier terminology for the category called "Charges for the use of intellectual property n.i.e" in the revised and updated data shown in Tables 7-15A/7-16A. Other categories differ in both title and content; see the Notes and Definitions.

[1]Contains goods that cannot be separately identified.

Table 7-14. U.S. Export and Import Price Indexes by End-Use Category

(2000 = 100, not seasonally adjusted.)

Year and month	Exports			Imports		
	All commodities	Agricultural	Nonagricultural	All commodities	Petroleum [1]	Nonpetroleum
1990	95.5	105.1	94.4	94.0	75.5	97.1
1991	96.3	103.4	95.4	94.2	67.3	98.7
1992	96.3	102.5	95.7	94.9	62.9	100.0
1993	96.9	104.4	96.2	94.6	57.7	100.6
1994	98.9	109.4	98.0	96.2	54.3	103.2
1995	103.9	119.0	102.5	100.6	59.8	107.2
1996	104.5	132.6	101.6	101.6	71.1	106.4
1997	103.1	120.6	101.3	99.1	66.0	104.1
1998	99.7	108.8	98.8	93.1	44.8	100.4
1999	98.4	101.1	98.2	93.9	60.1	99.0
2000	100.0	100.0	100.0	100.0	100.0	100.0
2001	99.2	101.2	99.0	96.5	82.8	98.5
2002	98.2	103.2	97.8	94.1	85.3	96.2
2003	99.7	112.3	98.8	96.9	103.2	97.3
2004	103.6	123.4	102.1	102.3	134.6	99.8
2005	106.9	121.0	105.9	110.0	185.1	102.5
2006	110.7	125.8	109.6	115.4	223.3	104.2
2007	116.1	150.9	113.6	120.2	249.1	107.0
2008	123.1	183.5	118.8	134.1	343.2	112.7
2009	117.4	160.0	114.3	118.6	219.9	108.0
2010	123.1	172.6	119.6	126.8	282.2	111.0
2011	133.0	211.0	127.5	140.6	385.1	115.9
2012	133.5	216.1	127.6	141.0	384.0	116.3
2013	133.0	219.7	126.7	139.5	374.2	115.6
2014	132.3	213.8	126.3	138.0	353.2	115.7
2015	123.9	185.4	119.3	123.9	190.8	112.5
2016	119.9	175.5	115.7	119.8	153.1	110.8
2017	122.8	178.2	118.6	123.3	193.9	112.0
2018	126.9	179.3	122.9	127.1	236.6	113.5
2019	125.9	178.5	121.8	125.5	230.4	112.3
2020	122.4	178.0	118.1	122.4	162.7	112.6
2021	139.4	221.6	133.2	133.2	261.2	118.9
2018						
January	125.6	178.5	121.5	126.5	229.6	113.3
February	125.8	179.5	121.7	126.8	227.1	113.7
March	126.3	185.2	121.8	126.5	221.6	113.7
April	126.9	183.1	122.6	127.1	231.2	113.8
May	127.8	186.0	123.3	128.2	248.4	113.9
June	128.0	184.2	123.7	128.2	255.4	113.5
July	127.4	174.7	123.8	128.1	256.8	113.4
August	127.3	175.4	123.6	127.6	251.5	113.1
September	127.3	173.2	123.8	127.7	251.5	113.2
October	127.9	173.0	124.4	128.3	258.9	113.4
November	126.9	176.0	123.1	126.2	220.2	113.5
December	126.1	182.6	121.7	124.4	186.4	113.7
2019						
January	125.3	178.7	121.2	124.6	200.9	113.0
February	126.1	179.0	122.1	125.9	221.3	113.2
March	127.0	180.7	122.9	126.6	235.5	113.2
April	127.1	178.1	123.2	126.8	246.3	112.7
May	126.7	176.2	122.9	127.0	255.7	112.4
June	126.0	180.5	121.8	125.6	236.6	112.0
July	126.2	180.8	122.0	125.6	237.3	111.9
August	125.5	176.5	121.6	124.9	226.7	111.8
September	125.1	173.6	121.4	125.0	228.8	111.8
October	125.1	176.5	121.1	124.5	223.4	111.7
November	125.2	180.7	121.0	124.7	225.3	111.8
December	125.0	180.5	120.7	125.0	227.0	112.0
2020						
January	125.8	184.2	121.4	125.2	227.9	112.1
February	124.3	178.8	120.1	124.3	207.5	112.3
March	122.5	176.3	118.4	121.3	151.3	112.1
April	118.2	170.4	114.3	118.2	102.3	111.5
May	118.2	169.7	114.3	119.0	117.1	111.6
June	120.3	172.4	116.3	120.6	142.6	111.9
July	121.5	175.2	117.4	122.1	166.1	112.1
August	122.1	171.3	118.4	123.2	171.7	113.0
September	122.8	176.1	118.7	123.4	161.2	113.7
October	123.0	182.2	118.5	123.3	160.9	113.6
November	124.0	188.5	119.1	123.4	165.0	113.6
December	125.5	190.3	120.6	124.6	179.0	114.1
2021						
January	128.9	201.8	123.4	126.5	196.8	115.1
February	131.0	207.3	125.3	128.0	217.9	115.7
March	134.3	212.3	128.4	129.9	237.1	116.7
April	135.9	213.8	130.0	131.1	243.0	117.6
May	139.0	226.9	132.4	132.8	255.3	118.8
June	140.6	230.0	133.9	134.2	267.6	119.6
July	142.1	226.4	135.7	134.6	273.4	119.7
August	142.4	228.1	135.9	134.3	267.0	119.7
September	142.8	224.7	136.6	134.9	276.4	119.9
October	145.5	227.2	139.3	136.9	305.4	120.7
November	146.5	229.7	140.2	137.9	309.1	121.5
December	144.2	231.2	137.6	137.4	285.4	122.0

[1]Petroleum and petroleum products.

NOTES AND DEFINITIONS, CHAPTER 7

This chapter presents data from two different data systems on international flows of goods, services, income payments, and financial transactions as they affect the U.S. economy. Tables 7-1 through 7-5 present data on the value, quantities, and prices of foreign transactions in the national income and product accounts (NIPAs). Tables 7-6 through 7-8 show foreign transactions and investment positions in current-dollar values as depicted in the U.S. international transactions accounts (ITAs). Both sets of accounts are prepared by the Bureau of Economic Analysis (BEA) and draw on the same original source data. The Census Bureau source data for exports and imports of goods and services are presented in greater detail in Tables 7-9 through 7-16. Table 7-17 shows selected summary values for export and import price indexes compiled by the Bureau of Labor Statistics (BLS).

Due to a few differences in concept, scope, and definitions, the aggregate values of international transactions in the NIPAs (shown in Tables 7-1 and 7-4) are not exactly equal to the values for similar concepts in the ITAs or the Census values that serve as their sources, shown in Tables 7-6 through 7-16. The principal sources of differences are as follows:

- The NIPAs cover only the 50 states and the District of Columbia. The ITAs include the U.S. territories and Puerto Rico as part of the U.S. economy.

- Gold is treated differently.

- Services without payment by financial intermediaries except life insurance carriers (imputed interest) is treated differently.

A reconciliation of the two sets of international accounts is published from time to time in the *Survey of Current Business*.

The conventions of presentation no longer differ between the two sets of international accounts. In all the tables that follow, as in their source documents, values of imports of goods and services and of all other transactions that result in a payment to the rest of the world—income payments to foreigners, net transfers to foreigners, and net acquisition of assets from abroad—are presented normally as positive. Where a minus sign does appear, it means that the usual direction of flow is reversed--for example, in the columns of the financial account in Table 7-6 labeled as "Net U.S. acquisition of financial assets," a minus sign would indicate net sales of such assets.

Tables 7-1 and 7-4

Foreign Transactions in the National Income and Product Accounts

SOURCE: U.S. DEPARTMENT OF COMMERCE, BUREAU OF ECONOMIC ANALYSIS

See the notes and definitions to Chapter 1 for an overview of the national income and product accounts (NIPAs).

Definitions

In accordance with the split between current and capital account, there are now two NIPA measures of the balance of international transactions.

The *balance on current account, national income and product accounts* is *current receipts from the rest of the world* minus *current payments to the rest of the world*. A negative value indicates that current payments exceed current receipts.

Net lending or net borrowing (-), national income and product accounts is equal to the balance on current account less capital account transactions with the rest of the world (net). Capital account transactions with the rest of the world (net) is not shown separately in Table 7-1 (for space reasons) but can be calculated from that table as the difference between net lending/borrowing and the current account balance. (A similar measure, a component of the ITAs, is shown explicitly in Table 7-6.) Capital account transactions with the rest of the world are cash or in-kind transfers linked to the acquisition or disposition of an existing, nonproduced, nonfinancial asset. In contrast, the current account is limited to flows associated with current production of goods and services.

Net lending or net borrowing provides an indirect measure of the net acquisition of foreign assets by U.S. residents less the net acquisition of U.S. assets by foreign residents. These asset flows are measured directly in the ITAs. See Table 7-6 and its notes and definitions for a more extensive discussion of the relationship between the balances on current and capital account and international asset flows.

Current receipts from the rest of the world is *exports of goods and services* plus *income receipts*.

Current payments to the rest of the world is *imports of goods and services* plus *income payments* plus *current taxes and transfer payments (net)*.

Exports and imports of goods and services. Goods, in general, are products that can be stored or inventoried. *Services*, in general, are products that cannot be stored and are consumed at the place and time of their purchase. Goods imports include expenditures abroad by U.S. residents, except for travel. Services include foreign travel by U.S. residents, expenditures in the United States by foreign travelers, and exports and imports of certain goods—primarily military equipment purchased and sold by the federal government. See the following paragraph for the definition of *travel*.

Table 7-4 shows values for selected components of total goods and services; the components shown will not add to the total because of omitted items. In the case of goods, a miscellaneous "other" category is not shown. In the case of services, only two components are shown in this table. One is *travel* (for all purposes including education), which does not include passenger fares but includes as exports spending by foreign tourists and students in the United States, and includes as imports all other spending abroad by tourists and students from the United States. The other component shown here is a category called *other business services*, which includes the professional and financial services (for example, computer services) that have accounted for a large part of the long-term growth in the service category. The remaining components of total services are transport (of both persons and goods), charges for the use of intellectual property not elsewhere classified, government goods and services not elsewhere classified, and a miscellaneous, smaller *other* category. They are shown separately in Tables 7-15 and 7-16.

Income receipts and payments. Income receipts—receipts from abroad of factor (labor or capital) income by U.S. residents—are analogous to exports and are combined with them to yield total *current receipts from the rest of the world. Income payments* by U.S. entities of factor income to entities abroad are analogous to imports.

Current taxes and transfer payments (net) consists of net payments between the United States and abroad that do not involve payment for the services of the labor or capital factors of production, purchase of currently-produced goods and services, or transfer of an existing asset. It includes net flows from persons, government, and business. The types of payments included are personal remittances from U.S. residents to the rest of the world, net of remittances from foreigners to U.S. residents; government grants; and transfer payments from businesses. Only the net payment to the rest of the world is shown. It usually appears in these accounts as a positive value, with transfers from the United States to abroad exceeding the reverse flow. An exception came in 1991, when U.S. allies in the Gulf War reimbursed the United States for the cost of the war, causing the only current-account surplus since 1981. This resulted in net payments to the United States from the rest of the world and appears as a negative entry in the net transfer payments column of the NIPA accounts.

Tables 7-2, 7-3 and 7-5

Chain-Type Quantity and Price Indexes for NIPA Foreign Transactions

These indexes represent the separation of the current-dollar values in Tables 7-1 and 7-4 into their real quantity and price trends components. (See the notes and definitions to Chapter 1 for a general explanation of chained-dollar estimates of real output and prices.) As those notes explain, quantity indexes are shown

instead of constant-dollar estimates, because BEA no longer publishes its real output estimates before 1999 in any detail in the constant-dollar form. Therefore, quantity indexes are the only comprehensive source of information about longer-term trends in real volumes.

Table 7-6 through 7-13

Exports and Imports of Goods and Services

SOURCES: U.S. DEPARTMENT OF COMMERCE, CENSUS BUREAU AND BUREAU OF ECONOMIC ANALYSIS

These tables present the source data used to build up the aggregate measures of goods and services flows shown in Tables 7-1 through 7-5. These data are compiled and published monthly, making trends evident before the publication of the quarterly aggregate estimates. They also provide more detail than the quarterly aggregates.

Monthly and annual data on exports and imports of *goods* are compiled by the Census Bureau from documents collected by the U.S. Customs Service. The Bureau of Economic Analysis (BEA) makes certain adjustments to these data (as described below) to place the estimates on a *balance of payments* basis—a basis consistent with the national and international accounts.

Data on exports and imports of *services* are prepared by BEA from a variety of sources. Monthly data on services are available from January 1992. Annual and quarterly data for earlier years are available as part of the international transactions accounts. Current data on goods and services are available each month in a joint Census Bureau-BEA press release.

In the case of some of the detailed breakdowns of exports and imports, such as by end-use categories, monthly data may not sum exactly to annual totals. This is due to later revisions, which are made only to annual data and are not allocated to monthly data. Also, the constant-dollar figures expressed in 2009 dollars are now calculated using chain weights. Therefore, the 2009-dollar detail will not add to the 2009-dollar totals.

In addition, monthly and annual data on exports and imports of goods for individual countries and various country groupings do not reflect subsequent revisions of annual total data. These country data are compiled by the Census Bureau for all countries, although this volume includes only a selection of the most significant countries and areas. The full set of data can be accessed on the Census Web site at <https://www.census.gov>.

Definitions: Goods

Goods: Census basis. The Census basis goods data are compiled from documents collected by the U.S. Customs Service. They reflect the movement of goods between foreign countries and the 50 states, the District of Columbia, Puerto Rico, the U.S. Virgin Islands, and U.S. Foreign Trade Zones. They include government and nongovernment shipments of goods, and exclude shipments between the United States and its territories and possessions; transactions with U.S. military, diplomatic, and consular installations abroad; U.S. goods returned to the United States by its armed forces; personal and household effects of travelers; and intransit shipments. The general import values reflect the total arrival of merchandise from foreign countries that immediately enters consumption channels, warehouses, or Foreign Trade Zones.

For *imports,* the value reported is the U.S. Customs Service appraised value of merchandise (generally, the price paid for merchandise for export to the United States). Import duties, freight, insurance, and other charges incurred in bringing merchandise to the United States are excluded.

Exports are valued at the f.a.s. (free alongside ship) value of merchandise at the U.S. port of export, based on the transaction price including inland freight, insurance, and other charges incurred in placing the merchandise alongside the carrier at the U.S. port of exportation.

Goods: balance of payments (BOP) basis. Goods on a Census basis are adjusted by BEA to goods on a BOP basis to bring the data in line with the concepts and definitions used to prepare the international and national accounts. In general, the adjustments include changes in ownership that occur without goods passing into or out of the customs territory of the United States. These adjustments are necessary to supplement coverage of the Census basis data, to eliminate duplication of transactions recorded elsewhere in the international accounts, and to value transactions according to a standard definition. With the June 4, 2013 release, improved BOP adjustments involving U.S. military transactions were introduced for data beginning with 1999.

The *export* adjustments include the following: (1) The deduction of *U.S. military sales contracts.* The Census Bureau has included these contracts in the goods data, but BEA includes them in the service category "Transfers Under U.S. Military Sales Contracts." BEA's source material for these contracts is more comprehensive but does not distinguish between goods and services. (2) The addition of *private gift parcels* mailed to foreigners by individuals through the U.S. Postal Service. Only commercial shipments are covered in Census goods exports. (3) The addition to *nonmonetary gold exports* of gold purchased by foreign official agencies from private dealers in the United States and held at the Federal Reserve Bank of New York. The Census data include only gold that leaves the customs territory. (4) *Smaller adjustments* includes deductions for repairs of goods, exposed motion picture film, and military grant aid, and additions for sales of fish in U.S. territorial waters, exports of electricity to Mexico, and vessels and oil rigs that change ownership without export documents being filed.

The *import* adjustments include the following: (1) On *inland freight in Canada*, the customs value for imports for certain Canadian goods is the point of origin in Canada. BEA makes an addition for the inland freight charges of transporting these Canadian goods to the U.S. border. (2) An addition is made to *nonmonetary gold imports* for gold sold by foreign official agencies to private purchasers out of stock held at the Federal Reserve Bank of New York. The Census Bureau data include only gold that enters the customs territory. (3) A deduction is made for *imports by U.S. military agencies*. The Census Bureau has included these contracts in the goods data, but BEA includes them in the service category "Direct Defense Expenditures." BEA's source material is more comprehensive but does not distinguish between goods and services. (4) *Smaller adjustments* includes deductions for repairs of goods and for exposed motion picture film and additions for imported electricity from Mexico, conversion of vessels for commercial use, and repairs to U.S. vessels abroad.

Definitions: Services

These statistics are estimates of service transactions between foreign countries and the 50 states, the District of Columbia, Puerto Rico, the U.S. Virgin Islands, and other U.S. territories and possessions. Transactions with U.S. military, diplomatic, and consular installations abroad are excluded because they are considered to be part of the U.S. economy.

In the 2014 comprehensive revision of the ITAs, new categories have been introduced in the services reports, beginning with January 1999. The 9 new categories, shown in Tables 7-11 and 7-12, are as follows:

Maintenance and repair services n.i.e. (not included elsewhere) were previously included in "other private services."

Transport includes the previous categories of "passenger fares" and "other transportation."

Travel for all purposes including education is broader than the previous "travel" category and now includes business travel, expenditures by border, seasonal, and other short-term workers, and personal travel including that related to health and education. As before, it consists of expenditures for food, lodging, recreation, gifts, and other items incidental to a foreign visit but not the actual transportation expenses.

Insurance services and *financial services* were previously included in other private services.

Charges for the use of intellectual property n.i.e. was previously named "royalties and license fees."

Telecommunications, computer, and information services and *other business services* were previously included in "other private services."

Government goods and services n.i.e. replaces the government categories in the previous system.

Earlier services definitions

Before 1999, services are classified in the broad categories described below. For six of these categories, the definitions are the same for imports and exports. For the seventh, the export category is "Transfers under U.S. Military Sales Contracts," while for imports, the category is "Direct Defense Expenditures."

Travel includes purchases of services and goods by U.S. travelers abroad and by foreign visitors to the United States. A traveler is defined as a person who stays for a period of less than one year in a country where the person is not a resident. Included are expenditures for food, lodging, recreation, gifts, and other items incidental to a foreign visit. Not included are the international costs of the travel itself, which are covered in *passenger fares* (see below).

Passenger fares consists of fares paid by residents of one country to residents in other countries. Receipts consist of fares received by U.S. carriers from foreign residents for travel between the United States and foreign countries and between two foreign points. Payments consist of fares paid by U.S. residents to foreign carriers for travel between the United States and foreign countries.

Other transportation includes charges for the transportation of goods by ocean, air, waterway, pipeline, and rail carriers to and from the United States. Included are freight charges, operating expenses that transportation companies incur in foreign ports, and payments for vessel charter and aircraft and freight car rentals.

Royalties and license fees consists of transactions with foreign residents involving intangible assets and proprietary rights, such as the use of patents, techniques, processes, formulas, designs, knowhow, trademarks, copyrights, franchises, and manufacturing rights. The term *royalties* generally refers to payments for the utilization of copyrights or trademarks, and the term *license fees* generally refers to payments for the use of patents or industrial processes.

Other private services includes transactions with "affiliated" foreigners for which no identification by type is available and transactions with unaffiliated foreigners.

The term "affiliated" refers to a direct investment relationship, which exists when a U.S. person has ownership or control (directly or indirectly) of 10 percent or more of a foreign business enterprise, or when a foreign person has a similar interest in a U.S. enterprise.

Transactions with "unaffiliated" foreigners in this "other private services" category consist of education services, financial services, insurance services, telecommunications services, and business, professional, and technical services. Included in the last group are advertising services; computer and data processing services; database and other information services; research, development, and testing services; management, consulting, and public relations services; legal services; construction, engineering, architectural, and mining services; industrial engineering services; installation, maintenance, and repair of equipment; and other services, including medical services and film and tape rental.

The insurance component of "other private services" was measured before the July 2003 revision as premiums less actual losses paid or recovered. Furthermore, catastrophic losses were entered immediately when the loss occurred, rather than when the insurance claim was actually paid out. This led to sharp swings for any month in which catastrophic losses occurred, such as Hurricane Katrina in August 2005 or the September 11, 2001, terror attacks. In the accounts as revised in July 2003 and presented here, insurance services are now measured as premiums less "normal" losses. Normal losses consist of a measure of expected regularly occurring losses based on six years of past experience plus an additional allowance for catastrophic loss. Catastrophic losses, when they occur, are added in equal increments to the estimate of regularly occurring losses over the 20 years following the occurrence. As adoption of this methodology introduces a difference between actual and normal losses, an amount equal to the difference is entered in the international accounts as a capital account transaction.

Transfers under U.S. military sales contracts (exports only) includes exports in which U.S. government military agencies participate. This category has included both goods, such as equipment, and services, such as repair services and training, that could not be separately identified. In the 2010 and 2013 annual revisions, more precise breakdowns between goods and services in this category were introduced and incorporated as revised estimates of services and of the BOP goods adjustment, beginning with the data for 2007. Transfers of goods and services under U.S. military grant programs are included.

Direct defense expenditures (imports only) consists of expenditures incurred by U.S. military agencies abroad, including expenditures by U.S. personnel, payments of wages to foreign residents, construction expenditures, payments for foreign contractual services, and procurement of foreign goods. Improved breakdowns between goods and services are now incorporated beginning with statistics for 1999.

U.S. government miscellaneous services includes transactions of U.S. government nonmilitary agencies with foreign residents. Most of these transactions involve the provision of services to, or purchases of services from, foreigners. Transfers of some goods are also included.

Services estimates are based on quarterly, annual, and benchmark surveys and partial information generated from monthly reports. Service transactions are estimated at market prices. Estimates are seasonally adjusted when statistically significant seasonal patterns are present.

Definitions: Area groupings

The Census trade statistics for groups of countries present "groups as they were at the time of reporting", which means that as multinational organizations such as the European Union expand, the statistics for trade with that group include the added country only beginning with the year it entered the group. The European Union was expanded from 15 to 28 nations as of July 1, 2013, and data for that year are available for both the new and the old group; to provide historical perspective, they are both shown here, along with the historical data back to 1974 for the original group.

The *European Union* (EU) now includes 27 countries: Austria, Belgium, Bulgaria, Croatia, Cyprus, Czech Republic, Denmark, Estonia, Finland, France, Germany, Greece, Hungary, Ireland, Italy, Latvia, Lithuania, Luxembourg, Malta, Netherlands, Poland, Portugal, Romania, Slovakia, Slovenia, Spain, and Sweden. The United Kingdom withdrew from the European Union in late 2020.

In a referendum on June 23, 2016, a majority of British voters supported leaving the EU. On March 29, 2017, the United Kingdom government invoked Article 50 of the Treaty on European Union. The European Union (Withdrawal) Act 2018 declares "exit day" to be March 29, 2019.

The *Euro area* now includes Austria, Belgium, Cyprus, Estonia, Finland, France, Germany, Greece, Ireland, Italy, Luxembourg, Malta, the Netherlands, Portugal, Slovakia, Slovenia, and Spain. See the notes and definitions in Table 13-2 for further information about the euro.

With the June 3, 2016 International Trade and Services Annual Revision for 2015, the area grouping *Asian Newly Industrialized Countries (NICS)* has been removed from all relevant exhibits and publications and are listed separately as Hong Kong, South Korea, Singapore, and Taiwan. This group was initially called the *Four Asian Tigers.*

The *Organization of Petroleum Exporting Countries (OPEC)* currently consists of Algeria, Angola, Ecuador, Equatorial Guinea, Iran, Iraq, Kuwait, Libya, Nigeria, Qatar, Saudi Arabia, the United Arab Emirates, and Venezuela.

Notes on the data

U.S./Canada data exchange and substitution. The data for U.S. exports to Canada are derived from import data compiled by Canada. The use of Canada's import data to produce U.S. export data requires several alignments in order to compare the two series.

- *Coverage*: Canadian imports are based on country of origin. U.S. goods shipped from a third country are included, but U.S. exports exclude these foreign shipments. U.S. export coverage also excludes certain Canadian postal shipments.

- *Valuation*: Canadian imports are valued at their point of origin in the United States. However, U.S. exports are valued at the port of exit in the United States and include inland freight charges, making the U.S. export value slightly larger. Canada requires inland freight to be reported.

- *Re-exports*: U.S. exports include re-exports of foreign goods. Again, the aggregate U.S. export figure is slightly larger.

- *Exchange Rate*: Average monthly exchange rates are applied to convert the published data to U.S. currency.

End-use categories and seasonal adjustment of trade in goods. Goods are initially classified under the Harmonized System, which describes and measures the characteristics of goods traded. Combining trade into approximately 140 export and 140 import enduse categories makes it possible to examine goods according to their principal uses. These categories are used as the basis for computing the seasonal and working-day adjusted data. Adjusted data are then summed to the six end-use aggregates for publication.

The seasonal adjustment procedure is based on a model that estimates the monthly movements as percentages above or below the general level of each end-use commodity series (unlike other methods that redistribute the actual series values over the calendar year). Imports of petroleum and petroleum products are adjusted for the length of the month.

Data availability

Data are released monthly in a joint Census Bureau-BEA press release (FT-900), which is published about six weeks after the end of the month to which the data pertain. The release and historical data are available on the Census Bureau Web site at <https://www.census.gov/foreign-trade/index.html >.

Revisions

Data for recent years are normally revised annually. In some cases, revisions to annual totals are not distributed to monthly data; therefore, monthly data may not sum to the revised total shown. Data on trade in services may be subject to extensive revision as part of BEA's annual revision of the international transactions accounts (ITAs), usually released in July.

References

See the references for Table 7-6.

Table 7-14

Export and Import Price Indexes

SOURCE: U.S. DEPARTMENT OF LABOR, BUREAU OF LABOR STATISTICS

The International Price Program of the Bureau of Labor Statistics (BLS) collects price data for nonmilitary goods traded between the United States and the rest of the world and for selected transportation services in international markets. BLS aggregates the goods price data into export and import price indexes. Summary values of these price indexes for goods are presented in *Business Statistics*. For product and locality detail on international prices for both goods and services, see the *Handbook of U.S. Labor Statistics,* also published by Bernan Press.

Definitions

The *export* price index provides a measure of price change for all goods sold by U.S. residents (businesses and individuals located within the geographic boundaries of the United States, whether or not owned by U.S. citizens) to foreign buyers.

The *import* price index provides a measure of price change for goods purchased from other countries by U.S. residents.

Notes on the data

Published index series use a base year of 2012 = 100 whenever possible.

The product universe for both the import and export indexes includes raw materials, agricultural products, and manufactures. Price data are primarily collected by mail questionnaire, and directly from the exporter or importer in all but a few cases.

To the greatest extent possible, the data refer to prices at the U.S. border for exports and at either the foreign border or the U.S. border for imports. For nearly all products, the prices refer to transactions completed during the first week of the month and represent the actual price for which the product was bought or sold, including discounts, allowances, and rebates.

For the export price indexes, the preferred pricing basis is f.a.s. (free alongside ship) U.S. port of exportation. Where necessary, adjustments are made to reported prices to place them on this basis. An attempt is made to collect two prices for imports: f.o.b. (free on board) at the port of exportation and c.i.f. (cost, insurance, and freight) at the U.S. port of importation. Adjustments are made to account for changes in product characteristics in order to obtain a pure measure of price change.

The indexes are weighted indexes of the Laspeyres type. (See "General Notes" at the beginning of this volume for further explanation.) The values assigned to each weight category are based on trade value figures compiled by the Census Bureau. They are reweighted annually, with a two-year lag (as concurrent value data are not available) in revisions.

The merchandise price indexes are published using three different classification systems: the Harmonized System, the Bureau of Economic Analysis End-Use System, and the Standard International Trade Classification (SITC) system. The aggregate indexes shown here are from the End-Use System.

Data availability

Indexes are published monthly in a press release and a more detailed report. Indexes are published for detailed product categories, as well as for all commodities. Aggregate import indexes by country or region of origin also are available, as are indexes for selected categories of internationally traded services. Additional information is available from the Division of International Prices in the Bureau of Labor Statistics. Complete historical data are available on the BLS Web site at <https://www.bls.gov>.

References

The indexes are described in "BLS to Produce Monthly Indexes of Export and Import Prices," *Monthly Labor Review* (December 1988), and Chapter 15, "International Price Indexes," *BLS Handbook of Methods* Bulletin 2490 (April 1997).

CHAPTER 8: PRICES

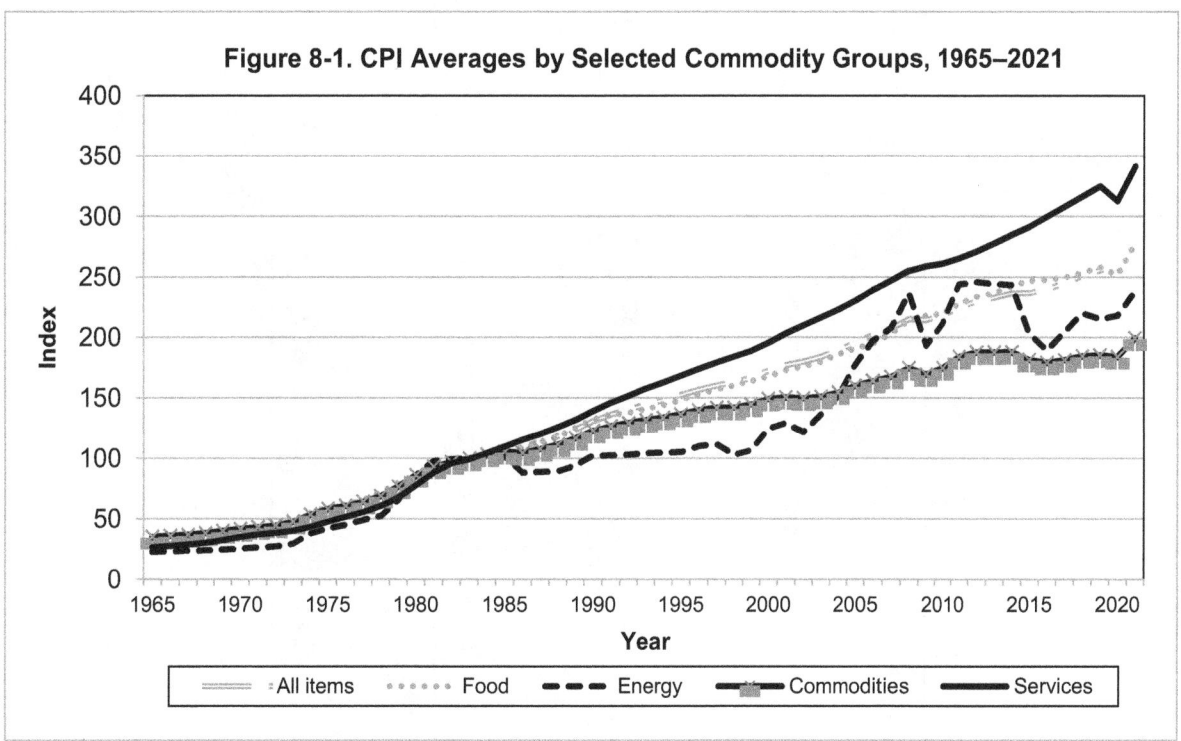

Figure 8-1. CPI Averages by Selected Commodity Groups, 1965–2021

- The publication of Consumer Price Index (CPI) began in 1919. After studying household expenditures, a market basket of eight groups was developed. These categories include food and beverages, housing, apparel, transportation, medical care, recreation, education and communication, other goods and services. In calculating the index, weights are determined by the importance of these purchases.

- Figure 8-1 shows selected CPI components fluctuation between 1965 to 2021. Two everyday items that are tracked are energy and food. Energy (i.e. gasoline, fuels oil) is the most volatile while food prices rise steadily. For example, the April 2020 the average price for gasoline was $1.93 by the end of December 2021, the price was $3.34 an increase of 73.0 percent. Gasoline prices soared to the highest amount of nearly $5.00 a gallon in July 2022. The BLS also computes a CPI which excludes energy and food items. (See Table 8-1 and Table 11-3 for the ever-fluctuating crude oil prices).

- The Bureau of Labor Statistics (BLS) collects prices for more than 200 categories arranged in eight major groups. (See Section 8b and Notes and Definitions for more information.) Consumer Price Index for All Urban Consumers (CPI-U) represents all goods and services purchased for consumption for day-to-day living expenditures. Inflation then, is the annual rate of change in this widely used measure of the general price level.

Table 8-1A. Summary Consumer Price Indexes: Recent Data

(Seasonally adjusted.)

Year and month	Consumer Price Index, 1982–1984 = 100						
	Urban wage earners and clerical workers (CPI-W), all items	All urban consumers (CPI-U)					
		All items	Food	Energy	All items less food and energy	Commodities	Services
1965	31.7	31.5	32.2	22.9	32.7	35.2	26.6
1966	32.6	32.4	33.8	23.3	33.5	36.1	27.6
1967	33.6	33.4	34.1	23.8	34.7	36.8	28.8
1968	35.0	34.8	35.3	24.2	36.3	38.1	30.3
1969	36.9	36.7	37.1	24.8	38.4	39.9	32.4
1970	39.0	38.8	39.2	25.5	40.8	41.7	35.0
1971	40.7	40.5	40.4	26.5	42.7	43.2	37.0
1972	42.1	41.8	42.1	27.2	44.0	44.5	38.4
1973	44.7	44.4	48.2	29.4	45.6	47.8	40.1
1974	49.6	49.3	55.1	38.1	49.4	53.5	43.8
1975	54.1	53.8	59.8	42.1	53.9	58.2	48.0
1976	57.2	56.9	61.6	45.1	57.4	60.7	52.0
1977	60.9	60.6	65.5	49.4	61.0	64.2	56.0
1978	65.6	65.2	72.0	52.5	65.5	68.8	60.8
1979	73.1	72.6	79.9	65.7	71.9	76.6	67.5
1980	82.9	82.4	86.8	86.0	80.8	86.0	77.9
1981	91.4	90.9	93.6	97.7	89.2	93.2	88.1
1982	96.9	96.5	97.4	99.2	95.8	97.0	96.0
1983	99.8	99.6	99.4	99.9	99.6	99.8	99.4
1984	103.3	103.9	103.2	100.9	104.6	103.2	104.6
1985	106.9	107.6	105.6	101.6	109.1	105.4	109.9
1986	108.6	109.6	109.0	88.2	113.5	104.4	115.4
1987	112.5	113.6	113.5	88.6	118.2	107.7	120.2
1988	117.0	118.3	118.2	89.3	123.4	111.5	125.7
1989	122.6	124.0	125.1	94.3	129.0	116.7	131.9
1990	129.0	130.7	132.4	102.1	135.5	122.8	139.2
1991	134.3	136.2	136.3	102.5	142.1	126.6	146.3
1992	138.2	140.3	137.9	103.0	147.3	129.1	152.0
1993	142.1	144.5	140.9	104.2	152.2	131.5	157.9
1994	145.6	148.2	144.3	104.6	156.5	133.8	163.1
1995	149.8	152.4	148.4	105.2	161.2	136.4	168.7
1996	154.1	156.9	153.3	110.1	165.6	139.9	174.1
1997	157.6	160.5	157.3	111.5	169.5	141.8	179.4
1998	159.7	163.0	160.7	102.9	173.4	141.9	184.2
1999	163.2	166.6	164.1	106.6	177.0	144.4	188.8
2000	168.9	172.2	167.8	124.6	181.3	149.2	195.3
2001	173.5	177.1	173.1	129.3	186.1	150.7	203.4
2002	175.9	179.9	176.2	121.7	190.5	149.7	209.8
2003	179.8	184.0	180.0	136.5	193.2	151.2	216.5
2004	184.5	188.9	186.2	151.4	196.6	154.7	222.8
2005	191.0	195.3	190.7	177.1	200.9	160.2	230.1
2006	197.1	201.6	195.2	196.9	205.9	164.0	238.9
2007	202.8	207.3	202.9	207.7	210.7	167.5	246.8
2008	211.1	215.3	214.1	236.7	215.6	174.8	255.5
2009	209.6	214.5	218.0	193.1	219.2	169.7	259.2
2010	214.0	218.1	219.6	211.4	221.3	174.6	261.3
2011	221.6	224.9	227.8	243.9	225.0	183.9	265.8
2012	226.2	229.6	233.8	246.1	229.8	187.6	271.4
2013	229.3	233.0	237.0	244.4	233.8	187.7	277.9
2014	232.8	236.7	242.7	243.6	237.9	187.9	285.1
2015	231.8	237.0	247.2	202.9	242.2	181.7	291.7
2016	234.1	240.0	247.9	189.5	247.6	179.2	299.9
2017	239.1	245.1	250.1	204.5	252.2	181.2	308.1
2018	245.1	251.1	253.6	219.9	257.6	184.6	316.6
2019	249.2	255.7	258.3	215.3	263.2	185.3	325.1
2020	243.0	248.8	252.0	217.7	255.1	183.9	312.8
2021	265.5	271.0	277.8	238.3	277.3	199.2	341.4
2020							
January	252.1	258.7	261.1	217.8	266.4	186.0	330.4
February	252.4	259.0	261.9	214.1	267.1	185.9	331.2
March	251.5	258.2	262.7	203.9	266.9	184.4	331.1
April	249.2	256.1	266.5	182.9	265.8	181.5	330.0
May	249.0	255.9	268.3	179.5	265.6	181.3	329.9
June	250.4	257.2	269.7	188.4	266.1	183.0	330.7
July	252.0	258.5	268.7	192.6	267.6	184.1	332.3
August	253.2	259.6	269.0	194.3	268.7	185.5	332.8
September	253.9	260.2	269.1	196.9	269.2	186.4	333.1
October	254.0	260.4	269.6	196.4	269.3	186.4	333.4
November	254.4	260.7	269.6	196.4	269.8	186.2	334.3
December	255.3	261.6	270.5	203.6	270.0	187.5	334.6
2021							
January	256.0	262.2	271.0	209.3	270.1	188.6	334.8
February	257.3	263.3	271.4	218.9	270.5	190.0	335.7
March	259.1	265.0	271.9	231.1	271.3	192.0	336.9
April	260.8	266.7	272.8	228.4	273.7	193.7	338.6
May	262.9	268.6	274.1	229.9	275.7	196.0	340.0
June	265.6	271.0	276.1	234.6	277.9	199.4	341.3
July	266.9	272.2	277.9	238.4	278.8	200.8	342.3
August	267.8	273.1	279.0	243.0	279.3	202.0	342.8
September	269.0	274.2	281.5	245.8	280.0	203.2	343.8
October	271.5	276.6	283.9	255.0	281.7	206.0	345.6
November	273.7	278.5	286.1	261.3	283.2	208.5	346.9
December	275.4	280.1	287.4	263.6	284.8	210.5	348.1

Table 8-1B. Summary Consumer Price Indexes: Historical Data, 1946 to Date

(Seasonally adjusted.)

Year and month	Urban wage earners and clerical workers (CPI-W), all items	Consumer Price Index, 1982–1984 = 100					
		All urban consumers (CPI-U)					
		All items	Food	Energy	All items less food and energy	Commod-ities	Services
1946	19.6	19.5	19.8	. . .	. . .	22.9	14.1
1947	22.5	22.3	24.1	. . .	. . .	27.6	14.7
1948	24.2	24.1	26.1	. . .	. . .	29.6	15.6
1949	24.0	23.8	25.0	. . .	. . .	28.8	16.4
1950	24.2	24.1	25.4	. . .	. . .	29.0	16.9
1951	26.1	26.0	28.2	. . .	. . .	31.6	17.8
1952	26.7	26.5	28.7	. . .	. . .	32.0	18.6
1953	26.9	26.7	28.3	. . .	. . .	31.9	19.4
1954	27.0	26.9	28.2	. . .	. . .	31.6	20.0
1955	26.9	26.8	27.8	. . .	. . .	31.3	20.4
1956	27.3	27.2	28.0	. . .	. . .	31.6	20.9
1957	28.3	28.1	28.9	21.5	28.9	32.6	21.8
1958	29.1	28.9	30.2	21.5	29.6	33.3	22.6
1959	29.3	29.1	29.7	21.9	30.2	33.3	23.3
1960	29.8	29.6	30.0	22.4	30.6	33.6	24.1
1961	30.1	29.9	30.4	22.5	31.0	33.8	24.5
1962	30.4	30.2	30.6	22.6	31.4	34.1	25.0
1963	30.8	30.6	31.1	22.6	31.8	34.4	25.5
1964	31.2	31.0	31.5	22.5	32.3	34.8	26.0
1950							
January	23.6	23.5	24.3	. . .	. . .	. . .	. . .
February	23.7	23.6	24.7	. . .	. . .	. . .	. . .
March	23.8	23.6	24.6	. . .	. . .	. . .	. . .
April	23.8	23.7	24.6	. . .	. . .	. . .	. . .
May	23.9	23.8	24.8	. . .	. . .	. . .	. . .
June	24.0	23.9	25.1	. . .	. . .	. . .	. . .
July	24.2	24.1	25.6	. . .	. . .	. . .	. . .
August	24.3	24.2	25.8	. . .	. . .	. . .	. . .
September	24.5	24.3	25.8	. . .	. . .	. . .	. . .
October	24.6	24.5	26.0	. . .	. . .	. . .	. . .
November	24.7	24.6	26.1	. . .	. . .	. . .	. . .
December	25.1	25.0	26.9	. . .	. . .	. . .	. . .
1951							
January	25.5	25.4	27.6	. . .	. . .	. . .	. . .
February	26.0	25.8	28.5	. . .	. . .	. . .	. . .
March	26.0	25.9	28.4	. . .	. . .	. . .	. . .
April	26.1	25.9	28.2	. . .	. . .	. . .	. . .
May	26.1	26.0	28.3	. . .	. . .	. . .	. . .
June	26.1	25.9	28.0	. . .	. . .	. . .	. . .
July	26.1	25.9	27.9	. . .	. . .	. . .	. . .
August	26.0	25.9	27.8	. . .	. . .	. . .	. . .
September	26.2	26.0	27.9	. . .	. . .	. . .	. . .
October	26.3	26.2	28.4	. . .	. . .	. . .	. . .
November	26.5	26.3	28.6	. . .	. . .	. . .	. . .
December	26.6	26.5	28.9	. . .	. . .	. . .	. . .
1952							
January	26.6	26.5	28.9	. . .	. . .	. . .	. . .
February	26.6	26.4	28.6	. . .	. . .	. . .	. . .
March	26.5	26.4	28.5	. . .	. . .	. . .	. . .
April	26.6	26.5	28.7	. . .	. . .	. . .	. . .
May	26.6	26.5	28.7	. . .	. . .	. . .	. . .
June	26.7	26.5	28.6	. . .	. . .	. . .	. . .
July	26.8	26.7	28.9	. . .	. . .	. . .	. . .
August	26.8	26.7	28.9	. . .	. . .	. . .	. . .
September	26.8	26.6	28.7	. . .	. . .	. . .	. . .
October	26.8	26.7	28.8	. . .	. . .	. . .	. . .
November	26.8	26.7	28.8	. . .	. . .	. . .	. . .
December	26.9	26.7	28.6	. . .	. . .	. . .	. . .
1953							
January	26.8	26.6	28.4	. . .	. . .	. . .	. . .
February	26.7	26.6	28.3	. . .	. . .	. . .	. . .
March	26.8	26.6	28.3	. . .	. . .	. . .	. . .
April	26.8	26.7	28.1	. . .	. . .	. . .	. . .
May	26.9	26.7	28.2	. . .	. . .	. . .	. . .
June	26.9	26.8	28.4	. . .	. . .	. . .	. . .
July	26.9	26.8	28.2	. . .	. . .	. . .	. . .
August	27.0	26.9	28.3	. . .	. . .	. . .	. . .
September	27.0	26.9	28.4	. . .	. . .	. . .	. . .
October	27.1	27.0	28.4	. . .	. . .	. . .	. . .
November	27.0	26.9	28.1	. . .	. . .	. . .	. . .
December	27.0	26.9	28.3	. . .	. . .	. . .	. . .

. . . = Not available.

Table 8-1B. Summary Consumer Price Indexes: Historical Data, 1946 to Date—*Continued*

(Seasonally adjusted.)

Year and month	Urban wage earners and clerical workers (CPI-W), all items	Consumer Price Index, 1982–1984 = 100					
		All urban consumers (CPI-U)					
		All items	Food	Energy	All items less food and energy	Commod-ities	Services
1954							
January	27.1	26.9	28.5	. . .	. . .	. . .	. . .
February	27.1	27.0	28.5	. . .	. . .	. . .	. . .
March	27.1	26.9	28.4	. . .	. . .	. . .	. . .
April	27.0	26.9	28.4	. . .	. . .	. . .	. . .
May	27.1	26.9	28.4	. . .	. . .	. . .	. . .
June	27.1	26.9	28.4	. . .	. . .	. . .	. . .
July	27.0	26.9	28.4	. . .	. . .	. . .	. . .
August	27.0	26.9	28.3	. . .	. . .	. . .	. . .
September	27.0	26.8	28.0	. . .	. . .	. . .	. . .
October	26.9	26.7	27.9	. . .	. . .	. . .	. . .
November	26.9	26.8	27.9	. . .	. . .	. . .	. . .
December	26.9	26.8	27.8	. . .	. . .	. . .	. . .
1955							
January	26.9	26.8	27.8	. . .	. . .	. . .	. . .
February	27.0	26.8	28.0	. . .	. . .	. . .	. . .
March	26.9	26.8	28.0	. . .	. . .	. . .	. . .
April	26.9	26.8	28.0	. . .	. . .	. . .	. . .
May	26.9	26.8	27.9	. . .	. . .	. . .	. . .
June	26.9	26.7	27.7	. . .	. . .	. . .	. . .
July	26.9	26.8	27.7	. . .	. . .	. . .	. . .
August	26.9	26.7	27.6	. . .	. . .	. . .	. . .
September	27.0	26.9	27.8	. . .	. . .	. . .	. . .
October	27.0	26.8	27.7	. . .	. . .	. . .	. . .
November	27.0	26.9	27.6	. . .	. . .	. . .	. . .
December	27.0	26.9	27.6	. . .	. . .	. . .	. . .
1956							
January	27.0	26.8	27.5	. . .	. . .	31.2	20.7
February	27.0	26.9	27.5	. . .	. . .	31.1	20.7
March	27.1	26.9	27.5	. . .	. . .	31.2	20.7
April	27.1	26.9	27.6	. . .	. . .	31.3	20.8
May	27.2	27.0	27.8	. . .	. . .	31.4	20.8
June	27.3	27.2	28.1	. . .	. . .	31.5	20.9
July	27.4	27.3	28.4	. . .	. . .	31.8	20.9
August	27.5	27.3	28.2	. . .	. . .	31.7	21.0
September	27.5	27.4	28.2	. . .	. . .	31.8	21.1
October	27.7	27.5	28.3	. . .	. . .	32.0	21.1
November	27.7	27.5	28.4	. . .	. . .	32.0	21.2
December	27.8	27.6	28.5	. . .	. . .	32.1	21.3
1957							
January	27.8	27.7	28.4	21.3	28.5	32.1	21.4
February	28.0	27.8	28.7	21.4	28.6	32.3	21.4
March	28.0	27.9	28.6	21.5	28.7	32.3	21.6
April	28.1	27.9	28.6	21.6	28.8	32.4	21.6
May	28.2	28.0	28.7	21.6	28.8	32.4	21.7
June	28.3	28.1	28.9	21.6	28.9	32.5	21.8
July	28.4	28.2	29.1	21.5	29.0	32.6	21.8
August	28.4	28.3	29.4	21.4	29.0	32.8	21.9
September	28.5	28.3	29.2	21.4	29.1	32.8	22.0
October	28.5	28.3	29.2	21.4	29.2	32.7	22.1
November	28.6	28.4	29.2	21.5	29.3	32.8	22.2
December	28.6	28.5	29.2	21.5	29.3	32.9	22.2
1958							
January	28.8	28.6	29.8	21.6	29.3	33.1	22.3
February	28.9	28.7	29.9	21.3	29.4	33.2	22.4
March	29.0	28.9	30.5	21.4	29.5	33.4	22.4
April	29.1	28.9	30.6	21.4	29.5	33.5	22.5
May	29.1	28.9	30.5	21.5	29.5	33.5	22.6
June	29.1	28.9	30.3	21.5	29.6	33.4	22.6
July	29.1	28.9	30.2	21.6	29.6	33.3	22.7
August	29.1	28.9	30.1	21.7	29.6	33.3	22.7
September	29.1	28.9	30.0	21.7	29.7	33.3	22.8
October	29.1	28.9	30.0	21.7	29.7	33.2	22.8
November	29.1	29.0	30.0	21.4	29.8	33.3	22.8
December	29.1	29.0	29.9	21.4	29.9	33.3	22.8
1959							
January	29.2	29.0	30.0	21.4	29.9	33.3	22.9
February	29.2	29.0	29.8	21.6	29.9	33.3	23.0
March	29.1	29.0	29.7	21.7	30.0	33.2	23.0
April	29.1	29.0	29.5	21.8	30.0	33.2	23.1
May	29.2	29.0	29.5	21.8	30.1	33.3	23.2
June	29.3	29.1	29.7	21.9	30.2	33.3	23.2
July	29.3	29.2	29.6	21.8	30.2	33.3	23.3
August	29.3	29.2	29.6	21.9	30.2	33.3	23.4
September	29.4	29.3	29.7	21.9	30.3	33.5	23.5
October	29.5	29.4	29.7	22.2	30.4	33.5	23.6
November	29.5	29.4	29.7	22.2	30.4	33.5	23.6
December	29.6	29.4	29.6	22.3	30.5	33.5	23.7

. . . = Not available.

Table 8-1B. Summary Consumer Price Indexes: Historical Data, 1946 to Date—*Continued*

(Seasonally adjusted.)

Year and month	Urban wage earners and clerical workers (CPI-W), all items	Consumer Price Index, 1982–1984 = 100 — All urban consumers (CPI-U)					
		All items	Food	Energy	All items less food and energy	Commod-ities	Services
1960							
January	29.5	29.4	29.6	22.3	30.5	33.5	23.7
February	29.6	29.4	29.5	22.2	30.6	33.4	23.8
March	29.6	29.4	29.6	22.3	30.6	33.5	23.9
April	29.7	29.5	30.0	22.4	30.6	33.6	23.9
May	29.7	29.6	30.0	22.3	30.6	33.6	24.0
June	29.8	29.6	30.0	22.4	30.7	33.6	24.0
July	29.7	29.6	29.9	22.5	30.6	33.5	24.1
August	29.8	29.6	30.0	22.5	30.6	33.6	24.1
September	29.8	29.6	30.1	22.6	30.6	33.6	24.2
October	29.9	29.8	30.3	22.5	30.8	33.7	24.2
November	30.0	29.8	30.5	22.7	30.8	33.8	24.3
December	30.0	29.8	30.5	22.6	30.7	33.9	24.3
1961							
January	30.0	29.8	30.5	22.7	30.8	33.8	24.4
February	30.0	29.8	30.5	22.6	30.8	33.8	24.4
March	30.0	29.8	30.5	22.6	30.9	33.8	24.4
April	30.0	29.8	30.4	22.2	30.9	33.8	24.5
May	30.0	29.8	30.3	22.4	30.9	33.8	24.5
June	30.0	29.8	30.2	22.5	31.0	33.8	24.5
July	30.1	29.9	30.3	22.5	31.0	33.9	24.5
August	30.1	29.9	30.3	22.5	31.1	33.9	24.6
September	30.2	30.0	30.3	22.6	31.1	33.9	24.6
October	30.2	30.0	30.3	22.4	31.1	33.9	24.7
November	30.2	30.0	30.3	22.5	31.2	33.8	24.7
December	30.2	30.0	30.3	22.4	31.2	33.9	24.8
1962							
January	30.2	30.0	30.4	22.4	31.2	33.9	24.8
February	30.3	30.1	30.5	22.6	31.2	34.0	24.8
March	30.4	30.2	30.6	22.4	31.3	34.0	24.9
April	30.4	30.2	30.7	22.7	31.3	34.1	24.9
May	30.4	30.2	30.6	22.7	31.4	34.1	25.0
June	30.4	30.2	30.5	22.5	31.4	34.1	25.0
July	30.4	30.2	30.4	22.3	31.4	34.0	25.1
August	30.5	30.3	30.6	22.4	31.5	34.1	25.1
September	30.6	30.4	30.9	22.8	31.5	34.3	25.1
October	30.6	30.4	30.8	22.7	31.5	34.2	25.1
November	30.6	30.4	30.9	22.7	31.5	34.3	25.2
December	30.6	30.4	30.7	22.8	31.6	34.2	25.2
1963							
January	30.6	30.4	31.0	22.8	31.5	34.3	25.3
February	30.7	30.5	31.1	22.7	31.6	34.3	25.3
March	30.7	30.5	31.0	22.7	31.7	34.3	25.3
April	30.7	30.5	30.9	22.6	31.7	34.3	25.4
May	30.7	30.5	30.9	22.6	31.7	34.3	25.4
June	30.8	30.6	31.0	22.5	31.8	34.4	25.5
July	30.9	30.7	31.2	22.7	31.8	34.5	25.5
August	30.9	30.8	31.2	22.6	31.9	34.6	25.6
September	30.9	30.7	31.1	22.5	31.9	34.5	25.6
October	30.9	30.8	31.0	22.7	32.0	34.5	25.6
November	31.0	30.8	31.2	22.6	32.0	34.6	25.7
December	31.1	30.9	31.3	22.6	32.1	34.7	25.8
1964							
January	31.1	30.9	31.4	22.8	32.2	34.7	25.8
February	31.1	30.9	31.4	22.2	32.2	34.7	25.8
March	31.1	30.9	31.4	22.6	32.2	34.7	25.8
April	31.1	31.0	31.4	22.5	32.2	34.7	25.9
May	31.2	31.0	31.4	22.5	32.2	34.7	25.9
June	31.2	31.0	31.4	22.6	32.3	34.7	26.0
July	31.2	31.0	31.5	22.5	32.3	34.7	26.0
August	31.2	31.1	31.4	22.6	32.3	34.7	26.0
September	31.3	31.1	31.6	22.5	32.3	34.8	26.0
October	31.3	31.1	31.6	22.5	32.4	34.8	26.1
November	31.4	31.2	31.7	22.5	32.5	34.9	26.2
December	31.4	31.3	31.7	22.6	32.5	35.0	26.2
1965							
January	31.5	31.3	31.6	22.8	32.6	35.0	26.3
February	31.5	31.3	31.5	22.7	32.6	34.9	26.4
March	31.5	31.3	31.7	22.6	32.6	35.0	26.4
April	31.6	31.4	31.8	22.9	32.7	35.0	26.5
May	31.7	31.5	32.1	23.0	32.7	35.1	26.5
June	31.8	31.6	32.6	23.1	32.7	35.3	26.5
July	31.8	31.6	32.5	23.0	32.7	35.3	26.6
August	31.7	31.6	32.4	23.0	32.7	35.2	26.6
September	31.8	31.6	32.3	23.1	32.8	35.2	26.7
October	31.8	31.7	32.5	23.0	32.8	35.3	26.8
November	31.9	31.8	32.6	23.1	32.9	35.4	26.9
December	32.0	31.9	32.8	23.1	33.0	35.5	26.9

Table 8-1B. Summary Consumer Price Indexes: Historical Data, 1946 to Date—*Continued*

(Seasonally adjusted.)

Year and month	Urban wage earners and clerical workers (CPI-W), all items	Consumer Price Index, 1982–1984 = 100 All urban consumers (CPI-U)					
		All items	Food	Energy	All items less food and energy	Commod- ities	Services
1966							
January	32.1	31.9	33.0	23.1	33.0	35.6	27.0
February	32.3	32.1	33.5	23.2	33.1	35.8	27.0
March	32.4	32.2	33.8	23.2	33.1	35.9	27.1
April	32.5	32.3	33.8	23.2	33.3	36.0	27.3
May	32.5	32.4	33.7	23.2	33.4	36.0	27.4
June	32.6	32.4	33.7	23.3	33.5	36.0	27.5
July	32.6	32.5	33.5	23.4	33.6	36.1	27.7
August	32.8	32.7	34.0	23.3	33.7	36.2	27.7
September	32.9	32.8	34.1	23.4	33.8	36.4	27.9
October	33.0	32.9	34.2	23.4	34.0	36.4	28.0
November	33.1	32.9	34.1	23.5	34.0	36.4	28.2
December	33.1	32.9	34.0	23.5	34.1	36.4	28.2
1967							
January	33.1	32.9	33.9	23.6	34.2	36.4	28.3
February	33.2	33.0	33.8	23.7	34.2	36.4	28.4
March	33.2	33.0	33.8	23.6	34.3	36.4	28.5
April	33.3	33.1	33.7	23.9	34.4	36.4	28.6
May	33.3	33.1	33.7	23.9	34.5	36.5	28.6
June	33.5	33.3	34.0	23.8	34.6	36.6	28.8
July	33.6	33.4	34.1	23.8	34.7	36.8	28.8
August	33.7	33.5	34.3	23.9	34.9	37.0	28.9
September	33.8	33.6	34.3	24.0	35.0	37.0	29.0
October	33.9	33.7	34.4	23.9	35.1	37.1	29.2
November	34.0	33.9	34.5	24.0	35.2	37.2	29.2
December	34.1	34.0	34.6	23.9	35.4	37.4	29.4
1968							
January	34.3	34.1	34.6	24.0	35.5	37.5	29.5
February	34.4	34.2	34.8	24.1	35.7	37.6	29.6
March	34.5	34.3	34.9	24.1	35.8	37.7	29.8
April	34.6	34.4	35.0	24.0	35.9	37.8	29.9
May	34.7	34.5	35.1	24.1	36.0	37.8	30.0
June	34.9	34.7	35.2	24.2	36.2	38.0	30.2
July	35.0	34.9	35.3	24.2	36.4	38.1	30.4
August	35.2	35.0	35.4	24.3	36.5	38.3	30.6
September	35.3	35.1	35.6	24.3	36.7	38.4	30.7
October	35.5	35.3	35.9	24.3	36.9	38.6	30.9
November	35.6	35.4	35.9	24.4	37.1	38.7	31.0
December	35.8	35.6	36.0	24.3	37.2	38.8	31.2
1969							
January	35.9	35.7	36.1	24.4	37.3	38.9	31.4
February	36.0	35.8	36.1	24.4	37.6	39.0	31.5
March	36.3	36.1	36.2	24.7	37.8	39.3	31.8
April	36.5	36.3	36.4	24.9	38.1	39.4	32.0
May	36.6	36.4	36.6	24.8	38.1	39.5	32.2
June	36.8	36.6	37.0	25.0	38.3	39.8	32.3
July	37.0	36.8	37.3	24.9	38.5	39.9	32.5
August	37.1	36.9	37.5	24.9	38.7	40.1	32.7
September	37.3	37.1	37.7	25.0	38.9	40.2	33.0
October	37.5	37.3	37.8	25.0	39.1	40.4	33.1
November	37.7	37.5	38.2	25.0	39.2	40.6	33.3
December	37.9	37.7	38.6	25.1	39.4	40.8	33.5
1970							
January	38.1	37.9	38.7	25.1	39.6	41.0	33.8
February	38.3	38.1	38.9	25.1	39.8	41.2	34.0
March	38.5	38.3	38.9	25.0	40.1	41.2	34.4
April	38.7	38.5	39.0	25.5	40.4	41.4	34.6
May	38.8	38.6	39.2	25.4	40.5	41.5	34.8
June	39.0	38.8	39.2	25.3	40.8	41.6	35.0
July	39.1	38.9	39.2	25.5	40.9	41.7	35.2
August	39.2	39.0	39.2	25.4	41.1	41.8	35.4
September	39.4	39.2	39.4	25.6	41.3	42.0	35.6
October	39.6	39.4	39.5	25.9	41.5	42.2	35.8
November	39.8	39.6	39.5	26.0	41.8	42.3	36.0
December	40.0	39.8	39.5	26.2	42.0	42.5	36.2
1971							
January	40.1	39.9	39.4	26.3	42.1	42.5	36.4
February	40.2	39.9	39.5	26.2	42.2	42.6	36.5
March	40.2	40.0	39.8	26.2	42.2	42.7	36.5
April	40.4	40.1	40.1	26.1	42.4	42.9	36.6
May	40.5	40.3	40.3	26.2	42.6	43.1	36.7
June	40.7	40.5	40.5	26.3	42.8	43.2	37.0
July	40.9	40.6	40.6	26.3	42.9	43.3	37.1
August	41.0	40.7	40.6	26.8	43.0	43.4	37.3
September	41.0	40.8	40.6	26.9	43.0	43.4	37.4
October	41.1	40.9	40.7	27.0	43.1	43.5	37.5
November	41.2	41.0	40.9	26.9	43.2	43.5	37.6
December	41.4	41.1	41.3	27.0	43.3	43.8	37.7

Table 8-1B. Summary Consumer Price Indexes: Historical Data, 1946 to Date—*Continued*

(Seasonally adjusted.)

Year and month	Urban wage earners and clerical workers (CPI-W), all items	Consumer Price Index, 1982–1984 = 100 — All urban consumers (CPI-U)					
		All items	Food	Energy	All items less food and energy	Commodities	Services
1972							
January	41.5	41.2	41.1	27.0	43.5	43.8	37.9
February	41.6	41.4	41.7	26.8	43.6	44.0	38.0
March	41.7	41.4	41.6	26.9	43.6	44.0	38.1
April	41.7	41.5	41.6	26.9	43.8	44.1	38.2
May	41.8	41.6	41.7	27.0	43.9	44.2	38.3
June	41.9	41.7	41.9	27.0	44.0	44.3	38.4
July	42.1	41.8	42.1	27.1	44.1	44.5	38.5
August	42.2	41.9	42.2	27.3	44.3	44.5	38.6
September	42.3	42.1	42.5	27.6	44.3	44.8	38.7
October	42.5	42.2	42.8	27.7	44.4	44.9	38.8
November	42.6	42.4	43.0	27.9	44.4	45.1	38.9
December	42.8	42.5	43.2	27.8	44.6	45.2	39.0
1973							
January	43.0	42.7	44.0	27.9	44.6	45.5	39.1
February	43.2	43.0	44.6	28.2	44.8	45.9	39.2
March	43.6	43.4	45.8	28.3	45.0	46.4	39.4
April	43.9	43.7	46.5	28.6	45.1	46.8	39.5
May	44.2	43.9	47.1	28.8	45.3	47.2	39.6
June	44.4	44.2	47.6	29.2	45.4	47.5	39.8
July	44.5	44.2	47.7	29.2	45.5	47.5	39.9
August	45.3	45.0	50.5	29.4	45.7	48.7	40.2
September	45.4	45.2	50.4	29.4	46.0	48.7	40.5
October	45.8	45.6	50.7	30.3	46.3	49.0	41.0
November	46.2	45.9	51.4	31.5	46.5	49.5	41.3
December	46.5	46.3	51.9	32.5	46.7	49.9	41.5
1974							
January	47.0	46.8	52.5	34.1	46.9	50.5	41.8
February	47.6	47.3	53.6	35.4	47.2	51.3	42.0
March	48.1	47.8	54.2	36.9	47.6	51.9	42.4
April	48.3	48.1	54.1	37.6	47.9	52.1	42.6
May	48.8	48.6	54.5	38.3	48.5	52.7	43.1
June	49.2	49.0	54.5	38.6	49.0	53.1	43.5
July	49.6	49.3	54.3	38.9	49.5	53.3	44.0
August	50.2	49.9	55.1	39.2	50.2	54.1	44.5
September	50.9	50.6	56.2	39.3	50.7	54.8	45.0
October	51.3	51.0	56.8	39.2	51.2	55.3	45.4
November	51.8	51.5	57.5	39.4	51.6	55.8	45.8
December	52.2	51.9	58.2	39.6	52.0	56.3	46.2
1975							
January	52.6	52.3	58.4	40.0	52.3	56.7	46.5
February	52.9	52.6	58.5	40.3	52.8	56.9	46.9
March	53.1	52.8	58.4	40.6	53.0	57.1	47.0
April	53.3	53.0	58.3	41.0	53.3	57.2	47.3
May	53.4	53.1	58.6	41.3	53.5	57.5	47.5
June	53.8	53.5	59.2	41.7	53.8	57.9	47.8
July	54.3	54.0	60.3	42.5	54.0	58.6	48.0
August	54.5	54.2	60.3	42.8	54.2	58.7	48.3
September	54.9	54.6	60.7	43.2	54.5	59.0	48.7
October	55.2	54.9	61.3	43.5	54.8	59.4	49.0
November	55.6	55.3	61.7	43.9	55.2	59.7	49.6
December	55.9	55.6	62.1	44.1	55.5	59.9	49.9
1976							
January	56.2	55.8	61.9	44.5	55.9	60.0	50.5
February	56.2	55.9	61.3	44.4	56.2	59.9	50.8
March	56.3	56.0	60.9	44.1	56.5	59.8	51.1
April	56.5	56.1	60.9	43.9	56.7	59.9	51.3
May	56.7	56.4	61.1	44.1	57.0	60.2	51.4
June	57.0	56.7	61.3	44.4	57.2	60.4	51.7
July	57.3	57.0	61.6	44.8	57.6	60.7	52.1
August	57.6	57.3	61.8	45.2	57.9	61.0	52.4
September	57.9	57.6	62.1	45.7	58.2	61.3	52.8
October	58.2	57.9	62.4	46.1	58.5	61.6	53.1
November	58.4	58.1	62.3	46.8	58.7	61.7	53.4
December	58.7	58.4	62.5	47.5	58.9	62.0	53.7
1977							
January	59.1	58.7	62.7	48.1	59.3	62.3	54.1
February	59.6	59.3	63.9	48.1	59.7	63.0	54.4
March	59.9	59.6	64.2	48.4	60.0	63.2	54.8
April	60.3	60.0	65.0	48.6	60.3	63.7	55.2
May	60.6	60.2	65.3	48.9	60.6	63.9	55.4
June	60.9	60.5	65.7	48.9	61.0	64.2	55.8
July	61.2	60.8	65.9	49.1	61.2	64.4	56.3
August	61.4	61.1	66.2	49.5	61.5	64.6	56.6
September	61.7	61.3	66.4	49.8	61.8	64.8	56.9
October	61.9	61.6	66.6	50.5	62.0	65.0	57.2
November	62.3	62.0	67.1	51.3	62.3	65.5	57.6
December	62.6	62.3	67.4	51.6	62.7	65.7	57.9

Table 8-1B. Summary Consumer Price Indexes: Historical Data, 1946 to Date—*Continued*

(Seasonally adjusted.)

Year and month	Urban wage earners and clerical workers (CPI-W), all items	Consumer Price Index, 1982–1984 = 100					
		All urban consumers (CPI-U)					
		All items	Food	Energy	All items less food and energy	Commod-ities	Services
1978							
January	63.0	62.7	67.9	51.1	63.1	66.1	58.3
February	63.3	63.0	68.6	50.6	63.4	66.4	58.7
March	63.8	63.4	69.5	51.0	63.8	66.8	59.1
April	64.2	63.9	70.6	51.4	64.3	67.4	59.6
May	64.8	64.5	71.6	51.7	64.7	68.0	60.0
June	65.3	65.0	72.7	51.9	65.2	68.6	60.5
July	65.8	65.5	73.0	52.1	65.6	69.1	61.0
August	66.2	65.9	73.3	52.6	66.1	69.4	61.5
September	66.7	66.5	73.6	53.2	66.7	70.0	62.1
October	67.4	67.1	74.2	54.1	67.2	70.6	62.6
November	67.8	67.5	74.7	54.9	67.6	71.1	63.1
December	68.3	67.9	75.1	55.9	68.0	71.6	63.3
1979							
January	68.8	68.5	76.4	55.8	68.5	72.2	63.8
February	69.6	69.2	77.7	55.9	69.2	72.9	64.4
March	70.3	69.9	78.4	57.4	69.8	73.8	64.9
April	71.1	70.6	79.0	59.5	70.3	74.7	65.5
May	71.9	71.4	79.7	62.0	70.8	75.6	66.2
June	72.7	72.2	80.0	64.7	71.3	76.4	66.8
July	73.5	73.0	80.5	67.3	71.9	77.2	67.6
August	74.2	73.7	80.4	69.7	72.7	77.9	68.5
September	75.0	74.4	80.9	71.9	73.3	78.6	69.2
October	75.7	75.2	81.5	73.5	74.0	79.3	70.1
November	76.5	76.0	82.0	74.8	74.8	80.0	71.1
December	77.3	76.9	82.8	76.8	75.7	80.8	72.0
1980							
January	78.5	78.0	83.3	79.1	76.7	82.0	73.1
February	79.4	79.0	83.4	81.9	77.5	82.8	74.1
March	80.6	80.1	84.1	84.5	78.6	83.9	75.4
April	81.4	80.9	84.7	85.4	79.5	84.4	76.6
May	82.2	81.7	85.2	86.4	80.1	84.9	77.6
June	83.0	82.5	85.7	86.5	81.0	85.3	79.0
July	83.1	82.6	86.6	86.7	80.8	85.9	78.5
August	83.7	83.2	88.0	87.2	81.3	86.9	78.5
September	84.4	83.9	89.1	87.5	82.1	87.8	79.0
October	85.3	84.7	89.8	88.0	83.0	88.5	80.0
November	86.2	85.6	90.8	88.8	83.9	89.2	81.1
December	87.0	86.4	91.3	90.7	84.9	89.7	82.2
1981							
January	87.7	87.2	91.6	92.1	85.4	90.4	83.0
February	88.6	88.0	92.1	95.2	85.9	91.4	83.7
March	89.1	88.6	92.6	97.4	86.4	91.9	84.4
April	89.6	89.1	92.8	97.6	87.0	92.0	85.3
May	90.2	89.7	92.8	97.9	87.8	92.4	86.4
June	90.9	90.5	93.2	97.3	88.6	92.9	87.5
July	92.0	91.5	93.9	97.3	89.8	93.6	88.9
August	92.7	92.2	94.4	97.8	90.7	94.0	89.9
September	93.5	93.1	94.8	98.6	91.8	94.6	91.2
October	93.8	93.4	95.0	99.2	92.1	94.7	91.7
November	94.2	93.8	95.1	100.5	92.5	94.9	92.5
December	94.5	94.1	95.3	101.5	93.0	95.1	93.0
1982							
January	94.8	94.4	95.6	100.6	93.3	95.2	93.5
February	95.1	94.7	96.3	98.0	93.8	95.4	93.9
March	95.0	94.7	96.2	96.6	93.9	95.3	94.0
April	95.3	95.0	96.4	94.2	94.7	95.1	94.9
May	96.1	95.9	97.2	95.7	95.4	96.0	95.7
June	97.3	97.0	98.1	98.4	96.1	97.4	96.5
July	97.8	97.5	98.2	99.3	96.7	97.9	97.0
August	98.1	97.7	98.0	99.8	97.1	97.9	97.6
September	98.1	97.7	98.2	100.3	97.2	97.8	97.6
October	98.5	98.1	98.2	101.7	97.5	98.2	97.9
November	98.4	98.0	98.2	102.5	97.3	98.3	97.7
December	98.1	97.7	98.2	102.8	97.2	98.3	96.9
1983							
January	98.2	97.9	98.1	99.6	97.6	98.3	97.5
February	98.2	98.0	98.2	97.7	98.0	98.1	97.9
March	98.5	98.1	98.8	96.8	98.2	98.2	98.1
April	99.1	98.8	99.2	98.9	98.6	98.9	98.7
May	99.5	99.2	99.5	100.4	98.9	99.5	98.9
June	99.7	99.4	99.6	100.6	99.2	99.8	99.2
July	100.0	99.8	99.6	100.9	99.8	100.2	99.6
August	100.5	100.1	99.7	101.2	100.1	100.5	99.8
September	100.7	100.4	100.0	101.0	100.5	100.7	100.2
October	101.0	100.8	100.3	100.8	101.0	101.0	100.7
November	101.2	101.1	100.3	100.5	101.5	101.1	101.3
December	101.3	101.4	100.6	100.0	101.8	101.2	101.6

Table 8-1B. Summary Consumer Price Indexes: Historical Data, 1946 to Date—*Continued*

(Seasonally adjusted.)

Year and month	Urban wage earners and clerical workers (CPI-W), all items	Consumer Price Index, 1982–1984 = 100					
		All urban consumers (CPI-U)					
		All items	Food	Energy	All items less food and energy	Commod- ities	Services
1984							
January	101.8	102.1	102.0	100.2	102.5	101.9	102.1
February	102.0	102.6	102.7	101.4	102.8	102.4	102.6
March	102.0	102.9	102.9	101.4	103.2	102.6	103.0
April	102.2	103.3	102.9	101.7	103.7	102.9	103.5
May	102.5	103.5	102.7	101.6	104.1	103.0	103.9
June	102.7	103.7	103.1	100.8	104.5	103.1	104.2
July	103.2	104.1	103.3	100.5	105.0	103.2	104.9
August	104.1	104.4	103.9	100.1	105.4	103.4	105.4
September	104.5	104.7	103.8	100.6	105.8	103.6	105.9
October	104.7	105.1	104.0	101.1	106.2	103.9	106.3
November	104.8	105.3	104.1	100.8	106.4	103.9	106.7
December	104.9	105.5	104.5	100.1	106.8	103.9	107.1
1985							
January	105.2	105.7	104.7	100.3	107.1	104.1	107.4
February	105.7	106.3	105.2	100.3	107.7	104.7	107.9
March	106.1	106.8	105.5	101.3	108.1	105.1	108.4
April	106.4	107.0	105.4	102.3	108.4	105.4	108.7
May	106.6	107.2	105.2	102.2	108.8	105.2	109.4
June	106.9	107.5	105.5	102.2	109.1	105.3	109.8
July	107.0	107.7	105.5	102.2	109.4	105.3	110.3
August	107.1	107.9	105.6	101.2	109.8	105.2	110.7
September	107.3	108.1	105.8	101.2	110.0	105.4	111.0
October	107.7	108.5	105.8	101.2	110.5	105.6	111.5
November	108.2	109.0	106.5	101.8	111.1	106.1	112.1
December	108.7	109.5	107.3	102.4	111.4	106.6	112.5
1986							
January	109.1	109.9	107.5	102.6	111.9	106.9	113.1
February	108.8	109.7	107.3	99.5	112.2	106.0	113.5
March	108.1	109.1	107.5	92.6	112.5	104.5	114.1
April	107.7	108.7	107.7	87.2	112.9	103.3	114.6
May	107.8	109.0	108.2	87.2	113.1	103.5	114.8
June	108.3	109.4	108.3	88.8	113.4	103.8	115.5
July	108.3	109.5	109.1	85.6	113.8	103.7	115.7
August	108.4	109.6	110.1	83.6	114.2	103.6	116.1
September	108.8	110.0	110.2	84.4	114.6	104.0	116.5
October	108.9	110.2	110.5	82.8	115.0	104.0	116.9
November	109.2	110.4	111.1	82.1	115.3	104.2	117.2
December	109.5	110.8	111.4	82.5	115.6	104.5	117.5
1987							
January	110.2	111.4	111.8	85.4	115.9	105.5	117.9
February	110.7	111.8	112.2	87.4	116.2	106.1	118.3
March	111.1	112.2	112.4	87.6	116.6	106.5	118.6
April	111.6	112.7	112.6	87.6	117.3	106.9	119.2
May	111.9	113.0	113.2	87.1	117.7	107.2	119.6
June	112.4	113.5	113.9	88.5	117.9	107.7	120.0
July	112.7	113.8	113.7	89.2	118.3	108.0	120.3
August	113.2	114.3	113.9	90.5	118.7	108.5	120.9
September	113.6	114.7	114.3	90.3	119.2	108.8	121.4
October	113.9	115.0	114.5	89.6	119.8	109.0	121.8
November	114.2	115.4	114.5	90.0	120.1	109.3	122.2
December	114.4	115.6	115.1	89.5	120.4	109.3	122.6
1988							
January	114.7	116.0	115.6	88.8	120.9	109.5	123.0
February	114.9	116.2	115.6	88.7	121.2	109.5	123.5
March	115.2	116.5	115.8	88.4	121.7	109.8	123.9
April	115.8	117.2	116.4	88.8	122.3	110.5	124.4
May	116.2	117.5	116.9	88.5	122.7	110.7	124.8
June	116.6	118.0	117.6	88.9	123.2	111.2	125.4
July	117.3	118.5	118.8	89.4	123.6	111.9	125.8
August	117.7	119.0	119.4	90.1	124.0	112.2	126.4
September	118.2	119.5	120.1	89.8	124.7	112.8	126.9
October	118.6	119.9	120.3	89.8	125.2	113.0	127.5
November	118.9	120.3	120.5	89.8	125.6	113.3	127.9
December	119.3	120.7	121.1	89.6	126.0	113.5	128.4
1989							
January	119.9	121.2	121.6	90.3	126.5	114.1	128.9
February	120.3	121.6	122.5	90.8	126.9	114.5	129.4
March	120.9	122.2	123.2	91.8	127.4	115.1	130.0
April	121.9	123.1	123.9	96.6	127.8	116.5	130.5
May	122.5	123.7	124.7	97.4	128.3	117.1	131.1
June	122.8	124.1	125.1	96.9	128.8	117.2	131.6
July	123.2	124.5	125.6	96.7	129.2	117.3	132.3
August	123.2	124.5	125.9	94.9	129.5	117.0	132.8
September	123.4	124.8	126.3	93.8	129.9	117.2	133.1
October	123.9	125.4	126.8	94.4	130.6	117.8	133.7
November	124.4	125.9	127.4	93.9	131.1	118.1	134.3
December	124.9	126.3	127.8	94.2	131.6	118.4	134.9

Table 8-1B. Summary Consumer Price Indexes: Historical Data, 1946 to Date—*Continued*

(Seasonally adjusted.)

Year and month	Urban wage earners and clerical workers (CPI-W), all items	Consumer Price Index, 1982–1984 = 100					
		All urban consumers (CPI-U)					
		All items	Food	Energy	All items less food and energy	Commod-ities	Services
1990							
January	126.1	127.5	129.7	98.9	132.1	120.2	135.4
February	126.6	128.0	130.8	98.2	132.7	120.7	136.0
March	127.0	128.6	131.0	97.6	133.5	120.9	136.8
April	127.3	128.9	130.8	97.5	134.0	121.0	137.4
May	127.5	129.1	131.1	96.7	134.4	121.0	137.9
June	128.2	129.9	132.1	97.3	135.1	121.6	138.8
July	128.8	130.5	132.8	97.1	135.8	122.0	139.6
August	129.9	131.6	133.2	101.6	136.6	123.2	140.6
September	130.9	132.5	133.6	106.5	137.1	124.5	141.1
October	131.7	133.4	134.1	110.8	137.6	125.8	141.6
November	132.1	133.7	134.5	111.2	138.0	126.0	142.2
December	132.5	134.2	134.6	111.0	138.6	126.3	142.7
1991							
January	132.9	134.7	135.0	108.5	139.5	126.3	143.7
February	132.9	134.8	135.1	104.5	140.2	125.9	144.4
March	133.0	134.8	135.3	101.9	140.5	125.5	144.7
April	133.3	135.1	136.1	101.2	140.9	126.0	144.9
May	133.8	135.6	136.6	102.1	141.3	126.4	145.4
June	134.1	136.0	137.4	101.1	141.8	126.7	145.9
July	134.3	136.2	136.7	100.7	142.3	126.6	146.5
August	134.6	136.6	136.2	101.1	142.9	126.8	146.9
September	135.0	137.0	136.4	101.5	143.4	127.0	147.6
October	135.2	137.2	136.2	101.6	143.7	127.0	148.0
November	135.8	137.8	136.7	102.4	144.2	127.6	148.5
December	136.2	138.2	137.0	103.1	144.7	127.9	149.2
1992							
January	136.2	138.3	136.6	101.5	145.1	127.6	149.6
February	136.5	138.6	137.1	101.2	145.4	127.8	149.9
March	136.9	139.1	137.6	101.2	145.9	128.2	150.4
April	137.2	139.4	137.5	101.4	146.3	128.3	150.9
May	137.5	139.7	137.2	102.0	146.8	128.6	151.3
June	138.0	140.1	137.6	103.3	147.1	129.1	151.7
July	138.4	140.5	137.4	103.7	147.6	129.3	152.2
August	138.7	140.8	138.4	103.5	147.9	129.6	152.6
September	139.0	141.1	138.9	103.6	148.1	129.9	152.9
October	139.5	141.7	138.9	104.3	148.8	130.2	153.7
November	139.8	142.1	138.7	105.1	149.2	130.3	154.3
December	140.1	142.3	138.8	105.3	149.6	130.5	154.7
1993							
January	140.5	142.8	139.1	105.0	150.1	130.7	155.3
February	140.8	143.1	139.6	104.3	150.6	131.1	155.6
March	141.0	143.3	139.6	104.9	150.8	131.1	156.0
April	141.4	143.8	140.0	104.9	151.4	131.4	156.7
May	141.8	144.2	141.0	104.3	151.8	131.6	157.3
June	142.0	144.3	140.6	103.9	152.1	131.3	157.8
July	142.1	144.5	140.6	103.4	152.3	131.3	158.1
August	142.4	144.8	141.1	103.4	152.8	131.6	158.6
September	142.5	145.0	141.4	103.0	152.9	131.3	159.0
October	143.2	145.6	142.0	105.3	153.4	132.2	159.4
November	143.4	146.0	142.3	104.4	153.9	132.4	159.9
December	143.7	146.3	142.8	103.7	154.3	132.4	160.5
1994							
January	143.8	146.3	142.9	102.8	154.5	132.3	160.8
February	144.0	146.7	142.7	104.1	154.8	132.4	161.4
March	144.3	147.1	142.7	104.3	155.3	132.5	162.0
April	144.5	147.2	143.0	103.7	155.5	132.6	162.2
May	144.8	147.5	143.3	102.8	155.9	132.9	162.4
June	145.3	147.9	143.8	103.1	156.4	133.5	162.8
July	145.9	148.4	144.6	104.5	156.7	134.1	163.1
August	146.5	149.0	145.1	106.7	157.1	134.7	163.8
September	146.8	149.3	145.3	106.1	157.5	134.8	164.1
October	146.9	149.4	145.3	105.7	157.8	134.8	164.5
November	147.3	149.8	145.6	106.1	158.2	135.0	165.0
December	147.6	150.1	146.8	105.9	158.3	135.4	165.2
1995							
January	148.0	150.5	146.7	105.7	159.0	135.4	166.0
February	148.4	150.9	147.3	105.8	159.4	135.6	166.5
March	148.6	151.2	147.1	105.5	159.9	135.6	167.1
April	149.2	151.8	148.1	105.6	160.4	136.2	167.7
May	149.5	152.1	148.2	105.8	160.7	136.4	168.1
June	149.8	152.4	148.3	106.7	161.1	136.6	168.5
July	149.9	152.6	148.5	105.8	161.4	136.6	168.9
August	150.2	152.9	148.6	105.6	161.8	136.8	169.3
September	150.4	153.1	149.1	104.1	162.2	136.8	169.7
October	150.8	153.5	149.5	104.4	162.7	137.1	170.3
November	150.9	153.7	149.6	103.4	163.0	137.0	170.7
December	151.3	153.9	149.9	104.4	163.1	137.3	170.9

Table 8-1B. Summary Consumer Price Indexes: Historical Data, 1946 to Date—*Continued*

(Seasonally adjusted.)

Year and month	Urban wage earners and clerical workers (CPI-W), all items	Consumer Price Index, 1982–1984 = 100					
		All urban consumers (CPI-U)					
		All items	Food	Energy	All items less food and energy	Commod-ities	Services
1996							
January	152.0	154.7	150.4	106.9	163.7	138.2	171.5
February	152.3	155.0	150.8	107.1	164.0	138.3	172.0
March	152.9	155.5	151.4	108.3	164.4	139.0	172.4
April	153.4	156.1	152.0	111.2	164.6	139.6	172.8
May	153.8	156.4	151.9	112.0	165.0	139.7	173.4
June	154.0	156.7	152.9	110.3	165.4	139.8	173.8
July	154.3	157.0	153.4	110.1	165.7	139.8	174.4
August	154.5	157.2	153.9	109.7	166.0	139.8	174.9
September	154.9	157.7	154.6	109.8	166.5	140.3	175.4
October	155.4	158.2	155.5	110.5	166.8	140.8	175.8
November	155.9	158.7	156.1	111.8	167.2	141.4	176.3
December	156.3	159.1	156.3	113.9	167.4	141.7	176.7
1997							
January	156.6	159.4	155.9	115.2	167.8	141.8	177.3
February	156.9	159.7	156.5	115.0	168.1	142.1	177.6
March	156.9	159.8	156.6	113.0	168.4	141.8	178.0
April	157.0	159.9	156.5	111.0	168.9	141.6	178.4
May	157.0	159.9	156.6	108.8	169.2	141.4	178.7
June	157.3	160.2	156.9	110.0	169.4	141.5	179.2
July	157.4	160.4	157.2	109.1	169.7	141.4	179.7
August	157.8	160.8	157.7	110.9	169.8	141.9	179.9
September	158.2	161.2	158.0	112.4	170.2	142.2	180.4
October	158.4	161.5	158.3	111.8	170.6	142.2	180.9
November	158.6	161.7	158.6	111.4	170.8	142.1	181.4
December	158.6	161.8	158.7	109.8	171.2	142.1	181.7
1998							
January	158.8	162.0	159.5	107.5	171.6	142.0	182.1
February	158.7	162.0	159.4	105.1	171.9	141.8	182.3
March	158.7	162.0	159.7	103.3	172.2	141.4	182.8
April	158.8	162.2	159.7	102.4	172.5	141.3	183.3
May	159.3	162.6	160.3	103.2	172.9	141.7	183.7
June	159.5	162.8	160.2	103.6	173.2	141.8	184.0
July	159.8	163.2	160.6	103.3	173.5	142.1	184.3
August	160.0	163.4	161.0	102.1	174.0	142.2	184.7
September	160.1	163.5	161.1	101.3	174.2	142.0	185.1
October	160.5	163.9	162.0	101.5	174.4	142.3	185.5
November	160.7	164.1	162.2	101.1	174.8	142.2	186.0
December	161.1	164.4	162.4	100.1	175.4	142.5	186.4
1999							
January	161.4	164.7	163.0	99.7	175.6	142.8	186.6
February	161.3	164.7	163.3	99.2	175.6	142.4	186.9
March	161.4	164.8	163.3	100.4	175.7	142.4	187.4
April	162.4	165.9	163.5	105.5	176.3	144.0	187.9
May	162.6	166.0	163.8	104.9	176.5	143.9	188.1
June	162.6	166.0	163.7	104.5	176.6	143.8	188.3
July	163.3	166.7	163.9	106.7	177.1	144.5	188.9
August	163.8	167.1	164.2	109.5	177.3	145.0	189.3
September	164.6	167.8	164.6	111.8	177.8	145.9	189.8
October	164.9	168.1	165.0	112.0	178.1	146.1	190.2
November	165.1	168.4	165.3	111.5	178.4	145.9	190.9
December	165.6	168.8	165.5	113.8	178.7	146.5	191.2
2000							
January	166.0	169.3	165.6	115.0	179.3	146.7	192.0
February	166.7	170.0	166.2	118.8	179.4	147.6	192.5
March	167.8	171.0	166.5	124.3	180.0	149.1	193.1
April	167.6	170.9	166.7	120.9	180.3	148.5	193.5
May	167.9	171.2	167.3	120.0	180.7	148.5	194.0
June	169.0	172.2	167.4	126.8	181.1	149.6	194.9
July	169.5	172.7	168.3	127.3	181.5	149.8	195.7
August	169.3	172.7	168.7	123.8	181.9	149.2	196.3
September	170.3	173.6	168.9	129.2	182.3	150.4	196.9
October	170.5	173.9	169.0	129.6	182.6	150.1	197.7
November	170.8	174.2	169.2	129.2	183.1	150.3	198.1
December	171.2	174.6	170.0	130.1	183.3	150.4	198.8
2001							
January	172.2	175.6	170.3	135.0	183.9	150.6	200.6
February	172.5	176.0	171.2	134.1	184.4	150.8	201.2
March	172.6	176.1	171.7	131.7	184.7	150.5	201.6
April	173.0	176.4	172.1	132.3	185.1	150.9	202.0
May	174.0	177.3	172.4	138.4	185.3	151.9	202.7
June	174.2	177.7	173.1	136.9	186.0	151.9	203.5
July	173.8	177.4	173.6	129.6	186.4	150.9	203.8
August	173.8	177.4	174.0	127.3	186.7	150.4	204.4
September	174.7	178.1	174.2	130.9	187.1	151.6	204.5
October	173.9	177.6	174.8	122.9	187.4	150.3	204.8
November	173.7	177.5	174.9	116.9	188.1	149.2	205.6
December	173.4	177.4	174.7	113.9	188.4	148.3	206.1

Table 8-1B. Summary Consumer Price Indexes: Historical Data, 1946 to Date—*Continued*

(Seasonally adjusted.)

Year and month	Urban wage earners and clerical workers (CPI-W), all items	Consumer Price Index, 1982–1984 = 100					
		All urban consumers (CPI-U)					
		All items	Food	Energy	All items less food and energy	Commod-ities	Services
2002							
January	173.7	177.7	175.3	114.2	188.7	148.3	206.8
February	173.9	178.0	175.7	113.5	189.1	148.3	207.5
March	174.5	178.5	176.1	117.6	189.2	149.0	207.9
April	175.4	179.3	176.4	121.5	189.7	150.0	208.5
May	175.5	179.5	175.8	121.9	190.0	149.7	209.0
June	175.7	179.6	175.9	121.6	190.2	149.7	209.3
July	176.1	180.0	176.1	122.4	190.5	149.9	209.9
August	176.6	180.5	176.1	123.1	191.1	150.2	210.6
September	176.8	180.8	176.5	123.7	191.3	150.2	211.1
October	177.2	181.2	176.4	126.9	191.5	150.5	211.7
November	177.5	181.5	176.9	126.7	191.9	150.5	212.4
December	177.7	181.8	177.1	127.1	192.1	150.3	213.0
2003							
January	178.6	182.6	177.1	133.5	192.4	151.3	213.7
February	179.7	183.6	178.1	140.8	192.5	152.7	214.2
March	180.1	183.9	178.4	143.9	192.5	152.6	215.0
April	179.2	183.2	178.5	136.5	192.5	151.1	215.1
May	178.7	182.9	178.8	129.4	192.9	149.4	216.0
June	178.9	183.1	179.7	129.8	193.0	149.7	216.2
July	179.4	183.7	179.8	132.2	193.4	150.3	216.8
August	180.3	184.5	180.5	137.8	193.6	151.4	217.2
September	180.9	185.1	180.9	142.9	193.7	152.1	217.8
October	180.6	184.9	181.6	137.8	194.0	151.1	218.4
November	180.6	185.0	182.6	136.9	194.0	151.1	218.6
December	181.0	185.5	183.5	138.8	194.2	151.6	219.0
2004							
January	181.9	186.3	183.4	143.9	194.6	152.5	219.7
February	182.4	186.7	183.9	145.8	194.9	153.1	220.1
March	182.7	187.1	184.2	145.1	195.5	153.3	220.8
April	182.8	187.4	184.6	143.4	195.9	153.0	221.4
May	183.8	188.2	186.1	147.6	196.2	154.2	221.9
June	184.4	188.9	186.4	151.5	196.6	154.9	222.7
July	184.6	189.1	186.8	151.1	196.8	154.6	223.2
August	184.7	189.2	187.0	151.5	196.9	154.4	223.7
September	185.3	189.8	186.9	152.9	197.5	154.9	224.2
October	186.4	190.8	187.8	158.6	197.9	156.7	224.6
November	187.4	191.7	188.4	163.8	198.3	157.8	225.4
December	187.4	191.7	188.4	162.3	198.6	157.4	225.8
2005							
January	187.2	191.6	188.7	157.2	199.0	156.8	226.2
February	188.0	192.4	188.6	161.8	199.4	157.5	226.9
March	188.6	193.1	189.1	163.5	200.1	157.9	228.0
April	189.3	193.7	190.4	166.7	200.2	158.6	228.5
May	189.1	193.6	190.6	163.3	200.5	158.1	228.9
June	189.3	193.7	190.5	163.7	200.6	158.0	229.1
July	190.6	194.9	190.9	172.8	200.9	159.6	229.9
August	192.0	196.1	191.1	183.5	201.1	161.5	230.4
September	195.1	198.8	191.5	208.2	201.3	166.0	231.4
October	195.2	199.1	192.0	205.9	202.0	164.8	233.1
November	193.7	198.1	192.6	191.0	202.5	161.8	234.2
December	193.7	198.1	192.9	187.6	202.8	161.5	234.4
2006							
January	195.1	199.3	193.6	196.6	203.2	162.9	235.5
February	195.0	199.4	193.7	194.1	203.6	162.5	235.9
March	195.3	199.7	194.0	192.0	204.3	162.6	236.5
April	196.4	200.7	193.8	198.5	204.8	164.1	237.1
May	197.0	201.3	194.1	199.8	205.4	164.6	237.8
June	197.4	201.8	194.7	199.8	205.9	164.8	238.5
July	198.6	202.9	195.2	207.9	206.3	166.4	239.2
August	199.5	203.8	195.7	211.9	206.8	167.2	239.9
September	198.3	202.8	196.3	198.1	207.2	164.6	240.7
October	197.1	201.9	196.9	184.1	207.6	162.5	241.0
November	197.2	202.0	197.0	184.1	207.8	162.0	241.7
December	198.4	203.1	197.1	192.7	208.1	163.4	242.4
2007							
January	198.6	203.4	198.4	190.3	208.6	163.3	243.2
February	199.4	204.2	199.7	192.3	209.1	164.1	244.1
March	200.7	205.3	200.4	200.2	209.4	165.6	244.7
April	201.3	205.9	201.0	203.3	209.7	166.2	245.3
May	202.3	206.8	201.7	208.6	210.1	167.3	245.9
June	202.7	207.2	202.6	209.8	210.4	167.5	246.6
July	203.0	207.6	203.2	209.6	210.8	167.8	247.1
August	203.0	207.7	204.0	206.4	211.1	167.5	247.5
September	204.0	208.5	205.0	210.7	211.6	168.5	248.2
October	204.7	209.2	205.7	212.4	212.1	169.0	249.1
November	206.5	210.8	206.5	223.8	212.7	171.5	249.8
December	207.1	211.4	206.9	225.6	213.2	172.0	250.5

Table 8-1B. Summary Consumer Price Indexes: Historical Data, 1946 to Date—*Continued*

(Seasonally adjusted.)

Year and month	Urban wage earners and clerical workers (CPI-W), all items	Consumer Price Index, 1982–1984 = 100					
		All urban consumers (CPI-U)					
		All items	Food	Energy	All items less food and energy	Commod-ities	Services
2008							
January	207.9	212.2	208.1	226.8	213.8	172.7	251.3
February	208.4	212.6	208.9	229.7	213.9	173.0	251.8
March	209.2	213.4	209.3	233.3	214.4	173.7	252.9
April	209.8	214.0	211.1	234.8	214.6	174.1	253.6
May	211.1	215.2	212.0	243.9	214.9	175.5	254.7
June	213.7	217.5	213.3	262.1	215.4	178.8	255.8
July	215.5	219.1	215.4	271.1	216.0	180.7	257.1
August	215.0	218.7	216.5	262.6	216.4	179.6	257.6
September	215.1	218.9	217.8	260.1	216.7	179.8	257.6
October	212.7	217.0	218.7	238.1	216.8	175.8	257.7
November	207.9	213.1	219.1	195.2	216.9	168.0	257.8
December	205.9	211.4	219.1	176.6	216.9	164.5	258.0
2009							
January	206.5	212.0	219.2	178.8	217.3	165.3	258.4
February	207.4	212.8	219.0	184.9	217.8	166.8	258.7
March	207.1	212.6	218.5	178.8	218.3	166.2	258.7
April	207.4	212.7	218.2	177.1	218.7	166.5	258.7
May	207.8	213.0	217.8	179.7	218.9	167.2	258.6
June	209.9	214.7	217.8	196.9	219.2	170.7	258.7
July	210.0	214.7	217.4	195.6	219.3	170.5	258.7
August	210.9	215.5	217.4	201.5	219.5	171.3	259.3
September	211.3	215.9	217.3	202.8	219.9	171.9	259.6
October	211.9	216.5	217.5	204.6	220.5	172.7	260.0
November	212.7	217.1	217.6	210.3	220.6	173.8	260.2
December	213.0	217.3	217.9	210.3	220.8	174.2	260.3
2010							
January	213.4	217.5	218.5	212.8	220.6	174.9	259.8
February	213.3	217.3	218.6	209.6	220.7	174.3	260.0
March	213.3	217.4	219.0	209.3	220.8	174.1	260.3
April	213.2	217.4	219.2	209.2	220.8	173.9	260.7
May	212.9	217.3	219.3	206.6	221.0	173.4	260.9
June	212.9	217.2	219.3	203.8	221.2	172.9	261.2
July	213.5	217.6	219.2	206.9	221.4	173.4	261.5
August	213.9	217.9	219.5	208.8	221.5	173.8	261.7
September	214.3	218.3	220.2	209.8	221.7	174.4	261.9
October	215.1	219.0	220.5	216.7	221.8	175.7	262.1
November	215.5	219.6	220.9	219.5	222.1	176.5	262.4
December	216.9	220.5	221.2	227.1	222.3	177.9	262.7
2011							
January	217.5	221.2	222.5	229.3	222.8	178.9	263.2
February	218.2	221.9	223.5	232.1	223.2	179.8	263.7
March	219.5	223.0	225.2	240.1	223.5	181.8	264.1
April	220.8	224.1	226.1	248.0	223.7	183.5	264.5
May	221.6	224.8	226.9	250.7	224.2	184.5	264.9
June	221.5	224.8	227.5	245.5	224.7	184.1	265.3
July	222.1	225.4	228.5	246.2	225.2	184.6	266.0
August	222.8	226.1	229.6	246.9	225.9	185.3	266.7
September	223.4	226.6	230.7	248.6	226.1	185.8	267.1
October	223.5	226.8	230.9	246.7	226.5	185.7	267.5
November	224.0	227.2	231.1	247.6	226.9	186.2	267.8
December	223.9	227.2	231.6	243.4	227.4	185.7	268.5
2012							
January	224.5	227.8	232.2	244.9	227.9	186.5	268.9
February	225.1	228.3	232.1	248.9	228.0	187.4	269.0
March	225.7	228.8	232.6	249.7	228.5	187.9	269.6
April	226.0	229.2	233.0	249.7	228.9	188.1	270.1
May	225.4	228.7	233.2	241.8	229.2	186.8	270.4
June	225.0	228.5	233.7	235.9	229.6	185.8	271.0
July	224.9	228.6	233.8	233.6	230.0	185.5	271.4
August	226.4	229.9	234.2	245.0	230.2	187.5	272.1
September	227.7	231.0	234.4	253.0	230.7	189.1	272.7
October	228.4	231.6	234.8	256.0	231.0	189.8	273.2
November	227.8	231.2	235.3	248.8	231.3	188.5	273.8
December	227.7	231.2	235.7	244.7	231.7	187.7	274.4
2013							
January	228.1	231.7	236.0	245.0	232.2	188.0	275.1
February	229.6	232.9	236.0	255.7	232.6	189.9	275.8
March	228.8	232.3	236.2	246.6	232.8	188.1	276.2
April	228.1	231.8	236.7	240.5	232.8	186.8	276.5
May	228.3	231.9	236.5	240.5	233.0	186.5	277.0
June	228.8	232.4	237.0	242.7	233.4	187.1	277.4
July	229.2	232.9	237.2	243.0	233.9	187.3	278.1
August	229.8	233.5	237.5	244.8	234.3	187.8	278.7
September	229.8	233.5	237.5	242.7	234.7	187.4	279.4
October	229.9	233.7	237.8	242.0	234.9	187.2	279.8
November	230.4	234.1	237.9	242.7	235.4	187.5	280.3
December	231.0	234.7	238.2	245.7	235.8	188.2	280.9

Table 8-1B. Summary Consumer Price Indexes: Historical Data, 1946 to Date—*Continued*

(Seasonally adjusted.)

Year and month	Urban wage earners and clerical workers (CPI-W), all items	Consumer Price Index, 1982–1984 = 100					
		All urban consumers (CPI-U)					
		All items	Food	Energy	All items less food and energy	Commod-ities	Services
2014							
January	231.6	235.3	238.5	250.3	236.0	188.5	281.7
February	231.9	235.5	239.4	249.9	236.2	188.4	282.3
March	232.3	236.0	240.4	250.0	236.6	188.1	283.5
April	232.8	236.5	241.2	249.9	237.1	188.8	283.8
May	233.1	236.9	242.4	249.2	237.5	188.8	284.7
June	233.4	237.2	242.6	249.7	237.8	189.0	285.1
July	233.6	237.5	243.2	248.7	238.2	188.9	285.7
August	233.5	237.5	243.8	245.7	238.4	188.5	286.0
September	233.4	237.5	244.5	241.6	238.8	188.1	286.4
October	233.2	237.4	244.9	237.1	239.2	187.5	286.9
November	232.6	237.0	245.4	229.0	239.5	186.1	287.4
December	231.5	236.3	246.2	218.5	239.6	184.0	288.0
2015							
January	229.5	234.7	246.2	199.9	239.8	180.3	288.6
February	230.3	235.3	246.5	203.0	240.2	181.1	288.9
March	230.9	236.0	246.1	205.8	240.8	181.9	289.5
April	231.1	236.2	246.0	203.6	241.3	181.6	290.2
May	232.0	237.0	246.2	209.0	241.7	182.9	290.5
June	232.7	237.7	246.9	212.0	242.1	183.4	291.3
July	233.0	238.0	247.2	211.6	242.6	183.4	292.0
August	233.0	238.0	247.7	208.6	242.8	182.9	292.5
September	232.1	237.5	248.5	197.2	243.3	181.2	293.1
October	232.3	237.7	248.8	195.6	243.8	180.9	293.9
November	232.5	238.0	248.5	195.1	244.2	180.7	294.6
December	232.1	237.8	248.2	190.1	244.5	179.7	295.0
2016							
January	231.9	237.7	248.4	185.2	245.0	178.8	295.8
February	231.3	237.3	248.6	176.4	245.5	177.5	296.4
March	232.2	238.1	248.0	182.2	245.9	178.3	297.1
April	233.2	239.0	248.2	186.7	246.6	179.3	297.9
May	233.7	239.6	247.9	188.6	247.1	179.5	298.9
June	234.4	240.2	247.7	192.9	247.5	179.9	299.7
July	234.1	240.1	247.7	189.0	247.8	178.9	300.5
August	234.5	240.5	247.7	188.8	248.4	178.8	301.4
September	235.2	241.2	247.8	192.2	248.8	179.5	302.0
October	235.8	241.7	247.8	196.0	249.1	180.1	302.5
November	236.0	242.0	247.7	196.4	249.5	179.8	303.3
December	236.7	242.6	247.7	199.5	249.9	180.3	304.0
2017							
January	237.7	243.6	248.0	205.5	250.5	181.6	304.8
February	237.9	243.9	248.7	203.5	250.9	181.2	305.7
March	237.7	243.8	249.1	202.2	250.8	181.1	305.6
April	238.2	244.3	249.5	203.8	251.3	181.4	306.3
May	237.9	244.1	249.9	198.7	251.5	180.3	306.9
June	238.0	244.2	249.8	197.7	251.8	179.9	307.6
July	238.0	244.3	250.3	195.7	252.0	179.5	308.1
August	239.0	245.2	250.5	201.1	252.6	180.4	309.0
September	240.6	246.6	250.9	211.9	253.0	182.5	309.7
October	240.6	246.7	251.2	208.4	253.5	181.9	310.5
November	241.5	247.4	251.3	214.7	253.7	182.8	311.0
December	241.8	247.7	251.7	213.1	254.3	182.7	311.8
2018							
January	242.9	248.7	252.2	217.3	255.0	183.9	312.6
February	243.4	249.3	252.2	219.8	255.5	184.2	313.5
March	243.5	249.5	252.3	216.5	256.1	183.8	314.3
April	244.3	250.3	252.9	219.4	256.7	184.6	315.0
May	244.8	250.8	252.9	220.8	257.2	184.8	315.8
June	245.3	251.2	253.3	221.1	257.5	184.9	316.5
July	245.4	251.3	253.8	219.2	257.9	184.7	317.1
August	245.8	251.7	254.1	221.8	258.1	184.8	317.6
September	246.2	252.2	254.4	222.4	258.5	185.1	318.2
October	247.1	252.9	254.2	226.7	259.0	185.9	318.9
November	246.8	252.8	254.9	221.3	259.4	185.2	319.4
December	246.1	252.5	255.7	212.4	259.9	183.5	320.4
2019							
January	246.0	252.5	256.4	205.5	260.5	182.9	321.1
February	246.7	253.1	257.2	208.7	260.9	183.7	321.6
March	247.9	254.3	257.8	216.4	261.4	185.1	322.4
April	248.9	255.2	257.5	221.8	262.0	186.1	323.3
May	249.0	255.3	258.0	219.7	262.3	185.9	323.8
June	248.9	255.4	258.0	214.7	262.9	185.2	324.6
July	249.5	255.9	258.1	215.9	263.5	185.6	325.3
August	249.7	256.2	258.3	213.2	264.1	185.3	326.1
September	250.1	256.6	258.9	213.1	264.6	185.3	326.9
October	250.8	257.3	259.4	216.6	265.0	185.8	327.9
November	251.3	257.8	259.9	217.4	265.5	185.9	328.7
December	251.9	258.3	260.3	219.8	265.7	186.3	329.3

Table 8-1C. Consumer and Producer Price Indexes: Historical Data, 1913–1949

(Not seasonally adjusted.)

Year and month	Consumer price indexes, 1982–1984 =100				Producer Price Indexes for goods, 1982 = 100			
	All urban consumers (CPI-U)		Urban wage earners and clerical workers (CPI-W)		All commodities		Farm products	Industrial commodities
	Index	Percent change	Index	Percent change	Index	Percent change		
1913	9.9	. . .	10.0	. . .	12.0	. . .	18.0	11.9
1914	10.0	1.0	10.1	1.0	11.8	-1.7	17.9	11.3
1915	10.1	1.0	10.2	1.0	12.0	1.7	18.0	11.6
1916	10.9	7.9	11.0	7.8	14.7	22.5	21.3	15.0
1917	12.8	17.4	12.9	17.3	20.2	37.4	32.6	19.5
1918	15.1	18.0	15.1	17.1	22.6	11.9	37.4	21.1
1919	17.3	14.6	17.4	15.2	23.9	5.8	39.8	22.0
1920	20.0	15.6	20.1	15.5	26.6	11.3	38.0	27.4
1921	17.9	-10.5	18.0	-10.4	16.8	-36.8	22.3	17.8
1922	16.8	-6.1	16.9	-6.1	16.7	-0.6	23.7	17.4
1923	17.1	1.8	17.2	1.8	17.3	3.6	24.9	17.8
1924	17.1	0.0	17.2	0.0	16.9	-2.3	25.2	17.0
1925	17.5	2.3	17.6	2.3	17.8	5.3	27.7	17.5
1926	17.7	1.1	17.8	1.1	17.2	-3.4	25.3	17.0
1927	17.4	-1.7	17.5	-1.7	16.5	-4.1	25.1	16.0
1928	17.1	-1.7	17.2	-1.7	16.7	1.2	26.7	15.8
1929	17.1	0.0	17.2	0.0	16.4	-1.8	26.4	15.6
1930	16.7	-2.3	16.8	-2.3	14.9	-9.1	22.4	14.5
1931	15.2	-9.0	15.3	-8.9	12.6	-15.4	16.4	12.8
1932	13.7	-9.9	13.7	-10.5	11.2	-11.1	12.2	11.9
1933	13.0	-5.1	13.0	-5.1	11.4	1.8	13.0	12.1
1934	13.4	3.1	13.5	3.8	12.9	13.2	16.5	13.3
1935	13.7	2.2	13.8	2.2	13.8	7.0	19.8	13.3
1936	13.9	1.5	13.9	0.7	13.9	0.7	20.4	13.5
1937	14.4	3.6	14.4	3.6	14.9	7.2	21.8	14.5
1938	14.1	-2.1	14.2	-1.4	13.5	-9.4	17.3	13.9
1939	13.9	-1.4	14.0	-1.4	13.3	-1.5	16.5	13.9
1940	14.0	0.7	14.1	0.7	13.5	1.5	17.1	14.1
1941	14.7	5.0	14.8	5.0	15.1	11.9	20.8	15.1
1942	16.3	10.9	16.4	10.8	17.0	12.6	26.7	16.2
1943	17.3	6.1	17.4	6.1	17.8	4.7	30.9	16.5
1944	17.6	1.7	17.7	1.7	17.9	0.6	31.2	16.7
1945	18.0	2.3	18.1	2.3	18.2	1.7	32.4	17.0
1946	19.5	8.3	19.6	8.3	20.8	14.3	37.5	18.6
1947	22.3	14.4	22.5	14.8	25.6	23.1	45.1	22.7
1948	24.1	8.1	24.2	7.6	27.7	8.2	48.5	24.6
1949	23.8	-1.2	24.0	-0.8	26.3	-5.1	41.9	24.1
1913								
January	9.8	. . .	9.9	. . .	12.1	. . .	17.6	12.3
February	9.8	0.0	9.8	-1.0	12.0	-0.8	17.5	12.2
March	9.8	0.0	9.8	0.0	12.0	0.0	17.6	12.1
April	9.8	0.0	9.9	1.0	12.0	0.0	17.5	12.0
May	9.7	-1.0	9.8	-1.0	11.9	-0.8	17.4	11.9
June	9.8	1.0	9.8	0.0	11.9	0.0	17.6	11.8
July	9.9	1.0	9.9	1.0	12.0	0.8	18.1	11.8
August	9.9	0.0	10.0	1.0	12.0	0.0	18.2	11.7
September	10.0	1.0	10.0	0.0	12.2	1.7	18.8	11.8
October	10.0	0.0	10.1	1.0	12.2	0.0	18.8	11.8
November	10.1	1.0	10.1	0.0	12.1	-0.8	18.9	11.7
December	10.0	-1.0	10.1	0.0	11.9	-1.7	18.5	11.6
1914								
January	10.0	0.0	10.1	0.0	11.8	-0.8	18.4	11.5
February	9.9	-1.0	10.0	-1.0	11.8	0.0	18.3	11.5
March	9.9	0.0	10.0	0.0	11.7	-0.8	18.2	11.5
April	9.8	-1.0	9.9	-1.0	11.7	0.0	18.0	11.5
May	9.9	1.0	9.9	0.0	11.6	-0.9	18.0	11.4
June	9.9	0.0	10.0	1.0	11.6	0.0	18.1	11.3
July	10.0	1.0	10.1	1.0	11.6	0.0	18.0	11.2
August	10.2	2.0	10.2	1.0	12.0	3.4	18.3	11.2
September	10.2	0.0	10.3	1.0	12.1	0.8	17.9	11.3
October	10.1	-1.0	10.2	-1.0	11.7	-3.3	17.2	11.0
November	10.2	1.0	10.2	0.0	11.7	0.0	17.6	11.0
December	10.1	-1.0	10.2	0.0	11.6	-0.9	17.4	11.0
1915								
January	10.1	0.0	10.2	0.0	11.8	1.7	18.1	11.1
February	10.0	-1.0	10.1	-1.0	11.8	0.0	18.4	11.0
March	9.9	-1.0	10.0	-1.0	11.8	0.0	17.9	11.0
April	10.0	1.0	10.1	1.0	11.8	0.0	18.2	11.1
May	10.1	1.0	10.1	0.0	11.9	0.8	18.2	11.2
June	10.1	0.0	10.2	1.0	11.8	-0.8	17.7	11.4
July	10.1	0.0	10.2	0.0	11.9	0.8	18.1	11.5
August	10.1	0.0	10.2	0.0	11.8	-0.8	17.9	11.5
September	10.1	0.0	10.2	0.0	11.8	0.0	17.5	11.7
October	10.2	1.0	10.3	1.0	12.1	2.5	18.1	11.9
November	10.3	1.0	10.4	1.0	12.3	1.7	18.0	12.3
December	10.3	0.0	10.4	0.0	12.8	4.1	18.4	12.9

. . . = Not available.

Table 8-1C. Consumer and Producer Price Indexes: Historical Data, 1913–1949—*Continued*

(Not seasonally adjusted.)

Year and month	Consumer price indexes, 1982–1984 =100				Producer Price Indexes for goods, 1982 = 100			
	All urban consumers (CPI-U)		Urban wage earners and clerical workers (CPI-W)		All commodities		Farm products	Industrial commodities
	Index	Percent change	Index	Percent change	Index	Percent change		
1916								
January	10.4	1.0	10.5	1.0	13.3	3.9	19.4	13.6
February	10.4	0.0	10.5	0.0	13.5	1.5	19.4	14.0
March	10.5	1.0	10.6	1.0	13.9	3.0	19.4	14.4
April	10.6	1.0	10.7	0.9	14.1	1.4	19.6	14.6
May	10.7	0.9	10.7	0.0	14.2	0.7	19.8	14.7
June	10.8	0.9	10.9	1.9	14.3	0.7	19.7	14.8
July	10.8	0.0	10.9	0.0	14.4	0.7	20.3	14.6
August	10.9	0.9	11.0	0.9	14.7	2.1	21.7	14.6
September	11.1	1.8	11.2	1.8	15.0	2.0	22.6	14.8
October	11.3	1.8	11.3	0.9	15.7	4.7	23.7	15.5
November	11.5	1.8	11.5	1.8	16.8	7.0	25.3	16.8
December	11.6	0.9	11.6	0.9	17.1	1.8	25.0	17.7
1917								
January	11.7	0.9	11.8	1.7	17.6	2.9	26.2	18.3
February	12.0	2.6	12.0	1.7	18.0	2.3	27.2	18.6
March	12.0	0.0	12.1	0.8	18.5	2.8	28.6	18.8
April	12.6	5.0	12.6	4.1	19.7	6.5	31.6	19.0
May	12.8	1.6	12.9	2.4	20.8	5.6	33.6	19.8
June	13.0	1.6	13.0	0.8	21.0	1.0	33.8	20.4
July	12.8	-1.5	12.9	-0.8	21.2	1.0	34.0	20.7
August	13.0	1.6	13.1	1.6	21.5	1.4	34.6	20.7
September	13.3	2.3	13.3	1.5	21.3	-0.9	34.3	20.1
October	13.5	1.5	13.6	2.3	21.1	-0.9	35.2	19.1
November	13.5	0.0	13.6	0.0	21.2	0.5	36.0	19.2
December	13.7	1.5	13.8	1.5	21.2	0.0	35.6	19.5
1918								
January	14.0	2.2	14.0	1.4	21.6	1.9	37.0	19.9
February	14.1	0.7	14.2	1.4	21.1	-2.3	37.1	19.0
March	14.0	-0.7	14.1	-0.7	21.8	3.3	37.3	20.2
April	14.2	1.4	14.3	1.4	22.1	1.4	36.6	20.7
May	14.5	2.1	14.5	1.4	22.1	0.0	35.4	21.0
June	14.7	1.4	14.8	2.1	22.2	0.5	35.4	21.3
July	15.1	2.7	15.2	2.7	22.7	2.3	37.0	21.5
August	15.4	2.0	15.4	1.3	23.2	2.2	38.6	21.7
September	15.7	1.9	15.8	2.6	23.7	2.2	39.6	22.1
October	16.0	1.9	16.1	1.9	23.5	-0.8	38.2	22.1
November	16.3	1.9	16.3	1.2	23.5	0.0	38.0	22.1
December	16.5	1.2	16.6	1.8	23.5	0.0	38.1	21.8
1919								
January	16.5	0.0	16.6	0.0	23.2	-1.3	38.9	21.1
February	16.2	-1.8	16.2	-2.4	22.4	-3.4	37.5	20.6
March	16.4	1.2	16.5	1.9	22.6	0.9	38.5	20.1
April	16.7	1.8	16.8	1.8	22.9	1.3	40.0	20.0
May	16.9	1.2	17.0	1.2	23.3	1.7	40.9	20.2
June	16.9	0.0	17.0	0.0	23.4	0.4	39.6	21.1
July	17.4	3.0	17.5	2.9	24.3	3.8	41.5	22.1
August	17.7	1.7	17.8	1.7	24.9	2.5	41.3	23.1
September	17.8	0.6	17.9	0.6	24.3	-2.4	38.7	23.2
October	18.1	1.7	18.2	1.7	24.4	0.4	38.5	23.5
November	18.5	2.2	18.6	2.2	24.9	2.0	40.3	23.8
December	18.9	2.2	19.0	2.2	26.0	4.4	41.8	24.7
1920								
January	19.3	2.1	19.4	2.1	27.2	4.6	43.0	26.1
February	19.5	1.0	19.6	1.0	27.1	-0.4	41.2	27.1
March	19.7	1.0	19.8	1.0	27.3	0.7	41.5	27.7
April	20.3	3.0	20.4	3.0	28.5	4.4	42.5	28.7
May	20.6	1.5	20.7	1.5	28.8	1.1	42.8	29.0
June	20.9	1.5	21.0	1.4	28.7	-0.3	42.3	29.0
July	20.8	-0.5	20.9	-0.5	28.6	-0.3	40.5	29.5
August	20.3	-2.4	20.4	-2.4	27.8	-2.8	37.8	29.7
September	20.0	-1.5	20.1	-1.5	26.8	-3.6	36.4	28.5
October	19.9	-0.5	20.0	-0.5	24.9	-7.1	32.2	26.9
November	19.8	-0.5	19.9	-0.5	23.0	-7.6	30.0	24.5
December	19.4	-2.0	19.5	-2.0	20.8	-9.6	26.4	22.7
1921								
January	19.0	-2.1	19.1	-2.1	19.6	-5.8	25.6	21.1
February	18.4	-3.2	18.5	-3.1	18.1	-7.7	23.4	19.4
March	18.3	-0.5	18.4	-0.5	17.7	-2.2	22.7	18.7
April	18.1	-1.1	18.2	-1.1	17.0	-4.0	20.9	18.4
May	17.7	-2.2	17.8	-2.2	16.6	-2.4	21.0	17.9
June	17.6	-0.6	17.7	-0.6	16.1	-3.0	20.3	17.4
July	17.7	0.6	17.8	0.6	16.1	0.0	21.8	16.9
August	17.7	0.0	17.8	0.0	16.1	0.0	22.5	16.5
September	17.5	-1.1	17.6	-1.1	16.1	0.0	22.7	16.5
October	17.5	0.0	17.6	0.0	16.2	0.6	22.7	17.0
November	17.4	-0.6	17.5	-0.6	16.2	0.0	22.1	17.3
December	17.3	-0.6	17.4	-0.6	16.0	-1.2	22.2	17.0

Table 8-1C. Consumer and Producer Price Indexes: Historical Data, 1913–1949—*Continued*

(Not seasonally adjusted.)

Year and month	Consumer price indexes, 1982–1984 =100				Producer Price Indexes for goods, 1982 = 100			
	All urban consumers (CPI-U)		Urban wage earners and clerical workers (CPI-W)		All commodities		Farm products	Industrial commodities
	Index	Percent change	Index	Percent change	Index	Percent change		
1922								
January	16.9	-2.3	17.0	-2.3	15.7	-1.9	22.2	16.7
February	16.9	0.0	17.0	0.0	16.0	1.9	24.0	16.6
March	16.7	-1.2	16.8	-1.2	16.0	0.0	23.6	16.5
April	16.7	0.0	16.8	0.0	16.1	0.6	23.4	16.6
May	16.7	0.0	16.8	0.0	16.6	3.1	23.8	17.4
June	16.7	0.0	16.8	0.0	16.6	0.0	23.4	17.4
July	16.8	0.6	16.9	0.6	17.1	3.0	24.1	18.1
August	16.6	-1.2	16.7	-1.2	17.0	-0.6	23.0	18.2
September	16.6	0.0	16.7	0.0	17.1	0.6	23.3	18.2
October	16.7	0.6	16.8	0.6	17.2	0.6	23.8	17.9
November	16.8	0.6	16.9	0.6	17.3	0.6	24.7	17.7
December	16.9	0.6	17.0	0.6	17.3	0.0	25.0	17.7
1923								
January	16.8	-0.6	16.9	-0.6	17.6	1.7	25.1	18.2
February	16.8	0.0	16.9	0.0	17.8	1.1	25.3	18.6
March	16.8	0.0	16.9	0.0	18.0	1.1	25.3	18.8
April	16.9	0.6	17.0	0.6	17.9	-0.6	24.8	18.7
May	16.9	0.0	17.0	0.0	17.5	-2.2	24.4	18.3
June	17.0	0.6	17.1	0.6	17.3	-1.1	24.2	17.9
July	17.2	1.2	17.3	1.2	17.0	-1.7	23.7	17.6
August	17.1	-0.6	17.2	-0.6	16.9	-0.6	24.2	17.4
September	17.2	0.6	17.3	0.6	17.2	1.8	25.3	17.3
October	17.3	0.6	17.4	0.6	17.1	-0.6	25.4	17.1
November	17.3	0.0	17.4	0.0	17.0	-0.6	25.7	16.9
December	17.3	0.0	17.4	0.0	16.9	-0.6	25.5	16.9
1924								
January	17.3	0.0	17.4	0.0	17.2	1.8	25.6	17.4
February	17.2	-0.6	17.3	-0.6	17.2	0.0	25.0	17.6
March	17.1	-0.6	17.2	-0.6	17.0	-1.2	24.2	17.5
April	17.0	-0.6	17.1	-0.6	16.7	-1.8	24.6	17.3
May	17.0	0.0	17.1	0.0	16.5	-1.2	24.0	17.0
June	17.0	0.0	17.1	0.0	16.4	-0.6	23.8	16.7
July	17.1	0.6	17.2	0.6	16.5	0.6	24.9	16.6
August	17.0	-0.6	17.1	-0.6	16.7	1.2	25.7	16.6
September	17.1	0.6	17.2	0.6	16.7	0.0	25.3	16.6
October	17.2	0.6	17.3	0.6	16.9	1.2	26.0	16.6
November	17.2	0.0	17.3	0.0	17.1	1.2	26.2	16.8
December	17.3	0.6	17.4	0.6	17.5	2.3	27.3	17.1
1925								
January	17.3	0.0	17.4	0.0	17.7	1.1	28.7	17.3
February	17.2	-0.6	17.3	-0.6	17.9	1.1	28.4	17.7
March	17.3	0.6	17.4	0.6	17.9	0.0	28.5	17.5
April	17.2	-0.6	17.3	-0.6	17.5	-2.2	27.1	17.2
May	17.3	0.6	17.4	0.6	17.5	0.0	27.1	17.3
June	17.5	1.2	17.6	1.1	17.7	1.1	27.6	17.5
July	17.7	1.1	17.8	1.1	18.0	1.7	28.3	17.6
August	17.7	0.0	17.8	0.0	17.9	-0.6	28.1	17.4
September	17.7	0.0	17.8	0.0	17.8	-0.6	27.7	17.4
October	17.7	0.0	17.8	0.0	17.8	0.0	27.0	17.5
November	18.0	1.7	18.1	1.7	18.0	1.1	27.3	17.6
December	17.9	-0.6	18.0	-0.6	17.8	-1.1	26.6	17.6
1926								
January	17.9	0.0	18.0	0.0	17.8	0.0	27.1	17.5
February	17.9	0.0	18.0	0.0	17.6	-1.1	26.5	17.3
March	17.8	-0.6	17.9	-0.6	17.3	-1.7	25.7	17.1
April	17.9	0.6	18.0	0.6	17.3	0.0	26.0	17.0
May	17.8	-0.6	17.9	-0.6	17.3	0.0	25.8	17.0
June	17.7	-0.6	17.8	-0.6	17.3	0.0	25.5	17.0
July	17.5	-1.1	17.6	-1.1	17.1	-1.2	24.9	16.9
August	17.4	-0.6	17.5	-0.6	17.1	0.0	24.6	16.9
September	17.5	0.6	17.6	0.6	17.2	0.6	25.1	16.9
October	17.6	0.6	17.7	0.6	17.1	-0.6	24.7	16.9
November	17.7	0.6	17.8	0.6	17.0	-0.6	23.9	16.9
December	17.7	0.0	17.8	0.0	16.9	-0.6	24.0	16.7
1927								
January	17.5	-1.1	17.6	-1.1	16.4	-3.0	24.3	16.4
February	17.4	-0.6	17.5	-0.6	16.6	1.2	24.1	16.3
March	17.3	-0.6	17.4	-0.6	16.5	-0.6	23.8	16.1
April	17.3	0.0	17.4	0.0	16.3	-1.2	23.8	15.9
May	17.4	0.6	17.5	0.6	16.2	-0.6	24.3	15.9
June	17.6	1.1	17.7	1.1	16.2	0.0	24.3	15.9
July	17.3	-1.7	17.4	-1.7	16.2	0.0	24.6	15.9
August	17.2	-0.6	17.3	-0.6	16.4	1.2	25.8	15.9
September	17.3	0.6	17.4	0.6	16.6	1.2	26.7	16.0
October	17.4	0.6	17.5	0.6	16.7	0.6	26.5	15.9
November	17.3	-0.6	17.4	-0.6	16.6	-0.6	26.3	15.8
December	17.3	0.0	17.4	0.0	16.6	0.0	26.3	15.9

Table 8-1C. Consumer and Producer Price Indexes: Historical Data, 1913–1949—*Continued*

(Not seasonally adjusted.)

Year and month	Consumer price indexes, 1982–1984 =100				Producer Price Indexes for goods, 1982 = 100			
	All urban consumers (CPI-U)		Urban wage earners and clerical workers (CPI-W)		All commodities		Farm products	Industrial commodities
	Index	Percent change	Index	Percent change	Index	Percent change		
1928								
January	17.3	0.0	17.4	0.0	16.6	0.0	26.8	15.8
February	17.1	-1.2	17.2	-1.1	16.5	-0.6	26.4	15.8
March	17.1	0.0	17.2	0.0	16.5	0.0	26.1	15.8
April	17.1	0.0	17.2	0.0	16.7	1.2	27.1	15.8
May	17.2	0.6	17.3	0.6	16.8	0.6	27.7	15.8
June	17.1	-0.6	17.2	-0.6	16.7	-0.6	26.9	15.8
July	17.1	0.0	17.2	0.0	16.8	0.6	27.4	15.8
August	17.1	0.0	17.2	0.0	16.8	0.0	27.0	15.8
September	17.3	1.2	17.4	1.2	17.0	1.2	27.5	15.8
October	17.2	-0.6	17.3	-0.6	16.7	-1.8	26.1	15.8
November	17.2	0.0	17.3	0.0	16.5	-1.2	25.7	15.8
December	17.1	-0.6	17.2	-0.6	16.5	0.0	26.2	15.8
1929								
January	17.1	0.0	17.2	0.0	16.5	0.0	26.7	15.7
February	17.1	0.0	17.2	0.0	16.4	-0.6	26.6	15.6
March	17.0	-0.6	17.1	-0.6	16.6	1.2	27.1	15.7
April	16.9	-0.6	17.0	-0.6	16.5	-0.6	26.5	15.6
May	17.0	0.6	17.1	0.6	16.3	-1.2	25.8	15.6
June	17.1	0.6	17.2	0.6	16.4	0.6	26.1	15.6
July	17.3	1.2	17.4	1.2	16.6	1.2	27.1	15.6
August	17.3	0.0	17.4	0.0	16.6	0.0	27.1	15.5
September	17.3	0.0	17.4	0.0	16.6	0.0	26.9	15.6
October	17.3	0.0	17.4	0.0	16.4	-1.2	26.2	15.6
November	17.3	0.0	17.4	0.0	16.1	-1.8	25.5	15.5
December	17.2	-0.6	17.3	-0.6	16.1	0.0	25.7	15.4
1930								
January	17.1	-0.6	17.2	-0.6	15.9	-1.2	25.5	15.2
February	17.0	-0.6	17.1	-0.6	15.7	-1.3	24.7	15.1
March	16.9	-0.6	17.0	-0.6	15.5	-1.3	23.9	15.0
April	17.0	0.6	17.1	0.6	15.5	0.0	24.2	15.0
May	16.9	-0.6	17.0	-0.6	15.3	-1.3	23.5	14.9
June	16.8	-0.6	16.9	-0.6	15.0	-2.0	22.5	14.6
July	16.6	-1.2	16.7	-1.2	14.5	-3.3	21.0	14.4
August	16.5	-0.6	16.6	-0.6	14.5	0.0	21.4	14.2
September	16.6	0.6	16.7	0.6	14.5	0.0	21.5	14.2
October	16.5	-0.6	16.6	-0.6	14.3	-1.4	20.8	14.0
November	16.4	-0.6	16.5	-0.6	14.0	-2.1	20.0	13.8
December	16.1	-1.8	16.2	-1.8	13.7	-2.1	19.0	13.6
1931								
January	15.9	-1.2	16.0	-1.2	13.5	-1.5	18.4	13.4
February	15.7	-1.3	15.7	-1.9	13.2	-2.2	17.7	13.3
March	15.6	-0.6	15.6	-0.6	13.1	-0.8	17.8	13.1
April	15.5	-0.6	15.5	-0.6	12.9	-1.5	17.7	12.9
May	15.3	-1.3	15.4	-0.6	12.6	-2.3	16.9	12.8
June	15.1	-1.3	15.2	-1.3	12.4	-1.6	16.5	12.6
July	15.1	0.0	15.2	0.0	12.4	0.0	16.4	12.6
August	15.1	0.0	15.1	-0.7	12.4	0.0	16.1	12.6
September	15.0	-0.7	15.1	0.0	12.3	-0.8	15.3	12.6
October	14.9	-0.7	15.0	-0.7	12.1	-1.6	14.8	12.4
November	14.7	-1.3	14.8	-1.3	12.1	0.0	14.8	12.5
December	14.6	-0.7	14.7	-0.7	11.8	-2.5	14.1	12.3
1932								
January	14.3	-2.1	14.4	-2.0	11.6	-1.7	13.3	12.2
February	14.1	-1.4	14.2	-1.4	11.4	-1.7	12.8	12.1
March	14.0	-0.7	14.1	-0.7	11.4	0.0	12.7	12.0
April	13.9	-0.7	14.0	-0.7	11.3	-0.9	12.4	12.0
May	13.7	-1.4	13.8	-1.4	11.1	-1.8	11.8	11.9
June	13.6	-0.7	13.7	-0.7	11.0	-0.9	11.6	11.9
July	13.6	0.0	13.7	0.0	11.1	0.9	12.1	11.8
August	13.5	-0.7	13.5	-1.5	11.2	0.9	12.4	11.9
September	13.4	-0.7	13.5	0.0	11.3	0.9	12.4	11.9
October	13.3	-0.7	13.4	-0.7	11.1	-1.8	11.8	11.9
November	13.2	-0.8	13.3	-0.7	11.0	-0.9	11.8	11.9
December	13.1	-0.8	13.2	-0.8	10.8	-1.8	11.1	11.7
1933								
January	12.9	-1.5	13.0	-1.5	10.5	-2.8	10.8	11.4
February	12.7	-1.6	12.8	-1.5	10.3	-1.9	10.3	11.2
March	12.6	-0.8	12.7	-0.8	10.4	1.0	10.8	11.2
April	12.6	0.0	12.6	-0.8	10.4	0.0	11.2	11.1
May	12.6	0.0	12.7	0.8	10.8	3.8	12.7	11.3
June	12.7	0.8	12.8	0.8	11.2	3.7	13.4	11.7
July	13.1	3.1	13.2	3.1	11.9	6.3	15.2	12.3
August	13.2	0.8	13.3	0.8	12.0	0.8	14.6	12.6
September	13.2	0.0	13.3	0.0	12.2	1.7	14.4	13.0
October	13.2	0.0	13.3	0.0	12.3	0.8	14.1	13.1
November	13.2	0.0	13.3	0.0	12.3	0.0	14.3	13.1
December	13.2	0.0	13.2	-0.8	12.2	-0.8	14.0	13.2

Table 8-1C. Consumer and Producer Price Indexes: Historical Data, 1913–1949—*Continued*

(Not seasonally adjusted.)

Year and month	Consumer price indexes, 1982–1984 =100				Producer Price Indexes for goods, 1982 = 100			
	All urban consumers (CPI-U)		Urban wage earners and clerical workers (CPI-W)		All commodities		Farm products	Industrial commodities
	Index	Percent change	Index	Percent change	Index	Percent change		
1934								
January	13.2	0.0	13.3	0.8	12.4	1.6	14.8	13.3
February	13.3	0.8	13.4	0.8	12.7	2.4	15.5	13.4
March	13.3	0.0	13.4	0.0	12.7	0.0	15.5	13.4
April	13.3	0.0	13.4	0.0	12.7	0.0	15.1	13.4
May	13.3	0.0	13.4	0.0	12.7	0.0	15.1	13.4
June	13.4	0.8	13.4	0.0	12.9	1.6	16.0	13.3
July	13.4	0.0	13.4	0.0	12.9	0.0	16.3	13.3
August	13.4	0.0	13.5	0.7	13.2	2.3	17.6	13.3
September	13.6	1.5	13.7	1.5	13.4	1.5	18.5	13.3
October	13.5	-0.7	13.6	-0.7	13.2	-1.5	17.8	13.3
November	13.5	0.0	13.5	-0.7	13.2	0.0	17.8	13.3
December	13.4	-0.7	13.5	0.0	13.3	0.8	18.2	13.3
1935								
January	13.6	1.5	13.7	1.5	13.6	2.3	19.6	13.2
February	13.7	0.7	13.8	0.7	13.7	0.7	20.0	13.2
March	13.7	0.0	13.8	0.0	13.7	0.0	19.7	13.2
April	13.8	0.7	13.9	0.7	13.8	0.7	20.3	13.1
May	13.8	0.0	13.8	-0.7	13.8	0.0	20.3	13.2
June	13.7	-0.7	13.8	0.0	13.8	0.0	19.8	13.3
July	13.7	0.0	13.7	-0.7	13.7	-0.7	19.5	13.3
August	13.7	0.0	13.7	0.0	13.9	1.5	20.0	13.3
September	13.7	0.0	13.8	0.7	13.9	0.0	20.1	13.2
October	13.7	0.0	13.8	0.0	13.9	0.0	19.7	13.3
November	13.8	0.7	13.9	0.7	13.9	0.0	19.6	13.4
December	13.8	0.0	13.9	0.0	14.0	0.7	19.8	13.4
1936								
January	13.8	0.0	13.9	0.0	13.9	-0.7	19.7	13.4
February	13.8	0.0	13.8	-0.7	13.9	0.0	20.1	13.4
March	13.7	-0.7	13.8	0.0	13.7	-1.4	19.3	13.4
April	13.7	0.0	13.8	0.0	13.7	0.0	19.4	13.4
May	13.7	0.0	13.8	0.0	13.5	-1.5	19.0	13.4
June	13.8	0.7	13.9	0.7	13.7	1.5	19.7	13.4
July	13.9	0.7	14.0	0.7	13.9	1.5	20.5	13.5
August	14.0	0.7	14.1	0.7	14.0	0.7	21.2	13.5
September	14.0	0.0	14.1	0.0	14.0	0.0	21.2	13.5
October	14.0	0.0	14.1	0.0	14.0	0.0	21.2	13.6
November	14.0	0.0	14.1	0.0	14.2	1.4	21.5	13.8
December	14.0	0.0	14.1	0.0	14.5	2.1	22.4	14.0
1937								
January	14.1	0.7	14.2	0.7	14.8	2.1	23.1	14.2
February	14.1	0.0	14.2	0.0	14.9	0.7	23.1	14.3
March	14.2	0.7	14.3	0.7	15.1	1.3	23.8	14.5
April	14.3	0.7	14.4	0.7	15.2	0.7	23.3	14.7
May	14.4	0.7	14.4	0.0	15.1	-0.7	22.7	14.7
June	14.4	0.0	14.5	0.7	15.0	-0.7	22.3	14.6
July	14.5	0.7	14.5	0.0	15.2	1.3	22.6	14.7
August	14.5	0.0	14.6	0.7	15.1	-0.7	21.8	14.6
September	14.6	0.7	14.7	0.7	15.1	0.0	21.7	14.6
October	14.6	0.0	14.6	-0.7	14.7	-2.6	20.3	14.5
November	14.5	-0.7	14.5	-0.7	14.4	-2.0	19.1	14.3
December	14.4	-0.7	14.5	0.0	14.1	-2.1	18.4	14.2
1938								
January	14.2	-1.4	14.3	-1.4	14.0	-0.7	18.1	14.2
February	14.1	-0.7	14.2	-0.7	13.8	-1.4	17.6	14.1
March	14.1	0.0	14.2	0.0	13.7	-0.7	17.7	14.1
April	14.2	0.7	14.2	0.0	13.5	-1.5	17.2	14.0
May	14.1	-0.7	14.2	0.0	13.5	0.0	17.0	13.9
June	14.1	0.0	14.2	0.0	13.5	0.0	17.3	13.8
July	14.1	0.0	14.2	0.0	13.6	0.7	17.5	13.9
August	14.1	0.0	14.2	0.0	13.4	-1.5	17.0	13.9
September	14.1	0.0	14.2	0.0	13.5	0.7	17.2	13.9
October	14.0	-0.7	14.1	-0.7	13.4	-0.7	16.8	13.8
November	14.0	0.0	14.1	0.0	13.4	0.0	17.1	13.7
December	14.0	0.0	14.1	0.0	13.3	-0.7	17.0	13.6
1939								
January	14.0	0.0	14.0	-0.7	13.3	0.0	17.0	13.6
February	13.9	-0.7	14.0	0.0	13.3	0.0	16.9	13.6
March	13.9	0.0	13.9	-0.7	13.2	-0.8	16.6	13.7
April	13.8	-0.7	13.9	0.0	13.1	-0.8	16.1	13.7
May	13.8	0.0	13.9	0.0	13.1	0.0	16.1	13.7
June	13.8	0.0	13.9	0.0	13.0	-0.8	15.7	13.6
July	13.8	0.0	13.9	0.0	13.0	0.0	15.8	13.6
August	13.8	0.0	13.9	0.0	12.9	-0.8	15.4	13.6
September	14.1	2.2	14.2	2.2	13.6	5.4	17.3	14.0
October	14.0	-0.7	14.1	-0.7	13.7	0.7	16.9	14.2
November	14.0	0.0	14.1	0.0	13.6	-0.7	17.0	14.3
December	14.0	0.0	14.0	-0.7	13.7	0.7	17.1	14.3

Table 8-1C. Consumer and Producer Price Indexes: Historical Data, 1913–1949—*Continued*

(Not seasonally adjusted.)

Year and month	Consumer price indexes, 1982–1984 =100				Producer Price Indexes for goods, 1982 = 100			
	All urban consumers (CPI-U)		Urban wage earners and clerical workers (CPI-W)		All commodities		Farm products	Industrial commodities
	Index	Percent change	Index	Percent change	Index	Percent change		
1940								
January	13.9	-0.7	14.0	0.0	13.7	0.0	17.4	14.3
February	14.0	0.7	14.1	0.7	13.6	-0.7	17.3	14.2
March	14.0	0.0	14.1	0.0	13.5	-0.7	17.1	14.1
April	14.0	0.0	14.1	0.0	13.5	0.0	17.5	14.0
May	14.0	0.0	14.1	0.0	13.5	0.0	17.1	14.0
June	14.1	0.7	14.1	0.0	13.4	-0.7	16.7	14.0
July	14.0	-0.7	14.1	0.0	13.4	0.0	16.8	14.0
August	14.0	0.0	14.1	0.0	13.4	0.0	16.5	14.0
September	14.0	0.0	14.1	0.0	13.4	0.0	16.7	14.0
October	14.0	0.0	14.1	0.0	13.6	1.5	16.8	14.2
November	14.0	0.0	14.1	0.0	13.7	0.7	17.2	14.3
December	14.1	0.7	14.2	0.7	13.8	0.7	17.6	14.3
1941								
January	14.1	0.0	14.2	0.0	13.9	0.7	18.1	14.3
February	14.1	0.0	14.2	0.0	13.9	0.0	17.7	14.3
March	14.2	0.7	14.2	0.0	14.0	0.7	18.1	14.4
April	14.3	0.7	14.4	1.4	14.4	2.9	18.8	14.6
May	14.4	0.7	14.5	0.7	14.6	1.4	19.3	14.9
June	14.7	2.1	14.7	1.4	15.0	2.7	20.7	15.1
July	14.7	0.0	14.8	0.7	15.3	2.0	21.7	15.2
August	14.9	1.4	14.9	0.7	15.6	2.0	22.1	15.5
September	15.1	1.3	15.2	2.0	15.8	1.3	23.0	15.6
October	15.3	1.3	15.4	1.3	15.9	0.6	22.7	15.9
November	15.4	0.7	15.5	0.6	15.9	0.0	22.9	15.9
December	15.5	0.6	15.5	0.0	16.2	1.9	23.9	15.9
1942								
January	15.7	1.3	15.7	1.3	16.5	1.9	25.5	16.1
February	15.8	0.6	15.9	1.3	16.7	1.2	25.6	16.1
March	16.0	1.3	16.1	1.3	16.8	0.6	26.0	16.2
April	16.1	0.6	16.2	0.6	17.0	1.2	26.4	16.2
May	16.3	1.2	16.3	0.6	17.0	0.0	26.3	16.3
June	16.3	0.0	16.4	0.6	17.0	0.0	26.3	16.3
July	16.4	0.6	16.5	0.6	17.0	0.0	26.6	16.3
August	16.5	0.6	16.6	0.6	17.1	0.6	26.8	16.2
September	16.5	0.0	16.6	0.0	17.2	0.6	27.2	16.2
October	16.7	1.2	16.8	1.2	17.2	0.0	27.5	16.2
November	16.8	0.6	16.9	0.6	17.3	0.6	27.9	16.3
December	16.9	0.6	17.0	0.6	17.4	0.6	28.7	16.3
1943								
January	16.9	0.0	17.0	0.0	17.5	0.6	29.5	16.4
February	16.9	0.0	17.0	0.0	17.7	1.1	30.0	16.4
March	17.2	1.8	17.3	1.8	17.8	0.6	31.0	16.4
April	17.4	1.2	17.5	1.2	17.9	0.6	31.2	16.5
May	17.5	0.6	17.6	0.6	17.9	0.0	31.7	16.5
June	17.5	0.0	17.6	0.0	17.9	0.0	31.9	16.5
July	17.4	-0.6	17.5	-0.6	17.8	-0.6	31.5	16.5
August	17.3	-0.6	17.4	-0.6	17.8	0.0	31.2	16.5
September	17.4	0.6	17.5	0.6	17.8	0.0	31.0	16.5
October	17.4	0.0	17.5	0.0	17.8	0.0	30.9	16.5
November	17.4	0.0	17.5	0.0	17.7	-0.6	30.6	16.6
December	17.4	0.0	17.5	0.0	17.8	0.6	30.7	16.6
1944								
January	17.4	0.0	17.5	0.0	17.8	0.0	30.7	16.6
February	17.4	0.0	17.5	0.0	17.8	0.0	30.9	16.7
March	17.4	0.0	17.5	0.0	17.9	0.6	31.2	16.7
April	17.5	0.6	17.6	0.6	17.9	0.0	31.1	16.7
May	17.5	0.0	17.6	0.0	17.9	0.0	31.0	16.7
June	17.6	0.6	17.7	0.6	18.0	0.6	31.5	16.7
July	17.7	0.6	17.8	0.6	17.9	-0.6	31.3	16.7
August	17.7	0.0	17.8	0.0	17.9	0.0	30.9	16.8
September	17.7	0.0	17.8	0.0	17.9	0.0	31.0	16.8
October	17.7	0.0	17.8	0.0	17.9	0.0	31.2	16.8
November	17.7	0.0	17.8	0.0	18.0	0.6	31.4	16.8
December	17.8	0.6	17.9	0.6	18.0	0.0	31.6	16.8
1945								
January	17.8	0.0	17.9	0.0	18.1	0.6	31.9	16.8
February	17.8	0.0	17.9	0.0	18.1	0.0	32.1	16.9
March	17.8	0.0	17.9	0.0	18.1	0.0	32.1	16.9
April	17.8	0.0	17.9	0.0	18.2	0.6	32.5	16.9
May	17.9	0.6	18.0	0.6	18.3	0.5	32.8	16.9
June	18.1	1.1	18.2	1.1	18.3	0.0	32.9	16.9
July	18.1	0.0	18.2	0.0	18.3	0.0	32.5	17.0
August	18.1	0.0	18.2	0.0	18.2	-0.5	32.0	17.0
September	18.1	0.0	18.2	0.0	18.1	-0.5	31.4	17.0
October	18.1	0.0	18.2	0.0	18.2	0.6	32.1	17.0
November	18.1	0.0	18.2	0.0	18.4	1.1	33.1	17.0
December	18.2	0.6	18.3	0.5	18.4	0.0	33.2	17.1

Table 8-1C. Consumer and Producer Price Indexes: Historical Data, 1913–1949—*Continued*

(Not seasonally adjusted.)

Year and month	Consumer price indexes, 1982–1984 =100				Producer Price Indexes for goods, 1982 = 100			
	All urban consumers (CPI-U)		Urban wage earners and clerical workers (CPI-W)		All commodities		Farm products	Industrial commodities
	Index	Percent change	Index	Percent change	Index	Percent change		
1946								
January	18.2	0.0	18.3	0.0	18.4	0.0	32.7	17.1
February	18.1	-0.5	18.2	-0.5	18.5	0.5	33.0	17.2
March	18.3	1.1	18.4	1.1	18.8	1.6	33.6	17.4
April	18.4	0.5	18.5	0.5	19.0	1.1	34.1	17.5
May	18.5	0.5	18.6	0.5	19.1	0.5	34.7	17.7
June	18.7	1.1	18.8	1.1	19.4	1.6	35.4	18.0
July	19.8	5.9	19.9	5.9	21.5	10.8	39.6	18.6
August	20.2	2.0	20.3	2.0	22.2	3.3	40.6	19.0
September	20.4	1.0	20.5	1.0	21.4	-3.6	39.0	19.1
October	20.8	2.0	20.9	2.0	23.1	7.9	41.7	19.7
November	21.3	2.4	21.5	2.9	24.1	4.3	42.8	20.6
December	21.5	0.9	21.6	0.5	24.3	0.8	42.4	21.2
1947								
January	21.5	0.0	21.6	0.0	24.5	0.8	41.6	21.8
February	21.5	0.0	21.6	0.0	24.7	0.8	42.6	22.0
March	21.9	1.9	22.1	2.3	25.3	2.4	45.5	22.3
April	21.9	0.0	22.1	0.0	25.1	-0.8	44.0	22.4
May	21.9	0.0	22.0	-0.5	25.0	-0.4	43.6	22.3
June	22.0	0.5	22.2	0.9	25.0	0.0	43.8	22.4
July	22.2	0.9	22.4	0.9	25.3	1.2	44.3	22.5
August	22.5	1.4	22.6	0.9	25.6	1.2	44.8	22.8
September	23.0	2.2	23.1	2.2	26.1	2.0	46.6	23.1
October	23.0	0.0	23.1	0.0	26.4	1.1	47.4	23.3
November	23.1	0.4	23.3	0.9	26.7	1.1	47.7	23.6
December	23.4	1.3	23.6	1.3	27.2	1.9	50.1	23.9
1948								
January	23.7	1.3	23.8	0.8	27.7	1.8	51.2	24.3
February	23.5	-0.8	23.6	-0.8	27.2	-1.8	47.7	24.1
March	23.4	-0.4	23.6	0.0	27.2	0.0	47.6	24.1
April	23.8	1.7	23.9	1.3	27.4	0.7	48.3	24.3
May	23.9	0.4	24.1	0.8	27.5	0.4	49.4	24.3
June	24.1	0.8	24.2	0.4	27.7	0.7	50.4	24.4
July	24.4	1.2	24.5	1.2	28.0	1.1	50.2	24.6
August	24.5	0.4	24.6	0.4	28.2	0.7	49.6	24.9
September	24.5	0.0	24.6	0.0	28.1	-0.4	48.8	25.0
October	24.4	-0.4	24.5	-0.4	27.8	-1.1	46.9	25.0
November	24.2	-0.8	24.4	-0.4	27.8	0.0	46.3	25.1
December	24.1	-0.4	24.2	-0.8	27.6	-0.7	45.2	25.1
1949								
January	24.0	-0.4	24.2	0.0	27.3	-1.1	43.8	24.9
February	23.8	-0.8	23.9	-1.2	26.8	-1.8	42.0	24.7
March	23.8	0.0	24.0	0.4	26.8	0.0	42.7	24.6
April	23.9	0.4	24.0	0.0	26.5	-1.1	42.7	24.3
May	23.8	-0.4	24.0	0.0	26.3	-0.8	42.7	24.0
June	23.9	0.4	24.0	0.0	26.0	-1.1	41.8	23.8
July	23.7	-0.8	23.8	-0.8	26.0	0.0	41.7	23.7
August	23.8	0.4	23.9	0.4	26.0	0.0	41.7	23.8
September	23.9	0.4	24.0	0.4	26.1	0.4	41.8	23.8
October	23.7	-0.8	23.9	-0.4	26.0	-0.4	41.0	23.8
November	23.8	0.4	23.9	0.0	26.0	0.0	40.9	23.8
December	23.6	-0.8	23.8	-0.4	25.9	-0.4	40.3	23.8

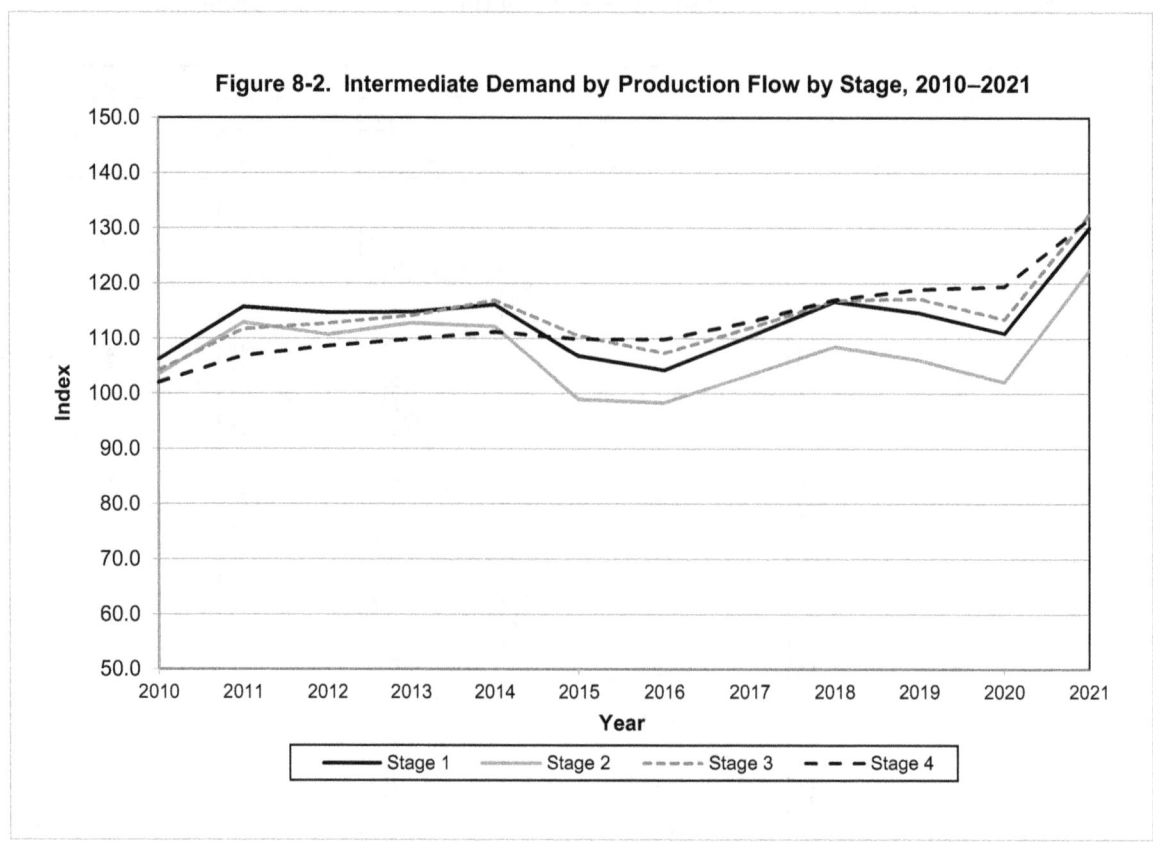

Figure 8-2. Intermediate Demand by Production Flow by Stage, 2010–2021

- The producer price index (PPI) measures inflation from the perspective of costs to industry or producers of products. Because it measures price changes before they reach consumers, some people see it as an earlier predictor of inflation than the CPI.

- Goods and services can be classified as final demand, i.e., sold to consumers, businesses, governments and imports or exports, while intermediate demand goods and services that are used as inputs into another goods and services. The production flow treatment of intermediate demand is a stage-based system of price indexes. As such, four stages of price indexes are reported, i.e., Stages 1 to 4 as shown in Figure 8-2. For example, Stage 1 includes oil and gas extraction which are sold to Stage 2 oil refineries. Refined oil and gas are then sold to Stage 3 gas-fired electric power plants so manufacturing companies can produce automobiles, etc.

- COVID-19 interrupted the whole economy with demand plummeting in 2020. Prices declined as demand decreased. However, demand for many products soared in 2021 and 2022 leading to much higher prices as supply chain disruptions led to less product being available.

- A broader system of the Producer Price Index, includes the Producer Price Index (PPI) Final Demand Intermediate Demand (FD-ID). This includes services and construction as well as goods and was introduced in 2014, featuring a more detailed representation by stages of production as well. However, these new measures only go back to November 2009. (Tables 8-5 and 8-6)

Table 8-2. Consumer Price Indexes and Purchasing Power of the Dollar

(1982–1984 = 100, seasonally adjusted, except as noted.)

Year and month	CPI-U, All items — Not seasonally adjusted	Seasonally adjusted — Index	Seasonally adjusted — Percent change from previous period	Total	Total food	Food at home — Total	Cereals and bakery products	Meats, poultry, fish, and eggs	Dairy and related products[1]	Fruits and vege-tables	Non-alcoholic beverages	Other food at home	Food away from home[1]	Alcoholic bever-ages
1975	53.8	53.8	9.1	60.2	59.8	61.8	62.9	67.0	62.6	56.9	41.3	55.4	54.5	65.9
1976	56.9	56.9	5.8	62.1	61.6	63.1	61.5	68.0	67.7	58.4	49.4	56.4	58.2	68.1
1977	60.6	60.6	6.5	65.8	65.5	66.8	62.5	67.4	69.5	63.8	74.4	68.4	62.6	70.0
1978	65.2	65.2	7.6	72.2	72.0	73.8	68.1	77.6	74.2	70.9	78.7	73.6	68.3	74.1
1979	72.6	72.6	11.3	79.9	79.9	81.8	74.9	89.0	82.8	76.6	82.6	79.0	75.9	79.9
1980	82.4	82.4	13.5	86.7	86.8	88.4	83.9	92.0	90.9	82.1	91.4	88.4	83.4	86.4
1981	90.9	90.9	10.3	93.5	93.6	94.8	92.3	96.0	97.4	92.0	95.3	94.9	90.9	92.5
1982	96.5	96.5	6.2	97.3	97.4	98.1	96.5	99.6	98.8	97.0	97.9	97.3	95.8	96.7
1983	99.6	99.6	3.2	99.5	99.4	99.1	99.6	99.2	100.0	97.3	99.8	99.5	100.0	100.4
1984	103.9	103.9	4.3	103.2	103.2	102.8	103.9	101.3	101.3	105.7	102.3	103.1	104.2	103.0
1985	107.6	107.6	3.6	105.6	105.6	104.3	107.9	100.1	103.2	108.4	104.3	105.7	108.3	106.4
1986	109.6	109.6	1.9	109.1	109.0	107.3	110.9	104.5	103.3	109.4	110.4	109.4	112.5	111.1
1987	113.6	113.6	3.6	113.5	113.5	111.9	114.8	110.5	105.9	119.1	107.5	110.5	117.0	114.1
1988	118.3	118.3	4.1	118.2	118.2	116.6	122.1	114.3	108.4	128.1	107.5	113.1	121.8	118.6
1989	124.0	124.0	4.8	124.9	125.1	124.2	132.4	121.3	115.6	138.0	111.3	119.1	127.4	123.5
1990	130.7	130.7	5.4	132.1	132.4	132.3	140.0	130.0	126.5	149.0	113.5	123.4	133.4	129.3
1991	136.2	136.2	4.2	136.8	136.3	135.8	145.8	132.6	125.1	155.8	114.1	127.3	137.9	142.8
1992	140.3	140.3	3.0	138.7	137.9	136.8	151.5	130.9	128.5	155.4	114.3	128.8	140.7	147.3
1993	144.5	144.5	3.0	141.6	140.9	140.1	156.6	135.5	129.4	159.0	114.6	130.5	143.2	149.6
1994	148.2	148.2	2.6	144.9	144.3	144.1	163.0	137.2	131.7	165.0	123.2	135.6	145.7	151.5
1995	152.4	152.4	2.8	148.9	148.4	148.8	167.5	138.8	132.8	177.7	131.7	140.8	149.0	153.9
1996	156.9	156.9	3.0	153.7	153.3	154.3	174.0	144.8	142.1	183.9	128.6	142.9	152.7	158.5
1997	160.5	160.5	2.3	157.7	157.3	158.1	177.6	148.5	145.5	187.5	133.4	147.3	157.0	162.8
1998	163.0	163.0	1.6	161.1	160.7	161.1	181.1	147.3	150.8	198.2	133.0	150.8	161.1	165.7
1999	166.6	166.6	2.2	164.6	164.1	164.2	185.0	147.9	159.6	203.1	134.3	153.5	165.1	169.7
2000	172.2	172.2	3.4	168.4	167.8	167.9	188.3	154.5	160.7	204.6	137.8	155.6	169.0	174.7
2001	177.1	177.1	2.8	173.6	173.1	173.4	193.8	161.3	167.1	212.2	139.2	159.6	173.9	179.3
2002	179.9	179.9	1.6	176.8	176.2	175.6	198.0	162.1	168.1	220.9	139.2	160.8	178.3	183.6
2003	184.0	184.0	2.3	180.5	180.0	179.4	202.8	169.3	167.9	225.9	139.8	162.6	182.1	187.2
2004	188.9	188.9	2.7	186.6	186.2	186.2	206.0	181.7	180.2	232.7	140.4	164.9	187.5	192.1
2005	195.3	195.3	3.4	191.2	190.7	189.8	209.0	184.7	182.4	241.4	144.4	167.0	193.4	195.9
2006	201.6	201.6	3.2	195.7	195.2	193.1	212.8	186.6	181.4	252.9	147.4	169.6	199.4	200.7
2007	207.3	207.3	2.8	203.3	202.9	201.2	222.1	195.6	194.8	262.6	153.4	173.3	206.7	207.0
2008	215.3	215.3	3.8	214.2	214.1	214.1	244.9	204.7	210.4	278.9	160.0	184.2	215.8	214.5
2009	214.5	214.5	-0.4	218.2	218.0	215.1	252.6	203.8	197.0	272.9	163.0	191.2	223.3	220.8
2010	218.1	218.1	1.6	220.0	219.6	215.8	250.4	207.7	199.2	273.5	161.6	191.1	226.1	223.3
2011	224.9	224.9	3.2	227.9	227.8	226.2	260.3	223.2	212.7	284.7	166.8	197.4	231.4	226.7
2012	229.6	229.6	2.1	233.7	233.8	231.8	267.7	231.0	217.3	282.8	168.6	204.8	238.0	230.8
2013	233.0	233.0	1.5	237.0	237.0	233.9	270.4	236.0	217.6	290.0	166.9	204.8	243.1	234.6
2014	236.7	236.7	1.6	242.4	242.7	239.5	271.1	253.0	225.3	294.4	166.0	206.2	249.0	237.3
2015	237.0	237.0	0.1	246.8	247.2	242.3	274.1	260.3	222.4	293.8	167.9	209.3	256.1	239.5
2016	240.0	240.0	1.3	247.7	247.9	239.1	273.1	247.7	217.3	296.3	167.3	209.5	262.7	242.5
2017	245.1	245.1	2.1	249.8	250.1	238.6	271.7	245.8	217.5	295.7	167.6	209.9	268.8	245.4
2018	251.1	251.1	2.4	253.3	253.6	239.7	272.8	248.9	216.5	297.8	167.6	210.2	275.9	249.1
2019	255.7	255.7	1.8	258.0	258.3	241.8	276.6	249.8	218.7	300.9	170.8	211.1	284.4	252.5
2020	258.8	258.8	1.2	266.6	267.2	250.2	282.6	265.2	228.3	305.0	176.9	217.3	293.9	257.2
2021	271.0	271.0	4.7	276.8	277.8	258.9	289.1	282.8	231.4	314.8	181.8	222.9	307.3	262.8
2020														
January	258.0	258.7	2.5	260.7	261.1	243.2	276.6	254.5	221.7	299.3	171.2	211.8	289.1	253.5
February	258.7	259.0	2.3	261.5	261.9	244.1	276.9	255.6	224.0	299.1	171.7	213.1	289.8	254.4
March	258.1	258.2	1.5	262.3	262.7	245.2	277.2	256.1	225.3	300.3	173.1	214.5	290.2	255.4
April	256.4	256.1	0.4	265.9	266.5	251.3	285.0	266.9	228.7	303.1	178.8	218.5	290.6	256.1
May	256.4	255.9	0.2	267.7	268.3	253.6	284.4	275.3	230.8	304.9	178.9	218.9	291.7	257.8
June	257.8	257.2	0.7	269.0	269.7	254.9	285.7	279.0	229.8	306.2	179.8	219.1	293.2	258.1
July	259.1	258.5	1.0	268.0	268.7	252.2	284.4	268.7	228.4	307.1	179.2	218.5	294.6	257.5
August	259.9	259.6	1.3	268.3	269.0	252.1	284.1	265.3	231.8	308.1	179.2	219.1	295.4	257.9
September	260.3	260.2	1.4	268.4	269.1	251.3	284.2	264.3	230.6	307.8	177.9	218.2	297.1	257.7
October	260.4	260.4	1.2	268.9	269.6	251.5	285.0	264.8	228.5	308.1	177.9	218.8	297.9	258.7
November	260.2	260.7	1.1	269.0	269.6	251.2	283.8	265.3	229.5	308.4	177.1	218.1	298.3	260.0
December	260.5	261.6	1.3	269.8	270.5	252.0	284.3	266.2	231.0	307.0	178.4	219.2	299.4	259.7
2021														
January	261.6	262.2	1.4	270.3	271.0	252.3	283.7	267.7	230.2	307.8	178.6	219.0	300.4	259.7
February	263.0	263.3	1.7	270.7	271.4	252.8	284.4	269.1	230.0	309.3	178.6	219.0	300.5	259.6
March	264.9	265.0	2.6	271.2	271.9	253.3	284.4	270.2	228.9	311.8	178.5	219.2	300.9	260.4
April	267.1	266.7	4.2	272.1	272.8	254.3	285.2	272.2	230.1	312.8	179.1	219.4	301.8	261.0
May	269.2	268.6	5.0	273.3	274.1	255.3	286.1	275.7	230.9	313.5	178.6	219.7	303.5	261.8
June	271.7	271.0	5.4	275.3	276.1	257.2	286.4	280.7	231.4	316.0	180.2	220.0	305.6	262.9
July	273.0	272.2	5.4	277.0	277.9	258.6	288.6	284.3	232.6	313.9	181.3	221.3	308.0	263.7
August	273.6	273.1	5.3	278.1	279.0	259.5	288.6	286.5	230.7	315.1	182.7	222.2	309.3	264.5
September	274.3	274.2	5.4	280.4	281.5	262.6	291.9	291.9	232.0	317.3	184.6	225.0	311.0	264.9
October	276.6	276.6	6.2	282.7	283.9	265.0	294.9	296.2	232.5	317.4	185.9	227.7	313.6	264.6
November	277.9	278.5	6.8	284.7	286.1	267.3	296.9	299.2	233.2	320.7	186.4	230.5	315.5	265.0
December	278.8	280.1	7.0	286.0	287.4	268.4	297.7	299.7	234.6	322.4	187.5	231.5	317.4	265.7

[1]Not seasonally adjusted.

Table 8-2. Consumer Price Indexes and Purchasing Power of the Dollar—*Continued*

(1982–1984 = 100, seasonally adjusted, except as noted.)

Year and month	Total	CPI-U, Housing											
		Shelter						Fuels and utilities				Household furnishings and operations	
		Total	Rent of shelter [2]	Rent of primary residence	Lodging away from home [3]	Owners' equivalent rent of primary residence [2]	Tenants' and household insur-ance [1,3]	Total	Fuels		Water and sewer and trash collection services [3]	Total	Household oper-ations [1,3]
									Fuel oil and other fuels	Energy services			
1975	50.7	48.8	. . .	58.0	. . .	. . .	. . .	45.4	36.4	40.1	. . .	63.4	. . .
1976	53.8	51.5	. . .	61.1	. . .	. . .	. . .	49.4	38.8	44.7	. . .	67.3	. . .
1977	57.4	54.9	. . .	64.8	. . .	. . .	. . .	54.7	43.9	50.5	. . .	70.4	. . .
1978	62.4	60.5	. . .	69.3	. . .	. . .	. . .	58.5	46.2	55.0	. . .	74.7	. . .
1979	70.1	68.9	. . .	74.3	. . .	. . .	. . .	64.8	62.4	61.0	. . .	79.9	. . .
1980	81.1	81.0	. . .	80.9	. . .	. . .	. . .	75.4	86.1	71.4	. . .	86.3	. . .
1981	90.4	90.5	. . .	87.9	. . .	. . .	. . .	86.4	104.6	81.9	. . .	93.0	. . .
1982	96.9	96.9	. . .	94.6	. . .	. . .	. . .	94.9	103.4	93.2	. . .	98.0	. . .
1983	99.5	99.1	102.7	100.1	. . .	102.5	. . .	100.2	97.2	101.5	. . .	100.2	. . .
1984	103.6	104.0	107.7	105.3	. . .	107.3	. . .	104.8	99.4	105.4	. . .	101.9	. . .
1985	107.7	109.8	113.9	111.8	. . .	113.2	. . .	106.5	95.9	107.1	. . .	103.8	. . .
1986	110.9	115.8	120.2	118.3	. . .	119.4	. . .	104.1	77.6	105.7	. . .	105.2	. . .
1987	114.2	121.3	125.9	123.1	. . .	124.8	. . .	103.0	77.9	103.8	. . .	107.1	. . .
1988	118.5	127.1	132.0	127.8	. . .	131.1	. . .	104.4	78.1	104.6	. . .	109.4	. . .
1989	123.0	132.8	138.0	132.8	. . .	137.4	. . .	107.8	81.7	107.5	. . .	111.2	. . .
1990	128.5	140.0	145.5	138.4	. . .	144.8	. . .	111.6	99.3	109.3	. . .	113.3	. . .
1991	133.6	146.3	152.1	143.3	. . .	150.4	. . .	115.3	94.6	112.6	. . .	116.0	. . .
1992	137.5	151.2	157.3	146.9	. . .	155.5	. . .	117.8	90.7	114.8	. . .	118.0	. . .
1993	141.2	155.7	162.0	150.3	. . .	160.5	. . .	121.3	90.3	118.5	. . .	119.3	. . .
1994	144.8	160.5	167.0	154.0	. . .	165.8	. . .	122.8	88.8	119.2	. . .	121.0	. . .
1995	148.5	165.7	172.4	157.8	. . .	171.3	. . .	123.7	88.1	119.2	. . .	123.0	. . .
1996	152.8	171.0	178.0	162.0	. . .	176.8	. . .	127.5	99.2	122.1	. . .	124.7	. . .
1997	156.8	176.3	183.4	166.7	. . .	181.9	. . .	130.8	99.8	125.1	. . .	125.4	. . .
1998	160.4	182.1	189.6	172.1	109.0	187.8	99.8	128.5	90.0	121.2	101.6	126.6	101.5
1999	163.9	187.3	195.0	177.5	112.3	192.9	101.3	128.8	91.4	120.9	104.0	126.7	104.5
2000	169.6	193.4	201.3	183.9	117.5	198.7	103.7	137.9	129.7	128.0	106.5	128.2	110.5
2001	176.4	200.6	208.9	192.1	118.6	206.3	106.2	150.2	129.3	142.4	109.6	129.1	115.6
2002	180.3	208.1	216.7	199.7	118.3	214.7	108.7	143.6	115.5	134.4	113.0	128.3	119.0
2003	184.8	213.1	221.9	205.5	119.3	219.9	114.8	154.5	139.5	145.0	117.2	126.1	121.8
2004	189.5	218.8	227.9	211.0	125.9	224.9	116.2	161.9	160.5	150.6	124.0	125.5	125.0
2005	195.7	224.4	233.7	217.3	130.3	230.2	117.6	179.0	208.6	166.5	130.3	126.1	130.3
2006	203.2	232.1	241.9	225.1	136.0	238.2	116.5	194.7	234.9	182.1	136.8	127.0	136.6
2007	209.6	240.6	250.8	234.7	142.8	246.2	117.0	200.6	251.5	186.3	143.7	126.9	140.6
2008	216.3	246.7	257.2	243.3	143.7	252.4	118.8	220.0	334.4	202.2	152.1	127.8	147.5
2009	217.1	249.4	259.9	248.8	134.2	256.6	121.5	210.7	239.8	193.6	161.1	128.7	150.3
2010	216.3	248.4	258.8	249.4	133.7	256.6	125.7	214.2	275.1	192.9	170.9	125.5	150.3
2011	219.1	251.6	262.2	253.6	137.4	259.6	127.4	220.4	337.1	194.4	179.6	124.9	151.8
2012	222.7	257.1	267.8	260.4	140.5	264.8	131.3	219.0	335.9	189.7	189.3	125.7	155.2
2013	227.4	263.1	274.0	267.7	142.4	270.7	135.4	225.2	332.0	194.8	197.6	124.8	157.6
2014	233.2	270.5	281.8	276.2	148.5	277.8	141.9	234.6	338.9	203.4	204.9	123.1	161.6
2015	238.1	278.8	290.4	286.0	153.0	285.9	146.4	230.1	256.2	198.7	214.0	122.6	166.9
2016	244.0	288.2	300.3	296.8	158.1	295.3	147.7	228.9	226.3	196.1	221.7	121.6	171.6
2017	251.2	297.8	310.3	308.1	159.4	305.1	148.8	237.3	254.4	202.7	229.1	120.7	176.3
2018	258.5	307.7	320.7	310.3	161.1	315.2	150.7	241.6	293.0	203.8	237.1	121.6	186.0
2019	266.0	318.1	331.6	351.1	165.9	325.6	151.8	242.6	280.8	203.5	244.7	123.8	194.5
2020	271.8	325.9	339.9	341.5	149.0	334.8	151.1	243.9	237.4	204.5	252.5	125.9	200.6
2021	280.7	334.6	349.1	349.1	163.4	343.4	150.7	260.5	302.8	218.8	252.5	131.6	212.8
2020													
January	269.8	323.4	337.2	337.6	162.7	331.4	151.3	244.1	279.5	204.2	248.6	124.1	197.8
February	270.4	324.4	338.3	338.5	166.6	332.1	151.7	243.3	266.1	203.5	249.6	124.3	199.1
March	270.3	324.5	338.5	339.5	156.2	332.9	150.8	242.4	242.2	203.2	250.3	124.4	199.3
April	270.3	324.5	338.4	340.3	144.8	333.5	151.2	241.6	220.4	203.0	250.6	124.8	199.3
May	270.8	325.2	339.2	341.1	144.3	334.3	150.4	241.4	214.1	202.8	251.1	125.2	199.2
June	271.3	325.5	339.5	341.6	144.3	334.6	150.4	242.3	224.2	203.4	251.7	125.6	199.4
July	271.8	326.2	340.2	342.3	145.0	335.3	150.9	242.5	229.7	203.2	252.5	126.0	200.1
August	272.5	326.7	340.7	342.6	145.7	335.8	150.8	242.9	236.6	202.9	253.8	127.2	201.0
September	272.9	327.0	341.1	343.0	145.5	336.2	150.8	245.0	230.9	205.4	254.3	127.1	201.7
October	273.1	327.4	341.4	343.5	142.4	336.8	151.2	245.4	227.8	205.9	254.8	126.8	202.4
November	273.8	327.8	341.8	343.7	145.4	337.0	151.6	247.2	230.6	207.7	255.6	127.6	201.7
December	274.3	328.2	342.2	344.1	145.4	337.5	151.8	248.9	246.2	208.8	256.5	127.9	205.7
2021													
January	274.6	328.6	342.7	344.5	143.9	338.0	152.5	249.3	258.1	208.5	248.6	127.7	207.1
February	275.2	329.1	343.4	345.1	141.7	338.8	150.7	251.6	280.9	210.0	249.6	127.7	207.7
March	276.1	330.0	344.3	345.7	146.4	339.5	150.5	253.2	285.9	211.5	250.3	128.3	208.0
April	277.4	331.3	345.6	346.4	155.6	340.3	150.6	255.1	283.3	213.8	250.6	129.2	209.1
May	278.7	332.3	346.8	347.3	157.6	341.3	150.4	256.8	289.4	215.4	251.1	130.9	215.7
June	279.8	333.8	348.3	348.1	165.9	342.4	150.6	258.3	296.6	216.7	251.7	130.7	213.7
July	280.9	335.3	349.9	348.8	175.5	343.4	150.7	260.0	300.5	218.2	252.5	130.7	214.1
August	282.0	335.9	350.5	349.9	170.7	344.4	150.4	262.5	304.7	220.7	253.8	132.3	215.6
September	283.5	337.3	352.0	351.4	170.9	345.9	150.9	265.3	315.2	223.3	254.3	133.6	215.1
October	285.5	338.9	353.5	352.8	174.4	347.4	150.5	270.9	337.9	228.8	254.8	134.7	216.2
November	286.8	340.5	355.1	354.2	177.7	348.9	150.1	271.5	342.3	229.3	255.6	135.8	218.7
December	288.3	342.0	356.5	355.5	180.6	350.4	150.4	272.2	339.0	229.9	256.5	137.3	. . .

[1] Not seasonally adjusted.
[2] December 1982 = 100.
[3] December 1997 = 100.
. . . = Not available.

Table 8-3. Alternative Measures of Total and Core Consumer Prices: Index Levels

(Various bases; monthly data seasonally adjusted, except as noted.)

Year and month	CPIs, all items				CPIs, all items less food and energy		
	CPI-U, 1982–1984 = 100	CPI-W, 1982–1984 = 100	CPI-U-RS, Dec. 1977 = 100, not seasonally adjusted	C-CPI-U, Dec. 1999 = 100, not seasonally adjusted	CPI-U, 1982–1984 = 100	CPI-U-RS, Dec. 1977 = 100, not seasonally adjusted	C-CPI-U, Dec. 1999 = 100, not seasonally adjusted
1975	53.8	54.1	. . .	. . .	53.8	. . .	. . .
1976	56.9	57.2	. . .	. . .	56.9	. . .	. . .
1977	60.6	60.9	. . .	. . .	60.6	. . .	. . .
1978	65.2	65.6	104.4	. . .	65.2	103.6	. . .
1979	72.6	73.1	114.3	. . .	72.6	111.0	. . .
1980	82.4	82.9	127.1	. . .	82.4	120.9	. . .
1981	90.9	91.4	139.1	. . .	90.9	132.2	. . .
1982	96.5	96.9	147.5	. . .	96.5	142.4	. . .
1983	99.6	99.8	153.8	. . .	99.6	150.4	. . .
1984	103.9	103.3	160.2	. . .	103.9	157.9	. . .
1985	107.6	106.9	165.7	. . .	107.6	164.8	. . .
1986	109.6	108.6	168.6	. . .	109.6	171.4	. . .
1987	113.6	112.5	174.4	. . .	113.6	178.1	. . .
1988	118.3	117.0	180.7	. . .	118.3	185.2	. . .
1989	124.0	122.6	188.6	. . .	124.0	192.6	. . .
1990	130.7	129.0	197.9	. . .	130.7	201.4	. . .
1991	136.2	134.3	205.1	. . .	136.2	209.9	. . .
1992	140.3	138.2	210.2	. . .	140.3	216.4	. . .
1993	144.5	142.1	215.5	. . .	144.5	222.5	. . .
1994	148.2	145.6	220.0	. . .	148.2	227.7	. . .
1995	152.4	149.8	225.3	. . .	152.4	233.4	. . .
1996	156.9	154.1	231.3	. . .	156.9	239.1	. . .
1997	160.5	157.6	236.3	. . .	160.5	244.4	. . .
1998	163.0	159.7	239.5	. . .	163.0	249.6	. . .
1999	166.6	163.2	244.6	. . .	166.6	254.6	. . .
2000	172.2	168.9	252.9	102.0	172.2	260.9	101.4
2001	177.1	173.5	260.1	104.3	177.1	267.9	103.5
2002	179.9	175.9	264.2	105.6	179.9	274.1	105.4
2003	184.0	179.8	270.2	107.8	184.0	278.1	106.6
2004	188.9	184.5	277.5	110.5	188.9	283.1	108.4
2005	195.3	191.0	286.9	113.7	195.3	289.2	110.4
2006	201.6	197.1	296.2	117.0	201.6	296.5	112.9
2007	207.3	202.8	304.6	120.0	207.3	303.4	115.0
2008	215.3	211.1	316.3	124.4	215.3	310.3	117.3
2009	214.5	209.6	315.2	123.9	214.5	315.6	119.1
2010	218.1	214.0	320.4	125.6	218.1	318.7	120.0
2011	224.9	221.6	330.5	129.5	224.9	324.0	121.9
2012	229.6	226.2	337.5	132.0	229.6	331.0	124.3
2013	233.0	229.3	342.5	. . .	233.0	337.0	. . .
2014	236.7	232.8	348.3	. . .	236.7	343.1	. . .
2015	237.0	231.8	348.9	. . .	237.0	349.7	. . .
2016	240.0	234.1	353.4	. . .	240.0	357.5	. . .
2017	245.1	239.1	361.0	. . .	245.1	364.2	. . .
2018	251.1	245.1	369.8	. . .	251.1	372.0	. . .
2019	255.7	249.2	376.5	. . .	255.7	380.1	. . .
2020	258.8	252.2	381.2	. . .	258.8	386.6	. . .
2021	271.0	265.5	399.0	. . .	271.0	400.3	. . .
2020							
January	258.7	252.1	379.9	144.8	266.4	384.2	139.7
February	259.0	252.4	381.0	145.2	267.1	386.0	140.3
March	258.2	251.5	380.1	144.9	266.9	386.0	140.4
April	256.1	249.2	377.6	144.1	265.8	384.3	139.8
May	255.9	249.0	377.6	144.0	265.6	383.9	139.5
June	257.2	250.4	379.7	144.8	266.1	384.6	139.8
July	258.5	252.0	381.6	145.7	267.6	386.6	140.7
August	259.6	253.2	382.8	146.3	268.7	388.1	141.4
September	260.2	253.9	383.3	146.4	269.2	388.5	141.5
October	260.4	254.0	383.5	146.4	269.3	388.9	141.5
November	260.7	254.4	383.2	146.2	269.8	389.1	141.6
December	261.6	255.3	383.6	146.4	270.0	388.8	141.5
2021							
January	262.2	256.0	385.2	147.1	270.1	389.6	141.9
February	263.3	257.3	387.3	147.8	270.5	390.9	142.3
March	265.0	259.1	390.0	148.7	271.3	392.4	142.8
April	266.7	260.8	393.2	149.9	273.7	395.6	143.9
May	268.6	262.9	396.4	151.0	275.7	398.3	144.8
June	271.0	265.6	400.0	152.3	277.9	401.7	145.9
July	272.2	266.9	402.0	153.1	278.8	403.0	146.5
August	273.1	267.8	402.8	153.3	279.3	403.5	146.6
September	274.2	269.0	403.9	153.7	280.0	404.1	146.8
October	276.6	271.5	407.2	155.0	281.7	406.6	147.7
November	278.5	273.7	409.2	155.7	283.2	408.2	148.3
December	280.1	275.4	410.5	156.1	284.8	409.9	148.8

. . . = Not available.

Table 8-4. Alternative Measures of Total and Core Consumer Prices: Inflation Rates

(Percent changes from year earlier, except as noted; monthly data seasonally adjusted, except as noted.)

Year and month	CPIs, all items				CPIs, all items less food and energy		
	CPI-U, 1982–1984 = 100	CPI-W, 1982–1984 = 100	CPI-U-RS, Dec. 1977 = 100, not seasonally adjusted	C-CPI-U, Dec. 1999 = 100, not seasonally adjusted	CPI-U, 1982–1984 = 100	CPI-U-RS, Dec. 1977 = 100, not seasonally adjusted	C-CPI-U, Dec. 1999 = 100, not seasonally adjusted
1975	9.1	9.1	. . .	. . .	9.1	. . .	. . .
1976	5.8	5.7	. . .	. . .	5.8	. . .	. . .
1977	6.5	6.5	. . .	. . .	6.5	. . .	. . .
1978	7.6	7.7	. . .	. . .	7.6	. . .	. . .
1979	11.3	11.4	9.5	. . .	11.3	7.1	. . .
1980	13.5	13.4	11.2	. . .	13.5	8.9	. . .
1981	10.3	10.3	9.4	. . .	10.3	9.3	. . .
1982	6.2	6.0	6.0	. . .	6.2	7.7	. . .
1983	3.2	3.0	4.3	. . .	3.2	5.6	. . .
1984	4.3	3.5	4.2	. . .	4.3	5.0	. . .
1985	3.6	3.5	3.4	. . .	3.6	4.4	. . .
1986	1.9	1.6	1.8	. . .	1.9	4.0	. . .
1987	3.6	3.6	3.4	. . .	3.6	3.9	. . .
1988	4.1	4.0	3.6	. . .	4.1	4.0	. . .
1989	4.8	4.8	4.4	. . .	4.8	4.0	. . .
1990	5.4	5.2	4.9	. . .	5.4	4.6	. . .
1991	4.2	4.1	3.6	. . .	4.2	4.2	. . .
1992	3.0	2.9	2.5	. . .	3.0	3.1	. . .
1993	3.0	2.8	2.5	. . .	3.0	2.8	. . .
1994	2.6	2.5	2.1	. . .	2.6	2.3	. . .
1995	2.8	2.9	2.4	. . .	2.8	2.5	. . .
1996	3.0	2.9	2.7	. . .	3.0	2.4	. . .
1997	2.3	2.3	2.2	. . .	2.3	2.2	. . .
1998	1.6	1.3	1.4	. . .	1.6	2.1	. . .
1999	2.2	2.2	2.1	. . .	2.2	2.0	. . .
2000	3.4	3.5	3.4	. . .	3.4	2.5	. . .
2001	2.8	2.7	2.8	2.3	2.8	2.7	2.1
2002	1.6	1.4	1.6	1.2	1.6	2.3	1.8
2003	2.3	2.2	2.3	2.1	2.3	1.5	1.1
2004	2.7	2.6	2.7	2.5	2.7	1.8	1.7
2005	3.4	3.5	3.4	2.9	3.4	2.2	1.8
2006	3.2	3.2	3.2	2.9	3.2	2.5	2.3
2007	2.8	2.9	2.8	2.5	2.8	2.3	1.8
2008	3.8	4.1	3.8	3.7	3.8	2.3	2.0
2009	-0.4	-0.7	-0.3	-0.5	-0.4	1.7	1.5
2010	1.6	2.1	1.6	1.4	1.6	1.0	0.7
2011	3.2	3.6	3.2	3.1	3.2	1.7	1.6
2012	2.1	2.1	2.1	1.9	2.1	2.2	2.0
2013	1.5	1.4	1.5	2.0	1.5	1.8	. . .
2014	1.6	1.5	1.7	. . .	1.6	1.8	. . .
2015	0.1	-0.4	0.2	. . .	0.1	1.9	. . .
2016	1.3	1.0	1.3	. . .	1.3	2.2	. . .
2017	2.1	2.1	2.2	. . .	2.1	1.9	. . .
2018	2.4	2.5	2.4	. . .	2.4	2.1	. . .
2019	1.8	1.7	1.8	. . .	1.8	2.2	. . .
2020	1.2	1.2	1.2	. . .	1.2	1.7	. . .
2021	4.7	5.3	4.7	. . .	4.7	3.5	. . .
2021							
January	1.4	1.5	1.4	1.3	1.4	1.4	1.1
February	1.7	2.0	1.7	2.0	1.3	1.3	1.4
March	2.7	3.0	2.6	3.2	1.7	1.7	2.1
April	4.2	4.7	4.1	4.1	3.0	2.9	3.1
May	4.9	5.6	5.0	4.3	3.8	3.8	3.6
June	5.3	6.1	5.3	4.5	4.4	4.4	3.7
July	5.3	5.9	5.3	4.7	4.2	[1]4.2	3.6
August	5.2	5.8	5.2	4.7	4.0	[1]4.0	3.6
September	5.4	5.9	5.4	5.0	4.0	[1]4.0	3.8
October	6.2	6.9	6.2	6.0	4.6	[1]4.6	4.4
November	6.8	7.6	6.8	6.3	5.0	[1]4.9	4.8
December	7.1	7.9	7.0	6.1	5.5	[1]5.4	4.9

[1]Interim values.
. . . = Not available.

Table 8-5. Producer Price Indexes for Goods and Services: Final Demand

(November 2009 =100, except as noted.)

Year and month	Final demand	Final demand goods			Final demand goods less food and energy			Final demand services				Final demand construction	Final demand less food and energy (April 2010 =100)
		Final demand goods	Final demand foods	Final demand energy goods	Total	Finished goods less foods and energy (1982 =100)		Final demand services	Final demand trade services	Final demand transportation and warehousing services	Final demand services less trade, transportation, and warehousing		
						Total	Private capital equipment						
NOT SEASONALLY ADJUSTED													
2010	101.8	102.8	103.7	107.2	101.4	173.6	157.3	101.3	101.7	103.2	100.9	100.3	103.2
2011	105.7	109.9	112.5	126.2	104.9	177.8	159.7	103.4	104.0	110.0	102.5	102.5	110.0
2012	107.7	111.7	115.9	126.3	106.8	182.4	162.8	105.4	106.7	114.2	103.9	105.5	114.2
2013	109.1	112.6	117.8	125.3	107.9	185.1	164.2	107.1	108.2	115.3	105.8	107.5	115.3
2014	110.9	114.0	121.6	124.2	109.5	188.6	166.4	109.0	110.2	117.7	107.5	110.6	117.7
2015	109.9	109.1	118.4	98.6	109.9	192.3	168.5	110.0	111.6	115.3	108.7	112.7	115.3
2016	110.4	107.6	115.1	90.4	110.7	195.3	169.3	111.5	113.1	113.5	110.6	114.0	113.5
2017	113.0	111.2	116.5	99.8	113.2	198.9	170.9	113.5	114.8	115.9	112.8	116.5	115.9
2018	116.2	115.0	116.7	110.0	116.0	203.4	173.6	116.5	116.9	122.0	115.8	121.2	122.0
2019	118.2	115.5	118.9	105.0	117.6	207.8	177.4	119.1	119.7	125.5	118.2	127.2	125.5
2020	118.4	113.8	120.4	91.5	118.5	210.2	179.3	120.2	121.7	121.2	119.5	130.2	121.2
2021	126.7	125.8	131.0	119.5	126.2	218.4	186.1	126.7	130.7	130.9	124.5	136.9	130.9
2018													
January	114.5	113.2	116.1	105.2	114.7	201.4	171.9	114.8	115.2	117.9	114.4	119.0	113.7
February	114.9	113.5	115.5	106.4	115.0	201.8	172.2	115.3	115.8	119.0	114.8	119.0	114.1
March	115.4	114.0	118.0	105.6	115.4	202.1	172.5	115.8	116.0	120.5	115.3	119.1	114.6
April	115.7	114.4	116.8	108.0	115.6	202.4	172.6	116.0	116.5	120.8	115.2	120.4	114.8
May	116.2	115.5	117.8	112.8	115.8	202.6	172.9	116.1	116.7	120.7	115.4	120.5	114.9
June	116.6	116.0	116.9	115.3	116.0	202.9	173.2	116.6	117.2	122.6	115.7	120.7	115.3
July	116.8	115.9	116.3	114.9	116.2	203.3	173.5	116.8	116.8	122.9	116.3	121.2	115.5
August	116.6	115.8	115.7	114.6	116.3	203.7	174.0	116.7	116.4	122.3	116.3	121.4	115.5
September	116.6	115.8	115.2	114.7	116.3	203.9	174.3	116.7	116.3	122.7	116.3	121.4	115.5
October	117.6	116.3	115.7	114.9	116.9	205.2	175.3	117.8	118.8	124.6	116.7	123.8	116.5
November	117.1	115.4	117.0	108.0	117.1	205.7	175.6	117.6	118.3	125.4	116.5	124.0	116.4
December	116.8	114.3	119.4	100.2	117.1	205.8	175.7	117.6	118.6	124.9	116.4	124.1	116.4
2019													
January	116.7	113.9	117.6	97.4	117.6	207.2	176.8	117.8	118.1	125.5	116.8	125.0	116.6
February	117.1	114.3	117.4	99.5	117.7	207.3	177.0	118.1	118.6	124.3	117.3	125.0	116.9
March	117.7	115.4	118.0	104.7	117.8	207.5	176.9	118.5	119.1	124.8	117.6	125.2	117.2
April	118.5	116.3	118.2	109.3	117.8	207.5	177.0	119.1	120.3	125.5	117.9	126.9	117.7
May	118.6	116.4	118.5	110.3	117.6	207.6	177.2	119.2	119.8	125.4	118.3	127.1	117.7
June	118.5	116.0	119.6	107.5	117.5	207.6	177.2	119.3	119.8	126.4	118.4	127.1	117.8
July	118.7	116.2	119.3	108.8	117.6	207.8	177.3	119.5	119.9	126.5	118.7	128.0	118.0
August	118.8	115.7	118.4	106.9	117.5	207.7	177.2	119.9	120.9	125.3	118.9	128.1	118.2
September	118.3	115.2	118.3	105.1	117.3	207.7	177.3	119.4	120.0	124.1	118.6	128.2	117.8
October	118.8	115.6	119.4	104.8	117.7	208.6	178.0	120.0	121.4	125.7	118.8	128.6	118.4
November	118.3	115.6	121.0	103.2	117.8	208.9	178.2	119.2	119.3	125.5	118.6	128.7	117.8
December	118.4	115.5	120.8	102.6	117.8	208.8	178.2	119.3	119.5	127.6	118.5	128.9	117.9
2020													
January	119.0	116.0	120.9	103.6	118.3	209.3	178.6	120.0	119.9	126.4	119.4	129.6	118.5
February	118.4	115.0	118.7	99.6	118.4	209.8	179.0	119.7	119.4	125.6	119.3	129.7	118.3
March	118.1	113.4	118.8	91.5	118.3	209.7	178.9	120.0	120.8	122.5	119.4	129.6	118.5
April	116.7	110.3	118.6	75.7	118.0	210.1	179.1	119.5	122.3	118.3	118.3	130.3	118.1
May	117.3	112.2	126.2	80.0	117.8	209.9	179.0	119.4	121.6	119.3	118.4	130.2	118.0
June	117.7	113.0	120.3	89.0	117.9	209.8	178.8	119.6	121.2	121.5	118.7	130.1	118.2
July	118.4	113.7	118.8	93.3	118.2	210.0	179.1	120.3	122.2	120.5	119.4	130.8	118.7
August	118.5	113.8	118.3	93.8	118.4	210.2	179.2	120.3	122.2	118.8	119.7	130.5	118.8
September	118.7	114.1	119.8	92.8	118.6	210.2	179.4	120.5	122.0	118.9	120.0	130.4	119.0
October	119.5	114.4	122.0	91.6	118.9	210.9	179.9	121.6	124.4	121.4	120.3	130.2	119.8
November	119.3	114.7	122.1	91.8	119.3	211.4	180.2	121.1	123.0	120.7	120.3	130.4	119.6
December	119.4	115.5	120.6	95.6	119.8	211.6	180.5	120.8	121.8	120.1	120.5	130.4	119.5
2021													
January	120.9	117.5	122.4	100.8	121.0	212.7	181.2	122.2	122.6	121.2	122.2	130.7	120.8
February	121.9	119.0	124.0	105.5	121.6	213.3	181.6	122.8	123.5	122.0	122.7	130.9	121.4
March	123.0	121.3	124.9	113.2	122.6	213.9	181.9	123.5	124.0	124.4	123.2	131.4	122.1
April	124.3	122.3	127.3	112.7	123.7	215.0	183.0	124.9	127.0	128.9	123.6	133.1	123.5
May	125.5	124.7	131.6	117.1	125.0	216.2	184.1	125.5	128.6	128.6	123.9	133.9	124.3
June	126.6	126.5	133.4	121.0	126.2	217.6	185.6	126.2	129.4	131.2	124.4	134.2	125.1
July	127.8	127.5	131.1	125.0	127.2	218.9	186.8	127.5	131.5	134.2	125.1	136.5	126.3
August	128.8	128.3	133.6	124.8	127.8	219.8	187.4	128.5	134.4	134.5	125.3	137.0	127.2
September	129.1	129.3	135.7	126.4	128.5	221.1	188.5	128.5	134.7	132.3	125.4	137.4	127.4
October	130.1	130.8	134.9	131.0	129.5	222.8	190.2	129.1	136.1	134.7	125.5	145.5	128.2
November	131.1	131.7	136.6	131.2	130.5	224.1	191.2	130.1	137.5	138.3	126.0	146.0	129.2
December	131.3	131.0	136.4	125.8	131.0	225.3	192.3	130.9	139.1	140.5	126.3	146.3	129.8

Table 8-5. Producer Price Indexes for Goods and Services: Final Demand—*Continued*

(November 2009 =100, except as noted.)

Year and month	Final demand	Final demand goods			Final demand goods less food and energy			Final demand services				Final demand construction	Final demand less food and energy (April 2010 =100)
		Final demand goods	Final demand foods	Final demand energy goods	Total	Finished goods less foods and energy (1982 =100)		Final demand services	Final demand trade services	Final demand transportation and warehousing services	Final demand services less trade, transportation, and warehousing services		
						Total	Private capital equipment						
SEASONALLY ADJUSTED													
2018													
January	114.8	113.7	116.8	108.1	114.5	200.9	171.6	115.0	115.7	117.9	114.5	119.0	113.8
February	115.1	114.1	116.2	109.8	114.8	201.3	172.0	115.3	115.8	119.3	114.7	119.0	114.1
March	115.4	114.3	118.5	107.2	115.2	201.9	172.4	115.6	115.8	120.1	115.1	119.1	114.4
April	115.5	114.4	116.8	108.2	115.5	202.3	172.6	115.7	115.9	120.2	115.2	120.4	114.6
May	115.9	115.0	117.0	110.6	115.7	202.6	172.9	116.1	116.6	120.8	115.4	120.5	114.9
June	116.3	115.1	115.5	111.9	116.0	203.0	173.4	116.6	117.4	121.8	115.7	120.7	115.3
July	116.4	115.2	115.7	111.3	116.3	203.6	173.7	116.7	117.1	122.3	116.0	121.2	115.5
August	116.5	115.4	115.3	112.0	116.4	204.1	174.4	116.7	116.7	122.4	116.2	121.4	115.5
September	116.7	115.6	115.2	112.7	116.6	204.4	174.7	116.8	116.3	123.8	116.4	121.4	115.6
October	117.5	116.5	116.1	115.4	116.9	205.1	175.1	117.6	118.1	124.6	116.7	123.8	116.3
November	117.3	115.7	117.5	109.3	117.1	205.6	175.4	117.8	118.2	125.6	116.8	124.0	116.5
December	117.3	115.1	119.9	103.6	117.2	205.8	175.6	118.0	119.1	125.3	116.8	124.1	116.7
2019													
January	117.0	114.3	118.4	99.6	117.4	206.7	176.5	118.0	118.6	125.6	116.9	125.0	116.8
February	117.3	114.8	118.1	102.4	117.5	206.9	176.7	118.1	118.6	124.9	117.2	125.0	116.9
March	117.7	115.6	118.5	105.8	117.7	207.3	176.9	118.3	118.9	124.5	117.4	125.2	117.0
April	118.3	116.3	118.2	109.6	117.7	207.5	177.0	118.8	119.7	124.8	117.9	126.9	117.5
May	118.4	115.9	117.6	108.2	117.6	207.6	177.2	119.2	119.7	125.4	118.3	127.1	117.7
June	118.2	115.3	118.2	104.7	117.5	207.8	177.3	119.3	120.1	125.5	118.3	127.1	117.8
July	118.4	115.5	118.7	105.4	117.6	208.0	177.5	119.4	120.2	125.9	118.5	128.0	117.9
August	118.6	115.2	118.0	104.5	117.6	208.1	177.6	119.9	121.2	125.5	118.7	128.1	118.2
September	118.3	115.1	118.4	103.3	117.6	208.2	177.7	119.5	120.0	125.1	118.8	128.2	118.0
October	118.7	115.7	119.9	105.3	117.7	208.5	177.8	119.8	120.7	125.6	118.8	128.6	118.2
November	118.5	115.9	121.5	104.3	117.8	208.8	178.0	119.3	119.2	125.6	118.8	128.7	117.9
December	118.9	116.3	121.3	106.5	117.8	208.8	178.1	119.8	120.0	127.8	118.9	128.9	118.2
2020													
January	119.3	116.5	121.6	106.3	118.1	208.8	178.3	120.2	120.4	126.6	119.5	129.6	118.6
February	118.6	115.6	119.4	102.8	118.2	209.4	178.7	119.6	119.5	126.5	119.1	129.7	118.3
March	118.1	113.5	119.4	92.0	118.2	209.5	178.8	119.8	120.6	122.5	119.3	129.6	118.4
April	116.6	110.4	118.6	76.5	117.9	210.0	179.2	119.2	121.6	117.7	118.2	130.3	117.9
May	117.2	111.9	124.9	79.4	117.8	209.8	179.0	119.3	121.5	119.2	118.4	130.2	117.9
June	117.5	112.4	118.9	87.0	117.9	209.9	179.0	119.6	121.5	120.6	118.7	130.1	118.1
July	118.2	113.1	118.2	90.5	118.2	210.3	179.3	120.2	122.5	119.9	119.2	130.8	118.7
August	118.4	113.5	117.8	91.7	118.5	210.6	179.5	120.3	122.4	118.9	119.6	130.5	118.8
September	118.7	114.0	119.9	91.5	118.7	210.7	179.7	120.6	121.9	119.7	120.1	130.4	119.1
October	119.4	114.6	122.5	92.0	118.9	210.8	179.7	121.4	123.7	121.3	120.3	130.2	119.7
November	119.4	115.0	122.6	92.8	119.3	211.4	180.1	121.2	122.8	120.8	120.5	130.4	119.6
December	119.8	116.2	121.1	98.8	119.9	211.6	180.3	121.2	122.2	120.2	120.9	130.4	119.8
2021													
January	121.2	118.0	123.2	103.3	120.8	212.2	180.9	122.4	123.1	121.4	122.3	130.7	120.9
February	122.1	119.7	124.7	109.1	121.4	213.0	181.4	122.8	123.5	122.8	122.5	130.9	121.3
March	122.9	121.3	125.4	113.3	122.5	213.8	181.9	123.3	123.7	124.4	123.1	131.4	122.0
April	124.1	122.3	127.2	113.0	123.7	215.0	183.0	124.6	126.3	128.2	123.5	133.1	123.2
May	125.3	124.0	130.4	114.7	125.0	216.2	184.1	125.5	128.6	128.4	123.8	133.9	124.2
June	126.3	125.6	131.5	118.0	126.2	217.7	185.7	126.2	129.6	130.2	124.3	134.2	125.0
July	127.5	126.6	130.3	120.6	127.2	219.1	187.0	127.4	131.8	133.5	124.9	136.5	126.2
August	128.6	127.8	133.0	122.2	128.0	220.2	187.7	128.5	134.6	134.6	125.2	137.0	127.2
September	129.2	129.3	135.8	125.2	128.7	221.6	188.8	128.6	134.5	133.2	125.6	137.4	127.5
October	130.0	131.0	135.6	131.5	129.5	222.8	190.0	128.9	135.2	134.7	125.5	145.5	128.0
November	131.3	132.2	137.3	132.6	130.6	224.1	191.1	130.2	137.1	138.4	126.3	146.0	129.2
December	132.0	132.1	137.1	130.8	131.1	225.3	192.1	131.3	139.7	140.6	126.7	146.3	130.2

Table 8-6. Producer Price Indexes for Goods and Services: Intermediate Demand

(November 2009 = 100, except as noted.)

Year and month	Intermediate demand by commodity type						Intermediate demand by production flow (Prices of inputs to indicated stage of production)			
	Processed goods (1982=100)	Unprocessed goods (1982=100)	Services	Construction	Processed materials less foods and energy (1982=100)	Unprocessed nonfood materials less energy (1982 =100)	Stage 4 intermediate demand	Stage 3 intermediate demand	Stage 2 intermediate demand	Stage 1 intermediate demand
NOT SEASONALLY ADJUSTED										
2010	183.4	212.2	101.1	101.1	180.8	329.1	102.0	104.2	103.5	106.2
2011	199.9	249.4	103.2	102.3	192.0	390.4	106.9	111.7	112.9	115.7
2012	200.7	241.4	105.3	103.8	192.6	369.6	108.6	112.7	110.7	114.7
2013	200.8	246.7	107.2	105.7	193.8	351.2	109.9	114.1	112.8	114.8
2014	201.9	249.3	108.9	108.0	195.2	345.7	111.2	116.9	112.2	116.1
2015	188.0	189.1	110.2	110.1	189.4	296.0	109.9	110.5	98.9	106.8
2016	182.2	173.4	112.1	111.7	186.9	288.0	109.8	107.3	98.3	104.2
2017	190.7	190.8	115.0	114.1	193.3	324.1	113.0	111.9	103.4	110.4
2018	200.9	200.1	118.6	116.2	201.8	340.7	117.0	116.9	108.5	116.7
2019	198.1	185.9	121.4	119.3	201.1	323.4	118.9	117.2	106.0	114.6
2020	192.5	167.6	121.9	119.8	198.9	346.0	119.4	113.5	102.0	111.0
2021	230.0	242.3	130.7	125.5	233.0	462.6	131.6	132.5	122.4	130.1
2018										
January	195.4	199.7	117.0	115.3	197.0	341.9	114.9	114.4	106.7	114.0
February	197.0	203.0	117.5	115.3	198.2	342.8	115.4	115.4	107.7	114.7
March	197.3	198.2	117.7	115.5	199.5	347.2	115.8	115.7	106.5	115.0
April	198.5	199.9	118.0	115.6	200.1	349.6	116.2	116.1	107.4	115.7
May	201.7	205.7	118.2	115.9	201.6	349.3	116.9	117.7	108.9	117.0
June	203.4	204.2	118.6	116.0	202.5	350.8	117.5	118.5	108.8	118.0
July	203.6	204.8	119.0	116.1	203.1	342.4	117.7	118.4	109.7	118.2
August	203.8	194.6	119.0	116.5	203.7	332.3	117.6	117.3	109.0	117.8
September	204.3	194.8	119.1	116.5	204.4	328.2	117.7	117.5	109.4	117.8
October	204.6	200.3	119.8	117.0	204.7	330.6	118.1	118.7	110.2	118.6
November	202.2	194.4	119.9	117.2	204.0	333.5	117.8	117.6	108.4	117.7
December	199.4	202.0	119.7	117.4	202.7	339.2	117.6	115.8	109.3	116.1
2019										
January	197.8	193.6	120.3	117.9	202.9	333.4	117.7	116.0	107.4	114.9
February	198.2	189.4	120.5	118.7	202.6	334.3	118.0	116.2	106.6	115.1
March	199.6	190.6	120.9	118.8	202.6	339.6	118.6	117.3	106.9	116.2
April	200.2	193.4	121.6	119.0	202.4	332.9	119.2	118.9	107.3	116.4
May	200.2	188.8	121.5	119.4	202.0	321.3	119.2	118.9	106.8	115.6
June	198.8	183.8	121.7	118.9	201.3	319.3	119.2	117.9	105.4	114.5
July	198.9	184.9	121.7	119.6	200.8	321.5	119.4	117.7	105.7	114.7
August	197.7	179.7	122.2	119.8	200.0	318.5	119.5	117.3	105.1	114.2
September	197.2	177.4	122.1	119.8	199.6	314.2	119.4	116.4	105.2	113.7
October	196.8	177.9	121.5	119.9	200.1	311.6	118.9	116.8	104.5	113.2
November	196.4	184.4	121.4	120.0	199.7	311.9	118.9	116.7	105.5	113.1
December	196.0	187.2	121.7	120.0	199.1	322.3	119.2	116.7	105.8	113.6
2020										
January	195.8	186.5	122.3	120.9	199.5	339.4	119.6	117.2	105.4	113.8
February	194.2	174.6	122.1	121.0	199.3	336.0	119.1	115.6	103.4	112.4
March	191.7	160.9	122.2	119.6	199.2	339.9	118.8	114.0	100.7	111.0
April	185.0	138.1	120.2	119.4	196.3	328.0	116.8	107.9	96.2	106.3
May	185.8	150.8	119.7	119.4	195.2	329.8	117.1	109.3	97.6	105.6
June	188.8	158.5	120.1	119.4	196.0	332.7	117.9	111.2	99.4	107.9
July	191.6	159.2	120.6	119.5	197.1	333.8	118.8	112.4	100.1	109.5
August	193.2	163.4	121.7	119.5	198.6	342.5	119.7	113.1	101.5	110.8
September	194.1	170.1	122.8	119.6	200.2	356.2	120.6	113.6	103.0	112.0
October	195.0	173.7	123.6	119.6	200.7	357.8	120.9	114.9	103.6	112.5
November	196.1	185.5	123.6	119.7	201.0	367.7	121.0	115.7	105.5	113.6
December	198.9	189.6	124.2	119.8	203.7	388.4	122.1	116.6	107.3	116.6
2021										
January	202.5	201.3	126.0	119.9	207.6	423.2	124.0	119.4	110.3	118.7
February	207.9	225.6	126.5	119.9	211.8	422.7	125.0	122.0	116.4	120.6
March	215.5	216.9	127.4	120.1	217.7	430.8	126.8	125.1	114.8	123.5
April	219.6	219.9	129.0	121.6	224.3	440.6	128.6	128.6	115.5	125.6
May	227.3	237.9	129.7	122.6	230.4	481.1	130.5	132.1	118.8	129.3
June	232.2	242.4	131.3	124.7	234.9	483.2	132.3	134.3	121.3	131.5
July	236.0	248.4	132.0	126.0	238.0	483.9	133.6	135.3	124.0	133.4
August	237.7	249.2	132.6	128.4	240.8	484.8	134.4	136.2	124.8	134.1
September	240.2	252.6	132.9	130.2	242.7	472.0	134.7	137.0	127.2	134.1
October	245.1	270.1	132.8	130.5	246.6	466.7	135.3	138.8	131.9	135.5
November	248.3	277.4	133.6	131.2	249.8	483.9	136.7	140.0	133.6	137.1
December	247.4	265.4	134.5	131.2	251.2	478.1	137.5	140.8	130.5	137.4

Table 8-6. Producer Price Indexes for Goods and Services: Intermediate Demand—*Continued*

(November 2009 = 100, except as noted.)

Year and month	Intermediate demand by commodity type						Intermediate demand by production flow (Prices of inputs to indicated stage of production)			
	Processed goods (1982=100)	Unprocessed goods (1982=100)	Services	Construction	Processed materials less foods and energy (1982=100)	Unprocessed nonfood materials less energy (1982 =100)	Stage 4 intermediate demand	Stage 3 intermediate demand	Stage 2 intermediate demand	Stage 1 intermediate demand
SEASONALLY ADJUSTED										
2018										
January	196.5	199.8	117.0	115.3	197.2	341.8	115.1	114.9	106.8	114.5
February	198.3	202.9	117.3	115.3	198.2	341.6	115.5	115.9	107.7	115.1
March	198.1	196.6	117.6	115.5	199.3	345.7	115.9	115.7	106.4	115.2
April	199.4	198.2	117.9	115.6	199.9	347.5	116.3	115.9	107.3	116.0
May	201.0	203.3	118.2	115.9	201.4	346.7	116.7	116.9	108.7	116.7
June	201.9	201.6	118.5	116.0	202.3	349.0	117.1	117.5	108.6	117.2
July	202.1	203.2	118.9	116.1	203.0	341.7	117.4	117.6	109.5	117.5
August	202.7	195.9	118.9	116.5	203.6	333.7	117.4	117.1	108.9	117.4
September	203.4	197.8	119.2	116.5	204.5	330.9	117.6	117.7	109.7	117.6
October	204.6	203.0	119.9	117.0	204.8	333.1	118.3	119.1	110.3	118.7
November	202.7	196.4	120.0	117.2	204.2	335.9	118.0	118.1	108.7	117.8
December	200.5	202.8	120.1	117.4	203.1	340.2	118.0	116.6	109.6	116.7
2019										
January	198.8	193.2	120.3	117.9	203.0	333.3	117.9	116.3	107.4	115.3
February	199.3	188.9	120.3	118.7	202.6	333.0	118.1	116.6	106.5	115.5
March	200.3	189.3	120.8	118.8	202.4	338.2	118.7	117.2	106.7	116.5
April	201.1	191.9	121.4	119.0	202.2	330.9	119.2	118.7	107.2	116.7
May	199.7	186.7	121.5	119.4	201.7	319.0	119.0	118.2	106.6	115.3
June	197.4	181.7	121.6	118.9	201.1	317.3	118.8	117.1	105.2	113.8
July	197.5	183.8	121.6	119.6	200.7	320.5	119.1	117.1	105.6	114.0
August	196.6	180.8	122.1	119.8	199.9	319.9	119.2	117.1	105.1	113.8
September	196.4	180.5	122.3	119.8	199.7	317.2	119.3	116.7	105.4	113.6
October	196.8	180.4	121.6	119.9	200.3	314.3	119.1	117.2	104.7	113.3
November	196.9	185.9	121.5	120.0	199.9	314.3	119.1	117.0	105.8	113.2
December	197.2	187.7	122.1	120.0	199.5	323.3	119.6	117.5	106.1	114.1
2020										
January	196.9	186.2	122.3	120.9	199.6	339.2	119.8	117.5	105.4	114.3
February	195.3	174.1	122.0	121.0	199.3	334.7	119.2	116.1	103.3	112.8
March	192.1	159.9	122.0	119.6	199.0	338.7	118.8	113.9	100.5	111.2
April	185.6	136.8	120.0	119.4	196.1	326.3	116.8	107.8	96.0	106.4
May	185.4	149.0	119.6	119.4	195.0	327.7	116.9	108.8	97.4	105.4
June	187.6	157.2	120.0	119.4	195.8	331.0	117.6	110.7	99.2	107.3
July	190.3	158.7	120.5	119.5	197.0	332.9	118.5	112.0	99.9	108.9
August	192.2	164.5	121.6	119.5	198.5	343.6	119.5	113.0	101.5	110.5
September	193.4	173.1	122.9	119.6	200.3	359.3	120.5	113.9	103.3	111.9
October	195.1	175.9	123.7	119.6	200.9	360.7	121.1	115.2	103.8	112.7
November	196.6	186.8	123.7	119.7	201.3	370.3	121.3	115.9	105.8	113.7
December	200.0	190.2	124.5	119.8	204.1	389.6	122.5	117.3	107.6	117.0
2021										
January	203.5	201.2	126.0	119.9	207.8	423.0	124.1	119.6	110.3	119.1
February	209.0	224.9	126.4	119.9	211.8	419.9	125.1	122.1	116.4	120.9
March	216.1	215.8	127.2	120.1	217.5	427.9	126.8	125.0	114.7	123.6
April	220.6	217.5	128.8	121.6	224.0	436.1	128.6	128.4	115.2	125.7
May	226.7	234.6	129.6	122.6	230.1	474.3	130.2	131.5	118.6	129.0
June	230.6	239.5	131.2	124.7	234.6	479.0	131.9	133.6	121.1	130.9
July	234.3	247.1	132.0	126.0	237.9	482.0	133.2	134.9	123.8	132.8
August	236.6	250.7	132.5	128.4	240.6	488.7	134.1	136.2	124.8	133.9
September	239.4	257.6	133.0	130.2	242.8	479.7	134.7	137.7	127.4	134.1
October	245.1	273.1	132.9	130.5	246.8	472.5	135.6	139.1	132.2	135.6
November	248.8	279.3	133.7	131.2	250.2	488.5	137.0	140.2	133.8	137.3
December	248.6	265.8	134.8	131.2	251.8	479.7	138.0	141.3	130.8	137.8

Table 8-7. Producer Price Indexes by Major Commodity Groups

(1982 = 100.)

Year and month	All commodities	Farm products	Processed foods and feeds	Industrial commodities													
				Total	Textile products and apparel	Hides, leather, and related products	Fuels and related products and power	Chemicals and allied products	Rubber and plastics products	Lumber and wood products	Pulp, paper, and allied products	Metals and metal products	Machinery and equipment	Furniture and household durables	Nonmetallic mineral products	Transportation equipment	Miscellaneous products
1950	27.3	44.0	33.2	25.0	50.2	32.9	12.6	30.4	35.6	31.4	25.7	22.0	22.6	40.9	23.5	. . .	28.6
1951	30.4	51.2	36.9	27.6	56.0	37.7	13.0	34.8	43.7	34.1	30.5	24.5	25.3	44.4	25.0	. . .	30.3
1952	29.6	48.4	36.4	26.9	50.5	30.5	13.0	33.0	39.6	33.2	29.7	24.5	25.3	43.5	25.0	. . .	30.2
1953	29.2	43.8	34.8	27.2	49.3	31.0	13.4	33.4	36.9	33.1	29.6	25.3	25.9	44.4	26.0	. . .	31.0
1954	29.3	43.2	35.4	27.2	48.2	29.5	13.2	33.8	37.5	32.5	29.6	25.5	26.3	44.9	26.6	. . .	31.3
1955	29.3	40.5	33.8	27.8	48.2	29.4	13.2	33.7	42.4	34.1	30.4	27.2	27.2	45.1	27.3	. . .	31.3
1956	30.3	40.0	33.8	29.1	48.2	31.2	13.6	33.9	43.0	34.6	32.4	29.6	29.3	46.3	28.5	. . .	31.7
1957	31.2	41.1	34.8	29.9	48.3	31.2	14.3	34.6	42.8	32.8	33.0	30.2	31.4	47.5	29.6	. . .	32.6
1958	31.6	42.9	36.5	30.0	47.4	31.6	13.7	34.9	42.8	32.5	33.4	30.0	32.1	47.9	29.9	. . .	33.3
1959	31.7	40.2	35.6	30.5	48.1	35.9	13.7	34.8	42.6	34.7	33.7	30.6	32.8	48.0	30.3	. . .	33.4
1960	31.7	40.1	35.6	30.5	48.6	34.6	13.9	34.8	42.7	33.5	34.0	30.6	33.0	47.8	30.4	. . .	33.6
1961	31.6	39.7	36.2	30.4	47.8	34.9	14.0	34.5	41.1	32.0	33.0	30.5	33.0	47.5	30.5	. . .	33.7
1962	31.7	40.4	36.5	30.4	48.2	35.3	14.0	33.9	39.9	32.2	33.4	30.2	33.0	47.2	30.5	. . .	33.9
1963	31.6	39.6	36.8	30.3	48.2	34.3	13.9	33.5	40.1	32.8	33.1	30.3	33.1	46.9	30.3	. . .	34.2
1964	31.6	39.0	36.7	30.5	48.5	34.4	13.5	33.6	39.6	33.5	33.0	31.1	33.3	47.1	30.4	. . .	34.4
1965	32.3	40.7	38.0	30.9	48.8	35.9	13.8	33.9	39.7	33.7	33.3	32.0	33.7	46.8	30.4	. . .	34.7
1966	33.3	43.7	40.2	31.5	48.9	39.4	14.1	34.0	40.5	35.2	34.2	32.8	34.7	47.4	30.7	. . .	35.3
1967	33.4	41.3	39.8	32.0	48.9	38.1	14.4	34.2	41.4	35.1	34.6	33.2	35.9	48.3	31.2	. . .	36.2
1968	34.2	42.3	40.6	32.8	50.7	39.3	14.3	34.1	42.8	39.8	35.0	34.0	37.0	49.7	32.4	. . .	37.0
1969	35.6	45.0	42.7	33.9	51.8	41.5	14.6	34.2	43.6	44.0	36.0	36.0	38.2	50.7	33.6	40.4	38.1
1970	36.9	45.8	44.6	35.2	52.4	42.0	15.3	35.0	44.9	39.9	37.5	38.7	40.0	51.9	35.3	41.9	39.8
1971	38.1	46.6	45.5	36.5	53.3	43.4	16.6	35.6	45.2	44.7	38.1	39.4	41.4	53.1	38.2	44.2	40.8
1972	39.8	51.6	48.0	37.8	55.5	50.0	17.1	35.6	45.3	50.7	39.3	40.9	42.3	53.8	39.4	45.5	41.5
1973	45.0	72.7	58.9	40.3	60.5	54.5	19.4	37.6	46.6	62.2	42.3	44.0	43.7	55.7	40.7	46.1	43.3
1974	53.5	77.4	68.0	49.2	68.0	55.2	30.1	50.2	56.4	64.5	52.5	57.0	50.0	61.8	47.8	50.3	48.1
1975	58.4	77.0	72.6	54.9	67.4	56.5	35.4	62.0	62.2	62.1	59.0	61.5	57.9	67.5	54.4	56.7	53.4
1976	61.1	78.8	70.8	58.4	72.4	63.9	38.3	64.0	66.0	72.2	62.1	65.0	61.3	70.3	58.2	60.5	55.6
1977	64.9	79.4	74.0	62.5	75.3	68.3	43.6	65.9	69.4	83.0	64.6	69.3	65.2	73.2	62.6	64.6	59.4
1978	69.9	87.7	80.6	67.0	78.1	76.1	46.5	68.0	72.4	96.9	67.7	75.3	70.3	77.5	69.6	69.5	66.7
1979	78.7	99.6	88.5	75.7	82.5	96.1	58.9	76.0	80.5	105.5	75.9	86.0	76.7	82.8	77.6	75.3	75.5
1980	89.8	102.9	95.9	88.0	89.7	94.7	82.8	89.0	90.1	101.5	86.3	95.0	86.0	90.7	88.4	82.9	93.6
1981	98.0	105.2	98.9	97.4	97.6	99.3	100.2	98.4	96.4	102.8	94.8	99.6	94.4	95.9	96.7	94.3	96.1
1982	100.0	100.0	100.0	100.0	100.0	100.0	100.0	100.0	100.0	100.0	100.0	100.0	100.0	100.0	100.0	100.0	100.0
1983	101.3	102.4	101.8	101.1	100.3	103.2	95.9	100.3	100.8	107.9	103.3	101.8	102.7	103.4	101.6	102.8	104.8
1984	103.7	105.5	105.4	103.3	102.7	109.0	94.8	102.9	102.3	108.0	110.3	104.8	105.1	105.7	105.4	105.2	107.0
1985	103.2	95.1	103.5	103.7	102.9	108.9	91.4	103.7	101.9	106.6	113.3	104.4	107.2	107.1	108.6	107.9	109.4
1986	100.2	92.9	105.4	100.0	103.2	113.0	69.8	102.6	101.9	107.2	116.1	103.2	108.8	108.2	110.0	110.5	111.6
1987	102.8	95.5	107.9	102.6	105.1	120.4	70.2	106.4	103.0	112.8	121.8	107.1	110.4	109.9	110.0	112.5	114.9
1988	106.9	104.9	112.7	106.3	109.2	131.4	66.7	116.3	109.3	118.9	130.4	118.7	113.2	113.1	111.2	114.3	120.2
1989	112.2	110.9	117.8	111.6	112.3	136.3	72.9	123.0	112.6	126.7	137.8	124.1	117.4	116.9	112.6	117.7	126.5
1990	116.3	112.2	121.9	115.8	115.0	141.7	82.3	123.6	113.6	129.7	141.2	122.9	120.7	119.2	114.7	121.5	134.2
1991	116.5	105.7	121.9	116.5	116.3	138.9	81.2	125.6	115.1	132.1	142.9	120.2	123.0	121.2	117.2	126.4	140.8
1992	117.2	103.6	122.1	117.4	117.8	140.4	80.4	125.9	115.1	146.6	145.2	119.2	123.4	122.2	117.3	130.4	145.3
1993	118.9	107.1	124.0	119.0	118.0	143.7	80.0	128.2	116.0	174.0	147.3	119.2	124.0	123.7	120.0	133.7	145.4
1994	120.4	106.3	125.5	120.7	118.3	148.5	77.8	132.1	117.6	180.0	152.5	124.8	125.1	126.1	124.2	137.2	141.9
1995	124.7	107.4	127.0	125.5	120.8	153.7	78.0	142.5	124.3	178.1	172.2	134.5	126.6	128.2	129.0	139.7	145.4
1996	127.7	122.4	133.3	127.3	122.4	150.5	85.8	142.1	123.8	176.1	168.7	131.0	126.5	130.4	131.0	141.7	147.7
1997	127.6	112.9	134.0	127.7	122.6	154.2	86.1	143.6	123.2	183.8	167.9	131.8	125.9	130.8	133.2	141.6	150.9
1998	124.4	104.6	131.6	124.8	122.9	148.0	75.3	143.9	122.6	179.1	171.7	127.8	124.9	131.3	135.4	141.2	156.0
1999	125.5	98.4	131.1	126.5	121.1	146.0	80.5	144.2	122.5	183.6	174.1	124.6	124.3	131.7	138.9	141.8	166.6
2000	132.7	99.5	133.1	134.8	121.4	151.5	103.5	151.0	125.5	178.2	183.7	128.1	124.0	132.6	142.5	143.8	170.8
2001	134.2	103.8	137.3	135.7	121.3	158.4	105.3	151.8	127.2	174.4	184.8	125.4	123.7	133.2	144.3	145.2	181.3
2002	131.1	99.0	136.2	132.4	119.9	157.6	93.2	151.9	126.8	173.3	185.9	125.9	122.9	133.5	146.2	144.6	182.4
2003	138.1	111.5	143.4	139.1	119.8	162.3	112.9	161.8	130.1	177.4	190.0	129.2	121.9	133.9	148.2	145.7	179.6
2004	146.7	123.3	151.2	147.6	121.0	164.5	126.9	174.4	133.8	195.6	195.7	149.6	122.1	135.1	153.2	148.6	183.2
2005	157.4	118.5	153.1	160.2	122.8	165.4	156.4	192.0	143.8	196.5	202.6	160.8	123.7	139.4	164.2	151.0	195.1
2006	164.7	117.0	153.8	168.8	124.5	168.4	166.7	205.8	153.8	194.4	209.8	181.6	126.2	142.6	179.9	152.6	205.6
2007	172.6	143.4	165.1	175.1	125.8	173.6	177.6	214.8	155.0	192.4	216.9	193.5	127.3	144.7	186.2	155.0	210.3
2008	189.6	161.3	180.5	192.3	128.9	173.1	214.6	245.5	165.9	191.3	226.8	213.0	129.7	148.9	197.1	158.6	216.6
2009	172.9	134.6	176.2	174.8	129.5	157.0	158.7	229.4	165.2	182.8	225.6	186.8	131.3	153.1	202.4	162.2	217.5
2010	184.7	151.0	182.3	187.0	131.7	181.4	185.8	246.6	170.7	192.7	236.9	207.6	131.1	153.2	201.8	163.4	221.5
2011	201.0	186.7	197.5	202.0	141.7	199.9	215.9	275.1	182.7	194.7	245.1	225.9	132.7	156.4	205.0	166.1	229.2
2012	202.2	192.5	205.2	202.1	142.2	202.3	212.1	276.6	186.9	201.6	244.2	219.9	134.2	160.6	211.0	169.8	235.6
2013	203.4	195.3	208.3	203.0	143.4	217.9	211.8	279.2	189.0	214.9	248.8	213.5	135.2	161.1	216.9	171.8	239.5
2014	205.3	197.4	216.5	204.1	145.5	229.1	209.8	280.9	190.2	224.2	250.5	215.0	136.2	163.2	223.7	174.1	243.0
2015	190.4	173.8	209.1	188.8	144.1	210.4	160.5	266.0	187.0	221.9	248.8	200.3	136.9	164.7	228.9	176.5	247.4
2016	185.4	157.0	203.5	184.6	143.3	195.1	145.9	265.1	184.6	222.7	247.7	194.3	136.9	165.1	233.3	177.4	252.1
2017	193.5	161.8	205.4	193.7	145.1	192.1	163.7	280.8	189.0	230.4	254.6	207.8	137.9	166.9	238.6	179.0	257.6
2018	202.0	160.9	206.1	203.7	149.3	180.4	181.6	295.1	195.1	243.9	260.0	223.6	140.3	171.6	247.3	181.2	264.0
2019	199.8	161.5	209.1	200.7	150.7	165.9	168.7	289.1	196.0	236.7	259.4	221.3	143.3	176.4	253.2	182.9	274.2
2020	194.4	157.9	212.0	193.9	149.4	157.1	144.0	279.8	194.2	254.5	259.9	219.9	144.9	179.1	257.5	183.8	281.6
2021	227.4	198.0	230.3	228.4	162.2	180.1	200.1	331.4	217.4	315.5	288.6	293.8	149.9	190.3	271.0	188.7	295.3

. . . = Not available.

NOTES AND DEFINITIONS

CHAPTER 8: PRICE INDEXES

This chapter presents price indexes (Consumer and Producer) from two major price collection systems, both conducted by the U.S. Bureau of Labor Statistics. Effective on February 26, 2015, the Bureau of Labor Statistics began utilizing a new estimation system for the Consumer Price Index. The new estimation system, the first major improvement to the existing system in over 25 years. This system is redesigned, state-of-the-art with improved flexibility and review capabilities.

In 2014 the Producer Price Index system was expanded to include services and construction as well as goods. A new index for "Final Demand" for goods, services and construction, with more than double the scope, is now presented alongside the familiar Finished Goods index. The expanded system is only available beginning in November 2009, and the historical Producer Price Indexes for goods—with data going back to 1913—are also maintained and carried forward. See the Notes and Definitions for Tables 8-5 through 8-7, below, for further information.

Tables 8-1 through 8-4

Average Price Data

SOURCES: U.S. DEPARTMENT OF LABOR, BUREAU OF LABOR STATISTICS (BLS) AND U.S. DEPARTMENT OF COMMERCE, BUREAU OF ECONOMIC ANALYSIS (BEA)

With the release of the Consumer Price Index (CPI) each month, the Bureau of Labor Statistics (BLS) also publishes average retail prices for select utility, automotive fuel, and food items. Although average prices are calculated from the price observations collected for the CPI, they serve a different purpose. The CPI measures price change while average prices provide estimates of price levels. Specifically, average prices are estimates of the average price paid by the consumer for a good or service.

At the U.S. level, the BLS publishes approximately 70 average prices for food items, 6 for utility gas (natural gas) and electricity, and 5 for automotive fuels. Average prices are estimates of the average price paid by the consumer, not estimates of price change. They provide an estimate of the price levels in a given month which cannot be determined from an index. Average prices can be used for comparing price levels of different items in the same month.

Consumer Price Indexes

The Consumer Price Index (CPI), which is compiled by the Bureau of Labor Statistics (BLS), was originally conceived as a statistical measure of the average change in the cost to consumers of a market basket of goods and services purchased by urban wage earners and clerical workers. In 1978, its scope was broadened to also provide a measure of the change in the cost of the average market basket for all urban consumers. There was still a demand for a wage-earner index, so both versions have been calculated and published since then. The most commonly cited measure in this system is the Consumer Price Index for All Urban Consumers (CPI-U). The wage-earner alternative, used according to law for calculating cost of living adjustments in many government programs, including Social Security, and also used by choice of the contracting parties in wage agreements, is called the Consumer Price Index for Urban Wage Earners and Clerical Workers (CPI-W). Both are presented by the BLS back to 1913, and reproduced in *Business Statistics*; however, the movements (percent changes) in the two indexes before 1978 are identical and are based on the wage-earner market basket. (The pre-1978 levels of the two indexes differ because of differences between 1978 and the reference base period.)

These CPIs have typically been called "cost-of-living" indexes, even though the original fixed market basket concept does not correspond to economists' definition of a cost-of- living index, which is the cost of maintaining a constant standard of living or level of satisfaction. In recent years, the concept measured in practice in the CPI has developed into something intended to be closer to the theoretical definition of a cost-of-living index. In addition, a new variation of the CPI—the Chained Consumer Price Index for All Urban Consumers (C-CPI-U)—is intended to provide an even closer approximation.

The reference base for the total BLS Consumer Price Index and most of its components is currently 1982–1984 = 100. However, new products that have been introduced into the index since January 1982 are shown on later reference bases, as is the entire C-CPI-U.

Price indexes for personal consumption expenditures (PCE) are calculated and published by the Bureau of Economic Analysis (BEA) as a part of the national income and product accounts (NIPAs). (See Chapters 1 and 4 and their notes and definitions.) Monthly, quarterly, and annual values are all available. The reference base for these indexes is the average in the NIPA base year, 2009. These indexes differ in a number of other respects from the CPIs, and are often emphasized by the Federal Reserve in its analyses of the nation's economy. The Federal Reserve is mandated to maximize employment (see Chapter 10) and maintain price stability as measured by the Consumer Price Index (CPI). The target inflation rate is 2 percent. Four important NIPA aggregate price indexes are shown in Tables 8-3 and 8-4 for convenient comparison with the CPIs. See the definitions for those tables for more information.

The CPI-U and the CPI-W

The *CPI-U*, which is displayed in Tables 8-1 through 8-4 and also provides all of the component category sub-indexes shown in Table 8-2, uses the consumption patterns for all urban consumers, who currently comprise about 89 percent of the population.

A slightly different index that is widely used for adjusting wages and government benefits is the *CPI-W*, of which the all-items total is shown in each of Tables 8-1 through 8-4. It represents the buying habits of only urban wage earners and clerical workers, who currently comprise about 28 percent of the population. The weights are derived from the same Consumer Expenditure Surveys (CES) used for the CPI-U weights, and are changed on the same schedule. However, they include only consumers from the specified categories instead of all urban consumers.

Beginning with February 2020, the weights in both indexes are based on consumer expenditures in the 2018-2019 period In February 2016, the weights in both indexes are based on consumer expenditures in the 2014-2015 period. In January 2012, the weights in both indexes are based on consumer expenditures in the 2009–2010 period. From January 2010 to December 2011, 2007–2008 weights were used; from January 2008 to December 2009, 2005–2006 weights; from January 2006 to December 2007, 2003–2004 weights; from January 2004 to December 2005, 2001–2002 weights; from January 2002 to December 2003, 1999–2000 weights; and from January 1998 to December 2001, 1993–1995 weights. The weights will continue to be updated at two-year intervals, with new weights introduced in the January indexes of each even-numbered year. Previously, new weights were introduced only at the time of a major revision, which translated into a lag of a decade or more.

Specifically, the CPI weights for 1964 through 1977 were derived from reported expenditures of a sample of wageearner and clericalworker families and individuals in 1960–1961 and adjusted for price changes between the survey dates and 1963. Weights for the 1978–1986 period were derived from a survey undertaken during the 1972–1974 period and adjusted for price change between the survey dates and December 1977. For 1987 through 1997, the spending patterns reflected in the CPI were derived from a survey undertaken during the 1982–1984 period. The reported expenditures were adjusted for price change between the survey dates and December 1986.

The CPI was overhauled and updated in the latest major revision, which took effect in January 1998. In addition, new products and improved methods are regularly introduced into the index, usually in January.

The latest change in methods was the introduction of a geometric mean formula for calculating many of the basic components of the index. Beginning with the index for January 1999, this formula is used for categories comprising approximately 61 percent of total consumer spending. The new formula allows for the possibility that some consumers may react to changing relative prices within a category by substituting items whose relative prices have declined for products whose relative prices have risen, while maintaining their overall level of satisfaction. The geometric mean formula is not used for a few categories in which consumer substitution in the short term is not feasible, currently housing rent and utilities.

The CPI-U was introduced in 1978. Before that time, only CPI-W data were available. The movements of the CPI-U before 1978 are therefore based on the changes in the CPI-W. However, the index levels are different because the two indexes differed in the 1982–1984 base period.

Because the official CPI-U and CPI-W are so widely used in "escalation"—the calculation of cost-of-living adjustments for wages and other private contracts, and for government payments and tax parameters—these price indexes are not retrospectively revised to incorporate new information and methods. (An exception is occasionally made for outright error, which happened in September 2000 and affected the data for January through August of that year.) Instead, the new information and methods of calculation are introduced in the current index and affect future index changes only. In Tables 8-3 and 8-4, PCE indexes, which are subject to routine revision, and special CPI indexes that have been retrospectively revised are presented. These indexes can be used by researchers to provide more consistent historical information.

Notes on the CPI data

The CPI is based on prices of food, clothing, shelter, fuel, utilities, transportation, medical care, and other goods and services that people buy for daytoday living. The quantity and quality of these priced items are kept essentially constant between revisions to ensure that only price changes will be measured. All taxes directly associated with the purchase and use of these items, such as sales and property taxes, are included in the index; the effects of income and payroll tax changes are not included.

Data are collected on about 80,000 individually defined goods and services from about 23,000 retail and service establishments and about 6,000 housing units in 75 urban areas across the country. These data are used to develop the U.S. city average.

Periodic major revisions of the indexes update the content and weights of the market basket of goods and services; update the statistical sample of urban areas, outlets, and unique items used in calculating the CPI; and improve the statistical methods used. In addition, retail outlets and items are resampled on a rotating 5-year basis. Adjustments for changing quality are made at times of major product changes, such as the annual auto model changeover. Other methodological changes are introduced from time to time.

The Consumer Expenditure Survey (CES) provides the weights—that is, the relative importance—used to combine the individual price changes into subtotals and totals. This survey is composed of two separate surveys: an interview survey and a diary survey, both of which are conducted by the Census Bureau for BLS. Each expenditure reported in the two surveys is classified into a series of detailed categories, which are then combined into expenditure classes and ultimately into major expenditure groups. CPI data as of 1998 are grouped into eight such categories: (1) food and beverages, (2) housing, (3) apparel, (4) transportation, (5) medical care, (6) entertainment (7) education and communication, and (8) other goods and services.

Seasonally adjusted national CPI indexes are published for selected series for which there is a significant seasonal pattern of price change. The factors currently in use were derived by the X13ARIMA-SEATS seasonal adjustment method. Some series with extreme or sharp movements are seasonally adjusted using Intervention Analysis Seasonal Adjustment. Seasonally adjusted indexes and seasonal factors for the preceding five years are updated annually based on data through the previous December. Due to these revisions, BLS advises against the use of seasonally adjusted data for escalation. Detailed descriptions of seasonal adjustment procedures are available upon request from BLS.

BLS estimates the "standard error"—the error due to collecting data from a sample instead of the universe—of the one-month percent change in the not-seasonally-adjusted U.S. all-items index in 2013 was 0.03 percentage point. This means that for the 2013 median 0.12 percent change in the All Items CPI-U, BLS is 95 percent confident that the actual percent change based on all retail prices would fall between 0.06 and 0.18 percent. Monthly percent changes in the seasonally adjusted indexes, in contrast, may be revised by 0.1 percentage point when reviewed at the end of the year, and occasionally by even more.

CPI Definitions

Definitions of the major CPI groupings were modified beginning with the data for January 1998. These modifications were carried back to 1993. The following definitions are the current definitions currently used for the CPI components.

The *food and beverage index* includes both food at home and food away from home (restaurant meals and other food bought and eaten away from home).

The *housing index* measures changes in rental costs and expenses connected with the acquisition and operation of a home. The CPIU, beginning with data for January 1983, and the CPIW, beginning with data for January 1985, reflect a change in the methodology used to compute the homeownership component. A rental equivalence measure replaced an assetprice approach, which included purchase prices and interest costs. The intent

of the change was to separate shelter costs from the investment component of homeownership, so that the index would only reflect the cost of the shelter services provided by owner-occupied homes. In addition to measures of the cost of shelter, the housing category includes insurance, fuel, utilities, and household furnishings and operations.

The *apparel index* includes the purchase of apparel and footwear.

The *private transportation index* includes prices paid by urban consumers for such items as new and used automobiles and other vehicles, gasoline, motor oil, tires, repairs and maintenance, insurance, registration fees, driver's licenses, parking fees, and the like. Auto finance charges, like mortgage interest payments, are considered to be a cost of asset acquisition, not of current consumption. Therefore, they are no longer included in the CPI. City bus, streetcar, subway, taxicab, intercity bus, airplane, and railroad coach fares are some of the components of the *public transportation index*.

The *medical care index* includes prices for professional medical services, hospital and related services, prescription and nonprescription drugs, and other medical care commodities. The weight for the portion of health insurance premiums that is used to cover the costs of these medical goods and services is distributed among the items; the weight for the portion of health insurance costs attributable to administrative expenses and profits of insurance providers constitutes a separate health insurance item. Effective with the January 1997 data, the method of calculating the hospital cost component was changed from the pricing of individual commodities and services to a more comprehensive cost-of-treatment approach.

Recreation includes components formerly listed in housing, apparel, entertainment, and "other goods and services."

Education and communication is a new group including components formerly categorized in housing and "other goods and services," such as college tuition and books, telephone and internet services, and computers.

Other goods and services now includes tobacco, personal care, and miscellaneous.

Table 8-2

Purchasing Power of the Dollar

SOURCE: U.S. DEPARTMENT OF LABOR, BUREAU OF LABOR STATISTICS (BLS)

The purchasing power of the dollar measures changes in the quantity of goods and services a dollar will buy at a particular date compared with a selected base date. It must be defined in terms of the following: (1) the specific commodities and services that are to be purchased with the dollar; (2) the market level (producer, retail, etc.) at which they are purchased; and (3) the dates for which the comparison is to be made. Thus, the purchasing power of the dollar for a selected period, compared with another period, may be measured in terms of a single commodity or a large group of commodities such as all goods and services purchased by consumers at retail.

The purchasing power of the dollar is computed by dividing the price index number for the base period by the price index number for the comparison date and expressing the result in dollars and cents. The base period is the period in which the price index equals 100; the average purchasing power in that base period—1982–1984 in the case of the measure shown here—is therefore $1.00.

Purchasing power estimates in terms of both the CPI-U and the CPI-W are calculated by BLS, based on indexes not adjusted for seasonal variation, and published in the CPI press release. The CPI-U version is shown here.

Alternative price measures in Tables 8-3 and 8-4

Table 8-3 shows the all-items CPI-U and CPI-W, along with a number of other indexes that various analysts of price trends have preferred as measures of the price level. Table 8-4 shows the inflation rates (percent changes in price levels) implied by each of the indexes in Table 8-3.

As food and energy prices are volatile and frequently determined by forces separate from monetary aggregate demand pressures, many analysts prefer an index of prices excluding those components. Indexes *excluding food and energy* are known as *core* indexes, and inflation rates calculated from them are known as *core inflation rates*.

The *CPI-U-X1* is a special experimental version of the CPI that researchers have used to provide a more historically consistent series. As explained above, the official CPI-U treated homeownership on an asset-price basis until January 1983. It then changed to a rental equivalence method. The CPI-U-X1 incorporates a rental equivalence approach to homeowners' costs for the years 1967–1982 as well. It is rebased to the December 1982 value of the CPI-U (1982–1984 = 100); thus, it is identical to the CPI-U in December 1982 and all subsequent periods. For this reason, it is not updated or published in the CPI news release or on the BLS Web site.

The *CPI-E* is an experimental re-weighting of components of the CPI-U to represent price change for the goods and services purchased by Americans age 62 years and over, who accounted for 16.5 percent of the total number of urban consumer units in the 2001–2002 CES.

BLS does not consider the CPI-E to be an ideal measure of price change for older Americans. Because the sample is small, the sampling error in the weights is greater than the error in the all-urban index. The products and outlets sampled are those characteristic of the general urban population rather than older residents. In addition, senior discounts are not included in the prices collected. Such discounts are included—appropriately—in the weights, which are based on the expenditures reported by the older consumers' households. Therefore, such discounts are only a problem if they do not move proportionately to general prices.

The *CPI-U-RS* is a "research series" CPI that retroactively incorporates estimates of the effects of most of the methodological changes implemented since 1978, including the rental equivalence method, new or improved quality adjustments, and improvement of formulas to eliminate bias and allow for some consumer substitution within categories. This index is calculated from 1977 onward. Its reference base is December 1977 = 100. Thus, although it generally shows less <u>increase</u> than the official index, its current <u>levels</u> are considerably higher because the earlier reference base period had lower prices. Unlike the official CPIs and the CPI-U-X1, its historical values will be revised each time a significant change is made in the calculation of the current index. This index is not seasonally adjusted and is not included in the CPI news release. It is available on the BLS Web site, along with an explanation and background material. The CPI-U-RS is used by BLS in the calculation of historical trends in real compensation per hour in its Productivity and Costs system; see Table 9-3 and its notes and definitions. It is also now used by the Census Bureau to convert household incomes into constant dollars, as seen in Chapter 3. And it is used by the editor in some analytical calculations in this volume.

The *C-CPI-U* (Chained Consumer Price Index for All Urban Consumers) is a new, supplemental index that has been published in the monthly CPI news release since August 2002. It is available only from December 1999 to date and is calculated with the base December 1999 = 100; it is not seasonally adjusted. It is designed to be a still-closer approximation to a true cost-of-living index than the CPI-U and the CPI-W, in that it assumes that consumers substitute between as well as within categories as relative prices change, in order to maintain a fixed basket of "consumer satisfaction."

The C-CPI-U is technically a "superlative" index, using a method known as the "Tornqvist formula" to incorporate the composition of consumer spending in the current period as well as in the earlier base period. (All of the other Consumer Price Indexes use a "Laspeyres" formula; see the General Notes at the beginning of this volume.) As it requires consumer expenditure data for the current as well as the earlier period, its final version can only be calculated after the expenditure data become available—about two years later—and is approximated in more recent periods by making more extensive use of the geometric mean formula (see above). With the release of January 2014 data, the indexes for 2012 were revised to their final form, and the initial indexes for 2013 were revised to "interim" levels, shown in Tables 8-3 and 8-4.

Personal consumption expenditure (PCE) chain-type price indexes are calculated by the Bureau of Economic Analysis (BEA) in the framework of the national income and product accounts (NIPAs). (See the notes and definitions for Chapters 1 and 4.) The scope of NIPA PCE is broader than the scope of the CPI. PCE includes the rural as well as the urban population and also covers the consumption spending of nonprofit entities. The CPI includes only consumer out-of-pocket cash spending, whereas PCE includes some imputed servi and includes expenditures financed by government and private insurance, particularly in the medical care area. For this reason, there is a large difference between the relatively small weight of medical care spending in the CPI and the markedly greater percentage of PCE that is accounted for by total medical care spending. Housing, on the other hand, has a somewhat smaller weight in PCE while all non-housing components have a higher weight. The reason for this is that the CES—the survey on which the CPI weights are based—tends to report housing expenditures accurately and somewhat underestimate other spending. This suggests that the weight of housing relative to all other products may be overestimated in the CPI but measured more correctly in the PCE price index.

PCE chain-type indexes use the expenditure weights of both the earlier and the later period to determine the aggregate price change between the two periods. (See the notes and definitions for Chapter 1, as well as the General Notes on index number formulas.) Thus, they are subject to revision as improved data on the composition of consumption spending become available, and in this respect resemble the C-CPI-U.

For a large share of PCE, the price movements for basic individual spending categories are determined by CPI components. Hence, the differences between the rates of change in the aggregate CPI and PCE indexes are largely the result of the different weights, but also reflect some alternative methodologies and the previously mentioned differences in scope.

Market-based PCE indexes are based on household expenditures for which there are observable price measures. They exclude most implicit prices (for example, the services furnished without payment by financial intermediaries) and they exclude items not deflated by a detailed component of either the Consumer Price Index (CPI) or the Producer Price Index (PPI). This means that the price observations that make up these new aggregate measures are all based on observed market transactions, making them "market-based price indexes." The imputed rent for owner-occupied housing is included in the market-based price index, since it is based on observed rentals of comparable homes. Household insurance premiums are also included in the market-based index, since they are deflated by the CPI for tenants' and household insurance. Excluded are services furnished without payment by financial intermediaries, most insurance purchases, expenses of NPISHs (nonprofit institutions serving households), legal gambling (illegal gambling is excluded from all measures), margins on used light motor vehicles, and expenditures by U.S. residents working and traveling abroad. Also excluded are medical, hospitalization, and income loss insurance; expense of handling life insurance; motor vehicle insurance; and workers' compensation.

The *inflation rates* shown in Table 8-4 are percent changes in the price indexes introduced in Table 8-3. For annual indexes, the rate is the percent change from the previous year. For monthly indexes, the rate is the percent change from the same month a year earlier. To give an indication of the longer-run implications of these different price indicators, comparisons of compound annual inflation rates, calculated by the editor, are also shown for the 1978–2013, 1983–2013, 2000–2013 and 2013-2015 periods, using the growth rate formula presented in the article at the beginning of this volume.

Data availability and references

The CPI-U, CPI-W, and C-CPI-U are initially issued in a press release two to three weeks after the end of the month for which the data were collected. This release and detailed and complete current and historical data on the CPI and its variants and components, along with extensive documentation, are available on the BLS Web site at <https://www.bls.gov/cpi>. Seasonal factors and seasonally adjusted indexes are revised once a year with the issuance of the January index.

Information available on the BLS Web site includes "Common Misconceptions about the Consumer Price Index: Questions and Answers;" another fact sheet on frequently asked questions; a fact sheet on seasonal adjustment; Chapter 17 of the *BLS Handbook of Methods*, entitled "The Consumer Price Index"; a section entitled "Note on Chained Consumer Price Index for All Urban Consumers"; and a number of explanatory CPI fact sheets on specific subjects.

As previously indicated, the CPI-U-X1 is not currently published because its recent values are identical to the CPI-U. The CPI-E is presented in articles in the CPI section of the BLS Web site, the most recent of which is "Experimental Consumer Price Index for Americans 62 Years of Age and Older, 1998-2005"; recent values are available by request from BLS. The CPI-U-RS is updated each month in a report entitled "CPI Research Series Using Current Methods" on the site. In both cases, the reports describe the indexes and provide references.

The monthly PCE indexes are included in the personal income report issued by BEA, which is published near the end of the following month. These indexes are revised month-by-month to reflect new information and annually to reflect the annual and quinquennial benchmarking of the NIPAs. The complete historical record can be found on the BEA Web site at <https://www.

bea.gov> in the Personal Income and Outlays section of the NIPA tables, in tables entitled "Price Indexes for Personal Consumption Expenditures by Major Type of Product."

Two special editions of the *Monthly Labor Review* were devoted to CPI issues. The December 1996 issue describes the subsequently implemented 1997 and 1998 revisions in a series of articles, and the December 1993 issue, entitled *The Anatomy of Price Change*, includes the following articles: "The Consumer Price Index: Underlying Concepts and Caveats"; "Basic Components of the CPI: Estimation of Price Changes"; "The Commodity Substitution Effect in CPI Data, 1982–1991"; and "Quality Adjustment of Price Indexes."

The new formula for calculating basic components is described in "Incorporating a Geometric Mean Formula into the CPI," *Monthly Labor Review* (October 1998). For a detailed discussion of the treatment of homeownership, see "Changing the Homeownership Component of the Consumer Price Index to Rental Equivalence," *CPI Detailed Report* (January 1983).

For a comprehensive professional review of CPI concepts and methodology, see Charles Schultze and Christopher Mackie, ed., *At What Price? Conceptualizing and Measuring Cost-of-Living and Price Indexes* (Washington, DC: National Academy Press, 2001). Earlier references include: "Using Survey Data to Assess Bias in the Consumer Price Index," *Monthly Labor Review* (April 1998); Joel Popkin, "Improving the CPI: The Record and Suggested Next Steps," *Business Economics*, Vol. XXXII, No. 3 (July 1997), pages 42–47; *Measurement Issues in the Consumer Price Index* (Bureau of Labor Statistics, U.S. Department of Labor, June 1997); *Toward a More Accurate Measure of the Cost of Living* (Final Report to the Senate Finance Committee from the Advisory Commission to Study the Consumer Price Index, December 4, 1996)—also known as the "Boskin Commission" report; and *Government Price Statistics* (U.S. Congress Joint Economic Committee, 87th Congress, 1st Session, January 24, 1961)—also known as the "Stigler Committee" report.

For an explanation of the differences between the CPI-U and the PCE index, see Clinton P. McCully, Brian C. Moyer, and Kenneth J. Stewart, "Comparing the Consumer Price Index and the Personal Consumption Expenditures Price Index," *Survey of Current Business,* November 2007, pp. 26-33.

Tables 8-1 and 8-5 through 8-7

Producer Price Indexes

SOURCE: U.S. DEPARTMENT OF LABOR, BUREAU OF LABOR STATISTICS (BLS)

The Bureau of Labor Statistics first compiled and published a "Wholesale Price Index," measuring prices of various goods from

the perspective of the seller, in 1902; it covered the years 1890-1901. Over the years this index was broadened and refined. In a major revamping in 1978, it was structured into an input-output format, differentiated between stages of processing, and renamed the Producer Price Index. The index for "Finished Goods," from the stage-of-processing system, became the featured "headline" number. Still, this index only covered goods.

The Producer Price Index (PPI) measures the average change over time in the selling prices that domestic producers receive for their output. The indexes of the Final Demand–Intermediate Demand (FD–ID) aggregation system, used to analyze the behavior of producer prices, measure final-demand inflation (price changes for goods, services, and construction sold for personal consumption, as capital investment, to government, and for export) and intermediate-demand inflation (price changes for goods, services, and construction sold to businesses as inputs to production).

New FD-ID system (Tables 8-5 and 8-6)

Over subsequent years the Bureau instituted collection of an increasing number of prices for services as well. All prices are collected within an industry input-output structure, with one of the most important purposes being to measure real output quantities by deflating industry outputs and inputs. In the new aggregation system introduced in February 2014, prices for goods, services, and construction have been integrated into a set of Final Demand-Intermediate Demand (FD-ID) indexes, organized by class of buyer, degree of fabrication, and stage of production. Its principal components are calculated beginning in November 2009 with that month as the reference base (i.e. November 2009 = 100). Components of the previous goods PPI system continue to be calculated on the base 1982 = 100 as well.

In the new FD-ID system, all products, including services and construction, are referred to as "commodities." In the old PPI system and in the CPI system, the term "commodities" refers to goods only; note, for example, how the CPI components are aggregated into summary measures of "commodities" [goods] and services, displaying different trends and behaviors. Unless and until these terminologies are reconciled, users need to be mindful of which system they are operating in.

More that 100,000 producer price quotations from over 25,000 establishment are collected each month; more than 10,000 indexes for individual products and groups of products are released each month. The prices are organized into three sets of PPIs: the FD-ID indexes; commodity indexes; and indexes for the net output of industries and their products.

Final demand. The final demand portion of the FD-ID structure measures price change for commodities sold for personal consumption, capital investment, government, and export. *Final demand trade services* measures changes in margins received by wholesalers and retailers. The other main components are *final demand goods, final demand transportation and warehousing services, other final demand services,* and *final demand construction.* The total index for final demand is now featured by BLS in its press release as its "headline number," replacing the previously featured Finished Goods index.

Intermediate demand. This portion of the system tracks price changes for goods, services, and construction products sold to businesses as inputs to production and not as capital investment. There are two parallel treatments.

The first treatment organizes intermediate demand commodities by type, including the distinction between *processed goods* and *unprocessed goods,* which is carried over from the older PPI goods system.

The second system organizes intermediate demand commodities into production stages, with the explicit goal of developing a forward-flow model of production and price change. For each production stage, the intermediate demand index measures the prices of inputs to the included industries. Many commodities, for example energy products, are sold to both final demand and various intermediate stages of production; their weight is allocated proportionately to all the consuming stages of production and their price movements are proportionately represented in each stage.

Industries assigned to *Stage 4* primarily produce final demand commodities. The intermediate demand index for Stage 4 measures inputs to those industries, such as motor vehicle parts, beef and veal, and long distance motor carrying.

Industries assigned to *Stage 3* produce the output sold to Stage 4, and therefore include motor vehicle parts and slaughtering. Examples of inputs to Stage 3 included in their intermediate demand index include slaughter steers and heifers, industrial electric power, steel plates, and temporary help services.

Industries assigned to *Stage 2* include petroleum refining, electricity, and insurance agencies. The goods and services that they purchase and that are included in their intermediate demand index include crude oil and business loans.

Industries assigned to *Stage 1* include oil and gas extraction, paper mills, and advertising services. Inputs to those industries include electric power and solid waste collection. According to BLS, "It should be noted that all inputs purchased by stage 1 industries are by definition produced either within stage 1 or by later stages of processing, leaving stage 1 less useful for price transmission analysis."

Commodity indexes

Aggregation by *commodity* organizes the price measures by similarity of product or end use, disregarding industry of origin. For the original Wholesale Price Index (goods only), this was the principal means of aggregation; in Table 8-1C, producer price indexes are shown for *farm products, industrial commodities,* and *"all commodities"* back to the year 1913. Table 8-7 shows 16 goods commodity groups from 1950 to date. Whatever their imperfections, these measures provide the longest historical perspective for producer prices.

The major goods commodity groups—particularly the totals for all commodities and industrial commodities—came under criticism in the energy price crisis of the early 1970s, for aggregating successive stages of processing of the same product (e.g. crude oil) and thus exaggerating price trends. As a result, the stage-of-processing grouping was introduced in 1978, and the finished goods components, in total and minus food and energy, became the headline Producer Price Indexes.

Stage of processing indexes

In the PPI for goods as reconstructed in 1978 and shown in Table 8-1B, the three major indexes are: (1) *finished goods,* or goods that will not undergo further processing and are ready for sale to the ultimate user (such as automobiles, meats, apparel, and machine tools, and also unprocessed foods such as eggs and fresh vegetables, that are ready for the consumer); (2) *processed goods for intermediate demand* (formerly *intermediate materials, supplies, and components*), or goods that have been processed but require further processing before they become finished goods (such as steel mill products, cotton yarns, lumber, and flour), as well as physically complete goods that are purchased by business firms as inputs for their operations (such as diesel fuel and paper boxes); and (3) *unprocessed goods for intermediate demand* (formerly *crude materials for further processing*), or goods entering the market for the first time that have not been manufactured or fabricated and are not sold directly to consumers (such as ores, scrap metals, crude petroleum, raw cotton, and livestock).

Notes on the data

The probability sample used for calculating the PPI provides more than 100,000 price quotations per month. To the greatest extent possible, prices used in calculating the PPI represent prices received by domestic producers in the first important commercial transaction for each commodity. These indexes attempt to measure only price changes (changes in receipts per unit of measurement not influenced by changes in quality, quantity sold, terms of sale, or level of distribution). Transaction prices are sought instead of list or book prices. Price data are collected monthly via Internet, mail, and fax. Prices are obtained directly from producing companies on a voluntary and confidential basis. Prices are generally reported for the Tuesday of the week containing the 13th day of the month. Samples are updated regularly.

The BLS revises the PPI weighting structure when data from economic censuses become available. Beginning with data for January 2012, the weights used to construct the PPI reflect 2007 shipments values as measured by the 2007 Economic Censuses. Data for January 2007 through December 2011 used 2002 values; 2002 through 2006, 1997 shipments values; 1996 through 2001, 1992 values; 1992 through 1995, 1987 values; 1987 through 1991, 1982 values; 1976 through 1986, 1972 values; and 1967 through 1975, 1963 values.

Price indexes are available in unadjusted form and are also adjusted for seasonal variation using the X-12-ARIMA method. Since January 1988, BLS has also used X-12-ARIMA Intervention Analysis Seasonal Adjustment for a small number of series to remove unusual values that might distort seasonal patterns before calculating the seasonal adjustment factors. Seasonal factors for the PPI are revised annually to take into account the most recent 12 months of data. Seasonally adjusted data for the previous 5 years are subject to these annual revisions.

The newer FD-ID indexes are only available beginning in November 2009. Hence, they only regard, so far, the recovery and expansion phase of a particularly severe business cycle; the editor suggests that up to now, both seasonal adjustments and broader inferences about relative price behavior are necessarily based on a short and possibly unrepresentative time period. Partly for that reason, we present both unadjusted and seasonally adjusted indexes in Tables 8-5 and 8-6.

Data availability and references

The indexes are initially issued in a press release two to three weeks after the end of the month for which the data were collected. Data are subsequently published in greater detail in a monthly BLS publication, *PPI Detailed Report*. Each month, data for the fourth previous month (both unadjusted and seasonally adjusted) are revised to reflect late reports and corrections.

The press release, the *PPI Detailed Report*, detailed and complete current and historical data, and extensive documentation are available at <https://www.bls.gov/ppi>. The items available on this Web site include Chapter 14 of the *BLS Handbook of Methods*, "Producer Price Indexes"; a selection of *Monthly Labor Review* articles on the PPI; and fact sheets on a number of issues and index components.

CHAPTER 9: EMPLOYMENT COSTS, PRODUCTIVITY, AND PROFITS

SECTION 9A: EMPLOYMENT COST INDEXES

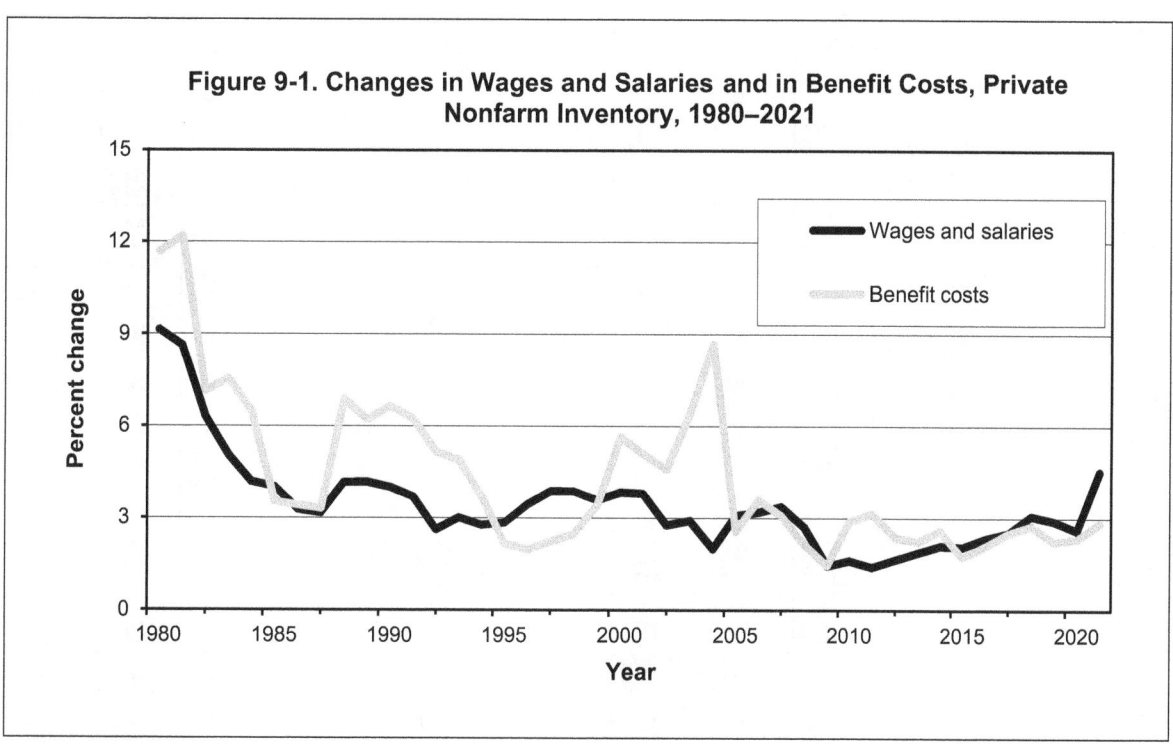

Figure 9-1. Changes in Wages and Salaries and in Benefit Costs, Private Nonfarm Inventory, 1980–2021

- The Employment Cost Index (ECI) measures the change in the cost of labor, free from the influence of employment shifts among occupations and industries. This cost of labor includes not only wages and salaries but also benefits. These benefits include vacations and sick leave, overtime, health insurance, and retirement. (See Chapter 8.)

- Analogous to the ECI is the Consumer Price Index (CPI), which holds the market basket constant in any individual time-period so as to reflect only an aggregate of price changes affecting individual defined products.

- SIC industrial classification began in 1930 when the U.S. was manufacturing-based. Changes to the economy to serviced-based could not be accommodated by SIC. Table 9-1 presents the ECI by the North American Industrial Classification (NAICS) while Table 9-2 presents the data for Standard Industrial Code (SIC). The NAICS system began with the North American Free Trade Agreement (NAFTA), instituted in 1994 with Canada and Mexico.

- From 2009 to 2021, total compensation for all civilian workers rose 33.2 percent. During this period, wages and salaries grew slightly less at 32.8 percent while total benefits grew more rapidly at 34.2 percent. Much of this increase was due to medical care costs. (See Table 9-1)

Table 9-1. Employment Cost Indexes, NAICS Basis

(December 2005 [not seasonally adjusted] = 100; annual values are for December, not seasonally adjusted; quarterly values, seasonally adjusted, except as noted.)

Year and month	All civilian workers [1]	State and local government workers	Private industry workers										Union [2]	Non-union [2]
			All private industry workers	By occupational group					By industry				
				Management, professional, and related	Sales and office	Natural resources, construction, and maintenance	Production, transportation, and material moving	Service occupations	Goods-producing industries		Service-providing		
									Total	Manufacturing			
TOTAL COMPENSATION													
2009	111.0	114.2	110.2	110.7	109.2	111.2	108.9	111.8	108.6	107.0	110.8	111.1	110.1
2010	113.2	116.2	112.5	113.0	111.6	113.3	111.5	113.5	111.1	110.0	113.0	114.8	112.1
2011	115.5	117.7	115.0	115.4	114.2	115.8	114.2	115.4	113.8	113.1	115.3	117.9	114.5
2012	117.7	119.9	117.1	117.7	116.3	117.8	116.0	117.4	115.6	114.9	117.6	120.5	116.6
2013	120.0	122.2	119.4	120.2	119.0	120.1	118.0	119.0	117.7	117.0	120.0	122.6	119.0
2014	122.7	124.7	122.2	123.0	121.9	123.2	120.6	121.1	120.3	119.8	122.8	126.7	121.5
2015	125.1	127.8	124.5	125.3	123.9	124.9	123.7	123.2	123.2	122.8	124.9	128.7	123.8
2016	127.9	130.9	127.2	127.4	126.8	127.7	127.0	127.2	125.8	125.5	127.7	130.6	126.6
2017	131.2	134.2	130.5	130.5	130.1	131.2	131.0	130.9	128.9	128.9	131.0	134.5	129.9
2018	135.0	137.7	134.4	133.8	135.0	134.5	134.7	135.6	131.9	131.6	135.2	138.8	133.7
2019	138.7	141.7	138.0	136.8	138.8	137.9	139.2	140.6	135.8	135.3	138.7	142.3	137.3
2020	142.2	144.9	141.6	139.5	143.2	141.3	143.8	145.6	138.9	138.5	142.4	146.3	140.9
2021	147.9	148.6	147.8	144.4	149.9	146.7	150.9	155.9	144.0	143.5	148.9	151.2	147.2
2010													
March	111.8	114.5	111.1	111.7	109.8	112.3	109.9	112.3	109.7	108.4	111.5	112.8	110.9
June	112.3	115.1	111.6	112.1	110.8	112.6	110.4	112.6	110.2	109.0	112.1	113.7	111.4
September	112.8	115.5	112.1	112.7	111.1	112.9	111.2	113.3	110.9	109.9	112.5	114.6	111.8
December	113.3	116.1	112.6	113.3	111.6	113.4	111.6	113.6	111.2	110.2	113.1	114.8	112.1
2011													
March	114.0	116.7	113.3	114.0	112.1	113.9	112.2	114.5	112.0	111.3	113.8	115.6	113.0
June	114.7	117.0	114.2	114.7	113.3	114.8	113.5	114.7	113.2	112.6	114.5	117.1	113.8
September	115.1	117.3	114.6	115.1	113.8	115.4	113.7	115.0	113.3	112.8	115.0	117.4	114.2
December	115.6	117.7	115.1	115.7	114.2	115.9	114.3	115.5	113.9	113.3	115.5	117.9	114.5
2012													
March	116.3	118.3	115.7	116.3	115.0	116.4	114.5	116.0	114.1	113.4	116.3	118.3	115.3
June	116.8	118.9	116.3	117.0	115.9	116.9	115.0	116.5	114.6	113.9	116.9	119.3	116.0
September	117.3	119.5	116.8	117.3	116.2	117.5	115.6	116.8	115.2	114.6	117.3	120.2	116.3
December	117.8	119.9	117.2	118.0	116.3	118.0	116.1	117.4	115.7	115.1	117.7	120.5	116.6
2013													
March	118.4	120.5	117.9	118.5	117.2	118.7	116.7	117.8	116.4	115.7	118.3	121.5	117.3
June	119.0	121.0	118.5	119.3	118.0	119.0	117.1	118.3	116.9	116.2	119.0	122.1	118.0
September	119.5	121.4	119.0	119.9	118.4	119.7	117.5	118.4	117.4	116.7	119.5	122.5	118.5
December	120.1	122.2	119.6	120.4	119.0	120.3	118.1	119.1	117.8	117.2	120.2	122.6	119.0
2014													
March	120.5	122.8	119.9	120.7	119.3	120.9	118.8	119.0	118.6	118.0	120.4	123.5	119.4
June	121.4	123.5	120.9	121.9	120.5	121.9	119.5	119.6	119.1	118.6	121.5	125.0	120.4
September	122.2	124.1	121.7	122.7	121.1	122.6	120.2	120.5	119.8	119.3	122.3	125.8	121.1
December	122.8	124.7	122.4	123.1	121.9	123.4	120.8	121.2	120.4	120.0	123.0	126.7	121.5
2015													
March	123.6	125.4	123.2	123.8	123.4	123.7	121.6	121.8	121.0	120.8	123.8	127.4	122.5
June	123.8	126.2	123.2	124.0	122.8	124.0	122.4	122.1	121.8	121.6	123.7	127.5	122.7
September	124.6	126.9	124.0	124.8	123.6	124.5	123.0	122.6	122.4	122.1	124.5	128.0	123.4
December	125.3	127.8	124.6	125.5	123.9	125.1	123.9	123.3	123.3	123.0	125.1	128.7	123.8
2016													
March	126.0	128.5	125.3	126.0	125.1	125.8	124.6	124.2	123.8	123.6	125.8	129.6	124.7
June	126.7	129.2	126.1	126.3	126.6	126.5	125.5	125.5	124.6	124.4	126.6	130.0	125.7
September	127.4	130.2	126.7	127.0	126.7	126.9	126.3	126.5	125.1	125.1	127.3	130.4	126.3
December	128.1	130.9	127.4	127.6	126.8	127.8	127.2	127.3	125.8	125.7	127.9	130.6	126.6
2017													
March	128.9	131.8	128.2	128.4	128.1	128.6	128.2	128.4	126.5	126.3	128.8	131.9	127.8
June	129.7	132.5	129.0	129.4	128.7	129.6	129.0	129.2	127.1	127.0	129.6	132.7	128.6
September	130.6	133.3	130.0	130.0	129.9	130.5	130.4	130.0	128.3	128.4	130.5	133.7	129.5
December	131.4	134.2	130.7	130.7	130.1	131.3	131.2	131.1	129.0	129.1	131.2	134.5	129.9
2018													
March	132.4	134.9	131.8	131.7	132.0	131.9	132.3	132.4	129.9	129.9	132.4	135.4	131.4
June	133.4	135.8	132.8	132.5	133.2	133.2	133.2	133.4	130.7	130.6	133.4	137.4	132.2
September	134.3	136.8	133.7	133.3	134.4	133.8	134.1	134.6	131.2	131.0	134.5	137.8	133.2
December	135.2	137.8	134.6	134.0	135.0	134.6	134.8	135.8	132.0	131.7	135.4	138.8	133.7
2019													
March	136.1	138.8	135.4	134.7	136.4	135.4	136.3	137.0	133.1	132.9	136.2	140.0	134.9
June	137.0	139.8	136.3	135.6	137.1	136.0	137.2	138.5	133.9	133.7	137.0	140.8	135.8
September	138.0	140.9	137.3	136.3	138.4	137.2	138.1	139.3	135.1	134.6	138.0	141.4	136.8
December	138.9	141.8	138.1	137.0	138.8	138.0	139.3	140.8	135.9	135.4	138.8	142.3	137.3
2020													
March	140.0	142.8	139.3	137.9	140.6	139.4	140.5	141.9	136.7	136.2	140.0	143.1	138.8
June	140.7	143.7	139.9	138.3	141.5	139.7	141.7	143.2	137.5	137.1	140.7	144.7	139.4
September	141.4	144.3	140.7	139.0	141.9	140.5	142.6	144.3	138.2	137.7	141.5	145.6	140.1
December	142.4	145.0	141.7	139.7	143.2	141.4	143.9	145.7	139.0	138.6	142.5	146.3	140.9
2021													
March	143.7	145.7	143.2	140.6	146.1	142.8	145.0	147.6	140.0	139.4	144.2	147.5	142.7
June	144.8	146.6	144.3	141.6	146.6	144.0	146.8	150.1	141.3	140.7	145.2	148.4	143.8
September	146.6	147.6	146.3	143.4	148.5	145.4	148.9	153.0	142.8	142.5	147.4	150.1	145.8
December	148.0	148.7	147.9	144.6	149.9	146.7	150.9	156.0	144.1	143.6	149.0	151.2	147.2

[1] Excludes farm workers, private household workers, and federal government employees.
[2] Not seasonally adjusted.

Table 9-1. Employment Cost Indexes, NAICS Basis—*Continued*

(December 2005 [not seasonally adjusted] = 100; annual values are for December, not seasonally adjusted; quarterly values, seasonally adjusted, except as noted.)

Year and month	All civilian workers [1]	State and local government workers	All private industry workers	Private industry workers								Union [2]	Non-union [2]
				By occupational group					By industry				
				Management, professional, and related	Sales and office	Natural resources, construction, and maintenance	Production, transportation, and material moving	Service occupations	Goods-producing industries		Service-providing		
									Total	Manufacturing			
WAGES AND SALARIES													
2009	111.2	112.5	110.8	111.5	109.4	112.0	109.6	112.3	110.0	108.9	111.1	110.9	110.9
2010	113.0	113.8	112.8	113.7	111.5	113.3	111.3	113.5	111.6	110.7	113.1	112.9	112.7
2011	114.6	114.9	114.6	115.5	113.6	115.4	112.8	115.1	113.5	112.7	114.9	114.9	114.6
2012	116.5	116.2	116.6	117.7	115.8	116.7	115.1	116.8	115.4	114.8	117.0	117.4	116.5
2013	118.7	117.5	119.0	120.2	118.4	118.8	117.2	118.3	117.6	117.2	119.4	119.8	118.9
2014	121.2	119.4	121.6	122.8	121.3	121.4	119.9	120.7	120.1	119.8	122.1	123.1	121.5
2015	123.7	121.6	124.2	125.6	123.5	123.5	122.8	122.8	123.2	123.0	124.5	125.5	124.0
2016	126.6	124.1	127.1	127.1	126.2	126.7	126.6	125.1	126.2	126.2	127.4	127.3	127.1
2017	129.8	126.7	130.6	131.1	129.8	130.4	130.7	131.3	129.3	129.3	131.0	130.9	130.6
2018	133.8	129.7	134.7	134.6	135.0	133.4	135.1	136.4	133.0	132.9	135.2	134.6	134.7
2019	137.7	133.0	138.7	137.7	139.2	137.4	140.5	142.2	137.5	137.1	139.1	139.2	138.7
2020	141.3	135.4	142.6	140.4	144.1	141.2	145.5	147.6	141.0	140.7	143.1	143.0	142.6
2021	147.7	139.0	149.7	145.8	151.9	147.2	153.9	159.5	146.6	146.4	150.5	148.6	149.8
2010													
March	111.7	112.8	111.4	112.3	109.8	112.6	109.9	112.5	110.5	109.3	111.7	111.5	111.4
June	112.1	113.2	111.9	112.8	110.5	112.8	110.3	112.8	110.9	109.9	112.2	112.1	111.9
September	112.5	113.3	112.3	113.4	110.8	113.0	111.0	113.2	111.4	110.5	112.6	112.7	112.4
December	113.0	113.8	112.9	113.9	111.5	113.3	111.3	113.5	111.7	110.9	113.2	112.9	112.7
2011													
March	113.4	114.1	113.2	114.4	111.8	113.8	111.6	114.2	112.2	111.5	113.6	113.6	113.2
June	113.9	114.4	113.7	114.8	112.5	114.5	112.0	114.3	112.7	111.9	114.1	114.0	113.8
September	114.3	114.5	114.2	115.2	113.1	115.0	112.4	114.6	113.1	112.5	114.6	114.6	114.3
December	114.7	114.8	114.7	115.7	113.7	115.4	112.9	115.1	113.6	113.0	115.0	114.9	114.6
2012													
March	115.3	115.2	115.3	116.3	114.5	115.7	113.7	115.4	114.0	113.5	115.7	115.6	115.2
June	115.8	115.6	115.8	116.9	115.0	116.0	114.0	115.9	114.4	113.9	116.2	116.2	115.9
September	116.2	115.8	116.3	117.2	115.7	116.4	114.6	116.2	115.0	114.5	116.7	116.9	116.3
December	116.6	116.1	116.7	117.8	115.9	116.8	115.2	116.8	115.5	115.0	117.1	117.4	116.5
2013													
March	117.2	116.4	117.4	118.5	116.7	117.3	115.8	117.2	116.1	115.6	117.7	118.4	117.2
June	117.7	116.7	118.0	119.3	117.1	117.6	116.2	117.7	116.7	116.3	118.3	119.0	117.9
September	118.2	116.9	118.4	119.7	117.7	118.4	116.6	117.6	117.3	116.8	118.8	119.6	118.4
December	118.8	117.4	119.1	120.3	118.6	118.9	117.3	118.3	117.7	117.4	119.5	119.8	118.9
2014													
March	119.1	117.8	119.4	120.6	118.6	119.5	118.0	118.4	118.2	118.0	119.7	120.5	119.2
June	119.8	118.2	120.2	121.7	119.5	120.0	118.7	119.0	118.9	118.7	120.6	121.2	120.2
September	120.7	118.8	121.1	122.5	120.3	120.7	119.5	120.1	119.5	119.3	121.5	122.1	121.0
December	121.3	119.4	121.8	122.8	121.5	121.5	120.0	120.8	120.2	120.0	122.2	123.1	121.5
2015													
March	122.1	120.0	122.6	123.5	123.2	121.8	120.7	121.5	120.9	120.8	123.1	123.7	122.4
June	122.4	120.6	122.8	124.1	122.1	122.6	121.5	121.6	121.7	121.6	123.2	124.5	122.7
September	123.1	121.0	123.6	125.0	123.0	123.0	122.1	122.2	122.4	122.3	124.0	124.8	123.6
December	123.8	121.5	124.3	125.7	123.8	123.6	123.0	122.9	123.3	123.2	124.6	125.5	124.0
2016													
March	124.5	122.1	125.1	126.5	124.4	124.5	123.8	123.8	124.0	123.9	125.4	126.4	125.0
June	125.4	122.7	126.0	126.8	126.2	125.4	124.9	125.2	124.8	124.8	126.4	126.8	126.0
September	126.0	123.4	126.6	127.6	126.2	125.8	125.8	126.4	125.4	125.7	127.0	127.2	126.6
December	126.7	124.0	127.3	128.2	126.4	126.8	126.8	127.3	126.3	126.4	127.6	127.3	127.1
2017													
March	127.5	124.8	128.2	129.0	127.6	127.7	127.9	128.4	127.1	127.0	128.5	128.6	128.2
June	128.3	125.3	129.0	130.0	128.2	128.6	128.8	129.3	127.8	127.8	129.4	129.2	129.1
September	129.2	125.9	129.9	130.4	129.5	129.6	130.1	130.2	128.7	128.7	130.3	129.9	130.0
December	130.0	126.5	130.8	131.2	130.0	130.5	130.9	131.5	129.5	129.5	131.2	130.9	130.6
2018													
March	131.0	127.1	131.9	132.3	131.7	131.1	132.2	132.8	130.4	130.3	132.4	131.6	132.1
June	131.9	127.8	132.8	133.0	132.8	131.9	133.2	134.0	131.3	131.2	133.2	132.7	132.9
September	133.0	128.7	134.0	133.9	134.3	132.5	134.4	135.3	132.2	132.0	134.5	133.5	134.1
December	133.9	129.5	134.9	134.7	135.1	133.4	135.3	136.6	133.1	133.0	135.4	134.6	134.7
2019													
March	134.8	130.3	135.8	135.4	136.4	134.2	137.0	138.1	134.2	134.2	136.3	135.7	136.0
June	135.7	131.0	136.8	136.3	137.1	135.3	137.9	139.7	135.2	135.1	137.2	137.0	136.9
September	136.9	132.2	138.0	137.1	138.8	136.6	139.1	140.6	136.5	136.1	138.4	138.1	138.0
December	137.8	132.9	138.9	137.9	139.4	137.5	140.6	142.4	137.6	137.3	139.3	139.2	138.7
2020													
March	139.1	133.7	140.3	139.0	141.4	139.2	142.0	143.7	138.6	138.3	140.8	140.2	140.4
June	139.6	134.5	140.8	139.3	142.1	139.3	143.1	144.9	139.4	139.1	141.3	141.2	140.9
September	140.3	134.6	141.6	139.9	142.6	140.3	144.2	146.2	140.1	139.9	142.1	142.2	141.6
December	141.4	135.3	142.8	140.6	144.2	141.2	145.6	147.8	141.0	140.8	143.3	143.0	142.6
2021													
March	142.9	135.9	144.5	141.6	147.5	142.9	147.0	149.9	142.1	141.8	145.1	144.5	144.6
June	144.1	136.7	145.8	142.8	148.2	144.2	149.4	153.0	143.8	143.5	146.4	145.9	145.9
September	146.2	137.9	148.1	144.8	150.4	145.7	151.6	156.2	145.1	145.1	148.9	147.2	148.3
December	147.7	138.8	149.8	145.9	152.0	147.2	154.0	159.7	146.7	146.5	150.6	148.6	149.8

[1] Excludes farm workers, private household workers, and federal government employees.
[2] Not seasonally adjusted.

Table 9-1. Employment Cost Indexes, NAICS Basis—*Continued*

(December 2005 [not seasonally adjusted] = 100; annual values are for December, not seasonally adjusted; quarterly values, seasonally adjusted, except as noted.)

Year and month	All civilian workers [1]	State and local government workers	All private industry workers	Management, professional, and related	Sales and office	Natural resources, construction, and maintenance	Production, transportation, and material moving	Service occupations	Goods-producing industries Total	Goods-producing industries Manufacturing	Service-providing	Union [2]	Non-union [2]
TOTAL BENEFITS													
2009	110.7	117.7	108.7	108.8	108.7	109.8	107.4	110.5	105.8	103.6	109.9	111.4	108.2
2010	113.9	121.1	111.9	111.2	111.8	113.5	112.0	113.5	110.1	108.8	112.6	117.9	110.6
2011	117.5	123.6	115.9	115.2	115.5	117.1	117.0	116.4	114.4	113.9	116.4	122.8	114.4
2012	120.3	127.8	118.2	117.9	117.6	120.6	118.0	119.2	116.0	115.0	119.1	125.6	116.7
2013	123.0	132.0	120.5	120.2	120.5	123.2	119.5	121.0	118.0	116.6	121.5	127.3	119.1
2014	126.2	135.8	123.5	123.4	123.4	127.4	122.1	122.2	120.7	119.8	124.6	132.6	121.7
2015	128.4	140.6	125.1	124.5	125.0	128.1	125.4	124.3	123.1	122.5	125.9	133.9	123.3
2016	131.1	145.0	127.3	126.0	128.4	130.1	127.9	127.1	124.9	124.3	128.3	136.1	125.5
2017	134.4	149.7	130.2	129.1	130.8	133.1	131.4	129.7	128.0	128.0	131.2	140.6	128.2
2018	138.1	154.4	133.6	132.1	135.3	137.1	133.8	132.8	129.6	129.1	135.1	145.7	131.2
2019	141.2	159.5	136.2	134.8	137.7	139.2	136.6	135.5	132.5	131.9	137.6	147.4	133.9
2020	144.5	164.4	139.1	137.2	140.9	141.8	140.5	138.8	134.9	134.3	140.6	151.5	136.6
2021	148.6	168.5	143.2	141.3	144.7	145.8	144.6	144.0	138.7	138.2	144.8	155.5	140.8
2010													
March	112.0	118.1	110.3	110.0	110.1	111.6	109.9	111.5	108.4	106.6	111.1	114.8	109.5
June	112.7	119.1	110.9	110.3	110.9	112.1	110.7	112.3	108.9	107.4	111.7	116.2	110.0
September	113.5	120.2	111.6	110.9	111.6	112.8	111.7	113.3	110.0	108.7	112.3	117.6	110.4
December	114.1	121.2	112.1	111.7	112.1	113.5	112.2	113.8	110.2	108.9	112.9	117.9	110.6
2011													
March	115.4	122.0	113.6	113.2	113.3	114.2	113.5	115.2	111.7	111.0	114.4	119.0	112.6
June	116.8	122.5	115.2	114.6	114.9	115.6	116.4	115.9	114.1	113.9	115.7	122.3	113.9
September	117.1	123.2	115.4	114.7	115.3	116.1	116.3	116.0	113.8	113.4	116.0	122.0	114.0
December	117.7	123.7	116.1	115.6	115.8	117.1	117.1	116.7	114.5	114.0	116.7	122.8	114.4
2012													
March	118.5	124.7	116.8	116.6	116.6	117.9	116.1	117.8	114.2	113.2	117.8	122.9	115.6
June	119.3	125.8	117.5	117.1	117.4	118.8	117.0	118.2	114.8	113.9	118.5	124.3	116.2
September	119.9	127.1	117.9	117.7	117.4	119.9	117.6	118.8	115.7	114.7	118.8	125.5	116.4
December	120.5	127.9	118.5	118.3	117.9	120.6	118.1	119.4	116.1	115.1	119.4	125.6	116.7
2013													
March	121.3	129.1	119.1	118.5	118.9	121.6	118.7	119.7	117.0	115.7	120.0	126.6	117.7
June	121.9	129.9	119.6	119.3	119.3	122.0	119.0	120.3	117.3	116.1	120.6	127.3	118.3
September	122.6	130.9	120.3	120.2	120.1	122.6	119.1	120.8	117.6	116.4	121.4	127.1	118.9
December	123.2	132.1	120.8	120.7	120.9	123.2	119.7	121.2	118.1	116.7	121.9	127.3	119.1
2014													
March	123.8	133.0	121.3	120.9	121.2	124.0	120.5	120.9	119.2	118.1	122.2	128.5	119.9
June	125.1	134.2	122.5	122.4	122.5	126.0	120.9	121.1	119.4	118.2	123.8	131.3	120.9
September	125.7	134.8	123.2	123.1	123.0	126.7	121.6	121.7	120.3	119.3	124.3	131.9	121.4
December	126.4	135.8	123.8	123.8	123.8	127.4	122.1	122.3	120.8	119.9	125.0	132.6	121.7
2015													
March	127.1	136.7	124.5	124.6	123.7	127.7	123.5	122.9	121.4	120.8	125.7	133.4	122.7
June	127.2	137.8	124.2	123.9	123.9	126.9	124.2	123.3	122.1	121.5	125.1	132.3	122.7
September	127.8	138.9	124.8	124.3	124.6	127.5	124.9	123.9	122.3	121.6	125.8	133.2	123.0
December	128.7	140.5	125.3	124.9	125.5	128.1	125.6	124.5	123.2	122.6	126.3	133.9	123.3
2016													
March	129.3	141.5	125.9	124.9	126.7	128.6	126.3	125.2	123.6	123.1	126.9	135.0	124.2
June	129.9	142.4	126.3	125.2	127.4	128.9	126.7	126.0	124.2	123.6	127.3	135.3	124.7
September	130.7	144.0	127.0	125.8	128.2	129.4	127.4	126.6	124.5	124.0	128.0	135.6	125.3
December	131.3	144.9	127.5	126.3	128.8	130.1	128.0	127.3	124.9	124.4	128.6	136.1	125.5
2017													
March	132.2	146.0	128.3	127.2	129.3	130.6	128.8	128.1	125.4	124.9	129.5	137.4	126.6
June	133.0	147.0	129.1	128.1	129.9	131.5	129.5	128.6	125.9	125.5	130.3	138.4	127.4
September	134.0	148.3	130.0	128.9	130.7	132.3	131.0	129.3	127.6	127.7	131.0	139.9	128.0
December	134.7	149.6	130.5	129.5	131.1	133.1	131.6	129.9	128.1	128.2	131.5	140.6	128.2
2018													
March	135.7	150.3	131.5	130.5	132.4	133.5	132.6	131.1	128.9	129.0	132.6	141.7	129.6
June	136.9	151.6	132.7	131.5	133.9	136.1	133.3	131.5	129.6	129.6	133.9	145.1	130.5
September	137.5	152.9	133.2	131.7	134.7	136.4	133.5	132.4	129.2	128.9	134.7	144.9	130.9
December	138.4	154.3	133.9	132.4	135.6	137.1	133.9	132.9	129.7	129.3	135.4	145.7	131.2
2019													
March	139.3	155.8	134.6	133.1	136.3	137.9	134.9	133.4	130.7	130.4	136.1	146.9	132.3
September	140.0	157.1	135.1	133.8	136.9	137.6	135.7	134.5	131.5	131.0	136.5	147.0	133.0
December	140.8	158.2	135.8	134.5	137.5	138.6	136.1	134.9	132.3	131.7	137.2	146.9	133.6
December	141.5	159.4	136.4	135.1	138.0	139.2	136.7	135.6	132.7	132.0	137.8	147.4	133.9
2020													
March	142.2	160.8	136.8	135.2	138.5	139.8	137.5	136.2	132.9	132.2	138.3	148.0	134.7
June	143.2	162.0	137.8	136.1	139.5	140.6	138.9	137.4	133.8	133.3	139.3	150.3	135.6
September	144.0	163.3	138.5	136.9	140.1	141.1	139.5	138.1	134.2	133.5	140.1	151.1	136.0
December	144.8	164.3	139.3	137.5	141.1	141.8	140.5	138.9	135.0	134.4	140.9	151.5	136.6
2021													
March	145.7	165.0	140.2	138.5	142.1	142.7	141.0	140.0	135.7	134.9	141.9	152.3	137.9
June	146.4	166.2	140.7	139.0	142.2	143.7	141.6	140.8	136.4	135.4	142.3	152.6	138.5
September	147.6	166.8	142.1	140.3	143.5	144.7	143.7	142.7	138.1	137.7	143.6	154.8	139.7
December	148.9	168.3	143.4	141.6	145.0	145.8	144.6	144.0	138.8	138.2	145.1	155.5	140.8

[1]Excludes farm workers, private household workers, and federal government employees.
[2]Not seasonally adjusted.

Table 9-2. Employment Cost Indexes, SIC Basis

(Not seasonally adjusted, December 2005 = 100; annual values are for December.)

Year	All civilian workers [1,2]	State and local government workers [2]	All private industry workers [2]	Private industry workers excluding sales occupations	Production and nonsupervisory occupations	White-collar occupations	Blue-collar occupations	Service occupations [2]	Total [2]	Construction [2]	Manufacturing [2]	Total [2]	Transportation and utilities	Wholesale trade	Retail trade	Finance, insurance, and real estate [2]	Services
TOTAL COMPENSATION																	
1979	. . .	. . .	32.8	32.5	. . .	31.2	35.0	33.9	33.7	. . .	33.1	32.0	. . .	. . .	. . .	. . .	. . .
1980	. . .	. . .	35.9	35.9	. . .	34.2	38.5	37.1	37.0	. . .	36.4	35.1	. . .	. . .	. . .	. . .	. . .
1981	39.0	36.8	39.5	39.4	40.1	37.6	42.2	40.5	40.7	. . .	40.0	38.6	. . .	. . .	. . .	. . .	. . .
1982	41.5	39.4	42.0	42.0	42.8	40.1	44.7	43.9	43.2	. . .	42.4	41.1	. . .	. . .	. . .	. . .	. . .
1983	43.9	41.8	44.4	44.4	45.2	42.7	47.0	46.3	45.3	. . .	44.6	43.8	. . .	. . .	. . .	. . .	. . .
1984	46.2	44.6	46.6	46.7	47.3	44.8	49.0	49.4	47.4	. . .	46.9	46.0	. . .	. . .	. . .	. . .	. . .
1985	48.2	47.1	48.4	48.3	49.1	47.0	50.5	50.9	49.0	50.8	48.4	48.1	50.6	. . .	52.4	44.7	46.1
1986	49.9	49.6	49.9	49.9	50.5	48.6	51.9	52.4	50.5	52.3	50.0	49.6	51.8	48.5	53.5	46.1	48.1
1987	51.7	51.8	51.6	51.7	52.2	50.4	53.5	53.7	52.1	54.2	51.5	51.4	53.3	50.4	54.8	47.0	50.5
1988	54.2	54.7	54.1	54.1	54.8	52.9	55.9	56.5	54.4	56.5	53.8	54.0	54.9	52.5	58.0	50.0	53.5
1989	56.9	58.1	56.7	56.5	57.6	55.7	58.2	59.0	56.7	59.0	56.3	56.8	56.9	57.1	59.9	52.7	56.4
1990	59.7	61.5	59.3	59.3	60.1	58.4	60.7	61.8	59.4	60.9	59.1	59.4	59.1	58.2	62.5	54.9	59.9
1991	62.3	63.7	61.9	62.0	62.7	61.0	63.4	64.7	62.1	63.3	61.9	61.9	61.7	60.7	65.2	57.2	62.5
1992	64.4	66.0	64.1	64.2	64.9	63.1	65.6	66.7	64.5	65.4	64.3	63.9	63.9	62.5	66.9	57.9	65.2
1993	66.7	67.9	66.4	66.6	67.3	65.4	68.1	68.8	67.0	67.1	66.9	66.2	66.1	64.4	68.9	60.5	67.5
1994	68.7	69.9	68.5	68.6	69.2	67.5	70.0	70.8	69.0	69.6	69.0	68.1	68.7	66.4	70.8	61.8	69.4
1995	70.6	72.0	70.2	70.4	71.0	69.4	71.7	72.1	70.7	71.1	70.8	70.0	71.2	69.4	72.3	64.0	70.9
1996	72.6	73.9	72.4	72.4	73.1	71.7	73.6	74.2	72.7	72.9	72.9	72.3	73.4	71.5	75.1	65.5	73.1
1997	75.0	75.6	74.9	74.9	75.4	74.4	75.5	77.2	74.5	74.8	74.6	75.1	75.5	73.8	77.7	69.9	75.9
1998	77.6	77.8	77.5	77.2	78.1	77.3	77.6	79.4	76.5	77.4	76.6	78.0	78.4	78.0	80.0	74.1	78.2
1999	80.2	80.5	80.2	80.0	80.4	79.9	80.2	82.1	79.1	79.9	79.2	80.6	80.1	81.1	83.0	77.1	80.9
2000	83.6	82.9	83.6	83.6	84.0	83.6	83.6	85.3	82.6	84.6	82.3	84.2	83.5	84.4	86.4	81.0	84.5
2001	87.0	86.4	87.1	87.0	87.4	87.1	86.7	89.1	85.7	88.2	85.3	87.8	87.5	87.2	90.3	83.9	88.3
2002	90.0	89.9	90.0	89.9	90.2	89.9	89.8	92.0	88.9	91.0	88.5	90.5	91.0	91.1	91.9	87.6	90.7
2003	93.5	92.9	93.6	93.6	93.6	93.6	93.4	94.9	92.4	94.1	92.2	94.2	94.0	94.0	94.9	94.1	94.0
2004	96.9	96.1	97.1	97.2	97.2	96.9	97.5	97.7	96.8	96.4	96.7	97.3	97.6	96.5	97.1	96.7	97.5
2005	100.0	100.0	100.0	100.0	100.0	100.0	100.0	100.0	100.0	100.0	100.0	100.0	100.0	100.0	100.0	100.0	100.0
WAGES AND SALARIES																	
1979	. . .	. . .	36.1	36.1	36.8	34.1	39.4	37.9	38.2	41.4	37.5	34.9	39.1	33.7	39.7	32.8	31.7
1980	. . .	. . .	39.4	39.3	40.3	37.1	43.1	41.0	41.8	45.0	41.0	38.0	43.5	37.1	42.5	35.2	34.5
1981	42.3	40.1	42.8	42.9	43.9	40.4	46.8	44.4	45.4	49.0	44.5	41.4	47.1	40.0	45.6	38.8	38.1
1982	45.0	42.7	45.5	45.6	46.7	43.1	49.4	48.2	48.0	51.5	47.0	44.2	50.5	42.5	47.5	41.3	41.2
1983	47.3	45.0	47.8	47.9	48.9	45.7	51.3	50.4	49.9	53.0	49.0	46.7	53.0	45.1	49.5	44.3	43.9
1984	49.4	47.7	49.8	50.1	50.8	47.6	53.1	53.5	51.8	53.7	51.2	48.7	54.8	47.6	52.0	43.9	46.7
1985	51.5	50.3	51.8	51.9	52.9	50.0	55.0	54.8	53.6	55.3	53.0	51.0	56.9	49.7	54.5	47.9	48.4
1986	53.3	53.0	53.5	53.6	54.3	51.7	56.4	56.2	55.3	56.7	54.8	52.5	57.9	51.5	55.7	49.2	50.3
1987	55.2	55.2	55.2	55.5	56.0	53.6	58.1	57.6	57.1	58.6	56.6	54.3	59.1	53.6	57.2	49.8	53.0
1988	57.5	57.9	57.5	57.5	58.4	56.1	59.9	60.1	58.9	60.7	58.3	56.9	60.6	55.6	60.1	52.9	55.6
1989	60.1	61.0	59.9	59.8	61.0	58.7	62.0	62.3	61.2	62.8	60.6	59.5	62.2	60.7	62.0	55.7	58.3
1990	62.6	64.2	62.3	62.4	63.2	61.2	64.2	64.8	63.4	64.1	63.1	61.8	64.3	61.2	64.2	57.6	61.6
1991	64.9	66.4	64.6	64.7	65.4	63.5	66.4	67.4	65.8	66.0	65.6	64.1	66.6	63.6	66.6	59.6	63.8
1992	66.6	68.4	66.3	66.5	67.2	65.2	68.1	68.8	67.6	67.3	67.6	65.7	68.7	65.5	68.2	59.5	66.0
1993	68.7	70.2	68.3	68.5	69.2	67.4	70.0	70.3	69.6	68.6	69.7	67.8	70.9	67.1	70.2	62.1	68.0
1994	70.6	72.4	70.2	70.5	71.1	69.3	72.0	72.4	71.7	70.8	71.8	69.6	73.5	69.1	71.9	62.8	70.0
1995	72.7	74.7	72.2	72.5	73.0	71.3	74.1	74.0	73.7	72.5	73.9	71.7	76.0	72.4	73.6	65.1	71.7
1996	75.1	76.8	74.7	74.9	75.5	73.8	76.3	76.6	76.0	74.6	76.3	74.2	78.1	74.7	76.8	67.2	74.2
1997	77.9	78.9	77.6	77.7	78.3	77.0	78.8	79.9	78.3	77.1	78.6	77.4	80.7	77.0	79.7	71.8	77.5
1998	80.8	81.3	80.6	80.4	81.4	80.3	81.3	82.4	81.1	79.9	81.3	80.5	83.0	81.5	82.2	76.9	80.1
1999	83.6	84.2	83.5	83.4	83.8	83.1	84.0	85.1	83.8	82.5	84.1	83.4	84.8	84.5	85.2	79.8	83.0
2000	86.7	87.0	86.7	86.7	87.1	86.4	87.1	88.3	87.1	86.9	87.1	86.6	87.5	87.4	88.6	83.4	86.3
2001	90.0	90.2	90.0	90.0	90.4	89.6	90.5	91.8	90.2	90.4	90.2	89.9	91.7	89.3	91.9	85.8	90.0
2002	92.6	93.1	92.4	92.5	92.6	92.0	93.0	94.1	92.9	92.8	93.0	92.3	94.7	92.8	93.2	89.4	92.0
2003	95.2	95.0	95.2	95.4	95.1	95.2	95.2	96.2	95.1	95.1	95.2	95.3	96.2	95.3	95.5	95.9	94.8
2004	97.5	97.0	97.5	97.8	97.5	97.5	97.6	97.9	97.4	97.0	97.5	97.7	98.6	96.6	97.2	97.7	97.8
2005	100.0	100.0	100.0	100.0	100.0	100.0	100.0	100.0	100.0	100.0	100.0	100.0	100.0	100.0	100.0	100.0	100.0

[1]Excludes farm workers, private household workers, and federal government employees.
[2]Roughly continuous and comparable with new NAICS-based series. See notes and definitions for more information.
. . . = Not available.

Table 9-2. Employment Cost Indexes, SIC Basis—*Continued*

(Not seasonally adjusted, December 2005 = 100; annual values are for December.)

Year	All civilian workers [1,2]	State and local government workers [2]	All private industry workers [2]	Private industry workers excluding sales occupations	Production and nonsupervisory occupations	White-collar occupations	Blue-collar occupations	Service occupations [2]	Goods-producing industries			Service-providing industries					
									Total [2]	Construction [2]	Manufacturing [2]	Total [2]	Transportation and utilities	Wholesale trade	Retail trade	Finance, insurance, and real estate [2]	Services
TOTAL BENEFITS																	
1979	. . .	. . .	25.7	. . .	. . .	24.7	27.4	. . .	26.0	. . .	25.8	25.4	. . .	. . .	. . .	. . .	. . .
1980	. . .	. . .	28.7	. . .	. . .	27.7	30.4	. . .	28.8	. . .	28.5	28.6	. . .	. . .	. . .	. . .	. . .
1981	31.8	. . .	32.2	. . .	. . .	31.1	34.0	. . .	32.4	. . .	32.1	31.9	. . .	. . .	. . .	. . .	. . .
1982	34.2	. . .	34.5	. . .	. . .	33.3	36.5	. . .	34.8	. . .	34.4	34.1	. . .	. . .	. . .	. . .	. . .
1983	36.8	. . .	37.1	. . .	. . .	35.8	39.1	. . .	37.2	. . .	36.9	36.8	. . .	. . .	. . .	. . .	. . .
1984	39.3	. . .	39.5	. . .	. . .	38.3	41.4	. . .	39.6	. . .	39.3	39.4	. . .	. . .	. . .	. . .	. . .
1985	40.8	. . .	40.9	. . .	. . .	40.0	42.5	41.2	40.8	. . .	40.4	40.9	. . .	. . .	. . .	. . .	. . .
1986	42.4	. . .	42.3	. . .	. . .	41.4	43.8	42.9	42.0	. . .	41.6	42.5	. . .	. . .	. . .	. . .	. . .
1987	44.0	. . .	43.7	. . .	. . .	42.9	45.3	43.9	43.2	. . .	42.7	44.2	. . .	. . .	. . .	. . .	. . .
1988	47.0	. . .	46.7	. . .	. . .	45.6	48.6	47.4	46.3	. . .	46.0	47.1	. . .	. . .	. . .	. . .	. . .
1989	50.1	52.2	49.6	. . .	. . .	48.6	51.2	50.5	48.8	. . .	48.7	50.2	. . .	. . .	. . .	. . .	. . .
1990	53.5	55.8	52.9	. . .	. . .	52.0	54.4	53.8	52.3	. . .	52.1	53.4	. . .	. . .	. . .	. . .	. . .
1991	56.5	58.0	56.2	. . .	. . .	55.2	57.8	57.7	55.5	. . .	55.2	56.7	. . .	. . .	. . .	. . .	. . .
1992	59.5	61.1	59.1	. . .	. . .	57.8	61.0	61.0	58.7	. . .	58.3	59.4	. . .	. . .	. . .	. . .	. . .
1993	62.2	62.9	62.0	. . .	. . .	60.5	64.4	64.4	62.0	. . .	61.8	62.0	. . .	. . .	. . .	. . .	. . .
1994	64.4	64.6	64.3	. . .	. . .	63.2	66.2	66.0	64.1	. . .	63.9	64.4	. . .	. . .	. . .	. . .	. . .
1995	65.8	66.3	65.7	. . .	. . .	64.8	67.2	66.6	65.2	. . .	65.0	66.0	. . .	. . .	. . .	. . .	. . .
1996	67.1	67.8	67.0	. . .	. . .	66.2	68.4	67.3	66.4	. . .	66.5	67.3	. . .	. . .	. . .	. . .	. . .
1997	68.5	68.6	68.5	. . .	. . .	68.0	69.4	69.6	67.3	. . .	67.4	69.2	. . .	. . .	. . .	. . .	. . .
1998	70.3	70.7	70.2	. . .	. . .	69.9	70.7	70.9	68.1	. . .	67.9	71.4	. . .	. . .	. . .	. . .	. . .
1999	72.6	72.7	72.6	. . .	. . .	72.3	73.0	73.4	70.5	. . .	70.3	73.8	. . .	. . .	. . .	. . .	. . .
2000	76.2	74.4	76.7	. . .	. . .	76.5	76.9	76.6	74.3	. . .	73.6	78.1	. . .	. . .	. . .	. . .	. . .
2001	80.2	78.5	80.6	. . .	. . .	81.1	79.5	81.3	77.3	. . .	76.3	82.5	. . .	. . .	. . .	. . .	. . .
2002	84.2	83.3	84.4	. . .	. . .	84.6	83.8	85.7	81.3	. . .	80.4	86.1	. . .	. . .	. . .	. . .	. . .
2003	89.5	88.4	89.8	. . .	. . .	89.7	89.8	91.3	87.4	. . .	86.7	91.2	. . .	. . .	. . .	. . .	. . .
2004	95.7	94.3	96.0	. . .	. . .	95.3	97.3	97.1	95.7	. . .	95.3	96.2	. . .	. . .	. . .	. . .	. . .
2005	100.0	100.0	100.0	. . .	. . .	100.0	100.0	100.0	100.0	. . .	100.0	100.0	. . .	. . .	. . .	. . .	. . .

[1] Excludes farm workers, private household workers, and federal government employees.
[2] Roughly continuous and comparable with new NAICS-based series. See notes and definitions for more information.
. . . = Not available.

SECTION 9B: PRODUCTIVITY AND RELATED DATA

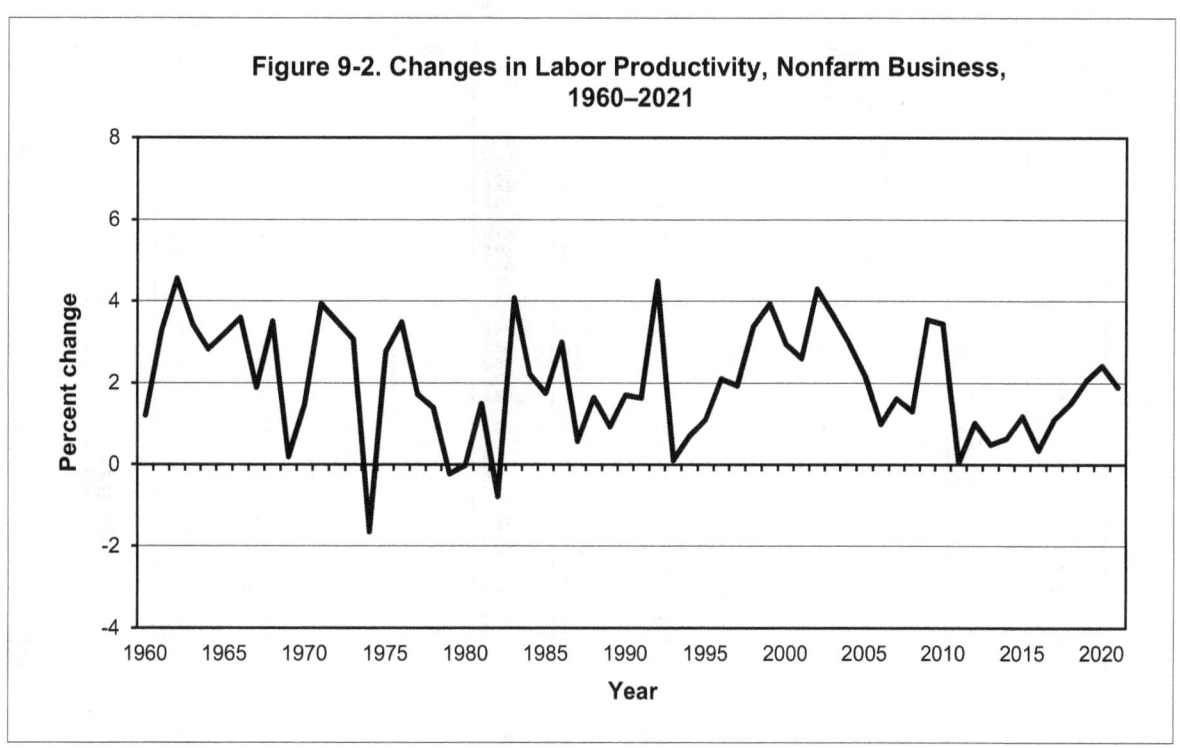

Figure 9-2. Changes in Labor Productivity, Nonfarm Business, 1960–2021

- As Figure 9-2 demonstrates, the rate of change in U.S. nonfarm labor productivity has often been quite variable from year to year. Up through the 1980s, productivity tended to decline (growth rates were less than zero) in recession years but rebound sharply in recovery. Firms often expected these declines in demand to be temporary so they therefore held on to their experienced workers in order to be prepared for the recovery. (Table 9-3A and B)

- As the U.S. economy has become more service-oriented and less dependent on manufacturing, labor has become less dominant. The lag between compensation and productivity mainly reflects a decline to unprecedented levels in the labor share of the total value of sector output. (Table 9-3A)

- Corporate profits are one of the most closely watched U.S. economic indicators. Profitability provides a summary measure of corporate financial health and thus serves as an essential indicator of economic performance. The estimates of corporate profits are an integral part of the national income and product accounts (NIPAs), a set of accounts prepared by the Bureau of Economic Analysis (BEA) that provides a logical and consistent framework for presenting statistics on U.S. economic activity. See Chapter 1 for in-depth information on NIPA accounting. (Table 9-4).

Table 9-3A. Productivity and Related Data: Recent Data

(2012 = 100, seasonally adjusted.)

Year and quarter	Business sector														
	Output per hour of all persons	Output	Hours of all persons	Employ-ment	Average weekly hours	Unit labor costs	Compen-sation per hour	Real hourly compen-sation	Labor share	Unit nonlabor payments	Implicit price deflator	Current dollar output	Compen-sation	Nonlabor payments	Output per job
1960	31.0	17.6	56.7	50.2	112.9	23.0	7.1	50.5	115.8	15.9	19.9	3.5	4.0	2.8	35.0
1961	32.1	17.9	55.8	49.7	112.4	23.1	7.4	52.0	115.2	16.1	20.0	3.6	4.1	2.9	36.1
1962	33.6	19.1	56.8	50.3	113.0	23.1	7.7	53.7	114.0	16.6	20.2	3.9	4.4	3.2	37.9
1963	34.9	20.0	57.2	50.6	113.2	23.0	8.0	54.9	112.9	17.0	20.4	4.1	4.6	3.4	39.4
1964	36.0	21.2	58.9	51.5	114.4	23.1	8.3	56.2	112.1	17.4	20.6	4.4	4.9	3.7	41.2
1965	37.3	22.7	60.9	53.0	114.9	23.1	8.6	57.4	110.5	18.1	20.9	4.8	5.3	4.1	42.9
1966	38.8	24.3	62.5	54.6	114.5	23.7	9.2	59.5	110.6	18.5	21.4	5.2	5.8	4.5	44.5
1967	39.7	24.8	62.3	55.3	112.7	24.5	9.7	61.0	111.2	18.8	22.0	5.4	6.1	4.7	44.8
1968	41.1	26.0	63.3	56.4	112.1	25.5	10.5	63.1	111.5	19.5	22.9	6.0	6.6	5.1	46.1
1969	41.3	26.8	64.9	58.2	111.5	27.1	11.2	64.1	113.5	19.8	23.9	6.4	7.3	5.3	46.1
1970	42.2	26.8	63.6	58.0	109.6	28.6	12.1	65.2	114.7	20.2	24.9	6.7	7.7	5.4	46.2
1971	43.9	27.8	63.4	58.1	109.1	29.1	12.8	66.2	112.2	21.9	26.0	7.2	8.1	6.1	47.9
1972	45.4	29.7	65.4	59.8	109.2	30.0	13.6	68.2	111.6	22.9	26.9	8.0	8.9	6.8	49.6
1973	46.7	31.7	67.9	62.4	108.7	31.4	14.7	69.3	111.1	24.2	28.3	9.0	10.0	7.7	50.8
1974	45.9	31.2	68.0	63.4	107.3	34.9	16.0	68.2	112.6	26.0	31.0	9.7	10.9	8.1	49.3
1975	47.6	30.9	65.0	61.5	105.8	37.3	17.8	69.2	109.7	29.8	34.0	10.5	11.6	9.2	50.3
1976	49.1	33.0	67.2	63.4	106.0	39.0	19.2	70.7	109.0	31.7	35.8	11.8	12.9	10.5	52.1
1977	50.0	34.9	69.8	66.1	105.5	41.4	20.7	71.7	109.2	33.5	37.9	13.2	14.5	11.7	52.8
1978	50.6	37.1	73.4	69.8	105.2	44.4	22.5	72.6	109.4	35.7	40.6	15.1	16.5	13.3	53.2
1979	50.7	38.5	75.9	72.5	104.7	48.6	24.6	72.7	110.6	38.0	43.9	16.9	18.7	14.6	53.1
1980	50.7	38.1	75.2	72.6	103.5	53.8	27.3	72.4	112.4	40.2	47.9	18.2	20.5	15.3	52.5
1981	51.8	39.2	75.7	73.4	103.2	57.6	29.8	72.4	110.3	45.4	52.3	20.5	22.6	17.8	53.5
1982	51.5	38.1	74.0	72.2	102.5	62.3	32.1	73.4	112.7	46.2	55.2	21.0	23.7	17.6	52.8
1983	53.3	40.1	75.3	72.8	103.4	62.9	33.5	73.5	109.9	50.0	57.2	23.0	25.2	20.1	55.1
1984	54.8	43.7	79.7	76.5	104.2	63.8	35.0	73.7	108.5	52.5	58.8	25.7	27.9	22.9	57.1
1985	56.0	45.7	81.6	78.4	104.0	65.6	36.8	74.9	108.6	53.8	60.4	27.6	30.0	24.6	58.3
1986	57.6	47.4	82.2	79.7	103.2	67.4	38.8	77.7	110.1	53.3	61.2	29.0	31.9	25.2	59.4
1987	58.0	49.1	84.7	81.8	103.4	69.5	40.3	78.0	111.5	53.2	62.4	30.6	34.1	26.1	60.0
1988	58.8	51.2	87.0	84.3	103.1	72.1	42.4	79.3	112.1	54.4	64.3	32.9	36.9	27.8	60.7
1989	59.5	53.1	89.3	86.2	103.6	73.5	43.7	78.2	110.1	58.1	66.7	35.4	39.0	30.9	61.7
1990	60.7	54.0	88.9	86.7	102.5	76.5	46.5	79.2	111.0	59.2	68.9	37.2	41.3	32.0	62.2
1991	61.7	53.7	87.0	85.4	101.9	78.8	48.6	80.0	111.1	60.8	70.9	38.1	42.3	32.6	62.8
1992	64.6	55.9	86.6	84.9	102.0	80.0	51.6	82.9	110.9	62.0	72.1	40.3	44.7	34.7	65.9
1993	64.6	57.5	89.0	86.7	102.6	81.0	52.4	82.0	109.9	64.4	73.7	42.4	46.6	37.0	66.3
1994	65.0	60.3	92.8	89.7	103.5	81.2	52.7	80.9	108.1	67.2	75.1	45.3	48.9	40.5	67.2
1995	65.5	62.1	94.9	92.2	103.0	82.5	54.0	80.9	108.0	68.5	76.4	47.5	51.3	42.6	67.4
1996	67.1	65.0	97.0	94.2	102.9	83.5	56.0	81.7	107.5	70.1	77.6	50.5	54.3	45.6	69.0
1997	68.5	68.4	99.9	96.8	103.2	85.0	58.2	83.1	107.9	70.8	78.7	53.9	58.1	48.4	70.7
1998	70.9	72.2	101.9	98.8	103.1	87.0	61.7	86.9	110.2	68.7	79.0	57.0	62.8	49.6	73.1
1999	73.8	76.4	103.5	100.4	103.1	87.6	64.6	89.2	110.4	68.9	79.4	60.6	66.9	52.6	76.1
2000	76.1	79.8	104.9	102.1	102.7	90.9	69.1	92.3	112.4	68.0	80.9	64.5	72.5	54.3	78.1
2001	78.1	80.3	102.8	101.4	101.4	92.6	72.3	93.8	112.6	68.9	82.2	66.0	74.3	55.4	79.2
2002	81.4	81.7	100.3	99.2	101.1	90.8	73.9	94.4	109.6	72.6	82.8	67.6	74.1	59.3	82.3
2003	84.5	84.2	99.7	99.0	100.7	90.8	76.7	95.8	108.0	75.5	84.1	70.8	76.5	63.6	85.1
2004	87.2	87.9	100.9	100.3	100.6	92.1	80.3	97.6	106.9	78.6	86.2	75.8	81.0	69.1	87.7
2005	89.1	91.4	102.6	102.1	100.4	93.4	83.2	97.9	105.1	83.1	88.8	81.2	85.3	75.9	89.5
2006	90.0	94.4	104.9	104.1	100.7	96.0	86.4	98.4	105.1	85.4	91.4	86.2	90.6	80.6	90.6
2007	91.4	96.4	105.5	105.0	100.5	98.8	90.3	100.0	105.7	86.7	93.5	90.1	95.2	83.6	91.8
2008	92.5	95.6	103.3	103.5	99.8	100.3	92.8	99.0	105.7	87.9	94.8	90.6	95.8	84.0	92.3
2009	95.9	92.0	96.0	97.7	98.3	97.6	93.6	100.2	102.9	91.4	94.9	87.3	89.8	84.1	94.2
2010	99.1	95.0	95.9	96.5	99.3	96.1	95.3	100.3	100.1	95.9	96.0	91.2	91.3	91.2	98.4
2011	99.1	96.9	97.8	98.1	99.7	98.2	97.3	99.4	100.0	98.2	98.2	95.2	95.2	95.2	98.8
2012	100.0	100.0	100.0	100.0	100.0	100.0	100.0	100.0	100.0	100.0	100.0	100.0	100.0	100.0	100.0
2013	100.9	102.5	101.6	101.7	99.9	100.5	101.4	99.9	99.1	102.7	101.5	104.0	103.0	105.2	100.7
2014	101.4	105.5	104.0	103.9	100.1	102.6	104.0	100.8	99.5	103.8	103.2	108.8	108.2	109.5	101.5
2015	102.5	109.1	106.5	106.4	100.0	104.5	107.0	103.5	100.7	102.7	103.7	113.1	113.9	112.0	102.5
2016	102.9	111.1	108.0	108.4	99.7	105.2	108.2	103.3	100.7	103.5	104.5	116.1	116.9	115.0	102.5
2017	104.0	114.1	109.7	110.1	99.6	107.7	112.0	104.7	101.3	104.5	106.3	121.3	122.8	119.3	103.6
2018	105.7	118.1	111.7	112.1	99.7	109.7	115.9	105.7	101.0	107.1	108.6	128.2	129.5	126.5	105.3
2019	107.7	121.2	112.5	113.4	99.2	111.7	120.3	107.8	101.4	108.3	110.2	133.5	135.3	131.2	106.8
2020	110.4	116.0	105.1	106.1	99.0	116.5	128.6	113.9	105.3	103.1	110.6	128.3	135.2	119.6	109.3
2021	112.5	124.4	110.6	110.4	100.2	120.9	136.0	115.1	104.6	108.7	115.6	143.8	150.5	135.2	112.7
2019															
1st quarter	106.8	119.8	112.2	112.9	99.3	112.1	119.7	108.3	102.5	106.0	109.4	131.1	134.3	127.0	106.1
2nd quarter	107.7	120.8	112.2	113.1	99.2	111.3	120.0	107.7	101.1	108.6	110.2	133.1	134.5	131.3	106.9
3rd quarter	108.0	121.8	112.7	113.7	99.1	111.1	120.0	107.3	100.7	109.4	110.4	134.4	135.3	133.3	107.1
4th quarter	108.4	122.3	112.9	113.9	99.1	112.1	121.5	108.0	101.2	109.0	110.8	135.5	137.2	133.3	107.4
2020															
1st quarter	107.9	120.2	111.4	112.9	98.7	115.0	124.1	109.9	103.8	105.3	110.8	133.1	138.2	126.6	106.4
2nd quarter	110.3	107.2	97.2	99.1	98.0	117.9	130.1	116.2	107.7	98.6	109.5	117.3	126.4	105.7	108.1
3rd quarter	112.3	117.5	104.7	105.4	99.4	114.7	128.8	113.8	103.5	105.8	110.8	130.3	134.8	124.4	111.6
4th quarter	111.3	119.3	107.2	107.2	100.0	118.5	131.9	115.8	106.5	102.0	111.3	132.7	141.3	121.7	111.3
2021															
1st quarter	111.9	121.6	108.7	108.3	100.4	117.7	131.7	114.6	104.5	106.1	112.6	137.0	143.2	129.1	112.3
2nd quarter	112.8	124.1	110.0	109.7	100.2	119.5	134.8	115.0	104.2	108.5	114.6	142.2	148.2	134.5	113.1
3rd quarter	111.8	124.6	111.5	111.1	100.3	122.6	137.0	115.0	105.3	108.4	116.4	145.0	152.8	135.1	112.1
4th quarter	113.5	127.3	112.2	112.4	99.8	123.8	140.5	115.7	104.5	111.7	118.5	150.8	157.6	142.1	113.2

Table 9-3A. Productivity and Related Data: Recent Data—*Continued*

(2012 = 100, seasonally adjusted.)

Year and quarter	Output per hour of all persons	Output	Hours of all persons	Employ-ment	Average weekly hours	Unit labor costs	Compen-sation per hour	Real hourly compen-sation	Labor share	Unit nonlabor payments	Implicit price deflator	Current dollar output	Compen-sation	Nonlabor payments	Output per job
1960	33.0	17.3	52.5	45.9	114.4	22.7	7.5	52.9	116.0	15.5	19.5	3.4	3.9	2.7	37.8
1961	34.1	17.7	52.0	45.5	114.1	22.7	7.7	54.2	115.2	15.8	19.7	3.5	4.0	2.8	38.9
1962	35.6	18.9	53.1	46.4	114.5	22.5	8.0	55.8	113.6	16.4	19.8	3.8	4.3	3.1	40.8
1963	36.9	19.8	53.7	46.9	114.5	22.5	8.3	56.9	112.7	16.7	20.0	4.0	4.5	3.3	42.2
1964	37.9	21.1	55.7	48.1	115.9	22.6	8.6	57.9	111.5	17.2	20.3	4.3	4.8	3.6	43.9
1965	39.1	22.6	57.9	49.8	116.3	22.6	8.8	58.9	110.2	17.8	20.5	4.6	5.1	4.0	45.5
1966	40.5	24.3	59.9	51.7	115.8	23.1	9.4	60.6	110.1	18.2	21.0	5.1	5.6	4.4	46.9
1967	41.3	24.7	59.9	52.6	113.8	24.0	9.9	62.2	111.0	18.6	21.6	5.3	5.9	4.6	47.0
1968	42.7	26.0	60.9	53.8	113.2	25.0	10.7	64.2	111.0	19.3	22.5	5.9	6.5	5.0	48.4
1969	42.8	26.8	62.7	55.7	112.4	26.6	11.4	65.1	113.3	19.4	23.5	6.3	7.1	5.2	48.1
1970	43.4	26.8	61.7	55.8	110.6	28.1	12.2	65.8	114.4	20.0	24.5	6.6	7.5	5.3	48.0
1971	45.2	27.8	61.6	55.9	110.0	28.6	12.9	67.0	112.0	21.6	25.6	7.1	8.0	6.0	49.7
1972	46.7	29.7	63.5	57.6	110.1	29.5	13.8	69.1	111.9	22.3	26.4	7.8	8.7	6.6	51.5
1973	48.2	31.8	66.1	60.2	109.7	30.8	14.8	70.0	112.8	22.8	27.3	8.7	9.8	7.2	52.9
1974	47.4	31.3	66.2	61.2	108.1	34.3	16.2	69.0	113.7	24.8	30.1	9.4	10.7	7.8	51.2
1975	48.7	30.8	63.3	59.4	106.6	36.8	17.9	69.9	110.5	28.8	33.3	10.3	11.4	8.9	51.9
1976	50.4	33.0	65.6	61.4	106.7	38.4	19.3	71.2	109.2	31.0	35.1	11.6	12.7	10.2	53.8
1977	51.3	34.9	68.2	64.2	106.1	40.8	20.9	72.4	109.3	32.8	37.3	13.0	14.3	11.5	54.4
1978	52.0	37.3	71.7	67.8	105.8	43.7	22.7	73.4	109.9	34.7	39.8	14.8	16.3	12.9	55.0
1979	51.9	38.5	74.3	70.7	105.1	48.0	24.9	73.4	111.3	36.8	43.1	16.6	18.5	14.2	54.5
1980	51.8	38.2	73.7	70.9	103.9	53.1	27.6	73.2	112.6	39.5	47.2	18.0	20.3	15.1	53.9
1981	52.6	39.1	74.3	71.7	103.6	57.4	30.2	73.3	111.0	44.4	51.7	20.2	22.4	17.3	54.5
1982	52.2	37.9	72.6	70.6	102.8	62.1	32.4	74.2	113.1	45.6	54.9	20.8	23.5	17.3	53.7
1983	54.3	40.2	74.0	71.3	103.9	62.3	33.9	74.3	109.7	49.7	56.8	22.9	25.1	20.0	56.4
1984	55.5	43.6	78.6	75.1	104.6	63.6	35.3	74.4	108.9	51.7	58.4	25.5	27.7	22.5	58.1
1985	56.5	45.6	80.6	77.2	104.3	65.6	37.0	75.5	108.9	53.2	60.2	27.4	29.9	24.2	59.0
1986	58.2	47.3	81.2	78.6	103.3	67.3	39.2	78.4	110.3	52.9	61.0	28.9	31.8	25.0	60.1
1987	58.5	49.0	83.7	80.8	103.6	69.5	40.7	78.7	111.7	52.7	62.2	30.5	34.0	25.8	60.6
1988	59.5	51.2	86.1	83.4	103.3	71.9	42.8	79.9	112.1	54.0	64.1	32.8	36.8	27.7	61.4
1989	60.0	53.1	88.5	85.3	103.7	73.3	44.0	78.7	110.4	57.5	66.4	35.3	38.9	30.5	62.3
1990	61.1	53.9	88.3	85.9	102.8	76.4	46.6	79.5	111.2	58.7	68.7	37.0	41.2	31.6	62.8
1991	62.1	53.6	86.3	84.5	102.2	78.7	48.9	80.4	111.2	60.6	70.8	37.9	42.2	32.4	63.4
1992	64.9	55.7	85.9	84.0	102.3	80.0	51.9	83.3	111.1	61.6	72.0	40.1	44.6	34.3	66.3
1993	64.9	57.5	88.5	86.0	102.9	80.9	52.5	82.3	109.8	64.3	73.7	42.3	46.5	37.0	66.8
1994	65.4	60.1	91.9	88.8	103.5	81.2	53.1	81.4	108.1	67.2	75.1	45.1	48.8	40.4	67.7
1995	66.1	62.2	94.1	91.4	103.0	82.3	54.4	81.5	107.7	68.8	76.4	47.5	51.1	42.7	68.0
1996	67.5	65.0	96.3	93.5	102.9	83.4	56.3	82.1	107.6	69.8	77.4	50.3	54.2	45.3	69.5
1997	68.8	68.3	99.3	96.2	103.3	85.0	58.5	83.5	107.8	70.8	78.8	53.8	58.0	48.4	71.0
1998	71.1	72.2	101.4	98.3	103.2	86.9	61.8	87.2	109.9	68.9	79.1	57.1	62.7	49.7	73.4
1999	73.9	76.3	103.3	100.1	103.1	87.5	64.7	89.3	109.9	69.4	79.6	60.8	66.8	53.0	76.2
2000	76.1	79.7	104.7	101.9	102.7	91.0	69.3	92.4	112.1	68.5	81.2	64.7	72.5	54.5	78.2
2001	78.1	80.2	102.7	101.3	101.4	92.6	72.3	93.8	112.2	69.5	82.5	66.2	74.2	55.7	79.2
2002	81.5	81.6	100.1	99.0	101.1	90.8	74.0	94.5	109.1	73.3	83.2	67.9	74.1	59.8	82.4
2003	84.4	84.1	99.6	98.9	100.6	90.9	76.7	95.8	107.7	75.9	84.3	70.9	76.4	63.8	85.0
2004	87.0	87.7	100.9	100.3	100.6	92.2	80.2	97.6	106.9	78.6	86.3	75.7	80.9	69.0	87.5
2005	88.9	91.2	102.6	102.1	100.4	93.6	83.1	97.8	104.9	83.6	89.2	81.3	85.3	76.2	89.2
2006	89.8	94.2	104.9	104.2	100.8	96.2	86.3	98.4	104.8	86.1	91.8	86.5	90.6	81.1	90.4
2007	91.2	96.3	105.6	105.1	100.5	98.8	90.1	99.8	105.5	87.0	93.7	90.2	95.2	83.8	91.7
2008	92.4	95.5	103.4	103.6	99.8	100.3	92.7	98.9	105.6	88.2	95.0	91.8	95.8	84.2	92.2
2009	95.7	91.8	96.0	97.7	98.3	97.8	93.5	100.1	102.5	92.2	95.4	87.6	89.8	84.7	94.0
2010	99.0	94.8	95.8	96.5	99.3	96.3	95.3	100.4	99.9	96.5	96.4	91.4	91.3	91.5	98.3
2011	99.0	96.8	97.8	98.0	99.7	98.4	97.4	99.5	100.2	98.0	98.2	95.1	95.2	94.9	98.7
2012	100.0	100.0	100.0	100.0	100.0	100.0	100.0	100.0	100.0	100.0	100.0	100.0	100.0	100.0	100.0
2013	100.5	102.2	101.7	101.9	99.9	100.7	101.2	101.2	99.8	99.3	102.4	101.4	103.7	103.0	104.6	100.4
2014	101.1	105.3	104.1	104.0	100.1	102.9	104.0	100.8	99.6	103.9	103.3	108.8	108.3	109.3	101.2
2015	102.3	108.8	106.4	106.4	100.0	104.8	107.2	103.7	100.7	103.1	104.1	113.3	114.1	112.2	102.3
2016	102.7	110.8	107.9	108.3	99.6	105.6	108.4	103.5	100.5	104.4	105.0	116.4	117.0	115.7	102.3
2017	103.8	113.8	109.7	110.1	99.6	108.0	112.1	104.8	101.1	105.2	106.8	121.6	123.0	119.8	103.4
2018	105.3	117.8	111.8	112.2	99.7	110.1	116.0	105.9	100.9	107.9	109.1	128.6	129.7	127.1	105.0
2019	107.5	121.0	112.6	113.5	99.2	112.0	120.5	108.0	101.1	109.2	110.8	134.1	135.6	132.2	106.6
2020	110.1	115.7	105.1	106.1	99.0	117.1	128.9	114.1	105.2	103.8	111.3	128.8	135.5	120.2	109.0
2021	112.2	124.2	110.7	110.5	100.2	121.4	136.2	115.2	104.8	108.6	115.8	143.9	150.8	134.9	112.4
2019															
1st quarter	106.5	119.6	112.3	113.1	99.3	112.5	119.9	108.4	102.2	106.9	110.1	131.7	134.6	127.9	105.8
2nd quarter	107.5	120.7	112.3	113.2	99.2	111.7	120.1	107.8	100.8	109.6	110.8	133.7	134.8	132.3	106.6
3rd quarter	107.8	121.6	112.8	113.8	99.1	111.5	120.2	107.5	100.4	110.4	111.0	135.0	135.6	134.3	106.9
4th quarter	108.2	122.2	112.9	114.0	99.1	112.5	121.7	108.2	101.0	109.9	111.4	136.1	137.5	134.3	107.2
2020															
1st quarter	107.5	119.9	111.5	113.0	98.7	115.6	124.3	110.2	103.7	106.0	111.4	133.6	138.6	127.1	106.1
2nd quarter	110.2	106.9	97.0	99.0	98.0	118.5	130.5	116.7	107.4	99.8	110.3	117.9	126.6	106.6	108.0
3rd quarter	111.8	117.2	104.8	105.4	99.4	115.3	129.0	113.9	103.3	106.8	111.6	130.8	135.1	125.1	111.1
4th quarter	111.1	118.9	107.1	107.2	99.9	119.1	132.2	116.2	106.5	102.4	111.8	133.0	141.6	121.9	111.0
2021															
1st quarter	111.7	121.4	108.7	108.4	100.3	118.3	132.1	114.8	104.6	106.4	113.1	137.3	143.5	129.2	112.0
2nd quarter	112.6	123.9	110.0	109.8	100.2	119.9	135.0	115.2	104.5	108.1	114.8	142.2	148.6	134.0	112.8
3rd quarter	111.4	124.5	111.7	111.3	100.4	123.0	137.1	115.0	105.6	108.0	116.5	145.0	153.1	134.5	111.9
4th quarter	113.2	127.2	112.4	112.6	99.8	124.2	140.6	115.7	104.6	111.5	118.7	151.0	158.0	141.9	112.9

Table 9-3B. Productivity and Related Data: Historical Data

(2012 = 100, seasonally adjusted.)

Year and quarter	Business sector								Nonfarm business sector							
	Output per hour of all persons	Output	Hours of all persons	Compen-sation per hour	Real compen-sation per hour	Unit labor costs	Unit nonlabor pay-ments	Implicit price deflator	Output per hour of all persons	Output	Hours of all persons	Compen-sation per hour	Real compen-sation per hour	Unit labor costs	Unit nonlabor pay-ments	Implicit price deflator
1947	20.4	11.2	54.7	3.6	33.9	17.7	11.8	15.1	20.4	11.2	54.7	3.6	33.9	16.4	11.3	14.2
1948	21.3	11.7	55.1	3.9	34.0	18.4	13.0	16.0	21.3	11.7	55.1	3.9	34.0	17.4	12.2	15.1
1949	21.8	11.6	53.3	4.0	34.9	18.2	12.9	15.9	21.8	11.6	53.3	4.0	34.9	17.3	12.5	15.2
1950	23.6	12.7	54.1	4.2	36.9	18.0	13.5	16.1	23.6	12.7	54.1	4.2	36.9	17.2	13.1	15.4
1951	24.3	13.6	55.8	4.7	37.5	19.2	14.9	17.3	24.3	13.6	55.8	4.7	37.5	18.2	14.1	16.4
1952	25.0	14.0	55.9	4.9	39.1	19.7	14.6	17.5	25.0	14.0	55.9	4.9	39.1	18.9	14.0	16.8
1953	25.9	14.7	56.6	5.3	41.2	20.2	14.3	17.6	25.9	14.7	56.6	5.3	41.2	19.5	14.0	17.1
1954	26.5	14.5	54.7	5.4	42.3	20.4	14.2	17.7	26.5	14.5	54.7	5.4	42.3	19.7	14.0	17.2
1955	27.6	15.7	56.8	5.6	43.5	20.1	15.2	18.0	27.6	15.7	56.8	5.6	43.5	19.6	14.9	17.5
1956	27.7	16.0	57.6	5.9	45.7	21.4	14.9	18.5	27.7	16.0	57.6	5.9	45.7	20.9	14.6	18.2
1957	28.6	16.3	56.8	6.3	47.1	22.1	15.4	19.1	28.6	16.3	56.8	6.3	47.1	21.5	15.1	18.7
1958	29.4	16.0	54.3	6.6	47.8	22.4	15.7	19.5	29.4	16.0	54.3	6.6	47.8	21.9	15.3	19.0
1959	30.5	17.2	56.5	6.9	49.4	22.5	16.1	19.7	30.5	17.2	56.5	6.9	49.4	22.0	15.9	19.3
1947																
1st quarter	20.4	10.8	46.3	3.7	35.9	16.0	11.6	14.6	23.3	10.8	46.3	3.7	35.9	16.0	10.8	13.7
2nd quarter	20.5	11.0	46.3	3.8	36.2	16.0	11.5	14.8	23.8	11.0	46.3	3.8	36.2	16.0	11.2	13.9
3rd quarter	20.3	10.7	46.4	3.9	36.5	17.0	11.8	15.2	23.1	10.7	46.4	3.9	36.5	17.0	11.4	14.5
4th quarter	20.5	11.3	46.9	4.0	36.3	16.7	12.3	15.7	24.0	11.3	46.9	4.0	36.3	16.7	11.7	14.5
1948																
1st quarter	21.0	11.4	47.2	4.1	36.4	17.0	12.8	15.8	24.1	11.4	47.2	4.1	36.4	17.0	11.8	14.7
2nd quarter	21.4	11.3	47.1	4.2	36.3	17.3	13.2	15.9	24.1	11.3	47.1	4.2	36.3	17.3	12.0	15.0
3rd quarter	21.3	11.4	47.5	4.2	36.4	17.6	13.2	16.2	24.1	11.4	47.5	4.2	36.4	17.6	12.3	15.3
4th quarter	21.5	11.4	47.0	4.3	37.1	17.7	12.9	16.2	24.2	11.4	47.0	4.3	37.1	17.7	12.6	15.5
1949																
1st quarter	21.4	11.3	46.2	4.3	37.7	17.6	13.0	16.1	24.5	11.3	46.2	4.3	37.7	17.6	12.5	15.4
2nd quarter	21.5	11.2	45.5	4.3	37.8	17.5	12.8	15.9	24.7	11.2	45.5	4.3	37.8	17.5	12.3	15.2
3rd quarter	22.1	11.4	45.0	4.3	38.2	17.1	13.0	15.8	25.3	11.4	45.0	4.3	38.2	17.1	12.7	15.2
4th quarter	22.1	11.3	44.8	4.3	38.2	17.1	12.7	15.8	25.2	11.3	44.8	4.3	38.2	17.1	12.5	15.1
1950																
1st quarter	23.1	11.7	45.1	4.4	39.3	17.0	12.9	15.7	26.0	11.7	45.1	4.4	39.3	17.0	12.8	15.2
2nd quarter	23.4	12.2	46.3	4.5	39.9	17.2	13.0	15.8	26.3	12.2	46.3	4.5	39.9	17.2	12.8	15.2
3rd quarter	23.8	12.8	47.7	4.6	39.9	17.1	13.8	16.2	26.9	12.8	47.7	4.6	39.9	17.1	13.2	15.4
4th quarter	23.9	13.0	48.2	4.7	40.1	17.5	14.3	16.5	27.0	13.0	48.2	4.7	40.1	17.5	13.4	15.7
1951																
1st quarter	23.9	13.2	49.0	4.8	39.4	17.9	14.9	17.1	27.0	13.2	49.0	4.8	39.4	17.9	13.9	16.2
2nd quarter	24.0	13.3	49.4	4.9	39.9	18.4	14.7	17.3	26.9	13.3	49.4	4.9	39.9	18.4	13.8	16.4
3rd quarter	24.7	13.4	48.9	5.0	40.4	18.2	15.0	17.3	27.5	13.4	48.9	5.0	40.4	18.2	14.3	16.5
4th quarter	24.6	13.5	48.9	5.1	40.6	18.5	15.0	17.5	27.6	13.5	48.9	5.1	40.6	18.5	14.2	16.6
1952																
1st quarter	24.7	13.6	49.2	5.1	40.8	18.6	14.8	17.4	27.7	13.6	49.2	5.1	40.8	18.6	14.1	16.6
2nd quarter	24.9	13.6	49.0	5.2	41.0	18.7	14.5	17.4	27.7	13.6	49.0	5.2	41.0	18.7	13.9	16.6
3rd quarter	25.0	13.6	49.4	5.3	41.3	19.1	14.6	17.6	27.5	13.6	49.4	5.3	41.3	19.1	13.9	16.8
4th quarter	25.4	14.3	50.7	5.4	42.2	19.1	14.5	17.6	28.1	14.3	50.7	5.4	42.2	19.1	14.1	16.9
1953																
1st quarter	25.8	14.5	51.2	5.4	42.9	19.2	14.4	17.6	28.4	14.5	51.2	5.4	42.9	19.2	14.0	17.0
2nd quarter	26.0	14.6	51.3	5.5	43.2	19.4	14.4	17.6	28.4	14.6	51.3	5.5	43.2	19.4	14.1	17.1
3rd quarter	26.0	14.5	50.8	5.6	43.5	19.5	14.2	17.7	28.5	14.5	50.8	5.6	43.5	19.5	14.1	17.1
4th quarter	25.9	14.2	50.0	5.6	43.8	19.8	14.2	17.7	28.4	14.2	50.0	5.6	43.8	19.8	13.8	17.1
1954																
1st quarter	25.9	14.1	49.3	5.7	44.1	19.9	14.1	17.7	28.5	14.1	49.3	5.7	44.1	19.9	13.7	17.2
2nd quarter	26.3	14.1	49.0	5.7	44.2	19.8	14.0	17.7	28.7	14.1	49.0	5.7	44.2	19.8	13.9	17.2
3rd quarter	26.7	14.3	48.8	5.7	44.7	19.6	14.4	17.7	29.2	14.3	48.8	5.7	44.7	19.6	14.1	17.2
4th quarter	27.1	14.6	49.4	5.8	45.3	19.5	14.4	17.7	29.6	14.6	49.4	5.8	45.3	19.5	14.3	17.3
1955																
1st quarter	27.5	15.1	50.2	5.8	45.5	19.3	15.2	17.8	30.1	15.1	50.2	5.8	45.5	19.3	14.8	17.4
2nd quarter	27.8	15.4	50.8	5.9	45.9	19.4	15.1	17.8	30.2	15.4	50.8	5.9	45.9	19.4	14.8	17.4
3rd quarter	27.7	15.6	51.4	6.0	46.7	19.7	15.2	18.0	30.4	15.6	51.4	6.0	46.7	19.7	14.9	17.6
4th quarter	27.5	15.7	52.0	6.0	47.0	19.9	15.3	18.2	30.2	15.7	52.0	6.0	47.0	19.9	15.0	17.8
1956																
1st quarter	27.4	15.6	52.3	6.1	47.7	20.5	14.9	18.3	29.9	15.6	52.3	6.1	47.7	20.5	14.6	17.9
2nd quarter	27.6	15.7	52.4	6.2	48.3	20.8	14.7	18.4	30.0	15.7	52.4	6.2	48.3	20.8	14.5	18.0
3rd quarter	27.6	15.7	52.2	6.3	48.6	21.1	15.0	18.7	30.0	15.7	52.2	6.3	48.6	21.1	14.6	18.3
4th quarter	28.2	15.9	52.5	6.4	49.0	21.2	15.1	18.7	30.3	15.9	52.5	6.4	49.0	21.2	14.7	18.4
1957																
1st quarter	28.4	16.1	52.5	6.5	49.3	21.3	15.3	19.0	30.7	16.1	52.5	6.5	49.3	21.3	15.1	18.6
2nd quarter	28.4	16.0	52.4	6.6	49.3	21.6	15.3	19.1	30.6	16.0	52.4	6.6	49.3	21.6	15.0	18.7
3rd quarter	28.7	16.2	52.2	6.7	49.6	21.6	15.6	19.2	31.0	16.2	52.2	6.7	49.6	21.6	15.2	18.8
4th quarter	29.0	15.9	51.1	6.8	50.0	21.8	15.3	19.2	31.1	15.9	51.1	6.8	50.0	21.8	15.0	18.8
1958																
1st quarter	28.8	15.3	49.9	6.8	49.4	22.1	15.3	19.4	30.7	15.3	49.9	6.8	49.4	22.1	14.8	18.9
2nd quarter	29.2	15.4	49.2	6.8	49.5	21.9	15.7	19.4	31.3	15.4	49.2	6.8	49.5	21.9	15.2	18.9
3rd quarter	29.7	15.9	49.8	7.0	50.7	22.0	15.7	19.5	31.9	15.9	49.8	7.0	50.7	22.0	15.3	19.0
4th quarter	30.0	16.4	50.5	7.0	50.9	21.7	16.2	19.6	32.4	16.4	50.5	7.0	50.9	21.7	15.8	19.1
1959																
1st quarter	30.3	16.7	51.5	7.1	51.3	21.9	16.0	19.6	32.4	16.7	51.5	7.1	51.3	21.9	15.8	19.2
2nd quarter	30.4	17.2	52.5	7.1	51.6	21.8	16.2	19.6	32.7	17.2	52.5	7.1	51.6	21.8	15.9	19.3
3rd quarter	30.6	17.2	52.3	7.2	51.6	21.9	16.2	19.7	32.8	17.2	52.3	7.2	51.6	21.9	16.0	19.3
4th quarter	30.6	17.1	52.4	7.3	51.8	22.2	16.0	19.8	32.7	17.1	52.4	7.3	51.8	22.2	15.8	19.4

Table 9-3B. Productivity and Related Data: Historical Data—*Continued*

(2012 = 100, seasonally adjusted.)

Year and quarter	Business sector								Nonfarm business sector							
	Output per hour of all persons	Output	Hours of all persons	Compensation per hour	Real compensation per hour	Unit labor costs	Unit nonlabor payments	Implicit price deflator	Output per hour of all persons	Output	Hours of all persons	Compensation per hour	Real compensation per hour	Unit labor costs	Unit nonlabor payments	Implicit price deflator
1960																
1st quarter	31.5	17.6	52.7	7.4	52.9	22.2	16.2	19.8	33.5	17.6	52.7	7.4	52.9	22.2	15.9	19.5
2nd quarter	30.8	17.4	52.8	7.5	52.9	22.7	15.8	19.9	32.9	17.4	52.8	7.5	52.9	22.7	15.4	19.5
3rd quarter	31.0	17.4	52.5	7.5	53.2	22.7	16.0	19.9	33.1	17.4	52.5	7.5	53.2	22.7	15.5	19.6
4th quarter	30.7	17.0	52.0	7.5	53.1	23.1	15.6	20.0	32.7	17.0	52.0	7.5	53.1	23.1	15.2	19.6
1961																
1st quarter	31.1	17.1	51.7	7.6	53.5	23.0	15.7	20.0	33.1	17.1	51.7	7.6	53.5	23.0	15.3	19.7
2nd quarter	32.1	17.5	51.6	7.7	54.2	22.7	16.1	20.0	34.0	17.5	51.6	7.7	54.2	22.7	15.8	19.7
3rd quarter	32.5	17.9	51.9	7.8	54.4	22.5	16.4	20.1	34.6	17.9	51.9	7.8	54.4	22.5	16.1	19.7
4th quarter	32.8	18.3	52.5	7.8	54.7	22.5	16.5	20.1	34.9	18.3	52.5	7.8	54.7	22.5	16.1	19.7
1962																
1st quarter	33.2	18.7	52.7	8.0	55.4	22.4	16.7	20.2	35.4	18.7	52.7	8.0	55.4	22.4	16.4	19.8
2nd quarter	33.3	18.8	53.4	8.0	55.5	22.7	16.5	20.2	35.3	18.8	53.4	8.0	55.5	22.7	16.2	19.9
3rd quarter	33.9	19.1	53.2	8.1	55.8	22.5	16.8	20.3	35.9	19.1	53.2	8.1	55.8	22.5	16.5	19.9
4th quarter	34.2	19.1	52.9	8.1	56.1	22.5	16.7	20.3	36.1	19.1	52.9	8.1	56.1	22.5	16.5	19.9
1963																
1st quarter	34.3	19.3	53.2	8.2	56.5	22.7	16.8	20.3	36.3	19.3	53.2	8.2	56.5	22.7	16.5	20.0
2nd quarter	34.5	19.6	53.6	8.3	56.7	22.6	16.9	20.3	36.5	19.6	53.6	8.3	56.7	22.6	16.6	20.0
3rd quarter	35.4	20.1	53.7	8.3	56.9	22.3	17.2	20.4	37.4	20.1	53.7	8.3	56.9	22.3	17.0	20.0
4th quarter	35.4	20.2	54.1	8.4	57.4	22.6	17.3	20.5	37.4	20.2	54.1	8.4	57.4	22.6	16.9	20.1
1964																
1st quarter	35.8	20.8	55.2	8.4	57.1	22.4	17.5	20.5	37.7	20.8	55.2	8.4	57.1	22.4	17.3	20.2
2nd quarter	35.9	21.0	55.4	8.5	57.7	22.5	17.4	20.6	37.9	21.0	55.4	8.5	57.7	22.5	17.3	20.2
3rd quarter	36.3	21.4	55.8	8.6	58.3	22.5	17.5	20.6	38.3	21.4	55.8	8.6	58.3	22.5	17.4	20.3
4th quarter	36.1	21.4	56.3	8.7	58.4	22.9	17.3	20.7	37.9	21.4	56.3	8.7	58.4	22.9	17.1	20.4
1965																
1st quarter	36.7	22.0	57.2	8.7	58.5	22.7	17.8	20.8	38.5	22.0	57.2	8.7	58.5	22.7	17.6	20.5
2nd quarter	36.7	22.3	57.8	8.8	58.5	22.7	17.8	20.9	38.6	22.3	57.8	8.8	58.5	22.7	17.6	20.5
3rd quarter	37.7	22.8	57.9	8.9	58.9	22.5	18.3	20.9	39.4	22.8	57.9	8.9	58.9	22.5	18.0	20.6
4th quarter	38.2	23.4	58.4	9.0	59.5	22.5	18.6	21.1	40.1	23.4	58.4	9.0	59.5	22.5	18.3	20.7
1966																
1st quarter	38.9	24.1	59.3	9.2	60.0	22.6	18.7	21.2	40.7	24.1	59.3	9.2	60.0	22.6	18.3	20.7
2nd quarter	38.7	24.2	59.9	9.3	60.4	23.1	18.4	21.3	40.4	24.2	59.9	9.3	60.4	23.1	18.1	20.9
3rd quarter	38.8	24.4	60.2	9.4	60.7	23.3	18.5	21.5	40.5	24.4	60.2	9.4	60.7	23.3	18.2	21.1
4th quarter	39.1	24.5	60.0	9.6	61.0	23.5	18.7	21.7	40.8	24.5	60.0	9.6	61.0	23.5	18.5	21.3
1967																
1st quarter	39.5	24.6	59.9	9.7	61.7	23.6	18.8	21.8	41.1	24.6	59.9	9.7	61.7	23.6	18.6	21.4
2nd quarter	39.8	24.6	59.6	9.9	62.3	23.9	18.7	21.9	41.2	24.6	59.6	9.9	62.3	23.9	18.5	21.6
3rd quarter	39.9	24.8	59.8	10.0	62.6	24.1	18.9	22.1	41.5	24.8	59.8	10.0	62.6	24.1	18.6	21.7
4th quarter	40.0	25.0	60.0	10.1	62.7	24.4	19.1	22.3	41.6	25.0	60.0	10.1	62.7	24.4	18.8	21.9
1968																
1st quarter	40.9	25.6	60.1	10.4	63.8	24.5	19.4	22.5	42.5	25.6	60.1	10.4	63.8	24.5	19.2	22.2
2nd quarter	41.3	26.0	60.7	10.6	64.2	24.6	19.7	22.8	42.9	26.0	60.7	10.6	64.2	24.6	19.5	22.4
3rd quarter	41.3	26.2	61.1	10.7	64.4	25.0	19.5	22.9	42.9	26.2	61.1	10.7	64.4	25.0	19.3	22.6
4th quarter	41.3	26.3	61.5	11.0	64.8	25.6	19.5	23.3	42.8	26.3	61.5	11.0	64.8	25.6	19.3	22.9
1969																
1st quarter	41.4	26.8	62.1	11.1	64.9	25.7	20.0	23.5	43.2	26.8	62.1	11.1	64.9	25.7	19.8	23.1
2nd quarter	41.4	26.8	62.7	11.3	65.0	26.4	19.8	23.8	42.8	26.8	62.7	11.3	65.0	26.4	19.5	23.4
3rd quarter	41.5	27.0	63.0	11.5	65.2	26.8	19.8	24.0	42.9	27.0	63.0	11.5	65.2	26.8	19.5	23.6
4th quarter	41.4	26.8	62.8	11.7	65.5	27.5	19.6	24.3	42.7	26.8	62.8	11.7	65.5	27.5	19.2	23.9
1970																
1st quarter	41.6	26.8	62.5	11.9	65.6	27.9	19.6	24.6	42.8	26.8	62.5	11.9	65.6	27.9	19.3	24.1
2nd quarter	42.0	26.8	61.7	12.1	65.7	27.9	20.3	24.9	43.4	26.8	61.7	12.1	65.7	27.9	20.0	24.5
3rd quarter	42.8	27.1	61.4	12.3	66.1	27.9	20.6	25.0	44.1	27.1	61.4	12.3	66.1	27.9	20.3	24.6
4th quarter	42.5	26.6	60.9	12.4	65.8	28.5	20.6	25.3	43.7	26.6	60.9	12.4	65.8	28.5	20.4	25.0
1971																
1st quarter	43.7	27.5	61.2	12.7	66.6	28.2	21.6	25.6	45.0	27.5	61.2	12.7	66.6	28.2	21.3	25.2
2nd quarter	43.8	27.7	61.4	12.9	67.0	28.5	21.9	25.9	45.1	27.7	61.4	12.9	67.0	28.5	21.6	25.5
3rd quarter	44.3	28.0	61.4	13.1	67.3	28.7	22.3	26.1	45.6	28.0	61.4	13.1	67.3	28.7	22.0	25.8
4th quarter	43.9	28.0	62.1	13.1	67.2	29.1	22.0	26.3	45.2	28.0	62.1	13.1	67.2	29.1	21.6	25.9
1972																
1st quarter	44.4	28.8	62.8	13.5	68.5	29.5	22.2	26.6	45.9	28.8	62.8	13.5	68.5	29.5	21.9	26.2
2nd quarter	45.5	29.6	63.2	13.7	68.9	29.2	22.9	26.7	46.8	29.6	63.2	13.7	68.9	29.2	22.5	26.3
3rd quarter	45.6	29.9	63.6	13.9	69.2	29.4	23.2	27.0	47.0	29.9	63.6	13.9	69.2	29.4	22.5	26.4
4th quarter	46.1	30.5	64.2	14.1	69.8	29.7	23.5	27.3	47.4	30.5	64.2	14.1	69.8	29.7	22.5	26.6
1973																
1st quarter	47.0	31.6	65.2	14.5	70.6	29.8	23.7	27.5	48.5	31.6	65.2	14.5	70.6	29.8	22.7	26.8
2nd quarter	47.1	32.0	65.9	14.7	70.1	30.3	24.2	27.9	48.5	32.0	65.9	14.7	70.1	30.3	22.9	27.1
3rd quarter	46.4	31.9	66.3	14.9	69.9	31.1	24.3	28.5	48.1	31.9	66.3	14.9	69.9	31.1	22.6	27.4
4th quarter	46.6	31.9	66.7	15.2	69.6	31.9	25.0	29.1	47.8	31.9	66.7	15.2	69.6	31.9	23.0	28.0
1974																
1st quarter	46.0	31.6	66.4	15.6	69.1	32.7	25.1	29.8	47.7	31.6	66.4	15.6	69.1	32.7	23.5	28.7
2nd quarter	46.1	31.6	66.6	16.0	69.0	33.7	25.7	30.5	47.5	31.6	66.6	16.0	69.0	33.7	24.6	29.7
3rd quarter	45.7	31.2	66.3	16.5	69.2	35.0	26.1	31.5	47.1	31.2	66.3	16.5	69.2	35.0	25.0	30.7
4th quarter	46.1	31.0	65.2	16.9	68.9	35.6	27.6	32.5	47.5	31.0	65.2	16.9	68.9	35.6	26.3	31.6

Table 9-3B. Productivity and Related Data: Historical Data—*Continued*

(2012 = 100, seasonally adjusted.)

Year and quarter	Business sector								Nonfarm business sector							
	Output per hour of all persons	Output	Hours of all persons	Compensation per hour	Real compensation per hour	Unit labor costs	Unit nonlabor payments	Implicit price deflator	Output per hour of all persons	Output	Hours of all persons	Compensation per hour	Real compensation per hour	Unit labor costs	Unit nonlabor payments	Implicit price deflator
1975																
1st quarter	46.8	30.2	63.2	17.4	69.6	36.4	28.5	33.3	47.9	30.2	63.2	17.4	69.6	36.4	27.6	32.6
2nd quarter	47.5	30.4	62.6	17.8	70.2	36.6	29.3	33.7	48.6	30.4	62.6	17.8	70.2	36.6	28.5	33.1
3rd quarter	48.0	31.1	63.2	18.1	70.0	36.8	30.6	34.3	49.2	31.1	63.2	18.1	70.0	36.8	29.4	33.6
4th quarter	48.2	31.7	64.2	18.4	69.9	37.4	31.0	34.9	49.3	31.7	64.2	18.4	69.9	37.4	29.8	34.1
1976																
1st quarter	48.8	32.6	65.3	18.8	70.4	37.6	31.3	35.2	50.0	32.6	65.3	18.8	70.4	37.6	30.5	34.5
2nd quarter	49.2	33.0	65.3	19.1	71.1	37.9	31.6	35.5	50.5	33.0	65.3	19.1	71.1	37.9	30.9	34.9
3rd quarter	49.2	33.2	65.6	19.5	71.5	38.6	31.8	36.0	50.6	33.2	65.6	19.5	71.5	38.6	31.1	35.3
4th quarter	49.5	33.5	65.9	19.9	71.9	39.3	32.3	36.6	50.7	33.5	65.9	19.9	71.9	39.3	31.7	36.0
1977																
1st quarter	49.8	34.0	66.6	20.3	72.0	39.8	32.9	37.2	51.1	34.0	66.6	20.3	72.0	39.8	32.2	36.5
2nd quarter	49.9	34.8	67.9	20.7	72.2	40.5	33.3	37.7	51.3	34.8	67.9	20.7	72.2	40.5	32.7	37.1
3rd quarter	50.6	35.6	68.6	21.1	72.6	40.8	33.8	38.1	51.8	35.6	68.6	21.1	72.6	40.8	33.4	37.6
4th quarter	50.0	35.4	69.3	21.5	72.8	42.1	34.1	38.9	51.1	35.4	69.3	21.5	72.8	42.1	33.3	38.2
1978																
1st quarter	49.8	35.6	69.6	22.1	73.6	43.2	33.8	39.4	51.2	35.6	69.6	22.1	73.6	43.2	32.9	38.7
2nd quarter	50.8	37.4	71.7	22.5	73.2	43.0	35.7	40.2	52.2	37.4	71.7	22.5	73.2	43.0	34.6	39.4
3rd quarter	51.0	37.7	72.3	22.9	73.3	43.8	36.3	40.9	52.2	37.7	72.3	22.9	73.3	43.8	35.3	40.1
4th quarter	51.1	38.4	73.1	23.5	73.7	44.6	37.1	41.7	52.5	38.4	73.1	23.5	73.7	44.6	36.1	40.9
1979																
1st quarter	50.9	38.4	73.7	24.1	73.9	46.2	36.9	42.5	52.1	38.4	73.7	24.1	73.9	46.2	35.6	41.6
2nd quarter	50.8	38.4	73.9	24.6	73.6	47.4	38.0	43.6	52.0	38.4	73.9	24.6	73.6	47.4	36.8	42.8
3rd quarter	50.8	38.7	74.6	25.2	73.3	48.5	38.6	44.5	51.9	38.7	74.6	25.2	73.3	48.5	37.4	43.7
4th quarter	50.7	38.8	74.7	25.8	73.3	49.7	38.8	45.3	51.8	38.8	74.7	25.8	73.3	49.7	37.7	44.5
1980																
1st quarter	51.0	38.8	74.6	26.5	73.0	50.9	39.5	46.3	52.1	38.8	74.6	26.5	73.0	50.9	38.8	45.6
2nd quarter	50.5	37.7	73.2	27.2	73.2	52.8	39.4	47.3	51.6	37.7	73.2	27.2	73.2	52.8	39.3	46.9
3rd quarter	50.6	37.7	72.8	27.9	73.3	54.0	40.3	48.4	51.8	37.7	72.8	27.9	73.3	54.0	39.5	47.7
4th quarter	51.1	38.6	73.8	28.7	73.5	54.8	42.0	49.6	52.3	38.6	73.8	28.7	73.5	54.8	40.8	48.7
1981																
1st quarter	52.0	39.4	74.3	29.4	73.4	55.4	44.6	50.9	53.1	39.4	74.3	29.4	73.4	55.4	43.6	50.2
2nd quarter	51.6	39.0	74.3	29.9	73.2	57.1	44.8	51.9	52.4	39.0	74.3	29.9	73.2	57.1	43.7	51.3
3rd quarter	52.3	39.3	74.3	30.6	73.4	57.8	46.4	52.8	52.9	39.3	74.3	30.6	73.4	57.8	45.2	52.3
4th quarter	51.7	38.7	73.9	31.1	73.3	59.4	46.1	53.6	52.4	38.7	73.9	31.1	73.3	59.4	45.4	53.3
1982																
1st quarter	51.4	37.9	72.7	31.9	74.4	61.2	45.2	54.3	52.1	37.9	72.7	31.9	74.4	61.2	44.5	53.9
2nd quarter	51.5	38.1	73.0	32.2	74.2	61.7	46.1	54.9	52.1	38.1	73.0	32.2	74.2	61.7	45.5	54.6
3rd quarter	51.5	37.9	72.5	32.7	74.1	62.5	46.7	55.7	52.2	37.9	72.5	32.7	74.1	62.5	45.9	55.3
4th quarter	52.0	37.8	71.8	33.1	74.3	62.9	47.4	56.2	52.7	37.8	71.8	33.1	74.3	62.9	46.9	55.9
1983																
1st quarter	52.4	38.5	72.2	33.5	74.7	62.7	48.4	56.6	53.4	38.5	72.2	33.5	74.7	62.7	47.6	56.2
2nd quarter	53.3	39.8	73.1	33.8	74.5	62.0	49.7	57.0	54.5	39.8	73.1	33.8	74.5	62.0	49.2	56.4
3rd quarter	53.6	40.8	74.6	34.0	74.2	62.1	50.9	57.5	54.8	40.8	74.6	34.0	74.2	62.1	51.0	57.3
4th quarter	54.0	41.8	76.0	34.4	74.3	62.4	51.3	57.9	55.0	41.8	76.0	34.4	74.3	62.4	51.3	57.6
1984																
1st quarter	54.3	42.8	77.4	34.8	74.2	62.9	51.9	58.3	55.3	42.8	77.4	34.8	74.2	62.9	51.0	57.7
2nd quarter	54.8	43.6	78.4	35.1	74.2	63.2	52.6	58.7	55.6	43.6	78.4	35.1	74.2	63.2	51.8	58.3
3rd quarter	55.1	44.0	78.8	35.6	74.7	63.8	52.8	59.1	55.8	44.0	78.8	35.6	74.7	63.8	52.1	58.7
4th quarter	55.2	44.3	79.3	35.9	74.7	64.3	53.0	59.4	55.9	44.3	79.3	35.9	74.7	64.3	52.2	59.0
1985																
1st quarter	55.5	44.8	79.9	36.4	75.0	64.9	53.7	60.0	56.1	44.8	79.9	36.4	75.0	64.9	53.0	59.7
2nd quarter	55.7	45.2	80.4	36.7	75.1	65.3	53.8	60.3	56.2	45.2	80.4	36.7	75.1	65.3	53.3	60.1
3rd quarter	56.6	45.9	80.7	37.3	75.7	65.4	54.4	60.6	57.0	45.9	80.7	37.3	75.7	65.4	54.1	60.5
4th quarter	56.8	46.4	81.1	38.0	76.4	66.4	53.6	60.8	57.2	46.4	81.1	38.0	76.4	66.4	53.1	60.6
1986																
1st quarter	57.3	46.8	80.9	38.5	77.1	66.6	53.9	61.0	57.9	46.8	80.9	38.5	77.1	66.6	53.6	61.0
2nd quarter	57.7	47.1	80.7	39.0	78.4	66.8	53.7	61.2	58.3	47.1	80.7	39.0	78.4	66.8	53.4	61.0
3rd quarter	58.0	47.5	81.1	39.5	78.9	67.4	53.5	61.3	58.6	47.5	81.1	39.5	78.9	67.4	52.9	61.1
4th quarter	57.9	47.8	81.7	40.0	79.5	68.4	52.6	61.5	58.5	47.8	81.7	40.0	79.5	68.4	52.1	61.3
1987																
1st quarter	57.6	48.2	82.7	40.2	78.9	69.0	52.6	61.8	58.2	48.2	82.7	40.2	78.9	69.0	52.1	61.7
2nd quarter	58.0	48.8	83.2	40.5	78.7	69.1	53.3	62.2	58.6	48.8	83.2	40.5	78.7	69.1	52.8	62.0
3rd quarter	58.1	49.1	83.8	40.9	78.7	69.8	53.5	62.7	58.6	49.1	83.8	40.9	78.7	69.8	53.1	62.5
4th quarter	58.6	50.1	84.7	41.4	79.0	69.9	53.8	62.9	59.2	50.1	84.7	41.4	79.0	69.9	53.3	62.7
1988																
1st quarter	58.7	50.3	84.7	42.1	79.8	70.9	53.7	63.5	59.4	50.3	84.7	42.1	79.8	70.9	53.1	63.1
2nd quarter	58.8	51.2	85.9	42.6	80.0	71.5	53.9	64.0	59.5	51.2	85.9	42.6	80.0	71.5	53.5	63.7
3rd quarter	59.0	51.4	86.2	43.1	80.0	72.2	54.8	64.8	59.7	51.4	86.2	43.1	80.0	72.2	54.3	64.5
4th quarter	59.1	52.1	87.1	43.4	79.9	72.6	55.5	65.3	59.8	52.1	87.1	43.4	79.9	72.6	55.6	65.2
1989																
1st quarter	59.3	52.7	88.0	43.6	79.3	72.8	56.9	65.9	59.9	52.7	88.0	43.6	79.3	72.8	56.1	65.5
2nd quarter	59.6	53.0	88.3	43.7	78.5	72.9	58.4	66.6	60.1	53.0	88.3	43.7	78.5	72.9	57.9	66.3
3rd quarter	59.8	53.4	88.5	44.1	78.6	73.2	58.9	67.0	60.3	53.4	88.5	44.1	78.6	73.2	58.6	66.8
4th quarter	59.9	53.4	88.5	44.8	79.0	74.2	58.5	67.4	60.4	53.4	88.5	44.8	79.0	74.2	58.0	67.2

Table 9-3B. Productivity and Related Data: Historical Data—*Continued*

(2012 = 100, seasonally adjusted.)

Year and quarter	Business sector								Nonfarm business sector							
	Output per hour of all persons	Output	Hours of all persons	Compensation per hour	Real compensation per hour	Unit labor costs	Unit nonlabor payments	Implicit price deflator	Output per hour of all persons	Output	Hours of all persons	Compensation per hour	Real compensation per hour	Unit labor costs	Unit nonlabor payments	Implicit price deflator
1990																
1st quarter	60.5	54.1	88.8	45.6	79.3	74.9	59.2	68.1	60.9	54.1	88.8	45.6	79.3	74.9	58.5	67.8
2nd quarter	60.9	54.2	88.4	46.5	80.1	75.9	59.3	68.8	61.3	54.2	88.4	46.5	80.1	75.9	58.8	68.5
3rd quarter	61.3	54.1	87.9	47.2	79.9	76.6	59.7	69.3	61.5	54.1	87.9	47.2	79.9	76.6	59.2	69.0
4th quarter	60.6	53.3	87.5	47.5	79.3	78.0	59.1	69.8	60.9	53.3	87.5	47.5	79.3	78.0	58.8	69.7
1991																
1st quarter	60.7	53.0	86.7	47.8	79.3	78.2	60.2	70.4	61.1	53.0	86.7	47.8	79.3	78.2	60.0	70.3
2nd quarter	61.7	53.5	86.2	48.7	80.5	78.5	60.8	70.8	62.1	53.5	86.2	48.7	80.5	78.5	60.6	70.7
3rd quarter	62.2	53.9	86.1	49.3	80.9	78.7	61.4	71.2	62.6	53.9	86.1	49.3	80.9	78.7	61.3	71.2
4th quarter	62.5	54.0	85.9	50.0	81.4	79.4	61.3	71.5	62.9	54.0	85.9	50.0	81.4	79.4	61.0	71.4
1992																
1st quarter	63.9	54.8	85.4	51.2	83.1	79.9	61.1	71.6	64.2	54.8	85.4	51.2	83.1	79.9	60.7	71.5
2nd quarter	64.4	55.5	85.7	51.7	83.3	79.9	61.8	71.9	64.7	55.5	85.7	51.7	83.3	79.9	61.3	71.8
3rd quarter	65.0	56.1	85.9	52.3	83.7	80.1	62.3	72.2	65.3	56.1	85.9	52.3	83.7	80.1	61.8	72.2
4th quarter	65.4	56.8	86.4	52.6	83.6	80.1	63.4	72.7	65.7	56.8	86.4	52.6	83.6	80.1	63.2	72.7
1993																
1st quarter	63.9	56.8	87.2	52.2	82.5	80.2	64.1	73.2	65.1	56.8	87.2	52.2	82.5	80.2	64.2	73.2
2nd quarter	64.4	57.1	88.2	52.6	82.5	81.3	63.8	73.6	64.7	57.1	88.2	52.6	82.5	81.3	63.8	73.7
3rd quarter	65.0	57.7	88.7	52.6	82.3	80.9	64.7	74.0	65.0	57.7	88.7	52.6	82.3	80.9	64.7	73.9
4th quarter	65.4	58.4	89.5	53.0	82.3	81.2	65.5	74.4	65.3	58.4	89.5	53.0	82.3	81.2	65.2	74.3
1994																
1st quarter	65.2	59.0	90.1	52.7	81.6	80.5	67.0	74.6	65.5	59.0	90.1	52.7	81.6	80.5	66.8	74.5
2nd quarter	65.1	60.0	91.6	53.1	81.8	81.1	66.9	74.9	65.5	60.0	91.6	53.1	81.8	81.1	66.8	74.9
3rd quarter	64.8	60.4	92.6	53.1	81.2	81.5	67.3	75.3	65.1	60.4	92.6	53.1	81.2	81.5	67.3	75.3
4th quarter	65.4	61.2	93.0	53.5	81.4	81.3	68.3	75.6	65.8	61.2	93.0	53.5	81.4	81.3	68.5	75.7
1995																
1st quarter	65.3	61.6	93.5	53.9	81.4	81.7	68.2	76.0	65.9	61.6	93.5	53.9	81.4	81.7	68.6	76.0
2nd quarter	65.5	61.8	93.3	54.3	81.5	82.0	68.6	76.3	66.2	61.8	93.3	54.3	81.5	82.0	69.0	76.4
3rd quarter	65.5	62.5	94.4	54.6	81.5	82.5	68.8	76.6	66.2	62.5	94.4	54.6	81.5	82.5	69.0	76.6
4th quarter	66.0	63.0	94.6	55.0	81.8	82.7	69.1	76.9	66.6	63.0	94.6	55.0	81.8	82.7	69.1	76.8
1996																
1st quarter	66.5	63.5	94.8	55.6	82.1	83.1	69.5	77.2	67.0	63.5	94.8	55.6	82.1	83.1	69.2	77.0
2nd quarter	67.2	64.7	95.7	56.2	82.1	83.0	70.5	77.6	67.6	64.7	95.7	56.2	82.1	83.0	69.9	77.3
3rd quarter	67.5	65.5	96.5	56.6	82.4	83.4	70.3	77.7	67.9	65.5	96.5	56.6	82.4	83.4	70.1	77.6
4th quarter	67.6	66.3	97.6	56.9	82.2	83.8	70.7	78.1	67.9	66.3	97.6	56.9	82.2	83.8	70.5	78.0
1997																
1st quarter	67.4	66.7	98.4	57.6	82.6	84.9	70.4	78.6	67.8	66.7	98.4	57.6	82.6	84.9	70.1	78.5
2nd quarter	68.5	68.0	98.9	58.1	83.2	84.5	71.2	78.6	68.8	68.0	98.9	58.1	83.2	84.5	71.3	78.7
3rd quarter	69.1	69.0	99.5	58.7	83.7	84.6	71.7	78.9	69.4	69.0	99.5	58.7	83.7	84.6	71.8	79.0
4th quarter	69.5	69.7	99.9	59.7	84.7	85.7	70.6	79.1	69.7	69.7	99.9	59.7	84.7	85.7	70.7	79.2
1998																
1st quarter	69.9	70.5	100.6	60.7	86.0	86.6	69.5	79.1	70.1	70.5	100.6	60.7	86.0	86.6	69.6	79.2
2nd quarter	70.2	71.3	101.1	61.5	86.9	87.2	68.7	79.2	70.5	71.3	101.1	61.5	86.9	87.2	69.0	79.3
3rd quarter	71.2	72.3	101.2	62.5	87.9	87.5	68.9	79.4	71.5	72.3	101.2	62.5	87.9	87.5	69.2	79.5
4th quarter	71.8	73.8	102.5	62.9	88.1	87.3	69.1	79.4	72.0	73.8	102.5	62.9	88.1	87.3	69.3	79.5
1999																
1st quarter	72.9	74.6	102.3	64.0	89.3	87.7	68.9	79.5	73.0	74.6	102.3	64.0	89.3	87.7	69.2	79.6
2nd quarter	73.0	75.3	102.9	64.2	89.0	87.8	69.0	79.6	73.1	75.3	102.9	64.2	89.0	87.8	69.5	79.9
3rd quarter	73.7	76.5	103.5	64.8	89.1	87.8	69.4	79.8	73.8	76.5	103.5	64.8	89.1	87.8	70.1	80.1
4th quarter	74.8	77.9	104.0	66.1	90.2	88.2	69.7	80.1	75.0	77.9	104.0	66.1	90.2	88.2	70.4	80.5
2000																
1st quarter	74.7	78.4	104.9	68.2	92.1	91.3	66.4	80.4	74.8	78.2	104.6	68.4	92.4	91.4	66.9	80.7
2nd quarter	76.2	80.1	105.1	68.4	91.7	89.8	69.2	80.8	76.3	80.0	104.9	68.5	91.9	89.9	69.7	81.1
3rd quarter	76.2	80.1	105.1	69.7	92.6	91.5	67.9	81.2	76.3	80.0	104.8	69.9	92.8	91.6	68.5	81.5
4th quarter	77.1	80.7	104.6	70.2	92.6	91.0	69.2	81.5	77.1	80.5	104.5	70.3	92.7	91.1	69.7	81.8
2001																
1st quarter	76.8	80.2	104.5	71.8	93.8	93.6	66.9	81.9	76.7	80.1	104.4	71.9	93.9	93.6	67.4	82.2
2nd quarter	78.0	80.7	103.5	72.2	93.6	92.5	69.2	82.3	78.0	80.7	103.4	72.1	93.6	92.4	69.7	82.6
3rd quarter	78.5	80.2	102.2	72.3	93.5	92.2	70.0	82.5	78.5	80.1	102.1	72.2	93.4	92.0	70.5	82.7
4th quarter	79.5	80.4	101.1	72.9	94.4	91.7	70.6	82.5	79.5	80.2	101.0	72.9	94.4	91.7	71.3	82.9
2002																
1st quarter	80.9	81.2	100.3	73.2	94.4	90.4	72.5	82.6	81.2	81.3	100.1	73.2	94.5	90.2	73.2	82.8
2nd quarter	81.3	81.7	100.5	73.8	94.5	90.9	72.3	82.7	81.3	81.6	100.3	73.9	94.6	90.9	73.2	83.2
3rd quarter	82.0	82.1	100.1	74.2	94.5	90.5	73.3	83.0	81.9	81.9	100.0	74.3	94.6	90.6	74.0	83.4
4th quarter	81.9	82.2	100.3	74.4	94.2	90.8	73.7	83.3	81.9	82.0	100.1	74.4	94.3	90.9	74.3	83.7
2003																
1st quarter	82.8	82.6	99.8	74.9	93.8	90.4	74.8	83.6	82.7	82.4	99.6	74.9	93.9	90.5	75.5	84.0
2nd quarter	84.1	83.5	99.2	76.3	95.8	90.8	74.6	83.7	83.8	83.2	99.3	76.2	95.7	90.9	75.2	84.1
3rd quarter	85.7	85.3	99.6	77.3	96.3	90.2	76.1	84.1	85.7	85.2	99.5	77.3	96.4	90.3	76.5	84.3
4th quarter	86.4	86.5	100.1	78.3	97.2	90.7	76.3	84.4	86.5	86.5	100.0	78.4	97.3	90.7	76.5	84.5
2004																
1st quarter	86.4	86.8	100.4	78.3	96.4	90.6	78.3	85.2	86.2	86.5	100.4	78.3	96.3	90.8	78.3	85.4
2nd quarter	87.1	87.5	100.5	79.8	97.4	91.7	78.3	85.8	87.0	87.4	100.4	79.8	97.4	91.7	78.2	85.8
3rd quarter	87.5	88.5	101.2	81.2	98.5	92.8	77.8	86.2	87.4	88.3	101.1	81.2	98.5	92.9	77.9	86.4
4th quarter	88.2	89.5	101.4	81.8	98.2	92.7	79.6	87.0	87.8	89.2	101.6	81.6	97.9	92.9	79.8	87.2

Table 9-3B. Productivity and Related Data: Historical Data—*Continued*

(2012 = 100, seasonally adjusted.)

Year and quarter	Business sector								Nonfarm business sector							
	Output per hour of all persons	Output	Hours of all persons	Compensation per hour	Real compensation per hour	Unit labor costs	Unit nonlabor payments	Implicit price deflator	Output per hour of all persons	Output	Hours of all persons	Compensation per hour	Real compensation per hour	Unit labor costs	Unit nonlabor payments	Implicit price deflator
2005																
1st quarter	89.1	90.6	101.7	82.3	98.2	92.3	81.6	87.6	88.8	90.4	101.8	82.1	98.1	92.5	82.0	87.9
2nd quarter	88.7	91.0	102.5	82.6	97.9	93.0	82.2	88.3	88.6	90.8	102.4	82.6	98.0	93.2	82.6	88.6
3rd quarter	89.5	91.9	102.8	83.6	97.7	93.5	83.5	89.1	89.3	91.7	102.7	83.6	97.8	93.7	84.0	89.5
4th quarter	89.7	92.6	103.2	84.3	97.5	93.9	84.5	89.8	89.4	92.4	103.3	84.2	97.4	94.2	85.1	90.2
2006																
1st quarter	90.3	94.1	104.2	86.0	99.0	95.2	84.1	90.3	90.0	93.9	104.4	85.8	98.9	95.4	84.8	90.8
2nd quarter	90.2	94.3	104.6	85.9	98.1	95.3	85.5	91.0	89.9	94.1	104.7	85.9	98.0	95.6	86.2	91.5
3rd quarter	89.9	94.5	105.1	86.1	97.3	95.8	86.0	91.5	89.6	94.3	105.2	86.0	97.3	96.0	86.7	92.0
4th quarter	90.6	95.5	105.5	87.5	99.4	96.7	85.2	91.6	90.4	95.4	105.5	87.6	99.4	96.8	85.8	92.0
2007																
1st quarter	90.9	95.8	105.5	89.8	100.9	98.8	84.3	92.5	90.7	95.7	105.5	89.7	100.9	98.9	84.7	92.8
2nd quarter	91.2	96.5	105.8	89.9	99.9	98.5	86.1	93.1	91.0	96.5	106.0	89.6	99.7	98.5	86.6	93.3
3rd quarter	92.1	97.1	105.4	90.3	99.7	98.0	87.7	93.5	91.9	97.1	105.7	90.0	99.4	97.9	88.2	93.7
4th quarter	92.8	97.6	105.2	91.1	99.5	98.2	88.0	93.8	92.7	97.6	105.3	91.0	99.3	98.2	88.2	93.9
2008																
1st quarter	92.1	96.6	104.9	92.0	99.4	99.9	86.3	94.0	91.9	96.6	105.0	91.9	99.2	100.0	86.4	94.1
2nd quarter	93.0	97.1	104.3	92.2	98.2	99.1	88.5	94.4	92.9	97.0	104.4	92.1	98.1	99.1	88.7	94.6
3rd quarter	93.2	96.2	103.2	93.0	97.6	99.8	89.1	95.1	93.1	96.2	103.3	92.9	97.5	99.8	89.5	95.3
4th quarter	92.7	93.4	100.7	93.9	100.8	101.3	87.2	95.1	92.6	93.2	100.7	93.8	100.8	101.4	87.8	95.5
2009																
1st quarter	93.6	91.9	98.1	91.5	99.0	97.7	91.8	95.1	93.4	91.7	98.2	91.4	98.9	97.9	92.8	95.7
2nd quarter	95.5	91.7	96.0	93.7	100.8	98.1	90.3	94.7	95.4	91.5	95.9	93.7	100.8	98.3	91.2	95.2
3rd quarter	96.9	92.1	95.1	94.3	100.6	97.3	91.4	94.7	96.6	91.8	95.0	94.2	100.5	97.5	92.3	95.2
4th quarter	98.5	93.3	94.8	94.9	100.5	96.4	93.3	95.0	98.2	93.1	94.8	94.8	100.4	96.6	93.9	95.4
2010																
1st quarter	98.9	93.7	94.8	94.3	99.6	95.4	95.5	95.4	98.7	93.6	94.8	94.3	99.6	95.5	96.2	95.8
2nd quarter	99.0	94.8	95.8	95.1	100.6	96.1	95.5	95.8	98.8	94.6	95.7	95.2	100.6	96.3	96.1	96.2
3rd quarter	99.6	95.8	96.3	95.6	100.8	96.0	96.0	96.0	99.4	95.6	96.3	95.6	100.8	96.2	96.6	96.4
4th quarter	99.9	96.5	96.6	96.1	100.4	96.1	97.3	96.6	99.8	96.4	96.6	96.1	100.5	96.3	97.5	96.8
2011																
1st quarter	99.2	96.0	96.8	97.8	101.1	98.5	95.7	97.3	99.1	95.9	96.7	97.9	101.3	98.8	95.4	97.3
2nd quarter	99.3	96.9	97.6	97.1	99.3	97.8	98.0	97.9	99.2	96.9	97.6	97.2	99.4	98.0	97.9	97.9
3rd quarter	98.9	96.9	98.0	97.8	99.4	98.9	98.2	98.6	98.8	96.9	98.0	97.9	99.5	99.1	97.9	98.6
4th quarter	99.6	98.4	98.7	96.6	97.7	96.9	101.3	98.8	99.5	98.2	98.7	96.6	97.7	97.1	101.3	98.9
2012																
1st quarter	99.9	99.5	99.6	98.9	99.4	98.9	99.7	99.3	99.9	99.4	99.5	98.9	99.5	99.0	99.7	99.3
2nd quarter	100.2	100.0	99.8	99.3	99.7	99.1	100.5	99.7	100.3	100.0	99.7	99.4	99.8	99.1	100.6	99.8
3rd quarter	100.1	100.2	100.1	99.5	99.4	99.5	101.3	100.3	100.1	100.2	100.1	99.5	99.4	99.4	101.3	100.3
4th quarter	99.8	100.3	100.5	102.3	101.5	102.5	98.4	100.7	99.8	100.4	100.6	102.1	101.4	102.4	98.3	100.6
2013																
1st quarter	100.7	101.5	100.8	100.9	99.7	100.2	102.0	101.0	100.4	101.4	101.0	100.7	99.5	100.3	101.5	100.8
2nd quarter	100.5	101.7	101.2	101.6	100.5	101.2	101.2	101.2	100.0	101.4	101.4	101.4	100.3	101.4	100.7	101.1
3rd quarter	100.8	102.7	101.9	101.3	99.6	100.5	103.1	101.6	100.4	102.4	102.0	101.2	99.5	100.7	102.8	101.6
4th quarter	101.6	103.8	102.2	102.0	99.9	100.4	104.3	102.1	101.2	103.6	102.3	101.9	99.8	100.6	104.4	102.3
2014																
1st quarter	100.7	103.3	102.6	104.0	101.3	103.3	101.5	102.5	100.3	103.1	102.8	103.9	101.1	103.6	101.5	102.7
2nd quarter	101.6	105.1	103.4	103.5	100.2	101.9	104.7	103.1	101.3	104.9	103.5	103.4	100.1	102.1	104.6	103.2
3rd quarter	102.4	106.7	104.3	104.0	100.4	101.6	105.9	103.5	102.2	106.5	104.3	104.1	100.5	101.8	106.0	103.6
4th quarter	101.8	107.5	105.5	105.0	101.7	103.1	103.9	103.4	101.7	107.3	105.4	105.2	101.8	103.4	104.0	103.7
2015																
1st quarter	102.9	108.7	105.7	106.3	103.6	103.4	102.8	103.1	102.7	108.5	105.6	106.6	103.8	103.7	103.2	103.5
2nd quarter	103.3	109.6	106.1	107.3	103.8	103.8	103.4	103.6	103.1	109.4	106.0	107.4	104.0	104.2	103.8	104.0
3rd quarter	103.3	110.0	106.5	107.6	103.7	104.1	103.6	103.9	103.1	109.8	106.4	107.8	103.9	104.5	104.0	104.3
4th quarter	102.9	110.1	107.0	107.5	103.6	104.5	102.8	103.8	102.7	109.9	106.9	107.8	103.9	104.9	103.3	104.2
2016																
1st quarter	103.2	110.8	107.4	107.6	103.7	104.2	102.7	103.6	103.0	110.5	107.3	107.8	104.0	104.6	103.5	104.1
2nd quarter	103.1	111.2	107.9	107.8	103.1	104.6	104.1	104.4	102.9	110.8	107.7	108.1	103.4	105.0	104.8	104.9
3rd quarter	103.4	111.9	108.2	108.3	103.1	104.7	104.6	104.7	103.3	111.5	108.0	108.6	103.4	105.1	105.5	105.3
4th quarter	104.4	112.8	108.0	109.8	103.9	105.1	105.1	105.1	104.0	112.5	108.1	109.7	103.9	105.5	106.1	105.8
2017																
1st quarter	104.5	113.4	108.6	110.7	104.1	105.9	105.2	105.6	104.2	113.1	108.5	110.8	104.2	106.3	105.9	106.2
2nd quarter	104.2	114.0	109.4	111.2	104.4	106.8	104.7	105.9	104.0	113.7	109.3	111.4	104.6	107.2	105.4	106.4
3rd quarter	105.1	115.0	109.4	112.7	105.3	107.3	105.3	106.4	104.8	114.8	109.5	112.8	105.4	107.6	106.1	107.0
4th quarter	105.5	116.3	110.3	114.2	105.9	108.3	105.5	107.1	105.3	116.1	110.3	114.4	106.1	108.7	106.2	107.6
2018																
1st quarter	106.1	117.6	110.9	115.0	105.7	108.4	106.6	107.6	105.8	117.3	110.9	115.1	105.8	108.8	107.4	108.2
2nd quarter	106.4	118.5	111.4	115.3	105.4	108.4	108.7	108.5	106.0	118.2	111.5	115.4	105.5	108.9	109.5	109.1
3rd quarter	106.6	119.1	111.8	116.6	106.2	109.4	108.1	108.9	106.3	118.9	111.8	116.8	106.4	109.9	109.0	109.5
4th quarter	106.7	119.6	112.0	117.1	106.2	109.7	108.7	109.3	106.4	119.3	112.1	117.3	106.3	110.2	109.5	109.9

Table 9-4. Corporate Profits with Inventory Valuation Adjustment by Industry Group, NAICS Basis

(Billions of dollars, quarterly data are at seasonally adjusted annual rates.)   NIPA Table 6.16D

Year and quarter	Total	Domestic industries			Nonfinancial		Manufacturing						
		Financial						Durable goods					
		Total	Federal Reserve banks	Other financial	Total	Utilities	Total	Fabricated metal products	Machinery	Computer and electronic products	Electrical equipment, appliances, and components	Motor vehicles, bodies and trailers, and parts	Other durable goods
2002	797.4	640.6	23.5	241.9	375.3	10.5	78.3	9.9	2.9	-25.0	-0.8	-3.1	19.5
2003	955.7	796.7	20.0	282.7	494.0	13.2	123.9	8.9	2.8	-6.1	2.7	7.9	15.5
2004	1 217.5	1 022.4	20.0	326.0	676.3	21.1	186.2	12.6	8.3	1.2	0.4	-4.6	35.2
2005	1 629.2	1 403.4	26.5	383.0	993.9	32.4	279.7	19.0	16.4	15.5	-0.6	1.6	61.4
2006	1 812.2	1 572.5	33.8	379.3	1 159.4	55.2	352.9	19.3	20.8	28.5	11.7	-6.9	67.6
2007	1 708.3	1 370.5	36.0	264.2	1 070.3	49.6	321.1	21.4	23.4	24.3	-0.7	-16.3	67.1
2008	1 344.5	954.3	35.1	59.5	859.7	30.4	240.0	15.7	18.0	27.7	5.0	-39.2	39.5
2009	1 470.1	1 121.3	47.3	315.3	758.7	23.4	164.7	11.8	9.6	27.1	9.2	-54.8	33.0
2010	1 786.4	1 400.6	71.6	334.3	994.8	30.6	281.8	15.4	17.3	48.4	10.1	-10.9	43.4
2011	1 750.2	1 337.7	76.0	302.4	959.3	10.2	296.0	16.5	25.8	37.8	4.9	-0.3	49.7
2012	2 144.7	1 739.3	71.7	410.6	1 256.9	13.8	403.0	24.0	33.5	52.9	12.0	23.0	60.1
2013	2 165.9	1 767.1	79.7	351.1	1 336.3	28.3	446.9	25.3	36.5	58.7	20.4	21.5	66.6
2014	2 266.6	1 861.7	103.5	379.6	1 378.6	32.8	458.7	24.1	35.5	60.3	14.2	32.0	68.1
2015	2 184.6	1 789.4	100.7	346.5	1 342.1	20.2	427.2	25.0	24.3	68.4	24.1	26.8	66.1
2016	2 138.8	1 718.9	92.0	365.4	1 261.5	9.4	336.8	23.9	19.1	50.8	5.7	29.6	65.7
2017	2 147.9	1 649.0	78.2	357.4	1 213.3	14.0	316.8	22.6	23.0	50.5	6.3	13.3	63.9
2018	2 211.3	1 689.6	68.0	382.3	1 239.3	22.0	346.7	19.5	15.7	65.1	11.3	-2.3	69.1
2019	2 254.6	1 741.2	64.1	469.0	1 208.0	7.7	355.7	21.9	25.8	61.9	4.3	4.5	65.0
2020	2 165.9	1 711.2	92.9	409.6	1 208.7	10.4	328.8	22.7	27.9	67.0	6.6	5.6	58.9
2021	2 753.8	2 262.3	113.9	460.3	1 688.1	18.3	477.1	23.6	30.3	99.3	5.1	-7.7	96.0
2020													
1st quarter	2 081.9	1 602.8	81.6	404.5	1 116.8	0.6	340.9	24.1	24.4	64.4	2.3	7.9	57.6
2nd quarter	1 864.0	1 455.7	89.7	410.9	955.1	11.1	246.9	11.5	18.4	63.4	6.3	6.6	26.8
3rd quarter	2 360.5	1 906.0	106.1	396.4	1 403.6	10.4	362.3	27.2	36.4	63.0	10.4	8.9	76.4
4th quarter	2 357.2	1 880.1	94.4	426.6	1 359.1	19.6	365.3	27.7	32.3	77.0	7.2	-1.1	74.8
2021													
1st quarter	2 461.8	1 995.4	83.9	436.0	1 475.6	20.9	401.9	26.6	32.5	93.1	7.1	-3.0	78.4
2nd quarter	2 747.7	2 287.6	114.4	462.5	1 710.7	11.9	450.5	25.3	33.1	97.8	4.0	-10.7	98.6
3rd quarter	2 873.9	2 362.6	128.7	468.8	1 765.1	20.4	500.4	13.4	20.2	111.7	5.3	-14.3	103.7
4th quarter	2 931.6	2 403.5	128.5	473.8	1 801.2	19.9	555.6	28.9	35.4	94.4	4.0	-2.7	103.2

Year and quarter	Domestic industries—Continued										Rest of the world, net
	Nonfinancial—Continued										
	Manufacturing—Continued										
	Nondurable goods					Wholesale trade	Retail trade	Transportation and warehousing	Information	Other nonfinancial	
	Total	Food and beverage and tobacco products	Petroleum and coal products	Chemical products	Other nondurable goods						
2002	74.9	26.7	4.8	30.7	12.8	53.5	83.3	-6.5	5.0	151.2	156.8
2003	92.3	25.6	26.7	31.8	8.1	56.6	87.9	4.4	28.1	179.9	158.9
2004	133.0	26.2	50.8	39.4	16.6	72.7	94.0	12.0	61.6	228.8	195.1
2005	166.3	29.2	80.0	36.2	20.9	96.0	123.3	28.4	100.7	333.5	225.7
2006	211.8	34.6	82.0	68.8	26.4	105.0	133.6	40.8	115.2	356.8	239.7
2007	201.9	31.3	76.1	70.8	23.7	102.8	119.4	23.3	120.5	333.6	337.8
2008	173.3	31.5	85.0	51.5	5.3	92.7	82.2	29.3	98.8	286.3	390.2
2009	128.9	45.0	10.4	55.2	18.2	88.9	107.9	21.7	87.0	265.1	348.8
2010	158.1	45.1	26.2	63.4	23.5	99.3	115.9	44.6	102.3	320.4	385.8
2011	161.6	40.0	47.5	53.2	20.9	97.2	115.1	30.6	95.7	314.5	412.6
2012	197.5	44.7	57.7	63.5	31.5	137.9	155.7	54.4	112.0	380.1	405.4
2013	217.8	55.6	53.9	75.0	33.3	146.4	153.3	45.2	137.6	378.6	398.8
2014	224.5	58.3	65.5	72.2	28.4	150.6	157.3	55.7	126.6	397.0	404.9
2015	192.6	69.0	19.6	65.5	38.4	152.4	169.3	61.0	135.5	376.4	395.2
2016	141.9	69.2	-30.4	64.7	38.4	127.9	175.2	64.6	157.8	389.8	419.9
2017	137.3	60.4	-5.1	55.7	26.3	123.3	149.6	59.4	139.1	411.2	498.9
2018	168.3	50.6	31.5	55.0	31.2	114.5	148.1	48.6	140.3	419.1	521.7
2019	172.3	55.2	16.7	68.0	32.4	117.8	159.1	37.6	127.8	402.3	513.4
2020	140.4	74.8	-37.9	74.6	29.0	123.7	218.5	19.2	134.9	373.1	454.7
2021	230.6	89.4	2.8	99.3	39.1	141.5	281.8	48.3	171.4	549.9	491.5
2020											
1st quarter	160.3	65.4	1.2	69.8	23.9	131.9	171.2	22.8	126.5	322.9	479.1
2nd quarter	113.8	76.2	-45.6	70.3	13.0	101.4	209.7	6.5	112.0	267.6	408.3
3rd quarter	140.0	78.7	-55.6	78.6	38.3	125.4	250.2	22.7	143.4	489.2	454.5
4th quarter	147.3	78.7	-51.7	79.6	40.7	136.2	242.9	24.8	157.7	412.5	477.0
2021											
1st quarter	167.2	79.3	-21.0	72.9	36.0	112.6	280.2	34.5	161.0	464.4	466.4
2nd quarter	202.3	75.1	2.7	90.7	33.8	137.6	307.6	64.4	175.5	563.3	460.2
3rd quarter	260.4	101.3	11.2	107.7	40.1	155.4	270.2	47.4	176.8	594.5	511.3
4th quarter	292.5	102.0	18.2	125.9	46.5	160.4	269.1	46.7	172.4	577.1	528.0

NOTES AND DEFINITIONS, CHAPTER 9

General note on data on compensation per hour

This chapter includes two data series with similar names—the Employment Cost Index for total compensation and the *Index of Compensation* per hour—that often display different behavior. Both are compiled and published by the Bureau of Labor Statistics (BLS), but the definitions, sources, and methods of compilation are different. Users should be aware of these differences and of the consequent differences in the appropriate uses and interpretations for each of the two series.

The *Employment Cost Index (ECI)* (Tables 9-1 and 9-2) measures changes in hourly compensation for "all civilian workers", which is not quite as broad as it sounds, as it excludes federal government workers, farm workers, and private household workers. Indexes are also published for subgroups including state and local workers, "all private industry" (again excluding farm and private household workers), and a number of industry and occupational subgroups.

The Employment Cost Index (ECI) data from the National Compensation Survey (NCS) are used for a variety of reasons, by both the private and public sectors. Some examples include: military pay adjustments, federal pay adjustments, Medicare reimbursement adjustments, contract escalator clauses, labor cost adjustments, and collective bargaining negotiations.

The ECI is calculated and published separately for *total compensation* and for the two components of hourly compensation, *wages and salaries* and the employer cost of employee *benefits*. It is constructed by analogy with the Consumer Price Index (CPI); that is, it holds the composition of employment constant in order to isolate hourly compensation trends that take place for individual occupations, which are then aggregated, using fixed relative importance weights. The ECI is based on a sample survey and may be revised from time to time, due to updated classification, weighting, and seasonal adjustments. However, it is not subject to major benchmark revision of the underlying wage, salary, and benefit rate observations. By design, it excludes any representation of employee stock options. As it is based on a sample survey, the ECI is measured "from the bottom up," aggregating from individual employers' reports to higher levels. The ECI is frequently and appropriately used as the best available measure of the general trend of wages and of the extent of inflationary pressure exerted on prices by labor costs.

The *compensation per hour* component of the report on "Productivity and Costs" (Table 9-3) is calculated and published for total compensation in total business, nonfarm business, nonfinancial corporations, and manufacturing. The nonfarm business category is similar in scope to the "all private industry" category in the ECI. The measures in Table 9-3, however, are compiled "from the top down," starting with aggregate estimates of compensation

and hours, then dividing the former by the latter. Compensation per hour is affected by changes in the composition of employment. If the composition of employment shifts toward a larger proportion of higher-paid employees and/or industries, compensation per hour will rise even if there is no increase in hourly compensation for any individual worker.

In addition, *compensation per hour* includes the value of exercised stock options as expensed by companies. Also included are other transitory payments, many of which may be of little relevance to the typical worker or to ongoing production costs. These values are not reported immediately. Instead, they are incorporated when later, more comprehensive reports are received. This process can lead to dramatic revisions in compensation per hour and in the unit labor costs index, which is based on compensation. For example, the fourth-quarter 2004 increase in compensation per hour in nonfarm business was initially reported at an annual rate of 3.1 percent. Four months later, the reported rate for the same time period was 10.2 percent. The rate of increase from a year earlier was revised from 3.6 to 5.9 percent. According to then-Federal Reserve Chairman Alan Greenspan, in testimony before the Joint Economic Committee on June 9, 2005, this reflected "a large but apparently transitory surge in bonuses and the proceeds of stock option exercises," not a potentially inflationary acceleration in the rate of labor compensation increase. More recently, it was reported in August 2009 that "first-quarter unit labor costs were revised to negative 2.7% from positive 3%." (*Wall Street Journal,* August 12, 2009, p. A2.)

These characteristics suggest that *compensation per hour* should not be considered a reliable or appropriate indicator of wage or compensation trends for typical workers. It is useful in conjunction with the productivity series, because aggregate productivity is subject to the same composition shifts—higher-productivity industries also tend to have higher-paid employees. Hence, the measure of *unit labor costs* (derived by dividing compensation per hour by output per hour in this system) is not distorted when the composition of output shifts toward higher-productivity industries. The shift affects the numerator and denominator of the ratio similarly. However, both compensation and unit labor costs can still be distorted by transitory payments, such as those discussed above.

There are other, probably less important differences between the two measures. Compensation per hour refers to the entire quarter, while the ECI is observed in the terminal month of each quarter. Tips and other forms of compensation not provided by employers are included in hourly compensation but not in the ECI. The ECI excludes persons working for token wages, business owners and others who set their own wage, and family workers who do not earn a market wage; all of these workers are included in the productivity and cost accounts. Hourly compensation excludes employees of nonprofit institutions serving individuals—about

10 percent of private workers (mostly in education and medical care) who are within the scope of the ECI. Hourly compensation measures include an estimate for the unincorporated self-employed, who are assumed to earn the same hourly compensation as other employees in the sector. Implicitly, unpaid family workers also are included in the hourly compensation measures with the assumption that their hourly compensation is zero. Both of these groups are also excluded from the ECI.

Tables 9-1 and 9-2

Employment Cost Indexes

SOURCE: U.S. DEPARTMENT OF LABOR, BUREAU OF LABOR STATISTICS (BLS)

The Employment Cost Index (ECI) is a quarterly measure of the change in the cost of labor, independent of the influence of employment shifts among occupations and industries. It uses a fixed market basket of labor—similar in concept to the Consumer Price Index's fixed market basket of goods and services—to measure changes over time in employer costs of employing labor. Data are quarterly in all cases and are reported for the final month of each quarter. These measures are expressed as indexes, with the not-seasonally-adjusted value for December 2005 set at 100.

Care should be used in comparing the ECI with other data sets. The "all private industry" category in the ECI excludes farm and household workers (it is sometimes, and more precisely, called "private nonfarm industry"), and the "all civilian workers" category excludes federal government, farm, and household workers.

The data for 1979 through 2019, which are presented in Table 9-2 and are the official ECI measures for that time period, were based on the 1987 Standard Industrial Classification (SIC) and 2010 Occupational Classification System (OCS).

For over 60 years, the Standard Industrial Classification (SIC) system served as the structure for the collection, presentation, and analysis of the U.S. economy. The SIC system was developed in the 1930s at a time when manufacturing dominated the U.S. economy. Developments in information services, new forms of health care provision, expansion of services, and high-tech manufacturing are examples of industrial changes that could not be incorporated under the SIC system.

Currently the ECI is compiled based on the 2012 North American Industry Classification System (NAICS) and the 2010 Standard Occupational Classification Manual (SOC). These data, along with comparable data for 2004 through 2019, are shown in Table 9-1.

Developed in cooperation with Canada and Mexico, the North American Industry Classification System (NAICS) represents one of the most profound changes for statistical programs focusing on emerging economic activities. NAICS uses a production-oriented conceptual framework to group establishments into industries based on the activity in which they are primarily engaged. Establishments using similar raw material inputs, similar capital equipment, and similar labor are classified in the same industry. In other words, establishments that do similar things in similar ways are classified together. NAICS was introduced in 1997 and is periodically revised to reflect changes in the industrial structure of the U.S. and North American economy.

For certain broad categories shown in this volume—indicated by footnote 2 in Table 9-2—the old SIC categories are roughly comparable and continuous with the data for 2006 and subsequent years. (However, they differ slightly on overlap dates, and should be "linked" if a continuous time series is desired; see the article at the beginning of this volume.) Many of the new industry and occupational categories are not continuous with the old series shown here, and some of the old categories are not being continued because BLS finds them obsolete and no longer meaningful.

Definitions

Total compensation comprises wages, salaries, and the employer's costs for employee benefits. Excluded from wages and salaries and employee benefits are the value of stock option exercises and items such as payment-in-kind, free room and board, and tips.

Wages and salaries consists of straight-time earnings per hour before payroll deductions, including production bonuses, incentive earnings, commissions, and cost-of-living adjustments. These wage rates exclude premium pay for overtime and for work on weekends and holidays, shift differentials, and nonproduction bonuses such as lump-sum payments provided in lieu of wage increases. According to BLS, wages and salaries are about 70 percent of total compensation.

Benefits includes the cost to employers for paid leave—vacations, holidays, sick leave, and other leave; for supplemental pay—premium pay for work in addition to the regular work schedule (such as overtime, weekends, and holidays), shift differentials, and nonproduction bonuses (such as referral bonuses and lump-sum payments provided in lieu of wage increases); for insurance benefits—life, health, short-term disability, and long-term disability; for retirement and savings benefits—defined benefit and defined contribution plans; and for legally required benefits—Social Security, Medicare, federal and state unemployment insurance, and workers' compensation. Severance pay and supplemental unemployment benefit (SUB) plans are included in the data through December 2005 but were dropped beginning with the March 2006 data. The combined cost of these two benefits accounted for less than one-tenth of one percent of compensation, and according to BLS, dropping these benefits has had virtually no impact on the index. According to BLS, benefit costs are about 30 percent of total compensation.

Civilian workers are private industry workers, as defined below, and workers in state and local government. Federal workers are not included.

Private industry workers are paid workers in private industry excluding farms and private households. To be included in the ECI, employees in occupations must receive cash payments from the establishment for services performed and the establishment must pay the employer's portion of Medicare taxes on that individual's wages. Major exclusions from the survey are the self-employed, individuals who set their own pay (for example, proprietors, owners, major stockholders, and partners in unincorporated firms), volunteers, unpaid workers, family members being paid token wages, individuals receiving long-term disability compensation, and U.S. citizens working overseas.

Private industry workers excluding incentive paid occupations is a new category introduced in the 2006 revision to eliminate the quarter-to-quarter variability related to the way workers (for example, salespersons working on commission) are paid. (The category *private industry workers excluding sales occupations* was intended to serve a similar purpose in the previous SIC-based classification system, but was much less accurate in separately identifying workers with highly variable compensation.)

Goods-producing industries include mining, construction, and manufacturing.

Service-providing industries include the following NAICS industries: wholesale trade; retail trade; transportation and warehousing; utilities; information; finance and insurance; real estate and rental and leasing; professional, scientific, and technical services; management of companies and enterprises; administrative and support and waste management and remediation services; education services; health care and social assistance; arts, entertainment, and recreation; accommodation and food services; and other services, except public administration.

Notes on the data

Employee benefit costs are calculated as cents per hour worked.

The July 2019 data were collected from probability samples of approximately 25,600 occupational observations in about 6,300 sample establishments in private industry, and approximately 7800 occupations within about 1,400 establishments in state and local governments. The private industry sample is rotated over approximately five years. The state and local government sample is replaced less frequently; the latest sample was introduced in September 2007.

Currently, the sample establishments are classified in industry categories based on the NAICS. Within an establishment, specific job categories are selected and classified into approximately

800 occupational classifications according to the SOC. Similar procedures were followed under the previous classification systems. Data are collected each quarter for the pay periods including the 12th day of March, June, September, and December.

Aggregate indexes are calculated using fixed employment weights. Beginning with December 2013, estimates are based on 2012 employment weight, using Occupational Employment counts. From March 2006 through June 2018, ECI weights were based on fixed employment counts for 2012 from the BLS Occupational Employment Statistics survey. Employment data from the 2012 Survey were introduced in December 2013. ECI measures were based on 1990 employment counts from March 1995 through December 2005 and 1980 census employment counts from June 1986 through December 1994. Prior to June 1986, they were based on 1970 census employment counts.

Use of fixed weights ensures that changes in the indexes reflect only changes in hourly compensation, not employment shifts among industries or occupations with different levels of wages and compensation. This feature distinguishes the ECI from other compensation series such as average hourly earnings (see Chapter 10 and its notes and definitions) and the compensation per hour component of the productivity series (see Table 9-3 and its notes and definitions, and the general note above), each of which is affected by such employment shifts.

Data availability

Data for wages and salaries for the private nonfarm economy are available beginning with the data for 1975; data for compensation begin with the 1980 data. The series for state and local government and for the civilian nonfarm economy begin with the 1981 data. All series are available on the BLS Web site at <https://www.bls.gov>.

Wage and salary change and compensation cost change data also are available by major occupational and industry groups, as well as by region and collective bargaining status. Information on wage and salary change is available from 1975 to the present for most of these series. Compensation cost change data are available from 1980 to the present for most series. For 10 occupational and industry series, benefit cost change data are available from the early 1980s to the present. For state and local governments and the civilian economy (state and local governments plus private industry), wage and salary change and compensation cost change data are available for major occupational and industry series. BLS provides data for all these series from June 1981 to the present.

Updates are available about four weeks after the end of the reference quarter. Reference quarters end in March, June, September, and December. Seasonal adjustment factors and seasonally adjusted indexes are released in late April.

References

Explanatory notes, including references, are included in a Technical Note in each quarter's ECI news release, and can be found on the BLS Web site, in the PDF version of the release.

More detailed information on the ECI is available from Chapter 8, "National compensation measures," (www.bls.gov/opub/hom/pdf/homch8.pdf) from the BLS Handbook of Methods, and several articles published in the *Monthly Labor Review* and *Compensation and Working Conditions.* The articles and other descriptive pieces are available at www.bls.gov/ect/#publications, by calling (202) 691-6199, or sending e-mail to NCSinfo@bls.gov.

Table 9-3A and 9-3B

Productivity and Related Data

The indexes of productivity and costs for the entire postwar period, 1947 through 2019, have been revised to reflect the 2013 and 2014 comprehensive revisions of the National Income and Product Accounts (NIPAs).

Productivity is a measure of economic efficiency that shows how effectively economic inputs are converted into goods and services. Therefore, productivity measures relate real physical output to real input. They encompass a family of measures that includes single-factor input measures, such as output per unit of labor input or output per unit of capital input, as well as measures of multifactor productivity—that is, output per unit of combined labor and capital inputs. The indexes published in this book are indexes of labor productivity expressed in terms of output per hour of labor input. (A larger group of BLS productivity measures can be found in Bernan Press's *Handbook of U.S. Labor Statistics.*) All data are presented as indexes with a base of 2012 = 100.

Labor productivity is then the efficiency at which labor hours are utilized in producing output of goods and services, measured as output per hour of labor. (Also known as output per hour, or output per hour of all persons.)

Definitions

Current dollar output is the current-dollar value of the goods and services produced in the specified sector. *Output* is the constant-dollar value of the same goods and services, derived as current-dollar output divided by the sector *implicit price deflator* (the ratio of the current-dollar value of a series to its corresponding chained-dollar value, multiplied by 100.)

All these data are derived from components of the NIPAs; see Notes on the data below, and for general information on the NIPAs, see the Notes and Definitions to Chapter 1.

Output per hour of all persons (labor productivity) is the value of goods and services in constant dollars produced per hour of labor input. By definition, nonfinancial corporations include no self-employed persons. Productivity in this sector is expressed as *output per hour of all employees. Output per person* is output divided by the index for employment instead of by the index for hours of all persons.

Compensation is the total value of the wages and salaries of employees, plus employers' contributions for social insurance and private benefit plans, plus wages, salaries, and supplementary payments for the self-employed. *Compensation per hour* is compensation divided by *hours of all persons.* Included in compensation is the value of exercised stock options that companies report as a charge against earnings. Stock option values are reported with a delay; consequently, recent values are estimated based on extrapolation. They are revised to actual values when the data become available; sometimes the revisions are very large. The labor compensation of proprietors cannot be explicitly identified and must be estimated. This is done by assuming that proprietors have the same hourly compensation as employees in the same sector. The quarterly labor productivity and cost measures do not contain estimates of compensation for unpaid family workers.

Real compensation per hour is compensation per hour deflated by the Consumer Price Index Research Series (CPI-U-RS) for the period 1978 through 2019 (For current quarters, before the CPI-U-RS becomes available, changes in the CPI-U are used.) Changes in the Consumer Price Index for Urban Wage Earners and Clerical Workers (CPI-W) are used for data before 1978, as there was no CPI-U (or CPIU-RS) for that period. See the Notes and Definitions to Chapter 8 for explanation of the CPI-U, the CPI-W, and the CPI-U-RS.

Unit labor costs represent the cost of labor required to produce one unit of output. Unit labor costs also describe the relationship between compensation per hour worked (hourly compensation) and real output per hour worked (labor productivity). When hourly compensation growth outpaces productivity, units labor costs increase. Alternatively, when productivity growth exceeds hourly compensation, unit labor costs decrease.

Unit nonlabor payments include profits, depreciation, interest, rental income of persons, and indirect taxes per unit of output. They are computed by subtracting current-dollar compensation of all persons from current-dollar value of output, providing the data for the index of total *nonlabor payments,* which is then divided by output.

Unit nonlabor costs are available for nonfinancial corporations only. They contain all the components of unit nonlabor payments except unit profits (and rental income of persons, which is zero by definition for nonfinancial corporations).

Unit profits, the other component of unit nonlabor payments, are also only available for nonfinancial corporations.

Labor hours are measured as annual hours worked by all employed in an industry. Data on industry and hours come primarily from the BLS Current Employment Statistics (CES) survey and Current Population Survey (CPS). Definitions and data for these data sources are fund in Chapter 10.

Hours of all persons (labor input) consists of the total hours at work (*employment* multiplied by *average weekly hours*) of payroll workers, self-employed persons, and unpaid family workers. For the nonfinancial corporations data, there are no self-employed persons; the data represent *employee hours*.

Labor share is the total dollar amount of labor compensation divided by the total current-dollar value of output.

Notes on the data

Output for the business sector is equal to constant-dollar gross domestic product minus: the rental value of owner-occupied dwellings, the output of nonprofit institutions, the output of paid employees of private households, and general government output. The measures are derived from national income and product account (NIPA) data supplied by the U.S. Department of Commerce's Bureau of Economic Analysis (BEA). For manufacturing, BLS produces annual estimates of sectoral output. Quarterly manufacturing output indexes derived from the Federal Reserve Board of Governors' monthly indexes of industrial production (see Chapter 2) are adjusted to these annual measures by the BLS, and are also used to project the quarterly values in the current period.

Nonfinancial corporate output consists of business output minus unincorporated businesses and those corporations classified as offices of bank holding companies, offices of other holding companies, or offices in the finance and insurance sector.. Unit profits and unit nonlabor costs can be calculated separately for this sector and are shown in this table.

Compensation and hours data are developed from BLS and BEA data. The primary source for hours and employment is BLS's Current Employment Statistics (CES) program (see the notes and definitions for Chapter 10). Other data sources are the Current Population Survey (CPS) and the National Compensation Survey (NCS). Weekly paid hours are adjusted to hours at work using the NCS. For paid employees, hours at work differ from hours paid, in that they exclude paid vacation and holidays, paid sick leave, and other paid personal or administrative leave.

Although the labor productivity measures relate output to labor input, they do not measure the contribution of labor or any other specific factor of production. Instead, they reflect the joint effect of many influences, including changes in technology; capital investment; level of output; utilization of capacity, energy, and materials; the organization of production; managerial skill; and the characteristics and efforts of the work force.

Revisions

Data for recent years are revised frequently to take account of revisions in the output and labor input measures that underlie the estimates. Customarily, all revisions to source data are reflected in the release following the source data revision. Data in this volume were released July 30, 2019, and reflect the midyear 2017 revisions to the NIPAs and all revisions in labor input and compensation available up to that release date, including the annual benchmark revision of the CES and updated seasonal factors.

Data availability

Series are available quarterly and annually. Quarterly measures are based entirely on seasonally adjusted data. For some detailed manufacturing series (not shown here), only annual averages are available. Productivity indexes are published early in the second and third months of each quarter, reflecting new data for preceding quarters. Complete historical data are available on the BLS Web site at <https://www.bls.gov>.

BLS also publishes productivity estimates for a number of individual industries. A release entitled "Productivity and Costs by Industry" is available on the BLS Web site at <https://www.bls.gov>.

References

Further information is available in the Technical Notes and footnotes on the most current monthly release, available on the Web site, and from the following sources: Chapter 10, "Productivity Measures: Business Sector and Major Subsectors," *BLS Handbook of Methods*—Bulletin 2490 (April 1997) and the following *Monthly Labor Review* articles: "Alternative Measures of Supervisory Employee Hours and Productivity Growth" (April 2004); "Possible Measurement Bias in Aggregate Productivity Growth" (February 1999); "Improvements to the Quarterly Productivity Measures" (October 1995); "Hours of Work: A New Base for BLS Productivity Statistics" (February 1990); and "New Sector Definitions for Productivity Series" (October 1976).

Table 9-4

Corporate Profits with Inventory Valuation Adjustment by Industry Group

SOURCE: U.S. DEPARTMENT OF COMMERCE, BUREAU OF ECONOMIC ANALYSIS

Corporate profits is one of the most closely watched U.S. economic indicator. Profitability provides a summary measure of corporate financial health and thus serves as an essential indicator of economic performance. Profits are a source of retained earnings, providing much of the funding for capital investments that raise productive capacity. The estimates of profits and of related measures may also be used to evaluate the effects on corporations of changes in policy or in economic conditions.

Corporate profits represents the portion of the total income earned from current production that is accounted for by U.S. corporations. The estimates of corporate profits are an integral part of the national income and product accounts (NIPAs), a set of accounts prepared by the Bureau of Economic Analysis (BEA) that provides a logical and consistent framework for presenting statistics on U.S. economic activity.

These profits measures are derived from the NIPAs and classified according to the NAICS. See the notes and definitions to Chapter 1 for definitions, data availability, and references. Note that this industry breakdown of profits incorporates the inventory valuation adjustment (IVA), which eliminates any capital gain element in profits arising from changes in the prices at which inventories are valued, but does <u>not</u> incorporate the capital consumption adjustment (CCAdj), which adjusts historical costs of fixed capital to replacement costs and uses actual rather than tax-based service lives. This is because the CCAdj is calculated by BEA at an aggregate level, whereas the IVA is calculated at an industry level.

CHAPTER 10: EMPLOYMENT, HOURS, AND EARNINGS

SECTION 10A: LABOR FORCE, EMPLOYMENT, AND UNEMPLOYMENT

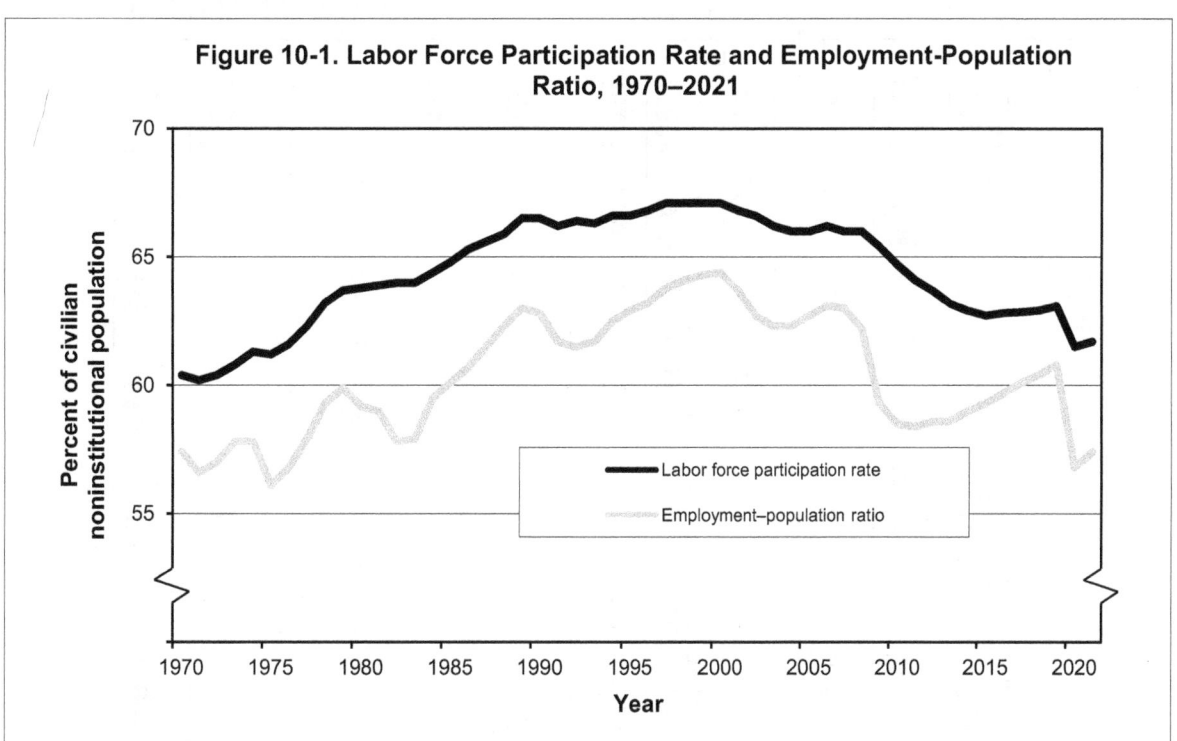

Figure 10-1. Labor Force Participation Rate and Employment-Population Ratio, 1970–2021

- The National Bureau of Economic Research (NBER) announced on July 19, 2021 that the 2020 economy fell into a recession in February 2020 due to the coronavirus pandemic. This induced steep job losses, pushed unemployment to its highest level in decades, and resulted in the shrinkage of the labor force. By April 2020, the shortest recession in the history of the United States ended.

- Two labor force measurements that are not commonly discussed are labor force participation rate and employment/population rate. The labor force participation rate (LFPR) is the civilian labor force (employed and actively looking for a job) divided by the civilian labor force. The employment-population ratio measures the civilian labor force currently employed against the total working-working age population. See Figure 10-1.

- Over the past few decades, participation and population rates have fallen in the United States faster than in other countries. The main factor for the declining rates is the aging U.S. population. Older Americans are less likely than younger ones to be in the labor force; this demographic shift reduced overall labor participation. The labor force participation rate declined from 63.1 percent in 2019 to 61.7 percent in 2020 and remained stable at 61.7 percent in 2021. (Table 10-1)

Table 10-1A. Summary Labor Force, Employment, and Unemployment: Recent Data

(Thousands of persons, percent, seasonally adjusted, except as noted.)

Year and month	Civilian noninstitutional population [1]	Civilian labor force		Employment, thousands of persons						Employment-population ratio, percent	Unemployment		
		Thousands of persons	Participation rate (percent)	Total	By age and sex			By industry			Thousands of persons		Rate (percent)
					Men, 20 years and over	Women, 20 years and over	Both sexes, 16 to 19 years	Agri-cultural	Nonagri-cultural		Total	Unemployed 15 weeks and over	
1970	137 085	82 771	60.4	78 678	45 581	26 952	6 144	3 463	75 215	57.4	4 093	663	4.9
1971	140 216	84 382	60.2	79 367	45 912	27 246	6 208	3 394	75 972	56.6	5 016	1 187	5.9
1972	144 126	87 034	60.4	82 153	47 130	28 276	6 746	3 484	78 669	57.0	4 882	1 167	5.6
1973	147 096	89 429	60.8	85 064	48 310	29 484	7 271	3 470	81 594	57.8	4 365	826	4.9
1974	150 120	91 949	61.3	86 794	48 922	30 424	7 448	3 515	83 279	57.8	5 156	955	5.6
1975	153 153	93 775	61.2	85 846	48 018	30 726	7 104	3 408	82 438	56.1	7 929	2 505	8.5
1976	156 150	96 158	61.6	88 752	49 190	32 226	7 336	3 331	85 421	56.8	7 406	2 366	7.7
1977	159 033	99 009	62.3	92 017	50 555	33 775	7 688	3 283	88 734	57.9	6 991	1 942	7.1
1978	161 910	102 251	63.2	96 048	52 143	35 836	8 070	3 387	92 661	59.3	6 202	1 414	6.1
1979	164 863	104 962	63.7	98 824	53 308	37 434	8 083	3 347	95 477	59.9	6 137	1 241	5.8
1980	167 745	106 940	63.8	99 303	53 101	38 492	7 710	3 364	95 938	59.2	7 637	1 871	7.1
1981	170 130	108 670	63.9	100 397	53 582	39 590	7 225	3 368	97 030	59.0	8 273	2 285	7.6
1982	172 271	110 204	64.0	99 526	52 891	40 086	6 549	3 401	96 125	57.8	10 678	3 485	9.7
1983	174 215	111 550	64.0	100 834	53 487	41 004	6 342	3 383	97 450	57.9	10 717	4 210	9.6
1984	176 383	113 544	64.4	105 005	55 769	42 793	6 444	3 321	101 685	59.5	8 539	2 737	7.5
1985	178 206	115 461	64.8	107 150	56 562	44 154	6 434	3 179	103 971	60.1	8 312	2 305	7.2
1986	180 587	117 834	65.3	109 597	57 569	45 556	6 472	3 163	106 434	60.7	8 237	2 232	7.0
1987	182 753	119 865	65.6	112 440	58 726	47 074	6 640	3 208	109 232	61.5	7 425	1 983	6.2
1988	184 613	121 669	65.9	114 968	59 781	48 383	6 805	3 169	111 800	62.3	6 701	1 610	5.5
1989	186 393	123 869	66.5	117 342	60 837	49 745	6 759	3 199	114 142	63.0	6 528	1 375	5.3
1990	189 164	125 840	66.5	118 793	61 678	50 535	6 581	3 223	115 570	62.8	7 047	1 525	5.6
1991	190 925	126 346	66.2	117 718	61 178	50 634	5 906	3 269	114 449	61.7	8 628	2 357	6.8
1992	192 805	128 105	66.4	118 492	61 496	51 328	5 669	3 247	115 245	61.5	9 613	3 408	7.5
1993	194 838	129 200	66.3	120 259	62 355	52 099	5 805	3 115	117 144	61.7	8 940	3 094	6.9
1994	196 814	131 056	66.6	123 060	63 294	53 606	6 161	3 409	119 651	62.5	7 996	2 860	6.1
1995	198 584	132 304	66.6	124 900	64 085	54 396	6 419	3 440	121 460	62.9	7 404	2 363	5.6
1996	200 591	133 943	66.8	126 708	64 897	55 311	6 500	3 443	123 264	63.2	7 236	2 316	5.4
1997	203 133	136 297	67.1	129 558	66 284	56 613	6 661	3 399	126 159	63.8	6 739	2 062	4.9
1998	205 220	137 673	67.1	131 463	67 135	57 278	7 051	3 378	128 085	64.1	6 210	1 637	4.5
1999	207 753	139 368	67.1	133 488	67 761	58 555	7 172	3 281	130 207	64.3	5 880	1 480	4.2
2000	212 577	142 583	67.1	136 891	69 634	60 067	7 189	2 464	134 427	64.4	5 692	1 318	4.0
2001	215 092	143 734	66.8	136 933	69 776	60 417	6 740	2 299	134 635	63.7	6 801	1 752	4.7
2002	217 570	144 863	66.6	136 485	69 734	60 420	6 332	2 311	134 174	62.7	8 378	2 904	5.8
2003	221 168	146 510	66.2	137 736	70 415	61 402	5 919	2 275	135 461	62.3	8 774	3 378	6.0
2004	223 357	147 401	66.0	139 252	71 572	61 773	5 907	2 232	137 020	62.3	8 149	3 072	5.5
2005	226 082	149 320	66.0	141 730	73 050	62 702	5 978	2 197	139 532	62.7	7 591	2 619	5.1
2006	228 815	151 428	66.2	144 427	74 431	63 834	6 162	2 206	142 221	63.1	7 001	2 266	4.6
2007	231 867	153 124	66.0	146 047	75 337	64 799	5 911	2 095	143 952	63.0	7 078	2 303	4.6
2008	233 788	154 287	66.0	145 362	74 750	65 039	5 573	2 168	143 194	62.2	8 924	3 188	5.8
2009	235 801	154 142	65.4	139 877	71 341	63 699	4 837	2 103	137 775	59.3	14 265	7 272	9.3
2010	237 830	153 889	64.7	139 064	71 230	63 456	4 378	2 206	136 858	58.5	14 825	8 786	9.6
2011	239 618	153 617	64.1	139 869	72 182	63 360	4 327	2 254	137 615	58.4	13 747	8 077	8.9
2012	243 284	154 975	63.7	142 469	73 403	64 640	4 426	2 186	140 283	58.6	12 506	6 996	8.1
2013	245 679	155 389	63.2	143 929	74 176	65 295	4 458	2 130	141 799	58.6	11 460	6 117	7.4
2014	247 947	155 922	62.9	146 305	75 471	66 287	4 548	2 237	144 068	59.0	9 617	4 714	6.2
2015	250 801	157 130	62.7	148 834	76 776	67 323	4 734	2 422	146 411	59.3	8 296	3 595	5.3
2016	253 538	159 187	62.8	151 436	78 084	68 387	4 965	2 460	148 976	59.7	7 751	3 163	4.9
2017	255 079	160 320	62.9	153 337	78 919	69 344	5 074	2 454	150 883	60.1	6 982	2 704	4.4
2018	257 791	162 075	62.9	155 761	80 211	70 424	5 126	2 425	153 336	60.4	6 314	2 268	3.9
2019	259 175	163 539	63.1	157 538	80 917	71 470	5 150	2 425	155 113	60.8	6 001	2 126	3.7
2020	260 329	160 742	61.7	147 795	76 227	66 873	4 695	2 349	145 446	56.8	12 947	4 511	8.1
2021	261 445	161 204	61.7	152 581	78 216	69 099	5 266	2 291	150 290	58.4	8 623	4 501	5.3
2020													
January	259 502	164 479	63.4	158 653	81 310	72 040	5 303	2 384	156 141	61.1	5 826	2 064	3.5
February	259 628	164 583	63.4	158 866	81 224	72 244	5 397	2 468	156 240	61.2	5 717	1 914	3.5
March	259 758	162 764	62.7	155 599	79 828	70 661	5 110	2 386	153 084	59.9	7 165	1 930	4.4
April	259 896	156 358	60.2	133 320	70 006	59 969	3 345	2 385	131 023	51.3	23 038	1 717	14.7
May	260 047	158 122	60.8	137 182	71 760	61 592	3 830	2 319	134 988	52.8	20 940	2 199	13.2
June	260 204	159 834	61.4	142 218	73 668	64 285	4 265	2 265	140 039	54.7	17 616	3 268	11.0
July	260 373	160 015	61.5	143 727	74 184	65 142	4 401	2 165	141 493	55.2	16 288	7 989	10.2
August	260 558	160 707	61.7	147 176	75 873	66 610	4 692	2 185	145 252	56.5	13 532	8 134	8.4
September	260 742	160 153	61.4	147 569	76 195	66 402	4 972	2 280	145 417	56.6	12 584	7 358	7.9
October	260 925	160 834	61.6	149 719	76 947	67 638	5 134	2 488	147 315	57.4	11 115	6 211	6.9
November	261 085	160 539	61.5	149 761	76 753	67 902	5 107	2 456	147 142	57.4	10 777	5 808	6.7
December	261 230	160 671	61.5	149 883	76 949	67 933	5 000	2 448	147 199	57.4	10 789	5 542	6.7
2021													
January	260 851	160 184	61.4	150 004	77 185	67 776	5 043	2 454	147 404	57.5	10 180	5 382	6.4
February	260 918	160 359	61.5	150 367	77 203	68 005	5 158	2 307	147 887	57.6	9 992	5 539	6.2
March	261 003	160 631	61.5	150 940	77 262	68 486	5 192	2 227	148 550	57.8	9 691	5 572	6.0
April	261 103	160 978	61.7	151 259	77 423	68 436	5 399	2 275	148 978	57.9	9 719	5 348	6.0
May	261 210	160 801	61.6	151 550	77 489	68 633	5 428	2 291	149 381	58.0	9 251	4 995	5.8
June	261 338	161 114	61.6	151 612	77 665	68 747	5 200	2 309	149 564	58.0	9 502	5 311	5.9
July	261 469	161 375	61.7	152 704	78 135	69 306	5 264	2 289	150 498	58.4	8 671	4 615	5.4
August	261 611	161 505	61.7	153 167	78 480	69 390	5 297	2 307	151 146	58.5	8 339	4 353	5.2
September	261 766	161 471	61.7	153 806	78 952	69 555	5 298	2 247	151 686	58.8	7 666	3 711	4.7
October	261 908	161 610	61.7	154 234	79 164	69 790	5 281	2 296	152 070	58.9	7 375	3 340	4.6
November	262 029	162 126	61.9	155 324	79 736	70 257	5 331	2 212	152 933	59.3	6 802	3 063	4.2
December	262 136	162 294	61.9	155 975	79 892	70 795	5 287	2 308	153 409	59.5	6 319	2 788	3.9

[1] Not seasonally adjusted.

Table 10-1B. Summary Labor Force, Employment, and Unemployment: Historical Data

(Thousands of persons, percent, seasonally adjusted, except as noted.)

Year and month	Civilian noninstitutional population [1]	Civilian labor force — Thousands of persons	Civilian labor force — Participation rate (percent)	Employment — Total	Employment By age and sex — Men, 20 years and over	Employment By age and sex — Women, 20 years and over	Employment By age and sex — Both sexes, 16 to 19 years	Employment By industry — Agricultural	Employment By industry — Nonagricultural	Employment-population ratio, percent	Unemployment — Total	Unemployment — Unemployed 15 weeks and over	Unemployment — Rate (percent) [2]
14 Years and Over													
1929	...	49 180	...	47 630	...	...	...	10 450	37 180	...	1 550	...	3.2
1930	...	49 820	...	45 480	...	...	...	10 340	35 140	...	4 340	...	8.7
1931	...	50 420	...	42 400	...	...	...	10 290	32 110	...	8 020	...	15.9 (15.3)
1932	...	51 000	...	38 940	...	...	...	10 170	28 770	...	12 060	...	23.6 (22.5)
1933	...	51 590	...	38 760	...	...	...	10 090	28 670	...	12 830	...	24.9 (20.6)
1934	...	52 230	...	40 890	...	...	...	9 900	30 990	...	11 340	...	21.7 (16.0)
1935	...	52 870	...	42 260	...	...	...	10 110	32 150	...	10 610	...	20.1 (14.2)
1936	...	53 440	...	44 410	...	...	...	10 000	34 410	...	9 030	...	16.9 (9.9)
1937	...	54 000	...	46 300	...	...	...	9 820	36 480	...	7 700	...	14.3 (9.1)
1938	...	54 610	...	44 220	...	...	...	9 690	34 530	...	10 390	...	19.0 (12.5)
1939	...	55 230	...	45 750	...	...	...	9 610	36 140	...	9 480	...	17.2 (11.3)
1940	99 840	55 640	55.7	47 520	...	...	...	9 540	37 980	47.6	8 120	...	14.6 (9.5)
1941	99 900	55 910	56.0	50 350	...	...	...	9 100	41 250	50.4	5 560	...	9.9 (6.0)
1942	98 640	56 410	57.2	53 750	...	...	...	9 250	44 500	54.5	2 660	...	4.7 (3.1)
1943	94 640	55 540	58.7	54 470	...	...	...	9 080	45 390	57.6	1 070	...	1.9 (1.8)
1944	93 220	54 630	58.6	53 960	...	...	...	8 950	45 010	57.9	670	...	1.2
1945	94 090	53 860	57.2	52 820	...	...	...	8 580	44 240	56.1	1 040	...	1.9
1946	103 070	57 520	55.8	55 250	...	...	...	8 320	46 930	53.6	2 270	...	3.9
1947	106 018	60 168	56.8	57 812	...	...	...	8 256	49 557	54.5	2 356	...	3.9
16 Years and Over													
1947	101 827	59 350	58.3	57 038	...	...	...	7 890	49 148	56.0	2 311	...	3.9
1948	103 068	60 621	58.8	58 343	39 382	14 936	4 026	7 629	50 714	56.6	2 276	309	3.8
1949	103 994	61 286	58.9	57 651	38 803	15 137	3 712	7 658	49 993	55.4	3 637	684	5.9
1950	104 995	62 208	59.2	58 918	39 394	15 824	3 703	7 160	51 758	56.1	3 288	782	5.3
1951	104 621	62 017	59.2	59 961	39 626	16 570	3 767	6 726	53 235	57.3	2 055	303	3.3
1952	105 231	62 138	59.0	60 250	39 578	16 958	3 719	6 500	53 749	57.3	1 883	232	3.0
1953	107 056	63 015	58.9	61 179	40 296	17 164	3 720	6 260	54 919	57.1	1 834	210	2.9
1954	108 321	63 643	58.8	60 109	39 634	17 000	3 475	6 205	53 904	55.5	3 532	812	5.5
1955	109 683	65 023	59.3	62 170	40 526	18 002	3 642	6 450	55 722	56.7	2 852	702	4.4
1956	110 954	66 552	60.0	63 799	41 216	18 767	3 818	6 283	57 514	57.5	2 750	533	4.1
1957	112 265	66 929	59.6	64 071	41 239	19 052	3 778	5 947	58 123	57.1	2 859	560	4.3
1958	113 727	67 639	59.5	63 036	40 411	19 043	3 582	5 586	57 450	55.4	4 602	1 452	6.8
1959	115 329	68 369	59.3	64 630	41 267	19 524	3 838	5 565	59 065	56.0	3 740	1 040	5.5
1960	117 245	69 628	59.4	65 778	41 543	20 105	4 129	5 458	60 318	56.1	3 852	957	5.5
1961	118 771	70 459	59.3	65 746	41 342	20 296	4 108	5 200	60 546	55.4	4 714	1 532	6.7
1962	120 153	70 614	58.8	66 702	41 815	20 693	4 195	4 944	61 759	55.5	3 911	1 119	5.5
1963	122 416	71 833	58.7	67 762	42 251	21 257	4 255	4 687	63 076	55.4	4 070	1 088	5.7
1964	124 485	73 091	58.7	69 305	42 886	21 903	4 516	4 523	64 782	55.7	3 786	973	5.2
1951													
January	104 844	61 941	59.1	59 636	39 595	16 279	3 762	6 828	52 808	56.9	2 305	438	3.7
February	104 604	61 778	59.1	59 661	39 695	16 257	3 709	6 738	52 923	57.0	2 117	386	3.4
March	104 629	62 526	59.8	60 401	40 013	16 557	3 831	6 858	53 543	57.7	2 125	355	3.4
April	104 541	61 808	59.1	59 889	39 804	16 426	3 659	6 722	53 167	57.3	1 919	294	3.1
May	104 491	62 044	59.4	60 188	39 752	16 581	3 855	6 752	53 436	57.6	1 856	269	3.0
June	104 488	61 615	59.0	59 620	39 538	16 368	3 714	6 529	53 091	57.1	1 995	258	3.2
July	104 504	62 106	59.4	60 156	39 483	16 898	3 775	6 601	53 555	57.6	1 950	260	3.1
August	104 536	61 927	59.2	59 994	39 508	16 665	3 821	6 790	53 204	57.4	1 933	249	3.1
September	104 588	61 780	59.1	59 713	39 416	16 504	3 793	6 558	53 155	57.1	2 067	223	3.3
October	104 690	62 204	59.4	60 010	39 555	16 674	3 781	6 636	53 374	57.3	2 194	269	3.5
November	104 740	62 014	59.2	59 836	39 504	16 669	3 663	6 699	53 137	57.1	2 178	316	3.5
December	104 810	62 457	59.6	60 497	39 691	16 946	3 860	7 065	53 432	57.7	1 960	269	3.1
1952													
January	104 862	62 432	59.5	60 460	39 714	17 001	3 745	7 148	53 312	57.7	1 972	282	3.2
February	104 868	62 419	59.5	60 462	39 772	16 935	3 755	7 020	53 442	57.7	1 957	248	3.1
March	104 860	61 721	58.9	59 908	39 580	16 627	3 701	6 468	53 440	57.1	1 813	234	2.9
April	104 906	61 720	58.8	59 909	39 542	16 659	3 708	6 525	53 384	57.1	1 811	242	2.9
May	104 996	62 058	59.1	60 195	39 588	16 844	3 763	6 334	53 861	57.3	1 863	219	3.0
June	105 118	62 103	59.1	60 219	39 558	16 837	3 824	6 529	53 690	57.3	1 884	210	3.0
July	105 246	61 962	58.9	59 971	39 496	16 778	3 697	6 334	53 637	57.0	1 991	194	3.2
August	105 346	61 877	58.7	59 790	39 289	16 867	3 634	6 174	53 616	56.8	2 087	211	3.4
September	105 436	62 457	59.2	60 521	39 386	17 477	3 658	6 537	53 984	57.4	1 936	249	3.1
October	105 591	61 971	58.7	60 132	39 451	17 032	3 649	6 363	53 769	56.9	1 839	230	3.0
November	105 706	62 491	59.1	60 748	39 549	17 450	3 749	6 509	54 239	57.5	1 743	216	2.8
December	105 812	62 621	59.2	60 954	40 011	17 181	3 762	6 361	54 593	57.6	1 667	238	2.7
1953													
January	106 594	63 439	59.5	61 600	40 256	17 482	3 862	6 642	54 958	57.8	1 839	268	2.9
February	106 678	63 520	59.5	61 884	40 546	17 321	4 017	6 463	55 421	58.0	1 636	208	2.6
March	106 744	63 657	59.6	62 010	40 648	17 397	3 965	6 420	55 590	58.1	1 647	213	2.6
April	106 826	63 167	59.1	61 444	40 346	17 242	3 856	6 362	55 082	57.5	1 723	180	2.7
May	106 910	62 615	58.6	61 019	40 323	16 983	3 713	5 937	55 082	57.1	1 596	176	2.5
June	106 978	63 063	58.9	61 456	40 358	17 301	3 797	6 361	55 095	57.4	1 607	213	2.5
July	107 034	63 057	58.9	61 397	40 378	17 341	3 678	6 267	55 130	57.4	1 660	168	2.6
August	107 132	62 816	58.6	61 151	40 352	17 108	3 691	6 319	54 832	57.1	1 665	177	2.7
September	107 253	62 727	58.5	60 906	40 192	17 063	3 651	6 198	54 708	56.8	1 821	178	2.9
October	107 383	62 867	58.5	60 893	40 155	17 236	3 502	6 096	54 797	56.7	1 974	190	3.1
November	107 504	62 949	58.6	60 738	40 163	16 974	3 601	6 345	54 393	56.5	2 211	259	3.5
December	107 623	62 795	58.3	59 977	39 885	16 599	3 493	5 929	54 048	55.7	2 818	309	4.5

[1]Not seasonally adjusted.
[2]In 1930 through 1943, the official BLS data count persons on work relief as unemployed. The unemployment rates for those years shown in parentheses count persons on work relief as employed, which is more consistent with the postwar practice. See notes and definitions.
. . . = Not available.

Table 10-1B. Summary Labor Force, Employment, and Unemployment: Historical Data—*Continued*

(Thousands of persons, percent, seasonally adjusted, except as noted.)

Year and month	Civilian noninsti-tutional popu-lation [1]	Civilian labor force		Employment, thousands of persons						Employ-ment-population ratio, percent	Unemployment		
		Thousands of persons	Participa-tion rate (percent)	Total	By age and sex			By industry			Thousands of persons		Rate (percent) [2]
					Men, 20 years and over	Women, 20 years and over	Both sexes, 16 to 19 years	Agri-cultural	Nonagri-cultural		Total	Unem-ployed 15 weeks and over	
1954													
January	107 763	63 101	58.6	60 024	39 834	16 574	3 616	6 073	53 951	55.7	3 077	372	4.9
February	107 880	63 994	59.3	60 663	39 899	17 162	3 602	6 590	54 073	56.2	3 331	532	5.2
March	107 987	63 793	59.1	60 186	39 497	17 022	3 667	6 395	53 791	55.7	3 607	765	5.7
April	108 080	63 934	59.2	60 185	39 613	17 015	3 557	6 142	54 043	55.7	3 749	774	5.9
May	108 184	63 675	58.9	59 908	39 467	16 975	3 466	6 210	53 698	55.4	3 767	879	5.9
June	108 267	63 343	58.5	59 792	39 476	16 894	3 422	6 162	53 630	55.2	3 551	880	5.6
July	108 344	63 302	58.4	59 643	39 467	16 777	3 399	6 222	53 421	55.0	3 659	932	5.8
August	108 440	63 707	58.7	59 853	39 582	16 868	3 403	6 087	53 766	55.2	3 854	1 002	6.0
September	108 546	64 209	59.2	60 282	39 702	17 133	3 447	6 453	53 829	55.5	3 927	1 017	6.1
October	108 668	63 936	58.8	60 270	39 618	17 209	3 443	6 242	54 028	55.5	3 666	1 009	5.7
November	108 798	63 759	58.6	60 357	39 745	17 213	3 399	5 934	54 423	55.5	3 402	975	5.3
December	108 892	63 312	58.1	60 116	39 763	17 121	3 232	5 848	54 268	55.2	3 196	827	5.0
1955													
January	109 059	63 910	58.6	60 753	39 937	17 375	3 441	6 113	54 640	55.7	3 157	882	4.9
February	109 078	63 696	58.4	60 727	39 964	17 413	3 350	5 854	54 873	55.7	2 969	826	4.7
March	109 254	63 882	58.5	60 964	40 111	17 415	3 438	6 242	54 722	55.8	2 918	816	4.6
April	109 377	64 564	59.0	61 515	40 120	17 867	3 528	6 363	55 152	56.2	3 049	811	4.7
May	109 544	64 381	58.8	61 634	40 410	17 665	3 559	6 327	55 307	56.3	2 747	734	4.3
June	109 680	64 482	58.8	61 781	40 444	17 837	3 500	6 243	55 538	56.3	2 701	668	4.2
July	109 792	65 145	59.3	62 513	40 751	18 123	3 639	6 438	56 075	56.9	2 632	640	4.0
August	109 882	65 581	59.7	62 797	40 747	18 377	3 673	6 575	56 222	57.1	2 784	535	4.2
September	109 977	65 628	59.7	62 950	40 920	18 285	3 745	6 819	56 131	57.2	2 678	558	4.1
October	110 085	65 821	59.8	62 991	40 858	18 327	3 806	6 728	56 263	57.2	2 830	572	4.3
November	110 177	66 037	59.9	63 257	40 936	18 422	3 899	6 655	56 602	57.4	2 780	564	4.2
December	110 296	66 445	60.2	63 684	41 063	18 630	3 991	6 653	57 031	57.7	2 761	581	4.2
1956													
January	110 390	66 419	60.2	63 753	41 203	18 691	3 859	6 590	57 163	57.8	2 666	561	4.0
February	110 478	66 124	59.9	63 518	41 175	18 582	3 761	6 457	57 061	57.5	2 606	545	3.9
March	110 582	66 175	59.8	63 411	41 199	18 496	3 716	6 221	57 190	57.3	2 764	521	4.2
April	110 650	66 264	59.9	63 614	41 289	18 629	3 696	6 460	57 154	57.5	2 650	476	4.0
May	110 810	66 722	60.2	63 861	41 166	18 844	3 851	6 375	57 486	57.6	2 861	506	4.3
June	110 903	66 702	60.1	63 820	41 196	18 748	3 876	6 335	57 485	57.5	2 882	516	4.3
July	111 019	66 752	60.1	63 800	41 216	18 718	3 866	6 320	57 480	57.5	2 952	523	4.4
August	111 099	66 673	60.0	63 972	41 265	18 864	3 843	6 280	57 692	57.6	2 701	543	4.1
September	111 222	66 714	60.0	64 079	41 221	19 019	3 839	6 375	57 704	57.6	2 635	577	3.9
October	111 335	66 546	59.8	63 975	41 261	18 928	3 786	6 137	57 838	57.5	2 571	530	3.9
November	111 432	66 657	59.8	63 796	41 208	18 846	3 742	5 997	57 799	57.3	2 861	575	4.3
December	111 526	66 700	59.8	63 910	41 192	18 859	3 859	5 806	58 104	57.3	2 790	567	4.2
1957													
January	111 626	66 428	59.5	63 632	41 168	18 740	3 724	5 790	57 842	57.0	2 796	509	4.2
February	111 711	66 879	59.9	64 257	41 341	19 115	3 801	6 125	58 132	57.5	2 622	530	3.9
March	111 824	66 913	59.8	64 404	41 500	19 066	3 838	5 963	58 441	57.6	2 509	514	3.7
April	111 933	66 647	59.5	64 047	41 345	18 937	3 765	5 836	58 211	57.2	2 600	516	3.9
May	112 031	66 695	59.5	63 985	41 334	18 897	3 754	5 999	57 986	57.1	2 710	538	4.1
June	112 172	67 052	59.8	64 196	41 411	18 973	3 812	6 002	58 194	57.2	2 856	526	4.3
July	112 317	67 336	60.0	64 540	41 472	19 262	3 806	6 401	58 139	57.5	2 796	535	4.2
August	112 421	66 706	59.3	63 959	41 243	19 020	3 696	5 898	58 061	56.9	2 747	542	4.1
September	112 554	67 064	59.6	64 121	41 213	19 116	3 792	5 728	58 393	57.0	2 943	559	4.4
October	112 710	67 066	59.5	64 046	41 069	19 160	3 817	5 875	58 171	56.8	3 020	650	4.5
November	112 874	67 123	59.5	63 669	40 853	19 082	3 734	5 686	57 983	56.4	3 454	674	5.1
December	113 013	67 398	59.6	63 922	40 884	19 285	3 753	6 037	57 885	56.6	3 476	731	5.2
1958													
January	113 138	67 095	59.3	63 220	40 617	19 035	3 568	5 831	57 389	55.9	3 875	879	5.8
February	113 234	67 201	59.3	62 898	40 336	18 951	3 611	5 654	57 244	55.5	4 303	1 005	6.4
March	113 337	67 223	59.3	62 731	40 180	18 968	3 583	5 561	57 170	55.3	4 492	1 128	6.7
April	113 415	67 647	59.6	62 631	40 129	18 969	3 533	5 602	57 029	55.2	5 016	1 387	7.4
May	113 534	67 895	59.8	62 874	40 253	18 978	3 643	5 647	57 227	55.4	5 021	1 493	7.4
June	113 647	67 674	59.5	62 730	40 208	19 008	3 514	5 510	57 220	55.2	4 944	1 677	7.3
July	113 727	67 824	59.6	62 745	40 270	19 039	3 436	5 525	57 220	55.2	5 079	1 796	7.5
August	113 835	68 037	59.8	63 012	40 343	19 103	3 566	5 673	57 339	55.4	5 025	1 888	7.4
September	113 977	68 002	59.7	63 181	40 564	19 033	3 584	5 453	57 728	55.4	4 821	1 795	7.1
October	114 138	68 045	59.6	63 475	40 699	19 091	3 685	5 563	57 912	55.6	4 570	1 708	6.7
November	114 283	67 658	59.2	63 470	40 684	19 157	3 629	5 571	57 899	55.5	4 188	1 570	6.2
December	114 429	67 740	59.2	63 549	40 666	19 170	3 713	5 521	58 028	55.5	4 191	1 490	6.2
1959													
January	114 582	67 936	59.3	63 868	40 769	19 292	3 807	5 481	58 387	55.7	4 068	1 396	6.0
February	114 712	67 649	59.0	63 684	40 699	19 167	3 818	5 429	58 255	55.5	3 965	1 277	5.9
March	114 849	68 068	59.3	64 267	41 079	19 379	3 809	5 677	58 590	56.0	3 801	1 210	5.6
April	114 986	68 339	59.4	64 768	41 419	19 498	3 851	5 893	58 875	56.3	3 571	1 039	5.2
May	115 144	68 178	59.2	64 699	41 355	19 565	3 779	5 792	58 907	56.2	3 479	965	5.1
June	115 287	68 278	59.2	64 849	41 387	19 658	3 804	5 712	59 137	56.3	3 429	963	5.0
July	115 429	68 539	59.4	65 011	41 596	19 595	3 820	5 564	59 447	56.3	3 528	889	5.1
August	115 555	68 432	59.2	64 844	41 485	19 568	3 791	5 442	59 402	56.1	3 588	889	5.2
September	115 668	68 545	59.3	64 770	41 351	19 531	3 888	5 447	59 323	56.0	3 775	895	5.5
October	115 798	68 821	59.4	64 911	41 362	19 702	3 847	5 355	59 556	56.1	3 910	883	5.7
November	115 916	68 533	59.1	64 530	41 062	19 594	3 874	5 480	59 050	55.7	4 003	982	5.8
December	116 040	68 994	59.5	65 341	41 651	19 717	3 973	5 458	59 883	56.3	3 653	920	5.3

[1] Not seasonally adjusted.
[2] In 1930 through 1943, the official BLS data count persons on work relief as unemployed. The unemployment rates for those years shown in parentheses count persons on work relief as employed, which is more consistent with the postwar practice. See notes and definitions.

Table 10-1B. Summary Labor Force, Employment, and Unemployment: Historical Data—*Continued*

(Thousands of persons, percent, seasonally adjusted, except as noted.)

Year and month	Civilian noninsti- tutional popu- lation [1]	Civilian labor force		Employment, thousands of persons						Employ- ment- population ratio, percent	Unemployment		
		Thousands of persons	Participa- tion rate (percent)	Total	By age and sex			By industry			Thousands of persons		Rate (percent) [2]
					Men, 20 years and over	Women, 20 years and over	Both sexes, 16 to 19 years	Agri- cultural	Nonagri- cultural		Total	Unem- ployed 15 weeks and over	
1960													
January	116 594	68 962	59.1	65 347	41 637	19 686	4 024	5 458	59 889	56.0	3 615	915	5.2
February	116 702	68 949	59.1	65 620	41 729	19 765	4 126	5 443	60 177	56.2	3 329	841	4.8
March	116 827	68 899	58.5	64 673	41 320	19 388	3 965	4 959	59 714	55.4	3 726	959	5.4
April	116 910	69 579	59.5	65 959	41 641	20 110	4 208	5 471	60 488	56.4	3 620	896	5.2
May	117 033	69 626	59.5	66 057	41 668	20 186	4 203	5 359	60 698	56.4	3 569	797	5.1
June	117 167	69 934	59.7	66 168	41 553	20 290	4 325	5 416	60 752	56.5	3 766	854	5.4
July	117 281	69 745	59.5	65 909	41 490	20 257	4 162	5 542	60 367	56.2	3 836	921	5.5
August	117 431	69 841	59.5	65 895	41 503	20 316	4 076	5 520	60 375	56.1	3 946	927	5.6
September	117 521	70 151	59.7	66 267	41 604	20 493	4 170	5 755	60 512	56.4	3 884	982	5.5
October	117 643	69 884	59.4	65 632	41 464	20 076	4 092	5 436	60 196	55.8	4 252	1 189	6.1
November	117 829	70 439	59.8	66 109	41 543	20 384	4 182	5 513	60 596	56.1	4 330	1 223	6.1
December	118 001	70 395	59.7	65 778	41 416	20 332	4 030	5 622	60 156	55.7	4 617	1 142	6.6
1961													
January	118 155	70 447	59.6	65 776	41 363	20 325	4 088	5 422	60 354	55.7	4 671	1 328	6.6
February	118 250	70 420	59.6	65 588	41 177	20 392	4 019	5 472	60 116	55.5	4 832	1 416	6.9
March	118 358	70 703	59.7	65 850	41 273	20 459	4 118	5 406	60 444	55.6	4 853	1 463	6.9
April	118 503	70 267	59.3	65 374	41 206	20 145	4 023	5 037	60 337	55.2	4 893	1 598	7.0
May	118 638	70 452	59.4	65 449	41 139	20 261	4 049	5 099	60 350	55.2	5 003	1 686	7.1
June	118 767	70 878	59.7	65 993	41 349	20 446	4 198	5 220	60 773	55.6	4 885	1 651	6.9
July	118 889	70 536	59.3	65 608	41 245	20 252	4 111	5 153	60 455	55.2	4 928	1 830	7.0
August	119 006	70 534	59.3	65 852	41 362	20 279	4 211	5 366	60 486	55.3	4 682	1 649	6.6
September	119 107	70 217	59.0	65 541	41 400	20 112	4 029	5 021	60 520	55.0	4 676	1 531	6.7
October	119 202	70 492	59.1	65 919	41 509	20 338	4 072	5 203	60 716	55.3	4 573	1 481	6.5
November	119 153	70 376	59.1	66 081	41 556	20 330	4 195	5 090	60 991	55.5	4 295	1 388	6.1
December	119 214	70 077	58.8	65 900	41 534	20 287	4 079	4 992	60 908	55.3	4 177	1 361	6.0
1962													
January	119 300	70 189	58.8	66 108	41 547	20 501	4 060	5 094	61 014	55.4	4 081	1 235	5.8
February	119 360	70 409	59.0	66 538	41 745	20 693	4 100	5 289	61 249	55.7	3 871	1 244	5.5
March	119 476	70 414	58.9	66 443	41 696	20 567	4 230	5 157	61 336	55.7	3 921	1 162	5.6
April	119 702	70 278	58.7	66 372	41 647	20 567	4 158	5 009	61 363	55.4	3 906	1 122	5.6
May	119 813	70 551	58.9	66 688	41 847	20 558	4 283	4 964	61 724	55.7	3 863	1 134	5.5
June	119 943	70 514	58.8	66 670	41 761	20 547	4 362	4 943	61 727	55.6	3 844	1 079	5.5
July	120 128	70 302	58.5	66 483	41 671	20 592	4 220	4 840	61 643	55.3	3 819	1 049	5.4
August	120 323	70 981	59.0	66 968	41 900	20 841	4 227	4 866	62 102	55.7	4 013	1 081	5.7
September	120 653	71 153	59.0	67 192	42 020	20 982	4 190	4 867	62 325	55.7	3 961	1 096	5.6
October	120 856	70 917	58.7	67 114	42 086	20 856	4 172	4 816	62 298	55.5	3 803	1 022	5.4
November	121 045	70 871	58.5	66 847	41 985	20 794	4 068	4 831	62 016	55.2	4 024	1 051	5.7
December	121 236	70 854	58.4	66 947	41 934	20 831	4 182	4 647	62 300	55.2	3 907	1 068	5.5
1963													
January	121 463	71 146	58.6	67 072	41 938	20 933	4 201	4 882	62 190	55.2	4 074	1 122	5.7
February	121 633	71 262	58.6	67 024	41 876	21 046	4 102	4 652	62 372	55.1	4 238	1 137	5.9
March	121 824	71 423	58.6	67 351	42 047	21 162	4 142	4 696	62 655	55.3	4 072	1 087	5.7
April	121 986	71 697	58.8	67 642	42 131	21 281	4 230	4 670	62 972	55.5	4 055	1 071	5.7
May	122 162	71 832	58.8	67 615	42 145	21 225	4 245	4 729	62 886	55.3	4 217	1 157	5.9
June	122 352	71 626	58.5	67 649	42 268	21 185	4 196	4 642	63 007	55.3	3 977	1 067	5.6
July	122 521	71 956	58.7	67 905	42 427	21 268	4 210	4 694	63 211	55.4	4 051	1 070	5.6
August	122 667	71 786	58.5	67 908	42 400	21 185	4 323	4 604	63 304	55.4	3 878	1 114	5.4
September	122 821	72 131	58.7	68 174	42 500	21 317	4 357	4 650	63 524	55.5	3 957	1 069	5.5
October	123 014	72 281	58.8	68 294	42 437	21 456	4 401	4 702	63 592	55.5	3 987	1 071	5.5
November	123 192	72 418	58.8	68 267	42 415	21 553	4 299	4 694	63 573	55.4	4 151	1 054	5.7
December	123 360	72 188	58.5	68 213	42 427	21 481	4 305	4 629	63 584	55.3	3 975	1 007	5.5
1964													
January	123 560	72 356	58.6	68 327	42 510	21 462	4 355	4 603	63 724	55.3	4 029	1 057	5.6
February	123 707	72 683	58.8	68 751	42 579	21 652	4 520	4 563	64 188	55.6	3 932	1 015	5.4
March	123 857	72 713	58.7	68 763	42 600	21 685	4 478	4 366	64 397	55.5	3 950	1 039	5.4
April	124 019	73 274	59.1	69 356	42 885	22 110	4 361	4 414	64 942	55.9	3 918	934	5.3
May	124 204	73 395	59.1	69 631	43 025	22 103	4 503	4 603	65 028	56.1	3 764	975	5.1
June	124 386	73 032	58.7	69 218	42 760	21 995	4 463	4 556	64 662	55.6	3 814	1 047	5.2
July	124 567	73 007	58.6	69 399	42 998	21 846	4 555	4 591	64 808	55.7	3 608	1 002	4.9
August	124 731	73 118	58.6	69 463	42 963	22 002	4 498	4 573	64 890	55.7	3 655	934	5.0
September	124 920	73 290	58.7	69 578	43 009	21 863	4 706	4 619	64 959	55.7	3 712	917	5.1
October	125 108	73 308	58.6	69 582	43 023	21 984	4 575	4 550	65 032	55.6	3 726	903	5.1
November	125 291	73 286	58.5	69 735	43 171	21 954	4 610	4 496	65 239	55.7	3 551	922	4.8
December	125 468	73 465	58.6	69 814	43 109	22 136	4 569	4 322	65 492	55.6	3 651	873	5.0
1965													
January	125 647	73 569	58.6	69 997	43 237	22 282	4 478	4 271	65 726	55.7	3 572	793	4.9
February	125 810	73 857	58.7	70 127	43 279	22 276	4 572	4 322	65 805	55.7	3 730	919	5.1
March	125 985	73 949	58.7	70 439	43 370	22 373	4 696	4 318	66 121	55.9	3 510	796	4.7
April	126 155	74 228	58.8	70 633	43 397	22 416	4 820	4 424	66 209	56.0	3 595	796	4.8
May	126 320	74 466	59.0	71 034	43 579	22 494	4 961	4 724	66 310	56.2	3 432	736	4.6
June	126 499	74 412	58.8	71 025	43 487	22 759	4 779	4 444	66 581	56.1	3 387	786	4.6
July	126 573	74 761	59.1	71 460	43 489	22 841	5 130	4 390	67 070	56.5	3 301	683	4.4
August	126 756	74 616	58.9	71 362	43 447	22 783	5 132	4 355	67 007	56.3	3 254	733	4.4
September	126 906	74 502	58.7	71 286	43 371	22 684	5 231	4 271	67 015	56.2	3 216	732	4.3
October	127 043	74 838	58.9	71 695	43 461	22 819	5 415	4 418	67 277	56.4	3 143	672	4.2
November	127 171	74 797	58.8	71 724	43 447	22 829	5 448	4 093	67 631	56.4	3 073	645	4.1
December	127 294	75 093	59.0	72 062	43 513	22 983	5 566	4 159	67 903	56.6	3 031	659	4.0

[1]Not seasonally adjusted.
[2]In 1930 through 1943, the official BLS data count persons on work relief as unemployed. The unemployment rates for those years shown in parentheses count persons on work relief as employed, which is more consistent with the postwar practice. See notes and definitions.

Table 10-1B. Summary Labor Force, Employment, and Unemployment: Historical Data—*Continued*

(Thousands of persons, percent, seasonally adjusted, except as noted.)

Year and month	Civilian noninsti- tutional popu- lation [1]	Civilian labor force		Employment, thousands of persons						Employ- ment- population ratio, percent	Unemployment		
					By age and sex			By industry			Thousands of persons		
		Thousands of persons	Participa- tion rate (percent)	Total	Men, 20 years and over	Women, 20 years and over	Both sexes, 16 to 19 years	Agri- cultural	Nonagri- cultural		Total	Unem- ployed 15 weeks and over	Rate (percent) [2]
1966													
January	127 394	75 186	59.0	72 198	43 495	23 098	5 605	4 077	68 121	56.7	2 988	623	4.0
February	127 514	74 954	58.8	72 134	43 528	23 089	5 517	4 078	68 056	56.6	2 820	594	3.8
March	127 626	75 075	58.8	72 188	43 576	23 109	5 503	4 069	68 119	56.6	2 887	583	3.8
April	127 744	75 338	59.0	72 510	43 679	23 227	5 604	4 108	68 402	56.8	2 828	575	3.8
May	127 879	75 447	59.0	72 497	43 710	23 282	5 505	3 930	68 567	56.7	2 950	534	3.9
June	127 983	75 647	59.1	72 775	43 662	23 359	5 754	3 967	68 808	56.9	2 872	475	3.8
July	128 102	75 736	59.1	72 860	43 574	23 422	5 864	3 920	68 940	56.9	2 876	427	3.8
August	128 240	76 046	59.3	73 146	43 636	23 605	5 905	3 921	69 225	57.0	2 900	464	3.8
September	128 359	76 056	59.3	73 258	43 718	23 881	5 659	3 952	69 306	57.1	2 798	488	3.7
October	128 494	76 199	59.3	73 401	43 776	23 881	5 744	3 912	69 489	57.1	2 798	494	3.7
November	128 627	76 610	59.6	73 840	43 804	24 130	5 906	3 945	69 895	57.4	2 770	464	3.6
December	128 730	76 641	59.5	73 729	43 820	24 025	5 884	3 906	69 823	57.3	2 912	488	3.8
1967													
January	128 909	76 639	59.5	73 671	44 029	23 872	5 770	3 890	69 781	57.1	2 968	489	3.9
February	129 032	76 521	59.3	73 606	43 997	23 919	5 690	3 723	69 883	57.0	2 915	459	3.8
March	129 190	76 328	59.1	73 439	43 922	23 832	5 685	3 757	69 682	56.8	2 889	436	3.8
April	129 344	76 777	59.4	73 882	44 061	24 161	5 660	3 748	70 134	57.1	2 895	428	3.8
May	129 515	76 773	59.3	73 844	44 100	24 172	5 572	3 658	70 186	57.0	2 929	417	3.8
June	129 722	77 270	59.6	74 278	44 230	24 303	5 745	3 689	70 589	57.3	2 992	422	3.9
July	129 918	77 464	59.6	74 520	44 364	24 416	5 740	3 833	70 687	57.4	2 944	412	3.8
August	130 187	77 712	59.7	74 767	44 410	24 600	5 757	3 963	70 804	57.4	2 945	441	3.8
September	130 392	77 812	59.7	74 854	44 535	24 683	5 636	3 851	71 003	57.4	2 958	448	3.8
October	130 582	78 194	59.9	75 051	44 610	24 802	5 639	4 008	71 043	57.5	3 143	472	4.0
November	130 754	78 191	59.8	75 125	44 625	24 914	5 586	3 933	71 192	57.5	3 066	490	3.9
December	130 936	78 491	59.9	75 473	44 719	25 104	5 650	4 076	71 397	57.6	3 018	485	3.8
1968													
January	131 112	77 578	59.2	74 700	44 606	24 581	5 513	3 908	70 792	57.0	2 878	503	3.7
February	131 277	78 230	59.6	75 229	44 659	24 881	5 689	3 959	71 270	57.3	3 001	468	3.8
March	131 412	78 256	59.6	75 379	44 663	25 019	5 697	3 904	71 475	57.4	2 877	447	3.7
April	131 553	78 270	59.5	75 561	44 753	25 072	5 736	3 875	71 686	57.4	2 709	393	3.5
May	131 712	78 847	59.9	76 107	44 841	25 513	5 753	3 814	72 293	57.8	2 740	395	3.5
June	131 872	79 120	60.0	76 182	44 914	25 466	5 802	3 806	72 376	57.8	2 938	405	3.7
July	132 053	78 970	59.8	76 087	44 935	25 347	5 805	3 820	72 267	57.6	2 883	426	3.7
August	132 251	78 811	59.6	76 043	44 897	25 201	5 945	3 736	72 307	57.5	2 768	393	3.5
September	132 446	78 858	59.5	76 172	44 893	25 445	5 834	3 758	72 414	57.5	2 686	375	3.4
October	132 617	78 913	59.5	76 224	44 884	25 475	5 865	3 741	72 483	57.5	2 689	386	3.4
November	132 903	79 209	59.6	76 494	44 996	25 674	5 824	3 758	72 736	57.6	2 715	357	3.4
December	133 120	79 463	59.7	76 778	45 262	25 712	5 804	3 746	73 032	57.7	2 685	351	3.4
1969													
January	133 324	79 523	59.6	76 805	45 154	25 777	5 874	3 704	73 101	57.6	2 718	339	3.4
February	133 465	80 019	60.0	77 327	45 339	26 092	5 896	3 770	73 557	57.9	2 692	358	3.4
March	133 639	80 079	59.9	77 367	45 305	26 115	5 947	3 668	73 699	57.9	2 712	353	3.4
April	133 821	80 281	60.0	77 523	45 262	26 233	6 028	3 629	73 894	57.9	2 758	386	3.4
May	134 027	80 125	59.8	77 412	45 278	26 283	5 851	3 706	73 706	57.8	2 713	387	3.4
June	134 213	80 696	60.1	77 880	45 313	26 429	6 138	3 663	74 217	58.0	2 816	368	3.5
July	134 414	80 827	60.1	77 959	45 305	26 516	6 138	3 548	74 411	58.0	2 868	377	3.5
August	134 597	81 106	60.3	78 250	45 513	26 556	6 181	3 613	74 637	58.1	2 856	373	3.5
September	134 774	81 290	60.3	78 250	45 447	26 572	6 231	3 551	74 699	58.1	3 040	391	3.7
October	135 012	81 494	60.4	78 445	45 488	26 658	6 299	3 517	74 928	58.1	3 049	374	3.7
November	135 239	81 397	60.2	78 541	45 505	26 652	6 384	3 477	75 064	58.1	2 856	392	3.5
December	135 489	81 624	60.2	78 740	45 577	26 832	6 331	3 409	75 331	58.1	2 884	413	3.5
1970													
January	135 713	81 981	60.4	78 780	45 654	26 908	6 218	3 422	75 358	58.0	3 201	431	3.9
February	135 957	82 151	60.4	78 698	45 627	26 828	6 243	3 439	75 259	57.9	3 453	470	4.2
March	136 179	82 498	60.6	78 863	45 668	26 933	6 262	3 499	75 364	57.9	3 635	534	4.4
April	136 416	82 727	60.6	78 930	45 679	27 114	6 137	3 568	75 362	57.9	3 797	602	4.6
May	136 686	82 483	60.3	78 564	45 666	26 739	6 159	3 547	75 017	57.5	3 919	591	4.8
June	136 928	82 484	60.2	78 413	45 554	26 904	5 955	3 555	74 858	57.3	4 071	657	4.9
July	137 196	82 901	60.4	78 726	45 516	27 083	6 127	3 517	75 209	57.4	4 175	662	5.0
August	137 455	82 880	60.3	78 624	45 495	27 011	6 118	3 418	75 206	57.2	4 256	705	5.1
September	137 717	82 954	60.2	78 498	45 535	26 784	6 179	3 451	75 047	57.0	4 456	788	5.4
October	137 988	83 276	60.4	78 685	45 508	27 058	6 119	3 337	75 348	57.0	4 591	771	5.5
November	138 264	83 548	60.4	78 650	45 540	27 020	6 090	3 372	75 278	56.9	4 898	871	5.9
December	138 529	83 670	60.4	78 594	45 466	27 038	6 090	3 380	75 214	56.7	5 076	1 102	6.1
1971													
January	138 795	83 850	60.4	78 864	45 527	27 173	6 164	3 393	75 471	56.8	4 986	1 113	5.9
February	139 021	83 603	60.1	78 700	45 455	27 040	6 205	3 288	75 412	56.6	4 903	1 068	5.9
March	139 285	83 575	60.0	78 588	45 520	26 967	6 101	3 356	75 232	56.4	4 987	1 098	6.0
April	139 566	83 946	60.1	78 987	45 789	26 984	6 214	3 574	75 413	56.6	4 959	1 149	5.9
May	139 826	84 135	60.2	79 139	45 917	27 056	6 166	3 449	75 690	56.6	4 996	1 173	5.9
June	140 090	83 706	59.8	78 757	45 879	27 013	5 865	3 334	75 423	56.2	4 949	1 167	5.9
July	140 343	84 340	60.1	79 305	46 000	27 054	6 251	3 386	75 919	56.5	5 035	1 251	6.0
August	140 596	84 673	60.2	79 539	46 041	27 171	6 327	3 395	76 144	56.6	5 134	1 261	6.1
September	140 869	84 731	60.1	79 689	46 090	27 390	6 209	3 367	76 322	56.6	5 042	1 239	6.0
October	141 146	84 872	60.1	79 918	46 132	27 538	6 248	3 405	76 513	56.6	4 954	1 268	5.8
November	141 393	85 458	60.4	80 297	46 209	27 721	6 367	3 410	76 887	56.8	5 161	1 277	6.0
December	141 666	85 625	60.4	80 471	46 280	27 791	6 400	3 371	77 100	56.8	5 154	1 283	6.0

[1] Not seasonally adjusted.
[2] In 1930 through 1943, the official BLS data count persons on work relief as unemployed. The unemployment rates for those years shown in parentheses count persons on work relief as employed, which is more consistent with the postwar practice. See notes and definitions.

Table 10-1B. Summary Labor Force, Employment, and Unemployment: Historical Data—*Continued*

(Thousands of persons, percent, seasonally adjusted, except as noted.)

Year and month	Civilian noninsti- tutional popu- lation [1]	Civilian labor force		Employment, thousands of persons						Employ- ment- population ratio, percent	Unemployment		
					By age and sex			By industry			Thousands of persons		Rate (percent) [2]
		Thousands of persons	Participa- tion rate (percent)	Total	Men, 20 years and over	Women, 20 years and over	Both sexes, 16 to 19 years	Agri- cultural	Nonagri- cultural		Total	Unem- ployed 15 weeks and over	
1972													
January	142 736	85 978	60.2	80 959	46 471	27 956	6 532	3 366	77 593	56.7	5 019	1 257	5.8
February	143 017	86 036	60.2	81 108	46 600	28 016	6 492	3 358	77 750	56.7	4 928	1 292	5.7
March	143 263	86 611	60.5	81 573	46 821	28 126	6 626	3 438	78 135	56.9	5 038	1 232	5.8
April	143 483	86 614	60.4	81 655	46 863	28 114	6 678	3 382	78 273	56.9	4 959	1 203	5.7
May	143 760	86 809	60.4	81 887	46 950	28 184	6 753	3 412	78 475	57.0	4 922	1 168	5.7
June	144 033	87 006	60.4	82 083	47 147	28 175	6 761	3 402	78 681	57.0	4 923	1 141	5.7
July	144 285	87 143	60.4	82 230	47 244	28 225	6 761	3 461	78 769	57.0	4 913	1 154	5.6
August	144 522	87 517	60.6	82 578	47 321	28 382	6 875	3 603	78 975	57.1	4 939	1 156	5.6
September	144 761	87 392	60.4	82 543	47 394	28 417	6 732	3 568	78 975	57.0	4 849	1 131	5.5
October	144 988	87 491	60.3	82 616	47 354	28 438	6 824	3 634	78 982	57.0	4 875	1 123	5.6
November	145 211	87 592	60.3	82 990	47 529	28 567	6 894	3 517	79 473	57.2	4 602	1 040	5.3
December	145 446	87 943	60.5	83 400	47 747	28 698	6 955	3 596	79 804	57.3	4 543	1 006	5.2
1973													
January	145 720	87 487	60.0	83 161	47 701	28 596	6 864	3 456	79 705	57.1	4 326	947	4.9
February	145 943	88 364	60.5	83 912	47 884	28 995	7 033	3 415	80 497	57.5	4 452	894	5.0
March	146 230	88 846	60.8	84 452	48 117	29 110	7 225	3 469	80 983	57.8	4 394	889	4.9
April	146 459	89 018	60.8	84 559	48 098	29 304	7 157	3 407	81 152	57.7	4 459	809	5.0
May	146 719	88 977	60.6	84 648	48 068	29 432	7 148	3 376	81 272	57.7	4 329	816	4.9
June	146 981	89 548	60.9	85 185	48 244	29 505	7 436	3 509	81 676	58.0	4 363	779	4.9
July	147 233	89 604	60.9	85 299	48 452	29 592	7 255	3 540	81 759	57.9	4 305	756	4.8
August	147 471	89 509	60.7	85 204	48 353	29 578	7 273	3 425	81 779	57.8	4 305	788	4.8
September	147 731	89 838	60.8	85 488	48 408	29 710	7 370	3 342	82 146	57.9	4 350	785	4.8
October	147 980	90 131	60.9	85 987	48 631	29 885	7 471	3 424	82 563	58.1	4 144	793	4.6
November	148 219	90 716	61.2	86 320	48 764	30 071	7 485	3 593	82 727	58.2	4 396	832	4.8
December	148 479	90 890	61.2	86 401	48 902	29 991	7 508	3 658	82 743	58.2	4 489	767	4.9
1974													
January	148 753	91 199	61.3	86 555	49 107	29 893	7 555	3 756	82 799	58.2	4 644	799	5.1
February	148 982	91 485	61.4	86 754	49 057	30 146	7 551	3 824	82 930	58.2	4 731	829	5.2
March	149 225	91 453	61.3	86 819	48 986	30 293	7 540	3 726	83 093	58.2	4 634	849	5.1
April	149 478	91 287	61.1	86 669	48 853	30 376	7 440	3 582	83 087	58.0	4 618	889	5.1
May	149 750	91 596	61.2	86 891	49 039	30 424	7 428	3 529	83 362	58.0	4 705	880	5.1
June	150 012	91 868	61.2	86 941	48 946	30 512	7 483	3 386	83 555	58.0	4 927	926	5.4
July	150 248	92 212	61.4	87 149	48 883	30 869	7 397	3 436	83 713	58.0	5 063	924	5.5
August	150 493	92 059	61.2	87 037	48 950	30 662	7 425	3 429	83 608	57.8	5 022	960	5.5
September	150 753	92 488	61.4	87 051	48 978	30 569	7 504	3 460	83 591	57.7	5 437	1 021	5.9
October	151 009	92 518	61.3	86 995	48 959	30 570	7 466	3 431	83 564	57.6	5 523	1 072	6.0
November	151 256	92 766	61.3	86 626	48 833	30 424	7 369	3 405	83 221	57.3	6 140	1 128	6.6
December	151 494	92 780	61.2	86 144	48 458	30 431	7 255	3 361	82 783	56.9	6 636	1 326	7.2
1975													
January	151 755	93 128	61.4	85 627	48 086	30 343	7 198	3 401	82 226	56.4	7 501	1 555	8.1
February	151 990	92 776	61.0	85 256	47 927	30 215	7 114	3 361	81 895	56.1	7 520	1 841	8.1
March	152 217	93 165	61.2	85 187	47 776	30 334	7 077	3 358	81 829	56.0	7 978	2 074	8.6
April	152 443	93 399	61.3	85 189	47 759	30 410	7 020	3 315	81 874	55.9	8 210	2 442	8.8
May	152 704	93 884	61.5	85 451	47 835	30 483	7 133	3 560	81 891	56.0	8 433	2 643	9.0
June	152 976	93 575	61.2	85 355	47 754	30 618	6 983	3 368	81 987	55.8	8 220	2 843	8.8
July	153 309	94 021	61.3	85 894	48 050	30 794	7 050	3 457	82 437	56.0	8 127	2 943	8.6
August	153 580	94 162	61.3	86 234	48 239	30 966	7 029	3 429	82 805	56.1	7 928	2 862	8.4
September	153 848	94 202	61.2	86 279	48 126	30 979	7 174	3 508	82 771	56.1	7 923	2 906	8.4
October	154 082	94 267	61.2	86 370	48 165	31 121	7 084	3 397	82 973	56.1	7 897	2 689	8.4
November	154 338	94 250	61.1	86 456	48 203	31 135	7 118	3 331	83 125	56.0	7 794	2 789	8.3
December	154 589	94 409	61.1	86 665	48 266	31 268	7 131	3 259	83 406	56.1	7 744	2 868	8.2
1976													
January	154 853	94 934	61.3	87 400	48 592	31 595	8 967	3 387	84 013	56.4	7 534	2 713	7.9
February	155 066	94 998	61.3	87 672	48 721	31 680	8 981	3 304	84 368	56.5	7 326	2 519	7.7
March	155 306	95 215	61.3	87 985	48 836	31 842	9 007	3 296	84 689	56.7	7 230	2 441	7.6
April	155 529	95 746	61.6	88 416	49 097	31 951	9 151	3 438	84 978	56.8	7 330	2 210	7.7
May	155 765	95 847	61.5	88 794	49 193	32 147	9 155	3 367	85 427	57.0	7 053	2 115	7.4
June	156 026	95 885	61.5	88 563	49 010	32 267	8 943	3 310	85 253	56.8	7 322	2 332	7.6
July	156 276	96 583	61.8	89 093	49 236	32 334	9 204	3 358	85 735	57.0	7 490	2 316	7.8
August	156 525	96 741	61.8	89 223	49 417	32 437	9 168	3 380	85 843	57.0	7 518	2 378	7.8
September	156 779	96 553	61.6	89 173	49 485	32 390	8 968	3 278	85 895	56.9	7 380	2 296	7.6
October	156 993	96 704	61.6	89 274	49 524	32 412	9 054	3 316	85 958	56.9	7 430	2 292	7.7
November	157 235	97 254	61.9	89 634	49 561	32 753	9 055	3 263	86 371	57.0	7 620	2 354	7.8
December	157 438	97 348	61.8	89 803	49 599	32 914	9 011	3 251	86 552	57.0	7 545	2 375	7.8
1977													
January	157 688	97 208	61.6	89 928	49 738	32 872	9 025	3 185	86 743	57.0	7 280	2 200	7.5
February	157 913	97 785	61.9	90 342	49 838	32 997	9 198	3 222	87 120	57.2	7 443	2 174	7.6
March	158 131	98 115	62.0	90 808	50 031	33 246	9 257	3 212	87 596	57.4	7 307	2 057	7.4
April	158 371	98 330	62.1	91 271	50 185	33 470	9 289	3 313	87 958	57.6	7 059	1 936	7.2
May	158 657	98 665	62.2	91 754	50 280	33 851	9 279	3 432	88 322	57.8	6 911	1 928	7.0
June	158 928	99 093	62.4	91 959	50 544	33 678	9 525	3 340	88 619	57.9	7 134	1 918	7.2
July	159 185	98 913	62.1	92 084	50 597	33 749	9 377	3 247	88 837	57.8	6 829	1 907	6.9
August	159 430	99 366	62.3	92 441	50 745	33 809	9 550	3 260	89 181	58.0	6 925	1 836	7.0
September	159 674	99 453	62.3	92 702	50 825	34 218	9 340	3 201	89 501	58.1	6 751	1 853	6.8
October	159 915	99 815	62.4	93 052	51 046	34 187	9 441	3 272	89 780	58.2	6 763	1 789	6.8
November	160 129	100 576	62.8	93 761	51 316	34 536	9 551	3 375	90 386	58.6	6 815	1 804	6.8
December	160 376	100 491	62.7	94 105	51 492	34 668	9 406	3 320	90 785	58.7	6 386	1 717	6.4

[1] Not seasonally adjusted.
[2] In 1930 through 1943, the official BLS data count persons on work relief as unemployed. The unemployment rates for those years shown in parentheses count persons on work relief as employed, which is more consistent with the postwar practice. See notes and definitions.

Table 10-1B. Summary Labor Force, Employment, and Unemployment: Historical Data—*Continued*

(Thousands of persons, percent, seasonally adjusted, except as noted.)

Year and month	Civilian noninsti-tutional popu-lation [1]	Civilian labor force		Employment, thousands of persons						Employ-ment-population ratio, percent	Unemployment		
		Thousands of persons	Participa-tion rate (percent)	Total	By age and sex			By industry			Thousands of persons		Rate (percent) [2]
					Men, 20 years and over	Women, 20 years and over	Both sexes, 16 to 19 years	Agri-cultural	Nonagri-cultural		Total	Unem-ployed 15 weeks and over	
1978													
January	160 617	100 873	62.8	94 384	51 542	34 948	9 473	3 434	90 950	58.8	6 489	1 643	6.4
February	160 831	100 837	62.7	94 519	51 578	35 118	9 448	3 320	91 199	58.8	6 318	1 584	6.3
March	161 038	101 092	62.8	94 755	51 635	35 310	9 441	3 351	91 404	58.8	6 337	1 531	6.3
April	161 263	101 574	63.0	95 394	51 912	35 546	9 518	3 349	92 045	59.2	6 180	1 502	6.1
May	161 518	101 896	63.1	95 769	52 050	35 597	9 668	3 325	92 444	59.3	6 127	1 420	6.0
June	161 794	102 371	63.3	96 343	52 240	35 828	9 781	3 483	92 860	59.5	6 028	1 352	5.9
July	162 034	102 399	63.2	96 090	52 190	35 764	9 749	3 441	92 649	59.3	6 309	1 373	6.2
August	162 259	102 511	63.2	96 431	52 228	35 856	9 903	3 401	93 030	59.4	6 080	1 242	5.9
September	162 502	102 795	63.3	96 670	52 284	36 274	9 700	3 400	93 270	59.5	6 125	1 308	6.0
October	162 783	103 080	63.3	97 133	52 448	36 525	9 727	3 409	93 724	59.7	5 947	1 319	5.8
November	163 017	103 562	63.5	97 485	52 802	36 559	9 704	3 284	94 201	59.8	6 077	1 242	5.9
December	163 272	103 809	63.6	97 581	52 807	36 686	9 708	3 396	94 185	59.8	6 228	1 269	6.0
1979													
January	163 516	104 057	63.6	97 948	53 072	36 697	9 749	3 305	94 643	59.9	6 109	1 250	5.9
February	163 726	104 502	63.8	98 329	53 233	36 904	9 762	3 373	94 956	60.1	6 173	1 297	5.9
March	164 027	104 589	63.8	98 480	53 120	37 159	9 751	3 368	95 112	60.0	6 109	1 365	5.8
April	164 162	104 172	63.5	98 103	53 085	36 944	9 652	3 291	94 812	59.8	6 069	1 272	5.8
May	164 459	104 171	63.3	98 331	53 178	37 134	9 553	3 272	95 059	59.8	5 840	1 239	5.6
June	164 720	104 638	63.5	98 679	53 309	37 221	9 664	3 331	95 348	59.9	5 959	1 171	5.7
July	164 970	105 002	63.6	99 006	53 384	37 514	9 606	3 335	95 671	60.0	5 996	1 123	5.7
August	165 198	105 096	63.6	98 776	53 336	37 548	9 456	3 374	95 402	59.8	6 320	1 203	6.0
September	165 431	105 530	63.8	99 340	53 510	37 798	9 623	3 371	95 969	60.0	6 190	1 172	5.9
October	165 813	105 700	63.7	99 404	53 478	37 931	9 574	3 325	96 079	59.9	6 296	1 219	6.0
November	166 051	105 812	63.7	99 574	53 435	38 065	9 599	3 436	96 138	60.0	6 238	1 239	5.9
December	166 300	106 258	63.9	99 933	53 555	38 259	9 690	3 400	96 533	60.1	6 325	1 277	6.0
1980													
January	166 544	106 562	64.0	99 879	53 501	38 367	9 590	3 316	96 563	60.0	6 683	1 353	6.3
February	166 759	106 697	64.0	99 995	53 686	38 389	9 501	3 397	96 598	60.0	6 702	1 358	6.3
March	166 984	106 442	63.7	99 713	53 353	38 406	9 500	3 418	96 295	59.7	6 729	1 457	6.3
April	167 197	106 591	63.8	99 233	53 035	38 427	9 272	3 326	95 907	59.4	7 358	1 694	6.9
May	167 407	106 929	63.9	98 945	52 915	38 335	9 457	3 382	95 563	59.1	7 984	1 740	7.5
June	167 643	106 780	63.7	98 682	52 712	38 312	9 438	3 296	95 386	58.9	8 098	1 760	7.6
July	167 932	107 159	63.8	98 796	52 733	38 374	9 499	3 319	95 477	58.8	8 363	1 995	7.8
August	168 103	107 105	63.7	98 824	52 815	38 511	9 247	3 234	95 590	58.8	8 281	2 162	7.7
September	168 297	107 098	63.6	99 077	52 866	38 595	9 289	3 443	95 634	58.9	8 021	2 309	7.5
October	168 503	107 405	63.7	99 317	53 094	38 620	9 319	3 372	95 945	58.9	8 088	2 306	7.5
November	168 695	107 568	63.8	99 545	53 210	38 795	9 246	3 396	96 149	59.0	8 023	2 329	7.5
December	168 883	107 352	63.6	99 634	53 333	38 737	9 175	3 492	96 142	59.0	7 718	2 406	7.2
1981													
January	169 104	108 026	63.9	99 955	53 392	39 042	9 300	3 429	96 526	59.1	8 071	2 389	7.5
February	169 280	108 242	63.9	100 191	53 445	39 280	9 257	3 345	96 846	59.2	8 051	2 344	7.4
March	169 453	108 553	64.1	100 571	53 662	39 464	9 212	3 365	97 206	59.4	7 982	2 276	7.4
April	169 641	108 925	64.2	101 056	53 886	39 628	9 289	3 529	97 527	59.6	7 869	2 231	7.2
May	169 829	109 222	64.3	101 048	53 879	39 759	9 160	3 369	97 679	59.5	8 174	2 221	7.5
June	170 042	108 396	63.7	100 298	53 576	39 682	8 780	3 334	96 964	59.0	8 098	2 250	7.5
July	170 246	108 556	63.8	100 693	53 814	39 683	8 839	3 296	97 397	59.1	7 863	2 166	7.2
August	170 399	108 725	63.8	100 689	53 718	39 723	8 931	3 379	97 310	59.1	8 036	2 241	7.4
September	170 593	108 294	63.5	100 064	53 625	39 342	8 835	3 361	96 703	58.7	8 230	2 261	7.6
October	170 809	109 024	63.8	100 378	53 482	39 843	8 851	3 412	96 966	58.8	8 646	2 303	7.9
November	170 996	109 236	63.9	100 207	53 335	39 908	8 852	3 415	96 792	58.6	9 029	2 345	8.3
December	171 166	108 912	63.6	99 645	53 149	39 708	8 602	3 227	96 418	58.2	9 267	2 374	8.5
1982													
January	171 335	109 089	63.7	99 692	53 103	39 821	8 676	3 393	96 299	58.2	9 397	2 409	8.6
February	171 489	109 467	63.8	99 762	53 172	39 859	8 697	3 375	96 387	58.2	9 705	2 758	8.9
March	171 667	109 567	63.8	99 672	53 054	39 936	8 550	3 372	96 300	58.1	9 895	2 965	9.0
April	171 844	109 820	63.9	99 576	53 081	39 848	8 605	3 351	96 225	57.9	10 244	3 086	9.3
May	172 026	110 451	64.2	100 116	53 234	40 121	8 753	3 434	96 682	58.2	10 335	3 276	9.4
June	172 190	110 081	63.9	99 543	52 933	40 219	8 293	3 331	96 212	57.8	10 538	3 451	9.6
July	172 364	110 342	64.0	99 493	52 896	40 228	8 380	3 402	96 091	57.7	10 849	3 555	9.8
August	172 511	110 514	64.1	99 633	52 797	40 336	8 514	3 408	96 225	57.8	10 881	3 696	9.8
September	172 690	110 721	64.1	99 504	52 760	40 275	8 469	3 385	96 119	57.6	11 217	3 889	10.1
October	172 881	110 744	64.1	99 215	52 624	40 105	8 499	3 489	95 726	57.4	11 529	4 185	10.4
November	173 058	111 050	64.2	99 112	52 537	40 111	8 520	3 510	95 602	57.3	11 938	4 485	10.8
December	173 199	111 083	64.1	99 032	52 497	40 164	8 397	3 414	95 618	57.2	12 051	4 662	10.8
1983													
January	173 354	110 695	63.9	99 161	52 487	40 268	8 335	3 439	95 722	57.2	11 534	4 668	10.4
February	173 505	110 634	63.8	99 089	52 453	40 336	8 159	3 382	95 707	57.1	11 545	4 641	10.4
March	173 656	110 587	63.8	99 179	52 615	40 368	8 098	3 360	95 819	57.1	11 408	4 612	10.3
April	173 794	110 828	63.8	99 560	52 814	40 542	8 094	3 341	96 219	57.3	11 268	4 370	10.2
May	173 953	110 790	63.7	99 642	52 922	40 538	8 006	3 328	96 314	57.3	11 154	4 538	10.1
June	174 125	111 879	64.3	100 633	53 515	40 695	8 448	3 462	97 171	57.8	11 246	4 470	10.1
July	174 306	111 756	64.1	101 208	53 835	41 041	8 207	3 481	97 727	58.1	10 548	4 329	9.4
August	174 440	112 231	64.3	101 608	53 837	41 314	8 379	3 502	98 106	58.2	10 623	4 070	9.5
September	174 602	112 298	64.3	102 016	53 983	41 650	8 147	3 347	98 669	58.4	10 282	3 854	9.2
October	174 779	111 926	64.0	102 039	54 146	41 597	8 010	3 303	98 736	58.4	9 887	3 648	8.8
November	174 951	112 228	64.1	102 729	54 499	41 788	8 075	3 291	99 438	58.7	9 499	3 535	8.5
December	175 121	112 327	64.1	102 996	54 662	41 852	8 089	3 332	99 664	58.8	9 331	3 379	8.3

[1]Not seasonally adjusted.
[2]In 1930 through 1943, the official BLS data count persons on work relief as unemployed. The unemployment rates for those years shown in parentheses count persons on work relief as employed, which is more consistent with the postwar practice. See notes and definitions.

Table 10-1B. Summary Labor Force, Employment, and Unemployment: Historical Data—*Continued*

(Thousands of persons, percent, seasonally adjusted, except as noted.)

Year and month	Civilian noninsti-tutional popu-lation [1]	Civilian labor force		Employment, thousands of persons						Employ-ment-population ratio, percent	Unemployment		
					By age and sex			By industry			Thousands of persons		Rate (percent) [2]
		Thousands of persons	Participa-tion rate (percent)	Total	Men, 20 years and over	Women, 20 years and over	Both sexes, 16 to 19 years	Agri-cultural	Nonagri-cultural		Total	Unem-ployed 15 weeks and over	
1984													
January	175 533	112 209	63.9	103 201	54 975	41 812	7 965	3 293	99 908	58.8	9 008	3 254	8.0
February	175 679	112 615	64.1	103 824	55 213	42 196	7 958	3 353	100 471	59.1	8 791	2 991	7.8
March	175 824	112 713	64.1	103 967	55 281	42 328	7 926	3 233	100 734	59.1	8 746	2 881	7.8
April	175 969	113 098	64.3	104 336	55 373	42 512	7 988	3 291	101 045	59.3	8 762	2 858	7.7
May	176 123	113 649	64.5	105 193	55 661	43 071	7 944	3 343	101 850	59.7	8 456	2 884	7.4
June	176 284	113 817	64.6	105 591	55 996	42 944	8 131	3 383	102 208	59.9	8 226	2 612	7.2
July	176 440	113 972	64.6	105 435	55 921	42 979	8 045	3 344	102 091	59.8	8 537	2 638	7.5
August	176 583	113 682	64.4	105 163	55 930	42 885	7 809	3 286	101 877	59.6	8 519	2 604	7.5
September	176 763	113 857	64.4	105 490	56 095	42 967	7 951	3 393	102 097	59.7	8 367	2 538	7.3
October	176 956	114 019	64.4	105 638	56 183	43 052	7 862	3 194	102 444	59.7	8 381	2 526	7.4
November	177 135	114 170	64.5	105 972	56 274	43 244	7 844	3 394	102 578	59.8	8 198	2 438	7.2
December	177 306	114 581	64.6	106 223	56 313	43 472	7 933	3 385	102 838	59.9	8 358	2 401	7.3
1985													
January	177 384	114 725	64.7	106 302	56 184	43 589	8 036	3 317	102 985	59.9	8 423	2 284	7.3
February	177 516	114 876	64.7	106 555	56 216	43 787	8 020	3 317	103 238	60.0	8 321	2 389	7.2
March	177 667	115 328	64.9	106 989	56 356	44 035	8 062	3 250	103 739	60.2	8 339	2 394	7.2
April	177 799	115 331	64.9	106 936	56 374	44 000	7 958	3 306	103 630	60.1	8 395	2 393	7.3
May	177 944	115 234	64.8	106 932	56 531	43 905	7 966	3 280	103 652	60.1	8 302	2 292	7.2
June	178 096	114 965	64.6	106 505	56 288	43 958	7 680	3 161	103 344	59.8	8 460	2 310	7.4
July	178 263	115 320	64.7	106 807	56 435	43 975	8 013	3 143	103 664	59.9	8 513	2 329	7.4
August	178 405	115 291	64.6	107 095	56 655	44 103	7 714	3 121	103 974	60.0	8 196	2 258	7.1
September	178 572	115 905	64.9	107 657	56 845	44 395	7 818	3 064	104 593	60.3	8 248	2 242	7.1
October	178 770	116 145	65.0	107 847	56 969	44 565	7 889	3 051	104 796	60.3	8 298	2 295	7.1
November	178 940	116 135	64.9	108 007	56 972	44 617	7 852	3 062	104 945	60.4	8 128	2 207	7.0
December	179 112	116 354	65.0	108 216	56 995	44 889	7 826	3 141	105 075	60.4	8 138	2 208	7.0
1986													
January	179 670	116 682	64.9	108 887	57 637	44 944	7 704	3 287	105 600	60.6	7 795	2 089	6.7
February	179 821	116 882	65.0	108 480	57 269	44 804	7 895	3 083	105 397	60.3	8 402	2 308	7.2
March	179 985	117 220	65.1	108 837	57 353	44 960	7 977	3 200	105 637	60.5	8 383	2 261	7.2
April	180 148	117 316	65.1	108 952	57 358	45 081	8 058	3 153	105 799	60.5	8 364	2 162	7.1
May	180 311	117 528	65.2	109 089	57 287	45 289	7 997	3 150	105 939	60.5	8 439	2 232	7.2
June	180 503	118 084	65.4	109 576	57 471	45 621	8 024	3 193	106 383	60.7	8 508	2 320	7.2
July	180 682	118 129	65.4	109 810	57 514	45 837	7 914	3 141	106 669	60.8	8 319	2 269	7.0
August	180 828	118 150	65.3	110 015	57 597	45 926	7 920	3 082	106 933	60.8	8 135	2 276	6.9
September	180 997	118 395	65.4	110 085	57 630	45 972	7 945	3 171	106 914	60.8	8 310	2 318	7.0
October	181 186	118 516	65.4	110 273	57 660	46 046	7 977	3 128	107 145	60.9	8 243	2 188	7.0
November	181 363	118 634	65.4	110 475	57 941	46 070	7 891	3 220	107 255	60.9	8 159	2 202	6.9
December	181 547	118 611	65.3	110 728	58 185	46 132	7 769	3 148	107 580	61.0	7 883	2 161	6.6
1987													
January	181 827	118 845	65.4	110 953	58 264	46 219	7 861	3 143	107 810	61.0	7 892	2 168	6.6
February	181 998	119 122	65.5	111 257	58 279	46 444	7 969	3 208	108 049	61.1	7 865	2 117	6.6
March	182 179	119 270	65.5	111 408	58 362	46 549	7 913	3 214	108 194	61.2	7 862	2 070	6.6
April	182 344	119 336	65.4	111 794	58 503	46 746	7 916	3 246	108 548	61.3	7 542	2 091	6.3
May	182 533	120 008	65.7	112 434	58 713	47 052	8 075	3 345	109 089	61.6	7 574	2 104	6.3
June	182 703	119 644	65.5	112 246	58 581	47 102	7 857	3 216	109 030	61.4	7 398	2 087	6.2
July	182 885	119 902	65.6	112 634	58 740	47 229	7 911	3 235	109 399	61.6	7 268	1 921	6.1
August	183 002	120 318	65.7	113 057	58 810	47 322	8 232	3 112	109 945	61.8	7 261	1 878	6.0
September	183 161	120 011	65.5	112 909	58 964	47 285	7 945	3 189	109 720	61.6	7 102	1 866	5.9
October	183 311	120 509	65.7	113 282	59 073	47 533	8 074	3 219	110 063	61.8	7 227	1 794	6.0
November	183 470	120 540	65.7	113 505	59 210	47 622	8 002	3 145	110 360	61.9	7 035	1 797	5.8
December	183 620	120 729	65.7	113 793	59 217	47 781	8 092	3 213	110 580	62.0	6 936	1 767	5.7
1988													
January	183 822	120 969	65.8	114 016	59 346	47 862	8 110	3 247	110 769	62.0	6 953	1 714	5.7
February	183 969	121 156	65.9	114 227	59 535	47 919	8 025	3 201	111 026	62.1	6 929	1 738	5.7
March	184 111	120 913	65.7	114 037	59 393	48 090	7 854	3 169	110 868	61.9	6 876	1 744	5.7
April	184 232	121 251	65.8	114 650	59 832	48 147	7 937	3 224	111 426	62.2	6 601	1 563	5.4
May	184 374	121 071	65.7	114 292	59 644	47 946	7 912	3 121	111 171	62.0	6 779	1 647	5.6
June	184 562	121 473	65.8	114 927	59 751	48 146	8 193	3 111	111 816	62.3	6 546	1 531	5.4
July	184 729	121 665	65.9	115 060	59 888	48 186	8 198	3 060	112 000	62.3	6 605	1 601	5.4
August	184 830	122 125	66.1	115 282	59 877	48 467	8 201	3 119	112 163	62.4	6 843	1 639	5.6
September	184 962	121 960	65.9	115 356	59 980	48 511	8 124	3 165	112 191	62.4	6 604	1 569	5.4
October	185 114	122 206	66.0	115 638	60 023	48 859	7 961	3 231	112 407	62.5	6 568	1 562	5.4
November	185 244	122 637	66.2	116 100	60 042	49 254	7 904	3 241	112 859	62.7	6 537	1 468	5.3
December	185 402	122 622	66.1	116 104	60 059	49 257	7 966	3 194	112 910	62.6	6 518	1 490	5.3
1989													
January	185 644	123 390	66.5	116 708	60 477	49 529	8 019	3 287	113 421	62.9	6 682	1 480	5.4
February	185 777	123 135	66.3	116 776	60 588	49 497	7 871	3 234	113 542	62.9	6 359	1 304	5.2
March	185 897	123 227	66.3	117 022	60 795	49 503	7 809	3 198	113 824	62.9	6 205	1 353	5.0
April	186 024	123 565	66.4	117 097	60 764	49 565	7 929	3 162	113 935	62.9	6 468	1 397	5.2
May	186 181	123 474	66.3	117 099	60 795	49 583	7 890	3 125	113 974	62.9	6 375	1 348	5.2
June	186 329	123 995	66.5	117 418	61 054	49 542	8 094	3 068	114 350	63.0	6 577	1 300	5.3
July	186 483	123 967	66.5	117 472	60 947	49 693	7 961	3 227	114 245	63.0	6 495	1 435	5.2
August	186 598	124 166	66.5	117 655	60 915	49 804	8 126	3 284	114 371	63.1	6 511	1 302	5.2
September	186 726	123 944	66.4	117 354	60 668	50 015	7 870	3 219	114 135	62.8	6 590	1 360	5.3
October	186 871	124 211	66.5	117 581	60 958	49 871	7 940	3 215	114 366	62.9	6 630	1 392	5.3
November	187 017	124 637	66.6	117 912	60 958	50 221	7 964	3 132	114 780	63.0	6 725	1 418	5.4
December	187 165	124 497	66.5	117 830	61 068	50 116	7 851	3 188	114 642	63.0	6 667	1 375	5.4

[1]Not seasonally adjusted.
[2]In 1930 through 1943, the official BLS data count persons on work relief as unemployed. The unemployment rates for those years shown in parentheses count persons on work relief as employed, which is more consistent with the postwar practice. See notes and definitions.

Table 10-1B. Summary Labor Force, Employment, and Unemployment: Historical Data—*Continued*

(Thousands of persons, percent, seasonally adjusted, except as noted.)

Year and month	Civilian noninstitutional population [1]	Civilian labor force Thousands of persons	Participation rate (percent)	Employment Total	Men, 20 years and over	Women, 20 years and over	Both sexes, 16 to 19 years	Agricultural	Nonagricultural	Employment-population ratio, percent	Unemployment Total	Unemployed 15 weeks and over	Rate (percent) [2]
1990													
January	188 413	125 833	66.8	119 081	61 742	50 436	8 103	3 210	115 871	63.2	6 752	1 412	5.4
February	188 516	125 710	66.7	119 059	61 805	50 438	8 015	3 188	115 871	63.2	6 651	1 350	5.3
March	188 630	125 801	66.7	119 203	61 832	50 463	8 061	3 260	115 943	63.2	6 598	1 331	5.2
April	188 778	125 649	66.6	118 852	61 579	50 457	7 987	3 231	115 621	63.0	6 797	1 376	5.4
May	188 913	125 893	66.6	119 151	61 778	50 646	7 911	3 266	115 885	63.1	6 742	1 415	5.4
June	189 058	125 573	66.4	118 983	61 762	50 550	7 783	3 245	115 738	62.9	6 590	1 436	5.2
July	189 188	125 732	66.5	118 810	61 683	50 514	7 777	3 192	115 618	62.8	6 922	1 534	5.5
August	189 342	125 990	66.5	118 802	61 715	50 635	7 708	3 197	115 605	62.7	7 188	1 607	5.7
September	189 528	125 892	66.4	118 524	61 608	50 587	7 575	3 206	115 318	62.5	7 368	1 695	5.9
October	189 710	125 995	66.4	118 536	61 606	50 616	7 565	3 270	115 266	62.5	7 459	1 689	5.9
November	189 872	126 070	66.4	118 306	61 545	50 541	7 506	3 189	115 117	62.3	7 764	1 831	6.2
December	190 017	126 142	66.4	118 241	61 506	50 530	7 516	3 245	114 996	62.2	7 901	1 804	6.3
1991													
January	190 163	125 955	66.2	117 940	61 383	50 472	7 478	3 208	114 732	62.0	8 015	1 866	6.4
February	190 271	126 020	66.2	117 755	61 117	50 523	7 405	3 270	114 485	61.9	8 265	1 955	6.6
March	190 381	126 238	66.3	117 652	61 144	50 422	7 447	3 177	114 475	61.8	8 586	2 137	6.8
April	190 517	126 548	66.4	118 109	61 280	50 760	7 381	3 241	114 868	62.0	8 439	2 206	6.7
May	190 650	126 176	66.2	117 440	61 052	50 457	7 303	3 275	114 165	61.6	8 736	2 252	6.9
June	190 800	126 331	66.2	117 639	61 147	50 585	7 248	3 300	114 339	61.7	8 692	2 533	6.9
July	190 946	126 154	66.1	117 568	61 179	50 636	7 138	3 319	114 249	61.6	8 586	2 388	6.8
August	191 116	126 150	66.0	117 484	61 122	50 601	7 105	3 313	114 171	61.5	8 666	2 460	6.9
September	191 302	126 650	66.2	117 928	61 279	50 864	7 123	3 319	114 609	61.6	8 722	2 497	6.9
October	191 497	126 642	66.1	117 800	61 174	50 811	7 185	3 289	114 511	61.5	8 842	2 638	7.0
November	191 657	126 701	66.1	117 770	61 201	50 759	7 169	3 296	114 474	61.4	8 931	2 718	7.0
December	191 798	126 664	66.0	117 466	61 074	50 728	7 104	3 146	114 320	61.2	9 198	2 892	7.3
1992													
January	191 953	127 261	66.3	117 978	61 116	51 095	7 138	3 155	114 823	61.5	9 283	3 060	7.3
February	192 067	127 207	66.2	117 753	61 062	51 033	7 083	3 239	114 514	61.3	9 454	3 182	7.4
March	192 204	127 604	66.4	118 144	61 363	51 204	6 998	3 236	114 908	61.5	9 460	3 196	7.4
April	192 354	127 841	66.5	118 426	61 468	51 323	6 910	3 245	115 181	61.6	9 415	3 130	7.4
May	192 503	128 119	66.6	118 375	61 513	51 245	7 028	3 213	115 162	61.5	9 744	3 444	7.6
June	192 663	128 459	66.7	118 419	61 537	51 383	7 137	3 297	115 122	61.5	10 040	3 758	7.8
July	192 826	128 563	66.7	118 713	61 641	51 458	7 087	3 285	115 428	61.6	9 850	3 614	7.7
August	193 018	128 613	66.6	118 826	61 681	51 386	7 194	3 279	115 547	61.6	9 787	3 579	7.6
September	193 229	128 501	66.5	118 720	61 663	51 359	7 216	3 274	115 446	61.4	9 781	3 504	7.6
October	193 442	128 026	66.2	118 628	61 550	51 373	6 985	3 254	115 374	61.3	9 398	3 505	7.3
November	193 621	128 441	66.3	118 876	61 644	51 535	7 164	3 207	115 669	61.4	9 565	3 397	7.4
December	193 784	128 554	66.3	118 997	61 721	51 524	7 174	3 259	115 738	61.4	9 557	3 651	7.4
1993													
January	193 962	128 400	66.2	119 075	61 895	51 505	7 089	3 222	115 853	61.4	9 325	3 346	7.3
February	194 108	128 458	66.2	119 275	61 963	51 573	7 144	3 125	116 150	61.4	9 183	3 190	7.1
March	194 248	128 598	66.2	119 542	62 007	51 808	7 132	3 119	116 423	61.5	9 056	3 115	7.0
April	194 398	128 584	66.1	119 474	62 032	51 732	7 091	3 074	116 400	61.5	9 110	3 014	7.1
May	194 549	129 264	66.4	120 115	62 309	51 996	7 244	3 100	117 015	61.7	9 149	3 101	7.1
June	194 719	129 411	66.5	120 290	62 409	52 183	7 114	3 108	117 182	61.8	9 121	3 141	7.0
July	194 882	129 397	66.4	120 467	62 497	52 088	7 205	3 126	117 341	61.8	8 930	3 046	6.9
August	195 063	129 619	66.4	120 856	62 634	52 294	7 264	3 026	117 830	62.0	8 763	3 026	6.8
September	195 259	129 268	66.2	120 554	62 437	52 241	7 180	3 174	117 380	61.7	8 714	3 042	6.7
October	195 444	129 573	66.3	120 823	62 614	52 379	7 171	3 084	117 739	61.8	8 750	3 029	6.8
November	195 625	129 711	66.3	121 169	62 732	52 531	7 248	3 157	118 012	61.9	8 542	2 986	6.6
December	195 794	129 941	66.4	121 464	62 760	52 813	7 178	3 116	118 348	62.0	8 477	2 968	6.5
1994													
January	195 953	130 596	66.6	121 966	62 798	53 052	7 486	3 302	118 664	62.2	8 630	3 060	6.6
February	196 090	130 669	66.6	122 086	62 708	53 266	7 457	3 339	118 747	62.3	8 583	3 118	6.6
March	196 213	130 400	66.5	121 930	62 780	53 099	7 381	3 354	118 576	62.1	8 470	3 055	6.5
April	196 363	130 621	66.5	122 290	62 906	53 274	7 551	3 428	118 862	62.3	8 331	2 921	6.4
May	196 510	130 779	66.6	122 864	63 116	53 624	7 466	3 409	119 455	62.5	7 915	2 836	6.1
June	196 693	130 561	66.4	122 634	63 041	53 393	7 527	3 299	119 335	62.3	7 927	2 735	6.1
July	196 859	130 652	66.4	122 706	63 034	53 531	7 453	3 333	119 373	62.3	7 946	2 822	6.1
August	197 043	131 275	66.6	123 342	63 294	53 744	7 619	3 451	119 891	62.6	7 933	2 750	6.0
September	197 248	131 421	66.6	123 687	63 631	53 991	7 352	3 430	120 257	62.7	7 734	2 746	5.9
October	197 430	131 744	66.7	124 112	63 818	54 071	7 543	3 490	120 622	62.9	7 632	2 955	5.8
November	197 607	131 891	66.7	124 516	64 080	54 168	7 423	3 574	120 942	63.0	7 375	2 666	5.6
December	197 765	131 951	66.7	124 721	64 359	54 054	7 599	3 577	121 144	63.1	7 230	2 488	5.5
1995													
January	197 753	132 038	66.8	124 663	64 185	54 087	7 650	3 519	121 144	63.0	7 375	2 396	5.6
February	197 886	132 115	66.8	124 928	64 378	54 226	7 659	3 620	121 308	63.1	7 187	2 345	5.4
March	198 007	132 108	66.7	124 955	64 321	54 141	7 742	3 634	121 321	63.1	7 153	2 287	5.4
April	198 148	132 590	66.9	124 945	64 165	54 366	7 774	3 566	121 379	63.1	7 645	2 473	5.8
May	198 286	131 851	66.5	124 421	63 829	54 272	7 664	3 349	121 072	62.7	7 430	2 577	5.6
June	198 452	131 949	66.5	124 522	63 992	54 020	7 850	3 461	121 061	62.7	7 427	2 266	5.6
July	198 615	132 343	66.6	124 816	63 962	54 476	7 798	3 379	121 437	62.8	7 527	2 311	5.7
August	198 801	132 336	66.6	124 852	63 875	54 434	7 910	3 374	121 478	62.8	7 484	2 391	5.7
September	199 005	132 611	66.6	125 133	64 179	54 507	7 825	3 285	121 848	62.9	7 478	2 306	5.6
October	199 192	132 716	66.6	125 388	64 272	54 692	7 774	3 438	121 950	62.9	7 328	2 272	5.5
November	199 355	132 614	66.5	125 188	63 931	54 850	7 765	3 338	121 850	62.8	7 426	2 339	5.6
December	199 508	132 511	66.4	125 088	64 041	54 674	7 768	3 352	121 736	62.7	7 423	2 331	5.6

[1]Not seasonally adjusted.
[2]In 1930 through 1943, the official BLS data count persons on work relief as unemployed. The unemployment rates for those years shown in parentheses count persons on work relief as employed, which is more consistent with the postwar practice. See notes and definitions.

Table 10-1B. Summary Labor Force, Employment, and Unemployment: Historical Data—*Continued*

(Thousands of persons, percent, seasonally adjusted, except as noted.)

Year and month	Civilian noninsti-tutional popu-lation [1]	Civilian labor force Thousands of persons	Civilian labor force Participa-tion rate (percent)	Total	Men, 20 years and over	Women, 20 years and over	Both sexes, 16 to 19 years	Agri-cultural	Nonagri-cultural	Employ-ment-population ratio, percent	Unemployment Total	Unem-ployed 15 weeks and over	Rate (percent) [2]
1996													
January	199 634	132 616	66.4	125 125	64 180	54 580	7 733	3 483	121 642	62.7	7 491	2 371	5.6
February	199 772	132 952	66.6	125 639	64 398	54 844	7 688	3 547	122 092	62.9	7 313	2 307	5.5
March	199 921	133 180	66.6	125 862	64 506	54 994	7 673	3 489	122 373	63.0	7 318	2 454	5.5
April	200 101	133 409	66.7	125 994	64 481	55 067	7 774	3 406	122 588	63.0	7 415	2 455	5.6
May	200 278	133 667	66.7	126 244	64 683	55 034	7 841	3 473	122 771	63.0	7 423	2 403	5.6
June	200 459	133 697	66.7	126 602	64 940	55 177	7 739	3 424	123 178	63.2	7 095	2 355	5.3
July	200 641	134 284	66.9	126 947	65 068	55 362	7 859	3 433	123 514	63.3	7 337	2 297	5.5
August	200 847	134 054	66.7	127 172	65 216	55 525	7 731	3 395	123 777	63.3	6 882	2 267	5.1
September	201 060	134 515	66.9	127 536	65 169	55 669	7 935	3 448	124 088	63.4	6 979	2 220	5.2
October	201 273	134 921	67.0	127 890	65 460	55 750	7 980	3 463	124 427	63.5	7 031	2 268	5.2
November	201 463	135 007	67.0	127 771	65 320	55 896	7 875	3 356	124 415	63.4	7 236	2 159	5.4
December	201 636	135 113	67.0	127 860	65 435	55 849	7 883	3 445	124 415	63.4	7 253	2 124	5.4
1997													
January	202 285	135 456	67.0	128 298	65 679	56 024	7 930	3 449	124 849	63.4	7 158	2 162	5.3
February	202 388	135 400	66.9	128 298	65 758	55 955	7 948	3 353	124 945	63.4	7 102	2 140	5.2
March	202 513	135 891	67.1	128 891	65 974	56 270	7 951	3 419	125 472	63.6	7 000	2 110	5.2
April	202 674	136 016	67.1	129 143	66 092	56 347	7 974	3 462	125 681	63.7	6 873	2 176	5.1
May	202 832	136 119	67.1	129 464	66 328	56 446	7 964	3 437	126 027	63.8	6 655	2 121	4.9
June	203 000	136 211	67.1	129 412	66 308	56 573	7 849	3 409	126 003	63.7	6 799	2 085	5.0
July	203 166	136 477	67.2	129 822	66 422	56 785	7 975	3 422	126 400	63.9	6 655	2 119	4.9
August	203 364	136 618	67.2	130 010	66 508	56 852	7 922	3 359	126 651	63.9	6 608	2 004	4.8
September	203 570	136 675	67.1	130 019	66 483	56 931	7 873	3 392	126 627	63.9	6 656	2 074	4.9
October	203 767	136 633	67.1	130 179	66 511	56 982	7 876	3 312	126 867	63.9	6 454	1 950	4.7
November	203 941	136 961	67.2	130 653	66 765	57 039	8 042	3 386	127 267	64.1	6 308	1 817	4.6
December	204 098	137 155	67.2	130 679	66 643	57 219	7 923	3 405	127 274	64.0	6 476	1 901	4.7
1998													
January	204 238	137 095	67.1	130 726	66 750	56 941	8 171	3 299	127 389	64.0	6 368	1 833	4.6
February	204 400	137 112	67.1	130 807	66 856	56 992	8 137	3 284	127 522	64.0	6 306	1 809	4.6
March	204 546	137 236	67.1	130 814	66 721	57 080	8 235	3 146	127 650	64.0	6 422	1 772	4.7
April	204 731	137 150	67.0	131 209	67 151	57 074	8 071	3 334	127 852	64.1	5 941	1 476	4.3
May	204 899	137 372	67.0	131 325	67 164	57 155	8 228	3 360	127 959	64.1	6 047	1 490	4.4
June	205 085	137 455	67.0	131 244	67 054	57 156	8 268	3 380	127 874	64.0	6 212	1 613	4.5
July	205 270	137 588	67.0	131 329	67 119	57 192	8 221	3 455	127 913	64.0	6 259	1 577	4.5
August	205 479	137 570	67.0	131 390	66 985	57 332	8 289	3 509	127 970	63.9	6 179	1 626	4.5
September	205 699	138 286	67.2	131 986	67 254	57 520	8 489	3 500	128 399	64.2	6 300	1 688	4.6
October	205 919	138 279	67.2	131 999	67 433	57 529	8 347	3 593	128 389	64.1	6 280	1 582	4.5
November	206 104	138 381	67.1	132 280	67 591	57 638	8 269	3 375	128 897	64.2	6 100	1 590	4.4
December	206 270	138 634	67.2	132 602	67 548	57 840	8 340	3 246	129 320	64.3	6 032	1 559	4.4
1999													
January	206 719	139 003	67.2	133 027	67 679	58 256	8 367	3 233	129 802	64.4	5 976	1 490	4.3
February	206 873	138 967	67.2	132 856	67 498	58 129	8 399	3 246	129 647	64.2	6 111	1 551	4.4
March	207 036	138 730	67.0	132 947	67 660	58 132	8 343	3 238	129 656	64.2	5 783	1 472	4.2
April	207 236	138 959	67.1	132 955	67 542	58 260	8 334	3 336	129 615	64.2	6 004	1 480	4.3
May	207 427	139 107	67.1	133 311	67 539	58 440	8 454	3 335	129 937	64.3	5 796	1 505	4.2
June	207 632	139 329	67.1	133 378	67 700	58 641	8 175	3 386	129 982	64.2	5 951	1 624	4.3
July	207 828	139 439	67.1	133 414	67 731	58 490	8 306	3 346	130 146	64.2	6 025	1 513	4.3
August	208 038	139 430	67.0	133 591	67 768	58 707	8 208	3 234	130 366	64.2	5 838	1 455	4.2
September	208 265	139 622	67.0	133 707	67 882	58 735	8 323	3 173	130 434	64.2	5 915	1 449	4.2
October	208 483	139 771	67.0	133 993	67 840	58 921	8 394	3 229	130 758	64.3	5 778	1 438	4.1
November	208 666	140 025	67.1	134 309	68 094	59 018	8 358	3 343	130 989	64.4	5 716	1 378	4.1
December	208 832	140 177	67.1	134 523	68 217	59 056	8 370	3 260	131 257	64.4	5 653	1 375	4.0
2000													
January	211 410	142 267	67.3	136 559	69 419	59 842	8 360	2 613	133 863	64.6	5 708	1 380	4.0
February	211 576	142 456	67.3	136 598	69 505	59 887	8 359	2 731	133 912	64.6	5 858	1 300	4.1
March	211 772	142 434	67.3	136 701	69 482	59 977	8 355	2 579	134 022	64.6	5 733	1 312	4.0
April	212 018	142 751	67.3	137 270	69 519	60 358	8 458	2 505	134 806	64.7	5 481	1 261	3.8
May	212 242	142 388	67.1	136 630	69 399	59 951	8 344	2 480	134 144	64.4	5 758	1 325	4.0
June	212 466	142 591	67.1	136 940	69 629	60 027	8 308	2 445	134 528	64.5	5 651	1 242	4.0
July	212 677	142 278	66.9	136 531	69 525	60 011	8 078	2 408	134 196	64.2	5 747	1 343	4.0
August	212 916	142 514	66.9	136 662	69 823	59 719	8 280	2 433	134 311	64.2	5 853	1 394	4.1
September	213 163	142 518	66.9	136 893	69 700	60 083	8 176	2 384	134 489	64.2	5 625	1 290	3.9
October	213 405	142 622	66.8	137 088	69 762	60 238	8 124	2 319	134 808	64.2	5 534	1 337	3.9
November	213 540	142 962	66.9	137 322	69 910	60 269	8 211	2 330	134 921	64.3	5 639	1 315	3.9
December	213 736	143 248	67.0	137 614	69 939	60 503	8 258	2 389	135 194	64.4	5 634	1 329	3.9
2001													
January	213 888	143 800	67.2	137 778	70 064	60 609	8 243	2 360	135 304	64.4	6 023	1 372	4.2
February	214 110	143 701	67.1	137 612	69 959	60 615	8 154	2 370	135 291	64.3	6 089	1 491	4.2
March	214 305	143 924	67.2	137 783	69 881	60 902	8 120	2 350	135 372	64.3	6 141	1 521	4.3
April	214 525	143 569	66.9	137 299	69 916	60 523	7 970	2 336	135 036	64.0	6 271	1 499	4.4
May	214 732	143 318	66.7	137 092	69 865	60 509	7 760	2 353	134 735	63.8	6 226	1 502	4.3
June	214 950	143 357	66.7	136 873	69 690	60 371	7 942	2 082	134 755	63.7	6 484	1 532	4.5
July	215 180	143 654	66.8	137 071	69 808	60 480	7 929	2 295	134 858	63.7	6 583	1 653	4.6
August	215 420	143 284	66.5	136 241	69 585	60 301	7 531	2 305	133 944	63.2	7 042	1 861	4.9
September	215 665	143 989	66.8	136 846	69 933	60 265	7 836	2 322	134 558	63.5	7 142	1 950	5.0
October	215 903	144 086	66.7	136 392	69 621	60 168	7 858	2 327	134 098	63.2	7 694	2 082	5.3
November	216 117	144 240	66.7	136 238	69 444	60 174	7 873	2 203	133 955	63.0	8 003	2 318	5.5
December	216 315	144 305	66.7	136 047	69 551	60 095	7 712	2 293	133 751	62.9	8 258	2 444	5.7

[1]Not seasonally adjusted.
[2]In 1930 through 1943, the official BLS data count persons on work relief as unemployed. The unemployment rates for those years shown in parentheses count persons on work relief as employed, which is more consistent with the postwar practice. See notes and definitions.

Table 10-1B. Summary Labor Force, Employment, and Unemployment: Historical Data—*Continued*

(Thousands of persons, percent, seasonally adjusted, except as noted.)

Year and month	Civilian noninstitutional population [1]	Civilian labor force Thousands of persons	Civilian labor force Participation rate (percent)	Employment Total	Men, 20 years and over	Women, 20 years and over	Both sexes, 16 to 19 years	Agricultural	Nonagricultural	Employment-population ratio, percent	Unemployment Total	Unemployed 15 weeks and over	Rate (percent) [2]
2002													
January	216 506	143 883	66.5	135 701	69 308	60 032	7 619	2 385	133 233	62.7	8 182	2 578	5.7
February	216 663	144 653	66.8	136 438	69 534	60 479	7 650	2 397	134 127	63.0	8 215	2 608	5.7
March	216 823	144 481	66.6	136 177	69 480	60 190	7 802	2 368	133 816	62.8	8 304	2 719	5.7
April	217 006	144 725	66.7	136 126	69 574	60 204	7 621	2 371	133 833	62.7	8 599	2 852	5.9
May	217 198	144 938	66.7	136 539	69 981	60 226	7 588	2 260	134 278	62.9	8 399	2 967	5.8
June	217 407	144 808	66.6	136 415	69 769	60 297	7 617	2 161	134 135	62.7	8 393	3 023	5.8
July	217 630	144 803	66.5	136 413	69 806	60 290	7 591	2 324	134 107	62.7	8 390	2 966	5.8
August	217 866	145 009	66.6	136 705	69 937	60 560	7 477	2 127	134 593	62.7	8 304	2 887	5.7
September	218 107	145 552	66.7	137 302	70 207	60 679	7 667	2 285	135 102	63.0	8 251	2 971	5.7
October	218 340	145 314	66.6	137 008	69 948	60 663	7 537	2 471	134 580	62.7	8 307	3 042	5.7
November	218 548	145 041	66.4	136 521	69 615	60 697	7 487	2 261	134 171	62.5	8 520	3 062	5.9
December	218 741	145 066	66.3	136 426	69 620	60 667	7 385	2 352	134 071	62.4	8 640	3 271	6.0
2003													
January	219 897	145 937	66.4	137 417	69 919	61 406	7 358	2 337	135 045	62.5	8 520	3 166	5.8
February	220 114	146 100	66.4	137 482	70 262	61 159	7 322	2 234	135 306	62.5	8 618	3 161	5.9
March	220 317	146 022	66.3	137 434	70 243	61 317	7 143	2 263	135 232	62.4	8 588	3 161	5.9
April	220 540	146 474	66.4	137 633	70 311	61 374	7 223	2 150	135 561	62.4	8 842	3 348	6.0
May	220 768	146 500	66.4	137 544	70 215	61 393	7 228	2 183	135 370	62.3	8 957	3 318	6.1
June	221 014	147 056	66.5	137 790	70 159	61 747	7 268	2 185	135 419	62.3	9 266	3 552	6.3
July	221 252	146 485	66.2	137 474	70 190	61 437	7 150	2 187	135 242	62.1	9 011	3 633	6.2
August	221 507	146 445	66.1	137 549	70 237	61 442	7 035	2 313	135 200	62.1	8 896	3 557	6.1
September	221 779	146 530	66.1	137 609	70 631	61 119	7 112	2 349	135 355	62.0	8 921	3 486	6.1
October	222 039	146 716	66.1	137 984	70 685	61 451	7 060	2 479	135 571	62.1	8 732	3 451	6.0
November	222 279	147 000	66.1	138 424	70 935	61 494	7 112	2 373	136 003	62.3	8 576	3 420	5.8
December	222 509	146 729	65.9	138 411	71 170	61 396	6 978	2 243	136 145	62.2	8 317	3 366	5.7
2004													
January	222 161	146 842	66.1	138 472	71 318	61 183	7 194	2 196	136 228	62.3	8 370	3 364	5.7
February	222 357	146 709	66.0	138 542	71 122	61 514	7 077	2 210	136 362	62.3	8 167	3 248	5.6
March	222 544	146 944	66.0	138 453	71 155	61 534	6 930	2 180	136 302	62.2	8 491	3 314	5.8
April	222 757	146 850	65.9	138 680	71 121	61 647	7 093	2 241	136 474	62.3	8 170	2 971	5.6
May	222 967	147 065	66.0	138 852	71 180	61 762	7 126	2 300	136 556	62.3	8 212	3 103	5.6
June	223 196	147 460	66.1	139 174	71 562	61 793	7 007	2 237	136 748	62.4	8 286	3 130	5.6
July	223 422	147 692	66.1	139 556	71 780	61 884	7 166	2 222	137 354	62.5	8 136	2 918	5.5
August	223 677	147 564	66.0	139 573	71 808	61 836	7 123	2 333	137 230	62.4	7 990	2 846	5.4
September	223 941	147 415	65.8	139 487	71 744	61 859	7 056	2 251	137 323	62.3	7 927	2 910	5.4
October	224 192	147 793	65.9	139 732	71 860	61 942	7 180	2 216	137 598	62.3	8 061	3 041	5.5
November	224 422	148 162	66.0	140 231	72 110	62 088	7 216	2 206	137 978	62.5	7 932	2 960	5.4
December	224 640	148 059	65.9	140 125	72 058	62 136	7 202	2 171	137 947	62.4	7 934	2 927	5.4
2005													
January	224 837	148 029	65.8	140 245	72 063	62 260	7 071	2 112	138 111	62.4	7 784	2 851	5.3
February	225 041	148 364	65.9	140 385	72 299	62 253	7 073	2 129	138 267	62.4	7 980	2 896	5.4
March	225 236	148 391	65.9	140 654	72 478	62 222	7 185	2 180	138 462	62.4	7 737	2 817	5.2
April	225 441	148 926	66.1	141 254	72 860	62 483	7 190	2 248	138 992	62.7	7 672	2 678	5.2
May	225 670	149 261	66.1	141 609	73 133	62 557	7 201	2 225	139 379	62.8	7 651	2 683	5.1
June	225 911	149 238	66.1	141 714	73 223	62 516	7 140	2 302	139 276	62.7	7 524	2 405	5.0
July	226 153	149 432	66.1	142 026	73 337	62 691	7 150	2 308	139 789	62.8	7 406	2 449	5.0
August	226 421	149 779	66.2	142 434	73 513	62 844	7 240	2 183	140 277	62.9	7 345	2 569	4.9
September	226 693	149 954	66.1	142 401	73 333	63 035	7 141	2 181	140 276	62.8	7 553	2 537	5.0
October	226 959	150 001	66.1	142 548	73 445	63 127	7 124	2 191	140 435	62.8	7 453	2 492	5.0
November	227 204	150 065	66.0	142 499	73 341	63 127	7 265	2 174	140 299	62.7	7 566	2 486	5.0
December	227 425	150 030	66.0	142 752	73 467	63 209	7 139	2 094	140 635	62.8	7 279	2 429	4.9
2006													
January	227 553	150 214	66.0	143 150	73 892	63 151	7 197	2 164	140 933	62.9	7 064	2 270	4.7
February	227 763	150 641	66.1	143 457	73 972	63 304	7 298	2 178	141 254	63.0	7 184	2 546	4.8
March	227 975	150 813	66.2	143 741	74 228	63 353	7 342	2 153	141 604	63.1	7 072	2 373	4.7
April	228 199	150 881	66.1	143 761	74 204	63 413	7 198	2 249	141 388	63.0	7 120	2 353	4.7
May	228 428	151 069	66.1	144 089	74 229	63 656	7 215	2 194	141 859	63.1	6 980	2 303	4.6
June	228 671	151 354	66.2	144 353	74 261	63 866	7 393	2 256	142 019	63.1	7 001	2 127	4.6
July	228 912	151 377	66.1	144 202	74 011	64 030	7 324	2 278	142 066	63.0	7 175	2 289	4.7
August	229 167	151 716	66.2	144 625	74 384	64 139	7 266	2 240	142 440	63.1	7 091	2 293	4.7
September	229 420	151 662	66.1	144 815	74 866	63 922	7 196	2 182	142 661	63.1	6 847	2 231	4.5
October	229 675	152 041	66.2	145 314	74 833	64 298	7 289	2 183	143 222	63.3	6 727	2 062	4.4
November	229 905	152 406	66.3	145 534	74 962	64 328	7 331	2 164	143 350	63.3	6 872	2 159	4.5
December	230 108	152 732	66.4	145 970	75 232	64 518	7 287	2 233	143 716	63.4	6 762	2 083	4.4
2007													
January	230 650	153 144	66.4	146 028	75 238	64 621	7 240	2 214	143 785	63.3	7 116	2 156	4.6
February	230 834	152 983	66.3	146 057	75 239	64 750	7 133	2 295	143 741	63.3	6 927	2 211	4.5
March	231 034	153 051	66.2	146 320	75 386	64 928	7 061	2 178	144 153	63.3	6 731	2 255	4.4
April	231 253	152 435	65.9	145 586	75 342	64 366	6 985	2 069	143 385	63.0	6 850	2 281	4.5
May	231 480	152 670	66.0	145 903	75 386	64 724	6 888	2 081	143 773	63.0	6 766	2 231	4.4
June	231 713	153 041	66.0	146 063	75 327	64 788	7 109	1 946	144 112	63.0	6 979	2 281	4.6
July	231 958	153 054	66.0	145 905	75 247	64 766	6 953	2 016	144 041	62.9	7 149	2 364	4.7
August	232 211	152 749	65.8	145 682	75 195	64 838	6 714	1 863	143 865	62.7	7 067	2 333	4.6
September	232 461	153 414	66.0	146 244	75 273	65 086	7 001	2 095	144 148	62.9	7 170	2 355	4.7
October	232 715	153 183	65.8	145 946	75 146	64 842	7 039	2 121	143 926	62.7	7 237	2 300	4.7
November	232 939	153 835	66.0	146 595	75 683	64 985	7 071	2 148	144 413	62.9	7 240	2 366	4.7
December	233 156	153 918	66.0	146 273	75 510	64 910	7 032	2 219	144 018	62.7	7 645	2 501	5.0

[1] Not seasonally adjusted.
[2] In 1930 through 1943, the official BLS data count persons on work relief as unemployed. The unemployment rates for those years shown in parentheses count persons on work relief as employed, which is more consistent with the postwar practice. See notes and definitions.

Table 10-1B. Summary Labor Force, Employment, and Unemployment: Historical Data—*Continued*

(Thousands of persons, percent, seasonally adjusted, except as noted.)

Year and month	Civilian noninstitutional population [1]	Civilian labor force		Employment, thousands of persons						Employment-population ratio, percent	Unemployment		
		Thousands of persons	Participation rate (percent)	Total	By age and sex			By industry			Thousands of persons		Rate (percent) [2]
					Men, 20 years and over	Women, 20 years and over	Both sexes, 16 to 19 years	Agricultural	Nonagricultural		Total	Unemployed 15 weeks and over	
2008													
January	232 616	154 063	66.2	146 378	75 551	65 058	7 015	2 205	144 168	62.9	7 685	2 540	5.0
February	232 809	153 653	66.0	146 156	75 450	65 021	6 820	2 190	143 943	62.8	7 497	2 446	4.9
March	232 995	153 908	66.1	146 086	75 294	65 074	6 813	2 172	143 871	62.7	7 822	2 491	5.1
April	233 198	153 769	65.9	146 132	75 182	65 107	6 947	2 115	143 874	62.7	7 637	2 687	5.0
May	233 405	154 303	66.1	145 908	74 953	65 137	7 182	2 113	143 737	62.5	8 395	2 780	5.4
June	233 627	154 313	66.1	145 737	74 975	65 169	6 925	2 127	143 629	62.4	8 575	2 913	5.6
July	233 864	154 469	66.1	145 532	74 950	65 103	6 909	2 134	143 519	62.2	8 937	3 114	5.8
August	234 107	154 641	66.1	145 203	74 658	65 008	6 801	2 148	143 086	62.0	9 438	3 420	6.1
September	234 360	154 570	66.0	145 076	74 456	65 078	6 850	2 231	142 796	61.9	9 494	3 626	6.1
October	234 612	154 876	66.0	144 802	74 263	65 103	6 793	2 199	142 689	61.7	10 074	3 990	6.5
November	234 828	154 639	65.9	144 100	73 943	64 885	6 612	2 207	141 962	61.4	10 538	3 923	6.8
December	235 035	154 655	65.8	143 369	73 311	64 813	6 601	2 209	141 139	61.0	11 286	4 547	7.3
2009													
January	234 739	154 210	65.7	142 152	72 724	64 209	5 218	2 147	140 029	60.6	12 058	4 764	7.8
February	234 913	154 538	65.8	141 640	72 260	64 195	5 185	2 130	139 493	60.3	12 898	5 455	8.3
March	235 086	154 133	65.6	140 707	71 629	64 027	5 051	2 031	138 664	59.9	13 426	5 886	8.7
April	235 271	154 509	65.7	140 656	71 599	64 021	5 036	2 146	138 437	59.8	13 853	6 385	9.0
May	235 452	154 747	65.7	140 248	71 410	63 807	5 031	2 145	138 036	59.6	14 499	7 022	9.4
June	235 655	154 716	65.7	140 009	71 326	63 747	4 937	2 165	137 841	59.4	14 707	7 837	9.5
July	235 870	154 502	65.5	139 901	71 273	63 761	4 867	2 126	137 819	59.3	14 601	7 839	9.5
August	236 087	154 307	65.4	139 492	71 111	63 633	4 749	2 088	137 371	59.1	14 814	7 828	9.6
September	236 322	153 827	65.1	138 818	70 844	63 324	4 649	2 033	136 734	58.7	15 009	8 402	9.8
October	236 550	153 784	65.0	138 432	70 713	63 275	4 445	2 039	136 483	58.5	15 352	8 648	10.0
November	236 743	153 878	65.0	138 659	70 774	63 422	4 463	2 098	136 640	58.6	15 219	8 755	9.9
December	236 924	153 111	64.6	138 013	70 479	63 086	4 449	2 087	135 904	58.3	15 098	8 835	9.9
2010													
January	236 832	153 404	64.8	138 451	70 506	63 515	4 430	2 131	136 390	58.5	14 953	8 903	9.7
February	236 998	153 720	64.9	138 599	70 601	63 505	4 493	2 307	136 333	58.5	15 121	8 933	9.8
March	237 159	153 964	64.9	138 752	70 876	63 378	4 498	2 211	136 588	58.5	15 212	9 096	9.9
April	237 329	154 642	65.2	139 309	71 356	63 416	4 537	2 288	136 966	58.7	15 333	9 133	9.9
May	237 499	154 106	64.9	139 247	71 378	63 436	4 433	2 197	136 998	58.6	14 858	8 892	9.6
June	237 690	153 631	64.6	139 148	71 353	63 555	4 240	2 140	136 975	58.5	14 483	8 898	9.4
July	237 890	153 706	64.6	139 179	71 457	63 415	4 307	2 172	136 934	58.5	14 527	8 704	9.5
August	238 099	154 087	64.7	139 427	71 607	63 420	4 400	2 163	137 187	58.6	14 660	8 405	9.5
September	238 322	153 971	64.6	139 393	71 592	63 533	4 268	2 161	137 209	58.5	14 578	8 444	9.5
October	238 530	153 631	64.4	139 111	71 432	63 382	4 297	2 338	136 891	58.3	14 520	8 617	9.5
November	238 715	154 127	64.6	139 030	71 140	63 494	4 396	2 191	136 872	58.2	15 097	8 697	9.8
December	238 889	153 639	64.3	139 266	71 470	63 493	4 302	2 186	137 072	58.3	14 373	8 549	9.4
2011													
January	238 704	153 198	64.2	139 287	71 544	63 413	4 330	2 270	137 036	58.4	13 910	8 430	9.1
February	238 851	153 280	64.2	139 422	71 819	63 281	4 322	2 266	137 182	58.4	13 858	8 213	9.0
March	239 000	153 403	64.2	139 655	71 834	63 461	4 360	2 260	137 471	58.4	13 748	8 184	9.0
April	239 146	153 566	64.2	139 622	71 946	63 373	4 302	2 143	137 438	58.4	13 944	8 007	9.1
May	239 313	153 526	64.2	139 653	72 120	63 267	4 266	2 230	137 395	58.4	13 873	8 189	9.0
June	239 489	153 379	64.0	139 409	71 999	63 134	4 276	2 253	137 136	58.2	13 971	8 107	9.1
July	239 671	153 309	64.0	139 524	72 008	63 293	4 223	2 225	137 215	58.2	13 785	8 151	9.0
August	239 871	153 724	64.1	139 904	72 217	63 339	4 348	2 344	137 470	58.3	13 820	8 214	9.0
September	240 071	154 059	64.2	140 154	72 409	63 372	4 372	2 232	137 904	58.4	13 905	8 282	9.0
October	240 269	153 940	64.1	140 335	72 415	63 540	4 381	2 211	138 283	58.4	13 604	7 808	8.8
November	240 441	154 072	64.1	140 747	72 861	63 489	4 396	2 251	138 500	58.5	13 326	7 713	8.6
December	240 584	153 927	64.0	140 836	73 039	63 406	4 390	2 362	138 454	58.5	13 090	7 555	8.5
2012													
January	242 269	154 328	63.7	141 677	73 083	64 219	4 375	2 211	139 437	58.5	12 650	7 467	8.2
February	242 435	154 826	63.9	141 943	73 103	64 436	4 403	2 193	139 782	58.5	12 883	7 373	8.3
March	242 604	154 811	63.8	142 079	73 181	64 521	4 377	2 246	139 888	58.6	12 732	7 216	8.2
April	242 784	154 565	63.7	141 963	73 131	64 456	4 376	2 203	139 712	58.5	12 603	7 056	8.2
May	242 966	154 946	63.8	142 257	73 245	64 600	4 412	2 278	139 980	58.6	12 689	7 069	8.2
June	243 155	155 134	63.8	142 432	73 294	64 629	4 509	2 221	140 246	58.6	12 702	7 170	8.2
July	243 354	154 970	63.7	142 272	73 301	64 456	4 515	2 212	140 020	58.5	12 698	6 946	8.2
August	243 566	154 669	63.5	142 204	73 197	64 644	4 364	2 106	140 017	58.4	12 464	6 848	8.1
September	243 772	155 018	63.6	142 947	73 677	64 857	4 414	2 178	140 773	58.6	12 070	6 728	7.8
October	243 983	155 507	63.7	143 369	73 923	64 980	4 466	2 176	141 279	58.8	12 138	6 795	7.8
November	244 174	155 279	63.6	143 233	73 807	64 962	4 465	2 126	141 110	58.7	12 045	6 563	7.8
December	244 350	155 485	63.6	143 212	73 924	64 901	4 387	2 066	141 121	58.6	12 273	6 634	7.9
2013													
January	244 663	155 699	63.6	143 384	74 084	64 790	4 510	2 057	141 234	58.6	12 315	6 573	7.9
February	244 828	155 511	63.5	143 464	74 183	64 911	4 370	2 070	141 393	58.6	12 047	6 485	7.7
March	244 995	155 099	63.3	143 393	74 190	64 838	4 365	2 020	141 350	58.5	11 706	6 355	7.5
April	245 175	155 359	63.4	143 676	74 161	65 148	4 368	2 048	141 604	58.6	11 683	6 329	7.5
May	245 363	155 609	63.4	143 919	74 137	65 323	4 459	2 081	141 860	58.7	11 690	6 287	7.5
June	245 552	155 822	63.5	144 075	74 265	65 340	4 470	2 091	142 021	58.7	11 747	6 218	7.5
July	245 756	155 693	63.4	144 285	74 301	65 514	4 470	2 171	142 081	58.7	11 408	6 031	7.3
August	245 959	155 435	63.2	144 179	74 015	65 743	4 421	2 205	141 918	58.6	11 256	5 973	7.2
September	246 168	155 473	63.2	144 270	74 115	65 539	4 580	2 208	142 058	58.6	11 203	5 927	7.2
October	246 381	154 625	62.8	143 485	73 808	65 229	4 448	2 208	141 449	58.2	11 140	5 824	7.2
November	246 567	155 284	63.0	144 443	74 373	65 547	4 523	2 139	142 317	58.6	10 841	5 786	7.0
December	246 745	154 937	62.8	144 586	74 467	65 617	4 502	2 229	142 337	58.6	10 351	5 530	6.7

[1]Not seasonally adjusted.
[2]In 1930 through 1943, the official BLS data count persons on work relief as unemployed. The unemployment rates for those years shown in parentheses count persons on work relief as employed, which is more consistent with the postwar practice. See notes and definitions.

Table 10-1B. Summary Labor Force, Employment, and Unemployment: Historical Data—*Continued*

(Thousands of persons, percent, seasonally adjusted, except as noted.)

Year and month	Civilian noninstitutional population [1]	Civilian labor force — Thousands of persons	Civilian labor force — Participation rate (percent)	Employment — Total	Employment — Men, 20 years and over	Employment — Women, 20 years and over	Employment — Both sexes, 16 to 19 years	Employment — Agricultural	Employment — Nonagricultural	Employment-population ratio, percent	Unemployment — Total	Unemployment — Unemployed 15 weeks and over	Unemployment — Rate (percent) [2]
2014													
January	230 244	149 943	65.1	140 818	74 905	65 913	4 388	1 999	141 527	58.1	10 280	5 392	6.6
February	230 421	150 207	65.2	140 989	74 820	66 168	4 312	1 973	142 160	58.3	10 387	5 657	6.7
March	230 600	150 488	65.3	141 293	75 284	66 009	4 504	2 008	143 082	58.7	10 384	5 708	6.6
April	230 787	149 878	64.9	141 239	75 163	66 076	4 485	2 048	143 718	58.9	9 696	5 139	6.2
May	230 978	150 006	64.9	141 323	75 159	66 164	4 545	2 101	144 297	59.1	9 761	4 898	6.3
June	231 178	150 059	64.9	141 771	75 504	66 267	4 476	2 288	144 815	59.4	9 453	4 448	6.1
July	231 394	150 396	65.0	141 881	75 631	66 250	4 520	2 403	144 862	59.4	9 648	4 452	6.2
August	231 607	150 441	65.0	141 956	75 668	66 289	4 495	2 472	144 175	59.1	9 568	4 321	6.1
September	231 831	150 200	64.8	142 081	75 889	66 192	4 527	2 482	144 459	59.1	9 237	4 242	5.9
October	232 049	150 377	64.8	142 488	75 928	66 560	4 772	2 517	145 419	59.5	8 983	4 251	5.7
November	232 243	150 627	64.9	142 569	75 675	66 894	4 762	2 332	145 335	59.3	9 071	4 144	5.8
December	232 432	150 383	64.7	142 658	76 026	66 632	4 784	2 220	144 970	59.1	8 688	3 922	5.6
2015													
January	249 723	157 022	62.9	148 061	75 364	66 894	4 294	2 234	144 317	59.3	8 962	4 250	5.7
February	249 899	156 771	62.7	148 108	75 671	67 058	4 389	2 234	144 884	59.3	8 663	4 248	5.5
March	250 080	156 781	62.7	148 244	76 122	67 022	4 491	2 405	145 230	59.3	8 538	4 064	5.4
April	250 266	157 043	62.8	148 522	76 749	67 303	4 536	2 294	146 293	59.3	8 521	3 802	5.4
May	250 455	157 447	62.9	148 792	77 137	67 493	4 718	2 431	146 918	59.4	8 655	3 851	5.5
June	250 663	156 993	62.6	148 742	77 315	67 003	5 327	2 703	146 942	59.3	8 251	3 369	5.3
July	250 876	157 125	62.6	148 890	77 541	66 485	5 696	2 601	147 121	59.3	8 235	3 245	5.2
August	251 096	157 109	62.6	149 092	77 311	66 874	5 042	2 539	146 689	59.4	8 017	3 318	5.1
September	251 325	156 809	62.4	148 932	77 110	67 394	4 476	2 471	146 509	59.3	7 877	3 207	5.0
October	251 541	157 123	62.5	149 255	77 258	67 885	4 574	2 518	147 198	59.3	7 869	3 301	5.0
November	251 747	157 358	62.5	149 419	76 911	68 335	4 520	2 363	147 404	59.4	7 939	3 256	5.0
December	251 936	157 957	62.7	150 030	76 827	68 131	4 745	2 273	147 430	59.6	7 927	3 231	5.0
2016													
January	252 397	158 362	62.7	150 533	76 644	67 904	4 490	2 200	146 838	59.6	7 829	3 297	4.9
February	252 577	158 888	62.9	151 043	77 148	68 305	4 608	2 274	147 787	59.8	7 845	3 525	4.9
March	252 768	159 278	63.0	151 301	77 639	68 451	4 648	2 491	148 247	59.9	7 977	3 651	5.0
April	252 969	158 938	62.8	151 028	78 028	68 346	4 701	2 478	148 597	59.7	7 910	3 499	5.0
May	253 174	158 510	62.6	151 058	78 241	68 496	4 857	2 620	148 974	59.7	7 451	3 113	4.7
June	253 397	158 889	62.7	151 090	78 673	67 769	5 548	2 661	149 329	59.6	7 799	2 970	4.9
July	253 620	159 295	62.8	151 546	78 695	67 702	6 040	2 597	149 840	59.8	7 749	3 060	4.9
August	253 854	159 508	62.8	151 655	78 562	67 776	5 466	2 718	149 086	59.7	7 853	2 942	4.9
September	254 091	159 830	62.9	151 926	78 459	68 709	4 810	2 526	149 451	59.8	7 904	3 004	4.9
October	254 321	159 643	62.8	151 902	78 538	68 997	4 800	2 408	149 927	59.7	7 740	3 087	4.8
November	254 540	159 456	62.6	152 048	78 405	69 203	4 778	2 366	150 020	59.7	7 409	2 859	4.6
December	254 742	159 640	62.7	152 111	77 984	68 984	4 831	2 180	149 617	59.7	7 529	2 945	4.7
2017													
January	254 082	159 718	62.9	152 076	78 448	68 572	5 056	2 225	149 851	59.9	7 642	3 055	4.8
February	254 246	159 997	62.9	152 511	78 515	68 978	5 018	2 262	150 249	60.0	7 486	2 813	4.7
March	254 414	160 235	63.0	153 064	78 548	69 337	5 179	2 441	150 623	60.2	7 171	2 725	4.5
April	254 588	160 181	62.9	153 161	78 839	69 218	5 104	2 587	150 574	60.2	7 021	2 719	4.4
May	254 767	159 729	62.7	152 892	78 794	69 087	5 010	2 564	150 328	60.0	6 837	2 788	4.3
June	254 957	160 214	62.8	153 250	78 753	69 289	5 209	2 612	150 638	60.1	6 964	2 652	4.3
July	255 151	160 467	62.9	153 511	78 863	69 586	5 062	2 506	151 005	60.2	6 956	2 779	4.3
August	255 357	160 598	62.9	153 471	78 887	69 502	5 082	2 508	150 963	60.1	7 127	2 802	4.4
September	255 562	161 082	63.0	154 324	79 393	69 692	5 238	2 367	151 957	60.4	6 759	2 695	4.2
October	255 766	160 371	62.7	153 846	79 248	69 576	5 022	2 559	151 287	60.2	6 524	2 500	4.1
November	255 949	160 533	62.7	153 917	79 324	69 665	4 928	2 451	151 466	60.1	6 616	2 514	4.1
December	256 109	160 597	62.7	154 021	79 431	69 614	4 977	2 368	151 653	60.1	6 576	2 397	4.1
2018													
January	256 780	161 123	62.7	154 495	82 915	72 238	5 143	2 480	2 480	60.2	6 641	2 387	4.1
February	256 934	161 900	63.0	155 174	83 258	72 595	5 178	2 450	2 450	60.4	6 687	2 336	4.1
March	257 097	161 646	62.9	155 266	83 149	72 580	5 123	2 331	2 331	60.4	6 486	2 237	4.0
April	257 272	161 551	62.8	155 363	83 163	72 558	5 074	2 312	2 312	60.3	6 335	2 330	3.9
May	257 454	161 667	62.8	155 688	83 257	72 590	5 079	2 353	2 353	60.4	6 128	2 164	3.8
June	257 642	162 129	62.9	155 768	83 103	73 155	5 131	2 363	2 363	60.4	6 537	2 329	4.0
July	257 843	162 209	62.9	156 186	83 019	73 295	5 125	2 493	2 493	60.5	6 245	2 377	3.9
August	258 066	161 802	62.7	155 567	83 044	73 153	4 892	2 346	2 346	60.3	6 197	2 247	3.8
September	258 290	162 055	62.7	155 948	83 104	73 107	5 108	2 478	2 478	60.4	5 986	2 240	3.7
October	258 514	162 694	62.9	156 306	83 277	73 442	5 258	2 418	2 418	60.6	6 112	2 229	3.8
November	258 708	162 821	62.9	156 598	83 408	73 478	5 221	2 556	2 556	60.6	6 018	2 124	3.7
December	258 888	163 240	63.1	156 745	83 500	73 769	5 226	2 522	2 522	60.6	6 294	2 203	3.9
2019													
January	258 239	163 142	63.2	156 627	80 474	67 776	5 166	2 546	154 112	60.7	6 516	2 156	4.0
February	258 392	163 047	63.1	156 866	80 677	68 005	5 012	2 488	154 354	60.7	6 181	2 207	3.8
March	258 537	162 935	63.0	156 741	80 570	68 486	5 181	2 336	154 346	60.6	6 194	2 242	3.8
April	258 693	162 546	62.8	156 696	80 609	68 436	4 942	2 389	154 369	60.6	5 850	2 087	3.6
May	258 861	162 782	62.9	156 844	80 761	68 633	4 990	2 423	154 486	60.6	5 938	2 120	3.6
June	259 037	163 133	63.0	157 148	80 780	68 747	5 188	2 330	154 835	60.7	5 985	2 189	3.7
July	259 225	163 373	63.0	157 346	80 975	69 306	5 265	2 400	155 035	60.7	6 027	2 079	3.7
August	259 432	163 894	63.2	157 895	81 046	69 390	5 166	2 414	155 546	60.9	5 999	2 082	3.7
September	259 638	164 051	63.2	158 298	81 146	69 555	5 126	2 416	155 816	61.0	5 753	2 124	3.5
October	259 845	164 401	63.3	158 544	81 196	69 790	5 195	2 473	155 970	61.0	5 857	2 144	3.6
November	260 020	164 347	63.2	158 536	81 377	70 257	5 277	2 356	156 167	61.0	5 811	2 083	3.5
December	260 181	164 556	63.2	158 803	81 390	70 795	5 240	2 533	156 241	61.0	5 753	1 998	3.5

[1] Not seasonally adjusted.
[2] In 1930 through 1943, the official BLS data count persons on work relief as unemployed. The unemployment rates for those years shown in parentheses count persons on work relief as employed, which is more consistent with the postwar practice. See notes and definitions.

Table 10-2. Labor Force and Employment by Major Age and Sex Groups

(Thousands of persons, percent, seasonally adjusted.)

Year and month	Civilian labor force (thousands)			Participation rate (percent)			Employment (thousands)			Employment-population ratio, percent		
	Men, 20 years and over	Women, 20 years and over	Both sexes, 16 to 19 years	Men, 20 years and over	Women, 20 years and over	Both sexes, 16 to 19 years	Men, 20 years and over	Women, 20 years and over	Both sexes, 16 to 19 years	Men, 20 years and over	Women, 20 years and over	Both sexes, 16 to 19 years
1970	47 220	28 301	7 249	82.6	43.3	49.9	45 581	26 952	6 144	79.7	41.2	42.3
1971	48 009	28 904	7 470	82.1	43.3	49.7	45 912	27 246	6 208	78.5	40.9	41.3
1972	49 079	29 901	8 054	81.6	43.7	51.9	47 130	28 276	6 746	78.4	41.3	43.5
1973	49 932	30 991	8 507	81.3	44.4	53.7	48 310	29 484	7 271	78.6	42.2	45.9
1974	50 879	32 201	8 871	81.0	45.3	54.8	48 922	30 424	7 448	77.9	42.8	46.0
1975	51 494	33 410	8 870	80.3	46.0	54.0	48 018	30 726	7 104	74.8	42.3	43.3
1976	52 288	34 814	9 056	79.8	47.0	54.5	49 190	32 226	7 336	75.1	43.5	44.2
1977	53 348	36 310	9 351	79.7	48.1	56.0	50 555	33 775	7 688	75.6	44.8	46.1
1978	54 471	38 128	9 652	79.8	49.6	57.8	52 143	35 836	8 070	76.4	46.6	48.3
1979	55 615	39 708	9 638	79.8	50.6	57.9	53 308	37 434	8 083	76.5	47.7	48.5
1980	56 455	41 106	9 378	79.4	51.3	56.7	53 101	38 492	7 710	74.6	48.1	46.6
1981	57 197	42 485	8 988	79.0	52.1	55.4	53 582	39 590	7 225	74.0	48.6	44.6
1982	57 980	43 699	8 526	78.7	52.7	54.1	52 891	40 086	6 549	71.8	48.4	41.5
1983	58 744	44 636	8 171	78.5	53.1	53.5	53 487	41 004	6 342	71.4	48.8	41.5
1984	59 701	45 900	7 943	78.3	53.7	53.9	55 769	42 793	6 444	73.2	50.1	43.7
1985	60 277	47 283	7 901	78.1	54.7	54.5	56 562	44 154	6 434	73.3	51.0	44.4
1986	61 320	48 589	7 926	78.1	55.5	54.7	57 569	45 556	6 472	73.3	52.0	44.6
1987	62 095	49 783	7 988	78.0	56.2	54.7	58 726	47 074	6 640	73.8	53.1	45.5
1988	62 768	50 870	8 031	77.9	56.8	55.3	59 781	48 383	6 805	74.2	54.0	46.8
1989	63 704	52 212	7 954	78.1	57.7	55.9	60 837	49 745	6 759	74.5	54.9	47.5
1990	64 916	53 131	7 792	78.2	58.0	53.7	61 678	50 535	6 581	74.3	55.2	45.3
1991	65 374	53 708	7 265	77.7	57.9	51.6	61 178	50 634	5 906	72.7	54.6	42.0
1992	66 213	54 796	7 096	77.7	58.5	51.3	61 496	51 328	5 669	72.1	54.8	41.0
1993	66 642	55 388	7 170	77.3	58.5	51.5	62 355	52 099	5 805	72.3	55.0	41.7
1994	66 921	56 655	7 481	76.8	59.3	52.7	63 294	53 606	6 161	72.6	56.2	43.4
1995	67 324	57 215	7 765	76.7	59.4	53.5	64 085	54 396	6 419	73.0	56.5	44.2
1996	68 044	58 094	7 806	76.8	59.9	52.3	64 897	55 311	6 500	73.2	57.0	43.5
1997	69 166	59 198	7 932	77.0	60.5	51.6	66 284	56 613	6 661	73.7	57.8	43.4
1998	69 715	59 702	8 256	76.8	60.4	52.8	67 135	57 278	7 051	73.9	58.0	45.1
1999	70 194	60 840	8 333	76.7	60.7	52.0	67 761	58 555	7 172	74.0	58.5	44.7
2000	72 010	62 301	8 271	76.7	60.6	52.0	69 634	60 067	7 189	74.2	58.4	45.2
2001	72 816	63 016	7 902	76.5	60.6	49.6	69 776	60 417	6 740	73.3	58.1	42.3
2002	73 630	63 648	7 585	76.3	60.5	47.4	69 734	60 420	6 332	72.3	57.5	39.6
2003	74 623	64 716	7 170	75.9	60.6	44.5	70 415	61 402	5 919	71.7	57.5	36.8
2004	75 364	64 923	7 114	75.8	60.3	43.9	71 572	61 773	5 907	71.9	57.4	36.4
2005	76 443	65 714	7 164	75.8	60.4	43.7	73 050	62 702	5 978	72.4	57.6	36.5
2006	77 562	66 585	7 281	75.9	60.5	43.7	74 431	63 834	6 162	72.9	58.0	36.9
2007	78 596	67 516	7 012	75.9	60.6	41.3	75 337	64 799	5 911	72.8	58.2	34.8
2008	79 047	68 382	6 858	75.7	60.9	40.2	74 750	65 039	5 573	71.6	57.9	32.6
2009	78 897	68 856	6 390	74.8	60.8	37.5	71 341	63 699	4 837	67.6	56.2	28.4
2010	78 994	68 990	5 906	74.1	60.3	34.9	71 230	63 456	4 378	66.8	55.5	25.9
2011	79 080	68 810	5 727	73.4	59.8	34.1	72 182	63 360	4 327	67.0	55.0	25.8
2012	79 387	69 765	5 823	73.0	59.3	34.3	73 403	64 640	4 426	67.5	55.0	26.1
2013	79 744	69 860	5 785	72.5	58.8	34.5	74 176	65 295	4 458	67.4	54.9	26.6
2014	80 056	70 212	5 654	71.9	58.5	34.0	75 471	66 287	4 548	67.8	55.2	27.3
2015	80 735	70 695	5 700	71.7	58.2	34.3	76 776	67 323	4 734	68.1	55.4	28.5
2016	81 759	71 538	5 889	71.7	58.3	35.2	78 084	68 387	4 965	68.5	55.7	29.7
2017	82 206	72 213	5 901	71.6	58.5	35.2	78 919	69 344	5 074	68.8	56.1	30.3
2018	83 188	73 002	5 885	71.6	58.5	35.1	80 211	70 424	5 126	69.0	56.4	30.6
2019	83 737	73 906	5 896	71.6	58.9	35.3	80 917	71 470	5 150	69.2	56.9	30.9
2020	82 345	72 677	5 720	70.1	57.6	34.5	76 227	66 873	4 695	64.8	53.0	28.3
2021	82 518	72 724	5 962	69.8	57.3	36.2	78 216	69 099	5 266	66.2	54.5	32.0
2020												
January	83 989	74 448	6 041	71.7	59.2	36.3	81 310	72 040	5 303	69.4	57.3	29.2
February	83 933	74 567	6 083	71.6	59.3	36.6	81 224	72 244	5 397	69.3	57.4	30.2
March	83 218	73 604	5 942	71.0	58.5	35.8	79 828	70 661	5 110	68.1	56.1	29.0
April	80 479	70 915	4 965	68.6	56.3	30.0	70 006	59 969	3 345	59.7	47.6	19.1
May	81 128	71 486	5 508	69.1	56.7	33.2	71 760	61 592	3 830	61.1	48.9	22.7
June	81 933	72 398	5 503	69.7	57.4	33.2	73 668	64 285	4 265	62.7	51.0	29.5
July	81 820	72 739	5 456	69.6	57.6	33.0	74 184	65 142	4 401	63.1	51.6	32.3
August	82 410	72 677	5 620	70.0	57.5	34.0	75 873	66 610	4 692	64.5	52.7	30.5
September	82 241	71 986	5 925	69.8	56.9	35.8	76 195	66 402	4 972	64.7	52.5	28.9
October	82 498	72 374	5 961	70.0	57.2	36.0	76 947	67 638	5 134	65.3	53.5	30.2
November	82 226	72 388	5 925	69.7	57.2	35.8	76 753	67 902	5 107	65.1	53.6	29.6
December	82 236	72 494	5 940	69.7	57.2	35.9	76 949	67 933	5 000	65.2	53.6	29.0
2021												
January	82 191	72 087	5 906	69.7	57.0	35.8	77 185	67 776	5 043	65.5	53.6	27.9
February	82 114	72 255	5 989	69.6	57.1	36.4	77 203	68 005	5 158	65.5	53.7	29.1
March	82 048	72 635	5 948	69.6	57.4	36.1	77 262	68 486	5 192	65.5	54.1	29.7
April	82 384	72 486	6 107	69.8	57.2	37.1	77 423	68 436	5 399	65.6	54.0	31.1
May	82 297	72 499	6 005	69.7	57.2	36.5	77 489	68 633	5 428	65.6	54.2	32.4
June	82 499	72 756	5 859	69.8	57.4	35.6	77 665	68 747	5 200	65.7	54.2	36.2
July	82 544	72 934	5 897	69.8	57.5	35.9	78 135	69 306	5 264	66.1	54.6	38.9
August	82 672	72 862	5 971	69.9	57.4	36.3	78 480	69 390	5 297	66.4	54.7	34.7
September	82 851	72 644	5 976	70.0	57.2	36.3	78 952	69 555	5 298	66.7	54.8	31.0
October	82 703	72 929	5 978	69.8	57.4	36.3	79 164	69 790	5 281	66.9	54.9	31.2
November	83 007	73 134	5 985	70.1	57.5	36.4	79 736	70 257	5 331	67.3	55.3	31.0
December	82 902	73 455	5 936	69.9	57.8	36.1	79 892	70 795	5 287	67.4	55.7	30.8

Table 10-3. Employment by Type of Job

(Thousands of persons, seasonally adjusted, except as noted.)

Year and month	Agricultural	By class of worker — Nonagricultural industries								Multiple jobholders		Employed and at work part-time	
		Total	Wage and salary				Self-employed (unincor-porated)	Unpaid family workers [1]		Total (thousands)	Percent of total employed	Economic reasons	Non-economic reasons
			Total	Government	Private industries								
					Private house-holds [1]	Other private industries							
1970	3 463	75 215	69 491	12 431	. . .	. . .	5 221	502	. . .	. . .	2 446	9 999
1971	3 394	75 972	70 120	12 799	. . .	. . .	5 327	522	. . .	. . .	2 688	10 152
1972	3 484	78 669	72 785	13 393	. . .	. . .	5 365	519	. . .	. . .	2 648	10 612
1973	3 470	81 594	75 580	13 655	. . .	. . .	5 474	540	. . .	. . .	2 554	10 972
1974	3 515	83 279	77 094	14 124	. . .	. . .	5 697	489	. . .	. . .	2 988	11 153
1975	3 408	82 438	76 249	14 675	. . .	. . .	5 705	483	. . .	. . .	3 804	11 228
1976	3 331	85 421	79 175	15 132	. . .	. . .	5 783	464	. . .	. . .	3 607	11 607
1977	3 283	88 734	82 121	15 361	. . .	. . .	6 114	498	. . .	. . .	3 608	12 120
1978	3 387	92 661	85 753	15 525	. . .	. . .	6 429	479	. . .	. . .	3 516	12 650
1979	3 347	95 477	88 222	15 635	. . .	. . .	6 791	463	. . .	. . .	3 577	12 893
1980	3 364	95 938	88 525	15 912	. . .	. . .	7 000	413	. . .	. . .	4 321	13 067
1981	3 368	97 030	89 543	15 689	. . .	. . .	7 097	390	. . .	. . .	4 768	13 025
1982	3 401	96 125	88 462	15 516	. . .	. . .	7 262	401	. . .	. . .	6 170	12 953
1983	3 383	97 450	89 500	15 537	. . .	. . .	7 575	376	. . .	. . .	6 266	12 911
1984	3 321	101 685	93 565	15 770	. . .	. . .	7 785	335	. . .	. . .	5 744	13 169
1985	3 179	103 971	95 871	16 031	. . .	. . .	7 811	289	. . .	. . .	5 590	13 489
1986	3 163	106 434	98 299	16 342	. . .	. . .	7 881	255	. . .	. . .	5 588	13 935
1987	3 208	109 232	100 771	16 800	. . .	. . .	8 201	260	. . .	. . .	5 401	14 395
1988	3 169	111 800	103 021	17 114	. . .	. . .	8 519	260	. . .	. . .	5 206	14 963
1989	3 199	114 142	105 259	17 469	. . .	. . .	8 605	279	. . .	. . .	4 894	15 393
1990	3 223	115 570	106 598	17 769	. . .	. . .	8 719	253	. . .	. . .	5 204	15 341
1991	3 269	114 449	105 373	17 934	. . .	. . .	8 851	226	. . .	. . .	6 161	15 172
1992	3 247	115 245	106 437	18 136	. . .	. . .	8 575	233	. . .	. . .	6 520	14 918
1993	3 115	117 144	107 966	18 579	. . .	. . .	8 959	218	. . .	. . .	6 481	15 240
1994	3 409	119 651	110 517	18 293	. . .	. . .	9 003	131	7 260	5.9	4 625	17 638
1995	3 440	121 460	112 448	18 362	. . .	. . .	8 902	110	7 693	6.2	4 473	17 734
1996	3 443	123 264	114 171	18 217	. . .	. . .	8 971	122	7 832	6.2	4 315	17 770
1997	3 399	126 159	116 983	18 131	. . .	. . .	9 056	120	7 955	6.1	4 068	18 149
1998	3 378	128 085	119 019	18 383	. . .	. . .	8 962	103	7 926	6.0	3 665	18 530
1999	3 281	130 207	121 323	18 903	. . .	. . .	8 790	95	7 802	5.8	3 357	18 758
2000	2 464	134 427	125 114	19 248	718	105 148	9 205	108	7 604	5.6	3 227	18 814
2001	2 299	134 635	125 407	19 335	694	105 378	9 121	107	7 357	5.4	3 715	18 790
2002	2 311	134 174	125 156	19 636	757	104 764	8 923	95	7 291	5.3	4 213	18 843
2003	2 275	135 461	126 015	19 634	764	105 616	9 344	101	7 315	5.3	4 701	19 014
2004	2 232	137 020	127 463	19 983	779	106 701	9 467	90	7 473	5.4	4 567	19 380
2005	2 197	139 532	129 931	20 357	812	108 761	9 509	93	7 546	5.3	4 350	19 491
2006	2 206	142 221	132 449	20 337	803	111 309	9 685	87	7 576	5.2	4 162	19 591
2007	2 095	143 952	134 283	21 003	813	112 467	9 557	112	7 655	5.2	4 401	19 756
2008	2 168	143 194	133 882	21 258	805	111 819	9 219	93	7 620	5.2	5 875	19 343
2009	2 103	137 775	128 713	21 178	783	106 752	8 995	66	7 271	5.2	8 913	18 710
2010	2 206	136 858	127 914	21 003	667	106 244	8 860	84	6 878	4.9	8 874	18 251
2011	2 254	137 615	128 934	20 536	722	107 676	8 603	78	6 880	4.9	8 560	18 334
2012	2 186	140 283	131 452	20 360	738	110 355	8 749	81	6 943	4.9	8 122	18 806
2013	2 130	141 799	133 111	20 247	723	112 141	8 619	70	7 002	4.9	7 935	18 903
2014	2 237	144 068	135 402	20 135	820	114 456	8 602	64	7 146	4.9	7 213	19 489
2015	2 422	146 411	137 678	20 601	798	116 279	8 665	68	7 262	4.9	6 371	20 018
2016	2 460	148 975	140 161	20 630	724	118 807	8 715	65	7 531	5.0	5 843	20 680
2017	2 457	150 875	142 090	20 834	657	120 600	8 734	52	7 545	4.9	5 186	20 557
2018	2 425	153 336	144 326	20 942	777	122 607	8 941	69	7 769	5.0	6 788	19 370
2019	2 425	155 106	146 256	20 976	821	124 462	8 799	53	8 050	5.1	4 329	21 058
2020	2 348	145 443	136 879	20 598	654	116 306	8 511	55	6 687	4.5	7 126	17 960
2021	2 294	150 290	140 991	20 660	659	120 330	9 227	67	7 007	4.6	4 914	19 727
2020												
January	2 405	156 217	147 434	21 460	125 147	801	8 846	50	8 083	5.1	4 130	21 669
February	2 455	156 240	147 439	21 054	125 323	781	8 893	45	8 181	5.2	4 304	21 801
March	2 352	153 093	144 327	21 147	122 327	712	8 799	37	7 358	4.7	5 728	19 987
April	2 379	130 982	123 374	19 268	103 600	492	7 523	23	5 360	4.0	10 739	11 986
May	2 303	134 904	126 840	19 749	106 551	498	7 928	41	5 509	4.0	10 486	14 073
June	2 257	139 840	131 306	20 765	110 114	564	8 316	64	6 114	4.3	8 939	16 718
July	2 158	141 455	132 763	20 479	111 741	708	8 462	82	6 569	4.5	8 336	17 383
August	2 194	145 216	136 168	20 988	114 440	715	8 788	77	6 541	4.4	7 439	18 257
September	2 270	145 454	136 493	20 466	115 601	683	8 675	54	6 482	4.4	6 197	18 589
October	2 515	147 255	138 539	20 678	117 304	636	8 690	70	6 866	4.6	6 552	19 029
November	2 432	147 314	138 891	20 418	117 902	626	8 570	45	6 690	4.5	6 582	18 182
December	2 461	147 351	138 971	20 709	117 472	636	8 638	66	6 496	4.3	6 082	17 846
2021												
January	2 454	146 037	138 964	20 653	117 992	622	8 750	71	6 535	4.4	5 940	18 424
February	2 307	147 338	139 265	20 809	118 226	604	8 827	72	6 787	4.5	6 099	18 458
March	2 227	148 384	139 504	20 617	118 663	650	9 248	80	7 004	4.7	5 823	19 128
April	2 275	148 964	139 915	20 424	119 287	602	8 992	75	6 883	4.6	5 245	19 220
May	2 291	149 442	139 967	20 475	119 334	586	9 265	94	7 249	4.8	5 267	19 362
June	2 309	149 885	140 111	20 552	119 474	654	9 162	71	6 987	4.6	4 616	20 122
July	2 289	151 195	140 699	20 760	119 966	679	9 555	67	7 013	4.6	4 450	20 051
August	2 307	150 847	141 225	20 762	120 347	733	9 496	60	6 783	4.4	4 481	20 330
September	2 247	151 754	141 756	20 514	121 909	768	9 424	53	7 032	4.6	4 450	20 335
October	2 296	152 548	142 194	20 511	122 175	766	9 465	68	7 166	4.6	4 398	20 539
November	2 212	153 603	143 816	20 750	123 416	654	9 256	47	7 180	4.6	4 266	20 441
December	2 308	153 479	144 474	21 097	123 172	585	9 282	43	7 461	4.8	3 929	20 315

[1] Not seasonally adjusted.
. . . = Not available.

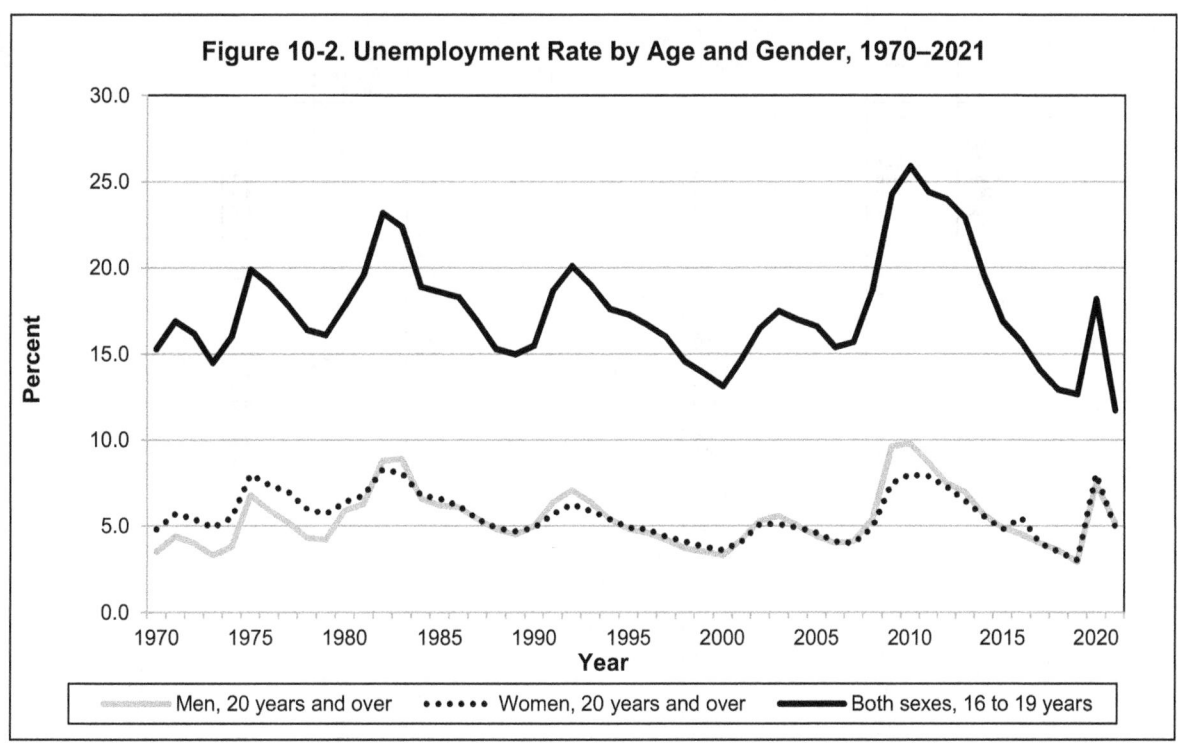

- As the pandemic spread nationwide in mid-March 2020, many businesses, schools and governments abruptly closed. Unemployment rose to 14.7 percent, more than three-fold increase between March and April 2020. Unemployment continued to decline throughout 2021 and 2022. (Tables 10-04 and 10-05)

- One of the most iconic graphs early in the pandemic was from the Department of Labor's, Employment and Training Administration. The severity of the pandemic was illustrated in a stark chart. Unemployment compensation claims rose from 212,200 in February 2020 to 2.3 million in March, nearly 4.7 million in April then slowly declining the remainder of the year. By December 2021, claims fell to approximately 222,000. See Table 10-6. Unemployment compensation, established with the Social Security Act of 1935, is a Federal-State program that provides financial assistance to recently unemployed workers. (Table 10-6)

- Figure 10-2 depicts the unemployment rates by age and gender. Just in two months during the pandemic, from February 2020 to April 2020, the unemployment rate for women 20 years and over increased from 3.1 percent to 15.4 percent while the unemployment rate for men 20 years and over increased from 3.2 percent to 13.0 percent. (See Table 10-4).

- Although unemployment by race have varied over the decades, Blacks and Hispanics have typically experienced higher unemployment than Whites and Asians. In 2021, the unemployment rate for Blacks was 8.6 percent compared with 4.7 percent for Whites and 6.8 percent for Hispanics. The unemployment rate for Asians was 5.0 percent. (Table 10-4)

Table 10-4. Unemployment by Demographic Group

(Unemployment in thousands of persons and as a percent of the civilian labor force in group, seasonally adjusted, except as noted.)

Year and month	Unemployment (thousands of persons)				Unemployment rate (percent)							
						By age and sex			By race			
	Total	Men, 20 years and over	Women, 20 years and over	Both sexes, 16 to 19 years	All civilian workers	Men, 20 years and over	Women, 20 years and over	Both sexes, 16 to 19 years	White	Black or African American	Asian [1]	Hispanic or Latino ethnicity
1970	4 093	1 638	1 349	1 106	4.9	3.5	4.8	15.3	4.5	. . .	. . .	. . .
1971	5 016	2 097	1 658	1 262	5.9	4.4	5.7	16.9	5.4	. . .	. . .	. . .
1972	4 882	1 948	1 625	1 308	5.6	4.0	5.4	16.2	5.1	10.4	. . .	. . .
1973	4 365	1 624	1 507	1 235	4.9	3.3	4.9	14.5	4.3	9.4	. . .	7.5
1974	5 156	1 957	1 777	1 422	5.6	3.8	5.5	16.0	5.0	10.5	. . .	8.1
1975	7 929	3 476	2 684	1 767	8.5	6.8	8.0	19.9	7.8	14.8	. . .	12.2
1976	7 406	3 098	2 588	1 719	7.7	5.9	7.4	19.0	7.0	14.0	. . .	11.5
1977	6 991	2 794	2 535	1 663	7.1	5.2	7.0	17.8	6.2	14.0	. . .	10.1
1978	6 202	2 328	2 292	1 583	6.1	4.3	6.0	16.4	5.2	12.8	. . .	9.1
1979	6 137	2 308	2 276	1 555	5.8	4.2	5.7	16.1	5.1	12.3	. . .	8.3
1980	7 637	3 353	2 615	1 669	7.1	5.9	6.4	17.8	6.3	14.3	. . .	10.1
1981	8 273	3 615	2 895	1 763	7.6	6.3	6.8	19.6	6.7	15.6	. . .	10.4
1982	10 678	5 089	3 613	1 977	9.7	8.8	8.3	23.2	8.6	18.9	. . .	13.8
1983	10 717	5 257	3 632	1 829	9.6	8.9	8.1	22.4	8.4	19.5	. . .	13.7
1984	8 539	3 932	3 107	1 499	7.5	6.6	6.8	18.9	6.5	15.9	. . .	10.7
1985	8 312	3 715	3 129	1 468	7.2	6.2	6.6	18.6	6.2	15.1	. . .	10.5
1986	8 237	3 751	3 032	1 454	7.0	6.1	6.2	18.3	6.0	14.5	. . .	10.6
1987	7 425	3 369	2 709	1 347	6.2	5.4	5.4	16.9	5.3	13.0	. . .	8.8
1988	6 701	2 987	2 487	1 226	5.5	4.8	4.9	15.3	4.7	11.7	. . .	8.2
1989	6 528	2 867	2 467	1 194	5.3	4.5	4.7	15.0	4.5	11.4	. . .	8.0
1990	7 047	3 239	2 596	1 212	5.6	5.0	4.9	15.5	4.8	11.4	. . .	8.2
1991	8 628	4 195	3 074	1 359	6.8	6.4	5.7	18.7	6.1	12.5	. . .	10.0
1992	9 613	4 717	3 469	1 427	7.5	7.1	6.3	20.1	6.6	14.2	. . .	11.6
1993	8 940	4 287	3 288	1 365	6.9	6.4	5.9	19.0	6.1	13.0	. . .	10.8
1994	7 996	3 627	3 049	1 320	6.1	5.4	5.4	17.6	5.3	11.5	. . .	9.9
1995	7 404	3 239	2 819	1 346	5.6	4.8	4.9	17.3	4.9	10.4	. . .	9.3
1996	7 236	3 146	2 783	1 306	5.4	4.6	4.8	16.7	4.7	10.5	. . .	8.9
1997	6 739	2 882	2 585	1 271	4.9	4.2	4.4	16.0	4.2	10.0	. . .	7.7
1998	6 210	2 580	2 424	1 205	4.5	3.7	4.1	14.6	3.9	8.9	. . .	7.2
1999	5 880	2 433	2 285	1 162	4.2	3.5	3.8	13.9	3.7	8.0	. . .	6.4
2000	5 692	2 376	2 235	1 081	4.0	3.3	3.6	13.1	3.5	7.6	3.6	5.7
2001	6 801	3 040	2 599	1 162	4.7	4.2	4.1	14.7	4.2	8.6	4.5	6.6
2002	8 378	3 896	3 228	1 253	5.8	5.3	5.1	16.5	5.1	10.2	5.9	7.5
2003	8 774	4 209	3 314	1 251	6.0	5.6	5.1	17.5	5.2	10.8	6.0	7.7
2004	8 149	3 791	3 150	1 208	5.5	5.0	4.9	17.0	4.8	10.4	4.4	7.0
2005	7 591	3 392	3 013	1 186	5.1	4.4	4.6	16.6	4.4	10.0	4.0	6.0
2006	7 001	3 131	2 751	1 119	4.6	4.0	4.1	15.4	4.0	8.9	3.0	5.2
2007	7 078	3 259	2 718	1 101	4.6	4.1	4.0	15.7	4.1	8.3	3.2	5.6
2008	8 924	4 297	3 342	1 285	5.8	5.4	4.9	18.7	5.2	10.1	4.0	7.6
2009	14 265	7 555	5 157	1 552	9.3	9.6	7.5	24.3	8.5	14.8	7.3	12.1
2010	14 825	7 763	5 534	1 528	9.6	9.8	8.0	25.9	8.7	16.0	7.5	12.5
2011	13 747	6 898	5 450	1 400	8.9	8.7	7.9	24.4	7.9	15.8	7.0	11.5
2012	12 506	5 984	5 125	1 397	8.1	7.5	7.3	24.0	7.2	13.8	5.9	10.3
2013	11 460	5 568	4 565	1 327	7.4	7.0	6.5	22.9	6.5	13.1	5.2	9.1
2014	9 617	4 585	3 926	1 106	6.2	5.7	5.6	19.6	5.3	11.3	5.0	7.4
2015	8 296	3 959	3 371	966	5.3	4.9	4.8	16.9	4.6	9.6	3.8	6.6
2016	7 751	3 675	3 151	925	4.9	4.5	5.5	15.7	4.3	8.4	3.6	5.8
2017	6 973	3 220	2 865	831	4.4	4.0	4.0	14.1	3.8	7.5	3.4	5.1
2018	6 306	2 971	2 575	760	3.9	3.6	3.5	12.9	3.5	6.5	3.0	4.7
2019	5 989	2 209	2 012	746	3.7	2.9	3.0	12.6	3.3	6.1	2.7	4.3
2020	12 948	6 118	5 804	1 025	8.1	7.5	8.0	18.2	7.3	11.5	8.7	10.5
2021	8 626	4 302	3 625	699	5.4	5.2	5.0	11.7	4.7	8.6	5.0	6.8
2020												
January	5 826	2 679	2 409	739	3.5	3.2	3.2	12.2	3.1	6.3	3.0	4.3
February	5 717	2 709	2 323	685	3.5	3.2	3.1	11.3	3.0	6.0	2.5	4.4
March	7 165	3 390	2 943	832	4.4	4.1	4.0	14.0	3.9	6.8	4.1	5.9
April	23 038	10 474	10 945	1 619	14.7	13.0	15.4	32.6	14.1	16.6	14.4	18.8
May	20 940	9 368	9 894	1 678	13.2	11.5	13.8	30.5	12.3	16.8	14.8	17.6
June	17 616	8 265	8 113	1 238	11.0	10.1	11.2	22.5	10.0	15.2	13.8	14.5
July	16 288	7 636	7 597	1 055	10.2	9.3	10.4	19.3	9.2	14.4	11.9	12.8
August	13 532	6 536	6 067	929	8.4	7.9	8.3	16.5	7.4	12.8	10.6	10.6
September	12 584	6 046	5 584	953	7.9	7.4	7.8	16.1	7.0	12.1	8.9	10.4
October	11 115	5 551	4 735	828	6.9	6.7	6.5	13.9	6.0	10.9	7.6	8.9
November	10 777	5 474	4 486	818	6.7	6.7	6.2	13.8	6.0	10.4	6.8	8.6
December	10 789	5 287	4 561	940	6.7	6.4	6.3	15.8	6.1	10.0	6.1	9.4
2021												
January	10 180	5 006	4 311	863	6.4	6.1	6.0	14.6	5.7	9.2	6.6	8.6
February	9 992	4 911	4 250	831	6.2	6.0	5.9	13.9	5.5	9.8	5.1	8.4
March	9 691	4 786	4 149	756	6.0	5.8	5.7	12.7	5.3	9.5	5.9	7.7
April	9 719	4 961	4 050	708	6.0	6.0	5.6	11.6	5.3	9.7	5.7	7.7
May	9 251	4 808	3 866	578	5.8	5.8	5.3	9.6	5.1	9.1	5.5	7.1
June	9 502	4 834	4 008	660	5.9	5.9	5.5	11.3	5.3	9.2	5.7	7.2
July	8 671	4 410	3 628	633	5.4	5.3	5.0	10.7	4.8	8.2	5.2	6.4
August	8 339	4 192	3 472	675	5.2	5.1	4.8	11.3	4.5	8.7	4.5	6.2
September	7 666	3 899	3 089	678	4.7	4.7	4.3	11.3	4.2	7.8	4.2	6.1
October	7 375	3 539	3 139	697	4.6	4.3	4.3	11.7	3.9	7.8	4.2	5.7
November	6 802	3 272	2 876	654	4.2	3.9	3.9	10.9	3.7	6.5	3.9	5.2
December	6 319	3 010	2 660	649	3.9	3.6	3.6	10.9	3.2	7.1	3.8	4.9

[1] Not seasonally adjusted.
. . . = Not available.

Table 10-5. Unemployment Rates and Related Data

(Seasonally adjusted, except as noted.)

Year and month	Unemployment rates by marital status (percent of labor force in group)			Unemployment rates by reason for unemployment (percent of total civilian labor force in group.)					Duration of unemployment		Alternative measures of labor under-utilization (percent)		
	Married men, spouse present	Married women, spouse present	Women who maintain families[1]	Total	Job losers and persons who completed temporary jobs	Job leavers	Reentrants	New entrants	Average (mean) weeks unemployed	Median weeks unemployed	Including discouraged workers (U-4)	Including all marginally attached workers (U-5)	Including marginally attached and under-employed (U-6)
1970	2.6	4.9	5.4	4.9	2.2	0.7	1.5	0.6	8.6	4.9	. . .	. . .	. . .
1971	3.2	5.7	7.3	5.9	2.8	0.7	1.7	0.7	11.3	6.3	. . .	. . .	. . .
1972	2.8	5.4	7.2	5.6	2.4	0.7	1.7	0.8	12.0	6.2	. . .	. . .	. . .
1973	2.3	4.7	7.1	4.9	1.9	0.8	1.5	0.7	10.0	5.2	. . .	. . .	. . .
1974	2.7	5.3	7.0	5.6	2.4	0.8	1.6	0.7	9.8	5.2	. . .	. . .	. . .
1975	5.1	7.9	10.0	8.5	4.7	0.9	2.0	0.9	14.2	8.4	. . .	. . .	. . .
1976	4.2	7.1	10.1	7.7	3.8	0.9	2.0	0.9	15.8	8.2	. . .	. . .	. . .
1977	3.6	6.5	9.4	7.1	3.2	0.9	2.0	1.0	14.3	7.0	. . .	. . .	. . .
1978	2.8	5.5	8.5	6.1	2.5	0.9	1.8	0.9	11.9	5.9	. . .	. . .	. . .
1979	2.8	5.1	8.3	5.8	2.5	0.8	1.7	0.8	10.8	5.4	. . .	. . .	. . .
1980	4.2	5.8	9.2	7.1	3.7	0.8	1.8	0.8	11.9	6.5	. . .	. . .	. . .
1981	4.3	6.0	10.4	7.6	3.9	0.8	1.9	0.9	13.7	6.9	. . .	. . .	. . .
1982	6.5	7.4	11.7	9.7	5.7	0.8	2.2	1.1	15.6	8.7	. . .	. . .	. . .
1983	6.5	7.0	12.2	9.6	5.6	0.7	2.2	1.1	20.0	10.1	. . .	. . .	. . .
1984	4.6	5.7	10.3	7.5	3.9	0.7	1.9	1.0	18.2	7.9	. . .	. . .	. . .
1985	4.3	5.6	10.4	7.2	3.6	0.8	2.0	0.9	15.6	6.8	. . .	. . .	. . .
1986	4.4	5.2	9.8	7.0	3.4	0.9	1.8	0.9	15.0	6.9	. . .	. . .	. . .
1987	3.9	4.3	9.2	6.2	3.0	0.8	1.6	0.8	14.5	6.5	. . .	. . .	. . .
1988	3.3	3.9	8.1	5.5	2.5	0.8	1.5	0.7	13.5	5.9	. . .	. . .	. . .
1989	3.0	3.7	8.1	5.3	2.4	0.8	1.5	0.5	11.9	4.8	. . .	. . .	. . .
1990	3.4	3.8	8.3	5.6	2.7	0.8	1.5	0.5	12.0	5.3	. . .	. . .	. . .
1991	4.4	4.5	9.3	6.8	3.7	0.8	1.7	0.6	13.7	6.8	. . .	. . .	. . .
1992	5.1	5.0	10.0	7.5	4.2	0.8	1.8	0.7	17.7	8.7	. . .	. . .	. . .
1993	4.4	4.6	9.7	6.9	3.8	0.8	1.7	0.7	18.0	8.3	. . .	. . .	. . .
1994	3.7	4.1	8.9	6.1	2.9	0.6	2.1	0.5	18.8	9.2	6.5	7.4	10.9
1995	3.3	3.9	8.0	5.6	2.6	0.6	1.9	0.4	16.6	8.3	5.9	6.7	10.1
1996	3.0	3.6	8.2	5.4	2.5	0.6	1.9	0.4	16.7	8.3	5.7	6.5	9.7
1997	2.7	3.1	8.1	4.9	2.2	0.6	1.7	0.4	15.8	8.0	5.2	5.9	8.9
1998	2.4	2.9	7.2	4.5	2.1	0.5	1.5	0.4	14.5	6.7	4.7	5.4	8.0
1999	2.2	2.7	6.4	4.2	1.9	0.6	1.4	0.3	13.4	6.4	4.4	5.0	7.4
2000	2.0	2.7	5.9	4.0	1.8	0.5	1.4	0.3	12.6	5.9	4.2	4.8	7.0
2001	2.7	3.1	6.6	4.7	2.4	0.6	1.4	0.3	13.1	6.8	4.9	5.6	8.1
2002	3.6	3.7	8.0	5.8	3.2	0.6	1.6	0.4	16.6	9.1	6.0	6.7	9.6
2003	3.8	3.7	8.5	6.0	3.3	0.6	1.7	0.4	19.2	10.1	6.3	7.0	10.1
2004	3.1	3.5	8.0	5.5	2.8	0.6	1.6	0.5	19.6	9.8	5.8	6.5	9.6
2005	2.8	3.3	7.8	5.1	2.5	0.6	1.6	0.4	18.4	8.9	5.4	6.1	8.9
2006	2.4	2.9	7.1	4.6	2.2	0.5	1.5	0.4	16.8	8.3	4.9	5.5	8.2
2007	2.5	2.8	6.5	4.6	2.3	0.5	1.4	0.4	16.8	8.5	4.9	5.5	8.3
2008	3.4	3.6	8.0	5.8	3.1	0.6	1.6	0.5	17.9	9.4	6.1	6.8	10.5
2009	6.6	5.5	11.5	9.3	5.9	0.6	2.1	0.7	24.4	15.1	9.7	10.5	16.2
2010	6.8	5.9	12.3	9.6	6.0	0.6	2.3	0.8	33.0	21.4	10.3	11.1	16.7
2011	5.8	5.6	12.4	8.9	5.3	0.6	2.2	0.8	39.3	21.4	9.5	10.4	15.9
2012	4.9	5.3	11.4	8.1	4.4	0.6	2.2	0.8	39.4	19.3	8.6	9.5	14.7
2013	4.3	4.6	10.2	7.4	3.9	0.6	2.1	0.8	36.5	17.0	7.9	8.8	13.8
2014	3.4	3.8	8.6	6.2	3.1	0.5	1.8	0.7	33.7	14.0	6.6	7.5	12.0
2015	2.8	3.1	7.4	5.3	2.6	0.5	1.6	0.6	29.2	11.6	5.7	6.4	10.4
2016	2.7	3.0	6.8	4.9	2.3	0.5	1.5	0.5	27.5	10.6	5.2	5.9	9.6
2017	2.4	2.7	6.2	4.4	2.1	0.5	1.3	0.4	25.0	10.0	4.6	5.3	8.5
2018	2.0	2.4	5.4	3.9	1.8	0.5	1.2	0.4	22.7	9.3	4.1	4.8	7.7
2019	1.8	2.2	5.0	3.7	1.7	0.5	1.1	0.4	21.6	9.1	3.9	4.5	7.2
2020	4.9	6.3	9.6	8.1	6.1	0.4	1.2	0.3	16.5	9.7	8.4	9.2	13.6
2021	3.2	3.4	7.1	5.3	3.2	0.5	1.4	0.3	28.7	16.5	5.6	6.4	9.4
2020													
January	1.7	2.1	5.4	3.5	1.6	0.5	1.1	0.3	22.0	9.7	3.7	4.3	6.9
February	1.9	2.2	4.1	3.5	1.6	0.5	1.1	0.3	20.8	9.0	3.7	4.3	7.0
March	2.2	3.0	5.3	4.4	2.6	0.4	1.1	0.3	16.9	5.3	4.7	5.2	8.8
April	9.6	13.1	15.9	14.7	13.2	0.4	1.0	0.3	7.2	1.5	15.0	16.0	22.9
May	8.2	11.5	15.8	13.2	11.6	0.3	1.0	0.3	10.5	7.4	13.6	14.5	21.2
June	6.8	9.0	13.1	11.0	8.9	0.4	1.4	0.4	14.2	13.1	11.4	12.4	18.0
July	6.1	8.6	12.4	10.2	8.1	0.4	1.4	0.3	16.8	14.7	10.5	11.3	16.5
August	4.9	6.5	10.4	8.4	6.4	0.4	1.3	0.3	19.8	16.5	8.7	9.6	14.3
September	4.8	5.9	10.0	7.9	5.6	0.5	1.3	0.3	21.3	18.0	8.2	9.0	12.8
October	4.2	4.8	8.6	6.9	4.8	0.5	1.3	0.3	22.0	19.4	7.3	8.0	12.1
November	4.1	4.5	7.7	6.7	4.6	0.4	1.2	0.4	23.5	19.2	7.1	7.9	12.0
December	4.1	4.7	7.2	6.7	4.6	0.5	1.4	0.3	23.7	17.9	7.1	8.0	11.7
2021													
January	4.0	4.4	8.3	6.4	4.3	0.4	1.2	0.3	26.1	16.0	6.7	7.5	11.1
February	3.8	4.3	7.7	6.2	4.1	0.4	1.3	0.4	27.8	17.9	6.5	7.3	11.1
March	3.2	3.8	8.0	6.0	3.9	0.5	1.4	0.3	29.4	19.1	6.3	7.1	10.7
April	3.8	3.8	7.3	6.0	3.9	0.5	1.3	0.4	28.5	19.4	6.4	7.1	10.3
May	3.5	3.7	6.6	5.8	3.6	0.5	1.4	0.3	29.4	19.3	6.1	6.9	10.1
June	3.7	3.7	8.1	5.9	3.6	0.6	1.4	0.3	31.6	19.6	6.2	7.0	9.8
July	3.3	3.3	8.5	5.4	3.0	0.6	1.4	0.3	29.4	14.4	5.7	6.5	9.2
August	3.2	2.9	7.9	5.2	2.7	0.5	1.5	0.3	29.4	14.2	5.4	6.1	8.8
September	2.8	2.8	6.8	4.7	2.5	0.5	1.4	0.3	28.3	13.7	5.0	5.8	8.5
October	2.5	3.0	5.9	4.6	2.3	0.5	1.4	0.3	26.9	13.0	4.8	5.5	8.2
November	2.3	2.8	4.8	4.2	2.1	0.5	1.3	0.3	29.1	13.4	4.5	5.1	7.7
December	1.9	2.5	5.6	3.9	1.9	0.4	1.3	0.3	28.6	12.9	4.2	4.9	7.3

[1]Not seasonally adjusted.
. . . = Not available.

Table 10-6. Insured Unemployment

(Averages of weekly data; thousands of persons, except as noted.)

Year and month	State programs, seasonally adjusted			Federal programs, not seasonally adjusted			
				Initial claims		Persons claiming benefits	
	Initial claims	Insured unemployment	Insured unemployment rate (percent) [1]	Federal employees	Newly discharged veterans	Federal employees	Newly discharged veterans
1980	488	3 365	3.9	...	...	...	...
1981	451	3 032	3.5	...	...	...	...
1982	586	4 094	4.7	...	...	...	...
1983	441	3 337	3.9	...	...	...	...
1984	374	2 452	2.8	...	...	...	...
1985	392	2 584	2.9	...	...	...	...
1986	378	2 632	2.8	2	2.5	21	17.5
1987	325	2 273	2.4	2	2.6	21	17.7
1988	309	2 075	2.1	2	2.7	23	18.1
1989	330	2 174	2.1	2	2.3	22	15.1
1990	385	2 539	2.4	2	2.5	24	18.4
1991	447	3 338	3.2	3	2.9	31	22.7
1992	409	3 208	3.1	3	5.0	32	60.6
1993	344	2 768	2.6	3	3.9	32	54.4
1994	340	2 667	2.5	3	3.0	32	37.5
1995	359	2 590	2.4	5	2.5	32	29.6
1996	352	2 552	2.3	7	2.1	29	24.2
1997	322	2 300	2.0	2	1.8	24	19.6
1998	317	2 213	1.9	2	1.4	19	15.6
1999	298	2 186	1.8	1	1.2	17	14.2
2000	299	2 112	1.7	2	1.0	19	12.5
2001	406	3 016	2.4	1	1.2	18	14.0
2002	404	3 570	2.8	1	1.2	18	16.2
2003	402	3 532	2.8	2	1.5	18	19.8
2004	342	2 930	2.3	2	1.9	18	26.9
2005	331	2 660	2.1	1	2.0	17	27.6
2006	312	2 456	1.9	1	2.0	15	26.3
2007	321	2 548	1.9	1	1.7	15	22.8
2008	418	3 337	2.5	1	1.6	15	22.2
2009	574	5 808	4.4	2	2.0	20	30.4
2010	459	4 544	3.6	3	2.6	28	39.2
2011	409	3 744	3.0	2	2.6	31	39.1
2012	374	3 319	2.6	1	2.6	20	39.7
2013	343	2 978	2.3	4	2.3	22	34.8
2014	308	2 590	2.2	1	1.8	16	26.0
2015	278	2 267	1.7	1	1.4	13	19.4
2016	263	2 136	1.6	1	1.4	11	13.8
2017	245	1 961	1.4	1	0.8	11	10.2
2018	220	1 756	1.2	1	0.6	9	7.4
2019	218	1 701	1.2	2	0.5	11	6.0
2020	1 380	10 329	7.1	1	1.0	1	1.0
2021	4 768	32 256	2.3	1	0.6	12	6.7
2019							
January	220	1 717	1.2	14	0.6	37	7.0
February	225	1 723	1.2	1	0.5	13	6.3
March	218	1 734	1.2	1	0.5	11	6.0
April	216	1 678	1.2	1	0.5	9	5.8
May	218	1 690	1.2	1	0.5	7	5.6
June	221	1 691	1.2	1	0.5	7	5.5
July	214	1 698	1.2	1	0.5	7	5.6
August	216	1 699	1.2	1	0.5	7	5.6
September	213	1 678	1.2	1	0.5	7	5.8
October	215	1 694	1.2	1	0.5	7	5.8
November	215	1 690	1.2	1	0.4	9	6.3
December	226	1 736	1.2	1	0.5	11	6.6
2020							
January	211	1 742	1.2	1	0.6	1	0.6
February	212	1 715	1.2	1	0.6	1	0.6
March	2 344	3 612	2.5	1	0.6	1	0.6
April	4 668	16 913	11.6	1	0.9	1	0.9
May	2 148	20 363	13.9	2	1.2	2	1.2
June	1 476	17 853	12.3	1	1.3	1	1.3
July	1 384	16 669	11.4	2	1.4	2	1.5
August	919	14 048	9.6	1	1.4	1	1.4
September	851	11 830	8.1	1	1.4	1	1.4
October	789	7 828	5.3	1	1.3	1	1.3
November	735	5 991	4.1	1	1.0	1	1.0
December	823	5 385	3.7	2	1.0	2	1.0
2021							
January	828	4 945	3.5	3	1.2	19	9.1
February	755	4 432	3.1	1	0.7	20	8.6
March	669	3 975	2.8	1	0.6	18	8.1
April	589	3 788	2.7	1	0.6	15	7.6
May	469	3 622	2.6	1	0.5	12	7.0
June	420	3 280	2.3	1	0.5	11	6.5
July	409	2 998	2.2	1	0.5	10	6.3
August	399	2 789	2.0	1	0.5	9	6.0
September	370	2 682	2.0	1	0.5	8	5.5
October	308	2 397	2.8	1	0.5	8	5.2
November	257	2 087	1.6	1	0.4	8	4.9
December	222	1 857	1.4	1	0.4	10	4.6

[1] Insured unemployed as a percent of employment covered by state programs.

... = Not available.

SECTION 10B: PAYROLL EMPLOYMENT, HOURS, AND EARNINGS FROM THE CURRENT EMPLOYMENT STATISTICS SURVEY

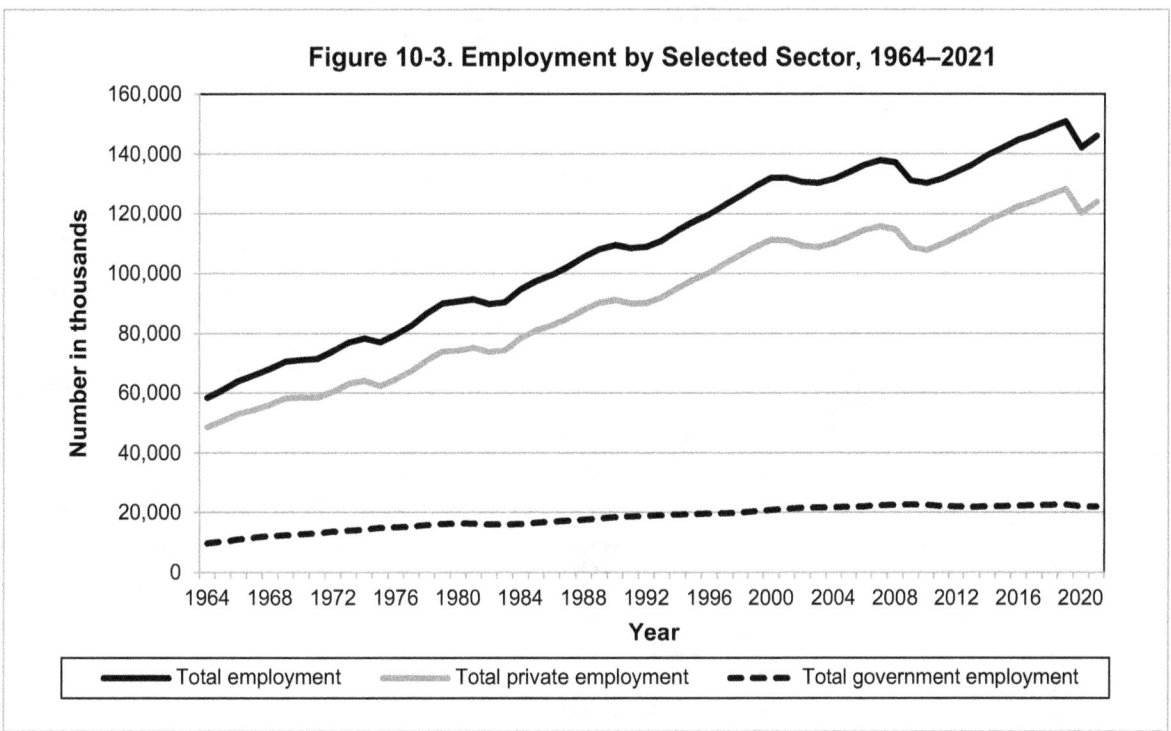

Figure 10-3. Employment by Selected Sector, 1964–2021

- Figure 10-3 illustrates employment by total, private and government. As shown in the figure, private employment follows the total trends. However, government employment has remained steady at approximately 22 million. Nonfarm employment includes wage and salary workers but not self-employed persons and unpaid family members working in a family business. The Bureau of Labor Statistics use 'non-farm' employment which excludes farm employees. (Table 10-7)

- COVID-19 caused considerable disruption on the labor force. All industries suffered employment declines between March and April 2020. In 2020, leisure and hospitality industry experienced the largest decline in employment, dropping 19.3 percent followed by mining and logging at 15.6 percent. In 2021, employment increased in most industries, although mining and logging continued to decrease. (Table 10–7).

- The U.S. economy continues to be service-oriented rather than production of goods. Chapter 7 shows the United States still exports more goods than services. Manufacturing, once the economic engine of the economy, lost 22.3 percent of its workforce in the last 57 years. More and more employees work in the Services subsector of Professional and Business Services, which includes lawyers, architects, engineers, and computer designers. Between 1964–2021, nonfarm payroll employment increased nearly three-fold. (Table 10-7)

- The diffusion index indicates the percentage of private industries in which employment is higher than six months earlier. Diffusion indexes measure the extent to which expansion or contraction have spread throughout the economy; indexes below 50 percent indicate recession. This index reached a low of 7.2 in both April and May 2020—lower than the lowest points reached in any of the previous four recessions (1980, 1981–1982, 1990–1991, and 2001), and thus indicating the most widespread and pervasive decline in 56 years. By December 2021, this index recovered to 83.2, higher any annual amount. (Tables 10-7).

Table 10-7. Nonfarm Payroll Employment by NAICS Supersector

(Thousands; seasonally adjusted, except as noted.)

Year and month	Total	Private								Service-providing				
		Total	Goods-producing						Total	Private				
			Total	Mining and logging	Construc-tion	Manufacturing				Total	Trade, transportation, and utilities			
						Total	Durable	Nondurable			Total	Wholesale trade	Retail trade
1964	58 391	48 680	19 733	697	3 148	15 888	9 414	6 474	38 658	28 947	11 660	2 835	5 978
1965	60 874	50 683	20 595	694	3 284	16 617	9 973	6 644	40 279	30 089	12 121	2 945	6 264
1966	64 020	53 110	21 740	690	3 371	17 680	10 803	6 878	42 280	31 370	12 593	3 057	6 532
1967	65 931	54 406	21 882	679	3 305	17 897	10 952	6 945	44 049	32 524	12 932	3 134	6 713
1968	68 023	56 050	22 292	671	3 410	18 211	11 137	7 074	45 731	33 759	13 315	3 212	6 979
1969	70 512	58 181	22 893	683	3 637	18 573	11 396	7 177	47 619	35 288	13 833	3 320	7 297
1970	71 006	58 318	22 179	677	3 654	17 848	10 762	7 086	48 827	36 139	14 124	3 392	7 465
1971	71 335	58 323	21 602	658	3 770	17 174	10 229	6 944	49 734	36 721	14 298	3 398	7 659
1972	73 798	60 333	22 299	672	3 957	17 669	10 630	7 039	51 499	38 034	14 767	3 521	8 041
1973	76 912	63 050	23 450	693	4 167	18 589	11 414	7 176	53 462	39 600	15 327	3 661	8 374
1974	78 389	64 086	23 364	755	4 095	18 514	11 432	7 082	55 025	40 721	15 670	3 795	8 539
1975	77 069	62 250	21 318	802	3 608	16 909	10 266	6 643	55 751	40 932	15 583	3 782	8 604
1976	79 502	64 501	22 025	832	3 662	17 531	10 640	6 891	57 477	42 476	16 105	3 891	8 970
1977	82 593	67 334	22 972	865	3 940	18 167	11 132	7 035	59 620	44 362	16 741	4 025	9 363
1978	86 826	71 014	24 156	902	4 322	18 932	11 770	7 162	62 670	46 858	17 633	4 248	9 882
1979	89 933	73 865	24 997	1 008	4 562	19 426	12 220	7 206	64 936	48 869	18 276	4 452	10 185
1980	90 533	74 158	24 263	1 077	4 454	18 733	11 679	7 054	66 270	49 895	18 387	4 524	10 249
1981	91 297	75 117	24 118	1 180	4 304	18 634	11 611	7 023	67 179	50 999	18 577	4 600	10 369
1982	89 689	73 706	22 550	1 163	4 024	17 363	10 610	6 753	67 138	51 156	18 430	4 541	10 377
1983	90 295	74 284	22 110	997	4 065	17 048	10 326	6 722	68 186	52 174	18 642	4 525	10 640
1984	94 548	78 389	23 435	1 014	4 501	17 920	11 050	6 870	71 113	54 954	19 624	4 753	11 227
1985	97 532	81 000	23 585	974	4 793	17 819	11 034	6 784	73 947	57 415	20 350	4 878	11 738
1986	99 500	82 661	23 318	829	4 937	17 552	10 795	6 757	76 182	59 343	20 765	4 899	12 082
1987	102 116	84 960	23 470	771	5 090	17 609	10 767	6 842	78 647	61 490	21 271	4 966	12 422
1988	105 378	87 838	23 909	770	5 233	17 906	10 969	6 938	81 469	63 929	21 942	5 115	12 812
1989	108 051	90 124	24 045	750	5 309	17 985	11 004	6 981	84 006	66 079	22 477	5 245	13 112
1990	109 526	91 112	23 723	765	5 263	17 695	10 737	6 958	85 803	67 389	22 633	5 230	13 186
1991	108 425	89 879	22 588	739	4 780	17 068	10 220	6 848	85 837	67 291	22 247	5 147	12 900
1992	108 799	90 012	22 095	689	4 608	16 799	9 946	6 853	86 704	67 918	22 091	5 072	12 831
1993	110 931	91 942	22 219	666	4 779	16 774	9 901	6 872	88 712	69 723	22 343	5 056	13 024
1994	114 393	95 118	22 774	659	5 095	17 020	10 132	6 889	91 619	72 344	23 090	5 208	13 494
1995	117 400	97 968	23 156	641	5 274	17 241	10 373	6 868	94 245	74 812	23 793	5 393	13 900
1996	119 828	100 289	23 409	637	5 536	17 237	10 486	6 751	96 419	76 880	24 197	5 481	14 116
1997	122 941	103 278	23 886	654	5 813	17 419	10 705	6 714	99 055	79 392	24 656	5 622	14 393
1998	126 146	106 237	24 354	645	6 149	17 560	10 911	6 649	101 792	81 883	25 139	5 752	14 613
1999	129 228	108 921	24 465	598	6 545	17 322	10 831	6 491	104 763	84 456	25 722	5 848	14 974
2000	132 011	111 221	24 649	599	6 787	17 263	10 877	6 386	107 362	86 572	26 174	5 888	15 284
2001	132 073	110 955	23 873	606	6 826	16 441	10 336	6 105	108 200	87 082	25 931	5 728	15 242
2002	130 634	109 121	22 557	583	6 716	15 259	9 485	5 774	108 077	86 564	25 442	5 606	15 029
2003	130 331	108 748	21 816	572	6 735	14 509	8 964	5 546	108 515	86 931	25 228	5 556	14 922
2004	131 769	110 148	21 882	591	6 976	14 315	8 925	5 390	109 887	88 266	25 470	5 608	15 063
2005	134 005	112 201	22 190	628	7 336	14 227	8 956	5 271	111 814	90 010	25 959	5 764	15 280
2006	136 398	114 424	22 530	684	7 691	14 155	8 981	5 174	113 867	91 894	26 276	5 905	15 353
2007	137 936	115 718	22 233	724	7 630	13 879	8 808	5 071	115 703	93 485	26 630	6 015	15 520
2008	137 170	114 661	21 335	767	7 162	13 406	8 463	4 943	115 835	93 326	26 293	5 943	15 283
2009	131 233	108 678	18 558	694	6 016	11 847	7 284	4 564	112 675	90 121	24 906	5 587	14 522
2010	130 275	107 785	17 751	705	5 518	11 528	7 064	4 464	112 524	90 034	24 636	5 452	14 440
2011	131 842	109 756	18 047	788	5 533	11 726	7 273	4 453	113 795	91 708	25 065	5 543	14 668
2012	134 104	112 184	18 420	848	5 646	11 927	7 470	4 457	115 683	93 763	25 476	5 667	14 841
2013	136 368	114 504	18 700	868	5 827	12 006	7 543	4 463	117 668	95 804	25 870	5 747	15 077
2014	139 578	117 670	19 360	904	6 231	12 225	7 708	4 517	120 218	98 310	26 490	5 824	15 414
2015	142 253	120 196	19 614	778	6 490	12 346	7 769	4 577	122 639	100 582	26 938	5 843	15 631
2016	144 882	122 566	19 718	661	6 727	12 330	7 693	4 637	125 164	102 848	27 322	5 878	15 887
2017	146 608	124 258	20 048	676	6 969	12 440	7 741	4 699	126 768	104 174	27 393	5 814	15 846
2018	148 908	126 454	20 704	727	7 288	12 688	7 946	4 742	128 205	105 750	27 607	5 841	15 786
2019	150 939	128 346	21 067	735	7 492	12 840	8 059	4 781	129 873	107 279	27 715	5 903	15 644
2020	142 252	120 344	20 076	620	7 274	12 182	7 581	4 601	122 117	100 268	26 589	5 641	14 856
2021	146 102	124 102	20 324	566	7 412	12 346	7 677	4 670	125 777	103 778	27 718	5 679	15 410

Table 10-7. Nonfarm Payroll Employment by NAICS Supersector—*Continued*

(Thousands; seasonally adjusted, except as noted.)

Year and month	Service-providing—*Continued*													Diffusion index, 6-month span, private nonfarm [2]
	Private—*Continued*						Government							
								Federal		State		Local		
	Information	Financial activities	Professional and business services	Education and health services	Leisure and hospitality	Other services	Total	Total	Department of Defense [1]	Total	Education	Total	Education	
1964	1 766	2 811	4 154	3 438	3 772	1 346	9 711	2 463	676	1 856	609	5 392	2 839	. . .
1965	1 824	2 878	4 323	3 587	3 951	1 404	10 191	2 495	679	1 996	679	5 700	3 031	. . .
1966	1 908	2 961	4 536	3 770	4 127	1 475	10 910	2 690	741	2 141	775	6 080	3 297	. . .
1967	1 955	3 087	4 739	3 986	4 269	1 558	11 525	2 852	802	2 302	873	6 371	3 490	. . .
1968	1 991	3 234	4 937	4 191	4 453	1 638	11 972	2 871	801	2 442	958	6 660	3 649	. . .
1969	2 048	3 404	5 175	4 428	4 670	1 731	12 330	2 893	815	2 533	1 042	6 904	3 785	. . .
1970	2 041	3 532	5 287	4 577	4 789	1 789	12 687	2 865	756	2 664	1 104	7 158	3 912	. . .
1971	2 009	3 651	5 348	4 675	4 914	1 827	13 012	2 828	731	2 747	1 149	7 437	4 091	. . .
1972	2 056	3 784	5 544	4 863	5 121	1 900	13 465	2 815	720	2 859	1 188	7 790	4 262	. . .
1973	2 135	3 920	5 796	5 092	5 341	1 990	13 862	2 794	696	2 923	1 205	8 146	4 433	. . .
1974	2 160	4 023	5 997	5 322	5 471	2 078	14 303	2 858	698	3 039	1 267	8 407	4 584	. . .
1975	2 061	4 047	6 056	5 497	5 544	2 144	14 820	2 882	704	3 179	1 323	8 758	4 722	. . .
1976	2 111	4 155	6 310	5 756	5 794	2 244	15 001	2 863	693	3 273	1 371	8 865	4 786	. . .
1977	2 185	4 348	6 611	6 052	6 065	2 359	15 258	2 859	676	3 377	1 385	9 023	4 859	. . .
1978	2 287	4 599	6 997	6 427	6 411	2 505	15 812	2 893	661	3 474	1 367	9 446	4 958	. . .
1979	2 375	4 843	7 339	6 768	6 631	2 637	16 068	2 894	649	3 541	1 378	9 633	4 989	. . .
1980	2 361	5 025	7 571	7 077	6 721	2 755	16 375	3 000	645	3 610	1 398	9 765	5 090	. . .
1981	2 382	5 163	7 809	7 364	6 840	2 865	16 180	2 922	655	3 640	1 420	9 619	5 095	. . .
1982	2 317	5 209	7 875	7 526	6 874	2 924	15 982	2 884	690	3 640	1 433	9 458	5 049	. . .
1983	2 253	5 334	8 065	7 781	7 078	3 021	16 011	2 915	699	3 662	1 450	9 434	5 020	. . .
1984	2 398	5 553	8 493	8 211	7 489	3 186	16 159	2 943	716	3 734	1 488	9 482	5 076	. . .
1985	2 437	5 815	8 900	8 679	7 869	3 366	16 533	3 014	738	3 832	1 540	9 687	5 221	. . .
1986	2 445	6 128	9 241	9 086	8 156	3 523	16 838	3 044	736	3 893	1 561	9 901	5 358	. . .
1987	2 507	6 385	9 639	9 543	8 446	3 699	17 156	3 089	736	3 967	1 586	10 100	5 469	. . .
1988	2 585	6 500	10 121	10 096	8 778	3 907	17 540	3 124	719	4 076	1 621	10 339	5 590	. . .
1989	2 622	6 562	10 588	10 652	9 062	4 116	17 927	3 136	735	4 182	1 668	10 609	5 740	. . .
1990	2 688	6 614	10 881	11 024	9 288	4 261	18 415	3 196	722	4 305	1 730	10 914	5 902	. . .
1991	2 677	6 561	10 746	11 556	9 256	4 249	18 545	3 110	702	4 355	1 768	11 081	5 994	43.6
1992	2 641	6 559	11 001	11 948	9 437	4 240	18 787	3 111	702	4 408	1 799	11 267	6 076	61.6
1993	2 668	6 742	11 527	12 362	9 732	4 350	18 989	3 063	670	4 488	1 834	11 438	6 206	72.5
1994	2 738	6 910	12 207	12 872	10 100	4 428	19 275	3 018	657	4 576	1 882	11 682	6 329	81.4
1995	2 843	6 866	12 878	13 360	10 501	4 572	19 432	2 949	627	4 635	1 919	11 849	6 453	70.5
1996	2 940	7 018	13 497	13 761	10 777	4 690	19 539	2 877	597	4 606	1 911	12 056	6 592	78.5
1997	3 084	7 255	14 371	14 185	11 018	4 825	19 664	2 806	588	4 582	1 904	12 276	6 759	81.0
1998	3 218	7 565	15 183	14 570	11 232	4 976	19 909	2 772	550	4 612	1 922	12 525	6 921	70.2
1999	3 419	7 753	15 994	14 939	11 543	5 087	20 307	2 769	525	4 709	1 983	12 829	7 120	70.5
2000	3 630	7 783	16 704	15 252	11 862	5 168	20 790	2 865	510	4 786	2 031	13 139	7 294	58.9
2001	3 629	7 900	16 514	15 814	12 036	5 258	21 118	2 764	504	4 905	2 113	13 449	7 479	32.4
2002	3 395	7 956	16 016	16 398	11 986	5 372	21 513	2 766	499	5 029	2 243	13 718	7 654	38.0
2003	3 188	8 078	16 029	16 835	12 173	5 401	21 583	2 761	486	5 002	2 255	13 820	7 709	40.5
2004	3 118	8 105	16 440	17 230	12 493	5 409	21 621	2 730	473	4 982	2 238	13 909	7 765	61.0
2005	3 038	8 197	16 954	18 154	12 816	5 395	21 804	2 732	493	5 032	2 260	14 041	7 856	64.5
2006	3 032	8 367	17 566	18 099	13 110	5 438	21 974	2 732	491	5 075	2 293	14 167	7 913	60.1
2007	2 984	8 348	17 942	18 613	13 427	5 494	22 218	2 734	496	5 122	2 318	14 362	7 987	57.2
2008	2 804	8 206	17 735	19 156	13 436	5 515	22 509	2 762	519	5 177	2 354	14 571	8 084	27.3
2009	2 707	7 838	16 579	19 550	13 077	5 367	22 555	2 832	545	5 169	2 360	14 554	8 079	19.2
2010	2 674	7 695	16 728	19 889	13 049	5 331	22 490	2 977	559	5 137	2 373	14 376	8 013	62.8
2011	2 676	7 697	17 332	20 228	13 353	5 360	22 086	2 859	552	5 078	2 374	14 150	7 873	73.8
2012	2 706	7 784	17 932	20 698	13 768	5 430	21 920	2 820	537	5 055	2 389	14 045	7 778	62.2
2013	2 726	7 880	18 560	21 102	14 242	5 464	21 864	2 766	524	5 048	2 393	14 050	7 783	63.0
2014	2 750	8 006	19 189	21 541	14 775	5 575	21 908	2 736	526	5 043	2 379	14 129	7 847	78.5
2015	2 794	8 149	19 705	22 140	15 266	5 620	22 057	2 761	529	5 086	2 407	14 210	7 865	64.5
2016	2 814	8 324	20 279	22 745	15 684	5 708	22 316	2 811	527	5 101	2 423	14 404	7 968	63.2
2017	2 839	8 451	20 508	23 188	16 051	5 770	22 350	2 805	531	5 165	2 479	14 379	7 922	70.2
2018	2 860	8 590	20 950	23 638	16 295	5 831	22 455	2 800	543	5 173	2 487	14 481	7 963	69.8
2019	2 860	8 746	21 313	24 177	16 576	5 893	22 594	2 834	543	5 177	2 484	14 583	8 010	63.2
2020	2 698	8 727	20 253	23 234	13 369	5 396	21 908	2 929	560	5 074	2 380	13 905	7 572	37.6
2021	2 830	8 775	21 238	23 666	14 094	5 455	21 999	2 886	564	5 209	2 535	13 905	7 577	76.6

[1]Not seasonally adjusted.
[2]See notes and definitions for explanation. September value used to represent year.
. . . = Not available.

Table 10-7. Nonfarm Payroll Employment by NAICS Supersector—*Continued*

(Thousands; seasonally adjusted, except as noted.)

Year and month	Total	Private								Service-providing				
			Goods-producing								Private				
		Total	Total	Mining and logging	Construc-tion	Manufacturing			Total	Total	Trade, transportation, and utilities			
						Total	Durable	Nondurable			Total	Wholesale trade	Retail trade
2017														
January	145 628	121 206	19 854	648	6 840	12 366	7 702	4 664	125 774	103 458	27 358	5 802	15 918
February	145 818	121 781	19 916	655	6 881	12 380	7 698	4 682	125 902	103 576	27 342	5 805	15 882
March	145 960	122 369	19 954	659	6 902	12 393	7 705	4 688	126 006	103 677	27 340	5 807	15 865
April	146 165	123 365	19 986	670	6 916	12 400	7 708	4 692	126 179	103 844	27 342	5 807	15 848
May	146 388	124 260	20 015	675	6 931	12 409	7 717	4 692	126 373	104 026	27 359	5 807	15 835
June	146 585	125 307	20 062	678	6 962	12 422	7 725	4 697	126 523	104 163	27 380	5 813	15 835
July	146 768	125 388	20 072	681	6 968	12 423	7 718	4 705	126 696	104 322	27 378	5 815	15 822
August	146 913	125 471	20 154	685	7 002	12 467	7 753	4 714	126 759	104 449	27 398	5 817	15 827
September	147 012	124 852	20 177	687	7 013	12 477	7 765	4 712	126 835	104 502	27 424	5 816	15 821
October	147 153	125 444	20 209	688	7 031	12 490	7 776	4 714	126 944	104 583	27 441	5 821	15 817
November	147 353	125 885	20 266	693	7 068	12 505	7 795	4 710	127 087	104 708	27 458	5 821	15 824
December	147 529	125 769	20 316	692	7 091	12 533	7 818	4 715	127 213	104 829	27 471	5 824	15 810
2018														
January	147 662	123 187	20 356	698	7 102	12 556	7 838	4 718	127 306	104 938	27 444	5 822	15 781
February	148 064	123 952	20 473	705	7 186	12 582	7 861	4 721	127 591	105 181	27 517	5 825	15 820
March	148 289	124 585	20 515	712	7 195	12 608	7 887	4 721	127 774	105 353	27 574	5 837	15 836
April	148 468	125 525	20 576	721	7 223	12 632	7 906	4 726	127 892	105 457	27 578	5 814	15 834
May	148 801	126 511	20 658	726	7 271	12 661	7 922	4 739	128 143	105 684	27 625	5 820	15 843
June	148 984	127 565	20 716	732	7 291	12 693	7 943	4 750	128 268	105 791	27 607	5 825	15 798
July	149 050	127 588	20 762	732	7 316	12 714	7 961	4 753	128 288	105 839	27 613	5 838	15 781
August	149 269	127 725	20 809	740	7 345	12 724	7 971	4 753	128 460	105 991	27 665	5 856	15 783
September	149 326	127 078	20 850	741	7 366	12 743	7 988	4 755	128 476	105 992	27 640	5 853	15 738
October	149 471	127 689	20 886	744	7 380	12 762	8 009	4 753	128 585	106 102	27 636	5 857	15 705
November	149 573	128 061	20 890	737	7 379	12 774	8 018	4 756	128 683	106 210	27 681	5 864	15 724
December	149 821	127 978	20 930	741	7 396	12 793	8 034	4 759	128 891	106 382	27 649	5 869	15 704
2019														
January	150 100	125 501	20 999	743	7 434	12 822	8 062	4 760	129 101	106 582	27 696	5 878	15 683
February	150 124	125 891	20 962	739	7 402	12 821	8 062	4 759	129 162	106 633	27 670	5 886	15 661
March	150 348	126 473	20 983	737	7 427	12 819	8 055	4 764	129 365	106 804	27 659	5 883	15 648
April	150 636	127 469	21 032	738	7 470	12 824	8 053	4 771	129 604	107 005	27 701	5 888	15 645
May	150 713	128 227	21 043	738	7 484	12 821	8 046	4 775	129 670	107 074	27 707	5 890	15 619
June	150 843	129 240	21 074	735	7 510	12 829	8 046	4 783	129 769	107 172	27 706	5 883	15 585
July	150 921	129 333	21 084	730	7 522	12 832	8 047	4 785	129 837	107 280	27 732	5 890	15 589
August	151 081	129 397	21 077	723	7 527	12 827	8 039	4 788	130 004	107 405	27 728	5 887	15 588
September	151 244	128 839	21 080	720	7 540	12 820	8 032	4 788	130 164	107 509	27 738	5 888	15 582
October	151 337	129 440	21 028	721	7 543	12 764	7 979	4 785	130 309	107 629	27 755	5 896	15 591
November	151 589	129 900	21 055	707	7 536	12 812	8 021	4 791	130 534	107 820	27 735	5 892	15 560
December	151 789	129 789	21 017	693	7 529	12 795	8 011	4 784	130 772	108 041	27 801	5 896	15 608
2020														
January	152 128	127 405	21 045	684	7 577	12 784	8 004	4 780	131 083	108 299	27 842	5 898	15 594
February	152 504	127 874	21 095	686	7 624	12 785	8 007	4 778	131 409	108 530	27 832	5 893	15 597
March	151 006	126 825	20 939	673	7 549	12 717	7 965	4 752	130 067	107 242	27 720	5 875	15 511
April	130 513	108 013	18 554	615	6 516	11 423	7 068	4 355	111 959	90 055	24 673	5 488	13 352
May	133 155	111 762	19 258	595	7 007	11 656	7 203	4 453	113 897	92 476	25 053	5 503	13 689
June	137 660	117 211	19 737	581	7 166	11 990	7 460	4 530	117 923	96 507	26 030	5 545	14 496
July	139 048	118 713	19 793	570	7 198	12 025	7 492	4 533	119 255	97 744	26 322	5 528	14 744
August	140 713	119 600	19 835	563	7 222	12 050	7 489	4 561	120 878	98 915	26 725	5 540	15 044
September	141 632	119 988	19 899	561	7 243	12 095	7 520	4 575	121 733	99 810	26 830	5 566	15 054
October	142 279	121 433	19 973	556	7 295	12 122	7 530	4 592	122 306	100 535	26 976	5 575	15 113
November	142 612	121 957	20 024	554	7 313	12 157	7 559	4 598	122 588	100 890	27 065	5 584	15 111
December	142 497	121 619	20 101	554	7 357	12 190	7 580	4 610	122 396	100 705	27 158	5 598	15 170
2021														
January	143 017	119 314	20 090	546	7 360	12 184	7 572	4 612	122 927	101 139	27 279	5 612	15 243
February	143 727	120 136	20 072	542	7 308	12 222	7 600	4 622	123 655	101 850	27 403	5 622	15 292
March	144 431	121 165	20 227	551	7 408	12 268	7 626	4 642	124 204	102 345	27 503	5 636	15 328
April	144 694	122 117	20 187	554	7 393	12 240	7 593	4 647	124 507	102 597	27 527	5 647	15 338
May	145 141	123 111	20 209	560	7 381	12 268	7 616	4 652	124 932	102 956	27 538	5 656	15 313
June	145 698	124 593	20 232	566	7 378	12 288	7 632	4 656	125 466	103 441	27 661	5 676	15 381
July	146 387	125 471	20 314	569	7 395	12 350	7 680	4 670	126 073	103 997	27 735	5 694	15 398
August	146 904	125 653	20 362	574	7 397	12 391	7 710	4 681	126 542	104 446	27 807	5 699	15 434
September	147 328	125 444	20 416	576	7 427	12 413	7 725	4 688	126 912	104 801	27 907	5 704	15 493
October	148 005	126 847	20 499	578	7 455	12 466	7 766	4 700	127 506	105 412	28 013	5 716	15 537
November	148 652	127 659	20 598	582	7 502	12 514	7 785	4 729	128 054	105 940	28 084	5 731	15 556
December	149 240	127 922	20 691	590	7 546	12 555	7 816	4 739	128 549	106 408	28 163	5 750	15 595

Table 10-7. Nonfarm Payroll Employment by NAICS Supersector—*Continued*

(Thousands; seasonally adjusted, except as noted.)

Year and month	Information	Financial activities	Professional and business services	Education and health services	Leisure and hospitality	Other services	Total	Federal Total	Federal Department of Defense [1]	State Total	State Education	Local Total	Local Education	Diffusion index, 6-month span, private nonfarm [2]
2017														
January	2 824	8 397	20 328	22 946	15 874	5 731	22 316	2 813	531	5 156	2 471	14 347	7 919	63.1
February	2 815	8 397	20 346	23 016	15 917	5 743	22 326	2 812	530	5 160	2 473	14 354	7 922	65.0
March	2 812	8 409	20 375	23 051	15 941	5 749	22 329	2 810	529	5 163	2 475	14 356	7 924	68.2
April	2 807	8 425	20 407	23 103	16 006	5 754	22 335	2 798	528	5 169	2 484	14 368	7 922	67.0
May	2 804	8 435	20 469	23 147	16 046	5 766	22 347	2 808	526	5 181	2 499	14 358	7 924	65.4
June	2 808	8 450	20 504	23 167	16 087	5 767	22 360	2 805	526	5 174	2 490	14 381	7 923	70.3
July	2 809	8 463	20 545	23 232	16 122	5 773	22 374	2 806	526	5 178	2 491	14 390	7 918	72.5
August	2 816	8 472	20 584	23 255	16 150	5 774	22 310	2 802	526	5 169	2 479	14 339	7 871	67.4
September	2 813	8 481	20 579	23 287	16 140	5 778	22 333	2 799	526	5 144	2 458	14 390	7 915	71.3
October	2 812	8 479	20 619	23 309	16 133	5 790	22 361	2 802	524	5 152	2 466	14 407	7 931	69.7
November	2 812	8 489	20 635	23 352	16 160	5 802	22 379	2 791	525	5 161	2 475	14 427	7 940	65.2
December	2 817	8 496	20 673	23 384	16 183	5 805	22 384	2 794	527	5 159	2 471	14 431	7 942	64.3
2018														
January	2 818	8 501	20 721	23 442	16 200	5 812	22 368	2 799	524	5 148	2 478	14 421	7 929	65.8
February	2 813	8 528	20 771	23 500	16 234	5 818	22 410	2 791	524	5 151	2 478	14 468	7 967	68.4
March	2 824	8 537	20 819	23 530	16 248	5 821	22 421	2 792	525	5 157	2 481	14 472	7 967	73.2
April	2 838	8 546	20 869	23 547	16 251	5 828	22 435	2 793	528	5 169	2 481	14 473	7 969	72.5
May	2 837	8 572	20 924	23 590	16 293	5 843	22 459	2 791	530	5 182	2 489	14 486	7 972	74.4
June	2 840	8 591	20 963	23 617	16 329	5 844	22 477	2 796	530	5 182	2 487	14 499	7 982	77.5
July	2 842	8 600	20 980	23 644	16 335	5 825	22 449	2 800	531	5 179	2 485	14 470	7 950	74.0
August	2 843	8 612	21 016	23 693	16 337	5 825	22 469	2 802	532	5 182	2 490	14 485	7 959	73.8
September	2 839	8 631	21 047	23 707	16 296	5 832	22 484	2 806	534	5 187	2 497	14 491	7 964	70.3
October	2 851	8 640	21 073	23 751	16 316	5 835	22 483	2 805	534	5 183	2 495	14 495	7 963	69.9
November	2 851	8 650	21 089	23 768	16 336	5 835	22 473	2 808	536	5 165	2 477	14 500	7 964	62.9
December	2 853	8 660	21 118	23 854	16 398	5 850	22 509	2 809	538	5 174	2 489	14 526	7 984	64.6
2019														
January	2 843	8 672	21 098	23 906	16 511	5 856	22 519	2 809	537	5 169	2 486	14 541	7 999	66.0
February	2 836	8 684	21 140	23 936	16 507	5 860	22 529	2 812	538	5 177	2 492	14 540	7 995	67.2
March	2 848	8 704	21 168	23 996	16 546	5 883	22 561	2 813	539	5 179	2 495	14 569	8 017	68.6
April	2 846	8 724	21 215	24 058	16 565	5 896	22 599	2 821	540	5 178	2 500	14 600	8 036	68.6
May	2 853	8 738	21 247	24 082	16 553	5 894	22 596	2 828	541	5 182	2 500	14 586	8 012	67.0
June	2 873	8 749	21 294	24 128	16 529	5 893	22 597	2 834	544	5 186	2 499	14 577	7 982	65.4
July	2 868	8 771	21 318	24 177	16 519	5 895	22 557	2 831	545	5 200	2 508	14 526	7 938	63.3
August	2 868	8 786	21 337	24 234	16 558	5 894	22 599	2 855	543	5 220	2 525	14 524	7 943	63.1
September	2 872	8 785	21 350	24 279	16 591	5 894	22 655	2 853	545	5 224	2 527	14 578	7 989	56.6
October	2 873	8 797	21 360	24 312	16 647	5 885	22 680	2 838	546	5 238	2 537	14 604	8 013	54.9
November	2 883	8 814	21 393	24 390	16 699	5 906	22 714	2 842	554	5 247	2 546	14 625	8 029	58.6
December	2 894	8 821	21 396	24 437	16 771	5 921	22 731	2 836	554	5 247	2 549	14 648	8 040	50.6
2020														
January	2 897	8 837	21 371	24 531	16 881	5 940	22 784	2 855	553	5 264	2 560	14 665	8 036	54.3
February	2 903	8 870	21 393	24 598	16 983	5 951	22 879	2 861	558	5 310	2 606	14 708	8 064	55.9
March	2 898	8 851	21 308	24 360	16 245	5 860	22 825	2 877	559	5 247	2 542	14 701	8 061	39.3
April	2 642	8 590	19 091	21 759	8 780	4 520	21 904	2 875	558	5 091	2 393	13 938	7 642	7.2
May	2 606	8 607	19 294	22 149	10 011	4 756	21 421	2 877	559	5 080	2 389	13 464	7 331	7.2
June	2 624	8 623	19 651	22 699	11 791	5 089	21 416	2 882	558	5 076	2 386	13 458	7 336	7.4
July	2 617	8 623	19 836	22 889	12 232	5 225	21 511	2 907	561	5 084	2 388	13 520	7 376	9.2
August	2 640	8 647	20 026	23 088	12 513	5 276	21 963	3 156	563	5 114	2 414	13 693	7 491	8.6
September	2 698	8 675	20 154	23 184	12 946	5 323	21 923	3 122	564	5 102	2 399	13 699	7 401	9.2
October	2 698	8 696	20 374	23 277	13 179	5 335	21 771	2 982	564	5 077	2 375	13 712	7 389	76.8
November	2 706	8 709	20 525	23 346	13 209	5 330	21 698	2 894	565	5 077	2 377	13 727	7 394	81.1
December	2 719	8 721	20 689	23 350	12 749	5 319	21 691	2 893	565	5 080	2 379	13 718	7 398	75.0
2021														
January	2 745	8 732	20 800	23 378	12 877	5 328	21 788	2 886	566	5 154	2 457	13 748	7 440	77.0
February	2 758	8 724	20 902	23 454	13 270	5 339	21 805	2 888	566	5 157	2 463	13 760	7 450	76.8
March	2 768	8 733	21 021	23 541	13 423	5 356	21 859	2 888	567	5 170	2 479	13 801	7 482	78.7
April	2 788	8 747	20 943	23 582	13 631	. . .	21 910	2 895	567	5 173	2 482	13 842	7 515	76.2
May	2 803	8 747	21 023	23 620	13 830	5 395	21 976	2 889	566	5 231	2 545	13 856	7 541	74.4
June	2 820	8 745	21 084	23 640	14 054	5 437	22 025	2 885	566	5 251	2 572	13 889	7 586	73.6
July	2 841	8 772	21 226	23 699	14 251	5 473	22 076	2 887	565	5 241	2 570	13 948	7 645	76.4
August	2 866	8 781	21 309	23 728	14 453	5 502	22 096	2 886	564	5 226	2 561	13 984	7 665	75.8
September	2 874	8 794	21 383	23 737	14 587	5 519	22 111	2 885	563	5 224	2 563	14 002	7 636	73.8
October	2 886	8 817	21 619	23 805	14 728	5 544	22 094	2 880	564	5 224	2 567	13 990	7 633	74.6
November	2 904	8 849	21 730	23 874	14 919	5 580	22 114	2 884	560	5 220	2 571	14 010	7 659	79.1
December	2 913	8 863	21 821	23 939	15 105	5 604	22 141	2 876	557	5 237	2 596	14 028	7 677	83.2

[1]Not seasonally adjusted.
[2]See notes and definitions for explanation. September value used to represent year.
. . . = Not available.

Table 10-8. Employment, Hours, and Earnings, Total Nonfarm and Manufacturing, Historical Annual and Monthly

(Wage and salary workers on nonfarm payrolls, seasonally adjusted.)

Year and month	All wage and salary workers (thousands)					Production and nonsupervisory workers on private payrolls							
	Total	Private			Service-providing	Number (thousands)		Average hours per week		Average hourly earnings, dollars		Average weekly earnings, dollars	
		Total	Goods-producing			Total private	Manufac-turing	Total private	Manufac-turing	Total private	Manufac-turing	Total private	Manufac-turing
			Total	Manufac-turing									
1939	30 645	26 606	11 511	9 450	19 134	...	8 163	...	37.7	...	0.49	...	18.47
1940	32 407	28 156	12 378	10 099	20 029	...	8 737	...	38.2	...	0.53	...	20.25
1941	36 600	31 874	14 940	12 121	21 660	...	10 641	...	40.7	...	0.61	...	24.83
1942	40 213	34 621	17 275	14 030	22 938	...	12 447	...	43.2	...	0.74	...	31.97
1943	42 574	36 353	18 738	16 153	23 837	...	14 407	...	45.1	...	0.86	...	38.79
1944	42 006	35 819	17 981	15 903	24 026	...	14 031	...	45.4	...	0.91	...	41.31
1945	40 510	34 428	16 308	14 255	24 203	...	12 445	...	43.6	...	0.90	...	39.24
1946	41 759	36 054	16 122	13 513	25 637	...	11 781	...	40.4	...	0.95	...	38.38
1947	43 945	38 379	17 314	14 287	26 631	...	12 453	...	40.5	...	1.10	...	44.55
1948	44 954	39 213	17 579	14 324	27 376	...	12 383	...	40.1	...	1.20	...	48.12
1949	43 843	37 893	16 464	13 281	27 379	...	11 355	...	39.2	...	1.25	...	49.00
1950	45 287	39 167	17 343	14 013	27 945	...	12 032	...	40.6	...	1.32	...	53.59
1951	47 930	41 427	18 703	15 070	29 227	...	12 808	...	40.7	...	1.45	...	59.02
1952	48 909	42 182	18 928	15 291	29 981	...	12 797	...	40.8	...	1.53	...	62.42
1953	50 310	43 552	19 733	16 131	30 577	...	13 437	...	40.6	...	1.63	...	66.18
1954	49 093	42 235	18 515	15 002	30 578	...	12 300	...	39.7	...	1.66	...	65.90
1955	50 744	43 722	19 234	15 524	31 510	...	12 735	...	40.8	...	1.74	...	70.99
1956	52 473	45 087	19 799	15 858	32 674	...	12 869	...	40.5	...	1.84	...	74.52
1957	52 959	45 235	19 669	15 798	33 290	...	12 640	...	39.9	...	1.93	...	77.01
1958	51 426	43 480	18 319	14 656	33 107	...	11 532	...	39.2	...	1.99	...	78.01
1959	53 374	45 182	19 163	15 325	34 211	...	12 089	...	40.3	...	2.08	...	83.82
1960	54 296	45 832	19 182	15 438	35 114	...	12 074	...	39.8	...	2.15	...	85.57
1961	54 105	45 399	18 647	15 011	35 458	...	11 612	...	39.9	...	2.20	...	87.78
1962	55 659	46 655	19 203	15 498	36 455	...	11 986	...	40.5	...	2.27	...	91.94
1963	56 764	47 423	19 385	15 631	37 379	...	12 051	...	40.6	...	2.34	...	95.00
1964	58 391	48 680	19 733	15 888	38 658	40 575	12 298	38.5	40.8	2.53	2.41	97.41	98.33
1952													
January	48 298	41 709	18 719	15 067	29 579	...	12 675	...	40.8	...	1.49	...	60.79
February	48 522	41 872	18 813	15 105	29 709	...	12 689	...	40.8	...	1.49	...	60.79
March	48 504	41 842	18 775	15 127	29 729	...	12 695	...	40.6	...	1.51	...	61.31
April	48 616	41 954	18 806	15 162	29 810	...	12 713	...	40.3	...	1.51	...	60.85
May	48 645	41 951	18 784	15 143	29 861	...	12 676	...	40.5	...	1.51	...	61.16
June	48 286	41 574	18 419	14 828	29 867	...	12 353	...	40.6	...	1.51	...	61.31
July	48 144	41 407	18 268	14 707	29 876	...	12 233	...	40.2	...	1.50	...	60.30
August	48 923	42 205	18 928	15 279	29 995	...	12 764	...	40.7	...	1.53	...	62.27
September	49 319	42 585	19 206	15 553	30 113	...	13 007	...	41.1	...	1.55	...	63.71
October	49 598	42 782	19 312	15 690	30 286	...	13 122	...	41.2	...	1.56	...	64.27
November	49 816	43 015	19 473	15 843	30 343	...	13 262	...	41.2	...	1.58	...	65.10
December	50 164	43 229	19 610	15 973	30 554	...	13 375	...	41.2	...	1.58	...	65.10
1953													
January	50 145	43 351	19 721	16 067	30 424	...	13 447	...	41.1	...	1.59	...	65.35
February	50 339	43 542	19 841	16 158	30 498	...	13 529	...	41.0	...	1.61	...	66.01
March	50 475	43 691	19 909	16 270	30 566	...	13 620	...	41.2	...	1.61	...	66.33
April	50 432	43 662	19 908	16 293	30 524	...	13 629	...	40.9	...	1.62	...	66.26
May	50 491	43 774	19 930	16 341	30 561	...	13 645	...	41.0	...	1.62	...	66.42
June	50 522	43 788	19 909	16 343	30 613	...	13 636	...	40.9	...	1.63	...	66.67
July	50 536	43 813	19 910	16 353	30 626	...	13 653	...	40.7	...	1.64	...	66.75
August	50 487	43 733	19 834	16 278	30 653	...	13 564	...	40.7	...	1.64	...	66.75
September	50 365	43 616	19 726	16 151	30 639	...	13 419	...	40.1	...	1.65	...	66.17
October	50 242	43 478	19 578	15 981	30 664	...	13 244	...	40.1	...	1.65	...	66.17
November	49 907	43 158	19 315	15 728	30 592	...	12 990	...	40.0	...	1.65	...	66.00
December	49 702	42 959	19 173	15 581	30 529	...	12 847	...	39.7	...	1.65	...	65.51
1954													
January	49 468	42 708	18 963	15 440	30 505	...	12 706	...	39.5	...	1.65	...	65.18
February	49 382	42 599	18 880	15 307	30 502	...	12 593	...	39.7	...	1.65	...	65.51
March	49 158	42 362	18 748	15 197	30 410	...	12 493	...	39.6	...	1.65	...	65.34
April	49 178	42 372	18 602	15 065	30 576	...	12 361	...	39.7	...	1.65	...	65.51
May	48 965	42 136	18 476	14 974	30 489	...	12 282	...	39.7	...	1.67	...	66.30
June	48 896	42 050	18 400	14 910	30 496	...	12 220	...	39.7	...	1.67	...	66.30
July	48 835	41 967	18 280	14 799	30 555	...	12 121	...	39.7	...	1.66	...	65.90
August	48 825	41 933	18 251	14 772	30 574	...	12 089	...	39.8	...	1.66	...	66.07
September	48 882	41 988	18 261	14 805	30 621	...	12 104	...	39.9	...	1.66	...	66.23
October	48 944	42 044	18 321	14 841	30 623	...	12 142	...	39.7	...	1.67	...	66.30
November	49 178	42 214	18 438	14 913	30 740	...	12 206	...	40.1	...	1.68	...	67.37
December	49 331	42 374	18 508	14 967	30 823	...	12 254	...	40.1	...	1.68	...	67.37
1955													
January	49 497	42 544	18 609	15 034	30 888	...	12 309	...	40.4	...	1.69	...	68.28
February	49 644	42 721	18 726	15 138	30 918	...	12 408	...	40.6	...	1.70	...	69.02
March	49 963	43 025	18 910	15 258	31 053	...	12 524	...	40.7	...	1.71	...	69.60
April	50 247	43 288	19 067	15 375	31 180	...	12 626	...	40.8	...	1.71	...	69.77
May	50 512	43 521	19 223	15 493	31 289	...	12 731	...	41.1	...	1.73	...	71.10
June	50 790	43 770	19 331	15 585	31 459	...	12 810	...	40.8	...	1.73	...	70.58
July	50 985	43 936	19 376	15 614	31 609	...	12 818	...	40.7	...	1.75	...	71.23
August	51 111	44 088	19 432	15 679	31 679	...	12 866	...	40.7	...	1.76	...	71.63
September	51 262	44 195	19 427	15 668	31 835	...	12 830	...	40.7	...	1.77	...	72.04
October	51 431	44 313	19 482	15 740	31 949	...	12 896	...	41.0	...	1.77	...	72.57
November	51 592	44 509	19 554	15 813	32 038	...	12 967	...	41.1	...	1.78	...	73.16
December	51 805	44 673	19 608	15 859	32 197	...	13 009	...	40.9	...	1.78	...	72.80

. . . = Not available.

Table 10-8. Employment, Hours, and Earnings, Total Nonfarm and Manufacturing, Historical Annual and Monthly—*Continued*

(Wage and salary workers on nonfarm payrolls, seasonally adjusted.)

Year and month	All wage and salary workers (thousands)					Production and nonsupervisory workers on private payrolls							
	Total	Private			Service-providing	Number (thousands)		Average hours per week		Average hourly earnings, dollars		Average weekly earnings, dollars	
		Total	Goods-producing			Total private	Manufac-turing	Total private	Manufac-turing	Total private	Manufac-turing	Total private	Manufac-turing
			Total	Manufac-turing									
1956													
January	51 975	44 808	19 665	15 882	32 310	. . .	13 011	. . .	40.8	. . .	1.78	. . .	72.62
February	52 167	44 955	19 731	15 889	32 436	. . .	12 986	. . .	40.7	. . .	1.79	. . .	72.85
March	52 295	45 043	19 691	15 829	32 604	. . .	12 905	. . .	40.6	. . .	1.80	. . .	73.08
April	52 375	45 099	19 811	15 909	32 564	. . .	12 970	. . .	40.5	. . .	1.82	. . .	73.71
May	52 506	45 139	19 825	15 893	32 681	. . .	12 925	. . .	40.4	. . .	1.83	. . .	73.93
June	52 584	45 217	19 905	15 835	32 679	. . .	12 836	. . .	40.3	. . .	1.83	. . .	73.75
July	51 954	44 549	19 390	15 468	32 564	. . .	12 435	. . .	40.3	. . .	1.82	. . .	73.35
August	52 630	45 179	19 922	15 893	32 708	. . .	12 860	. . .	40.3	. . .	1.85	. . .	74.56
September	52 601	45 120	19 860	15 863	32 741	. . .	12 822	. . .	40.5	. . .	1.87	. . .	75.74
October	52 781	45 262	19 918	15 937	32 863	. . .	12 908	. . .	40.6	. . .	1.88	. . .	76.33
November	52 822	45 269	19 886	15 916	32 936	. . .	12 864	. . .	40.4	. . .	1.88	. . .	75.95
December	52 930	45 346	19 926	15 957	33 004	. . .	12 882	. . .	40.6	. . .	1.91	. . .	77.55
1957													
January	52 888	45 268	19 833	15 970	33 055	. . .	12 881	. . .	40.4	. . .	1.90	. . .	76.76
February	53 097	45 451	19 933	15 998	33 164	. . .	12 885	. . .	40.5	. . .	1.91	. . .	77.36
March	53 157	45 485	19 936	15 994	33 221	. . .	12 855	. . .	40.4	. . .	1.92	. . .	77.57
April	53 238	45 537	19 887	15 970	33 351	. . .	12 811	. . .	40.0	. . .	1.91	. . .	76.40
May	53 149	45 436	19 834	15 931	33 315	. . .	12 762	. . .	40.0	. . .	1.92	. . .	76.80
June	53 066	45 364	19 777	15 873	33 289	. . .	12 697	. . .	40.0	. . .	1.92	. . .	76.80
July	53 123	45 369	19 735	15 854	33 388	. . .	12 669	. . .	40.0	. . .	1.93	. . .	77.20
August	53 126	45 369	19 728	15 867	33 398	. . .	12 673	. . .	40.0	. . .	1.94	. . .	77.60
September	52 932	45 183	19 545	15 710	33 387	. . .	12 528	. . .	39.7	. . .	1.95	. . .	77.42
October	52 765	44 997	19 421	15 599	33 344	. . .	12 437	. . .	39.4	. . .	1.96	. . .	77.22
November	52 559	44 790	19 260	15 466	33 299	. . .	12 301	. . .	39.2	. . .	1.96	. . .	76.83
December	52 385	44 539	19 111	15 332	33 274	. . .	12 170	. . .	39.1	. . .	1.95	. . .	76.25
1958													
January	52 077	44 256	18 902	15 130	33 175	. . .	11 969	. . .	38.9	. . .	1.95	. . .	75.86
February	51 576	43 744	18 529	14 908	33 047	. . .	11 757	. . .	38.7	. . .	1.95	. . .	75.47
March	51 300	43 452	18 335	14 670	32 965	. . .	11 532	. . .	38.8	. . .	1.96	. . .	76.05
April	51 027	43 159	18 120	14 506	32 907	. . .	11 373	. . .	38.9	. . .	1.96	. . .	76.24
May	50 913	43 019	18 008	14 414	32 905	. . .	11 294	. . .	38.9	. . .	1.97	. . .	76.63
June	50 912	42 986	17 984	14 408	32 928	. . .	11 300	. . .	39.1	. . .	1.98	. . .	77.42
July	51 037	43 065	18 038	14 450	32 999	. . .	11 349	. . .	39.3	. . .	1.98	. . .	77.81
August	51 231	43 219	18 147	14 524	33 084	. . .	11 412	. . .	39.5	. . .	2.01	. . .	79.40
September	51 506	43 490	18 331	14 658	33 175	. . .	11 556	. . .	39.5	. . .	2.00	. . .	79.00
October	51 486	43 455	18 218	14 503	33 268	. . .	11 394	. . .	39.6	. . .	2.00	. . .	79.20
November	51 944	43 916	18 610	14 827	33 334	. . .	11 702	. . .	39.9	. . .	2.03	. . .	81.00
December	52 088	43 988	18 592	14 877	33 496	. . .	11 743	. . .	39.9	. . .	2.04	. . .	81.40
1959													
January	52 480	44 375	18 796	14 998	33 684	. . .	11 849	. . .	40.2	. . .	2.04	. . .	82.01
February	52 687	44 571	18 890	15 115	33 797	. . .	11 950	. . .	40.3	. . .	2.05	. . .	82.62
March	53 016	44 884	19 069	15 259	33 947	. . .	12 078	. . .	40.4	. . .	2.07	. . .	83.63
April	53 320	45 178	19 269	15 385	34 051	. . .	12 185	. . .	40.5	. . .	2.08	. . .	84.24
May	53 549	45 396	19 378	15 487	34 171	. . .	12 277	. . .	40.7	. . .	2.08	. . .	84.66
June	53 679	45 536	19 462	15 554	34 217	. . .	12 330	. . .	40.6	. . .	2.09	. . .	84.85
July	53 803	45 630	19 529	15 623	34 274	. . .	12 366	. . .	40.3	. . .	2.09	. . .	84.23
August	53 334	45 153	19 049	15 202	34 285	. . .	11 936	. . .	40.4	. . .	2.07	. . .	83.63
September	53 429	45 190	19 052	15 254	34 377	. . .	11 984	. . .	40.4	. . .	2.08	. . .	84.03
October	53 359	45 094	18 925	15 158	34 434	. . .	11 864	. . .	40.1	. . .	2.07	. . .	83.01
November	53 635	45 351	19 108	15 300	34 527	. . .	11 991	. . .	39.9	. . .	2.07	. . .	82.59
December	54 175	45 807	19 425	15 573	34 750	. . .	12 254	. . .	40.3	. . .	2.11	. . .	85.03
1960													
January	54 274	45 967	19 491	15 687	34 783	. . .	12 362	. . .	40.6	. . .	2.13	. . .	86.48
February	54 513	46 187	19 605	15 765	34 908	. . .	12 434	. . .	40.3	. . .	2.14	. . .	86.24
March	54 458	45 933	19 373	15 707	35 085	. . .	12 362	. . .	40.0	. . .	2.14	. . .	85.60
April	54 812	46 278	19 446	15 654	35 366	. . .	12 299	. . .	40.0	. . .	2.14	. . .	85.60
May	54 473	46 041	19 374	15 575	35 099	. . .	12 218	. . .	40.1	. . .	2.14	. . .	85.81
June	54 347	45 915	19 240	15 466	35 107	. . .	12 102	. . .	39.9	. . .	2.14	. . .	85.39
July	54 304	45 862	19 170	15 413	35 134	. . .	12 047	. . .	39.9	. . .	2.14	. . .	85.39
August	54 271	45 799	19 105	15 360	35 166	. . .	11 986	. . .	39.7	. . .	2.15	. . .	85.36
September	54 228	45 734	19 057	15 330	35 171	. . .	11 956	. . .	39.4	. . .	2.16	. . .	85.10
October	54 144	45 642	18 952	15 231	35 192	. . .	11 846	. . .	39.7	. . .	2.16	. . .	85.75
November	53 962	45 446	18 799	15 112	35 163	. . .	11 726	. . .	39.3	. . .	2.15	. . .	84.50
December	53 744	45 147	18 548	14 947	35 196	. . .	11 556	. . .	38.4	. . .	2.16	. . .	82.94
1961													
January	53 683	45 119	18 508	14 863	35 175	. . .	11 473	. . .	39.3	. . .	2.16	. . .	84.89
February	53 556	44 969	18 418	14 801	35 138	. . .	11 414	. . .	39.4	. . .	2.16	. . .	85.10
March	53 662	45 051	18 438	14 802	35 224	. . .	11 410	. . .	39.5	. . .	2.16	. . .	85.32
April	53 626	44 997	18 432	14 825	35 194	. . .	11 444	. . .	39.5	. . .	2.18	. . .	86.11
May	53 785	45 121	18 523	14 932	35 262	. . .	11 544	. . .	39.7	. . .	2.19	. . .	86.94
June	53 977	45 289	18 618	14 981	35 359	. . .	11 593	. . .	40.0	. . .	2.20	. . .	88.00
July	54 123	45 399	18 640	15 029	35 483	. . .	11 639	. . .	40.0	. . .	2.21	. . .	88.40
August	54 298	45 534	18 725	15 093	35 573	. . .	11 701	. . .	40.1	. . .	2.22	. . .	89.02
September	54 388	45 592	18 730	15 080	35 658	. . .	11 679	. . .	39.5	. . .	2.20	. . .	86.90
October	54 522	45 717	18 805	15 143	35 717	. . .	11 731	. . .	40.3	. . .	2.23	. . .	89.87
November	54 743	45 931	18 927	15 259	35 816	. . .	11 842	. . .	40.7	. . .	2.23	. . .	90.76
December	54 871	46 035	18 981	15 309	35 890	. . .	11 872	. . .	40.4	. . .	2.24	. . .	90.50

. . . = Not available.

Table 10-8. Employment, Hours, and Earnings, Total Nonfarm and Manufacturing, Historical Annual and Monthly—*Continued*

(Wage and salary workers on nonfarm payrolls, seasonally adjusted.)

Year and month	All wage and salary workers (thousands)					Production and nonsupervisory workers on private payrolls							
	Total	Private			Service-providing	Number (thousands)		Average hours per week		Average hourly earnings, dollars		Average weekly earnings, dollars	
		Total	Goods-producing			Total private	Manufac-turing	Total private	Manufac-turing	Total private	Manufac-turing	Total private	Manufac-turing
			Total	Manufac-turing									
1962													
January	54 891	46 040	18 936	15 322	35 955	. . .	11 865	. . .	40.0	. . .	2.25	. . .	90.00
February	55 187	46 309	19 109	15 411	36 078	. . .	11 950	. . .	40.4	. . .	2.26	. . .	91.30
March	55 276	46 375	19 109	15 451	36 167	. . .	11 970	. . .	40.6	. . .	2.26	. . .	91.76
April	55 602	46 680	19 258	15 524	36 344	. . .	12 034	. . .	40.6	. . .	2.26	. . .	91.76
May	55 627	46 669	19 253	15 513	36 374	. . .	12 011	. . .	40.6	. . .	2.27	. . .	92.16
June	55 644	46 644	19 186	15 518	36 458	. . .	12 006	. . .	40.5	. . .	2.26	. . .	91.53
July	55 746	46 720	19 248	15 522	36 498	. . .	12 004	. . .	40.5	. . .	2.27	. . .	91.94
August	55 838	46 775	19 251	15 517	36 587	. . .	11 990	. . .	40.5	. . .	2.28	. . .	92.34
September	55 977	46 888	19 305	15 568	36 672	. . .	12 033	. . .	40.5	. . .	2.28	. . .	92.34
October	56 041	46 927	19 301	15 569	36 740	. . .	12 034	. . .	40.3	. . .	2.29	. . .	92.29
November	56 056	46 911	19 260	15 530	36 796	. . .	11 977	. . .	40.5	. . .	2.29	. . .	92.75
December	56 028	46 902	19 219	15 520	36 809	. . .	11 961	. . .	40.3	. . .	2.29	. . .	92.29
1963													
January	56 116	46 912	19 257	15 545	36 859	. . .	11 974	. . .	40.5	. . .	2.30	. . .	93.15
February	56 230	46 999	19 228	15 542	37 002	. . .	11 965	. . .	40.5	. . .	2.31	. . .	93.56
March	56 322	47 077	19 233	15 564	37 089	. . .	11 990	. . .	40.5	. . .	2.32	. . .	93.96
April	56 580	47 316	19 343	15 602	37 237	. . .	12 029	. . .	40.5	. . .	2.32	. . .	93.96
May	56 616	47 328	19 399	15 641	37 217	. . .	12 066	. . .	40.5	. . .	2.33	. . .	94.37
June	56 658	47 356	19 371	15 624	37 287	. . .	12 050	. . .	40.7	. . .	2.34	. . .	95.24
July	56 794	47 460	19 423	15 646	37 371	. . .	12 080	. . .	40.6	. . .	2.35	. . .	95.41
August	56 910	47 542	19 437	15 644	37 473	. . .	12 060	. . .	40.6	. . .	2.34	. . .	95.00
September	57 077	47 660	19 483	15 674	37 594	. . .	12 088	. . .	40.6	. . .	2.36	. . .	95.82
October	57 284	47 805	19 517	15 714	37 767	. . .	12 131	. . .	40.7	. . .	2.36	. . .	96.05
November	57 255	47 771	19 456	15 675	37 799	. . .	12 072	. . .	40.7	. . .	2.37	. . .	96.46
December	57 360	47 863	19 493	15 712	37 867	. . .	12 108	. . .	40.6	. . .	2.38	. . .	96.63
1964													
January	57 487	47 925	19 406	15 715	38 081	39 913	12 132	38.2	40.1	2.50	2.38	95.50	95.44
February	57 751	48 170	19 570	15 742	38 181	40 123	12 165	38.5	40.7	2.50	2.38	96.25	96.87
March	57 898	48 287	19 587	15 770	38 311	40 171	12 190	38.5	40.6	2.50	2.38	96.25	96.63
April	57 922	48 278	19 593	15 785	38 329	40 209	12 211	38.6	40.7	2.52	2.40	97.27	97.68
May	58 089	48 419	19 630	15 812	38 459	40 332	12 231	38.6	40.8	2.52	2.40	97.27	97.92
June	58 221	48 552	19 682	15 839	38 539	40 448	12 255	38.6	40.8	2.53	2.41	97.66	98.33
July	58 413	48 736	19 740	15 887	38 673	40 624	12 309	38.5	40.8	2.53	2.41	97.41	98.33
August	58 619	48 887	19 810	15 948	38 809	40 771	12 354	38.5	40.9	2.55	2.42	98.18	98.98
September	58 903	49 117	19 903	16 073	38 960	41 026	12 479	38.5	40.9	2.55	2.44	98.18	99.80
October	58 794	48 949	19 723	15 821	39 071	40 828	12 224	38.5	40.7	2.55	2.40	98.18	97.68
November	59 217	49 338	20 026	16 096	39 191	41 157	12 477	38.6	41.0	2.56	2.42	98.82	99.22
December	59 421	49 524	20 111	16 176	39 310	41 307	12 551	38.7	41.2	2.58	2.44	99.85	100.53
1965													
January	59 583	49 646	20 173	16 245	39 410	41 453	12 603	38.7	41.3	2.58	2.45	99.85	101.19
February	59 800	49 826	20 216	16 291	39 584	41 583	12 644	38.7	41.3	2.59	2.46	100.23	101.60
March	60 003	49 993	20 292	16 353	39 711	41 674	12 701	38.7	41.3	2.60	2.47	100.62	102.01
April	60 259	50 208	20 317	16 418	39 942	41 885	12 752	38.7	41.2	2.60	2.47	100.62	101.76
May	60 492	50 398	20 444	16 477	40 048	42 044	12 792	38.8	41.3	2.62	2.49	101.66	102.84
June	60 690	50 562	20 522	16 554	40 168	42 183	12 854	38.6	41.2	2.62	2.49	101.13	102.59
July	60 963	50 762	20 611	16 669	40 352	42 364	12 962	38.6	41.2	2.63	2.49	101.52	102.59
August	61 228	50 957	20 726	16 732	40 502	42 537	12 994	38.5	41.1	2.64	2.50	101.64	102.75
September	61 490	51 152	20 808	16 802	40 682	42 726	13 046	38.6	41.1	2.65	2.51	102.29	103.16
October	61 718	51 340	20 895	16 864	40 823	42 871	13 100	38.5	41.2	2.66	2.52	102.41	103.82
November	61 997	51 561	21 021	16 962	40 976	43 045	13 175	38.6	41.3	2.67	2.52	103.06	104.08
December	62 321	51 822	21 151	17 051	41 170	43 270	13 243	38.6	41.3	2.68	2.53	103.45	104.49
1966													
January	62 528	51 987	21 214	17 143	41 314	43 401	13 301	38.6	41.5	2.68	2.54	103.45	105.41
February	62 796	52 185	21 315	17 288	41 481	43 552	13 426	38.7	41.7	2.69	2.56	104.10	106.75
March	63 192	52 500	21 515	17 400	41 677	43 801	13 508	38.7	41.6	2.70	2.56	104.49	106.50
April	63 436	52 677	21 568	17 517	41 868	43 959	13 598	38.7	41.8	2.71	2.58	104.88	107.84
May	63 711	52 890	21 675	17 625	42 036	44 138	13 678	38.5	41.5	2.72	2.58	104.72	107.07
June	64 110	53 208	21 846	17 733	42 264	44 390	13 753	38.5	41.4	2.72	2.58	104.72	106.81
July	64 301	53 327	21 872	17 760	42 429	44 484	13 758	38.4	41.2	2.74	2.60	105.22	107.12
August	64 507	53 501	21 972	17 882	42 535	44 596	13 843	38.4	41.4	2.75	2.61	105.60	108.05
September	64 644	53 581	21 948	17 886	42 696	44 659	13 841	38.3	41.2	2.76	2.63	105.71	108.36
October	64 854	53 727	21 991	17 956	42 863	44 789	13 906	38.4	41.3	2.77	2.64	106.37	109.03
November	65 019	53 816	21 988	17 981	43 031	44 834	13 918	38.3	41.2	2.78	2.65	106.47	109.18
December	65 200	53 944	22 008	17 998	43 192	44 916	13 906	38.2	40.9	2.78	2.64	106.20	107.98
1967													
January	65 407	54 092	22 057	18 033	43 350	45 051	13 925	38.3	41.1	2.79	2.65	106.86	108.92
February	65 428	54 075	21 987	17 978	43 441	44 967	13 853	37.9	40.4	2.81	2.67	106.50	107.87
March	65 530	54 133	21 919	17 940	43 611	44 991	13 797	37.9	40.5	2.81	2.67	106.50	108.14
April	65 467	54 032	21 842	17 878	43 625	44 871	13 712	37.8	40.4	2.82	2.68	106.60	108.27
May	65 619	54 145	21 779	17 832	43 840	44 961	13 664	37.8	40.4	2.83	2.69	106.97	108.68
June	65 750	54 216	21 761	17 812	43 989	45 004	13 632	37.8	40.4	2.84	2.69	107.35	108.68
July	65 887	54 343	21 772	17 784	44 115	45 105	13 602	37.8	40.5	2.86	2.71	108.11	109.76
August	66 142	54 552	21 887	17 905	44 255	45 267	13 681	37.8	40.6	2.87	2.73	108.49	110.84
September	66 164	54 541	21 775	17 794	44 389	45 236	13 559	37.8	40.6	2.88	2.73	108.86	110.84
October	66 225	54 583	21 779	17 800	44 446	45 278	13 587	37.8	40.6	2.89	2.74	109.24	111.24
November	66 703	55 008	21 996	17 985	44 707	45 701	13 777	37.9	40.6	2.91	2.75	110.29	111.65
December	66 900	55 165	22 037	18 025	44 863	45 800	13 782	37.7	40.7	2.92	2.77	110.08	112.74

. . . = Not available.

Table 10-8. Employment, Hours, and Earnings, Total Nonfarm and Manufacturing, Historical Annual and Monthly—*Continued*

(Wage and salary workers on nonfarm payrolls, seasonally adjusted.)

Year and month	All wage and salary workers (thousands)					Production and nonsupervisory workers on private payrolls							
		Private			Service-providing	Number (thousands)		Average hours per week		Average hourly earnings, dollars		Average weekly earnings, dollars	
	Total	Total	Goods-producing			Total private	Manufac-turing	Total private	Manufac-turing	Total private	Manufac-turing	Total private	Manufac-turing
			Total	Manufac-turing									
1968													
January	66 805	55 011	21 917	18 040	44 888	45 655	13 798	37.6	40.4	2.94	2.81	110.54	113.52
February	67 215	55 396	22 117	18 054	45 098	45 980	13 793	37.8	40.8	2.95	2.82	111.51	115.06
March	67 295	55 453	22 119	18 067	45 176	46 041	13 803	37.7	40.8	2.97	2.84	111.97	115.87
April	67 555	55 677	22 207	18 131	45 348	46 239	13 858	37.6	40.3	2.98	2.85	112.05	114.86
May	67 653	55 748	22 255	18 190	45 398	46 267	13 900	37.7	40.9	3.00	2.87	113.10	117.38
June	67 904	55 917	22 264	18 228	45 640	46 402	13 921	37.8	40.9	3.01	2.88	113.78	117.79
July	68 125	56 107	22 329	18 265	45 796	46 563	13 953	37.7	40.8	3.03	2.89	114.23	117.91
August	68 328	56 286	22 350	18 254	45 978	46 670	13 903	37.7	40.7	3.03	2.89	114.23	117.62
September	68 487	56 420	22 390	18 252	46 097	46 792	13 914	37.7	40.9	3.06	2.92	115.36	119.43
October	68 720	56 619	22 419	18 293	46 301	46 990	13 974	37.7	41.0	3.07	2.94	115.74	120.54
November	68 985	56 878	22 512	18 346	46 473	47 244	14 028	37.5	40.9	3.09	2.96	115.88	121.06
December	69 246	57 101	22 617	18 410	46 629	47 385	14 044	37.5	40.7	3.11	2.97	116.63	120.88
1969													
January	69 438	57 229	22 644	18 432	46 794	47 529	14 086	37.7	40.8	3.12	2.99	117.62	121.99
February	69 700	57 476	22 755	18 502	46 945	47 696	14 134	37.5	40.4	3.14	3.00	117.75	121.20
March	69 905	57 676	22 813	18 558	47 092	47 852	14 169	37.6	40.8	3.15	3.01	118.44	122.81
April	70 072	57 827	22 815	18 554	47 257	47 959	14 144	37.7	41.0	3.17	3.03	119.51	124.23
May	70 328	58 044	22 899	18 588	47 429	48 122	14 161	37.6	40.7	3.19	3.04	119.94	123.73
June	70 636	58 277	22 981	18 640	47 655	48 329	14 206	37.5	40.7	3.20	3.05	120.00	124.14
July	70 729	58 389	22 990	18 642	47 739	48 435	14 194	37.5	40.6	3.22	3.08	120.75	125.05
August	71 006	58 633	23 111	18 767	47 895	48 616	14 287	37.5	40.6	3.24	3.10	121.50	125.86
September	70 917	58 538	22 988	18 620	47 929	48 524	14 159	37.5	40.6	3.26	3.12	122.25	126.67
October	71 120	58 690	22 976	18 613	48 144	48 669	14 174	37.4	40.5	3.28	3.13	122.67	126.77
November	71 087	58 639	22 840	18 467	48 247	48 589	14 035	37.5	40.5	3.29	3.14	123.38	127.17
December	71 240	58 763	22 884	18 485	48 356	48 638	14 013	37.5	40.6	3.30	3.15	123.75	127.89
1970													
January	71 176	58 680	22 726	18 424	48 450	48 564	13 964	37.3	40.4	3.31	3.16	123.46	127.66
February	71 304	58 786	22 747	18 361	48 557	48 600	13 897	37.3	40.2	3.33	3.17	124.21	127.43
March	71 452	58 849	22 738	18 360	48 714	48 690	13 917	37.2	40.1	3.35	3.19	124.62	127.92
April	71 348	58 643	22 552	18 207	48 796	48 480	13 785	37.0	39.8	3.36	3.19	124.32	126.96
May	71 123	58 455	22 336	18 029	48 787	48 287	13 616	37.0	39.8	3.38	3.22	125.06	128.16
June	71 029	58 362	22 241	17 930	48 788	48 225	13 554	36.9	39.8	3.39	3.24	125.09	128.95
July	71 053	58 356	22 195	17 877	48 858	48 243	13 527	37.0	40.0	3.41	3.25	126.17	130.00
August	70 933	58 222	22 105	17 779	48 828	48 088	13 449	37.0	39.8	3.43	3.26	126.91	129.75
September	70 948	58 207	21 988	17 692	48 960	48 101	13 401	36.8	39.6	3.45	3.29	126.96	130.28
October	70 519	57 726	21 477	17 173	49 042	47 619	12 905	36.8	39.5	3.46	3.26	127.33	128.77
November	70 409	57 579	21 345	17 024	49 064	47 466	12 781	36.7	39.5	3.47	3.26	127.35	128.77
December	70 790	57 945	21 673	17 309	49 117	47 778	13 062	36.8	39.5	3.50	3.32	128.80	131.14
1971													
January	70 866	57 988	21 594	17 280	49 272	47 859	13 069	36.8	39.9	3.52	3.36	129.54	134.06
February	70 806	57 929	21 514	17 216	49 292	47 779	13 033	36.7	39.7	3.54	3.39	129.92	134.58
March	70 859	57 951	21 491	17 154	49 368	47 819	12 984	36.7	39.8	3.56	3.39	130.65	134.92
April	71 037	58 092	21 552	17 149	49 485	47 966	12 993	36.8	39.9	3.57	3.41	131.38	136.06
May	71 247	58 277	21 645	17 225	49 602	48 153	13 081	36.7	40.0	3.60	3.43	132.12	137.20
June	71 253	58 245	21 568	17 139	49 685	48 108	13 012	36.8	39.9	3.62	3.45	133.22	137.66
July	71 315	58 304	21 564	17 126	49 751	48 169	13 001	36.7	40.0	3.63	3.46	133.22	138.40
August	71 370	58 329	21 570	17 115	49 800	48 164	12 993	36.7	39.8	3.66	3.48	134.32	138.50
September	71 617	58 549	21 650	17 154	49 967	48 363	13 038	36.7	39.7	3.67	3.48	134.69	138.16
October	71 642	58 527	21 604	17 126	50 038	48 305	13 027	36.8	39.9	3.68	3.50	135.42	139.65
November	71 846	58 698	21 684	17 166	50 162	48 441	13 064	36.9	40.0	3.69	3.49	136.16	139.60
December	72 108	58 918	21 741	17 202	50 367	48 613	13 078	36.9	40.2	3.73	3.55	137.64	142.71
1972													
January	72 445	59 179	21 865	17 283	50 580	49 035	13 173	36.9	40.2	3.80	3.57	140.22	143.51
February	72 652	59 354	21 915	17 361	50 737	49 143	13 235	36.9	40.4	3.82	3.61	140.96	145.84
March	72 945	59 616	22 036	17 447	50 909	49 437	13 316	36.9	40.4	3.84	3.63	141.70	146.65
April	73 163	59 805	22 099	17 508	51 064	49 562	13 373	36.9	40.5	3.86	3.65	142.43	147.83
May	73 467	60 051	22 222	17 602	51 245	49 745	13 451	36.8	40.5	3.87	3.67	142.42	148.64
June	73 760	60 355	22 282	17 641	51 478	49 995	13 475	36.9	40.6	3.88	3.68	143.17	149.41
July	73 708	60 226	22 162	17 556	51 546	49 844	13 387	36.8	40.5	3.90	3.69	143.52	149.45
August	74 138	60 400	22 400	17 741	51 738	50 155	13 562	36.8	40.6	3.92	3.73	144.26	151.44
September	74 263	60 688	22 456	17 774	51 807	50 226	13 572	36.9	40.6	3.94	3.75	145.39	152.25
October	74 673	61 067	22 613	17 893	52 060	50 552	13 681	37.0	40.7	3.97	3.78	146.89	153.85
November	74 967	61 324	22 688	18 005	52 279	50 789	13 783	36.9	40.7	3.98	3.79	146.86	154.25
December	75 270	61 586	22 772	18 158	52 498	51 054	13 902	36.8	40.6	4.01	3.83	147.57	155.50
1973													
January	75 621	61 931	22 955	18 276	52 666	51 349	14 006	36.8	40.4	4.03	3.86	148.30	155.94
February	76 017	62 306	23 160	18 410	52 857	51 685	14 127	36.9	40.9	4.04	3.87	149.08	158.28
March	76 285	62 540	23 262	18 493	53 023	51 901	14 181	37.0	40.9	4.06	3.88	150.22	158.69
April	76 455	62 678	23 316	18 530	53 139	51 983	14 192	36.9	40.8	4.08	3.91	150.55	159.53
May	76 646	62 829	23 382	18 564	53 264	52 082	14 217	36.9	40.7	4.10	3.93	151.29	159.95
June	76 887	63 015	23 485	18 606	53 402	52 233	14 253	36.9	40.7	4.12	3.95	152.03	160.77
July	76 911	63 046	23 522	18 598	53 389	52 240	14 232	36.9	40.7	4.15	3.98	153.14	161.99
August	77 166	63 262	23 559	18 629	53 607	52 394	14 251	36.9	40.6	4.16	4.00	153.50	162.40
September	77 276	63 384	23 548	18 609	53 728	52 410	14 213	36.8	40.7	4.19	4.03	154.19	164.02
October	77 606	63 629	23 641	18 702	53 965	52 655	14 289	36.7	40.6	4.21	4.05	154.51	164.43
November	77 912	63 877	23 719	18 773	54 193	52 845	14 342	36.9	40.6	4.23	4.07	156.09	165.24
December	78 035	63 965	23 779	18 820	54 256	52 954	14 386	36.7	40.6	4.25	4.09	155.98	166.05

Table 10-8. Employment, Hours, and Earnings, Total Nonfarm and Manufacturing, Historical Annual and Monthly—*Continued*

(Wage and salary workers on nonfarm payrolls, seasonally adjusted.)

Year and month	All wage and salary workers (thousands)					Production and nonsupervisory workers on private payrolls							
		Private			Service-providing	Number (thousands)		Average hours per week		Average hourly earnings, dollars		Average weekly earnings, dollars	
	Total	Total	Goods-producing			Total private	Manufac-turing	Total private	Manufac-turing	Total private	Manufac-turing	Total private	Manufac-turing
			Total	Manufac-turing									
1974													
January	78 104	64 014	23 709	18 788	54 395	52 896	14 340	36.6	40.5	4.26	4.10	155.92	166.05
February	78 254	64 119	23 718	18 727	54 536	52 970	14 269	36.6	40.4	4.29	4.13	157.01	166.85
March	78 296	64 144	23 687	18 700	54 609	52 951	14 223	36.6	40.4	4.31	4.15	157.75	167.66
April	78 382	64 191	23 670	18 702	54 712	53 006	14 225	36.4	39.5	4.34	4.16	157.98	164.32
May	78 547	64 326	23 635	18 688	54 912	53 094	14 199	36.5	40.3	4.39	4.25	160.24	171.28
June	78 602	64 363	23 591	18 690	55 011	53 106	14 197	36.5	40.2	4.43	4.30	161.70	172.86
July	78 635	64 347	23 462	18 656	55 173	53 046	14 152	36.5	40.1	4.45	4.33	162.43	173.63
August	78 619	64 291	23 396	18 570	55 223	53 026	14 089	36.5	40.2	4.49	4.38	163.89	176.08
September	78 611	64 189	23 274	18 492	55 337	52 915	14 025	36.4	40.0	4.53	4.42	164.89	176.80
October	78 629	64 145	23 118	18 364	55 511	52 835	13 884	36.3	40.0	4.56	4.48	165.53	179.20
November	78 261	63 729	22 773	18 077	55 488	52 411	13 607	36.1	39.5	4.57	4.49	164.98	177.36
December	77 657	63 098	22 303	17 693	55 354	51 856	13 259	36.1	39.3	4.61	4.52	166.42	177.64
1975													
January	77 297	62 673	21 974	17 344	55 323	51 438	12 933	36.1	39.2	4.61	4.54	166.42	177.97
February	76 919	62 172	21 512	17 004	55 407	50 934	12 622	35.9	38.9	4.63	4.58	166.22	178.16
March	76 649	61 895	21 274	16 853	55 375	50 665	12 483	35.7	38.8	4.66	4.63	166.36	179.64
April	76 461	61 666	21 109	16 759	55 352	50 442	12 407	35.8	39.0	4.66	4.63	166.83	180.57
May	76 623	61 796	21 097	16 746	55 526	50 557	12 406	35.9	39.0	4.68	4.65	168.01	181.35
June	76 520	61 736	21 018	16 690	55 502	50 537	12 371	35.9	39.2	4.72	4.68	169.45	183.46
July	76 769	61 908	20 981	16 678	55 788	50 729	12 374	35.9	39.4	4.73	4.71	169.81	185.57
August	77 155	62 285	21 176	16 824	55 979	51 070	12 538	36.1	39.7	4.77	4.75	172.20	188.58
September	77 230	62 406	21 284	16 904	55 946	51 182	12 617	36.1	39.8	4.79	4.78	172.92	190.24
October	77 535	62 635	21 384	16 984	56 151	51 375	12 687	36.1	39.9	4.81	4.80	173.64	191.52
November	77 680	62 777	21 442	17 025	56 238	51 456	12 700	36.1	39.9	4.85	4.83	175.09	192.72
December	78 018	63 072	21 602	17 140	56 416	51 759	12 811	36.2	40.2	4.87	4.86	176.29	195.37
1976													
January	78 506	63 537	21 799	17 287	56 707	52 182	12 945	36.3	40.3	4.90	4.90	177.87	197.47
February	78 817	63 836	21 893	17 384	56 924	52 430	13 030	36.3	40.4	4.94	4.94	179.32	199.58
March	79 049	64 062	21 980	17 470	57 069	52 615	13 092	36.0	40.2	4.96	4.98	178.56	200.20
April	79 292	64 307	22 050	17 541	57 242	52 812	13 160	36.0	39.6	4.98	4.98	179.28	197.21
May	79 311	64 340	21 988	17 513	57 323	52 802	13 130	36.1	40.3	5.02	5.04	181.22	203.11
June	79 376	64 413	21 982	17 521	57 394	52 830	13 121	36.1	40.2	5.04	5.07	181.94	203.81
July	79 547	64 554	21 988	17 524	57 559	52 975	13 124	36.1	40.3	5.07	5.11	183.03	205.93
August	79 704	64 697	22 038	17 596	57 666	53 072	13 195	36.0	40.2	5.12	5.16	184.32	207.43
September	79 892	64 921	22 142	17 665	57 750	53 268	13 253	36.0	40.2	5.15	5.20	185.40	209.04
October	79 905	64 877	22 037	17 548	57 868	53 164	13 109	35.9	40.0	5.17	5.19	185.60	207.60
November	80 237	65 164	22 207	17 682	58 030	53 362	13 199	35.9	40.1	5.21	5.25	187.04	210.53
December	80 448	65 373	22 261	17 719	58 187	53 542	13 230	35.9	39.9	5.23	5.29	187.76	211.07
1977													
January	80 692	65 636	22 320	17 803	58 372	53 755	13 305	35.6	39.4	5.26	5.35	187.26	210.79
February	80 988	65 932	22 478	17 843	58 510	54 016	13 331	36.0	40.2	5.30	5.36	190.80	215.47
March	81 391	66 341	22 672	17 941	58 719	54 389	13 424	35.9	40.3	5.33	5.40	191.35	217.62
April	81 729	66 654	22 807	18 024	58 922	54 672	13 490	36.0	40.4	5.37	5.45	193.32	220.18
May	82 089	66 957	22 919	18 107	59 170	54 940	13 567	36.0	40.5	5.40	5.49	194.40	222.35
June	82 488	67 281	23 046	18 192	59 442	55 194	13 622	36.0	40.5	5.43	5.54	195.48	224.37
July	82 836	67 537	23 106	18 259	59 730	55 396	13 670	35.9	40.4	5.46	5.58	196.01	225.43
August	83 074	67 746	23 124	18 276	59 950	55 543	13 679	35.9	40.4	5.48	5.61	196.73	226.64
September	83 532	68 129	23 244	18 334	60 288	55 858	13 714	35.9	40.4	5.51	5.65	197.81	228.26
October	83 794	68 331	23 279	18 356	60 515	56 003	13 722	36.0	40.6	5.56	5.69	200.16	231.01
November	84 173	68 658	23 371	18 419	60 802	56 281	13 771	35.9	40.5	5.59	5.72	200.68	231.66
December	84 408	68 870	23 371	18 531	61 037	56 465	13 861	35.8	40.4	5.61	5.75	200.84	232.30
1978													
January	84 595	68 984	23 374	18 593	61 221	56 547	13 917	35.3	39.5	5.66	5.83	199.80	230.29
February	84 948	69 277	23 453	18 639	61 495	56 768	13 950	35.6	39.9	5.69	5.86	202.56	233.81
March	85 461	69 730	23 649	18 699	61 812	57 176	13 992	35.8	40.5	5.73	5.88	205.13	238.14
April	86 163	70 366	24 008	18 772	62 155	57 711	14 037	35.8	40.4	5.79	5.93	207.28	239.57
May	86 509	70 675	24 082	18 848	62 427	57 941	14 096	35.8	40.4	5.82	5.96	208.36	240.78
June	86 951	71 099	24 238	18 919	62 713	58 262	14 129	35.9	40.6	5.87	6.01	210.73	244.01
July	87 205	71 304	24 300	18 951	62 905	58 422	14 152	35.9	40.6	5.90	6.06	211.81	246.04
August	87 481	71 590	24 374	19 006	63 107	58 626	14 187	35.8	40.5	5.93	6.09	212.29	246.65
September	87 618	71 799	24 444	19 068	63 174	58 819	14 241	35.8	40.5	5.97	6.15	213.73	249.08
October	87 954	72 096	24 548	19 142	63 406	59 017	14 291	35.8	40.5	6.03	6.20	215.87	251.10
November	88 391	72 497	24 678	19 257	63 713	59 377	14 388	35.7	40.6	6.06	6.26	216.34	254.16
December	88 673	72 762	24 758	19 334	63 915	59 599	14 459	35.7	40.5	6.10	6.31	217.77	255.56
1979													
January	88 810	72 873	24 740	19 388	64 070	59 659	14 497	35.6	40.4	6.14	6.36	218.58	256.94
February	89 054	73 107	24 784	19 409	64 270	59 840	14 501	35.7	40.5	6.18	6.40	220.63	259.20
March	89 480	73 524	24 998	19 453	64 482	60 216	14 526	35.8	40.6	6.22	6.45	222.68	261.87
April	89 418	73 441	24 958	19 450	64 460	60 069	14 515	35.3	39.3	6.22	6.43	219.57	252.70
May	89 791	73 801	25 071	19 509	64 720	60 369	14 551	35.6	40.2	6.28	6.52	223.57	262.10
June	90 109	74 064	25 161	19 553	64 948	60 583	14 566	35.6	40.2	6.32	6.56	224.99	263.71
July	90 215	74 065	25 163	19 531	65 052	60 559	14 536	35.6	40.2	6.36	6.59	226.42	264.92
August	90 297	74 068	25 059	19 406	65 238	60 517	14 397	35.6	40.1	6.40	6.63	227.84	265.86
September	90 325	74 197	25 088	19 442	65 237	60 631	14 440	35.6	40.1	6.45	6.67	229.62	267.47
October	90 482	74 346	25 038	19 390	65 444	60 748	14 384	35.6	40.2	6.47	6.71	230.33	269.74
November	90 576	74 403	24 947	19 299	65 629	60 781	14 295	35.6	40.1	6.51	6.74	231.76	270.27
December	90 673	74 493	24 970	19 301	65 703	60 863	14 300	35.5	40.1	6.57	6.80	233.24	272.68

Table 10-8. Employment, Hours, and Earnings, Total Nonfarm and Manufacturing, Historical Annual and Monthly—*Continued*

(Wage and salary workers on nonfarm payrolls, seasonally adjusted.)

Year and month	All wage and salary workers (thousands)					Production and nonsupervisory workers on private payrolls							
		Private				Number (thousands)		Average hours per week		Average hourly earnings, dollars		Average weekly earnings, dollars	
	Total	Total	Goods-producing		Service-providing	Total private	Manufacturing	Total private	Manufacturing	Total private	Manufacturing	Total private	Manufacturing
			Total	Manufacturing									
1980													
January	90 802	74 601	24 949	19 282	65 853	60 899	14 241	35.4	40.0	6.57	6.82	232.58	272.80
February	90 882	74 656	24 874	19 219	66 008	60 966	14 170	35.4	40.1	6.63	6.88	234.70	275.89
March	90 994	74 698	24 818	19 217	66 176	60 990	14 165	35.3	39.9	6.70	6.95	236.51	277.31
April	90 850	74 267	24 507	18 973	66 343	60 544	13 914	35.2	39.8	6.72	6.97	236.54	277.41
May	90 419	73 965	24 234	18 726	66 185	60 198	13 632	35.1	39.3	6.76	7.02	237.28	275.89
June	90 099	73 658	23 968	18 490	66 131	59 895	13 405	35.0	39.2	6.82	7.10	238.70	278.32
July	89 837	73 419	23 698	18 276	66 139	59 698	13 227	34.9	39.1	6.86	7.16	239.41	279.96
August	90 097	73 687	23 860	18 414	66 237	59 913	13 349	35.1	39.5	6.91	7.24	242.54	285.98
September	90 210	73 880	23 931	18 445	66 279	60 079	13 396	35.1	39.6	6.95	7.30	243.95	289.08
October	90 491	74 105	24 012	18 506	66 479	60 244	13 437	35.2	39.8	7.02	7.38	247.10	293.72
November	90 748	74 357	24 123	18 601	66 625	60 455	13 528	35.3	39.9	7.09	7.47	250.28	298.05
December	90 943	74 570	24 182	18 640	66 761	60 611	13 550	35.3	40.1	7.13	7.52	251.69	301.55
1981													
January	91 037	74 677	24 152	18 639	66 885	60 715	13 545	35.4	40.1	7.19	7.58	254.53	303.96
February	91 105	74 759	24 118	18 613	66 987	60 742	13 518	35.2	39.8	7.23	7.62	254.50	303.28
March	91 210	74 918	24 203	18 647	67 007	60 881	13 550	35.3	40.0	7.29	7.68	257.34	307.20
April	91 283	75 023	24 151	18 711	67 132	60 979	13 594	35.3	40.1	7.33	7.76	258.75	311.18
May	91 293	75 095	24 148	18 766	67 145	60 981	13 633	35.3	40.2	7.37	7.81	260.16	313.96
June	91 490	75 331	24 290	18 789	67 200	61 141	13 632	35.2	40.0	7.42	7.85	261.18	314.00
July	91 602	75 427	24 302	18 785	67 300	61 228	13 629	35.2	39.9	7.46	7.89	262.59	314.81
August	91 566	75 456	24 258	18 748	67 308	61 223	13 573	35.2	40.0	7.53	7.97	265.06	318.80
September	91 479	75 448	24 210	18 712	67 269	61 241	13 565	35.0	39.6	7.57	8.03	264.95	317.99
October	91 380	75 311	24 051	18 566	67 329	61 074	13 399	35.1	39.6	7.59	8.06	266.41	319.18
November	91 171	75 093	23 875	18 409	67 296	60 825	13 235	35.1	39.4	7.64	8.08	268.16	318.35
December	90 893	74 820	23 656	18 223	67 237	60 520	13 033	34.9	39.2	7.64	8.09	266.64	317.13
1982													
January	90 567	74 526	23 362	18 047	67 205	60 218	12 874	34.1	37.3	7.72	8.26	263.25	308.10
February	90 562	74 551	23 361	17 981	67 201	60 285	12 831	35.1	39.6	7.73	8.21	271.32	325.12
March	90 432	74 408	23 214	17 857	67 218	60 150	12 727	34.9	39.1	7.76	8.24	270.82	322.18
April	90 152	74 142	22 996	17 683	67 156	59 877	12 566	34.8	39.1	7.77	8.28	270.40	323.75
May	90 107	74 104	22 884	17 588	67 223	59 851	12 506	34.8	39.1	7.83	8.33	272.48	325.70
June	89 864	73 848	22 643	17 430	67 221	59 599	12 365	34.8	39.2	7.85	8.37	273.18	328.10
July	89 522	73 632	22 434	17 278	67 088	59 422	12 261	34.8	39.2	7.89	8.40	274.57	329.28
August	89 364	73 434	22 268	17 160	67 096	59 213	12 153	34.7	39.0	7.94	8.43	275.52	328.77
September	89 183	73 260	22 146	17 074	67 037	59 078	12 104	34.8	39.0	7.94	8.45	276.31	329.55
October	88 906	72 950	21 879	16 853	67 027	58 761	11 880	34.6	38.9	7.96	8.44	275.42	328.32
November	88 783	72 806	21 736	16 722	67 047	58 625	11 766	34.6	39.0	7.98	8.46	276.11	329.94
December	88 769	72 788	21 688	16 690	67 081	58 599	11 746	34.7	39.0	8.02	8.49	278.29	331.11
1983													
January	88 993	72 970	21 757	16 705	67 236	58 828	11 783	34.8	39.3	8.06	8.52	280.49	334.84
February	88 918	72 914	21 676	16 706	67 242	58 803	11 794	34.5	39.3	8.10	8.59	279.45	337.59
March	89 090	73 085	21 649	16 711	67 441	58 971	11 817	34.7	39.6	8.10	8.59	281.07	340.16
April	89 366	73 376	21 729	16 794	67 637	59 214	11 894	34.8	39.7	8.13	8.61	282.92	341.82
May	89 643	73 638	21 829	16 885	67 814	59 458	11 987	34.9	40.0	8.17	8.64	285.13	345.60
June	90 022	74 002	21 949	16 960	68 073	59 819	12 054	34.9	40.1	8.19	8.66	285.83	347.27
July	90 440	74 429	22 103	17 059	68 337	60 203	12 155	34.9	40.3	8.23	8.71	287.23	351.01
August	90 132	74 116	22 207	17 118	67 925	59 834	12 200	34.9	40.3	8.20	8.71	286.18	351.01
September	91 247	75 205	22 381	17 255	68 866	60 859	12 318	35.0	40.6	8.26	8.76	289.10	355.66
October	91 518	75 532	22 546	17 367	68 972	61 108	12 408	35.2	40.6	8.31	8.80	292.51	357.28
November	91 871	75 874	22 698	17 479	69 173	61 392	12 503	35.1	40.6	8.32	8.84	292.03	358.90
December	92 227	76 219	22 803	17 551	69 424	61 680	12 553	35.1	40.5	8.33	8.87	292.38	359.24
1984													
January	92 673	76 663	22 942	17 630	69 731	61 925	12 617	35.1	40.6	8.06	8.91	294.14	361.75
February	93 154	77 129	23 116	17 728	70 008	62 342	12 703	35.3	41.1	8.10	8.92	295.46	366.61
March	93 429	77 399	23 209	17 806	70 220	62 531	12 768	35.1	40.7	8.10	8.96	295.19	364.67
April	93 792	77 717	23 305	17 872	70 487	62 817	12 814	35.2	40.8	8.13	8.98	297.44	366.38
May	94 100	77 997	23 389	17 916	70 711	63 029	12 840	35.1	40.7	8.17	8.99	296.24	365.89
June	94 479	78 352	23 497	17 967	70 982	63 313	12 871	35.1	40.6	8.19	9.03	297.65	366.62
July	94 792	78 620	23 571	18 013	71 221	63 532	12 901	35.1	40.6	8.23	9.05	299.05	367.43
August	95 034	78 810	23 608	18 034	71 426	63 670	12 906	35.0	40.5	8.20	9.09	298.20	368.15
September	95 344	79 089	23 617	18 019	71 727	63 889	12 880	35.1	40.5	8.26	9.12	300.46	369.36
October	95 630	79 356	23 626	18 024	72 004	64 100	12 868	34.9	40.5	8.31	9.15	298.40	370.58
November	95 979	79 668	23 639	18 016	72 340	64 343	12 846	35.0	40.4	8.32	9.19	299.95	371.28
December	96 107	79 825	23 673	18 023	72 434	64 460	12 848	35.1	40.5	8.33	9.22	302.21	373.41
1985													
January	96 373	80 037	23 672	18 009	72 701	64 678	12 833	34.9	40.3	8.61	9.27	300.49	373.58
February	96 497	80 148	23 621	17 966	72 876	64 775	12 784	34.8	40.1	8.64	9.29	300.67	372.53
March	96 843	80 448	23 661	17 939	73 182	65 026	12 758	34.9	40.4	8.67	9.32	302.58	376.53
April	97 039	80 609	23 644	17 886	73 395	65 133	12 701	34.9	40.5	8.69	9.35	303.28	378.68
May	97 313	80 839	23 632	17 855	73 681	65 328	12 673	34.9	40.4	8.70	9.37	303.63	378.55
June	97 459	80 961	23 592	17 819	73 867	65 403	12 635	34.9	40.5	8.74	9.39	305.03	380.30
July	97 649	81 029	23 549	17 776	74 100	65 450	12 596	34.8	40.4	8.74	9.42	304.15	380.57
August	97 842	81 223	23 546	17 756	74 296	65 633	12 593	34.8	40.6	8.77	9.43	305.20	382.86
September	98 045	81 407	23 528	17 718	74 517	65 769	12 556	34.8	40.6	8.80	9.44	306.24	383.26
October	98 233	81 579	23 529	17 708	74 704	65 900	12 556	34.8	40.7	8.79	9.46	305.89	385.02
November	98 442	81 768	23 520	17 697	74 922	66 089	12 545	34.8	40.7	8.82	9.49	306.94	386.24
December	98 609	81 915	23 518	17 693	75 091	66 219	12 550	34.9	40.9	8.87	9.55	309.56	390.60

Table 10-8. Employment, Hours, and Earnings, Total Nonfarm and Manufacturing, Historical Annual and Monthly—Continued

(Wage and salary workers on nonfarm payrolls, seasonally adjusted.)

Year and month	All wage and salary workers (thousands)					Production and nonsupervisory workers on private payrolls							
	Total	Private			Service-providing	Number (thousands)		Average hours per week		Average hourly earnings, dollars		Average weekly earnings, dollars	
		Total	Goods-producing			Total private	Manufac-turing	Total private	Manufac-turing	Total private	Manufac-turing	Total private	Manufac-turing
			Total	Manufac-turing									
1986													
January	98 734	82 019	23 530	17 686	75 204	66 316	12 546	35.0	40.7	8.85	9.53	309.75	387.87
February	98 841	82 082	23 485	17 663	75 356	66 387	12 530	34.8	40.7	8.88	9.56	309.02	389.09
March	98 935	82 180	23 428	17 624	75 507	66 425	12 498	34.8	40.7	8.89	9.58	309.37	389.91
April	99 122	82 357	23 427	17 616	75 695	66 554	12 495	34.7	40.5	8.89	9.56	308.48	387.18
May	99 249	82 459	23 349	17 593	75 900	66 635	12 474	34.8	40.7	8.90	9.59	309.72	390.31
June	99 155	82 376	23 263	17 530	75 892	66 558	12 424	34.7	40.7	8.91	9.58	309.18	389.91
July	99 473	82 694	23 235	17 497	76 238	66 829	12 389	34.6	40.6	8.92	9.60	308.63	389.76
August	99 587	82 787	23 225	17 489	76 362	66 927	12 399	34.7	40.7	8.94	9.61	310.22	391.13
September	99 934	83 024	23 216	17 498	76 718	67 133	12 411	34.6	40.7	8.94	9.60	309.32	390.72
October	100 120	83 151	23 208	17 477	76 912	67 230	12 396	34.6	40.6	8.96	9.62	310.02	390.57
November	100 306	83 301	23 204	17 472	77 102	67 368	12 407	34.7	40.7	9.00	9.64	312.30	392.35
December	100 511	83 490	23 237	17 478	77 274	67 517	12 425	34.6	40.8	9.01	9.66	311.75	394.13
1987													
January	100 683	83 638	23 232	17 465	77 451	67 638	12 405	34.7	40.8	9.02	9.67	312.99	394.54
February	100 915	83 879	23 296	17 499	77 619	67 869	12 438	34.9	41.2	9.05	9.69	315.85	399.23
March	101 164	84 100	23 307	17 507	77 857	68 015	12 446	34.7	41.0	9.07	9.71	314.73	398.11
April	101 502	84 393	23 342	17 525	78 160	68 261	12 465	34.7	40.8	9.08	9.71	315.08	396.17
May	101 728	84 616	23 390	17 542	78 338	68 467	12 481	34.8	41.0	9.11	9.73	317.03	398.93
June	101 900	84 776	23 390	17 537	78 510	68 579	12 482	34.7	40.9	9.11	9.74	316.12	398.37
July	102 247	85 087	23 455	17 593	78 792	68 819	12 521	34.7	41.0	9.12	9.74	316.46	399.34
August	102 418	85 246	23 506	17 630	78 912	68 941	12 560	34.9	40.9	9.18	9.80	320.38	400.82
September	102 646	85 511	23 566	17 691	79 080	69 164	12 614	34.7	40.8	9.19	9.85	318.89	401.88
October	103 138	85 869	23 655	17 729	79 483	69 442	12 637	34.8	41.1	9.22	9.84	320.86	404.42
November	103 370	86 071	23 711	17 775	79 659	69 621	12 678	34.8	41.0	9.27	9.87	322.60	404.67
December	103 664	86 317	23 772	17 809	79 892	69 852	12 707	34.6	41.0	9.28	9.89	321.09	405.49
1988													
January	103 758	86 393	23 668	17 790	80 090	69 859	12 684	34.6	41.1	9.29	9.91	321.43	407.30
February	104 211	86 822	23 769	17 823	80 442	70 255	12 706	34.7	41.1	9.29	9.92	322.36	407.71
March	104 487	87 040	23 824	17 844	80 663	70 397	12 712	34.5	40.9	9.31	9.94	321.20	406.55
April	104 732	87 280	23 880	17 874	80 852	70 604	12 733	34.6	41.0	9.36	9.99	323.86	409.59
May	104 961	87 480	23 896	17 892	81 065	70 749	12 747	34.6	41.0	9.41	10.02	325.59	410.82
June	105 324	87 809	23 951	17 916	81 373	71 031	12 767	34.6	41.1	9.42	10.04	325.93	412.64
July	105 546	88 052	23 966	17 926	81 580	71 235	12 774	34.7	41.1	9.45	10.05	327.92	413.06
August	105 670	88 126	23 926	17 891	81 744	71 287	12 752	34.5	40.9	9.46	10.07	326.37	411.86
September	106 009	88 375	23 942	17 914	82 067	71 487	12 764	34.5	41.0	9.51	10.12	328.10	414.92
October	106 277	88 607	23 987	17 966	82 290	71 680	12 812	34.7	41.1	9.56	10.16	331.73	417.58
November	106 616	88 870	24 030	18 003	82 586	71 902	12 851	34.5	41.1	9.58	10.19	330.51	418.81
December	106 906	89 170	24 054	18 025	82 852	72 175	12 864	34.6	40.9	9.60	10.20	332.16	417.18
1989													
January	107 168	89 394	24 097	18 057	83 071	72 393	12 882	34.7	41.1	9.65	10.23	334.86	420.45
February	107 426	89 614	24 080	18 055	83 346	72 577	12 880	34.5	41.2	9.68	10.26	333.96	422.71
March	107 619	89 797	24 069	18 060	83 550	72 695	12 878	34.5	41.1	9.70	10.29	334.65	422.92
April	107 792	89 952	24 100	18 055	83 692	72 819	12 867	34.6	41.1	9.75	10.28	337.35	422.51
May	107 910	90 034	24 089	18 040	83 821	72 889	12 852	34.4	41.0	9.73	10.30	334.71	422.30
June	108 026	90 114	24 052	18 013	83 974	72 941	12 822	34.4	40.9	9.77	10.33	336.09	422.50
July	108 066	90 161	24 027	17 980	84 039	72 972	12 790	34.5	40.9	9.82	10.36	338.79	423.72
August	108 115	90 126	24 048	17 964	84 067	72 940	12 790	34.5	40.9	9.83	10.39	339.14	424.95
September	108 365	90 338	24 000	17 922	84 365	73 114	12 745	34.4	40.8	9.87	10.41	339.53	424.73
October	108 476	90 443	23 997	17 895	84 479	73 211	12 723	34.6	40.8	9.93	10.43	343.58	425.54
November	108 753	90 696	24 009	17 886	84 744	73 427	12 713	34.4	40.7	9.93	10.44	341.59	424.91
December	108 849	90 774	23 949	17 881	84 900	73 504	12 705	34.3	40.5	9.98	10.49	342.31	424.85
1990													
January	109 199	91 048	23 982	17 797	85 217	73 750	12 738	34.4	40.5	10.02	10.52	344.69	426.06
February	109 435	91 258	24 071	17 893	85 364	73 944	12 848	34.4	40.6	10.07	10.64	346.41	431.98
March	109 644	91 350	24 023	17 868	85 621	73 997	12 821	34.4	40.6	10.11	10.70	347.78	434.42
April	109 686	91 309	23 966	17 845	85 720	73 963	12 804	34.3	40.5	10.12	10.68	347.12	432.54
May	109 839	91 240	23 888	17 797	85 951	73 863	12 755	34.3	40.6	10.16	10.74	348.49	436.04
June	109 856	91 300	23 849	17 776	86 007	73 856	12 739	34.4	40.7	10.20	10.78	350.88	438.75
July	109 824	91 264	23 746	17 704	86 078	73 814	12 673	34.2	40.6	10.22	10.81	349.52	438.89
August	109 616	91 159	23 648	17 649	85 968	73 741	12 624	34.3	40.5	10.24	10.80	351.23	437.40
September	109 518	91 081	23 571	17 609	85 947	73 633	12 596	34.2	40.5	10.28	10.86	351.58	439.83
October	109 367	90 924	23 473	17 577	85 894	73 499	12 577	34.1	40.4	10.30	10.92	351.23	441.17
November	109 214	90 764	23 283	17 428	85 931	73 345	12 439	34.2	40.2	10.32	10.88	352.94	437.38
December	109 166	90 698	23 203	17 395	85 963	73 267	12 415	34.2	40.3	10.34	10.93	353.63	440.48
1991													
January	109 055	90 581	23 061	17 330	85 994	73 153	12 351	34.1	40.2	10.38	10.97	353.96	440.99
February	108 734	90 252	22 900	17 211	85 834	72 859	12 242	34.1	40.1	10.39	10.97	354.30	439.90
March	108 574	90 086	22 779	17 140	85 795	72 705	12 191	34.0	40.0	10.41	11.00	354.98	440.00
April	108 364	89 879	22 687	17 093	85 677	72 534	12 157	34.0	40.1	10.46	11.05	355.64	443.11
May	108 249	89 751	22 618	17 070	85 631	72 457	12 148	34.1	40.2	10.49	11.09	357.71	445.82
June	108 334	89 773	22 571	17 044	85 763	72 455	12 135	34.1	40.5	10.51	11.13	358.39	450.77
July	108 292	89 694	22 507	17 015	85 785	72 430	12 130	34.1	40.5	10.54	11.18	359.41	452.79
August	108 310	89 743	22 493	17 025	85 817	72 485	12 153	34.1	40.6	10.56	11.18	360.10	453.91
September	108 336	89 793	22 466	17 010	85 870	72 497	12 140	34.1	40.6	10.58	11.21	360.78	455.13
October	108 357	89 764	22 418	16 999	85 939	72 471	12 138	34.1	40.6	10.59	11.25	361.12	456.75
November	108 296	89 669	22 316	16 961	85 980	72 397	12 102	34.1	40.7	10.61	11.26	361.80	458.28
December	108 328	89 687	22 274	16 916	86 054	72 434	12 075	34.1	40.7	10.64	11.27	362.82	458.69

Table 10-8. Employment, Hours, and Earnings, Total Nonfarm and Manufacturing, Historical Annual and Monthly—*Continued*

(Wage and salary workers on nonfarm payrolls, seasonally adjusted.)

Year and month	All wage and salary workers (thousands)					Production and nonsupervisory workers on private payrolls							
	Total	Private			Service-providing	Number (thousands)		Average hours per week		Average hourly earnings, dollars		Average weekly earnings, dollars	
		Total	Goods-producing			Total private	Manufac-turing	Total private	Manufac-turing	Total private	Manufac-turing	Total private	Manufac-turing
			Total	Manufac-turing									
1992													
January	108 369	89 681	22 213	16 839	86 156	72 474	12 013	34.1	40.6	10.64	11.24	362.82	456.34
February	108 311	89 622	22 142	16 829	86 169	72 456	12 015	34.1	40.7	10.67	11.30	363.85	459.91
March	108 365	89 650	22 127	16 805	86 238	72 482	12 006	34.1	40.7	10.69	11.32	364.53	460.72
April	108 519	89 780	22 132	16 831	86 387	72 629	12 029	34.3	40.9	10.72	11.36	367.70	464.62
May	108 649	89 896	22 135	16 835	86 514	72 741	12 046	34.3	40.9	10.74	11.39	368.38	465.85
June	108 715	89 953	22 097	16 826	86 618	72 784	12 042	34.2	40.8	10.77	11.41	368.33	465.53
July	108 793	89 976	22 074	16 819	86 719	72 809	12 049	34.2	40.8	10.79	11.43	369.02	466.34
August	108 925	90 042	22 045	16 783	86 880	72 877	12 020	34.2	40.8	10.81	11.46	369.70	467.57
September	108 959	90 130	22 020	16 761	86 939	72 978	12 002	34.3	40.7	10.82	11.45	371.13	466.02
October	109 139	90 311	22 029	16 751	87 110	73 143	11 999	34.2	40.8	10.85	11.47	371.07	467.98
November	109 272	90 431	22 042	16 758	87 230	73 297	12 012	34.2	40.9	10.87	11.49	371.75	469.94
December	109 495	90 617	22 076	16 769	87 419	73 464	12 031	34.2	40.9	10.89	11.51	372.44	470.76
1993													
January	109 794	90 893	22 133	16 791	87 661	73 741	12 060	34.3	41.1	10.93	11.55	374.90	474.71
February	110 044	91 142	22 188	16 805	87 856	73 996	12 072	34.3	41.1	10.95	11.57	375.59	475.53
March	109 994	91 087	22 142	16 795	87 852	73 922	12 074	34.1	40.8	10.99	11.58	374.76	472.46
April	110 296	91 358	22 131	16 772	88 165	74 143	12 056	34.4	41.4	10.99	11.63	378.06	481.48
May	110 568	91 617	22 189	16 766	88 379	74 398	12 056	34.3	41.0	11.01	11.65	377.64	477.65
June	110 749	91 780	22 165	16 742	88 584	74 506	12 039	34.3	40.9	11.03	11.68	378.33	477.71
July	111 055	91 995	22 183	16 739	88 872	74 701	12 043	34.4	41.1	11.05	11.69	380.12	480.46
August	111 206	92 178	22 203	16 741	89 003	74 874	12 050	34.3	41.1	11.07	11.72	379.70	481.69
September	111 448	92 407	22 252	16 769	89 196	75 071	12 080	34.4	41.3	11.10	11.76	381.84	485.69
October	111 733	92 691	22 306	16 778	89 427	75 314	12 092	34.4	41.3	11.13	11.79	382.87	486.93
November	111 984	92 916	22 347	16 800	89 637	75 537	12 119	34.4	41.3	11.15	11.83	383.56	488.58
December	112 314	93 205	22 413	16 815	89 901	75 788	12 140	34.4	41.4	11.18	11.88	384.59	491.83
1994													
January	112 595	93 448	22 465	16 855	90 130	75 987	12 181	34.4	41.4	11.20	11.90	385.28	492.66
February	112 781	93 631	22 451	16 862	90 330	76 157	12 198	34.2	40.9	11.25	11.97	384.75	489.57
March	113 242	94 052	22 550	16 897	90 692	76 531	12 234	34.5	41.7	11.25	11.95	388.13	498.32
April	113 586	94 363	22 641	16 933	90 945	76 821	12 276	34.5	41.8	11.27	11.96	388.82	499.93
May	113 921	94 657	22 704	16 962	91 217	77 096	12 304	34.5	41.8	11.29	11.98	389.51	500.76
June	114 238	94 964	22 764	17 010	91 474	77 348	12 351	34.5	41.8	11.31	12.00	390.20	501.60
July	114 610	95 309	22 807	17 026	91 803	77 651	12 367	34.6	41.8	11.34	12.03	392.36	502.85
August	114 896	95 590	22 876	17 081	92 020	77 894	12 428	34.5	41.7	11.36	12.06	391.92	502.90
September	115 247	95 910	22 948	17 115	92 299	78 162	12 459	34.5	41.6	11.39	12.09	392.96	502.94
October	115 458	96 114	22 974	17 144	92 484	78 344	12 489	34.5	41.8	11.43	12.12	394.34	506.62
November	115 869	96 502	23 050	17 186	92 819	78 696	12 529	34.5	41.8	11.45	12.15	395.03	507.87
December	116 165	96 777	23 095	17 217	93 070	78 967	12 558	34.5	41.8	11.47	12.17	395.72	508.71
1995													
January	116 501	97 104	23 147	17 262	93 354	79 199	12 593	34.5	41.8	11.48	12.20	396.06	509.96
February	116 697	97 290	23 103	17 265	93 594	79 332	12 602	34.4	41.7	11.53	12.24	396.63	510.41
March	116 907	97 480	23 151	17 263	93 756	79 509	12 600	34.4	41.5	11.55	12.24	397.32	507.96
April	117 069	97 635	23 174	17 278	93 895	79 648	12 608	34.3	41.0	11.56	12.25	396.51	502.25
May	117 049	97 631	23 120	17 259	93 929	79 654	12 590	34.2	41.1	11.59	12.28	396.38	504.71
June	117 286	97 841	23 137	17 247	94 149	79 823	12 574	34.3	41.2	11.63	12.31	398.91	507.17
July	117 380	97 943	23 119	17 218	94 261	79 901	12 538	34.3	41.1	11.67	12.39	400.28	509.23
August	117 634	98 205	23 164	17 240	94 470	80 152	12 566	34.3	41.2	11.69	12.40	400.97	510.88
September	117 875	98 445	23 208	17 247	94 667	80 352	12 567	34.3	41.2	11.73	12.41	402.34	511.29
October	118 031	98 567	23 206	17 216	94 825	80 466	12 535	34.3	41.2	11.75	12.44	403.03	512.53
November	118 175	98 712	23 200	17 209	94 975	80 536	12 515	34.3	41.3	11.78	12.45	404.05	514.19
December	118 320	98 854	23 209	17 231	95 111	80 688	12 551	34.2	40.9	11.81	12.49	403.90	510.84
1996													
January	118 316	98 866	23 196	17 208	95 120	80 649	12 517	33.8	39.7	11.86	12.60	400.87	500.22
February	118 739	99 254	23 280	17 229	95 459	81 015	12 533	34.3	41.3	11.87	12.56	407.14	518.73
March	118 993	99 461	23 276	17 193	95 717	81 190	12 488	34.3	41.1	11.89	12.50	407.83	513.75
April	119 158	99 643	23 316	17 204	95 842	81 361	12 505	34.2	41.2	11.95	12.69	408.69	522.83
May	119 486	99 957	23 358	17 222	96 128	81 634	12 518	34.3	41.4	11.97	12.71	410.57	526.19
June	119 769	100 241	23 399	17 226	96 370	81 828	12 522	34.4	41.5	12.03	12.76	413.83	529.54
July	120 015	100 468	23 418	17 223	96 597	82 027	12 517	34.3	41.4	12.05	12.80	413.32	529.92
August	120 199	100 695	23 479	17 255	96 720	82 235	12 546	34.4	41.5	12.09	12.82	415.90	532.03
September	120 410	100 843	23 497	17 252	96 913	82 338	12 544	34.4	41.6	12.13	12.85	417.27	534.56
October	120 665	101 111	23 546	17 268	97 119	82 593	12 559	34.4	41.4	12.15	12.83	417.96	531.16
November	120 961	101 396	23 584	17 277	97 377	82 778	12 560	34.4	41.5	12.20	12.88	419.68	534.52
December	121 143	101 572	23 598	17 284	97 545	82 944	12 571	34.4	41.7	12.24	12.95	421.06	540.02
1997													
January	121 363	101 770	23 618	17 297	97 745	83 092	12 579	34.3	41.4	12.29	12.99	421.55	537.79
February	121 675	102 077	23 686	17 316	97 989	83 371	12 592	34.4	41.6	12.31	12.99	423.46	540.38
March	121 990	102 382	23 739	17 340	98 251	83 610	12 613	34.5	41.8	12.36	13.04	426.42	545.07
April	122 286	102 683	23 765	17 349	98 521	83 864	12 618	34.5	41.8	12.39	13.03	427.46	544.65
May	122 546	102 945	23 809	17 362	98 737	84 100	12 633	34.6	41.7	12.43	13.07	430.08	545.02
June	122 814	103 154	23 834	17 387	98 980	84 220	12 647	34.3	41.6	12.46	13.09	427.38	544.54
July	123 111	103 425	23 862	17 389	99 249	84 465	12 645	34.5	41.6	12.50	13.10	431.25	544.96
August	123 093	103 476	23 952	17 452	99 141	84 425	12 699	34.6	41.7	12.57	13.17	434.92	549.19
September	123 585	103 906	23 996	17 465	99 589	84 802	12 711	34.6	41.7	12.60	13.18	435.96	549.61
October	123 929	104 191	24 053	17 513	99 876	85 023	12 746	34.6	41.8	12.66	13.29	438.04	555.52
November	124 235	104 474	24 112	17 556	100 123	85 223	12 777	34.5	41.8	12.71	13.33	438.50	557.19
December	124 549	104 783	24 184	17 588	100 365	85 441	12 800	34.6	42.0	12.75	13.35	441.15	560.70

Table 10-8. Employment, Hours, and Earnings, Total Nonfarm and Manufacturing, Historical Annual and Monthly—*Continued*

(Wage and salary workers on nonfarm payrolls, seasonally adjusted.)

Year and month	All wage and salary workers (thousands)					Production and nonsupervisory workers on private payrolls							
	Total	Private			Service-providing	Number (thousands)		Average hours per week		Average hourly earnings, dollars		Average weekly earnings, dollars	
		Total	Goods-producing			Total private	Manufac-turing	Total private	Manufac-turing	Total private	Manufac-turing	Total private	Manufac-turing
			Total	Manufac-turing									
1998													
January	124 812	105 042	24 262	17 619	100 550	85 602	12 818	34.6	41.9	12.79	13.34	442.53	558.95
February	125 016	105 230	24 283	17 627	100 733	85 774	12 828	34.5	41.7	12.83	13.39	442.64	558.36
March	125 164	105 372	24 264	17 637	100 900	85 809	12 822	34.5	41.6	12.87	13.43	444.02	558.69
April	125 442	105 626	24 340	17 637	101 102	86 025	12 814	34.4	41.2	12.92	13.40	444.45	552.08
May	125 844	105 969	24 361	17 624	101 483	86 297	12 790	34.5	41.5	12.97	13.45	447.47	558.18
June	126 076	106 197	24 387	17 608	101 689	86 459	12 769	34.4	41.4	12.99	13.43	446.86	556.00
July	126 205	106 275	24 238	17 422	101 967	86 471	12 558	34.5	41.4	13.01	13.34	448.85	552.28
August	126 544	106 585	24 420	17 563	102 124	86 763	12 702	34.5	41.4	13.07	13.46	450.92	557.24
September	126 752	106 767	24 419	17 557	102 333	86 914	12 715	34.3	41.3	13.11	13.52	449.67	558.38
October	126 954	106 953	24 406	17 512	102 548	87 074	12 673	34.5	41.4	13.15	13.52	453.68	559.73
November	127 231	107 187	24 394	17 465	102 837	87 248	12 634	34.4	41.4	13.17	13.54	453.05	560.56
December	127 596	107 517	24 454	17 449	103 142	87 497	12 625	34.5	41.5	13.21	13.56	455.75	562.74
1999													
January	127 702	107 618	24 401	17 427	103 301	87 551	12 605	34.4	41.3	13.27	13.59	456.49	561.27
February	128 120	107 976	24 434	17 395	103 686	87 874	12 575	34.4	41.4	13.30	13.63	457.52	564.28
March	128 227	108 059	24 378	17 368	103 849	87 943	12 562	34.3	41.3	13.33	13.69	457.22	565.40
April	128 597	108 360	24 425	17 344	104 172	88 167	12 540	34.4	41.3	13.38	13.73	460.27	567.05
May	128 808	108 579	24 445	17 333	104 363	88 347	12 534	34.3	41.4	13.42	13.80	460.31	571.32
June	129 089	108 817	24 434	17 295	104 655	88 530	12 503	34.3	41.3	13.47	13.86	462.02	572.42
July	129 414	109 075	24 474	17 308	104 940	88 730	12 525	34.4	41.4	13.51	13.91	464.74	575.87
August	129 569	109 194	24 467	17 287	105 102	88 839	12 502	34.4	41.5	13.53	13.94	465.43	578.51
September	129 772	109 368	24 485	17 281	105 287	89 000	12 495	34.3	41.4	13.61	13.99	466.82	579.19
October	130 177	109 720	24 505	17 272	105 672	89 305	12 484	34.4	41.4	13.64	13.99	469.22	579.19
November	130 466	109 970	24 561	17 282	105 905	89 523	12 488	34.4	41.4	13.66	14.01	469.90	580.01
December	130 772	110 232	24 582	17 280	106 190	89 760	12 490	34.4	41.4	13.70	14.06	471.28	582.08
2000													
January	131 005	110 434	24 628	17 284	106 377	89 909	12 491	34.4	41.5	13.75	14.13	473.00	586.40
February	131 124	110 525	24 609	17 285	106 515	89 956	12 481	34.4	41.5	13.80	14.14	474.72	586.81
March	131 596	110 863	24 705	17 302	106 891	90 237	12 490	34.4	41.4	13.85	14.17	476.44	586.64
April	131 888	111 086	24 688	17 298	107 200	90 473	12 477	34.4	41.6	13.89	14.23	477.82	591.97
May	132 105	110 958	24 647	17 279	107 458	90 351	12 464	34.3	41.2	13.94	14.22	478.14	585.86
June	132 061	111 174	24 672	17 296	107 389	90 532	12 468	34.3	41.3	13.99	14.30	479.86	590.59
July	132 236	111 369	24 717	17 322	107 519	90 654	12 474	34.3	41.5	14.02	14.33	480.89	594.70
August	132 230	111 393	24 683	17 287	107 547	90 680	12 431	34.2	41.0	14.06	14.36	480.85	588.76
September	132 353	111 618	24 642	17 230	107 711	90 856	12 382	34.3	41.1	14.12	14.40	484.32	591.84
October	132 351	111 608	24 638	17 217	107 713	90 838	12 357	34.3	41.1	14.17	14.48	486.03	595.13
November	132 556	111 796	24 623	17 202	107 933	90 962	12 336	34.2	41.1	14.23	14.52	486.67	596.77
December	132 709	111 905	24 575	17 181	108 134	90 985	12 307	34.0	40.4	14.28	14.50	485.52	585.80
2001													
January	132 698	111 863	24 533	17 104	108 165	90 992	12 229	34.2	40.6	14.29	14.48	488.72	587.89
February	132 789	111 883	24 474	17 028	108 315	90 933	12 155	34.0	40.5	14.36	14.55	488.24	589.28
March	132 747	111 802	24 409	16 938	108 338	90 875	12 085	34.1	40.5	14.42	14.58	491.72	590.49
April	132 463	111 471	24 254	16 802	108 209	90 652	11 982	34.0	40.4	14.45	14.63	491.30	591.05
May	132 410	111 381	24 119	16 661	108 291	90 548	11 859	34.0	40.4	14.50	14.69	493.00	593.48
June	132 299	111 162	23 965	16 515	108 334	90 352	11 739	34.0	40.3	14.54	14.74	494.36	594.02
July	132 177	110 992	23 837	16 382	108 340	90 239	11 632	34.0	40.6	14.55	14.82	494.70	601.69
August	132 028	110 810	23 667	16 232	108 361	90 094	11 495	33.9	40.3	14.59	14.85	494.60	598.46
September	131 771	110 529	23 537	16 117	108 234	89 835	11 400	33.8	40.2	14.63	14.89	494.49	598.58
October	131 454	110 179	23 378	15 972	108 076	89 558	11 286	33.7	40.1	14.66	14.89	494.04	597.09
November	131 142	109 816	23 209	15 825	107 933	89 238	11 175	33.8	40.1	14.71	14.96	497.20	599.90
December	130 982	109 627	23 094	15 711	107 888	89 127	11 081	33.8	40.2	14.75	15.01	498.55	603.40
2002													
January	130 852	109 475	22 961	15 587	107 891	89 121	10 993	33.7	40.1	14.76	15.04	497.41	603.10
February	130 736	109 346	22 876	15 515	107 860	89 064	10 951	33.8	40.3	14.78	15.12	499.56	609.34
March	130 717	109 286	22 786	15 443	107 931	89 019	10 901	33.9	40.5	14.82	15.15	502.40	613.58
April	130 623	109 180	22 689	15 392	107 934	88 867	10 859	33.9	40.6	14.84	15.17	503.08	615.90
May	130 634	109 120	22 604	15 337	108 030	88 726	10 824	33.9	40.6	14.88	15.24	504.43	618.74
June	130 684	109 135	22 578	15 298	108 106	88 637	10 797	33.9	40.7	14.94	15.27	506.47	621.49
July	130 590	109 046	22 521	15 256	108 069	88 482	10 764	33.8	40.4	14.98	15.30	506.32	618.12
August	130 587	108 998	22 449	15 171	108 138	88 423	10 697	33.9	40.5	15.02	15.34	509.18	621.27
September	130 501	108 955	22 397	15 119	108 104	88 395	10 668	33.9	40.5	15.06	15.37	510.53	622.49
October	130 628	109 069	22 325	15 060	108 303	88 481	10 631	33.8	40.3	15.12	15.45	511.06	622.64
November	130 615	109 034	22 282	14 992	108 333	88 425	10 583	33.8	40.4	15.15	15.48	512.07	625.39
December	130 472	108 884	22 189	14 912	108 283	88 244	10 523	33.8	40.5	15.20	15.54	513.76	629.37
2003													
January	130 580	108 954	22 146	14 866	108 434	88 275	10 484	33.8	40.3	15.22	15.58	514.44	627.87
February	130 444	108 820	22 023	14 781	108 421	88 147	10 416	33.6	40.3	15.29	15.63	513.74	629.89
March	130 232	108 622	21 945	14 721	108 287	87 845	10 357	33.8	40.4	15.27	15.64	516.13	631.86
April	130 177	108 582	21 864	14 609	108 313	87 824	10 256	33.6	40.1	15.28	15.63	513.41	626.76
May	130 196	108 629	21 832	14 557	108 364	87 816	10 218	33.7	40.2	15.33	15.69	516.62	630.74
June	130 194	108 588	21 788	14 493	108 406	87 790	10 165	33.6	40.3	15.36	15.72	516.10	633.52
July	130 191	108 558	21 708	14 402	108 483	87 767	10 093	33.6	40.1	15.40	15.76	517.44	631.98
August	130 149	108 593	21 706	14 376	108 443	87 823	10 084	33.7	40.2	15.42	15.78	519.65	634.36
September	130 254	108 750	21 700	14 347	108 554	87 932	10 059	33.6	40.5	15.41	15.83	517.78	641.12
October	130 454	108 896	21 691	14 334	108 763	88 015	10 054	33.7	40.6	15.42	15.83	519.65	642.70
November	130 474	108 939	21 688	14 316	108 786	88 077	10 039	33.8	40.9	15.47	15.90	522.89	650.31
December	130 588	109 042	21 703	14 300	108 885	88 148	10 031	33.6	40.7	15.47	15.92	519.79	647.94

Table 10-8. Employment, Hours, and Earnings, Total Nonfarm and Manufacturing, Historical Annual and Monthly—*Continued*

(Wage and salary workers on nonfarm payrolls, seasonally adjusted.)

Year and month	All wage and salary workers (thousands)					Production and nonsupervisory workers on private payrolls							
	Total	Private			Service-providing	Number (thousands)		Average hours per week		Average hourly earnings, dollars		Average weekly earnings, dollars	
		Total	Goods-producing			Total private	Manufacturing	Total private	Manufacturing	Total private	Manufacturing	Total private	Manufacturing
			Total	Manufacturing									
2004													
January	130 769	109 231	21 715	14 290	109 054	88 225	10 027	33.7	40.9	15.51	15.95	522.69	652.36
February	130 825	109 275	21 693	14 279	109 132	88 266	10 012	33.8	41.0	15.53	15.98	524.91	655.18
March	131 142	109 554	21 758	14 287	109 384	88 511	10 025	33.7	40.9	15.56	16.01	524.37	654.81
April	131 411	109 797	21 802	14 315	109 609	88 775	10 060	33.7	40.7	15.59	16.05	525.38	653.24
May	131 694	110 080	21 881	14 342	109 813	89 056	10 091	33.8	41.1	15.63	16.07	528.29	660.48
June	131 793	110 192	21 885	14 332	109 908	89 221	10 087	33.6	40.8	15.67	16.11	526.51	657.29
July	131 848	110 242	21 900	14 330	109 948	89 338	10 095	33.7	40.8	15.69	16.12	528.75	657.70
August	131 937	110 311	21 944	14 345	109 993	89 477	10 115	33.7	40.8	15.73	16.20	530.10	660.96
September	132 093	110 458	21 957	14 331	110 136	89 656	10 104	33.7	40.7	15.78	16.29	531.79	663.00
October	132 447	110 791	22 004	14 332	110 443	89 967	10 103	33.8	40.6	15.81	16.27	534.38	660.56
November	132 503	110 811	21 997	14 307	110 506	89 992	10 078	33.7	40.5	15.84	16.30	533.81	660.15
December	132 624	110 931	22 005	14 287	110 619	90 155	10 063	33.8	40.6	15.86	16.34	536.07	663.40
2005													
January	132 774	111 039	21 958	14 257	110 816	90 236	10 045	33.7	40.7	15.90	16.38	535.83	666.67
February	133 032	111 288	22 036	14 273	110 996	90 484	10 052	33.8	40.6	15.93	16.44	538.43	667.46
March	133 156	111 416	22 066	14 269	111 090	90 647	10 056	33.7	40.4	15.97	16.44	538.19	664.18
April	133 518	111 764	22 136	14 250	111 382	90 980	10 048	33.8	40.4	16.00	16.46	540.80	664.98
May	133 690	111 909	22 172	14 256	111 518	91 098	10 061	33.7	40.4	16.04	16.53	540.55	667.81
June	133 942	112 179	22 185	14 227	111 757	91 372	10 047	33.7	40.4	16.08	16.54	541.90	668.22
July	134 296	112 439	22 205	14 226	112 091	91 606	10 039	33.7	40.5	16.15	16.57	544.26	671.09
August	134 498	112 635	22 228	14 203	112 270	91 792	10 043	33.7	40.5	16.17	16.63	544.93	673.52
September	134 566	112 721	22 226	14 175	112 340	91 895	10 046	33.8	40.7	16.19	16.59	547.22	675.21
October	134 655	112 826	22 292	14 192	112 363	92 036	10 073	33.8	41.0	16.28	16.69	550.26	684.29
November	134 993	113 134	22 357	14 187	112 636	92 358	10 093	33.8	40.9	16.30	16.68	550.94	682.21
December	135 149	113 270	22 376	14 193	112 773	92 520	10 112	33.8	40.8	16.35	16.68	552.63	680.54
2006													
January	135 429	113 582	22 467	14 210	112 962	92 826	10 153	33.8	41.0	16.42	16.70	555.00	684.70
February	135 737	113 859	22 535	14 209	113 202	93 115	10 164	33.8	41.1	16.48	16.70	557.02	686.37
March	136 047	114 144	22 572	14 214	113 475	93 412	10 174	33.8	41.1	16.54	16.72	559.05	687.19
April	136 205	114 286	22 631	14 226	113 574	93 584	10 190	33.9	41.3	16.63	16.75	563.76	691.78
May	136 244	114 318	22 597	14 203	113 647	93 653	10 179	33.8	41.2	16.65	16.77	562.77	690.92
June	136 325	114 403	22 598	14 213	113 727	93 728	10 190	33.9	41.2	16.72	16.78	566.81	691.34
July	136 520	114 547	22 590	14 188	113 930	93 864	10 177	33.9	41.4	16.77	16.78	568.50	694.69
August	136 694	114 683	22 572	14 159	114 122	94 010	10 158	33.8	41.2	16.82	16.83	568.52	693.40
September	136 843	114 761	22 537	14 125	114 306	94 058	10 120	33.8	41.1	16.87	16.83	570.21	691.71
October	136 852	114 784	22 456	14 075	114 396	94 109	10 071	33.9	41.2	16.93	16.91	573.93	696.69
November	137 063	114 980	22 408	14 041	114 655	94 284	10 047	33.8	41.0	16.97	16.92	573.59	693.72
December	137 249	115 161	22 405	14 015	114 844	94 488	10 041	33.9	41.1	17.04	16.99	577.66	698.29
2007													
January	137 477	115 382	22 439	14 008	115 038	94 682	10 036	33.8	41.0	17.09	17.01	577.64	697.41
February	137 558	115 427	22 334	13 997	115 224	94 717	10 035	33.7	40.9	17.15	17.05	577.96	697.35
March	137 793	115 644	22 391	13 970	115 402	94 954	10 011	33.9	41.3	17.22	17.10	583.76	706.23
April	137 842	115 667	22 350	13 945	115 492	95 023	10 006	33.8	41.3	17.27	17.20	583.73	710.36
May	137 993	115 800	22 323	13 929	115 670	95 198	10 007	33.8	41.2	17.33	17.23	585.75	709.88
June	138 069	115 862	22 323	13 911	115 746	95 309	9 996	33.9	41.4	17.42	17.29	590.54	715.81
July	138 038	115 867	22 277	13 889	115 761	95 399	9 990	33.8	41.3	17.46	17.29	590.15	714.08
August	138 015	115 789	22 165	13 828	115 850	95 339	9 944	33.8	41.3	17.50	17.35	591.50	716.56
September	138 095	115 816	22 093	13 790	116 002	95 437	9 933	33.8	41.3	17.56	17.37	593.53	717.38
October	138 174	115 877	22 056	13 764	116 118	95 540	9 911	33.8	41.2	17.58	17.36	594.20	715.23
November	138 284	115 950	22 015	13 757	116 269	95 609	9 920	33.8	41.3	17.63	17.44	595.89	720.27
December	138 392	116 016	21 976	13 746	116 416	95 706	9 924	33.8	41.1	17.69	17.44	597.92	716.78
2008													
January	138 403	116 015	21 947	13 725	116 456	95 728	9 914	33.7	41.1	17.73	17.50	597.50	719.25
February	138 324	115 907	21 897	13 696	116 427	95 640	9 888	33.7	41.2	17.80	17.57	599.86	723.88
March	138 275	115 832	21 820	13 659	116 455	95 606	9 866	33.8	41.3	17.88	17.63	604.34	728.12
April	138 035	115 585	21 681	13 599	116 354	95 413	9 810	33.7	41.1	17.92	17.63	603.90	724.59
May	137 858	115 375	21 599	13 564	116 259	95 225	9 779	33.7	41.0	17.98	17.69	605.93	725.29
June	137 687	115 170	21 483	13 504	116 204	95 042	9 721	33.7	41.0	18.03	17.75	607.61	727.75
July	137 491	114 923	21 360	13 430	116 131	94 852	9 655	33.6	40.9	18.10	17.80	608.16	728.02
August	137 213	114 646	21 250	13 358	115 963	94 614	9 586	33.7	40.9	18.18	17.80	612.67	728.02
September	136 753	114 216	21 101	13 275	115 652	94 281	9 504	33.6	40.5	18.20	17.83	611.52	722.12
October	136 272	113 723	20 895	13 147	115 377	93 870	9 384	33.5	40.5	18.25	17.90	611.38	724.95
November	135 545	112 985	20 623	13 034	114 922	93 169	9 290	33.4	40.1	18.31	17.95	611.55	719.80
December	134 839	112 283	20 322	12 850	114 517	92 598	9 137	33.3	39.8	18.38	18.00	612.05	716.40
2009													
January	134 055	111 476	19 889	12 561	114 166	91 894	8 889	33.2	39.7	18.40	18.01	610.88	715.00
February	133 312	110 736	19 575	12 380	113 737	91 286	8 741	33.3	39.6	18.44	18.09	614.05	716.36
March	132 512	109 952	19 227	12 208	113 285	90 613	8 592	33.1	39.3	18.50	18.13	612.35	712.51
April	131 817	109 140	18 894	12 030	112 923	89 911	8 453	33.1	39.5	18.52	18.16	613.01	717.32
May	131 475	108 858	18 655	11 862	112 820	89 700	8 311	33.0	39.3	18.53	18.14	611.49	712.90
June	131 008	108 432	18 422	11 726	112 586	89 311	8 203	33.0	39.6	18.56	18.18	612.48	719.93
July	130 668	108 147	18 278	11 668	112 390	89 102	8 172	33.1	39.9	18.59	18.29	615.33	729.77
August	130 485	107 948	18 151	11 626	112 334	88 934	8 148	33.1	40.0	18.67	18.32	617.98	732.80
September	130 244	107 793	18 043	11 591	112 201	88 817	8 133	33.1	40.0	18.70	18.42	618.97	736.80
October	130 045	107 521	17 915	11 538	112 130	88 578	8 100	33.0	40.2	18.74	18.38	618.42	738.88
November	130 057	107 524	17 869	11 509	112 188	88 606	8 079	33.3	40.5	18.80	18.42	626.04	746.01
December	129 788	107 306	17 792	11 475	111 996	88 532	8 050	33.2	40.6	18.83	18.42	625.16	747.85

Table 10-8. Employment, Hours, and Earnings, Total Nonfarm and Manufacturing, Historical Annual and Monthly—*Continued*

(Wage and salary workers on nonfarm payrolls, seasonally adjusted.)

Year and month	All wage and salary workers (thousands)					Production and nonsupervisory workers on private payrolls							
	Total	Private			Service-providing	Number (thousands)		Average hours per week		Average hourly earnings, dollars		Average weekly earnings, dollars	
		Total	Goods-producing			Total private	Manufac-turing	Total private	Manufac-turing	Total private	Manufac-turing	Total private	Manufac-turing
			Total	Manufac-turing									
2010													
January	129 790	107 299	17 707	11 460	112 083	88 503	8 034	33.3	40.8	18.88	18.43	628.70	751.94
February	129 698	107 222	17 627	11 453	112 071	88 431	8 032	33.1	40.5	18.91	18.47	625.92	748.04
March	129 879	107 361	17 672	11 453	112 207	88 565	8 027	33.3	41.0	18.91	18.47	629.70	757.27
April	130 110	107 541	17 729	11 489	112 381	88 706	8 050	33.4	41.1	18.96	18.51	633.26	760.76
May	130 650	107 654	17 742	11 525	112 908	88 772	8 078	33.4	41.4	19.01	18.58	634.93	769.21
June	130 511	107 771	17 763	11 545	112 748	88 871	8 100	33.3	41.0	19.02	18.58	633.37	761.78
July	130 427	107 858	17 777	11 561	112 650	88 945	8 106	33.4	41.1	19.04	18.63	635.94	765.69
August	130 422	108 002	17 793	11 553	112 629	89 046	8 099	33.5	41.2	19.11	18.65	640.19	768.38
September	130 357	108 110	17 787	11 563	112 570	89 138	8 098	33.5	41.5	19.11	18.72	640.19	776.88
October	130 625	108 328	17 801	11 562	112 824	89 306	8 096	33.5	41.2	19.20	18.73	643.20	771.68
November	130 750	108 463	17 827	11 585	112 923	89 434	8 103	33.5	41.3	19.21	18.76	643.54	774.79
December	130 822	108 556	17 796	11 595	113 026	89 535	8 117	33.5	41.3	19.22	18.79	643.87	776.03
2011													
January	130 841	108 583	17 784	11 621	113 057	89 523	8 133	33.4	41.1	19.32	18.89	645.29	776.38
February	131 053	108 838	17 844	11 654	113 209	89 726	8 160	33.5	41.4	19.31	18.91	646.89	782.87
March	131 288	109 096	17 906	11 675	113 382	89 960	8 183	33.5	41.4	19.31	18.90	646.89	782.46
April	131 602	109 418	17 957	11 704	113 645	90 220	8 212	33.6	41.4	19.36	18.91	650.50	782.87
May	131 703	109 574	18 007	11 713	113 696	90 364	8 218	33.6	41.5	19.41	18.92	652.18	785.18
June	131 939	109 775	18 045	11 727	113 894	90 533	8 228	33.6	41.4	19.41	18.90	652.18	782.46
July	131 999	109 950	18 094	11 746	113 905	90 702	8 244	33.7	41.4	19.47	18.93	656.14	783.70
August	132 125	110 108	18 120	11 764	114 005	90 835	8 259	33.5	41.3	19.47	18.90	652.25	780.57
September	132 358	110 375	18 167	11 769	114 191	91 068	8 266	33.6	41.3	19.48	18.91	654.53	780.98
October	132 562	110 564	18 188	11 780	114 374	91 233	8 274	33.7	41.5	19.56	18.98	659.17	787.67
November	132 694	110 723	18 187	11 770	114 507	91 423	8 268	33.6	41.5	19.56	18.96	657.22	786.84
December	132 896	110 942	18 244	11 802	114 652	91 626	8 295	33.7	41.6	19.56	19.00	659.17	790.40
2012													
January	133 250	111 304	18 304	11 838	114 946	91 934	8 322	33.8	41.8	19.59	19.02	662.14	795.04
February	133 512	111 565	18 334	11 860	115 178	92 212	8 352	33.7	41.7	19.59	19.00	660.18	792.30
March	133 752	111 809	18 372	11 898	115 380	92 378	8 386	33.7	41.6	19.64	19.02	661.87	791.23
April	133 834	111 903	18 384	11 916	115 450	92 478	8 399	33.7	41.7	19.68	19.09	663.22	796.05
May	133 934	112 023	18 386	11 927	115 548	92 604	8 411	33.6	41.6	19.68	19.04	661.25	792.06
June	134 007	112 077	18 411	11 936	115 596	92 657	8 412	33.7	41.7	19.72	19.08	664.56	795.64
July	134 159	112 246	18 447	11 964	115 712	92 781	8 438	33.7	41.7	19.74	19.11	665.24	796.89
August	134 331	112 415	18 459	11 960	115 872	92 916	8 429	33.6	41.5	19.74	19.05	663.26	790.58
September	134 518	112 593	18 461	11 954	116 057	93 065	8 419	33.7	41.5	19.78	19.06	666.59	790.99
October	134 677	112 774	18 472	11 961	116 205	93 248	8 426	33.6	41.5	19.79	19.09	664.94	792.24
November	134 833	112 950	18 477	11 950	116 356	93 377	8 411	33.6	41.5	19.84	19.13	666.62	793.90
December	135 072	113 185	18 532	11 960	116 540	93 562	8 415	33.8	41.7	19.90	19.13	672.62	797.72
2013													
January	135 263	113 394	18 580	11 983	116 683	93 659	8 422	33.6	41.7	19.94	19.17	669.98	799.39
February	135 541	113 660	18 638	11 996	116 903	93 870	8 421	33.8	41.8	19.99	19.21	675.66	802.98
March	135 680	113 810	18 660	11 999	117 020	94 001	8 409	33.8	41.9	20.01	19.21	676.34	804.90
April	135 871	114 002	18 653	12 000	117 218	94 155	8 414	33.7	41.8	20.04	19.23	675.35	803.81
May	136 093	114 229	18 691	12 000	117 402	94 302	8 402	33.7	41.8	20.05	19.23	675.69	803.81
June	136 274	114 434	18 724	12 004	117 550	94 488	8 398	33.7	41.8	20.12	19.28	678.04	805.90
July	136 386	114 571	18 705	11 984	117 681	94 638	8 383	33.5	41.7	20.14	19.26	674.69	803.14
August	136 628	114 797	18 756	12 014	117 872	94 813	8 406	33.6	41.9	20.17	19.31	677.71	809.09
September	136 815	114 980	18 810	12 032	118 005	94 956	8 426	33.7	41.9	20.23	19.33	681.75	809.93
October	137 040	115 210	18 857	12 056	118 183	95 178	8 450	33.6	41.9	20.25	19.35	680.40	810.77
November	137 304	115 461	18 911	12 079	118 393	95 397	8 464	33.7	42.0	20.31	19.39	684.45	814.38
December	137 373	115 553	18 881	12 083	118 492	95 461	8 468	33.6	41.9	20.34	19.46	683.42	815.37
2014													
January	137 548	115 734	18 937	12 081	118 611	95 590	8 468	33.5	41.6	20.39	19.46	683.07	809.54
February	137 714	115 889	18 988	12 106	118 726	95 744	8 497	33.4	41.6	20.50	19.49	684.70	810.78
March	137 968	116 135	19 037	12 120	118 931	95 991	8 510	33.7	42.0	20.50	19.53	690.85	820.26
April	138 293	116 440	19 104	12 134	119 189	96 211	8 525	33.7	41.9	20.51	19.48	691.19	816.21
May	138 511	116 679	19 142	12 146	119 369	96 423	8 532	33.7	42.1	20.54	19.51	692.20	821.37
June	138 837	116 942	19 195	12 170	119 642	96 642	8 558	33.7	42.1	20.57	19.54	693.21	822.63
July	139 069	117 168	19 264	12 189	119 805	96 817	8 580	33.7	41.9	20.61	19.59	694.56	820.82
August	139 257	117 402	19 316	12 208	119 941	96 981	8 594	33.7	42.0	20.67	19.60	696.58	823.20
September	139 566	117 669	19 371	12 226	120 195	97 158	8 598	33.7	42.2	20.67	19.59	696.58	826.70
October	139 818	117 901	19 419	12 259	120 399	97 333	8 623	33.7	42.1	20.70	19.65	697.59	827.27
November	140 109	118 177	19 456	12 284	120 653	97 536	8 646	33.8	42.2	20.76	19.65	701.69	829.23
December	140 377	118 430	19 481	12 292	120 896	97 738	8 652	33.8	42.1	20.70	19.63	699.66	826.42
2015													
January	140 568	118 608	19 500	12 292	121 068	97 844	8 645	33.8	42.0	20.80	19.65	703.04	825.30
February	140 839	118 861	19 537	12 301	121 302	98 040	8 655	33.8	42.0	20.80	19.73	703.04	828.66
March	140 910	118 940	19 505	12 312	121 405	98 133	8 660	33.7	41.9	20.88	19.77	703.66	828.36
April	141 194	119 189	19 553	12 318	121 641	98 266	8 660	33.6	41.8	20.91	19.80	702.58	827.64
May	141 525	119 513	19 580	12 333	121 945	98 565	8 683	33.6	41.8	20.99	19.86	705.26	830.15
June	141 699	119 684	19 591	12 334	122 108	98 711	8 691	33.7	41.8	21.01	19.90	708.04	831.82
July	142 001	119 951	19 626	12 349	122 375	98 834	8 702	33.7	41.8	21.03	19.94	708.71	833.49
August	142 126	120 066	19 629	12 345	122 497	98 969	8 690	33.7	41.8	21.08	19.98	710.40	835.16
September	142 281	120 241	19 641	12 354	122 640	99 121	8 697	33.7	41.7	21.11	20.08	711.41	837.34
October	142 587	120 531	19 680	12 362	122 907	99 351	8 708	33.7	41.8	21.19	20.05	714.10	838.09
November	142 824	120 743	19 711	12 357	123 113	99 509	8 698	33.7	41.8	21.20	20.06	714.44	838.51
December	143 097	121 000	19 738	12 362	123 359	99 707	8 696	33.8	41.8	21.24	20.11	717.91	840.60

Table 10-8. Employment, Hours, and Earnings, Total Nonfarm and Manufacturing, Historical Annual and Monthly—*Continued*

(Wage and salary workers on nonfarm payrolls, seasonally adjusted.)

Year and month	All wage and salary workers (thousands)					Production and nonsupervisory workers on private payrolls							
		Private			Service-providing	Number (thousands)		Average hours per week		Average hourly earnings, dollars		Average weekly earnings, dollars	
	Total	Total	Goods-producing			Total private	Manufac-turing	Total private	Manufac-turing	Total private	Manufac-turing	Total private	Manufac-turing
			Total	Manufac-turing									
2016													
January	143 170	121 052	19 730	12 379	123 440	99 756	8 705	33.7	41.9	21.31	20.16	718.15	844.70
February	143 433	121 289	19 728	12 367	123 705	99 907	8 691	33.6	41.9	21.34	20.19	717.02	845.96
March	143 662	121 482	19 716	12 345	123 946	100 066	8 677	33.6	41.8	21.40	20.27	719.04	847.29
April	143 849	121 663	19 728	12 349	124 121	100 158	8 672	33.6	41.8	21.45	20.38	720.72	851.88
May	143 891	121 694	19 689	12 332	124 202	100 195	8 651	33.6	41.8	21.47	20.41	721.39	853.14
June	144 158	121 974	19 709	12 351	124 449	100 414	8 674	33.6	41.8	21.53	20.48	723.41	856.06
July	144 512	122 227	19 757	12 369	124 755	100 623	8 690	33.6	42.0	21.58	20.49	725.09	860.58
August	144 647	122 379	19 732	12 348	124 915	100 742	8 662	33.6	41.8	21.61	20.56	726.10	859.41
September	144 916	122 613	19 762	12 347	125 154	100 935	8 658	33.6	41.9	21.64	20.55	727.10	861.05
October	145 061	122 769	19 789	12 347	125 272	101 065	8 651	33.6	41.9	21.70	20.59	729.12	862.72
November	145 212	122 922	19 808	12 342	125 404	101 246	8 651	33.6	41.8	21.72	20.60	729.79	861.08
December	145 442	123 134	19 825	12 356	125 617	101 472	8 661	33.5	41.9	21.76	20.63	728.96	864.40
2017													
January	145 627	123 325	19 865	12 369	125 762	101 643	8 671	33.6	41.9	21.81	20.62	732.82	863.98
February	145 815	123 496	19 928	12 384	125 887	101 779	8 688	33.6	41.9	21.86	20.64	734.50	864.82
March	145 944	123 619	19 964	12 395	125 980	101 914	8 699	33.5	41.8	21.88	20.69	732.98	864.84
April	146 141	123 811	19 985	12 400	126 156	102 061	8 709	33.7	41.9	21.93	20.76	739.04	869.84
May	146 296	123 964	20 007	12 406	126 289	102 175	8 708	33.6	41.9	21.97	20.80	738.19	871.52
June	146 512	124 166	20 050	12 418	126 462	102 342	8 713	33.7	42.0	22.03	20.86	742.41	876.12
July	146 727	124 368	20 056	12 417	126 671	102 499	8 715	33.7	42.0	22.08	20.92	744.10	878.64
August	146 911	124 554	20 135	12 461	126 776	102 649	8 745	33.6	42.0	22.11	20.95	742.90	879.90
September	146 929	124 563	20 161	12 470	126 768	102 672	8 756	33.6	41.9	22.20	21.01	745.92	880.32
October	147 196	124 827	20 206	12 492	126 990	102 899	8 771	33.7	42.0	22.18	21.08	747.47	885.36
November	147 421	125 028	20 273	12 514	127 148	103 022	8 783	33.8	42.0	22.23	21.11	751.37	886.62
December	147 551	125 170	20 326	12 541	127 225	103 133	8 805	33.7	41.8	22.30	21.21	751.51	886.58
2018													
January	147 672	125 317	20 371	12 558	127 301	103 253	8 817	33.6	41.8	22.36	21.29	751.30	889.92
February	148 078	125 672	20 494	12 588	127 584	103 518	8 827	33.8	42.2	22.40	21.33	757.12	900.13
March	148 254	125 850	20 530	12 611	127 724	103 677	8 842	33.7	42.2	22.49	21.39	757.91	902.66
April	148 391	125 977	20 577	12 632	127 814	103 772	8 863	33.8	42.4	22.55	21.47	762.19	910.33
May	148 669	126 238	20 648	12 658	128 021	104 031	8 869	33.8	42.0	22.61	21.43	764.22	900.06
June	148 888	126 429	20 698	12 687	128 190	104 173	8 902	33.8	42.1	22.67	21.48	766.25	904.31
July	149 024	126 562	20 739	12 706	128 285	104 262	8 916	33.8	42.2	22.71	21.45	767.60	905.19
August	149 268	126 778	20 791	12 719	128 477	104 426	8 918	33.8	42.2	22.79	21.55	770.30	909.41
September	149 348	126 859	20 834	12 740	128 514	104 504	8 934	33.7	42.1	22.86	21.62	770.38	910.20
October	149 549	127 064	20 884	12 764	128 665	104 658	8 951	33.7	42.0	22.90	21.70	771.73	911.40
November	149 683	127 197	20 897	12 784	128 786	104 741	8 965	33.7	42.0	23.00	21.78	775.10	914.76
December	149 865	127 370	20 948	12 805	128 917	104 907	8 983	33.7	42.0	23.09	21.82	778.13	916.44
2019													
January	150 134	127 628	21 023	12 825	129 111	105 168	8 998	33.8	42.0	23.11	21.84	781.12	917.28
February	150 135	127 622	20 994	12 830	129 141	105 109	9 000	33.6	41.7	23.19	21.91	779.18	913.65
March	150 282	127 754	21 011	12 827	129 271	105 217	8 992	33.7	41.7	23.28	21.96	784.54	915.73
April	150 492	127 939	21 039	12 829	129 453	105 335	8 979	33.7	41.6	23.33	21.96	786.22	913.54
May	150 577	128 026	21 050	12 829	129 527	105 399	8 970	33.6	41.5	23.42	22.04	786.91	914.66
June	150 759	128 206	21 076	12 838	129 683	105 503	8 968	33.6	41.6	23.47	22.14	788.59	921.02
July	150 953	128 366	21 085	12 845	129 868	105 604	8 967	33.5	41.5	23.54	22.19	788.59	920.89
August	151 160	128 523	21 087	12 848	130 073	105 731	8 968	33.6	41.5	23.64	22.22	794.30	922.13
September	151 368	128 718	21 106	12 851	130 262	105 885	8 968	33.6	41.5	23.70	22.26	796.32	923.79
October	151 553	128 908	21 086	12 810	130 467	105 992	8 931	33.6	41.4	23.76	22.30	798.34	923.22
November	151 814	129 155	21 131	12 868	130 683	106 156	8 978	33.5	41.4	23.81	22.39	797.64	926.95
December	151 998	129 319	21 136	12 866	130 862	106 300	8 980	33.6	41.4	23.84	22.44	801.02	929.02
2020													
January	152 234	129 445	21 096	12 792	131 138	106 444	8 916	33.6	41.4	23.88	22.41	802.37	927.77
February	152 523	129 688	21 137	12 799	131 386	106 651	8 932	33.7	41.7	23.96	22.50	807.45	938.25
March	150 840	128 066	20 949	12 718	129 891	105 083	8 860	33.4	41.3	24.15	22.58	806.61	932.55
April	130 161	108 335	18 571	11 414	111 590	87 038	7 776	33.5	38.5	25.16	22.72	842.86	874.72
May	132 994	111 680	19 262	11 657	113 732	90 011	7 962	34.1	39.4	25.01	22.76	852.84	896.74
June	137 840	116 487	19 767	11 999	118 073	94 400	8 326	33.9	39.9	24.77	22.62	839.70	902.54
July	139 566	118 010	19 827	12 037	119 739	95 920	8 354	34.0	40.7	24.67	22.84	838.78	929.59
August	141 149	119 076	19 880	12 068	121 269	96 836	8 364	34.0	41.1	24.81	22.87	843.54	939.96
September	141 865	120 008	19 971	12 123	121 894	97 686	8 390	34.1	41.2	24.79	23.01	845.34	948.01
October	142 545	120 962	20 078	12 155	122 467	98 541	8 406	34.2	41.3	24.83	22.99	849.19	949.49
November	142 809	121 321	20 146	12 196	122 663	98 926	8 441	34.2	41.3	24.93	23.10	852.61	954.03
December	142 503	121 047	20 228	12 231	122 275	98 617	8 471	34.2	41.3	25.15	23.12	860.13	954.86
2021													
January	143 017	121 229	20 090	12 184	121 139	98 703	8 457	34.4	41.6	25.18	23.27	866.19	968.03
February	143 727	121 922	20 072	12 222	121 850	99 159	8 477	34.1	41.5	25.26	23.39	861.37	970.69
March	144 431	122 572	20 227	12 268	122 345	99 573	8 518	34.4	41.7	25.35	23.40	872.04	975.78
April	144 694	122 784	20 187	12 240	122 597	99 820	8 467	34.4	41.6	25.49	23.48	876.86	976.77
May	145 141	123 165	20 209	12 268	122 956	100 217	8 502	34.3	41.5	25.67	23.64	880.48	981.06
June	145 698	123 673	20 232	12 288	123 441	100 715	8 528	34.3	41.3	25.81	23.77	885.28	981.70
July	146 387	124 311	20 314	12 350	123 997	101 314	8 584	34.3	41.5	25.96	23.89	890.43	991.44
August	146 904	124 808	20 362	12 391	124 446	101 731	8 626	34.2	41.4	26.10	24.03	892.62	994.84
September	147 328	125 217	20 416	12 413	124 801	102 152	8 641	34.3	41.4	26.26	24.10	900.72	997.74
October	148 005	125 911	20 499	12 466	125 412	102 682	8 693	34.2	41.3	26.42	24.17	903.56	998.22
November	148 652	126 538	20 598	12 514	125 940	103 155	8 731	34.2	41.4	26.55	24.24	908.01	1 003.54
December	149 240	127 099	20 691	12 555	106 408	103 605	8 771	34.1	41.4	26.74	24.38	911.83	1 009.33

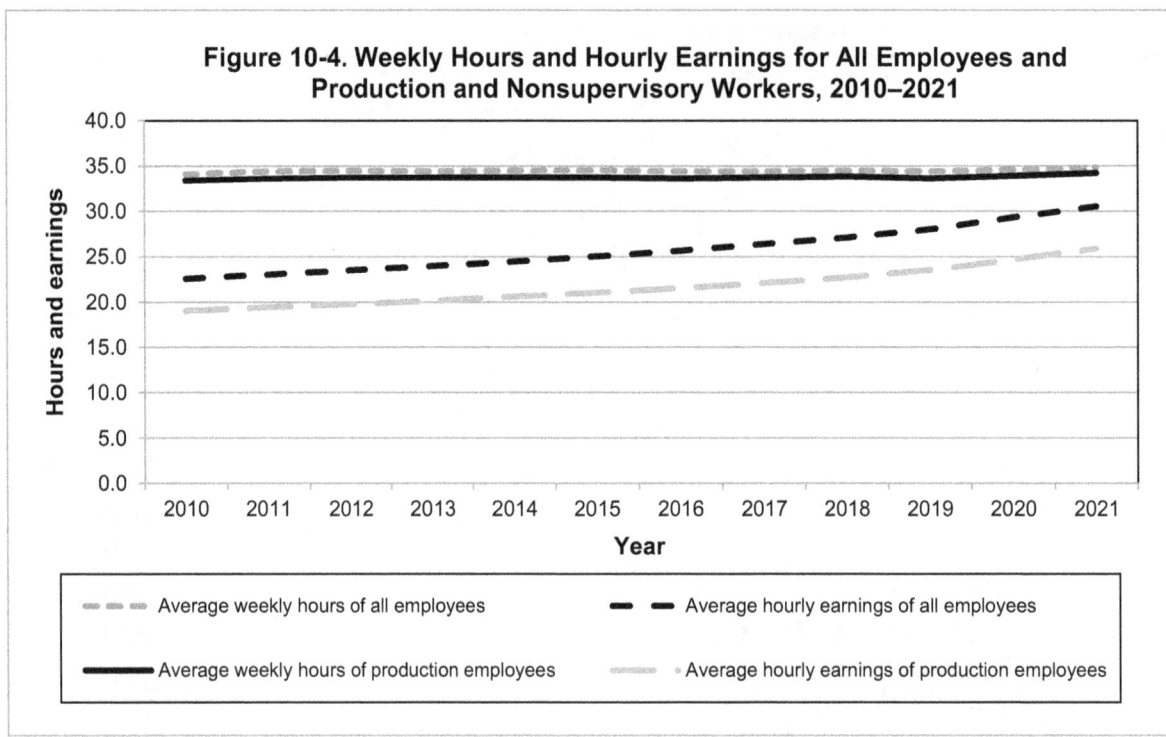

Figure 10-4. Weekly Hours and Hourly Earnings for All Employees and Production and Nonsupervisory Workers, 2010–2021

- The payroll survey (Current Employment Statistics) began in March 2006 collecting more comprehensive hours and earnings data for all nonfarm jobs (See Notes and Definitions section to learn what farm employment is.) For production and nonsupervisory workers, hours and weekly data has been collected for decades. Figure 10-4 displays hourly earnings and hours per week for both nonfarm workers and production and nonsupervisory employees.

- Miners and loggers continued to work the most hours during the pandemic, averaging at 44.4 hours a week in 2020 and 45.1 hours in 2021. At the other end, workers in leisure and hospitality averaged the least amount of hours in 2020 at 25.5 and 26.2 hours in 2021. (Table 10-9)

- In 2021, workers in information had the highest weekly earnings at $1,644.33 followed by workers in financial activities at $1,506.90. Workers in leisure and hospitality continued to have the lowers earnings at $481.15. (Table 10-12)

- The index of aggregate hours can point to an upcoming recession. As the index falls, fewer hours are being used for the production of goods and services. Even though employment is up, hours are not up proportionally. This reflects the trend to part-time workers and the reduction of hours for part-time workers. (Table 10-15).

Table 10-9. Average Weekly Hours of All Employees on Private Nonfarm Payrolls by NAICS Supersector

(Hours per week, seasonally adjusted.)

Year and month	Total private	Mining and logging	Construction	Manufacturing		Trade, transportation, and utilities			Information	Financial activities	Professional and business services	Education and health services	Leisure and hospitality	Other services
				Average weekly hours	Overtime hours	Total	Wholesale trade	Retail trade						
2010	34.1	43.4	37.8	40.2	3.0	34.2	38.1	31.4	36.5	36.9	35.4	32.7	25.7	31.6
2011	34.4	44.5	38.3	40.5	3.2	34.6	38.6	31.6	36.6	37.3	35.7	32.7	25.9	31.7
2012	34.5	44.0	38.7	40.7	3.3	34.6	38.7	31.7	36.6	37.4	36.0	32.8	26.1	31.6
2013	34.4	43.9	39.0	40.8	3.4	34.5	38.7	31.4	36.7	37.1	36.1	32.7	26.0	31.7
2014	34.5	34.5	39.0	41.0	3.5	34.5	38.9	31.3	36.8	37.3	36.3	32.7	26.2	31.8
2015	34.5	44.0	39.2	40.8	3.3	34.6	38.9	31.4	36.2	37.6	36.2	32.8	26.3	31.9
2016	34.4	43.4	39.0	40.7	3.3	34.3	38.9	31.0	36.0	37.5	36.1	32.9	26.1	31.9
2017	34.4	45.1	39.1	40.8	3.4	34.4	39.0	31.0	36.2	37.5	36.1	32.9	26.1	31.8
2018	34.5	46.0	39.2	40.9	3.5	34.5	39.0	31.0	36.1	37.6	36.1	32.9	26.1	31.8
2019	34.4	46.2	39.3	40.5	3.3	34.2	38.9	30.6	36.3	37.6	36.2	33.0	25.9	31.9
2020	34.6	44.4	38.9	39.9	2.9	34.2	38.5	30.8	36.6	37.6	36.4	33.2	25.5	32.2
2021	34.8	45.1	39.0	40.4	3.2	34.5	39.2	30.8	37.0	37.6	36.7	33.4	26.2	32.4
2017														
January	34.4	44.2	38.9	40.8	3.3	34.3	38.9	30.9	36.5	37.2	36.1	33.1	25.7	31.8
February	34.3	44.4	39.0	40.7	3.2	34.2	38.9	30.8	36.3	37.4	36.1	32.8	25.7	31.7
March	34.3	45.1	38.9	40.6	3.3	34.2	38.9	30.9	36.3	37.4	35.9	32.7	25.9	31.6
April	34.4	44.9	39.1	40.7	3.3	34.5	39.0	31.2	36.3	37.4	36.1	33.0	26.3	32.0
May	34.4	45.4	39.2	40.8	3.3	34.4	39.0	31.0	36.2	37.4	36.1	32.7	26.0	31.7
June	34.4	45.0	39.1	40.8	3.3	34.4	39.1	30.9	36.2	37.6	36.1	32.8	26.3	31.8
July	34.4	45.6	39.0	41.0	3.4	34.4	39.2	30.9	36.2	37.5	36.0	33.1	26.8	32.1
August	34.4	45.1	39.0	40.8	3.4	34.4	39.1	30.9	36.1	37.5	36.0	32.8	26.4	31.9
September	34.4	45.4	39.0	40.8	3.3	34.3	39.0	30.9	36.2	37.5	36.0	32.8	25.8	31.5
October	34.4	45.3	39.2	41.0	3.5	34.4	39.0	31.0	36.1	37.5	36.0	33.1	26.4	31.9
November	34.5	45.7	39.5	41.0	3.5	34.6	39.1	31.3	36.0	37.6	36.2	32.9	25.9	31.6
December	34.5	45.6	39.1	40.8	3.4	34.6	39.3	31.2	36.2	37.6	36.0	32.9	25.8	31.7
2018														
January	34.4	45.5	38.8	40.7	3.5	34.5	39.0	31.1	35.9	37.5	35.9	32.8	25.3	31.3
February	34.5	45.9	39.3	41.0	3.6	34.6	39.0	31.2	36.0	37.6	36.2	32.9	25.9	31.6
March	34.5	45.8	39.2	40.9	3.6	34.5	39.0	31.2	36.1	37.5	36.1	32.7	26.0	31.5
April	34.5	46.1	39.4	41.1	3.6	34.5	39.0	31.0	36.0	37.6	36.1	33.1	26.2	32.0
May	34.5	46.2	39.5	40.9	3.4	34.6	39.1	31.1	35.9	37.6	36.1	32.8	26.1	31.6
June	34.6	46.4	39.2	40.9	3.5	34.6	39.2	31.1	35.7	37.7	36.2	32.9	26.4	31.8
July	34.5	46.1	39.4	41.0	3.5	34.5	39.1	31.0	36.0	37.6	36.2	33.1	26.8	32.2
August	34.5	46.1	39.1	41.0	3.5	34.5	39.1	30.9	36.1	37.6	36.1	32.9	26.5	32.0
September	34.5	46.0	39.0	40.9	3.5	34.4	39.0	30.9	36.2	37.6	36.1	33.2	26.1	32.1
October	34.5	46.0	38.9	40.8	3.5	34.4	38.9	30.8	36.2	37.7	36.2	32.8	25.9	31.8
November	34.4	46.0	38.9	40.8	3.5	34.4	38.9	30.9	36.2	37.6	36.1	32.9	25.7	31.8
December	34.5	46.2	39.3	40.9	3.5	34.3	39.0	30.6	36.4	37.6	36.2	33.2	26.0	32.1
2019														
January	34.5	46.4	39.7	40.8	3.5	34.3	39.0	30.7	36.2	37.7	36.3	32.9	25.4	31.6
February	34.4	46.2	38.8	40.7	3.4	34.3	39.0	30.7	36.2	37.7	36.2	32.9	25.8	31.7
March	34.5	46.6	39.3	40.7	3.4	34.3	39.0	30.7	36.3	37.7	36.2	32.8	26.0	31.8
April	34.4	46.5	39.1	40.6	3.3	34.3	39.0	30.7	36.1	37.6	36.2	32.9	25.8	31.8
May	34.4	46.5	39.1	40.6	3.3	34.2	38.9	30.6	36.3	37.6	36.2	32.9	25.8	31.7
June	34.4	46.5	39.4	40.7	3.3	34.3	38.9	30.7	36.4	37.5	36.2	33.3	26.5	32.2
July	34.3	46.3	39.1	40.4	3.3	34.2	38.8	30.7	36.2	37.6	36.1	32.9	26.2	31.9
August	34.4	46.3	39.3	40.5	3.2	34.2	38.9	30.6	36.5	37.7	36.2	32.9	26.2	32.0
September	34.4	46.3	39.8	40.5	3.2	34.3	38.9	30.7	36.6	37.6	36.1	33.2	26.0	32.0
October	34.4	46.2	39.3	40.3	3.2	34.2	38.9	30.6	36.5	37.6	36.1	32.9	25.7	31.8
November	34.3	45.8	39.0	40.5	3.2	34.0	38.9	30.3	36.3	37.7	36.1	33.0	25.6	31.8
December	34.3	45.8	38.9	40.4	3.2	34.2	38.8	30.6	36.2	37.5	36.1	33.2	25.8	32.0
2020														
January	34.3	45.6	39.1	40.4	3.1	34.1	38.8	30.4	36.1	37.6	36.1	32.9	25.2	31.6
February	34.4	45.4	39.4	40.6	3.1	34.2	38.7	30.7	36.3	37.6	36.3	33.2	25.8	32.0
March	34.1	44.9	39.0	40.4	3.0	34.1	38.7	30.6	36.3	37.6	36.1	33.0	24.4	31.6
April	34.2	42.8	37.8	38.0	2.0	33.8	37.7	30.5	36.5	37.6	35.9	32.6	24.1	32.2
May	34.7	43.1	38.9	38.7	2.4	34.3	38.0	31.2	36.6	37.7	36.4	32.8	25.9	32.6
June	34.6	43.5	38.9	39.1	2.5	34.3	38.3	31.1	36.5	37.5	36.4	33.1	25.9	32.5
July	34.6	44.0	39.0	39.7	3.0	34.2	38.3	30.7	36.2	37.6	36.4	33.3	25.8	32.1
August	34.7	44.3	39.0	40.0	3.0	34.3	38.5	30.8	36.7	37.6	36.5	33.6	26.4	32.6
September	34.8	44.3	38.9	40.2	3.0	34.4	38.6	30.9	36.7	37.7	36.5	33.4	25.8	32.2
October	34.8	44.7	38.9	40.5	3.2	34.5	38.7	30.9	36.9	37.7	36.7	33.4	25.9	32.3
November	34.8	45.0	39.0	40.3	3.1	34.5	38.7	30.9	37.0	37.7	36.6	33.7	25.6	32.6
December	34.7	44.9	39.1	40.1	3.2	34.2	38.7	30.5	37.0	37.8	36.7	33.5	24.9	32.3
2021														
January	35.0	45.4	39.2	40.5	3.2	34.5	39.1	30.7	37.4	37.7	36.9	33.6	25.1	32.3
February	34.6	44.8	38.5	40.4	3.2	34.2	38.7	30.5	37.2	37.7	36.5	33.2	25.1	32.0
March	34.9	45.6	39.4	40.5	3.3	34.5	39.1	30.7	37.1	37.7	36.7	33.3	26.2	32.4
April	34.9	45.2	39.0	40.4	3.2	34.7	39.2	31.0	37.2	37.6	36.7	33.2	26.5	32.4
May	34.9	45.1	39.0	40.4	3.3	34.7	39.2	30.9	37.1	37.6	36.6	33.5	26.7	32.7
June	34.8	45.3	38.7	40.3	3.2	34.6	39.2	30.8	37.1	37.6	36.6	33.3	26.7	32.3
July	34.8	45.1	38.8	40.5	3.2	34.5	39.3	30.8	37.0	37.6	36.7	33.3	26.8	32.2
August	34.7	44.7	38.8	40.4	3.2	34.4	39.1	30.7	37.0	37.5	36.5	33.6	26.8	32.5
September	34.8	45.4	39.5	40.4	3.3	34.4	39.3	30.7	36.7	37.6	36.7	33.3	26.0	32.1
October	34.8	44.8	38.8	40.3	3.2	34.5	39.4	30.8	36.9	37.5	36.7	33.3	26.1	32.3
November	34.8	45.0	39.0	40.3	3.3	34.5	39.2	31.1	36.8	37.4	36.7	33.4	26.0	32.3
December	34.8	44.9	39.2	40.4	3.2	34.6	39.2	31.3	36.9	37.5	36.7	33.4	25.8	32.1

Table 10-10. Indexes of Aggregate Weekly Hours of All Employees on Private Nonfarm Payrolls by NAICS Supersector

(2007 =100, seasonally adjusted.)

Year and month	Total private	Mining and logging	Construction	Manu-facturing	Trade, transportation, and utilities			Information	Financial activities	Profes-sional and business services	Education and health services	Leisure and hospitality	Other services
					Total	Wholesale trade	Retail trade						
2010	92.4	96.3	72.0	83.4	91.9	90.8	92.1	90.5	93.3	93.2	106.7	95.9	97.3
2011	94.7	110.2	72.9	85.3	94.3	93.5	94.1	89.6	93.9	97.4	108.7	98.8	98.1
2012	97.0	116.6	75.2	87.3	95.9	95.6	95.4	89.3	94.9	101.4	111.1	102.4	98.9
2013	99.0	119.2	78.6	88.2	97.1	96.9	96.2	90.6	95.9	105.0	112.6	105.7	100.5
2014	101.4	125.3	82.6	89.8	98.9	98.5	97.6	91.4	97.3	108.6	114.5	109.7	102.1
2015	103.8	112.3	87.2	90.4	101.2	99.2	99.6	91.0	100.0	111.7	118.0	113.5	103.3
2016	105.4	92.4	90.3	90.4	101.7	99.5	99.7	91.2	101.8	114.3	121.4	116.2	104.7
2017	107.3	96.2	93.7	91.3	102.8	100.6	99.8	92.5	103.7	116.0	124.5	119.4	105.7
2018	109.5	105.0	98.4	93.4	103.9	100.6	99.3	93.5	105.8	118.7	127.2	121.2	106.9
2019	110.8	106.9	101.5	93.6	103.4	101.4	97.3	94.8	107.9	120.9	130.3	122.5	108.3
2020	104.4	86.6	97.6	87.4	99.3	95.7	92.8	90.1	107.6	115.6	126.0	97.3	100.1
2021	108.5	80.2	99.6	89.8	104.4	98.1	96.5	95.7	108.1	122.1	129.1	105.3	101.8
2017													
January	106.5	90.0	91.7	90.8	102.4	99.6	99.9	94.1	102.3	115.1	123.3	117.8	104.7
February	106.3	91.4	92.5	90.6	102.0	99.6	99.3	93.3	102.9	115.2	123.6	117.6	105.3
March	106.5	93.4	92.6	90.5	102.0	99.6	99.5	93.2	103.0	114.7	123.8	118.3	105.4
April	106.9	94.5	93.2	90.8	102.9	99.9	100.4	93.1	103.2	115.5	123.7	119.7	105.5
May	107.1	96.3	93.7	91.1	102.7	99.9	99.7	92.7	103.4	115.9	124.0	119.0	105.7
June	107.3	95.9	93.8	91.2	102.8	100.3	99.4	92.8	104.1	116.1	124.5	119.3	105.7
July	107.4	97.6	93.7	91.6	102.8	100.5	99.3	92.9	104.0	116.0	124.8	119.6	105.5
August	107.6	97.1	94.1	91.5	102.8	100.3	99.3	92.8	104.1	116.2	124.9	119.8	105.5
September	107.4	98.0	94.3	91.6	102.6	100.1	99.3	93.0	104.2	116.2	124.7	119.7	105.6
October	107.8	97.9	95.0	92.1	103.0	100.1	99.6	92.7	104.2	116.4	125.2	120.1	105.8
November	108.2	99.5	96.2	92.2	103.7	100.4	100.6	92.5	104.6	117.1	125.4	120.8	106.0
December	108.4	99.2	95.6	92.0	103.7	101.0	100.2	93.1	104.7	116.7	125.6	120.5	106.4
2018													
January	108.2	99.8	95.0	91.9	103.3	100.2	99.7	92.4	104.5	116.6	125.9	120.2	105.9
February	108.8	101.7	97.4	92.8	103.9	100.2	100.2	92.5	105.1	117.9	126.6	120.9	106.7
March	109.0	102.5	97.2	92.8	103.8	100.4	100.3	93.1	104.9	117.8	126.4	121.0	106.4
April	109.2	104.4	98.1	93.4	103.8	100.0	99.7	93.3	105.3	118.1	126.5	121.0	106.9
May	109.4	105.4	99.0	93.2	104.3	100.4	100.1	93.0	105.6	118.4	126.7	121.3	106.8
June	109.6	106.7	98.5	93.4	104.2	100.7	99.8	92.6	106.1	119.0	127.3	121.6	107.2
July	109.6	106.0	99.4	93.8	103.9	100.7	99.3	93.4	106.0	119.1	127.0	121.2	106.8
August	109.8	107.2	99.0	93.9	104.1	101.0	99.0	93.7	106.1	119.0	127.7	121.7	106.8
September	109.9	107.1	99.0	93.8	103.7	100.7	98.8	93.9	106.3	119.1	127.4	120.9	107.3
October	110.0	107.5	99.0	93.7	103.7	100.5	98.2	94.3	106.7	119.6	127.6	121.5	107.3
November	109.8	106.5	98.9	93.8	103.9	100.6	98.7	94.3	106.6	119.4	127.7	121.2	107.3
December	110.3	107.6	100.2	94.1	103.5	101.0	97.6	94.8	106.7	119.9	128.5	121.6	107.6
2019													
January	110.5	108.3	101.7	94.1	103.7	101.1	97.8	94.0	107.1	120.1	128.8	123.0	107.7
February	110.2	107.3	99.0	93.9	103.6	101.3	97.6	93.8	107.3	120.0	129.0	122.5	107.8
March	110.7	107.9	100.6	93.9	103.5	101.2	97.6	94.4	107.5	120.1	129.3	122.7	108.2
April	110.6	107.8	100.7	93.7	103.7	101.3	97.5	93.8	107.5	120.4	129.6	122.4	108.1
May	110.6	107.8	100.9	93.6	103.4	101.1	97.1	94.6	107.7	120.6	129.8	121.9	108.1
June	110.7	107.4	102.0	93.9	103.7	101.0	97.2	95.5	107.5	120.9	130.0	122.1	108.4
July	110.9	106.2	101.4	93.3	103.5	100.8	97.2	94.8	108.1	120.7	130.3	121.6	108.4
August	111.0	105.2	102.0	93.5	103.5	101.0	96.9	95.6	108.5	121.1	130.6	122.4	108.4
September	111.0	104.8	103.4	93.4	103.8	101.0	97.1	96.0	108.2	120.8	130.4	122.6	108.1
October	111.1	104.7	102.2	92.5	103.6	101.2	96.9	95.8	108.4	120.9	131.0	123.0	108.2
November	111.0	101.8	101.3	93.3	102.9	101.1	95.7	95.6	108.9	121.1	131.4	123.4	108.6
December	111.1	99.7	101.0	93.0	103.7	100.9	97.0	95.7	108.4	121.1	131.7	123.5	108.6
2020													
January	111.4	98.0	102.1	92.9	103.6	100.9	96.3	95.5	108.9	121.0	132.2	124.8	109.3
February	111.9	97.9	103.5	93.4	103.9	100.6	97.2	96.2	109.3	121.8	132.9	125.0	109.5
March	109.7	95.0	101.5	92.4	103.1	100.3	96.4	96.1	109.0	120.6	131.3	111.2	105.8
April	93.2	82.7	84.9	78.1	91.0	91.3	82.7	88.1	105.8	107.5	116.2	60.6	83.9
May	97.3	80.6	94.0	81.2	93.8	92.2	86.7	87.1	106.3	110.1	119.0	74.0	89.7
June	101.0	79.4	96.1	84.3	97.4	93.7	91.5	87.5	106.0	112.2	123.1	86.1	95.1
July	102.1	78.8	96.8	85.9	98.2	93.4	91.9	86.5	106.2	113.2	124.8	88.6	96.7
August	103.4	78.4	97.1	86.7	100.0	94.1	94.1	88.5	106.5	114.6	125.9	92.5	98.3
September	104.6	78.1	97.1	87.5	100.7	94.8	94.5	90.4	107.2	115.3	126.4	96.4	99.4
October	105.6	78.1	97.8	88.3	101.5	95.2	94.8	90.9	107.4	117.2	127.3	98.1	99.7
November	105.6	78.3	98.3	88.1	101.9	95.3	94.8	91.4	107.6	117.8	127.3	96.5	99.6
December	105.2	78.2	99.2	87.9	101.3	95.6	94.0	91.9	108.0	119.1	127.7	91.7	99.4
2021													
January	106.5	77.9	99.5	88.8	102.7	96.8	95.0	93.8	107.9	120.3	128.6	94.8	100.1
February	105.9	76.3	97.0	88.8	102.3	96.0	94.7	93.7	107.8	119.6	127.5	95.8	99.1
March	107.4	79.0	100.6	89.4	103.5	97.2	95.6	93.8	107.9	121.0	128.8	100.3	100.7
April	107.6	78.7	99.4	89.0	104.2	97.6	96.6	94.7	107.8	120.5	128.2	103.5	100.5
May	107.9	79.4	99.2	89.2	104.3	97.8	96.1	95.0	107.8	120.6	128.8	104.2	101.1
June	108.0	80.6	98.4	89.1	104.4	98.1	96.2	95.5	107.7	121.0	128.9	105.9	101.3
July	108.6	80.6	98.9	90.0	104.4	98.7	96.3	96.0	108.1	122.1	129.2	107.3	101.9
August	108.7	80.6	98.9	90.1	104.4	98.3	96.2	96.8	107.9	122.0	129.4	108.5	102.1
September	109.4	82.2	101.1	90.2	104.7	98.9	96.6	96.3	108.3	123.0	129.1	109.0	102.8
October	110.0	81.4	99.7	90.4	105.5	99.3	97.2	97.3	108.3	124.4	129.8	110.5	103.6
November	110.5	82.3	100.9	90.7	105.7	99.1	98.2	97.6	108.4	125.0	130.2	111.5	103.9
December	111.0	83.2	102.0	91.3	106.3	99.4	99.1	98.2	108.9	125.6	130.6	112.5	104.4

Table 10-11. Average Hourly Earnings of All Employees on Private Nonfarm Payrolls by NAICS Supersector

(Dollars, seasonally adjusted.)

Year and month	Total private	Mining and logging	Construc-tion	Manu-facturing	Trade, transportation, and utilities			Information	Financial activities	Profes-sional and business services	Education and health services	Leisure and hospitality	Other services
					Total	Wholesale trade	Retail trade						
2010	22.57	27.39	25.19	23.31	19.65	26.13	15.56	30.53	27.21	27.24	22.81	13.08	20.16
2011	23.04	28.10	25.41	23.69	20.04	26.38	15.86	31.59	27.76	27.76	23.47	13.23	20.50
2012	23.50	28.76	25.73	23.92	20.50	26.89	16.30	31.83	29.26	28.13	24.05	13.37	20.85
2013	23.96	29.73	26.12	24.35	20.97	27.64	16.62	32.90	30.15	28.52	24.44	13.50	21.40
2014	24.47	30.78	26.69	24.81	21.39	28.09	17.00	34.01	30.76	29.28	24.74	13.91	21.98
2015	25.02	31.15	27.37	25.25	21.83	28.65	17.52	35.14	31.52	30.08	25.24	14.32	22.48
2016	25.65	32.09	28.11	25.99	22.33	29.50	17.87	36.65	32.29	30.80	25.75	14.86	23.05
2017	26.40	32.60	28.90	26.57	22.80	30.10	18.16	37.87	34.29	31.59	26.31	15.46	23.97
2018	27.10	32.54	29.88	27.04	23.34	30.46	18.77	39.96	34.76	32.56	27.02	15.98	24.55
2019	28.00	33.81	30.75	27.70	24.22	31.37	19.68	42.18	35.93	33.68	27.63	16.56	25.23
2020	29.30	34.68	31.61	28.75	25.19	32.31	20.82	43.73	37.71	35.13	28.43	17.13	26.56
2021	30.53	34.90	32.81	29.64	26.23	33.60	21.84	44.35	40.05	36.49	29.99	18.28	27.57
2017													
January	26.02	32.87	28.49	26.35	22.59	29.91	18.01	37.00	32.62	31.27	26.01	15.21	23.54
February	26.09	32.54	28.49	26.36	22.62	30.01	18.01	37.48	31.69	31.36	26.11	15.25	26.62
March	30.01	32.54	28.55	26.37	22.63	29.93	18.01	37.50	32.82	31.35	26.06	15.33	23.50
April	26.18	32.45	28.52	26.58	22.64	29.95	18.05	37.95	32.89	31.53	26.17	15.35	23.55
May	26.21	32.39	28.69	26.49	22.73	30.03	18.11	38.06	32.98	31.52	26.20	15.40	23.56
June	26.25	32.48	28.82	26.51	22.76	30.07	18.13	38.30	33.11	31.51	26.22	15.44	23.55
July	23.39	32.95	28.94	26.69	22.86	30.15	18.20	38.56	33.22	31.69	26.39	15.45	23.71
August	26.43	32.57	29.00	26.56	22.89	30.14	18.27	34.48	33.31	31.79	26.44	15.49	23.79
September	26.55	32.58	29.19	26.68	22.95	30.25	18.27	38.90	33.44	32.00	26.50	15.55	23.91
October	26.51	32.66	29.10	26.75	22.90	30.02	18.26	38.30	38.30	31.85	26.48	15.55	23.92
November	26.54	32.57	29.71	26.71	22.96	30.22	18.28	38.47	38.47	31.19	26.51	15.60	23.99
December	26.63	32.59	29.24	26.74	23.04	30.50	18.34	38.59	38.59	32.04	26.58	15.88	24.04
2018													
January	26.71	32.29	29.36	26.84	22.98	30.07	18.42	39.06	34.23	32.10	26.69	15.74	24.25
February	26.75	32.19	29.53	26.84	23.04	30.13	18.47	39.15	34.25	32.10	26.71	15.75	24.25
March	26.84	32.39	29.47	26.89	23.09	30.15	18.49	39.30	34.39	32.25	26.85	15.81	24.41
April	26.90	32.36	29.67	26.95	23.13	30.11	18.60	39.46	34.46	32.28	26.84	15.86	24.46
May	26.99	32.26	29.72	26.97	23.24	30.31	18.70	39.55	34.67	32.40	26.95	15.89	24.51
June	27.05	32.53	29.79	27.03	23.27	30.51	18.68	39.73	34.68	32.50	27.00	15.95	24.52
July	27.11	32.49	29.92	27.03	23.32	30.47	18.76	39.75	34.81	32.61	27.05	16.00	24.55
August	27.23	32.67	30.02	27.11	23.46	30.59	18.87	40.04	34.92	32.82	27.13	16.05	24.59
September	27.30	32.94	30.15	27.14	23.51	30.70	18.92	40.50	35.02	32.82	27.15	16.08	24.68
October	27.35	32.72	30.23	27.16	23.58	30.73	19.02	40.68	34.96	32.89	27.22	16.14	24.74
November	27.43	32.84	30.26	27.24	23.63	30.82	19.07	41.02	35.31	32.93	27.27	16.21	24.80
December	27.53	32.77	30.42	27.33	23.79	30.92	19.23	41.29	35.37	32.99	27.32	16.27	24.88
2019													
January	27.58	32.74	30.32	27.27	23.80	30.83	19.34	41.78	35.39	33.07	27.42	16.28	24.97
February	27.69	32.95	30.45	27.43	23.93	30.99	19.42	41.77	35.51	33.23	27.46	16.38	25.00
March	27.76	32.96	30.50	27.46	24.02	31.26	19.44	41.96	35.54	33.33	27.52	16.40	25.05
April	27.81	33.33	30.63	27.48	24.01	31.12	19.48	41.97	35.73	33.43	27.49	16.45	25.09
May	27.87	33.47	30.70	27.57	24.13	31.30	19.55	42.00	35.82	33.52	27.43	16.51	25.16
June	27.96	33.65	30.74	27.68	24.20	31.38	19.65	41.84	35.91	33.63	27.54	16.55	25.18
July	28.05	34.11	30.75	27.75	24.28	31.39	19.73	42.26	35.93	33.75	27.64	16.59	25.21
August	28.16	34.15	30.87	27.81	24.38	31.62	19.79	42.80	36.19	33.86	27.71	16.62	25.30
September	28.16	34.44	30.87	27.88	24.38	31.56	19.84	42.28	36.03	33.94	27.74	16.67	25.32
October	28.24	34.72	30.98	27.91	24.44	31.66	19.89	42.30	36.14	34.04	27.85	16.70	25.39
November	28.34	34.57	31.09	28.02	24.52	31.74	20.00	42.58	36.40	34.17	27.87	16.76	25.48
December	28.37	34.57	31.15	28.14	24.50	31.61	20.04	42.57	36.53	34.23	27.86	16.77	25.55
2020													
January	28.43	34.24	31.23	28.18	24.60	31.73	20.12	42.85	36.64	34.31	27.86	16.85	25.54
February	28.51	34.41	31.36	28.23	24.65	31.81	20.18	42.95	36.85	34.43	27.90	16.90	25.59
March	28.74	34.43	31.37	28.37	24.76	31.88	20.33	43.25	36.90	34.52	28.05	16.89	25.78
April	30.07	34.74	31.38	29.31	25.62	32.45	21.10	43.66	37.37	35.83	28.41	18.00	27.79
May	29.74	34.87	31.50	29.06	25.34	32.44	20.77	43.62	37.65	35.51	28.52	17.44	27.50
June	29.35	34.94	31.63	28.64	25.02	32.25	20.64	43.51	37.88	35.22	28.51	17.02	26.91
July	29.37	34.84	31.74	28.81	25.30	32.42	20.99	44.09	37.77	35.13	28.55	16.92	26.72
August	29.47	34.80	31.82	28.95	25.41	32.49	21.19	44.00	38.10	35.29	28.64	17.06	26.59
September	29.50	34.89	31.82	28.90	25.55	32.52	21.44	43.93	38.21	35.35	28.70	17.10	26.58
October	29.52	34.89	31.87	28.86	25.41	32.66	21.11	44.77	38.66	35.38	28.72	17.12	26.51
November	29.61	34.47	31.97	28.99	25.47	32.76	21.15	44.40	38.79	35.44	28.86	17.09	26.69
December	29.91	34.67	32.09	29.00	25.67	32.87	21.33	44.28	39.06	35.59	29.45	17.15	26.85
2021													
January	29.93	34.41	32.16	29.07	25.69	32.99	21.37	44.36	39.28	35.59	29.31	17.20	26.90
February	30.04	34.53	32.27	29.18	25.71	33.13	21.32	44.66	39.58	35.77	29.40	17.40	27.10
March	30.06	34.30	32.24	29.20	25.83	33.20	21.50	44.06	39.77	35.80	29.46	17.60	27.22
April	30.20	34.72	32.56	29.35	25.98	33.32	21.64	44.25	39.84	36.08	29.65	17.80	26.99
May	30.36	34.71	32.74	29.53	26.16	33.46	21.82	44.20	40.05	36.27	29.74	18.01	27.30
June	30.52	34.79	32.85	29.62	26.29	33.56	21.90	44.28	40.10	36.50	29.90	18.47	27.55
July	30.67	35.06	32.94	29.80	26.41	33.77	21.95	44.28	40.22	36.71	30.09	18.60	27.71
August	30.76	35.25	33.08	29.86	26.45	33.84	22.01	44.30	40.11	36.87	30.25	18.70	27.94
September	30.92	35.25	33.22	30.02	26.57	33.98	22.14	44.30	40.30	37.01	30.55	18.82	28.03
October	31.11	35.30	33.41	30.14	26.67	34.17	22.22	44.60	40.55	37.29	30.71	19.19	28.21
November	31.23	35.58	33.44	30.24	26.79	34.19	22.33	44.57	40.70	37.48	30.88	19.28	28.29
December	31.38	35.66	33.62	30.35	27.00	34.42	22.50	44.96	40.65	37.68	31.01	19.40	28.42

Table 10-12. Average Weekly Earnings of All Employees on Private Nonfarm Payrolls by NAICS Supersector

(Dollars, seasonally adjusted.)

Year and month	Total private	Mining and logging	Construction	Manu-facturing	Trade, transportation, and utilities			Information	Financial activities	Profes-sional and business services	Education and health services	Leisure and hospitality	Other services
					Total	Wholesale trade	Retail trade						
2010	769.97	1 189.32	952.78	937.34	672.58	994.71	487.66	1 114.65	1 004.14	963.57	744.85	336.83	637.65
2011	791.55	1 250.91	973.85	958.84	692.51	1 019.05	500.75	1 156.56	1 039.70	991.87	767.52	342.67	649.87
2012	810.46	1 263.98	997.01	974.15	709.33	1 041.41	515.81	1 166.45	1 093.00	1 013.76	786.46	349.12	659.49
2013	825.05	1 306.59	1 018.26	994.42	723.49	1 070.34	522.12	1 206.64	1 119.77	1 029.13	798.94	350.89	679.08
2014	845.06	1 380.80	1 040.75	1 016.42	738.34	1 092.30	532.49	1 250.30	1 146.48	1 061.92	808.79	364.19	698.71
2015	864.21	1 371.13	1 040.85	1 016.42	738.22	1 092.30	532.57	1 252.44	1 146.22	1 062.48	827.85	364.07	698.41
2016	881.55	1 389.27	1 100.51	1 057.73	766.83	1 144.62	553.98	1 315.24	1 207.97	1 109.64	845.72	387.19	735.14
2017	957.02	1 457.34	1 127.89	1 083.50	724.65	1 170.88	562.92	1 384.56	1 244.13	1 140.15	865.68	402.63	753.54
2018	934.47	1 495.12	1 171.46	1 106.11	804.72	1 188.67	581.34	1 441.00	1 306.82	1 176.41	889.48	416.25	780.61
2019	962.93	1 563.06	1 207.85	1 122.97	828.17	1 221.40	602.71	1 532.05	1 352.03	1 218.47	911.94	428.81	804.04
2020	1 015.05	1 534.69	1 231.12	1 146.16	863.67	1 245.51	641.99	1 602.29	1 424.46	1 278.12	947.17	435.67	858.02
2021	1 065.32	1 577.07	1 281.96	1 199.73	907.44	1 318.75	675.04	1 644.33	1 506.90	1 341.54	1 004.88	481.15	894.53
2017													
January	896.81	1 433.89	1 118.38	1 074.07	775.87	1 168.44	555.02	1 363.55	1 230.38	1 127.52	858.36	397.28	750.48
February	1 096.74	1 457.22	1 105.27	1 071.43	776.55	1 164.67	557.13	1 363.43	1 221.20	1 136.52	858.03	398.32	749.65
March	1 107.44	1 467.90	1 119.16	1 082.21	781.43	1 168.83	563.16	1 377.95	1 232.63	1 135.44	860.66	400.90	751.88
April	1 106.64	1 472.27	1 124.26	1 077.33	782.60	1 171.56	561.72	1 384.48	1 232.70	1 133.64	861.65	401.18	749.84
May	906.32	1 455.66	1 127.25	1 082.83	784.32	1 176.52	562.65	1 392.83	1 240.80	1 139.32	863.95	402.20	752.52
June	909.42	1 492.64	1 130.38	1 091.21	786.04	1 178.87	563.89	1 397.19	1 243.50	1 141.84	867.57	402.98	736.66
July	907.82	1 461.94	1 129.44	1 079.77	787.07	1 128.47	563.93	1 391.74	1 247.25	1 141.92	869.22	402.22	755.89
August	912.63	1 471.26	1 132.18	1 089.77	789.48	1 183.17	563.62	1 390.08	1 254.75	1 150.20	871.52	404.56	758.26
September	911.60	1 471.26	1 134.12	1 094.08	787.42	1 171.17	565.75	1 393.19	1 261.88	1 146.96	871.19	407.41	757.95
October	915.63	1 415.34	1 141.72	1 092.85	75.32	1 183.45	571.23	1 388.52	1 267.87	1 150.51	874.48	407.44	766.19
November	919.08	1 473.37	1 157.75	1 092.22	794.88	1 190.79	570.37	1 404.56	1 279.90	1 150.56	879.45	411.08	770.20
December	962.74	1 461.16	1 129.08	1 084.34	720.09	1 171.45	563.50	1 386.14	1 246.62	1 141.31	866.92	403.23	754.50
2018													
January	918.82	1 459.51	1 147.98	1 095.07	792.81	1 172.73	572.86	1 398.35	1 287.05	1 152.39	878.10	409.24	768.73
February	922.88	1 477.52	1 160.53	1 100.44	794.88	1 175.07	574.42	1 409.40	1 287.80	1 162.02	881.43	411.08	768.73
March	925.98	1 480.22	1 158.17	1 099.80	796.61	1 178.87	575.04	1 414.80	1 289.63	1 167.45	883.37	412.64	773.80
April	928.05	1 485.32	1 169.00	1 104.95	797.99	1 174.29	576.60	1 424.51	1 295.70	1 165.31	885.72	412.36	777.83
May	931.16	1 487.19	1 173.94	1 100.38	801.78	1 185.12	579.70	1 423.80	1 303.59	1 172.88	889.35	414.73	776.97
June	933.23	1 509.39	1 167.77	1 105.53	805.14	1 192.94	582.82	1 422.33	1 307.44	1 176.50	891.00	416.30	779.74
July	935.30	1 491.29	1 178.85	1 108.23	806.87	1 188.33	583.44	1 431.00	1 305.38	1 180.48	889.95	417.60	780.69
August	939.44	1 506.09	1 176.78	1 111.51	809.37	1 196.07	583.08	1 445.44	1 312.99	1 184.80	895.29	418.91	781.96
September	941.85	1 515.24	1 178.87	1 110.03	808.74	1 197.30	584.63	1 470.15	1 313.25	1 184.80	893.24	418.08	784.82
October	943.58	1 508.39	1 172.92	1 108.13	811.15	1 195.40	585.82	1 472.62	1 321.49	1 190.62	895.54	421.25	789.21
November	943.59	1 507.36	1 171.06	1 111.39	815.24	1 201.98	589.26	1 480.82	1 327.66	1 188.77	897.18	419.84	791.12
December	949.79	1 513.97	1 201.59	1 117.80	816.00	1 205.88	588.44	1 498.83	1 329.91	1 190.94	901.56	423.02	793.67
2019													
January	951.51	1 519.14	1 209.77	1 112.62	816.34	1 202.37	593.74	1 512.44	1 334.20	1 200.44	904.86	424.91	796.54
February	952.54	1 525.59	1 181.46	1 116.40	818.41	1 208.61	594.25	1 512.07	1 338.73	1 202.93	906.18	425.88	795.00
March	957.72	1 535.94	1 201.70	1 117.62	823.89	1 219.14	596.81	1 523.15	1 339.86	1 209.88	908.16	428.04	801.60
April	956.66	1 559.84	1 200.70	1 115.69	823.54	1 213.68	598.04	1 519.31	1 347.02	1 210.17	907.17	426.06	800.37
May	958.73	1 549.66	1 200.37	1 119.34	827.66	1 217.57	600.19	1 528.80	1 346.83	1 213.42	905.19	427.61	802.60
June	961.82	1 558.00	1 208.08	1 123.81	827.64	1 220.68	603.26	1 522.98	1 346.63	1 217.41	908.82	428.65	803.24
July	962.12	1 575.88	1 202.33	1 121.10	827.95	1 217.93	603.74	1 529.81	1 347.38	1 218.38	912.12	428.02	804.20
August	968.70	1 577.73	1 216.28	1 126.31	833.80	1 230.02	605.57	1 562.20	1 364.36	1 225.73	914.43	428.80	804.54
September	968.70	1 591.13	1 225.54	1 129.14	833.80	1 227.68	609.09	1 543.22	1 354.73	1 225.23	915.42	431.75	805.18
October	971.46	1 600.59	1 217.51	1 124.77	835.85	1 234.74	608.63	1 539.72	1 362.48	1 228.84	919.05	430.86	809.94
November	972.06	1 579.85	1 215.62	1 132.01	833.68	1 237.86	606.00	1 545.65	1 372.28	1 233.54	922.50	432.41	812.81
December	973.09	1 583.31	1 214.85	1 136.86	835.45	1 226.47	613.22	1 545.29	1 369.88	1 235.70	919.38	432.67	812.49
2020													
January	975.15	1 564.99	1 219.53	1 139.68	839.20	1 230.74	612.56	1 547.25	1 378.42	1 240.04	919.05	436.93	815.68
February	982.46	1 567.21	1 236.37	1 148.17	845.08	1 232.60	622.29	1 562.35	1 386.69	1 251.26	925.15	435.76	826.85
March	981.74	1 548.15	1 224.99	1 147.76	847.04	1 235.30	625.16	1 570.34	1 387.06	1 247.26	928.29	405.36	817.56
April	1 026.34	1 486.02	1 185.03	1 113.02	865.96	1 224.12	644.47	1 594.32	1 402.48	1 286.30	926.72	435.12	881.31
May	1 030.94	1 502.04	1 223.79	1 123.07	868.13	1 233.48	646.46	1 599.79	1 414.88	1 291.84	936.99	451.70	893.69
June	1 015.86	1 516.85	1 229.63	1 120.22	857.16	1 235.94	640.35	1 588.85	1 417.13	1 279.46	947.20	437.25	868.32
July	1 017.59	1 526.36	1 237.86	1 142.96	863.55	1 240.92	645.01	1 600.04	1 419.78	1 276.55	954.91	430.28	857.39
August	1 022.96	1 530.57	1 241.37	1 156.80	869.51	1 252.41	651.73	1 619.20	1 437.82	1 284.44	957.58	439.26	860.15
September	1 026.95	1 536.32	1 237.02	1 161.38	875.48	1 256.04	658.79	1 615.90	1 446.55	1 288.82	958.58	443.96	864.11
October	1 030.60	1 547.96	1 238.58	1 168.83	875.27	1 263.94	651.37	1 646.48	1 460.12	1 295.14	962.79	444.74	863.46
November	1 031.82	1 543.05	1 246.05	1 168.70	878.37	1 268.59	653.84	1 644.65	1 464.65	1 293.08	966.60	436.22	869.62
December	1 038.22	1 546.81	1 253.16	1 163.30	879.28	1 272.07	651.79	1 638.36	1 477.98	1 303.22	982.22	431.42	878.04
2021													
January	1 047.55	1 562.21	1 260.67	1 177.34	886.31	1 289.91	656.06	1 659.06	1 480.86	1 313.27	987.75	443.76	876.94
February	1 039.38	1 546.94	1 242.40	1 178.87	879.28	1 282.13	650.26	1 661.35	1 492.17	1 305.61	979.02	440.22	872.62
March	1 049.09	1 564.08	1 270.26	1 182.60	891.14	1 298.12	660.05	1 634.63	1 499.33	1 313.86	986.91	461.12	887.37
April	1 053.98	1 569.34	1 269.84	1 185.74	901.51	1 306.14	670.84	1 646.10	1 497.98	1 324.14	987.35	473.48	874.48
May	1 059.56	1 565.42	1 276.86	1 193.01	907.75	1 311.63	674.24	1 639.82	1 505.88	1 327.48	993.32	475.46	887.25
June	1 062.10	1 575.99	1 271.30	1 193.69	909.63	1 315.55	674.52	1 642.79	1 507.76	1 335.90	998.66	487.61	889.87
July	1 067.32	1 581.21	1 278.07	1 206.90	911.15	1 327.16	676.06	1 638.36	1 512.27	1 347.26	1 005.01	491.04	895.03
August	1 067.37	1 575.68	1 283.50	1 206.34	909.88	1 323.14	675.71	1 639.10	1 504.13	1 345.76	1 010.35	491.81	899.67
September	1 076.02	1 600.35	1 312.19	1 212.81	914.01	1 335.41	679.70	1 625.81	1 515.28	1 358.27	1 017.32	493.08	905.37
October	1 082.63	1 581.44	1 296.31	1 214.64	920.12	1 346.30	684.38	1 645.74	1 520.63	1 368.54	1 025.71	504.70	914.00
November	1 086.80	1 601.10	1 304.16	1 218.67	924.26	1 340.25	694.46	1 640.18	1 522.18	1 375.52	1 031.39	505.14	913.77
December	1 092.02	1 601.13	1 317.90	1 226.14	934.20	1 349.26	704.25	1 659.02	1 524.38	1 382.86	1 035.73	506.34	917.97

Table 10-13. Production and Nonsupervisory Workers on Private Nonfarm Payrolls by NAICS Supersector

(Thousands, seasonally adjusted.)

Year and month	Total private	Mining and logging	Construc-tion	Manu-facturing	Trade, transportation, and utilities			Information	Financial activities	Profes-sional and business services	Education and health services	Leisure and hospitality	Other services
					Total	Wholesale trade	Retail trade						
1965	42 302	523	2 906	12 905	10 702	. . .	. . .	1 268	2 434	3 515	3 443	3 443	1 161
1966	44 292	517	2 977	13 703	11 095	. . .	. . .	1 334	2 492	3 715	3 623	3 607	1 230
1967	45 185	501	2 903	13 714	11 369	. . .	. . .	1 365	2 585	3 890	3 818	3 734	1 306
1968	46 519	491	2 986	13 908	11 688	. . .	. . .	1 394	2 700	4 067	4 008	3 898	1 379
1969	48 246	501	3 177	14 147	12 152	. . .	. . .	1 438	2 841	4 252	4 196	4 089	1 452
1970	48 180	496	3 158	13 490	12 388	. . .	. . .	1 422	2 922	4 321	4 305	4 185	1 494
1971	48 151	474	3 238	13 034	12 502	. . .	. . .	1 392	2 978	4 354	4 372	4 286	1 521
1972	49 971	494	3 425	13 497	12 954	2 920	7 257	1 437	3 066	4 518	4 531	4 467	1 583
1973	52 235	502	3 576	14 227	13 437	3 041	7 551	1 504	3 164	4 748	4 747	4 664	1 666
1974	52 846	550	3 469	14 040	13 700	3 148	7 673	1 516	3 217	4 907	4 941	4 766	1 740
1975	51 010	581	2 990	12 576	13 578	3 121	7 714	1 416	3 227	4 939	5 088	4 821	1 795
1976	52 916	606	2 999	13 127	14 038	3 212	8 048	1 459	3 300	5 153	5 309	5 046	1 880
1977	55 207	636	3 209	13 591	14 579	3 323	8 396	1 514	3 452	5 404	5 561	5 284	1 978
1978	58 188	658	3 544	14 150	15 329	3 509	8 861	1 586	3 645	5 717	5 874	5 588	2 099
1979	60 404	737	3 760	14 458	15 843	3 667	9 113	1 650	3 825	5 993	6 158	5 772	2 209
1980	60 377	785	3 623	13 667	15 907	3 708	9 158	1 626	3 957	6 197	6 447	5 850	2 318
1981	60 967	861	3 469	13 492	16 004	3 753	9 238	1 633	4 052	6 396	6 700	5 944	2 414
1982	59 475	834	3 208	12 315	15 821	3 662	9 254	1 564	4 055	6 421	6 822	5 976	2 458
1983	60 018	698	3 240	12 121	15 999	3 639	9 494	1 502	4 128	6 581	7 045	6 161	2 542
1984	63 333	714	3 614	12 821	16 797	3 821	9 964	1 631	4 289	6 918	7 385	6 491	2 672
1985	65 456	686	3 868	12 648	17 427	3 935	10 399	1 660	4 476	7 258	7 789	6 817	2 827
1986	66 825	577	3 984	12 449	17 769	3 941	10 704	1 663	4 698	7 532	8 130	7 066	2 957
1987	68 725	541	4 088	12 537	18 196	3 989	10 986	1 717	4 861	7 859	8 513	7 310	3 104
1988	71 059	545	4 199	12 765	18 771	4 132	11 306	1 775	4 894	8 256	8 985	7 587	3 280
1989	72 960	526	4 257	12 805	19 230	4 235	11 565	1 807	4 931	8 648	9 465	7 833	3 459
1990	73 721	538	4 115	12 669	19 032	4 198	11 308	1 866	4 973	8 889	9 784	8 299	3 555
1991	72 567	515	3 674	12 164	18 640	4 122	11 008	1 871	4 914	8 748	10 257	8 247	3 539
1992	72 854	478	3 546	12 020	18 506	4 071	10 931	1 871	4 924	8 971	10 607	8 406	3 526
1993	74 671	462	3 704	12 070	18 752	4 072	11 104	1 896	5 084	9 451	10 961	8 667	3 623
1994	77 478	461	3 973	12 361	19 392	4 196	11 502	1 928	5 220	10 078	11 397	8 979	3 689
1995	79 943	458	4 113	12 567	19 984	4 361	11 841	2 007	5 199	10 645	11 829	9 330	3 812
1996	81 888	461	4 325	12 532	20 325	4 423	12 057	2 096	5 322	11 161	12 195	9 565	3 907
1997	84 313	479	4 546	12 673	20 698	4 523	12 274	2 181	5 482	11 896	12 566	9 780	4 013
1998	86 516	473	4 807	12 729	21 059	4 605	12 440	2 217	5 692	12 566	12 903	9 947	4 124
1999	88 647	438	5 105	12 524	21 576	4 673	12 772	2 351	5 818	13 184	13 217	10 216	4 219
2000	90 543	446	5 295	12 428	21 965	4 686	13 040	2 502	5 819	13 790	13 487	10 516	4 296
2001	90 202	457	5 332	11 677	21 709	4 555	12 952	2 531	5 888	13 588	13 986	10 662	4 373
2002	88 645	436	5 196	10 768	21 337	4 474	12 774	2 398	5 964	13 049	14 471	10 576	4 449
2003	87 938	420	5 123	10 189	21 078	4 396	12 655	2 347	6 052	12 911	14 726	10 666	4 426
2004	89 212	440	5 309	10 072	21 319	4 444	12 788	2 371	6 052	13 287	14 984	10 955	4 425
2005	91 401	473	5 611	10 060	21 830	4 584	13 030	2 386	6 127	13 854	15 359	11 263	4 438
2006	93 727	519	5 903	10 137	22 166	4 724	13 110	2 399	6 312	14 446	15 783	11 568	4 494
2007	95 203	547	5 883	9 975	22 546	4 851	13 317	2 403	6 365	14 784	16 261	11 861	4 578
2008	94 610	574	5 521	9 629	22 337	4 822	13 134	2 388	6 320	14 585	16 777	11 873	4 606
2009	89 556	510	4 567	8 322	21 116	4 506	12 472	2 240	6 066	13 520	17 166	11 560	4 488
2010	88 875	525	4 172	8 077	20 874	4 378	12 425	2 170	5 942	13 699	17 452	11 507	4 458
2011	90 537	594	4 184	8 228	21 234	4 443	12 647	2 148	5 900	14 251	17 736	11 772	4 491
2012	92 715	641	4 246	8 400	21 617	4 562	12 793	2 164	5 986	14 802	18 165	12 154	4 541
2013	94 580	639	4 401	8 412	21 882	4 632	12 921	2 178	6 064	15 351	18 519	12 579	4 558
2014	96 794	658	4 631	8 568	22 281	4 707	13 113	2 221	6 157	15 795	18 859	12 981	4 642
2015	98 783	592	4 866	8 683	22 629	4 702	13 264	2 226	6 278	16 133	19 337	13 360	4 678
2016	100 531	476	5 062	8 666	22 882	4 696	13 424	2 235	429	16 479	19 839	13 749	4 715
2017	102 331	504	5 186	8 728	23 121	4 742	13 491	2 205	6 569	16 875	20 320	14 047	4 771
2018	104 310	544	5 437	8 899	23 386	4 698	13 521	2 275	6 638	17 121	20 788	14 384	4 839
2019	105 617	540	5 583	8 975	23 438	4 739	13 349	2 301	6 768	17 335	21 233	14 568	4 876
2020	98 013	440	5 385	8 433	22 426	4 487	12 663	2 140	6 678	16 265	20 348	11 503	4 395
2021	101 069	418	5 483	8 583	23 403	4 515	13 141	2 243	6 622	17 070	20 670	12 164	4 412
2020													
January	106 444	496	5 672	8 916	23 555	4 724	13 313	2 334	6 848	17 390	21 528	14 804	4 901
February	106 651	496	5 709	8 932	23 575	4 721	13 323	2 338	6 870	17 414	21 572	14 846	4 899
March	105 083	478	5 598	8 860	23 441	4 702	13 215	2 327	6 843	17 260	21 350	14 125	4 801
April	87 038	433	4 726	7 776	20 550	4 346	11 232	2 091	6 589	15 158	18 970	7 121	3 624
May	90 011	420	5 155	7 962	20 901	4 368	11 579	2 047	6 585	15 307	19 314	8 478	3 842
June	94 400	422	5 321	8 326	21 796	4 404	12 344	2 051	6 594	15 596	19 806	10 316	4 172
July	95 920	421	5 374	8 354	22 032	4 394	12 548	2 058	6 586	15 764	20 049	10 963	4 319
August	96 836	421	5 378	8 364	22 371	4 409	12 791	2 065	6 602	15 940	20 226	11 097	4 372
September	97 686	422	5 380	8 390	22 491	4 436	12 832	2 103	6 628	16 079	20 279	11 489	4 425
October	98 541	421	5 415	8 406	22 684	4 444	12 923	2 088	6 648	16 322	20 333	11 755	4 469
November	98 926	428	5 432	8 441	22 859	4 447	12 921	2 084	6 671	16 414	20 381	11 753	4 463
December	98 617	426	5 463	8 471	22 855	4 453	12 936	2 092	6 667	16 534	20 370	11 287	4 452
2021													
January	98 703	392	5 467	8 457	23 033	4 458	12 962	2 163	6 610	16 689	20 474	11 106	4 312
February	99 159	393	5 409	8 477	23 093	4 463	12 996	2 176	6 607	16 704	20 517	11 478	4 305
March	99 573	403	5 497	8 518	23 177	4 482	13 022	2 191	6 610	16 752	20 561	11 563	4 301
April	99 820	408	5 466	8 467	23 194	4 487	13 048	2 203	6 611	16 789	20 592	11 777	4 313
May	100 217	414	5 456	8 502	23 249	4 501	13 088	2 214	6 608	16 863	20 633	11 940	4 338
June	100 715	419	5 451	8 528	23 366	4 512	13 158	2 235	6 596	16 953	20 668	12 113	4 386
July	101 314	425	5 449	8 584	23 456	4 530	13 185	2 258	6 616	17 077	20 703	12 311	4 435
August	101 731	428	5 461	8 626	23 495	4 531	13 196	2 281	6 623	17 207	20 723	12 410	4 477
September	102 152	428	5 482	8 641	23 579	4 535	13 238	2 285	6 628	17 349	20 725	12 538	4 497
October	102 682	431	5 502	8 693	23 648	4 544	13 264	2 291	6 639	17 506	20 781	12 669	4 522
November	103 155	435	5 563	8 731	23 738	4 562	13 253	2 308	6 652	17 462	20 809	12 936	4 521
December	103 605	444	5 588	8 771	23 811	4 576	13 286	2 312	6 669	17 491	20 856	13 122	4 541

. . . = Not available.

Table 10-14. Average Weekly Hours of Production and Nonsupervisory Workers on Private Nonfarm Payrolls by NAICS Supersector

(Hours per week, seasonally adjusted.)

Year and month	Total private	Mining and logging	Construction	Manufacturing Average weekly hours	Manufacturing Overtime hours	Trade, transportation, and utilities Total	Trade, transportation, and utilities Wholesale trade	Trade, transportation, and utilities Retail trade	Information	Financial activities	Professional and business services	Education and health services	Leisure and hospitality	Other services
1965	38.6	43.7	37.9	41.2	3.6	39.6	...	...	38.3	37.1	37.3	35.2	32.5	36.1
1966	38.5	44.1	38.1	41.4	3.9	39.1	...	...	38.3	37.2	37.0	34.9	31.9	35.8
1967	37.9	43.9	38.1	40.6	3.3	38.5	...	...	37.6	36.9	36.6	34.5	31.3	35.4
1968	37.7	44.0	37.8	40.7	3.6	38.2	...	...	37.6	36.8	36.3	34.1	30.8	35.0
1969	37.5	44.3	38.4	40.6	3.6	37.9	...	...	37.6	36.9	36.3	34.1	30.4	35.0
1970	37.0	43.9	37.8	39.8	2.9	37.6	...	...	37.2	36.6	35.9	33.8	30.0	34.7
1971	36.7	43.7	37.6	39.9	2.9	37.4	...	...	37.0	36.4	35.5	33.3	29.9	34.2
1972	36.9	44.1	37.0	40.6	3.4	37.4	39.8	35.1	37.3	36.4	35.5	33.3	29.7	34.2
1973	36.9	43.8	37.2	40.7	3.8	37.2	39.6	34.8	37.3	36.4	35.5	33.3	29.4	34.1
1974	36.4	43.7	37.1	40.0	3.2	36.8	39.2	34.3	37.0	36.3	35.3	33.1	29.1	33.9
1975	36.0	43.7	36.9	39.5	2.6	36.4	39.1	34.0	36.6	36.2	35.1	33.0	28.8	33.8
1976	36.0	44.2	37.3	40.1	3.1	36.3	39.1	33.8	36.7	36.2	34.9	32.7	28.5	33.6
1977	35.9	44.7	37.0	40.3	3.4	36.0	39.2	33.3	36.8	36.2	34.7	32.5	28.1	33.4
1978	35.8	44.9	37.3	40.4	3.6	35.6	39.2	32.7	36.8	36.1	34.6	32.3	27.7	33.2
1979	35.6	44.7	37.5	40.2	3.3	35.4	39.2	32.4	36.6	35.9	34.4	32.2	27.4	33.0
1980	35.2	44.9	37.5	39.6	2.8	35.0	38.8	31.9	36.4	36.0	34.3	32.1	27.0	33.0
1981	35.2	45.1	37.4	39.8	2.8	35.0	38.9	31.9	36.3	36.0	34.3	32.1	26.9	33.0
1982	34.7	44.1	37.2	38.9	2.3	34.6	38.7	31.7	35.8	36.0	34.2	32.1	26.8	33.0
1983	34.9	43.9	37.6	40.1	2.9	34.6	38.8	31.6	36.2	35.9	34.4	32.1	26.8	33.0
1984	35.1	44.6	38.2	40.6	3.4	34.7	38.9	31.6	36.6	36.2	34.3	32.0	26.7	32.9
1985	34.9	44.6	38.2	40.5	3.3	34.4	38.8	31.2	36.5	36.1	34.2	31.9	26.4	32.8
1986	34.7	43.6	37.9	40.7	3.4	34.1	38.7	31.0	36.4	36.1	34.3	32.0	26.2	32.9
1987	34.7	43.5	38.2	40.9	3.7	34.1	38.5	31.0	36.5	36.0	34.3	32.0	26.3	32.8
1988	34.6	43.3	38.2	41.0	3.8	33.8	38.5	30.9	36.1	35.6	34.2	32.0	26.3	32.9
1989	34.5	44.1	38.3	40.9	3.8	33.8	38.4	30.7	36.1	35.6	34.2	32.0	26.1	32.9
1990	34.3	45.0	38.3	40.5	3.9	33.7	38.4	30.6	35.8	35.5	34.2	31.9	26.0	32.8
1991	34.1	45.3	38.1	40.4	3.8	33.6	38.5	30.4	35.6	35.4	34.0	31.9	25.6	32.7
1992	34.2	44.6	38.0	40.7	4.0	33.8	38.6	30.7	35.8	35.6	34.0	32.0	25.7	32.6
1993	34.3	44.9	38.4	41.1	4.4	34.1	38.5	30.7	36.0	35.5	34.0	32.0	25.9	32.6
1994	34.5	45.3	38.8	41.7	5.0	34.3	38.8	30.9	36.0	35.5	34.1	32.0	26.0	32.7
1995	34.3	45.3	38.8	41.3	4.7	34.1	38.6	30.8	36.0	35.5	34.1	32.0	25.9	32.6
1996	34.3	46.0	38.9	41.3	4.8	34.1	38.7	30.7	36.3	35.5	34.1	31.9	25.9	32.5
1997	34.5	46.2	38.9	41.7	5.1	34.2	38.8	30.9	36.3	35.8	34.3	32.2	26.1	32.7
1998	34.5	44.9	38.8	41.4	4.9	34.1	38.7	30.9	36.6	36.0	34.3	32.2	26.2	32.6
1999	34.3	44.2	39.0	41.4	4.9	33.9	38.6	30.8	36.7	35.8	34.4	32.1	26.1	32.5
2000	34.3	44.4	39.2	41.3	4.7	33.8	38.8	30.7	36.8	35.9	34.5	32.2	26.1	32.5
2001	33.9	44.6	38.7	40.3	4.0	33.5	38.4	30.7	36.9	35.8	34.2	32.3	25.8	32.3
2002	33.9	43.2	38.4	40.5	4.2	33.6	38.0	30.9	36.5	35.6	34.2	32.4	25.8	32.1
2003	33.7	43.6	38.4	40.4	4.2	33.5	37.9	30.9	36.2	35.6	34.1	32.3	25.6	31.4
2004	33.7	44.5	38.3	40.8	4.6	33.5	37.8	30.7	36.3	35.6	34.2	32.4	25.7	31.0
2005	33.8	45.6	38.6	40.7	4.6	33.4	37.7	30.6	36.5	36.0	34.3	32.6	25.7	30.9
2006	33.9	45.6	39.0	41.1	4.4	33.4	38.0	30.5	36.6	35.8	34.6	32.5	25.7	30.9
2007	33.8	45.9	39.0	41.2	4.2	33.3	38.2	30.2	36.5	35.9	34.8	32.5	25.5	30.9
2008	33.6	45.1	38.5	40.8	3.7	33.1	38.3	30.0	36.7	35.9	34.8	32.4	25.2	30.8
2009	33.1	43.2	37.6	39.8	2.9	32.8	37.7	29.9	36.6	36.1	34.7	32.2	24.8	30.5
2010	33.4	44.6	38.4	41.1	3.8	33.3	37.9	30.2	36.3	36.2	35.1	32.0	24.8	30.7
2011	33.6	46.7	39.0	41.4	4.1	33.7	38.5	30.5	36.2	36.4	35.2	32.2	24.8	30.8
2012	33.7	46.6	39.3	41.7	4.2	33.8	38.7	30.6	36.0	36.8	35.3	32.3	25.0	30.7
2013	33.7	45.9	39.6	41.8	4.3	33.7	38.7	30.2	35.9	36.7	35.4	32.1	25.0	30.8
2014	33.7	47.3	39.6	42.0	4.5	33.6	38.6	30.0	35.9	36.7	35.6	32.0	25.1	30.7
2015	33.7	45.8	39.6	41.8	4.3	33.7	38.6	30.1	35.7	37.1	35.5	32.1	25.1	30.7
2016	33.6	45.3	39.7	41.9	4.3	33.5	38.6	29.7	35.5	36.9	35.4	32.2	24.9	30.8
2017	33.7	46.1	39.7	41.9	4.3	33.8	39.0	30.2	35.8	37.0	35.4	32.2	24.9	30.7
2018	33.8	46.8	40.0	42.2	4.6	33.9	38.9	30.4	35.6	37.0	35.4	32.2	24.9	30.8
2019	33.6	46.9	39.8	41.6	4.3	33.8	38.7	30.3	35.3	36.9	35.4	32.2	24.7	30.8
2020	33.9	44.9	39.2	40.7	3.7	34.1	38.2	30.8	36.0	37.1	35.8	32.5	24.1	31.2
2021	34.2	46.5	39.5	41.4	4.1	34.3	38.8	30.8	36.5	37.2	36.2	32.6	24.9	31.4
2020														
January	33.6	46.0	39.6	41.3	3.9	34.0	38.5	30.5	35.2	36.9	35.5	32.2	24.7	30.9
February	33.7	45.9	39.8	41.6	4.0	34.0	38.5	30.5	35.4	36.8	35.6	32.3	24.6	30.9
March	33.4	45.6	39.4	41.3	3.9	34.0	38.3	30.6	35.5	36.8	35.5	32.3	22.7	30.6
April	33.5	43.0	38.2	38.4	2.8	33.6	37.0	30.5	35.6	36.9	35.2	31.8	22.2	31.2
May	34.1	43.8	39.4	39.4	3.2	34.3	37.6	31.3	35.8	36.9	35.8	32.1	24.3	31.8
June	34.0	44.1	39.4	39.9	3.4	34.1	38.0	30.9	36.1	36.9	35.8	32.4	24.2	31.5
July	34.0	44.3	39.5	40.7	3.7	34.2	38.1	31.0	35.8	37.1	35.9	32.5	24.0	31.2
August	34.2	45.0	39.4	41.0	3.7	34.2	38.2	31.0	36.3	37.1	36.0	32.7	24.5	31.4
September	34.2	44.9	39.1	41.2	3.8	34.4	38.5	31.0	36.4	37.2	36.0	32.7	24.8	31.5
October	34.3	45.3	39.3	41.3	4.0	34.5	38.5	31.0	36.4	37.3	36.1	32.8	24.6	31.4
November	34.3	45.9	39.4	41.3	4.0	34.5	38.4	31.1	36.8	37.2	36.2	32.8	24.4	31.5
December	34.2	45.8	39.7	41.4	4.1	34.0	38.5	30.4	36.5	37.3	36.2	32.9	24.0	31.4
2021														
January	34.4	46.5	39.9	41.6	4.1	34.5	38.8	31.0	36.5	37.5	36.4	32.9	24.6	31.5
February	34.1	45.3	38.9	41.5	4.2	34.3	38.5	30.9	36.5	37.4	36.0	32.6	24.1	31.1
March	34.4	46.7	39.9	41.7	4.1	34.5	38.9	31.0	36.3	37.4	36.3	32.7	24.8	31.6
April	34.4	46.7	39.7	41.6	4.3	34.6	38.9	31.0	36.7	37.4	36.2	32.7	25.2	31.5
May	34.3	46.5	39.6	41.5	4.2	34.4	38.9	30.9	36.9	37.4	36.3	32.7	25.1	31.5
June	34.3	47.0	39.1	41.3	4.1	34.3	38.9	30.7	36.7	37.4	36.3	32.8	25.1	31.5
July	34.3	46.4	39.5	41.5	4.1	34.4	39.1	30.8	36.7	37.4	36.3	32.7	25.2	31.4
August	34.2	46.2	39.4	41.4	4.1	34.3	38.9	30.7	36.9	37.3	36.2	32.6	25.0	31.2
September	34.3	47.2	40.4	41.4	4.1	34.3	39.1	30.7	36.5	37.3	36.4	32.6	25.0	31.4
October	34.2	46.7	39.5	41.3	4.0	34.4	39.2	30.8	36.3	37.4	36.3	32.6	25.0	31.4
November	34.2	47.0	39.7	41.4	4.1	34.2	39.1	30.7	36.5	37.3	36.4	32.5	25.0	31.4
December	34.1	46.4	39.9	41.4	4.1	34.1	39.1	30.6	36.5	37.4	36.3	32.6	24.9	31.4

... = Not available.

Table 10-15. Indexes of Aggregate Weekly Hours of Production and Nonsupervisory Workers on Private Nonfarm Payrolls by NAICS Supersector

(2002 = 100, seasonally adjusted.)

Year and month	Total private	Mining and logging	Construction	Manu-facturing	Trade, transportation, and utilities			Information	Financial activities	Profes-sional and business services	Education and health services	Leisure and hospitality	Other services
					Total	Wholesale trade	Retail trade						
1965	54.4	121.6	55.2	122.1	59.1	. . .	. . .	55.5	42.6	29.5	25.9	41.0	29.4
1966	56.8	121.1	56.8	130.2	60.6	. . .	. . .	58.3	43.6	30.9	27.0	42.2	30.9
1967	57.0	117.0	55.4	127.8	61.2	. . .	. . .	58.6	44.9	31.9	28.1	42.9	32.4
1968	58.4	114.9	56.5	130.1	62.4	. . .	. . .	59.9	46.8	33.1	29.1	44.0	33.9
1969	60.3	118.1	61.0	131.9	64.4	. . .	. . .	61.8	49.4	34.6	30.5	45.6	35.6
1970	59.4	115.7	59.8	123.3	65.0	. . .	. . .	60.4	50.3	34.8	31.0	46.1	36.3
1971	59.0	109.9	61.0	119.3	65.2	. . .	. . .	58.7	51.1	34.7	31.1	46.9	36.5
1972	61.4	115.6	63.4	125.7	67.6	68.4	64.4	61.1	52.5	36.0	32.2	48.5	37.9
1973	64.2	117.0	66.7	132.9	69.7	71.0	66.4	64.1	54.2	37.8	33.7	50.3	39.9
1974	64.2	127.7	64.5	129.0	70.3	72.7	66.7	64.0	54.9	38.8	34.9	50.8	41.4
1975	61.2	134.9	55.2	113.9	69.1	71.8	66.4	59.1	55.0	38.9	35.8	50.9	42.6
1976	63.5	142.4	56.0	120.8	71.1	73.9	68.8	61.2	56.2	40.4	37.0	52.8	44.3
1977	66.1	151.1	59.4	125.8	73.2	76.7	70.7	63.5	58.8	42.1	38.5	54.4	46.3
1978	69.3	156.9	66.2	131.3	76.3	81.0	73.4	66.6	62.0	44.3	40.4	56.6	48.8
1979	71.6	175.2	70.6	133.3	78.4	84.6	74.7	69.0	64.7	46.3	42.2	57.9	51.2
1980	70.8	187.2	68.0	124.4	77.8	84.8	74.0	67.5	67.0	47.7	44.1	57.8	53.6
1981	71.4	206.2	64.9	123.1	78.1	86.0	74.5	67.7	68.6	49.2	45.8	58.7	55.8
1982	68.8	195.5	59.7	109.9	76.5	83.5	74.2	64.0	68.6	49.3	46.7	58.7	56.8
1983	69.8	162.8	61.0	111.6	77.3	83.3	76.0	62.1	69.8	50.7	48.3	60.4	58.9
1984	74.1	169.3	69.1	119.6	81.4	87.5	79.8	68.0	73.0	53.3	50.4	63.6	61.7
1985	76.0	162.7	73.9	117.5	83.7	89.9	82.2	69.1	76.1	55.7	53.0	66.0	65.0
1986	77.3	133.5	75.5	116.3	84.6	89.9	83.9	69.1	79.9	57.9	55.4	67.9	68.1
1987	79.5	125.2	78.1	117.8	86.7	90.5	86.3	71.5	82.3	60.4	58.0	70.5	71.5
1988	81.9	125.6	80.4	120.3	88.7	93.6	88.5	73.1	82.0	63.4	61.3	73.0	75.6
1989	83.9	123.2	81.7	120.3	90.7	95.9	90.0	74.4	82.6	66.4	64.6	74.9	79.7
1990	84.2	128.6	78.8	117.7	89.7	95.0	87.5	76.2	83.1	68.1	66.6	78.9	81.8
1991	82.4	123.8	70.1	112.8	87.6	93.4	84.8	76.1	82.0	66.7	69.7	77.3	81.1
1992	83.0	113.3	67.5	112.4	87.4	92.5	85.1	76.5	82.4	68.4	72.4	79.2	80.6
1993	85.3	110.3	71.3	113.9	89.2	92.5	86.3	78.0	84.9	72.0	74.8	82.1	82.8
1994	89.1	111.0	77.3	118.3	92.7	95.8	89.8	79.2	87.2	77.0	77.8	85.5	84.5
1995	91.4	110.3	79.9	119.0	95.2	99.3	92.3	82.5	86.9	81.3	80.6	88.5	87.0
1996	93.6	112.7	84.3	118.8	96.7	100.7	93.7	86.9	89.0	85.3	82.9	90.7	89.1
1997	97.0	117.6	88.6	121.4	98.9	103.4	95.9	90.4	92.3	91.5	86.2	93.4	91.9
1998	99.4	112.8	93.4	121.1	100.4	104.9	97.2	92.6	96.4	96.7	88.6	95.5	94.3
1999	101.4	102.9	99.7	119.0	102.0	106.3	99.5	98.5	98.0	101.6	90.4	97.8	96.2
2000	103.5	105.1	104.0	117.7	103.6	107.1	101.3	105.0	98.4	106.5	92.6	100.5	97.8
2001	102.0	108.3	103.2	108.1	101.6	102.9	100.5	106.7	99.2	104.0	96.5	100.6	99.0
2002	100.0	100.0	100.0	100.0	100.0	100.0	100.0	100.0	100.0	100.0	100.0	100.0	100.0
2003	98.7	97.4	98.4	94.5	98.6	98.0	98.9	97.0	101.3	98.7	101.7	100.0	97.4
2004	100.2	104.0	101.7	94.3	99.6	98.7	99.4	98.2	101.3	101.8	103.8	103.0	96.1
2005	102.8	114.7	108.3	93.9	101.6	101.6	100.8	99.4	103.7	106.4	107.0	106.2	96.2
2006	105.8	125.8	115.4	95.6	103.2	105.5	101.1	100.2	106.3	112.2	109.6	108.8	97.4
2007	107.4	133.5	114.7	94.4	104.8	108.9	101.8	100.1	107.6	115.4	113.2	110.8	99.3
2008	106.0	137.6	106.5	90.2	103.2	108.3	99.8	100.0	106.8	114.0	116.5	109.7	99.5
2009	98.8	117.2	85.9	76.1	96.7	99.5	94.3	93.5	103.1	105.3	118.3	105.1	96.0
2010	99.0	124.5	80.2	76.2	96.8	97.4	95.0	90.0	101.3	107.7	119.8	104.6	96.0
2011	101.4	147.4	81.7	78.3	99.7	100.2	97.7	88.9	101.1	112.6	122.3	106.9	96.8
2012	104.3	158.7	83.6	80.3	101.8	103.5	98.9	88.9	103.7	117.3	125.4	111.3	97.7
2013	106.1	155.0	87.7	80.9	102.6	104.8	98.8	89.8	104.7	121.4	126.6	115.2	98.7
2014	108.6	164.3	92.0	82.6	104.4	106.4	99.5	90.5	106.5	125.9	128.5	119.3	99.9
2015	110.9	144.1	96.5	83.3	106.3	106.4	101.0	90.8	109.6	128.3	132.3	122.7	100.7
2016	112.5	113.4	100.9	83.3	106.9	106.2	101.1	91.4	111.6	130.2	136.1	125.6	101.8
2017	114.9	120.2	104.0	84.0	109.2	107.8	103.1	92.6	114.3	132.6	139.8	128.7	102.9
2018	117.2	134.5	108.8	86.1	110.8	108.3	103.6	93.0	116.0	135.2	142.7	130.6	104.4
2019	118.3	133.3	111.2	85.6	110.9	108.5	102.1	93.0	117.5	137.0	145.7	131.9	105.3
2020	110.7	101.5	105.4	78.8	107.4	101.6	98.8	88.7	116.2	130.7	141.1	99.9	95.1
2021	115.3	103.2	108.5	81.6	112.3	104.1	102.4	93.4	116.1	138.1	143.9	111.1	97.1
2020													
January	119.0	119.3	112.0	84.5	111.7	107.8	102.3	93.4	118.7	137.2	148.0	134.4	106.1
February	119.6	120.3	113.3	85.1	111.7	107.8	102.4	94.2	119.1	137.2	148.7	134.7	106.0
March	116.9	117.3	110.8	84.1	111.2	106.9	102.0	94.3	118.6	135.5	147.1	118.4	103.0
April	97.4	99.6	90.6	68.7	97.0	95.6	87.0	85.2	114.3	119.1	128.9	58.8	78.8
May	102.3	97.3	101.7	71.9	100.8	97.5	92.1	84.2	114.3	122.7	132.4	74.5	85.0
June	106.8	96.1	104.4	76.1	104.4	99.1	96.7	85.3	114.5	125.7	137.0	88.6	91.0
July	108.3	94.4	104.6	77.8	106.2	99.2	98.9	84.9	114.9	127.8	138.9	92.2	93.0
August	110.1	94.9	105.2	78.6	108.0	99.8	101.0	86.6	115.0	130.0	141.0	95.5	94.6
September	111.2	94.7	104.7	79.2	109.0	101.0	101.0	88.3	115.6	131.5	141.6	100.7	96.0
October	112.3	95.1	106.3	79.5	109.8	101.1	101.2	88.2	116.0	133.7	142.5	101.6	96.3
November	112.8	96.3	107.1	79.8	110.7	101.0	101.6	89.3	115.9	134.3	142.9	102.0	95.9
December	112.2	96.1	108.5	80.3	109.3	101.5	99.4	89.0	116.2	134.5	143.5	96.6	95.1
2021													
January	113.1	96.9	109.2	80.8	111.1	102.6	101.7	90.1	116.7	135.8	143.6	100.1	95.3
February	112.7	94.6	105.4	80.8	110.8	102.0	101.6	90.7	116.3	134.5	142.6	101.3	93.9
March	114.1	100.0	109.8	81.5	111.8	103.5	102.2	90.8	116.4	136.0	143.4	105.0	95.3
April	114.4	101.3	108.7	80.9	112.2	103.6	102.4	92.3	116.4	135.9	143.6	108.7	95.3
May	114.5	102.3	108.2	81.0	111.8	103.9	102.3	93.2	116.3	136.9	143.9	109.8	95.8
June	115.1	104.6	106.7	80.9	112.1	104.2	102.2	93.6	116.1	137.6	144.5	111.4	96.9
July	115.8	104.8	107.8	81.8	112.8	105.1	102.8	94.6	116.5	138.6	144.3	113.6	97.7
August	115.9	105.1	107.7	82.0	112.7	104.6	102.5	96.1	116.3	139.3	144.0	113.6	98.0
September	116.8	107.4	110.9	82.1	113.1	105.2	102.8	95.2	116.4	141.2	144.1	114.8	99.0
October	117.0	107.0	108.8	82.4	113.8	105.7	103.4	94.9	116.9	142.1	144.4	116.0	99.6
November	117.6	108.6	110.6	83.0	113.5	105.9	103.0	96.2	116.8	142.1	144.2	118.5	99.6
December	117.7	109.5	111.6	83.4	113.5	106.2	102.9	96.3	117.4	142.0	145.0	119.7	100.0

. . . = Not available.

Table 10-16. Average Hourly Earnings of Production and Nonsupervisory Workers on Private Nonfarm Payrolls by NAICS Supersector

(Dollars, seasonally adjusted.)

Year and month	Total private	Mining and logging	Construc-tion	Manu-facturing	Trade, transportation, and utilities			Information	Financial activities	Profes-sional and business services	Education and health services	Leisure and hospitality	Other services
					Total	Wholesale trade	Retail trade						
1965	2.63	2.87	3.23	2.49	2.94	. . .	. . .	4.47	2.38	3.28	2.12	1.17	1.25
1966	2.73	3.00	3.41	2.60	3.04	. . .	. . .	4.56	2.47	3.39	2.23	1.26	1.37
1967	2.85	3.14	3.63	2.71	3.15	. . .	. . .	4.68	2.58	3.51	2.36	1.37	1.49
1968	3.03	3.30	3.92	2.89	3.32	. . .	. . .	4.85	2.75	3.65	2.49	1.53	1.62
1969	3.22	3.54	4.30	3.07	3.48	. . .	. . .	5.05	2.92	3.84	2.68	1.69	1.81
1970	3.41	3.77	4.74	3.24	3.65	. . .	. . .	5.25	3.07	4.04	2.88	1.82	2.01
1971	3.63	3.99	5.17	3.45	3.86	. . .	. . .	5.53	3.23	4.26	3.11	1.95	2.24
1972	3.91	4.28	5.55	3.70	4.23	4.57	3.52	5.87	3.37	4.50	3.33	2.08	2.46
1973	4.14	4.59	5.89	3.97	4.46	4.79	3.69	6.17	3.55	4.72	3.54	2.20	2.67
1974	4.44	5.09	6.29	4.31	4.74	5.10	3.92	6.52	3.80	5.01	3.82	2.40	2.95
1975	4.74	5.68	6.78	4.71	5.01	5.44	4.15	6.92	4.08	5.29	4.09	2.58	3.21
1976	5.06	6.19	7.17	5.10	5.31	5.74	4.37	7.37	4.30	5.60	4.39	2.78	3.51
1977	5.44	6.70	7.56	5.55	5.66	6.11	4.66	7.84	4.58	5.95	4.72	3.03	3.84
1978	5.88	7.44	8.11	6.05	6.10	6.60	5.01	8.34	4.93	6.32	5.07	3.33	4.19
1979	6.34	8.20	8.71	6.57	6.55	7.11	5.35	8.86	5.31	6.71	5.44	3.63	4.56
1980	6.84	8.97	9.37	7.15	7.03	7.67	5.72	9.47	5.82	7.22	5.93	3.98	5.05
1981	7.43	9.89	10.24	7.87	7.54	8.27	6.10	10.21	6.34	7.80	6.49	4.36	5.61
1982	7.86	10.64	11.04	8.36	7.90	8.80	6.35	10.76	6.82	8.30	7.00	4.63	6.11
1983	8.20	11.14	11.36	8.70	8.22	9.25	6.61	11.18	7.32	8.70	7.39	4.89	6.51
1984	8.49	11.54	11.56	9.05	8.44	9.59	6.74	11.50	7.65	8.98	7.66	4.99	6.79
1985	8.73	11.87	11.75	9.40	8.59	9.86	6.84	11.81	7.97	9.28	7.97	5.10	7.10
1986	8.92	12.14	11.92	9.60	8.73	10.05	6.94	12.08	8.37	9.56	8.24	5.20	7.38
1987	9.14	12.17	12.15	9.77	8.91	10.30	7.03	12.36	8.73	9.86	8.56	5.30	7.69
1988	9.44	12.45	12.52	10.05	9.14	10.69	7.24	12.63	9.07	10.23	8.95	5.50	8.08
1989	9.81	12.90	12.98	10.35	9.45	11.10	7.47	12.99	9.54	10.70	9.45	5.76	8.58
1990	10.20	13.40	13.42	10.77	9.82	11.55	7.71	13.40	9.98	11.15	9.98	6.02	9.08
1991	10.51	13.82	13.65	11.13	10.07	11.92	7.89	13.90	10.43	11.51	10.48	6.22	9.39
1992	10.77	14.09	13.81	11.40	10.29	12.18	8.12	14.29	10.86	11.80	10.86	6.36	9.66
1993	11.05	14.12	14.04	11.70	10.53	12.55	8.36	14.86	11.38	11.97	11.20	6.48	9.90
1994	11.34	14.41	14.38	12.04	10.79	12.90	8.62	15.32	11.84	12.16	11.48	6.62	10.18
1995	11.65	14.78	14.73	12.34	11.08	13.31	8.85	15.68	12.31	12.54	11.78	6.79	10.51
1996	12.04	15.09	15.11	12.75	11.44	13.77	9.21	16.30	12.75	13.01	12.15	6.99	10.85
1997	12.51	15.57	15.67	13.14	11.88	14.38	9.60	17.14	13.28	13.58	12.53	7.32	11.29
1998	13.01	16.20	16.23	13.45	12.37	15.03	10.06	17.67	14.00	14.28	12.96	7.67	11.79
1999	13.48	16.33	16.80	13.85	12.80	15.59	10.45	18.40	14.55	14.86	13.40	7.96	12.26
2000	14.01	16.55	17.48	14.32	13.28	16.24	10.87	19.07	15.04	15.53	13.91	8.32	12.73
2001	14.54	17.00	18.00	14.76	13.68	16.74	11.30	19.80	15.65	16.34	14.58	8.57	13.27
2002	14.96	17.19	18.52	15.29	13.99	16.94	11.67	20.20	16.25	16.82	15.15	8.81	13.72
2003	15.36	17.56	18.95	15.74	14.31	17.33	11.90	21.01	17.21	17.22	15.56	9.00	13.84
2004	15.68	18.07	19.23	16.14	14.55	17.62	12.09	21.40	17.58	17.49	16.07	9.15	13.98
2005	16.12	18.72	19.46	16.56	14.90	18.13	12.36	22.06	17.98	18.09	16.62	9.38	14.34
2006	16.74	19.90	20.02	16.81	15.36	18.87	12.58	23.23	18.83	19.14	17.28	9.75	14.77
2007	17.41	20.97	20.95	17.26	15.74	19.54	12.76	23.96	19.67	20.16	17.99	10.41	15.42
2008	18.06	22.50	21.87	17.75	16.13	20.08	12.87	24.78	20.32	21.19	18.73	10.84	16.09
2009	18.60	23.29	22.66	18.24	16.44	20.78	13.02	25.45	20.90	22.36	19.34	11.12	16.59
2010	19.04	23.82	23.22	18.61	16.78	21.46	13.25	25.87	21.55	22.80	19.95	11.31	17.06
2011	19.43	24.50	23.65	18.93	17.10	21.88	13.52	26.62	21.93	23.14	20.60	11.45	17.32
2012	19.73	25.79	23.97	19.08	17.38	22.13	13.82	27.04	22.82	23.31	20.91	11.62	17.59
2013	20.13	26.80	24.22	19.30	17.69	22.52	14.03	27.98	23.87	23.74	21.29	11.78	18.00
2014	20.60	26.84	24.67	19.56	18.21	23.14	14.40	28.70	24.71	24.31	21.64	12.09	18.51
2015	21.03	26.48	25.20	19.91	18.61	23.52	14.83	29.05	25.34	24.81	22.09	12.41	19.01
2016	21.53	26.97	25.97	20.44	18.93	24.07	15.05	30.05	26.12	25.43	22.52	12.85	19.36
2017	22.05	27.44	26.74	20.90	19.29	24.58	15.33	30.74	26.57	26.05	23.03	13.38	20.10
2018	22.71	28.27	27.55	21.54	19.88	25.17	15.91	31.97	26.93	26.82	23.64	13.87	20.78
2019	23.51	29.92	28.52	22.15	20.63	26.06	16.62	33.93	27.68	27.79	24.34	14.50	21.40
2020	24.68	30.42	29.21	22.80	21.41	26.81	17.60	35.74	29.09	29.25	25.40	14.71	22.58
2021	25.89	31.08	30.48	23.80	22.41	27.76	18.54	36.82	30.34	30.56	27.12	16.17	23.65
2020													
January	23.91	30.28	28.95	22.47	20.92	26.25	16.98	34.55	28.22	28.38	24.73	14.89	21.82
February	24.03	30.80	29.18	22.55	21.02	26.32	17.07	34.80	28.38	28.47	24.86	14.96	21.94
March	24.19	30.78	29.12	22.61	21.07	26.53	17.15	34.95	28.46	28.57	25.02	14.69	22.12
April	25.12	30.93	28.63	22.73	21.61	26.87	17.65	35.58	28.76	29.83	25.28	14.64	23.46
May	24.98	30.54	28.92	22.77	21.61	26.91	17.82	35.52	29.04	29.65	25.36	14.58	23.14
June	24.79	30.50	29.25	22.60	21.62	26.89	18.04	35.72	29.04	29.40	25.37	14.54	22.66
July	24.70	30.39	29.33	22.81	21.24	26.88	17.47	36.01	29.18	29.31	25.40	14.50	22.64
August	24.81	30.25	29.43	22.85	21.52	26.94	17.68	36.24	29.34	29.42	25.47	14.65	22.54
September	24.80	30.18	29.11	23.00	21.43	26.93	17.77	36.29	29.49	29.46	25.57	14.74	22.65
October	24.84	30.11	29.31	22.99	21.51	26.97	17.81	36.54	29.60	29.35	25.65	14.76	22.69
November	24.92	29.75	29.49	23.11	21.57	27.10	17.86	36.36	29.66	29.39	25.82	14.73	22.84
December	25.18	30.06	29.63	23.18	21.76	27.14	17.97	36.25	29.75	29.59	26.29	14.72	22.99
2021													
January	25.18	30.28	29.71	23.27	21.75	27.27	17.97	36.66	29.90	29.65	26.12	14.85	22.98
February	25.26	30.46	29.82	23.39	21.75	27.30	18.00	36.93	29.97	29.81	26.25	15.07	23.07
March	25.35	30.47	29.84	23.40	21.84	27.34	18.13	36.88	30.07	29.91	26.41	15.28	23.37
April	25.49	30.79	30.12	23.48	22.01	27.35	18.38	36.96	29.90	30.14	26.62	15.59	23.42
May	25.67	30.87	30.27	23.64	22.19	27.50	18.43	36.90	30.30	30.33	26.77	15.86	23.50
June	25.81	30.92	30.43	23.77	22.31	27.60	18.52	37.13	30.32	30.50	26.95	16.15	23.58
July	25.96	31.19	30.61	23.89	22.52	27.94	18.61	36.82	30.39	30.65	27.16	16.35	23.67
August	26.10	31.54	30.76	24.03	22.56	27.91	18.61	36.62	30.51	30.82	27.38	16.49	23.86
September	26.26	31.37	30.76	24.10	22.71	28.08	18.70	36.65	30.54	31.01	27.67	16.65	23.91
October	26.42	31.30	30.95	24.17	22.85	28.20	18.92	36.91	30.73	31.29	27.79	16.90	24.07
November	26.55	31.74	31.04	24.24	23.05	28.26	18.99	36.87	30.90	31.46	27.97	16.95	24.19
December	26.74	32.09	31.25	24.38	23.27	28.49	19.17	36.97	30.98	31.65	28.20	17.16	24.28

. . . = Not available.

Table 10-17. Average Weekly Earnings of Production and Nonsupervisory Workers on Private Nonfarm Payrolls by NAICS Supersector

(Dollars, seasonally adjusted.)

Year and month	Total private	Mining and logging	Construction	Manu-facturing	Trade, transportation, and utilities			Information	Financial activities	Professional and business services	Education and health services	Leisure and hospitality	Other services
					Total	Wholesale trade	Retail trade						
1965	101.54	125.48	122.35	102.69	116.36	. . .	. . .	171.24	88.50	122.30	74.84	38.06	45.30
1966	105.23	132.50	130.11	107.47	118.78	. . .	. . .	174.52	91.83	125.53	78.04	40.34	48.94
1967	108.14	137.76	138.55	109.85	121.57	. . .	. . .	176.09	95.35	128.34	81.34	43.06	52.69
1968	113.98	145.26	148.22	117.73	126.69	. . .	. . .	182.65	101.18	132.47	85.02	47.07	56.81
1969	120.80	157.11	164.88	124.74	132.13	. . .	. . .	190.18	107.91	139.37	91.46	51.29	63.44
1970	125.91	165.82	179.11	128.84	137.15	. . .	. . .	195.24	112.32	144.76	97.23	54.57	69.67
1971	133.35	174.18	194.70	137.59	144.11	. . .	. . .	204.50	117.60	151.51	103.57	58.39	76.58
1972	143.99	188.76	205.04	150.23	158.09	181.58	123.57	218.72	122.86	159.88	111.12	61.78	84.14
1973	152.71	201.43	219.32	161.59	165.61	189.93	128.16	230.48	129.32	167.40	117.85	64.92	91.06
1974	161.76	222.24	233.24	172.37	174.18	200.13	134.63	241.07	137.71	176.47	126.50	69.90	99.98
1975	170.45	248.38	249.70	185.69	182.61	212.46	141.33	253.21	147.75	185.81	134.83	74.49	108.67
1976	182.36	273.69	267.00	204.41	192.40	224.27	147.55	270.80	155.54	195.61	143.47	79.47	117.85
1977	195.34	299.46	279.61	224.01	203.51	239.18	154.84	288.29	165.47	206.78	153.38	85.20	128.12
1978	210.17	334.27	302.27	244.49	217.18	258.36	164.07	306.71	177.96	218.42	163.48	92.16	138.74
1979	225.46	366.58	326.55	263.99	232.01	278.35	173.50	324.51	190.72	231.16	174.80	99.47	150.47
1980	240.83	402.51	351.49	283.35	246.25	297.85	182.57	344.38	209.21	247.64	190.16	107.52	166.32
1981	261.29	446.10	382.75	312.74	263.58	321.69	194.29	370.36	228.21	267.46	208.00	117.49	184.77
1982	272.98	469.10	410.39	325.07	273.74	340.26	201.06	385.82	245.16	284.11	224.53	124.14	201.49
1983	286.34	488.89	427.00	348.89	284.42	359.20	209.12	404.89	262.83	298.74	237.40	130.82	214.87
1984	298.08	514.77	441.28	367.77	292.64	373.01	213.14	420.45	276.50	308.24	245.16	133.49	223.33
1985	304.37	529.62	448.35	380.60	295.47	382.44	213.69	430.86	287.66	317.41	254.19	134.71	232.81
1986	309.69	529.20	451.22	390.46	297.73	388.96	214.83	439.84	302.32	327.36	263.41	136.34	242.33
1987	317.33	529.72	463.78	400.00	303.76	396.62	218.36	450.77	314.01	337.91	273.49	139.45	252.58
1988	326.50	539.63	478.74	412.62	309.24	410.94	223.97	455.59	322.87	350.23	286.57	144.51	265.83
1989	338.42	568.55	497.43	423.58	319.07	426.64	229.45	468.77	339.46	366.27	302.70	150.29	282.09
1990	349.63	602.43	513.43	436.01	331.24	443.61	235.72	479.50	354.63	381.01	318.90	156.32	297.88
1991	358.46	625.46	520.41	449.74	338.71	458.48	240.23	495.14	369.57	391.49	334.10	159.20	306.75
1992	368.17	628.94	525.13	464.43	348.17	469.59	249.71	511.95	386.31	401.16	347.64	163.70	315.08
1993	378.74	634.77	539.81	480.80	358.70	483.54	256.91	535.19	403.68	406.60	358.34	167.54	322.69
1994	391.07	653.13	558.53	501.98	369.63	499.98	265.85	551.21	420.08	414.59	367.50	172.27	332.44
1995	399.93	670.40	571.57	509.26	378.04	514.18	272.68	564.92	437.23	427.16	376.77	175.74	342.36
1996	413.06	695.04	588.48	526.52	389.77	532.16	282.76	592.45	453.02	443.31	387.45	181.02	352.68
1997	431.75	720.07	609.48	548.36	406.55	558.06	296.04	622.37	475.03	466.13	403.42	190.66	368.63
1998	448.47	727.19	629.75	557.24	422.40	581.48	310.43	646.52	504.00	490.53	417.47	200.82	384.25
1999	463.09	721.77	655.11	573.25	433.44	601.78	321.74	675.47	520.73	511.39	429.76	208.05	398.77
2000	480.90	734.88	685.78	590.92	448.78	630.09	333.48	700.92	540.42	535.56	447.80	217.20	413.30
2001	493.53	757.96	695.86	595.15	458.58	642.08	346.31	731.18	560.46	558.32	471.33	220.73	428.64
2002	506.48	741.97	711.82	618.62	469.97	643.40	360.92	737.94	579.08	575.00	490.38	227.31	439.87
2003	517.68	765.94	727.00	636.03	480.00	656.36	367.28	760.84	611.99	587.68	503.05	230.49	434.41
2004	528.65	804.01	735.55	658.49	487.37	665.96	371.23	776.72	625.50	597.88	521.06	234.86	433.04
2005	543.94	853.87	750.37	673.34	497.07	683.99	377.58	805.11	646.51	619.65	541.40	241.36	443.40
2006	566.94	907.95	781.59	690.88	512.82	717.42	383.25	850.64	673.66	662.80	561.02	250.34	456.50
2007	589.09	962.63	816.23	711.53	524.57	747.08	385.18	874.45	706.52	701.42	585.44	265.54	477.06
2008	607.10	1 014.69	842.61	724.46	534.44	768.14	386.44	908.78	729.64	738.31	607.82	273.39	495.57
2009	615.82	1 006.67	851.76	726.12	540.19	782.62	388.74	931.08	754.90	776.30	622.30	275.95	506.26
2010	636.02	1 063.11	891.83	765.18	558.05	814.04	400.38	939.85	780.25	799.43	639.37	280.87	523.70
2011	652.72	1 144.64	921.84	784.29	575.88	842.06	412.29	964.85	798.68	814.74	663.04	283.82	532.63
2012	665.54	1 201.69	942.14	794.67	587.09	857.06	422.35	973.52	839.84	823.37	674.48	290.54	539.46
2013	677.62	1 229.70	958.72	807.41	595.36	871.89	423.44	1 003.65	875.04	839.86	683.24	294.31	553.77
2014	694.74	1 270.91	977.11	822.03	611.77	894.06	431.97	1 030.17	908.15	865.25	692.56	303.81	568.92
2015	708.70	1 211.91	998.02	832.22	626.54	907.72	446.01	1 038.10	939.46	879.63	709.25	311.32	583.54
2016	723.20	1 221.69	1 031.88	855.77	633.77	929.09	447.69	1 068.23	962.95	899.79	723.91	319.67	595.68
2017	742.48	1 265.92	1 061.98	876.10	652.11	957.95	463.10	1 100.03	982.09	922.51	741.55	332.54	617.91
2018	766.99	1 322.45	1 108.59	908.01	674.74	979.82	483.03	1 139.52	997.26	949.18	761.86	345.21	640.70
2019	790.44	1 402.39	1 135.73	921.87	697.95	1 007.42	503.06	1 198.97	1 020.44	984.35	783.66	358.27	659.07
2020	837.39	1 365.39	1 145.52	928.94	730.52	1 023.97	542.14	1 288.27	1 078.50	1 047.43	824.72	354.77	705.74
2021	886.06	1 443.70	1 203.77	985.92	769.17	1 078.17	571.02	1 342.87	1 130.07	1 105.72	885.33	402.79	742.14
2020													
January	803.38	1 392.88	1 146.42	928.01	711.28	1 010.63	517.89	1 216.16	1 041.32	1 007.49	796.31	367.78	674.24
February	809.81	1 413.72	1 161.36	938.08	714.68	1 013.32	520.64	1 231.92	1 044.38	1 013.53	802.98	368.02	677.95
March	807.95	1 403.57	1 147.33	933.79	716.38	1 016.10	524.79	1 240.73	1 047.33	1 014.24	808.15	333.46	676.87
April	841.52	1 329.99	1 093.67	872.83	726.10	994.19	538.33	1 266.65	1 061.24	1 050.02	803.90	325.01	731.95
May	851.82	1 337.65	1 139.45	897.14	741.22	1 011.82	557.77	1 271.62	1 071.58	1 061.47	814.06	354.29	735.85
June	842.86	1 345.05	1 152.45	901.74	737.24	1 021.82	557.44	1 289.49	1 071.58	1 052.52	821.99	351.87	713.79
July	839.80	1 346.28	1 158.54	928.37	726.41	1 024.13	541.57	1 289.16	1 082.58	1 052.23	825.50	348.00	706.37
August	848.50	1 361.25	1 159.54	936.85	735.98	1 029.11	548.08	1 315.51	1 088.51	1 059.12	832.87	358.93	707.76
September	848.16	1 355.08	1 138.20	947.60	737.19	1 036.81	550.87	1 320.96	1 097.03	1 060.56	836.14	365.55	713.48
October	852.01	1 363.98	1 151.88	949.49	742.10	1 038.35	552.11	1 330.06	1 104.08	1 059.54	841.32	363.10	712.47
November	854.76	1 365.53	1 161.91	954.44	744.17	1 040.64	555.45	1 338.05	1 103.35	1 063.92	846.90	359.41	719.46
December	861.16	1 376.75	1 176.31	959.65	739.84	1 044.89	546.29	1 323.13	1 109.68	1 071.16	864.94	353.28	721.89
2021													
January	866.19	1 408.02	1 185.43	968.03	750.38	1 058.08	557.07	1 338.09	1 121.25	1 079.26	859.35	365.31	723.87
February	861.37	1 379.84	1 160.00	970.69	746.03	1 051.05	556.20	1 347.95	1 120.88	1 073.16	855.75	363.19	717.48
March	872.04	1 422.95	1 190.62	975.78	753.48	1 063.53	562.03	1 338.74	1 124.62	1 085.73	863.61	378.94	738.49
April	876.86	1 437.89	1 195.76	976.77	761.55	1 063.92	569.78	1 356.43	1 118.26	1 091.07	870.47	392.87	737.73
May	880.48	1 435.46	1 198.69	981.06	763.34	1 069.75	569.49	1 361.61	1 133.22	1 100.98	875.38	398.09	740.25
June	885.28	1 453.24	1 189.81	981.70	765.23	1 073.64	568.56	1 362.67	1 133.97	1 107.15	883.96	405.37	742.77
July	890.43	1 447.22	1 209.10	991.44	774.69	1 092.45	573.19	1 351.29	1 136.59	1 112.60	888.13	412.02	743.24
August	892.62	1 457.15	1 211.94	994.84	773.81	1 085.70	571.33	1 351.28	1 138.02	1 115.68	892.59	412.25	744.43
September	900.72	1 480.66	1 242.70	997.74	778.95	1 097.93	574.09	1 337.73	1 139.14	1 128.76	902.04	416.25	750.77
October	903.56	1 461.71	1 222.53	998.22	786.04	1 105.44	582.74	1 339.83	1 149.30	1 135.83	905.95	422.50	755.80
November	908.01	1 491.78	1 232.29	1 003.54	788.31	1 104.97	582.99	1 345.76	1 152.57	1 145.14	909.03	423.75	759.57
December	911.83	1 488.98	1 246.88	1 009.33	793.51	1 113.96	586.60	1 349.41	1 158.65	1 148.90	919.32	427.28	762.39

. . . = Not available.

SECTION 10-C: OTHER SIGNIFICANT LABOR MARKET DATA

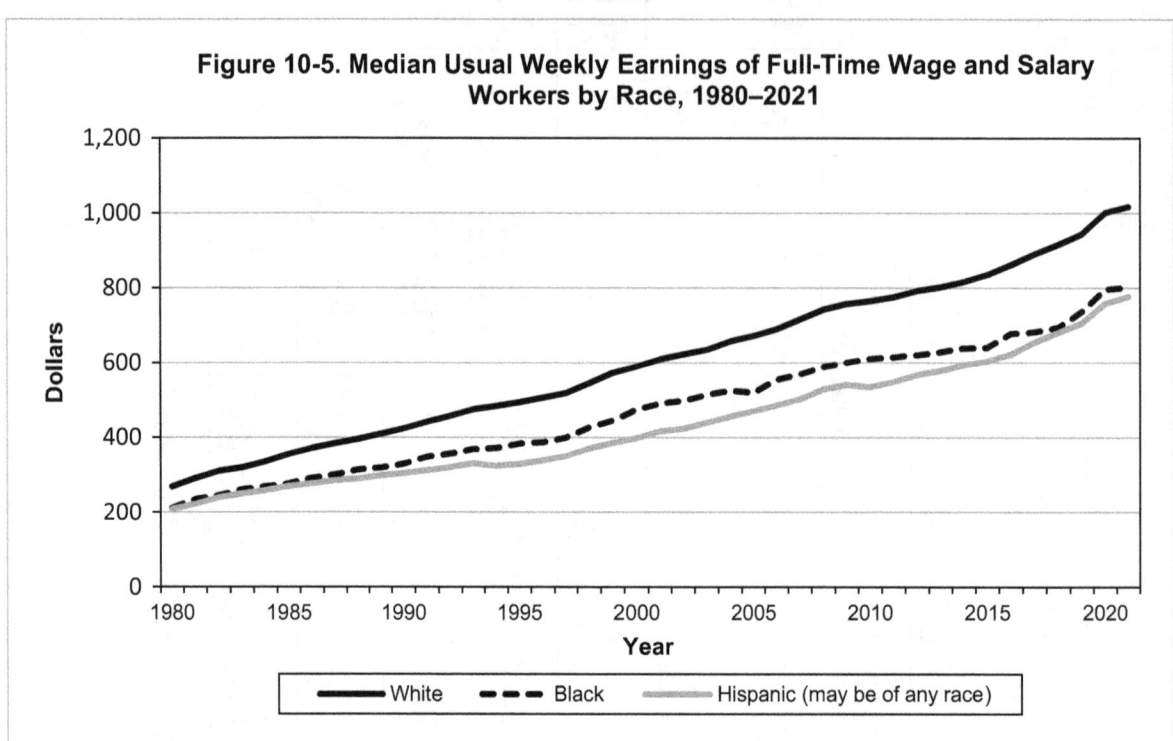

Figure 10-5. Median Usual Weekly Earnings of Full-Time Wage and Salary Workers by Race, 1980–2021

- This section of *Business Statistics* includes indicators of hours and earnings from the Current Population Statistics (household) survey that are more appropriate than similarly named indicators produced by the payroll survey and shown in the previous section. It also incorporates annual employment data from the Bureau of Economic Analysis, produced as part of the National Income and Product Accounts (NIPA), that provide a consistent historical record of U.S. employment from 1929 through 2021.

- The gender pay gap is illustrated in Table 10-19. As women entered the workforce at higher rates in the 1970s, this pay gap began to shrink. However, in 2021 women still only earned 83.1 percent of what men earned. It would take women 42 extra days of work to earn what men earned.

- In 2021, Asians had the highest median usual weekly earnings of all races at $1,315 followed by Whites at $1,018, Blacks at $801, and Hispanics at $777. In 2000, the gap between Asian and Hispanic workers was $216. By 2021, it increased to $538. (Table 10-19).

Table 10-18. Hours at Work, Current Population Survey

(Hours per week.)

Year and month	Hours per person, all industries				Hours per person, nonagricultural industries	
					All workers	
	Total	Men	Women	Persons who usually work full-time	Total	Usually work full-time
1948	42.8	. . .	. . .	. . .	41.6	. . .
1949	42.1	. . .	. . .	. . .	40.9	. . .
1950	41.7	. . .	. . .	. . .	40.7	. . .
1951	42.2	. . .	. . .	. . .	41.3	. . .
1952	42.4	. . .	. . .	. . .	41.6	. . .
1953	41.9	. . .	. . .	. . .	41.1	. . .
1954	40.9	. . .	. . .	. . .	40.0	. . .
1955	41.6	. . .	. . .	. . .	40.9	. . .
1956	41.5	43.8	36.5	. . .	40.9	. . .
1957	41.0	43.4	36.1	. . .	40.5	. . .
1958	40.6	42.9	35.8	. . .	40.1	. . .
1959	40.5	42.8	35.6	. . .	40.0	. . .
1960	40.5	43.0	35.4	. . .	40.0	. . .
1961	40.5	43.0	35.3	. . .	40.1	. . .
1962	40.5	43.2	35.2	. . .	40.1	. . .
1963	40.4	43.2	35.1	. . .	40.1	. . .
1964	40.0	43.2	34.7	. . .	39.7	. . .
1965	40.5	42.8	35.1	. . .	40.2	. . .
1966	40.4	43.3	35.2	. . .	40.1	. . .
1967	40.4	43.2	35.2	. . .	40.0	. . .
1968	40.1	43.3	34.9	. . .	39.7	. . .
1969	39.9	43.0	34.9	. . .	39.5	. . .
1970	39.1	42.9	34.2	. . .	38.7	. . .
1971	39.3	42.0	34.3	. . .	38.9	. . .
1972	39.4	42.2	34.5	. . .	39.0	. . .
1973	39.3	42.3	34.4	. . .	39.0	. . .
1974	39.0	42.4	34.3	. . .	38.7	. . .
1975	38.7	42.0	34.1	. . .	38.4	. . .
1976	38.7	41.6	34.1	. . .	38.4	. . .
1977	38.8	41.7	34.2	. . .	38.5	. . .
1978	39.0	41.9	34.5	. . .	38.7	. . .
1979	38.9	42.1	34.5	. . .	38.6	. . .
1980	38.5	42.0	34.5	. . .	38.3	. . .
1981	38.1	41.5	34.1	. . .	37.9	. . .
1982	38.0	41.1	34.1	. . .	37.7	. . .
1983	38.3	40.9	34.5	. . .	38.1	. . .
1984	38.8	41.2	34.9	. . .	38.6	. . .
1985	39.0	41.8	35.2	. . .	38.9	. . .
1986	39.1	42.0	35.4	. . .	38.9	. . .
1987	39.0	42.1	35.3	. . .	38.8	. . .
1988	39.4	42.0	35.7	. . .	39.3	. . .
1989	39.6	42.4	35.8	. . .	39.4	. . .
1990	39.4	42.6	35.8	. . .	39.3	. . .
1991	39.2	42.3	35.8	. . .	39.1	. . .
1992	38.9	42.0	35.6	. . .	38.8	. . .
1993	39.4	41.7	36.0	. . .	39.3	. . .
1994	39.2	42.2	35.5	43.4	39.1	43.3
1995	39.3	42.2	35.6	43.4	39.2	43.2
1996	39.3	42.3	35.7	43.3	39.2	43.2
1997	39.5	42.3	36.0	43.4	39.4	43.3
1998	39.3	42.4	35.8	43.2	39.2	43.1
1999	39.6	42.2	36.2	43.4	39.5	43.3
2000	39.7	42.4	36.4	43.4	39.6	43.3
2001	39.2	42.5	36.1	42.9	39.2	42.8
2002	39.2	41.9	36.0	42.9	39.1	42.8
2003	39.0	41.8	35.9	42.9	39.0	42.7
2004	39.0	41.7	35.9	42.9	39.0	42.8
2005	39.2	41.7	36.1	42.9	39.1	42.8
2006	39.2	41.8	36.2	42.9	39.2	42.8
2007	39.2	41.8	36.1	42.8	39.1	42.7
2008	38.9	41.7	36.1	42.6	38.8	42.5
2009	37.9	41.3	35.3	41.9	37.8	41.8
2010	38.2	40.2	35.5	42.2	38.1	42.2
2011	38.3	40.5	35.6	42.4	38.2	42.3
2012	38.5	40.6	35.8	42.5	38.4	42.4
2013	38.6	40.8	36.0	42.6	38.5	42.5
2014	38.6	40.9	35.9	42.5	38.6	42.5
2015	38.6	41.0	35.9	42.4	38.5	42.3
2016	38.7	40.9	36.2	42.5	38.7	42.4
2017	38.7	41.0	36.2	42.4	38.6	42.3
2018	38.9	40.9	36.4	42.5	38.9	42.1
2019	39.0	41.0	36.6	42.6	38.9	42.5
2020	38.2	40.1	36.1	41.5	38.0	42.0
2021	38.7	40.5	36.6	42.0	38.7	42.1

. . . = Not available.

Table 10-19 Median Usual Weekly Earnings of Full-Time Wage and Salary Workers

(Current dollars, [second quartile] except as noted; not seasonally adjusted.)

Year and quarter	Sex and age						Race and ethnicity			
	Men, 16 years and over			Women, 16 years and over			White	Black or African American	Asian	Hispanic or Latino ethnicity
	16 to 24 years	25 to 54 years	55 years and over	16 to 24 years	25 to 54 years	55 years and over				
1985	241	. . .	. . .	211	. . .	. . .	356	277	. . .	270
1986	246	. . .	. . .	219	. . .	. . .	371	291	. . .	277
1987	257	. . .	. . .	227	. . .	. . .	384	301	. . .	285
1988	262	. . .	. . .	235	. . .	. . .	395	314	. . .	290
1989	271	. . .	. . .	246	. . .	. . .	409	319	. . .	298
1990	282	. . .	. . .	254	. . .	. . .	424	329	. . .	304
1991	285	. . .	. . .	266	. . .	. . .	442	348	. . .	312
1992	284	. . .	. . .	267	. . .	. . .	458	357	. . .	321
1993	288	. . .	. . .	273	. . .	. . .	475	369	. . .	331
1994	294	. . .	. . .	276	. . .	. . .	484	371	. . .	324
1995	303	. . .	. . .	275	. . .	. . .	494	383	. . .	329
1996	307	. . .	. . .	284	. . .	. . .	506	387	. . .	339
1997	317	. . .	. . .	292	. . .	. . .	519	400	. . .	351
1998	334	. . .	. . .	305	. . .	. . .	545	426	. . .	370
1999	356	. . .	. . .	324	. . .	. . .	573	445	. . .	385
2000	375	690	714	344	519	497	590	474	615	399
2001	391	717	742	353	547	519	610	491	639	417
2002	391	727	773	367	571	556	623	498	658	424
2003	398	736	797	371	584	584	636	514	693	440
2004	400	755	816	375	599	601	657	525	708	456
2005	409	763	829	381	610	619	672	520	753	471
2006	418	784	870	395	624	641	690	554	784	486
2007	443	809	902	409	644	657	716	569	830	503
2008	461	843	920	420	666	687	742	589	861	529
2009	458	857	944	424	683	706	757	601	880	541
2010	443	854	961	422	700	716	765	611	855	535
2011	455	864	976	421	713	738	775	615	866	549
2012	468	890	987	416	719	752	792	621	920	568
2013	479	891	999	423	733	766	802	629	942	578
2014	493	899	1 007	451	746	773	816	639	953	594
2015	510	921	1 054	450	757	774	835	641	993	604
2016	512	943	1 082	486	778	801	862	678	1 021	624
2017	547	977	1 084	499	801	843	890	682	1 043	655
2018	569	1 005	1 123	528	825	847	916	694	1 093	681
2019	607	1 046	1 150	541	864	869	945	736	1 181	706
2020	622	1 127	1 205	589	928	945	1 003	796	1 303	759
2021	649	1 144	1 224	604	954	955	1 018	801	1 315	777
2014										
1st quarter	480	925	979	434	750	767	819	646	955	593
2nd quarter	481	914	993	449	744	768	802	649	954	588
3rd quarter	498	920	1 034	448	743	778	816	638	945	598
4th quarter	508	929	1 019	469	749	784	823	621	959	600
2015										
1st quarter	491	944	1 029	461	757	768	835	650	966	590
2nd quarter	497	942	1 032	444	753	782	829	647	965	601
3rd quarter	517	946	1 069	442	757	781	829	624	974	602
4th quarter	543	958	1 092	453	764	768	847	643	1 091	624
2016										
1st quarter	511	963	1 102	488	771	821	857	673	1 032	612
2nd quarter	505	967	1 049	470	774	785	854	677	1 021	618
3rd quarter	510	971	1 095	480	782	793	854	685	1 010	632
4th quarter	522	977	1 084	506	788	810	881	675	1 022	646
2017										
1st quarter	558	998	1 045	489	795	828	894	679	1 019	649
2nd quarter	524	995	1 046	496	811	859	886	689	1 103	657
3rd quarter	527	995	1 125	500	797	859	887	696	1 010	655
4th quarter	581	998	1 116	512	799	818	891	666	1 061	657
2018										
1st quarter	563	1 001	1 097	545	819	819	911	696	1 066	675
2nd quarter	528	991	1 117	511	811	868	907	683	1 083	674
3rd quarter	575	1 012	1 111	515	845	826	915	686	1 128	689
4th quarter	609	1 014	1 166	539	825	873	931	712	1 095	684
2019										
1st quarter	605	1 034	1 149	539	841	859	935	737	1 157	696
2nd quarter	601	1 035	1 141	522	852	871	933	724	1 152	696
3rd quarter	601	1 047	1 143	538	883	854	943	727	1 247	718
4th quarter	621	1 066	1 168	566	881	892	967	756	1 166	712
2020										
1st quarter	593	1 109	1 197	582	894	895	980	775	1 221	721
2nd quarter	640	1 136	1 191	594	948	977	1 017	805	1 336	786
3rd quarter	631	1 149	1 231	583	942	942	1 008	813	1 392	785
4th quarter	625	1 115	1 202	596	929	965	1 007	792	1 261	742
2021										
1st quarter	634	1 142	1 194	593	937	954	1 006	799	1 286	750
2nd quarter	643	1 138	1 224	596	945	941	1 012	799	1 281	779
3rd quarter	656	1 149	1 216	603	962	953	1 024	799	1 309	779
4th quarter	662	1 148	1 262	623	972	971	1 030	805	1 384	799

. . . = Not available.

CHAPTER 10. NOTES AND DEFINITION

General note on monthly employment data

This chapter presents data from two different data sets that measure employment monthly. Both are compiled and published by the Bureau of Labor Statistics (BLS), but each set has different characteristics. Users should be aware of these dissimilarities and the consequent differences in the appropriate uses and interpretations of data from the two systems.

One set of monthly employment estimates comes from the Current Population Survey (CPS), a large sample survey of approximately 60,000 U.S. households. The numbers in the sample are expanded to match the latest estimates of the total U.S. population. These are the most comprehensive estimates in their scope—that is, in the universe that they are designed to measure. These estimates represent all civilian workers, including the following groups that are excluded by definition from the other set of estimates: all farm workers; domestic household workers (house cleaners, gardeners, nannies, etc.); nonagricultural, non-incorporated self-employed workers; and nonagricultural unpaid family workers. See Notes and Definitions from Chapter 3 for the impact of gathering data for the CPS system.

This **household survey** (CPS) is designed to measure the labor force status of the civilian noninstitutional population with demographic detail. The national unemployment rate is the best-known statistic produced from the household survey. The survey also provides a measure of employed people, one that includes agricultural workers and the self-employed. A representative sample of U.S. households provides the information for the household survey.

However, official CPS data are characterized by periodic discontinuities, which occur when new benchmarks for Census measures of the total population are introduced. These updates take place in a single month—usually January—and the official data for previous months are typically not modified to provide a smooth transition. Therefore, shorter-term comparisons (for a year or two or for a business cycle phase) will be misleading if such a discontinuity is included in the period. A recent example will illustrate. Beginning with January 2019, the updated controls decreased the estimated size of the civilian noninstitutional population 16 years and over by 811,000, the civilian labor force by 524,000, employment by 507,000, unemployment by 17,000, and the number of persons not in the labor force by 287,000. The total unemployment rate, the labor force participation rate, and the employment-population ratio were not affected. Such discontinuities occur throughout the history of the series.

The CPS is a count of persons employed, rather than a count of jobs. A person is counted as employed in this data set only once, no matter how many jobs he or she may hold. The CPS count is limited to persons 16 years of age and over.

The second set of employment estimates—the payroll survey—comes from a very large sample survey of about 131,000 business and government employers at approximately 670,000 worksites, the Current Employment Statistics (CES) survey. It is benchmarked annually to a survey of all employers. Benchmark data are introduced with a smooth adjustment back to the previous benchmark, thus preserving the continuity of the series and making it more appropriate for measurement of employment change over a year or two, a business cycle, or other short- to medium-length periods. This sample is much larger than the CPS sample, including about one-third of all nonfarm payroll employees, and consequently the threshold of statistical significance for changes is lower.

Data collection for the establishment survey (called the Current Employment Statistics (CES) was impacted by the pandemic. Approximately one-fifth of the establishments are assigned to four regional data collection centers for collection. Although these centers were closed during the collection period, interviewers at these centers worked remotely to collect data by telephone. Additionally, the Bureau of Labor Statistics (BLS) encouraged businesses to report their data electronically.

The **payroll survey** (CES) is designed to measure employment, hours, and earnings in the nonfarm sector, with industry and geographic detail. The survey is best known for providing a highly reliable gauge of monthly change in nonfarm payroll employment. A representative sample of businesses in the U.S. provides the data for the payroll survey.

Over recent years, benchmark revisions to payroll survey employment have ranged in magnitude from an upward revision of 0.6 percent, in 2006, to the March 2009 benchmark, which reduced the seasonally adjusted level of payroll employment in that month by 902,000 persons, or 0.7 percent. The most recent revision increased the level of employment in March 2019 deceased employment by 489,000, or 0.3. percent. In absolute terms (that is, disregarding the sign), revisions have ranged from 0.1 to 0.7 percentage points over the latest 13 years and averaged 0.195 percentage points. Within that range, relatively large upward revisions have been seen for strong economies, and relatively large downward revisions for weak ones.

The scope of the CES survey is smaller than that of the CPS survey, as it is limited to wage and salary workers on nonfarm payrolls. There is also a significant definitional difference, because the CES survey is a count of jobs. Thus, a person with more than one nonfarm wage or salary job is counted as employed in each job. In addition, workers are not classified by age; as a result, there may be some workers younger than 16 years old in the job count.

Persons with a job but not at work (absent due to bad weather, work stoppages, personal reasons, and the like) are included in the household survey. However, they are excluded from the payroll survey if on leave without pay for the entire payroll period.

In addition to the differences in definitions and scope between the two series, there are also differences in sample design, collection methodology, and the sampling variability inherent in the surveys.

The payroll survey provides the most reliable and detailed information on employment by industry (for example, the data shown in Table 15-1). In addition, it provides data on weekly hours per job and hourly and weekly earnings per job.

The CPS employment estimates provide information not collected in the CES on employment by demographic characteristics, such as age, race, and Hispanic ethnicity; by education levels; and by occupation. A few of these tabulations are shown in *Business Statistics*. Many more breakdowns, in richer detail, can be found in the *Handbook of U.S. Labor Statistics*, also published by Bernan Press.

The differences between the two employment measurement systems are discussed in an article on the BLS Web site, "Employment from the BLS household and payroll surveys: summary of recent trends," which is updated monthly along with the release of the monthly data,and can be found under "Publications" on the CPS homepage at https://www.bls.gov. This article also includes references to further relevant studies.

Additional information on how COVID-19 impacted the CPS or CES can be found here: https://www.bls.gov/covid19/effects-of-covid-19-pandemic-and-response-on-the-employment-situation-news-release.htm

Additional annual employment data

In addition to the CPS and CES monthly and annual data series, a third set of historical, annual-only estimates of employment is presented at the end of this chapter. These estimates of "full-time and part-time employees" by industry are compiled by the U.S. Department of Commerce, Bureau of Economic Analysis, as part of the National Income and Product Accounts (NIPAs). These estimates provide the most comprehensive and consistent employment estimates for the years before 1948.

Further detail on the historical and other characteristics of all of these employment series is presented below in the notes associated with specific data tables.

Tables 10-1 through 10-5

Labor Force, Employment, and Unemployment

SOURCE: U.S. DEPARTMENT OF LABOR, BUREAU OF LABOR STATISTICS (BLS)

Labor force, employment, and unemployment data are derived from the Current Population Survey (CPS), a sample survey of households conducted each month by the Census Bureau for the Bureau of Labor Statistics (BLS). The data pertain to the U.S. civilian noninstitutional population age 16 years and over.

Due to changes in questionnaire design and survey methodology, data for 1994 and subsequent years are not fully comparable with data for 1993 and earlier years. Additionally, discontinuities in the reported number of persons in the population, and consequently in the estimated numbers of employed and unemployed persons and the number of persons in the labor force, are introduced whenever periodic updates are made to U.S. population estimates.

For example, population controls based on Census 2000 were introduced beginning with the data for January 2000. These data are therefore not comparable with data for December 1999 and earlier. Data for 1990 through 1999 incorporate 1990 census–based population controls and are not comparable with the preceding years. An additional large population adjustment was introduced in January 2004, making the data from that time forward not comparable with data for December 2003 and earlier; further adjustments have been made in each subsequent January and other discontinuities have been introduced in various earlier years, usually with January data. See "Notes on the Data," below, for information on adjustments in other years, including the incorporation of the 2010 Census count beginning in January 2012.

For the most part, these population adjustments distort comparisons involving the numbers of persons in the population, labor force, and employment. They generally have negligible effects on the percentages that comprise the most important features of the CPS: the unemployment rates, the labor force participation rates, and the employment-population ratios.

Beginning with the data for January 2000, data classified by industry and occupation use the North American Industry Classification System (NAICS) and the 2000 Standard Occupational Classification System. This creates breaks in the time series between December 1999 and January 2000 for occupational and industry data at all levels of aggregation. Since the recent history is so short, most CPS industry and occupation data have been dropped from *Business Statistics* in favor of other important and economically meaningful data for which a longer consistent history can be supplied. However, detailed employment data by occupation and industry can be found in Bernan Press's *Handbook of U.S. Labor Statistics.*

Pre-1948 data

The Census Bureau began the survey of households that provides labor force data in 1942, and the Census of Population supplied data for 1940. For the years before that, annual data for labor force, employment, and unemployment are retrospective estimates. The 1929-1947 estimates were made by BLS. The 1890-1929 estimates shown in Table 10-1B were made by Stanley Lebergott. Both of those used trend interpolation of labor force participation between Census years, and the Census and Lebergott estimates are identical in 1929.

From 1929 to 1947, the data collected pertained to persons 14 years of age and over. From 1947 to the present the survey pertains to persons 16 years of age and over. Table 10-1C shows summary data for both age definitions in the overlap year, 1947. In that year, the unemployment rates are the same (3.9 percent) for both age definitions. However, the labor force participation rate and the employment/population ratio are higher when the 14- and 15-year-olds are excluded. Naturally, the raw numbers for population, labor force, and employment are smaller when the 14- and 15-year-olds are excluded.

The 1940 Census and the BLS data for 1931 through 1942 did not treat government work relief employment as employment; persons engaged in such work were counted as unemployed. In the labor force survey used today, anyone who worked for pay or profit is counted as employed (see the definitions below). Therefore, today's survey would count work relief as employment and not unemployment, and the BLS figures for the period before 1942 are not consistent with today's unemployment rates. Michael Darby, a former member of NBER, calculated an alternative unemployment rate in which such workers are counted as employed, and this rate is shown in parentheses in Table 10-1B. BLS counts employment in nonprofit and private groups that provide relief under the "emergency and other relief services" industry (also referred to in some BLS data as the "community food and housing, and emergency and other relief services" industry). This employment is usually found in the "Other Services' of the NAICS supersector.

Race and ethnic origin

Data for two broad racial categories were made available beginning in 1954: *White* and *Black and other.* The latter included

Asians and all other "nonwhite" races, and was discontinued after 2002. Data for *Blacks* only are available beginning with 1972; this category is now called *Black or African American.* Data for *Asians* are shown beginning with 2000. Persons in the remaining race categories—American Indian or Alaska Native, Native Hawaiian or Other Pacific Islanders, and persons who selected more than one race category when that became possible, beginning in 2003 (see below)—are included in the estimates of total employment and unemployment, but are not shown separately because their numbers are too small to yield quality estimates.

Hispanic or Latino ethnicity, previously labeled *Hispanic origin*, is not a racial category and is established in a survey question separate from the question about race. Persons of Hispanic or Latino ethnicity may be of any race.

In January 2003, changes that affected classification by race and Hispanic ethnicity were introduced. These changes caused discontinuities in race and ethnic group data between December 2002 and January 2003.

- Individuals in the sample are now asked whether they are of Hispanic ethnicity <u>before</u> being asked about their race. Prior to 2003, individuals were asked their ethnic origin <u>after</u> they were asked about their race. Furthermore, respondents are now asked directly if they are Spanish, Hispanic, or Latino. Previously, they were identified based on their or their ancestors' country of origin.

- Individuals in the sample are now allowed to choose more than one race category. Before 2003, they were required to select a single primary race. This change had no impact on the size of the overall civilian noninstitutional population and labor force. It did reduce the population and labor force levels of Whites and Blacks beginning in January 2003, as individuals who reported more than one race are now excluded from those groups.

BLS has estimated, based on a special survey, that these changes reduced the population and labor force levels for Whites by about 950,000 and 730,000 persons, respectively, and for Blacks by about 320,000 and 240,000 persons, respectively, while having little or no impact on either of their unemployment rates. The changes did not affect the size of the Hispanic population or labor force, but they did cause an increase of about half a percentage point in the Hispanic unemployment rate.

Definitions

The employment status of the civilian population is surveyed each month with respect to a specific week in mid-month—not for the entire month. This is known as the "reference week." For a precise definition and explanation of the reference week, see Notes on the Data, which follows these definitions.

The *civilian noninstitutional population* comprises all civilians 16 years of age and over who are not inmates of penal or mental institutions, sanitariums, or homes for the aged, infirm, or needy. A recent example will illustrate. Benchmark population updates does occur annually. For example, in January 2019, the updated controls decreased the estimated size of the civilian noninstitutional population 16 years and over by 811,000, the civilian labor force by 524,000, employment by 507,000, unemployment by 17,000, and the number of persons not in the labor force by 287,000. The total unemployment rate, the labor force participation rate, and the employment-population ratio were not affected. Such discontinuities occur throughout the history of the series.

Civilian employment includes those civilians who (1) worked for pay or profit at any time during the Sunday-through-Saturday week that includes the 12th day of the month (the reference week), or who worked for 15 hours or more as an unpaid worker in a family-operated enterprise; or (2) were temporarily absent from regular jobs because of vacation, illness, industrial dispute, bad weather, or similar reasons. Each employed person is counted only once; those who hold more than one job are counted as being in the job at which they worked the greatest number of hours during the reference week.

Unemployed persons are all civilians who were not employed (according to the above definition) during the reference week, but who were available for work—except for temporary illness—and who had made specific efforts to find employment sometime during the previous four weeks. Persons who did not look for work because they were on layoff are also counted as unemployed.

The *civilian labor force* comprises all civilians classified as employed or unemployed.

Civilians 16 years of age and over in the noninstitutional population who are not classified as employed or unemployed are defined as *not in the labor force*. This group includes those engaged in own-home housework; in school; unable to work because of longterm illness, retirement, or age; seasonal workers for whom the reference week fell in an "off" season (if not qualifying as unemployed by looking for a job); persons who became discouraged and gave up the search for work; and the voluntarily idle. Also included are those doing only incidental work (less than 15 hours) in a family-operated business during the reference week.

The civilian *labor force participation rate* represents the percentage of the civilian noninstitutional population (age 16 years and over) that is in the civilian labor force. This rate includes people who have stopped looking for a job while the unemployment figure does not. Thus a low unemployment rate while the labor force participation rate is also low points to a structural problem in the labor market. When former workers become discouraged and stop looking for work, this shrinks the labor force.

The *employment-population ratio* represents the percentage of the civilian noninstitutional population (age 16 years and over) that is employed. This is traditionally called a "ratio," although it is also traditionally expressed as a percent and therefore would be more appropriately called a "rate," as is the case with the labor force participation rate. Factors that change the rate are population demographics such as baby boomers are retiring and younger individuals chose to stay in college longer.

Employment is shown by *class of worker*, including a breakdown of total employment into *agricultural* and *nonagricultural* industries. Employment in *nonagricultural industries* includes *wage and salary workers*, the *self-employed*, and *unpaid family workers*.

Wage and salary workers receive wages, salaries, commissions, tips, and/or pay-in-kind. This category includes owners of self-owned incorporated businesses.

Self-employed workers are those who work for profit or for fees in their own business, profession, trade, or farm. This category includes only the unincorporated; a person whose business is incorporated is considered to be a wage and salary worker since he or she is a paid employee of a corporation, even if he or she is the corporation's president and sole employee. These categories are now labeled "Self-employed workers, unincorporated" to clarify this definition.

Wage and salary employment comprises *government* and *private industry* wage and salary workers. Domestic workers and other employees of *private households*, who are not included in the payroll employment series, are shown separately from *all other private industries*. The series for *government* and *other private industries* wage and salary workers are the closest in scope to similar categories in the payroll employment series.

Multiple jobholders are employed persons who, during the reference week, either had two or more jobs as a wage and salary worker, were self-employed and also held a wage and salary job, or worked as an unpaid family worker and also held a wage and salary job. This category does not include self-employed persons with multiple businesses or persons with multiple jobs as unpaid family workers. For purposes of industry and occupational classification, multiple jobholders are counted as being in the job at which they worked the greatest number of hours during the reference week.

Employed and at work part time does not include employed persons who were absent from their jobs during the entire reference week for reasons such as vacation, illness, or industrial dispute.

At work part time for economic reasons ("involuntary" part time) refers to individuals who worked 1 to 34 hours during the reference week because of slack work, unfavorable business conditions, an inability to find full-time work, or seasonal declines in demand. To be included in this category, workers must also indicate that they want and are available for full-time work.

At work part time for noneconomic reasons ("voluntary" part time) refers to persons who usually work part time and were at work for 1 to 34 hours during the reference week for reasons such as illness, other medical limitations, family obligations, education, retirement, Social Security limits on earnings, or working in an industry where the workweek is less than 35 hours. It also includes respondents who gave an economic reason but were not available for, or did not want, full-time work. At work part time for noneconomic reasons excludes persons who usually work full time, but who worked only 1 to 34 hours during the reference week for reasons such as holidays, illnesses, and bad weather.

The *long-term unemployed* are persons currently unemployed (searching or on layoff) who have been unemployed for 15 consecutive weeks or longer. If a person ceases to look for work for two weeks or more, or becomes temporarily employed, the continuity of longterm unemployment is broken. If he or she starts searching for work or is laid off again, the monthly CPS will record the length of his or her unemployment from the time the search recommenced or since the latest layoff.

The civilian *unemployment rate* is the number of unemployed as a percentage of the civilian labor force. The unemployment rates for groups within the civilian population (such as males age 20 years and over) are the number of unemployed in a group as a percent of that group's labor force.

Unemployment rates by reason provides a breakdown of the total unemployment rate. Each unemployed person is classified into one of four groups.

Job losers and persons who completed temporary jobs includes persons on temporary layoff, permanent job losers, and persons who completed temporary jobs and began looking for work after those jobs ended. These three categories are shown separately without seasonal adjustment in the BLS's "Employment Situation" news release and on its Web site. They are combined, under the title shown here, for the purpose of seasonal adjustment. This is the category of unemployment that responds most strongly to the business cycle.

Job leavers terminated their employment voluntarily and immediately began looking for work.

Reentrants are persons who previously worked, but were out of the labor force prior to beginning their current job search.

New entrants are persons searching for a first job who have never worked.

Each of these categories is expressed as a proportion of the entire civilian labor force, so that the sum of the four rates equals the unemployment rate for all civilian workers, except for possible discrepancies due to rounding or separate seasonal adjustment.

Median and average weeks unemployed are summary measures of the length of time that persons classified as unemployed have been looking for work. For persons on layoff, the duration represents the number of full weeks of the layoff. The *average (mean)* number of weeks is computed by aggregating all the weeks of unemployment experienced by all unemployed persons during their current spell of unemployment and dividing by the number of unemployed. The average can be distorted by what is called "top coding" because the length of unemployment is reported in ranges, including a top range of "over __ weeks", rather than exact numbers. See the paragraph below for further explanation. The *median* number of weeks unemployed is the number of weeks of unemployment experienced by the person at the midpoint of the distribution of all unemployed persons, as ranked by duration of unemployment, and is not distorted by top coding. Like medians in other economic time series, it is likely to be a better measure of typical experience.

Beginning with the data for January 2011 and phasing in through April 2011, respondents could report unemployment durations of up to 5 years; before that time, the "top code" was up to 2 years. This change caused a sharp increase in January 2011 and continued rises through April for *average weeks unemployed.* It did not affect total unemployment, total long-term unemployment, or the *median weeks unemployed.* Comparisons of the average weeks statistics on the old and new basis are available on the BLS Web site.

Alternative measures of labor underutilization are calculated by BLS and published in the monthly Employment Situation release. They measure alternative concepts of unused working capacity, and are numbered "U-1" through "U-6" in order of increasing breadth of the definition of underutilization.

"U-1" is persons unemployed 15 weeks or longer, as a percent of the civilian labor force. It is not shown in *Business Statistics.*

"U-2" is job losers and persons who completed temporary jobs, as a percent of the civilian labor force; it is shown in *Business Statistics* in the fifth column of Table 10-5.

"U-3" is the official rate, described above and shown in the final columns of Tables 10-1, the fifth column of Table 10-4, and the fourth column of Table 10-5.

"U-4" through "U-6" are shown in the last three columns of Table 10-5. They are based on additional labor force status questions, now included in the CPS survey, that were introduced beginning in 1994. U-4 and U-5 are increasingly broader rates of unemployment, while U-6 can be described as an "unemployment and underemployment rate."

"U-4" adds discouraged workers to unemployment and the labor force. Discouraged workers are persons not in the officially defined labor force who have given a job-market-related reason for not looking currently for a job—for example, they have not looked for a job because they believed that no jobs were available.

"U-5" adds both discouraged workers and all other "marginally attached" workers to unemployment and the labor force. "Marginally attached" workers are all persons who currently are neither working nor looking for work but indicate that they want and are available for a job and have looked for work sometime in the recent past.

"U-6" adds persons employed part time for economic reasons, as shown in Table 10-3, to the number of persons counted as unemployed in "U-5", with the same labor force definition as in "U-5." This statistic, which measures a combination of unemployment and underemployment, is often cited in media reports on the employment situation.

For more information, see "BLS introduced new range of alternative unemployment measures" in the October 1995 issue of the *Monthly Labor Review.*

Notes on the data

The CPS data are collected by trained interviewers from about 60,000 sample households selected to represent the U.S. civilian noninstitutional population. The sample size has fluctuated between 50,000 and 60,000 households In January 1996, the size was reduced to 50,00 due to budgetary reasons. The sample size was increased back to 60,000 households, beginning with the data for July 2001, as part of a plan to meet the requirements of the State Children's Health Insurance Program legislation. The CPS provides data for other data series in addition to the BLS employment status data, such as household income and poverty) and health insurance (see Chapter 3).

The employment status data are based on the activity or status reported for the calendar week, Sunday through Saturday, that includes the 12th day of the month (the reference week). This specification is chosen so as to avoid weeks that contain major holidays. Households are interviewed in the week following the reference week. Sample households are phased in and out of the sample on a rotating basis. Consequently, three-fourths of the sample is the same for any two consecutive months. One-half of the sample is the same as the sample in the same month a year earlier.

Data relating to 1994 and subsequent years are not strictly comparable with data for 1993 and earlier years because of the major 1994 redesign of the survey questionnaire and collection methodology. The redesign included new and revised questions for the classification of individuals as employed or unemployed, the collection of new data on multiple jobholding, a change in the definition of discouraged workers, and the implementation of a more completely automated data collection.

The 1994 redesign of the CPS was the most extensive since 1967. However, there are many other significant periods of year-to-year noncomparability in the labor force data. These typically result from the introduction of new decennial census data into the CPS estimation procedures, expansions of the sample, or other improvements made to increase the reliability of the estimates. Each change introduces a new discontinuity, usually between December of the previous year and January of the newly altered year. The discontinuities are usually minor or negligible with respect to figures expressed as nationwide percentages (such as the unemployment rate or the labor force participation rate), but can be significant with respect to levels (such as labor force and employment in thousands of persons).

For further information on changes to the CPS, see "Publications and Other Documentation" at https://www.bls.gov/cps.

The monthly labor force, employment, and unemployment data are seasonally adjusted by the X-12-ARIMA method. All seasonally adjusted civilian labor force and unemployment rate statistics, as well as major employment and unemployment estimates, are computed by aggregating independently adjusted series. For example, the seasonally adjusted level of total unemployment is the sum of the seasonally adjusted levels of unemployment for the four age/sex groups (men and women age 16 to 19 years, and men and women age 20 years and over). Seasonally adjusted employment is the sum of the seasonally adjusted levels of employment for the same four groups. The seasonally adjusted civilian labor force is the sum of all eight components. Finally, the seasonally adjusted civilian worker unemployment rate is calculated by taking total seasonally adjusted unemployment as a percent of the total seasonally adjusted civilian labor force.

To minimize subsequent revisions, BLS uses a concurrent technique that estimates factors for the latest month using the most recent data. Then, seasonal adjustment factors are fully revised at the end of each year to reflect recent experience. The revisions also affect the preceding four years. An article describing the seasonal adjustment methodology for the household survey data is available at https://www.bls.gov/cps/cpsrs2010.pdf.

Breakdowns other than the basic age/sex classification described above—such as the employment data by class of worker in Table 10-3—will not necessarily add to totals because of independent seasonal adjustment.

Data availability

Data for each month are usually released on the first Friday of the following month in the "Employment Situation" press release, which also includes data from the establishment survey (Tables 10-7 through 10-17 and Chapter 15). (The release date actually is determined by the timing of the survey week.) The press release and data are available on the BLS Web site at <https://www.bls. gov>. The *Monthly Labor Review*, also available online at the

BLS Web site, features frequent articles analyzing developments in the labor force, employment, and unemployment.

Monthly and annual data on the current basis are available beginning with 1948. Historical unadjusted data are published in *Labor Force Statistics Derived from the Current Population Survey* (BLS Bulletin 2307). Historical seasonally adjusted data are available from BLS upon request. Complete historical data are available on the BLS Web site at <https://www.bls.gov/cps>.

Seasonal adjustment factors are revised each year for the five previous years, with the release of December data in early January. New population controls are introduced with the release of January data in early February.

BLS annual data for 1940 through 1947 are published on their Web site at <https://www.bls.gov>. The data for 1929 through 1939 were published in *Employment and Earnings,* May 1972, and in U.S. Commerce Department, Bureau of Economic Analysis, *Long-Term Economic Growth, 1860–1970*, June 1973, p. 163. The Lebergott estimates are also found in the latter volume.

The Darby alternative unemployment rate is found in Michael Darby, "Three-and-a-Half Million U.S. Employees Have Been Mislaid," *Journal of Political Economy,* February 1976, v. 84, no. 1. It is also displayed and discussed in Robert A. Margo, "Employment and Unemployment in the 1930s," *Journal of Economic Perspectives*, v. 7, no. 2, Spring 1993.

References

Comprehensive descriptive material can be found at <https://www.bls.gov/cps> under the "Publications and Other Documentation" section. Historical background on the CPS, as well as a description of the 1994 redesign, can be found in three articles from the September 1993 edition of *Monthly Labor Review*: "Why Is It Necessary to Change?"; "Redesigning the Questionnaire"; and "Evaluating Changes in the Estimates." The redesign is also described in the February 1994 issue of *Employment and Earnings.* See also Chapter 1, "Labor Force Data Derived from the Current Population Survey," *BLS Handbook of Methods*, Bulletin 2490 (April 1997).

Table 10-6

Insured Unemployment

SOURCE: U.S. DEPARTMENT OF LABOR, EMPLOYMENT AND TRAINING ADMINISTRATION

Definitions

State programs of unemployment insurance cover operations of regular programs under state unemployment insurance laws. In 1976, the law was amended to extend coverage to include virtually all state and local government employees, as well as many agricultural and domestic workers. (This took effect on January 1, 1978.) Benefits under state programs are financed by taxes levied by the states on employers.

An *initial claim* is the first claim in a benefit year filed by a worker after losing his or her job, or the first claim filed at the beginning of a subsequent period of unemployment in the same benefit year. The initial claim establishes the starting date for any insured unemployment that may result if the claimant is unemployed for one week or longer. Transitional claims (filed by claimants as they start a new benefit year in a continuing spell of unemployment) are excluded; therefore, these data more closely represent instances of new unemployment and are widely followed as a leading indicator of job market conditions.

Insured unemployment and *persons claiming benefits* both describe the average number of persons receiving benefits in the indicated month or year.

The *insured unemployment rate* for state programs is the level of insured unemployment as a percentage of employment covered by state programs.

Monthly averages in this book are averages, calculated by the editor, of the weekly data published by the Employment and Training Administration. Annual data are averages of the monthly data.

Data availability

Data are published in weekly press releases from the Employment and Training Administration. These releases are available on their Web site at <https://www.doleta.gov> under "Labor Market Data," as are historical data, under the category "UI/Program Statistics."

Tables 10-7, 10-8, 10-13, 15-1, and 15-2

Nonfarm Payroll Employment

SOURCE: U.S. DEPARTMENT OF LABOR, BUREAU OF LABOR STATISTICS (BLS)

These nonfarm employment data, as well as the hours and earnings data in Tables 10-8 through 10-12, 10-14 through 10-17, and 15-3 through 15-6, are compiled from payroll records. Information is reported monthly on a voluntary basis to BLS and its cooperating state agencies by a large sample of establishments, representing all industries except farming. These data, formally known as the Current Employment Statistics (CES) survey, are often referred to as the "establishment data" or the "payroll data." They are also known as the BLS-790 survey.

The survey, originally based on a stratified quota sample, has been replaced on a phased-in basis by a stratified probability sample. The new sampling procedure went into effect for wholesale trade in June 2000; for mining, construction, and manufacturing in June 2001; and for retail trade, transportation and public utilities, and finance, insurance, and real estate in June 2002. The phase-in was completed in June 2003, upon its extension to the service industries. The phase-in schedule was slightly different for the state and area series.

The sample has always been very large. Currently, it includes approximately 131,000 businesses and government agencies covering about 670,000 individual worksites, which account for about one-third of total benchmark employment of payroll workers. The sample is drawn from a sampling frame of over 10.2 million unemployment insurance tax accounts.

Data are classified according to the North American Industry Classification System. BLS has reconstructed historical time series to conform with NAICS, to ensure that all published series have a NAICS-based history extending back to at least January 1990. NAICS-based history extends back to January 1939 for total nonfarm and other high-level aggregates. For more detailed series, the starting date for NAICS data varies depending on the extent of the definitional changes between the old Standard Industrial Classification (SIC) and NAICS.

Definitions

An *establishment* is an economic unit, such as a factory, store, or professional office, that produces goods or services at a single location and is engaged in one type of economic activity.

Employment comprises all persons who received pay (including holiday and sick pay) for any part of the payroll period that includes the 12th day of the month. The definition of the payroll period for each reporting respondent is that used by the employer; it could be weekly, biweekly, monthly, or other. Included are all fulltime and parttime workers in nonfarm establishments, including salaried officers of corporations. Persons holding more than one job are counted in each establishment that reports them. Not covered are proprietors, the selfemployed, unpaid volunteer and family workers, farm workers, domestic workers in households, and military personnel. Employees of the Central Intelligence Agency, the Defense Intelligence Agency, the National Geospatial-Intelligence Agency, and the National Security Agency are not included.

Persons on an establishment payroll who are on paid sick leave (when pay is received directly from the employer), on paid holiday or vacation, or who work during a portion of the pay period despite being unemployed or on strike during the rest of the period, are counted as employed. Not counted as employed are persons who are laid off, on leave without pay, on strike for the entire period, or hired but not paid during the period.

Intermittent workers are counted if they performed any service during the month. BLS considers regular fulltime teachers (private and government) to be employed during the summer vacation period, regardless of whether they are specifically paid during those months.

The *government* division includes federal, state, and local activities such as legislative, executive, and judicial functions, as well as the U.S. Postal Service and all governmentowned and governmentoperated business enterprises, establishments, and institutions (arsenals, navy yards, hospitals, state-owned utilities, etc.), and government force account construction. However, as indicated earlier, members of the armed forces and employees of certain national-security-related agencies are not included.

The monthly *diffusion index of employment change*, currently based on 271 private nonfarm NAICS industries, represents the percentage of those industries in which the seasonally adjusted level of employment in that month was higher than six months earlier, plus one-half of the percentage of industries with unchanged employment. Therefore, the diffusion index reported for September represents the change from March to September. *Business Statistics* uses the September value to represent the year as a whole, since it spans the year's midpoint. Diffusion indexes measure the dispersion of economic gains and losses, with values below 50 percent associated with recessions. The current NAICS-based series begins with January 1991. For October 1976 through December 1990, an earlier series is available based on 347 SIC industries (there are more industries using the older classification system because in SIC manufacturing industries were represented in greater detail). September values from this series are used here to represent the years 1977 through 1990.

Production and nonsupervisory workers include all *production and related workers* in mining and manufacturing; *construction workers* in construction; and *nonsupervisory workers* in transportation, communication, electric, gas, and sanitary services; wholesale and retail trade; finance, insurance, and real estate; and services. These groups account for about four-fifths of the total employment on private nonagricultural payrolls. Previously, this category was called "production or nonsupervisory workers." The definitions have not changed.

Production and related workers include working supervisors and all nonsupervisory workers (including group leaders and trainees) engaged in fabricating, processing, assembling, inspecting, receiving, storing, handling, packing, warehousing, shipping, trucking, hauling, maintenance, repair, janitorial, guard services, product development, auxiliary production for plant's own use (such as a power plant), record keeping, and other services closely associated with these production operations.

Construction workers include the following employees in the construction division of the NAICS: working supervisors, qualified craft workers, mechanics, apprentices, laborers, and the like, who are engaged in new work, alterations, demolition, repair, maintenance, and other tasks, whether working at the site of construction or working in shops or yards at jobs (such as precutting and preassembling) ordinarily performed by members of the construction trades.

Nonsupervisory employees include employees (not above the working supervisory level) such as office and clerical workers, repairers, salespersons, operators, drivers, physicians, lawyers, accountants, nurses, social workers, research aides, teachers, drafters, photographers, beauticians, musicians, restaurant workers, custodial workers, attendants, line installers and repairers, laborers, janitors, guards, and other employees at similar occupational levels whose services are closely associated with those of the employees listed.

Notes on the data

Benchmark adjustments. The establishment survey data are adjusted annually to comprehensive counts of employment, called "benchmarks." Benchmark information on employment by industry is compiled by state agencies from reports of establishments covered under state unemployment insurance laws; these form an annual compilation of administrative data known as the ES-202. These tabulations cover about 97 percent of all employees on nonfarm payrolls. Benchmark data for the residual are obtained from alternate sources, primarily from Railroad Retirement Board records and the Census Bureau's *County Business Patterns*. The latest benchmark adjustment, which is incorporated into the data in this volume, increased the employment level in the benchmark month March 2018 by 135,000 jobs, which was 0.1 percent.

The estimates for the benchmark month are compared with new benchmark levels for each industry. If revisions are necessary, the monthly series of estimates between benchmark periods are adjusted by graduated amounts between the new benchmark and the preceding one ("wedged back"), and the new benchmark level for each industry is then carried forward month by month based on the sample.

More specifically, the month-to-month changes for each estimation cell are based on changes in a matched sample for that cell, plus an estimate of net business births and deaths. The matched sample for each pair of months consists of establishments that have reported data for both months (which automatically excludes establishments that have gone out of business by the second month). Since new businesses are not immediately incorporated into the sample, a model-based estimate of net business births and deaths in that estimating cell is added. The birth/death adjustment factors are re-estimated quarterly based on the Quarterly Census of Employment and Wages.

Not-seasonally-adjusted data for all months since the last benchmark date are subject to revision.

Beginning in 1959, the data include Alaska and Hawaii. This inclusion resulted in an increase of 212,000 (0.4 percent) in total nonfarm employment for the March 1959 benchmark month.

Seasonal adjustment. The seasonal movements that recur periodically—such as warm and cold weather, holidays, and vacations—are generally the largest single component of monthtomonth changes in employment. After adjusting the data to remove such seasonal variation, basic trends become more evident. BLS uses X-12-ARIMA software to produce seasonal factors and perform concurrent seasonal adjustment, using the most recent 10 years of data. New factors are developed each month adding the most current data.

For most series, a special procedure called REGARIMA (regression with autocorrelated errors) is used before calculating the seasonal factors; this adjusts for the length of the interval (which can be either four or five weeks) between the survey weeks. REGARIMA has also been used to isolate extreme weather effects that distort the measurement of seasonal patterns in the construction industry, and to identify variations in local government employment due to the presence or absence of election poll workers.

Seasonal adjustment factors are directly applied to the component levels. Seasonally adjusted totals for employment series are then obtained by aggregating the seasonally adjusted components directly, while hours and earnings series represent weighted averages of the seasonally adjusted component series. Seasonally adjusted data are not published for a small number of series characterized by small seasonal components relative to their trend and/or irregular components. However, these series are used in aggregating to broader seasonally adjusted levels.

Revisions of the seasonally adjusted data, usually for the most recent five-year period, are made once a year coincident with the benchmark revisions. This means that these revisions typically extend back farther than the benchmark revisions.

Data availability

Employment data by industry division are available beginning with 1919. Data for each month usually are released on the first Friday of the following month in a press release that also contains data from the household survey (Tables 10-1 through 10-5). (The release date actually is determined by the timing of the survey week.) The *Monthly Labor Review* frequently contains articles analyzing developments in the labor force, employment, and unemployment. The *Monthly Labor Review*, press releases, and complete historical data are available on the BLS Web site at <https://www.bls.gov>.

Benchmark revisions and revised seasonally adjusted data for recent years are made each year with the release of January data in early February. Before 2004, the benchmark revisions were not made until June; the acceleration is due to earlier availability of the benchmark UI (ES-202) data.

References

References can be found at <https://www.bls.gov/ces> under the headings "Special Notices," "Benchmark Information," and "Technical Notes." Extensive changes incorporated in June 2003 are described in "Recent Changes in the National Current Employment Statistics Survey," *Monthly Labor Review*, June 2003. The latest benchmark revision is discussed in an article available on the Website. See also Chapter 2, "Employment, Hours, and Earnings from the Establishment Survey," *BLS Handbook of Methods*, Bulletin 2490 (April 1997).

Tables 10-8 through 10-10, 10-14, 10-15, 15-3 and 15-6

Average Hours Per Week; Aggregate Employee Hours

SOURCE: U.S. DEPARTMENT OF LABOR, BUREAU OF LABOR STATISTICS (BLS)

See the notes and definitions to Tables 10-7 and related tables for an overall description of the "establishment" or "payroll" survey that is the source of these earnings data.

Hours and earnings have been reported for production and non-supervisory workers, as defined above, since the inception of the CES. Beginning with data for March 2006, such data have also been collected for all payroll employees. With sufficient history for calculation of seasonal adjustment factors, BLS began publishing all-employee hours and earnings in February 2010, and these new data are presented in *Business Statistics* Tables 10-9 through 10-12.

Definitions

Average weekly hours represents the average hours paid per worker during the pay period that includes the 12th of the month. Included are hours paid for holidays and vacations, as well as those paid for sick leave when pay is received directly from the firm.

Average weekly hours are different from standard or scheduled hours. Factors such as unpaid absenteeism, labor turnover, part-time work, and work stoppages can cause average weekly hours to be lower than scheduled hours of work for an establishment.

An important characteristic of these data is that average weekly hours pertain to jobs, not to persons; thus, a person with half-time jobs in two different establishments is represented in this series as two jobs that have 20-hour workweeks, not as one person with a 40-hour workweek.

Overtime hours represent the portion of average weekly hours worked in excess of regular hours, for which overtime premiums were paid. Weekend and holiday hours are included only if overtime premiums were paid. Hours for which only shift differential, hazard, incentive, or other similar types of premiums were paid are excluded.

Aggregate hours provide measures of changes over time in labor input to the industry, in index-number form.

Indexes of aggregate weekly hours are calculated by dividing the current month's aggregate hours by the average of the 12 monthly figures, for the base year. The index of aggregate hours paints a good picture of the stall in the recovery. Employment is up, but hours are not up proportionally. This reflects the trend to part-time workers and the reduction of hours in part-time workers. For the series covering production and nonsupervisory workers, the base period is 2002; for the all-employee series, the base period is 2007.

Notes on the data

Benchmark adjustments. Independent benchmarks are not available for the hours and earnings series. However, at the time of the annual adjustment of the employment series to new benchmarks, the levels of hours and earnings may be affected by the revised employment weights (which are used in computing the industry averages for hours and earnings), as well as by the changes in seasonal adjustment factors introduced with the benchmark revision.

Method of computing industry series. "Average weekly hours" for individual industries are computed by dividing worker hours (reported by establishments classified in each industry) by the number of workers reported for the same establishments. Estimates for divisions and major industry groups are averages (weighted by employment) of the figures for component industries.

Seasonal adjustment. Hours and earnings series are seasonally adjusted by applying factors directly to the corresponding unadjusted series. Data for some industries are not seasonally adjusted because the seasonal component is small relative to the trendcycle and/or irregular components. Consequently, they cannot be separated with sufficient precision.

Special adjustments are made to average weekly hours to account for the presence or absence of religious holidays in the April survey reference period and the occasional occurrence of Labor Day in the September reference period. In addition, REGARIMA modeling is used prior to seasonal adjustment to correct for reporting and processing errors associated with the number of weekdays in a month (rather than to correct for the 4- and 5-week effect, which is less significant for hours than it is for employment). This is of particular importance for average weekly hours in the service-providing industries other than retail trade. For this reason, BLS advises that calculations of over-the-year changes (for example, the change for the current month from a year earlier) should use seasonally adjusted data, since the actual not-seasonally-adjusted monthly data may be distorted.

Data availability

See data availability for Tables 10-7 and related, above.

References

See references for Tables 10-7 and related, above.

Tables 10-8, 10-11, 10-12, 10-16, 10-17, 15-4, and 15-5

Hourly and Weekly Earnings

SOURCE: U.S. DEPARTMENT OF LABOR, BUREAU OF LABOR STATISTICS (BLS)

See the notes and definitions to Tables 10-8 and related for an overall description of the "establishment" or "payroll" survey that is the source of these earnings data.

Hours and earnings have been reported for production and non-supervisory workers, as defined above, since the inception of the CES. Beginning with data for March 2006, such data have also been collected for all payroll employees. With sufficient history for calculation of seasonal adjustment factors, BLS began publishing all-employee hours and earnings in February 2010, and these data are presented in new *Business Statistics* Tables 10-9 through 10-12.

Definitions

Earnings are the payments that workers receive during the survey period (before deductions for taxes and other items), including premium pay for overtime or late-shift work but excluding irregular bonuses and other special payments. After being previously excluded, tips were asked to be reported beginning in September 2005. This made little difference in most industries, and BLS asserts that many respondents had already been including tips. In two industries, full-service restaurants and cafeterias, there was a substantial difference, and the historical earnings data for those industries have been reconstructed to reflect the new higher level of earnings.

Notes on the data

The hours and earnings series are based on reports of gross payroll and corresponding paid hours for full and parttime workers who received pay for any part of the pay period that included the 12th of the month.

Total payrolls are before deductions, such as for the employee share of oldage and unemployment insurance, group insurance, withholding taxes, bonds, and union dues. The payroll figures also include pay for overtime, holidays, vacations, and sick leave (paid directly by the employer for the period reported). Excluded from the payroll figures are fringe benefits (health and other types of insurance and contributions to retirement, paid by the employer, and the employer share of payroll taxes), bonuses (unless earned and paid regularly each pay period), other pay not earned in the pay period reported (retroactive pay), and the value of free rent, fuel, meals, or other payment-in-kind.

Average hourly earnings data reflect not only changes in basic hourly and incentive wage rates, but also such variable factors as premium pay for overtime and lateshift work and changes in output of workers paid on an incentive basis. Shifts in the volume of employment between relatively highpaid and lowpaid work also affect the general average of hourly earnings.

Averages of hourly earnings should not be confused with wage rates, which represent the rates stipulated for a given unit of work or time, while earnings refer to the actual return to the worker for a stated period of time. The earnings series do not represent total labor cost to the employer because of the inclusion of tips and the exclusion of irregular bonuses, retroactive items, the cost of employer-provided benefits, and payroll taxes paid by employers.

Average weekly earnings are not the amounts available to workers for spending, since they do not reflect deductions such as income taxes and Social Security taxes. It is also important to understand that average weekly earnings represent earnings per job, not per worker (since a worker may have more than one job) and not per family (since a family may have more than one worker). A person with two half-time jobs will be reflected as two earners with low weekly earnings rather than as one person with the total earnings from his or her two jobs.

Method of computing industry series. Average hourly earnings are obtained by dividing the reported total worker payroll by total worker hours. Estimates for both hours and hourly earnings for nonfarm divisions and major industry groups are employment-weighted averages of the figures for component industries.

Average weekly earnings are computed by multiplying average hourly earnings by average weekly hours. In addition to the factors mentioned above, which exert varying influences upon average hourly earnings, average weekly earnings are affected by changes in the length of the workweek, parttime work, work stoppages, labor turnover, and absenteeism. Persistent longterm uptrends in the proportion of parttime workers in retail trade and many of the service industries have reduced average workweeks (as measured here), and have similarly affected the average weekly earnings series.

Benchmark adjustments. Independent benchmarks are not available for the hours and earnings series. At the time of the annual adjustment of the employment series to new benchmarks, the levels of hours and earnings may be affected by the revised employment weights (which are used in computing the industry averages for hours and earnings), as well as by the changes in seasonal adjustment factors that were also introduced with the benchmark revision.

Seasonal adjustment. Hours and earnings series are seasonally adjusted by applying factors directly to the corresponding unadjusted series; seasonally adjusted average weekly earnings are the product of seasonally adjusted hourly earnings and weekly hours.

REGARIMA modeling is used to correct for reporting and processing errors associated with variations in the number of weekdays in a month (rather than for the 4- and 5-week effect, which is less significant for earnings than for employment). This is of particular importance for average hourly earnings in wholesale trade, financial activities, professional and business services, and other services. For this reason, BLS advises that calculations of over-the-year changes, for example the change for the current month from a year earlier, should use seasonally adjusted data, since the actual not seasonally adjusted monthly data may be distorted.

Data availability

See data availability for Tables 10-7 and related, above.

References

See references for Tables 10-7 and related, above.

Table 10-18

Hours at Work, Current Population Survey

This table presents annual average measures of hours worked per week reported by workers in the Current Population Survey, in response to questions asking for the hours worked in the survey week by each worker in the household on all his or her jobs combined. These measures are not published in regular BLS reports but are available on request. *Business Statistics* obtained these numbers from BLS staff and presents them here in annual average form.

Do CPS respondents overestimate the number of hours they work? One study made that claim, but a careful re-examination of the data by Harley Frazis and Jay Stewart in the June 2014 *Monthly Labor Review* indicates that respondents slightly under-report the hours that they actually worked during the reference week. (On the other hand, the authors also note that the reference week overestimates the average for the entire month because of the absence of holidays.) (*Monthly Labor Review* is available online at www.bls.gov.) In any event, the CPS data give a more accurate picture of <u>trends</u> in the workweeks of typical American workers than does the establishment (CES) survey.

Table 10-19

Median Usual Weekly Earnings of Full-Time Wage and Salary Workers

SOURCE: U.S. DEPARTMENT OF LABOR, BUREAU OF LABOR STATISTICS

These data are from the Current Population Survey, which was described in the notes to Tables 10-1 through 10-6. Because they are earnings per worker, not per job, and are limited to full-time workers, the data are not distorted by the increasing proportion of part-time workers, as the CES earnings data are.

Definitions

Full-time wage and salary workers are those workers reported as "employed" in the CPS who receive wages, salaries, commissions, tips, pay in kind, or piece rates, and usually work 35 hours or more per week at their sole or principal job. Both private-sector and public-sector employees are included. All self-employed persons are excluded (even those whose businesses are incorporated).

Usual weekly earnings are earnings before taxes and other deductions and include any overtime pay, commissions, or tips usually received. In the case of multiple jobholders they refer to the main job. The wording of the question was changed in January 1994 to better deal with persons who found it easier to report earnings on other than a weekly basis. Such reports are then converted to the weekly equivalent. According to BLS, "the term 'usual' is as perceived by the respondent. If the respondent asks for a definition of usual, interviewers are instructed to define the term as more than half the weeks worked during the past 4 or 5 months."

The *median* is the amount that divides a given earnings distribution into two equal groups, one having earnings above the median and the other having earnings below the median.

Race and ethnicity. See the notes to Tables 10-1 through 10-6 for the definitions of these categories.

Data availability

These data become available about 3 weeks after the end of each quarter in the "Usual Weekly Earnings of Wage and Salary Workers" press release, available on the BLS Web site at <https://www.bls.gov/cps>. Recent data are available at that location. Also available are greater detail by demographic and age groups, by occupation, by union status, and by education; distributional data, by deciles and quartiles; and earnings for part-time workers. Also available are earnings in 1982 dollars using the CPI-U. (In the opinion of the editor, these give a less accurate depiction of longer-term trends, which is why *Business Statistics* provides the CPI-U-RS data explained above.) Historical data are available upon request from BLS by telephone at (202) 691-6555.

CHAPTER 11: ENERGY

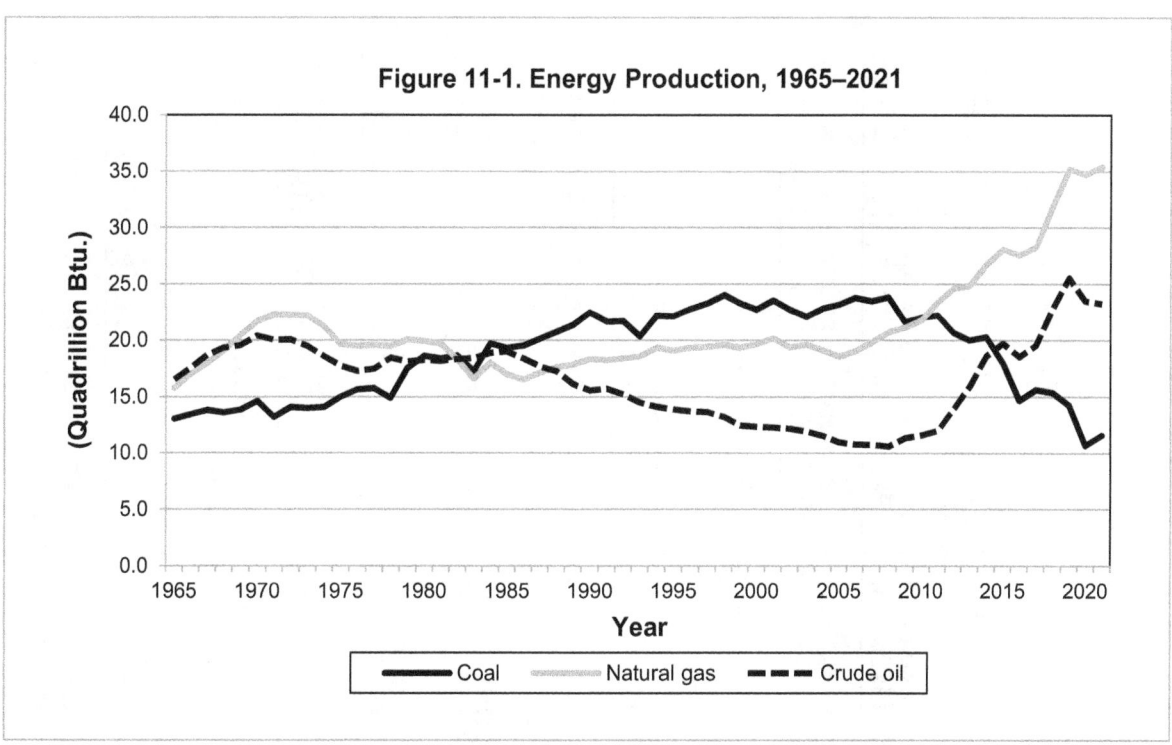

Figure 11-1. Energy Production, 1965–2021

- As the war in Ukraine, COVID-19 and supply chain disturbances continue, the global economy becomes even more unstable. Supply chain disturbances refers to the network of organizations, people, activities, information, and resources involved in delivering a product or service to a consumer.

- Demand for coal has been declining since 1998, with production declining from 24.045 quadrillion Btu to 11.613 quadrillion Btu in 2021, a loss of 52 percent. Although production has been declining, it did increase 8.5 percent in 2021. In contrast, renewable energy, such as hydropower, wind and solar, has been rising since the 1960s with the biggest boost in the 2000s. From 1965 through 2021 total production of renewable energy has more than tripled. (Table 11-1)

- Of note, renewable energy production first passed coal production in 2020 at 11.687 Q Btu for renewable energy compared with 10.703 Q Btu for coal production. Renewable energy continued to outpace coal production in 2021 at 12.320 Q Btu and 11.613 Q Btu respectively. (Table 11-1 and Figure 11-1)

- During the COVID lockdowns, consumption of energy products declined 7.4 percent from 2019 to 2020 but increased 4.7 percent the following year in 2021. The residential and commercial sector consumed the largest amount of energy in 2021 at 39.3 percent, followed by the industrial sector at 33.0 percent and the transportation sector at 27.7 percent. (Table 11-1)

Table 11-1. Energy Supply and Consumption

(Quadrillion Btu.)

Year and month	Imports	Exports	Production, by source									Consumption, by end-use sector			
			Total	Fossil fuels					Nuclear electric power	Renew-able energy, total	Total	Residential and commercial	Industrial	Transport-ation
				Total	Coal	Natural gas	Crude oil	Natural gas plant liquids							
1965	5.892	1.829	50.644	47.205	13.055	15.775	16.521	1.853	0.043	3.396	53.953	16.485	25.035	12.432
1966	6.146	1.829	53.507	50.011	13.468	17.011	17.561	1.971	0.064	3.432	56.949	17.493	26.356	13.100
1967	6.159	2.115	56.347	52.568	13.825	17.943	18.651	2.148	0.088	3.690	58.895	18.539	26.604	13.752
1968	6.905	1.998	58.188	54.274	13.609	19.068	19.308	2.289	0.142	3.773	62.401	19.666	27.869	14.866
1969	7.676	2.126	60.501	56.252	13.863	20.446	19.556	2.386	0.154	4.095	65.597	21.003	29.087	15.507
1970	8.342	2.632	63.462	59.152	14.607	21.666	20.401	2.478	0.239	4.070	67.817	22.113	29.605	16.098
1971	9.535	2.151	62.686	58.011	13.186	22.280	20.033	2.513	0.413	4.262	69.261	22.968	29.562	16.730
1972	11.387	2.118	63.870	58.904	14.092	22.208	20.041	2.564	0.584	4.382	72.660	24.041	30.901	17.717
1973	14.613	2.033	63.528	58.207	13.992	22.187	19.493	2.535	0.910	4.411	75.645	24.441	32.591	18.613
1974	14.304	2.203	62.308	56.294	14.074	21.210	18.575	2.435	1.272	4.742	73.922	24.049	31.753	18.120
1975	14.032	2.323	61.284	54.697	14.989	19.640	17.729	2.338	1.900	4.687	71.930	24.307	29.379	18.245
1976	16.760	2.172	61.522	54.684	15.654	19.480	17.262	2.288	2.111	4.727	75.931	25.474	31.356	19.101
1977	19.948	2.052	61.970	55.059	15.755	19.565	17.454	2.286	2.702	4.209	77.913	25.870	32.221	19.822
1978	19.106	1.920	63.060	55.031	14.910	19.485	18.434	2.202	3.024	5.005	79.905	26.645	32.643	20.617
1979	19.460	2.855	65.851	57.952	17.540	20.076	18.104	2.232	2.776	5.123	80.810	26.461	33.878	20.472
1980	15.796	3.695	67.147	58.979	18.598	19.908	18.249	2.225	2.739	5.428	78.023	26.332	31.994	19.697
1981	13.719	4.307	66.910	58.488	18.377	19.699	18.146	2.266	3.008	5.414	76.055	25.878	30.663	19.514
1982	11.861	4.608	66.527	57.416	18.639	18.319	18.309	2.149	3.131	5.980	73.042	26.392	27.561	19.089
1983	11.752	3.693	64.066	54.368	17.247	16.593	18.392	2.136	3.203	6.496	72.913	26.364	27.372	19.177
1984	12.471	3.786	68.800	58.809	19.719	18.008	18.848	2.234	3.553	6.438	76.569	27.404	29.509	19.656
1985	11.781	4.196	67.661	57.502	19.325	16.980	18.992	2.204	4.076	6.084	76.339	27.493	28.758	20.088
1986	14.151	4.021	67.030	56.539	19.509	16.541	18.376	2.113	4.380	6.111	76.596	27.582	28.226	20.789
1987	15.398	3.812	67.506	57.131	20.141	17.136	17.675	2.179	4.754	5.622	79.012	28.210	29.333	21.469
1988	17.296	4.366	68.890	57.846	20.738	17.599	17.279	2.231	5.587	5.457	82.657	29.711	30.628	22.318
1989	18.766	4.661	69.285	57.448	21.360	17.847	16.117	2.123	5.602	6.235	84.748	30.987	31.283	22.479
1990	18.817	4.752	70.668	58.523	22.488	18.326	15.571	2.138	6.104	6.040	84.427	30.258	31.750	22.419
1991	18.335	5.141	70.321	57.831	21.636	18.229	15.701	2.265	6.422	6.068	84.381	30.920	31.343	22.118
1992	19.372	4.937	69.914	57.615	21.694	18.375	15.223	2.323	6.479	5.821	85.726	30.797	32.514	22.415
1993	21.218	4.227	68.273	55.780	20.336	18.584	14.494	2.366	6.410	6.082	87.260	32.029	32.560	22.671
1994	22.307	4.035	70.683	58.002	22.202	19.348	14.103	2.349	6.694	5.987	88.990	32.208	33.463	23.319
1995	22.180	4.496	71.129	57.496	22.130	19.082	13.887	2.398	7.075	6.557	90.929	33.207	33.910	23.812
1996	23.633	4.613	72.435	58.338	22.790	19.344	13.723	2.480	7.087	7.011	93.932	34.675	34.838	24.419
1997	25.119	4.493	72.420	58.806	23.310	19.394	13.658	2.445	6.597	7.017	94.502	34.644	35.135	24.723
1998	26.473	4.237	72.827	59.266	24.045	19.613	13.235	2.372	7.068	6.493	94.925	34.920	34.780	25.225
1999	27.152	3.669	71.686	57.560	23.295	19.341	12.451	2.473	7.610	6.516	96.540	35.931	34.693	25.916
2000	28.865	3.962	71.271	57.307	22.735	19.662	12.358	2.551	7.862	6.102	98.701	37.597	34.589	26.515
2001	30.052	3.731	71.675	58.485	23.547	20.166	12.282	2.491	8.029	5.162	96.070	37.175	32.653	26.242
2002	29.331	3.608	70.653	56.777	22.732	19.382	12.160	2.502	8.145	5.731	97.530	38.132	32.590	26.808
2003	31.007	4.013	69.885	55.983	22.094	19.633	11.960	2.296	7.960	5.943	97.836	38.466	32.489	26.881
2004	33.492	4.351	70.170	55.884	22.852	19.074	11.550	2.408	8.223	6.063	100.000	38.738	33.444	27.826
2005	34.659	4.462	69.377	54.995	23.185	18.556	10.974	2.280	8.161	6.221	100.100	39.467	32.374	28.261
2006	34.649	4.727	70.678	55.877	23.790	19.022	10.767	2.299	8.215	6.587	99.392	38.379	32.317	28.697
2007	34.679	5.338	71.338	56.369	23.493	19.786	10.741	2.349	8.459	6.511	100.890	39.773	32.306	28.815
2008	32.970	6.949	73.146	57.527	23.851	20.703	10.613	2.359	8.426	7.192	98.754	40.071	31.261	27.421
2009	29.690	6.920	72.593	56.612	21.624	21.139	11.340	2.508	8.355	7.626	93.943	38.971	28.380	26.592
2010	29.866	8.176	74.909	58.159	22.038	21.806	11.610	2.705	8.434	8.315	97.507	39.955	30.577	26.975
2011	28.748	10.373	78.100	60.529	22.221	23.406	12.012	2.890	8.269	9.310	96.865	39.365	30.896	26.603
2012	27.068	11.267	79.254	62.296	20.677	24.610	13.847	3.162	8.062	8.896	94.384	37.294	30.958	26.132
2013	24.623	11.788	81.866	64.184	20.001	24.859	15.872	3.451	8.244	9.438	97.131	38.982	31.531	26.618
2014	23.241	12.270	87.757	69.622	20.286	26.718	18.613	4.005	8.338	9.798	98.292	39.710	31.702	26.880
2015	23.794	12.902	88.295	70.190	17.946	28.067	19.701	4.476	8.337	9.768	97.405	38.774	31.375	27.256
2016	25.378	14.119	84.337	65.430	14.667	27.576	18.522	4.665	8.427	10.480	97.388	38.209	31.366	27.813
2017	25.458	17.946	88.129	68.447	15.625	28.289	19.546	4.987	8.419	11.263	97.659	37.787	31.821	28.051
2018	24.833	21.224	95.780	75.758	15.363	31.882	22.786	5.727	8.438	11.584	101.240	39.949	32.785	28.507
2019	22.865	23.476	101.430	81.354	14.256	35.187	25.559	6.352	8.452	11.632	100.460	39.087	32.706	28.673
2020	19.988	23.463	95.672	75.734	10.703	34.724	23.501	6.805	8.251	11.687	92.978	37.302	31.234	24.442
2021	21.434	25.246	97.768	77.320	11.613	35.408	23.239	7.061	8.129	12.320	97.333	38.294	32.105	26.933
2020														
January	1.871	2.175	8.768	7.011	1.112	3.064	2.256	0.580	0.775	0.982	8.976	3.916	2.785	2.274
February	1.727	2.089	8.129	6.454	0.949	2.863	2.117	0.526	0.689	0.986	8.371	3.563	2.641	2.166
March	1.782	2.236	8.497	6.833	0.921	3.066	2.261	0.585	0.669	0.996	7.887	3.124	2.703	2.060
April	1.507	1.880	7.783	6.241	0.787	2.889	2.034	0.532	0.618	0.923	6.518	2.651	2.300	1.567
May	1.651	1.694	7.488	5.794	0.744	2.808	1.713	0.529	0.672	1.022	6.829	2.619	2.416	1.794
June	1.705	1.659	7.627	5.885	0.791	2.756	1.779	0.560	0.702	1.039	7.273	2.834	2.454	1.985
July	1.692	1.874	8.013	6.293	0.864	2.898	1.933	0.598	0.725	0.995	8.057	3.280	2.617	2.159
August	1.613	1.877	7.973	6.298	0.950	2.889	1.863	0.596	0.721	0.955	8.003	3.152	2.679	2.172
September	1.545	1.853	7.700	6.129	0.903	2.798	1.856	0.572	0.687	0.885	7.296	2.692	2.529	2.075
October	1.578	1.975	7.755	6.196	0.899	2.870	1.837	0.590	0.620	0.939	7.475	2.694	2.658	2.123
November	1.596	1.957	7.847	6.221	0.886	2.863	1.899	0.574	0.645	0.981	7.582	2.909	2.670	2.002
December	1.720	2.194	8.093	6.378	0.897	2.963	1.955	0.563	0.730	0.985	8.710	3.871	2.776	2.064
2021														
January	1.770	2.129	8.242	6.487	0.976	2.983	1.951	0.576	0.749	1.006	8.873	4.089	2.758	2.026
February	1.565	1.720	6.847	5.307	0.823	2.504	1.557	0.423	0.658	0.882	8.072	3.937	2.287	1.848
March	1.780	2.031	8.288	6.525	1.022	2.967	1.969	0.568	0.665	1.097	8.112	3.304	2.610	2.198
April	1.702	2.166	7.949	6.312	0.909	2.901	1.917	0.585	0.596	1.041	7.449	2.682	2.600	2.167
May	1.800	2.100	8.335	6.572	0.976	2.990	2.000	0.607	0.662	1.101	7.705	2.670	2.720	2.316
June	1.888	2.188	8.122	6.396	0.980	2.900	1.927	0.589	0.690	1.036	8.012	2.977	2.721	2.315
July	1.876	2.117	8.303	6.593	0.976	3.012	1.999	0.606	0.719	0.991	8.337	3.209	2.728	2.400
August	1.845	2.188	8.366	6.632	1.006	3.030	1.977	0.619	0.726	1.008	8.483	3.255	2.818	2.410
September	1.828	1.933	8.004	6.360	1.000	2.912	1.853	0.596	0.674	0.970	7.707	2.799	2.639	2.268
October	1.749	2.131	8.331	6.725	0.984	3.072	2.033	0.635	0.595	1.011	7.684	2.667	2.681	2.336
November	1.773	2.170	8.328	6.629	0.983	3.017	2.009	0.620	0.655	1.044	8.135	3.103	2.730	2.301
December	1.859	2.373	8.653	6.781	0.978	3.119	2.047	0.637	0.739	1.133	8.763	3.604	2.811	2.348

Table 11-2. Energy Consumption Per Dollar of Real Gross Domestic Product

Year	Primary energy consumption (quadrillion Btu)			Gross domestic product (billions of chained [2012] dollars)	Energy consumption per real dollar of GDP		
	Total	Petroleum and natural gas	Other energy		Total	Petroleum and natural gas	Other energy
1950	34.599	19.267	15.332	2 291.1	15.12	8.42	6.70
1951	36.954	21.456	15.497	2 475.4	14.95	8.68	6.26
1952	36.726	22.484	14.243	2 576.7	14.27	8.74	5.53
1953	37.641	23.439	14.202	2 697.5	13.97	8.70	5.27
1954	36.614	24.144	12.470	2 681.9	13.67	9.02	4.65
1955	40.178	26.223	13.955	2 873.2	14.00	9.14	4.86
1956	41.722	27.519	14.203	2 934.4	14.24	9.40	4.84
1957	41.754	28.089	13.665	2 996.2	13.96	9.39	4.56
1958	41.609	29.154	12.455	2 974.0	14.01	9.82	4.19
1959	43.423	30.997	12.426	3 180.2	13.68	9.77	3.91
1960	45.041	32.259	12.782	3 262.1	13.83	9.91	3.92
1961	45.691	33.096	12.595	3 345.7	13.68	9.91	3.77
1962	47.775	34.728	13.047	3 550.7	13.48	9.80	3.68
1963	49.589	36.049	13.540	3 705.3	13.41	9.75	3.66
1964	51.755	37.530	14.226	3 918.8	13.23	9.60	3.63
1965	53.953	38.953	15.001	4 173.4	12.95	9.35	3.60
1966	56.949	41.331	15.618	4 448.7	12.82	9.31	3.51
1967	58.895	43.219	15.676	4 570.7	12.90	9.46	3.43
1968	62.401	46.176	16.225	4 795.4	13.02	9.64	3.39
1969	65.596	48.999	16.598	4 945.2	13.28	9.92	3.36
1970	67.817	51.294	16.523	4 954.4	13.70	10.36	3.34
1971	69.260	53.008	16.253	5 117.6	13.55	10.37	3.18
1972	72.660	55.617	17.043	5 386.7	13.50	10.34	3.17
1973	75.652	57.318	18.334	5 690.9	13.31	10.08	3.22
1974	73.929	55.153	18.776	5 660.1	13.08	9.76	3.32
1975	71.931	52.647	19.284	5 648.5	12.75	9.33	3.42
1976	75.939	55.487	20.452	5 952.8	12.77	9.33	3.44
1977	77.920	57.013	20.907	6 228.1	12.53	9.17	3.36
1978	79.907	57.920	21.987	6 572.8	12.17	8.82	3.35
1979	80.812	57.741	23.070	6 780.9	11.93	8.53	3.40
1980	78.021	54.394	23.627	6 763.5	11.55	8.05	3.50
1981	76.057	51.631	24.426	6 935.2	10.98	7.46	3.52
1982	73.046	48.535	24.511	6 810.1	10.74	7.14	3.60
1983	72.915	47.218	25.698	7 122.3	10.25	6.64	3.61
1984	76.571	49.386	27.185	7 637.7	10.04	6.48	3.56
1985	76.334	48.570	27.764	7 956.2	9.61	6.12	3.49
1986	76.599	48.742	27.857	8 231.7	9.32	5.93	3.39
1987	79.008	50.457	28.551	8 516.4	9.29	5.93	3.35
1988	82.659	52.621	30.038	8 872.2	9.33	5.94	3.39
1989	84.740	53.766	30.974	9 198.0	9.22	5.85	3.37
1990	84.433	53.103	31.330	9 371.5	9.02	5.68	3.35
1991	84.380	52.822	31.558	9 361.3	9.03	5.65	3.37
1992	85.725	54.181	31.544	9 691.1	8.86	5.60	3.26
1993	87.266	54.817	32.449	9 957.7	8.78	5.52	3.26
1994	88.983	56.181	32.802	10 358.9	8.61	5.44	3.17
1995	90.931	57.012	33.918	10 637.0	8.56	5.37	3.19
1996	93.935	58.674	35.261	11 038.3	8.52	5.33	3.20
1997	94.507	59.288	35.219	11 529.2	8.21	5.15	3.06
1998	94.920	59.550	35.370	12 045.8	7.89	4.95	2.94
1999	96.545	60.641	35.903	12 623.4	7.66	4.82	2.85
2000	98.702	61.976	36.727	13 138.0	7.53	4.73	2.80
2001	96.064	60.856	35.208	13 263.4	7.25	4.60	2.65
2002	97.535	61.628	35.908	13 488.4	7.24	4.58	2.66
2003	97.835	61.538	36.297	13 865.5	7.06	4.44	2.62
2004	100.002	63.062	36.940	14 399.7	6.95	4.38	2.56
2005	100.102	62.782	37.320	14 901.3	6.72	4.22	2.50
2006	99.392	61.969	37.423	15 315.9	6.49	4.05	2.44
2007	100.894	63.030	37.863	15 623.9	6.46	4.04	2.42
2008	98.754	60.612	38.142	15 643.0	6.34	3.89	2.44
2009	93.943	58.195	35.748	15 236.3	6.19	3.84	2.35
2010	97.514	59.895	37.619	15 649.0	6.25	3.85	2.40
2011	96.872	59.594	37.278	15 891.5	6.11	3.77	2.34
2012	94.387	59.922	34.465	16 254.0	5.83	3.71	2.12
2013	97.130	61.203	35.927	16 553.3	5.89	3.72	2.17
2014	98.297	62.041	36.257	16 932.1	5.82	3.68	2.13
2015	97.407	63.559	33.847	17 390.3	5.60	3.67	1.93
2016	97.384	64.112	33.271	17 680.3	5.52	3.64	1.87
2017	97.660	64.098	33.562	18 079.1	5.41	3.56	1.85
2018	101.235	68.045	33.190	18 606.8	5.44	2.05	1.78
2019	100.471	69.118	31.352	19 032.7	5.28	2.14	1.65
2020	92.974	63.871	29.103	18 384.7	5.06	2.09	1.58
2021	97.331	66.413	30.918	19 427.3	5.01	3.42	1.59

Table 11-3. Petroleum and Petroleum Products—Prices, Imports, Domestic Production, and Stocks

(Not seasonally adjusted.)

Year and month	Crude oil futures price (dollars per barrel) Current dollars	2009 dollars	Imports Total energy-related petroleum products (thousands of barrels)	Crude petroleum Thousands of barrels Total	Average per day	Unit price (dollars per barrel)	Supply (thousands of barrels per day) Petroleum and products Exports	Imports	Net imports	Domestic production Crude oil	Natural gas plant liquids	Stocks (end of period, millions of barrels) Crude oil and petroleum products	Crude petroleum Non-SPR	Strategic petroleum reserve
1983	30.66	69.52	. . .	1 293 819	3 545	29.51	739	5 051	4 312	8 688	1 559	1 454	344	379
1984	29.44	63.41	. . .	1 319 683	3 616	27.68	722	5 437	4 715	8 879	1 630	1 556	345	451
1985	27.89	57.07	. . .	1 260 856	3 454	26.20	781	5 067	4 286	8 971	1 609	1 519	321	493
1986	15.05	29.56	. . .	1 634 567	4 478	13.90	785	6 224	5 439	8 680	1 551	1 593	331	512
1987	19.15	36.38	. . .	1 744 977	4 781	16.80	764	6 678	5 914	8 349	1 595	1 607	349	541
1988	15.96	29.10	. . .	1 887 860	5 172	13.69	815	7 402	6 587	8 140	1 625	1 597	330	560
1989	19.58	34.69	. . .	2 146 552	5 881	16.49	859	8 061	7 202	7 613	1 546	1 581	341	580
1990	24.50	42.53	. . .	2 216 604	6 073	19.75	857	8 018	7 161	7 355	1 559	1 621	323	586
1991	21.50	37.24	2 828 953	2 146 064	5 880	17.46	1 001	7 627	6 626	7 417	1 659	1 617	325	569
1992	20.58	34.37	2 947 582	2 294 570	6 269	16.80	950	7 888	6 938	7 171	1 697	1 592	318	575
1993	18.48	29.82	3 257 008	2 543 374	6 968	15.13	1 003	8 620	7 618	6 847	1 736	1 647	335	587
1994	17.19	26.71	3 416 045	2 704 196	7 409	14.23	942	8 996	8 054	6 662	1 727	1 653	337	592
1995	18.40	27.76	3 361 882	2 767 312	7 582	15.81	949	8 835	7 886	6 560	1 762	1 563	303	592
1996	22.03	32.11	3 622 385	2 893 647	7 906	18.98	981	9 478	8 498	6 465	1 830	1 507	284	566
1997	20.61	28.95	3 802 574	3 069 430	8 409	17.67	1 003	10 162	9 158	6 452	1 817	1 560	305	563
1998	14.40	19.20	4 088 027	3 242 711	8 884	11.49	945	10 708	9 764	6 252	1 759	1 647	324	571
1999	19.30	24.44	4 081 181	3 228 092	8 844	15.76	940	10 852	9 912	5 881	1 850	1 493	284	567
2000	30.26	36.47	4 314 825	3 399 239	9 288	26.44	1 040	11 459	10 419	5 822	1 911	1 468	286	541
2001	25.95	30.48	4 475 026	3 471 067	9 510	21.40	971	11 871	10 900	5 801	1 868	1 586	312	550
2002	26.15	29.95	4 337 075	3 418 022	9 364	22.61	984	11 530	10 546	5 744	1 880	1 548	278	599
2003	30.99	34.41	4 654 638	3 676 005	10 071	26.98	1 027	12 264	11 238	5 649	1 719	1 568	269	638
2004	41.47	44.35	4 917 591	3 820 979	10 440	34.48	1 048	13 145	12 097	5 441	1 809	1 645	286	676
2005	56.70	58.57	5 004 339	3 754 671	10 287	46.81	1 165	13 714	12 549	5 181	1 717	1 682	308	685
2006	66.25	66.42	4 880 734	3 734 226	10 231	58.01	1 317	13 707	12 390	5 088	1 739	1 703	296	689
2007	72.41	71.01	4 807 811	3 690 568	10 111	64.28	1 433	13 468	12 036	5 077	1 783	1 648	268	697
2008	99.75	98.15	4 613 444	3 590 628	9 810	95.22	1 802	12 915	11 114	5 000	1 784	1 719	308	702
2009	62.09	62.09	4 266 007	3 314 787	9 082	56.93	2 024	11 691	9 667	5 350	1 910	1 758	307	727
2010	79.61	78.11	4 279 611	3 377 077	9 252	74.67	2 353	11 793	9 441	5 482	2 074	1 772	312	727
2011	95.11	91.25	4 164 117	3 321 918	9 101	99.82	2 986	11 436	8 450	5 645	2 216	1 725	308	696
2012	94.15	89.03	3 847 545	3 097 407	8 463	101.11	3 205	10 598	7 393	6 497	2 408	1 779	338	695
2013	98.05	91.17	3 549 945	2 813 770	7 709	96.95	3 621	9 859	6 237	7 465	2 606	1 728	327	696
2014	92.91	84.12	3 381 460	2 700 939	7 400	91.23	4 176	9 240	5 064	8 753	3 015	1 825	361	691
2015	48.79	44.54	3 384 807	2 661 968	7 293	47.26	4 738	9 449	4 650	9 408	3 342	1 982	449	695
2016	43.32	39.20	3 576 378	2 806 413	7 689	36.00	5 261	10 055	2 480	8 857	3 509	2 030	485	695
2017	50.80	45.09	3 639 778	2 883 753	7 901	45.97	6 343	10 075	3 723	9 355	3 736	1 895	421	662
2018	64.81	60.27	3 464 237	2 694 326	7 382	58.22	7 588	9 928	2 340	10 962	4 349	1 912	442	649
2019	56.99	51.97	3 116 908	2 374 322	6 505	53.30	8 499	9 943	594	12 232	4 813	1 916	443	635
2020	61.65	54.77	2 719 832	2 087 168	5 718	36.66	8 508	7 857	-651	11 313	5 161	1 982	485	658
2021	115.53	93.68	2 198 997	2 198 997	6 025	60.40	103 522	101 575	-162	11 177	5 390	1 077	455	622
2020														
January	57.52	47.19	256 779	198 338	6 400	52.24	9 228	9 768	-649	12 785	5 206	1 075	440	635
February	50.54	41.51	236 244	183 257	6 319	48.54	9 589	8 671	-1 108	12 826	5 052	1 088	453	635
March	29.21	25.65	244 125	187 756	6 057	40.53	9 522	8 905	-1 162	12 816	5 253	1 118	483	635
April	16.55	16.56	205 548	159 479	53	25.65	8 353	9 525	-1 112	11 911	4 934	1 167	529	638
May	28.56	26.33	217 732	172 384	5 561	22.78	7 112	9 893	650	9 711	4 745	1 170	522	648
June	38.81	33.35	229 229	180 788	6 062	27.69	7 608	9 297	760	10 420	5 195	1 189	533	656
July	40.71	35.01	226 286	172 283	5 558	33.14	8 485	9 601	-639	10 956	5 368	1 176	520	656
August	42.34	36.08	224 011	169 412	5 465	37.56	8 550	9 387	-1 100	10 558	5 351	1 152	504	648
September	39.63	33.40	216 120	158 489	5 283	37.60	8 315	8 712	-756	10 868	5 308	1 140	498	642
October	39.40	33.12	221 117	164 429	5 304	36.37	8 389	8 599	-1 013	10 413	5 297	1 132	494	639
November	40.94	34.63	217 308	166 803	5 560	35.70	7 913	8 103	-297	11 121	5 321	1 139	501	638
December	47.02	40.15	225 982	173 698	5 603	38.30	8 924	9 159	-1 186	11 084	5 058	1 124	485	638
2021														
January	52.00	43.52	224 189	170 100	5 487	42.50	8 729	7 915	-814	11 056	5 188	1 114	476	638
February	59.04	50.07	199 581	153 581	5 485	46.37	7 661	7 648	-13	9 773	4 215	1 131	493	638
March	62.33	50.55	244 814	182 265	5 880	51.54	7 679	8 288	609	11 160	5 116	1 140	502	638
April	61.72	49.83	232 822	173 972	5 799	56.03	9 110	8 267	-843	11 230	5 443	1 123	490	633
May	65.17	52.87	248 271	176 880	5 706	58.91	8 270	8 569	299	11 334	5 461	1 104	477	628
June	71.38	57.57	269 569	200 280	6 676	60.66	9 262	9 298	37	11 288	5 474	1 069	448	621
July	72.49	58.65	253 596	189 905	6 123	65.24	8 647	8 796	149	11 330	5 455	1 060	439	621
August	67.73	54.40	257 133	194 749	6 282	65.06	8 897	8 712	-184	11 206	5 568	1 043	422	621
September	71.65	57.40	258 048	195 795	6 527	64.43	7 807	8 931	1 124	10 851	5 540	1 038	420	618
October	81.48	64.80	234 679	175 722	5 668	68.77	8 660	8 122	-538	11 526	5 713	1 047	437	611
November	79.15	63.00	249 837	193	6 448	72.38	9 182	8 472	-710	11 769	5 768	1 035	434	601
December	71.71	57.89	246 242	192 405	6 207	67.60	9 618	8 556	-1 062	11 604	5 733	1 015	421	594

. . . = Not available.

NOTES AND DEFINITIONS, CHAPTER 11

Tables 11-1 and 11-2

Energy Supply and Consumption

SOURCES: U.S. DEPARTMENT OF ENERGY, ENERGY INFORMATION ADMINISTRATION; U.S. DEPARTMENT OF COMMERCE, BUREAU OF ECONOMIC ANALYSIS

Definitions

The *British thermal unit (Btu)* is a measure used to combine data for different energy sources into a consistent aggregate. It is the amount of energy required to raise the temperature of 1 pound of water 1 degree Fahrenheit when the water is near a temperature of 39.2 degrees Fahrenheit. To illustrate one of the factors used to convert volumes to Btu, conventional motor gasoline has a heat content of 5.253 million Btu per barrel. For further information, see the Energy Information Administration's *Monthly Energy Review*, Appendix A.

Production: Crude oil Is defined as the quantities of oil extracted from the ground after the removal of inert matter or impurities. It includes crude oil, natural gas liquids (NGLs), additives, and lease condensates.

Renewable energy, total includes conventional hydroelectric power, geothermal, solar thermal and photovoltaic, wind, and biomass. Hydroelectric power includes conventional electrical utility and industrial generation. Biomass includes wood, waste, and alcohol fuels (ethanol blended into motor gasoline).

The sum of domestic energy *production* and net imports of energy (*imports* minus *exports*) does not exactly equal domestic energy *consumption*. The difference is attributed to inventory changes; losses and gains in conversion, transportation, and distribution; the addition of blending compounds; shipments of anthracite to U.S. armed forces in Europe; and adjustments to account for discrepancies between reporting systems.

Consumption by end-use sector is based on total, not net, consumption--that is, each sector's consumption includes its electricity purchases as well as its own energy production. Consumption of energy sources are categorized into three sectors: (A) residential/commercial; (B) industrial and (C) transportation. Historically, residential/commercial consumption has been the largest sector at around 40 percent, Industrial at 30 percent and transportation at 25 percent.

Electric utilities are not treated as a separate end-use sector. However, they are counted as primary producers in the production accounts, which measure only primary production. As a result, total national supply and consumption are in rough balance, though components may not add to exact totals, not only because of the miscellaneous adjustments described above, but also because of different sector-specific conversion factors.

References and notes on the data

All of these data are published each month in Tables 1.1, 1.2, 1.7, and 2.1 in the *Monthly Energy Review*. Annual data before 1973 are published in the *Annual Energy Review*. These two publications are no longer published in printed form but are available, along with all current and historical data, on the EIA Web site at <https://www.eia.doe.gov>.

The real gross domestic product (GDP) data used to calculate energy consumption per dollar of real GDP are from the Bureau of Economic Analysis; see Table 1-2 and the applicable notes and definitions in this volume of *Business Statistics*. The GDP numbers shown in this table reflect the comprehensive revision of July 2013, the most recent review, which increased the overall level of GDP by including as investment research, development, and creation of intellectual property. This changed the average level of the energy-to-GDP ratio but had little effect on its downward trend. The GDP estimate shown here also reflects subsequent revisions and updates made through June 2020.

TABLE 11-3

Petroleum and Petroleum Products—Prices, Imports, Domestic Production, and Stocks

SOURCES: FUTURES PRICES—U.S. DEPARTMENT OF ENERGY, ENERGY INFORMATION ADMINISTRATION (EIA), AND U.S. DEPARTMENT OF COMMERCE, BUREAU OF ECONOMIC ANALYSIS; IMPORTS—U.S. DEPARTMENT OF COMMERCE, CENSUS BUREAU (SEE NOTES AND DEFINITIONS FOR TABLES 7-9 THROUGH 7-14); SUPPLY (NET IMPORTS AND DOMESTIC PRODUCTION) AND STOCKS—EIA.

Definitions and notes on the data

The *crude oil futures price* in *current dollars per barrel* is the price for next-month delivery in Cushing, Oklahoma (a pipeline hub), of light, sweet crude oil, as determined by trading on the New York Mercantile Exchange (NYMEX). Official daily closing prices are reported each day at 2:30 p.m., and are tabulated weekly in Table 13 of *EIA's Weekly Petroleum Status Report*. The monthly averages shown in this volume are the average prices for the nearest future from each trading day of the month. For example, for most days in January, the futures contract priced will be for February; for the last few days in January, the February contract will have expired and the March contract will be quoted. The annual averages are averages of the monthly averages.

The *crude oil futures price* in *2012 dollars* is calculated by the editors, by dividing each month's current-dollar price by that month's chain price index for total personal consumption expenditures (PCE), with the price index average for the year 2012 set at 1.0000. The PCE chain price index is compiled by the Bureau of Economic Analysis (BEA). It is described in the notes and definitions for Chapter 1 and is also presented in Chapter 8, Table 8-2, and discussed in its notes and definitions.

The import data in Columns 3 through 6 of this table are those published as Exhibit 17, "Imports of Energy-related Petroleum Products, including Crude Petroleum," in the monthly Census-BEA foreign trade press release, FT900. *Total energy-related petroleum products* includes the following North American Industry Classification System (NAICS) commodity groupings: crude oil, petroleum preparations, and liquefied propane and butane gas.

The data in Columns 7 through 11, on exports, imports, and net imports (imports minus exports) of petroleum and products and domestic production of crude oil and natural gas plant liquids (all expressed as thousands of barrels per day), and in Columns 12 through 14, depicting stocks of crude oil in millions of barrels, are derived from the Department of Energy's weekly petroleum supply reporting system. They are published in EIA's *Monthly Energy Review*, Tables 3.1 and 3.4, which can be reached by searching the Web site. Stock totals are as of the end of the period. Geographic coverage includes the 50 states and the District of Columbia.

Data availability

Data on futures prices, petroleum supply and stocks are available from the EIA Web site at <https://www.eia.doe.gov>, under the categories "Publications and Reports/Monthly Energy Review" and "Petroleum/Weekly Petroleum Status Report." The *Monthly Energy Review* is no longer published in printed form.

The import data are available in the FT900 report from the Census Bureau at www.census.gov. See the notes and definitions for Tables 7-9 through 7-14 for further information.

CHAPTER 12: MONEY, INTEREST, ASSETS, LIABILITIES, AND ASSET PRICES

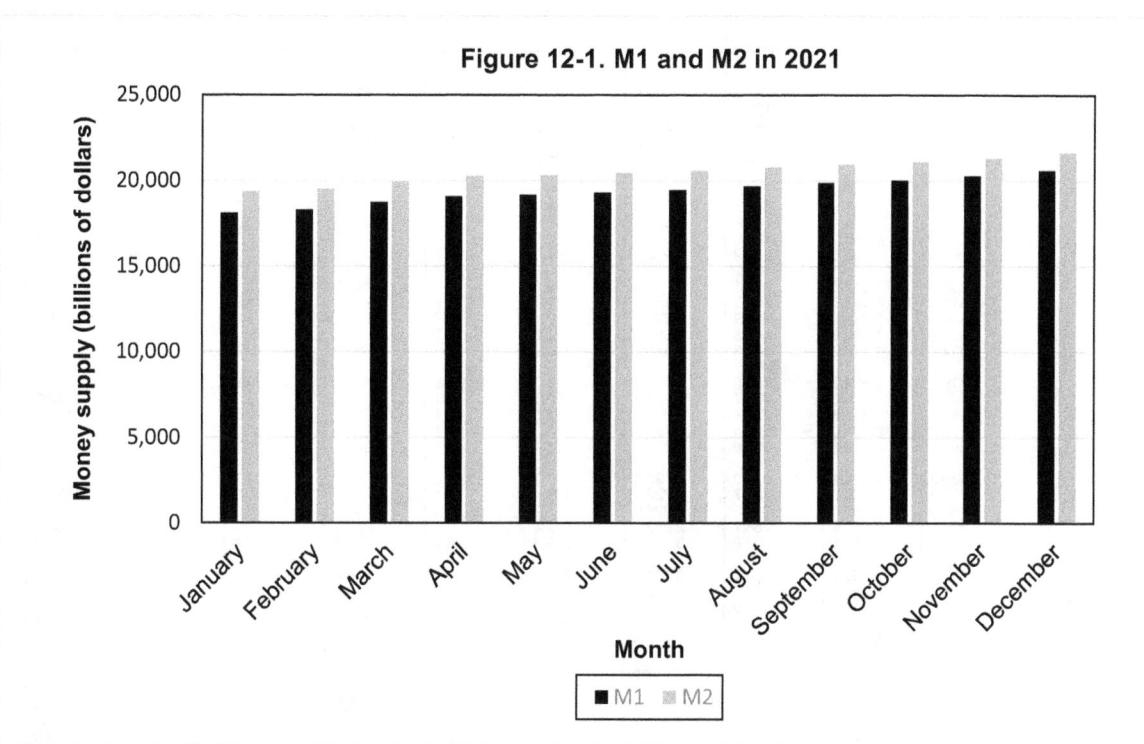

Figure 12-1. M1 and M2 in 2021

- The United States' money supply has changed greatly from gold and silver coins to demand deposits then debit cards. Before 2020, the money supply (M1) consisted of currency in circulation, traveler's checks, demand deposits, deposits at commercial banks, and thrift institutions. M2 includes M1 plus savings deposits and small-denomination time-deposits. (Tables 12-1, 12-2 and Figure 12-1).

- The money supply is now composed of three components: currency in circulation, total other checkable deposits, and other liquid deposits. With all these changes, M1 is significantly higher in 2021 than 2019 because savings deposits are now combined with other deposits. (Table 12-1)

- The Federal Reserve Board of Governors (FED) announced on March 15, 2020 that required reserve ratios were reduced to zero with no plans to re-institute them. In addition, the FED now classifies savings as transactions, thus these actions are added together into the new category now called "other liquid deposits. Another change was that separate deposits in thrift institutions and commercial banks do not have to be reported individually. Instead, they are combined into "other checkable deposits total." (Table 12-1)

Table 12-1A. Money Stock Measures and Components of M1: Recent Data

(Billions of dollars, monthly data are averages of daily figures, annual data are for December.)

Year and month	Not seasonally adjusted		Seasonally adjusted								
								Other checkable deposits			
	M1	M2	M1	M2	Currency	Traveler's checks	Demand deposits	At commercial banks	At thrift institutions	Total	Other liquid deposits
1965	172.6	463.1	167.8	459.2	36.0	0.5	131.3	0.0	0.1	0.1	...
1966	176.9	483.7	172.0	480.2	38.0	0.6	133.4	0.0	0.1	0.1	...
1967	188.4	528.0	183.3	524.8	40.0	0.6	142.5	0.0	0.1	0.1	...
1968	202.8	569.7	197.4	566.8	43.0	0.7	153.6	0.0	0.1	0.1	...
1969	209.3	590.1	203.9	587.9	45.7	0.8	157.3	0.0	0.1	0.1	...
1970	220.1	627.8	214.4	626.5	48.6	0.9	164.7	0.0	0.1	0.1	...
1971	234.5	711.2	228.3	710.3	52.0	1.0	175.1	0.0	0.2	0.2	...
1972	256.1	803.1	249.2	802.3	56.2	1.2	191.6	0.0	0.2	0.2	...
1973	270.2	856.5	262.9	855.5	60.8	1.4	200.3	0.0	0.3	0.3	...
1974	281.8	903.5	274.2	902.1	67.0	1.7	205.1	0.2	0.4	0.4	...
1975	295.3	1 017.8	287.1	1 016.2	72.8	2.1	211.3	0.4	0.5	0.9	...
1976	314.5	1 153.5	306.2	1 152.0	79.5	2.6	221.5	1.3	1.4	2.7	...
1977	340.0	1 273.0	330.9	1 270.3	87.4	2.9	236.4	1.8	2.3	4.2	...
1978	367.9	1 370.8	357.3	1 366.0	96.0	3.3	249.5	5.3	3.1	8.5	...
1979	393.2	1 479.0	381.8	1 473.7	104.8	3.5	256.6	12.7	4.2	16.9	...
1980	419.5	1 604.8	408.5	1 599.8	115.3	3.9	261.2	20.8	7.3	28.2	...
1981	447.0	1 760.3	436.7	1 755.5	122.5	4.1	231.4	63.0	15.6	79.0	...
1982	485.8	1 913.8	474.8	1 905.9	132.5	4.1	234.1	80.5	23.6	104.6	...
1983	533.3	2 134.0	521.4	2 123.5	146.2	4.7	238.5	97.3	34.8	132.9	...
1984	564.6	2 318.5	551.6	2 306.4	156.1	5.0	243.4	104.7	42.4	148.4	...
1985	633.3	2 504.1	619.8	2 492.1	167.7	5.6	266.9	124.7	54.9	181.2	...
1986	739.8	2 740.7	724.7	2 728.0	180.4	6.1	302.9	161.0	74.2	237.4	...
1987	765.4	2 838.3	750.2	2 826.4	196.7	6.6	287.7	178.2	81.0	261.8	...
1988	803.1	3 000.6	786.7	2 988.2	212.0	7.0	287.1	192.5	88.1	283.5	...
1989	810.6	3 165.6	792.9	3 152.5	222.3	6.9	278.6	197.4	87.7	288.2	...
1990	842.7	3 285.1	824.7	3 271.8	246.5	7.7	276.8	208.7	85.0	297.0	...
1991	915.6	3 386.4	897.0	3 372.2	267.1	7.7	289.6	241.6	90.9	336.3	...
1992	1 045.6	3 441.3	1 024.9	3 424.7	292.1	8.2	340.0	280.8	103.8	388.9	...
1993	1 153.3	3 495.1	1 129.6	3 474.5	321.6	8.0	385.4	302.6	112.0	419.4	...
1994	1 174.5	3 507.8	1 150.7	3 486.4	354.5	8.6	383.6	297.4	106.6	408.4	...
1995	1 152.7	3 653.3	1 127.5	3 629.5	372.8	9.0	389.0	249.0	107.6	360.5	...
1996	1 105.8	3 839.8	1 081.3	3 818.6	394.6	8.8	402.1	172.1	103.6	279.1	...
1997	1 097.5	4 055.1	1 072.5	4 032.9	425.3	8.4	393.5	148.4	96.7	247.9	...
1998	1 121.2	4 399.6	1 095.0	4 375.2	460.4	8.5	376.3	143.9	105.9	252.7	...
1999	1 148.2	4 664.5	1 122.2	4 638.0	517.9	8.6	352.5	139.7	103.6	246.0	...
2000	1 111.7	4 953.0	1 088.6	4 925.0	531.3	8.3	310.5	133.2	105.4	241.2	...
2001	1 208.5	5 465.0	1 183.2	5 433.8	581.2	8.0	336.3	142.2	115.6	261.1	...
2002	1 245.5	5 804.0	1 220.2	5 772.0	626.2	7.8	306.9	154.4	125.0	283.8	...
2003	1 332.5	6 098.6	1 306.2	6 067.3	662.4	7.7	325.9	175.3	134.8	315.2	...
2004	1 401.5	6 447.4	1 376.0	6 418.3	697.9	7.6	342.8	187.1	140.7	332.5	...
2005	1 397.2	6 708.9	1 374.3	6 681.9	724.7	7.2	324.2	180.6	137.7	322.5	...
2006	1 387.7	7 100.1	1 366.6	7 071.6	750.3	6.7	304.8	176.3	128.5	308.6	...
2007	1 394.9	7 504.2	1 373.4	7 471.6	760.6	6.3	301.7	171.9	132.9	309.2	...
2008	1 632.3	8 231.5	1 601.7	8 192.1	816.2	5.5	469.9	177.1	133.0	314.9	...
2009	1 724.6	8 543.7	1 692.8	8 496.0	863.7	5.1	445.9	229.1	149.0	384.1	...
2010	1 871.4	8 857.6	1 836.7	8 801.8	918.8	4.7	516.5	233.3	163.4	402.3	...
2011	2 208.1	9 729.2	2 165.7	9 660.1	1 001.9	4.3	751.6	231.1	176.0	411.5	...
2012	2 509.7	10 531.4	2 460.7	10 459.7	1 090.3	3.8	927.2	243.2	196.7	443.8	...
2013	2 715.7	11 104.3	2 664.3	11 028.8	1 160.2	3.5	1 034.6	255.6	210.7	471.2	...
2014	2 992.0	11 760.0	2 940.9	11 681.5	1 252.9	2.9	1 200.6	265.2	219.7	489.5	...
2015	3 141.1	12 427.3	3 095.8	12 344.0	1 339.6	2.5	1 238.9	276.6	238.2	519.2	...
2016	3 384.0	13 299.9	3 340.9	13 209.6	1 421.2	2.2	1 370.4	288.8	258.4	550.7	...
2017	3 652.7	13 945.0	3 610.6	13 852.3	1 525.4	1.9	1 489.2	306.4	287.0	596.7	...
2018	3 800.7	14 448.8	3 763.4	14 358.8	1 625.5	1.7	1 504.4	333.4	293.7	634.2	...
2019	4 043.3	15 412.5	4 007.1	15 319.1	1 712.9	...	1 615.0	367.2	306.8	681.1	...
2020	17 949.3	19 247.9	17 834.4	19 124.8	1 975.9	...	3 296.9	...	...	...	12 561.6
2021	20 591.3	21 660.4	20 430.7	21 490.0	2 133.2	...	4 696.7	...	...	...	13 600.8
2020											
January	3 983.5	15 397.1	3 993.6	15 401.8	1 722.5	...	1 595.8	...	...	675.3	...
February	3 942.0	15 383.1	4 002.9	15 458.7	1 730.1	...	1 591.8	...	...	681.1	...
March	4 290.0	16 056.1	4 261.9	15 988.6	1 753.3	...	1 814.2	...	...	694.5	...
April	4 851.5	17 102.4	4 779.8	17 002.5	1 787.1	...	1 996.2	...	...	996.4	...
May	16 170.7	17 766.9	16 232.9	17 835.2	1 819.8	...	2 121.2	...	...	...	12 291.9
June	16 544.5	18 103.7	16 563.5	18 129.3	1 849.5	...	2 210.9	...	...	...	12 503.1
July	16 746.4	18 252.8	16 763.8	18 277.8	1 876.6	...	2 254.6	...	...	...	12 632.7
August	16 869.1	18 319.2	16 896.7	18 357.4	1 904.5	...	2 293.9	...	...	...	12 698.3
September	17 136.8	18 543.1	17 161.5	18 575.2	1 922.7	...	2 418.4	...	...	...	12 820.3
October	17 321.5	18 689.1	17 365.3	18 735.7	1 941.6	...	2 441.6	...	...	...	12 982.2
November	17 642.4	18 980.6	17 626.7	18 969.8	1 958.1	...	2 791.2	...	...	...	12 877.5
December	17 949.3	19 247.9	17 834.4	19 124.8	1 975.9	...	3 296.9	...	...	...	12 561.6
2021											
January	18 085.1	19 371.9	18 107.0	19 372.6	1 997.2	...	3 392.6	...	...	...	12 717.2
February	18 263.5	19 523.9	18 367.6	19 615.4	2 014.3	...	3 595.2	...	...	...	12 758.1
March	18 721.1	19 946.0	18 641.1	19 853.6	2 028.2	...	3 739.4	...	...	...	12 873.5
April	19 085.5	20 270.0	18 927.4	20 110.5	2 057.2	...	3 744.1	...	...	...	13 126.1
May	19 169.7	20 319.5	19 259.5	20 418.6	2 063.5	...	4 010.3	...	...	...	13 185.7
June	19 310.4	20 440.7	19 319.6	20 460.2	2 070.2	...	4 247.7	...	...	...	13 001.7
July	19 459.4	20 571.8	19 497.4	20 620.8	2 076.7	...	4 374.1	...	...	...	13 046.6
August	19 683.6	20 777.9	19 746.4	20 853.3	2 084.9	...	4 489.6	...	...	...	13 172.0
September	19 874.1	20 957.8	19 898.8	20 992.3	2 092.8	...	4 502.9	...	...	...	13 303.1
October	20 021.0	21 098.0	20 063.6	21 144.0	2 104.2	...	4 595.1	...	...	...	13 364.3
November	20 267.3	21 334.5	20 279.8	21 349.3	2 118.2	...	4 676.8	...	...	...	13 484.8
December	20 591.3	21 660.4	20 430.7	21 490.0	2 133.2	...	4 696.7	...	...	...	13 600.8

. . . = Not available.

Table 12-1B. Money Stock, Historical: 1892–1924

(Not seasonally adjusted, millions of dollars.)

Classification	1892	1893	1894	1895	1896	1897	1898	1899	1900	1901	1902
June 30											
Currency outside banks	1 015	1 081	972	971	974	1 013	1 150	1 181	1 331	1 395	1 431
Demand deposits adjusted	2 880	2 766	2 807	2 960	2 839	2 871	3 432	4 162	4 420	5 204	5 719
M1	3 895	3 847	3 779	3 931	3 813	3 884	4 582	5 343	5 751	6 599	7 150
Time deposits	1 929	2 007	1 994	2 088	2 220	2 305	2 397	2 617	3 015	3 315	3 565
M2	5 824	5 854	5 773	6 019	6 033	6 189	6 979	7 960	8 766	9 914	10 715
December 31											
Currency outside banks	. . .	. . .	. . .	. . .	. . .	. . .	. . .	. . .	. . .	. . .	. . .
Demand deposits adjusted	. . .	. . .	. . .	. . .	. . .	. . .	. . .	. . .	. . .	. . .	. . .
M1	. . .	. . .	. . .	. . .	. . .	. . .	. . .	. . .	. . .	. . .	. . .
Time deposits	. . .	. . .	. . .	. . .	. . .	. . .	. . .	. . .	. . .	. . .	. . .
M2	. . .	. . .	. . .	. . .	. . .	. . .	. . .	. . .	. . .	. . .	. . .

Classification	1903	1904	1905	1906	1907	1908	1909	1910	1911	1912	1913
June 30											
Currency outside banks	1 543	1 562	1 629	1 759	1 700	1 711	1 691	1 725	1 709	1 762	1 858
Demand deposits adjusted	5 962	6 256	7 069	7 504	7 872	7 384	7 768	8 254	8 668	9 156	9 140
M1	7 505	7 818	8 698	9 263	9 572	9 095	9 459	9 979	10 377	10 918	10 998
Time deposits	3 800	4 045	4 464	4 769	5 350	5 493	6 265	6 944	7 337	7 889	8 356
M2	11 305	11 863	13 162	14 032	14 922	14 588	15 724	16 923	17 714	18 807	19 354
December 31											
Currency outside banks	. . .	. . .	. . .	. . .	. . .	. . .	. . .	. . .	. . .	. . .	. . .
Demand deposits adjusted	. . .	. . .	. . .	. . .	. . .	. . .	. . .	. . .	. . .	. . .	. . .
M1	. . .	. . .	. . .	. . .	. . .	. . .	. . .	. . .	. . .	. . .	. . .
Time deposits	. . .	. . .	. . .	. . .	. . .	. . .	. . .	. . .	. . .	. . .	. . .
M2	. . .	. . .	. . .	. . .	. . .	. . .	. . .	. . .	. . .	. . .	. . .

Classification	1914	1915	1916	1917	1918	1919	1920	1921	1922	1923	1924
June 30											
Currency outside banks	1 533	1 575	1 876	2 276	3 298	3 593	4 105	3 677	3 346	3 739	3 650
Demand deposits adjusted	10 082	9 828	11 973	13 501	14 843	17 624	19 616	17 113	18 045	18 958	19 412
M1	11 615	11 403	13 849	15 777	18 141	21 217	23 721	20 790	21 391	22 697	23 062
Time deposits	8 350	9 231	10 313	11 543	11 717	13 423	15 834	16 583	17 437	19 722	21 259
M2	19 965	20 634	24 162	27 320	29 858	34 640	39 555	37 373	48 828	42 419	44 321
December 31											
Currency outside banks	. . .	. . .	. . .	. . .	. . .	. . .	. . .	. . .	. . .	3 726	3 696
Demand deposits adjusted	. . .	. . .	. . .	. . .	. . .	. . .	. . .	. . .	. . .	19 144	20 898
M1	. . .	. . .	. . .	. . .	. . .	. . .	. . .	. . .	. . .	22 870	24 594
Time deposits	. . .	. . .	. . .	. . .	. . .	. . .	. . .	. . .	. . .	20 379	22 232
M2	. . .	. . .	. . .	. . .	. . .	. . .	. . .	. . .	. . .	43 249	46 826

. . . = Not available.

Table 12-1C. Money Stock, Historical: January 1947–January 1959

(Averages of daily figures; seasonally adjusted, billions of dollars.)

Year and month	Money stock (M1)			Time deposits adjusted	M2 (M1 plus time deposits)
	Total	Currency component	Demand deposit component		
1947					
January	109.5	26.7	82.8	33.3	142.8
February	109.7	26.7	83.0	33.5	143.2
March	110.3	26.7	83.7	33.6	143.9
April	111.1	26.6	84.5	33.7	144.8
May	111.7	26.6	85.1	33.8	145.5
June	112.1	26.6	85.5	33.9	146.0
July	112.2	26.5	85.7	34.0	146.2
August	112.6	26.5	86.1	34.4	147.0
September	113.0	26.7	86.3	34.7	147.7
October	112.9	26.5	86.4	35.0	147.9
November	113.3	26.5	86.8	35.2	148.5
December	113.1	26.4	86.7	35.4	148.5
1948					
January	113.4	26.4	87.0	35.5	148.9
February	113.2	26.3	86.8	35.7	148.9
March	112.6	26.2	86.4	35.7	148.3
April	112.3	26.1	86.3	35.7	148.0
May	112.1	26.0	86.0	35.7	147.8
June	112.0	26.0	86.0	35.8	147.8
July	112.2	26.0	86.2	35.8	148.0
August	112.3	26.0	86.2	35.9	148.2
September	112.2	26.0	86.2	35.9	148.1
October	112.1	26.0	86.1	35.9	148.0
November	111.8	26.0	85.9	36.0	147.8
December	111.5	25.8	85.8	36.0	147.5
1949					
January	111.2	25.7	85.5	36.1	147.3
February	111.2	25.7	85.5	36.1	147.3
March	111.2	25.7	85.6	36.1	147.3
April	113.3	25.7	85.6	36.2	149.5
May	111.5	25.7	85.8	36.3	147.8
June	111.3	25.6	85.7	36.4	147.7
July	111.2	25.5	85.7	36.4	147.6
August	111.0	25.5	85.6	36.4	147.4
September	110.9	25.3	85.6	36.4	147.3
October	110.9	25.3	85.6	36.4	147.3
November	111.0	25.2	85.8	36.4	147.4
December	111.2	25.1	86.0	36.4	147.6
1950					
January	111.5	25.1	86.4	36.4	147.9
February	112.1	25.1	86.9	36.6	148.7
March	112.5	25.2	87.3	36.6	149.1
April	113.2	25.3	88.0	36.7	149.9
May	113.7	25.2	88.5	36.9	150.6
June	114.1	25.1	89.0	36.9	151.0
July	114.6	25.0	89.6	36.8	151.4
August	115.0	24.9	90.1	36.7	151.7
September	115.2	24.9	90.3	36.6	151.8
October	115.7	24.9	90.8	36.5	152.2
November	115.9	24.9	90.9	36.6	152.5
December	116.2	25.0	91.2	36.7	152.9
1951					
January	116.7	25.0	91.7	36.7	153.4
February	117.1	25.1	92.0	36.6	153.7
March	117.6	25.2	92.4	36.6	154.2
April	117.8	25.2	92.6	36.7	154.5
May	118.2	25.3	92.8	36.8	155.0
June	118.6	25.4	93.2	36.9	155.5
July	119.1	25.6	93.4	37.2	156.3
August	119.6	25.7	93.8	37.4	157.0
September	120.4	25.8	94.5	37.7	158.1
October	121.0	26.0	95.1	37.8	158.8
November	122.0	26.0	96.0	38.0	160.0
December	122.7	26.1	96.5	38.2	160.9
1952					
January	123.1	26.2	96.9	38.4	161.5
February	123.6	26.3	97.3	38.7	162.3
March	123.8	26.4	97.5	38.9	162.7
April	124.1	26.4	97.6	39.1	163.2
May	124.5	26.5	98.0	39.3	163.8
June	125.0	26.7	98.4	39.5	164.5
July	125.3	26.7	98.6	39.7	165.0
August	125.7	26.8	98.9	40.0	165.7
September	126.4	26.9	99.4	40.3	166.7
October	126.7	27.0	99.7	40.5	167.2
November	127.1	27.2	99.9	40.9	168.0
December	127.4	27.3	100.1	41.1	168.5

Table 12-1C. Money Stock, Historical: January 1947–January 1959—*Continued*

(Averages of daily figures; seasonally adjusted, billions of dollars.)

Year and month	Money stock (M1)			Time deposits adjusted	M2 (M1 plus time deposits)
	Total	Currency component	Demand deposit component		
1953					
January	127.3	27.4	99.9	41.4	168.7
February	127.4	27.5	99.9	41.6	169.0
March	128.0	27.6	100.4	41.9	169.9
April	128.3	27.7	100.7	42.1	170.4
May	128.5	27.7	100.7	42.4	170.9
June	128.5	27.7	100.7	42.6	171.1
July	128.6	27.8	100.8	42.9	171.5
August	128.7	27.8	100.9	43.2	171.9
September	128.6	27.8	100.8	43.5	172.1
October	128.7	27.8	100.9	43.9	172.6
November	128.7	27.8	100.9	44.2	172.9
December	128.8	27.7	101.1	44.5	173.3
1954					
January	129.0	27.7	101.3	44.8	173.8
February	129.1	27.7	101.5	45.2	174.3
March	129.2	27.6	101.6	45.6	174.8
April	128.6	27.6	101.0	46.1	174.7
May	129.7	27.6	102.1	46.5	176.2
June	129.9	27.5	102.3	46.8	176.7
July	130.3	27.5	102.8	47.3	177.6
August	130.7	27.5	103.2	47.8	178.5
September	130.9	27.4	103.5	47.9	178.8
October	131.5	27.4	104.1	48.1	179.6
November	132.1	27.4	104.7	48.2	180.3
December	132.3	27.4	104.9	48.3	180.6
1955					
January	133.0	27.4	105.6	48.5	181.5
February	133.9	27.5	106.4	48.7	182.6
March	133.6	27.5	106.0	48.8	182.4
April	133.9	27.5	106.3	49.0	182.9
May	134.6	27.6	107.0	49.0	183.6
June	134.4	27.6	106.8	49.2	183.6
July	134.8	27.7	107.2	49.3	184.1
August	134.8	27.7	107.0	49.3	184.1
September	135.0	27.7	107.3	49.6	184.6
October	135.2	27.8	107.4	49.7	184.9
November	134.9	27.8	107.1	49.9	184.8
December	135.2	27.8	107.4	50.0	185.2
1956					
January	135.5	27.9	107.7	49.9	185.4
February	135.5	27.9	107.7	49.9	185.4
March	135.7	27.9	107.8	50.1	185.8
April	136.0	27.9	108.1	50.3	186.3
May	135.8	27.9	107.9	50.4	186.2
June	136.0	27.9	108.1	50.7	186.7
July	136.0	28.0	108.0	50.9	186.9
August	135.7	28.0	107.8	51.2	186.9
September	136.2	28.0	108.2	51.5	187.7
October	136.3	28.0	108.2	51.6	187.9
November	136.6	28.1	108.4	51.8	188.4
December	136.9	28.2	108.7	51.9	188.8
1957					
January	136.9	28.2	108.6	52.6	189.5
February	136.8	28.2	108.6	53.1	189.9
March	136.9	28.2	108.7	53.7	190.6
April	136.9	28.2	108.7	54.0	190.9
May	137.0	28.2	108.8	54.5	191.5
June	136.9	28.3	108.6	54.8	191.7
July	137.0	28.3	108.7	55.3	192.3
August	137.1	28.3	108.8	55.7	192.8
September	136.8	28.3	108.4	56.1	192.9
October	136.5	28.3	108.2	56.6	193.1
November	136.3	28.3	108.0	57.0	193.3
December	135.9	28.3	107.6	57.4	193.3
1958					
January	135.5	28.3	107.2	57.6	193.1
February	136.2	28.2	107.9	59.2	195.4
March	136.5	28.2	108.3	60.5	197.0
April	137.0	28.2	108.7	61.5	198.5
May	137.5	28.3	109.2	62.3	199.8
June	138.4	28.3	110.1	63.2	201.6
July	138.4	28.4	110.0	64.0	202.4
August	139.1	28.4	110.7	64.6	203.7
September	139.5	28.5	111.1	64.8	204.3
October	140.1	28.5	111.6	64.9	205.0
November	140.9	28.5	112.4	65.2	206.1
December	141.1	28.6	112.6	65.4	206.5
1959					
January	142.2	28.7	113.5	66.3	208.5

Table 12-2. Components of Non-M1 M2

(Billions of dollars, seasonally adjusted; monthly data are averages of daily figures, annual data are for December.)

Year and month	Savings deposits				Small-denomination time deposits			Retail money funds	Total non-M1 M2
	At commercial banks	At thrift institutions	Total	Other liquid deposits	At commercial banks	At thrift institutions	Total		
1965	92.4	164.5	256.9	...	26.7	7.8	33.6	...	290.5
1966	89.9	163.3	253.1	...	38.7	16.3	53.4	...	306.5
1967	94.1	169.6	263.7	...	50.7	27.1	75.6	...	339.3
1968	96.1	172.8	268.9	...	63.5	37.1	97.8	...	366.7
1969	93.8	169.8	263.7	...	71.6	48.8	117.4	...	381.1
1970	98.6	162.3	261.0	...	79.3	71.9	148.8	...	409.8
1971	112.8	179.4	292.2	...	94.7	95.1	186.8	...	479.0
1972	124.8	196.6	321.4	...	108.2	123.5	228.3	...	549.7
1973	128.0	198.7	326.8	...	116.8	149.0	262.3	0.1	589.1
1974	136.8	201.8	338.6	...	123.1	164.8	284.8	1.4	623.4
1975	161.2	227.6	388.9	...	142.3	195.5	334.9	2.3	723.8
1976	201.8	251.4	453.2	...	155.5	235.2	388.1	1.7	841.3
1977	218.8	273.4	492.2	...	167.5	278.0	443.3	1.6	935.5
1978	216.5	265.4	481.9	...	185.1	335.8	519.4	5.4	1 001.3
1979	195.0	228.8	423.8	...	235.5	398.7	633.1	32.2	1 056.9
1980	185.7	214.5	400.3	...	286.2	442.3	727.9	60.3	1 128.2
1981	159.0	184.9	343.9	...	347.7	475.4	823.0	149.1	1 166.9
1982	190.1	210.0	400.1	...	379.9	471.0	851.4	179.4	1 251.5
1983	363.2	321.7	684.9	...	350.9	433.1	784.8	133.5	1 469.7
1984	389.3	315.4	704.7	...	387.9	500.9	889.7	161.9	1 594.4
1985	456.6	358.6	815.3	...	386.4	499.3	886.4	171.4	1 701.7
1986	533.5	407.4	940.9	...	369.4	489.0	858.4	203.6	1 799.3
1987	534.8	402.6	937.4	...	391.7	529.3	920.1	216.9	1 857.5
1988	542.4	383.9	926.4	...	451.2	585.9	1 035.0	236.9	1 961.4
1989	541.1	352.6	893.7	...	533.8	617.6	1 148.1	313.2	2 041.8
1990	581.3	341.6	922.9	...	610.7	562.6	1 170.9	349.5	2 093.8
1991	664.8	379.6	1 044.5	...	602.2	463.1	1 063.0	364.6	2 107.5
1992	754.2	433.1	1 187.2	...	508.1	359.7	865.8	344.6	2 053.0
1993	785.3	434.0	1 219.3	...	467.9	313.5	779.7	344.5	1 999.0
1994	752.8	398.5	1 151.3	...	503.6	313.9	815.8	367.8	1 967.1
1995	774.8	361.0	1 135.9	...	575.8	356.5	930.8	434.9	2 066.7
1996	906.0	368.7	1 274.8	...	594.2	353.7	947.0	515.1	2 221.8
1997	1 022.5	378.7	1 401.2	...	625.5	342.2	967.5	591.8	2 368.7
1998	1 187.4	416.1	1 603.6	...	626.4	324.9	951.8	724.9	2 555.4
1999	1 288.9	451.2	1 740.2	...	636.9	318.3	956.0	820.4	2 696.2
2000	1 425.3	454.3	1 879.6	...	700.8	345.3	1 047.0	911.7	2 926.6
2001	1 740.3	571.2	2 311.5	...	636.0	338.5	975.0	966.7	3 286.5
2002	2 057.9	713.1	2 771.0	...	591.3	303.5	894.6	888.9	3 665.6
2003	2 335.2	823.6	3 158.8	...	541.9	276.2	817.9	786.7	3 976.7
2004	2 633.9	872.7	3 506.6	...	552.3	276.1	828.4	709.4	4 335.0
2005	2 777.2	825.0	3 602.2	...	647.2	346.5	994.2	713.7	4 596.4
2006	2 913.1	779.9	3 693.0	...	781.4	424.6	1 207.9	808.2	4 900.9
2007	3 042.7	823.5	3 866.2	...	859.4	416.5	1 279.1	959.0	5 145.3
2008	3 323.1	765.3	4 088.4	...	1 079.6	378.0	1 461.3	1 048.5	5 549.7
2009	3 978.9	833.0	4 812.0	...	868.6	319.0	1 190.3	808.4	6 002.3
2010	4 412.3	919.2	5 331.5	...	663.9	270.5	933.7	704.9	6 265.2
2011	5 037.6	996.0	6 033.6	...	548.3	228.6	774.6	694.1	6 808.2
2012	5 727.5	955.8	6 683.3	...	469.0	176.8	642.5	673.6	7 325.8
2013	6 108.1	1 020.1	7 128.2	...	425.9	144.5	566.0	671.5	7 694.2
2014	6 495.8	1 077.2	7 573.0	...	391.4	132.0	518.3	650.4	8 091.3
2015	7 026.4	1 143.3	8 169.7	...	302.6	110.6	420.8	671.9	8 590.5
2016	7 556.1	1 258.4	8 814.5	...	251.6	101.8	363.5	704.3	9 178.0
2017	7 813.1	1 297.2	9 110.3	...	302.5	111.7	426.7	719.6	9 537.0
2018	7 926.4	1 334.6	9 260.9	...	425.4	107.6	546.6	811.5	9 807.5
2019	8 418.1	1 347.7	9 765.8	...	458.7	121.3	596.5	982.7	10 362.3
2020	...	...	...	12 618.4	...	...	248.5	1 050.1	248.5
2021	...	...	...	13 687.9	...	...	86.6	982.5	86.6
2020									
January	...	...	9 849.5	...	...	...	579.4	993.0	10 428.9
February	...	...	9 927.2	...	...	...	549.1	984.8	10 476.3
March	...	...	10 191.9	...	...	...	516.1	1 027.8	10 708.0
April	...	...	10 633.4	...	...	...	497.9	1 091.7	11 131.3
May	...	...	...	12 219.8	...	...	480.8	1 115.4	480.8
June	...	...	...	12 469.4	...	...	452.1	1 107.1	452.1
July	...	...	...	12 599.8	...	...	418.5	1 087.8	418.5
August	...	...	...	12 684.4	...	...	381.4	1 068.7	381.4
September	...	...	...	12 818.2	...	...	350.0	1 056.3	350.0
October	...	...	...	12 948.1	...	...	314.8	1 052.9	314.8
November	...	...	...	12 929.8	...	...	276.6	1 061.6	276.6
December	...	...	...	12 618.4	...	...	248.5	1 050.1	248.5
2021									
January	...	...	...	12 728.0	...	...	229.8	1 057.0	229.8
February	...	...	...	12 732.8	...	...	210.2	1 050.2	210.2
March	...	...	...	12 932.1	...	...	192.5	1 032.5	192.5
April	...	...	...	13 180.7	...	...	174.4	1 010.1	174.4
May	...	...	...	13 076.0	...	...	163.2	986.6	163.2
June	...	...	...	12 964.9	...	...	154.6	975.7	154.6
July	...	...	...	12 987.6	...	...	144.1	968.4	144.1
August	...	...	...	13 145.4	...	...	130.8	963.5	130.8
September	...	...	...	13 322.4	...	...	118.7	965.0	118.7
October	...	...	...	13 350.5	...	...	107.8	969.2	107.8
November	...	...	...	13 535.2	...	...	97.7	969.5	97.7
December	...	...	...	13 687.9	...	...	86.6	982.5	86.6

. . . = Not available.

Figure 12-2. S&P Stock Price Index and FHFA House Price Index, 1975–2021

- The Federal Reserve used similar tools from the Great Recession to recover from the COVID-19 pandemic which precipitated business closures, event cancelations, schools closing, and work-at-home policies. From March 2020 to March 2022, the federal funds rates was kept at a near-zero range. In July 2022, the Federal Reserve instituted a three-quarter point rate hike to help slow inflation. They continue to evaluate economic conditions each time they meet.

- While the federal funds rate most directly impacts what banks charge each other for short-term loans, it feeds into a multitude of consumer products such as adjustable mortgages, auto loans, and credit cards. (Table 12-2 and Figure 12-2).

- U.S. net worth is a concept that measures the total nonfinancial worth, including land, machines and patent rights, of the U.S. as a whole. Household net worth tripled between 2003 to 2021. (Table 12-5)

Table 12-3. Consumer Credit

(Outstanding at end of period, billions of dollars.)

Year and month	Seasonally adjusted Total	By major credit type Revolving	By major credit type Non-revolving	Not seasonally adjusted Total [1]	By major holder Depository institutions	By major holder Finance companies [2]	By major holder Credit unions	By major holder Federal government [2]	By major holder Nonfinancial businesses	By major holder Securitized pools [3]
1970	131.6	5.0	126.6	133.7	70.1	27.6	13.0	0.0	23.0	0.0
1971	146.9	8.2	138.7	149.2	79.0	29.2	14.8	0.0	26.2	0.0
1972	166.2	9.4	156.8	168.8	92.1	31.9	17.0	0.0	27.8	0.0
1973	190.1	11.3	178.7	193.0	108.1	35.4	19.6	0.0	29.8	0.0
1974	198.9	13.2	185.7	201.9	112.1	36.1	21.9	0.0	31.8	0.0
1975	204.0	14.5	189.5	207.0	116.2	32.6	25.7	0.0	32.6	0.0
1976	225.7	16.5	209.2	229.0	128.9	33.7	31.2	0.0	35.2	0.0
1977	260.6	37.4	223.1	264.9	152.1	37.3	37.6	0.5	37.4	0.0
1978	306.1	45.7	260.4	311.3	179.6	44.4	45.2	0.9	41.2	0.0
1979	348.6	53.6	295.0	354.6	205.7	55.4	47.4	1.5	44.6	0.0
1980	351.9	55.0	297.0	358.0	202.9	62.2	44.1	2.6	46.2	0.0
1981	371.3	60.9	310.4	377.9	208.2	70.1	46.7	4.8	48.1	0.0
1982	389.8	66.3	323.5	396.7	217.5	75.3	48.8	6.4	48.7	0.0
1983	437.1	79.0	358.0	444.9	245.2	83.3	56.1	4.6	55.7	0.0
1984	517.3	100.4	416.9	526.6	303.1	89.9	67.9	5.6	60.2	0.0
1985	599.7	124.5	475.2	610.6	354.8	111.7	74.0	6.8	63.3	0.0
1986	654.8	141.1	513.7	666.4	383.1	134.0	77.1	8.2	64.0	0.0
1987	686.3	160.9	525.5	698.6	399.4	140.0	81.0	10.0	68.1	0.0
1988	731.9	184.6	547.3	745.2	427.6	144.7	88.3	13.2	71.4	0.0
1989	794.6	211.2	583.4	809.3	470.9	158.5	91.7	16.0	72.2	47.3
1990	808.2	238.6	569.6	824.4	476.4	160.2	91.6	19.2	77.0	76.7
1991	798.0	263.8	534.3	815.6	476.1	153.5	90.3	21.1	74.6	103.0
1992	806.1	278.4	527.7	824.8	472.1	158.0	91.7	24.2	78.8	120.3
1993	865.7	309.9	555.7	886.2	509.1	162.0	101.6	27.2	86.3	130.5
1994	997.3	365.6	631.7	1 021.2	588.4	178.3	119.6	37.2	97.6	146.1
1995	1 140.7	443.9	696.8	1 168.2	689.2	201.5	131.9	43.5	102.0	213.1
1996	1 253.4	507.5	745.9	1 273.9	763.8	214.0	144.1	51.4	100.5	273.5
1997	1 324.8	540.0	784.8	1 344.2	784.3	240.7	152.4	57.2	109.6	320.5
1998	1 421.0	581.4	839.6	1 441.3	852.7	267.8	155.4	64.9	100.6	393.9
1999	1 531.1	610.7	920.4	1 553.6	902.1	305.7	167.9	81.8	96.1	456.7
2000	1 717.0	682.6	1 034.3	1 741.3	976.7	379.9	184.4	96.7	103.6	528.4
2001	1 867.9	714.8	1 153.0	1 891.8	1 039.3	453.1	189.6	111.9	98.0	597.8
2002	1 972.1	750.9	1 221.2	1 997.0	1 080.2	502.8	195.7	117.3	101.0	630.4
2003	2 077.4	768.3	1 309.1	2 102.9	1 122.1	601.5	205.9	102.9	70.6	594.8
2004	2 192.2	799.6	1 392.7	2 220.1	1 186.6	665.0	215.4	86.1	67.0	571.5
2005	2 290.9	829.5	1 461.4	2 320.6	1 242.3	691.9	228.6	89.8	68.0	609.9
2006	2 456.7	923.9	1 532.8	2 456.7	1 252.9	728.0	236.1	108.7	56.3	617.2
2007	2 609.5	1 001.6	1 607.9	2 609.5	1 340.2	776.5	236.6	115.7	58.0	652.5
2008	2 643.8	1 004.0	1 639.8	2 643.8	1 397.1	734.8	236.2	135.2	51.6	610.2
2009	2 555.0	916.1	1 638.9	2 555.0	1 328.3	627.4	237.1	232.6	47.0	572.5
2010	2 646.8	839.1	1 807.7	2 646.8	1 225.0	715.8	226.5	363.8	44.4	50.3
2011	2 756.2	840.2	1 916.1	2 756.2	1 229.4	697.0	223.0	494.8	45.0	46.2
2012	2 912.9	840.0	2 072.9	2 912.9	1 256.1	688.6	243.6	622.2	44.2	50.0
2013	3 090.5	854.1	2 236.3	3 090.5	1 311.2	688.2	265.6	735.5	38.1	49.1
2014	3 309.5	887.4	2 422.2	3 309.5	1 383.4	693.6	301.0	846.2	37.7	49.8
2015	3 400.2	898.1	2 502.1	3 400.2	1 454.6	561.3	352.6	949.7	37.1	26.4
2016	3 636.4	960.1	2 676.3	3 636.4	1 562.6	548.4	396.7	1 049.3	38.2	30.5
2017	3 830.8	1 016.8	2 813.9	3 830.8	1 633.2	541.3	439.3	1 145.6	36.2	21.4
2018	4 007.0	1 053.8	2 953.2	4 007.0	1 687.4	534.4	481.2	1 236.3	36.5	5.5
2019	4 192.2	1 092.0	3 100.2	4 192.2	1 774.1	537.7	498.0	1 319.2	35.8	3.1
2020	4 184.9	974.6	3 210.3	4 184.9	1 687.5	551.4	505.1	1 381.0	35.8	1.9
2021	4 431.3	1 041.7	3 389.6	4 431.3	1 827.2	577.5	532.0	1 436.4	35.8	1.4
2020										
January	4 207.7	1 096.3	3 111.4	4 194.7	1 754.1	535.2	497.2	1 345.6	35.5	3.0
February	4 221.4	1 100.1	3 121.3	4 180.1	1 739.8	531.1	496.4	1 351.0	35.1	2.9
March	4 208.2	1 082.6	3 125.6	4 147.8	1 712.7	528.5	495.2	1 350.6	34.7	2.8
April	4 147.0	1 028.3	3 118.7	4 086.5	1 656.1	526.6	491.5	1 352.2	34.7	2.7
May	4 127.3	1 001.8	3 125.5	4 080.8	1 643.5	530.3	492.1	1 354.8	34.7	2.6
June	4 137.2	991.4	3 145.8	4 097.2	1 646.9	536.4	498.3	1 355.8	34.8	2.5
July	4 152.2	989.6	3 162.5	4 110.2	1 650.1	541.6	501.8	1 357.1	34.8	2.4
August	4 146.8	980.9	3 165.9	4 125.5	1 648.3	544.6	501.5	1 371.5	35.0	2.3
September	4 161.8	982.7	3 179.1	4 142.7	1 651.4	548.6	503.9	1 379.4	35.0	2.2
October	4 167.8	979.1	3 188.8	4 144.4	1 651.6	549.2	503.9	1 380.5	35.1	2.1
November	4 172.2	973.1	3 199.1	4 159.8	1 664.0	551.8	504.0	1 380.4	35.4	2.0
December	4 184.9	974.6	3 210.3	4 184.9	1 687.5	551.4	505.1	1 381.0	35.8	1.9
2021										
January	4 195.7	972.0	3 223.7	4 180.9	1 659.1	556.6	503.5	1 402.2	35.5	1.9
February	4 213.5	973.3	3 240.2	4 171.4	1 643.7	554.4	506.5	1 407.8	35.0	1.9
March	4 228.6	972.9	3 255.6	4 167.2	1 635.1	560.5	502.9	1 410.1	34.7	1.9
April	4 247.4	975.1	3 272.3	4 186.1	1 645.5	567.7	503.4	1 411.2	34.6	1.8
May	4 274.1	980.4	3 293.7	4 228.0	1 674.4	570.3	512.5	1 412.7	34.7	1.8
June	4 297.4	989.2	3 308.2	4 259.1	1 702.6	572.3	512.4	1 413.9	34.8	1.7
July	4 313.3	994.6	3 318.7	4 273.0	1 712.4	572.7	514.6	1 415.4	34.8	1.6
August	4 331.5	1 000.7	3 330.9	4 311.0	1 730.5	574.1	519.1	1 429.4	35.0	1.6
September	4 355.2	1 009.7	3 345.5	4 337.4	1 743.3	578.0	522.0	1 436.4	35.0	1.5
October	4 376.4	1 018.5	3 357.9	4 353.0	1 757.6	576.6	523.4	1 437.7	35.1	1.5
November	4 408.3	1 033.6	3 374.7	4 396.4	1 796.2	576.9	528.6	1 436.7	35.4	1.4
December	4 431.3	1 041.7	3 389.6	4 431.3	1 827.2	577.5	532.0	1 436.4	35.8	1.4

[1]Includes nonprofit and educational institutions, not shown.
[2]Student Loan Marketing Association (Sallie Mae) included in federal government sector until end of 2004, and in finance companies since then.
[3]Outstanding balances of pools upon which securities have been issued; these balances are no longer carried on the balance sheets of the loan originators.
. . . = Not available.

Table 12-4. Selected Stock and Housing Market Data

Year and month	Stock price indexes			FHFA House Price Indexes			
				House Price Index (purchases and refinance)		Purchase-Only Index	
	Dow Jones industrials (30 stocks)	Standard and Poor's composite (500 stocks) (1941–1943 = 10)	Nasdaq composite (Feb. 5, 1971 = 100)	Level at end of period (1980:I = 100)	Appreciation from same quarter one year earlier (percent)	Level at end of period (1991:I = 100)	Appreciation from same quarter one year earlier (percent)
1965	910.88	88.17	. . .	. . .	. . .	. . .	. . .
1966	873.60	85.26	. . .	. . .	. . .	. . .	. . .
1967	879.12	91.93	. . .	. . .	. . .	. . .	. . .
1968	906.00	98.70	. . .	. . .	. . .	. . .	. . .
1969	876.72	97.84	. . .	. . .	. . .	. . .	. . .
1970	753.19	83.22	. . .	. . .	. . .	. . .	. . .
1971	884.76	98.29	107.44	. . .	. . .	. . .	. . .
1972	950.71	109.20	128.52	. . .	. . .	. . .	. . .
1973	923.88	107.43	109.90	. . .	. . .	. . .	. . .
1974	759.37	82.85	76.29	. . .	. . .	. . .	. . .
1975	802.49	86.16	77.20	62.22	. . .	. . .	. . .
1976	974.92	102.01	89.90	67.26	8.10	. . .	. . .
1977	894.63	98.20	98.71	77.19	14.76	. . .	. . .
1978	820.23	96.02	117.53	87.50	13.36	. . .	. . .
1979	844.40	103.01	136.57	98.24	12.27	. . .	. . .
1980	891.41	118.78	168.61	104.61	6.48	. . .	. . .
1981	932.92	128.05	203.18	107.49	2.75	. . .	. . .
1982	884.36	119.71	188.97	111.71	3.93	. . .	. . .
1983	1 190.34	160.41	285.43	117.65	5.32	. . .	. . .
1984	1 178.48	160.46	248.88	123.16	4.68	. . .	. . .
1985	1 328.23	186.84	290.19	130.20	5.72	. . .	. . .
1986	1 792.76	236.34	366.96	139.69	7.29	. . .	. . .
1987	2 275.99	286.83	402.57	147.31	5.45	. . .	. . .
1988	2 060.82	265.79	374.43	155.59	5.62	. . .	. . .
1989	2 508.91	322.84	437.81	164.31	5.60	. . .	. . .
1990	2 678.94	334.59	409.17	166.31	1.22	. . .	. . .
1991	2 929.33	376.18	491.69	171.50	3.12	101.47	. . .
1992	3 284.29	415.74	599.26	175.62	2.40	104.19	2.68
1993	3 522.06	451.41	715.16	180.29	2.66	107.02	2.72
1994	3 793.77	460.42	751.65	183.11	1.56	110.03	2.81
1995	4 493.76	541.72	925.19	191.44	4.55	112.96	2.66
1996	5 742.89	670.50	1 164.96	196.29	2.53	116.05	2.74
1997	7 441.15	873.43	1 469.49	204.90	4.39	119.84	3.27
1998	8 625.52	1 085.50	1 794.91	215.28	5.07	126.64	5.67
1999	10 464.88	1 327.33	2 728.15	225.89	4.93	134.42	6.14
2000	10 786.85	1 320.28	2 470.52	241.88	7.08	143.75	6.94
2001	10 021.50	1 148.08	1 950.40	259.09	7.12	153.44	6.74
2002	8 341.63	879.82	1 335.51	276.47	6.71	165.15	7.63
2003	10 453.92	1 111.92	2 003.37	295.77	6.98	178.07	7.82
2004	10 783.01	1 211.92	2 175.44	326.35	10.34	196.13	10.14
2005	10 717.50	1 248.29	2 205.32	363.02	11.24	216.10	10.18
2006	12 463.15	1 418.30	2 415.29	379.46	4.53	222.19	2.82
2007	13 264.82	1 468.36	2 652.28	375.18	-1.13	216.13	-2.73
2008	8 776.39	903.25	1 577.03	348.37	-7.15	194.31	-10.10
2009	10 428.05	1 115.10	2 269.15	330.29	-5.19	189.42	-2.52
2010	11 577.51	1 257.64	2 652.87	324.21	-1.84	181.84	-4.00
2011	12 217.56	1 257.60	2 605.15	313.44	-3.32	177.18	-2.56
2012	13 104.14	1 426.19	3 019.51	315.31	0.60	185.61	4.76
2013	16 576.66	1 848.36	4 176.59	329.03	4.35	198.09	6.72
2014	17 823.07	2 058.90	4 736.05	345.90	5.13	207.15	4.57
2015	17 425.03	2 043.94	5 007.41	363.40	5.06	218.37	5.42
2016	19 762.60	2 238.83	5 383.12	383.27	5.47	231.28	5.91
2017	24 719.22	2 673.61	6 903.39	404.19	5.46	245.69	6.23
2018	23 327.46	2 506.85	6 635.28	423.99	4.90	259.60	5.66
2019	28 538.44	3 230.78	8 972.60	445.30	5.03	273.81	5.47
2020	30 606.48	3 756.07	12 888.28	473.02	6.23	304.36	11.16
2021	36 338.30	4 766.18	15 644.97	557.93	17.95	358.25	17.71
2020							
January	28 256.03	3 225.52	9 150.94	. . .	. . .	. . .	. . .
February	25 409.36	2 954.22	8 567.37	. . .	. . .	. . .	. . .
March	21 917.16	2 584.59	7 700.10	450.42	5.07	278.83	6.26
April	24 345.72	2 912.43	8 889.55	. . .	. . .	. . .	. . .
May	25 383.11	3 044.31	9 489.87	. . .	. . .	. . .	. . .
June	25 812.88	3 100.29	10 058.77	454.83	4.36	285.50	5.73
July	26 428.32	3 271.12	10 745.27	. . .	. . .	. . .	. . .
August	28 430.05	3 500.31	11 775.46	. . .	. . .	. . .	. . .
September	27 781.70	3 363.00	11 167.51	462.80	4.86	295.04	8.18
October	26 501.60	3 269.96	10 911.59	. . .	. . .	. . .	. . .
November	29 638.64	3 621.63	12 198.74	. . .	. . .	. . .	. . .
December	30 606.48	3 756.07	12 888.28	473.02	6.23	304.36	11.16
2021							
January	29 982.62	3 714.24	13 070.69	. . .	. . .	. . .	. . .
February	30 932.37	3 811.15	13 192.35	. . .	. . .	. . .	. . .
March	32 981.55	3 972.89	13 246.87	484.29	7.52	315.40	13.12
April	33 874.85	4 181.17	13 962.68	. . .	. . .	. . .	. . .
May	34 529.45	4 204.11	13 748.74	. . .	. . .	. . .	. . .
June	34 502.51	4 297.50	14 503.95	511.22	12.40	336.16	17.74
July	34 935.47	4 395.26	14 672.68	. . .	. . .	. . .	. . .
August	35 360.73	4 522.68	15 259.24	. . .	. . .	. . .	. . .
September	33 843.92	4 307.54	14 448.58	539.60	16.59	349.88	18.59
October	35 819.56	4 605.38	15 498.39	. . .	. . .	. . .	. . .
November	34 483.72	4 567.00	15 537.69	. . .	. . .	. . .	. . .
December	36 338.30	4 766.18	15 644.97	557.93	17.95	358.25	17.71

. . . = Not available.

Table 12-5. Derivation of U.S. Net Wealth

(Billions of dollars, amounts outstanding at the end of period.)

Year and month	Household net worth	Growth of domestic nonfinancial debt				
		Total	households	Business	State and local governments	Federal
2003	49 426	8.0	11.8	2.2	8.3	10.9
2004	55 951	9.0	11.1	5.6	11.4	9.0
2005	61 789	8.6	10.6	8.1	5.8	6.6
2006	66 073	8.4	10.5	9.8	3.9	3.9
2007	66 499	8.1	7.2	12.4	6.0	4.7
2008	56 292	5.8	0.0	5.7	1.4	21.4
2009	60 347	3.7	0.5	-3.9	4.7	20.4
2010	67 129	4.4	-0.6	-0.8	2.7	18.5
2011	67 900	3.7	0.1	2.5	-1.0	10.8
2012	71 911	4.7	0.5	5.6	-0.1	10.1
2013	80 525	4.2	2.3	4.9	-0.2	6.7
2014	86 525	3.8	1.2	6.8	-2.3	5.4
2015	89 621	4.4	2.3	7.0	0.5	5.0
2016	94 707	4.4	3.1	5.1	1.0	5.6
2017	103 415	4.2	3.9	6.1	0.0	3.7
2018	104 130	4.7	3.1	4.5	-1.2	7.6
2019	116 777	4.7	3.3	4.8	0.0	6.6
2020	131 343	12.3	3.8	8.9	2.9	24.1
2021	150 290	6.2	3.5	4.5	1.9	7.2
2014						
1st quarter	80 940	4.1	1.9	6.1	-1.7	5.7
2nd quarter	82 627	4.2	5.2	5.1	0.1	3.5
3rd quarter	82 520	4.5	3.0	5.9	-1.7	6.0
4th quarter	84 189	4.7	2.2	7.0	1.5	5.9
2015						
1st quarter	85 798	2.7	2.0	7.4	1.6	-0.3
2nd quarter	86 434	4.4	3.8	8.0	0.5	2.7
3rd quarter	85 249	2.7	1.3	5.5	0.2	2.1
4th quarter	87 287	7.8	3.8	5.6	-1.2	15.4
2016						
1st quarter	86 811	5.5	2.5	9.2	0.7	6.2
2nd quarter	87 532	4.6	4.4	4.2	2.2	5.7
3rd quarter	89 750	5.0	3.5	6.1	0.8	6.3
4th quarter	91 583	3.1	3.7	2.4	0.4	3.6
2017						
1st quarter	95 101	3.2	3.7	5.9	-2.2	1.7
2nd quarter	97 272	4.7	3.9	6.6	-0.9	4.9
3rd quarter	98 866	4.9	2.7	6.2	-0.6	6.9
4th quarter	100 926	3.3	5.1	3.6	3.5	1.3
2018						
1st quarter	106 792	6.7	3.0	3.9	-3.2	14.3
2nd quarter	108 507	4.0	3.6	3.3	-0.4	5.7
3rd quarter	110 594	4.3	3.4	4.3	-1.4	5.9
4th quarter	107 219	3.4	2.8	4.8	-1.5	3.7
2019						
1st quarter	111 132	5.9	2.2	6.7	-0.7	9.6
2nd quarter	113 446	3.5	4.3	4.2	-1.8	3.1
3rd quarter	114 304	5.9	3.3	5.9	0.9	8.9
4th quarter	117 878	3.3	3.6	2.2	2.9	4.2
2020						
1st quarter	110 449	11.7	3.6	18.9	1.0	14.1
2nd quarter	118 430	26.7	-0.1	15.2	3.5	62.5
3rd quarter	122 774	4.1	5.5	0.1	5.6	6.0
4th quarter	131 343	5.1	6.1	0.5	1.5	8.4
2021						
1st quarter	136 636	6.8	6.7	4.6	3.4	9.0
2nd quarter	142 307	6.5	7.7	1.8	3.2	9.6
3rd quarter	144 992	2.6	6.2	4.7	1.9	-1.3
4th quarter	150 290	8.2	8.0	6.7	-0.9	10.8

NOTES AND DEFINITIONS, CHAPTER 12

The Federal Reserve's mission is to promote the goals of maximum employment and stables prices by using these monetary policy tools. Monetary policy in the United States comprises the Federal Reserve's actions and communications to promote maximum employment, stable prices, and moderate long-term interest rates–the three economic goals the Congress has instructed the Federal Reserve to pursue.

When the financial crisis started in 2007, the Federal Reserve used Monetary tools in accordance to their mission: reducing interest rates to near-zero and increasing the money supply with its Qualitative Easing policy.

As home-owners defaulted on their sub-prime mortgages in 2007 to 2009, the Federal Reserve played an important role in turning the economy around. One such program was Quantitative Easing where the Fed purchased financial assets in addition to conventional easing, which has consisted of reducing short-term interest rates to near zero and supporting that rate level with purchases and sales of short-term securities on the open market. In addition, the Federal Reserve began an initiative to provide a richer and more detailed picture of financial intermediation and interconnections.

Quantitative easing policy was discontinued in late 2014. By then the federal reserve had bought $4.5 trillion worth of bonds over five years. The goal of the program during the Great Recession was to lower interest rates and increase the money supply. In addition, the Fed held its benchmark rate to 0.25 which is effectively zero. This policy remained in place for seven years, until December 2015.

The Federal Reserve Board announced on August 1, 2014 the Enhanced Financial Accounts (EFA) initiative which is an ambitious and long-term effort to enhance the "Financial Accounts" (FA) by providing additional detail and disaggregation, higher-frequency data, and additional documentation and analysis of financial data, in order to improve the picture of financial intermediation and activity in the United States. These large-scale and fundamental improvements will expand the detail, dimensionality, and scope of the FA in order to improve the overall picture of financial intermediation and activity in the United States.

In early 2020, the Federal Reserve began lowering interest rates again and increasing money supply through purchasing bank's bond in response to the spreading coronavirus. States issued stay-at-home orders which effectively closed many nonessential businesses. Unemployment compensation requests soared to 36 million by mid-May 2020.

Interest rates were kept near zero for nearly two years.

Most of the data in this chapter are found on the Federal Reserve Board Web site, <http://www.federalreserve.gov>. Current releases and most historical data are found at that site by selecting Economic Research & Data/Statistical Releases and Historical Data and then selecting the appropriate report. This is the location for all data not otherwise specified.

Historical data not found online are taken from two printed volumes of statistical data that were published by the Board of Governors of the Federal Reserve System: *Banking and Monetary Statistics,* 1943, and *Banking and Monetary Statistics, 1941-1970,* 1976. These will be referred to as *B&MS* 1943 and *B&MS* 1976.

Tables 12-1 and 12-2

Money Stock Measures and Components

SOURCE: BOARD OF GOVERNORS OF THE FEDERAL RESERVE SYSTEM

Monetary policy includes monitoring two different measures – M1 and M2. M1 consists of the most liquid forms of money such as demand deposits. M2 includes M1 and short term savings. Estimates of these measures are published weekly. The monthly data are averages of daily figures. In addition, these measures are revised in subsequent releases.

The Federal Reserve Board ceased publication of the M3 aggregate on March 23, 2006. Weekly publication was also discontinued for the following components of M3: large-denomination time deposits, repurchase agreements (RPs), and Eurodollars. The Board continues to publish institutional money market mutual funds as a memorandum item in this release. Measures of large-denomination time deposits continue to be published in the Financial Accounts (Z.1 release) and in the H.8 release weekly for commercial banks.

The Board stated that "M3 does not appear to convey any additional information about economic activity that is not already embodied in M2 and has not played a role in the monetary policy process for many years. Consequently, the Board judged that the costs of collecting the underlying data and publishing M3 outweigh the benefits." M3 included Individual Retirement Acts (IRA) and Keogh retirement plans designed for self-employed individuals. ("Discontinuance of M3," H.6, Money Stock Measures [November 10, 2005, revised March 9, 2006]. [Accessed November 6, 2006.]

Definitions

M1 consists of (1) currency, (2) traveler's checks of nonbank issuers, (3) demand deposits, and (4) other checkable deposits.

M2 consists of M1 plus savings deposits (including money market deposit accounts), smalldenomination time deposits, and balances in retail money market mutual funds.

Currency consists of paper notes and coins outside the U.S. Treasury, the Federal Reserve Banks, and the vaults of depository institutions.

Traveler's checks is the outstanding amount of U.S. dollar-denominated traveler's checks of nonbank issuers. Traveler's checks issued by depository institutions are included in demand deposits.

Demand deposits consists of funds at domestically chartered commercial banks, U.S. branches and agencies of foreign banks, and Edge Act corporations (excluding those amounts held by depository institutions, the U.S. government, and foreign banks and official institutions) less cash items in the process of collection and Federal Reserve float

Other checkable deposits at commercial banks consists of negotiable order of withdrawal (NOW) and automatic transfer service (ATS) balances at domestically chartered commercial banks, U.S. branches and agencies of foreign banks, and Edge Act corporations.

Other checkable deposits at thrift Other liquid deposits consist of negotiable order of withdrawal (NOW) and automatic transfer service (ATS) balances at depository institutions, share draft accounts at credit unions, demand deposits at thrift institutions, and savings deposits, including money market deposit accounts.

Savings deposits includes money market deposit accounts and other savings deposits at *commercial banks* and *thrift institutions*.

Small time deposits are deposits issued at *commercial banks* and *thrift institutions* in amounts less than $100,000. All Individual Retirement Account (IRA) and Keogh account balances at commercial banks and thrift institutions are subtracted from small time deposits.

Retail money funds are investment funds with capital invested by individual investors. Also IRA and Keogh account balances are excluded.

Institutional money funds are included in the money stock report for informational purposes. They are not part of M1 or M2.

Notes on the data

Seasonal adjustment. Seasonally adjusted M1 is calculated by summing currency, traveler's checks, demand deposits, and other checkable deposits (each seasonally adjusted separately). Seasonally adjusted M2 is computed by adjusting each of its nonM1 components and then adding this result to seasonally adjusted M1.

Revisions. Money stock measures are revised frequently and have a benchmark and seasonal factor review in the middle of the year; this review typically extends back a number of years. The

monetary aggregates were redefined in major revisions introduced in 1980.

Historical: 1892–1946. These data are from *B&MS* 1943 and *B&MS* 1976. They pertain only to the last day of June and, after 1922, the last day of December, the "call dates" on which banks reported to the federal government. For more data and analysis concerning monetary developments in this period, including monthly money supply estimates, see Milton Friedman and Anna Jacobson Schwartz, *A Monetary History of the United States, 1867–1960,* Princeton, Princeton University Press, 1963. In Table 12-1B, *Demand deposits adjusted* refers to the elimination of interbank and U.S. government deposits and cash items in process of collection, not to seasonal adjustment, which is not applicable to call report data because they are only reported once or twice a year. The editor has retitled as *M1* the "Total" money stock shown in the source document, and has added time deposits to it in order to approximate *M2*, which is not shown in the source document.

Historical: January 1947-January 1959. These data are not currently maintained online and are found in *B&MS* 1976. They are not continuous with the current data series; for that reason the values for January 1959 are shown so that users can link to the current data. The *demand deposit component* includes demand deposits held in commercial banks by individuals, partnerships, and corporations both domestic and foreign, and demand deposits held by nonbank financial institutions and foreign banks. Note that this includes demand deposit liabilities to foreign governments, central banks, and international institutions—said to be "relatively small" in the source document. *Time deposits adjusted* is time and savings deposits at commercial banks, other than large negotiable certificates of deposit (CDs), and excluding all deposits due to the U.S. government and domestic commercial banks. The editor has added this to the *Money stock (M1)* to approximate *M2*, which is not shown as such in the source document, over this period.

Data availability

Estimates are released weekly in Federal Reserve Statistical Release H.6, "Money Stock Measures." Current and historical data are available on the Federal Reserve Web site.

References

Board of Governors of the Federal Reserve System, *The Federal Reserve System: Purposes and Functions,* available online at <http://www.federalreserve.gov> in the category "About the Fed/ Features," includes a chapter discussing monetary policy and the monetary aggregates and a glossary of terms as an appendix.

An explanation of the 1980 redefinition of the monetary aggregates is found in the *Federal Reserve Bulletin* for February 1980.

Table 12-3

Consumer Credit

SOURCE: BOARD OF GOVERNORS OF THE FEDERAL RESERVE SYSTEM

The consumer credit series cover most shortand intermediate-term credit extended to individuals through regular business channels, excluding loans secured by real estate (such as first and second mortgages and home equity credit). In October 2003, the scope of this survey was expanded to incorporate student loans extended by the federal government and by SLM Holding Corporation (SLM), the parent company of Sallie Mae (Student Loan Marketing Association). The historical data have been revised back to 1977 to reflect this inclusion.

Consumer credit is categorized by major types of credit and by major holders.

Definitions and notes on the data

The major types of consumer credit are *revolving* and *nonrevolving*.

Revolving credit includes credit arising from purchases on credit card plans of retail stores and banks, cash advances and check credit plans of banks, and some overdraft credit arrangements.

Nonrevolving credit includes automobile loans, mobile home loans, and all other loans not included in revolving credit, such as student loans, boats, trailers, or vacations. These loans may be secured or unsecured.

Debt secured by real estate (including first liens, junior liens, and home equity loans) is excluded. Credit extended to governmental agencies and nonprofit or charitable organizations, as well as credit extended to business or to individuals exclusively for business purposes, is excluded.

Categories of *holders* include *U.S.-chartered depository institutions* (comprising commercial banks and savings institutions), *finance companies, credit unions, federal government, nonfinancial businesses*, and *pools of securitized assets*. The Student Loan Marketing Association (Sallie Mae) is included in "Federal government" until the end of 2004, at which time it became fully privatized. Beginning with the end of 2004, Sallie Mae is included in "Finance companies." Retailers and gasoline companies are included in the nonfinancial businesses category.

Federal government includes student loans originated by the Department of Education under the Federal Direct Loan Program and the Perkins Loan Program, as well as Federal Family Education Loan Program loans that the government purchased under the Ensuring Continued Access to Student Loans Act.

Pools of securitized assets comprises the outstanding balances of pools upon which securities have been issued; these balances are no longer carried on the balance sheets of the loan originators.

Data availability

Current data are available monthly in the Federal Reserve Statistical Release G.19, "Consumer Credit," available along with all current and historical data on the Federal Reserve website. In the autumn of each year there is a revision of several years of past data reflecting benchmarking and seasonal factor review.

Tables 12- 4

Stock Prices and Housing Market Data

SOURCES: DOW JONES, INC.; STANDARD AND POOR'S CORPORATION; NASDAQ; NEW YORK STOCK EXCHANGE; FEDERAL HOUSING FINANCE AGENCY

Definitions and notes on the data

Stock price indexes and yields.

The *Dow Jones industrial* average is an average price of 30 stocks compiled by Dow Jones, Inc.

The *Standard and Poor's composite* is an index of the prices of 500 stocks that are weighted by the volume of shares outstanding, accounting for about 90 percent of New York Stock Exchange value, with a base of 1941–1943 = 10, compiled by Standard and Poor's Corporation. (Before February 1957, these data are based on a conversion of an earlier 90-stock index, and are obtained from *B&MS* 1943 and 1976.)

The *Nasdaq composite index* is an average price of over 5,000 stocks traded on the Nasdaq exchange.

The *fixed-rate first mortgage* rates are primary market contract interest rates on commitments for fixedrate conventional 30-year first mortgages. The rates are obtained by the Federal Reserve from the Federal Home Loan Mortgage Corporation (FHLMC, or Freddie Mac).

The Federal Housing Finance Agency (FHFA) (formerly Federal Housing Enterprise Oversight (OFHEO) House Price Index is a broad economic measure of the movement of single-family house and repeat-sales in the United States. The FHFA HPI index measures changes in single-family house prices based on data covering all 50 states and over 400 American cities. Extending back to the mid-1970s, the HPIs are built on tens of millions of home sales and offer insights about house price fluctuations at national, census division, state metro area, county, ZIP code, and census tract levels.

FHFA publishes Purchase-Only Indexes for the house purchase subgroup of new mortgage transactions, excluding refinancing transactions. Nation-wide, this index is based on millions of transactions over the latest 27 years. While this is still a very large statistical base, it is subject to somewhat greater revision and is less reliable for smaller geographical areas.

The FHFA HPI is a weighted, repeat-sales index, meaning that it measures average price changes in repeat sales or refinancing's on the same properties. This information is obtained by reviewing repeat mortgage transactions on single-family properties whose mortgages have been purchased or securitized by Fannie Mae or Freddie Mac since January 1975. In addition the repeat-sales technique helps to control for differences in the quality of the houses comprising the sample and is the reason the FHFA HPI is referred to as a "constant quality" index or as "all-transactions" house price index. Appraisal values from refinance mortgages are added to the purchase-only data sample.

The FHFA price indexes are subject to revision for preceding quarters and years, because each new transaction, when reported, affects the rate of price change for all periods since the last time that the property involved in the new transaction changed hands or was refinanced. In 2006, the purchase-only index was the largest index since 1991. However by 2019, this index rose 24.1 percent.

The national conforming loan limit for mortgages that finance single-family one-unit properties increased from $33,000 in the early 1970s to $417,000 for 2006-2008, with limits 50 percent higher for four statutorily-designated high cost areas: Alaska, Hawaii, Guam, and the U.S. Virgin Islands. Since 2008, various legislative acts increased the loan limits in certain high-cost areas in the United States. While some of the legislative initiatives established temporary limits for loans originated in select time periods, a permanent formula was established under the Housing and Economic Recovery Act of 2008 (HERA). The 2019 loan limits have been set under the HERA formula.

The FHFA indexes do not come from a random sample of house prices, and users need to consider possible sources of bias. Expensive houses are under-represented in general because the transactions are limited to conforming mortgages. This is important if the price trends for expensive houses are different.

Analysis of purchase-only and refinance indexes illustrated that these two indexes behave similarly even there was some questions that they behaved differently. Between the end of 1991 and the peak at the end of 2006, the total House Price Index rose 121 percent, identical with the Purchase-Only Index. Between 2006 and 2015, the house price index fell 3.9 percent. This index has improved over 12 percent from 2016 and 2019. The prices

of purchased homes fell 4.0 percent from 2006 and 2014 while between 2015 and 2019 these prices increased 25.9 percent.

In addition to these government-supplied measures, new privately-developed house price indexes–not available for publication in *Business Statistics*–are now receiving regular media attention, and even provide the basis for a futures contract trading on the Chicago Mercantile Exchange. Standard & Poor's now issues S&P/Case-Shiller® Home Price Indexes each month. They cover resales only for houses at all price ranges, based on information obtained from county assessor and recorder offices. They are value-weighted, meaning that price trends for more expensive homes have greater influence on changes in the index. (The FHFA index weights price trends equally for all properties.) S&P/Case-Shiller data are only collected for 20 major metropolitan statistical areas. Series description and data can be found at <https://www.homeprice.standardandpoors.com>.

Table 12-5

Derivation of U.S. Net Wealth

SOURCE: BOARD OF GOVERNORS OF THE FEDERAL RESERVE SYSTEM.

The Z-1 *Financial Accounts* provide information on macro-financial flows and aggregate balance sheets for major sectors of the economy, including households, financial institutions, nonfinancial businesses, governments, and the international sector. The *Financial Accounts* also make up the financial component of the *Integrated Macroeconomic Accounts*, which are published jointly with the Bureau of Economic Analysis and which relate production, income, and saving from the *National Income and Product Accounts* to changes in net worth and financial transactions across the major economic sectors of the U.S. economy. The basic framework of the FA allows understanding of the economic relationships underlying the major sections of the economy, as well as for monitoring the effects of macro-financial developments in the United States and globally.

Researchers and analysts have used the Financial Accounts to investigates the causes and consequences of the financial crisis and to create and analyze indicators of financial stability. However, they were not originally designed to be a comprehensive source of data for all the complex financial relationships and transactions whose importance to the macro-economy were made clear during the financial crisis of 2007-2009.

A new table on the derivation on U.S. net worth has been added to the summary section of the "Financial Accounts." The calculation of U.S. net worth (table 12.7) Household Net Worth and Growth of Domestic Nonfinancial Debt includes the value of nonfinancial assets (real estate, equipment, intellectual property products, consumer durables and inventories) held by households and nonprofit organizations and noncorporate businesses. The measure of U.S. net worth includes the market value of domestic nonfinancial and financial corporations and is adjusted to reflect U.S. financial claims on the rest of the world.

Taking all this together, net U.S worth is defined as the value of tangible assets controlled by households and nonprofits, noncorporate business, and government sectors of the U.S. economy, plus the market value of domestic nonfinancial and financial corporations, net of U.S. financial obligations to the rest of the world.

Changes in net worth consist of transactions, revaluations, and other volume changes. Corporate equity and debt securities include directly and indirectly held securities. Real estate is the value of owner-occupied real estate. Other includes equity in noncorporate businesses, consumer durable goods, fixed assets of nonprofit organizations, and all other financial assets apart from corporate equities and debt securities, net of liabilities, as shown on table B.101 Balance Sheet of Households and Nonprofit Organizations.

Definitions and notes on the data

The concept of *U.S. net worth* ignores all domestic financial intermediation and just counts the value of the land, machines, houses, cars, etc., plus intangible worth but does not include financial worth.

Household net worth is the value of net worth for the household and nonprofit organizations sector, as reported on table B.101 in the *Financial Accounts*. Net worth is calculated as the difference between a sector's total assets, including both financial and nonfinancial assets, and liabilities (debts owed to other sectors) and does include financial worth.

*Noncorporate business*es includes both sole proprietorships and partnerships, including noncorporate farms.

Debt equates to the sum of debt securities and loans.

Domestic Nonfinancial entities include households, corporations, nonfarm noncorporate businesses, farm business, federal, state and local governments.

Domestic Nonfinancial assets include housing, property, automobiles, equipment, business equity, intellectual properties such as patents, copyrights and trademarks.

For corporate *businesses,* worth is the market value of their outstanding equity shares and is used to better capture the value of intangible assets, such as intellectual property.

A *corporation* is formed under state law by the filing of articles of incorporation with the state.

Federal Government consists of all federal government agencies and funds included in the unified budget. However, the District of Columbia government is included in the state and local sector.

Nonprofits include private foundations and organizations that are tax-exempt under Sections 501(c)(3) through 501(c)(9) of the Internal Revenue Code. Does not include religious organizations or organizations with less than $25,000 in gross annual receipts.

Revision

Data shown for the most recent quarters are based on preliminary and potentially incomplete information. Nonetheless, when source data are revised or estimation methods are improved, all data are subject to revision. There is no specific revision schedule; rather, data are revised on an ongoing basis.

Data availability

The "Financial Accounts" are published online and in print four times per year, about 10 weeks following the end of each calendar quarter. The publication with series mnemonics and the guide are available online: www.federalreserve.gov/releases/Z1.

CHAPTER 13: INTERNATIONAL COMPARISONS

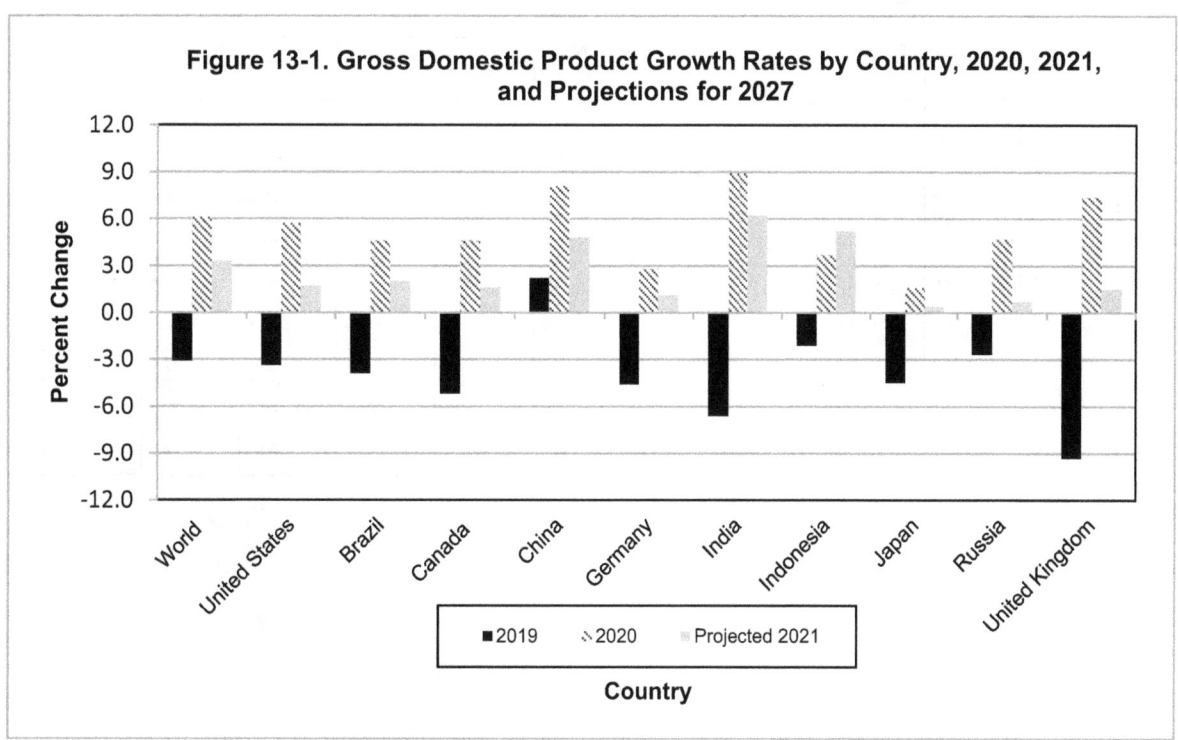

Figure 13-1. Gross Domestic Product Growth Rates by Country, 2020, 2021, and Projections for 2027

- The World Economic Outlook (WEO), published by The International Monetary Fund (IMF) revised their economic forecast in April 2022. They are projecting global growth at 3.6 percent in 2022 and 2023, down 0.8 percent and 0.2 percent percentage points from their forecast in January. The decline is largely due to Russia's invasion of Ukraine. It is expected that both countries will experience large contractions in their GDP. (Table 13-1)

- While inflation has increased rapidly in many countries in 2021 and 2022, it is projected that inflation will slow to 2.0 percent in the United States in 2027. In addition, unemployment is expected to decline in many countries by 2027. (Table 13-1)

- Five of the six major currencies listed in Table 13-2 including the Canadian dollar, the Euro, the Japanese yen, the British pound, and the Swiss franc are all major industrial countries whose currencies are freely traded on world markets. The other currency listed is the Chinese yuan, which is not freely traded. China can control the international values of their currencies (through, for example, direct capital controls) and keep their currencies from appreciating relative to the dollar to maintain their competitiveness in the U.S. market. (Table 13-2)

Table 13-1 International Comparisons: Percent Change in Real GDP, Consumer Prices, Current Account Balances, and Unemployment Rate, 2020, 2021, and Projected 2027

(Percent, dollar.)

Country	Gross domestic product, constant prices			Inflation, average consumer prices			Current account balance (billions of U.S.dollars)			Unemployment rate		
	2020	2021	Projected 2027	2020	2021	Projected 2027	2020	2021	Projected 2027	2020	2021	Projected 2027
WORLD	-3.1	6.1	3.3	3.2	4.7	3.2	367.9	744.6	323.5	. . .	. . .	. . .
Euro Area	-6.4	5.3	1.3	0.3	2.6	1.9	250.0	345.2	479.3	8.0	7.7	6.8
Germany	-4.6	2.8	1.1	0.4	3.2	2.0	272.5	314.0	369.3	3.8	3.5	3.1
United Kingdom	-9.3	7.4	1.5	0.9	2.6	2.0	-69.0	-82.5	-161.0	4.5	4.5	4.2
Brazil	-3.9	4.6	2.0	3.2	8.3	3.0	-24.5	-27.9	-52.4	13.8	14.2	10.4
Canada	-5.2	4.6	1.6	0.7	3.4	2.0	-29.4	1.2	-51.0	9.6	7.4	5.0
China	2.2	8.1	4.8	2.4	0.9	2.0	248.8	317.3	120.1	4.2	4.0	3.6
India	-6.6	8.9	6.2	6.2	5.5	6.1	24.0	-49.3	-128.0	. . .	. . .	. . .
Indonesia	-2.1	3.7	5.2	2.0	1.6	2.9	-4.4	3.3	-28.1	7.1	6.5	5.1
Japan	-4.5	1.6	0.4	0.0	-0.3	1.0	148.8	141.7	202.0	2.8	2.8	2.4
Russia	-2.7	4.7	0.7	3.4	6.7	4.0	36.0	122.0	56.3	5.8	4.8	4.7
UNITED STATES	-3.4	5.7	1.7	1.2	4.7	2.0	-616.0	-806.0	-636.0	8.1	5.4	4.0

. . . = Not available.

Table 13-2 Foreign Exchange Rates

(Not seasonally adjusted.)

Year and month	Foreign currency per U.S. dollar					
	Canadian dollar	Chinese yuan	European currency unit	Japananese yen	Switzerland franc	British pound
1971	1.0099	. . .	. . .	347.79	4.1171	2.4442
1972	0.9907	. . .	. . .	303.12	3.8186	2.5034
1973	1.0002	. . .	. . .	271.31	3.1688	2.4525
1974	0.9780	. . .	. . .	291.84	2.9805	2.3403
1975	1.0175	. . .	. . .	296.78	2.5839	2.2217
1976	0.9863	. . .	. . .	296.45	2.5002	1.8048
1977	1.0633	. . .	. . .	268.62	2.4065	1.7449
1978	1.1405	. . .	. . .	210.39	1.7907	1.9184
1979	1.1713	. . .	. . .	219.02	1.6644	2.1224
1980	1.1693	. . .	. . .	226.63	1.6772	2.3246
1981	1.1990	1.7100	. . .	220.63	1.9675	2.0243
1982	1.2344	1.8979	. . .	249.06	2.0319	1.7480
1983	1.2325	1.9810	. . .	237.55	2.1007	1.5159
1984	1.2952	2.3303	. . .	237.46	2.3500	1.3368
1985	1.3659	2.9434	. . .	238.47	2.4552	1.2974
1986	1.3896	3.4616	. . .	168.35	1.7979	1.4677
1987	1.3259	3.7314	. . .	144.60	1.4918	1.6398
1988	1.2306	3.7314	. . .	128.17	1.4643	1.7813
1989	1.1842	3.7673	. . .	138.07	1.6369	1.6382
1990	1.1668	4.7921	. . .	145.00	1.3901	1.7841
1991	1.1460	5.3337	. . .	134.59	1.4356	1.7674
1992	1.2085	5.5206	. . .	126.78	1.4064	1.7663
1993	1.2902	5.7795	. . .	111.08	1.4781	1.5016
1994	1.3664	8.6397	. . .	102.18	1.3667	1.5319
1995	1.3725	8.3700	. . .	93.96	1.1812	1.5785
1996	1.3638	8.3389	. . .	108.78	1.2361	1.5607
1997	1.3849	8.3193	. . .	121.06	1.4514	1.6376
1998	1.4836	8.3008	. . .	130.99	1.4506	1.6573
1999	1.4858	8.2783	1.0653	113.73	1.5045	1.6172
2000	1.4855	8.2784	0.9232	107.80	1.6904	1.5156
2001	1.5487	8.2770	0.8952	121.57	1.6891	1.4396
2002	1.5704	8.2771	0.9454	125.22	1.5567	1.5025
2003	1.4008	8.2772	1.1321	115.94	1.3450	1.6347
2004	1.3017	8.2768	1.2438	108.15	1.2428	1.8330
2005	1.2115	8.1936	1.2449	110.11	1.2459	1.8204
2006	1.1340	7.9723	1.2563	116.31	1.2532	1.8434
2007	1.0734	7.6058	1.3711	117.76	1.1999	2.0020
2008	1.0660	6.9477	1.4726	103.39	1.0816	1.8545
2009	1.1412	6.8307	1.3935	93.68	1.0860	1.5661
2010	1.0298	6.7696	1.3261	87.78	1.0432	1.5452
2011	0.9887	6.4630	1.3931	79.70	0.8862	1.6043
2012	0.9995	6.3093	1.2859	79.82	0.9377	1.5853
2013	1.0300	6.1478	1.3281	97.60	0.9269	1.5642
2014	1.1043	6.1620	1.3297	105.74	0.9147	1.6484
2015	1.2791	6.2827	1.1096	121.05	0.9628	1.5284
2016	1.3243	6.6400	1.1072	108.66	0.9848	1.3555
2017	1.2984	6.7569	1.1301	112.10	0.9842	1.2890
2018	1.2957	6.6090	1.1817	110.40	0.9784	1.3363
2019	1.3269	6.9081	1.1194	109.02	0.9937	1.2768
2020	1.3422	6.9042	1.1410	106.78	0.9389	1.2829
2021	1.2533	6.4508	1.1830	109.84	0.9144	1.3764
2020						
January	1.3089	6.9184	1.1098	109.27	0.9698	1.3076
February	1.3286	6.9967	1.0911	110.03	0.9762	1.2953
March	1.3960	7.0205	1.1046	107.67	0.9593	1.2369
April	1.4048	7.0708	1.0871	107.74	0.9701	1.2420
May	1.3972	7.1016	1.0907	107.20	0.9692	1.2302
June	1.3552	7.0816	1.1259	107.58	0.9513	1.2523
July	1.3497	7.0041	1.1488	106.68	0.9327	1.2701
August	1.3229	6.9270	1.1831	106.01	0.9099	1.3143
September	1.3230	6.8106	1.1785	105.59	0.9149	1.2947
October	1.3218	6.7254	1.1768	105.21	0.9124	1.2980
November	1.3073	6.6029	1.1826	104.41	0.9110	1.3198
December	1.2809	6.5393	1.2168	103.80	0.8884	1.3434
2021						
January	1.2725	6.4672	1.2178	103.79	0.8865	1.3641
February	1.2696	6.4601	1.2094	105.38	0.8979	1.3867
March	1.2569	6.5109	1.1902	108.70	0.9298	1.3863
April	1.2494	6.5186	1.1965	109.04	0.9218	1.3845
May	1.2125	6.4321	1.2146	109.11	0.9027	1.4084
June	1.2220	6.4250	1.2048	110.11	0.9078	1.4025
July	1.2530	6.4763	1.1821	110.21	0.9174	1.3808
August	1.2599	6.4768	1.1767	109.85	0.9147	1.3797
September	1.2671	6.4563	1.1765	110.16	0.9228	1.3732
October	1.2434	6.4172	1.1600	113.12	0.9227	1.3701
November	1.2567	6.3889	1.1416	113.97	0.9213	1.3463
December	1.2800	6.3693	1.1301	113.83	0.9210	1.3303

. . . = Not available.

NOTES AND DEFINITIONS, CHAPTER 13

Table 13-1

International Comparisons: Gross Domestic Product Growth, Unemployment Rates, Inflation and Current Account Balances

SOURCE: APRIL AND JULY 2021 WORLD ECONOMIC OUTLOOK, PUBLISHED BY THE INTERNATIONAL MONETARY FUND

The United States trades with many countries for both goods and services. Specific countries include neighbors Canada and Mexico, European countries Germany and the United Kingdom; plus, Asian nations such as China, Japan, and India and finally Russia. Table 13-1 provides international comparisons of these nations in terms of major economic indicators.

The IMF was established in 1944 in the aftermath of the Great Depression of the 1930s. 44 founding member countries sought to build a framework for international economic cooperation. Today, its membership embraces 190 countries, with staff drawn from 150 nations.

Definitions and notes on the data

The basic measure of the overall health of an economy is the *gross domestic product* (GDP). It is the market value of all goods and services produced by labor and property located in the United States. *Real GDP* is an inflation-adjusted measure that reflects the value of all goods and services produced by an economy each year, expressed in base-year prices. See chapter 1 for in depth and historical data of GDP and its components plus notes and definitions at the end of the chapter.

The *unemployment rate* represents the number unemployed as a percent of the labor force. See Chapter 10.

The *Consumer Price Index* (CPI) measures the change in prices paid by consumers for goods and services. *Inflation/deflation* is the change over time of the CPI. See Chapter 8 for more information on the CPI and inflation.

Current *account is all transactions other than those in the financial and capital items. The major* classification are goods and services, income and current transfers. The focus of the Balance of Payment (BOP) is on transactions (between an economy and the rest of the world) in goods, services, and income. Chapter 7 provides much more historical and current data.

Table 13-1 presents the current account balance as a percent of GDP. This measure provides an indication on the level of international competitiveness of a country. Usually, countries recording a strong current account surplus have an economy heavily dependent on exports revenues, with high savings ratings but weak domestic demand. On the other hand, countries recording a current account deficit have strong imports, a low saving rates and high personal consumption rates as a percentage of disposable incomes. See Chapter 7 for International Trade information, Chapter 1 for GDP and its components and Chapter 4 for savings data and personal consumption expenditures. (PCE)

References and notes on the data

The International Monetary Fund (IMF) publishes the World Economic Outlook (WEO) on mostly annual basis with updates if there are major changes in the world economy. Tables appear in the first chapter's Annex.

Table 13-2

Foreign Exchange Rates

SOURCE: BOARD OF GOVERNORS OF THE FEDERAL RESERVE SYSTEM

Definitions and notes on the data

The price of a nation's currency in terms of another currency. An *exchange rate* thus has two components, the domestic currency and a foreign currency, and can be quoted either directly or indirectly. In a direct quotation, the price of a unit of foreign currency is expressed in terms of the domestic currency. In an indirect quotation, the price of a unit of domestic currency is expressed in terms of the foreign currency.

This table measures the U.S. dollar relative to the currencies of some important individual countries and relative to average values for major groups of countries. In *Business Statistics,* all these measures are defined as the foreign currency price of the U.S. dollar. When the measure is relatively high, the dollar is relatively strong—but less competitive (in the sense of price competition)—and the other currency or group of currencies named in the measure is relatively weak and more competitive.

For consistency, this definition is used in Business Statistics even in the case of currencies that are commonly quoted in the financial press and elsewhere as dollars per foreign currency unit instead of foreign currency units per dollar. Notably, this is the case for the euro and for the British pound.

The definition of the dollar's value used in *Business Statistics* is the most useful for economic analysis from the U.S. point of view and for foreign tourists in the United States. For American tourists overseas, it is easier to use the inverse of this measure, the value of the other currency; for example, the traveler in Paris can more easily translate prices into dollars by multiplying by the dollar value of the euro than by dividing by the euro value of the dollar.

The foreign exchange rates shown are averages of the daily noon buying rates for cable transfers in New York City certified for customs purposes by the Federal Reserve Bank of New York.

The introduction of the euro was in January 1999 as the common currency for 11 European countries and marked a major change in the international currency system. Over time, the Eurozone has increased to 19 countries - Austria, Belgium, Cyprus, Estonia, Finland, France, Germany, Greece, Ireland, Italy, Latvia, Lithuania, Luxembourg, Malta, Netherlands, Portugal, Slovakia, Slovenia and Spain. In addition, the euro is also the national currency in Monaco, the Vatican City and San Marino, and is the de facto currency in Andorra, Kosovo, and Montenegro. The values of the currencies of these countries no longer fluctuate relative to each other, but the value of the euro still fluctuates relative to the dollar and to currencies for countries outside the EMU. The currency and coins of the individual countries continued to circulate from 1999 through the end of 2001, but in January 2002, new euro currency and coins were introduced, replacing the currency and coins of the individual countries. Once a country has entered the monetary union, its values relative to the dollar will continue to fluctuate—but only due to fluctuations in the value of the euro relative to the dollar.

There is no fully satisfactory historical equivalent to the euro. For comparisons over time, the Federal Reserve Board uses a "restated German mark," derived simply by dividing each historical value of the mark by the euro conversion factor, 1.95583. The G-10 dollar index described below includes five of the currencies that later merged into the euro, but also includes the currencies of Canada, Japan, the United Kingdom, Switzerland, and Sweden.

Data availability and references

Current press releases, historical data, and information on weights and methods for exchange rates and exchange rate indexes are available on the Federal Reserve Web site at <https://www.federalreserve.gov/>; go to Data, then "Foreign Exchange Rates H10/G5," and select DDP, the new Data Download Program. The dollar value indexes are described in the article "Indexes of the Foreign Exchange Value of the Dollar," *Federal Reserve Bulletin* (Winter 2005), also available on the Federal Reserve Web site.

Additional information on exchange rates can be found on the Federal Reserve Bank of St. Louis Web site at <https://www.stls.frb.org/fred/data/exchange.html>.

PART B: INDUSTRY PROFILES

CHAPTER 14: PRODUCT AND INCOME BY INDUSTRY

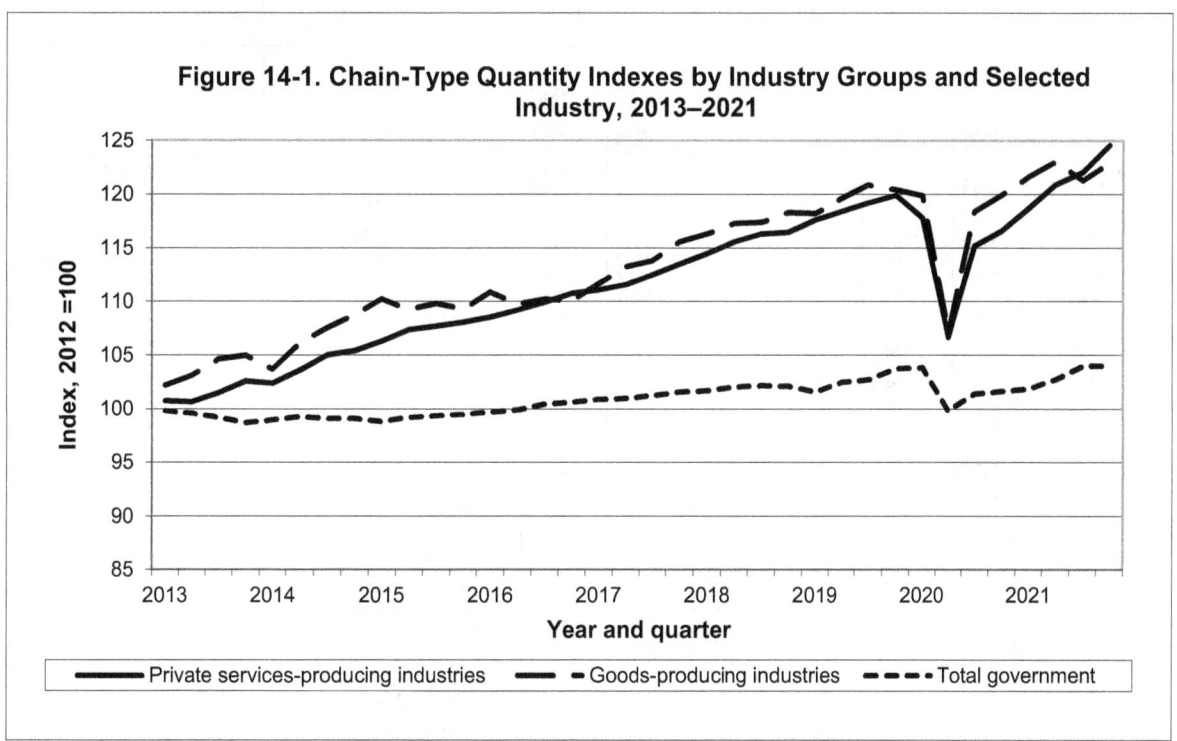

Figure 14-1. Chain-Type Quantity Indexes by Industry Groups and Selected Industry, 2013–2021

- Private services-producing industries, which accounted for 70.3 percent of total GDP in 2021, typically display less cyclical swing and more real growth than the goods sector, which was 17.6 percent of the total. Government production—the other 12.1 percent of total GDP—was comparatively stable, but this is an incomplete measurement of the counter-cyclical impact of government, as it does not include the effects of changes in tax receipts and payments. (Tables 14-1 and 14-2)

- Table 14-3 can be used to assess the share of each industry group in total gross domestic factor income and the shares paid to employees and accruing to land and capital in each industry. For these purposes factor income is a better measure than the BEA definition of value added because value added includes, but factor income excludes, taxes on production and imports.

- In private goods-producing industries in 2020, employee compensation was 52.0 percent of gross factor income, while in the less capital-intensive private services-producing industries (excluding real estate and rental and leasing), compensation was 54.9 percent of total value. (Table 14-3)

- BEA publishes quarterly measures of GDP by industrial origin, in both current-dollar and real (quantity) terms. Industry output, sometimes referred to as "gross product originating in the industry," is here termed "value added".

Table 14-1. Gross Domestic Product (Value Added) by Industry

(Billions of dollars.)

Year	Total gross domestic product	Private industries												
		Total	Agriculture, forestry, fishing, and hunting	Mining	Utilities	Construction	Manufacturing		Wholesale trade	Retail trade	Transportation and warehousing	Information	Finance and insurance	Real estate and rental and leasing
							Durable goods	Nondurable goods						
2000	10 251.0	8 927.9	98.3	110.5	180.1	461.2	924.6	625.2	622.5	685.4	307.8	471.2	744.4	1 230.3
2001	10 581.9	9 189.0	99.8	123.9	181.3	486.4	833.3	640.3	613.7	709.4	308.0	502.3	800.3	1 329.1
2002	10 929.1	9 454.7	95.9	112.4	177.6	493.5	832.8	635.6	613.1	732.6	305.6	550.5	811.1	1 398.9
2003	11 456.5	9 904.1	114.6	138.9	183.9	525.2	863.1	660.9	641.4	769.5	321.4	564.8	846.2	1 448.0
2004	12 217.2	10 585.9	143.8	166.4	199.1	584.6	905.0	702.8	697.1	795.5	352.0	620.3	877.2	1 515.6
2005	13 039.2	11 328.9	129.5	225.4	197.9	651.6	956.3	736.2	754.7	840.6	375.6	642.0	981.5	1 629.9
2006	13 815.6	12 023.6	126.4	273.1	226.7	697.1	1 004.2	789.3	811.4	869.8	410.3	651.9	1 050.3	1 694.9
2007	14 474.2	12 587.2	145.5	314.1	231.9	715.7	1 031.0	814.7	858.2	869.4	414.0	707.5	1 041.6	1 824.0
2008	14 769.9	12 788.3	146.0	392.5	241.7	649.3	1 000.2	801.8	884.8	848.8	427.0	743.8	887.3	1 928.9
2009	14 478.1	12 433.0	129.1	275.4	257.8	565.4	880.4	820.5	833.8	827.3	404.4	721.4	981.0	1 922.2
2010	15 049.0	12 941.0	144.9	306.4	279.1	525.7	965.5	834.3	890.0	852.1	433.5	754.9	1 006.2	1 984.2
2011	15 599.7	13 462.7	179.2	357.8	288.3	525.6	1 017.9	855.7	937.1	873.1	452.5	763.0	1 033.5	2 047.3
2012	16 254.0	14 094.5	178.7	360.5	280.7	554.9	1 065.2	869.5	1 000.3	910.0	473.3	762.7	1 172.4	2 116.8
2013	16 843.2	14 630.7	214.3	387.8	286.9	588.7	1 104.5	892.8	1 042.2	950.6	492.1	831.4	1 156.5	2 205.5
2014	17 550.7	15 279.3	198.9	417.0	298.3	637.7	1 135.6	917.9	1 089.6	975.1	522.5	844.4	1 296.0	2 264.7
2015	18 206.0	15 866.6	180.1	261.7	299.2	695.3	1 184.4	946.6	1 143.6	1 020.3	566.1	907.8	1 384.5	2 329.3
2016	18 695.1	16 310.9	165.8	218.1	302.0	747.7	1 187.8	915.1	1 135.8	1 053.0	582.4	970.3	1 475.0	2 408.3
2017	19 479.6	17 032.6	175.9	276.9	311.6	800.6	1 235.4	963.8	1 165.7	1 081.6	609.4	1 004.7	1 512.1	2 508.2
2018	20 527.2	17 980.9	175.6	320.1	319.0	847.1	1 298.9	1 035.3	1 217.4	1 119.7	648.1	1 064.6	1 626.7	2 631.0
2019	21 372.6	18 750.8	162.6	295.7	333.3	903.6	1 327.9	1 043.0	1 275.0	1 166.7	685.7	1 134.5	1 682.9	2 768.7
2020	20 893.7	18 223.1	174.5	182.1	341.7	895.9	1 268.8	1 003.1	1 243.3	1 202.2	572.0	1 167.9	1 787.7	2 804.4
2021	22 996.1	20 223.5	246.4	283.7	380.6	958.8	1 385.7	1 177.6	1 383.0	1 385.5	642.6	1 300.7	1 949.5	2 935.5
2013														
1st quarter	16 629.1	14 434.6	217.3	371.0	288.3	572.7	1 092.8	891.2	1 030.4	944.4	484.6	814.8	1 119.4	2 173.7
2nd quarter	16 699.6	14 492.1	223.6	384.1	287.2	580.1	1 093.6	876.3	1 028.2	943.9	485.4	823.3	1 137.8	2 181.2
3rd quarter	16 911.1	14 696.0	220.9	402.7	283.8	595.5	1 109.9	885.2	1 047.3	955.0	492.7	832.7	1 156.1	2 225.9
4th quarter	17 133.1	14 900.0	195.4	393.3	288.4	606.4	1 121.7	918.5	1 063.1	959.0	505.8	854.6	1 212.4	2 241.2
2014														
1st quarter	17 144.3	14 896.9	195.3	412.7	301.4	616.4	1 103.1	894.7	1 050.6	952.0	499.2	835.7	1 239.5	2 228.4
2nd quarter	17 462.7	15 202.0	211.0	435.8	295.8	630.7	1 123.0	917.0	1 076.2	969.7	516.4	842.8	1 296.3	2 254.7
3rd quarter	17 743.2	15 464.6	194.6	432.2	298.1	644.8	1 156.3	933.0	1 110.4	983.5	532.5	847.7	1 312.3	2 283.7
4th quarter	17 852.5	15 553.8	194.8	387.4	298.1	658.6	1 160.0	926.9	1 121.4	995.3	541.9	851.4	1 335.7	2 292.1
2015														
1st quarter	17 991.3	15 673.4	179.7	290.4	299.8	673.7	1 177.7	940.9	1 135.1	1 001.5	553.6	878.8	1 372.4	2 304.5
2nd quarter	18 193.7	15 859.3	179.7	279.2	297.1	690.0	1 182.2	952.0	1 151.5	1 012.4	561.7	897.6	1 417.6	2 316.8
3rd quarter	18 307.0	15 958.8	183.3	251.4	303.0	703.4	1 191.6	962.7	1 145.4	1 031.1	573.3	918.2	1 373.4	2 340.4
4th quarter	18 332.1	15 974.8	177.8	225.7	297.0	714.2	1 186.1	930.8	1 142.3	1 036.3	575.8	936.6	1 374.5	2 355.4
2016														
1st quarter	18 425.3	16 060.3	170.4	196.8	295.2	730.9	1 185.4	912.2	1 137.1	1 045.4	575.1	959.9	1 390.4	2 379.2
2nd quarter	18 611.6	16 234.8	170.3	211.9	298.2	739.1	1 183.8	919.9	1 133.2	1 048.5	582.0	964.1	1 454.6	2 404.2
3rd quarter	18 775.5	16 383.7	165.5	222.8	307.4	750.0	1 187.9	915.7	1 135.1	1 055.6	581.0	976.7	1 511.8	2 414.2
4th quarter	18 968.0	16 564.8	157.2	240.9	307.1	770.7	1 194.1	912.5	1 138.0	1 062.6	591.5	980.4	1 543.2	2 435.5
2017														
1st quarter	19 153.9	16 735.3	181.0	262.2	305.5	787.6	1 208.0	936.6	1 145.6	1 070.2	597.9	985.4	1 504.0	2 465.5
2nd quarter	19 322.9	16 889.6	178.9	270.1	314.2	792.1	1 222.9	949.1	1 159.1	1 075.2	607.2	995.9	1 478.8	2 495.7
3rd quarter	19 558.7	17 103.3	170.4	274.3	310.7	804.1	1 242.1	968.1	1 169.4	1 085.4	612.2	1 010.2	1 517.1	2 519.7
4th quarter	19 883.0	17 402.0	173.4	300.9	316.0	818.7	1 268.7	1 001.5	1 188.6	1 095.8	620.2	1 027.3	1 548.4	2 551.8
2018														
1st quarter	20 143.7	17 634.7	178.2	308.0	318.3	832.5	1 280.0	1 013.4	1 194.2	1 107.9	633.3	1 030.2	1 587.9	2 585.1
2nd quarter	20 492.5	17 956.7	182.7	322.6	321.0	843.2	1 295.1	1 035.0	1 213.1	1 121.0	643.0	1 069.0	1 632.8	2 619.7
3rd quarter	20 659.1	18 096.7	170.2	328.8	314.4	850.5	1 304.8	1 036.3	1 220.4	1 124.2	650.0	1 078.3	1 666.2	2 643.5
4th quarter	20 813.3	18 235.5	171.4	321.2	322.5	862.3	1 315.6	1 056.4	1 242.1	1 125.6	666.2	1 080.9	1 620.0	2 675.8
2019														
1st quarter	21 001.6	18 413.4	159.7	302.1	323.9	887.1	1 325.8	1 016.4	1 262.8	1 142.2	676.4	1 098.4	1 644.6	2 711.7
2nd quarter	21 289.3	18 685.0	158.8	305.6	330.1	901.1	1 330.9	1 042.6	1 268.0	1 160.7	684.5	1 133.8	1 676.1	2 755.6
3rd quarter	21 505.0	18 871.3	163.3	288.1	337.7	911.4	1 325.8	1 052.7	1 283.1	1 179.8	692.0	1 146.6	1 680.0	2 794.9
4th quarter	21 694.5	19 033.4	168.4	286.9	341.4	914.8	1 329.1	1 060.5	1 286.1	1 183.9	689.9	1 159.2	1 730.8	2 812.5
2020														
1st quarter	21 481.4	18 784.2	183.8	236.6	328.2	914.3	1 308.0	1 050.8	1 280.9	1 185.6	660.5	1 158.9	1 715.1	2 827.7
2nd quarter	19 477.4	16 846.5	140.2	126.6	337.3	851.6	1 134.5	917.0	1 136.5	1 101.6	499.2	1 120.6	1 751.1	2 740.6
3rd quarter	21 138.6	18 469.7	172.9	170.7	353.4	898.2	1 314.0	1 018.8	1 275.8	1 262.0	555.0	1 186.6	1 802.9	2 824.3
4th quarter	21 477.6	18 792.2	201.2	194.5	348.0	919.3	1 318.9	1 025.9	1 279.9	1 259.6	573.4	1 205.5	1 881.9	2 824.8
2021														
1st quarter	22 038.2	19 332.8	214.4	243.7	374.6	941.2	1 346.9	1 096.7	1 319.4	1 331.5	594.2	1 240.0	1 892.6	2 857.3
2nd quarter	22 741.0	19 998.2	254.7	265.5	366.4	951.0	1 375.2	1 149.5	1 377.3	1 397.5	619.8	1 296.6	1 936.3	2 908.6
3rd quarter	23 202.3	20 396.4	261.7	289.4	379.9	951.1	1 380.7	1 190.2	1 390.6	1 379.1	658.3	1 305.5	1 965.7	2 955.0
4th quarter	24 002.8	21 166.6	255.0	336.1	401.6	991.9	1 440.0	1 274.2	1 444.6	1 434.1	698.0	1 360.6	2 003.6	3 021.1

Table 14-1. Gross Domestic Product (Value Added) by Industry—*Continued*

(Billions of dollars.)

Year	Professional, scientific, and technical services	Management of companies and enterprises	Administrative and waste management services	Educational services	Health care and social assistance	Arts, entertainment, and recreation	Accommodation and food services	Other services except government	Total government	Federal	State and local	Private goods-producing industries	Private services-producing industries	Information-communications-technology-producing industries[1]
2000	651.7	171.1	282.1	95.2	600.1	386.5	287.5	279.7	1 323.0	423.5	899.5	2 219.9	6 708.0	632.8
2001	686.7	173.6	295.0	101.7	648.1	390.7	294.0	265.5	1 392.9	430.4	962.5	2 183.7	7 005.3	610.2
2002	714.7	175.0	300.2	106.5	700.5	413.5	309.7	284.9	1 474.4	462.5	1 011.9	2 170.2	7 284.6	620.9
2003	741.3	185.6	320.5	116.8	746.0	432.1	321.1	283.8	1 552.3	498.9	1 053.5	2 302.8	7 601.3	653.1
2004	792.3	203.1	345.5	129.0	798.2	461.1	343.3	297.2	1 631.3	525.5	1 105.8	2 502.7	8 083.2	706.2
2005	852.1	214.1	379.8	133.2	837.0	481.1	358.9	310.6	1 710.3	551.3	1 159.0	2 698.9	8 630.0	755.4
2006	917.0	230.4	399.1	142.9	892.4	511.4	381.0	325.0	1 792.0	575.5	1 216.4	2 890.1	9 133.5	795.1
2007	985.4	251.1	430.8	151.5	936.5	533.6	396.2	330.5	1 887.1	601.9	1 285.2	3 021.1	9 566.0	853.1
2008	1 082.8	256.4	438.8	167.8	1 017.2	542.9	399.6	330.3	1 981.6	632.2	1 349.4	2 989.8	9 798.4	905.0
2009	1 030.9	245.0	412.3	188.2	1 078.8	533.0	388.5	326.4	2 045.1	663.3	1 381.7	2 670.7	9 762.3	888.3
2010	1 065.1	265.3	438.0	199.0	1 112.3	556.2	403.8	328.2	2 108.0	697.4	1 410.5	2 776.8	10 164.2	939.1
2011	1 127.2	277.9	455.0	206.3	1 149.9	581.9	423.2	333.5	2 137.1	712.3	1 424.8	2 936.1	10 526.5	977.7
2012	1 191.8	302.1	474.9	214.2	1 195.1	622.7	451.0	348.6	2 159.5	713.9	1 445.6	3 028.8	11 065.7	989.3
2013	1 210.7	319.6	489.8	217.6	1 230.8	652.3	474.5	356.7	2 212.5	703.8	1 508.7	3 188.0	11 442.7	1 065.2
2014	1 269.0	332.8	518.4	226.2	1 266.4	691.9	502.6	376.8	2 271.4	715.8	1 555.5	3 307.1	11 972.2	1 097.6
2015	1 349.2	347.9	540.6	233.4	1 337.8	747.0	553.5	391.6	2 339.4	731.3	1 608.2	3 268.2	12 598.4	1 183.6
2016	1 395.5	350.9	559.7	246.2	1 406.4	790.5	583.2	400.5	2 384.2	743.0	1 641.2	3 234.5	13 076.4	1 255.6
2017	1 458.5	372.7	603.0	249.2	1 461.5	828.2	611.3	413.5	2 447.1	761.7	1 685.3	3 452.7	13 579.9	1 318.3
2018	1 559.4	392.4	635.1	261.1	1 523.0	869.6	639.6	436.5	2 546.3	789.4	1 756.9	3 677.0	14 303.9	1 424.8
2019	1 645.0	411.8	674.5	275.0	1 596.4	914.2	673.2	454.4	2 621.8	811.5	1 810.3	3 732.8	15 018.0	1 515.3
2020	1 627.8	410.5	651.6	251.3	1 547.3	672.1	508.7	419.0	2 670.6	848.4	1 822.3	3 524.4	14 698.7	1 574.3
2021	1 779.9	434.2	759.3	257.6	1 675.3	839.6	643.8	447.9	2 772.6	881.5	1 891.1	4 052.2	16 171.3	. . .
2013														
1st quarter	1 204.1	313.9	480.7	215.0	1 223.6	643.1	468.2	353.6	2 194.4	706.5	1 487.9	3 145.0	11 289.6	. . .
2nd quarter ...	1 199.6	319.6	485.4	216.1	1 226.1	646.4	470.9	354.3	2 207.5	704.1	1 503.4	3 157.6	11 334.4	. . .
3rd quarter ...	1 211.0	321.0	493.6	218.0	1 232.8	655.2	477.0	356.8	2 215.1	698.4	1 516.7	3 214.2	11 481.8	. . .
4th quarter ...	1 228.2	324.0	499.4	221.5	1 240.6	664.4	481.9	362.0	2 233.1	706.3	1 526.8	3 235.2	11 664.8	. . .
2014														
1st quarter	1 231.7	333.2	503.5	222.1	1 242.2	669.9	483.8	365.2	2 247.4	710.9	1 536.5	3 222.2	11 674.7	. . .
2nd quarter ...	1 249.0	327.7	515.7	225.5	1 254.7	686.2	497.2	374.0	2 260.7	713.7	1 547.0	3 317.5	11 884.5	. . .
3rd quarter ...	1 291.0	330.9	523.9	228.2	1 277.4	701.6	510.0	382.5	2 278.6	717.5	1 561.1	3 360.9	12 103.7	. . .
4th quarter ...	1 304.5	339.5	530.5	228.9	1 291.4	709.9	519.3	385.5	2 298.7	721.2	1 577.5	3 327.7	12 226.1	. . .
2015														
1st quarter	1 325.5	346.7	533.8	230.3	1 312.1	728.4	537.6	388.3	2 318.0	726.7	1 591.3	3 262.5	12 410.9	. . .
2nd quarter ...	1 342.6	348.2	537.0	231.5	1 328.6	741.6	549.2	392.0	2 334.4	729.4	1 605.0	3 283.2	12 576.1	. . .
3rd quarter ...	1 361.1	347.7	543.7	233.9	1 349.2	753.7	559.6	392.3	2 348.2	733.2	1 614.9	3 292.4	12 666.4	. . .
4th quarter ...	1 367.8	348.9	547.8	238.2	1 361.3	764.3	567.4	394.0	2 357.2	735.8	1 621.4	3 234.6	12 740.3	. . .
2016														
1st quarter	1 384.8	347.8	550.8	242.7	1 383.0	775.8	574.3	397.5	2 365.0	737.4	1 627.6	3 195.7	12 864.6	. . .
2nd quarter ...	1 390.6	349.4	554.5	246.1	1 401.7	783.7	579.3	399.2	2 376.8	740.4	1 636.4	3 225.0	13 009.8	. . .
3rd quarter ...	1 394.3	351.3	560.1	246.5	1 409.4	797.2	586.7	401.7	2 391.8	745.0	1 646.8	3 241.8	13 141.9	. . .
4th quarter ...	1 412.3	355.3	573.5	249.6	1 431.7	805.3	592.6	403.4	2 403.2	749.2	1 654.0	3 275.4	13 289.4	. . .
2017														
1st quarter	1 426.1	361.6	586.7	248.6	1 443.5	813.3	601.7	406.1	2 418.6	754.0	1 664.6	3 375.4	13 359.9	. . .
2nd quarter ...	1 447.3	367.5	598.6	247.8	1 455.6	823.7	609.6	409.8	2 433.4	757.9	1 675.4	3 413.2	13 476.4	. . .
3rd quarter ...	1 468.4	374.0	608.8	249.3	1 466.5	836.1	614.6	416.4	2 455.4	763.8	1 691.5	3 459.1	13 644.3	. . .
4th quarter ...	1 492.3	387.7	617.9	251.1	1 480.4	839.6	619.5	421.7	2 481.0	771.1	1 709.8	3 563.2	13 838.8	. . .
2018														
1st quarter	1 524.3	385.9	621.3	255.4	1 501.4	849.6	627.8	427.9	2 509.0	779.1	1 729.9	3 612.1	14 022.6	. . .
2nd quarter ...	1 560.1	387.2	630.4	259.1	1 517.0	869.1	636.5	435.5	2 535.8	786.8	1 749.0	3 678.6	14 278.1	. . .
3rd quarter ...	1 571.3	398.0	637.6	262.4	1 526.6	874.4	641.6	439.0	2 562.4	793.5	1 768.9	3 690.5	14 406.2	. . .
4th quarter ...	1 581.9	398.6	651.2	267.7	1 547.1	885.1	652.4	443.7	2 577.9	798.3	1 779.6	3 727.0	14 508.5	. . .
2019														
1st quarter	1 614.4	409.7	660.7	271.6	1 568.7	891.7	658.8	445.5	2 588.2	803.4	1 784.7	3 691.2	14 722.2	. . .
2nd quarter ...	1 633.6	412.9	670.7	275.7	1 587.8	906.1	669.6	450.1	2 604.2	807.0	1 797.2	3 739.1	14 946.0	. . .
3rd quarter ...	1 659.4	411.2	680.5	277.1	1 605.8	924.8	681.4	457.1	2 633.7	814.3	1 819.4	3 741.4	15 130.0	. . .
4th quarter ...	1 672.6	413.5	685.9	275.8	1 623.2	934.2	683.1	464.9	2 661.1	821.0	1 840.0	3 759.6	15 273.8	. . .
2020														
1st quarter	1 669.3	412.0	676.7	271.9	1 598.9	849.2	620.3	455.5	2 697.2	831.1	1 866.1	3 693.6	15 090.6	. . .
2nd quarter ...	1 548.3	399.1	588.9	240.1	1 371.6	473.7	365.9	368.1	2 630.9	843.1	1 787.8	3 169.9	13 676.6	. . .
3rd quarter ...	1 632.1	403.7	656.2	250.7	1 591.9	677.3	526.5	423.3	2 668.9	858.5	1 810.4	3 574.5	14 895.2	. . .
4th quarter ...	1 661.3	427.0	684.5	242.5	1 626.8	688.1	522.2	429.0	2 685.4	860.7	1 824.7	3 659.8	15 132.4	. . .
2021														
1st quarter	1 702.9	431.1	720.3	247.7	1 636.5	716.1	543.2	425.8	2 705.4	866.5	1 838.9	3 842.8	15 490.0	. . .
2nd quarter ...	1 754.4	431.7	739.0	254.3	1 656.7	820.5	635.1	443.2	2 742.7	875.1	1 867.6	3 995.9	16 002.4	. . .
3rd quarter ...	1 798.7	438.3	768.1	261.4	1 680.7	887.1	683.0	454.9	2 806.0	886.4	1 919.5	4 073.1	16 323.3	. . .
4th quarter ...	1 863.4	435.7	810.0	266.8	1 727.4	934.7	713.9	467.9	2 836.2	897.8	1 938.4	4 297.1	16 869.5	. . .

[1]Consists of computer and electronic products manufacturing; publishing, including software; information and data processing services; and computer systems design and related services.
. . . = Not available.

Table 14-2. Chain-Type Quantity Indexes for Value Added by Industry

(New Series, 2012 = 100.)

Year	Total gross domestic product	Private industries					Manufacturing							
		Total	Agriculture, forestry, fishing, and hunting	Mining	Utilities	Construction	Durable goods	Nondurable goods	Wholesale trade	Retail trade	Transportation and warehousing	Information	Finance and insurance	Real estate and rental and leasing
2000	80.8	80.7	89.7	65.1	91.9	140.8	70.5	110.9	80.3	90.1	89.5	55.3	78.1	72.6
2001	81.6	81.3	86.6	75.5	76.5	138.2	66.1	109.9	81.7	93.5	83.7	58.7	82.0	76.3
2002	83.0	82.7	89.8	77.6	79.2	133.7	67.5	109.2	82.7	97.6	80.7	64.3	81.5	77.3
2003	85.3	85.0	97.1	68.8	77.8	136.1	72.6	112.6	87.1	102.7	83.6	66.4	80.3	78.8
2004	88.6	88.6	105.0	69.2	82.5	140.9	77.8	120.4	91.1	104.4	90.5	74.0	81.0	80.7
2005	91.7	91.9	109.8	70.3	78.3	141.5	83.1	118.3	95.3	107.8	94.9	79.0	88.2	85.1
2006	94.2	94.9	111.6	81.2	83.4	138.7	89.6	122.1	98.1	108.7	100.5	81.8	91.3	86.3
2007	96.1	96.6	99.3	87.6	85.2	134.5	93.8	124.2	101.4	105.2	99.8	89.9	88.0	91.1
2008	96.2	96.3	99.4	84.8	89.5	121.3	94.3	117.7	101.7	101.3	98.9	95.7	76.8	94.5
2009	93.7	93.3	110.5	97.0	84.4	104.0	80.6	114.1	89.2	96.8	92.7	93.0	94.8	92.1
2010	96.3	95.9	107.2	86.0	94.9	98.8	91.0	112.1	94.5	99.0	97.4	98.6	91.3	96.1
2011	97.8	97.5	103.1	89.4	98.7	97.3	97.2	104.8	96.6	99.3	99.3	100.2	91.7	98.3
2012	100.0	100.0	100.0	100.0	100.0	100.0	100.0	100.0	100.0	100.0	100.0	100.0	100.0	100.0
2013	101.8	101.9	116.1	103.7	98.8	102.4	102.4	103.7	102.1	103.0	101.4	108.9	94.5	102.3
2014	104.2	104.6	116.7	115.0	94.9	104.3	103.9	105.5	106.0	105.0	104.4	111.6	99.4	102.9
2015	107.0	107.8	124.2	125.2	94.9	109.0	105.5	106.1	110.6	108.9	107.1	123.1	102.8	102.6
2016	108.8	109.7	131.3	118.5	100.0	113.2	105.7	105.1	109.2	112.9	108.7	134.0	104.4	103.3
2017	111.2	112.5	129.3	120.9	101.2	117.2	110.1	107.5	109.7	116.7	113.5	142.5	102.7	105.2
2018	114.5	116.1	133.1	121.1	100.9	120.0	115.4	111.0	111.0	120.4	117.5	153.6	102.6	108.1
2019	117.1	119.0	125.0	135.4	102.1	121.6	116.3	114.3	110.4	123.4	119.6	164.3	104.3	110.5
2020	113.1	114.5	142.5	121.6	106.4	117.2	110.6	113.9	108.4	119.8	103.6	170.0	107.4	109.0
2021	119.5	121.7	135.8	114.7	100.4	120.9	120.7	120.2	111.4	122.3	106.4	192.4	117.5	112.1
2013														
1st quarter	101.2	101.1	109.1	101.2	101.6	101.9	102.1	101.6	101.4	103.5	101.1	106.6	93.4	101.4
2nd quarter ..	101.3	101.2	117.7	102.3	99.2	101.8	101.6	103.0	100.9	102.7	100.3	107.4	94.0	101.6
3rd quarter ...	102.1	102.2	120.3	103.8	98.3	103.3	102.6	105.0	102.4	102.7	101.1	109.2	93.9	103.0
4th quarter ...	102.8	103.1	117.4	107.7	95.9	102.6	103.0	105.1	103.6	103.3	103.1	112.3	96.6	103.2
2014														
1st quarter	102.5	102.7	116.0	105.0	92.6	102.8	101.5	103.7	102.5	103.7	102.8	109.5	97.0	102.7
2nd quarter ..	103.8	104.1	116.9	110.9	94.2	104.3	103.2	106.3	104.7	105.1	103.4	111.2	99.7	102.7
3rd quarter ...	105.0	105.6	116.8	117.8	96.5	104.3	105.6	105.7	108.2	105.9	105.8	112.2	99.7	103.2
4th quarter ...	105.5	106.1	117.1	126.2	96.2	106.0	105.3	106.2	108.7	105.0	105.7	113.4	101.2	102.9
2015														
1st quarter	106.3	107.1	122.2	132.9	89.9	107.0	105.6	107.5	110.0	106.8	104.6	118.2	103.0	102.8
2nd quarter ..	106.9	107.8	121.9	119.4	95.3	109.1	105.4	106.6	111.1	108.7	106.7	121.1	105.2	102.4
3rd quarter ...	107.3	108.1	125.5	123.6	97.3	109.8	105.8	106.1	111.2	109.8	108.6	124.6	101.4	102.6
4th quarter ...	107.4	108.3	127.1	124.7	97.2	110.4	105.2	104.1	109.9	110.2	108.7	128.6	101.7	102.7
2016														
1st quarter	108.1	109.0	132.7	133.1	98.3	112.7	105.6	104.7	108.2	111.9	106.6	132.1	101.3	103.0
2nd quarter ..	108.4	109.3	130.9	115.9	99.3	112.2	105.0	105.7	108.9	112.1	108.7	133.0	103.6	103.5
3rd quarter ...	109.0	110.0	131.5	112.8	101.5	113.1	106.0	105.8	110.0	113.4	108.7	135.1	105.8	103.4
4th quarter ...	109.6	110.6	129.9	112.2	101.0	114.7	106.2	104.3	109.5	114.3	111.0	135.8	107.0	103.5
2017														
1st quarter	110.1	111.2	133.0	114.1	99.6	116.8	107.5	105.6	109.5	114.7	112.2	138.6	104.5	104.3
2nd quarter ..	110.7	111.9	130.5	120.9	101.6	116.4	108.9	108.5	109.4	115.9	113.5	140.8	101.2	105.1
3rd quarter ...	111.5	112.8	126.5	125.0	100.7	116.7	110.7	107.4	109.7	117.9	113.6	143.9	102.5	105.3
4th quarter ...	112.6	113.9	127.1	123.7	103.0	119.0	113.3	108.6	110.3	118.2	114.6	146.9	102.6	105.9
2018														
1st quarter	113.4	114.9	131.2	118.9	100.5	120.3	114.7	109.3	111.2	120.2	117.3	148.6	102.3	107.2
2nd quarter ..	114.4	115.9	135.5	121.9	103.7	119.7	115.2	110.8	110.5	119.7	117.1	153.8	103.1	108.1
3rd quarter ...	114.9	116.6	133.2	120.3	99.4	120.0	115.4	111.4	111.3	121.5	117.5	155.3	104.3	108.2
4th quarter ...	115.2	116.9	132.6	123.5	99.8	119.9	116.5	112.4	110.8	120.1	118.3	156.7	100.8	109.1
2019														
1st quarter	115.9	117.7	123.5	131.9	98.2	121.6	116.3	109.9	111.4	122.1	118.4	159.2	103.6	109.6
2nd quarter ..	116.8	118.7	124.1	134.9	103.7	121.8	116.4	113.6	109.4	122.7	119.4	163.7	104.1	110.3
3rd quarter ...	117.6	119.6	124.6	138.7	100.5	121.9	116.2	117.3	110.3	124.1	120.7	166.0	103.5	110.9
4th quarter ...	118.1	120.0	127.8	136.2	106.0	121.1	116.4	116.5	110.7	124.6	119.9	168.1	106.1	111.0
2020														
1st quarter	116.6	118.2	145.2	137.4	106.1	119.8	114.3	116.0	111.6	122.4	117.0	167.4	102.6	110.8
2nd quarter ..	106.2	106.8	132.1	120.1	106.8	110.7	98.4	105.8	101.0	111.3	90.3	164.7	105.3	107.0
3rd quarter ...	114.2	115.8	146.4	114.5	107.9	117.7	114.0	116.7	110.6	122.8	102.9	173.5	108.5	109.2
4th quarter ...	115.5	117.3	146.2	114.5	104.8	120.7	115.8	116.9	110.3	122.9	104.1	174.4	113.3	108.9
2021														
1st quarter	117.2	119.3	140.9	113.5	102.5	122.5	119.4	117.9	111.2	127.8	106.3	180.5	115.3	110.3
2nd quarter ..	119.2	121.4	136.0	115.5	103.4	124.5	120.7	119.9	112.2	122.8	103.7	190.9	116.3	111.7
3rd quarter ...	119.8	121.9	132.8	113.2	99.0	119.9	119.9	119.8	109.9	118.3	106.7	194.6	118.5	112.3
4th quarter ...	121.9	124.3	133.6	116.4	96.8	117.0	122.7	123.3	112.3	120.4	109.0	203.7	119.7	114.2

Table 14-2. Chain-Type Quantity Indexes for Value Added by Industry—*Continued*

(New Series, 2012 = 100.)

Year	Private industries—*Continued*								Government			Private goods-producing industries	Private services-producing industries	Information-communi-cations-technology-producing industries[1]
	Profes-sional, scientific, and technical services	Manage-ment of companies and enterprises	Adminis-trative and waste manage-ment services	Educational services	Health care and social assistance	Arts, entertain-ment, and recreation	Accom-modation and food services	Other services except govern-ment	Total govern-ment	Federal	State and local			
2000	70.8	91.9	71.1	71.2	69.9	90.3	94.2	123.7	91.6	87.4	93.7	93.4	77.2	38.7
2001	73.2	95.7	72.2	73.1	71.6	87.2	91.7	111.6	92.5	86.3	95.7	91.0	78.6	40.3
2002	74.9	94.8	71.9	73.5	74.9	89.6	93.7	114.7	94.2	88.0	97.3	91.2	80.4	42.7
2003	76.0	98.0	77.1	77.1	77.8	91.9	95.8	111.5	95.3	89.7	98.2	94.6	82.4	47.5
2004	78.6	92.4	81.1	81.7	81.3	96.0	100.5	112.9	96.2	91.3	98.7	100.2	85.4	54.4
2005	81.6	92.4	88.1	80.3	83.3	96.3	100.9	113.7	97.1	91.9	99.7	102.6	89.1	61.4
2006	84.8	92.0	90.2	82.3	86.9	98.9	103.6	114.3	97.6	92.3	100.3	107.2	91.6	68.0
2007	88.1	89.8	95.3	83.6	87.5	98.4	102.4	111.7	98.6	93.1	101.4	108.8	93.3	76.3
2008	94.9	90.3	95.3	89.0	93.0	96.2	98.9	107.6	100.5	95.5	103.0	104.6	94.1	84.6
2009	89.5	83.3	87.6	96.1	95.4	90.6	91.5	101.1	100.6	98.1	101.8	97.4	92.2	84.6
2010	91.8	89.3	93.7	99.0	96.2	94.2	94.7	99.3	101.1	100.4	101.4	98.5	95.2	92.5
2011	95.8	92.9	96.9	99.8	98.1	97.6	98.4	98.5	100.8	100.5	100.9	98.7	97.2	97.6
2012	100.0	100.0	100.0	100.0	100.0	100.0	100.0	100.0	100.0	100.0	100.0	100.0	100.0	100.0
2013	100.2	104.9	101.4	98.4	101.7	102.1	102.1	99.2	99.3	97.7	100.1	103.7	101.4	108.2
2014	104.5	112.0	105.3	99.4	103.7	105.7	105.5	102.0	99.1	97.1	100.0	106.5	104.1	113.1
2015	109.1	114.9	106.8	100.2	108.2	109.0	110.7	102.6	99.2	97.2	100.2	109.6	107.3	125.4
2016	112.3	116.4	107.1	103.0	111.2	110.9	112.0	101.8	100.2	98.1	101.2	110.2	109.6	136.6
2017	116.1	124.9	113.9	101.5	113.8	113.6	114.4	102.4	101.2	98.7	102.3	113.6	112.2	147.3
2018	123.1	133.9	118.6	104.0	117.1	115.7	115.6	105.8	102.0	99.3	103.3	117.3	115.7	. . .
2019	128.4	143.5	122.8	106.8	120.4	118.0	117.7	105.8	102.6	100.0	103.9	119.8	118.8	173.5
2020	126.0	145.6	115.8	94.8	113.7	82.9	85.1	92.7	101.7	102.9	101.2	116.3	114.0	181.7
2021	137.7	158.5	133.3	95.3	120.3	99.4	102.0	95.3	103.2	103.2	103.2	122.2	121.6	. . .
2013														
1st quarter	99.9	101.2	100.1	97.9	101.4	101.0	102.4	99.3	99.8	99.0	100.2	102.2	100.7	. . .
2nd quarter ..	99.2	103.6	100.9	97.9	101.5	101.2	101.6	98.7	99.6	98.3	100.2	103.1	100.7	. . .
3rd quarter ...	100.2	106.5	102.0	98.2	101.8	101.2	101.8	98.9	99.2	97.3	100.1	104.6	101.5	. . .
4th quarter ...	101.4	108.4	102.8	99.4	102.2	103.9	102.7	99.7	98.7	96.1	99.9	105.0	102.6	. . .
2014														
1st quarter	101.7	112.5	103.5	98.4	102.3	105.3	103.4	99.8	98.9	97.5	99.7	103.7	102.4	. . .
2nd quarter ..	103.2	110.7	105.2	99.2	102.9	106.3	104.8	101.7	99.2	97.2	100.2	106.1	103.6	. . .
3rd quarter ...	106.3	112.0	106.0	100.1	104.3	107.2	106.6	103.3	99.1	96.9	100.1	107.6	105.0	. . .
4th quarter ...	106.8	112.8	106.6	99.9	105.3	106.7	107.2	103.4	99.1	96.7	100.2	108.7	105.4	. . .
2015														
1st quarter	107.7	114.6	106.9	100.0	107.0	104.6	109.4	103.2	98.8	97.1	99.6	110.2	106.3	. . .
2nd quarter ..	108.5	114.7	106.6	99.6	107.7	103.8	110.5	103.1	99.2	97.2	100.2	109.2	107.3	. . .
3rd quarter ...	109.7	115.1	107.1	99.9	108.7	104.3	111.4	102.2	99.3	97.2	100.4	109.8	107.7	. . .
4th quarter ...	110.3	115.4	106.8	101.4	109.2	105.1	111.5	102.0	99.5	97.3	100.5	109.3	108.0	. . .
2016														
1st quarter	111.9	115.1	106.3	102.7	110.5	106.2	111.5	102.1	99.7	97.6	100.7	110.8	108.5	. . .
2nd quarter ..	112.0	115.5	106.1	103.4	111.2	106.8	111.2	101.7	99.9	98.0	100.9	109.8	109.2	. . .
3rd quarter ...	112.0	116.5	107.0	102.7	111.1	108.2	112.1	101.9	100.5	98.3	101.5	110.2	109.9	. . .
4th quarter ...	113.2	118.5	109.0	103.1	112.2	111.1	113.1	101.6	100.6	98.4	101.7	110.1	110.7	. . .
2017														
1st quarter	113.7	120.3	111.4	101.9	112.9	108.7	114.3	101.4	100.9	98.6	102.0	111.6	111.1	. . .
2nd quarter ..	115.4	122.7	113.2	101.2	113.7	110.5	114.5	101.7	101.0	98.5	102.2	113.3	111.6	. . .
3rd quarter ...	116.8	125.2	114.6	101.4	114.0	114.0	114.3	102.8	101.2	98.8	102.4	113.8	112.5	. . .
4th quarter ...	118.6	131.6	116.2	101.4	114.7	113.5	114.4	103.7	101.6	99.0	102.8	115.6	113.5	. . .
2018														
1st quarter	120.8	130.2	116.6	102.7	116.3	113.2	113.8	104.8	101.7	99.1	102.9	116.3	114.5	. . .
2nd quarter ..	122.9	131.5	117.4	103.3	116.6	117.5	115.4	105.9	102.1	99.4	103.3	117.3	115.6	. . .
3rd quarter ...	123.8	136.1	119.0	104.2	117.3	116.9	115.6	106.0	102.2	99.6	103.4	117.4	116.3	. . .
4th quarter ...	124.7	137.8	121.3	105.6	118.1	116.8	117.5	106.5	102.1	99.2	103.5	118.3	116.4	. . .
2019														
1st quarter	126.3	142.1	121.6	106.6	119.4	116.6	116.9	105.7	101.6	98.3	103.2	118.2	117.6	. . .
2nd quarter ..	127.5	143.3	122.4	107.7	120.1	117.1	117.5	105.3	102.5	100.1	103.6	119.6	118.4	. . .
3rd quarter ...	129.6	143.7	123.4	107.3	120.8	120.4	119.2	106.1	102.7	100.6	103.7	120.9	119.2	. . .
4th quarter ...	130.3	144.9	123.6	105.9	121.2	121.5	117.4	106.0	103.7	101.1	105.0	120.4	119.9	. . .
2020														
1st quarter	129.6	144.5	121.8	103.6	118.7	108.9	105.0	102.1	103.8	101.7	104.9	119.9	117.8	. . .
2nd quarter ..	119.9	141.1	104.3	90.7	101.0	50.1	61.1	81.8	99.8	102.6	98.6	107.2	106.6	. . .
3rd quarter ...	126.4	143.5	115.7	94.1	116.4	70.5	88.4	93.1	101.4	103.8	100.3	118.4	115.2	. . .
4th quarter ...	128.0	153.3	121.2	90.7	118.9	78.0	85.8	93.6	101.6	103.3	100.9	119.9	116.6	. . .
2021														
1st quarter	131.1	156.2	127.2	92.5	118.1	84.3	88.2	91.5	101.9	103.2	101.3	121.6	118.7	. . .
2nd quarter ..	135.9	157.1	130.2	94.6	119.8	87.5	103.4	95.2	102.7	103.3	102.5	123.0	120.9	. . .
3rd quarter ...	139.9	160.1	135.1	96.5	120.6	95.7	107.8	96.7	104.0	103.4	104.4	121.3	122.1	. . .
4th quarter ...	144.0	160.4	141.0	97.5	122.8	101.0	108.6	97.7	104.0	103.1	104.5	122.9	124.6	. . .

[1]Consists of computer and electronic products manufacturing; publishing, including software; information and data processing services; and computer systems design and related services.
. . . = Not available.

Table 14-3. Gross Domestic Factor Income by Industry

(Billions of current dollars.)

NAICS industry	2008	2009	2010	2011	2012	2013	2014	2015	2016	2017	2018	2019	2020
Gross domestic factor income, total	13 772.7	13 509.6	14 041.7	14 556.0	15 175.9	15 714.2	16 368.0	16 988.0	17 445.2	18 173.1	19 128.7	19 913.1	20 120.5
Compensation of employees	8 068.7	7 767.2	7 933.0	8 234.0	8 575.4	8 843.6	9 259.7	9 709.5	9 977.1	10 436.7	10 969.8	11 459.4	11 580.1
Gross operating surplus	5 704.0	5 742.4	6 108.7	6 322.0	6 600.5	6 870.6	7 108.3	7 278.5	7 468.1	7 736.4	8 158.9	8 453.7	8 540.4
Private industries	11 770.7	11 442.0	11 913.0	12 396.2	12 993.9	13 477.2	14 071.4	14 624.1	15 035.1	15 700.8	16 555.6	17 263.7	17 405.0
Compensation of employees	6 475.5	6 126.3	6 241.3	6 532.0	6 871.6	7 095.3	7 468.7	7 863.2	8 089.7	8 499.8	8 953.5	9 383.6	9 453.5
Gross operating surplus	5 295.2	5 315.7	5 671.7	5 864.2	6 122.3	6 381.9	6 602.7	6 760.9	6 945.4	7 201.0	7 602.1	7 880.1	7 951.5
Agriculture, forestry, fishing, and hunting	147.5	130.9	146.5	178.5	177.7	213.0	194.8	177.8	166.4	174.4	176.1	171.3	209.5
Compensation of employees	42.1	42.3	41.4	41.2	48.1	48.9	51.0	50.6	53.7	56.2	55.1	56.2	59.4
Gross operating surplus	105.4	88.6	105.1	137.3	129.6	164.1	143.8	127.2	112.7	118.2	121.0	115.1	150.1
Mining	350.3	245.9	273.4	320.2	320.5	346.1	370.9	222.0	180.7	237.9	275.9	251.2	144.0
Compensation of employees	72.8	64.7	69.2	80.3	90.5	93.5	101.1	91.9	74.5	76.9	84.8	86.2	70.9
Gross operating surplus	277.5	181.2	204.2	239.9	230.0	252.6	269.8	130.1	106.2	161.0	191.1	165.0	73.1
Utilities	188.5	202.9	222.6	230.6	222.1	228.0	239.4	240.5	242.0	249.8	254.9	266.8	276.1
Compensation of employees	66.3	66.8	67.7	71.2	69.8	72.8	75.2	77.6	81.4	81.6	84.5	87.9	93.8
Gross operating surplus	122.2	136.1	154.9	159.4	152.3	155.2	164.2	162.9	160.6	168.2	170.4	178.9	182.3
Construction	641.4	558.2	518.6	518.4	547.5	580.8	629.3	686.4	738.2	790.5	836.3	891.9	956.0
Compensation of employees	433.9	368.4	343.8	347.3	365.9	388.0	422.4	458.5	485.9	520.4	558.2	597.3	595.8
Gross operating surplus	207.5	189.8	174.8	171.1	181.6	192.8	206.9	227.9	252.3	270.1	278.1	294.6	360.2
Durable goods manufacturing	974.7	854.6	940.5	992.9	1 040.1	1 076.0	1 106.5	1 154.4	1 158.9	1 205.3	1 267.5	1 294.3	1 279.3
Compensation of employees	615.5	539.2	546.2	578.7	604.4	612.0	638.6	662.7	666.0	694.8	732.3	747.5	735.8
Gross operating surplus	359.2	315.4	394.3	414.2	435.7	464.0	467.9	491.7	492.9	510.5	535.2	546.8	543.5
Nondurable goods manufacturing	762.4	771.5	783.6	802.5	816.0	837.5	863.3	891.5	859.5	905.6	976.7	984.1	967.6
Compensation of employees	316.4	296.0	301.0	303.7	312.6	319.8	334.5	343.7	347.2	358.5	368.9	381.0	388.3
Gross operating surplus	446.0	475.5	482.6	498.8	503.4	517.7	528.8	547.8	512.3	547.1	607.8	603.1	579.3
Wholesale trade	713.1	675.8	719.8	752.2	807.9	840.0	881.9	933.3	922.9	942.0	969.3	996.3	1 014.2
Compensation of employees	435.7	405.1	412.3	436.2	457.7	467.6	489.9	509.8	511.0	532.9	545.5	558.6	563.1
Gross operating surplus	277.4	270.7	307.5	316.0	350.2	372.4	392.0	423.5	411.9	409.1	423.8	437.7	451.1
Retail trade	670.4	661.5	673.8	686.1	715.5	745.5	761.3	803.6	830.4	848.9	877.0	916.0	1 005.3
Compensation of employees	500.9	474.3	478.9	495.7	510.1	526.7	545.5	573.6	587.7	606.8	628.1	652.0	671.3
Gross operating surplus	169.5	187.2	194.9	190.4	205.4	218.8	215.8	230.0	242.7	242.1	248.9	264.0	334.0
Transportation and warehousing	401.0	378.0	408.2	425.2	445.1	460.8	489.4	531.2	545.9	570.1	606.2	641.4	581.9
Compensation of employees	255.6	241.1	245.5	259.9	274.8	283.4	296.8	320.0	332.5	352.5	379.8	409.4	411.4
Gross operating surplus	145.4	136.9	162.7	165.3	170.3	177.4	192.6	211.2	213.4	217.6	226.4	232.0	170.5
Information	699.2	677.5	710.6	717.9	717.5	784.6	795.5	852.7	914.1	945.5	1 001.1	1 070.6	1 117.9
Compensation of employees	257.8	251.5	248.6	260.1	271.6	286.5	304.4	318.7	329.0	348.8	376.8	400.2	426.7
Gross operating surplus	441.4	426.0	462.0	457.8	445.9	498.1	491.1	534.0	585.1	596.7	624.3	670.4	691.2
Finance and insurance	843.7	937.4	962.3	988.5	1 127.3	1 108.5	1 238.4	1 321.1	1 408.6	1 454.2	1 552.1	1 618.9	1 723.6
Compensation of employees	612.1	548.0	573.3	606.5	630.1	641.3	681.1	715.7	734.1	787.6	819.1	852.0	913.8
Gross operating surplus	231.6	389.4	389.0	382.0	497.2	467.2	557.3	605.4	674.5	666.6	733.0	766.9	809.8
Real estate and rental and leasing	1 712.7	1 695.8	1 757.2	1 817.5	1 884.3	1 966.3	2 014.3	2 070.8	2 138.8	2 224.7	2 334.5	2 449.8	2 496.6
Compensation of employees	110.3	103.7	103.8	106.4	114.3	118.9	126.4	136.7	140.7	148.7	159.1	169.5	169.8
Gross operating surplus	1 602.4	1 592.1	1 653.4	1 711.1	1 770.0	1 847.4	1 887.9	1 934.1	1 998.1	2 076.0	2 175.4	2 280.3	2 326.8
Professional, scientific, and technical services	1 052.7	1 008.3	1 041.5	1 102.1	1 164.6	1 180.0	1 236.1	1 314.2	1 358.6	1 420.2	1 519.0	1 601.7	1 652.1
Compensation of employees	693.5	669.4	682.7	727.1	776.7	801.5	848.9	909.4	939.1	990.5	1 059.7	1 130.0	1 176.9
Gross operating surplus	359.2	338.9	358.8	375.0	387.9	378.5	387.2	404.8	419.5	429.7	459.3	471.7	475.2
Management of companies and enterprises	247.2	236.6	257.1	269.7	293.8	311.2	324.5	339.4	342.2	363.6	383.1	401.8	403.5
Compensation of employees	221.1	207.9	227.2	237.9	259.4	275.0	287.4	302.3	304.6	324.5	342.2	359.0	359.2
Gross operating surplus	26.1	28.7	29.9	31.8	34.4	36.2	37.1	37.1	37.6	39.1	40.9	42.8	44.3
Administrative and waste management services	429.3	403.0	428.1	444.6	464.1	478.4	506.4	528.3	546.9	589.3	620.6	659.1	667.9
Compensation of employees	314.1	289.2	306.5	321.9	341.3	353.7	376.7	398.1	409.9	439.4	464.2	489.0	489.6
Gross operating surplus	115.2	113.8	121.6	122.7	122.8	124.7	129.7	130.2	137.0	149.9	156.4	170.1	178.3
Educational services	160.9	180.6	191.2	198.5	206.3	209.5	218.1	225.1	237.3	240.0	251.5	264.6	245.9
Compensation of employees	129.4	139.9	145.5	152.8	161.4	165.2	174.9	180.4	190.5	192.4	202.2	213.2	214.6
Gross operating surplus	31.5	40.7	45.7	45.7	44.9	44.3	43.2	44.7	46.8	47.6	49.3	51.4	31.3
Health care and social assistance	993.9	1 054.4	1 087.7	1 129.3	1 171.4	1 206.6	1 241.9	1 310.8	1 377.1	1 429.8	1 489.3	1 561.0	1 625.6
Compensation of employees	824.6	862.4	888.5	922.0	963.6	997.3	1 028.3	1 085.1	1 136.5	1 187.0	1 247.2	1 309.2	1 351.2
Gross operating surplus	169.3	192.0	199.2	207.3	207.8	209.3	213.6	225.7	240.6	242.8	242.1	251.8	274.4
Arts, entertainment, and recreation	127.8	129.4	136.9	142.7	154.3	159.8	170.7	174.1	187.0	195.2	206.8	217.1	149.7
Compensation of employees	80.6	78.6	79.4	81.5	86.1	89.7	96.7	100.9	108.1	113.3	120.3	125.5	102.0
Gross operating surplus	47.2	50.8	57.5	61.2	68.2	70.1	74.0	73.2	78.9	81.9	86.5	91.6	47.7
Accommodation and food services	340.9	331.0	342.9	363.8	388.5	407.9	432.5	476.4	501.6	523.9	545.9	577.4	468.7
Compensation of employees	252.5	242.8	248.3	262.4	282.5	295.8	316.2	340.9	362.0	381.1	402.2	423.3	328.1
Gross operating surplus	88.4	88.2	94.6	101.4	106.0	112.1	116.3	135.5	139.6	142.8	143.7	154.1	140.6
Other services, except government	312.8	308.8	310.4	315.2	329.6	336.8	356.3	370.3	378.2	389.8	411.8	428.3	419.7
Compensation of employees	240.1	235.1	231.7	239.3	250.9	257.9	272.8	286.4	295.3	305.7	323.3	336.5	331.9
Gross operating surplus	72.7	73.7	78.7	75.9	78.7	78.9	83.5	83.9	82.9	84.1	88.5	91.8	87.8
Government	2 002.0	2 067.6	2 128.8	2 159.8	2 182.0	2 237.1	2 296.6	2 364.0	2 410.1	2 472.4	2 573.1	2 649.5	2 715.5
Compensation of employees	1 593.2	1 640.9	1 691.7	1 702.0	1 703.8	1 748.4	1 791.0	1 846.3	1 887.4	1 937.0	2 016.3	2 075.8	2 126.6
Gross operating surplus	408.8	426.7	437.1	457.8	478.2	488.7	505.6	517.7	522.7	535.4	556.8	573.7	588.9
Addenda:													
Private goods-producing industries	2 876.5	2 560.9	2 662.6	2 812.3	2 901.6	3 053.4	3 164.7	3 132.1	3 103.5	3 313.6	3 532.6	3 592.8	3 556.3
Compensation of employees	1 480.8	1 310.5	1 301.5	1 351.1	1 421.4	1 462.2	1 547.5	1 607.4	1 627.2	1 706.8	1 799.3	1 868.2	1 850.1
Gross operating surplus	1 395.7	1 250.4	1 361.1	1 461.2	1 480.2	1 591.2	1 617.2	1 524.7	1 476.3	1 606.8	1 733.3	1 724.6	1 706.2
Private services-producing industries	8 894.2	8 881.1	9 250.4	9 584.0	10 092.3	10 423.8	10 906.7	11 491.9	11 931.6	12 387.1	13 023.0	13 670.9	13 848.7
Compensation of employees	4 994.7	4 815.8	4 939.8	5 180.9	5 450.1	5 633.1	5 921.2	6 255.8	6 462.5	6 792.9	7 154.2	7 515.4	7 603.4
Gross operating surplus	3 899.5	4 065.3	4 310.6	4 403.1	4 642.2	4 790.7	4 985.5	5 236.1	5 469.1	5 594.2	5 868.8	6 155.5	6 245.3
Information-communications-technology-producing industries [1]	860.2	844.4	894.6	932.0	943.1	1 017.3	1 047.0	1 126.5	1 197.5	1 257.0	1 358.5	1 448.5	1 532.0
Compensation of employees	422.2	410.6	423.0	453.6	483.8	501.4	536.2	571.7	597.1	641.5	692.6	739.1	797.0
Gross operating surplus	438.0	433.8	471.6	478.4	459.3	515.9	510.8	554.8	600.4	615.5	665.9	709.4	735.0

[1] Consists of computer and electronic products manufacturing; publishing, including software; information and data processing services; and computer systems design and related services.

NOTES AND DEFINITIONS, CHAPTER 14

Tables 14-1 through 14-3

Gross Domestic Product (VALUE ADDED) and Gross Factor Income by Industry

SOURCE: U.S. DEPARTMENT OF COMMERCE, BUREAU OF ECONOMIC ANALYSIS (BEA)

In the introduction to the notes and definitions for Chapter 1, it was observed that gross domestic product (GDP), while primarily measured as the sum of final demands for goods and services, is also the sum of the values created by each industry in the economy. In this chapter, selected data are presented from the industry accounts in the national income and product accounts (NIPAs). The industry accounts measure the contribution of each major industry to GDP.

In recent years, estimates of GDP by industry have been prepared using a methodology integrated with annual input-output accounts in order to produce estimates of gross industry output, industry input, and the difference between the two—industry value added—with greater consistency and timeliness than was previously possible. The current integrated industry accounts also include a wealth of related information too extensive for inclusion here, such as quantity and price indexes for gross output and intermediate inputs, cost per unit of real value added allocated to the three components of value added, and components of domestic supply (domestic output, imports, exports, and inventory change).

The most precise estimates of GDP by NAICS industry begin with 1997, but the annual series were extended back to 1947, using approximations of current methods in earlier years when the source data were less comprehensive and were initially compiled on the older SIC classifications. Table 14-1B presents this "old series" current-dollar GDP for NAICS industry groups from 1947 through 2009; Table 14-2B presents "old series" indexes of real value added for each industry group.

The 2019 comprehensive benchmark revision incorporated three major types of revisions: 1) statistical changes to introduce new and improved technologies and newly available source data; 2) changes in definitions to more accurately portray the evolving U.S. economy to more accurately portray the evolving U.S. economy and to provide consistent comparisons with data for other national economies; and 3) changes in presentations to reflect the definitional and statistical changes, where necessary, or to provide additional data or perspective for users. Also output and price measures will be expressed with 2012 equal to 100. The estimates for most tables showing real, or chained-dollar, estimates will begin with 2002.

In Table 14-3, the editor presents a measure derived from the components of current-dollar value added as published by BEA. This measure, "gross domestic factor income," enables users to obtain a clearer picture of the quantitative impact of each industry on the economy's factors of production and of the shares of capital and labor in each industry.

The 2004 revision incorporated a change in terminology. An industry's contribution to total GDP, formerly referred to as "gross product originating" (GPO) or "gross product by industry," is now called "value added." This is consistent with the use of the term "value added" in most economic writing. However, it should not be confused with a concept known as "Census value added," which is used in U.S. censuses and surveys of manufactures. Census value added is calculated at the individual establishment level and, for that reason, does not exclude purchased business services. This means that census value added, while still an important gauge of relative importance, is not a true measure of economic value added.

Definitions and notes on the data

An industry's *gross domestic product (value added)*, formerly *GPO*, is equal to the market value of its gross output (which consists of the value, including taxes, of sales or receipts and other operating income plus the value of inventory change) minus the value of its intermediate inputs (energy, raw materials, semi finished goods, and services that are purchased from domestic industries or from foreign sources).

In concept, this is also equal to the sum of *compensation of employees, taxes on production and imports less subsidies,* and *gross operating surplus.* (See Chapter 1 and its notes and definitions for more information.)

The GDP data from 1997 forward are not comparable with the "old series" data for earlier years presented in Tables 14-1B and 14-2B, the major reason being that they do not reflect the conceptual revisions introduced in the comprehensive 2018 revision of the NIPAs (see the Notes and Definitions to Chapter 1). In particular, the new data include, while the old data exclude, the capitalized values of research and development, intellectual property, and all real estate transfer costs. This does not change labor compensation values--the associated workers were always included; it was just that their costs were taken to be written off in the first year. But it does increase across the board the non-labor share of the total value of output, by the amount of capital consumption and net investment. This is seen in labor compensation shares derived from Table 14-3, compared with those that would have been calculated on the old basis last year.

Compensation of employees consists of wage and salary accruals and supplements to wages and salaries. This approximates the labor share of production, subject to the note below about proprietors' income.

Taxes on production and imports less subsidies. Although this is shown in BEA source data as a single net line item, it represents two separate components.

Taxes on production and imports are included in the market value of the goods and services sold to final consumers and therefore in the consumer valuation of those goods. Since they are not part of the payments to the labor and capital inputs in the producing industries, they must be <u>added</u> to the sum of the returns to those inputs in order to account for the total value to consumers. Taxes that fall into this classification include property taxes, sales and excise taxes, and Customs duties.

BEA allocates these taxes to the industry level at which they are assessed by law. Most sales taxes are considered by BEA to be part of the value added by retail trade. Some sales taxes, most fuel taxes, and all customs duties are allocated by BEA to wholesale trade. Residential real property taxes, including those on owner-occupied dwellings, are allocated by BEA to the real estate industry.

Subsidies to business by government are included in the labor and/or capital payments made by that industry. Since they are payments to the industry in addition to the market values paid by consumers, they are *subtracted* from the values of the labor and capital inputs to make them consistent with the market values as defined in value added. The role of subsidies is obvious in the source data for the agricultural sector, where the net "taxes on production and imports less subsidies" has a negative sign: farm subsidies more than offset this industry's taxes on production and imports, which mainly consist of property taxes, since sales, excise, and import taxes are not levied on farms.

For private sector businesses, *gross operating surplus* consists of business income (corporate profits before tax, proprietors' income, and rental income of persons), net interest and miscellaneous payments, business current transfer payments (net), and capital consumption allowances. For government, households, and institutions, it consists of consumption of fixed capital and (for government) government enterprises' current surplus. This approximates the share of the value of production ascribable to capital and land as measured in the NIPAs accounts; however, as BEA notes, "an unknown portion [of proprietors' income] reflects the labor contribution of proprietors." (*Survey of Current Business*, June 2004, p. 27, footnote 7.) Another aspect to be noted is that gross operating surplus includes the return to owner-occupied housing in the real estate sector. Because there is in the NIPAs no employee compensation attributed to owner-occupied housing, the capital share in that industry as measured by gross operating surplus is very large.

Quantity indexes for value added. Measures of the constant-dollar change in each industry's gross output minus its intermediate input use are calculated by BEA, using a Fisher index-number formula which incorporates weights from two adjacent years. The changes for successive years are chained together in indexes, with the value for the year 2012 set at 100. The indexes are multiplied by 2012 current-dollar value added to provide estimates of value added in "chained 2012 dollars," but because the actual weights used change from year to year, components in chained 2012 dollars typically do not add up to total GDP in 2009 dollars—and do not contain any information not already summarized in the indexes. For that reason, only the indexes are published here.

Gross domestic factor income (not a category published as such in the NIPAs) is calculated by the editor as the sum of "compensation of employees" and "gross operating surplus," which the same as value added minus "taxes on production and imports less subsidies." The effect of this procedure is to take out the specified taxes, and to leave in the subsidies embedded in the employee compensation and gross operating surplus components. The editor believes that this provides a valuable alternative basis for assessing the importance of different industries in the economy, by measuring the value paid for by its labor and capital inputs, and for calculating the shares of labor and capital in each industry's output. The components shown in this table are found on the BEA website in a table entitled "Components of Value Added by Industry."

The editor's reasoning is based on the facts that more than half of these taxes are sales, excise, and import taxes, and the assignment of these taxes to industries is economically arbitrary. BEA assigns them to the industry with the legal liability to pay, not to the entity bearing the major incidence of the tax. Yet economists have demonstrated that most of the burdens of sales and excise taxes and import duties are not borne by the factors in the legally liable industry; instead, they are passed on to consumers. In addition, because the wholesale and retail trade industries are classified as "services-producing," BEA's allocation of those taxes has a very peculiar result: taxes on goods are represented as paid by "service" industries. The process adopted instead by the editor in Table 14-3, which excludes these taxes and focuses on "gross domestic factor income," has the effect (for example) of keeping the wholesale trade industry from appearing to be both larger and more heavily taxed than it really is.

Private goods-producing industries consists of agriculture, forestry, fishing, and hunting; mining; construction; and manufacturing.

Private services-producing industries consists of utilities; wholesale trade; retail trade; transportation and warehousing; information; finance, insurance, real estate, rental, and leasing; professional and business services; educational services, health care, and social assistance; arts, entertainment, recreation, accommodation, and food services; and other services, except government.

Information-communications-technology-producing industries is a category that cuts across the goods and services framework, consisting of computer and electronic products manufacturing; publishing industries (which includes software) from the information sector; information and data processing services; and computer systems design and related services.

Data availability and references

The comprehensive revision of the industry accounts from 1997 forward and the new quarterly statistics are described in "Industry Economic Accounts: Results of the Comprehensive Revision, Revised Statistics for 1997-2012" (*Survey of Current Business*, February 2014); "New Quarterly Statistics Detail Industries' Economic Performance," BEA news release, April 25, 2014; and "Prototype Quarterly Statistics on U.S. GDP by Industry, 2007-2011," June 2012, a "BEA Briefing." All are available on the BEA website, https://www.bea.gov. To access the historical data at <https://www.bea.gov>, click on "Annual Industry Accounts" and click on "Interactive Tables" under "Gross Domestic Product (GDP) by Industry."

"Old basis" annual GDP by industry data shown here were recalculated back to 1947 consistent with the 2009 comprehensive revision of the NIPAs. They were most recently presented and described in "Annual Industry Statistics: Revised Statistics for 2009-2011," *Survey of Current Business*, December 2012.

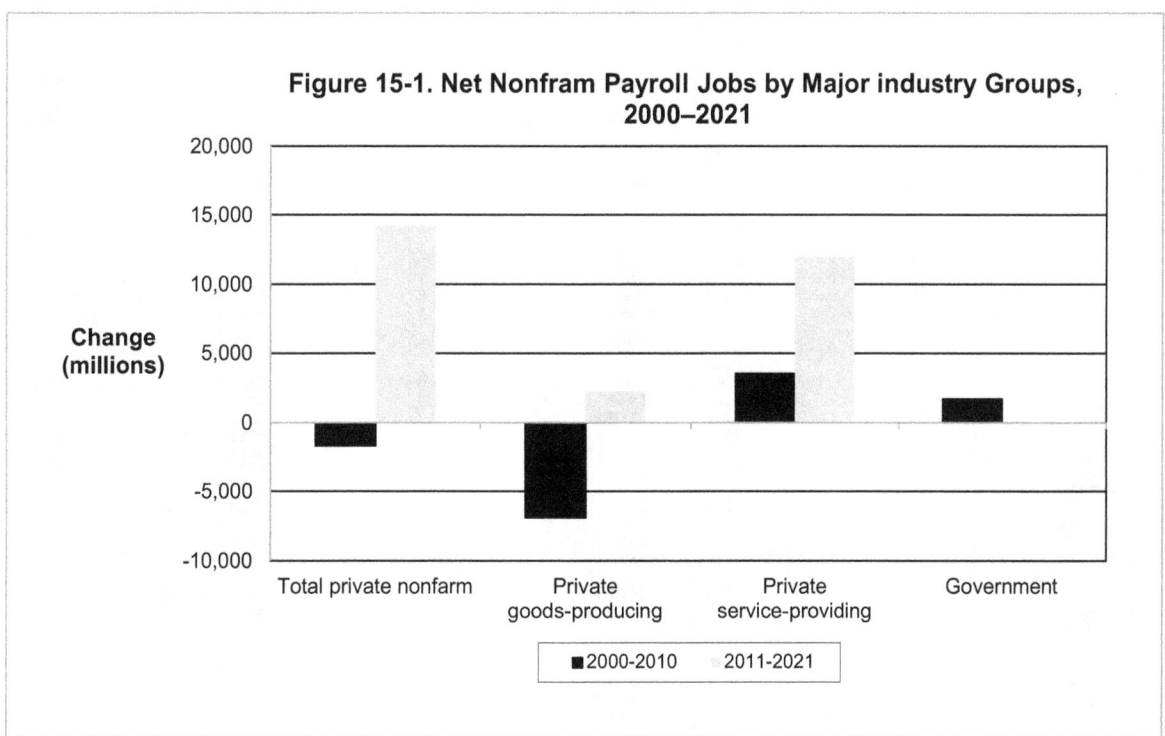

Figure 15-1. Net Nonfram Payroll Jobs by Major industry Groups, 2000–2021

- In 2021, total nonfarm employment increased 2.8 percent after decreasing 5.8 percent in 2020 due to the global pandemic. For nine consecutive years, from 2011 to 2019, employment increased. From 2020 to 2021, it increased 1.5 percent in goods-producing industries, 3.0 percent in service-providing industries, and .09 percent in the government. (Table 15-1)

- The recession that began in 2020 was much shorter than the Great Recession. According to the National Bureau of Economic Research, the most recent recession began in February 2022 and was over two months later in April 2022. In contrast, the Great Recession last 18 months. (Table 15-1)

- From 2000 to 2021, the number of service-providing jobs increased 17 percent while goods-producing employment declined 17.5 percent during the same period. (Table 15-1)

- The average workweek for production and nonsupervisory workers continued to increase in 2021 for the second consecutive year. In 2021, goods-producing workers averaged 40.9 hours per week while those in the private-service providing industry averaged far less at 33.1 hours. (Table 15-3)

- Average hourly earnings for production and nonsupervisory workers in 2021 ranged from a low of $16.17 in the leisure and hospitality sector to $39.97 in utilities. (Table 15-4)

Table 15-1. Nonfarm Employment by Sector and Industry

(Wage and salary workers on nonfarm payrolls, thousands.)

Industry	2000	2001	2002	2003	2004	2005	2006	2007	2008	2009	2010
TOTAL NONFARM	132 011	132 073	130 634	130 331	131 769	134 034	136 435	137 981	137 224	131 296	130 345
Total Private	111 221	110 955	109 121	108 748	110 148	112 230	114 462	115 763	114 714	108 741	107 855
Goods-Producing	24 649	23 873	22 557	21 816	21 882	22 190	22 530	22 233	21 335	18 558	17 751
Mining and logging	599	606	583	572	591	628	684	724	767	694	705
Logging	79.0	73.5	70.4	69.4	67.6	65.2	64.4	60.1	56.6	50.4	49.7
Mining	520.2	532.5	512.2	502.7	523.0	562.2	619.7	663.8	709.8	643.3	654.8
Oil and gas extraction	124.9	123.7	121.9	120.2	123.4	125.7	134.5	146.2	160.5	159.8	158.7
Mining, except oil and gas [1]	224.8	218.7	210.6	202.7	205.1	212.8	220.3	223.4	226.0	208.3	204.5
Coal mining	72.2	74.3	74.4	70.0	70.6	73.9	78.0	77.2	81.2	81.5	80.8
Support activities for mining	170.6	190.1	179.8	179.8	194.6	223.7	264.9	294.3	323.4	275.2	291.6
Construction	6 787	6 826	6 716	6 735	6 976	7 336	7 691	7 630	7 162	6 016	5 518
Construction of buildings	1 632.5	1 588.9	1 574.8	1 575.8	1 630.0	1 711.9	1 804.9	1 774.2	1 641.7	1 357.2	1 229.7
Heavy and civil engineering	937.0	953.0	930.6	903.1	907.4	951.2	985.1	1 005.4	964.5	851.3	825.1
Specialty trade contractors	4 217.0	4 283.9	4 210.4	4 255.7	4 438.6	4 673.1	4 901.1	4 850.2	4 555.8	3 807.9	3 463.4
Manufacturing	17 263	16 441	15 259	14 509	14 315	14 227	14 155	13 879	13 406	11 847	11 528
Durable goods	10 877	10 336	9 485	8 964	8 925	8 956	8 981	8 808	8 463	7 284	7 064
Wood products	615.4	576.3	557.0	539.5	551.6	561.0	560.6	517.1	457.7	360.2	342.1
Nonmetallic mineral products	554.2	544.5	516.0	494.2	505.5	505.3	509.6	500.5	465.0	394.3	370.9
Primary metals	621.8	570.9	509.4	477.4	466.8	466.0	464.0	455.8	442.0	362.1	362.3
Fabricated metal products	1 752.6	1 676.4	1 548.5	1 478.9	1 497.1	1 522.0	1 553.1	1 562.8	1 527.5	1 311.6	1 281.7
Machinery	1 457.0	1 370.6	1 231.8	1 151.6	1 145.2	1 165.5	1 183.2	1 187.1	1 187.6	1 028.6	996.1
Computer and electronic products [1]	1 820.0	1 748.8	1 507.2	1 355.2	1 322.8	1 316.4	1 307.5	1 272.5	1 244.2	1 136.9	1 094.6
Computer and peripheral equipment	301.9	286.2	250.0	224.0	210.0	205.1	196.2	186.2	183.2	166.4	157.6
Communications equipment	238.6	225.4	179.0	149.2	143.0	141.4	136.2	128.1	127.3	120.5	117.4
Semiconductors and electronic components	676.3	645.4	524.5	461.1	454.1	452.0	457.9	447.5	431.8	378.1	369.4
Electronic instruments	487.7	483.6	456.8	435.4	436.9	441.0	444.5	443.2	441.0	421.6	406.4
Electrical equipment and appliances	590.9	556.9	496.5	459.6	445.1	433.5	432.7	429.4	424.3	373.6	359.5
Transportation equipment [1]	2 057.1	1 939.1	1 830.0	1 775.1	1 766.7	1 772.3	1 768.9	1 711.9	1 608.0	1 347.9	1 333.1
Motor vehicles and parts	1 313.6	1 212.9	1 151.2	1 125.3	1 112.8	1 096.7	1 070.0	994.2	875.5	664.1	678.5
Furniture and related products	680.1	642.9	604.7	573.7	574.1	566.3	558.3	529.4	478.0	384.3	357.2
Miscellaneous manufacturing	728.0	709.5	683.3	658.3	650.6	647.2	643.7	641.7	628.9	584.4	566.8
Nondurable goods [1]	6 386	6 105	5 774	5 546	5 390	5 271	5 174	5 071	4 943	4 564	4 464
Food manufacturing	1 553.1	1 551.2	1 525.7	1 517.5	1 493.7	1 477.6	1 479.4	1 484.1	1 480.9	1 456.4	1 450.6
Textile mills	378.2	332.9	290.9	261.3	236.9	217.6	195.0	169.7	151.2	124.4	119.0
Textile product mills	229.6	217.0	204.2	187.7	183.2	176.4	166.7	157.7	147.2	125.7	119.0
Apparel	483.5	415.2	350.0	303.9	278.0	250.5	232.4	214.6	199.0	167.5	156.6
Paper and paper products	604.7	577.6	546.6	516.2	495.5	484.2	470.5	458.2	444.9	407.0	394.7
Printing and related support activities	806.8	768.3	706.6	680.4	662.6	646.3	634.4	622.0	594.1	521.9	487.6
Petroleum and coal products	123.2	121.1	118.1	114.3	111.7	112.1	113.2	114.5	117.4	115.3	113.9
Chemicals	980.4	959.0	927.5	906.1	887.0	872.1	865.9	860.9	847.1	804.1	786.5
Plastics and rubber products	950.9	896.2	846.8	814.3	804.7	802.3	785.5	757.2	729.4	624.9	624.8
Service-Providing	107 362	108 200	108 077	108 515	109 887	111 843	113 905	115 748	115 889	112 739	112 594
Private Service-Providing	86 572	87 082	86 564	86 931	88 266	90 039	91 931	93 530	93 380	90 184	90 104
Trade, transportation, and utilities	26 174	25 931	25 442	25 228	25 470	25 892	26 206	26 556	26 219	24 834	24 565
Wholesale trade	5 888.4	5 728.0	5 605.5	5 556.4	5 607.8	5 705.7	5 841.9	5 948.4	5 874.9	5 520.9	5 386.5
Durable goods	3 342.4	3 221.4	3 103.7	3 044.5	3 062.5	3 118.8	3 202.7	3 257.3	3 190.6	2 944.0	2 848.3
Nondurable goods	2 131.1	2 097.3	2 084.6	2 079.9	2 091.1	2 109.2	2 133.9	2 160.7	2 148.2	2 063.3	2 025.7
Electronic markets, agents, and brokers	414.9	409.3	417.3	432.1	454.2	477.8	505.3	530.4	536.1	513.7	512.5
Retail trade	15 283.6	15 242.4	15 029.0	14 921.7	15 062.7	15 284.5	15 358.5	15 525.5	15 288.8	14 527.9	14 446.0
Motor vehicle and parts dealers [1]	1 846.9	1 854.6	1 879.4	1 882.9	1 902.3	1 918.6	1 909.7	1 908.3	1 831.2	1 637.5	1 629.2
Automobile dealers	1 216.5	1 225.1	1 252.8	1 254.4	1 257.3	1 261.4	1 246.7	1 242.2	1 176.7	1 018.2	1 011.5
Furniture and home furnishings stores	543.5	541.2	538.7	547.3	563.4	576.1	586.9	574.6	531.1	449.2	437.9
Electronics and appliance stores	647.7	633.0	595.2	574.4	572.0	585.5	581.1	583.1	570.2	516.3	523.0
Building material and garden supply stores	1 142.7	1 152.3	1 177.1	1 185.7	1 227.8	1 276.8	1 324.8	1 310.1	1 248.8	1 156.4	1 132.6
Food and beverage stores	2 993.0	2 950.5	2 881.6	2 838.4	2 821.6	2 817.8	2 821.1	2 843.6	2 862.0	2 830.0	2 808.2
Health and personal care stores	927.6	951.5	938.8	938.1	941.1	953.7	961.1	993.1	1 002.8	986.0	980.5
Gasoline stations	935.7	925.3	895.9	882.0	875.6	871.1	864.1	861.5	842.4	825.5	819.3
Clothing and clothing accessories stores	1 321.6	1 321.1	1 312.5	1 304.5	1 364.3	1 414.6	1 450.9	1 500.0	1 468.0	1 363.9	1 352.5
Sporting goods, hobby, book, and music stores	602.7	601.1	591.8	584.7	585.9	597.9	606.0	623.3	621.9	589.2	579.1
General merchandise stores [1]	2 819.8	2 842.2	2 812.0	2 822.4	2 863.0	2 934.3	2 935.0	3 020.6	3 025.6	2 966.2	2 997.7
Department stores	1 739.5	1 752.5	1 668.5	1 605.2	1 589.8	1 579.5	1 541.5	1 575.0	1 524.1	1 456.9	1 485.2
Miscellaneous store retailers	1 007.1	993.3	959.5	930.7	913.5	899.9	881.0	865.4	842.5	782.4	761.5
Nonstore retailers	495.3	476.3	446.7	430.5	432.3	438.2	436.7	442.1	442.3	425.4	424.8

[1] Includes other industries, not shown separately.

Table 15-1. Nonfarm Employment by Sector and Industry—*Continued*

(Wage and salary workers on nonfarm payrolls, thousands.)

Industry	2011	2012	2013	2014	2015	2016	2017	2018	2019	2020	2021
TOTAL NONFARM	131 914	134 157	136 364	138 940	141 825	144 336	146 608	148 908	150 905	142 186	146 124
Total Private	109 828	112 237	114 511	117 058	119 796	122 112	124 258	126 454	128 292	120 200	124 119
Goods-Producing	18 047	18 420	18 738	19 226	19 610	19 750	20 084	20 704	21 037	20 023	20 325
Mining and logging	788	848	863	891	813	668	676	727	727	600	566
Logging	48.7	50.8	51.8	52.0	52.4	51.0	49.6	49.5	49.0	46.4	46.1
Mining	739.2	797.2	811.0	838.5	760.4	616.8	626.1	677.8	678.0	552.9	519.6
Oil and gas extraction	172.0	187.4	193.5	197.7	193.4	169.8	143.9	142.3	143.6	129.8	117.7
Mining, except oil and gas [1]	218.4	218.7	209.6	207.2	197.8	180.9	185.8	191.3	190.4	176.3	174.8
Coal mining	87.3	84.7	78.1	73.2	64.2	50.8	51.5	51.6	50.5	39.8	36.6
Support activities for mining	348.8	391.1	407.9	433.6	369.2	266.2	296.4	344.2	344.0	246.8	227.1
Construction	5 533	5 646	5 856	6 151	6 461	6 728	6 969	7 288	7 493	7 257	7 413
Construction of buildings	1 222.1	1 240.2	1 285.9	1 358.0	1 423.7	1 493.2	1 545.2	1 625.3	1 661.0	1 606.2	1 647.7
Heavy and civil engineering	836.8	868.3	885.0	912.3	937.6	951.6	996.4	1 050.7	1 082.2	1 045.7	1 040.5
Specialty trade contractors	3 474.4	3 537.1	3 684.4	3 880.6	4 099.7	4 283.0	4 427.2	4 612.5	4 750.0	4 604.9	4 725.1
Manufacturing	11 726	11 927	12 020	12 185	12 336	12 354	12 439	12 688	12 817	12 167	12 346
Durable goods	7 273	7 470	7 548	7 674	7 765	7 714	7 741	7 946	8 039	7 573	7 676
Wood products	337.1	339.1	353.2	371.6	382.5	392.7	397.0	406.0	408.7	396.0	409.7
Nonmetallic mineral products	366.6	365.3	373.4	384.1	398.0	406.1	409.8	416.5	419.0	399.3	402.0
Primary metals	388.3	402.0	395.3	398.7	394.0	374.5	371.3	380.2	387.3	353.5	350.4
Fabricated metal products	1 347.3	1 409.8	1 432.3	1 454.2	1 457.8	1 421.5	1 425.2	1 469.6	1 485.6	1 386.0	1 383.9
Machinery	1 055.8	1 098.5	1 104.5	1 127.3	1 120.8	1 076.5	1 079.1	1 116.9	1 126.6	1 055.0	1 053.2
Computer and electronic products [1]	1 103.5	1 089.0	1 065.6	1 048.7	1 052.8	1 048.4	1 039.2	1 054.1	1 075.1	1 063.1	1 058.3
Computer and peripheral equipment	157.4	157.4	157.5	159.8	160.3	162.7	155.6	156.6	160.7	159.7	157.6
Communications equipment	115.3	108.2	101.1	93.2	88.4	86.2	86.7	84.9	84.3	85.6	85.3
Semiconductors and electronic components	383.4	383.1	374.9	367.4	369.5	367.3	362.1	368.9	375.7	368.7	368.3
Electronic instruments	404.2	399.7	393.7	390.8	398.9	396.8	400.5	410.1	422.0	417.7	416.8
Electrical equipment and appliances	366.1	373.2	374.1	377.8	383.7	382.8	386.3	399.6	402.8	384.4	393.9
Transportation equipment [1]	1 381.5	1 461.1	1 508.8	1 559.0	1 604.9	1 630.3	1 643.2	1 702.3	1 729.3	1 590.9	1 639.6
Motor vehicles and parts	717.7	777.3	824.8	872.1	913.7	944.3	963.4	998.4	993.5	887.5	957.7
Furniture and related products	353.1	351.4	359.9	370.3	381.0	389.8	394.9	392.7	387.5	359.2	374.9
Miscellaneous manufacturing	573.7	580.1	580.5	581.9	589.9	590.9	594.5	608.2	617.7	585.9	609.7
Nondurable goods [1]	4 453	4 457	4 472	4 512	4 571	4 640	4 699	4 742	4 778	4 594	4 671
Food manufacturing	1 458.8	1 468.8	1 473.7	1 484.4	1 511.8	1 556.5	1 598.0	1 620.8	1 645.0	1 615.0	1 637.7
Textile mills	120.1	118.7	117.2	117.0	116.6	114.5	112.6	111.8	108.4	95.7	98.1
Textile product mills	117.6	116.3	114.4	115.0	116.1	116.2	116.2	116.0	113.4	102.5	103.4
Apparel	151.7	148.0	144.7	140.1	136.5	130.9	119.3	113.8	110.1	90.1	91.9
Paper and paper products	387.4	379.8	378.0	373.3	372.7	370.8	366.2	365.5	365.3	354.8	348.7
Printing and related support activities	471.8	461.8	452.0	453.7	450.3	447.6	440.2	432.3	425.1	375.3	367.4
Petroleum and coal products	111.8	112.1	110.4	111.6	112.9	112.5	114.6	115.2	114.3	107.6	105.6
Chemicals	783.6	783.3	792.7	803.0	807.3	811.9	823.8	835.3	851.0	845.4	869.0
Plastics and rubber products	635.2	645.1	659.2	674.3	689.4	702.4	716.9	730.3	731.6	706.9	724.0
Service-Providing	113 867	115 737	117 626	119 713	122 215	124 586	126 524	128 205	129 867	122 163	125 799
Private Service-Providing	91 781	93 817	95 773	97 832	100 186	102 362	104 174	105 750	107 254	100 177	103 794
Trade, transportation, and utilities	24 990	25 399	25 783	26 303	26 806	27 179	27 393	27 607	27 723	26 687	27 707
Wholesale trade	5 474.7	5 595.2	5 660.3	5 739.5	5 780.4	5 786.9	5 813.5	5 840.9	5 888.6	5 632.7	5 677.9
Durable goods	2 905.2	2 977.9	3 012.7	3 056.0	3 079.6	3 082.5	3 108.3	3 148.7	3 201.9	3 081.1	3 121.4
Nondurable goods	2 040.5	2 070.8	2 091.8	2 121.0	2 137.2	2 145.2	2 152.8	2 151.4	2 162.3	2 064.5	2 074.7
Electronic markets, agents, and brokers	528.9	546.6	555.9	562.5	563.6	559.2	552.5	540.7	524.4	487.1	481.8
Retail trade	14 673.7	14 846.8	15 084.7	15 363.4	15 610.9	15 831.6	15 845.7	15 786.3	15 619.9	14 871.4	15 396.0
Motor vehicle and parts dealers [1]	1 691.2	1 737.0	1 793.1	1 862.2	1 929.0	1 979.6	2 004.6	2 015.2	2 026.3	1 896.7	1 940.3
Automobile dealers	1 056.9	1 095.5	1 138.4	1 187.9	1 238.7	1 279.0	1 293.3	1 296.6	1 300.3	1 202.7	1 223.2
Furniture and home furnishings stores	438.9	439.4	445.8	455.9	466.8	470.9	476.2	477.2	473.5	404.0	441.9
Electronics and appliance stores	528.1	508.1	497.3	497.8	523.0	522.4	503.3	490.6	474.6	425.2	424.0
Building material and garden supply stores	1 146.6	1 175.1	1 208.5	1 229.0	1 235.3	1 267.8	1 276.7	1 302.7	1 292.4	1 358.8	1 399.2
Food and beverage stores	2 822.8	2 861.3	2 929.7	3 004.0	3 062.3	3 090.3	3 086.2	3 072.9	3 071.9	3 106.1	3 129.8
Health and personal care stores	980.9	997.9	1 015.8	1 022.5	1 033.7	1 053.3	1 066.7	1 063.0	1 043.4	964.0	1 029.2
Gasoline stations	831.0	843.5	866.3	881.3	905.3	923.1	929.8	931.6	946.8	927.4	939.2
Clothing and clothing accessories stores	1 360.9	1 391.4	1 390.9	1 370.4	1 353.7	1 359.3	1 374.4	1 358.5	1 292.1	950.4	1 032.6
Sporting goods, hobby, book, and music stores	577.9	582.2	602.5	618.8	623.2	620.4	606.4	573.3	552.0	472.1	527.0
General merchandise stores [1]	3 085.2	3 065.4	3 060.4	3 102.0	3 131.4	3 169.4	3 125.9	3 097.7	3 028.8	3 031.5	3 092.7
Department stores	1 521.7	1 439.0	1 334.0	1 335.3	1 312.5	1 267.2	1 173.6	1 137.7	1 063.3	931.0	937.0
Miscellaneous store retailers	772.4	794.0	802.5	818.3	828.0	831.8	828.4	834.5	842.9	746.8	805.1
Nonstore retailers	437.9	451.6	471.9	501.3	519.3	543.2	567.2	569.2	575.2	588.4	635.0

[1] Includes other industries, not shown separately.

Table 15-1. Nonfarm Employment by Sector and Industry—*Continued*

(Wage and salary workers on nonfarm payrolls, thousands.)

Industry	2000	2001	2002	2003	2004	2005	2006	2007	2008	2009	2010
Transportation and warehousing	4 400.7	4 361.2	4 211.7	4 172.7	4 235.6	4 348.0	4 457.0	4 528.0	4 495.9	4 224.8	4 179.2
Air transportation	614.4	615.3	563.5	528.3	514.5	500.8	487.0	491.8	490.7	462.8	458.3
Rail transportation	205.6	198.1	186.7	184.2	190.9	192.6	192.4	197.6	195.4	184.6	183.0
Water transportation	56.0	54.0	52.6	54.5	56.4	60.6	62.7	65.5	67.1	63.4	62.3
Truck transportation	1 406.1	1 387.1	1 339.6	1 325.9	1 352.1	1 397.9	1 436.2	1 439.6	1 389.4	1 268.6	1 250.8
Transit and ground passenger transportation	376.3	379.8	386.4	388.8	391.9	396.4	406.5	419.4	430.4	428.3	436.2
Pipeline transportation	46.0	45.4	41.7	40.2	38.4	37.8	38.7	39.9	41.7	42.6	42.3
Scenic and sightseeing transportation	27.5	29.1	25.6	26.6	27.2	28.8	27.5	28.6	28.0	27.6	27.3
Support activities for transportation	546.4	548.7	534.7	530.6	545.6	562.8	581.2	595.0	602.9	558.9	552.9
Couriers and messengers	605.0	587.0	560.9	561.7	556.6	571.4	582.4	580.7	573.4	546.3	528.1
Warehousing and storage	517.5	516.9	519.9	531.9	562.0	598.9	642.5	669.8	676.9	641.7	638.1
Utilities	601	599	596	577	564	554	548	553	559	560	553
Information	3 630	3 629	3 395	3 188	3 118	3 061	3 038	3 032	2 984	2 804	2 707
Publishing industries, except Internet	1 035.0	1 020.7	964.1	924.8	909.1	904.1	902.4	901.2	880.4	796.4	759.0
Motion picture and sound recording industries	382.6	376.8	387.9	376.2	385.0	377.5	375.7	380.6	371.3	357.6	370.2
Broadcasting, except Internet	343.5	344.6	334.1	324.3	325.0	327.7	328.3	325.2	318.7	300.5	290.3
Telecommunications	1 396.6	1 423.9	1 280.9	1 166.8	1 115.1	1 071.3	1 047.6	1 030.6	1 019.4	965.7	902.9
Data processing, hosting, and related services	315.7	316.8	303.9	280.0	267.1	262.5	263.2	267.8	260.3	248.5	243.0
Other information services [1]	157.1	146.5	123.6	115.9	116.9	117.7	120.8	126.3	133.5	135.0	141.7
Internet publishing and broadcasting	110.8	100.4	76.3	67.2	66.1	67.2	69.1	72.9	80.6	83.3	92.0
Financial activities	7 783	7 900	7 956	8 078	8 105	8 197	8 367	8 348	8 206	7 838	7 695
Finance and insurance	5 772.8	5 862.0	5 922.2	6 020.5	6 019.4	6 062.9	6 194.0	6 179.1	6 076.3	5 843.9	5 761.0
Monetary authorities–central bank	22.8	23.0	23.4	22.6	21.8	20.8	21.2	21.6	22.4	21.0	20.0
Credit intermediation and related activities [1]	2 547.8	2 597.7	2 686.0	2 792.4	2 817.0	2 869.0	2 924.9	2 866.3	2 732.7	2 590.2	2 550.0
Depository credit intermediation [1]	1 722.8	1 743.6	1 776.1	1 794.4	1 796.7	1 814.3	1 846.9	1 864.4	1 852.0	1 787.9	1 762.9
Commercial banking	1 325.2	1 334.4	1 355.8	1 361.5	1 361.1	1 375.5	1 401.9	1 425.0	1 424.3	1 378.6	1 366.3
Securities, commodity contracts, investments, and funds and trusts	851.1	879.0	836.4	803.9	813.1	834.2	868.9	899.6	916.2	862.1	850.4
Insurance carriers and related activities	2 351.1	2 362.3	2 376.4	2 401.5	2 367.5	2 338.9	2 379.1	2 391.6	2 405.1	2 370.6	2 340.6
Real estate and rental and leasing	2 010.6	2 038.4	2 033.3	2 057.5	2 085.5	2 133.5	2 172.5	2 169.1	2 129.6	1 994.0	1 933.8
Real estate	1 316.0	1 343.4	1 356.6	1 387.1	1 418.7	1 460.8	1 499.0	1 500.4	1 485.0	1 420.2	1 395.7
Rental and leasing services	666.8	666.3	649.1	643.1	641.1	645.8	645.5	640.3	616.9	547.3	513.5
Lessors of nonfinancial intangible assets	27.8	28.7	27.6	27.3	25.7	26.9	28.1	28.4	27.7	26.5	24.6
Professional and business services	16 704	16 514	16 016	16 029	16 440	17 003	17 619	17 998	17 792	16 634	16 783
Professional and technical services [1]	6 732.1	6 901.3	6 680.6	6 637.0	6 784.2	7 064.5	7 399.3	7 704.5	7 845.3	7 552.9	7 485.8
Legal services	1 065.7	1 091.3	1 115.3	1 142.1	1 163.1	1 168.0	1 173.2	1 175.4	1 161.5	1 124.9	1 114.2
Accounting and bookkeeping services	866.9	872.7	837.8	815.9	806.5	849.9	889.7	936.6	951.8	914.9	887.2
Architectural and engineering services	1 238.5	1 275.3	1 246.7	1 227.6	1 258.9	1 311.7	1 386.6	1 433.1	1 440.2	1 325.5	1 276.2
Computer systems design and related services	1 258.7	1 302.2	1 157.4	1 121.6	1 153.9	1 201.0	1 290.8	1 378.7	1 446.3	1 429.0	1 455.5
Management and technical consulting services	694.3	736.5	730.3	742.5	789.4	852.6	916.6	984.8	1 034.8	1 026.5	1 031.1
Management of companies and enterprises	1 799.7	1 782.7	1 709.3	1 691.5	1 729.0	1 763.8	1 816.1	1 872.0	1 910.1	1 872.4	1 877.8
Administrative and waste services	8 171.9	7 829.6	7 625.6	7 700.9	7 927.3	8 174.7	8 403.2	8 421.6	8 036.8	7 208.5	7 419.1
Administrative and support services [1]	7 859.0	7 512.3	7 307.3	7 378.8	7 598.7	7 837.0	8 055.1	8 066.6	7 680.0	6 856.8	7 061.8
Employment services [1]	3 850.0	3 468.9	3 274.0	3 327.3	3 456.4	3 607.8	3 681.9	3 547.1	3 134.1	2 481.8	2 723.5
Temporary help services	2 636.1	2 338.1	2 194.1	2 224.7	2 387.7	2 549.9	2 638.0	2 598.1	2 349.0	1 823.8	2 094.2
Business support services	788.1	781.2	758.0	751.3	759.5	768.2	794.8	819.5	834.4	822.1	810.7
Services to buildings and dwellings	1 570.5	1 606.2	1 606.1	1 636.1	1 693.7	1 737.5	1 801.4	1 849.5	1 839.8	1 753.3	1 745.0
Waste management and remediation services	312.9	317.3	318.3	322.1	328.6	337.6	348.1	355.0	356.8	351.7	357.3
Education and health services	15 252	15 814	16 398	16 835	17 230	17 676	18 154	18 676	19 228	19 630	19 975
Educational services	2 390.4	2 511.0	2 643.0	2 695.0	2 763.0	2 836.0	2 901.0	2 941.0	3 040.0	3 090.0	3 155.0
Health care and social assistance	12 861.1	13 302.9	13 755.2	14 139.6	14 467.8	14 840.4	15 253.2	15 734.5	16 188.2	16 539.9	16 820.0
Health care	10 857.8	11 188.1	11 536.0	11 817.1	12 055.3	12 313.9	12 601.8	12 946.8	13 289.9	13 543.0	13 776.9
Ambulatory health care services [1]	4 320.3	4 461.5	4 633.2	4 786.4	4 952.3	5 113.5	5 285.8	5 473.5	5 646.6	5 793.4	5 974.7
Offices of physicians	1 801.1	1 870.9	1 926.3	1 960.2	2 004.6	2 049.4	2 102.5	2 155.1	2 205.0	2 231.0	2 263.9
Outpatient care centers	425.2	440.0	454.5	469.0	493.7	517.3	537.9	558.4	580.8	605.6	648.7
Home health care services	633.3	638.6	679.8	732.6	776.6	821.0	865.6	913.8	961.4	1 027.1	1 084.6
Hospitals	3 954.3	4 050.9	4 159.6	4 244.6	4 284.7	4 345.4	4 423.4	4 515.0	4 627.3	4 667.4	4 678.5
Nursing and residential care facilities [1]	2 583.2	2 675.8	2 743.3	2 786.2	2 818.4	2 855.0	2 892.5	2 958.3	3 016.1	3 082.2	3 123.7
Nursing care facilities	1 513.6	1 546.8	1 573.2	1 579.8	1 576.9	1 577.4	1 581.4	1 602.6	1 618.7	1 644.9	1 657.1
Social assistance [1]	2 003.3	2 114.7	2 219.2	2 322.5	2 412.5	2 526.5	2 651.4	2 787.7	2 898.3	2 996.9	3 043.1
Child day care services	695.8	714.6	744.1	755.3	764.7	789.7	818.3	850.4	859.4	852.8	848.0

[1]Includes other industries, not shown separately.

Table 15-1. Nonfarm Employment by Sector and Industry—*Continued*

(Wage and salary workers on nonfarm payrolls, thousands.)

Industry	2011	2012	2013	2014	2015	2016	2017	2018	2019	2020	2021
Transportation and warehousing	4 289.3	4 403.7	4 486.0	4 648.6	4 858.6	5 003.5	5 178.2	5 426.4	5 664.9	5 639.6	6 091.9
Air transportation	456.9	459.2	444.3	444.2	458.6	477.5	491.5	496.9	504.9	441.2	475.3
Rail transportation	192.9	195.1	195.6	199.7	203.7	183.6	181.9	181.7	174.3	150.4	146.2
Water transportation	61.3	63.9	65.3	67.3	65.8	65.6	65.0	65.1	66.6	60.0	56.4
Truck transportation	1 301.0	1 349.8	1 382.6	1 417.7	1 452.7	1 448.1	1 457.0	1 496.2	1 528.8	1 471.3	1 514.2
Transit and ground passenger transportation	446.9	447.5	455.6	473.7	485.0	490.2	494.9	494.7	493.9	370.3	374.7
Pipeline transportation	42.9	43.6	44.5	47.0	49.7	49.8	48.8	49.7	51.5	51.1	49.9
Scenic and sightseeing transportation	27.5	28.0	29.1	30.6	32.9	34.5	35.2	34.6	35.5	21.3	22.6
Support activities for transportation	572.9	590.7	609.2	636.9	663.1	677.9	700.6	729.3	753.8	701.3	722.3
Couriers and messengers	529.2	534.1	543.9	576.5	612.8	644.8	676.1	739.5	826.9	967.3	1 082.2
Warehousing and storage	657.9	691.9	716.0	754.8	834.3	931.6	1 027.3	1 138.8	1 228.7	1 405.4	1 648.2
Utilities	553	553	552	552	556	556	555	553	549	543	541
Information	2 674	2 676	2 706	2 726	2 750	2 794	2 814	2 839	2 864	2 720	2 831
Publishing industries, except Internet	748.6	739.5	732.7	726.9	726.5	730.3	728.6	738.5	764.8	768.0	790.8
Motion picture and sound recording industries	362.1	362.3	370.5	379.3	397.9	426.1	432.6	441.3	437.8	301.0	370.8
Broadcasting, except Internet	283.2	285.1	283.7	282.8	276.7	270.5	268.0	269.8	266.9	247.0	236.3
Telecommunications	873.6	856.8	853.2	838.5	810.9	801.1	780.8	749.7	714.6	687.9	666.8
Data processing, hosting, and related services	245.8	254.9	269.6	279.5	296.2	303.9	318.0	331.0	343.2	361.7	388.3
Other information services [1]	160.0	177.2	196.2	219.0	241.4	262.3	285.8	308.8	336.8	355.0	378.3
Internet publishing and broadcasting	109.6	125.2	142.3	163.3	184.3	203.5	223.8	245.1	271.4	290.9	311.7
Financial activities	7 697	7 784	7 886	7 977	8 123	8 287	8 451	8 590	8 754	8 704	8 777
Finance and insurance	5 769.0	5 828.4	5 886.1	5 930.9	6 034.9	6 148.1	6 261.9	6 337.0	6 433.3	6 489.0	6 519.4
Monetary authorities–central bank	18.3	17.5	18.0	18.2	18.0	18.6	19.2	19.6	19.8	20.4	20.9
Credit intermediation and related activities [1]	2 554.1	2 583.3	2 614.1	2 564.0	2 570.7	2 609.7	2 644.9	2 651.2	2 648.9	2 667.8	2 706.9
Depository credit intermediation [1]	1 770.0	1 774.1	1 768.6	1 735.7	1 717.2	1 732.3	1 748.0	1 759.1	1 776.4	1 771.7	1 741.5
Commercial banking	1 375.4	1 381.3	1 373.7	1 348.3	1 338.3	1 361.5	1 375.0	1 381.4	1 392.8	1 388.3	1 358.6
Securities, commodity contracts, investments, and funds and trusts	860.1	859.3	865.0	882.9	907.8	927.1	938.3	953.6	962.3	964.9	990.0
Insurance carriers and related activities	2 336.4	2 368.3	2 388.9	2 465.8	2 538.3	2 592.7	2 659.6	2 712.7	2 802.3	2 835.9	2 801.7
Real estate and rental and leasing	1 927.4	1 955.2	2 000.2	2 045.7	2 088.4	2 138.8	2 189.2	2 253.3	2 320.7	2 214.9	2 257.4
Real estate	1 400.8	1 420.0	1 458.7	1 487.1	1 517.1	1 556.8	1 605.5	1 662.9	1 717.7	1 696.4	1 747.2
Rental and leasing services	502.2	511.0	517.7	535.0	547.5	558.3	560.1	567.2	579.9	496.4	489.7
Lessors of nonfinancial intangible assets	24.4	24.2	23.7	23.7	23.8	23.8	23.7	23.3	23.0	22.1	20.5
Professional and business services	17 389	17 992	18 575	19 124	19 695	20 114	20 508	20 950	21 274	20 314	21 250
Professional and technical services [1]	7 712.5	7 940.5	8 169.9	8 385.5	8 658.4	8 880.8	9 057.8	9 281.7	9 535.7	9 435.2	9 882.7
Legal services	1 115.7	1 124.0	1 128.5	1 119.0	1 118.6	1 123.7	1 136.8	1 142.0	1 150.7	1 128.5	1 154.8
Accounting and bookkeeping services	899.6	909.7	932.3	949.3	969.3	981.4	996.6	1 003.8	1 020.8	993.9	1 048.9
Architectural and engineering services	1 294.3	1 323.4	1 346.5	1 376.2	1 401.6	1 404.6	1 435.3	1 474.4	1 514.5	1 503.5	1 545.0
Computer systems design and related services	1 542.6	1 628.4	1 709.5	1 797.8	1 915.8	1 993.2	2 051.2	2 118.0	2 194.6	2 196.5	2 301.3
Management and technical consulting services	1 098.2	1 152.4	1 215.2	1 267.7	1 318.1	1 394.2	1 433.1	1 481.5	1 534.6	1 527.9	1 634.3
Management of companies and enterprises	1 939.3	2 029.3	2 109.0	2 174.6	2 213.6	2 251.6	2 308.1	2 373.9	2 419.8	2 350.0	2 337.5
Administrative and waste services	7 737.3	8 021.8	8 296.5	8 564.1	8 823.3	8 981.2	9 141.5	9 294.3	9 318.9	8 529.0	9 029.3
Administrative and support services [1]	7 372.0	7 649.9	7 919.1	8 178.0	8 426.8	8 577.1	8 726.3	8 858.0	8 867.6	8 082.0	8 573.0
Employment services [1]	2 943.2	3 135.2	3 269.7	3 408.1	3 528.3	3 537.9	3 595.1	3 656.6	3 617.6	3 117.3	3 563.0
Temporary help services	2 313.6	2 496.0	2 617.6	2 760.8	2 877.6	2 889.1	2 939.7	2 988.5	2 950.2	2 522.4	2 903.2
Business support services	816.7	830.7	858.3	879.7	895.9	912.0	904.4	895.3	875.7	815.3	810.1
Services to buildings and dwellings	1 788.6	1 830.0	1 884.7	1 943.9	2 006.6	2 062.8	2 111.2	2 144.8	2 173.7	2 101.0	2 152.6
Waste management and remediation services	365.3	371.9	377.5	386.1	396.5	404.1	415.2	436.3	451.3	447.0	456.3
Education and health services	20 318	20 769	21 086	21 439	22 029	22 639	23 188	23 638	24 163	23 275	23 673
Educational services	3 250.0	3 341.0	3 354.0	3 417.0	3 472.0	3 570.0	3 668.0	3 715.0	3 741.0	3 478.0	3 589.0
Health care and social assistance	17 068.6	17 428.1	17 731.1	18 022.2	18 557.4	19 068.8	19 519.6	19 922.6	20 421.1	19 796.3	20 083.9
Health care	14 025.9	14 281.6	14 491.5	14 676.5	15 042.3	15 413.5	15 716.6	15 964.3	16 269.1	15 849.6	16 023.6
Ambulatory health care services [1]	6 136.2	6 306.5	6 476.5	6 631.5	6 855.5	7 080.0	7 297.3	7 477.4	7 704.4	7 498.2	7 874.7
Offices of physicians	2 294.6	2 339.8	2 378.0	2 411.2	2 471.0	2 526.5	2 581.4	2 615.8	2 673.2	2 631.6	2 739.1
Outpatient care centers	670.2	699.0	731.1	763.7	805.7	853.0	897.2	931.4	969.1	970.3	996.7
Home health care services	1 140.3	1 185.0	1 230.3	1 262.4	1 314.7	1 365.3	1 419.6	1 467.0	1 518.5	1 494.6	1 514.3
Hospitals	4 721.7	4 779.0	4 785.8	4 786.8	4 895.8	5 015.2	5 071.8	5 129.8	5 189.7	5 137.4	5 126.1
Nursing and residential care facilities [1]	3 168.1	3 196.2	3 229.2	3 258.2	3 290.9	3 318.3	3 347.5	3 357.2	3 375.0	3 214.0	3 022.8
Nursing care facilities	1 669.6	1 662.8	1 653.8	1 650.3	1 648.3	1 641.5	1 627.1	1 606.8	1 596.3	1 499.3	1 374.6
Social assistance [1]	3 042.6	3 146.5	3 239.6	3 345.6	3 515.1	3 655.3	3 803.0	3 958.3	4 152.0	3 946.7	4 060.3
Child day care services	849.4	851.3	843.3	854.0	878.0	911.2	943.1	972.7	1 021.2	861.4	886.3

[1] Includes other industries, not shown separately.

Table 15-1. Nonfarm Employment by Sector and Industry—*Continued*

(Wage and salary workers on nonfarm payrolls, thousands.)

Industry	2000	2001	2002	2003	2004	2005	2006	2007	2008	2009	2010
Leisure and hospitality	11 862	12 036	11 986	12 173	12 493	12 816	13 110	13 427	13 436	13 077	13 049
Arts, entertainment, and recreation	1 787.9	1 824.4	1 782.6	1 812.9	1 849.6	1 892.3	1 928.5	1 969.2	1 970.1	1 915.5	1 913.3
Performing arts and spectator sports	381.8	382.3	363.7	371.7	367.5	376.3	398.5	405.0	405.7	396.8	406.2
Museums, historical sites, zoos, and parks	110.4	115.0	114.0	114.7	118.3	120.7	123.8	130.3	131.6	129.4	127.7
Amusements, gambling, and recreation	1 295.7	1 327.1	1 305.0	1 326.5	1 363.8	1 395.3	1 406.3	1 433.9	1 432.8	1 389.2	1 379.4
Accommodation and food services	10 073.5	10 211.3	10 203.2	10 359.8	10 643.2	10 923.0	11 181.1	11 457.4	11 466.3	11 161.9	11 135.4
Accommodation	1 884.4	1 852.2	1 778.6	1 775.4	1 789.5	1 818.6	1 832.1	1 866.9	1 868.7	1 763.0	1 759.6
Food services and drinking places	8 189.1	8 359.1	8 424.6	8 584.4	8 853.7	9 104.4	9 349.0	9 590.4	9 597.5	9 398.9	9 375.8
Other services	5 168	5 258	5 372	5 401	5 409	5 395	5 438	5 494	5 515	5 367	5 331
Repair and maintenance	1 241.5	1 256.5	1 246.9	1 233.6	1 228.8	1 236.0	1 248.5	1 253.4	1 227.0	1 150.4	1 138.8
Personal and laundry services	1 242.9	1 255.0	1 257.2	1 263.5	1 272.9	1 276.6	1 288.4	1 309.7	1 322.6	1 280.6	1 265.3
Membership associations and organizations	2 683.3	2 746.4	2 867.8	2 903.6	2 907.5	2 882.2	2 901.2	2 931.1	2 965.7	2 936.0	2 926.4
Government	20 790	21 118	21 513	21 583	21 621	21 804	21 974	22 218	22 509	22 555	22 490
Federal	2 865.0	2 764.0	2 766.0	2 761.0	2 730.0	2 732.0	2 732.0	2 734.0	2 762.0	2 832.0	2 977.0
Federal, except U.S. Postal Service	1 984.8	1 891.0	1 923.8	1 952.4	1 947.5	1 957.3	1 962.6	1 964.7	2 014.4	2 128.5	2 318.1
U.S. Postal Service	879.7	873.0	842.4	808.6	782.1	774.2	769.7	769.1	747.4	703.4	658.5
State government	4 786.0	4 905.0	5 029.0	5 002.0	4 982.0	5 032.0	5 075.0	5 122.0	5 177.0	5 169.0	5 137.0
State government education	2 030.6	2 112.9	2 242.8	2 254.7	2 238.1	2 259.9	2 292.5	2 317.5	2 354.4	2 360.2	2 373.1
State government, excluding education	2 755.9	2 791.8	2 786.3	2 747.6	2 743.9	2 771.6	2 782.0	2 804.3	2 822.5	2 808.8	2 764.1
Local government	13 139.0	13 449.0	13 718.0	13 820.0	13 909.0	14 041.0	14 167.0	14 362.0	14 571.0	14 554.0	14 376.0
Local government education	7 293.9	7 479.3	7 654.4	7 709.4	7 765.2	7 856.1	7 913.0	7 986.8	8 083.9	8 078.8	8 013.4
Local government, excluding education	5 844.6	5 970.0	6 063.2	6 110.2	6 144.1	6 184.6	6 253.8	6 375.5	6 486.5	6 474.9	6 362.9

¹Includes other industries, not shown separately.

Table 15-1. Nonfarm Employment by Sector and Industry—*Continued*

(Wage and salary workers on nonfarm payrolls, thousands.)

Industry	2011	2012	2013	2014	2015	2016	2017	2018	2019	2020	2021
Leisure and hospitality	13 353	13 768	14 254	14 696	15 160	15 660	16 051	16 295	16 586	13 148	14 101
Arts, entertainment, and recreation	1 919.1	1 968.6	2 029.7	2 103.1	2 166.4	2 251.5	2 333.2	2 382.5	2 436.9	1 773.2	1 979.3
Performing arts and spectator sports	394.2	402.4	419.2	443.3	450.4	464.4	493.8	506.4	518.9	336.3	381.0
Museums, historical sites, zoos, and parks	132.7	136.1	140.3	146.9	153.0	159.6	165.6	169.5	172.6	138.1	138.8
Amusements, gambling, and recreation	1 392.2	1 430.1	1 470.2	1 512.9	1 563.1	1 627.5	1 673.8	1 706.6	1 745.4	1 298.8	1 459.5
Accommodation and food services	11 433.6	11 799.7	12 224.2	12 592.9	12 993.8	13 408.4	13 717.9	13 912.9	14 148.8	11 374.7	12 121.4
Accommodation	1 800.5	1 825.1	1 864.9	1 894.5	1 923.0	1 960.3	2 002.9	2 034.7	2 082.4	1 471.1	1 470.6
Food services and drinking places	9 633.1	9 974.6	10 359.2	10 698.3	11 070.8	11 448.1	11 715.0	11 878.2	12 066.4	9 903.6	10 650.8
Other services	5 360	5 430	5 483	5 567	5 622	5 691	5 770	5 831	5 891	5 329	5 456
Repair and maintenance	1 168.7	1 194.0	1 216.6	1 242.1	1 277.2	1 293.1	1 310.6	1 326.7	1 346.9	1 281.0	1 349.6
Personal and laundry services	1 288.6	1 313.6	1 341.7	1 371.2	1 405.0	1 444.3	1 478.4	1 506.6	1 535.0	1 239.4	1 354.6
Membership associations and organizations	2 903.0	2 922.4	2 924.6	2 953.6	2 939.5	2 953.3	2 981.0	2 997.9	3 008.7	2 808.4	2 751.4
Government	22 086	21 920	21 853	21 882	22 029	22 224	22 350	22 455	22 613	21 986	22 005
Federal	2 859.0	2 820.0	2 769.0	2 733.0	2 757.0	2 795.0	2 805.0	2 800.0	2 831.0	2 930.0	2 886.0
Federal, except U.S. Postal Service	2 227.6	2 209.2	2 174.5	2 140.4	2 160.0	2 185.8	2 189.4	2 191.8	2 224.0	2 328.0	2 279.6
U.S. Postal Service	630.9	611.2	594.9	593.0	596.9	608.8	615.4	608.5	607.2	602.3	606.0
State government	5 078.0	5 055.0	5 046.0	5 050.0	5 077.0	5 110.0	5 165.0	5 173.0	5 206.0	5 135.0	5 207.0
State government education	2 374.0	2 388.5	2 393.3	2 389.3	2 401.4	2 429.2	2 478.7	2 486.9	2 515.2	2 435.9	2 533.9
State government, excluding education	2 703.7	2 666.4	2 652.8	2 660.5	2 675.6	2 680.9	2 686.4	2 686.4	2 690.9	2 699.0	2 673.0
Local government	14 150.0	14 045.0	14 037.0	14 098.0	14 195.0	14 319.0	14 379.0	14 481.0	14 576.0	13 921.0	13 912.0
Local government education	7 872.5	7 777.9	7 776.7	7 814.9	7 870.9	7 905.1	7 921.5	7 963.0	8 000.9	7 581.2	7 586.0
Local government, excluding education	6 277.7	6 266.8	6 260.1	6 283.4	6 324.0	6 414.1	6 457.5	6 518.0	6 574.9	6 339.6	6 326.1

¹Includes other industries, not shown separately.

Table 15-2. Production and Nonsupervisory Workers on Private Nonfarm Payrolls by Industry

(Wage and salary workers on nonfarm payrolls, thousands.)

Industry	2000	2001	2002	2003	2004	2005	2006	2007	2008	2009	2010
Total Private	90 534	90 200	88 649	87 948	89 230	91 426	93 759	95 243	94 660	89 616	88 940
Goods-Producing	18 169	17 466	16 400	15 732	15 821	16 145	16 559	16 405	15 724	13 399	12 774
Mining and logging	446	457	436	420	440	473	519	547	574	510	525
Construction	5 295	5 332	5 196	5 123	5 309	5 611	5 903	5 883	5 521	4 567	4 172
Manufacturing	12 428	11 677	10 768	10 189	10 072	10 060	10 137	9 975	9 629	8 322	8 077
Durable goods	7 659	7 164	6 530	6 152	6 140	6 220	6 355	6 250	5 975	4 990	4 829
Wood products	507	470	450	434	445	454	451	407	358	278	269
Nonmetallic mineral products	440	427	399	375	388	387	391	384	363	303	284
Primary metals	490	447	396	370	364	363	363	358	348	272	275
Fabricated metal products	1 326	1 254	1 147	1 092	1 109	1 129	1 162	1 171	1 143	960	935
Machinery	961	891	787	732	730	749	770	774	772	641	616
Computer and electronic products	949	876	744	673	656	700	756	744	730	654	629
Electrical equipment and appliances	433	402	352	320	307	300	303	305	305	266	251
Transportation equipment [1]	1 498	1 399	1 310	1 269	1 265	1 277	1 304	1 274	1 177	948	937
Motor vehicles and parts	1 073	987	931	906	903	894	873	804	696	510	525
Furniture and related products	544	509	475	444	444	436	433	409	364	284	263
Miscellaneous manufacturing	510	490	469	442	432	424	423	425	416	382	370
Nondurable goods [1]	4 769	4 513	4 238	4 037	3 932	3 841	3 782	3 725	3 653	3 332	3 248
Food manufacturing	1 228	1 221	1 202	1 192	1 178	1 170	1 172	1 184	1 184	1 161	1 152
Textile mills	315	276	242	217	194	174	158	137	122	99	96
Textile product mills	183	174	162	148	147	143	135	123	115	98	92
Apparel	404	341	286	242	219	193	182	173	163	132	120
Paper and paper products	468	446	421	393	374	365	357	350	344	313	302
Printing and related support activities	576	544	493	471	460	447	447	443	424	369	342
Chemicals	588	562	532	525	520	510	508	504	512	479	474
Plastics and rubber products	753	704	662	633	626	620	608	592	572	476	472
Private Service-Providing	72 365	72 734	72 249	72 216	73 409	75 282	77 200	78 838	78 936	76 217	76 166
Trade, transportation, and utilities	21 923	21 665	21 292	21 029	21 268	21 776	22 109	22 486	22 277	21 059	20 816
Wholesale trade	4 651	4 520	4 437	4 358	4 402	4 538	4 676	4 799	4 768	4 453	4 324
Retail trade	13 043	12 955	12 777	12 658	12 792	13 033	13 114	13 322	13 139	12 476	12 430
Transportation and warehousing	3 743	3 707	3 599	3 550	3 624	3 761	3 876	3 922	3 920	3 678	3 618
Utilities	485	483	478	464	450	443	443	444	450	451	444
Information	2 502	2 531	2 398	2 347	2 371	2 386	2 399	2 403	2 388	2 240	2 170
Financial activities	5 819	5 888	5 964	6 052	6 052	6 127	6 312	6 365	6 320	6 066	5 942
Professional and business services	13 819	13 617	13 080	12 942	13 321	13 892	14 487	14 828	14 631	13 565	13 744
Education and health services	13 491	13 998	14 491	14 753	15 018	15 401	15 832	16 318	16 842	17 240	17 531
Leisure and hospitality	10 516	10 662	10 576	10 666	10 955	11 263	11 568	11 861	11 873	11 560	11 507
Other services	4 296	4 373	4 449	4 426	4 425	4 438	4 494	4 578	4 606	4 488	4 458

[1]Includes other industries, not shown separately.

Table 15-2. Production and Nonsupervisory Workers on Private Nonfarm Payrolls by Industry
—Continued

(Wage and salary workers on nonfarm payrolls, thousands.)

Industry	2011	2012	2013	2014	2015	2016	2017	2018	2019	2020	2021
Total Private	90 605	92 766	94 573	96 688	98 769	100 555	102 411	104 169	105 570	97 901	101 089
Goods-Producing	13 005	13 287	13 481	13 858	14 141	14 215	14 450	14 876	15 073	14 217	14 488
Mining and logging	594	641	636	653	592	471	490	541	535	425	418
Construction	4 184	4 246	4 423	4 640	4 866	5 074	5 230	5 437	5 579	5 369	5 487
Manufacturing	8 228	8 400	8 422	8 565	8 683	8 670	8 730	8 898	8 959	8 423	8 583
Durable goods	4 986	5 152	5 185	5 282	5 350	5 303	5 315	5 464	5 532	5 131	5 247
Wood products	269	272	283	298	306	309	311	319	321	310	321
Nonmetallic mineral products	278	273	275	280	297	306	305	311	312	296	298
Primary metals	301	317	306	310	307	293	292	295	302	272	269
Fabricated metal products	994	1 050	1 063	1 071	1 069	1 036	1 045	1 087	1 106	1 016	1 012
Machinery	662	700	699	716	711	686	691	716	709	641	657
Computer and electronic products	630	628	610	589	594	596	598	612	638	640	634
Electrical equipment and appliances	248	249	245	248	258	259	253	261	262	248	258
Transportation equipment [1]	972	1 024	1 053	1 103	1 139	1 150	1 149	1 188	1 199	1 080	1 143
Motor vehicles and parts	556	598	642	690	718	739	753	780	768	663	732
Furniture and related products	260	259	266	276	284	286	290	290	288	261	271
Miscellaneous manufacturing	373	380	386	390	384	382	381	384	394	368	384
Nondurable goods [1]	3 241	3 248	3 237	3 283	3 333	3 367	3 415	3 434	3 427	3 292	3 336
Food manufacturing	1 158	1 169	1 169	1 176	1 189	1 212	1 251	1 272	1 290	1 274	1 290
Textile mills	98	96	92	91	90	90	88	87	85	73	75
Textile product mills	89	85	83	86	88	89	89	85	78	70	75
Apparel	112	109	106	103	104	99	88	82	74	65	67
Paper and paper products	295	288	279	277	277	275	278	275	271	262	256
Printing and related support activities	327	316	310	312	310	312	305	296	285	254	253
Chemicals	480	491	490	497	507	516	525	546	559	537	540
Plastics and rubber products	482	487	497	518	532	536	543	548	548	519	530
Private Service-Providing	77 600	79 479	81 093	82 830	84 628	86 340	87 961	89 293	90 497	83 683	86 601
Trade, transportation, and utilities	21 174	21 554	21 811	22 217	22 566	22 842	23 094	23 348	23 451	22 503	23 401
Wholesale trade	4 388	4 505	4 563	4 638	4 644	4 634	4 661	4 688	4 728	4 481	4 515
Retail trade	12 652	12 798	12 928	13 112	13 269	13 433	13 486	13 488	13 332	12 671	13 131
Transportation and warehousing	3 693	3 810	3 875	4 022	4 207	4 328	4 500	4 728	4 952	4 920	5 324
Utilities	441	441	445	446	447	447	447	444	440	432	430
Information	2 148	2 164	2 194	2 209	2 226	2 252	2 268	2 286	2 305	2 157	2 243
Financial activities	5 900	5 986	6 068	6 155	6 278	6 430	6 571	6 654	6 774	6 661	6 624
Professional and business services	14 298	14 851	15 352	15 818	16 183	16 455	16 751	17 079	17 301	16 326	17 076
Education and health services	17 818	18 230	18 505	18 827	19 337	19 859	20 365	20 763	21 221	20 385	20 673
Leisure and hospitality	11 772	12 154	12 590	12 968	13 360	13 782	14 139	14 334	14 571	11 311	12 172
Other services	4 491	4 541	4 573	4 637	4 678	4 720	4 775	4 828	4 874	4 339	4 413

[1] Includes other industries, not shown separately.

Table 15-3. Average Weekly Hours of Production and Nonsupervisory Workers on Private Nonfarm Payrolls by Industry

(Hours.)

Industry	2000	2001	2002	2003	2004	2005	2006	2007	2008	2009	2010
Total Private	34.3	33.9	33.9	33.7	33.7	33.8	33.9	33.8	33.6	33.1	33.4
Goods-Producing	40.7	39.9	39.9	39.8	40.0	40.1	40.5	40.6	40.2	39.2	40.4
Mining and logging	44.4	44.6	43.2	43.6	44.5	45.6	45.6	45.9	45.1	43.2	44.6
Construction	39.2	38.7	38.4	38.4	38.3	38.6	39.0	39.0	38.5	37.6	38.4
Manufacturing	41.3	40.3	40.5	40.4	40.8	40.7	41.1	41.2	40.8	39.8	41.1
Overtime hours	4.7	4.0	4.2	4.2	4.6	4.6	4.4	4.2	3.7	2.9	3.8
Durable goods	41.8	40.6	40.8	40.8	41.3	41.1	41.4	41.5	41.1	39.8	41.4
Overtime hours	4.8	3.9	4.2	4.3	4.7	4.6	4.4	4.2	3.7	2.7	3.8
Wood products	41.0	40.2	39.9	40.4	40.7	40.0	39.8	39.4	38.6	37.4	39.1
Nonmetallic mineral products	41.6	41.6	42.0	42.2	42.4	42.2	43.0	42.3	42.1	40.8	41.7
Primary metals	44.2	42.4	42.4	42.3	43.1	43.1	43.6	42.9	42.2	40.7	43.7
Fabricated metal products	41.9	40.6	40.6	40.7	41.1	41.0	41.4	41.6	41.3	39.4	41.4
Machinery	42.3	40.9	40.5	40.8	42.0	42.1	42.4	42.6	42.3	40.1	42.1
Computer and electronic products	41.4	39.8	39.7	40.4	40.4	40.0	40.5	40.6	41.0	40.4	40.9
Electrical equipment and appliances	41.6	39.8	40.1	40.6	40.7	40.6	41.0	41.2	40.9	39.3	41.1
Transportation equipment [1]	43.3	41.9	42.5	41.9	42.5	42.4	42.7	42.8	42.0	41.2	42.9
Motor vehicles and parts	43.3	41.7	42.6	42.0	42.6	42.3	42.2	42.3	41.4	40.1	43.4
Furniture and related products	39.2	38.3	39.2	38.9	39.5	39.2	38.8	39.2	38.1	37.7	38.5
Miscellaneous manufacturing	39.0	38.8	38.7	38.4	38.5	38.7	38.7	38.9	38.9	38.5	38.7
Nondurable goods [1]	4.5	4.1	4.2	4.1	4.4	4.4	4.4	4.1	3.7	3.2	3.8
Overtime hours	4.5	4.1	4.2	4.1	4.4	4.4	4.4	4.1	3.7	3.2	3.8
Food manufacturing	40.1	39.6	39.6	39.3	39.3	39.0	40.1	40.7	40.5	40.0	40.7
Textile mills	41.4	40.0	40.6	39.1	40.1	40.3	40.6	40.3	38.7	37.7	41.2
Textile product mills	38.7	38.4	39.0	39.4	38.7	38.9	39.8	39.7	38.6	37.9	39.0
Apparel	35.7	36.0	36.7	35.6	36.1	35.8	36.5	37.2	36.4	36.0	36.6
Paper and paper products	42.8	42.1	41.8	41.5	42.1	42.5	42.9	43.1	42.9	41.8	42.9
Printing and related support activities	39.2	38.7	38.4	38.2	38.4	38.4	39.2	39.1	38.3	38.0	38.2
Chemicals	42.2	41.9	42.3	42.4	42.8	42.3	42.5	41.9	41.5	41.4	42.2
Plastics and rubber products	40.8	40.0	40.6	40.4	40.4	40.0	40.7	41.3	41.0	40.2	41.9
Private Service-Providing	32.7	32.5	32.5	32.3	32.3	32.4	32.4	32.4	32.3	32.1	32.2
Trade, transportation, and utilities	33.8	33.5	33.6	33.5	33.5	33.4	33.4	33.3	33.1	32.8	33.3
Wholesale trade	38.8	38.4	38.0	37.9	37.8	37.7	38.0	38.2	38.3	37.7	37.9
Retail trade	30.7	30.7	30.9	30.9	30.7	30.6	30.5	30.2	30.0	29.9	30.2
Transportation and warehousing	37.3	36.6	36.7	36.7	37.2	37.0	36.8	36.9	36.4	36.0	37.1
Utilities	42.0	41.4	40.9	41.1	40.9	41.1	41.4	42.4	42.7	42.0	42.0
Information	36.8	36.9	36.5	36.2	36.3	36.5	36.6	36.5	36.7	36.6	36.3
Financial activities	35.9	35.8	35.6	35.6	35.6	36.0	35.8	35.9	35.9	36.1	36.2
Professional and business services	34.5	34.2	34.2	34.1	34.2	34.3	34.6	34.8	34.8	34.7	35.1
Education and health services	32.2	32.3	32.4	32.3	32.4	32.6	32.5	32.5	32.4	32.2	32.0
Leisure and hospitality	26.1	25.8	25.8	25.6	25.7	25.7	25.7	25.5	25.2	24.8	24.8
Other services	32.5	32.3	32.1	31.4	31.0	30.9	30.9	30.9	30.8	30.5	30.7

[1]Includes other industries, not shown separately.

Table 15-3. Average Weekly Hours of Production and Nonsupervisory Workers on Private Nonfarm Payrolls by Industry—*Continued*

(Hours.)

Industry	2011	2012	2013	2014	2015	2016	2017	2018	2019	2020	2021
Total Private	33.6	33.7	33.7	33.7	33.7	33.6	33.7	33.8	33.6	33.9	34.2
Goods-Producing	40.9	41.1	41.3	41.5	41.2	41.2	41.3	41.5	41.1	40.3	40.9
Mining and logging	46.7	46.6	45.9	47.3	45.8	45.3	46.1	46.8	46.9	44.9	46.5
Construction	39.0	39.3	39.6	39.6	39.6	39.7	39.7	40.0	39.8	39.2	39.5
Manufacturing	41.4	41.7	41.8	42.0	41.8	41.9	41.9	42.2	41.6	40.7	41.4
Overtime hours	4.1	4.2	4.3	4.5	4.3	4.3	4.3	4.6	4.3	3.7	4.1
Durable goods	41.9	42.0	42.2	42.5	42.1	42.3	42.3	42.5	42.0	40.9	41.5
Overtime hours	4.2	4.3	4.4	4.7	4.3	4.5	4.4	4.7	4.3	3.7	4.1
Wood products	39.7	41.1	42.7	42.0	41.3	41.8	42.1	41.9	41.5	41.7	42.1
Nonmetallic mineral products	42.3	42.2	42.5	43.3	42.4	42.0	42.9	44.2	43.8	43.4	42.6
Primary metals	44.6	43.8	43.8	44.2	43.8	43.4	43.1	44.6	43.8	42.1	43.2
Fabricated metal products	42.0	42.0	42.2	42.6	42.3	42.1	42.2	42.2	41.7	40.7	41.4
Machinery	43.2	42.8	42.9	43.0	41.9	42.1	42.7	42.7	42.4	41.0	41.6
Computer and electronic products	40.5	40.4	40.5	40.8	40.9	41.2	41.2	40.9	40.5	40.0	40.3
Electrical equipment and appliances	40.8	41.6	41.8	41.7	42.2	42.9	43.1	42.6	41.4	40.7	42.2
Transportation equipment [1]	43.2	43.8	43.6	43.6	43.7	44.1	43.9	44.4	43.4	41.6	42.2
Motor vehicles and parts	43.4	44.2	43.7	43.8	44.1	44.7	44.0	44.7	43.4	42.3	42.0
Furniture and related products	39.9	40.0	40.3	40.9	39.8	40.0	39.3	39.3	39.4	39.6	39.5
Miscellaneous manufacturing	38.9	39.2	40.1	40.2	40.1	40.8	39.9	39.5	39.7	38.4	39.6
Nondurable goods [1]	4.0	4.1	4.3	4.3	4.3	4.1	4.2	4.4	4.2	3.8	4.1
Overtime hours	4.0	4.1	4.3	4.3	4.3	4.1	4.2	4.4	4.2	3.8	4.1
Food manufacturing	40.2	40.6	40.8	40.8	41.0	41.4	41.7	42.0	41.5	41.3	41.5
Textile mills	41.7	42.6	41.5	41.5	42.5	41.2	40.6	42.3	43.5	43.7	46.2
Textile product mills	39.1	39.7	38.4	38.0	37.0	37.7	38.4	39.3	37.8	38.5	39.5
Apparel	38.2	37.1	38.1	38.5	38.2	36.4	36.5	37.7	37.0	36.6	38.7
Paper and paper products	42.9	42.9	43.1	43.7	43.0	42.7	42.5	43.1	42.1	42.4	43.5
Printing and related support activities	38.0	38.5	38.6	39.0	39.8	39.2	39.5	39.3	38.8	38.1	39.1
Chemicals	42.5	42.4	42.9	42.7	42.6	41.8	41.7	42.1	41.8	40.9	41.3
Plastics and rubber products	42.0	41.8	41.9	42.3	42.5	42.4	42.5	42.1	41.0	39.5	40.6
Private Service-Providing	32.4	32.5	32.4	32.4	32.4	32.3	32.4	32.5	32.4	32.8	33.1
Trade, transportation, and utilities	33.7	33.8	33.7	33.6	33.7	33.5	33.8	33.9	33.8	34.1	34.3
Wholesale trade	38.5	38.7	38.7	38.6	38.6	38.6	39.0	38.9	38.7	38.2	38.8
Retail trade	30.5	30.6	30.2	30.0	30.1	29.7	30.2	30.4	30.3	30.8	30.8
Transportation and warehousing	37.8	38.0	38.5	38.4	38.7	38.8	38.4	38.4	37.9	38.3	38.5
Utilities	42.1	41.1	41.7	42.3	42.4	42.5	42.5	42.7	42.4	42.6	42.5
Information	36.2	36.0	35.9	35.9	35.7	35.5	35.8	35.6	35.3	36.0	36.5
Financial activities	36.4	36.8	36.7	36.7	37.1	36.9	37.0	37.0	36.9	37.1	37.2
Professional and business services	35.2	35.3	35.4	35.6	35.5	35.4	35.4	35.4	35.4	35.8	36.2
Education and health services	32.2	32.3	32.1	32.0	32.1	32.2	32.2	32.2	32.2	32.5	32.6
Leisure and hospitality	24.8	25.0	25.0	25.1	25.1	24.9	24.9	24.9	24.7	24.1	24.9
Other services	30.8	30.7	30.8	30.7	30.7	30.8	30.7	30.8	30.8	31.2	31.4

[1] Includes other industries, not shown separately.

Table 15-4. Average Hourly Earnings of Production and Nonsupervisory Workers on Private Nonfarm Payrolls by Industry

(Dollars.)

Industry	2000	2001	2002	2003	2004	2005	2006	2007	2008	2009	2010
Total Private	14.01	14.54	14.96	15.36	15.68	16.12	16.74	17.41	18.06	18.60	19.04
Goods-Producing	15.27	15.78	16.33	16.80	17.19	17.60	18.02	18.67	19.33	19.90	20.28
Mining and logging	16.55	17.00	17.19	17.56	18.07	18.72	19.90	20.97	22.50	23.29	23.82
Construction	17.48	18.00	18.52	18.95	19.23	19.46	20.02	20.95	21.87	22.66	23.22
Manufacturing	14.32	14.76	15.29	15.74	16.14	16.56	16.81	17.26	17.75	18.24	18.61
Excluding overtime [1]	13.55	14.06	14.54	14.96	15.29	15.68	15.96	16.43	16.97	17.59	17.78
Durable goods	14.93	15.38	16.02	16.45	16.82	17.33	17.68	18.20	18.70	19.36	19.81
Wood products	11.63	11.99	12.33	12.71	13.03	13.16	13.39	13.68	14.19	14.92	14.85
Nonmetallic mineral products	14.53	14.86	15.39	15.76	16.25	16.61	16.59	16.93	16.90	17.28	17.48
Primary metals	16.64	17.06	17.68	18.13	18.57	18.94	19.36	19.66	20.19	20.10	20.13
Fabricated metal products	13.77	14.19	14.68	15.01	15.31.	15.80	16.17	16.53	16.99	17.48	17.94
Machinery	15.21	15.48	15.92	16.29	16.67	17.02	17.20	17.72	17.97	18.38	18.96
Computer and electronic products	14.73	15.42	16.20	16.68	17.27	18.39	18.94	19.94	21.04	21.87	22.78
Electrical equipment and appliances	13.23	13.78	13.98	14.36	14.90	15.24	15.53	15.93	15.78	16.27	16.87
Transportation equipment [2]	18.89	19.47	20.63	21.22	21.48	22.09	22.41	23.03	23.85	24.98	25.23
Motor vehicles and parts	19.11	19.66	21.09	21.68	21.71	22.26	22.13	22.00	22.21	21.86	22.02
Furniture and related products	11.73	12.14	12.62	12.99	13.16	13.45	13.80	14.32	14.54	15.04	15.06
Miscellaneous manufacturing	11.93	12.45	12.91	13.30	13.84	14.07	14.36	14.66	15.20	16.13	16.56
Nondurable goods [2]	13.31	13.75	14.15	14.63	15.05	15.27	15.33	15.67	16.15	16.56	16.80
Food manufacturing	11.77	12.18	12.55	12.80	12.98	13.04	13.13	13.55	14.00	14.39	14.41
Textile mills	11.23	11.40	11.73	11.99	12.13	12.38	12.55	13.00	13.58	13.71	13.56
Textile product mills	10.31	10.49	10.85	11.15	11.31	11.61	11.86	11.78	11.73	11.44	11.79
Apparel	8.61	8.83	9.11	9.58	9.77	10.26	10.65	11.05	11.40	11.37	11.43
Paper and paper products	15.91	16.38	16.85	17.33	17.91	17.99	18.01	18.44	18.89	19.29	20.04
Printing and related support activities	14.09	14.48	14.93	15.37	15.71	15.74	15.80	16.15	16.75	16.75	16.91
Chemicals	17.09	17.57	17.97	18.50	19.17	19.67	19.60	19.55	19.50	20.30	21.07
Plastics and rubber products	12.70	13.21	13.55	14.18	14.59	14.80	14.97	15.39	15.85	16.01	15.71
Private Service-Providing	13.62	14.18	14.58	14.98	15.28	15.72	16.40	17.09	17.75	18.33	18.78
Trade, transportation, and utilities	13.28	13.68	13.99	14.31	14.55	14.90	15.36	15.74	16.13	16.44	16.78
Wholesale trade	16.24	16.74	16.94	17.33	17.62	18.13	18.87	19.54	20.08	20.78	21.46
Retail trade	10.87	11.30	11.67	11.90	12.09	12.36	12.58	12.76	12.87	13.02	13.25
Transportation and warehousing	15.00	15.27	15.71	16.20	16.46	16.65	17.21	17.67	18.36	18.74	19.10
Utilities	22.75	23.58	23.96	24.77	25.61	26.68	27.40	27.88	28.83	29.48	30.04
Information	19.07	19.80	20.20	21.01	21.40	22.06	23.23	23.96	24.78	25.45	25.87
Financial activities	15.04	15.65	16.25	17.21	17.58	17.98	18.83	19.67	20.32	20.90	21.55
Professional and business services	15.53	16.34	16.82	17.22	17.49	18.09	19.14	20.16	21.19	22.36	22.80
Education and health services	13.91	14.58	15.15	15.56	16.07	16.62	17.28	17.99	18.73	19.34	19.95
Leisure and hospitality	8.32	8.57	8.81	9.00	9.15	9.38	9.75	10.41	10.84	11.12	11.31
Other services	12.73	13.27	13.72	13.84	13.98	14.34	14.77	15.42	16.09	16.59	17.06

[1]Derived by assuming that overtime hours are paid at the rate of time and one-half.
[2]Includes other industries, not shown separately.

Table 15-4. Average Hourly Earnings of Production and Nonsupervisory Workers on Private Nonfarm Payrolls by Industry—*Continued*

(Dollars.)

Industry	2011	2012	2013	2014	2015	2016	2017	2018	2019	2020	2021
Total Private	19.43	19.73	20.13	20.60	21.03	21.53	22.05	22.71	23.51	24.68	25.89
Goods-Producing	20.67	20.94	21.24	21.59	21.96	22.58	23.18	24.00	24.75	25.41	26.49
Mining and logging	24.50	25.79	26.80	26.84	26.48	26.97	27.44	28.27	29.92	30.42	31.08
Construction	23.65	23.97	24.22	24.67	25.20	25.97	26.74	27.75	28.52	29.21	30.48
Manufacturing	18.93	19.08	19.30	19.56	19.91	20.44	20.90	21.54	22.15	22.80	23.80
Excluding overtime [1]	18.03	18.16	18.34	18.57	18.93	19.43	19.87	20.42	21.07	21.80	22.68
Durable goods	20.11	20.18	20.35	20.66	20.97	21.48	21.89	22.51	23.08	23.76	24.83
Wood products	14.81	14.99	15.47	15.57	16.16	16.81	17.47	17.88	18.50	19.18	19.97
Nonmetallic mineral products	18.16	18.15	18.40	19.16	19.92	20.30	20.34	21.41	22.10	22.67	23.90
Primary metals	19.94	20.70	21.94	22.41	22.47	23.10	23.10	23.31	23.44	23.96	24.86
Fabricated metal products	18.13	18.26	18.35	18.68	19.02	19.66	20.15	20.55	21.29	22.16	23.04
Machinery	19.54	20.17	20.58	21.00	21.34	21.80	22.41	23.06	23.82	24.62	25.25
Computer and electronic products	23.32	23.34	23.41	23.36	23.30	24.27	24.58	25.09	25.20	25.59	27.00
Electrical equipment and appliances	17.96	18.03	18.04	18.28	18.85	19.29	19.72	20.59	20.42	20.59	22.14
Transportation equipment [2]	25.34	24.57	24.57	24.96	25.05	25.06	25.36	26.31	27.16	28.03	29.36
Motor vehicles and parts	21.93	21.27	21.08	21.38	21.49	21.59	21.72	22.76	23.51	23.80	25.24
Furniture and related products	15.24	15.46	15.59	15.67	16.09	16.82	17.52	17.87	18.34	19.01	19.67
Miscellaneous manufacturing	16.82	17.05	17.03	17.31	17.72	18.44	19.04	19.15	19.62	20.77	21.61
Nondurable goods [2]	17.06	17.29	17.56	17.75	18.16	18.74	19.32	19.95	20.60	21.28	22.19
Food manufacturing	14.63	15.02	15.44	15.55	15.90	16.52	16.92	17.49	18.19	18.90	19.96
Textile mills	13.79	13.51	13.90	14.15	14.72	15.71	15.97	16.46	16.59	17.46	18.85
Textile product mills	12.21	12.77	12.88	13.35	13.31	13.64	14.80	15.31	15.52	16.03	16.94
Apparel	11.96	12.89	13.21	13.51	13.65	13.73	14.35	15.33	15.92	16.90	17.46
Paper and paper products	20.28	20.42	20.32	20.35	21.46	21.71	21.75	21.89	22.47	23.32	23.33
Printing and related support activities	17.28	17.28	17.77	18.01	18.31	18.59	18.61	18.74	18.98	20.06	20.89
Chemicals	21.45	21.45	21.40	21.49	21.76	22.71	24.29	25.46	25.46	26.03	26.69
Plastics and rubber products	15.95	16.05	16.20	16.51	16.82	17.17	17.63	18.49	19.38	20.20	21.62
Private Service-Providing	19.17	19.48	19.90	20.39	20.83	21.31	21.82	22.44	23.25	24.53	25.77
Trade, transportation, and utilities	17.10	17.38	17.69	18.21	18.61	18.93	19.29	19.88	20.63	21.41	22.41
Wholesale trade	21.88	22.13	22.52	23.14	23.52	24.07	24.58	25.17	26.06	26.81	27.76
Retail trade	13.52	13.82	14.03	14.40	14.83	15.05	15.33	15.91	16.62	17.60	18.54
Transportation and warehousing	19.42	19.47	19.73	20.43	20.66	20.83	21.22	21.75	22.36	22.71	23.90
Utilities	30.82	31.61	32.27	32.86	34.02	35.33	36.22	36.76	36.91	38.46	39.97
Information	26.62	27.04	27.98	28.70	29.05	30.05	30.74	31.97	33.93	35.74	36.82
Financial activities	21.93	22.82	23.87	24.71	25.34	26.12	26.57	26.93	27.68	29.09	30.34
Professional and business services	23.14	23.31	23.74	24.31	24.81	25.43	26.05	26.82	27.79	29.25	30.56
Education and health services	20.60	20.91	21.29	21.64	22.09	22.52	23.03	23.64	24.34	25.40	27.12
Leisure and hospitality	11.45	11.62	11.78	12.09	12.41	12.85	13.38	13.87	14.50	14.71	16.17
Other services	17.32	17.59	18.00	18.51	19.01	19.36	20.10	20.78	21.40	22.58	23.65

[1]Derived by assuming that overtime hours are paid at the rate of time and one-half.
[2]Includes other industries, not shown separately.

Table 15-5. Average Weekly Earnings of Production and Nonsupervisory Workers on Private Nonfarm Payrolls by Industry

(Dollars.)

Industry	2000	2001	2002	2003	2004	2005	2006	2007	2008	2009	2010
Total Private	480.90	493.53	506.48	517.68	528.65	543.94	566.94	589.09	607.10	615.82	636.02
Goods-Producing	621.86	629.88	651.65	669.13	688.14	705.28	730.16	757.50	776.63	779.68	819.14
Mining and logging	734.88	757.96	741.97	765.94	804.01	853.87	907.95	962.63	1 014.69	1 006.67	1 063.11
Construction	685.78	695.86	711.82	727.00	735.55	750.37	781.59	816.23	842.61	851.76	891.83
Manufacturing	590.92	595.15	618.62	636.03	658.49	673.34	690.88	711.53	724.46	726.12	765.18
Durable goods	624.38	624.38	652.97	671.35	694.03	712.85	731.93	754.73	767.92	771.08	819.06
Wood products	476.97	481.36	491.96	514.06	530.12	526.65	533.00	539.30	547.65	557.68	580.65
Nonmetallic mineral products	604.76	618.91	647.00	664.96	688.33	700.63	712.67	716.78	711.11	705.54	728.22
Primary metals	734.83	723.86	749.17	767.15	799.69	815.90	843.79	843.42	851.12	817.70	880.46
Fabricated metal products	576.68	576.60	596.30	610.44	628.83	647.24	668.91	687.16	701.57	689.22	742.61
Machinery	643.94	632.72	645.38	664.44	699.45	716.13	728.81	754.34	760.27	738.06	797.62
Computer and electronic products	609.97	613.18	642.77	674.69	697.97	735.59	766.75	809.10	861.58	883.02	932.26
Electrical equipment and appliances	550.48	548.03	560.33	583.27	607.00	618.88	637.04	656.46	645.60	639.34	693.49
Transportation equipment [1]	817.56	816.74	877.50	889.42	912.56	937.72	957.47	986.75	1 000.87	1 028.51	1 081.60
Motor vehicles and parts	828.41	818.84	898.57	910.20	925.07	940.54	934.38	930.47	920.36	876.34	956.39
Furniture and related products	459.82	464.76	494.06	505.75	519.72	527.57	535.90	560.93	554.05	566.75	579.69
Miscellaneous manufacturing	464.80	483.07	499.01	510.54	533.27	545.01	555.87	570.12	591.95	620.74	640.85
Nondurable goods [1]	536.89	548.30	566.75	582.48	602.53	609.08	622.00	640.12	652.22	658.40	685.07
Food manufacturing	472.09	481.81	497.25	502.92	509.55	508.55	526.02	551.21	566.88	575.40	586.52
Textile mills	464.51	456.64	476.52	469.33	486.68	498.47	509.39	524.40	525.00	516.86	559.13
Textile product mills	398.93	402.53	423.05	438.67	437.89	451.36	472.10	467.80	453.06	433.09	459.46
Apparel	307.51	317.63	334.24	340.73	352.04	366.93	389.05	411.57	415.10	408.86	418.28
Paper and paper products	681.38	689.76	705.20	719.55	754.17	764.15	772.57	795.58	809.57	806.19	858.65
Printing and related support activities	552.15	560.89	573.05	587.58	603.97	604.73	618.92	632.02	642.50	635.68	646.11
Petroleum and coal products	721.41	735.57	759.56	784.26	819.93	831.79	833.84	819.51	809.29	841.18	888.25
Chemicals	517.60	528.95	550.06	572.60	590.08	591.68	608.69	635.57	649.41	643.81	658.39
Plastics and rubber products	445.66	460.97	473.61	484.32	493.95	509.00	532.11	554.05	573.23	587.37	604.91
Private Service-Providing	448.78	458.58	469.97	480.00	487.37	497.07	512.82	524.57	534.44	540.19	558.05
Trade, transportation, and utilities	630.09	642.08	643.40	656.36	665.96	683.99	717.42	747.08	768.14	782.62	814.04
Wholesale trade	333.48	346.31	360.92	367.28	371.23	377.58	383.25	385.18	386.44	388.74	400.38
Retail trade	559.63	559.22	576.77	594.70	611.99	615.26	633.23	651.78	667.57	674.19	707.93
Transportation and warehousing	955.09	977.25	979.26	1 017.44	1 048.01	1 095.91	1 135.57	1 182.65	1 230.65	1 239.34	1 262.89
Utilities	700.92	731.18	737.94	760.84	776.72	805.11	850.64	874.45	908.78	931.08	939.85
Information	540.42	560.46	579.08	611.99	625.50	646.51	673.66	706.52	729.64	754.90	780.25
Financial activities	535.56	558.32	575.00	587.68	597.88	619.65	662.80	701.42	738.31	776.30	799.43
Professional and business services	447.80	471.33	490.38	503.05	521.06	541.40	561.02	585.44	607.82	622.30	639.37
Education and health services	217.20	220.73	227.31	230.49	234.86	241.36	250.34	265.54	273.39	275.95	280.87
Leisure and hospitality	413.30	428.64	439.87	434.41	433.04	443.40	456.50	477.06	495.57	506.26	523.70

[1]Includes other industries, not shown separately.

Table 15-5. Average Weekly Earnings of Production and Nonsupervisory Workers on Private Nonfarm Payrolls by Industry—*Continued*

(Dollars.)

Industry	2011	2012	2013	2014	2015	2016	2017	2018	2019	2020	2021
Total Private	652.72	665.54	677.62	694.74	708.70	723.20	742.48	766.99	790.44	837.39	886.06
Goods-Producing	844.85	861.39	877.09	895.09	905.43	930.34	956.83	996.67	1 017.95	1 023.63	1 082.40
Mining and logging	1 144.64	1 201.69	1 229.70	1 270.91	1 211.91	1 221.69	1 265.92	1 322.45	1 402.39	1 365.39	1 443.70
Construction	921.84	942.14	958.72	977.11	998.02	1 031.88	1 061.98	1 108.59	1 135.73	1 145.52	1 203.77
Manufacturing	784.29	794.67	807.41	822.03	832.22	855.77	876.10	908.01	921.87	928.94	985.92
Durable goods	841.85	848.35	859.69	877.31	882.91	909.23	926.85	956.74	968.46	972.07	1 030.08
Wood products	587.77	615.91	661.23	653.87	666.82	703.34	735.06	749.60	767.71	799.15	840.21
Nonmetallic mineral products	768.35	766.16	782.69	829.79	844.77	852.66	873.01	947.10	968.08	983.01	1 018.56
Primary metals	889.34	907.23	960.61	991.13	984.77	1 003.42	995.41	1 038.42	1 026.93	1 007.46	1 072.81
Fabricated metal products	762.14	767.52	775.35	795.62	804.67	827.74	849.82	866.83	886.87	901.91	953.02
Machinery	843.10	863.99	883.03	903.42	894.61	918.23	957.16	985.50	1 010.06	1 009.82	1 051.28
Computer and electronic products	943.88	944.02	948.79	952.82	953.04	999.76	1 012.10	1 026.63	1 021.57	1 022.92	1 089.19
Electrical equipment and appliances	732.16	749.91	753.07	763.08	794.79	827.24	850.47	877.69	846.07	837.40	933.75
Transportation equipment [1]	1 094.46	1 075.00	1 070.88	1 088.27	1 094.01	1 105.96	1 113.99	1 167.96	1 178.81	1 165.23	1 239.89
Motor vehicles and parts	952.34	940.00	920.56	936.90	948.30	964.46	956.61	1 017.15	1 019.34	1 007.88	1 059.51
Furniture and related products	608.22	617.83	628.35	641.43	640.27	672.64	689.31	702.49	722.58	752.53	776.97
Miscellaneous manufacturing	654.90	668.95	682.97	695.67	709.56	751.91	759.06	756.91	778.42	797.76	856.42
Nondurable goods [1]	696.00	710.16	723.82	733.64	751.05	771.40	798.20	829.80	846.35	862.57	917.15
Food manufacturing	588.19	609.69	629.70	634.95	652.26	683.74	705.82	734.72	754.14	780.53	829.17
Textile mills	574.61	575.75	577.18	586.40	625.84	647.60	648.43	696.84	722.32	762.86	871.25
Textile product mills	477.49	507.00	494.76	507.19	493.03	513.89	568.47	602.46	587.20	617.57	668.33
Apparel	456.97	478.33	503.01	520.57	520.73	499.82	524.59	578.04	589.21	618.11	676.00
Paper and paper products	870.53	877.14	874.85	888.07	923.13	926.10	924.75	942.38	945.46	989.14	1 014.71
Printing and related support activities	655.81	665.45	685.33	701.55	729.57	728.41	734.43	736.06	736.74	764.71	817.37
Petroleum and coal products	910.88	910.02	918.69	917.96	927.83	950.00	1 012.35	1 071.90	1 064.44	1 063.37	1 101.19
Chemicals	669.70	670.94	678.38	697.81	713.84	728.44	750.04	778.83	794.71	797.23	878.29
Plastics and rubber products	620.78	632.87	644.65	661.42	675.83	689.13	707.04	728.42	752.56	805.56	853.00
Private Service-Providing	575.88	587.09	595.36	611.77	626.54	633.77	652.11	674.74	697.95	730.52	769.17
Trade, transportation, and utilities	842.06	857.06	871.89	894.06	907.72	929.09	957.95	979.82	1 007.42	1 023.97	1 078.17
Wholesale trade	412.29	422.35	423.44	431.97	446.01	447.69	463.10	483.03	503.06	542.14	571.02
Retail trade	734.06	739.12	758.79	785.50	800.14	807.25	813.69	835.39	847.97	870.19	920.68
Transportation and warehousing	1 296.92	1 298.23	1 344.70	1 388.91	1 444.03	1 502.09	1 540.27	1 569.38	1 566.91	1 639.19	1 699.88
Utilities	964.85	973.52	1 003.65	1 030.17	1 038.10	1 068.23	1 100.03	1 139.52	1 198.97	1 288.27	1 342.87
Information	798.68	839.84	875.04	908.15	939.46	962.95	982.09	997.26	1 020.44	1 078.50	1 130.07
Financial activities	814.74	823.37	839.86	865.25	879.63	899.79	922.51	949.18	984.35	1 047.43	1 105.72
Professional and business services	663.04	674.48	683.24	692.56	709.25	723.91	741.55	761.86	783.66	824.72	885.33
Education and health services	283.82	290.54	294.31	303.81	311.32	319.67	332.54	345.21	358.27	354.77	402.79
Leisure and hospitality	532.63	539.46	553.77	568.92	583.54	595.68	617.91	640.70	659.07	705.74	742.14

[1]Includes other industries, not shown separately.

Table 15-6. Indexes of Aggregate Weekly Hours of Production and Nonsupervisory Workers on Private Nonfarm Payrolls by Industry

(2002 = 100.)

Industry	2000	2001	2002	2003	2004	2005	2006	2007	2008	2009	2010
Total Private	103.5	102.0	100.0	98.7	100.2	102.8	105.8	107.4	106.0	98.8	99.0
Goods-Producing	113.1	106.5	100.0	95.7	96.8	98.9	102.5	101.7	96.5	80.2	78.9
Mining and logging	105.1	108.3	100.0	97.4	104.0	114.7	125.8	133.5	137.6	117.2	124.5
Construction	104.0	103.2	100.0	98.4	101.7	108.3	115.4	114.7	106.5	85.9	80.2
Manufacturing	117.7	108.1	100.0	94.5	94.3	93.9	95.6	94.4	90.2	76.1	76.2
Durable goods	120.4	109.3	100.0	94.3	95.2	96.1	98.9	97.4	92.2	74.7	75.0
Wood products	115.8	105.0	100.0	97.8	100.8	101.2	99.9	89.3	76.8	57.8	58.5
Nonmetallic mineral products	109.1	106.1	100.0	94.3	98.0	97.4	100.3	96.9	91.2	73.8	70.5
Primary metals	128.9	113.0	100.0	93.4	93.3	93.1	94.2	91.4	87.4	66.1	71.7
Fabricated metal products	119.2	109.3	100.0	95.3	97.7	99.3	103.1	104.5	101.3	81.3	83.1
Machinery	127.6	114.1	100.0	93.6	96.0	98.8	102.2	103.3	102.3	80.7	81.2
Computer and electronic products	133.1	117.9	100.0	92.1	89.8	94.8	103.6	102.2	101.2	89.4	87.2
Electrical equipment and appliances	127.7	113.4	100.0	92.0	88.7	86.4	88.0	89.1	88.5	74.1	73.2
Transportation equipment [1]	116.3	105.3	100.0	95.5	96.5	97.3	99.9	98.0	88.6	70.1	72.1
Motor vehicles and parts	117.3	103.6	100.0	95.9	97.0	95.2	92.9	85.8	72.7	51.6	57.5
Furniture and related products	114.7	104.8	100.0	93.0	94.3	91.9	90.4	86.1	74.6	57.6	54.4
Miscellaneous manufacturing	109.5	104.7	100.0	93.6	91.8	90.6	90.4	91.0	89.2	81.1	79.0
Nondurable goods [1]	113.3	106.0	100.0	94.7	92.7	90.3	90.4	89.7	86.9	78.1	78.0
Food manufacturing	103.4	101.4	100.0	98.4	97.1	95.8	98.6	101.1	100.6	97.5	98.5
Textile mills	132.4	112.2	100.0	86.3	79.0	71.3	65.1	56.3	47.9	37.8	40.2
Textile product mills	112.3	105.5	100.0	92.4	90.2	88.0	85.0	77.5	70.5	58.5	56.5
Apparel	137.5	117.1	100.0	81.9	75.1	65.7	63.4	61.5	56.7	45.4	42.0
Paper and paper products	113.5	106.6	100.0	92.5	89.2	88.0	86.9	85.8	83.5	74.2	73.5
Printing and related support activities	119.4	111.5	100.0	95.3	93.4	90.9	92.5	91.6	86.1	74.1	69.0
Petroleum and coal products	110.4	104.7	100.0	99.0	99.0	95.9	96.1	94.1	94.6	88.3	88.9
Chemicals	114.2	105.0	100.0	95.2	94.2	92.4	92.0	91.1	87.2	71.3	73.6
Plastics and rubber products	100.9	100.8	100.0	99.5	101.1	103.8	106.7	108.9	108.6	104.1	104.5
Private Service-Providing	103.6	101.6	100.0	98.6	99.6	101.6	103.2	104.8	103.2	96.7	96.8
Trade, transportation, and utilities	107.1	102.9	100.0	98.0	98.7	101.6	105.5	108.9	108.3	99.5	97.4
Wholesale trade	101.3	100.5	100.0	98.9	99.4	100.8	101.1	101.8	99.8	94.3	95.0
Retail trade	105.7	102.8	100.0	98.7	101.9	105.2	107.9	109.5	107.9	100.2	101.5
Transportation and warehousing	104.1	102.3	100.0	97.4	94.2	93.1	93.8	96.2	98.3	97.0	95.4
Utilities	105.0	106.7	100.0	97.0	98.2	99.4	100.2	100.1	100.0	93.5	90.0
Information	98.4	99.2	100.0	101.3	101.3	103.7	106.3	107.6	106.8	103.1	101.3
Financial activities	106.5	104.0	100.0	98.7	101.8	106.4	112.2	115.4	114.0	105.3	107.7
Professional and business services	92.6	96.5	100.0	101.7	103.8	107.0	109.6	113.2	116.5	118.3	119.8
Education and health services	100.5	100.6	100.0	100.0	103.0	106.2	108.8	110.8	109.7	105.1	104.6
Leisure and hospitality	97.8	99.0	100.0	97.4	96.1	96.2	97.4	99.3	99.5	96.0	96.0

[1]Includes other industries, not shown separately.

Table 15-6. Indexes of Aggregate Weekly Hours of Production and Nonsupervisory Workers on Private Nonfarm Payrolls by Industry—*Continued*

(2002 = 100.)

Industry	2011	2012	2013	2014	2015	2016	2017	2018	2019	2020	2021
Total Private	101.4	104.3	106.1	108.6	110.9	112.5	114.9	117.2	118.3	110.7	115.3
Goods-Producing	81.2	83.5	85.1	87.8	89.1	89.5	91.1	94.4	94.8	87.5	90.5
Mining and logging	147.4	158.7	155.0	164.3	144.1	113.4	120.2	134.5	133.3	101.5	103.2
Construction	81.7	83.6	87.7	92.0	96.5	100.9	104.0	108.8	111.2	105.4	108.5
Manufacturing	78.3	80.3	80.9	82.6	83.3	83.3	84.0	86.1	85.6	78.8	81.6
Durable goods	78.4	81.4	82.3	84.3	84.6	84.3	84.5	87.2	87.2	78.9	81.8
Wood products	59.3	62.2	67.3	69.6	70.2	72.0	72.9	74.4	74.2	71.8	75.2
Nonmetallic mineral products	70.1	68.9	69.7	72.4	75.0	76.7	78.1	82.1	81.6	76.5	75.8
Primary metals	80.1	82.7	79.8	81.7	80.1	75.8	74.9	78.4	78.8	68.1	69.2
Fabricated metal products	89.6	94.7	96.4	97.9	97.0	93.6	94.6	98.4	98.9	88.7	89.8
Machinery	89.6	94.0	94.0	96.6	93.4	90.6	92.5	95.9	94.3	82.4	85.7
Computer and electronic products	86.4	86.0	83.7	81.4	82.3	83.1	83.4	84.9	87.6	86.7	86.7
Electrical equipment and appliances	71.6	73.4	72.4	73.5	77.2	78.6	77.3	78.8	77.0	71.6	77.1
Transportation equipment [1]	75.3	80.4	82.4	86.3	89.3	91.1	90.6	94.7	93.4	80.6	86.6
Motor vehicles and parts	60.9	66.6	70.7	76.2	79.8	83.2	83.6	87.9	84.0	70.7	77.4
Furniture and related products	55.8	55.6	57.6	60.7	60.8	61.6	61.3	61.3	61.0	55.5	57.5
Miscellaneous manufacturing	80.0	82.2	85.3	86.3	84.9	85.8	83.8	83.7	86.3	77.9	83.9
Nondurable goods [1]	77.9	78.6	78.6	80.0	81.2	81.6	83.1	84.2	82.9	78.6	81.2
Food manufacturing	97.7	99.6	100.1	100.8	102.4	105.3	109.5	112.2	112.3	110.5	112.5
Textile mills	41.6	41.7	39.0	38.4	39.1	37.8	36.3	37.4	37.6	32.5	35.2
Textile product mills	55.2	53.3	50.5	51.5	51.5	53.3	54.1	53.2	46.8	42.8	46.9
Apparel	40.7	38.4	38.5	38.0	37.8	34.3	30.5	29.4	26.2	22.6	24.8
Paper and paper products	71.9	70.0	68.2	68.5	67.5	66.6	67.0	67.1	64.8	62.9	63.2
Printing and related support activities	65.6	64.3	63.2	64.2	65.2	64.6	63.7	61.4	58.5	51.2	52.3
Petroleum and coal products	90.6	92.6	93.6	94.4	96.1	96.1	97.4	102.3	103.9	97.6	99.1
Chemicals	75.3	75.8	77.4	81.4	84.0	84.7	86.0	85.9	83.7	76.3	80.1
Plastics and rubber products	107.0	110.0	112.0	114.5	117.0	118.9	121.5	123.5	124.8	117.1	122.1
Private Service-Providing	99.7	101.8	102.6	104.4	106.3	106.9	109.2	110.8	110.9	107.4	112.3
Trade, transportation, and utilities	100.2	103.5	104.8	106.4	106.4	106.2	107.8	108.3	108.5	101.6	104.1
Wholesale trade	97.7	98.9	98.8	99.5	101.0	101.1	103.1	103.6	102.1	98.8	102.4
Retail trade	105.7	109.5	112.8	117.0	123.3	126.9	130.6	137.4	142.1	142.7	155.3
Transportation and warehousing	94.9	92.6	94.9	96.3	97.0	97.1	97.2	96.9	95.6	94.1	93.6
Utilities	88.9	88.9	89.8	90.5	90.8	91.4	92.6	93.0	93.0	88.7	93.4
Information	101.1	103.7	104.7	106.5	109.6	111.6	114.3	116.0	117.5	116.2	116.1
Financial activities	112.6	117.3	121.4	125.9	128.3	130.2	132.6	135.2	137.0	130.7	138.1
Professional and business services	122.3	125.4	126.6	128.5	132.3	136.1	139.8	142.7	145.7	141.1	143.9
Education and health services	106.9	111.3	115.2	119.3	122.7	125.6	128.7	130.6	131.9	99.9	111.1
Leisure and hospitality	96.8	97.7	98.7	99.9	100.7	101.8	102.9	104.4	105.3	95.1	97.1

[1]Includes other industries, not shown separately.

NOTES AND DEFINITIONS, CHAPTER 15

Tables 15-1 through 15-6

Employment, Hours, and Earnings by NAICS Industry

SOURCE: U.S. DEPARTMENT OF LABOR, BUREAU OF LABOR STATISTICS

See the notes and definitions for Tables 10-8 through 10-18 regarding definitions of *employment, production and nonsupervisory workers, average weekly hours, overtime hours, average hourly earnings, average weekly earnings*, and the *indexes of aggregate weekly hours*. Availability and reference information is also provided in those notes and definitions.

Definitions

The North American Industry Classification System (NAICS) is the standard used by Federal statistical agencies in classifying business establishments for the purpose of collecting, analyzing, and publishing statistical data related to the U.S. business economy. NAICS defines industries according to a consistent principle: businesses that use similar production processes are grouped together.

NAICS is the product of a cooperative effort on the part of the statistical agencies of the United States, Canada, and Mexico. This system is the hierarchical, numerical system used by the Federal government to classify businesses by industry, in order to collect, analyze, and publish statistical data related to the U.S. business economy.

There are 20 high-level industrial sections and are listed below.

Sector	Description
11	Agriculture, Forestry, Fishing and Hunting
21	Mining, Quarrying, and Oil and Gas Extraction
22	Utilities
23	Construction
31-33	Manufacturing
42	Wholesale Trade
44-45	Retail Trade
48-49	Transportation and Warehousing
51	Information
52	Finance and Insurance
53	Real Estate and Rental and Leasing
54	Professional, Scientific, and Technical Services
55	Management of Companies and Enterprises
56	Administrative and Support and Waste Management and Remediation Services
61	Educational Services
62	Health Care and Social Assistance
71	Arts, Entertainment, and Recreation
72	Accommodation and Food Services
81	Other Services (except Public Administration)
92	Public Administration *(not covered in economic census)*

CHAPTER 16: KEY SECTOR STATISTICS

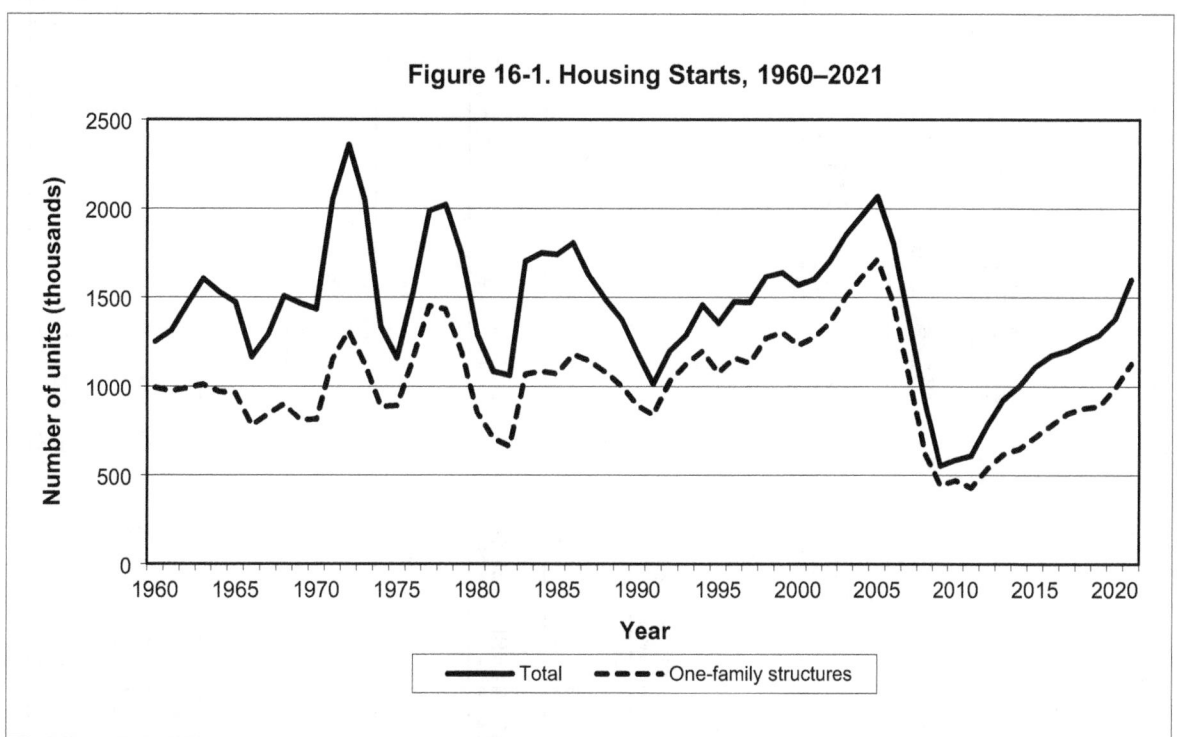

Figure 16-1. Housing Starts, 1960–2021

- The housing sector and associated financial excesses had the leading role in the boom and bust cycle of 2001–2009. In 2005, as shown in Figure 16-1, nearly 2.1 million housing units were started, the highest since 1972. Of those, 1.7 million were one-family homes, an all-time record. By 2009, both total and single-family starts had plunged to the lowest levels of their 50-year history. With very modest recovery in the years following 2009, starts remained at levels once viewed as recessionary. By 2021, the housing starts nearly tripled the 2009 low—to 1.6 million. (Table 16-2)

- New orders for nondefense capital goods excluding aircraft and parts at U.S. manufacturing firms is a widely followed advance indicator for production of investment goods. The value of such orders fell significantly from 2000 to 2002 and again from 2007 to 2009. The recovery in the four years following 2009 was faster than it was in the four years following 2002. The value of new orders in 2013 surpassed the peak in 2008 but declined nearly thirteen percent from 2013 to 2020. In 2021, nondefense capital goods, excluding aircraft and parts, increased 12.4 percent. (Table 16-5)

- E-commerce grew from 3.6 percent of total retail sales at the beginning of 2008 to 14.9 percent (seasonally adjusted) at the beginning of 2021. E-commerce was one sector of the economy that grew significantly during the global pandemic. E-commerce sales increased from 11.9 percent of sales in the first quarter of 2020 to 16.4 percent of sales in the second quarter of 2020. (Table 16-9)

- Sales of new passenger cars dropped to its lowest rate in decades in 2021, marking seven consecutive years in which sales have declined. (Table 16-7)

Table 16-1. New Construction Put in Place

(Billions of dollars, monthly data are at seasonally adjusted annual rates.)

Year and month	Total	Private Total¹	Residential	Office	Commercial Total¹	Commercial Multi-retail	Health care	Educational	Amusement and recreation	Transportation	Communication	Power	Manufacturing
1980	273.9	210.3	100.4	...	...	...	...	...	...	...	...	...	...
1981	289.1	224.4	99.2	...	...	...	...	...	...	...	...	...	...
1982	279.3	216.3	84.7	...	...	...	...	...	...	...	...	...	...
1983	311.9	248.4	125.8	...	...	...	...	...	...	...	...	...	...
1984	370.2	300.0	155.0	...	...	...	...	...	...	...	...	...	...
1985	403.4	325.6	160.5	...	...	...	...	...	...	...	...	...	...
1986	433.5	348.9	190.7	...	...	...	...	...	...	...	...	...	...
1987	446.6	356.0	199.7	...	...	...	...	...	...	...	...	...	...
1988	462.0	367.3	204.5	...	...	...	...	...	...	...	...	...	...
1989	477.5	379.3	204.3	...	...	...	...	...	...	...	...	...	...
1990	476.8	369.3	191.1	...	...	...	...	...	...	...	...	...	...
1991	432.6	322.5	166.3	...	...	...	...	...	...	...	...	...	...
1992	463.7	347.8	199.4	...	...	...	...	...	...	...	...	...	...
1993	485.5	358.2	208.2	20.0	34.4	11.5	14.9	4.8	4.6	4.7	9.8	23.6	23.4
1994	531.9	401.5	241.0	20.4	39.6	12.2	15.4	5.0	5.1	4.7	10.1	21.0	28.8
1995	548.7	408.7	228.1	23.0	44.1	12.0	15.3	5.7	5.9	4.8	11.1	22.0	35.4
1996	599.7	453.0	257.5	26.5	49.4	13.3	15.4	7.0	7.0	5.8	11.8	17.4	38.1
1997	631.9	478.4	264.7	32.8	53.1	12.2	17.4	8.8	8.5	6.2	12.5	16.4	37.6
1998	688.5	533.7	296.3	40.4	55.7	13.3	17.7	9.8	8.6	7.3	12.5	21.7	40.5
1999	744.6	575.5	326.3	45.1	59.4	15.2	18.4	9.8	9.6	6.5	18.4	22.0	35.1
2000	802.8	621.4	346.1	52.4	64.1	14.9	19.5	11.7	8.8	6.9	18.8	29.3	37.6
2001	840.2	638.3	364.4	49.7	63.6	16.4	19.5	12.8	7.8	7.1	19.6	31.5	37.8
2002	847.9	634.4	402.0	44.3	62.5	15.6	27.1	73.9	17.3	25.8	18.5	36.8	22.9
2003	891.5	675.4	451.3	39.4	61.5	15.4	29.3	74.3	16.8	24.7	14.6	41.5	21.5
2004	991.4	771.2	538.4	42.4	67.1	18.8	32.2	74.3	16.7	25.1	15.5	35.6	23.4
2005	1 116.8	882.7	624.6	37.3	66.6	22.8	28.5	12.8	7.5	7.1	18.8	29.2	28.4
2006	1 161.3	905.9	607.8	45.7	73.4	29.2	32.0	13.8	9.3	8.7	22.2	33.7	32.3
2007	1 148.0	858.9	488.8	53.8	85.9	34.8	35.6	16.7	10.2	9.0	27.5	54.1	40.2
2008	1 077.3	768.6	359.2	55.5	82.7	32.0	38.4	18.6	10.5	9.9	26.3	69.2	53.6
2009	911.8	596.9	252.8	37.3	51.1	18.4	35.3	16.9	8.4	9.1	19.7	76.1	57.4
2010	813.0	509.0	245.7	24.4	37.2	12.5	29.6	13.4	6.5	9.9	17.7	66.1	40.6
2011	791.2	504.8	247.0	23.7	39.2	13.4	28.9	14.1	6.7	9.5	17.5	64.3	39.8
2012	854.4	575.1	273.7	27.4	44.3	14.9	31.4	16.6	6.2	10.9	16.0	86.4	46.8
2013	914.6	643.9	329.6	30.1	50.9	16.7	29.7	16.9	6.9	11.0	17.6	81.3	51.8
2014	1 015.3	739.2	377.5	38.9	60.9	19.5	28.9	16.6	7.7	12.2	17.1	98.2	60.1
2015	1 140.2	846.4	431.8	47.9	64.5	20.0	30.9	17.7	10.0	13.6	21.5	99.5	82.4
2016	1 223.7	926.7	479.4	59.8	75.5	22.4	31.8	20.0	12.6	13.1	22.0	102.3	78.9
2017	1 279.8	983.3	539.0	59.9	84.5	24.0	33.5	21.2	14.5	14.8	23.6	89.8	70.0
2018	1 333.2	1 023.0	557.6	66.8	82.8	20.8	34.0	22.3	15.7	17.9	24.3	94.4	72.0
2019	1 391.0	1 046.7	546.6	77.5	80.3	14.6	36.8	21.6	15.8	17.2	22.1	110.4	80.5
2020	1 469.2	1 107.9	628.9	75.3	82.7	10.7	38.3	18.3	13.4	15.9	22.4	107.9	71.8
2021	1 591.7	1 245.4	776.2	70.7	87.6	10.1	38.8	15.9	11.8	15.1	21.7	105.9	78.1
2019													
January	1 304.4	983.1	519.6	72.6	77.5	16.3	35.5	22.3	15.7	19.6	22.3	83.7	77.7
February	1 321.9	989.4	520.0	72.2	75.8	15.6	35.4	22.0	16.1	18.7	21.8	88.2	81.5
March	1 335.7	1 001.6	521.7	74.2	76.3	15.4	36.1	22.4	16.1	18.0	22.4	94.2	82.3
April	1 363.6	1 010.0	527.3	75.3	75.1	14.0	35.2	21.7	16.0	15.9	22.4	100.1	82.3
May	1 368.7	1 024.1	532.9	76.4	77.4	15.0	35.7	21.3	15.6	16.8	21.9	107.6	80.7
June	1 385.3	1 041.9	541.7	75.3	80.4	15.1	36.2	21.1	15.6	16.6	21.8	113.2	81.3
July	1 409.1	1 061.5	552.0	80.7	80.8	14.6	37.1	21.7	15.2	16.9	21.8	115.8	81.1
August	1 419.3	1 073.5	556.7	82.7	82.0	13.9	36.3	22.0	16.0	17.6	22.2	119.3	80.4
September	1 427.9	1 076.4	559.6	79.5	82.3	14.0	37.4	21.9	15.9	17.8	22.2	122.6	80.3
October	1 429.8	1 080.8	561.3	80.2	84.0	14.0	37.6	21.3	15.9	17.0	22.0	124.2	79.3
November	1 450.2	1 099.1	572.4	80.6	86.9	14.5	39.2	21.1	16.3	16.4	21.9	124.5	81.5
December	1 458.5	1 101.5	581.5	79.5	83.9	13.0	39.3	20.8	15.5	16.0	22.8	125.6	78.8
2020													
January	1 486.4	1 118.5	591.5	82.1	88.3	12.8	39.1	20.5	15.1	16.1	22.6	127.4	77.5
February	1 501.6	1 130.2	609.7	81.9	88.3	12.9	39.1	20.1	15.1	16.5	22.4	122.6	76.2
March	1 507.1	1 132.4	617.6	83.0	87.9	12.4	39.9	19.8	15.1	16.4	22.7	117.4	76.3
April	1 452.4	1 086.2	597.7	76.5	85.8	11.6	38.7	18.4	13.9	16.3	22.9	109.7	71.8
May	1 437.7	1 063.3	584.2	75.9	84.1	10.7	37.8	18.6	13.5	16.1	22.6	105.6	71.5
June	1 435.0	1 070.9	590.4	76.3	84.9	10.2	39.3	18.5	12.7	16.2	22.5	106.2	70.9
July	1 439.6	1 083.6	608.6	74.3	81.2	10.0	38.9	18.4	13.0	16.1	22.7	105.3	72.8
August	1 455.0	1 098.9	632.7	73.0	79.2	10.1	38.2	17.6	12.7	15.4	22.4	104.2	72.1
September	1 459.3	1 107.1	648.3	72.5	78.2	9.9	36.9	17.3	12.6	15.5	22.6	102.6	69.1
October	1 471.7	1 120.1	664.1	71.3	79.9	9.7	37.7	17.1	12.7	15.4	21.9	99.9	69.7
November	1 487.2	1 131.8	684.5	69.5	78.7	9.4	37.1	17.1	12.4	15.3	21.6	98.1	68.0
December	1 504.2	1 147.0	704.8	69.0	77.2	9.3	36.5	16.6	11.8	15.5	21.8	100.0	65.9
2021													
January	1 549.8	1 194.6	731.2	71.3	80.3	9.1	38.9	15.9	11.7	15.9	21.9	109.0	70.8
February	1 533.3	1 187.6	729.3	68.2	80.6	8.6	36.6	15.7	11.4	15.8	21.9	110.3	71.2
March	1 548.6	1 203.7	745.0	69.3	82.1	8.6	36.8	15.7	11.4	15.2	22.1	108.0	71.4
April	1 553.5	1 209.8	752.8	69.4	83.1	9.4	37.8	15.3	11.0	14.5	21.7	106.3	72.0
May	1 564.2	1 223.1	762.9	69.8	85.0	9.7	38.0	14.8	11.5	15.5	21.6	104.8	75.3
June	1 579.3	1 240.7	780.7	69.9	85.7	9.9	38.3	14.7	11.3	15.6	21.6	105.2	74.6
July	1 581.1	1 239.3	775.9	70.0	87.3	10.4	39.6	15.1	11.7	15.1	21.5	105.6	74.6
August	1 596.8	1 249.6	780.5	71.7	89.6	10.4	38.9	15.5	12.0	14.8	21.6	104.3	78.6
September	1 612.3	1 264.7	791.1	71.3	90.7	10.8	39.2	16.2	12.0	14.6	21.6	104.9	81.6
October	1 626.4	1 273.7	795.3	71.2	90.7	10.9	39.0	16.5	12.5	14.5	21.8	104.7	85.5
November	1 643.0	1 290.8	801.6	72.0	94.9	10.8	40.2	17.0	12.4	15.2	21.9	104.5	89.1
December	1 668.7	1 319.7	827.4	72.9	96.6	11.5	40.6	18.1	12.6	15.1	21.8	104.5	88.1

¹Includes categories not shown separately.
. . . = Not available.

Table 16-1. New Construction Put in Place—*Continued*

(Billions of dollars, monthly data are at seasonally adjusted annual rates.)

Year and month	Total	Public													Federal
		State and local													
		Total [1]	Residential	Office	Health care	Educational	Public safety	Amusement and recreation	Transportation	Power	Highway and street	Sewage and waste disposal	Water supply		
1980	63.6	54.0	...	...	...	...	...	...	...	...	...	...	...		9.6
1981	64.7	54.3	...	...	...	...	...	...	...	...	...	...	...		10.4
1982	63.1	53.1	...	...	...	...	...	...	...	...	...	...	...		10.0
1983	63.5	52.9	...	...	...	...	...	...	...	...	...	...	...		10.6
1984	70.2	59.0	...	...	...	...	...	...	...	...	...	...	...		11.2
1985	77.8	65.8	...	...	...	...	...	...	...	...	...	...	...		12.0
1986	84.6	72.2	...	...	...	...	...	...	...	...	...	...	...		12.4
1987	90.6	76.6	...	...	...	...	...	...	...	...	...	...	...		14.1
1988	94.7	82.5	...	...	...	...	...	...	...	...	...	...	...		12.3
1989	98.2	86.0	...	...	...	...	...	...	...	...	...	...	...		12.2
1990	107.5	95.4	...	...	...	...	...	...	...	...	...	...	...		12.1
1991	110.1	97.3	...	...	...	...	...	...	...	...	...	...	...		12.8
1992	115.8	101.5	...	...	...	...	...	...	...	...	...	...	...		14.4
1993	127.4	112.9	3.4	2.8	2.3	24.2	4.6	4.3	9.8	7.4	34.5	11.2	6.4		14.4
1994	130.4	116.0	4.2	3.0	2.4	25.3	4.5	4.7	9.2	5.1	37.3	12.0	6.4		14.4
1995	140.0	124.3	4.5	3.3	2.6	27.5	5.0	5.1	9.6	5.7	38.6	13.0	7.3		15.8
1996	146.7	131.4	3.7	3.6	2.8	31.0	5.5	5.0	10.4	4.8	40.6	13.6	7.7		15.3
1997	153.4	139.4	3.3	3.8	2.9	34.3	5.6	5.7	10.3	4.4	44.4	13.1	8.1		14.1
1998	154.8	140.5	3.2	3.7	2.3	35.1	6.1	6.2	10.5	2.8	45.4	13.2	8.9		14.3
1999	169.1	155.1	3.2	3.6	2.5	39.8	6.2	7.2	11.4	2.9	51.0	14.5	9.6		14.0
2000	181.3	167.2	3.0	4.5	2.8	46.8	5.9	7.6	13.0	5.5	51.6	14.0	9.5		14.2
2001	201.9	186.8	3.5	5.6	2.9	52.8	6.1	9.1	15.9	5.3	56.4	14.2	11.4		15.1
2002	213.4	196.9	3.8	6.3	3.5	59.5	6.0	9.2	17.3	3.8	56.7	15.3	11.7		16.6
2003	216.1	198.2	3.7	6.1	4.0	59.3	5.8	8.4	16.5	6.8	56.3	15.6	11.7		17.9
2004	220.2	201.8	4.1	6.0	5.0	59.7	5.5	7.8	16.4	7.0	57.4	17.1	12.0		18.3
2005	234.2	216.9	4.0	5.2	5.1	65.8	6.0	7.3	16.3	8.3	63.2	18.3	13.5		17.3
2006	255.4	237.8	4.3	5.6	5.6	69.8	6.6	9.4	17.7	7.8	71.0	21.5	14.3		17.6
2007	289.1	268.5	5.1	7.2	7.0	78.4	8.4	10.7	21.1	11.4	75.5	23.3	15.0		20.6
2008	308.7	285.0	4.9	8.5	7.0	84.5	9.7	10.9	23.2	11.0	80.4	24.1	16.0		23.7
2009	314.9	286.5	5.8	9.2	6.8	83.7	9.4	10.6	25.5	11.8	81.3	23.5	14.8		28.4
2010	304.0	272.8	7.6	8.3	6.2	71.9	7.6	9.7	26.5	10.8	81.3	24.6	14.4		31.1
2011	286.4	254.8	6.0	7.4	7.0	68.0	7.2	8.5	23.3	9.5	78.4	21.2	13.4		31.7
2012	279.3	252.4	4.7	6.1	7.0	65.6	7.6	8.9	24.8	9.8	79.7	20.9	12.7		26.9
2013	270.7	247.0	4.5	5.2	6.9	60.0	6.6	8.1	25.9	11.0	80.6	21.0	12.9		23.7
2014	276.1	253.7	4.1	5.4	6.2	61.2	6.4	8.7	27.8	10.7	84.0	21.9	12.7		22.4
2015	293.8	271.2	6.0	5.9	5.5	65.8	5.9	10.0	29.4	10.3	90.8	23.4	12.8		22.5
2016	297.0	274.7	5.9	5.7	5.7	69.9	5.8	10.7	27.9	8.5	92.1	23.2	13.6		22.2
2017	296.5	275.3	6.2	6.0	6.4	74.0	6.2	11.6	29.3	5.4	88.3	22.4	13.7		21.3
2018	310.2	288.2	5.8	6.9	6.5	77.2	7.1	11.9	32.8	4.6	90.4	23.2	14.9		22.0
2019	344.3	318.1	6.1	8.1	6.5	85.2	8.1	14.2	37.6	7.1	97.5	25.0	15.6		26.3
2020	361.2	331.0	8.2	9.4	7.0	87.5	9.0	13.6	40.6	6.7	98.2	25.6	17.8		30.3
2021	346.3	321.7	8.1	8.5	7.7	81.0	8.1	12.8	37.7	8.5	98.5	26.8	18.0		24.5
2019															
January	321.4	296.6	5.3	7.1	6.2	82.2	7.2	12.3	35.0	6.2	91.4	23.2	13.3		24.8
February	332.5	306.6	5.6	7.1	6.1	82.4	7.6	13.8	35.1	6.2	99.2	22.8	14.2		26.0
March	334.1	309.5	5.5	7.3	6.4	82.4	7.1	14.0	35.4	5.3	99.9	24.1	15.1		24.6
April	353.5	327.6	5.8	7.3	6.4	84.6	7.4	14.1	36.6	7.0	112.0	24.3	15.5		25.9
May	344.6	319.9	5.6	7.5	6.4	83.4	7.8	14.1	37.9	6.9	102.9	25.6	15.0		24.7
June	343.4	317.1	6.0	7.6	6.3	83.3	7.6	14.9	37.8	6.4	99.3	25.3	15.3		26.3
July	347.6	321.3	5.8	8.4	6.6	85.2	8.3	14.4	38.9	7.3	97.9	25.4	15.7		26.3
August	345.8	320.0	6.4	8.6	6.7	85.1	8.5	14.7	38.9	7.9	95.3	25.6	15.2		25.9
September	351.5	324.8	6.7	8.8	6.5	87.0	8.2	14.1	37.8	8.0	97.0	27.2	16.3		26.7
October	349.0	321.4	6.9	8.6	6.7	90.2	8.9	14.2	37.5	7.7	91.4	24.8	16.9		27.5
November	351.2	322.6	6.7	8.7	6.7	89.4	9.0	14.7	39.1	7.8	89.9	25.4	17.7		28.6
December	356.9	328.2	7.2	9.2	6.9	87.3	8.9	14.9	40.0	8.4	95.6	25.7	16.9		28.7
2020															
January	367.9	338.1	8.2	9.4	6.5	89.3	9.3	14.9	41.5	7.4	100.7	25.9	17.8		29.8
February	371.4	341.7	8.2	9.6	6.8	90.7	9.5	14.8	41.0	7.9	102.6	25.5	17.5		29.7
March	374.7	344.7	8.0	9.6	6.8	91.6	9.8	13.8	40.7	8.1	106.4	25.0	17.5		30.0
April	366.2	333.3	7.5	9.2	6.8	90.7	9.7	13.0	39.3	7.0	100.0	25.3	17.8		32.9
May	374.4	342.2	8.0	9.4	7.0	93.9	9.7	13.2	42.0	6.8	101.8	25.1	18.0		32.2
June	364.2	331.1	8.1	9.7	6.8	87.5	9.2	13.3	40.5	5.9	98.5	26.1	18.3		33.0
July	356.0	322.6	8.4	9.7	6.8	83.5	9.2	13.4	39.9	6.0	93.3	26.5	18.3		33.4
August	356.2	324.3	8.3	9.5	7.2	83.2	8.5	13.8	42.5	6.2	94.3	25.3	18.2		31.8
September	352.2	322.4	8.4	9.5	7.4	84.6	8.4	13.8	41.1	6.2	92.1	26.0	17.8		29.8
October	351.7	324.9	8.3	9.0	7.4	83.5	8.4	13.5	39.2	6.3	98.5	25.4	17.8		26.8
November	355.4	328.9	8.5	9.1	7.1	86.6	8.4	13.0	39.1	6.5	100.4	25.8	17.1		26.5
December	357.2	331.1	8.3	8.8	7.3	87.3	8.2	13.3	40.5	6.6	100.9	25.8	16.8		26.0
2021															
January	355.1	328.5	8.6	8.7	7.4	88.5	8.6	13.4	38.1	7.5	98.6	25.6	16.8		26.6
February	345.6	320.1	8.2	8.7	7.2	86.3	8.5	12.8	37.6	7.6	95.0	25.1	16.7		25.5
March	344.9	320.0	8.2	8.8	7.6	84.2	8.4	13.0	38.0	7.6	94.7	25.7	17.5		24.9
April	343.8	321.2	8.0	8.6	7.6	83.0	8.3	13.2	38.1	7.6	96.0	27.0	17.8		22.5
May	341.1	319.1	8.1	8.3	7.6	81.1	8.2	13.0	37.7	7.6	96.8	26.7	17.7		22.0
June	338.6	315.2	8.2	8.3	7.4	78.4	8.4	12.7	38.0	8.3	93.7	27.3	18.0		23.4
July	341.8	318.6	8.2	8.5	7.9	77.3	8.2	12.3	37.8	9.4	97.0	27.2	18.2		23.2
August	347.2	323.1	8.1	8.2	8.1	78.7	8.2	12.4	37.9	9.3	99.9	27.7	18.8		24.1
September	347.6	324.0	8.1	8.4	7.9	80.5	7.9	12.5	37.9	9.0	100.1	27.6	18.9		23.6
October	352.7	326.0	8.2	8.5	7.8	80.4	7.8	12.6	37.9	9.5	102.4	26.9	18.5		26.7
November	352.2	325.9	7.7	8.5	8.0	80.5	7.8	12.9	37.7	9.6	102.6	27.0	18.2		26.3
December	349.0	323.7	7.8	8.5	8.0	79.7	7.4	12.8	37.0	8.8	103.8	26.9	17.9		25.3

[1]Includes categories not shown separately.
. . . = Not available.

Table 16-2. Housing Starts and Building Permits; New House Sales and Prices

	Housing starts and building permits										New house sales and prices			
	New private housing units (thousands)									Shipments of manufactured homes (thousands, seasonally adjusted annual rate)	Seasonally adjusted		Median sales price (dollars)	Price index (2005 = 100)
	Started (not seasonally adjusted)			Seasonally adjusted annual rate										
				Started			Authorized by building permits				Sold (thousands, annual rate)	For sale, end-of-period (thousands)		
Year and month	Total [1]	One-family structures	Five units or more	Total [1]	One-family structures	Five units or more	Total [1]	One-family structures	Five units or more					
1980	1 292	852	331	1 292	852	331	1 191	710	366	222	545	342	64 600	38.9
1981	1 084	705	288	1 084	705	288	986	564	319	241	436	278	68 900	42.0
1982	1 062	663	320	1 062	663	320	1 000	546	366	240	412	255	69 300	43.0
1983	1 703	1 068	522	1 703	1 068	522	1 605	901	570	296	623	304	75 300	43.9
1984	1 750	1 084	544	1 750	1 084	544	1 682	922	617	295	639	358	79 900	45.7
1985	1 742	1 072	576	1 742	1 072	576	1 733	957	657	284	688	350	84 300	46.2
1986	1 805	1 179	542	1 805	1 179	542	1 769	1 078	583	244	750	361	92 000	48.0
1987	1 621	1 146	409	1 621	1 146	409	1 535	1 024	421	233	671	370	104 500	50.6
1988	1 488	1 081	348	1 488	1 081	348	1 456	994	386	218	676	371	112 500	52.5
1989	1 376	1 003	318	1 376	1 003	318	1 338	932	340	198	650	366	120 000	54.6
1990	1 193	895	260	1 193	895	260	1 111	794	263	188	534	321	122 900	55.7
1991	1 014	840	138	1 014	840	138	949	754	152	171	509	284	120 000	56.4
1992	1 200	1 030	139	1 200	1 030	139	1 095	911	138	211	610	267	121 500	57.2
1993	1 288	1 126	133	1 288	1 126	133	1 199	987	160	254	666	295	126 500	59.4
1994	1 457	1 198	224	1 457	1 198	224	1 372	1 068	241	304	670	340	130 000	62.9
1995	1 354	1 076	244	1 354	1 076	244	1 333	997	272	340	667	374	133 900	64.3
1996	1 477	1 161	271	1 477	1 161	271	1 426	1 069	290	363	757	326	140 000	66.0
1997	1 474	1 134	296	1 474	1 134	296	1 441	1 062	310	354	804	287	146 000	67.5
1998	1 617	1 271	303	1 617	1 271	303	1 612	1 188	355	373	886	300	152 500	69.2
1999	1 641	1 302	307	1 641	1 302	307	1 664	1 247	351	348	880	315	161 000	72.8
2000	1 569	1 231	299	1 569	1 231	299	1 592	1 198	329	250	877	301	169 000	75.6
2001	1 603	1 273	293	1 603	1 273	293	1 637	1 236	335	193	908	310	175 200	77.9
2002	1 705	1 359	308	1 705	1 359	308	1 748	1 333	341	169	973	344	187 600	81.4
2003	1 848	1 499	315	1 848	1 499	315	1 889	1 461	346	131	1 086	377	195 000	86.0
2004	1 956	1 611	303	1 956	1 611	303	2 070	1 613	366	131	1 203	431	221 000	92.8
2005	2 068	1 716	311	2 068	1 716	311	2 155	1 682	389	147	1 283	515	240 900	100.0
2006	1 801	1 465	293	1 801	1 465	293	1 839	1 378	384	117	1 051	537	246 500	104.7
2007	1 355	1 046	277	1 355	1 046	277	1 398	980	359	96	776	496	247 900	104.9
2008	906	622	266	906	622	266	905	576	295	82	485	352	232 100	99.5
2009	554	445	97	554	445	97	583	441	121	50	375	232	216 700	95.1
2010	587	471	104	587	471	104	605	447	135	50	323	188	221 800	95.0
2011	609	431	167	609	431	167	624	418	184	52	306	150	227 200	94.3
2012	781	535	234	781	535	234	830	519	285	55	368	148	245 200	97.6
2013	925	618	294	925	618	294	991	621	341	60	429	186	268 900	104.7
2014	1 003	648	342	1 003	648	342	1 052	640	382	64	437	212	288 500	110.2
2015	1 112	715	386	1 112	715	386	1 183	696	455	71	501	235	294 200	112.9
2016	1 174	782	381	1 174	782	381	1 207	751	421	81	561	257	307 800	120.4
2017	1 203	849	343	1 203	849	343	1 282	820	425	93	613	294	323 100	126.8
2018	1 250	876	360	1 250	876	360	1 329	855	434	97	617	348	326 400	132.4
2019	1 290	888	389	1 290	888	389	1 386	862	481	95	683	327	321 500	135.5
2020	1 380	991	377	1 380	991	377	1 471	979	445	94	822	302	336 900	140.0
2021	1 601	1 127	462	1 601	1 127	462	1 737	1 115	569	106	771	391	397 100	161.3
2019														
January	87	64	22	1 232	925	291	1 253	792	416	88	599	345	305 400	. . .
February	80	55	25	1 129	777	347	1 311	804	470	90	638	340	320 800	. . .
March	98	70	28	1 200	838	357	1 317	824	455	91	702	337	310 600	129.9
April	117	82	33	1 280	883	375	1 330	808	475	92	698	334	339 000	. . .
May	118	78	39	1 308	859	437	1 349	841	472	93	620	335	312 700	. . .
June	115	83	31	1 235	863	361	1 303	853	403	94	753	330	311 800	133.9
July	114	84	29	1 232	890	330	1 363	857	460	96	674	328	308 300	. . .
August	121	81	39	1 370	901	454	1 485	899	543	97	699	324	327 000	. . .
September	113	79	34	1 297	919	367	1 461	898	526	98	719	323	315 700	137.7
October	115	77	37	1 328	896	420	1 520	924	549	99	714	321	322 400	. . .
November	103	68	34	1 343	905	419	1 497	932	525	100	694	321	328 000	. . .
December	108	69	38	1 538	1 007	511	1 439	921	474	98	688	323	329 500	137.1
2020														
January	113	67	45	1 569	968	592	1 493	955	495	100	708	327	328 900	. . .
February	112	73	37	1 571	1 038	514	1 457	996	415	104	690	328	331 800	. . .
March	105	74	30	1 270	888	369	1 383	897	440	96	610	331	328 200	135.7
April	85	63	21	938	688	235	1 084	679	372	73	582	325	310 100	. . .
May	95	68	27	1 055	750	297	1 256	756	458	80	706	312	317 100	. . .
June	119	87	31	1 269	900	362	1 338	867	431	86	922	299	341 100	137.5
July	139	94	44	1 510	1 002	498	1 553	1 000	505	97	1 007	290	329 800	. . .
August	123	92	28	1 376	1 026	329	1 520	1 062	405	95	1 036	283	325 500	. . .
September	126	95	31	1 461	1 115	340	1 614	1 131	437	96	991	284	344 400	142.4
October	131	100	30	1 530	1 174	341	1 599	1 137	403	100	1 001	281	346 900	. . .
November	118	88	29	1 541	1 166	359	1 682	1 144	482	101	851	289	350 800	. . .
December	115	90	25	1 651	1 308	333	1 730	1 213	468	104	871	300	365 300	144.6
2021														
January	115	78	36	1 602	1 117	472	1 843	1 217	568	107	911	304	373 200	. . .
February	102	75	27	1 430	1 053	364	1 743	1 132	561	100	768	310	362 000	. . .
March	141	103	36	1 711	1 243	446	1 773	1 204	510	109	881	309	359 600	152.5
April	136	97	37	1 505	1 061	430	1 765	1 152	564	102	809	317	376 600	. . .
May	146	101	44	1 605	1 110	485	1 691	1 138	494	105	740	330	390 400	. . .
June	154	112	42	1 664	1 165	488	1 661	1 091	521	105	714	346	374 700	159.1
July	144	105	38	1 573	1 124	438	1 655	1 051	549	104	726	362	406 000	. . .
August	140	98	41	1 576	1 095	474	1 772	1 061	668	105	686	374	404 300	. . .
September	135	94	41	1 559	1 094	455	1 615	1 054	513	105	732	375	413 200	165.0
October	134	92	41	1 563	1 079	474	1 698	1 077	569	108	671	387	427 300	. . .
November	131	91	38	1 706	1 220	469	1 729	1 111	570	111	756	390	430 300	. . .
December	124	83	41	1 768	1 212	553	1 896	1 118	710	109	839	389	410 000	175.8

[1]Includes structures with 2 to 4 units, not shown separately.
. . . = Not available.

Table 16-3. Manufacturers' Shipments

(Millions of dollars, seasonally adjusted.)

Year and month	Total	Total durable goods [1]	Total nondurable goods [1]	Construction materials and supplies	Information technology industries	Capital goods Total	Nondefense Total	Nondefense Excluding aircraft and parts	Defense	Consumer goods Total	Consumer goods Durable	Consumer goods Nondurable
1994	3 238 112	1 764 061	1 474 051	332 734	264 092	616 435	538 203	512 327	78 232	1 192 098	314 931	877 167
1995	3 479 677	1 902 815	1 576 862	353 198	291 885	666 167	590 578	565 729	75 589	1 256 611	324 036	932 575
1996	3 597 188	1 978 597	1 618 591	371 401	311 028	704 635	630 932	605 295	73 703	1 292 955	328 402	964 553
1997	3 834 699	2 147 384	1 687 315	399 880	349 846	779 232	702 971	665 074	76 261	1 358 516	360 193	998 323
1998	3 899 813	2 231 588	1 668 225	418 756	362 564	821 736	747 046	695 717	74 690	1 351 812	373 404	978 408
1999	4 031 887	2 326 736	1 705 151	434 138	374 384	839 754	768 799	713 042	70 955	1 424 828	412 646	1 012 182
2000	4 208 584	2 373 688	1 834 896	444 812	399 751	875 396	808 345	757 617	67 051	1 500 532	391 463	1 109 069
2001	3 970 499	2 174 406	1 796 093	424 517	353 237	801 999	728 495	678 288	73 504	1 480 495	367 522	1 112 973
2002	3 914 723	2 123 621	1 791 102	424 008	284 799	728 585	652 342	609 595	76 243	1 494 575	395 953	1 098 622
2003	4 015 388	2 142 589	1 872 799	429 183	274 829	719 602	634 273	600 616	85 329	1 584 329	418 821	1 165 508
2004	4 308 970	2 264 667	2 044 303	463 148	287 837	752 905	661 740	629 146	91 165	1 700 835	419 182	1 281 653
2005	4 742 077	2 424 844	2 317 233	509 865	295 447	821 906	730 368	686 939	91 538	1 895 119	422 555	1 472 564
2006	5 015 552	2 562 194	2 453 358	546 866	319 890	884 199	794 638	744 282	89 561	1 980 031	421 860	1 558 171
2007	5 319 457	2 687 028	2 632 429	560 208	322 846	936 404	836 426	768 662	99 978	2 106 081	421 822	1 684 259
2008	5 468 994	2 616 667	2 852 327	543 819	319 032	955 412	840 250	774 775	115 162	2 254 007	357 546	1 896 461
2009	4 423 779	2 056 829	2 366 950	426 663	271 678	820 521	697 469	642 555	123 052	1 849 113	268 036	1 581 077
2010	4 911 277	2 280 712	2 630 565	443 880	270 118	858 123	727 818	674 747	130 305	2 058 913	323 432	1 735 481
2011	5 491 894	2 479 086	3 012 808	471 598	274 110	923 876	803 248	740 848	120 628	2 373 512	344 299	2 029 213
2012	5 696 728	2 627 582	3 069 146	500 848	272 578	1 000 565	884 994	799 591	115 591	2 437 147	373 352	2 063 795
2013	5 814 127	2 698 831	3 115 296	523 741	271 471	1 010 075	893 660	800 926	116 415	2 496 007	401 442	2 094 565
2014	5 889 007	2 797 291	3 091 716	548 111	265 000	1 022 566	909 950	807 734	112 616	2 499 624	427 266	2 072 358
2015	5 533 033	2 781 867	2 751 166	554 163	258 289	995 652	883 796	779 425	111 856	2 257 336	457 847	1 799 489
2016	5 363 596	2 716 122	2 647 474	554 018	256 501	951 323	834 891	727 502	116 432	2 187 429	471 353	1 716 076
2017	5 548 795	2 767 416	2 781 379	574 239	256 478	978 816	854 811	736 908	124 005	2 273 113	453 465	1 819 648
2018	5 890 664	2 928 056	2 962 608	607 949	263 462	1 029 474	903 094	784 070	126 380	2 433 606	475 039	1 958 567
2019	5 734 457	2 860 508	2 873 949	606 324	265 742	989 920	859 230	785 582	130 690	2 384 474	470 492	1 913 982
2020	5 221 323	2 631 788	2 589 535	592 693	260 119	914 888	769 750	717 520	145 138	2 132 974	436 181	1 696 793
2021	5 797 752	2 923 246	2 874 506	678 285	276 049	1 025 396	866 833	793 194	158 563	2 391 626	477 697	1 913 929
2018												
January	481 905	238 242	243 663	49 380	21 693	84 030	73 251	63 408	10 779	199 583	38 616	160 967
February	483 979	239 796	244 183	49 792	21 349	83 927	73 609	63 923	10 318	200 503	39 342	161 161
March	485 700	242 030	243 670	50 092	21 393	86 235	76 148	63 747	10 087	199 574	39 117	160 457
April	485 591	241 434	244 157	50 530	21 832	82 537	71 480	64 856	11 057	201 362	40 686	160 676
May	491 462	242 493	248 969	51 036	21 745	85 758	75 206	64 903	10 552	202 299	37 426	164 873
June	494 268	244 563	249 705	51 028	21 891	86 492	76 088	65 722	10 404	204 158	39 135	165 023
July	493 100	243 499	249 601	51 267	22 386	83 618	73 198	66 516	10 420	205 013	39 804	165 209
August	496 827	246 033	250 794	51 208	22 217	86 647	76 210	66 098	10 437	205 892	39 771	166 121
September	498 944	246 988	251 956	50 908	21 912	87 245	76 772	66 124	10 473	207 703	40 142	167 561
October	499 157	247 576	251 581	50 918	22 424	87 102	76 393	66 595	10 709	208 120	40 659	167 461
November	491 973	247 334	244 639	50 665	22 358	87 357	76 867	66 102	10 490	201 705	40 104	161 601
December	487 122	246 932	240 190	50 727	22 279	87 494	76 531	66 367	10 963	197 938	40 142	157 796
2019												
January	484 934	243 939	240 995	50 449	22 302	85 382	74 433	66 340	10 949	199 083	39 943	159 140
February	487 289	244 507	242 782	50 807	22 370	85 521	74 951	66 673	10 570	200 899	39 752	161 147
March	485 756	243 738	242 018	50 637	22 113	85 505	74 827	66 403	10 678	200 590	39 467	161 123
April	482 774	239 496	243 278	50 214	22 863	83 192	72 359	67 017	10 833	200 846	38 202	162 644
May	483 427	240 881	242 546	50 759	22 614	83 685	72 635	67 118	11 050	200 826	39 050	161 776
June	481 228	241 922	239 306	51 093	22 284	82 938	71 870	66 521	11 068	199 157	40 578	158 579
July	477 329	237 722	239 607	50 581	22 270	81 665	70 997	65 716	10 668	199 031	39 593	159 438
August	476 235	237 912	238 323	50 739	22 033	81 854	70 796	65 407	11 058	198 308	39 696	158 612
September	473 994	236 118	237 876	50 779	21 840	80 758	69 779	64 553	10 979	197 872	39 515	158 357
October	470 099	234 131	235 968	50 381	21 688	81 320	70 221	64 291	11 099	196 400	38 637	157 763
November	467 731	232 122	235 609	50 263	21 841	79 939	69 001	63 242	10 938	195 928	38 254	157 674
December	467 121	230 588	236 533	49 945	22 085	80 200	69 225	62 992	10 975	196 155	37 751	158 404
2020												
January	461 646	227 925	233 721	49 796	21 538	77 889	66 161	62 016	11 728	193 586	37 574	156 012
February	460 720	231 281	229 439	49 796	21 500	78 904	67 331	61 154	11 573	191 997	39 709	152 288
March	435 665	218 833	216 832	49 188	21 422	80 573	69 184	59 919	11 389	171 572	30 748	140 824
April	371 289	174 037	197 252	43 599	20 858	68 889	57 078	54 966	11 811	141 762	13 830	127 932
May	380 336	182 170	198 166	45 492	20 870	69 734	57 875	55 925	11 859	145 739	17 647	128 092
June	421 852	211 915	209 937	48 064	21 017	72 317	60 309	57 894	12 008	174 234	36 357	137 877
July	439 248	225 508	213 740	49 763	21 545	73 637	61 663	59 197	11 974	184 822	44 540	140 282
August	443 110	227 752	215 358	50 181	21 686	76 702	64 514	59 932	12 188	184 583	43 193	141 390
September	445 122	228 992	216 130	50 794	21 988	76 482	64 434	60 377	12 048	185 173	43 603	141 570
October	448 309	231 692	216 617	51 178	22 695	79 953	67 493	61 647	12 460	183 907	42 191	141 716
November	450 081	231 214	218 867	51 448	22 251	77 806	64 714	61 790	13 092	186 373	42 909	143 464
December	459 150	235 847	223 303	52 558	22 290	80 505	67 829	62 065	12 676	190 029	42 912	147 117
2021												
January	468 239	239 576	228 663	54 845	22 839	82 197	69 240	63 371	12 957	192 941	43 005	149 936
February	461 028	232 574	228 454	54 173	22 448	80 072	67 203	62 698	12 869	190 193	39 770	150 423
March	466 236	237 016	229 220	54 905	22 707	83 107	70 023	63 876	13 084	192 234	40 281	151 953
April	466 698	235 561	231 137	55 414	23 066	84 294	70 973	64 672	13 321	189 630	36 571	153 059
May	473 192	238 060	235 132	55 568	22 889	83 969	71 083	65 123	12 886	194 518	38 174	156 344
June	480 651	240 320	240 331	56 059	22 927	85 129	72 290	65 883	12 839	198 780	38 002	160 778
July	487 964	246 972	240 992	56 249	23 079	86 601	72 965	66 530	13 636	201 850	41 101	160 749
August	488 388	245 585	242 803	56 652	23 123	85 974	72 631	66 845	13 343	201 955	39 791	162 164
September	492 160	247 098	245 062	57 396	23 027	87 701	74 321	67 647	13 380	202 467	38 135	164 332
October	501 087	250 719	250 368	58 247	23 180	87 609	74 216	67 994	13 393	208 047	40 279	167 768
November	505 813	253 596	252 217	59 582	23 390	88 734	75 183	68 664	13 551	209 709	41 024	168 685
December	508 219	255 903	252 316	60 072	23 532	89 019	75 597	69 483	13 422	210 480	41 918	168 562

[1]Includes categories not shown separately.

Table 16-4. Manufacturers' Inventories

(Current cost basis, end of period; seasonally adjusted, millions of dollars.)

Year and month	Total	Total durable goods	Durables total by stage of fabrication			Total nondurable goods	Nondurables total by stage of fabrication		
			Materials and supplies	Work in process	Finished goods		Materials and supplies	Work in process	Finished goods
1994	399 934	253 095	78 482	106 521	68 092	146 839	57 113	24 444	65 282
1995	424 802	267 437	85 545	106 634	75 258	157 365	60 778	25 776	70 811
1996	430 366	272 428	86 265	110 527	75 636	157 938	59 157	26 485	72 296
1997	443 227	280 730	92 253	109 714	78 763	162 497	60 175	28 523	73 799
1998	448 373	290 071	93 406	114 928	81 737	158 302	58 156	27 049	73 097
1999	463 004	296 009	97 722	113 805	84 482	166 995	60 975	28 791	77 229
2000	480 748	306 002	105 848	110 909	89 245	174 746	61 465	30 090	83 191
2001	427 353	267 409	91 168	93 768	82 473	159 944	55 671	27 157	77 116
2002	423 028	260 476	88 445	92 343	79 688	162 552	56 571	28 133	77 848
2003	408 302	246 922	82 330	88 608	75 984	161 380	56 866	27 251	77 263
2004	441 222	264 895	92 122	90 934	81 839	176 327	61 917	30 341	84 069
2005	474 639	283 712	98 652	98 400	86 660	190 927	67 224	33 226	90 477
2006	523 476	317 406	111 687	106 352	99 367	206 070	70 601	37 548	97 921
2007	563 043	334 628	116 506	117 496	100 626	228 415	75 570	45 290	107 555
2008	543 273	329 781	117 709	110 840	101 232	213 492	72 866	41 193	99 433
2009	505 025	294 755	100 633	106 167	87 955	210 270	71 913	42 137	96 220
2010	553 726	321 441	106 899	122 157	92 385	232 285	76 592	45 922	109 771
2011	607 035	352 897	119 445	133 306	100 146	254 138	82 059	50 675	121 404
2012	625 053	367 239	125 078	138 678	103 483	257 814	83 428	51 144	123 242
2013	631 742	371 896	126 209	141 455	104 232	259 846	84 679	52 438	122 729
2014	642 655	389 626	133 674	146 856	109 096	253 029	83 976	49 304	119 749
2015	638 177	393 021	130 533	151 919	110 569	245 156	84 263	45 809	115 084
2016	635 825	380 414	126 405	143 349	110 660	255 411	85 211	47 177	123 023
2017	658 986	389 862	132 589	141 652	115 621	269 124	90 021	50 430	128 673
2018	677 472	408 998	144 771	141 495	122 732	268 474	92 018	48 435	128 021
2019	709 281	433 093	148 127	158 579	126 387	276 188	93 386	50 282	132 520
2020	696 711	428 088	146 398	163 314	118 376	268 623	93 786	46 342	128 495
2021	759 327	466 676	169 652	169 050	127 974	292 651	104 815	48 602	139 234
2018									
January	660 356	391 124	132 876	142 802	115 446	269 232	89 475	50 522	129 235
February	663 744	393 868	134 323	143 765	115 780	269 876	89 850	50 155	129 871
March	662 832	393 229	134 857	142 376	115 996	269 603	90 124	51 014	128 465
April	665 016	395 095	136 055	142 640	116 400	269 921	90 078	50 792	129 051
May	666 051	396 775	137 141	142 740	116 894	269 276	90 082	50 376	128 818
June	666 158	395 669	138 452	139 342	117 875	270 489	90 383	50 244	129 862
July	673 038	402 003	140 040	143 818	118 145	271 035	91 406	50 067	129 562
August	673 301	401 116	141 155	141 272	118 689	272 185	92 252	50 415	129 518
September	677 448	404 326	142 514	141 815	119 997	273 122	93 155	50 867	129 100
October	678 850	405 213	143 184	141 852	120 177	273 637	93 120	50 152	130 365
November	677 870	407 281	144 454	141 660	121 167	270 589	92 272	48 773	129 544
December	677 472	408 998	144 771	141 495	122 732	268 474	92 018	48 435	128 021
2019									
January	682 048	411 786	145 742	142 798	123 246	270 262	92 409	49 223	128 630
February	685 369	413 874	145 730	144 884	123 260	271 495	92 451	49 427	129 617
March	688 124	414 446	145 475	145 017	123 954	273 678	92 440	50 488	130 750
April	691 192	416 986	145 756	147 302	123 928	274 206	92 645	50 431	131 130
May	692 960	418 955	145 624	148 965	124 366	274 005	92 799	50 148	131 058
June	695 211	420 845	146 279	149 285	125 281	274 366	93 194	49 336	131 836
July	698 662	423 789	146 852	150 819	126 118	274 873	92 473	49 778	132 622
August	700 299	426 158	147 057	152 521	126 580	274 141	92 647	49 398	132 096
September	702 610	428 239	147 689	153 850	126 700	274 371	92 359	49 613	132 399
October	704 450	429 979	148 229	155 272	126 478	274 471	92 187	49 907	132 377
November	706 448	431 204	148 248	156 768	126 188	275 244	92 808	50 542	131 894
December	709 281	433 093	148 127	158 579	126 387	276 188	93 386	50 282	132 520
2020									
January	706 883	432 235	147 391	159 479	125 365	274 648	93 215	49 620	131 813
February	703 376	431 112	147 339	159 754	124 019	272 264	92 837	48 485	130 942
March	695 350	431 724	147 945	160 842	122 937	263 626	91 296	45 197	127 133
April	693 204	432 394	151 623	159 942	120 829	260 810	90 140	44 367	126 303
May	691 831	430 830	151 117	159 750	119 963	261 001	90 129	45 270	125 602
June	694 095	430 318	148 974	160 971	120 373	263 777	91 415	46 156	126 206
July	690 783	427 058	147 269	160 637	119 152	263 725	91 730	46 228	125 767
August	691 278	426 337	146 363	161 296	118 678	264 941	92 116	46 504	126 321
September	689 703	425 812	144 976	162 977	117 859	263 891	91 300	46 232	126 359
October	690 624	426 508	145 285	163 165	118 058	264 116	91 464	45 116	127 536
November	695 094	429 230	145 496	164 096	119 638	265 864	92 067	45 973	127 824
December	696 711	428 088	146 398	163 314	118 376	268 623	93 786	46 342	128 495
2021									
January	698 229	427 186	146 820	160 911	119 455	271 043	95 163	46 281	129 599
February	705 029	431 087	149 224	161 524	120 339	273 942	96 444	47 293	130 205
March	707 492	432 587	148 882	162 558	121 147	274 905	97 262	46 429	131 214
April	710 250	434 874	150 872	162 443	121 559	275 376	97 843	46 754	130 779
May	717 919	439 251	152 740	163 321	123 190	278 668	98 455	47 661	132 552
June	725 494	444 199	155 002	165 274	123 923	281 295	99 562	48 260	133 473
July	729 783	446 899	157 622	165 482	123 795	282 884	100 783	47 919	134 182
August	735 546	451 303	159 714	166 582	125 007	284 243	101 601	47 587	135 055
September	743 493	456 128	162 536	167 509	126 083	287 365	103 130	48 197	136 038
October	749 747	458 915	165 138	167 193	126 584	290 832	104 776	48 606	137 450
November	756 238	462 817	167 641	167 574	127 602	293 421	105 774	49 008	138 639
December	759 327	466 676	169 652	169 050	127 974	292 651	104 815	48 602	139 234

Table 16-4. Manufacturers' Inventories—*Continued*

(Current cost basis, end of period; seasonally adjusted, millions of dollars.)

Year and month	Construction materials and supplies	Information technology industries	By topical categories						
			Capital goods				Consumer goods		
			Total	Nondefense		Defense	Total	Durable	Nondurable
				Total	Excluding aircraft and parts				
1994	40 879	41 538	123 368	103 320	85 717	20 048	109 536	23 948	85 588
1995	43 420	46 936	129 709	111 563	94 673	18 146	116 404	25 316	91 088
1996	44 124	43 556	132 746	115 211	93 441	17 535	116 351	24 752	91 599
1997	45 725	48 094	137 556	122 598	98 870	14 958	119 660	24 905	94 755
1998	46 500	45 333	145 048	127 108	97 362	17 940	117 343	24 895	92 448
1999	48 541	46 174	146 244	126 278	99 610	19 966	124 220	26 097	98 123
2000	50 518	52 719	148 992	131 655	110 122	17 337	130 823	27 295	103 528
2001	46 341	42 967	128 670	114 908	93 305	13 762	121 377	25 410	95 967
2002	46 698	39 083	122 538	108 147	88 529	14 391	124 904	25 687	99 217
2003	45 448	35 222	114 917	99 119	81 660	15 798	125 052	25 017	100 035
2004	51 244	33 132	117 611	98 900	83 687	18 711	134 390	26 240	108 150
2005	55 094	39 215	127 158	110 573	92 903	16 585	145 446	28 104	117 342
2006	60 864	39 914	139 499	122 442	101 760	17 057	154 185	27 686	126 499
2007	62 522	38 748	150 191	131 347	104 706	18 844	172 565	27 729	144 836
2008	61 386	38 048	150 665	134 264	107 682	16 401	155 212	24 151	131 061
2009	50 915	36 649	145 498	125 685	97 529	19 813	159 016	21 207	137 809
2010	53 287	37 550	160 079	139 469	103 618	20 610	174 664	21 989	152 675
2011	57 661	39 635	174 551	154 445	113 807	20 106	188 238	22 900	165 338
2012	60 146	39 341	184 130	163 770	118 280	20 360	191 826	25 061	166 765
2013	61 243	38 281	186 541	166 294	117 513	20 247	193 642	26 157	167 485
2014	65 421	37 097	193 807	173 625	121 593	20 182	186 716	27 627	159 089
2015	64 349	37 619	201 172	179 548	119 684	21 624	183 933	28 602	155 331
2016	64 821	36 744	191 772	171 688	115 453	20 084	192 461	28 119	164 342
2017	68 402	36 631	188 551	167 562	118 982	20 989	202 378	29 291	173 087
2018	74 164	38 334	191 437	172 820	127 416	18 617	200 086	31 068	169 018
2019	75 192	39 732	212 688	192 287	129 527	20 401	212 339	33 908	178 431
2020	71 238	39 725	215 129	194 209	125 785	20 920	206 700	32 975	173 725
2021	82 864	42 326	226 321	204 374	138 916	21 947	227 692	40 402	187 290
2018									
January	68 714	36 675	188 969	168 286	119 369	20 683	203 179	29 483	173 696
February	69 263	36 970	190 466	169 855	120 285	20 611	203 421	29 502	173 919
March	69 701	36 836	189 303	168 960	120 353	20 343	203 367	29 681	173 686
April	70 445	36 970	189 636	169 742	121 205	19 894	203 177	29 727	173 450
May	70 990	37 282	189 456	169 655	121 599	19 801	203 019	30 195	172 824
June	71 705	37 325	187 319	167 277	122 428	20 042	202 967	29 982	172 985
July	72 425	37 310	191 088	171 271	123 078	19 817	203 075	30 232	172 843
August	72 944	37 459	188 728	169 459	123 683	19 269	204 226	30 567	173 659
September	73 823	37 832	190 431	171 278	125 061	19 153	204 769	30 470	174 299
October	73 781	37 987	190 853	171 765	125 759	19 088	205 076	30 545	174 531
November	74 017	38 128	191 304	172 363	126 681	18 941	202 226	30 889	171 337
December	74 164	38 334	191 437	172 820	127 416	18 617	200 086	31 068	169 018
2019									
January	74 400	38 580	193 401	174 429	128 241	18 972	201 904	31 539	170 365
February	74 485	38 784	194 612	175 587	128 269	19 025	204 125	32 043	172 082
March	74 479	38 948	196 205	176 789	128 771	19 416	206 187	32 029	174 158
April	74 399	38 945	198 082	178 485	128 800	19 597	207 517	32 567	174 950
May	74 523	39 065	200 034	180 342	128 909	19 692	207 632	32 954	174 678
June	74 801	39 183	201 287	181 368	129 033	19 919	207 970	33 125	174 845
July	75 167	39 317	204 038	183 837	129 959	20 201	208 875	33 396	175 479
August	75 309	39 458	206 134	186 107	129 951	20 027	208 676	33 583	175 093
September	75 364	39 602	207 721	187 456	130 116	20 265	209 477	33 800	175 677
October	75 465	39 590	209 739	189 151	130 152	20 588	210 009	33 970	176 039
November	75 297	39 561	210 669	189 993	129 546	20 676	211 107	34 039	177 068
December	75 192	39 732	212 688	192 287	129 527	20 401	212 339	33 908	178 431
2020									
January	75 208	39 575	212 647	192 060	128 869	20 587	211 065	33 655	177 410
February	74 755	39 537	212 340	191 751	128 161	20 589	208 738	33 447	175 291
March	74 549	39 598	213 086	192 609	128 328	20 477	200 128	33 033	167 095
April	74 639	39 783	213 961	193 274	128 737	20 687	196 937	32 240	164 697
May	73 509	39 910	214 043	193 371	128 250	20 672	197 576	32 385	165 191
June	72 296	40 028	215 571	194 666	127 637	20 905	201 540	32 828	168 712
July	70 742	39 918	215 868	195 118	126 962	20 750	201 991	32 628	169 363
August	70 351	39 892	215 574	194 566	126 393	21 008	203 199	32 364	170 835
September	70 156	39 849	216 039	194 830	125 817	21 209	201 897	32 221	169 676
October	70 284	39 803	215 635	194 459	125 440	21 176	202 210	32 603	169 607
November	70 638	39 710	216 737	195 815	125 709	20 922	204 888	33 500	171 388
December	71 238	39 725	215 129	194 209	125 785	20 920	206 700	32 975	173 725
2021									
January	71 574	39 839	212 753	191 643	126 331	21 110	208 973	33 266	175 707
February	72 436	39 926	213 829	192 486	127 026	21 343	212 506	34 296	178 210
March	73 540	39 934	214 310	193 013	127 172	21 297	214 354	35 723	178 631
April	74 350	40 106	214 500	193 128	127 742	21 372	215 337	37 001	178 336
May	75 451	40 321	215 596	194 185	129 304	21 411	218 450	37 637	180 813
June	76 704	40 482	217 593	196 422	130 400	21 171	220 509	38 290	182 219
July	77 618	40 690	218 149	196 774	130 997	21 375	220 703	38 197	182 506
August	78 529	40 851	219 844	198 245	132 274	21 599	221 877	39 315	182 562
September	79 686	41 283	221 558	199 934	134 137	21 624	224 861	40 194	184 667
October	80 896	41 504	222 628	200 872	135 455	21 756	227 205	39 890	187 315
November	81 827	41 943	224 639	202 766	137 279	21 873	229 148	40 277	188 871
December	82 864	42 326	226 321	204 374	138 916	21 947	227 692	40 402	187 290

Table 16-5. Manufacturers' New Orders

(Net, millions of dollars, seasonally adjusted.)

Year and month	Total [1]	Total durable goods [1]	Construction materials and supplies	Information technology industries	Capital goods Total	Nondefense Total	Nondefense Excluding aircraft and parts	Defense	Consumer goods Total	Consumer goods Durable	Consumer goods Nondurable
1995	3 426 503	1 849 641	355 161	297 605	680 857	612 132	576 769	68 725	1 256 721	324 146	932 575
1996	3 567 384	1 948 793	373 536	310 074	737 268	648 797	607 174	88 471	1 293 537	328 984	964 553
1997	3 779 835	2 092 520	403 860	352 700	792 859	728 362	676 119	64 497	1 360 010	361 687	998 323
1998	3 808 143	2 139 918	419 330	365 723	809 727	745 600	698 279	64 127	1 352 708	374 300	978 408
1999	3 957 242	2 252 091	435 034	389 160	840 603	772 703	728 089	67 900	1 425 617	413 435	1 012 182
2000	4 161 472	2 326 576	446 792	409 500	910 933	831 335	767 754	79 598	1 501 810	392 741	1 109 069
2001	3 868 855	2 072 762	420 817	336 935	775 315	691 552	656 944	83 763	1 477 201	364 228	1 112 973
2002	3 823 145	2 032 043	423 561	273 788	698 865	622 403	589 148	76 462	1 494 106	395 484	1 098 622
2003	3 975 812	2 103 013	431 569	282 289	737 032	636 821	608 175	100 211	1 585 029	419 521	1 165 508
2004	4 289 001	2 244 698	468 746	293 836	787 748	688 813	643 997	98 935	1 701 565	419 912	1 281 653
2005	4 764 032	2 446 799	516 797	300 367	896 672	814 286	703 796	82 386	1 894 021	421 457	1 472 564
2006	5 089 646	2 636 288	549 467	332 649	992 499	889 370	775 156	103 129	1 979 165	420 994	1 558 171
2007	5 397 027	2 764 598	564 717	324 248	1 061 415	957 485	786 665	103 930	2 105 784	421 525	1 684 259
2008	5 452 124	2 599 797	543 218	318 571	1 006 627	879 429	781 810	127 198	2 252 724	356 263	1 896 461
2009	4 205 737	2 265 032	413 497	265 602	690 674	587 116	608 664	103 558	1 848 693	267 616	1 581 077
2010	4 895 899	2 265 334	450 921	272 817	885 135	747 708	685 492	137 427	2 058 565	323 084	1 735 481
2011	5 511 660	2 498 852	471 284	286 080	994 126	861 040	765 584	133 086	2 373 717	344 504	2 029 213
2012	5 709 710	2 640 564	500 617	274 254	1 051 261	932 086	803 477	119 175	2 437 479	373 684	2 063 795
2013	5 898 932	2 783 636	524 553	256 251	1 134 933	1 035 998	807 568	98 935	2 496 304	401 739	2 094 565
2014	5 952 546	2 860 830	547 944	260 335	1 114 942	1 005 179	806 881	109 763	2 499 685	427 327	2 072 358
2015	5 433 340	2 682 174	554 821	250 876	950 523	844 588	761 235	105 935	2 257 164	457 675	1 799 489
2016	5 295 968	2 648 494	552 175	260 653	959 105	829 099	723 458	130 006	2 187 809	471 733	1 716 076
2017	5 492 320	2 710 941	575 439	261 257	999 429	873 987	742 671	125 442	2 273 215	453 567	1 819 648
2018	5 821 697	2 859 089	616 805	267 024	989 190	851 977	794 652	137 213	2 434 393	475 826	1 958 567
2019	5 538 188	2 664 239	609 899	274 364	837 600	705 588	789 816	132 012	2 383 923	469 941	1 913 982
2020	5 141 371	2 551 836	596 997	267 845	885 944	726 873	728 339	159 071	2 137 570	440 777	1 696 793
2021	5 818 472	2 943 966	699 068	286 199	1 069 823	911 622	818 637	158 201	2 393 551	479 622	1 913 929
2018											
January	469 569	225 906	49 807	21 465	76 069	66 645	63 816	9 424	199 801	38 834	160 967
February	478 323	234 140	50 800	21 603	81 163	72 898	65 257	8 265	200 542	39 381	161 161
March	486 328	242 658	51 291	21 579	88 259	78 163	64 073	10 096	199 801	39 344	160 457
April	483 649	239 492	51 720	22 065	82 520	71 877	65 444	10 643	201 470	40 794	160 676
May	489 577	240 608	51 990	22 248	85 047	72 628	66 748	12 419	202 325	37 452	164 873
June	492 979	243 274	51 665	22 331	86 030	73 160	67 678	12 870	204 308	39 285	165 023
July	484 186	234 585	52 013	22 828	77 438	67 756	68 406	9 682	205 162	39 953	165 209
August	494 902	244 108	51 785	22 558	87 571	73 425	67 270	14 146	205 771	39 650	166 121
September	496 790	244 834	51 286	21 931	84 215	70 509	67 127	13 706	207 723	40 162	167 561
October	491 304	239 723	51 654	23 027	81 796	69 943	67 931	11 853	208 240	40 779	167 461
November	476 292	231 653	51 313	22 709	76 142	65 145	65 255	10 997	201 610	40 009	161 601
December	478 638	238 448	51 316	22 539	83 029	70 338	65 773	12 691	197 821	40 025	157 796
2019											
January	470 023	229 028	51 131	22 794	75 453	64 257	67 110	11 196	199 007	39 867	159 140
February	466 237	223 455	51 103	22 718	68 248	59 907	66 772	8 341	200 752	39 605	161 147
March	475 062	233 044	50 650	23 308	79 205	66 757	67 615	12 448	200 427	39 304	161 123
April	467 207	223 929	50 524	23 773	71 542	60 538	67 038	11 004	200 812	38 168	162 644
May	460 025	217 479	50 843	23 340	66 206	55 384	66 680	10 822	200 842	39 066	161 776
June	458 859	219 553	51 657	23 241	63 877	56 407	66 243	7 470	199 167	40 588	158 579
July	464 846	225 239	51 017	23 128	72 837	63 101	65 872	9 736	199 033	39 595	159 438
August	462 869	224 546	51 306	22 603	71 554	59 778	65 829	11 776	198 267	39 655	158 612
September	459 825	221 949	50 707	22 756	69 357	56 784	65 203	12 573	197 802	39 445	158 357
October	458 943	222 975	50 293	22 507	74 144	60 044	65 207	14 100	196 395	38 632	157 763
November	448 388	212 779	50 901	22 106	62 571	55 498	63 805	7 073	195 962	38 288	157 674
December	451 857	215 324	50 148	22 567	67 154	51 115	62 950	16 039	196 084	37 680	158 404
2020											
January	459 272	225 551	50 154	22 226	78 319	66 139	62 298	12 180	193 750	37 738	156 012
February	460 927	231 488	49 753	22 105	83 479	68 019	61 245	15 460	192 149	39 861	152 288
March	416 951	200 119	48 202	21 898	67 966	51 631	60 715	16 335	171 934	31 110	140 824
April	356 382	159 130	42 318	21 712	61 081	49 209	55 545	11 872	141 836	13 904	127 932
May	377 550	179 384	44 924	21 484	71 920	58 158	56 463	13 762	146 179	18 087	128 092
June	408 711	198 774	48 659	21 537	63 572	50 934	58 548	12 638	174 622	36 745	137 877
July	431 781	218 041	50 120	22 372	70 956	57 556	60 095	13 400	185 317	45 035	140 282
August	436 444	221 086	50 973	22 258	74 132	60 258	60 687	13 874	185 009	43 619	141 390
September	441 723	225 593	51 836	22 448	76 786	65 920	62 159	10 866	185 618	44 048	141 570
October	446 352	229 735	52 311	23 130	81 524	67 947	62 801	13 577	184 302	42 586	141 716
November	447 337	228 470	52 748	22 862	78 146	65 024	62 967	13 122	186 871	43 407	143 464
December	454 763	231 460	54 251	23 172	77 952	65 918	63 944	12 034	190 775	43 658	147 117
2021											
January	465 947	237 284	56 522	23 298	82 117	66 787	64 750	15 330	193 281	43 345	149 936
February	465 933	237 479	56 499	23 465	85 358	71 693	64 562	13 665	190 496	40 073	150 423
March	470 612	241 392	57 820	23 159	87 932	73 169	65 886	14 763	192 580	40 627	151 953
April	467 703	236 566	58 300	23 631	86 231	73 943	67 955	12 288	189 922	36 863	153 059
May	476 677	241 545	58 280	23 610	87 698	75 503	66 882	12 195	194 796	38 452	156 344
June	486 157	245 826	57 862	23 821	92 238	78 939	68 158	13 299	199 124	38 346	160 778
July	487 733	246 741	57 343	23 657	88 597	75 198	68 660	13 399	202 044	41 295	160 749
August	493 380	250 577	58 688	24 145	93 093	80 322	69 530	12 771	201 998	39 834	162 164
September	491 911	246 849	58 883	23 978	90 258	76 768	69 298	13 490	202 591	38 259	164 332
October	500 871	250 503	58 942	23 900	91 379	77 973	70 632	13 406	207 808	40 040	167 768
November	506 291	254 074	59 949	25 030	93 838	80 981	71 135	12 857	209 508	40 823	168 685
December	508 780	256 464	61 478	24 645	91 116	80 389	71 199	10 727	210 583	42 021	168 562

[1] Includes categories not shown separately.

Table 16-6. Manufacturers' Unfilled Orders, Durable Goods Industries

(End of period, millions of dollars, seasonally adjusted.)

Year and month	Total [1]	Transportation equipment		Construction materials and supplies	Information technology industries	By topical categories				Consumer durable goods
		Nondefense aircraft and parts	Defense aircraft and parts			Capital goods				
						Total	Nondefense		Defense	
							Total	Excluding aircraft and parts		
1995	447 510	109 506	42 360	27 155	84 919	313 963	199 613	118 006	114 350	5 282
1996	489 147	130 580	45 203	29 436	84 227	346 596	217 605	120 276	128 991	5 821
1997	513 317	143 183	40 842	33 584	87 704	360 636	243 413	132 076	117 223	7 330
1998	496 363	137 228	37 711	34 268	90 930	348 398	241 565	134 417	106 833	8 262
1999	505 667	126 256	35 616	35 246	105 883	349 497	245 603	149 679	103 894	9 035
2000	549 507	138 159	42 421	37 405	115 679	384 834	268 323	159 844	116 511	10 349
2001	509 910	124 656	52 002	33 580	98 908	357 539	230 560	137 637	126 979	6 988
2002	479 610	114 352	57 383	33 233	88 083	327 423	200 536	117 571	126 887	6 593
2003	506 423	109 736	63 441	35 701	95 736	344 824	203 047	125 283	141 777	7 296
2004	558 457	122 946	56 998	41 467	101 278	378 930	229 584	140 211	149 346	8 205
2005	653 074	187 614	54 421	48 493	106 404	451 740	311 502	157 208	140 238	7 245
2006	795 263	264 577	58 648	50 972	119 047	557 632	404 587	188 224	153 045	6 443
2007	944 036	375 979	61 975	55 394	120 159	681 761	524 218	206 323	157 543	6 169
2008	994 104	416 404	71 589	54 682	119 729	735 435	563 945	213 446	171 490	4 639
2009	825 089	342 911	61 144	41 183	113 546	606 897	456 046	178 858	150 851	4 205
2010	871 076	349 923	61 939	48 404	116 251	635 475	476 681	190 027	158 794	3 726
2011	952 436	388 754	65 509	48 161	128 181	704 201	533 254	215 229	170 947	3 884
2012	1 013 511	443 127	75 090	48 053	129 980	754 564	580 861	219 344	173 703	4 166
2013	1 142 454	587 347	75 060	48 955	115 028	877 759	721 470	226 191	156 289	4 498
2014	1 252 331	692 786	73 773	48 847	110 664	969 144	815 373	225 324	153 771	4 534
2015	1 201 974	672 595	69 165	49 589	103 254	923 620	776 305	206 571	147 315	4 393
2016	1 184 562	661 262	73 684	47 700	107 381	931 538	771 315	202 528	160 223	4 769
2017	1 181 179	648 937	66 780	48 935	112 074	953 069	791 379	208 194	161 690	4 912
2018	1 166 296	590 399	68 096	58 024	115 478	913 906	742 113	218 611	171 793	5 636
2019	1 024 141	438 423	61 743	61 657	124 016	764 095	590 589	222 662	173 506	5 091
2020	999 281	383 453	59 260	66 049	131 560	736 537	548 717	233 247	187 820	9 676
2021	1 078 952	405 120	57 833	87 453	141 692	781 986	594 657	259 108	187 329	11 603
2018										
January	1 173 389	641 447	65 642	49 362	111 846	945 108	784 773	208 602	160 335	5 130
February	1 172 072	639 020	64 358	50 370	112 100	942 344	784 062	209 936	158 282	5 169
March	1 177 043	641 385	63 408	51 569	112 286	944 368	786 077	210 262	158 291	5 396
April	1 179 471	641 693	62 661	52 759	112 519	944 351	786 474	210 850	157 877	5 504
May	1 182 078	637 985	63 064	53 713	113 022	943 640	783 896	212 695	159 744	5 530
June	1 185 249	633 626	65 435	54 350	113 462	943 178	780 968	214 651	162 210	5 680
July	1 180 618	626 367	64 676	55 096	113 904	936 998	775 526	216 541	161 472	5 829
August	1 183 041	623 086	64 500	55 673	114 245	937 922	772 741	217 713	165 181	5 708
September	1 185 237	615 811	68 687	56 051	114 264	934 892	766 478	218 716	168 414	5 728
October	1 181 730	608 219	68 445	56 787	114 867	929 586	760 028	220 052	169 558	5 848
November	1 170 473	596 861	68 347	57 435	115 218	918 371	748 306	219 205	170 065	5 753
December	1 166 296	590 399	68 096	58 024	115 478	913 906	742 113	218 611	171 793	5 636
2019										
January	1 155 691	579 282	67 675	58 706	115 970	903 977	731 937	219 381	172 040	5 560
February	1 139 202	564 384	66 573	59 002	116 318	886 704	716 893	219 480	169 811	5 413
March	1 132 745	554 977	66 568	59 015	117 513	880 404	708 823	220 692	171 581	5 250
April	1 121 514	542 815	66 357	59 325	118 423	868 754	697 002	220 713	171 752	5 216
May	1 102 503	525 560	65 008	59 409	119 149	851 275	679 751	220 275	171 524	5 232
June	1 084 418	510 709	63 660	59 973	120 106	832 214	664 288	219 997	167 926	5 242
July	1 076 241	502 887	61 874	60 409	120 964	823 386	656 392	220 153	166 994	5 244
August	1 067 127	491 662	61 539	60 976	121 534	813 086	645 374	220 575	167 712	5 203
September	1 057 174	479 102	62 021	60 904	122 450	801 685	632 379	221 225	169 306	5 133
October	1 050 272	468 072	64 307	60 816	123 269	794 509	622 202	222 141	172 307	5 128
November	1 035 156	455 594	60 747	61 454	123 534	777 141	608 699	222 704	168 442	5 162
December	1 024 141	438 423	61 743	61 657	124 016	764 095	590 589	222 662	173 506	5 091
2020										
January	1 025 962	438 963	61 172	62 015	124 704	764 525	590 567	222 944	173 958	5 255
February	1 030 552	439 588	60 867	61 972	125 309	769 100	591 255	223 035	177 845	5 407
March	1 016 129	421 053	63 181	60 986	125 785	756 493	573 702	223 831	182 791	5 769
April	1 005 432	412 912	63 263	59 705	126 639	748 685	565 833	224 410	182 852	5 843
May	1 006 917	412 722	63 355	59 137	127 253	750 871	566 116	224 948	184 755	6 283
June	998 120	402 132	62 637	59 732	127 773	742 126	556 741	225 602	185 385	6 671
July	995 146	396 851	63 059	60 089	128 600	739 445	552 634	226 500	186 811	7 166
August	992 984	391 297	63 516	60 881	129 172	736 875	548 378	227 255	188 497	7 592
September	994 521	389 822	61 642	61 923	129 632	737 179	549 864	229 037	187 315	8 037
October	996 991	388 660	60 890	63 056	130 067	738 750	550 318	230 191	188 432	8 432
November	998 962	387 296	59 700	64 356	130 678	739 090	550 628	231 368	188 462	8 930
December	999 281	383 453	59 260	66 049	131 560	736 537	548 717	233 247	187 820	9 676
2021										
January	1 001 660	379 620	59 919	67 726	132 019	736 457	546 264	234 626	190 193	10 016
February	1 011 271	382 306	60 368	70 052	133 036	741 743	550 754	236 490	190 989	10 319
March	1 020 427	383 293	60 368	72 967	133 488	746 568	553 900	238 500	192 668	10 665
April	1 026 280	382 937	59 681	75 853	134 053	748 505	556 870	241 783	191 635	10 957
May	1 034 607	385 773	59 300	78 565	134 774	752 234	561 290	243 542	190 944	11 235
June	1 044 946	390 265	58 581	80 368	135 668	759 343	567 939	245 817	191 404	11 579
July	1 049 514	390 587	58 022	81 462	136 246	761 339	570 172	247 947	191 167	11 773
August	1 059 290	395 769	57 552	83 498	137 268	768 458	577 863	250 632	190 595	11 816
September	1 063 898	396 728	57 936	84 985	138 219	771 015	580 310	252 283	190 705	11 940
October	1 068 436	398 109	58 049	85 680	138 939	774 785	584 067	254 921	190 718	11 701
November	1 073 584	401 659	57 033	86 047	140 579	779 889	589 865	257 392	190 024	11 500
December	1 078 952	405 120	57 833	87 453	141 692	781 986	594 657	259 108	187 329	11 603

[1]Includes categories not shown separately.

Table 16-7. Motor Vehicle Sales and Inventories

(Units.)

Year and month	Retail sales of new passenger cars						Retail inventories of new domestic passenger cars (thousands of units, end of period)		
	Thousands of units, not seasonally adjusted			Millions of units, seasonally adjusted annual rate			Not seasonally adjusted	Seasonally adjusted	Inventory to sales ratio
	Total	Domestic	Foreign	Total	Domestic	Foreign			
1980	8 981.8	6 581.4	2 400.4	8.982	6.581	2.400	1 448.0	1 440.0	2.600
1981	8 534.3	6 208.8	2 325.5	8.534	6.209	2.326	1 471.0	1 495.0	3.600
1982	7 979.4	5 758.2	2 221.2	7.979	5.758	2.221	1 126.0	1 127.0	2.200
1983	9 178.6	6 793.0	2 385.6	9.179	6.793	2.386	1 352.0	1 350.0	2.000
1984	10 390.2	7 951.7	2 438.5	10.390	7.952	2.439	1 415.0	1 411.0	2.100
1985	10 978.4	8 204.7	2 773.7	10.978	8.205	2.774	1 630.0	1 619.0	2.500
1986	11 405.7	8 215.0	3 190.7	11.406	8.215	3.191	1 499.0	1 515.0	2.000
1987	10 170.9	7 080.9	3 090.0	10.171	7.081	3.090	1 680.0	1 716.0	2.800
1988	10 545.6	7 539.4	3 006.2	10.546	7.539	3.006	1 601.0	1 601.0	2.300
1989	9 776.8	7 078.1	2 698.7	9.777	7.078	2.699	1 669.0	1 687.0	3.100
1990	9 300.2	6 896.9	2 403.3	9.300	6.897	2.403	1 408.0	1 418.0	2.600
1991	8 175.0	6 136.9	2 038.1	8.175	6.137	2.038	1 283.0	1 296.0	2.600
1992	8 214.4	6 276.6	1 937.8	8.214	6.277	1.938	1 276.0	1 288.0	2.300
1993	8 517.7	6 734.0	1 783.7	8.518	6.734	1.784	1 364.9	1 377.3	2.359
1994	8 990.4	7 255.2	1 735.2	8.990	7.255	1.735	1 436.6	1 445.3	2.319
1995	8 620.4	7 114.1	1 506.3	8.620	7.114	1.506	1 618.5	1 629.8	2.565
1996	8 478.6	7 206.3	1 272.3	8.479	7.206	1.272	1 363.4	1 422.5	2.478
1997	8 217.7	6 862.3	1 355.4	8.218	6.862	1.355	1 329.9	1 399.7	2.368
1998	8 084.9	6 705.1	1 379.8	8.085	6.705	1.380	1 324.4	1 369.7	2.222
1999	8 637.7	6 918.8	1 718.9	8.638	6.919	1.719	1 367.6	1 406.6	2.369
2000	8 777.7	6 761.6	2 016.1	8.778	6.762	2.016	1 377.0	1 397.2	2.810
2001	8 352.1	6 254.4	2 097.7	8.352	6.254	2.098	955.7	976.9	2.267
2002	8 042.1	5 816.5	2 225.6	8.042	5.817	2.226	1 132.0	1 229.8	2.533
2003	7 555.6	5 472.6	2 083.0	7.556	5.473	2.083	1 115.8	1 227.1	2.713
2004	7 482.5	5 333.6	2 148.9	7.483	5.334	2.149	1 034.2	1 144.8	2.405
2005	7 660.4	5 473.6	2 186.8	7.660	5.474	2.187	930.6	1 012.2	2.289
2006	7 761.3	5 416.7	2 344.6	7.761	5.417	2.345	1 031.7	1 105.5	2.498
2007	7 562.1	5 197.1	2 365.0	7.562	5.197	2.365	906.8	985.3	2.272
2008	6 769.2	4 491.0	2 278.2	6.769	4.491	2.278	1 144.2	1 215.5	4.115
2009	5 401.5	3 558.4	1 843.1	5.402	3.558	1.843	686.4	733.2	2.162
2010	5 635.7	3 791.5	1 844.2	5.636	3.792	1.844	759.1	796.7	2.402
2011	6 092.9	4 146.0	1 946.9	6.093	4.146	1.947	813.0	806.7	2.255
2012	7 245.1	5 119.8	2 125.3	7.245	5.120	2.125	1 069.5	1 067.8	2.374
2013	7 586.4	5 433.2	2 153.2	7.586	5.433	2.153	1 259.3	1 231.0	2.812
2014	7 708.0	5 609.9	2 098.1	7.708	5.610	2.098	1 249.4	1 218.0	2.522
2015	7 528.5	5 595.1	1 933.4	7.529	5.595	1.933	1 178.6	1 156.0	2.600
2016	6 883.3	5 145.6	1 737.8	6.883	5.146	1.738	1 209.8	1 143.9	2.700
2017	6 089.2	4 593.0	1 496.2	6.089	4.593	1.496	967.6	862.8	2.444
2018	5 310.3	4 086.9	1 223.4	5.310	4.087	1.223	802.6	722.5	2.172
2019	4 719.7	3 543.9	1 175.8	4.720	3.544	1.176	579.0	496.2	1.743
2020	3 401.8	2 559.8	842.1	3.402	2.560	0.842	518.3	426.5	1.884
2021	3 350.0	2 375.7	974.3	3.350	2.376	0.974	114.9	81.5	0.487
2019									
January	353.6	277.2	76.4	5.241	4.068	1.173	838.3	746.1	2.201
February	365.5	284.5	81.1	4.814	3.685	1.129	839.7	728.5	2.372
March	483.0	371.9	111.1	4.922	3.773	1.150	786.6	707.2	2.249
April	395.6	295.2	100.4	4.760	3.581	1.179	748.3	698.6	2.341
May	455.0	339.5	115.5	4.802	3.567	1.235	695.6	691.9	2.328
June	440.0	322.1	117.9	4.902	3.584	1.318	698.0	690.5	2.312
July	382.9	277.5	105.4	4.692	3.448	1.244	643.3	670.3	2.333
August	434.2	322.2	112.0	4.609	3.410	1.199	612.7	650.2	2.288
September	339.5	255.0	84.4	4.596	3.459	1.137	637.4	642.9	2.230
October	343.8	254.7	89.1	4.395	3.238	1.157	640.4	601.5	2.229
November	352.6	261.4	91.3	4.401	3.283	1.118	627.9	568.9	2.079
December	374.1	282.9	91.3	4.502	3.431	1.070	579.0	532.2	1.861
2020									
January	293.2	223.6	69.6	4.342	3.292	1.050	607.4	524.5	1.912
February	346.5	267.0	79.5	4.272	3.227	1.044	630.9	512.8	1.907
March	264.7	208.1	56.6	2.847	2.232	0.614	665.9	584.1	3.140
April	166.4	124.9	41.5	1.932	1.458	0.474	576.6	537.7	4.425
May	258.5	181.5	77.0	2.661	1.863	0.798	451.9	457.7	2.948
June	251.2	178.3	72.9	2.890	2.054	0.835	459.9	452.0	2.641
July	292.6	217.4	75.2	3.487	2.627	0.860	474.0	500.7	2.287
August	299.8	226.7	73.1	3.469	2.642	0.828	473.7	512.8	2.330
September	304.8	233.9	71.0	3.731	2.833	0.898	508.2	505.3	2.140
October	313.6	240.1	73.5	3.806	2.901	0.905	542.1	506.0	2.093
November	277.6	211.0	66.7	3.741	2.864	0.877	545.8	487.0	2.040
December	332.9	247.4	85.6	3.644	2.723	0.922	518.3	469.5	2.070
2021									
January	250.0	180.9	69.1	3.798	2.727	1.072	509.3	441.3	1.942
February	258.8	184.5	74.3	3.447	2.413	1.034	492.4	402.1	1.999
March	362.5	259.1	103.4	3.845	2.733	1.113	418.3	356.1	1.564
April	350.3	245.0	105.3	4.104	2.903	1.201	347.2	310.9	1.285
May	379.7	264.8	114.9	3.931	2.728	1.203	255.5	251.9	1.108
June	314.9	216.7	98.1	3.652	2.521	1.132	212.7	196.9	0.937
July	304.7	209.8	94.9	3.494	2.442	1.052	149.0	143.2	0.704
August	254.2	172.9	81.4	3.076	2.116	0.960	134.2	125.6	0.712
September	222.8	153.5	69.3	2.745	1.861	0.884	105.8	82.7	0.533
October	208.8	155.0	53.9	2.608	1.931	0.678	114.2	83.7	0.520
November	204.8	156.3	48.5	2.705	2.073	0.632	108.7	73.0	0.422
December	238.6	177.2	61.4	2.686	2.009	0.678	114.9	81.5	0.487

Table 16-7. Motor Vehicle Sales and Inventories—*Continued*

(Units.)

Year and month	Retail sales of new trucks and buses								Unit sales of cars and light trucks (millions of units, seasonally adjusted annual rate)		
	Thousands of units, not seasonally adjusted				Millions of units, seasonally adjusted annual rate						
	Total	0–14,000 pounds		14,001 pounds and over	Total	0–14,000 pounds		14,001 pounds and over	Total	Domestic	Foreign
		Domestic	Foreign			Domestic	Foreign				
1980	2 487.4	1 731.1	484.6	271.7	2.487	1.731	0.485	0.272	11.193	8.313	2.885
1981	2 255.6	1 581.7	447.6	226.3	2.256	1.582	0.448	0.226	10.564	7.791	2.773
1982	2 562.8	1 967.5	410.4	184.9	2.563	1.968	0.410	0.185	10.363	7.726	2.632
1983	3 117.3	2 465.2	463.3	188.8	3.117	2.465	0.463	0.189	12.120	9.258	2.849
1984	4 093.1	3 207.2	607.7	278.2	4.093	3.207	0.608	0.278	14.199	11.159	3.046
1985	4 741.7	3 618.4	828.3	295.0	4.742	3.618	0.828	0.295	15.444	11.823	3.602
1986	4 912.1	3 671.4	967.2	273.5	4.912	3.671	0.967	0.274	16.051	11.886	4.158
1987	4 991.5	3 792.0	912.2	287.3	4.992	3.792	0.912	0.287	14.861	10.873	4.002
1988	5 231.9	4 199.7	697.9	334.3	5.232	4.200	0.698	0.334	15.436	11.739	3.704
1989	5 055.9	4 113.6	630.3	312.0	5.056	4.114	0.630	0.312	14.529	11.192	3.329
1990	4 837.0	3 956.8	602.7	277.5	4.837	3.957	0.603	0.278	13.862	10.854	3.006
1991	4 355.4	3 605.6	528.8	221.0	4.355	3.606	0.529	0.221	12.315	9.743	2.567
1992	4 892.2	4 247.0	395.9	249.3	4.892	4.247	0.396	0.249	12.860	10.524	2.334
1993	5 667.8	5 000.5	364.5	302.8	5.668	5.001	0.365	0.303	13.874	11.735	2.148
1994	6 407.3	5 658.2	396.3	352.8	6.407	5.658	0.396	0.353	15.044	12.913	2.132
1995	6 496.4	5 705.9	402.1	388.4	6.496	5.706	0.402	0.388	14.728	12.820	1.908
1996	6 977.6	6 179.8	438.7	359.1	6.978	6.180	0.439	0.359	15.097	13.386	1.711
1997	7 280.4	6 324.7	579.5	376.2	7.280	6.325	0.580	0.376	15.122	13.187	1.935
1998	7 882.4	6 802.0	656.1	424.3	7.882	6.802	0.656	0.424	15.543	13.507	2.036
1999	8 777.3	7 480.7	775.3	521.3	8.777	7.481	0.775	0.521	16.894	14.400	2.494
2000	9 033.9	7 719.7	852.3	461.9	9.034	7.720	0.852	0.462	17.350	14.481	2.868
2001	9 120.4	7 789.0	981.3	350.1	9.120	7.789	0.981	0.350	17.122	14.043	3.079
2002	9 096.5	7 707.8	1 066.3	322.4	9.097	7.708	1.066	0.322	16.817	13.524	3.292
2003	9 411.9	7 856.3	1 227.2	328.4	9.412	7.856	1.227	0.328	16.639	13.329	3.310
2004	9 815.8	8 138.0	1 246.2	431.6	9.816	8.138	1.246	0.432	16.866	13.472	3.395
2005	9 784.4	8 072.4	1 215.5	496.5	9.784	8.072	1.216	0.497	16.948	13.546	3.402
2006	9 287.0	7 396.0	1 346.6	544.4	9.287	7.396	1.347	0.544	16.505	12.813	3.691
2007	8 897.9	7 138.7	1 388.1	371.1	8.898	7.139	1.388	0.371	16.089	12.336	3.753
2008	15 408.6	5 329.2	9 780.9	298.5	15.409	5.329	9.781	0.299	13.195	9.820	12.059
2009	5 200.5	4 116.5	884.2	199.8	5.201	4.117	0.884	0.200	10.402	7.675	2.727
2010	6 136.6	5 020.3	898.7	217.6	6.137	5.020	0.899	0.218	11.556	8.812	2.743
2011	6 955.5	5 666.5	982.4	306.6	6.956	5.667	0.982	0.307	12.743	9.813	2.929
2012	7 534.3	6 127.3	1 060.7	346.3	7.534	6.127	1.061	0.346	14.435	11.247	3.186
2013	8 296.4	6 704.5	1 239.3	352.6	8.296	6.705	1.239	0.353	15.530	12.138	3.393
2014	9 151.9	7 384.3	1 359.9	407.7	9.152	7.384	1.360	0.408	16.452	12.994	3.458
2015	10 328.8	8 097.4	1 782.1	449.3	10.329	8.097	1.782	0.449	17.131	13.692	3.715
2016	10 995.0	8 436.2	2 157.7	401.0	10.995	8.436	2.158	0.401	17.465	13.582	3.895
2017	11 475.9	8 651.8	2 409.1	415.0	11.476	8.652	2.409	0.415	17.137	13.245	3.905
2018	12 402.5	9 153.4	2 761.3	487.9	12.403	9.153	2.761	0.488	17.214	13.240	3.985
2019	12 768.4	9 621.7	2 619.7	527.1	12.768	9.622	2.620	0.527	16.938	13.166	3.795
2020	11 479.5	8 614.8	2 455.2	409.5	11.480	8.615	2.455	0.410	14.472	11.175	3.297
2021	12 058.5	9 006.5	2 590.4	461.6	12.059	9.007	2.590	0.462	14.947	11.382	3.565
2019											
January	818.4	598.1	181.9	38.3	12.025	8.852	2.651	0.522	16.744	12.919	3.824
February	923.4	680.7	205.9	36.8	12.370	9.126	2.735	0.510	16.674	12.811	3.864
March	1 160.5	870.1	246.4	43.9	12.734	9.618	2.592	0.524	17.132	13.390	3.741
April	977.8	745.2	186.4	46.1	12.237	9.270	2.398	0.570	16.427	12.850	3.577
May	1 173.8	897.4	229.8	46.6	13.038	9.923	2.551	0.564	17.276	13.490	3.786
June	1 115.5	856.6	213.9	45.1	12.931	9.870	2.510	0.550	17.282	13.455	3.828
July	1 061.6	803.9	210.2	47.4	12.905	9.785	2.554	0.565	17.032	13.233	3.798
August	1 251.7	946.2	258.9	46.6	13.036	9.850	2.651	0.535	17.110	13.260	3.850
September	976.7	729.7	198.5	48.5	13.118	9.885	2.679	0.554	17.161	13.344	3.817
October	1 037.3	776.1	215.0	46.2	12.835	9.608	2.722	0.505	16.725	12.846	3.880
November	1 086.7	820.4	231.0	35.3	13.156	9.985	2.715	0.456	17.101	13.268	3.833
December	1 185.1	897.3	241.6	46.2	12.837	9.689	2.678	0.470	16.869	13.121	3.748
2020											
January	875.2	659.4	183.9	31.9	12.964	9.852	2.681	0.431	16.874	13.144	3.731
February	1 037.2	786.7	217.4	33.1	13.065	9.906	2.703	0.456	16.881	13.134	3.747
March	758.6	582.5	142.7	33.4	8.788	6.779	1.621	0.387	11.247	9.011	2.236
April	576.9	436.0	112.9	28.0	7.029	5.258	1.424	0.347	8.614	6.716	1.898
May	884.2	645.6	215.0	23.6	9.777	7.134	2.335	0.308	12.131	8.998	3.133
June	880.2	631.5	218.3	30.4	10.558	7.510	2.695	0.353	13.095	9.564	3.530
July	975.9	725.7	218.4	31.8	11.601	8.616	2.606	0.379	14.710	11.244	3.466
August	1 054.6	794.3	223.9	36.3	12.208	9.293	2.484	0.430	15.246	11.935	3.311
September	1 074.8	822.6	213.6	38.6	12.972	9.856	2.692	0.424	16.280	12.690	3.590
October	1 085.8	823.1	222.3	40.4	13.047	9.902	2.694	0.450	16.402	12.803	3.599
November	957.6	709.1	212.4	36.1	12.598	9.383	2.749	0.466	15.873	12.247	3.626
December	1 318.5	998.1	274.5	45.9	13.117	9.885	2.779	0.452	16.309	12.608	3.701
2021											
January	891.7	661.1	195.3	35.4	13.489	10.076	2.905	0.508	16.779	12.803	3.976
February	967.9	723.5	211.5	32.9	12.945	9.684	2.801	0.460	15.932	12.097	3.835
March	1 280.3	945.1	289.5	45.6	14.310	10.618	3.177	0.514	17.641	13.351	4.290
April	1 206.9	899.0	269.1	38.7	14.676	10.840	3.353	0.482	18.297	13.743	4.554
May	1 229.0	897.0	293.6	38.3	13.462	9.784	3.177	0.501	16.891	12.512	4.380
June	1 028.1	760.9	226.5	40.8	12.296	9.038	2.781	0.477	15.471	11.559	3.913
July	1 012.0	747.7	228.3	35.9	11.609	8.565	2.604	0.440	14.663	11.007	3.656
August	874.7	642.0	196.5	36.3	10.427	7.733	2.277	0.417	13.086	9.848	3.237
September	830.2	614.8	178.3	37.0	9.948	7.310	2.233	0.405	12.287	9.170	3.117
October	880.5	669.7	172.5	38.3	10.877	8.310	2.129	0.438	13.047	10.241	2.806
November	844.8	662.6	147.0	35.2	10.769	8.477	1.853	0.439	13.035	10.551	2.485
December	1 012.5	783.1	182.3	47.0	10.318	7.975	1.879	0.464	12.540	9.983	2.557

Table 16-8. Retail and Food Services Sales

(All retail establishments and food services; millions of dollars; not seasonally adjusted.)

Year and month	Retail and food services, total [1]	GAFO (department store type goods), total [2]	Motor vehicles and parts	Furniture and home furnishings	Electronics and appliances	Building materials and garden	Food and beverages	Health and personal care	Gasoline	Clothing and accessories	General merchandise	Nonstore retailers	Food services and drinking places
1995	2 450 628	650 040	579 715	63 470	64 770	164 561	390 386	101 632	181 113	131 333	300 498	103 516	233 012
1996	2 603 794	682 613	627 507	67 707	68 363	176 683	401 073	109 554	194 425	136 581	315 305	117 761	242 245
1997	2 726 131	713 387	653 817	72 715	70 061	191 063	409 373	118 670	199 700	140 293	331 363	126 190	257 364
1998	2 852 956	757 936	688 415	77 412	74 527	202 423	416 525	129 582	191 727	149 151	351 081	133 904	271 194
1999	3 086 990	815 665	764 204	84 294	78 977	218 290	433 699	142 697	159 751	380 179	151 797	283 900	
2000	3 287 537	862 739	796 210	91 170	82 206	228 994	444 764	155 233	249 816	167 674	404 228	180 453	304 261
2001	3 378 906	882 700	815 579	91 484	80 240	239 379	462 429	166 532	251 383	167 287	427 468	180 563	316 638
2002	3 459 077	912 707	818 811	94 438	83 740	248 539	464 856	179 983	250 619	172 304	446 520	189 279	330 525
2003	3 612 457	946 114	841 588	96 736	86 442	263 463	474 385	275 187	178 694	178 694	468 771	206 359	349 726
2004	3 846 605	1 003 891	866 372	103 757	93 896	295 274	490 380	324 006	324 006	190 253	497 382	228 977	373 557
2005	4 085 746	1 059 599	888 307	109 120	100 461	320 802	508 484	378 923	378 923	200 969	528 385	255 579	396 463
2006	4 294 359	1 110 155	899 997	112 795	105 477	334 130	525 232	421 976	421 976	213 189	554 256	284 343	422 786
2007	4 439 733	1 143 426	910 139	111 144	106 599	320 854	547 837	451 822	451 822	221 205	578 582	308 767	444 551
2008	4 391 580	1 136 376	785 865	98 720	105 317	301 833	569 276	246 573	503 639	215 583	595 041	319 152	456 265
2009	4 064 476	1 088 197	671 772	84 749	95 364	261 637	568 418	252 794	391 234	204 475	588 918	311 152	452 005
2010	4 284 968	1 114 374	742 913	85 205	97 396	260 566	580 530	260 435	448 349	213 286	603 757	340 957	466 920
2011	4 598 302	1 155 666	812 938	87 586	99 928	269 480	609 137	271 612	533 457	228 606	624 766	376 344	495 350
2012	4 826 390	1 191 843	886 494	91 542	102 060	281 533	628 205	274 000	555 419	239 493	642 313	408 171	524 161
2013	5 002 745	1 213 826	962 057	95 753	103 511	299 578	641 515	279 551	553 712	245 162	653 572	429 977	543 507
2014	5 217 301	1 241 577	1 026 740	100 551	102 844	313 527	670 473	294 566	546 962	251 336	670 608	464 167	576 650
2015	5 350 286	1 262 841	1 103 521	107 884	100 175	323 979	687 375	307 891	455 602	257 279	680 127	498 331	624 175
2016	5 505 963	1 267 817	1 151 720	112 320	93 963	337 699	702 020	318 928	435 967	435 967	682 698	544 316	657 867
2017	5 732 863	1 274 977	1 185 696	115 309	92 424	349 365	728 843	323 866	476 152	261 396	691 891	608 194	692 649
2018	5 987 445	1 298 225	1 204 941	119 026	94 105	367 655	749 867	279 613	522 921	267 482	707 088	675 816	732 020
2019	6 175 020	1 306 269	1 237 744	120 650	90 934	373 321	775 014	344 045	513 508	269 537	716 467	750 640	772 748
2020	6 219 613	1 229 215	1 208 304	113 023	75 978	422 211	850 215	351 257	428 076	201 422	730 570	978 306	649 220
2021	7 441 386	1 471 976	1 480 124	141 960	94 181	477 790	880 260	385 388	583 495	294 062	804 289	1 153 237	876 337

2019

Year and month	Retail and food services, total [1]	GAFO (department store type goods), total [2]	Motor vehicles and parts	Furniture and home furnishings	Electronics and appliances	Building materials and garden	Food and beverages	Health and personal care	Gasoline	Clothing and accessories	General merchandise	Nonstore retailers	Food services and drinking places
January	456 012	91 522	88 152	8 846	7 197	26 749	64 169	28 715	36 539	22 176	51 637	57 538	56 653
February	441 793	90 917	89 981	8 659	6 599	24 154	62 926	26 854	35 613	22 194	50 502	53 342	56 816
March	513 263	106 574	110 658	10 054	7 229	30 056	64 026	28 885	42 184	22 566	58 713	57 157	66 103
April	506 157	102 943	103 656	9 617	6 532	34 179	64 241	28 518	44 390	22 515	56 870	58 029	63 453
May	543 388	110 486	112 050	10 334	7 161	37 383	64 325	29 612	47 508	22 215	60 900	61 961	67 732
June	514 479	105 820	104 805	9 785	7 026	33 623	64 707	27 768	44 983	22 167	58 882	57 704	66 255
July	528 010	107 295	109 250	10 210	7 213	33 773	65 549	28 292	46 492	22 569	58 919	61 315	66 368
August	541 276	114 271	114 426	10 631	7 556	32 436	65 324	28 694	46 068	22 615	61 882	61 105	68 385
September	492 004	100 049	99 156	10 109	7 152	30 004	64 832	27 399	42 845	22 376	54 615	58 162	63 670
October	521 235	106 658	103 096	10 248	7 116	32 660	64 933	29 673	44 422	22 417	58 628	64 768	66 200
November	531 243	121 690	100 229	11 009	9 261	29 755	64 963	27 976	41 473	22 184	66 609	70 840	63 932
December	586 160	148 044	102 285	11 148	10 892	28 549	65 455	31 659	40 991	23 230	78 310	88 719	67 181

2020

Year and month	Retail and food services, total [1]	GAFO (department store type goods), total [2]	Motor vehicles and parts	Furniture and home furnishings	Electronics and appliances	Building materials and garden	Food and beverages	Health and personal care	Gasoline	Clothing and accessories	General merchandise	Nonstore retailers	Food services and drinking places
January	479 343	93 680	91 754	9 386	7 063	26 878	64 768	29 186	39 536	16 831	52 574	63 108	63 058
February	478 065	96 496	95 877	9 344	6 659	26 116	64 872	27 972	36 801	19 208	53 782	60 596	64 862
March	477 715	94 444	80 434	8 037	5 778	31 960	81 800	31 102	34 088	10 958	62 810	68 609	49 430
April	406 411	68 075	67 654	3 852	3 013	35 674	71 138	25 764	26 668	2 761	54 179	75 132	31 169
May	504 187	90 069	104 334	7 145	3 914	42 102	72 476	26 360	31 927	8 696	62 824	82 010	43 934
June	532 357	101 364	110 900	9 712	5 583	41 746	71 208	28 465	36 169	16 260	59 878	80 287	53 690
July	549 264	105 142	112 696	10 318	6 478	39 078	71 444	29 781	38 709	17 567	60 813	83 894	57 005
August	546 379	107 774	112 191	10 790	6 765	36 360	70 080	29 146	38 547	18 694	61 205	83 160	59 245
September	532 094	102 992	109 270	10 844	6 383	36 597	70 053	29 699	37 044	18 449	57 435	81 754	57 810
October	554 838	109 605	110 899	10 859	6 781	37 217	69 685	30 864	37 960	19 764	61 958	88 157	60 704
November	545 736	117 015	99 804	10 943	8 194	34 298	70 464	28 837	34 202	20 905	66 798	98 215	53 923
December	613 224	142 559	112 491	11 793	9 367	34 185	69 983	34 081	36 425	31 329	76 314	113 384	54 390

2021

Year and month	Retail and food services, total [1]	GAFO (department store type goods), total [2]	Motor vehicles and parts	Furniture and home furnishings	Electronics and appliances	Building materials and garden	Food and beverages	Health and personal care	Gasoline	Clothing and accessories	General merchandise	Nonstore retailers	Food services and drinking places
January	518 300	100 170	100 629	10 432	6 843	30 890	70 921	29 377	41 104	21 093	58 475	86 010	55 742
February	492 597	93 197	99 324	9 916	6 121	29 284	70 969	27 599	42 741	19 904	53 073	80 926	53 664
March	634 945	124 196	141 659	12 401	7 875	43 010	71 284	33 452	46 054	24 320	68 779	95 909	69 181
April	629 451	117 693	138 891	11 951	7 346	46 533	71 817	31 960	45 500	24 319	64 291	94 884	71 577
May	644 652	124 204	137 600	11 925	7 501	46 315	72 566	31 436	46 166	24 844	67 916	92 062	77 191
June	638 109	121 517	132 297	11 730	7 891	44 931	73 230	32 617	47 253	25 705	65 694	93 523	77 430
July	636 312	123 638	129 123	12 027	7 920	41 162	72 959	31 992	48 385	25 237	66 868	88 478	81 467
August	633 403	125 034	123 620	12 091	7 854	39 586	74 234	32 537	49 523	25 020	67 707	94 144	79 581
September	609 406	116 392	118 654	11 974	7 548	38 859	74 785	32 089	51 633	25 376	62 955	90 401	76 566
October	638 069	125 223	120 186	12 040	7 896	39 435	75 535	32 541	53 978	25 487	69 188	97 978	80 332
November	654 469	137 115	115 837	12 795	8 940	39 491	75 783	32 432	55 209	25 784	74 215	114 631	74 782
December	711 673	163 597	122 304	12 678	10 446	38 294	76 187	37 356	55 910	25 051	85 128	124 291	78 824

[1] Includes store categories not shown separately.
[2] Includes furniture, home furnishings, electronics, appliances, clothing, sporting goods, hobby, book, music, general merchandise, office supplies, stationery, and gifts.

Table 16-8. Retail and Food Services Sales—*Continued*

(All retail establishments and food services; millions of dollars; seasonally adjusted.)

Year and month	Total	Retail and food services — Retail (NAICS industry categories)										
		Total	GAFO (department store type goods) [2]	Motor vehicles and parts	Furniture and home furnishings	Electronics and appliances	Building materials and garden	Food and beverages — Total [1]	Groceries	Beer, wine, and liquor	Health and personal care	Gasoline
1995	2 450 628	2 217 613	650 040	579 715	63 470	64 770	164 561	390 386	356 409	22 007	101 632	181 113
1996	2 603 794	2 361 546	682 613	627 507	67 707	68 363	176 683	401 073	365 547	23 157	109 554	194 425
1997	2 726 131	2 468 765	713 387	653 817	72 715	70 061	191 063	409 373	372 570	24 081	118 670	199 700
1998	2 852 956	2 581 761	757 936	688 415	77 412	74 527	202 423	416 525	378 188	25 382	129 582	191 727
1999	3 086 990	2 803 088	815 665	764 204	84 294	78 977	218 290	433 699	394 250	26 476	142 697	212 524
2000	3 287 537	2 983 275	862 739	796 210	91 170	82 206	228 994	444 764	402 515	28 507	155 233	249 816
2001	3 378 906	3 062 267	882 700	815 579	91 484	80 240	239 379	462 429	418 127	29 621	166 532	251 383
2002	3 459 077	3 128 552	912 707	818 811	94 438	83 740	248 539	464 856	419 813	29 894	179 983	250 619
2003	3 612 457	3 262 731	946 114	841 588	96 736	86 442	263 463	474 385	427 987	30 469	275 187	178 694
2004	3 846 605	3 473 048	1 003 891	866 372	103 757	93 896	295 274	490 380	441 136	32 189	324 006	324 006
2005	4 085 746	3 689 283	1 059 599	888 307	109 120	100 461	320 802	508 484	457 667	33 567	378 923	378 923
2006	4 294 359	3 871 573	1 110 155	899 997	112 795	105 477	334 130	525 232	471 699	36 016	421 976	421 976
2007	4 439 733	3 995 182	1 143 426	910 139	111 144	106 599	320 854	547 837	491 360	38 128	451 822	451 822
2008	4 391 580	3 935 315	1 136 376	785 865	98 720	105 317	301 833	569 276	511 222	39 504	246 573	503 639
2009	4 064 476	3 612 471	1 088 197	671 772	84 749	95 364	261 637	568 418	510 033	40 245	252 794	391 234
2010	4 284 968	3 818 048	1 114 374	742 913	85 205	97 396	260 566	580 530	520 750	41 401	260 435	448 349
2011	4 598 302	4 102 952	1 155 666	812 938	87 586	99 928	269 480	609 137	547 476	42 392	271 612	533 457
2012	4 826 390	4 302 229	1 191 843	886 494	91 542	102 060	281 533	628 205	563 645	44 365	274 000	555 419
2013	5 002 745	4 459 238	1 213 826	962 057	95 753	103 511	299 578	641 515	641 515	45 647	279 551	553 712
2014	5 217 301	4 640 651	1 241 567	1 026 740	100 551	102 844	313 527	670 473	670 473	47 395	294 566	546 962
2015	5 350 286	4 726 111	1 262 841	1 103 521	107 884	100 175	323 979	687 375	687 375	49 156	307 891	455 602
2016	5 505 963	4 848 096	1 267 817	1 151 720	112 320	93 963	337 699	702 020	702 020	51 253	318 928	435 967
2017	5 732 863	5 040 214	1 274 977	1 185 696	115 309	92 424	349 365	728 843	728 843	52 622	323 866	476 152
2018	5 987 445	5 255 425	1 298 225	1 204 941	119 026	94 105	367 655	749 867	749 867	55 089	337 799	522 921
2019	6 175 020	5 402 272	1 306 269	1 237 744	120 650	90 934	373 321	775 014	775 014	56 982	344 045	513 508
2020	6 219 613	5 570 393	1 229 215	1 208 304	113 023	75 978	422 211	850 215	850 215	66 310	351 257	428 076
2021	7 441 386	6 565 049	1 471 976	1 480 124	141 960	94 181	477 790	880 260	880 260	70 164	385 388	583 495
2019												
January	501 305	439 793	108 042	99 646	9 851	7 689	32 154	64 169	57 507	4 684	28 629	40 109
February	503 037	440 875	107 673	100 952	9 862	7 568	30 626	62 926	56 290	4 677	28 875	41 996
March	509 552	446 954	108 442	103 572	9 935	7 593	30 931	64 026	57 371	4 692	28 827	43 001
April	510 367	447 230	109 089	102 246	10 007	7 560	30 931	64 241	57 585	4 669	28 719	43 734
May	512 883	448 985	108 687	102 877	10 062	7 634	30 522	64 325	57 682	4 684	28 862	43 625
June	513 694	448 992	108 615	102 878	10 119	7 587	30 499	64 707	58 025	4 728	28 805	42 238
July	518 670	453 667	109 978	103 345	10 139	7 682	31 160	65 549	58 772	4 788	28 665	42 850
August	521 158	455 967	109 529	105 732	10 134	7 586	31 675	65 324	58 543	4 796	28 580	42 735
September	517 755	452 048	108 649	103 485	10 253	7 633	31 213	64 832	58 062	4 783	28 600	42 589
October	519 519	453 451	108 739	103 340	10 136	7 444	31 212	64 933	58 132	4 798	28 809	43 254
November	521 774	455 933	108 804	105 719	10 203	7 505	31 251	64 963	58 160	4 825	28 576	43 246
December	525 903	458 923	110 529	103 750	10 034	7 564	31 690	65 455	58 630	4 882	28 267	44 459
2020												
January	524 063	456 113	110 222	102 930	10 406	7 514	32 196	64 768	57 998	4 881	28 983	43 351
February	526 174	457 898	110 075	103 495	10 257	7 399	32 331	64 872	58 024	4 871	29 290	42 010
March	480 150	432 392	97 192	76 157	7 981	6 063	32 213	81 800	74 190	5 641	30 733	34 537
April	407 025	375 918	71 562	66 241	3 959	3 487	31 885	71 138	64 225	5 185	26 103	26 068
May	483 066	442 045	87 918	97 963	7 095	4 222	36 135	72 476	64 804	5 671	26 413	29 535
June	525 093	472 249	104 118	106 961	9 860	5 971	36 238	71 208	63 505	5 666	28 579	33 677
July	536 087	481 169	105 989	105 832	10 126	6 877	36 034	71 444	63 727	5 680	30 173	35 448
August	540 078	482 391	105 454	107 235	10 641	6 875	36 741	70 080	62 269	5 765	29 802	36 194
September	551 871	492 700	110 662	111 028	10 747	6 783	36 910	70 053	62 182	5 751	30 274	36 714
October	550 049	490 826	109 447	110 462	10 657	6 991	36 498	69 685	61 887	5 681	30 170	36 926
November	543 834	486 833	107 447	108 927	10 472	6 705	36 557	70 464	62 705	5 692	29 698	36 193
December	542 942	488 876	107 296	111 086	10 446	6 478	36 528	69 983	62 328	5 580	29 948	39 293
2021												
January	572 822	513 269	116 878	115 032	11 855	7 382	38 682	70 921	62 919	5 884	29 977	41 104
February	562 686	503 650	110 991	111 776	11 243	7 068	36 997	70 969	63 026	5 811	29 740	42 741
March	626 527	559 161	125 666	130 528	12 040	8 161	41 284	71 284	63 134	5 943	32 383	46 054
April	628 942	558 423	124 770	136 019	12 096	8 463	41 752	71 817	63 692	5 905	32 414	45 500
May	620 075	547 116	122 645	129 730	11 961	8 092	39 900	72 566	64 466	5 858	31 499	46 166
June	626 999	550 638	124 255	126 897	11 884	8 476	38 863	73 230	65 060	5 892	32 847	47 253
July	620 648	543 355	123 456	120 869	11 849	8 417	38 717	72 959	64 978	5 711	32 678	48 385
August	624 738	546 946	123 636	119 191	11 889	7 990	39 079	74 234	66 186	5 776	32 866	49 523
September	630 905	552 617	124 520	120 345	11 855	7 987	39 167	74 785	66 731	5 798	32 710	51 633
October	640 899	562 296	125 805	122 668	12 064	8 191	40 093	75 535	67 458	5 849	32 444	53 978
November	644 741	565 690	125 124	123 671	12 025	7 227	40 880	75 783	67 550	5 897	32 793	55 209
December	634 393	556 810	122 100	120 807	11 219	7 224	41 207	76 187	68 035	5 852	32 797	55 910

[1] Includes store categories not shown separately.
[2] Includes furniture, home furnishings, electronics, appliances, clothing, sporting goods, hobby, book, music, general merchandise, office supplies, stationery, and gifts.

Table 16-9. Quarterly U.S. Retail Sales: Total and E-Commerce

Year and quarter	Retail sales (millions of dollars)		E-commerce as a percent of total sales	Percent change from prior quarter		Percent change from same quarter a year ago	
	Total	E-commerce		Total sales	E-commerce sales	Total sales	E-commerce sales
NOT SEASONALLY ADJUSTED							
2020							
1st quarter	1 257 773	147 588	11.7	-12.7	-16.7	2.1	20.4
2nd quarter	1 314 162	203 546	15.5	4.5	37.9	-3.8	53.4
3rd quarter	1 453 677	207 716	14.3	10.6	2.0	6.7	49.7
4rd quarter	1 544 781	256 597	16.6	6.3	23.5	7.2	44.7
2021							
1st quarter	1 467 255	216 742	14.8	-5.0	-15.5	16.7	46.9
2nd quarter	1 686 014	234 892	13.9	14.9	8.4	28.3	15.4
3rd quarter	1 641 507	227 234	13.8	-2.6	-3.3	12.9	9.4
4rd quarter	1 770 273	281 576	15.9	7.8	23.9	14.6	9.7
SEASONALLY ADJUSTED							
2008							
1st quarter	1 007 189	36 012	3.6	-0.8	0.6	2.2	13.5
2nd quarter	1 011 101	36 509	3.6	0.4	1.4	1.6	8.9
3rd quarter	999 159	36 287	3.6	-1.2	-0.6	-0.3	4.2
4th quarter	910 187	33 051	3.6	-8.9	-8.9	-10.3	-7.6
2009							
1st quarter	888 604	34 127	3.8	-2.4	3.3	-11.8	-5.2
2nd quarter	892 284	35 279	4.0	0.4	3.4	-11.8	-3.4
3rd quarter	912 858	37 400	4.1	2.3	6.0	-8.6	3.1
4th quarter	919 242	38 117	4.1	0.7	1.9	1.0	15.3
2010							
1st quarter	932 895	39 284	4.2	1.5	3.1	5.0	15.1
2nd quarter	949 252	41 301	4.4	1.8	5.1	6.4	17.1
3rd quarter	953 280	43 469	4.6	0.4	5.2	4.4	16.2
4th quarter	981 346	45 076	4.6	2.9	3.7	6.8	18.3
2011							
1st quarter	1 004 965	47 041	4.7	2.4	4.4	7.7	19.7
2nd quarter	1 020 669	48 864	4.8	1.6	3.9	7.5	18.3
3rd quarter	1 029 304	50 207	4.9	0.8	2.7	8.0	15.5
4th quarter	1 046 819	53 217	5.1	1.7	6.0	6.7	18.1
2012							
1st quarter	1 068 883	55 316	5.2	2.1	3.9	6.4	17.6
2nd quarter	1 064 937	56 593	5.3	-0.4	2.3	4.3	15.8
3rd quarter	1 073 919	58 589	5.5	0.8	3.5	4.3	16.7
4th quarter	1 089 173	60 884	5.6	1.4	3.9	4.0	14.4
2013							
1st quarter	1 108 854	62 310	5.6	1.8	2.3	3.7	12.6
2nd quarter	1 107 785	64 071	5.8	-0.1	2.8	4.0	13.2
3rd quarter	1 118 381	65 982	5.9	1.0	3.0	4.1	12.6
4rd quarter	1 124 053	68 408	6.1	0.5	3.7	3.2	12.4
2014							
1st quarter	1 134 311	70 372	6.2	0.9	2.9	2.3	12.9
2nd quarter	1 161 299	73 396	6.3	2.4	4.3	4.8	14.6
3rd quarter	1 169 158	75 811	6.5	0.7	3.3	4.5	14.9
4rd quarter	1 170 412	77 724	6.6	0.1	2.5	4.1	13.6
2015							
1st quarter	1 161 718	80 365	6.9	-0.7	3.4	2.4	14.2
2nd quarter	1 180 566	82 996	7.0	1.6	1.7	1.7	13.1
3rd quarter	1 191 950	85 775	7.2	1.0	3.3	1.9	13.1
4rd quarter	1 187 810	88 482	7.4	-0.3	3.2	1.5	13.8
2016							
1st quarter	1 189 684	91 385	7.7	0.2	3.3	2.4	13.7
2nd quarter	1 202 685	94 381	7.8	1.1	3.3	1.9	13.7
3rd quarter	1 213 893	97 174	8.0	0.9	3.0	1.8	13.3
4rd quarter	1 226 336	100 449	8.2	1.0	3.4	3.2	13.5
2017							
1st quarter	1 246 977	104 503	8.4	1.7	4.0	4.8	14.4
2nd quarter	1 247 336	108 728	8.7	0.0	4.0	3.7	15.2
3rd quarter	1 259 956	111 854	8.9	1.0	2.9	3.8	15.1
4rd quarter	1 291 752	117 867	9.1	2.5	5.4	5.3	17.3
2018							
1st quarter	1 299 655	121 808	9.4	0.6	3.3	4.2	16.6
2nd quarter	1 312 347	125 257	9.5	1.0	2.8	5.2	15.2
3rd quarter	1 319 644	128 222	9.7	0.6	2.4	4.7	14.6
4rd quarter	1 326 839	131 668	9.9	0.5	2.7	2.7	11.7
2019							
1st quarter	1 327 622	133 162	10.0	0.1	1.1	2.2	9.3
2nd quarter	1 345 207	138 200	10.3	1.3	3.8	2.5	10.3
3rd quarter	1 361 682	146 201	10.7	1.2	5.8	3.2	14.0
4rd quarter	1 368 307	152 210	11.1	0.5	4.1	3.1	15.6
2020							
1st quarter	1 346 403	159 853	11.9	-1.6	5.0	1.4	20.0
2nd quarter	1 290 212	211 004	16.4	-4.2	32.0	-4.1	52.7
3rd quarter	1 456 260	219 278	15.1	12.9	3.9	6.9	50.0
4rd quarter	1 466 535	221 421	15.1	0.7	1.0	7.2	45.5
2021							
1st quarter	1 575 288	234 440	14.9	7.4	5.9	17.0	46.7
2nd quarter	1 654 285	241 196	14.6	5.0	2.9	28.2	14.3
3rd quarter	1 642 918	240 368	14.6	-0.7	-0.3	12.8	9.6
4rd quarter	1 684 796	244 144	14.5	2.5	1.6	14.9	10.3

Table 16-10. Retail Inventories

(All retail stores; end of period, millions of dollars.)

Year and month	Not seasonally adjusted			Seasonally adjusted							General merchandise	
	Total	Excluding motor vehicles and parts	Motor vehicles and parts	Total	Excluding motor vehicles and parts	Motor vehicles and parts	Furniture, home furnishings, electronics, and appliances	Building materials and garden	Food and beverages	Clothing and accessories	Total	Department stores [1]
1995	317 304	220 921	96 383	322 216	228 842	93 374	21 817	26 337	28 718	29 298	59 530	43 455
1996	328 160	227 888	100 272	333 255	236 015	97 240	22 253	27 447	29 658	29 778	60 591	44 124
1997	338 790	234 270	104 520	343 825	242 518	101 307	22 109	28 897	29 891	31 079	60 715	44 309
1998	351 255	245 400	105 855	356 518	253 888	102 630	22 665	30 921	30 837	32 308	61 542	43 438
1999	378 813	259 879	118 934	384 078	268 567	115 511	24 096	33 005	32 635	33 735	64 297	43 835
2000	400 394	268 982	131 412	405 931	277 829	128 102	25 622	34 269	32 108	36 753	64 929	42 667
2001	387 859	266 370	121 489	393 638	274 796	118 842	24 497	34 235	33 165	35 627	64 790	40 464
2002	409 314	271 757	137 557	415 174	280 277	134 897	25 853	36 123	32 907	37 401	66 006	38 750
2003	425 748	277 471	148 277	431 199	285 668	145 531	27 152	37 398	32 504	38 503	66 655	36 823
2004	454 848	297 561	157 287	460 335	305 941	154 394	30 043	41 593	33 433	41 417	70 969	37 230
2005	465 842	310 275	155 567	471 700	318 933	152 767	31 960	45 072	33 794	43 003	74 220	38 071
2006	480 436	324 101	156 335	486 412	332 981	153 431	31 938	46 961	34 694	47 272	75 672	37 213
2007	494 526	334 715	159 811	500 578	343 565	157 013	32 476	49 074	36 472	47 381	75 899	36 466
2008	471 516	323 519	147 997	476 690	331 328	145 362	28 659	46 496	37 267	45 958	72 655	33 090
2009	423 628	308 806	114 822	428 550	315 644	112 906	26 467	42 662	37 236	40 855	69 456	30 817
2010	449 059	320 671	128 388	453 505	327 407	126 098	28 006	42 926	38 601	41 931	72 999	30 900
2011	465 329	331 539	133 790	471 394	339 350	132 044	26 684	43 356	40 194	44 400	76 774	31 374
2012	500 392	341 738	158 654	507 468	350 317	157 151	27 511	44 648	41 092	46 986	78 497	30 406
2013	538 307	357 923	180 384	545 124	366 834	178 290	27 578	47 267	42 653	50 220	81 433	30 394
2014	555 393	367 114	188 279	561 614	375 734	185 880	27 486	48 111	44 081	51 637	82 031	28 965
2015	582 344	381 115	201 229	587 997	389 569	198 428	27 332	49 600	45 479	53 304	83 940	29 204
2016	604 870	388 103	216 767	611 482	396 634	214 848	27 233	50 960	46 931	53 628	83 192	27 878
2017	616 891	394 474	222 417	625 389	403 356	222 033	27 798	52 273	48 814	53 386	80 869	25 939
2018	645 291	409 004	236 287	652 689	417 454	235 235	27 895	55 721	50 504	54 619	82 306	24 360
2019	647 655	415 181	232 474	653 710	422 910	230 800	26 910	57 797	51 740	53 281	80 234	21 829
2020	618 501	422 645	195 856	622 240	428 791	193 449	23 354	62 946	53 321	45 131	80 405	80 405
2021	645 073	480 730	164 343	649 163	487 186	161 977	28 675	74 215	55 349	48 412	92 392	92 392
2018												
January	620 764	394 550	226 214	626 491	403 565	222 926	27 569	52 503	49 103	53 458	80 884	26 072
February	627 329	398 166	229 163	629 449	404 848	224 601	27 794	53 085	49 402	54 069	81 140	26 108
March	629 133	400 690	228 443	628 487	404 189	224 298	27 774	53 259	48 870	53 769	80 697	25 469
April	631 674	401 432	230 242	631 706	406 268	225 438	27 656	53 488	48 487	54 165	81 434	25 876
May	628 182	400 066	228 116	633 933	407 302	226 631	27 519	53 859	48 893	53 764	82 149	25 936
June	628 121	400 933	227 188	635 981	408 959	227 022	27 364	54 583	49 165	53 843	81 843	25 741
July	621 793	400 267	221 526	637 772	409 492	228 280	27 534	54 894	49 307	53 712	82 029	25 569
August	630 324	406 713	223 611	642 150	410 870	231 280	27 671	55 419	49 758	53 761	82 456	25 429
September	643 534	417 884	225 650	644 142	410 989	233 153	27 643	55 503	49 631	53 507	82 365	25 421
October	673 665	440 150	233 515	648 039	414 076	233 963	28 465	55 574	49 834	54 189	83 032	25 566
November	675 746	438 018	237 728	645 211	410 818	234 393	27 356	55 507	50 022	53 747	81 288	24 323
December	645 291	409 004	236 287	652 689	417 454	235 235	27 895	55 721	50 504	54 619	82 306	24 360
2019												
January	652 273	410 857	241 416	656 362	419 356	237 006	28 262	56 518	50 505	54 908	82 856	24 285
February	659 225	415 803	243 422	658 994	421 335	237 659	28 702	56 137	50 678	54 997	83 510	24 295
March	658 750	418 065	240 685	659 317	421 749	237 568	28 342	56 392	50 567	54 742	83 346	24 133
April	662 260	418 485	243 775	660 903	422 666	238 237	28 353	56 917	51 034	54 597	82 910	23 703
May	658 081	416 579	241 502	662 887	423 393	239 494	28 136	57 019	51 233	54 540	82 203	23 552
June	652 793	414 298	238 495	662 943	423 093	239 850	27 841	56 931	51 364	54 099	82 341	23 433
July	649 069	414 170	234 899	665 308	423 461	241 847	27 525	57 380	51 427	54 181	82 190	23 245
August	650 048	417 642	232 406	665 118	423 346	241 772	27 102	57 597	51 594	54 071	81 925	23 155
September	664 461	430 468	233 993	665 337	423 753	241 584	27 024	58 141	51 321	53 892	82 356	23 182
October	690 873	452 181	238 692	665 009	426 252	238 757	27 321	58 591	51 768	53 764	81 966	23 066
November	686 997	451 090	235 907	658 631	424 972	233 659	27 061	58 307	51 829	53 549	81 270	22 472
December	647 655	415 181	232 474	653 710	422 910	230 800	26 910	57 797	51 740	53 281	80 234	21 829
2020												
January	650 994	416 837	234 157	653 395	424 324	229 071	27 042	57 430	52 299	53 074	80 621	21 930
February	651 488	418 217	233 271	651 650	423 285	228 365	26 673	57 213	51 862	52 878	80 131	21 768
March	662 142	417 796	244 346	660 553	420 250	240 303	26 511	57 212	48 633	54 014	78 903	21 696
April	638 462	412 492	225 970	636 048	415 773	220 275	25 228	55 706	50 184	52 811	76 126	20 368
May	589 860	400 566	189 294	598 023	408 265	189 758	23 710	54 150	50 335	50 917	74 337	19 615
June	573 057	396 685	176 372	581 159	404 434	176 725	22 768	54 644	51 152	48 212	72 729	18 292
July	574 290	397 957	176 333	587 087	406 525	180 562	22 307	55 818	51 571	47 018	73 099	17 968
August	580 378	404 174	176 204	594 272	410 649	183 623	22 533	57 111	52 177	46 135	74 990	18 319
September	606 119	423 035	183 084	605 279	417 055	188 224	22 775	58 588	52 630	45 223	76 772	18 458
October	636 214	445 999	190 215	613 520	422 541	190 979	23 439	61 322	52 960	45 349	78 830	18 612
November	642 369	447 395	194 974	617 005	423 302	193 703	23 334	62 110	53 050	45 119	79 056	18 503
December	618 501	422 645	195 856	622 240	428 791	193 449	23 354	62 946	53 321	45 131	80 405	18 277
2021												
January	617 888	422 881	195 007	623 659	430 983	192 676	24 138	63 327	53 115	45 323	79 854	18 288
February	623 023	432 947	190 076	624 830	437 577	187 253	25 082	64 757	53 474	45 122	81 117	18 602
March	618 551	439 013	179 538	616 719	440 402	176 317	25 313	65 401	54 498	44 845	80 671	18 309
April	608 572	440 804	167 768	606 706	443 312	163 394	25 630	65 959	54 534	45 892	81 373	18 490
May	594 373	439 973	154 400	601 974	447 464	154 510	25 858	67 189	54 484	45 825	82 370	18 718
June	596 602	442 307	154 295	604 947	450 630	154 317	26 101	68 324	54 373	45 358	83 136	19 101
July	592 591	441 987	150 604	607 510	452 597	154 913	26 604	69 100	54 779	44 910	84 495	19 678
August	596 874	449 331	147 543	610 025	456 877	153 148	26 869	69 305	54 696	45 163	85 122	19 916
September	612 261	467 318	144 943	609 602	460 837	148 765	27 435	69 977	55 175	45 679	86 300	20 507
October	633 152	487 715	145 437	610 365	463 549	146 816	27 211	70 924	54 905	46 454	86 889	20 409
November	650 382	496 799	153 583	622 331	470 189	152 142	27 068	72 317	55 177	47 212	87 972	20 563
December	645 073	480 730	164 343	649 163	487 186	161 977	28 675	74 215	55 349	48 412	92 392	21 488

[1]Excluding leased departments.

Table 16-11. Merchant Wholesalers—Sales and Inventories

(Millions of dollars.)

Year and month	Not seasonally adjusted						Seasonally adjusted					
	Sales			Inventories (current cost, end of period)			Sales			Inventories (current cost, end of period)		
	Total	Durable goods establishments	Nondurable goods establishments	Total	Durable goods establishments	Nondurable goods establishments	Total	Durable goods establishments	Nondurable goods establishments	Total	Durable goods establishments	Nondurable goods establishments
1995	2 158 980	1 141 701	1 017 279	239 275	151 709	87 566	2 158 980	1 141 701	1 017 279	238 392	154 089	84 303
1996	2 284 343	1 190 342	1 094 001	241 396	154 207	87 189	2 284 343	1 190 342	1 094 001	241 058	156 683	84 375
1997	2 377 845	1 256 384	1 121 461	258 900	165 371	93 529	2 377 845	1 256 384	1 121 461	258 454	168 089	90 365
1998	2 427 120	1 306 545	1 120 575	272 575	175 994	96 581	2 427 120	1 306 545	1 120 575	272 297	178 918	93 379
1999	2 599 159	1 406 371	1 192 788	290 382	187 738	102 644	2 599 159	1 406 371	1 192 788	290 182	190 899	99 283
2000	2 814 554	1 486 673	1 327 881	309 710	198 525	111 185	2 814 554	1 486 673	1 327 881	309 191	201 797	107 394
2001	2 785 152	1 422 195	1 362 957	298 577	182 521	116 056	2 785 152	1 422 195	1 362 957	297 536	185 517	112 019
2002	2 835 528	1 421 503	1 414 025	302 715	182 150	120 565	2 835 528	1 421 503	1 414 025	301 310	185 048	116 262
2003	2 978 282	1 466 158	1 512 124	310 115	186 435	123 680	2 978 282	1 466 158	1 512 124	308 274	189 325	118 949
2004	3 330 011	1 689 588	1 640 423	341 642	213 590	128 052	3 330 011	1 689 588	1 640 423	340 128	216 704	123 424
2005	3 638 496	1 830 347	1 808 149	369 380	233 199	136 181	3 638 496	1 830 347	1 808 149	367 978	236 438	131 540
2006	3 941 257	2 005 139	1 936 118	400 297	256 731	143 566	3 941 257	2 005 139	1 936 118	398 924	260 115	138 809
2007	4 223 473	2 101 969	2 121 504	426 254	263 195	163 059	4 223 473	2 101 969	2 121 504	424 344	266 628	157 716
2008	4 525 024	2 127 382	2 397 642	446 402	280 122	166 280	4 525 024	2 127 382	2 397 642	445 681	283 785	161 896
2009	3 830 607	1 746 786	2 083 821	399 918	233 088	166 830	3 830 607	1 746 786	2 083 821	397 806	236 547	161 259
2010	4 339 199	2 001 087	2 338 112	445 603	256 010	189 593	4 339 199	2 001 087	2 338 112	442 743	260 109	182 634
2011	4 887 628	2 232 235	2 655 393	491 217	284 834	206 383	4 887 628	2 232 235	2 655 393	488 255	289 164	199 091
2012	5 211 528	2 393 081	2 818 447	527 675	309 457	218 218	5 211 528	2 393 081	2 818 447	524 721	314 336	210 385
2013	5 404 157	2 474 299	2 929 858	551 698	325 739	225 959	5 404 157	2 474 299	2 929 858	550 594	331 465	219 129
2014	5 629 484	2 580 053	3 049 431	587 958	349 339	238 619	5 629 484	2 580 053	3 049 431	586 084	355 439	230 645
2015	5 387 234	2 553 528	2 833 706	599 549	351 684	247 865	5 387 234	2 553 528	2 833 706	597 666	358 109	239 557
2016	5 339 689	2 548 176	2 791 513	614 852	353 704	261 148	5 339 689	2 548 176	2 791 513	612 125	359 752	252 373
2017	5 700 968	2 732 543	2 968 425	637 025	370 398	266 627	5 700 968	2 732 543	2 968 425	633 371	376 211	257 160
2018	6 098 697	2 922 568	3 176 129	675 080	403 288	271 792	6 098 697	2 922 568	3 176 129	671 681	409 201	262 480
2019	6 071 354	2 906 314	3 165 040	684 218	405 669	278 549	6 071 354	2 906 314	3 165 040	680 181	411 097	269 084
2020	5 795 028	2 847 389	2 947 639	674 911	394 938	279 973	5 795 028	2 847 389	2 947 639	667 974	400 374	267 600
2021	7 103 559	3 431 117	3 672 442	795 937	472 710	323 227	7 103 559	3 431 117	3 672 442	789 049	479 349	309 700
2018												
January	470 037	221 316	248 721	648 189	374 333	273 856	492 837	234 685	258 152	639 156	376 041	263 115
February	443 755	210 240	233 515	651 543	379 511	272 032	499 182	239 138	260 044	643 772	380 017	263 755
March	515 750	248 966	266 784	654 179	381 946	272 233	497 866	238 507	259 359	645 441	382 014	263 427
April	495 832	234 519	261 313	647 594	382 333	265 261	502 653	240 788	261 865	645 325	381 852	263 473
May	546 071	252 492	293 579	640 065	382 768	257 297	515 736	244 698	271 038	645 550	382 979	262 571
June	523 878	250 720	273 158	637 930	385 485	252 445	511 861	243 343	268 518	646 219	385 993	260 226
July	506 205	239 842	266 363	640 045	391 297	248 748	513 733	244 985	268 748	648 511	387 781	260 730
August	538 780	260 463	278 317	642 577	392 750	249 827	515 764	246 986	268 778	654 800	391 339	263 461
September	498 506	242 553	255 953	654 020	396 998	257 022	515 336	246 574	268 762	658 744	394 581	264 163
October	549 930	265 491	284 439	664 677	402 037	262 640	515 008	246 383	268 625	663 055	400 464	262 591
November	512 839	249 862	262 977	668 733	402 091	266 642	510 621	247 326	263 295	664 743	402 676	262 067
December	497 114	246 104	251 010	675 080	403 288	271 792	506 052	248 652	257 400	671 681	409 201	262 480
2019												
January	479 820	230 717	249 103	687 724	410 052	277 672	500 478	242 833	257 645	676 852	411 886	264 966
February	448 387	215 174	233 213	688 601	412 399	276 202	505 011	244 395	260 616	679 946	413 224	266 722
March	513 233	247 042	266 191	688 281	413 072	275 209	509 842	244 304	265 538	679 516	412 788	266 728
April	516 449	242 448	274 001	688 519	418 081	270 438	507 000	240 935	266 065	686 757	417 344	269 413
May	538 328	251 492	286 836	681 749	417 806	263 943	510 395	243 745	266 650	688 318	418 594	269 724
June	505 438	243 786	261 652	680 243	419 175	261 068	507 691	243 634	264 057	689 372	419 849	269 523
July	516 305	244 215	272 090	679 702	421 941	257 761	510 047	242 452	267 595	688 311	418 449	269 862
August	517 016	248 265	268 751	676 178	420 012	256 166	507 227	241 930	265 297	688 099	418 834	269 265
September	500 968	244 585	256 383	677 928	420 289	257 639	506 455	242 176	264 279	683 620	418 043	265 577
October	534 913	258 789	276 124	683 306	417 289	266 017	500 077	239 654	260 423	681 040	415 964	265 076
November	493 955	236 877	257 078	685 625	412 963	272 662	505 270	243 070	262 200	681 093	412 952	268 141
December	506 542	242 924	263 618	684 218	405 669	278 549	502 513	238 176	264 337	680 181	411 097	269 084
2020												
January	485 094	227 408	257 686	685 590	407 192	278 398	505 928	238 880	267 048	674 602	408 885	265 717
February	454 787	216 698	238 089	678 263	404 891	273 372	504 203	242 699	261 504	669 498	405 213	264 285
March	495 337	239 400	255 937	671 285	406 996	264 289	477 078	229 861	247 217	664 175	406 476	257 699
April	403 917	191 201	212 716	666 409	405 705	260 704	396 020	190 317	205 703	664 221	405 344	258 877
May	417 736	201 985	215 751	651 210	397 916	253 294	420 344	207 920	212 424	656 490	398 280	258 210
June	486 407	242 315	244 092	640 011	391 179	248 832	462 108	228 034	234 074	649 791	391 775	258 016
July	491 225	242 676	248 549	640 745	392 397	248 348	485 762	240 612	245 150	649 334	389 957	259 377
August	486 578	242 806	243 772	640 044	393 506	246 538	494 668	245 007	249 661	652 615	392 538	260 077
September	506 447	256 745	249 702	651 084	395 643	255 441	496 103	246 861	249 242	657 518	393 865	263 653
October	529 289	268 264	261 025	668 022	397 396	270 626	508 331	255 695	252 636	664 616	396 066	268 550
November	498 295	249 861	248 434	671 325	398 536	272 789	509 783	256 079	253 704	666 145	398 452	267 693
December	539 916	268 030	271 886	674 911	394 938	279 973	519 238	255 922	263 316	667 974	400 374	267 600
2021												
January	494 242	243 103	251 139	690 877	403 387	287 490	542 833	270 101	272 732	676 463	404 137	272 326
February	480 345	231 598	248 747	693 491	407 264	286 227	538 296	261 181	277 115	682 344	407 200	275 144
March	603 509	292 966	310 543	699 699	411 928	287 771	561 839	272 111	289 728	688 911	410 934	277 977
April	584 958	282 498	302 460	700 502	414 818	285 684	572 105	279 544	292 561	695 058	413 990	281 068
May	575 585	276 425	299 160	700 318	420 403	279 915	577 663	284 029	293 634	707 666	420 744	286 922
June	621 597	305 742	315 855	704 649	426 514	278 135	591 824	288 193	303 631	716 330	427 105	289 225
July	598 213	286 802	311 411	710 678	435 979	274 699	605 575	292 126	313 449	721 918	433 008	288 910
August	607 511	297 046	310 465	715 106	440 905	274 201	600 616	290 853	309 763	731 050	439 540	291 510
September	620 778	304 155	316 623	732 401	445 889	286 512	609 626	292 084	317 542	740 256	444 001	296 255
October	627 881	298 806	329 075	760 855	455 020	305 835	622 134	294 768	327 366	756 562	453 461	303 101
November	636 562	299 247	337 315	775 573	465 110	310 463	632 425	298 108	334 317	770 056	465 304	304 752
December	652 378	312 729	339 649	795 937	472 710	323 227	633 158	300 527	332 631	789 049	479 349	309 700

. . . = Not available.

Table 16-12. Manufacturing and Trade Sales and Inventories

| Year and month | Sales, billions of dollars | | | | | Inventories, billions of dollars, end of period, seasonally adjusted | | | | Ratios, inventories to sales, seasonally adjusted [1] | | | |
| | Not seasonally adjusted, total | Seasonally adjusted | | | | Total | Manufacturing | Retail trade | Merchant wholesalers | Total | Manufacturing | Retail trade | Merchant wholesalers |
		Total	Manufacturing	Retail trade	Merchant wholesalers								
2000	10 006.4	10 006.4	4 202.4	2 979.4	2 817.1	1 195.9	480.7	406.0	309.2	1.41	1.35	1.59	1.29
2001	9 817.9	9 817.9	3 971.2	3 062.2	2 785.9	1 118.6	427.4	393.7	297.5	1.42	1.38	1.58	1.32
2002	9 878.8	9 878.8	3 917.4	3 129.6	2 834.5	1 139.5	423.0	415.2	301.3	1.36	1.29	1.55	1.26
2003	10 256.4	10 256.4	4 016.6	3 261.6	2 977.4	1 147.8	408.3	431.2	308.3	1.34	1.25	1.56	1.22
2004	11 112.0	11 112.0	4 295.3	3 460.9	3 315.6	1 241.7	441.2	460.4	340.1	1.30	1.19	1.56	1.17
2005	12 069.9	12 069.9	4 743.7	3 686.6	3 643.6	1 314.3	474.6	471.7	368.0	1.27	1.17	1.51	1.17
2006	12 828.4	12 828.4	5 016.8	3 876.6	3 946.0	1 408.8	523.5	486.4	398.9	1.28	1.20	1.49	1.17
2007	13 538.1	13 538.1	5 320.1	3 997.4	4 221.1	1 487.6	562.7	500.6	424.3	1.28	1.22	1.49	1.17
2008	13 929.3	13 929.3	5 448.0	4 226.3	4 507.3	1 465.7	543.3	476.7	445.7	1.47	1.42	1.62	1.38
2009	11 866.9	11 866.9	4 427.7	3 613.0	3 829.8	1 331.4	505.0	428.5	397.8	1.28	1.29	1.39	1.17
2010	13 068.5	13 068.5	4 914.3	3 816.6	4 334.7	1 450.0	553.7	453.5	442.7	1.27	1.28	1.38	1.17
2011	14 482.5	14 482.5	5 053.3	4 102.0	4 893.9	1 566.7	607.0	471.4	488.3	1.26	1.30	1.35	1.16
2012	15 210.5	15 210.5	5 691.9	4 297.0	5 202.6	1 657.1	625.2	507.2	524.7	1.29	1.30	1.39	1.19
2013	15 667.5	15 667.5	5 816.9	4 459.1	5 399.7	1 727.5	631.7	545.1	550.6	1.29	1.30	1.41	1.19
2014	16 159.1	16 159.1	5 889.7	4 635.2	5 622.3	1 790.4	642.7	561.6	586.1	1.32	1.31	1.43	1.22
2015	15 646.4	15 646.4	5 534.1	4 722.0	5 381.0	1 823.8	638.2	588.0	597.7	1.39	1.40	1.43	1.33
2016	15 551.4	15 551.4	5 352.9	4 832.6	5 328.7	1 859.4	635.8	611.5	612.1	1.42	1.42	1.50	1.36
2017	16 290.0	16 290.0	5 555.0	5 046.0	5 713.4	1 917.7	659.0	625.4	633.4	1.39	1.39	1.42	1.31
2018	17 244.8	17 244.8	5 890.0	5 258.5	6 096.6	2 001.8	677.5	652.7	671.7	1.36	1.37	1.46	1.28
2019	17 208.0	17 208.0	5 737.9	5 402.8	6 072.0	2 043.2	709.3	653.7	680.2	1.42	1.46	1.47	1.35
2020	16 586.7	16 586.7	5 216.5	5 559.4	5 779.6	1 986.9	696.7	622.2	668.0	1.44	1.61	1.34	1.38
2021	19 466.4	19 466.4	5 799.7	6 559.7	7 088.1	2 197.5	759.3	649.2	789.0	1.28	1.51	1.13	1.23
2017													
January	1 220.2	1 340.0	457.0	416.0	467.0	1 863.3	637.1	614.6	611.6	1.39	1.39	1.48	1.31
February	1 207.3	1 342.7	457.7	416.0	469.0	1 866.5	638.3	615.5	612.7	1.39	1.39	1.48	1.31
March	1 404.3	1 338.4	457.5	414.9	466.0	1 870.3	638.0	618.1	614.1	1.40	1.39	1.49	1.32
April	1 302.3	1 338.6	454.4	416.7	467.5	1 868.9	639.0	617.6	612.2	1.40	1.41	1.48	1.31
May	1 395.5	1 335.8	458.8	414.3	462.7	1 873.5	638.7	619.2	615.7	1.40	1.39	1.49	1.33
June	1 401.4	1 340.9	457.0	416.4	467.5	1 881.8	638.6	622.4	620.9	1.40	1.40	1.49	1.33
July	1 300.8	1 341.6	457.2	416.5	467.9	1 888.4	641.8	623.0	623.6	1.41	1.40	1.50	1.33
August	1 414.2	1 355.8	462.9	417.0	475.9	1 899.4	645.1	626.4	627.9	1.40	1.39	1.50	1.32
September	1 372.2	1 374.0	465.6	426.5	481.9	1 902.5	649.5	621.6	631.5	1.38	1.39	1.46	1.31
October	1 406.8	1 385.9	470.6	426.7	488.7	1 903.3	651.9	622.0	629.4	1.37	1.39	1.46	1.29
November	1 408.3	1 404.8	478.2	431.0	495.6	1 911.2	655.1	623.2	632.9	1.36	1.37	1.45	1.28
December	1 456.6	1 415.8	478.1	434.1	503.5	1 917.7	659.0	625.4	633.4	1.35	1.38	1.44	1.26
2018													
January	1 308.0	1 406.5	481.9	431.8	492.8	1 926.0	660.4	626.5	639.2	1.37	1.37	1.45	1.30
February	1 273.2	1 417.8	484.0	434.6	499.2	1 937.0	663.7	629.4	643.8	1.37	1.37	1.45	1.29
March	1 472.3	1 416.8	485.7	433.2	497.9	1 936.8	662.8	628.5	645.4	1.37	1.36	1.45	1.30
April	1 397.8	1 423.3	485.6	435.1	502.7	1 942.0	665.0	631.7	645.3	1.36	1.37	1.45	1.28
May	1 519.1	1 447.0	491.5	439.8	515.7	1 945.5	666.1	633.9	645.6	1.34	1.36	1.44	1.25
June	1 487.0	1 443.7	494.3	437.5	511.9	1 948.4	666.2	636.0	646.2	1.35	1.35	1.45	1.26
July	1 423.5	1 447.3	493.1	440.4	513.7	1 959.3	673.0	637.8	648.5	1.35	1.36	1.45	1.26
August	1 514.3	1 452.5	496.8	439.9	515.8	1 970.3	673.3	642.2	654.8	1.36	1.36	1.46	1.27
September	1 422.0	1 453.6	498.9	439.3	515.3	1 980.3	677.4	644.1	658.7	1.36	1.36	1.47	1.28
October	1 507.2	1 458.3	499.2	444.1	515.0	1 989.9	678.9	648.0	663.1	1.36	1.36	1.46	1.29
November	1 454.9	1 448.4	492.0	445.8	510.6	1 987.8	677.9	645.2	664.7	1.37	1.38	1.45	1.30
December	1 465.5	1 430.1	487.1	436.9	506.1	2 001.8	677.5	652.7	671.7	1.40	1.39	1.49	1.33
2019													
January	1 332.2	1 425.2	484.9	439.8	500.5	2 015.3	682.0	656.4	676.9	1.41	1.41	1.49	1.35
February	1 286.4	1 433.2	487.3	440.9	505.0	2 024.3	685.4	659.0	679.9	1.41	1.41	1.49	1.35
March	1 465.6	1 442.6	485.8	447.0	509.8	2 027.0	688.1	659.3	679.5	1.41	1.42	1.48	1.33
April	1 444.4	1 437.0	482.8	447.2	507.0	2 038.9	691.2	660.9	686.8	1.42	1.43	1.48	1.35
May	1 513.8	1 442.8	483.4	449.0	510.4	2 044.2	693.0	662.9	688.3	1.42	1.43	1.48	1.35
June	1 450.9	1 437.9	481.2	449.0	507.7	2 047.5	695.2	662.9	689.4	1.42	1.44	1.48	1.36
July	1 443.9	1 441.0	477.3	453.7	510.0	2 052.3	698.7	665.3	688.3	1.42	1.46	1.47	1.35
August	1 482.1	1 439.4	476.2	456.0	507.2	2 053.5	700.3	665.1	688.1	1.43	1.47	1.46	1.36
September	1 413.1	1 432.5	474.0	452.0	506.5	2 051.6	702.6	665.3	683.6	1.43	1.48	1.47	1.35
October	1 476.5	1 423.6	470.1	453.5	500.1	2 050.5	704.5	665.0	681.0	1.44	1.50	1.47	1.36
November	1 414.6	1 428.9	467.7	455.9	505.3	2 046.2	706.4	658.6	681.1	1.43	1.51	1.44	1.35
December	1 484.5	1 428.6	467.1	458.9	502.5	2 043.2	709.3	653.7	680.2	1.43	1.52	1.42	1.35
2020													
January	1 335.0	1 423.7	461.6	456.1	505.9	2 034.9	706.9	653.4	674.6	1.43	1.53	1.43	1.33
February	1 307.2	1 422.8	460.7	457.9	504.2	2 024.5	703.4	651.7	669.5	1.42	1.53	1.42	1.33
March	1 381.0	1 345.1	435.7	432.4	477.1	2 020.1	695.4	660.6	664.2	1.50	1.60	1.53	1.39
April	1 151.0	1 143.2	371.3	375.9	396.0	1 993.6	693.2	636.0	664.2	1.74	1.87	1.69	1.68
May	1 259.7	1 242.7	380.3	442.0	420.3	1 946.3	691.8	598.0	656.5	1.57	1.82	1.35	1.56
June	1 409.6	1 356.2	421.9	472.2	462.1	1 925.0	694.1	581.2	649.8	1.42	1.65	1.23	1.41
July	1 411.9	1 406.2	439.2	481.2	485.8	1 927.2	690.8	587.1	649.3	1.37	1.57	1.22	1.34
August	1 424.3	1 420.2	443.1	482.4	494.7	1 938.2	691.3	594.3	652.6	1.36	1.56	1.23	1.32
September	1 441.1	1 433.9	445.1	492.7	496.1	1 952.5	689.7	605.3	657.5	1.36	1.55	1.23	1.33
October	1 483.8	1 447.5	448.3	490.8	508.3	1 968.8	690.6	613.5	664.6	1.36	1.54	1.25	1.31
November	1 425.6	1 446.7	450.1	486.8	509.8	1 978.2	695.1	617.0	666.1	1.37	1.54	1.27	1.31
December	1 556.6	1 467.3	459.2	488.9	519.2	1 986.9	696.7	622.2	668.0	1.35	1.52	1.27	1.29
2021													
January	1 385.3	1 524.3	468.2	513.3	542.8	1 998.4	698.2	623.7	676.5	1.31	1.49	1.22	1.25
February	1 348.9	1 503.0	461.0	503.7	538.3	2 012.2	705.0	624.8	682.3	1.34	1.53	1.24	1.27
March	1 666.4	1 586.4	466.2	558.4	561.8	2 012.6	707.5	616.2	688.9	1.27	1.52	1.10	1.23
April	1 612.4	1 594.7	466.7	555.9	572.1	2 011.0	710.3	605.7	695.1	1.26	1.52	1.09	1.21
May	1 617.1	1 601.0	473.2	550.2	577.7	2 027.6	717.9	602.0	707.7	1.27	1.52	1.09	1.23
June	1 690.4	1 623.1	480.7	550.6	591.8	2 046.8	725.5	604.9	716.3	1.26	1.51	1.10	1.21
July	1 625.7	1 636.9	488.0	543.4	605.6	2 059.2	729.8	607.5	721.9	1.26	1.50	1.12	1.19
August	1 662.6	1 636.0	488.4	546.9	600.6	2 076.6	735.5	610.0	731.1	1.27	1.51	1.12	1.22
September	1 662.3	1 654.4	492.2	552.6	609.6	2 093.4	743.5	609.6	740.3	1.27	1.51	1.10	1.21
October	1 692.4	1 685.5	501.1	562.3	622.1	2 116.7	749.7	610.4	756.6	1.26	1.50	1.09	1.22
November	1 710.7	1 703.9	505.8	565.7	632.4	2 148.6	756.2	622.3	770.1	1.26	1.50	1.10	1.22
December	1 792.4	1 698.2	508.2	556.8	633.2	2 197.5	759.3	649.2	789.0	1.29	1.49	1.17	1.25

[1] Annual data are averages of monthly ratios.

Table 16-13. Real Manufacturing and Trade Sales and Inventories

(Billions of chained [2012] dollars, ratios; seasonally adjusted; annual sales figures are averages of seasonally adjusted monthly data.)

NIPA Tables 1BU, 2BU, 3BU

Year and month	Sales, monthly average				Inventories, end of period				Ratios, end-of-period inventories to monthly average sales			
	Total	Manufac-turing	Retail trade	Merchant wholesalers	Total	Manufac-turing	Retail trade	Merchant wholesalers	Total	Manufac-turing	Retail trade	Merchant wholesalers
2002	1 128.4	470.9	320.6	338.1	1 558.3	642.3	496.8	419.7	1.38	1.36	1.55	1.24
2003	1 150.6	471.9	332.8	345.9	1 570.5	631.6	515.8	421.3	1.37	1.34	1.55	1.22
2004	1 195.0	481.7	346.0	367.0	1 631.0	638.3	543.3	446.3	1.37	1.33	1.57	1.22
2005	1 248.2	503.5	358.9	385.9	1 689.2	665.4	549.3	472.6	1.35	1.32	1.53	1.23
2006	1 283.1	509.8	370.2	402.9	1 742.7	687.6	560.5	493.2	1.36	1.35	1.51	1.22
2007	1 311.3	522.0	375.4	414.0	1 781.6	709.1	568.2	502.9	1.36	1.36	1.51	1.22
2008	1 261.8	494.7	358.7	408.8	1 741.2	692.1	535.3	513.1	1.38	1.40	1.49	1.26
2009	1 144.5	428.0	338.5	377.6	1 604.0	662.5	478.7	462.6	1.40	1.55	1.41	1.23
2010	1 198.7	449.8	349.0	399.9	1 663.9	687.1	493.1	483.7	1.39	1.53	1.41	1.21
2011	1 238.6	465.5	359.8	413.3	1 709.4	711.7	494.6	503.1	1.38	1.53	1.38	1.22
2012	1 279.7	473.9	371.7	434.1	1 784.0	730.8	522.1	531.0	1.39	1.54	1.41	1.22
2013	1 319.9	483.2	387.1	449.6	1 878.7	758.4	558.9	561.2	1.42	1.57	1.44	1.25
2014	1 358.6	486.2	404.7	467.8	1 947.2	776.9	574.5	595.7	1.43	1.60	1.42	1.27
2015	1 389.5	482.4	428.6	478.8	2 042.7	815.3	604.2	623.0	1.47	1.69	1.41	1.30
2016	1 411.7	476.6	448.6	486.8	2 077.4	817.2	628.8	629.7	1.47	1.72	1.40	1.29
2017	1 443.4	477.3	465.4	501.3	2 116.4	822.3	645.6	646.3	1.47	1.72	1.39	1.29
2018	1 474.2	483.7	480.1	511.1	2 187.8	840.8	670.8	673.6	1.48	1.74	1.40	1.32
2019	1 483.7	472.2	498.4	514.8	2 256.5	887.8	681.5	685.4	1.52	1.88	1.37	1.33
2020	1 473.2	450.4	521.4	504.5	2 214.6	878.1	663.0	672.1	1.50	1.95	1.27	1.33
2021	1 565.2	451.2	577.8	541.4	2 200.5	842.8	643.9	714.7	1.41	1.87	1.11	1.32
2017												
January	1 431.6	478.9	458.0	495.2	2 079.8	816.5	633.7	627.7	1.45	1.71	1.38	1.27
February	1 428.3	476.9	458.5	493.3	2 078.4	814.5	634.2	627.7	1.46	1.71	1.38	1.27
March	1 425.5	475.2	458.3	492.4	2 076.9	810.3	635.4	629.0	1.46	1.71	1.39	1.28
April	1 422.9	470.4	460.4	492.6	2 074.7	810.4	635.6	626.5	1.46	1.72	1.38	1.27
May	1 427.9	474.8	461.0	492.6	2 078.1	808.5	637.2	630.0	1.46	1.70	1.38	1.28
June	1 432.7	473.2	464.1	495.9	2 084.8	807.3	639.7	635.3	1.46	1.71	1.38	1.28
July	1 438.2	473.1	465.7	500.1	2 090.5	810.2	640.3	637.6	1.45	1.71	1.38	1.28
August	1 445.6	476.5	464.3	505.4	2 099.6	813.1	643.0	641.0	1.45	1.71	1.39	1.27
September	1 452.4	476.5	469.6	507.0	2 104.1	817.9	639.8	644.2	1.45	1.72	1.36	1.27
October	1 460.5	480.0	471.4	509.7	2 103.7	818.6	641.4	641.5	1.44	1.71	1.36	1.26
November	1 473.1	486.1	474.9	512.7	2 111.8	820.4	644.0	645.2	1.43	1.69	1.36	1.26
December	1 482.7	486.1	478.1	519.1	2 116.4	822.3	645.6	646.3	1.43	1.69	1.35	1.25
2018												
January	1 465.4	486.4	473.9	505.6	2 124.7	824.1	646.9	651.4	1.45	1.69	1.37	1.29
February	1 469.8	486.0	475.9	508.5	2 135.9	826.9	651.1	655.5	1.45	1.70	1.37	1.29
March	1 467.3	485.4	475.4	507.1	2 134.1	825.1	650.2	656.5	1.45	1.70	1.37	1.29
April	1 467.0	483.4	476.3	508.0	2 138.2	827.8	652.6	655.5	1.46	1.71	1.37	1.29
May	1 475.6	481.3	480.8	514.3	2 137.9	827.3	654.1	654.1	1.45	1.72	1.36	1.27
June	1 473.8	483.9	479.0	511.5	2 139.8	828.1	656.5	652.7	1.45	1.71	1.37	1.28
July	1 475.2	481.3	482.6	512.2	2 148.1	833.5	657.9	654.1	1.46	1.73	1.36	1.28
August	1 482.3	485.4	481.8	515.9	2 157.0	834.9	660.0	659.6	1.46	1.72	1.37	1.28
September	1 481.9	485.9	480.9	515.8	2 163.8	839.4	660.5	661.5	1.46	1.73	1.37	1.28
October	1 478.8	483.4	485.0	511.2	2 172.9	841.5	663.7	665.3	1.47	1.74	1.37	1.30
November	1 477.1	479.7	488.9	509.6	2 171.1	838.8	663.1	666.7	1.47	1.75	1.36	1.31
December	1 476.5	482.4	481.4	513.6	2 187.8	840.8	670.8	673.6	1.48	1.74	1.39	1.31
2019												
January	1 484.5	482.7	489.5	513.4	2 203.3	847.2	673.6	679.9	1.48	1.76	1.38	1.32
February	1 483.8	483.4	488.2	513.1	2 214.7	851.9	677.1	683.1	1.49	1.76	1.39	1.33
March	1 483.4	476.2	493.7	515.0	2 218.6	857.4	675.6	683.2	1.50	1.80	1.37	1.33
April	1 469.2	469.0	492.6	509.2	2 224.7	860.4	674.3	687.7	1.51	1.84	1.37	1.35
May	1 473.4	468.7	494.5	511.9	2 229.5	862.5	675.5	689.2	1.51	1.84	1.37	1.35
June	1 485.6	473.0	497.6	516.6	2 234.8	866.2	676.7	689.6	1.50	1.83	1.36	1.34
July	1 485.1	469.2	501.6	516.2	2 242.7	871.7	678.2	690.5	1.51	1.86	1.35	1.34
August	1 493.2	470.7	505.7	518.8	2 246.2	874.6	677.8	691.6	1.50	1.86	1.34	1.33
September	1 491.3	470.3	501.8	521.1	2 249.4	878.7	680.4	688.2	1.51	1.87	1.36	1.32
October	1 482.1	467.4	503.5	513.3	2 250.7	881.6	681.0	686.1	1.52	1.89	1.35	1.34
November	1 488.1	467.2	505.8	517.2	2 252.5	884.3	680.4	685.9	1.51	1.89	1.35	1.33
December	1 485.1	468.4	506.8	512.0	2 256.5	887.8	681.5	685.4	1.52	1.90	1.35	1.34
2020												
January	1 486.5	463.8	508.9	516.1	2 255.7	885.6	686.2	681.9	1.52	1.91	1.35	1.32
February	1 491.7	467.6	509.4	517.0	2 256.3	883.7	691.2	679.1	1.51	1.89	1.36	1.31
March	1 432.3	448.2	486.4	499.8	2 255.0	876.1	698.7	677.1	1.57	1.95	1.44	1.36
April	1 267.3	397.0	434.9	437.5	2 241.5	877.9	680.6	680.9	1.77	2.21	1.57	1.56
May	1 368.6	401.5	509.9	461.0	2 208.6	881.6	650.1	676.3	1.61	2.20	1.28	1.47
June	1 473.4	442.8	538.6	495.5	2 193.6	888.4	638.3	667.2	1.49	2.01	1.19	1.35
July	1 512.2	459.5	541.2	514.8	2 189.0	881.8	643.5	663.5	1.45	1.92	1.19	1.29
August	1 515.4	460.5	540.4	517.9	2 193.1	880.4	646.9	665.3	1.45	1.91	1.20	1.29
September	1 524.6	462.0	549.8	516.3	2 199.2	876.3	653.8	668.2	1.44	1.90	1.19	1.29
October	1 539.6	465.4	551.6	526.2	2 208.5	875.3	658.1	673.8	1.44	1.88	1.19	1.28
November	1 536.7	466.7	546.6	526.9	2 210.3	878.6	658.3	672.1	1.44	1.88	1.20	1.28
December	1 530.6	469.8	539.0	524.9	2 214.6	878.1	663.0	672.1	1.45	1.87	1.23	1.28
2021												
January	1 579.3	472.6	574.3	536.6	2 216.7	874.9	663.6	676.8	1.40	1.85	1.16	1.26
February	1 531.2	456.3	552.8	526.0	2 214.0	873.3	664.5	674.9	1.45	1.91	1.20	1.28
March	1 591.8	455.6	607.5	535.4	2 200.5	869.3	654.7	675.1	1.38	1.91	1.08	1.26
April	1 585.1	449.8	604.3	537.8	2 181.8	862.4	642.9	675.1	1.38	1.92	1.06	1.26
May	1 551.4	443.9	585.1	528.5	2 172.8	859.9	635.1	676.3	1.40	1.94	1.09	1.28
June	1 559.3	446.2	583.1	535.9	2 167.7	857.3	633.3	675.7	1.39	1.92	1.09	1.26
July	1 558.8	448.6	569.0	545.8	2 154.6	850.7	629.1	673.4	1.38	1.90	1.11	1.23
August	1 556.1	446.3	573.8	541.1	2 150.4	846.6	626.0	676.7	1.38	1.90	1.09	1.25
September	1 563.1	446.8	574.2	547.1	2 151.9	847.2	621.9	681.6	1.38	1.90	1.08	1.25
October	1 570.4	448.4	577.7	549.5	2 163.7	848.1	620.5	694.2	1.38	1.89	1.07	1.26
November	1 572.5	447.9	576.7	552.9	2 174.3	846.4	625.8	701.6	1.38	1.89	1.09	1.27
December	1 562.9	451.7	554.6	559.9	2 200.5	842.8	643.9	714.7	1.41	1.87	1.16	1.28

Table 16-14. Selected Services—Quarterly Estimated Revenue for Employer Firms

(Millions of dollars.)

2012 NAICS code	Kind of business	4th quarter 2020	1st quarter 2021	2rd quarter 2021	3rd quarter 2021	4th quarter 2021	1st quarter 2022
SEASONALLY ADJUSTED							
51	**Information**	471 607	491 796	509 722	519 535	528 935	549 604
5112	Software publishers	94 875	100 239	105 045	107 930	109 874	116 535
512	Motion picture and sound recording industries	24 293	24 979	26 266	29 435	31 886	29 850
54	**Professional, Scientific, and Technical Services**	560 503	575 502	592 746	615 634	632 882	651 262
5411	Legal services	82 480	86 142	83 248	87 814	88 913	91 686
5412	Accounting, tax preparation, bookkeeping, and payroll services	44 836	44 633	46 478	49 214	52 553	52 658
56 pt	**Administrative and Support and Waste Management and Remediation Services**	272 969	289 291	302 945	322 009	334 501	347 905
5613	Employment services	110 225	120 878	126 262	133 076	142 764	149 409
5615	Travel arrangement and reservation services	8 375	10 318	15 459	20 125	20 472	19 961
562	Waste management and remediation services	29 009	29 891	30 482	31 793	33 183	33 850
622	**Hospitals**	325 596	323 109	335 849	340 575	342 949	328 179
NOT SEASONALLY ADJUSTED							
51	**Information**	-3	494 244	480 485	504 625	511 222	554 324
511	Publishing industries (except Internet)	-1	120 897	119 038	126 534	125 726	137 483
51111	Newspaper publishers	-10	6 006	5 526	5 715	5 680	6 306
51112	Periodical publishers	-10	6 514	5 621	5 966	6 224	6 658
5111 pt	Book, directory and mailing list, and other publishers	-16	9 328	8 053	9 283	10 641	10 250
5112	Software publishers	2	99 049	99 838	105 570	103 181	114 269
512	Motion picture and sound recording industries	-15	25 945	24 429	26 135	28 140	34 246
515	Broadcasting (except Internet)	-5	49 366	44 526	45 268	47 398	51 480
5151	Radio and television broadcasting	-5	25 551	21 823	22 186	23 441	25 682
5152	Cable and other subscription programming	-4	23 815	22 703	23 082	23 957	25 798
517	Telecommunications [1]	-2	166 364	162 019	164 203	164 682	171 358
5171	Wired telecommunications carriers	-1	79 539	78 200	78 914	78 358	79 042
5172	Wireless telecommunications carriers (except satellite)	-2	75 460	72 318	73 315	74 392	80 180
54	**Professional, Scientific, and Technical Services** [1]	-1	570 032	562 841	598 673	612 556	643 641
5411	Legal services	-15	91 718	78 217	81 333	88 253	98 516
5412	Accounting, tax preparation, bookkeeping, and payroll services	29	39 949	51 640	48 477	44 637	47 140
5413	Architectural, engineering, and related services	2	86 882	89 539	95 807	96 448	101 462
5415	Computer systems design and related services	-1	132 211	130 606	139 331	141 494	143 170
5416	Management, scientific, and technical consulting services	1	78 056	77 259	85 186	89 005	93 723
5417	Scientific research and development services	-6	60 023	57 307	63 348	64 190	65 103
5418	Advertising and related services	-6	43 325	40 335	44 014	46 507	51 445
56	**Administrative and Support and Waste Management and Remediation Services** [1]	-1	278 003	280 279	303 256	325 878	340 672
561	Administrative and support services	-1	249 081	251 554	272 408	293 195	307 489
5613	Employment services	-2	115 957	119 548	121 843	132 144	150 188
5615	Travel arrangement and reservation services	-5	8 015	9 699	16 031	21 433	19 633
562	Waste management and remediation services	-2	28 922	28 725	30 848	32 683	33 183
61	**Educational Services**	. . .	18 302	18 852	20 992	21 238	22 524
62	**Health Care and Social Asistance**	-4	767 410	740 913	777 469	774 516	805 500
71	**Arts, Entertainment, and Recreation**	-13	58 326	58 157	73 398	88 203	90 961
81	**Other services (Except Public Administration)**	-22	176 461	160 336	182 173	174 075	207 829

. . . = Not available.

[1]Includes components not shown separately.

NOTES AND DEFINITIONS, CHAPTER 16

Table 16-1

Construction Put in Place

SOURCE: U.S. DEPARTMENT OF COMMERCE, CENSUS BUREAU

The Census Bureau's estimates of the value of new construction put in place are intended to provide monthly estimates of the total dollar value of construction work done in the United States.

The United States Code, Title 13, authorizes the Survey of Construction and provides for voluntary responses. Construction statistics are collected from building permits, housing starts and housing completions.

Definitions and notes on the data

The estimates cover all construction work done each month on new private residential and nonresidential buildings and structures, public construction, and improvements to existing buildings and structures. Included are the cost of labor, materials, and equipment rental; cost of architectural and engineering work; overhead costs assigned to the project; interest and taxes paid during construction; and contractor's profits.

The total value put in place for a given period is the sum of the value of work done on all projects underway during this period, regardless of when work on each individual project was started or when payment was made to the contractors. For some categories, estimates are derived by distributing the total construction cost of the project by means of historic construction progress patterns. Published estimates represent payments made during a period for some categories.

The statistics on the value of construction put in place result from direct measurement and indirect estimation. A series results from direct measurement when it is based on reports of the actual value of construction progress or construction expenditures obtained in a complete census or a sample survey. All other series are developed by indirect estimation using related construction statistics. On an annual basis, estimates for series directly measured monthly, quarterly, or annually accounted for about 71 percent of total construction in 1998 (private multifamily residential, private residential improvements, private nonresidential buildings, farm nonresidential construction, public utility construction, all other private construction, and virtually all of public construction). On a monthly basis, directly measured data are available for about 55 percent of the value in place estimates.

Beginning in 1993, the Construction Expenditures Branch of the Census Bureau's Manufacturing and Construction Division began collecting these data using a new classification system, which bases project types on their end usage instead of on building/nonbuilding types. Data collection on this system for federal construction began in January 2002.

With the changes in project classifications, data presented in these tables for 1993 to date are not directly comparable with data for previous years, except at aggregate levels. For that reason, *Business Statistics* shows earlier historical data only at these aggregate levels. Although some categories, such as lodging, office, education, and religion, have the same names as categories in previously published data, there have been changes within the classifications that make these values non-comparable. For example, private medical office buildings were classified as "office" buildings previously, but are categorized as "health care" under the new classification.

The seasonally adjusted data are obtained by removing normal seasonal movement from the unadjusted data to bring out underlying trends and business cycles, which is accomplished by using the Census X-12-ARIMA method. Seasonal adjustment accounts for month-to-month variations resulting from normal or average changes in any phenomena affecting the data, such as weather conditions, the differing lengths of months, and the varying number of holidays, weekdays, and weekends within each month. It does not adjust for abnormal conditions within each month or for year-to-year variations in weather. The seasonally adjusted annual rate is the seasonally adjusted monthly rate multiplied by 12.

Residential consists of new houses, town houses, apartments, and condominiums for sale or rent; these dwellings are built by the owner or for the owner on contract. It includes improvements inside and outside residential structures, such as remodeling, additions, major replacements, and additions of swimming pools and garages. Manufactured housing, houseboats, and maintenance and repair work are not included.

Office includes general office buildings, administration buildings, professional buildings, and financial institution buildings. Office buildings at manufacturing sites are classified as *manufacturing,* but office buildings owned by manufacturing companies but not at such a site are included in the *office* category. In the state and local government category, *office* includes capitols, city halls, courthouses, and similar buildings.

Commercial includes buildings and structures used by the retail, wholesale, farm, and selected service industries. One of the subgroups of this category is *multi-retail,* which consists of department and variety stores, shopping centers and malls, and warehouse-type retail stores.

Health care includes hospitals, medical buildings, nursing homes, adult day-care centers, and similar institutions.

Educational includes schools at all levels, higher education facilities, trade schools, libraries, museums, and similar institutions.

Amusement and recreation includes theme and amusement parks, sports structures not located at educational institutions, fitness centers and health clubs, neighborhood centers, camps, movie theaters, and similar establishments.

Transportation includes airport facilities; rail facilities, track, and bridges; bus, rail, maritime, and air terminals; and docks, marinas, and similar structures.

Communication includes telephone, television, and radio distribution and maintenance structures.

Power includes electricity production and distribution and gas and crude oil transmission, storage, and distribution.

Manufacturing includes all buildings and structures at manufacturing sites but not the installation of production machinery or special-purpose equipment.

Included in *total private construction*, but not shown separately in these pages, are lodging facilities (hotels and motels), religious structures, and private public safety, sewage and waste disposal, water supply, highway and street, and conservation and development spending.

Included in *total state and local construction,* but not shown separately in these pages, are state and local construction of commercial buildings, conservation and development (dams, levees, jetties, and dredging), lodging, religious facilities, and communication structures.

Public safety includes correctional facilities, police and sheriffs' stations, fire stations, and similar establishments.

Highway and street includes pavement, lighting, retaining walls, bridges, tunnels, toll facilities, and maintenance and rest facilities.

Sewage and waste disposal includes sewage systems, solid waste disposal, and recycling.

Water supply includes water supply, transmission, and storage facilities.

Among the data sources for construction expenditures are the Census Bureau's Survey of Construction, Building Permits Survey, Consumer Expenditure Survey (conducted for the Bureau of Labor Statistics), Annual Capital Expenditures Survey, and Construction Progress Reporting Survey; also included are data from the F.W. Dodge Division of the McGraw-Hill Information Systems Company, the U.S. Department of Agriculture, and utility regulatory agencies.

Data availability

Each month's "Construction Spending" press release is released on the last workday of the following month. The release, more detailed data, and a discussion of methodologies can be found on the Census Bureau's Web site at <https://www.census.gov/constructionspending>. Current data at this site may reflect benchmarking since Table 16-1 was compiled.

Table 16-2

Housing Starts and Building Permits; New House Sales and Prices

SOURCES: U.S. DEPARTMENT OF COMMERCE, CENSUS BUREAU

These data are mainly found in two major Census Bureau reports, "New Residential Construction" and "New Residential Sales." They cover new housing units intended for occupancy and maintained by the occupants, excluding hotels, motels, and group residential structures. Manufactured home units are reported in a separate survey.

Definitions

A *housing unit* is a house, an apartment, or a group of rooms or single room intended for occupancy as separate living quarters. Occupants must live separately from other individuals in the building and have direct access to the housing unit from the outside of the building or through a common hall. Each apartment unit in an apartment building is counted as one housing unit. As of January 2000, a previous requirement for residents to have the capability to eat separately has been eliminated. (Based on the old definition, some senior housing projects were excluded from the multifamily housing statistics because individual units did not have their own eating facilities.) Housing starts exclude group quarters such as dormitories or rooming houses, transient accommodations such as motels, and manufactured homes. Publicly owned housing units are excluded, but units in structures built by private developers with subsidies or for sale to local public housing authorities are both classified as private housing.

The *start* of construction of a privately owned housing unit is when excavation begins for the footings or foundation of a building primarily intended as a housekeeping residential structure and designed for nontransient occupancy. All housing units in a multifamily building are defined as being started when excavation for the building begins.

One-family structures includes fully detached, semi-detached, row houses, and townhouses. In the case of attached units, each must be separated from the adjacent unit by a ground-to-roof wall to be classified as a one-unit structure and must not share facilities such as heating or water supply. Units built one on top of another and those built side-by-side without a ground-to-roof wall and/or with common facilities are classified by the number of units in the structure.

Apartment buildings are defined as buildings containing *five units or more.* The type of ownership is not the criterion—a condominium apartment building is not classified as one-family structures but as a multifamily structure.

A *manufactured* home is a moveable dwelling, 8 feet or more wide and 40 feet or more long, designed to be towed on its own chassis with transportation gear integral to the unit when it leaves the factory, and without need of a permanent foundation. Multiwides and expandable manufactured homes are included. Excluded are travel trailers, motor homes, and modular housing. The shipments figures are based on reports submitted by manufacturers on the number of homes actually shipped during the survey month. Shipments to dealers may not necessarily be placed for residential use in the same month as they are shipped. The number of manufactured "homes" used for nonresidential purposes (for example, those used for offices) is not known.

Units authorized by building permits represents the approximately 97 percent of housing in permit-requiring areas.

The *start* occurs when excavation begins for the footing or foundation. Starts are estimated for all areas, regardless of whether permits are required.

New house *sales* are reported only for new single-family residential structures. The sales transaction must intend to include both house and land. Excluded are houses built for rent, houses built by the owner, and houses built by a contractor on the owner's land. A sale is reported when a deposit is taken or a sales agreement is signed; this can occur prior to a permit being issued.

> Once the sale is reported, the sold housing unit drops out of the survey. Consequently, the Census Bureau does not find out if the sales contract is cancelled or if the house is ever resold. As a result, if conditions are worsening and cancellations are high, sales are temporarily overestimated. When conditions improve and the cancelled sales materialize as actual sales, the Census sales estimates are then underestimated because the case did not re-enter the survey. In the long run, cancellations do not cause the survey to overestimate or underestimate sales; but in the short run, cancellations and ultimate resales are not reflected in this survey, and fluctuations can appear less severe than in reality.

A house is *for sale* when a permit to build has been issued (or work begun in non-permit areas) and a sales contract has not been signed nor a deposit accepted.

The *sales price* used in this survey is the price agreed upon between the purchaser and the seller at the time the first sales contract is signed or deposit made. It includes the price of the improved lot. The *median sales price* is the sales price of the house that falls on the middle point of a distribution by price of the total number of houses sold. Half of the houses sold have a price lower than the median; half have a price higher than the median. Changes in the *sales price* data reflect changes in the distribution of houses by region, size, and the like, as well as changes in the prices of houses with identical characteristics.

The *price index* measures the change in price of a new single-family house of constant physical characteristics, using the characteristics of houses built in 2005. Characteristics held constant include floor area, whether inside or outside a metropolitan area, number of bedrooms, number of bathrooms, number of fireplaces, type of parking facility, type of foundation, presence of a deck, construction method, exterior wall material, type of heating, and presence of air-conditioning. The indexes are calculated separately for attached and detached houses and combined with base period weights. The price measured includes the value of the lot.

Notes on the data

Monthly permit authorizations are based on data collected by a mail survey from a sample of about 9,000 permit-issuing places, selected from and representing a universe of 20,000 such places in the United States. The remaining places are surveyed annually. Data for 2014 to the present includes approximately 20,100 places while data for 2004 to 2013 included 19,300 places.

Data for 1994 through 2003 represented 19,000 places; data for 1984 through 1993 represented 17,000 places; data for 1978 through 1983 represented 16,000 places; data for 1972 through 1977 represented 14,000 places; data for 1967 through 1971 represented 13,000 places; data for 1963 through 1966 represented 12,000 places; and data for 1959 through 1962 represented 10,000 places.

Housing starts and sales data are obtained from the Survey of Construction, for which Census Bureau field representatives sample both permit-issuing and non-permit-issuing places.

Effective with the January 2005 data release, the Survey of Construction implemented a new sample of building permit offices, replacing a previous sample selected in 1985. As a result, writes the Census Bureau, "Data users should use caution when analyzing year over year changes in housing prices and characteristics between 2004 and 2005." In the newer sample, land may be more abundant, lot sizes larger, and sales prices lower.

For 2004, the permit data were compiled for both the new 20,000 place universe and the old 19,000 place universe. Ratios of the new estimates to the old were calculated by state for total housing units, structures by number of units, and valuation. For the United States as a whole, the new estimate was 100.9 percent of the old estimate.

Effective with the data for April 2001, the Census Bureau made changes to the methodology used for new house sales, including discontinuing an adjustment for construction in areas in which building permits are required without a permit being issued. It was believed that such unauthorized construction has virtually ceased. The upward adjustment was not phased out but dropped completely in revised estimates as of January 1999. The total effect of these changes was to lower the number of sales by about 2.9 percent relative to those published for earlier years.

The data used in the price index are collected in the Survey of Construction, through monthly interviews with the builders or owners. The size of the sample is currently about 20,000 observations per year.

Data availability and references

Housing starts and building permit data have been collected monthly by the Bureau of the Census since 1959.

The monthly report for "New Residential Construction" (permits, starts, and completions) is issued in the middle of the following month. The monthly report and associated descriptions and historical data can be found at <https://www.census.gov/construction/nrc>.

The monthly report for "New Residential Sales" (sales, houses for sale, and prices) is issued toward the end of the following month. The monthly report and associated descriptions and historical data can be found at <https://www.census.gov/construction/nrs>.

The manufactured housing data (not seasonally adjusted) and background information can be found at <https://www.manufacturedhousing.org/statistics>. Data with and without seasonal adjustment can be found at <https://www.census.gov/construction/mhs>.

Data and background on the price index for new one-family houses can be found at <https://www.census/gov>, in the alphabetical index under the category "Construction price indexes."

Tables 16-3 through 16-6

Manufacturers' Shipments, Inventories, and Orders

SOURCE: U.S. DEPARTMENT OF COMMERCE, CENSUS BUREAU

These data are from the Census Bureau's monthly M3 survey, a sample-based survey that provides measures of changes in the value of domestic manufacturing activity and indications of future production commitments. The sample is not a probability sample. It includes approximately 4,300 reporting units, including companies with $500 million or more in annual shipments

and a selection of smaller companies. Currently, reported monthly data represent approximately 60 percent of shipments at the total manufacturing level.

One important technology industry, semiconductors, is represented in the shipments and inventories data in this report but not in new or unfilled orders. This affects the new and unfilled orders totals for computers and electronic products, durable goods industries, and total manufacturing. Based on shipments data, semiconductors accounted for about 15 percent of computers and electronic products, 3 percent of durable goods industries, and 1.5 percent of total manufacturing. Since semiconductors are intermediate materials and components rather than finished final products, the absence of these data does not distort new and unfilled orders data for important final demand categories, such as capital goods and information technology.

Definitions and notes on the data

Shipments. The value of shipments data represent net selling values, f.o.b. (free on board) plant, after discounts and allowances and excluding freight charges and excise taxes. For multi-establishment companies, the M3 reports are typically company- or division-level reports that encompass groups of plants or products. The data reported are usually net sales and receipts from customers and do not include the value of interplant transfers. The reported sales are used to calculate month-to-month changes that bring forward the estimates for the entire industry (that is, estimates of the statistical "universe") that have been developed from the Annual Survey of Manufactures (ASM). The value of products made elsewhere under contract from materials owned by the plant is also included in shipments, along with receipts for contract work performed for others, resales, miscellaneous activities such as the sale of scrap and refuse, and installation and repair work performed by employees of the plant.

Inventories. Inventories in the M3 survey are collected on a current cost or pre-LIFO (last in, first out) basis. As different inventory valuation methods are reflected in the reported data, the estimates differ slightly from replacement cost estimates. Companies using the LIFO method for valuing inventories report their pre-LIFO value; the adjustment to their base-period prices is excluded. In the ASM, inventories are collected according to this same definition.

Inventory data are requested from respondents by three stages of fabrication: finished goods, work in process, and raw materials and supplies. Response to the stage of fabrication inquiries is lower than for total inventories; not all companies keep their monthly data at this level of detail. It should be noted that a product considered to be a finished good in one industry, such as steel mill shapes, may be reported as a raw material in another industry, such as stamping plants. For some purposes, this difference in definitions is an advantage. When a factory accumulates inventory that it considers to be raw materials, it can be expected that that accumulation is intentional. But when a factory—whether a materials-making or a final-product producer—has a buildup of finished goods inventories, it may indicate involuntary accumulation as a result of sales falling short of expectations. Hence, the two types of accumulation can have different economic interpretations, even if they represent identical types of goods.

Like total inventories, stage of fabrication inventories are benchmarked to the ASM data. Stage of fabrication data are benchmarked at the major group level, as opposed to the level of total inventories, which is benchmarked at the individual industry level.

New orders (durable goods), as reported in the monthly survey, are net of order cancellations and include orders received and filled during the month as well as orders received for future delivery. They also include the value of contract changes that increase or decrease the value of the unfilled orders to which they relate. Orders are defined to include those supported by binding legal documents such as signed contracts, letters of award, or letters of intent, although this definition may not be strictly applicable in some industries.

New orders (nondurable goods) are equal to shipments, as order backlogs are not reported for these industries.

Unfilled orders (durable goods) includes new orders (as defined above) that have not been reflected as shipments. Generally, unfilled orders at the end of the reporting period are equal to unfilled orders at the beginning of the period plus net new orders received less net shipments.

Series are adjusted for seasonal variation and variation in the number of trading days in the month using the X-12-ARIMA version of the Census Bureau's seasonal adjustment program.

Benchmarking and revisions

The data shown in the volume have been benchmarked to the 2007 Economic Census and to ASMs through 2011. In each benchmark revision, new and unfilled orders are adjusted to be consistent with the benchmarked shipments and inventory data, seasonal adjustment factors are revised and updated, and other corrections are made.

Data availability and references

Data have been collected monthly since 1958.

The "Advance Report on Durable Goods Manufacturers' Shipments, Inventories and Orders" is available as a press release about 18 working days after the end of each month. It includes seasonally adjusted and not seasonally adjusted estimates of shipments, new orders, unfilled orders, and inventories for durable goods industries.

The monthly "Manufacturers' Shipments, Inventories, and Orders" report is released on the 23rd working day after the end of the month. Content includes revisions to the advance durable goods data, estimates for nondurable goods industries, tabulations by market category, and ratios of shipments to inventories and to unfilled orders. Revisions may affect selected data for the two previous months.

Press releases, historical data, descriptions of the survey, and documentation are available on the Census Bureau Web site at <https://www.census.gov>, under the category "Manufacturing" in the alphabetic listing there.

Table 16-7

Motor Vehicle Sales and Inventories

SOURCE: U.S. DEPARTMENT OF COMMERCE, BUREAU OF ECONOMIC ANALYSIS

The Bureau of Economic Analysis (BEA) collects data on retail sales and inventories of cars, trucks, and buses from data from the American Automobile Manufacturers Association, Ward's Automotive Reports, and other sources. Seasonal adjustments are recalculated annually. Data are available on the BEA Web site at <http://www.bea.gov> as a part of the national income and product accounts data set; they are found under the "Supplemental Estimates" heading. They are also available on the STAT-USA subscription Web site at <http://www.stat-usa.gov>.

Definitions

Product	Description
Autos	All passenger cars, including station wagons.
Light trucks	Sport utility vehicles. Prior to the 2003 Benchmark Revision light trucks were up to 10,000 pounds.
Heavy trucks	Trucks more than 14,000 pounds gross vehicle weight. Prior to the 2003 Benchmark Revision heavy trucks were more than 10,000 pounds
Domestic sales	United States (U.S.) sales of vehicles assembled in the U.S., Canada, and Mexico
Foreign sales	U.S. sales of vehicles produced elsewhere
Domestic auto production	Autos assembled in the U.S
Domestic auto inventories	U.S. inventories of vehicles assembled in the U.S., Canada, and Mexico.

Data Availability

Auto and truck sales are updated by the end of the third business day after the end of the month. Auto production and inventories are available by the end of the second week after the end of month.

Tables 16-8 and 16-10

Retail and food services Sales; Retail inventories

SOURCE: U.S. DEPARTMENT OF COMMERCE, CENSUS BUREAU

Every month, the Census Bureau prepares estimates of retail sales and inventories by kind of business, based on a mail-out/mail-back survey of about 5,500 retail businesses with paid employees.

In June 2019, the monthly retail sales estimate is based on the results of the 2017 Annual Trade Survey and the service annual service. The annual retail trade survey (ARTS) produces national estimates of total annual sales, e-commerce sales, sales taxes, end-of-year inventories, purchases, total operating expenses, gross margins, and end-of-year accounts receivable for retail businesses located in the united states.

Retail sales and inventories are now compiled using the new NAICS classification system, which replaced the old SIC system. Historical data have been restated on the NAICS basis back to January 1992. In NAICS, Eating and drinking places and Mobile food services have been reclassified out of retail trade and into sector 72, Accommodation and food services, which also includes Hotels. The retail sales survey still collects and publishes sales data for Food services and drinking places. It no longer includes them in the Retail total, but they are included in a new Retail and food services total.

Subtotals of durable and nondurable goods are no longer published. They were always imprecise for retail sales, since general merchandise stores (including department stores) were included in nondurable goods, yet obviously sold substantial quantities of durable goods.

Definitions

Sales is the value of merchandise sold for cash or credit at retail or wholesale. Services that are incidental to the sale of merchandise, and excise taxes that are paid by the manufacturer or wholesaler and passed along to the retailer, are also included. Sales are net, after deductions for refunds and merchandise returns. They exclude sales taxes collected directly from customers and paid directly to a local, state, or federal tax agency. The sales estimates include only sales by establishments primarily engaged in retail trade, and are not intended to measure the total sales for a given commodity or merchandise line.

Inventories is the value of stocks of goods held for sale through retail stores, valued at cost, as of the last day of the report period. Stocks may be held either at the store or at warehouses that maintain supplies primarily intended for distribution to retail stores within the organization.

Leased departments consists of the operations of one company conducted within the establishment of another company, such as jewelry counters or optical centers within department stores. The values for sales and inventories at department stores in Tables 16-9 and 16-10 exclude sales of leased departments.

GAFO (department store type goods) is a special aggregate grouping of sales at general merchandise stores and at other stores that sell merchandise normally sold in department stores—clothing and accessories, furniture and home furnishings, electronics, appliances, sporting goods, hobby, book, music, office supplies, stationery, and gifts.

Notes on the data

The data published here have been benchmarked to the 2012, 2007, 2002, 1997, and 1992 Economic Censuses and the Annual Retail Trade Surveys for 2012 and previous years. Each year, the monthly series are benchmarked to the latest annual survey and new factors are incorporated to adjust for seasonal, trading-day, and holiday variations, using the Census Bureau's X-12-ARIMA program.

The survey sample is stratified by kind of business and estimated sales. All firms with sales above applicable size cutoffs are included. Firms are selected randomly from the remaining strata. The sample used for the end-of-month inventory estimates is a sub-sample of the monthly sales sample, about one-third of the size of the whole sample.

New samples, designed to produce NAICS estimates, were introduced with the 1999 Annual Retail Trade Survey and the March 2001 Monthly Retail Trade Survey. On November 30, 2006, another new sample was introduced, affecting the data for September 2006 and the following months. The sample is updated quarterly to take account of business births and deaths.

Data availability and references

An "Advance Monthly Retail Sales" report is released about nine working days after the close of the reference month, based on responses from a sub-sample of the complete retail sample.

The revised and more complete monthly "Retail Trade, Sales, and Inventories" reports are released six weeks after the close of the reference month. They contain preliminary figures for the current month and final figures for the prior 12 months. Statistics include retail sales, inventories, and ratios of inventories to sales. Data are both seasonally adjusted and unadjusted.

The "Annual Benchmark Report for Retail Trade" is released each spring. It includes updated seasonal adjustment factors; revised and benchmarked monthly estimates of sales and inventories; monthly data for the most recent 10 or more years; detailed annual estimates and ratios for the United States by kind of business; and comparable prior-year statistics and year-to-year changes.

All data are available on the Census Bureau Web site at <https://www.census.gov/retail>.

Table 16-9

Quarterly Retail Sales: Total and E-Commerce

SOURCE: U.S. DEPARTMENT OF COMMERCE, CENSUS BUREAU

Beginning with the fourth quarter of 1999, the Census Bureau has conducted a quarterly survey of retail e-commerce sales from the Monthly Retail Trade Survey sample. (The monthly survey does not report electronic shopping separately; it is combined with mail order.)

E-commerce sales are the sales of goods and services in which an order is placed by the buyer or the price and terms of sale are negotiated over the Internet or an extranet, Electronic Data Interchange (EDI) network, electronic mail, or other online system. Payment may or may not be made online. The quarterly release is issued around the 20th of February, May, August, and November, and is available along with full historical data on the Census Bureau Web site at <https://www.census.gov>. It can be located under the heading "Retail" in the alphabetical Web site index, under "E" for "Economic data and information."

These estimates reflect the NAICS definition of retail sales, which excludes food service. Online travel services, financial brokers and dealers, and ticket sales agencies are not classified as retail and are not included in these estimates; they are, however, included in the annual survey of selected services.

Table 16-11

Merchant Wholesalers--Sales and Inventories

SOURCE: U.S. DEPARTMENT OF COMMERCE, CENSUS BUREAU

The Annual Wholesale Trade Survey (AWTS) produces national estimates of total annual sales, e-commerce sales, end-of-year inventories, inventories held outside of the United States,

purchases, total operating expenses, gross margins, and commissions (for electronic markets, agents, and brokers) for wholesale businesses located in the United States. The sample consists of about 8400 establishments, with a response rate of about 62 percent; missing reports are imputed based on reports of similar reporters.

These data are now based on the new NAICS classification system, which replaced the old SIC system. Historical data have been restated on the NAICS basis back to January 1992.

Classification changes in NAICS

NAICS shifts a significant number of businesses from the Wholesale to the Retail sector. An important new criterion for classification concerns whether or not the establishment is intended to solicit walk-in traffic. If it is, and if it uses mass-media advertising, it is now classified as Retail, even if it also serves business and institutional clients.

Definitions

Merchant wholesalers includes merchant wholesalers that take title of the goods they sell, as well as jobbers, industrial distributors, exporters, and importers. The survey does not cover marketing sales offices and branches of manufacturing, refining, and mining firms, nor does it include NAICS 4251: Wholesale Electronic Markets and Agents and Brokers.

Notes on the data

Inventories are valued using methods other than LIFO (last in, first out) in order to better reflect the current costs of goods held as inventory.

A survey has been conducted monthly since 1946. New samples are drawn every 5 years, most recently in 2009. The samples are updated every quarter to add new businesses and to drop companies that are no longer active.

Data availability and references

"Monthly Wholesale Trade, Sales and Inventories" reports are released six weeks after the close of the reference month. They contain preliminary current-month figures and final figures for the previous month. Statistics include sales, inventories, and stock/sale ratios, along with standard errors. Data are both seasonally adjusted and unadjusted.

The "Annual Benchmark Report for Wholesale Trade" is released each spring. It contains estimated annual sales, monthly and yearend inventories, inventory/sales ratios, purchases, gross margins, and gross margin/sales ratios by kind of business. Annual estimates are benchmarked to annual surveys and the most recent census of wholesale trade. Monthly sales and inventories estimates are revised consistent with the annual data, seasonal adjustment factors are updated, and revised data for both seasonally adjusted and unadjusted values are published.

Data and documentation are available on the Census Bureau Web site at <https://www.census.gov>, under "Economic Indicators" and in the alphabetic index under "E" for economic data.

Tables 16-12 and 16-13

Manufacturing and Trade Sales and Inventories

SOURCES: U.S. DEPARTMENT OF COMMERCE, CENSUS BUREAU (CURRENT-DOLLAR SERIES) AND U.S. DEPARTMENT OF COMMERCE, BUREAU OF ECONOMIC ANALYSIS (BEA; CONSTANT-DOLLAR SERIES)

The current-dollar data on which these tables are based bring together summary data from the separate series on manufacturers' shipments, inventories, and orders; merchant wholesalers' sales and inventories; and retail sales and inventories, all of which are included in this chapter. Generally, current-dollar inventories are collected on a current cost (or pre-LIFO [last in, first out]) basis. See the notes and definitions for Tables 16-3, 16-4, 16-8 16-10, and 16-11 for further information about these data.

Based on these current-dollar values and relevant price data, BEA makes estimates of real sales, inventories, and inventory-sales ratios. Note, however, that annual figures for sales are shown as annual totals in Table 16-12 but as averages of the monthly data in Table 16-13, reflecting the practices of the respective source agencies. Also note that constant-dollar detail may not add to constant-dollar totals because of the chain-weighting formula; see the discussion of chain-weighted measures in the notes and definitions for Chapter 1. The constant-dollar estimates shown in this volume of *Business Statistics* are stated in 2009 dollars.

Inventory values are as of the end of the month or year. In Table 16-13, annual values for monthly current-dollar inventory-sales ratios are averages of seasonally adjusted monthly ratios. However, for the real ratios in Table 16-14, annual figures for inventory-sales ratios are calculated by BEA as year-end (December) inventories divided by the monthly average of sales for the entire year; this means that the annual ratios will not be equivalent to averages of month ratios. In all cases, the ratios in these two tables (like those in Table 1-8) represent the number of months' sales on hand as inventory at the end of the reporting period.

Data availability

Sales, inventories, and inventory-sales ratios for manufacturers, merchant wholesalers, and retailers are published monthly by the

Census Bureau in a press release entitled "Manufacturing and Trade Inventories and Sales." Recent and historical data are available on the Census Bureau Web site at <https://www.census.gov/mtis/www/mtis.html>. They can also be found by going to the general Census website, <https://www.census.gov>, going to the alphabetical index, finding "Economic Data and Information" under "E" and then finding "Manufacturing and trade" under "Manufacturing" or "Sales."

Sales and inventories in constant dollars are available on the BEA Web site at <https://www.bea.gov>. To locate these data on that site, click on "National Economic Accounts." Scroll down to "Supplemental Estimates," click "Underlying Detail Tables," and then click on "List of Underlying Detail Tables." For the most recent data, if there is more than one table with the same title, select the last table listed.

Table 16-14

Selected Services, Quarterly: Estimated Revenue for Employer Firms

SOURCE: U.S. DEPARTMENT OF COMMERCE, CENSUS BUREAU

Census data on quarterly revenue for selected service industries are based on information collected from a probability sample that has been expanded over recent years to approximately 19,000 employer firms (firms with employees), chosen from the sample for the larger Service Annual Survey and expanded to represent totals—for employer firms only—for the selected industries. The sample is updated quarterly to account for business births, deaths, and other changes. Industries are defined according to the 2012 NAICS.

The scope of the survey and the size of the sample have increased several times since the inception of this survey in 2004. More industries are now available than are shown here in Table 16-15, which focuses on industries with a longer statistical history.

Definitions and notes on the data

These data are collected in current dollars only. See the Producer Price Indexes in Chapter 8 for indicators of price trends in various sectors.

Both taxable and tax-exempt firms are covered unless otherwise specified.

Generally, government enterprises are not within the scope (that is, the industries it is designed to cover) of the survey. *Utilities* excludes government-owned utilities and *Transportation and warehousing* excludes the U.S. Postal Service.

Private industries that are not within the scope of the survey are NAICS 482, rail transportation; 525, funds, trusts, and other financial vehicles; 51112, offices of notaries; 6111, 6112, and

6113, elementary, secondary, and post-secondary schools; 8131, religious organizations; 81393 (labor unions and similar), 81394 (political organizations, and 814 (private households).

Totals shown for sectors and subsectors may include data for kinds of business that are in the scope of the survey but are not shown separately in the detail beneath.

Data for selected industry groups are adjusted for seasonal variation using the Census Bureau's X-13 ARIMA-SEATS program.

Data availability and references

The quarterly release "U.S. Government Estimates of Quarterly Revenue for Selected Services" is available on the Census Web site at <https://www.census.gov/>, as "Quarterly Services Survey" listed under Q in the alphabetic index; historical, technical, and background information, including sampling errors, is also available there.

INDEX

CPSIA information can be obtained
at www.ICGtesting.com
Printed in the USA
BVHW060856300123
656870BV00005B/7